ESPN

BIG TEN
FOOTBALL

ENCYCLOPEDIA

Copyright © 2007 ESPN Books

Illustration credits
Helmets by Carey Chiselbrook; renderings by Mike Johnson of Chapel Design & Marketing Ltd.

Photography credits
Page 8: Courtesy of University of Minnesota Archives, University of Minnesota; page 10: AP Images; page 11: Courtesy of Fielding Yost Papers, Bentley Historical Library, University of Michigan; pages 12-13: Getty Images (2); page 288: Courtesy of Athletic Records Division, Bentley Historical Library, University of Michigan; page 290: Courtesy of the University of Illinois Archives; page 291: Getty Images; page 292: AP Images.

Cover design by Eric Baker Design Associates, Inc.

Book design and composition by Laura Smyth/Smythtype.

ISBN-13: 978-1-933060-49-1

ISBN-10: 1-933060-49-2

ESPN books are available for special promotions and premiums. For details contact Michael Rentas, Assistant Director, Inventory Operations, Hyperion, 77 W. 66th St., 11th Floor, New York, N.Y. 10023, or call 212-456-0133.

10 9 8 7 6 5 4 3 2 1

TABLE OF CONTENTS

EDITOR'S NOTE

BY MICHAEL MACCAMBRIDGE

On the first Saturday of September 2007, I was with my girlfriend, Ivy, at a Mexican resort in a remote town 90 minutes south of Cancún, about as far away from the world of big-time American sports as you can get. There was no Internet connection down there, no newspapers, and when you tried to use your cell phone, you were scolded in Spanish. But somehow, big news travels fast.

As we sat down at the bar to get our first drink of the evening, we met a rotund, smiling man named Joe who said he was from Pennsylvania. We'd just exchanged introductions when Joe blurted out excitedly, "So did you hear?!"

"What?"

"Michigan! Lost!" Then he paused to add the kicker, "*To Appalachian State!*"

Joe started laughing and ordered a drink that looked like a Jell-O parfait and tasted like an alcohol smoothie. It turned out Joe was a Penn State fan, and Appalachian State had made his day.

Wolverine fans have already heard quite enough about their historic misfortune, but I was reminded that day that while the universe of college football is a big one, people always keep the closest tabs on their neighbors.

That's why we created the *ESPN Big Ten Football Encyclopedia*. It's a condensed version of our best-selling 2005 tome, the *ESPN College Football Encyclopedia*, that focuses on the schools of the Big Ten and the neighboring Mid-American Conference.

Inside this book, you'll find much of the same material you found in the *CFE*, expanded and updated for this edition, including:

- A pair of new essays, by Chuck Culpepper on the strange history of the Big Ten and by Mark Wangrin on the on-again, off-again relationship between the Big Ten and the Rose Bowl.
- Capsule histories of every school in the Big Ten and the Mid-American Conference, along with a complete list of players from each school who were selected in the first round of pro football drafts dating back to 1936. We've also added entries for the best backfield and the best defense in each school's history, as well as a complete record of all the players at each school named to the College and Pro Football Halls of Fame.
- A new feature, called Record Book, which provides a long list of single-game, single-season, and career leaders for each Big Ten and MAC school, as well as an updated version of the list of annual rushing, passing, and receiving leaders that first appeared in the *ESPN College Football Encyclopedia*.
- All-time scores for each of the schools in the Big Ten and MAC.
- A thumbnail overview of every season in college football history, including Big Ten and MAC players who made consensus All-America teams and other award winners, conference standings and bowl results, all-conference teams, and NCAA individual and team statistical leaders. This provides a good snapshot of how Big Ten and MAC schools fared on the national stage.
- Scoring summaries, along with team and individual statistics, for every major college bowl game in which either a Big Ten or a MAC team participated.

Getting all this information together has been a labor of love. One of the things that makes college football so absorbing is the myriad local and regional variations in the game. Those very same qualities have made the sport resistant to systematic documentation, especially during its first century.

The *ESPN College Football Encyclopedia* was a landmark because it provided us with a vast database from which to begin our work on future editions. As with that book, we value your input. In a project this ambitious, there are bound to be mistakes. If you spot one, tell us (by e-mail at espnbigtenencyclopedia@espn.go.com), and we'll correct it in future editions of this book and the upcoming second edition of the *ESPN College Football Encyclopedia*, which should be coming to you within two seasons.

In the meantime, if you're a football fan from the Big Ten and you're trying to figure out the duration of Iowa's longest winning streak, or how many times George Webster won all-conference honors, or what Tom Brady's completion percentage was in college, or any of a million other indispensable pieces of information, chances are excellent that you'll find the answers right here within the pages of the *Big Ten Football Encyclopedia*.

How to Use This Book

Each team is profiled in a quick-read format, featuring entries on Tradition, Best Player, Best Team, Best Coach, etc.

Key data about the university and its football history

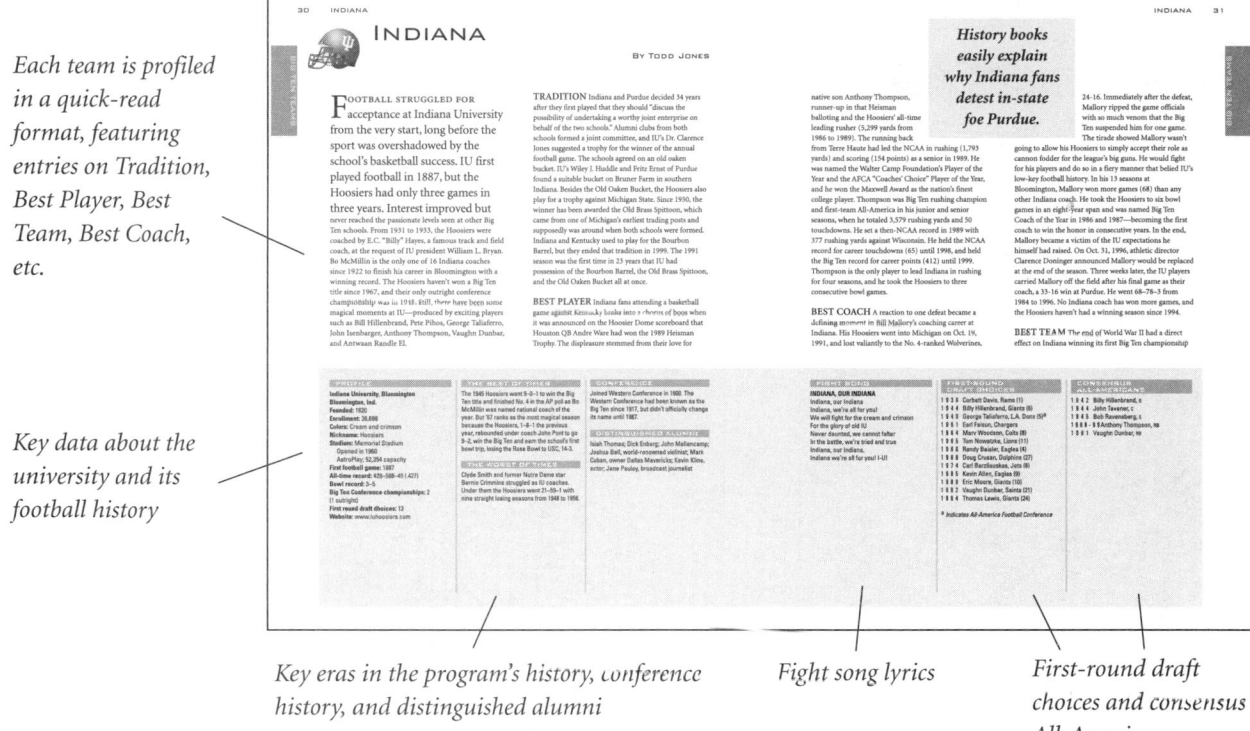

Key eras in the program's history, conference history, and distinguished alumni

Fight song lyrics

First-round draft choices and consensus All-Americans

Single-game, single-season, and career records for each school

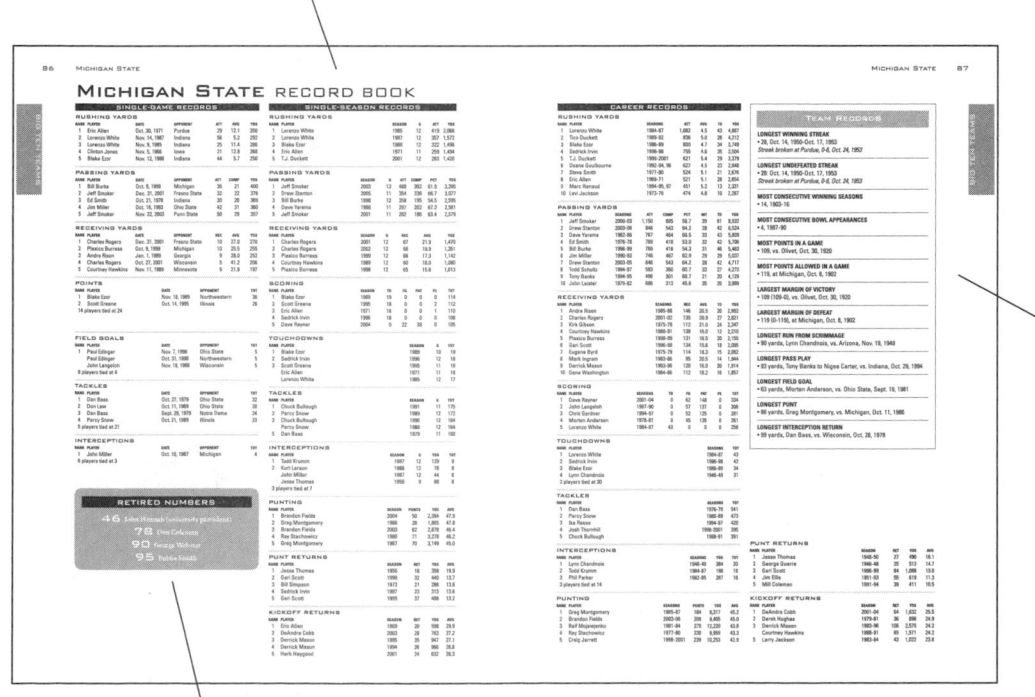

Team records include longest winning streak, most consecutive winning seasons, and largest margin of victory.

Retired numbers for each school

The bar charts illustrate a school's annual winning percentage dating back to 1936.

Each season is presented in detail, with date, site, opponent, and score. Season header includes overall record, with conference record in parentheses. Vertical bars denote conference games. At-a-glance results key shows bullets (•) for games won, equal signs (=) for ties, and blanks ( ) for losses. Shaded bars denote postseason games.

Each school's coaches are listed, with tenure, winning percentage, and overall win-loss record.

Where conference teams finished in final polls

Conference players and teams among NCAA statistical leaders

Conference standings

Bowl game appearances

Conference players named consensus All-Americans

All-conference teams

Conference players among the top 10 in Heisman Trophy voting

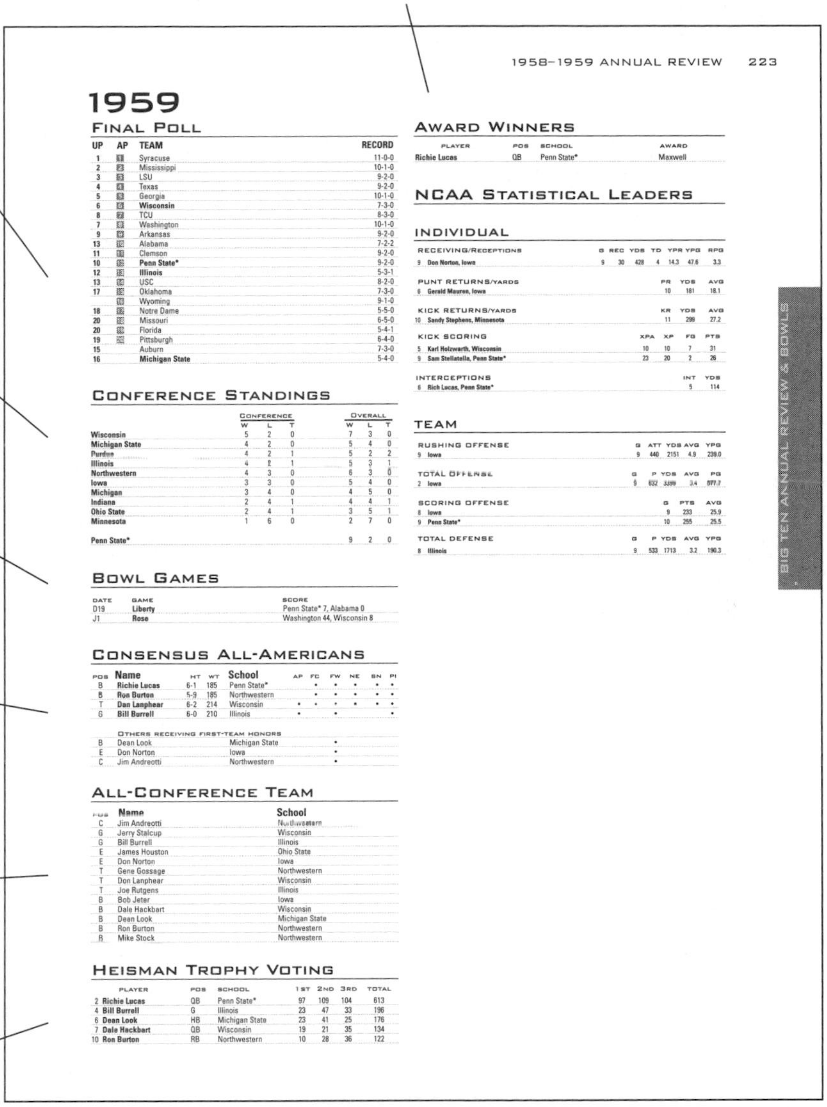

1959

FINAL POLL

UP	AP	TEAM	RECORD
1	1	Syracuse	11-0-0
2	2	Mississippi	10-1-0
3	3	LSU	9-2-0
4	4	Texas	9-2-0
5	5	Georgia	10-1-0
6	6	Wisconsin	7-3-0
8	7	TCU	8-3-0
7	8	Washington	10-1-0
9	9	Arkansas	9-2-0
13	10	Alabama	7-2-2
11	11	Clemson	9-2-0
10	12	Penn State*	9-2-0
13	13	Illinois	5-3-1
13	14	USC	8-2-0
17	15	Oklahoma	7-3-0
	16	Wyoming	9-1-0
18	17	Notre Dame	5-5-0
20	18	Missouri	6-5-0
20	19	Florida	5-4-1
19	20	Pittsburgh	6-4-0
15		Auburn	7-3-0
16		Michigan State	5-4-0

CONFERENCE STANDINGS

	CONFERENCE			OVERALL		
	W	L	T	W	L	T
Wisconsin	5	2	0	7	3	0
Michigan State	4	2	0	5	4	0
Purdue	4	2	1	5	2	2
Illinois	4	2	1	5	3	1
Northwestern	4	3	0	6	3	0
Iowa	3	3	0	5	4	0
Michigan	3	4	0	4	5	0
Indiana	2	4	1	4	4	1
Ohio State	2	4	1	3	5	1
Minnesota	1	6	0	2	7	0
Penn State*				9	2	0

BOWL GAMES

DATE	GAME	SCORE
D19	Liberty	Penn State* 7, Alabama 0
J1	Rose	Washington 44, Wisconsin 8

CONSENSUS ALL-AMERICANS

POS	Name	HT	WT	School	AP	FC	FW	NE	SN	PI
B	Richie Lucas	6-1	185	Penn State*	•	•	•	•	•	•
B	Ron Burton	5-9	185	Northwestern	•	•	•	•	•	•
T	Dan Lanphear	6-2	214	Wisconsin	•	•	•		•	•
G	Bill Burrell	6-0	210	Illinois	•	•	•		•	•

OTHERS RECEIVING FIRST-TEAM HONORS

B	Dean Look	Michigan State	•
E	Don Norton	Iowa	•
C	Jim Andreotti	Northwestern	•

ALL-CONFERENCE TEAM

POS	Name	School
C	Jim Andreotti	Northwestern
G	Jerry Stalcup	Wisconsin
G	Bill Burrell	Illinois
E	James Houston	Ohio State
E	Don Norton	Iowa
T	Gene Gossage	Northwestern
T	Don Lanphear	Wisconsin
T	Joe Rutgens	Illinois
B	Bob Jeter	Iowa
B	Dale Hackbart	Wisconsin
B	Dean Look	Michigan State
B	Ron Burton	Northwestern
B	Mike Stock	Northwestern

HEISMAN TROPHY VOTING

	PLAYER	POS	SCHOOL	1ST	2ND	3RD	TOTAL
2	Richie Lucas	QB	Penn State*	97	109	104	613
4	Bill Burrell	G	Illinois	23	47	33	196
6	Dean Look	HB	Michigan State	23	41	25	176
7	Dale Hackbart	QB	Wisconsin	19	21	35	134
10	Ron Burton	RB	Northwestern	10	28	36	122

AWARD WINNERS

PLAYER	POS	SCHOOL	AWARD
Richie Lucas	QB	Penn State*	Maxwell

NCAA STATISTICAL LEADERS

INDIVIDUAL

RECEIVING/RECEPTIONS

		G	REC	YDS	TD	YPR	YPG	RPG
9	Don Norton, Iowa	9	30	428	4	14.3	47.6	3.3

PUNT RETURNS/YARDS

		PR	YDS	AVG
9	Gerald Mauren, Iowa	10	181	18.1

KICK RETURNS/YARDS

		KR	YDS	AVG
10	Sandy Stephens, Minnesota	11	299	27.2

KICK SCORING

		XPA	XP	FG	PTS
5	Karl Holzwarth, Wisconsin	10	10	7	31
9	Sam Stellatella, Penn State*	23	20	2	26

INTERCEPTIONS

		INT	YDS
6	Rich Lucas, Penn State*	5	114

TEAM

RUSHING OFFENSE

		G	ATT	YDS	AVG	YPG
9	Iowa	9	440	2151	4.9	239.0

TOTAL OFFENSE

		G	P	YDS	AVG	YPG
2	Iowa	9	632	3399	3.4	877.7

SCORING OFFENSE

		G	PTS	AVG
8	Iowa	9	233	25.9
9	Penn State*	10	255	25.5

TOTAL DEFENSE

		G	P	YDS	AVG	YPG
8	Illinois	9	533	1713	3.2	190.3

BIG TEN ANNUAL REVIEW & BOWLS

ROSE BOWL

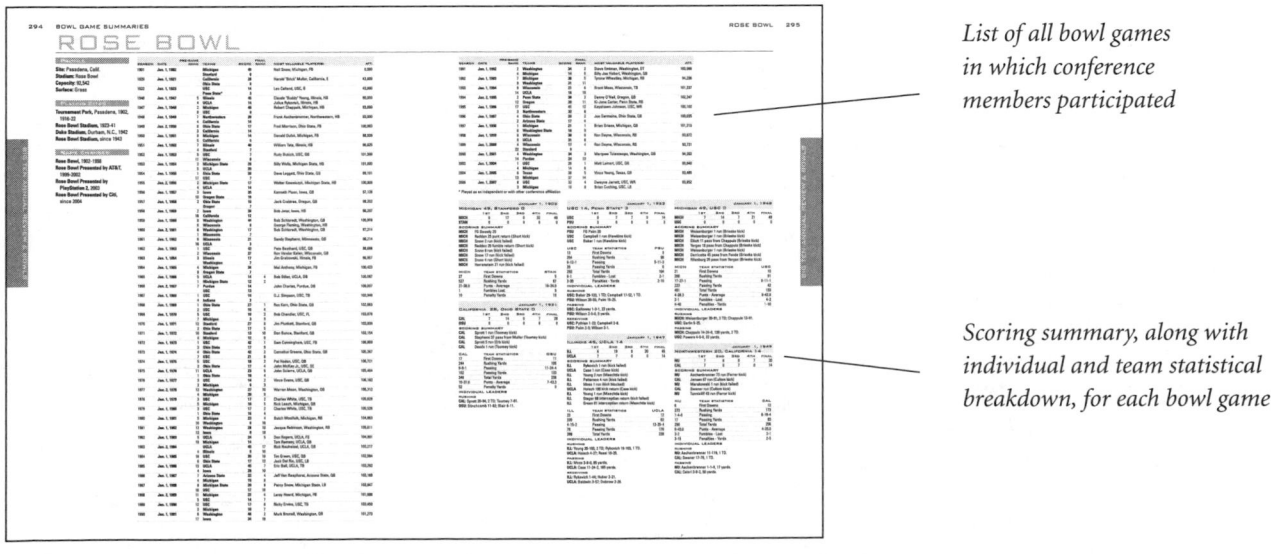

List of all bowl games in which conference members participated

Scoring summary, along with individual and team statistical breakdown, for each bowl game

The Once and Future Conference

Welcome to the crazy, mixed-up world of Big Ten football. No, really

BY CHUCK CULPEPPER

ON THE PLANET EARTH, IN THE WESTERN Hemisphere, in a northern midsection of the United States, there's an aged bedrock formation that goes by the name "Big Ten football." And the multitudes of the region long have gathered around this Big Ten football. And this Big Ten football long has epitomized the "Midwest," the "heartland"—even, to some, the "real America."

Long has the nation perceived in these people a certain sanity, stoicism, sturdiness. Long have they attracted such adjectives as "normal" and "corn-fed." Long has a football nation felt autumn in its corpuscles whenever it's Saturday and it's early afternoon and some Big Ten team on TV has begun the measured, prudent first-quarter act of establishing the running game.

Hatched in a Chicago hotel in 1896, the Big Ten has stood for common sense, stability, even a smidgeon of dullness for more than a century, which long has belied a truth strangely obvious: These people are thoroughly, unapologetically, vividly, gloriously, certifiably nuts about their football.

They're so wacko that sousaphone players at Ohio State sometimes compete before a panels of judges for the sacred honor of dotting the letter I in the word O-H-I-O on the football field. They're so strange that thousands of college students hop up and down in unison in a stadium in Madison, Wisconsin, in time to a song by an Irish-American hip-hop band, creating a mesmerizing lunacy rarely seen upon the Earth. They're so eccentric that the Iowa and Minnesota football teams strain and toil against each other every autumn so that one of them might, through sweat and drudgery and cunning and good fortune, wind up winning a statuette of a hog.

That's the Floyd of Rosedale. It's a replica of an actual hog from the 1930s. This hog apparently had a brother who doubled as a movie star in Will Rogers' *State Fair*. No, really. This hog—Floyd, not his brother—came along in 1935 to soothe the contempt between Iowa and Minnesota. No, really. Iowans had not appreciated some barbaric Minnesotan

Here piggy, piggy: Floyd of Rosedale's brother was the real ham.

tactics during the 1934 game, and Iowa governor Clyde Herring had dabbled in the rare act of gubernatorial riot incitement by noting that if the referees didn't quash such Minnesotan tactics, the Iowan crowd might.

No, really.

So the governors sought peace and wagered a hog, which Herring delivered to the office of Minnesota governor Floyd B. Olson after Minnesota's 13-6 victory.

Yet these people claim they're ordinary.

They're the Big Ten that boasted Fielding Yost, the early-20th-century Michigan coach who had the quirky vision that more than 100,000 people routinely would visit a football stadium to eyeball the exploits of a bunch of college students. They're the Big Ten of the orderly 1940s Ohio State coach Paul Brown, football's Rushmore figure who, rather revolutionarily, coached a bloody, gnarly, nasty sport while wearing such finery as Loden jackets with raglan sleeves. They're the Big Ten of Michigan State fans chanting "Kill, Bubba, kill" to 1960s defensive force, Bubba Smith, even after he graduated and was visiting. They're the Big Ten of Purdue Boilermakers who once went by unofficial nicknames such as grangers, pumpkin-shuckers, rail-splitters, cornfield sailors, blacksmiths, and foundry hands. They're the Big Ten that, since deciding to fully incorporate the kingdom of Pennsylvania State in a binge of capitalism in 1993, has, well, 11 members, yet goes by "Big Ten" while hiding the number 11 in the conference seal.

Yet these people claim to be normal.

This Big Ten started as seven in 1896, then went by Big Nine or Big Ten—or, for small patches, Big Eight—except for one epic 10-year stretch that began in 1969, when it also knew the common nickname Big Two, Little Eight. That's when a region of alleged calm and politeness endured a spate of dominance from Ohio State and Michigan and came to revere two unreconstructed grouches named Woody and Bo. One of them, Woody Hayes, used his position to see a larger picture and improve race relations at Ohio State. He also loathed Michigan

so much that he went for a two-point conversion to close a 50–14 win in 1968, explaining that he did so because he couldn't go for three. He also got so angry at the officials during the end of a 10–7 loss to Michigan in 1971 that he tore up some sideline markers.

Yet these people claim to be patient.

They had a behemoth of a fullback and tackle named Bronko Nagurski, said to be discovered by a Minnesota coach near the Canadian border hauling a plow without the help of a horse, a story that's surely untrue but certainly durable. They had a star quarterback at Northwestern, Otto Graham, who played football, basketball, baseball, and the cornet in the band. They had a star everything at the University of Chicago, Jay Berwanger, who won the first Heisman Trophy in 1935 yet met his university expenses by waiting tables, cleaning, operating elevators, and fixing leaky toilets.

The first of their many national stars, Harold "Red" Grange, famously scored four times in the first 12 minutes for the University of Illinois against Michigan on October 18, 1924, touchdowns covering 95, 67, 56, and 45 yards. He won the nickname Galloping Ghost from Chicago sportswriter Warren Brown, made the cover of *Time* magazine, and became the very first well-off professional player. Yet as he told the interviewer Robert Gallagher, he'd arrived at Illinois after 75 touchdowns at Wheaton (Illinois) High School and decided not to play football, having balked at the hugeness of the players. He changed his mind only when his Zeta Psi fraternity brothers hazed him with a wooden paddle.

Indeed, these people have bizarre rituals.

It's a quirky notion—that people from one institute of higher learning would crave beating the daylights out of people from another institute of higher learning in, well, games. The Midwest helped pioneer that craving way back in the 19th century, just after the East advanced the same notion. The idea that people would want these victories with such desperation that they'd hire non-student ringers in order to beat the hell out of the other university is unbelievable. The Big Ten harbored that, too, and that's why seven university presidents met at the Palmer House

> *Long has a football nation felt autumn in its corpuscles whenever it's Saturday and some Big Ten team on TV has begun the measured, prudent first-quarter act of establishing the running game.*

in Chicago in 1895 and again in 1896, trying to rein in this beast.

The idea that these athletic endeavors could be consolidated and monitored with something called a "conference" is ironic, to say the least. These presidents created the oldest official conference, banned professionals and coaches from playing, prohibited paying players, required players to live in residence at universities for at least six months—in short, they made academic institutions into supervisory agents for athletic teams. They called it the Intercollegiate Conference of Faculty Representatives—or, for short, Western Conference.

These peculiar habits of higher education began with a motley bunch of scholars who lacked a clue that football would play so well on TV, mostly because they, unimaginably, lacked TV. They began with an engineer (Purdue president James H. Smart, the ringleader), a future U.S. Court of Appeals judge who championed coeducation (Northwestern president Henry Wade Rogers), a former prodigy who entered college at age 10 and got his doctorate from Yale by his 19th birthday (University of Chicago president William Rainey Harper), a president beloved by students who called him Prexy (the University of Minnesota's Cyrus Northrop), a former superintendent of Cleveland schools and future commissioner of education for the state of New York (Andrew Sloan Draper of the University of Illinois), a former president of Cornell (Charles K. Adams, Wisconsin), and a former minister to China, future minister to Turkey, and future head of the Anglo-American International Commission on Canadian Fisheries (Michigan president James B. Angell).

The original meeting in 1895 also included a famous botanist (Dr. John M. Coulter, Lake Forest College), but the botanist didn't return for the January 1896 meeting, replaced by the former minister to China.

Even without a botanist, the league blossomed—Indiana and Iowa joined in 1899, for starters—sprouting all the bewildering vividness of humanity.

By 1901, the league had an icon, a Michigan coach who would become a lawyer, author, and businessman. This Yost brought along the avant-garde view that coaching could be a person's job and that it warranted a full

Chicago's Jay Berwanger strikes a Heisman pose. Sort of.

professor's salary. One hundred years later, no coach would yearn for a full professor's salary. Yost's 1901-04 teams won four national championships. His 1901 team outscored opponents 550–0 and beat Stanford 49-0 in a debut event called the Tournament of Roses in Pasadena. His 1901-05 teams outscored opponents 2,821-42 and never lost until Chicago beat Michigan 2-0 on November 30, 1905. Yet as his team made a 1903 trip to Minnesota, as John Woodford wrote for *Michigan Today*, Yost feared the enemy might try to infect Michigan's water supply, so he asked student manager Thomas B. Roberts to purchase a 30-cent, five-gallon water jug.

That was strange enough, but after Michigan abandoned the jug in the fan fracas after Minnesota's victorious 6-6 tie, the head of Minnesota's athletic department, L.J. Cooke, declined to return it. He wrote a letter to Michigan harrumphing, "You'll have to win it." That turn of

tomfoolery led to teams of grown young men playing a brutal game for a Little Brown Jug. That also led to representatives of Indiana and Purdue deciding they wanted to play for something by 1925, thus combing the farms of southern Indiana for just the right bucket, preferably a Civil War relic. This Old Oaken Bucket presaged the Slab of Bacon, for which Wisconsin and Minnesota fought annually from 1930 until the '40s, when it got lost in a post-game melee—remaining lost until 1994, when it turned up 46 years after the teams started playing for Paul Bunyan's Axe.

The Slab of Bacon preceded the aforementioned Floyd the hog. Floyd the hog in 1935 predated the Sweet Sioux, an 1833 carved statue of a Native American from a cigar store, for which Illinois and Northwestern began playing in 1945. Of course, after somebody stole the statue from its case one year later, they replaced it with the Sweet Sioux Tomahawk

and kept the latter even after recovering the former because the Tomahawk was easier to transport. That preceded Indiana and Michigan State deciding in 1950 to play for an Old Brass Spittoon. Then there's the foremost rivalry, the one that rivets the nation, in which Michigan and Ohio State play for … no particular trophy or trinket.

Yes, it's all senseless, wondrous, and quite likely true.

Even with the Big Ten still a pup in 1905, the citizens of the heartland loudly declared their loyalties. More than 20 football deaths in the country that season prompted concern, even from President Theodore Roosevelt. Some also fretted over football's influence on universities. Yet when the University of Wisconsin historian Frederick Jackson Turner suggested suspending the game for two years, students marched to his house and burned him in effigy. The heartland would have its football.

Northwestern did suspend football for 1906 and 1907, but restored it for 1908, ahead of schedule—Big Ten football's first instance of having to deal with conference fluctuations. Michigan withdrew from the conference in a snit in 1907. Ohio State joined in 1912. Michigan returned in 1917. The conference sailed on as football mushroomed in popularity and Yost foresaw crowds of 100,000 by the 1920s. Then, one day in 1939 served as a stage for behavior so abnormal that it cannot be explained.

On December 22, 1939, after 47 years of collegiate football, after a national championship in 1905 with that 2-0 win over Michigan, and after claiming the first Heisman Trophy with Berwanger, and after sporting the legendarily inventive coaching of Amos Alonzo Stagg, the University of Chicago made an announcement startling to any present-day American: It would take its big-time program and dissolve it. Its president, Robert Hutchins, claimed it constituted a campus distraction. He actually touted academics as his university's foremost mission, contradicting millions of citizens of the 20th and 21st centuries, who know that universities exist mainly to field football teams.

Out went the Chicago Maroons for good in 1946. In came the Michigan State Spartans in 1953. In came the Penn State Nittany Lions in 1993, lending more bedrock through the Rushmore surname Paterno, that coach, intellectual, and grump. All through those post-World War II decades, the Big Ten solidified as comfortable American bedrock despite some astonishingly weird counter-American bylaws. For instance, until a ruling on May 12, 1975, teams could not play in

Not a drop to drink: Fielding Yost feared Minnesota's drinking water.

any bowl game other than the Rose, meaning the conference refused to engage in utmost capitalism, an American shocker.

This meant that Michigan went 30–2–1 from 1972-74 yet played zero bowl games, and that the entire inexplicable era found its eccentric hilt in 1973. That November, Ohio State and Michigan entered their annual festival of contempt in Ann Arbor at 9–0 and 10–0. They then tied, 10-10, to reach 9–0–1 and 10–0–1. By bizarre decree from 1951, athletic directors still voted to determine the Rose Bowl participant, but this time those athletic directors faced a puzzler.

As the hearty citizens of a supposedly healthy region spent a Saturday night trying to guess how 10 suits might vote on a Sunday midday, many onlookers projected Michigan the election winner. They noted that, for one thing, Ohio State had played in the previous Rose Bowl, and thereby did those prognosticators employ the mental residue of another bizarre bylaw, one that had existed from 1951 to December 8, 1971. In that quite socialist bylaw, Big Ten teams could not play in successive Rose Bowls no matter how dominant their autumns. Mastodons like Michigan State in 1966 had played entire seasons pulverizing others and honing national title candidacy while realizing they would be spending New Year's Day on sofas.

With that restriction recently removed, the athletic directors voted 6–4 to send Ohio State to the Rose Bowl, with Michigan's one more win duly noted by all. An undefeated Michigan team saw no palm trees come holiday break, and the tie in 1973 led to that May 1975 decision, which helped detonate a strange rule and propel the 1975 Michigan team to the Orange Bowl after Ohio State claimed the Rose.

A large nation somehow found all of this only vaguely abnormal.

Yet the Big Ten's bouts of nonconformity, long amusing and wondrous, also tilted mildly toward the virtuous. While Big Ten integration in the early 20th century sorely lacked sufficiency by any standards, it did outpace the rest of the nation. Consider Iowa alone. Its halfback Carleton Holbrook in 1896 scored a touchdown even through derision from racist Missouri fans. Iowa cancelled its series with Missouri in 1910—yet to resume—after Missouri demanded that Iowa not bring a black player, and Missourians greeted the Iowa train menacingly to ensure he didn't come. Archie Alexander played tackle at Iowa from 1909 to 1911

before becoming a mathematician and engineer, studying bridges in London and accepting President Dwight Eisenhower's appointment as governor of the Virgin Islands. Another tackle, Duke Slater, became the first black All-America at Iowa, famously blocked three Notre Dame defenders at once in 1921, and wound up as that rare lineman with a campus building named for him. The 1920s Iowa guard, Harold Bradley, later reached the NFL.

When the dazzling back and kick returner Ozzie Simmons and his brother, Don, couldn't play college football in Texas in the early 1930s, they travelled by train to Iowa City, where they walked down the hallway and into the office of coach Ossie Solem, who overcame surprise and took them to practice, watched Ozzie return some punts, and then found them some quarters. When, shortly thereafter, the future dermatologist Homer Harris couldn't play at the University of Washington in his native Seattle, he, too, headed for Iowa, where he became the Big Ten's first black team captain, playing alongside the revered 1939 Heisman Trophy winner Nile Kinnick.

The conference's first black player, Bobby Marshall at Minnesota, played end but kicked a 60-yard field goal for a then-four points to beat Chicago 4-2 in 1906. The first black pro football coach, Fritz Pollard, stopped off to play for Northwestern in the mid-1910s before proceeding to Brown University.

They joined a century-plus procession of outright characters who made sane bedrock seem plenty lively. A coach named Duffy (Daugherty) led Michigan State to prominence in the 1960s and introduced the idea to a rapt nation that tying a game resembled "kissing your sister"— by 2007, a household phrase. A coach named Evy (Forest Evashevski) played at Michigan but then lit up Iowa in the 1950s with his Rose Bowls and his bombast that included storming fields after officials and feuding with his athletic director. A coach named Herbert (Crisler) led Michigan to a national championship in 1947 but went by the name Fritz only because Stagg nicknamed him after the violinist Fritz Kreisler during playing days at Chicago. The commonsensical city of Columbus, Ohio, had a coach nicknamed Close the Gates of Mercy because this Francis Schmidt, from the 1930s, specialized in razzle-dazzle plays and once beat Drake 85-7.

Amid all this regional shouting and noise, Minnesota won five national titles during the 1932-41 and 1945-50 reigns of Bernie Bierman, a coach so bashful that he used to

Please, Bubba, don't hurt 'em: Spartan eminence brawn, Bubba Smith.

spend halftimes reading instructions and corrections calmly from a piece of paper. And Northwestern, long on the low end of football scores, shockingly won the Big Ten in 1995 with a coach, Gary Barnett, who readied himself for the New Year's Day party by strolling around and around the Rose Bowl in a sort of New Age meditation.

Iowa in 1939 had a Heisman Trophy winner who scored a touchdown to beat Notre Dame, wowed the New York audience with an eloquent acceptance speech about World War II, and showed such multifaceted human promise that when this Nile Kinnick died in 1943, at age 24, in a military plane crash near Venezuela, a state mourned. Illinois in the early 1960s introduced to the American lexicon the proper noun that became a synonym for toughness. It's the familiar word "Butkus." After all the ruggedness, all the plodding of establishing running games that helped make the Big Ten the Big Ten, Michigan in 1997 boasted that rarest of players, a Charles Woodson so dazzling that he became the only person to fixate Heisman-voting eyes upon a defender (who also returned kicks and dabbled at wide receiver) and select accordingly.

A veritable Horse, Alan Ameche, thrilled 1950s Wisconsin. Quarterbacks came streaming out of Purdue and into the NFL, from Griese to Phipps to Dawson to Herrmann to Everett to Brees to Orton. An Anthony Carter of the early 1980s helped introduce Michigan and the country to the crucial concept of wide receivers who meant sheer danger. Ohio State helped affirm the huge importance of left tackles and pancake blocks to the life of a football village, when it kept track of the pancakes of a remarkable topographical formation named Orlando Pace.

By the early 21st century, Big Ten stadiums at Michigan, Ohio State, and Penn State welcomed more than 100,000 people on Saturdays as a routine matter, and Northwestern's Ryan Field seemed puny and intimate as the conference's smallest venue, holding 47,130. Minnesota long since played indoors. Wisconsin students forged a second decade of hopping after the third quarter.

The planet warmed in general, and the Big Ten thawed alongside. Long famous for close-to-the-vest, handoff football suitable for brutish late-season weather, it began to throw more on first down, the footballs especially airborne at Joe Tiller's Purdue. As the regions of the United States began to blur in distinctiveness and resemble each other ever more and shop at the same places and meet at standard

coffeehouses beneath green signs, old Big Ten reputations of plodding dullness faded.

While the league didn't tilt all the way amok, it did spew out 21st-century scores like Northwestern over Michigan by 54-51, Purdue over Michigan State by 45-42, Indiana over Minnesota by 51-43, Minnesota over Northwestern by 45-42, Northwestern over Wisconsin by 47-44, Michigan over Michigan State by 45-37, Penn State over Michigan State by 42-37, Northwestern over Wisconsin by 51-48. Michigan beat Minnesota by 38-35 in 2003 despite trailing 28-7 after three quarters. Michigan State beat Northwestern by 41-38 in 2006 despite trailing by 38-3 in the third quarter, for the largest comeback in NCAA Division I-A history. Then, when Ohio State and Michigan met as No. 1 and No. 2 for the first time in their history in 2006, a legacy of 10-10s and 12-10s and 10-7s gave way to this newfangled and defenseless 42-39 thing.

The conference upgraded its pizzazz quotient by necessity and wrung a Heisman Trophy in 2006 from an impressive young adult at Ohio State, quarterback Troy Smith, whose hybrid pass-run talent matched the national

Young gun: Buckeye Troy Smith stares down the modern Big Ten.

fashion. He'd throw it sometimes to the kind of breathtaking receiver-kick returner who'd become a must-have in the sport, Ted Ginn Jr.

In one sense, the Big Ten had gone from close-to-the-vest to sweater-vest, as a populous state, Ohio, came to regard that outdated garment as symbolic. This peculiarity centered on Jim Tressel, the coach who came from Youngstown State to Ohio State, donned a red sweater vest, and began winning. He won an unexpected 2002-03 national championship by curtailing a Miami, Florida, dynasty in something called double overtime. He won a very expected berth in the 2006-07 national championship game. He won with sturdy regularity, and some of the bizarre citizens of his city did respond with ritualistic furniture-burnings, attracting a nation of TV news trucks hooked on spectacle.

Big Ten fanatics mingled over the freshly invented Internet to reveal just how unhinged they had been all along. Some yearned to chuck Joe Paterno at Penn State after some clunker seasons, until he quelled that with a sudden title in 2005 at age 78 and three-quarters, dented only by a loss at Michigan on a melodramatic touchdown pass at 0:00. Paterno marched through his nadir and into his 80s still shy of retirement.

The mid-20th-century long gone, the Big Ten had so many bowl tie-ins (seven) that it had two in Orlando alone. In some years, the Big Ten would send teams all over the map except for the Rose, which quadrennially served as the national-title game. Before retiring, Barry Alvarez built Wisconsin into something reliably potent. Iowa became a hip pick for future supremacy. Illinois went to a Sugar Bowl, Iowa to an Orange, Northwestern to an Alamo, Minnesota to three Music Cities, plus an Insight, a Micron PC, and a Sun. Ohio State won the Fiesta Bowl—three times from 2003 to 2006.

And, because it wasn't quirky enough, the Big Ten even merged with the nation in one of humanity's most mystifying concoctions, something called the Bowl Championship Series. This intricate mathematical system designed to pinpoint a national title match proved adept at amplifying some of the seething, loathing, and class warfare that help make sports such pleasurable fodder—never more so than in 2006, when Ohio State and Michigan played the lead roles. It's complicated, and rational sorts from other lands would never understand it, but things ended with Michigan at No. 3 instead of No. 2, the Ohio State coach (Tressel) recusing himself from voting in the final coaches' poll because it would determine No. 1 Ohio State's national-championship opponent (which turned out to be Florida), and the Michigan coach (Lloyd Carr) criticizing the Ohio State coach for the recusing.

In this scenario, Michigan made off for the Rose Bowl as consolation, and the season added another case in a century-plus of weirdness that has spiced American life and that seven dignified university presidents in Chicago, led by an engineer, could never have imagined they'd prompt.

BIG TEN TEAMS

This section, the book's largest, contains historical essays and statistical data on each of the Big Ten's eleven universities.

Here's what you should know about information that appears in these pages:

- **Enrollment.** Undergraduate enrollment only.
- **National championships.** According to the NCAA's recognized list of consensus national champions since 1936 (the first year of the Associated Press poll).
- **Conference championships.** Overall and outright titles in the conference.
- **First-round draft choices.** Updated through the 2007 NFL draft.
- **Consensus All-Americans.** As designated by the NCAA. Because the NCAA recognizes multiple lists, it's quite common for a player to receive first-team All-America honors from one or more selectors and not be acknowledged as a consensus All-America.
- **All-time team.** Whenever a team recently selected by a respected authority was available, we included it.
- **All-time scores.** Compiled by BCS pollster Richard Billingsley, this section offers a bar chart for each school showing yearly winning percentage since 1936. (In calculating this percentage, a tie is treated as a half-win and a half-loss.) In the year-by-year summaries, the vertical lines beside opponents indicate a conference game. A bullet indicates a win, a blank indicates a loss, an equal sign indicates a tie. Conference affiliations are noted throughout.

In the early years, forfeits were not uncommon, frequently because of difficult travel arrangements. There were, however, instances where opponents did not agree on which team had forfeited. Since it's impossible to judge who did what 100 years after the fact, only the instances where *both* schools agreed are included.

American football evolved from rugby, and for over a decade it shared many of its predecessor's characteristics. Not until Walter Camp, the father of American football, established a point value system and rules of play (1878-82) did the sport assume the basic form we love today. Only games that were played by American football rules resulting in American point values are listed in this encyclopedia.

Billingsley and the ESPN research staff went to heroic lengths to determine, once and for all, the definitive final score for every disputed game. All games with disputed scores are footnoted, but we had to decide which outcome to record. If there was overwhelming evidence one way or another, through multiple reports or consensus, we selected the majority decision. Otherwise we granted the losing team the smallest margin of defeat.

- **Team record books.** Among the new features in the *ESPN Big Ten Football Encyclopedia* is this three-page section that includes significant single-game, single-season, and career records for each school. This section also incorporates the annual leaders in rushing, passing, and receiving, which now appear in an easier-to-read format. Due to recent changes in the NCAA's official record-keeping methodology, there is a great deal of disparity here. Before 2002, bowl game performances were not included in a school's rushing, passing, and receiving statistics. Some schools have yet to revise their numbers. Until all schools update their stats according to the NCAA model, records will skew to more recent performances, because today's players will be credited with stats from an extra game or two (in the case of conference championship games).

Another complication: Some schools identify as their receiving leader the player who gained the most yards in receptions, while others prefer the player who caught the most passes. When two players caught the same number of passes, we've listed the player who gained the most yards.

ILLINOIS

BY TODD JONES

ILLINOIS HAS HELPED SHAPE HOW we look at football. The Fighting Illini gave us the game's first superstar, a prototypical linebacker, and a player who came to define the autocratic professional coach. The trio—Red Grange, Dick Butkus, and George Halas, respectively—molded our perception of offense, defense, and coaching. The innovative Robert Zuppke coached Illinois to four national championships from 1914 to 1927 and created a standard of success in Champaign-Urbana. History reassures the future hopes of the Fighting Illini. As Ray Eliot, one of the school's great coaches, once told his players: "Anything you think you can do, you can do." It has all been done before at Illinois.

TRADITION Homecoming weekend originated at Illinois in 1910, created by undergraduates W. Elmer Ekblaw and C.F. "Dab" Williams. The first celebration was held Oct. 14-16, and the Fighting Illini beat Chicago 3-0 in a game that served as the weekend's main event.

Other schools adopted homecoming, as well as the idea of having cheerleaders perform acrobatic stunts. Robert "Red" Matthews created that role as an Illinois cheerleader from 1899 to 1900. Illinois has celebrated "Dad's Day" since 1920, when it crowns a "King Dad" (nominated by a student) on the field at halftime of one game each season. The Fighting Illini have three trophy games, the oldest dating to 1925, when they began competing against Ohio State for a wooden replica of a turtle known as the Illibuck Trophy. The Purdue Cannon has been up for grabs since 1943 whenever the Illini play the Boilermakers. In 1945, the winner of the Illinois-Northwestern game earned a bulky wooden Indian trophy called Sweet Sioux, but since 1947 the schools have played for the Tomahawk instead.

BEST PLAYER The man who would become one of sports' great legends arrived at Illinois in the fall of 1922. Harold "Red" Grange quit before his first practice ended, convinced he was too small, at 5'10" and 170 pounds, to play. He returned a day later and accepted No. 77 because all other jerseys had been given out, and Zuppke figured he may as well have two 7's because 7 is a winning dice roll. Three years later, the school retired that number after his final game. By then, people were writing poetry about the man Grantland Rice dubbed the Galloping Ghost.

Red Grange gave credibility to pro football as a Chicago Bear, but his fame began at Illinois.

Grange was as big a sports star in the Roaring Twenties as Babe Ruth and Jack Dempsey. The shy, modest, redheaded man from Wheaton, Ill., ran with the football like no one had before and few have since. He single-handedly gave credibility to pro football as a barnstorming member of the Chicago Bears, but his fame began at Illinois. There he gained 2,071 rushing yards, passed for 575 yards, and scored 31 touchdowns in 20 games over three seasons. With muscles toned from working on a hometown ice truck, the Wheaton Iceman ran with extraordinary speed, balance, and power. He was a natural athlete who ran the 100-yard dash in 9.81 seconds, long-jumped 23 feet, and high-jumped six feet. Grange rushed for 208 yards and three touchdowns against Nebraska in his first game as a sophomore, in 1923. A year later, he burst into stardom on Oct. 18, 1924, by scoring the first four times he touched the ball in the first 12 minutes against Michigan. He later scored a fifth touchdown and passed for a sixth against the school he had been asked to attend but didn't because he couldn't afford the out-of-state tuition. His legend became solidified in 1925 when the Eastern press saw him gain 363 total yards and score 3 TDs in a 24-2 win at powerful Penn. "This man Red Grange of Illinois is three or four men and a horse rolled into one," Damon Runyon wrote of the performance. A crowd of 85,000—then a college football record—turned out on Nov. 21, 1925, at Ohio State to see Grange play his final collegiate game. Two days later, he signed the richest pro football contract of the time, for $100,000, to play for the Bears, and, on Thanksgiving Day that same week, he made his pro debut before 36,000 at Wrigley Field. In 1999, an Associated Press panel voted Grange the fourth-best football player of the 20th century. He was a charter member of both the college and pro football halls of fame and a unanimous selection on the all-time All-America team.

BEST COACH He was born in Berlin, Germany, and never played varsity football. He looked out of place—a stubby 5'7" with a cowlick hanging on his youthful face—in such a bruising game. His mind, however, made up for what he lacked in physique. Robert Zuppke, who loved to paint, is remembered as one of football's most creative thinkers. He invented the huddle, the screen pass, the flea-flicker, spring practice, and the spiral snap from center. Zuppke named his offensive plays Razzle Dazzle and the Flying Trapeze, and once said his defense was "on loan

FIGHT SONG

ILLINOIS LOYALTY
We're loyal to you Illinois,
We're "Orange and Blue," Illinois,
We'll back you so stand
'Gainst the best in the land,
For we know you have sand, Illinois,
Rah! Rah!
So crack out that ball Illinois,
We're backing you all Illinois;
Our team is our fame protector,
On! boys, for we expect a vict'ry from you Illinois!
For honest Labor and for Learning we stand,
And unto thee we pledge our heart and hand,
Dear Alma Mater Illinois.

FIRST-ROUND DRAFT CHOICES

1944	Tony Butkovich, Rams (11)
1954	Stan Wallace, Bears (6)
1954	John Bauer, Browns (12)
1959	Rich Kreitling, Browns (11)
1961	Joe Rutgens, Redskins (3) and Raiders*
1965	Dick Butkus, Bears (3)
1965	George Donnelly, 49ers (13)
1966	Jim Grabowski, Dolphins (1) and Packers (9)*
1981	Dave Wilson (Saints)S
1983	Tony Eason, Patriots (15)
1988	Scott Davis, Raiders (25)
1990	Jeff George, Colts (1)
1991	Henry Jones, Bills (26)
1993	Brad Hopkins, Oilers (13)
1996	Kevin Hardy, Jaguars (2)
1996	Simeon Rice, Cardinals (3)

S Indicates NFL Supplemental Draft
*From 1960-1966, the NFL and the AFL held separate, competing drafts

CONSENSUS ALL-AMERICANS

1914	Perry Graves, E
1914	Ralph Chapman, G
1915	Bart Macomber, B
1918	John Depler, C
1920	Charles Carney, E
1923	James McMillen, G
1923-25	Red Grange, HB
1926	Bernie Shively, G
1946	Alex Agase, G
1951	Johnny Karras, B
1953	J.C. Caroline, B
1959	Bill Burrell, G
1963-64	Dick Butkus, C
1965	Jim Grabowski, FB
1984-85	David Williams, WR
1989-90	Moe Gardner, NT
1994	Dana Howard, LB
1995	Kevin Hardy, LB

from Barnum & Bailey." And he created all expectations for Illinois football. Grange and others who played for the Little Dutchman raved about his ability to inspire a team with motivational speeches. "Shoot at the moon," he often urged his team. Once, Zuppke even told his players that "the only man who comes out of the game today is a dead man." The Illini had won only one Big Ten title when he was hired in 1913, but they won seven in Zuppke's 29 seasons. He led Illinois to its only four national championships: 1914, 1919, 1923, and 1927.

BEST TEAM The 1914 Fighting Illini are revered for sharing the national championship with Army and Texas after going 7–0 and outscoring opponents 224-22. Zuppke once said he never had a quarterback as good as George "Potsy" Clark, and the team also had All-Americas in Perry Graves and Ralph Chapman. However, those who favor the modern era consider the 1951 squad the school's best. That team, led by fullback Bill Tate and linebacker Chuck Boerio, went 9–0–1, the school's last undefeated season, and outscored opponents 220-83. Only a 0-0 tie against Ohio State spoiled a perfect season. Despite being just 5'11" and 190 pounds, Boerio was first-team All-Big Ten on a defense that allowed league foes an average of five points per game. Besides winning the conference title, the Illini also defeated Syracuse and UCLA in the regular season. Illinois then beat Stanford 40-7 in the Rose Bowl in the first nationally televised college football game, on NBC. The Illini scored 34 unanswered points in the second half, and finished the game with a Rose Bowl record 360 rushing yards. Even so, Illinois finished #4 in the final AP poll.

BEST BACKFIELD An explosive offense powered Illinois to its last Big Ten championship, in 2001. The Illini went 10-2 and played in the Sugar Bowl because QB Kurt Kittner threw darts around the field while halfbacks Antoineo Harris and Rocky Harvey gave defenses something else to worry about by combining for over 1,200 rushing yards. Kittner completed 221 of 409 passes for 3,256 yards and a school-record 27 touchdowns. The senior threw 4 TD passes in games against Northwestern, Wisconsin, and in the Sugar Bowl loss to LSU. He passed for more than 260 yards in seven games, including 401 against Wisconsin, 387 against Northwestern (while completing 33 of 43 attempts), and 301 against Louisville.

COLLEGE FOOTBALL HALL OF FAME INDUCTEES		
NAME	YEARS	INDUCTED
Red Grange, HB	1923-25	1951
Ed Hall, COACH	1892-93	1951
Bob Zuppke, COACH	1913-41	1951
George Woodruff, COACH	1903	1963
Alex Agase, G	1941-43	1963
Chuck Carney, E	1918-1921	1966
Buddy Young, HB	1944, 1946	1968
Bart Macomber, HB	1914-16	1972
J.C. Caroline, HB	1953-54	1980
Bernie Shively, G	1924-26	1982
Dick Butkus, C/LB	1962-64	1983
Bob Blackman, COACH	1971-76	1987
Jim Grabowski, FB	1963-65	1995
Al Brosky, S	1950-52	1998
David Williams, WR	1983-85	2005

Kittner was second-team All-Big Ten behind the Conference's MVP, Indiana QB Antwaan Randle El. Kittner finished his career second on Illinois' all-time list with 8,722 career passing yards and a school-record 70 TD passes. While fullback Carey Davis cleared paths, Harris and Harvey split time at halfback, making for an effective duo. Harris rushed 169 times for 629 yards and six touchdowns. He ran for 201 yards against Louisville and 106 yards against Indiana. A year later, as a senior, Harris ran for a school-record 1,330 yards to finish second on the Illinois all-time rushing list with 2,985 yards. In 2001, Harvey chipped in with 620 yards on 145 carries and 4 TDs as a senior. He ranks fifth all time at Illinois with 2,711 rushing yards. The Illini averaged a school-record 32.5 points per game and 420.1 yards of offense, the third-highest total in school history, with Kittner, Harris, and Harvey wreaking havoc behind All-Big Ten linemen in guard Jay Kulaga, tackle Tony Pashos, and center Luke Butkus. Illinois totaled 5,041 yards in 12 games, gaining 570 yards in a game, against both Wisconsin and Northwestern.

BEST DEFENSE When you think defense at Illinois, you think of one player: Dick Butkus. He was All-America in 1963 and 1964, and was the Big Ten's MVP after leading the Illini to the 1963 Big Ten championship. Butkus defined the linebacker position, but also played center while helping the Illini win the 1964 Rose Bowl over Washington. He was National Player of the Year in 1964, as selected by the American Football Coaches Association, and third in the 1964 Heisman voting. Illinois retired his No. 50. Today, the Butkus Award, given to the nation's best linebacker, is named in his honor. And so it's appropriate that the Illini's best defense featured two players who won the Butkus Award: Dana Howard in 1994, and Kevin Hardy in 1995. They were half of a 1994 linebacker quartet—along with Simeon Rice and John Holecek—that ranks among the best in college football history. The foursome spearheaded an Illinois defense that shut out two opponents and held five others to 10 points or less in 1994. That season, opponents mustered only 13.0 points and 284.1 total yards per game, and 3.3 rushing yards per attempt. Howard set the Big Ten record for career tackles with 595—with four seasons of 100-plus stops—and earned consensus All-America honors as a senior in 1994. He led the team in tackles with 150 and was named Big Ten defensive player of the year for the second consecutive season. Howard was the first Illinois

player to win a major national award when he won the Butkus. Rice and Hardy, both juniors, joined Howard as first-team All-Big Ten members. The senior Holecek was named second-team All-Big Ten while making 101 tackles. Defensive back Antwoine Patton was honorable mention all-Big Ten, and Robert Crumpton led the team with four interceptions. Rice was second-team All-America in 1994 and the media chose him as the Big Ten lineman of the year for setting an Illinois record with 16 sacks, including five against Washington State and three against Northwestern. He also led the team that season in broken-up passes, with six. Rice's 44.5 career sacks are still a school record, as are his 69 career tackles for loss. He led the Illini in sacks four consecutive years, and was chosen by Arizona with the No. 3 overall pick of the 1996 NFL draft. That was one selection behind Hardy, who went No. 2 to Jacksonville. Hardy was a consensus All-America and Butkus winner in 1995 after finishing his career with 326 tackles, including 38 for a loss. Despite the four stellar linebackers, the Illini went just 6–5 during the 1994 regular season under Lou Tepper. They did, however, defeat East Carolina 30-0 in the Liberty Bowl as the defense made four interceptions and recovered a fumble.

PRO FOOTBALL HALL OF FAME INDUCTEES		
NAME	YEARS	INDUCTED
Red Grange, HB	1925-27, 1929-34	1963
George Halas, FOUNDER/OWNER/COACH	1920-1983	1963
Hugh Ray, RULES ADVISOR/SUPERVISOR OF OFFICIALS	1938-52	1966
Ray Nitschke, LB	1958-72	1978
Dick Butkus, LB	1965-73	1979
Bobby Mitchell, WR/HB	1958-68	1983

BIGGEST GAME Fans and the media greeted Illinois with little respect when it arrived for the 1947 Rose Bowl in Pasadena to fulfill the first contract calling to match the champions of the Big Ten and Pac-8. Many people wanted Pac-8 champ UCLA to play Army. Illinois coach Ray Eliot made his players read every negative article and convinced them they were playing for the Big Ten's pride, as well as their school's. UCLA, ranked #4 and favored by 11, led 7-6 after one quarter, but the Fighting Illini erupted for a 45-14 victory. Six different Illinois players scored TDs and the team set a Rose Bowl record with 326 rushing yards. Julius Rykovich and Buddy Young each gained 103 yards behind the blocking of All-America tackle Alex Agase, who had served at Okinawa during World War II. "You wanted an army. Well you got an army today," the Illinois players shouted at UCLA throughout the game.

BIGGEST UPSET Illinois' 14-9 victory over 40-point favorite Minnesota on Nov. 4, 1916, was so shocking, the headline on the *Chicago Herald*'s game story screamed: "Hold On Tight When You Read This!" The Gophers had five All-America candidates and had outscored opponents 236-14 while going 4–0. Illinois traveled to Minnesota with a 2–2 record, and Zuppke

allowed his players to go to a party the night before the game because they were going "to the slaughter [house]and to get murdered tomorrow." The next day, he delivered a passionate pregame speech. "I am Louis XIV, and you are my court," he told his players. "After us, the deluge. Let them eat their cake today. We'll live on bread." To that, halfback Joe Sternaman responded: "Come on, here's to the deluge!" The fired-up Illini went up 14-0 and held on despite using only 11 players, while 33 Gophers saw action. Minnesota was confused throughout the game by the underdog opponent's spread formation and wide splits on the line. When the game ended, injured Illinois player George Halas threw his crutches into the air in celebration. Up in the press box, Walter Camp said: "Will somebody please tell me how something like this could happen?"

HEARTBREAKER Illinois won the 1983 Big Ten championship by going 9–0 in league play, including victories over No. 4 Iowa, No. 6 Ohio State, and No. 8 Michigan. The Illini earned their first Rose Bowl berth in 20 years. Six players were named first-team All-Big Ten, including defensive tackle Don Thorp, the league's MVP. Mike White won the Big Ten's Coach of the Year honor. The storybook season, however, had an unhappy final chapter. UCLA, led by quarterback Rick Neuheisel, crushed the Illini 45-9 in the Rose Bowl. The Bruins scored 21 second-quarter points to lead 28-3 at halftime. UCLA gained 511 yards of total offense in the Rose Bowl's biggest margin of defeat in 23 years. Illinois finished 10–2.

WILDEST FINISH Another year, another loss in Ann Arbor. Or so it seemed on Oct. 23, 1993, when the Fighting Illini trailed the Wolverines 21-10 early in the fourth quarter and 21-17 with less than two minutes to play. Illinois linebacker Kevin Hardy, however, forced Michigan's Ricky Powers to fumble, and linebacker Simeon Rice recovered at the Wolverines' 44 with 1:13 remaining. Three completions later, the Illini faced fourth down and six. Johnny Johnson rolled left and split two defenders with a TD pass to tight end Jim Klein for a 24-21 lead. Michigan answered by driving to the Illini 25, but time ran out before the Wolverines could try a field goal. Maybe the pregame switch from orange to blue pants, in hopes of changing the team's luck, actually worked for Illinois.

BEST GOAL-LINE STAND Two different stands earned the Illini an 18-16 win at Ohio State on Oct. 10, 1992. Linebacker Dana Howard and safety Jeff Arneson

forced OSU's Eddie George, who won the Heisman three years later, to fumble on the Illini 1 on the game's opening series. Arneson recovered the ball and ran 96 yards for a touchdown. "I bit my mouth guard and ran as hard as I could," Arneson said. "It felt like I had a piano on my back at the end." Ohio State bounced back and led 16-15 early in the fourth quarter when it again had the ball on the Illini 1. But Howard and safety Tyrone Washington caused another George fumble. Illinois recovered, drove 86 yards, and ended the scoring with a game-winning Chris Richardson field goal.

"You wanted an army? Well, you got an army today."

BEST COMEBACK The Fighting Illini, a 24-point underdog, trailed 27-7 midway through the third period at No. 9 Michigan in 1999. Quarterback Kurt Kittner then rallied the Illini to four consecutive TDs. The last two scores came in the game's final 2:42 . First Kittner hit Rocky Harvey with a 59-yard TD pass, his fourth scoring toss of the day. Harvey followed with a 54-yard TD run. Tom Brady drove Michigan to within 16 yards of a touchdown, but Tony Francis intercepted his third-down pass near the goal line. Francis fumbled the ball into the end zone, and Illlinois safety Muhammad Abdullah fell on the ball. The Wolverines scored a safety on the play, but the Illini prevailed, 35-29.

STADIUM The 200 granite columns on the east and west sides of Memorial Stadium link fans to the past, which includes Red Grange running wild in the stadium's 1924 dedication game. Illinois athletic director George Huff pushed for a new stadium after the 1920 season. School president David Kinley agreed with the idea, saying he wanted one that could "bring a touch of Greek glory to the prairie." The wish came true when the 60,632-seat Memorial Stadium opened on Nov. 3, 1923, thanks to public donations that accounted for some $1.7 million of the stadium's $2.5 million cost. Zuppke suggested the new field honor the 184 Illinois students who died in World War I, so the names of those 183 men and one woman were etched on separate columns. Little changed about the stadium until 1966, when the playing field was named Zuppke Field. Memorial Stadium received $7 million worth of improvements in 1985— the year it hosted the first Farm Aid concert—and another $7 million in upgrades seven years later. It now seats 57,078. When the 2006 season ended, Illinois began a $116 million renovation that will enclose the stadium's north end with permanent seating for students and add new luxury box seating on the west side. The construction is due to be completed before 2008.

HALLOWED GROUND Grange Rock, a memorial to Red Grange, sits at the north end zone of Zuppke Field. The rock came from the same Indiana stone quarry that produced Memorial Stadium's granite columns. Ray Eliot, the coach known as Mr. Illini, is buried in Mt. Hope Cemetery, located across Fourth Street from Memorial Stadium.

RIVAL In basketball, it's simple: Illinois hates Indiana, and vice versa. All Fighting Illini football fans, however, don't aim their ill will at the same opponent. Some detest in-state rival Northwestern. The Illini have played the Wildcats 96 times, more than any other team, and hold a 51–42–5 lead in the series. Other Illinois fans can't stand Purdue, their closest geographical Big Ten opponent. And still other Illini fans consider Michigan the school's biggest rival, although the Wolverines don't share that feeling.

CONTROVERSY Ohio State trailed visiting Illinois 24-20 early in the fourth quarter in 1990 when Buckeye's kicker Tim Williams attempted a 51-yard field goal. Mel Agee blocked the kick. Illinois defensive tackle Mike Poloskey picked up the ball, began running and was tripped by Ohio State holder Kirk Herbstreit, now an ESPN college football analyst. Poloskey then pitched the ball to teammate Quintin Parker, who ran 43 yards for a TD. The Buckeyes protested that Poloskey had made an illegal forward lateral. Game officials huddled at midfield, discussed the matter, and signaled touchdown for Illinois. They're still grumbling about it in Columbus.

DUBIOUS DISTINCTION Illinois quarterback Dave Wilson filed a legal suit against the Big Ten in 1981 in response to the conference questioning his eligibility. The Big Ten answered on Aug. 6, 1981, by slapping the school with one-year sanctions for improprieties. League faculty representatives voted to prohibit the Illini from playing in a postseason bowl game that season and kept the school from sharing in conference television revenue. Illinois governor James Thompson then signed into law a bill creating a special lottery to help offset the university's estimated loss of $500,000 in TV money. The lottery netted Illinois $850,000. The next spring, the New Orleans Saints selected Wilson in the first round of the NFL draft.

NICKNAME The Illini Indians were the first inhabitants of what later became the state of Illinois. University officials adopted the name Illini because the word means "brave men." It's believed that *Chicago*

Tribune writer Harvey Woodruff first used the moniker Fighting Illini in an account of Illinois' 7-0 upset win at Ohio State in 1921.

MASCOT Chief Illiniwek was created when Ray Dvorak, assistant director of the Illinois marching band, proposed that an Illini Indian do a dance at halftime during a 1926 game against Penn. A student played the role of chief in war paint, feathered headdress, and buckskin regalia for 81 years. After two decades of pressure from activists who found the mascot offensive, the school announced in February of 2007 that it was doing away with Illiniwek. Two years earlier, the NCAA had barred Illinois from hosting postseason games because it deemed the mascot an offensive use of Native American imagery. The NCAA lifted the sanctions when Illinois announced it was dropping Chief Illiniwek. The school still uses the name Illini because it's short for Illlinois, and the nickname Fighting Illlini, because it's considered a reference to the team's competitive spirit. Chief Illiniwek, portrayed by graduate student Dan Maloney, performed for the final time in front of students and fans at halftime of a men's home basketball game against Michigan on Feb. 21, 2007.

ALL-TIME TEAM

In the fall of 1990, Illinois fans cast nearly 5,000 ballots to select the school's 25-man All-Century football team. The team was chosen as part of the university's celebration of 100 years of football.

FIRST TEAM

1923-25	Red Grange, HB
1962-64	Dick Butkus, LB/C
1963-65	Jim Grabowski, FB
1944, 1946	Buddy Young, HB
1955-57	Ray Nitschke, FB/LB
1981-82	Tony Eason, QB
1953-54	J.C. Caroline, HB
1973, 1975-76	Scott Studwell, LB
1917	George Halas, E
1987-90	Moe Gardner, NT

SECOND TEAM

1917-19	Burt Ingwersen, T
1932-34	Chuck Bennis, G
1941-42, 1946	Alex Agase, G
1946-48	Dike Eddleman, P
1949-51	John Karras, HB
1950-52	Al Brosky, DB
1959-60	Ed O'Bradovich, E/P
1968-70	Doug Dieken, TE
1973-76	Dan Beaver, PK
1980	Dave Wilson, QB
1980-82	Mike Bass, PK
1980-83	Don Thorp, DT
1982-85	Jim Juriga, G
1983-85	David Williams, WR
1988-89	Jeff George, QB

first half against Coe College. The other unit played the second half of each game. Illinois defeated Miami 20-7 and followed that with a 13-0 win over Coe College. Only 4,568 fans attended. The Illinois Athletic Association lost $3,600 after expenses.

LORE The greatest 12 minutes of individual performance in the history of college football occurred on Oct. 18, 1924. Illinois was dedicating its new Memorial Stadium against mighty Michigan. Red Grange returned the game's opening kickoff 95 yards for a touchdown. On Illinois' next possession, the junior ran around left end, cut back off tackle, and raced 67 yards for a score. Grange scored again when he ran 56 yards, cutting across the field after starting around the right end. Two minutes later, he ran 44 yards for yet another TD. In 12 minutes, he had scored all four times he touched the ball and totaled 265 yards. The crowd of 67,000 was roaring when Grange asked for a rest. He didn't return to play until the third quarter, then scored on a 13-yard run. He capped his day by throwing a TD pass. Grange totaled 402 yards, including 126 in kickoff returns. Illinois won, 39-14, to end Michigan's 22-game winning streak, and the legend of the Galloping Ghost was born.

UNIFORMS The University of Illinois convocation and faculty officially adopted orange and navy blue as the school's colors on Nov. 1, 1894. Those colors replaced Dartmouth green, which had been used to honor E.K. Hall, a Dartmouth graduate who served as Illinois football coach from 1892 to 1893. Illinois doesn't have a traditional logo and uniform design. Both have changed many times throughout the school's history.

QUIRK Illinois secured its second national championship in five years by winning 9-7 at Ohio State in the 1919 season finale. The victory came on a 25-yard field goal by Bob Fletcher, who had never attempted a field goal before. Zuppke asked him to kick with 12 seconds left because Fletcher's brother, Ralph, couldn't play due to an ankle injury . . . Illinois played a doubleheader on Oct. 1, 1932. Zuppke divided his team into two units and had one play the first half against Miami (Ohio) and the

NUMBERS Illinois running back Howard Griffith scored an NCAA-record 8 TDs against Southern Illinois on Sept. 22, 1990. Four of his touchdowns came in the fourth quarter ... Al Brosky set an NCAA record with an interception in 15 consecutive games (1950-52) and still holds the NCAA record with 29 career interceptions in 27 games. He never played pro football because of a back injury ... QB Dave Wilson set 44 different school, Big Ten, and NCAA records in a 49-42 loss at Ohio State on Nov. 8, 1980. The senior completed 43 of 69 passes to 10 different receivers for 621 yards and 6 TDs against an OSU defense ranked No. 1 in the conference against the pass ... Zero fans saw Illinois beat Municipal Pier 7-0 on Oct. 26, 1918. Spectators were not permitted at the game because of an influenza epidemic in Champaign-Urbana ... Jim Grabowski ran for a Big Ten-record 239 yards on 33 carries against Wisconsin on Nov. 14, 1964 ... The Illini entered 2007 with a six-game losing streak and 19

losses in their past 21 games. They've gone 13–45 since winning the Big Ten in 2001. They're 2–30 in Big Ten play since 2003 … Illinois has upset a No. 1-ranked opponent three times: 14-7 over Ohio State in 1950; 25-6 over Michigan in 1955; and 20-13 over Michigan State in 1956 … True freshman Isiah "Juice" Willliams rushed for 576 yards in 2006, the most ever by an Illinois QB in a season or career, while also completing a pass for 69 yards and another for 76 yards … The Illini led the Big Ten in rushing in 2006 with an average of 188.8 yards per game … "Champaign" Tony Eason holds the NCAA record for passing yards per game in a career with a 300.4 average during 1981 and 1982. He eclipsed 300 yards passing in a game 10 times … Wide receiver David Williams, twice a unanimous first-team All-America selection and a College Football Hall of Fame member, caught 101 passes in 1984. He had 208 receiving yards against Northwestern that season, and he

had 16 receptions in a 1985 game against Purdue. His 262 career receptions are 93 more than the next Illini receiver, Jason Dulick … Robert Holcombe ran for 315 yards against Minnesota in 1996 … Steve Weatherford set a school record in 2004 by averaging 45.4 yards per punt … John Sullivan made 34 tackles against Minnesota in a 1977 game … Tom O'Connell threw five touchdown passes in the first half against Washington in 1952 … Buddy Young had runs of 93 yards and 92 yards during the 1944 season … Dick Eddleman's punt returns of 92 and 89 yards in 1947 are still the two longest in Illini history … Pierre Thomas had two kickoff returns over 70 yards, including a 99-yarder against Western Michigan, in 2004.

QUOTE "We'll have the will to win, and if we go down, we'll go down fighting hard and clean. That's the Illinois way."—Ray Eliot

ILLINOIS ALL-TIME SCORES

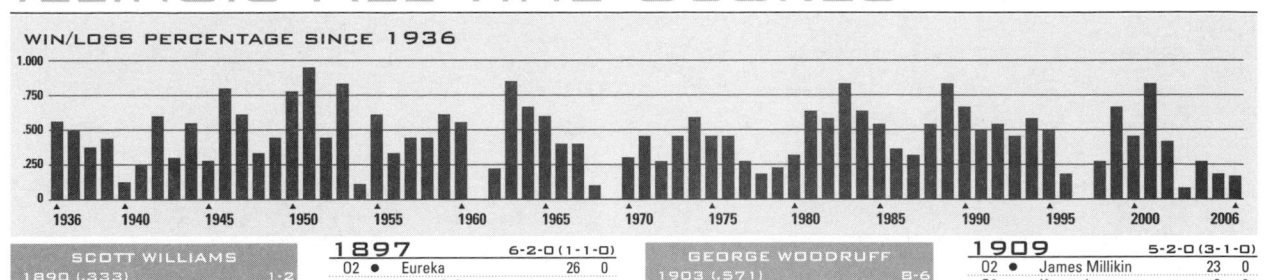

WIN/LOSS PERCENTAGE SINCE 1936

SCOTT WILLIAMS
1890 (.333)   1-2

1890   1-2-0
O2	at Ill. Wesleyan	0	16
N22	at Purdue	0	62
N27 ●	Ill. Wesleyan	12	6

ROBERT LACKEY
1891 (.833)   5-1

1891   5-1-0
O1	at Lake Forest	0	8
O17 ●	Bloomington	26	0
N7 ●	Eureka Coll.	40	0
N13 ●	Illinois Wesley	44	4
N21 ●	Knox Coll.	12	0
N26 ●	at Bloomington	20	12

E.K. HALL
1892-93 (.600)   10-6-4

1892   7-4-1
O8	Purdue	6	12
O12 =	Northwestern	16	16
O21 ●	at Washington, Mo.	22	0
O22 ●	Doane Coll. *OMA*	20	0
O24 ●	at Nebraska	0	6
O26 ●	at Baker U.	26	10
O27 ●	at Kansas	4	26
O29 ●	at Kansas City AC	42	0
N5 ●	Englewood HS	38	0
N16 ●	at Chicago	4	10
N18 ●	DePauw	34	0
N24 ●	Chicago	28	12

1893   3-2-3
S30 ●	Wabash	60	6
O7 ●	at DePauw	14	4
O21 =	at Northwestern	0	0
O28 ●	Chicago AA	4	10
N6 ●	Oberlin	24	34
N11 ●	Pastime AC *STL*	18	16
N25 =	at Purdue	26	26
N30 =	Lake Forest	10	10

LOUIS D. VAIL
1894 (.571)   4-3

1894   4-3-0
O6 ●	at Wabash	36	6
O13 ●	at Chicago AC	0	14
O20 ●	Lake Forest	54	6
N3 ●	Northwestern	66	0
N17 ●	Purdue	2	22
N24 ●	Indianapolis Artillery.	14	18
N29 ●	Pastime AC *STL*	10	0

GEORGE A. HUFF
1895-99 (.563)   21-16-3

1895   4-2-1
O5 ●	Wabash	48	0
O12 ●	at Chicago AC	0	8
O19 ●	Illinois College	79	0
O26 =	at Wisconsin	10	10
N2 ●	Lake Forest	38	0
N23 ●	Northwestern	38	4
N28 ●	at Purdue	2	6

1896–Present
BIG 10

1896   4-2-1 (0-2-1)
O3 ●	Lake Forest	38	0
O10 ●	Knox	70	4
O17 ●	Missouri *STL*	10	0
O21 ●	Oberlin	22	6
O31 |	at Chicago	0	12
N7 |	Northwestern	4	10
N25 = |	at Purdue	4	4

1897   6-2-0 (1-1-0)
O2 ●	Eureka	26	0
O9 ●	Phys. & Surg.	6	0
O16 ●	Lake Forest	36	0
O23 |	Purdue	34	4
O30 |	Chicago	12	18
N12 ●	Knox	64	0
N20 ●	Carlisle *CHI*	6	23
N25 ●	Eureka *PEO*	6	0

1898   4-5-0 (1-1-0)
S28 ●	Illinois Wesleyan	18	0
O1 ●	Phys. & Surg.	6	11
O8 ●	Notre Dame	0	5
O15 ●	DePauw	16	0
O22 ●	Alumni	10	6
N4 ●	Alumni	17	23
N12 |	Michigan *DET*	5	12
N19 |	Carlisle *CHI*	0	11
N24 ●	Minnesota	11	10

1899   3-5-1 (0-3-0)
S30 ●	Ill. Wesleyan	6	0
O7 ●	at Knox	5	0
O14 ●	Indiana	0	5
O28 ●	Michigan	0	5	*
N6 =	Alumni	0	0
N11 ●	Wisconsin *MIL*	0	23
N22 ●	Purdue	0	5
N25 ●	at St. Louis	29	0
N30 |	Iowa *RI*	0	58

FRED L. SMITH
1900 (.667)   7-3-2

1900   7-3-2 (1-3-2)
S29 ●	Rose Poly	26	0
O3 ●	DePauw	63	0
O6 ●	Illinois Wesleyan	21	0
O10 ●	Phys. & Surg.	6	0
O13 ●	Knox	16	0
O16 ●	Lombard	35	0
O20 =	at Northwestern	0	0
O27 |	Michigan *CHI*	0	12
N3 |	Purdue	17	5
N10 |	at Minnesota	0	23
N17 = |	Indiana *IND*	0	0
N24 |	at Wisconsin	0	27

EDGAR G. HOLT
1901-02 (.804)   18-4-1

1901   8-2-0 (4-2-0)
S28 ●	Englewood HS	39	0
O5 ●	Marion Sims	52	0
O11 ●	Phys. & Surg.	23	0
O12 ●	Washington, Mo.	21	0
O19 ●	at Chicago	24	0
O26 ●	Northwestern	11	17
N2 ●	Indiana *IND*	18	0
N9 ●	at Iowa	27	0
N16 ●	at Purdue	28	6
N28 ●	Minnesota	0	16

1902   10-2-1 (4-2-0)
S20 ●	North Div. HS	34	6
S27 ●	Englewood HS	45	0
O1 ●	Osteopaths	22	0
O4 ●	Monmouth	33	0
O8 ●	Haskell	24	10
O11 ●	Washington, Mo.	44	0
O18 ●	Purdue	29	5
O25 |	at Chicago	0	6
N1 ●	Indiana	47	0
N8 |	at Minnesota	5	17
N15 = |	at Ohio State	0	0
N22 ●	at Northwestern	17	0
N27 ●	Iowa	80	0

GEORGE WOODRUFF
1903 (.571)   8-6

1903   8-6-0 (1-5-0)
S19 ●	Englewood HS	45	5
S26 ●	Lombard	43	0
S30 ●	Osteopaths	36	0
O3 ●	Knox	29	5
O7 ●	Phys. & Surg.	40	0
O10 ●	Rush	64	0
O14 ●	Chicago Dental	54	0
O17 ●	at Purdue	24	0
O24 |	at Chicago	6	18
O31 |	Northwestern	11	12
N6 |	at Indiana	0	17
N14 |	Minnesota	0	32
N21 |	at Iowa	0	12
N26 |	at Nebraska	0	16

NO HEAD COACH

1904   9-2-1 (3-1-1)
S24 ●	North Central	10	0
S28 ●	Wabash	23	2
O1 ●	Knox	11	0
O5 ●	Phys. & Surg.	26	0
O8 ●	at Washington, Mo.	31	0
O15 ●	Indiana	10	0
O22 ●	at Purdue	24	6
O29 = |	at Chicago	6	6
N5 |	at Ohio State	46	0
N12 |	at Northwestern	6	12
N19 ●	Iowa	29	0
N24 |	at Nebraska	10	16

FRED LOWENTHAL
1905 (.556)   5-4

1905   5-4-0 (0-3-0)
S30 ●	Knox	6	0
O4 ●	Wabash	6	0
O7 ●	North Central	24	0
O14 ●	St. Louis	12	6
O21 |	Purdue	0	29
O28 ●	Phys. & Surg.	30	0
N4 |	Michigan	0	33
N18 |	at Chicago	0	44
N30 |	at Nebraska	6	24

JUSTA LINDGREN
1906 (.300)   1-3-1

1906   1-3-1 (1-3-0)
O13 =	Wabash	0	0
O27 |	at Michigan	9	28
N10 |	Wisconsin	6	16
N17 |	at Chicago	0	63
N25 ●	at Purdue	5	0

ARTHUR R. HALL
1907-12 (.713)   27-10-3

1907   3-2-0 (3-2-0)
O19 |	Chicago	6	42
O26 ●	at Wisconsin	15	4
N2 |	Purdue	21	4
N9 |	at Iowa	12	25
N22 |	at Indiana	10	6

1908   5-1-1 (4-1-0)
O3 ●	Monmouth	17	6
O10 ●	Marquette	6	6
O17 |	at Chicago	6	11
O31 |	Indiana	10	0
N7 |	Iowa	22	0
N14 |	at Purdue	15	6
N21 ●	Northwestern	64	8

1909   5-2-0 (3-1-0)
O2 ●	James Millikin	23	0
O9 ●	Kentucky	2	6
O16 |	at Chicago	8	14
O30 ● |	Purdue	24	6
N6 ●	Indiana	6	5
N13 ●	at Northwestern	35	0
N20 ●	at Syracuse	17	8

1910   7-0-0 (4-0-0)
O1 ●	James Millikin	13	0
O8 ●	Drake	29	0
O15 ●	Chicago	3	0
O29 ●	at Purdue	11	0
N5 ●	at Indiana	3	0
N12 ●	at Northwestern	27	0
N19 ●	Syracuse	3	0

1911   4-2-1 (2-2-1)
O7 ●	James Millikin	33	0
O14 ●	St. Louis	9	0
O21 |	at Chicago	0	24
N4 ●	Purdue	12	3
N11 =	at Indiana	0	0
N18 ●	Northwestern	27	13
N25 |	Minnesota	0	11

1912   3-3-1 (1-3-1)
O5 ●	Illinois Wesleyan	87	3
O12 ●	Washington, Mo.	13	0
O19 ●	Indiana	13	7
N2 |	at Minnesota	0	13
N9 = |	at Purdue	9	9
N16 |	Chicago	0	10
N23 |	at Northwestern	0	6

ROBERT C. ZUPPKE
1913-41 (.611)   131-81-13

1913   4-2-1 (2-2-1)
O4 ●	Kentucky	21	0
O11 ●	Missouri	24	7
O18 ●	Northwestern	37	0
O25 ●	at Indiana	10	0
N1 |	at Chicago	7	28
N15 = |	Purdue	0	0
N22 |	Minnesota	9	19

1914   7-0-0 (6-0-0)
O3 ●	Christian Brothers	37	0
O10 ●	Indiana	51	0
O17 ●	Ohio State	37	0
O24 ●	at Northwestern	33	0
O31 ●	at Minnesota	21	6
N14 ●	Chicago	21	7
N21 ●	at Wisconsin	24	9

1915   5-0-2 (3-0-2)
O2 ●	Haskell	36	0
O9 ●	Rolla Mines	75	7
O16 =	at Ohio State	3	3
O23 ●	Northwestern	36	6
N6 ●	Minnesota	6	6
N13 ●	Wisconsin	17	3
N20 ●	at Chicago	10	0

1916   3-3-1 (2-2-1)
O7 ●	Kansas	30	0
O14 ●	Colgate	3	15
O21 |	Ohio State	6	7
O28 |	at Purdue	14	7
N4 |	at Minnesota	14	9
N18 |	Chicago	7	20
N25 = |	at Wisconsin	0	0

1917   5-2-1 (2-2-1)
O6 ●	Kansas	22	0
O13 ●	Oklahoma	44	0
O20 ● |	Wisconsin	7	0
O27 |	Purdue	27	0
N3 |	at Chicago	0	0
N17 |	at Ohio State	0	13
N24 |	Minnesota	6	27
N29 ●	at Camp Funston	28	0

1918 — 5-2-0 (4-0-0)

Date		Opponent	Ill.	Opp.
O4	●	at Chanute Field	3	0
O12		Great Lakes NAS	0	7
O26		Municipal Pier	0	7
N2	● |	at Iowa	19	0
N9	● |	at Wisconsin	22	0
N16	● |	Ohio State	13	0
N23	● |	at Chicago	29	0

1919 — 6-1-0 (6-1-0)

Date		Opponent	Ill.	Opp.
O11	● |	at Purdue	14	7
O18	● |	Iowa	9	7
O25	|	Wisconsin	10	14
N1	● |	Chicago	10	0
N8	● |	at Minnesota	10	6
N15	● |	Michigan	29	7
N22	● |	at Ohio State	9	7

1920 — 5-2-0 (4-2-0)

Date		Opponent	Ill.	Opp.
O9	●	Drake	41	0
O16	● |	Iowa	20	3
O23	● |	at Michigan	7	6
O30	● |	Minnesota	17	7
N6	● |	at Chicago	3	0
N13	|	at Wisconsin	9	14
N20	|	Ohio State	0	7

1921 — 3-4-0 (1-4-0)

Date		Opponent	Ill.	Opp.
O8	●	South Dakota	52	0
O15	|	at Iowa	2	14
O22	|	Wisconsin	0	20
O29	|	Michigan	0	3
N5	●	DePauw	21	0
N12	|	Chicago	6	14
N19	● |	at Ohio State	7	0

1922 — 2-5-0 (2-4-0)

Date		Opponent	Ill.	Opp.
O14		Butler	7	10
O21	|	Iowa	7	8
O28	|	at Michigan	0	24
N4	● |	Northwestern	6	3
N11	● |	at Wisconsin	3	0
N18	|	at Chicago	0	9
N25	|	Ohio State	3	6

1923 — 8-0-0 (5-0-0)

Date		Opponent	Ill.	Opp.
O6	●	Nebraska	24	7
O13	●	Butler	21	7
O20	● |	at Iowa	9	6
O27	● |	Northwestern CHI	29	0
N3	● |	Chicago	7	0
N10	● |	Wisconsin	10	0
N17	●	Mississippi State	27	0
N24	● |	at Ohio State	9	0

1924 — 6-1-1 (3-1-1)

Date		Opponent	Ill.	Opp.
O4	●	at Nebraska	9	6
O11	●	Butler	40	10
O18	● |	Michigan	39	14
O25	●	DePauw	45	0
N1	● |	Iowa	36	0
N8	= |	at Chicago	21	21
N15	|	at Minnesota	7	20
N22	● |	Ohio State	7	0

1925 — 5-3-0 (2-2-0)

Date		Opponent	Ill.	Opp.
O3		Nebraska	0	14
O10	●	Butler	16	13
O17	|	at Iowa	10	12
O24	|	Michigan	0	3
O31	●	at Pennsylvania	24	2
N7	● |	Chicago	13	6
N14	●	Wabash	21	0
N21	● |	at Ohio State	14	9

1926 — 6-2-0 (2-2-0)

Date		Opponent	Ill.	Opp.
O2	●	Coe	27	0
O9	●	Butler	38	7
O16	● |	Iowa	13	6
O23	|	at Michigan	0	13
O30	●	Pennsylvania	3	0
N6	● |	at Chicago	7	0
N13	●	Wabash	27	13
N20	|	Ohio State	6	7

1927 — 7-0-1 (5-0-0)

Date		Opponent	Ill.	Opp.
O1	●	Bradley	19	0
O8	●	Butler	58	0
O15	=	Iowa State	12	12
O22	● |	at Northwestern	7	6
O29	● |	Michigan	14	0
N5	● |	at Iowa	14	0
N12	● |	Chicago	15	6
N19	● |	at Ohio State	13	0

1928 — 7-1-0 (4-1-0)

Date		Opponent	Ill.	Opp.
O6	●	Bradley	33	6
O13	●	Coe	31	0
O20	● |	Indiana	13	7
O27	● |	Northwestern	6	0
N3	|	at Michigan	0	3
N10	●	at Butler	14	0
N17	● |	at Chicago	40	0
N24	● |	Ohio State	8	0

1929 — 6-1-1 (3-1-1)

Date		Opponent	Ill.	Opp.
O5	●	Kansas	25	0
O12	●	Bradley	45	0
O20	= |	at Iowa	7	7
O26	● |	Michigan	14	0
N2	|	at Northwestern	0	7
N9	●	Army	17	7
N16	● |	Chicago	20	6
N23	● |	at Ohio State	27	0

1930 — 3-5-0 (1-4-0)

Date		Opponent	Ill.	Opp.
O4	●	Iowa State	7	0
O11	●	Butler	27	0
O18	|	Northwestern	0	32
O25	|	at Michigan	7	15
N1	|	Purdue	0	25
N8		Army BRNX	0	13
N15	● |	at Chicago	28	0
N22	|	Ohio State	9	12

1931 — 2-6-1 (0-6-1)

Date		Opponent	Ill.	Opp.
O3	●	St. Louis	20	6
O10	|	at Purdue	0	7
O17	●	Bradley	20	0
O24	|	Michigan	0	35
O31	|	at Northwestern	6	32
N7	|	Wisconsin	6	7
N14	|	Chicago	6	13
N21	|	at Ohio State	0	40
N26	= |	Indiana CHI	0	0

1932 — 5-4-0 (2-4-0)

Date		Opponent	Ill.	Opp.
O1	●	Miami (Ohio)	20	7
O1	●	Coe	13	0
O8	●	Bradley	20	0
O15	|	Northwestern	0	26
O22	|	at Michigan	0	32
O29	● |	at Chicago	13	7
N5	|	at Wisconsin	12	20
N12	● |	Indiana	18	6
N19	|	Ohio State	0	3

1933 — 5-3-0 (3-2-0)

Date		Opponent	Ill.	Opp.
S30	●	Drake	13	6
O7	●	at Washington, Mo.	21	6
O14	● |	Wisconsin	21	0
O21		Army CLEV	0	6
N4	|	Michigan	6	7
N11	● |	at Northwestern	3	0
N18	● |	Chicago	7	0
N25	|	at Ohio State	6	7

1934 — 7-1-0 (4-1-0)

Date		Opponent	Ill.	Opp.
S29	●	Bradley	40	7
O6	●	at Washington, Mo.	12	7
O13	● |	Ohio State	14	13
O27	● |	at Michigan	7	6
N3	●	Army	7	0
N10	● |	at Northwestern	14	3
N17	|	at Wisconsin	3	7
N24	● |	at Chicago	6	0

1935 — 3-5-0 (1-4-0)

Date		Opponent	Ill.	Opp.
S28		Ohio U.	0	6
O5	●	Washington, Mo.	28	6
O12	●	at USC	19	0
O26	|	Iowa	0	19
N2	|	at Northwestern	3	10
N9	● |	Michigan	3	0
N16	|	at Ohio State	0	6
N23	|	Chicago	6	7

1936 — 4-3-1 (2-2-1)

Date		Opponent	Ill.	Opp.
S26	●	DePaul	9	6
O3	●	Washington, Mo.	13	7
O10		USC	6	24
O17	= |	at Iowa	0	0
O24	|	Northwestern	2	13
O31	● |	at Michigan	9	6
N14	|	Ohio State	0	13
N21	● |	at Chicago	18	7

1937 — 3-3-2 (2-3-0)

Date		Opponent	Ill.	Opp.
S25	●	Ohio U.	20	6
O2	=	DePaul	0	0
O9	=	Notre Dame	0	0
O16	|	at Indiana	6	13
O30	|	Michigan	6	7
N6	● |	at Northwestern	6	0
N13	|	at Ohio State	0	19
N20	● |	Chicago	21	0

1938 — 3-5-0 (2-3-0)

Date		Opponent	Ill.	Opp.
S24		Ohio U.	0	6
O1	●	DePaul	44	7
O8	● |	Indiana	12	2
O15		at Notre Dame	6	14
O22	|	Northwestern	0	13
O29	|	at Michigan	0	14
N12	|	Ohio State	14	32
N19	● |	at Chicago	34	0

1939 — 3-4-1 (3-3-0)

Date		Opponent	Ill.	Opp.
S30	=	Bradley	0	0
O14		at USC	0	26
O21	|	Indiana	6	7
O28	|	at Northwestern	0	13
N4	● |	Michigan	16	7
N11	● |	Wisconsin	7	0
N18	|	at Ohio State	0	21
N25	● |	at Chicago	46	0

1940 — 1-7-0 (0-5-0)

Date		Opponent	Ill.	Opp.
O5	●	Bradley	31	0
O12		USC	7	13
O19	|	at Michigan	0	28
O26		Notre Dame	0	26
N2	|	at Wisconsin	6	13
N9	|	at Northwestern	14	32
N16	|	Ohio State	6	14
N23	|	at Iowa	7	18

1941 — 2-6-0 (0-5-0)

Date		Opponent	Ill.	Opp.
O4	●	Miami (Ohio)	45	0
O11	|	at Minnesota	6	34
O18	●	Drake	40	0
O25		at Notre Dame	14	49
N1	|	Michigan	0	20
N8	|	Iowa	0	21
N15	|	at Ohio State	7	12
N22	|	at Northwestern	0	27

RAY ELIOT
1942-59 (.530) 83-73-11

1942 — 6-4-0 (3-2-0)

Date		Opponent	Ill.	Opp.
S26	●	South Dakota	46	0
O3	●	Butler	67	0
O10	● |	Minnesota	20	13
O17	● |	at Iowa	12	7
O24		Notre Dame	14	21
O31	|	at Michigan	14	28
N7	● |	at Northwestern	14	7
N14	|	Ohio State CLEV	20	44
N21		Great Lakes NAS	0	6
N28	●	at Camp Grant	20	0

1943 — 3-7-0 (2-4-0)

Date		Opponent	Ill.	Opp.
S11		Camp Grant	0	23
S18		Iowa Pre-Flight	18	32
O2	|	at Purdue	21	40
O9	● |	at Wisconsin	25	7
O16	●	Pittsburgh	33	25
O23		at Notre Dame	0	47
O30	|	Michigan	6	42
N6	● |	at Iowa	19	10
N13	|	at Ohio State	26	29
N20	|	at Northwestern	6	53

1944 — 5-4-1 (3-3-0)

Date		Opponent	Ill.	Opp.
S16	●	Illinois St.	79	6
S23	● |	Indiana	26	18
S30	=	at Great Lakes NAS	26	26
O7	|	Purdue	19	35
O14	● |	Iowa	40	6
O21	●	at Pittsburgh	39	5
O28		Notre Dame	7	13
N11	|	at Michigan	0	14
N18	|	Ohio State CLEV	12	26
N25	● |	at Northwestern	25	6

1945 — 2-6-1 (1-4-1)

Date		Opponent	Ill.	Opp.
S22	●	Pittsburgh	23	6
S29		at Notre Dame	0	7
O6	|	Indiana	0	6
O20	= |	at Wisconsin	7	7
O27	|	Michigan	0	19
N3		Great Lakes NAS	6	12
N10	● |	Iowa	48	7
N17	|	at Ohio State	2	27
N24	|	at Northwestern	7	13

1946 — 8-2-0 (6-1-0)

Date		Opponent	Ill.	Opp.
S21	●	at Pittsburgh	33	7
S28		Notre Dame	6	26
O5	● |	Purdue	43	7
O12	|	at Indiana	7	14
O19	● |	Wisconsin	27	21
O26	● |	at Michigan	13	9
N2	● |	at Iowa	7	0
N16	● |	Ohio State	16	7
N23	● |	at Northwestern	20	0
		ROSE BOWL		
J1	●	UCLA	45	14

1947 — 5-3-1 (3-3-0)

Date		Opponent	Ill.	Opp.
S27	●	Pittsburgh	14	0
O4	● |	at Iowa	35	12
O11	=	Army BRNX	0	0
O18	● |	Minnesota	40	13
O25	|	at Purdue	7	14
N1	|	Michigan	7	14
N8	●	Western Michigan	60	14
N15	● |	at Ohio State	28	7
N22	|	Northwestern	13	28

1948 — 3-6-0 (2-5-0)

Date		Opponent	Ill.	Opp.
S25	●	Kansas State	40	0
O2	|	at Wisconsin	16	20
O9		Army	21	26
O16	|	at Minnesota	0	6
O23	● |	Purdue	10	6
O30	|	at Michigan	20	28
N6	● |	Iowa	14	0
N13	|	Ohio State	7	34
N20	|	at Northwestern	7	20

1949 — 3-4-2 (3-3-1)

Date		Opponent	Ill.	Opp.
S24	=	Iowa State	20	20
O1	= |	Wisconsin	13	13
O8	● |	at Iowa	20	14
O15		Missouri	20	27
O22	● |	at Purdue	19	0
O29	|	Michigan	0	13
N5	● |	Indiana	33	14
N12	|	at Ohio State	17	30
N19	|	Northwestern	7	9

1950 — 7-2-0 (4-2-0)

Date		Opponent	Ill.	Opp.
S30	●	Ohio U.	28	2
O7	|	Wisconsin	6	7
O13	●	at UCLA	14	6
O21	●	Washington	20	13
O28	● |	Indiana	20	0
N4	● |	at Michigan	7	0
N11	● |	at Iowa	21	7
N18	● |	Ohio State	14	7
N25	|	at Northwestern	7	14

1951 — 9-0-1 (5-0-1)

Date		Opponent	Ill.	Opp.
S29	●	UCLA	27	13
O6	● |	Wisconsin	14	10
O13	●	at Syracuse	41	20
O20	●	at Washington	27	20
O27	● |	at Indiana	21	0
N3	● |	Michigan	7	0
N10	● |	Iowa	40	13
N17	= |	at Ohio State	0	0
N24	● |	at Northwestern	3	0
		ROSE BOWL		
J1	●	Stanford	40	7

1952 — 4-5-0 (2-5-0)

Date		Opponent	Ill.	Opp.
S27	●	Iowa State	33	7
O4	|	at Wisconsin	6	20
O11	●	Washington	48	14
O18	|	at Minnesota	7	13
O25	|	Purdue	12	40
N1	● |	at Michigan	22	13
N8	● |	at Iowa	33	13
N15	|	Ohio State	7	27
N22	|	Northwestern	26	28

1953 — 7-1-1 (5-1-0)

Date		Opponent	Ill.	Opp.
S26	=	Nebraska	21	21
O3	●	Stanford	33	21
O10	● |	at Ohio State	41	20
O17	● |	Minnesota	27	7
O24	●	Syracuse	20	13
O31	● |	Purdue	21	0
N7	● |	Michigan	19	3
N14	|	at Wisconsin	7	34
N21	● |	at Northwestern	39	14

1954 1-8-0 (0-6-0)
S25 Penn State 12 14
O2 at Stanford 2 12
O9 | Ohio State 7 40
O16 | at Minnesota 6 19
O23 ● Syracuse 34 6
O30 | at Purdue 14 28
N6 | at Michigan 7 14
N13 | Wisconsin 14 27
N20 | Northwestern 7 20

1955 5-3-1 (3-3-1)
S24 ● at California 20 13
O1 ● Iowa State 40 0
O8 | at Ohio State 12 27
O15 ● | Minnesota 21 13
O22 | at Michigan State 7 21
O29 | Purdue 0 13
N5 ● | Michigan 25 6
N12 ● | at Wisconsin 17 14
N19 = | at Northwestern 7 7

1956 2-5-2 (1-4-2)
S29 ● California 32 20
O6 at Washington 13 28
O13 | Ohio State 6 26
O20 | at Minnesota 13 16
O27 ● | Michigan State 20 13
N3 = | at Purdue 7 7
N10 | at Michigan 7 17
N17 = | Wisconsin 13 13
N24 | at Northwestern 13 14

1957 4-5-0 (3-4-0)
S27 at UCLA 6 16
O5 ● Colgate 40 0
O12 | at Ohio State 7 21
O19 ● | Minnesota 34 13
O26 | at Michigan State 14 19
N2 | Purdue 6 21
N9 ● | Michigan 20 19
N16 | at Wisconsin 13 24
N23 ● | Northwestern 27 0

1958 4-5-0 (4-3-0)
S27 UCLA 14 18
O4 at Duke 13 15
O11 | Ohio State 13 19
O18 ● | at Minnesota 20 8
O25 ● | Michigan State 16 0
N1 | at Purdue 8 31
N8 ● | at Michigan 21 8
N15 | Wisconsin 12 31
N22 ● | Northwestern 27 20

1959 5-3-1 (4-2-1)
S26 | at Indiana 0 20
O3 ● Army 20 14
O10 ● | at Ohio State 9 0
O17 ● | Minnesota 14 6
O24 Penn State CLEV 9 20
O31 = | Purdue 7 7
N7 | Michigan 15 20
N14 ● | at Wisconsin 9 6
N21 ● | Northwestern 28 0

PETE ELLIOTT
1960-66 (.477) 31-34-1

1960 5-4-0 (3-4-0)
S24 ● | Indiana 17 6
O1 ● West Virginia 33 0
O8 | Ohio State 7 34
O15 | at Minnesota 10 21
O22 ● Penn State 10 8
O29 ● | at Purdue 14 12
N5 | at Michigan 7 8
N12 ● | Wisconsin 35 14
N19 | at Northwestern 7 14

1961 0-9-0 (0-7-0)
S30 Washington 7 20
O7 | Northwestern 7 28
O14 | at Ohio State 0 44
O21 | Minnesota 0 33
O28 at USC 10 14
N4 | Purdue 9 23
N11 | Michigan 6 38
N18 | at Wisconsin 7 55
N25 | at Michigan State 7 34

1962 2-7-0 (2-5-0)
S29 at Washington 7 28
O6 | at Northwestern 0 45
O13 | Ohio State 15 51
O20 | at Minnesota 0 17
O27 USC 16 28
N3 ● | at Purdue 14 10
N10 | at Michigan 10 14
N17 | Wisconsin 6 35
N24 ● | Michigan State 7 6

1963 8-1-1 (5-1-1)
S28 ● California 10 0
O5 ● | Northwestern 10 9
O12 = | at Ohio State 20 20
O19 ● | Minnesota 16 6
O25 ● at UCLA 18 12
N2 ● | Purdue 41 21
N9 | Michigan 8 14
N16 ● | at Wisconsin 17 7
N28 ● | at Michigan State 13 0
ROSE BOWL
J1 ● Washington 17 7

1964 6-3-0 (4-3-0)
S26 ● at California 20 14
O3 ● | at Northwestern 17 6
O10 | Ohio State 0 26
O17 ● | at Minnesota 14 0
O24 ● UCLA 26 7
O31 | at Purdue 14 26
N7 | at Michigan 6 21
N14 ● | Wisconsin 29 0
N21 ● | Michigan State 16 0

1965 6-4-0 (4-3-0)
S18 Oregon State 10 12
S25 ● SMU 42 0
O2 | at Michigan State 12 22
O9 | at Ohio State 14 28
O16 ● | Indiana 34 13
O23 ● Duke 28 14
O30 ● | Purdue 21 0
N6 | Michigan 3 23
N13 ● | at Wisconsin 51 0
N20 ● | at Northwestern 20 6

1966 4-6-0 (4-3-0)
S17 at SMU 7 26
S24 Missouri 14 21
O1 | Michigan State 10 26
O8 ● | Ohio State 10 9
O15 ● | at Indiana 24 10
O22 Stanford 3 6
O29 | at Purdue 21 25
N5 ● | at Michigan 28 21
N12 ● | Wisconsin 49 14
N19 | at Northwestern 7 35

JIM VALEK
1967-70 (.200) 8-32

1967 4-6-0 (3-4-0)
S23 at Florida 0 14
S30 ● Pittsburgh 34 6
O7 | Indiana 7 20
O14 | Minnesota 7 10
O21 Notre Dame 7 47
O28 ● | at Ohio State 17 13
N4 | Purdue 9 42
N11 | Michigan 14 21
N18 ● | at Northwestern 27 21
N25 ● | at Iowa 21 19

1968 1-9-0 (1-6-0)
S21 Kansas 7 47
S28 Missouri 0 44
O5 | at Indiana 14 28
O12 | at Minnesota 10 17
O19 at Notre Dame 8 58
O26 | Ohio State 24 31
N2 | at Purdue 17 35
N9 | at Michigan 0 36
N16 ● | Northwestern 14 0
N23 | Iowa 13 37

1969 0-10-0 (0-7-0)
S20 Washington State 18 19
S27 Missouri STL 6 37
O4 at Iowa State 20 48
O11 | Northwestern 6 10
O18 | at Indiana 20 41
O25 | at Ohio State 0 41
N1 | Purdue 22 49
N8 | Michigan 0 57
N15 | at Wisconsin 14 55
N22 | Iowa 0 40

1970 3-7-0 (1-6-0)
S19 ● Oregon 20 16
S26 Tulane 9 23
O3 ● Syracuse 27 0
O10 | at Northwestern 0 48
O17 | Indiana 24 30
O24 | Ohio State 29 48
O31 ● | at Purdue 23 21
N7 | at Michigan 0 42
N14 | Wisconsin 17 29
N21 | at Iowa 16 22

BOB BLACKMAN
1971-76 (.447) 29-36-1

1971 5-6-0 (5-3-0)
S11 | at Michigan State 0 10
S18 North Carolina 0 27
S25 at USC 0 28
O2 Washington 14 52
O9 | Ohio State 10 24
O16 | at Michigan 6 35
O23 ● | Purdue 21 7
O30 ● | Northwestern 24 7
N6 ● | at Indiana 22 21
N13 ● | at Wisconsin 35 27
N20 ● | Iowa 31 0

1972 3-8-0 (3-5-0)
S16 | Michigan State 0 24
S23 USC 20 55
S30 at Washington 11 31
O7 Penn State 17 35
O14 | at Ohio State 7 26
O21 | Michigan 7 31
O28 | at Purdue 14 20
N4 ● | at Northwestern 43 13
N11 ● | Indiana 37 20
N18 ● | Wisconsin 27 7
N25 | at Iowa 14 15

1973 5-6-0 (4-4-0)
S15 ● | at Indiana 28 14
S22 ● at California 27 7
S29 West Virginia 10 17
O6 Stanford 0 24
O13 ● | Purdue 15 13
O20 ● | at Michigan State 6 3
O27 ● | Iowa 50 0
N3 | Ohio State 0 30
N10 | at Michigan 6 21
N17 | Minnesota 16 19
N24 | at Northwestern 6 9

1974 6-4-1 (4-3-1)
S14 ● | Indiana 16 0
S21 ● at Stanford 41 7
S28 ● Washington State 21 19
O5 California 14 31
O12 ● | at Purdue 27 23
O19 = | Michigan State 21 21
O26 | at Iowa 12 14
N2 | at Ohio State 7 49
N9 | Michigan 6 14
N16 ● | at Minnesota 17 14
N23 ● | Northwestern 28 14

1975 5-6-0 (4-4-0)
S13 ● | at Iowa 27 12
S20 Missouri 20 30
S27 at Texas A&M 13 43
O4 ● Washington State 27 21
O11 ● | Minnesota 42 23
O18 | Purdue 24 26
O25 ● | at Michigan State 21 19
N1 | at Wisconsin 9 18
N8 | Ohio State 3 40
N15 | Michigan 15 21
N22 ● | at Northwestern 28 7

1976 5-6-0 (4-4-0)
S11 ● | Iowa 24 6
S18 ● at Missouri 31 6
S25 Baylor 19 34
O2 Texas A&M 7 14
O9 | at Minnesota 14 29
O16 ● | at Purdue 21 17
O23 | Michigan State 23 31
O30 ● | Wisconsin 31 25
N6 | at Ohio State 10 42
N13 | at Michigan 7 38
N20 ● | Northwestern 48 6

GARY MOELLER
1977-79 (.277) 6-24-3

1977 3-8-0 (2-6-0)
S10 | Michigan 9 37
S17 ● Missouri 11 7
S24 at Stanford 24 37
O1 Syracuse 20 30
O8 | at Wisconsin 0 26
O15 ● | at Purdue 29 22
O22 ● | Indiana 21 7
O29 | at Michigan State 20 49
N5 | Ohio State 0 35
N12 | Minnesota 0 21
N19 | at Northwestern 7 21

1978 1-8-2 (0-6-2)
S9 = | Northwestern 0 0
S16 | at Michigan 0 31
S23 Stanford 10 35
S30 ● at Syracuse 28 14
O7 at Missouri 3 45
O14 = | Wisconsin 20 20
O21 | Purdue 0 13
O28 | at Indiana 10 31
N4 | Michigan State 19 59
N11 | at Ohio State 7 45
N18 | at Minnesota 6 24

1979 2-8-1 (1-6-1)
S8 | at Michigan State 16 33
S15 Missouri 6 14
S22 ● at Air Force 27 19
S29 Navy 12 13
O6 | Iowa 7 13
O13 | at Purdue 14 28
O20 | Michigan 7 27
O27 = | at Minnesota 17 17
N3 | Ohio State 7 44
N10 | Indiana 14 45
N17 ● | at Northwestern 29 13

MIKE WHITE
1980-87 (.533) 47-41-3

1980 3-7-1 (3-5-0)
S6 ● | Northwestern 35 9
S13 ● | Michigan State 20 17
S20 at Missouri 7 52
S27 = Air Force 20 20
O4 Mississippi State 21 28
O11 ● | at Iowa 20 14
O18 | Purdue 20 45
O25 | at Michigan 14 45
N1 | Minnesota 18 21
N8 | at Ohio State 42 49
N15 | at Indiana 24 26

1981 7-4-0 (6-3-0)
S5 at Pittsburgh 6 26
S12 ● | at Michigan State 27 17
S19 ● Syracuse 17 14
O3 ● | Minnesota 38 29
O10 | at Purdue 20 44
O17 | at Ohio State 27 34
O24 ● | Wisconsin 23 21
O31 ● | Iowa 24 7
N7 | at Michigan 21 70
N14 ● | Indiana 35 14
N21 ● | at Northwestern 49 12

1982 7-5-0 (6-3-0)
S4 ● | Northwestern 49 13
S11 ● | Michigan State 23 16
S18 ● at Syracuse 47 10
S25 Pittsburgh 3 20
O2 ● | at Minnesota 42 24
O9 ● | Purdue 38 34
O16 | Ohio State 21 26
O23 ● | at Wisconsin 29 28
O30 | at Iowa 13 14
N6 | Michigan 10 16
N13 ● | at Indiana 48 7
LIBERTY BOWL
D29 Alabama 15 21

1983 10-2-0 (9-0-0)
S10 at Missouri 18 28
S17 ● Stanford 17 7
S24 ● | at Michigan State 20 10
O1 ● | Iowa 33 0
O8 ● | at Wisconsin 27 15
O15 ● | Ohio State 17 13
O22 ● | at Purdue 35 21
O29 ● | Michigan 16 6
N5 ● | at Minnesota 50 23
N12 ● | Indiana 49 21
N19 ● | at Northwestern 56 24
ROSE BOWL
J2 UCLA 9 45

1984 7-4-0 (6-3-0)
S1 ● | Northwestern 24 16
S8 ● Missouri 30 24
S15 at Stanford 19 34
S22 ● | Michigan State 40 7
S29 | at Iowa 16 21
O6 ● | Wisconsin 22 6
O13 | at Ohio State 38 45
O20 ● | Purdue 34 20
O27 | at Michigan 18 26
N3 ● | Minnesota 48 3
N10 ● | Indiana IND 34 7

BIG TEN TEAMS

1985 — 6-5-1 (5-2-1)

Date		Opponent		
S7		USC	10	20
S14	•	So. Illinois	28	25
S21		at Nebraska	25	52
O5	•	Ohio State	31	28
O12		at Purdue	24	30
O19	•	at Michigan State	30	17
O26	•	Wisconsin	38	25
N2	=	Michigan	3	3
N9		at Iowa	0	59
N16	•	Indiana	41	24
N23	•	at Northwestern	45	20
PEACH BOWL				
D31		Army	29	31

1986 — 4-7-0 (3-5-0)

Date		Opponent		
S6	•	Louisville	23	0
S13		at USC	16	31
S20		Nebraska	14	59
O4		at Ohio State	0	14
O11	•	Purdue	34	27
O18		Michigan State	21	29
O25		at Wisconsin	9	15
N1		at Michigan	13	69
N8	•	Iowa	20	16
N15	•	at Indiana	21	16
N22		Northwestern	18	23

1987 — 3-7-1 (2-5-1)

Date		Opponent		
S5		at North Carolina	14	34
S12		Arizona State	7	21
S19	•	East Carolina	20	10
O3		Ohio State	6	10
O10		at Purdue	3	9
O17	•	Wisconsin	16	14
O24	=	at Michigan State	14	14
O31	•	Minnesota	27	17
N7		at Indiana	22	34
N14		Michigan	14	17
N21		at Northwestern	10	28

JOHN MACKOVIC — 1988-91 (.649) — 30-16-1

1988 — 6-5-1 (5-2-1)

Date		Opponent		
S3		Washington State	7	44
S10		at Arizona State	16	21
S17	•	Utah	35	24
O1	•	at Ohio State	31	12
O8	•	Purdue	20	0
O15	•	at Wisconsin	34	6
O22	•	Michigan State	21	28
O29	=	at Minnesota	27	27
N5	•	Indiana	21	20
N12	•	at Michigan	9	38
N19	•	Northwestern	14	9
ALL-AMERICAN BOWL				
D29		Florida	10	14

1989 — 10-2-0 (7-1-0)

Date		Opponent		
S4	•	at USC	14	13
S16	•	at Colorado	7	38
S23	•	Utah State	41	2
O7	•	Ohio State	34	14
O14	•	at Purdue	14	2
O21	•	at Michigan State	14	10
O28	•	Wisconsin	32	9
N4	•	at Iowa	31	7
N11	•	Michigan	10	24
N18	•	Indiana	41	28
N25	•	at Northwestern	63	14
CITRUS BOWL				
J1	•	Virginia	31	21

1990 — 8-4-0 (6-2-0)

Date		Opponent		
S8		at Arizona	16	28
S15	•	Colorado	23	22
S22	•	So. Illinois	56	21
O6	•	at Ohio State	31	20
O13	•	Purdue	34	0
O20	•	Michigan State	15	13
O27	•	at Wisconsin	21	3
N3		Iowa	28	54
N10		at Michigan	17	22
N17	•	at Indiana	24	10
N24	•	Northwestern	28	23
HALL OF FAME BOWL				
J1		Clemson	0	30

1991 — 6-6-0 (4-4-0)

Date		Opponent		
A31		East Carolina	38	31
S14		at Missouri	19	23
S21	•	Houston	51	10
O5	•	Minnesota	24	3
O12	•	Ohio State	10	7
O19		at Iowa	21	24
O26		at Northwestern	11	17
N2	•	Wisconsin	22	6
N9	•	at Purdue	41	14
N16		Michigan	0	20
N23		at Michigan State	24	27
SUN BOWL				
D31		UCLA	3	6

LOU TEPPER — 1991-96 (.448) — 25-31-2

1992 — 6-5-1 (4-3-1)

Date		Opponent		
S5	•	Northern Illinois	30	14
S12	•	Missouri	24	17
S19		at Houston	13	31
O3		at Minnesota	17	18
O10	•	at Ohio State	18	16
O17		Iowa	14	24
O24		Northwestern	26	27
O31	•	at Wisconsin	13	12
N7	•	Purdue	20	17
N14	=	at Michigan	22	22
N21	•	Michigan State	14	10
HOLIDAY BOWL				
D30		Hawaii	17	27

1993 — 5-6-0 (5-3-0)

Date		Opponent		
S11		at Missouri	3	31
S18		Arizona	14	16
S25		Oregon	7	13
O2	•	at Purdue	28	10
O9		Ohio State	12	20
O16	•	at Iowa	49	3
O23	•	at Michigan	24	21
O30	•	Northwestern	20	13
N6	•	Minnesota	23	20
N13		at Penn State	14	28
N20		Wisconsin	10	35

1994 — 7-5-0 (4-4-0)

Date		Opponent		
S1		Washington State *CHI*	9	10
S10	•	Missouri	42	0
S17	•	Northern Illinois	34	10
O1		Purdue	16	22
O8	•	at Ohio State	24	10
O15	•	Iowa	47	7
O22		Michigan	14	19
O29	•	at Northwestern	28	7
N5	•	at Minnesota	21	17
N12		Penn State	31	35
N19		at Wisconsin	13	19
LIBERTY BOWL				
D31	•	East Carolina	30	0

1995 — 5-5-1 (3-4-1)

Date		Opponent		
S2		Michigan	14	38
S9		at Oregon	31	34
S16	•	Arizona	9	7
S23	•	East Carolina	7	0
O7	•	at Indiana	17	10
O14		Michigan State	21	27
O28	•	Northwestern	14	17
N4	•	at Iowa	26	7
N11	•	at Ohio State	3	41
N18	•	Minnesota	48	14
N25	=	at Wisconsin	3	3

1996 — 2-9 (1-7)

Date		Opponent		
A31		at Michigan	8	20
S7		USC	3	55
S14		at Arizona	0	41
S21	•	Akron	38	7
O5	•	Indiana	46	43
O12		at Michigan State	14	42
O26		at Northwestern	24	27
N2		Iowa	21	31
N9		Ohio State	0	48
N16		at Minnesota	21	23
N23		Wisconsin	15	35

RON TURNER — 1997-2004 (.380) — 35-57

1997 — 0-11 (0-8)

Date		Opponent		
S6		Southern Miss	7	24
S13		at Louisville	14	26
S20		Washington State	22	35
S27		at Iowa	10	38
O4		Penn State	6	41
O11		at Wisconsin	7	31
O25		Purdue	3	48
N1		at Indiana	6	23
N8		Northwestern	21	34
N15		at Ohio State	6	41
N22		Michigan State	17	27

1998 — 3-8 (2-6)

Date		Opponent		
S5		at Washington State	13	20
S12	•	Middle Tennessee	48	20
S19		Louisville	9	35
S26		Iowa	14	37
O3	•	at Northwestern	13	10
O10		Ohio State	0	41
O17		Wisconsin	3	37
O24		at Purdue	9	42
O31		at Penn State	0	27
N7	•	Indiana	31	16
N21		at Michigan State	9	41

1999 — 8-4 (4-4)

Date		Opponent		
S4	•	Arkansas State	41	3
S11	•	San Diego State	38	10
S18	•	at Louisville	41	36
S25		Michigan State	10	27
O2		at Indiana	31	34
O16		Minnesota	7	37
O23	•	at Michigan	35	29
O30		Penn State	7	35
N6	•	at Iowa	40	24
N13	•	at Ohio State	46	20
N20	•	Northwestern	29	7
MICRON PC BOWL				
D30	•	Virginia	63	21

2000 — 5-6 (2-6)

Date		Opponent		
S2	•	Middle Tennessee	35	6
S9	•	at San Diego State	49	13
S16		California	17	15
S30		at Minnesota	10	44
O14	•	Iowa	31	0
O21		at Penn State	25	39
O28		at Michigan State	10	14
N4	•	Indiana	42	35
N11		Ohio State	21	24
N18		at Northwestern	23	61

2001 — 10-2 (7-1)

Date		Opponent		
S1	•	at California	44	17
S8	•	Northern Illinois	17	12
S22		Louisville	34	10
S29		at Michigan	20	45
O6		Minnesota	25	14
O13		at Indiana	35	14
O20		Wisconsin	42	35
N3		at Purdue	38	13
N10		Penn State	33	28
N17		at Ohio State	34	22
N24	•	Northwestern	34	28
SUGAR BOWL				
J1		LSU	34	47

2002 — 5-7 (4-4)

Date		Opponent		
A31		Missouri *StL*	20	33
S7		at Southern Miss	20	23
S14	•	Arkansas State	59	7
S21		San Jose State	35	38
S28		Michigan	28	45
O3		at Minnesota	10	31
O12	•	Purdue	38	31
O26		Indiana	45	14
N2		at Penn State	7	18
N9	•	at Wisconsin	37	20
N16		Ohio State	16	23
N23	•	at Northwestern	31	24

2003 — 1-11 (0-8)

Date		Opponent		
A30		Missouri *StL*	15	22
S6	•	Illinois St.	49	22
S13		at UCLA	3	6
S20		California	24	31
S27		Wisconsin	20	38
O4		at Purdue	10	43
O11		Michigan State	14	49
O18		at Michigan	14	56
O25		Minnesota	10	36
N1		at Iowa	10	41
N8		at Indiana	14	17
N22		Northwestern	20	37

2004 — 3-8 (1-7)

Date		Opponent		
S4	•	Florida A&M	52	13
S11		UCLA	17	35
S18	•	Western Michigan	30	27
S25		Purdue	30	38
O2		at Wisconsin	7	24
O9		at Michigan State	25	38
O16		Michigan	19	30
O23		at Minnesota	0	45
O30		Iowa	13	23
N6	•	Indiana	26	22
N20		at Northwestern	21	28

RON ZOOK — 2005-Present (.174) — 4-19

2005 — 2-9 (0-8)

Date		Opponent		
S3	•	Rutgers	33	30
S10	•	San Jose State	40	19
S17		at California	20	35
S24		Michigan State	14	61
O1		at Iowa	7	35
O8		at Indiana	13	36
O22		Penn State	10	63
O29		Wisconsin	24	41
N5		at Ohio State	2	40
N12		at Purdue	3	37
N19		Northwestern	21	38

2006 — 2-10 (1-7)

Date		Opponent		
S2	•	Eastern Illinois	42	17
S9		Rutgers	0	33
S16		Syracuse	21	31
S23		Iowa	7	24
S30	•	Michigan State	23	20
O7		Indiana	32	34
O14		Ohio U.	17	20
O21		Penn State	12	26
O28		Wisconsin	24	30
N4		Ohio State	10	17
N11		Purdue	31	42
N18		Northwestern	16	27

Neutral Site key: *Clev* Cleveland, Ohio / *Brnx* Bronx, N.Y. / *Oma* Omaha, Neb. / *StL* St. Louis, Mo. / *Chi* Chicago, Ill. / *Peo* Peoria, Ill. / *Det* Detroit, Mich. / *Mil* Milwaukee, Wisc. / *RI* Rock Island, Ill. / *Ind* Indianapolis, Ind.

ƒ Forfeit   † Game Later Forfeited   # Disputed Victor   * Disputed Score || Designated Conference Game   2 Counted Twice in Conference Standings

ILLINOIS RECORD BOOK

SINGLE-GAME RECORDS

RUSHING YARDS

RANK	PLAYER	DATE	OPPONENT	ATT	AVG	YDS
1	Robert Holcombe	Nov. 16, 1996	Minnesota	43	7.3	315
2	Howard Griffith	Nov. 24, 1990	Northwestern	37	7.1	263
3	Jim Grabowski	Nov. 14, 1964	Wisconsin	33	7.2	239
4	Red Grange	Oct. 31, 1925	Pennsylvania	36	6.6	237
5	Rocky Harvey	Sept. 12, 1998	Middle Tennessee	24	9.0	215

PASSING YARDS

RANK	PLAYER	DATE	OPPONENT	ATT	COMP	YDS
1	Dave Wilson	Nov. 8, 1980	Ohio State	69	43	621
2	Tony Eason	Oct. 23, 1982	Wisconsin	51	37	479
3	Jason Verduzco	Sept. 14, 1991	Missouri	58	31	431
4	Jon Beutjer	Sept. 20, 2003	California	57	35	430
5	Jon Beutjer	Sept. 21, 2002	San Jose State	38	28	426

RECEIVING YARDS

RANK	PLAYER	DATE	OPPONENT	REC	AVG	YDS
1	David Williams	Sept. 1, 1984	Northwestern	11	18.9	208
2	Mike Sherrod	Nov. 15, 1980	Indiana	8	23.8	191
3	David Williams	Nov. 5, 1983	Minnesota	11	17.1	188
	Rex Smith	Nov. 8, 1952	Iowa	11	17.1	188
5	Walter Young	Jan. 1, 2002	LSU	6	29.7	178
	Brandon Lloyd	Sept. 1, 2001	California	8	22.2	178

POINTS

RANK	PLAYER	DATE	OPPONENT	TOT
1	Howard Griffith	Sept. 22, 1990	Southern Illinois	48
2	Red Grange	Oct. 18, 1924	Michigan	30
3	Antoineo Harris	Oct. 26, 2002	Indiana	24
	Lonnie Perrin	Nov. 22, 1976	Northwestern	24
	Mickey Bates	Oct. 10, 1953	Ohio State	24

FIELD GOALS

RANK	PLAYER	DATE	OPPONENT	TOT
1	Dan Beaver	Oct. 13, 1973	Purdue	5
	Mike Bass	Oct. 23, 1982	Wisconsin	5
	Chris White	Oct. 6, 1984	Wisconsin	5
	Doug Higgins	Oct. 20, 1990	Michigan State	5

TACKLES

RANK	PLAYER	DATE	OPPONENT	TOT
1	John Sullivan	Nov. 12, 1977	Minnesota	34
2	John Sullivan	Oct. 1, 1977	Syracuse	27
3	Bill Burrell	Oct. 31, 1959	Purdue	26
4	John Sullivan	Nov. 5, 1977	Ohio State	25
5	Dana Howard	Oct. 12, 1991	Ohio State	24

INTERCEPTIONS

RANK	PLAYER	DATE	OPPONENT	TOT
1	Mike Gow	Sept. 21, 1974	Stanford	4
2	Eugene Wilson	Nov. 10, 2001	Penn State	3
	Duane Lyle	Sept. 23, 1995	East Carolina	3
	Mike Gow	Nov. 17, 1973	Minnesota	3
	Phil Knell	Oct. 29, 1966	Purdue	3

RETIRED NUMBERS

50 Dick Butkus

77 Red Grange

SINGLE-SEASON RECORDS

RUSHING YARDS

RANK	PLAYER	SEASON	G	ATT	YDS
1	Antoineo Harris	2002	12	278	1,330
2	Robert Holcombe	1996	11	260	1,281
3	Jim Grabowski	1965	10	252	1,258
4	J.C. Caroline	1953	9	194	1,256
5	Robert Holcombe	1997	11	294	1,253

PASSING YARDS

RANK	PLAYER	SEASON	G	ATT	COMP	PCT	YDS
1	Tony Eason	1982	12	505	313	62.0	3,671
2	Tony Eason	1981	11	406	248	61.1	3,360
3	Jack Trudeau	1985	12	501	322	64.3	3,339
4	Kurt Kittner	2001	12	409	22	54.0	3,256
5	Dave Wilson	1980	10	463	245	52.9	3,154

RECEIVING YARDS

RANK	PLAYER	SEASON	G	REC	AVG	YDS
1	David Williams	1984	11	101	12.7	1,278
2	David Williams	1985	12	92	12.6	1,156
3	Mike Martin	1982	12	77	13.9	1,068
4	Brandon Lloyd	2001	12	65	16.3	1,062
5	Brandon Lloyd	2002	12	65	15.6	1,010

SCORING

RANK	PLAYER	SEASON	TD	FG	PAT	P2	TOT
1	Neil Rackers	1999	1	20	44	0	110
2	Mike Bass	1982	0	24	32	0	104
3	Chris White	1984	0	24	31	0	103
4	Howard Griffith	1990	15	0	0	0	90
5	Chris White	1983	0	14	39	0	81

TOUCHDOWNS

RANK	PLAYER	SEASON	G	TOT
1	Howard Griffith	1990	12	15
2	Red Grange	1924	6	13
	Buddy Young	1944	10	13
	John Karras	1951	10	13
	Robert Holcombe	1996	11	13

TACKLES

RANK	PLAYER	SEASON	G	TOT
1	John Sullivan	1977	11	202
2	Scott Studwell	1976	11	177
3	Darrick Brownlow	1988	12	166
4	Darrick Brownlow	1990	12	161
5	John Gillen	1978	11	155

INTERCEPTIONS

RANK	PLAYER	SEASON	G	YDS	TOT
1	Al Brosky	1951	10	197	11
	Al Brosky	1950	NA	96	11
3	Mike Gow	1973	11	142	10
4	George Donnelly	1964	9	54	8
	Al Brosky	1952	8	77	8

PUNTING

RANK	PLAYER	SEASON	PUNTS	YDS	AVG
1	Steve Weatherford	2004	57	2,589	45.4
2	Steve Weatherford	2003	46	2,045	44.5
3	Dike Eddleman	1948	59	2,535	43.0
4	Steve Weatherford	2005	67	2,856	42.6
5	Steve Fitts	1999	65	2,749	42.1

PUNT RETURNS

RANK	PLAYER	SEASON	RET	YDS	AVG
1	Gary Windy	1970	17	252	14.8
2	Red Grange	1923	15	212	14.1
3	Gary Voelker	1992	18	219	12.2

KICKOFF RETURNS

RANK	PLAYER	SEASON	RET	YDS	AVG
1	Darryl Usher	1987	15	445	29.7
2	Mike Bellamy	1989	16	459	28.7
3	Pierre Thomas	2004	25	677	27.1
4	Keith Jones	1986	15	398	26.5
5	Marshall Starks	1960	NA	NA	26.3

BIG TEN TEAMS

CAREER RECORDS

RUSHING YARDS

RANK	PLAYER	SEASONS	ATT	AVG	TD	YDS
1	Robert Holcombe	1994-97	943	4.4	25	4,105
2	Antoineo Harris	1999-2002	676	4.4	22	2,985
3	Thomas Rooks	1982-85	560	5.2	25	2,887
4	Jim Grabowski	1963-65	579	5.0	24	2,878
5	Rocky Harvey	1998-2001	545	5.0	20	2,711
6	Pierre Thomas	2003-06	453	5.6	20	2,545
7	Howard Griffith	1988-90	479	5.2	31	2,485
8	Keith Jones	1985-88	482	4.6	15	2,194
9	John Karras	1949-51	416	5.1	24	2,135
10	Chubby Phillips	1973-76	480	4.4	24	2,103

PASSING YARDS

RANK	PLAYER	SEASONS	ATT	COMP	PCT	INT	TD	YDS
1	Jack Trudeau	1981-85	1,245	797	64.0	43	55	8,725
2	Kurt Kittner	1998-2001	1,264	682	54.0	34	70	8,722
3	Jason Verduzco	1989-92	1,083	678	62.9	35	42	7,532
4	Tony Eason	1981-82	911	561	61.6	33	38	7,031
5	Johnny Johnson	1993-95	819	432	52.7	23	35	5,293
6	Jon Beutjer	2002-04	772	462	59.8	24	39	5,190
7	Jeff George	1988-89	789	474	60.1	22	31	5,189
8	Scott Weaver	1993-96	565	306	54.2	29	15	3,212
9	Dave Wilson	1980	463	245	52.9	15	19	3,154
10	Mike Wells	1970-72	507	231	45.6	15	19	2,750

RECEIVING YARDS

RANK	PLAYER	SEASONS	REC	AVG	TD	YDS
1	David Williams	1983-85	262	12.9	24	3,392
2	Brandon Lloyd	1999-2002	160	16.1	21	2,583
3	Walter Young	1999-2002	147	16.2	15	2,382
4	Mike Martin	1979-82	143	16.1	15	2,300
5	John Wright, Sr.	1965-67	159	14.4	12	2,284
6	Jason Dulick	1993-96	169	11.9	15	2,004
7	Shawn Wax	1987-90	101	16.0	12	1,614
8	Greg Lewis	1999-2002	103	14.1	12	1,456
9	Mike Bellamy	1988-89	90	16.1	10	1,453
10	Oliver Williams	1981-82	73	19.4	12	1,417

SCORING

RANK	PLAYER	SEASONS	TD	FG	PAT	P2	TOT
1	Chris White	1983-85	0	53	103	0	262
2	Chris Richardson	1991-94	0	52	103	0	259
3	Doug Higgins	1987-90	0	39	116	0	230
4	Mike Bass	1980-82	0	41	89	0	212

TOUCHDOWNS

RANK	PLAYER	SEASONS	G	TOT
1	Howard Griffith	1987-90	36	33
2	Red Grange	1923-25	21	31
3	Ty Douthard	1993-96	43	29
4	Robert Holcombe	1994-97	43	28
5	Thomas Rooks	1982-85	47	25

TACKLES

RANK	PLAYER	SEASONS	G	TOT
1	Dana Howard	1991-94	46	595
2	John Sullivan	1974-78	46	501
3	Darrick Brownlow	1987-90	47	483
4	John Gillen	1977-80	41	441
5	John Holecek	1991-94	38	436

INTERCEPTIONS

RANK	PLAYER	SEASONS	G	YDS	TOT
1	Al Brosky	1950-52	NA	356	30
2	Mike Gow	1972-74	53	284	19
3	Craig Soope	1982-85	31	272	13
	Mike Heaven	1981-84	46	106	13
	George Donnelly	1962-64	26	142	13

PUNTING

RANK	PLAYER	SEASONS	PUNTS	YDS	AVG
1	Steve Weatherford	2002-05	193	8,402	43.5
2	Steve Fitts	1998-2001	256	10,671	41.7
3	Ryan Tabloff	1996-97	84	3,437	40.9
4	Bill Brown	1958-60	33	1,313	40.3
5	J.C. Caroline	1953-54	26	1,030	39.7

PUNT RETURNS

RANK	PLAYER	SEASON	RET	YDS	AVG
1	Dike Eddleman	1946-48	18	387	21.5
2	Gary Windy	1970	17	252	14.8
3	Mike Gow	1972-74	62	650	10.5
4	Red Grange	1923-25	48	486	10.1
5	Eugene Wilson	1999-2002	93	896	9.6

KICKOFF RETURNS

RANK	PLAYER	SEASON	RET	YDS	AVG
1	Red Grange	1923-25	15	453	30.2
2	Mike Bellamy	1988-89	18	475	26.4
3	Pierre Thomas	2003	52	1,272	24.5
4	Bruce Beaman	1972-74	30	689	23.0
5	Ray Wilson	1983-86	22	503	22.9

TEAM RECORDS

LONGEST WINNING STREAK
- 13, Oct. 30, 1909-Oct. 14, 1911
Streak broken at Chicago, 0-24, Oct. 21, 1911
- 13, Oct. 6, 1923-Nov. 1, 1924
Streak broken at Chicago, 21-21, Nov. 8, 1924

LONGEST UNDEFEATED STREAK
- 15, Oct. 3, 1914-Oct. 7, 1916
Streak broken vs. Colgate, 3-15, Oct. 14, 1916

MOST CONSECUTIVE WINNING SEASONS
- 7 (twice), 1891-1897 and 1923-1929

MOST CONSECUTIVE BOWL APPEARANCES
- 5, 1988-1992

MOST POINTS IN A GAME
- 87, vs. Illinois Wesleyan, Oct. 5, 1912

MOST POINTS ALLOWED IN A GAME
- 70, vs. Michigan, Nov. 7, 1981

LARGEST MARGIN OF VICTORY
- 84 (87-3), vs. Illinois Wesleyan, Oct. 5, 1912

LARGEST MARGIN OF DEFEAT
- 58 (0-58), vs. Iowa, Nov. 30, 1899

LONGEST RUN FROM SCRIMMAGE
- 93 yards, Buddy Young, vs. Great Lakes, Sept. 30, 1944

LONGEST PASS PLAY
- 90 yards, Mike Taliaferro to Mike Yavorski, vs. Ohio State, Oct. 30, 1962

LONGEST FIELD GOAL
- 57 yards, Dan Beaver, vs. Purdue, Oct. 18, 1975

LONGEST PUNT
- 88 yards, Dike Eddleman, vs. Iowa, Nov. 6, 1948

LONGEST PUNT RETURN
- 92 yards, Dike Eddleman, vs. Western Michigan, Nov. 8, 1947

LONGEST INTERCEPTION RETURN
- 98 yards, by three players:
Julius Rykovich, vs. Ohio State, Nov. 16, 1946
Bruce Sullivan, vs. Michigan, Nov. 5, 1966
Willie Osley, vs. Washington, Oct. 2, 1971

ILLINOIS ANNUAL STATISTICAL LEADERS

YR	RUSHING	YDS	ATT	AVG	PASSING	ATT	CMP	PCT	YDS	RECEIVING	REC	YDS	AVG
1946	Buddy Young	456	NA	NA	Perry Moss	NA	23	NA	298	Bill Heiss	5	132	26.4
1947	Ruck Steger	447	125	3.6	Perry Moss	127	71	.56	719	Sam Zatkoff	13	147	11.3
1948	Ruck Steger	265	68	3.9	Bernie Krueger	106	52	.49	703	Walt Kersulis	22	329	15.0
1949	John Karras	826	127	6.5	Bernie Krueger	90	42	.47	477	Ronnie Clark	11	105	9.5
1950	Dick Raklovits	709	133	5.3	Fred Major	65	32	.49	464	Tony Klimek	13	200	15.4
1951	John Karras	716	159	4.5	Tom O'Connell	120	62	.52	692	Rex Smith	22	343	15.6
1952	Pete Bachouros	484	95	5.1	Tom O'Connell	224	133	.59	1,761	Rocky Ryan	45	714	15.9
1953	J.C. Caroline	1,256	194	6.5	Elry Falkenstein	72	36	.50	577	Rocky Ryan	16	308	19.3
1954	J.C. Caroline	440	93	4.7	Em Lindbeck	66	38	.58	476	Dean Renn	17	246	14.5
1955	Harry Jefferson	514	97	5.3	Em Lindbeck	86	39	.45	588	Bob DesEnfants	12	206	17.2
1956	Abe Woodson	599	110	5.4	Hiles Stout	39	20	.51	278	Abe Woodson	12	257	21.4
1957	Ray Nitschke	514	79	6.5	Tom Haller	100	51	.51	675	Rich Kreitling	12	203	16.9
1958	Marshall Starks	303	65	4.7	John Eastbrook	66	34	.52	656	Rich Kreitling	23	688	29.9
1959	Bill Brown	504	89	5.7	Mel Meyers	63	32	.51	495	John Counts	19	314	16.5
1960	Bill Brown	531	128	4.1	John Eastbrook	87	40	.46	538	Ed O'Bradovich	21	233	11.1
1961	Al Wheatland	230	73	3.2	Dave McGann	49	27	.55	269	Dick Newell	16	184	11.5
1962	Ken Zimmerman	225	55	4.1	Mike Taliaferro	212	80	.38	1,139	Jim Warren	18	230	12.8
1963	Jim Grabowski	616	141	4.4	Mike Taliaferro	87	35	.40	450	Jim Warren	10	121	12.1
1964	Jim Grabowski	1,004	186	5.4	Fred Custardo	159	86	.54	1,012	Bob Trumpy	28	428	15.3
1965	Jim Grabowski	1,258	252	5.0	Fred Custardo	170	90	.53	1,124	John Wright Sr.	47	755	16.1
1966	Bill Huston	420	89	4.7	Bob Naponic	162	70	.43	998	John Wright Sr.	60	831	13.9
1967	Rich Johnson	768	195	3.9	Dean Volkman	183	77	.42	1,005	John Wright Sr.	52	698	13.4
1968	Rich Johnson	973	186	5.2	Bob Naponic	213	83	.39	813	Doug Dieken	21	223	10.6
1969	Dave Jackson	465	118	3.9	Steve Livas	131	42	.32	705	Doug Dieken	29	486	16.8
1970	Darrell Robinson	749	193	3.9	Mike Wells	170	71	.42	906	Doug Dieken	39	537	13.8
1971	John Wilson	543	115	4.7	Mike Wells	179	84	.47	1,007	Garvin Roberson	28	372	13.3
1972	George Uremovich	611	152	4.0	Mike Wells	158	76	.48	837	Garvin Roberson	31	569	18.4
1973	George Uremovich	519	141	3.7	Jeff Hollenbach	178	78	.44	916	Garvin Roberson	25	416	16.6
1974	Chubby Phillips	772	175	4.4	Jeff Hollenbach	131	64	.49	1,037	Joe Smalzer	29	525	18.1
1975	Lonnie Perrin	907	171	5.3	Kurt Steger	166	80	.48	1,136	Jeff Chrystal	22	261	11.9
1976	James Coleman	687	170	4.0	Kurt Steger	187	87	.47	1,243	Frank Johnson	24	306	12.8
1977	James Coleman	715	143	5.0	Mike McCray	60	36	.60	418	Tom Schooley	15	231	15.4
1978	Wayne Strader	389	74	5.3	Rich Weiss	109	58	.53	665	Jeff Barnes	22	270	12.3
1979	Mike Holmes	792	147	5.4	Lawrence McCullough	228	130	.57	1,254	Mike Holmes	25	127	5.1
1980	Mike Holmes	305	69	4.4	Dave Wilson	463	245	.53	3,154	Greg Dentino	40	512	12.8
1981	Calvin Thomas	390	110	3.5	Tony Eason	406	248	.61	3,360	Darrell Smith	43	495	11.5
1982	Dwight Beverly	396	74	5.4	Tony Eason	505	313	.62	3,671	Mike Martin	77	1,068	13.9
1983	Thomas Rooks	863	156	5.5	Jack Trudeau	324	226	.70	2,624	David Williams	69	958	13.9
1984	Thomas Rooks	1,056	219	4.8	Jack Trudeau	378	247	.65	2,724	David Williams	101	1,278	12.7
1985	Thomas Rooks	753	133	5.7	Jack Trudeau	446	322	.72	3,339	David Williams	92	1,156	12.6
1986	Keith Jones	534	133	4.0	Shane Lamb	227	115	.51	1,414	Stephen Pierce	43	602	14.0
1987	Keith Jones	322	110	2.9	Scott Mohr	212	106	.50	1,436	Darryl Usher	43	723	16.8
1988	Keith Jones	1,196	206	5.8	Jeff George	366	232	.63	2,451	Keith Jones	48	388	8.1
1989	Howard Griffith	747	164	4.6	Jeff George	386	242	.63	2,738	Mike Bellamy	59	927	15.7
1990	Howard Griffith	1,115	201	5.5	Jason Verduzco	355	226	.64	2,567	Shawn Wax	60	863	14.4
1991	Kameno Bell	664	140	4.7	Jason Verduzco	420	252	.60	3,014	Kameno Bell	64	503	7.9
1992	Darren Boyer	593	157	3.8	Jason Verduzco	282	184	.65	1,779	John Wright Jr.	47	508	10.8
1993	Ty Douthard	599	153	3.9	Johnny Johnson	287	135	.47	1,688	Ty Douthard	43	406	9.4
1994	Ty Douthard	765	179	4.3	Johnny Johnson	333	198	.59	2,495	Jason Dulick	52	550	10.6
1995	Robert Holcombe	1,051	264	4.0	Johnny Johnson	199	99	.50	1,110	Jason Dulick	36	453	12.6
1996	Robert Holcombe	1,281	260	4.9	Scott Weaver	314	176	.56	1,701	Jason Dulick	53	614	11.6
1997	Robert Holcombe	1,253	294	4.3	Mark Hoekstra	219	115	.53	1,029	Robert Holcombe	35	277	7.9
1998	Rocky Harvey	634	134	4.7	Kurt Kittner	162	72	.44	782	Lenny Willis	26	301	11.6
1999	Steve Havard	790	179	4.4	Kurt Kittner	396	216	.55	2,702	Michael Dean	45	608	13.5
2000	Antoineo Harris	772	192	4.0	Kurt Kittner	297	173	.58	1,982	Greg Lewis	40	544	13.6
2001	Antoineo Harris	629	169	3.7	Kurt Kittner	409	221	.54	3,256	Brandon Lloyd	65	1,062	16.3
2002	Antoineo Harris	1,330	278	4.8	Jon Beutjer	327	193	.59	2,511	Brandon Lloyd	65	1,010	15.5
2003	E.B. Halsey	525	140	3.8	Jon Beutjer	257	162	.63	1,597	Kelvin Hayden	52	592	11.4
2004	Pierre Thomas	893	152	5.9	Jon Beutjer	188	107	.57	1,082	Kendrick Jones	47	687	14.6
2005	Pierre Thomas	664	127	5.2	Tim Brasic	337	206	.61	1,979	Kyle Hudson	31	469	15.1
2006	Pierre Thomas	755	131	5.8	Isiah Williams	261	103	.39	1,489	Kyle Hudson	30	403	13.4

Receiving leaders by receptions
All statistics include postseason

INDIANA

BY TODD JONES

FOOTBALL STRUGGLED FOR acceptance at Indiana University from the very start, long before the sport was overshadowed by the school's basketball success. IU first played football in 1887, but the Hoosiers had only three games in three years. Interest improved but never reached the passionate levels seen at other Big Ten schools. From 1931 to 1933, the Hoosiers were coached by E.C. "Billy" Hayes, a famous track and field coach, at the request of IU president William L. Bryan. Bo McMillin is the only one of 16 Indiana coaches since 1922 to finish his career in Bloomington with a winning record. The Hoosiers haven't won a Big Ten title since 1967, and their only outright conference championship was in 1945. Still, there have been some magical moments at IU—produced by exciting players such as Bill Hillenbrand, Pete Pihos, George Taliaferro, John Isenbarger, Anthony Thompson, Vaughn Dunbar, and Antwaan Randle El.

TRADITION Indiana and Purdue decided 34 years after they first played that they should "discuss the possibility of undertaking a worthy joint enterprise on behalf of the two schools." Alumni clubs from both schools formed a joint committee, and IU's Dr. Clarence Jones suggested a trophy for the winner of the annual football game. The schools agreed on an old oaken bucket. IU's Wiley J. Huddle and Purdue's Fritz Ernst found a suitable bucket on Bruner Farm in southern Indiana. Besides the Old Oaken Bucket, the Hoosiers also play for a trophy against Michigan State. Since 1950, the winner has been awarded the Old Brass Spittoon, which came from one of Michigan's earliest trading posts and has been around since both schools formed. Indiana and Kentucky used to play for the Bourbon Barrel, but they ended that tradition in 1999. The 1991 season was the first time in 23 years that IU had possession of the Bourbon Barrel, the Old Brass Spittoon, and the Old Oaken Bucket all at once.

BEST PLAYER Indiana fans attending a basketball game against Kentucky broke into a chorus of boos when it was announced on the Hoosier Dome scoreboard that Houston QB Andre Ware had won the 1989 Heisman Trophy. The displeasure stemmed from their love for

PROFILE

Indiana University, Bloomington
Bloomington, Ind.
Founded: 1820
Enrollment: 36,698
Colors: Cream and Crimson
Nickname: Hoosiers
Stadium: Memorial Stadium
Opened in 1960
AstroPlay; 52,354 capacity
First football game: 1887
All-time record: 428–588–45 (.427)
Bowl record: 3–5
Big Ten Conference championships: 2
(1 outright)
First-round draft choices: 13
Website: www.iuhoosiers.com

THE BEST OF TIMES

The 1945 Hoosiers went 9–0–1 to win the Big Ten title and finished No. 4 in the AP poll as Bo McMillin was named national coach of the year. But '67 ranks as the most magical season because the Hoosiers, 1–8–1 the previous year, rebounded under coach John Pont to go 9–2, win the Big Ten, and earn the school's first bowl trip, losing the Rose Bowl to USC, 14-3.

THE WORST OF TIMES

Clyde Smith and former Notre Dame star Bernie Crimmins struggled as IU coaches. Under them the Hoosiers went 21–59–1 with nine straight losing seasons from 1948 to 1956.

CONFERENCE

Indiana joined the Western Conference in 1900. The Western Conference has been known as the Big Ten since 1917, but didn't officially change its name until 1987.

DISTINGUISHED ALUMNI

Isiah Thomas; Dick Enberg; John Mellencamp; Joshua Bell, world-renowned violinist; Mark Cuban, owner Dallas Mavericks; Kevin Kline, actor; Jane Pauley, broadcast journalist

History books easily explain why Indiana fans detest in-state foe Purdue.

native son Anthony Thompson, runner-up in that Heisman balloting and the Hoosiers' all-time leading rusher (5,299 yards from 1986 to 1989). The running back from Terre Haute had led the NCAA in rushing (1,793 yards) and scoring (154 points) as a senior in 1989. He was named the Walter Camp Foundation's Player of the Year and the AFCA "Coaches' Choice" Player of the Year, and he won the Maxwell Award as the nation's finest college player. Thompson was Big Ten rushing champion and first-team All-America in his junior and senior seasons, when he totaled 3,579 rushing yards and 50 touchdowns. He set a then-NCAA record in 1989 with 377 rushing yards against Wisconsin. He held the NCAA record for career touchdowns (65) until 1998, and held the Big Ten record for career points (412) until 1999. Thompson is the only player to lead Indiana in rushing for four seasons, and he took the Hoosiers to three consecutive bowl games.

BEST COACH A reaction to one defeat became a defining moment in Bill Mallory's coaching career at Indiana. His Hoosiers went into Michigan on Oct. 19, 1991, and lost valiantly to the No. 4-ranked Wolverines,

24-16. Immediately after the defeat, Mallory ripped the game officials with so much venom that the Big Ten suspended him for one game. The tirade showed Mallory wasn't going to allow his Hoosiers to simply accept their role as fodder for the league's big guns. He would fight for his players and do so in a fiery manner that belied IU's low-key football history. In his 13 seasons at Bloomington, Mallory won more games (68) than any other Indiana coach. He took the Hoosiers to six bowl games in an eight-year span and was named Big Ten Coach of the Year in 1986 and 1987—becoming the first coach to win the honor in consecutive years. In the end, Mallory became a victim of IU expectations he himself had raised. On Oct. 31, 1996, athletic director Clarence Doninger announced Mallory would be replaced at the end of the season. Three weeks later, the IU players carried Mallory off the field after his final game as their coach, a 33-16 win at Purdue. He went 68–78–3 from 1984 to 1996. No Indiana coach has won more games, and the Hoosiers haven't had a winning season since 1994.

BEST TEAM The end of World War II had a direct effect on Indiana winning its first Big Ten championship

FIGHT SONG	FIRST-ROUND DRAFT CHOICES		CONSENSUS ALL-AMERICANS	
INDIANA, OUR INDIANA	1938	Corbett Davis, Rams (1)	1942	Billy Hillenbrand, B
Indiana, our Indiana	1944	Billy Hillenbrand, Giants (6)	1944	John Tavener, C
Indiana, we're all for you!	1949	George Taliaferro, L.A. Dons (5)[a]	1945	Bob Ravensberg, E
We will fight for the cream and crimson	1961	Earl Faison, Chargers	1988-89	Anthony Thompson, RB
For the glory of old IU	1964	Marv Woodson, Colts (8)	1991	Vaughn Dunbar, RB
Never daunted, we cannot falter	1965	Tom Nowatzke, Lions (11)		
In the battle, we're tried and true	1966	Randy Beisler, Eagles (4)		
Indiana, our Indiana,	1968	Doug Crusan, Dolphins (27)		
Indiana we're all for you! I-U!	1974	Carl Barzilauskas, Jets (6)		
	1985	Kevin Allen, Eagles (9)		
	1988	Eric Moore, Giants (10)		
	1992	Vaughn Dunbar, Saints (21)		
	1994	Thomas Lewis, Giants (24)		

[a] *All-America Football Conference*

in 1945, which is still the school's only outright conference title. Hoosiers coach Bo McMillin—a Texan who had signed a contract for $95,000 over 10 years—picked up two extra players after opening the season with a 13-7 win at Michigan. The military allowed Howard Brown, who was stationed in Europe, to return to Bloomington, Indiana, to play on 60 days' leave. The guard earned second-team All-America honors that season. Pete Pihos, an All-America end in 1943, returned to IU on permanent leave from the military. He earned All-America honors again, this time as a fullback, and finished sixth in the Heisman voting. Other top players were running back George Taliaferro, end Bob Ravensberg, guard Howard Brown, quarterback Ben Raimondi, tackle Russ Deal, and end Ted Kluszewski, later a major league baseball slugger. Northwestern tied IU 7-7 in Week 2, but the Hoosiers then won their final eight games. The final three wins were shutouts by a combined score of 94-0 over No. 20 Minnesota, Pittsburgh, and No. 18 Purdue. The Purdue game was scoreless at the half, but Raimondi threw TD passes to Kluszewski and Lou Mihajlovich and the Hoosiers pulled away for the 26-0 win. "This is the biggest thrill in my life," said McMillin, who was the QB on the Centre College team from Kentucky that ended Harvard's 25-game winning streak in 1921. McMillin was named national Coach of the Year. Indiana outscored its opponents 279-56 while going 9–0–1 as the only undefeated team in school history and finished No. 4 in the nation.

BEST BACKFIELD

While Anthony Thompson and QB Dave Schnell were a powerful duo in the late 1980s, the tandem of Antwaan Randle El and running back Levron Williams get the nod because of the quarterback's versatility. Randle El, dangerous throwing and running, was the Big Ten offensive Player of the Year in 2001 and finished sixth in the Heisman voting. He also earned the *Chicago Tribune*'s Silver Football award as the Big Ten's MVP after completing 118 of 231 passes for 1,664 yards and nine touchdowns, and rushing 188 times for 964 yards, an average of 5.1 per carry, and eight touchdowns. That same year, Williams was named third-team All-America and a unanimous first-team All-Big Ten pick after averaging 200.1 all-purpose yards per game, including 127.4 rushing. He averaged 6.6 yards on his 212 carries for a total of 1,401 rushing yards and 17 touchdowns. Williams also led the team in receptions with 26 for 289 yards and two scores. He scored a school-

record six TDs while rushing for 280 yards on 20 carries in a 63-32 win at Wisconsin and also ran for 251 yards against Michigan State. Both Williams (24.3 yards on kickoff returns) and Randle El (9.3 yards on 16 punt returns) chipped in on special teams, too. Running back Jeremi Johnson provided IU with a third threat in 2001 by averaging 5.7 yards per carry while rushing for 546 yards and seven touchdowns. Randle El, however, was the star. He finished his career with 3,895 rushing yards—more than any QB in Division I-A history—and 7,469 passing yards. In 44 career games he accounted for 86 touchdowns, scoring 45 of them himself rushing and receiving. Randle El finished fifth in the Division I-A total yardage list with 11,364 yards and is the only player in major college football history to record 2,500 total yards in four consecutive seasons. He is the only Division I-A player to pass for more than 6,000 yards and rush for more than 3,000. He was a second-round pick of the Pittsburgh Steelers as a wide receiver, and he threw a TD pass in their victory in Super Bowl XL.

BEST DEFENSE

Nothing suggested that Indiana coach John Pont's third IU team would be a defensive stalwart. The Hoosiers ended 1966 by yielding 88 points in their final two games, to Michigan State and Purdue, and an average of 22.9 for the season. The 1967 season, however, took on a different tone from the outset when the Hoosiers opened with a 12-10 win over Kentucky. Immediately noticeable was the help Doug Crusan provided on the defensive line. After playing offense throughout his career, the team captain switched to defense for his senior season. Crusan's move helped the Hoosiers win their first eight games while allowing more than 15 points just twice. They held Illinois and Arizona to seven points each, and limited Wisconsin to nine. A 33-7 loss at Minnesota proved to be just an off week. The Hoosiers earned a Rose Bowl trip a week later by holding No. 3 Purdue to two TDs in a 19-14 upset. Indiana's defense did its part in the Rose Bowl but still lost to eventual national champion USC, 14-3. For the season, the Hoosiers allowed 14.5 points per game. Senior linebacker Ken Kaczmarek, a South Bend, Ind., native, was named All-Big Ten and third-team All-America. The speedy Kaczmarek led the Hoosiers in tackles with 118, including nine for loss, intercepted two passes, and recovered one fumble. Fellow linebacker Jim Sniadecki was also named All-Big Ten. Crusan became the first IU defensive lineman to earn All-America honors when he

COLLEGE FOOTBALL HALL OF FAME INDUCTEES		
NAME	**YEARS**	**INDUCTED**
Pete Pihos, FB/E	1942-43, 1945-46	1966
Zora Clevenger, HB	1900-03	1968
Bill Ingram, COACH	1923-25	1973
George Taliaferro, HB	1945, 1947-48	1981
John Tavender, C	1941-44	1990
Anthony Thompson, RB	1986-89	2007

PRO FOOTBALL HALL OF FAME INDUCTEES		
NAME	**PRO YEARS**	**INDUCTED**
Pete Pihos, E	1947-55	1970

was named to the second team in 1967. He made 76 tackles, including three for a loss, broke up two passes, and recovered three fumbles. Miami drafted him in the first round, and Crusan moved back to offense. He was a tackle on the undefeated 1972 Dolphins, earning the first of his two Super Bowl rings.

BIGGEST GAME Indiana's first bowl game is still the school's only Rose Bowl appearance, and it came a season after a 1–8–1 finish. Pont took his surprising 9–1 team, along with 20,000 Indiana fans, to Pasadena to meet No. 1-ranked Southern California on New Year's Day 1968. For the first time, the Rose Bowl parade and game were being shown, via satellite, to other parts of the world. USC junior tailback O.J. Simpson thrilled the crowd of 102,946 by rushing for 128 yards and two TDs. His two-yard scoring run in the first quarter capped an 84-yard drive and put the Trojans ahead 7-0. Indiana drove inside the USC 10-yard line in the second quarter but had to settle for a 27-yard field goal by David Kornowa. Simpson added an eight-yard TD run to put USC up 14-3 in the third quarter. Indiana sophomore QB Harry Gonso, named the team's MVP for the season, struggled against the Trojans. The All-Big Ten pick gained just 15 yards on 11 carries and completed just 9 of 25 passes for 110 yards and one interception. All-America halfback John Isenbarger was held to 38 yards on 12 rushes. The Hoosiers mustered just 189 yards of offense while Southern California gained 317. In the end, a 14-3 loss couldn't dampen the memories of a storybook 1967 for Indiana. Pont was named college football's Coach of the Year.

BIGGEST UPSET The Hoosiers had won just 14 games from 1960 through 1966 when the unthinkable happened: They entered a game with a chance to earn a Rose Bowl berth. One year after going 1–8–1, Indiana entered the 1967 regular-season finale—the annual grudge game against Purdue—with an 8–1 record. The Hoosiers had earned the name the Cardiac Kids for winning six games by seven points or less, but their magic carpet ride was expected to end against Purdue. One week earlier, IU had lost 33-7 at Minnesota to fall from No. 5 to No. 14. The Boilermakers were the nation's No. 3-ranked team and came to Bloomington as 14-point favorites. They didn't, however, have an answer for Indiana running back Terry Cole. He rushed for 155 yards on 15 carries. Indiana won another thriller, 19-14, to earn its first bowl game berth as Big Ten champion.

HEARTBREAKER The Purdue game of 1980 still rankles the IU faithful. Indiana trailed 24-17 when it put together a 65-yard drive on its final possession of the game. The visiting Hoosiers converted three fourth-down situations. The third time was the charm, as quarterback

Tim Clifford threw a 10-yard touchdown pass to Steve Corso with seconds remaining. Indiana coach Lee Corso decided his team had come too far to settle for a tie. He ordered a two-point conversion attempt, but the pass was deflected incomplete. Purdue escaped with a 24-23 win.

WILDEST FINISH Indiana, missing five starters with injuries, played gallantly as homecoming opponent for Michigan in 1979. With IU trailing 21-14, quarterback Tim Clifford threw a two-yard TD pass to Dave Harangody with 55 seconds remaining in the game. Indiana radio announcer Don Fischer became so excited that he set himself on fire when cigarette ash burned the sleeve of his sport coat. He kept on announcing the game. An extra-point kick tied the score. Michigan took the kickoff, converted a fourth-down play from its own 31, survived an apparent interception two plays later when IU's Tim Wilbur couldn't get a foot inbounds, and drove to the Hoosier 45-yard line. Six seconds remained. Wolverine QB John Wangler then completed a pass to Anthony Carter near the 20. Indiana defenders Bart Ramsey and Stoner Gray hit the skinny freshman, but he bounced off and headed into the end zone. IU safety Tim Wilbur grabbed Carter but couldn't stop him. "Oh my God, Carter scored!" screamed Michigan radio announcer Bob Ufer as the Wolverines won 27-21.

BEST COMEBACK Iowa bolted to a 26-3 halftime lead over Indiana on Sept. 8, 1979. The Hawkeyes should have recalled their game against IU from two years earlier, when freshman QB Tim Clifford came off the bench and rallied the Hoosiers from a 14-point deficit to a 24-21 win. Now a junior, Clifford once again brought IU back against Iowa. He threw for two touchdowns, the second a 66-yarder to Lonnie Johnson with 58 seconds remaining. The Hoosiers pulled out a 30-26 victory. No other Indiana team has ever overcome such a large deficit to win.

STADIUM Jordan Field was home to the Hoosiers for 38 years before the original Memorial Stadium opened in 1925. Three years of fund-raising produced $250,000 to finance the building of that 22,000-seat horseshoe, named in honor of IU students and alumni who served in World War I. The Hoosiers played at Memorial Stadium for 35 years. Indiana began building new athletic facilities in the late 1950s on a 160-acre site on the northern edge of the campus. A $1.5 million football stadium opened in 1960 and was originally named Indiana University Stadium, although it was often referred to as the 17th Street Stadium. Indiana changed the official name to Memorial Stadium in 1971 to honor the school's veterans of World War I, World War II, and subsequent wars. The stadium capacity is 52,354.

RIVAL History books easily explain why Indiana fans detest in-state foe Purdue. The Boilermakers beat the Hoosiers 60-0 in their first game in 1891 and followed that up with a 68-0 win the next year and a 64-0 win the year after that. Indiana forfeited the 1894 game and lost two more to the Boilermakers before breaking through with a 17-5 win in 1899. The Hoosiers beat Purdue seven times from 1987 through 1996, but they have won just eight other times in the series since 1948, including one victory since 1997. No wonder the basketball rivalry is more intriguing.

INSPIRATION Terry Hoeppner coached the Hoosiers for only two seasons, but he had a profound impact on and transformed the mood around Indiana football. Hoeppner, a native of Woodburn, Ind., died June 19, 2007, from complications of a brain tumor. He was 59. "I think if you measure the man strictly by wins and losses, you're underselling a lot of attributes," said Indiana athletic director Rick Greenspan. "He has really touched a lot of people, inspired a lot of people, and his memory will live on in these players and other people for a long time." The Hoosiers went 9–14 and didn't play in a bowl game under Hoeppner, yet they benefited greatly from his charm, character, and charisma. His love for his home state and his folksy nature infused the program with energy as soon as he was hired in December 2004 after going 48–25 in six seasons with two bowl appearances at Miami of Ohio. His first year in Bloomington, home attendance improved 39% and IU student ticket sales went up 117%. Hoeppner created The Walk, a pregame ritual in which players stroll with fans through the tailgate parties in the parking lot on the way to the stadium. He also had a three-ton limestone rock placed in the back of the north end zone at Memorial Stadium so that his players could take pride in defending The Rock. In December 2005, doctors removed a tumor from Hoeppner's right temple. He underwent chemotherapy and radiation treatment, but needed a second surgery to remove a brain growth in September 2006. Three days later, he sneaked into Indiana's coaching booth to watch the Hoosiers play Southern Illinois. That same week, he also appeared before the school's board of trustees to lend support and endorse a $55 million facilities-upgrade plan. Hoeppner missed just two games after his second surgery, but his health deteriorated in the spring of 2007. He spent the last four months of his life on his third medical leave from the team. But he didn't burden his players with his battle and most were shocked to learn about his death, which came one week after IU announced that offensive coordinator and assistant head coach Bill Lynch would replace Hoeppner on an interim basis. Hoeppner died in the morning, and later that afternoon his wife, Jane, his mother, his sister, and two of his children attended a groundbreaking ceremony for the new athletic facilities. The ceremony turned into a warm tribute to Hoeppner. "He never quit. He just ran out of timeouts," Greenspan said.

DUBIOUS DISTINCTION The Big Ten suspended Indiana coach Phil Dickens for the 1957 season because the league said he offered players free room, board, tuition, and a monthly stipend. Bob Hicks served as acting coach and went 1–8. Dickens was reinstated but ran into further trouble. In March 1960, the NCAA put Indiana on four years' probation because of illegal payments to players in '57 and '59. The Big Ten added one year of conference probation for IU, disallowing any league win by the Hoosiers in 1960. It didn't really matter because Indiana went 0–7 in Big Ten play, anyway. After the scandal, the Hoosiers went 14–50–1 from 1960 to '66 and never finished better than ninth in the Big Ten during that span.

NICKNAME There are more than 30 theories about the origin of the word "Hoosier" but none of them is conclusive. Historians agree that the nickname for Indiana residents was popularized in the 1800s by novels, poetry, and newspaper articles. Former governor Robert D. Orr may have best summed up all the conjecture. In a 1987 letter to *The Wall Street Journal,* Orr wrote, "Those unfortunate souls who, for some reason, live elsewhere may continue to speculate as to the origin of our name; and we Hoosiers will continue to enjoy their doing so."

MASCOT Indiana doesn't have a mascot.

UNIFORMS Indiana officially made cream and crimson its school colors in 1888, but plain red and white have also been part of the uniforms. During the early 1960s, IU was one of the first schools to use something other than stripes or numerals on its helmets. From 1967 through 1996, the Hoosiers' headgear was varying shades of red and (except for 1983) sported a white block "I" on the side. They wore black helmets from 1997 to 2001, though when the team's fortunes didn't change, they switched back to crimson in 2002 with a white interlocking "IU" on the side.

QUIRK After an 18-0 loss to Notre Dame in the 1958 season opener, the Hoosiers decided to shake things up by discarding the crimson and cream and wearing light blue jerseys the next week at home against West Virginia. Indiana pulled off a 13-12 upset victory, prompting those jerseys to be worn at home the rest of the season. The Hoosiers finished 4–0 in blue.

LORE Lee Corso, now an ESPN college football analyst, went 41–68–2 but left them laughing during his 10

seasons as Indiana coach. Once, with his team mired in a losing streak, he emerged from a coffin on his coach's TV show and said, "We aren't dead yet." Corso also paused during a game against Ohio State to have his photograph taken with the scoreboard behind him showing the Hoosiers leading the Buckeyes. After a win over Purdue, he took the Old Oaken Bucket home and slept with it in his bed. "I've attended 150 banquets this winter and have been served chicken all 150 times," Corso once said. "I don't get a haircut anymore. I get plucked." Few were smiling, however, when his tenure as Hoosiers coach got off to a poor start on Sept. 15, 1973. Corso had his players warm up in the fieldhouse before the game and then board a double-decker bus to be driven onto the field. The team's bus was nearly late for the game's opening kickoff because of traffic. Illinois won 28-14.

NUMBERS Running back George Taliaferro was the first African-American drafted by an NFL team when he was selected in the 13th round in 1949 by the Chicago Bears ... IU beat Brigham Young 38-37 in the 1979 Holiday Bowl in a game that had 874 total yards of offense, 52 first downs, and eight lead changes ... Antwaan Randle El had 473 total yards of offense in a 51-43 win over Minnesota. He rushed for 210 yards and two TDs and threw for 263 yards and two scores while becoming only the fifth player in Division I-A history to rush for 200 yards and pass for 200 yards in the same game ... IU beat South Carolina 34-10 in the 1988 Liberty Bowl. The Hoosiers had 575 total yards of offense and held South Carolina to 153 ... Indiana signed 51 freshmen players in the fall of 1961 because the team didn't have many sophomores or juniors due to NCAA sanctions ... Indiana won its 1962 season opener over Kansas State 21-0 despite being penalized 16 times for 189 yards ... Duane Gunn opened a 1981 game at Syracuse with a 97-yard kickoff return for a TD. Indiana didn't score again and lost 21-7 ... Anthony Thompson scored four TDs in the first half as the Hoosiers beat Ohio State 41-7 in 1988 for their first win over the Buckeyes in Bloomington since 1904 ... Bo McMillin's 34–34–6 Big Ten record is the best winning percentage in conference play for an Indiana coach ... Vern Huffman, the Big Ten MVP in 1936, is the only Hoosier to be named All-America in both football and basketball ... Indiana defeated LSU 24-21 in 1977 after trailing 21-10 heading into the fourth quarter. It was the first time in 21 years the Hoosiers had erased a deficit of more than one TD in the fourth quarter to win ... Sam Wyche went 3–8 in 1983,

After a win over Purdue, coach Lee Corso took the Old Oaken Bucket home and slept with it.

his only season as Indiana coach, and left to become head coach of the Cincinnati Bengals ... Entering 2007, the Hoosiers have had 11 head coaches in the past 60 years and each of them left the school with a losing record ... The Hoosiers haven't gone to a bowl game since 1993—the longest bowl-less streak in the Big Ten— and haven't had a winning season since 1994 ... The Hoosiers rushed for 578 yards and produced a school-record 35 first downs in a 59-29 win at Kentucky in 1994. Freshman tailback Alex Smith ran for 221, Jermaine Chaney totaled 167, and Brett Law added 97 ... Smith rushed for a Big Ten freshman record 245 yards on 31 carries in IU's 33-29 win at Purdue ... True freshman safety Greg Yeldell intercepted three different Michigan passers in a 1998 game, tying the NCAA record for interceptions in a game by a freshman ... Indiana's 31-28 win over Iowa in 2006 was the Hoosiers' first in 19 years over a team ranked in the top 15 ... Marcus Thigpen tied a Big Ten record and set an IU record in 2006 with three kickoff returns for touchdowns in one season. His return average of 30.1 yards led the NCAA ... The Hoosiers' 30-24 win at Oregon in 2004 was their first road win over a ranked nonconference foe since 1973 ... Indiana's 10-0 win over No. 8-ranked Ohio State in 1937 was the Buckeyes' only Big Ten loss and cost them the conference championship ... Indiana's smallest home crowd in 40 years—22,232— saw a 30-21 win over Minnesota in 2004 ... Sophomore wide receiver James Hardy, a former basketball player for the Hoosiers, caught a school-record four TD passes in a 46-21 win over Michigan State in 2006, two weeks after he had three TD receptions in a 31-28 win over Iowa. His 10 TD catches that season led the Big Ten ... The Hoosiers blew a 24-0 second-quarter lead at Minnesota in 1978 and lost 32-31 on a last-second 31-yard field goal by Paul Rogind ... Entering 2007, the Hoosiers had gone 8–45 in road games the previous 10 seasons. They were 2–21 away from home from 2002 through 2005 ... Indiana passed for 345 yards in a 54-13 win over Nebraska in 1943 ... The Hoosiers upset No. 23 Wisconsin 32-29 in 2002 after trailing by 19 points in the second half ... IU and Ohio State played to a scoreless tie at Ohio Stadium in 1959 ... Indiana overcame a 21-3 deficit to grab a lead but lost to Tennessee 27-22 in the 1988 Peach Bowl ... Freshman QB Kellen Lewis completed 19 of 25 passes for 255 yards in a 31-28 win over Iowa in 2006 and was named *USA Today's* offensive Player of the Week. He had a streak of 146 consecutive passes without an interception. He also threw five TD passes in a 46-21 win over Michigan State and passed for 290 yards and rushed for 103 against

Purdue … The 1987 Hoosiers defeated Ohio State for the first time in 36 years and Michigan for the first time in 20 years. IU is 21–115–5 against the two Big Ten powers entering 2007 … IU overcame a 17-0 deficit at Wisconsin in 1991 to win 28-20 … Blake Powers threw a school-record 20 TD passes in 2005, but moved to tight end after the season … Tyson Beattie punted 208 times from 2003 through 2005 … Sophomore Brett Law rushed for 240 yards in a 20-10 win over Missouri in 1992 … John Paci threw a 99-yard TD pass to Thomas Lewis against Penn State in 1993 … In the four years he played at Indiana, Antwaan Randle El was the only Hoosier to be selected in the NFL draft. Pittsburgh took him in the second round in 2002 … Mike Dumas returned an interception 99 yards against Purdue in 1990 … Indiana's last first-round draft pick was in 1994: wide receiver Thomas Lewis to the New York Giants … An Indiana defensive player hasn't been taken in the first round of the NFL draft since Carl

Barzilauskas went to the New York Jets in 1974 … Vaughn Dunbar was All-America and finished sixth in the Heisman voting in 1991 while setting an IU record with 1,805 rushing yards. He ran for 265 yards on 33 carries in a 27-27 tie at Missouri that season … The Hoosiers trailed 28-7 with less than five minutes remaining in the third quarter, but rallied to defeat Illinois 34-31 in overtime on Oct. 2, 1999. One week later, IU wiped out a 14-0 deficit and totaled 543 yards of offense in a 34-17 win over Northwestern … Tim Clifford won the Big Ten MVP in 1979 while passing for 4,338 yards … IU enters 2007 with 192 Big Ten wins and 129 nonconference victories.

QUOTE "This has got to be the darkest day for Ohio State football since I've been associated with it." —Ohio State coach Earle Bruce after Indiana beat the Buckeyes 31-10 in 1987, the Hoosiers' first victory over Ohio State in 36 years

INDIANA ALL-TIME SCORES

WIN/LOSS PERCENTAGE SINCE 1936

A.B. WOODFORD
1887-88 (.250)　　　　0-1-1

1887　　　　0-1-0
UNK		Franklin *UNK*	8	10

1888　　　　0-0-1
O31	=	DePauw *UNK*	6	6

EVANS WOLLEN
1889 (.000)　　　　0-2

1889　　　　0-2-0
UNK		Wabash *UNK*	2	40
UNK		Depauw *IND*	5	10

1890
NO TEAM

BILLY HEROD
1891 (.167)　　　　1-5

1891　　　　1-5-0
UNK	●	Louisville AC *UNK*	30	0
UNK		Butler *UNK*	6	52
UNK		DePauw *UNK*	4	62
N14		at Purdue	0	60
UNK		Butler *UNK*	6	26
UNK		Wabash *UNK*	0	25

NO HEAD COACH

1892　　　　2-2-0
UNK	●	Butler *UNK*	11	10
N5		at Purdue	0	68
UNK	●	Wabash *UNK*	36	24
UNK		DePauw *UNK*	0	1 f

1893　　　　1-4-1
O14		at Purdue	0	64
UNK		Butler *UNK*	0	38
UNK	●	Danville AC *UNK*	18	0
O13		at DePauw	0	34
N30	=	at Kentucky	24	24
UNK		Wabash *UNK*	12	24

FERBERT & HUDDLESTON
1894 (.000)　　　　0-4

1894　　　　0-4-0
UNK		Butler *UNK*	0	58
O13		at DePauw	10	20
UNK		Wabash *UNK*	0	46
N24		at Purdue	0	1 f

OSGOOD & WREN
1895 (.563)　　　　4-3-1

1895　　　　4-3-1
UNK	●	Louisville AC *UNK*	36	0
UNK		Indianapolis *UNK*	8	16
UNK	●	Noblesville AC *UNK*	30	0
N4		at DePauw	0	14
N11	=	DePauw	14	14
UNK		Butler *UNK*	2	34
UNK	●	Rose Poly *UNK*	8	4
UNK	●	Wabash *UNK*	12	10

M.G. GONTERMAN
1896-97 (.781)　　　　12-3-1

1896　　　　6-2-0
UNK		DePauw *UNK*	4	22
UNK		Noblesville *UNK*	6	8
UNK		Knightstown *UNK*	50	0
UNK	●	Butler *UNK*	22	6
UNK		Cincinnati *UNK*	16	0
UNK		Wabash *UNK*	38	0
UNK	●	Louisville AC *UNK*	38	24
N21		at DePauw	12	0

1897　　　　6-1-1
UNK	=	Rose Poly	6	6
UNK	●	at Rose Poly	12	0
UNK	●	Bedford	40	0
UNK	●	Louisville Manual HS	30	0
O30		at Purdue	6	20
UNK	●	DePauw	18	0
UNK	●	Miami ,Ohio	22	6
UNK	●	DePauw	14	0

JAMES H. HORNE
1898-1904 (.602)　　　　33-21-5

1898　　　　4-1-2
UNK	●	Rose Poly	16	0
UNK	●	Indiana Training Sch	20	0
UNK	=	Cincinnati	0	0
N5	●	at Notre Dame	11	5
N7	●	at DePauw	32	0
N12		at Purdue	0	14
UNK	=	at Cincinnati	11	11

1899　　　　6-2-0
O7	●	Rose Poly	16	0
O14	●	at Illinois	5	0 *
O23		at Notre Dame	0	17
O28	●	at Vanderbilt	20	0
N4	●	Cincinnati	35	0
N11	●	DePauw	34	0
N18		at Northwestern	6	11
N30	●	at Purdue	17	5

1900-PRESENT
BIG 10

1900　　　　4-2-2 (1-2-1)
S29	=	Alumni	0	0
O6	●	Earlham	18	0
O13		at Northwestern	0	12
O20	●	Vinncennes	62	0
O25	●	Notre Dame	6	0
N3		at Michigan	0	12
N17	=	Illinois *IND*	0	0
N29		at Purdue	24	5

1901　　　　6-3-0 (1-2-0)
S28	●	Wabash	24	6
O5	●	Rose Poly	56	0
O12		at Michigan	0	33
O19	●	Franklin	76	0
O26		Purdue	11	6
N2		Illinois *IND*	0	18
N16		at Notre Dame	5	18
N23	●	at Ohio State	18	6
N28	●	DePauw	24	0

1902　　　　3-5-1 (0-4-0)
O4	●	Wabash	34	0
O11		at Michigan	0	60
O18	●	DePauw	16	5
O25		Notre Dame	5	11
N1		at Illinois	0	47
N8		at Chicago	0	39
N15		at Purdue	0	39
N22	●	Vinncennes	33	0
N27	=	at Ohio State	6	6

1903　　　　4-4-0 (1-2-0)
S26		Wabash	0	5
O3		at Chicago	0	34
O10	●	Earlham	39	0
O17		at Michigan	0	51
N6	●	Illinois	17	0
N14	●	DePauw	70	0
N21		at Transylvania, Ky	5	18
N28	●	at Ohio State	17	16

1904　　　　6-4-0 (0-3-0)
S24	●	Alumni	11	5
S28		Indiana Medical	12	0
O1		at Chicago	0	56
O8		Kentucky	0	12
O15		at Illinois	0	0
O22	●	at Washington, Mo.	22	6
O29	●	Ohio State	8	0
N5	●	at Wabash	4	0
N12		Purdue *IND*	0	27
N19	●	Kent	27	0

JAMES M. SHELDON
1905-13 (.570)　　　　35-26-3

1905　　　　8-1-1 (0-1-1)
S23	●	Alumni	5	0
S30	●	Butler	31	0
O7	●	Kentucky	29	0
O14		at Chicago	5	16
O21	●	Washington, Mo.	39	0
O28	=	Purdue *IND*	11	11
N4	●	Cincinnati	47	6
N11	●	Notre Dame	22	5
N18	●	Wabash	40	0
N30		at Ohio State	11	0

1906　　　　4-2-0 (0-2-0)
O13	●	Alumni	16	0
O20	●	at Wabash	12	5
O27		at Chicago	8	33
N3	●	DePauw	55	0
N10	●	Notre Dame *IND*	12	0
N24		at Minnesota	6	8

1907　　　　2-3-1 (0-3-0)
O5	●	DePauw	25	9
O12		at Chicago	6	27
O19	●	Alumni	40	0
N2	=	at Notre Dame	0	0
N9		at Wisconsin	8	11
N22		Illinois	6	10

1908　　　　3-4-0 (1-3-0)
S26	●	Alumni	11	0
O3	●	DePauw	16	0
O10		at Chicago	6	29
O17		Wisconsin	0	16
O31		at Illinois	0	10
N7		Notre Dame *IND*	0	11
N21	●	at Purdue	10	4

1909　　　　4-3-0 (1-3-0)
O2	●	DePauw	28	5
O9		at Chicago	0	28
O16	●	Lake Forest	27	5
O23		at Wisconsin	3	6
O30	●	at St. Louis	30	0
N6		at Illinois	5	6
N20	●	at Purdue	36	3

1910　　　　6-1-0 (3-1-0)
O1	●	DePauw	12	0
O8	●	at Chicago	6	0
O15	●	James Millikin	33	0
O22	●	Wisconsin *IND*	12	3
O29	●	Butler	33	0
N5		Illinois	0	3
N19	●	at Purdue	15	0

1911　　　　3-3-1 (0-3-1)
S30	●	DePauw	9	6
O7		at Chicago	6	23
O14	●	at Franklin	42	0
O21		at Northwestern	0	5
O28	●	Washington, Mo.	12	0
N11	=	Illinois	0	0
N25		Purdue	5	12

1912　　　　2-5-0 (0-5-0)
S28	●	DePauw	20	0
O5		at Chicago	0	13
O19		at Illinois	7	13
O26	●	Earlham	33	7
N2		Iowa	6	13
N9		Northwestern	6	21
N24		at Purdue	7	34

1913　　　　3-4-0 (2-4-0)
S27	●	DePauw	48	3
O4		at Chicago	7	21
O25		Illinois	0	10
N1	●	at Ohio State	7	6
N8		at Iowa	0	60
N15	●	at Northwestern	21	20
N23		Purdue	7	42

CLARENCE C. CHILDS
1914-15 (.464)　　　　6-7-1

1914　　　　3-4-0 (1-4-0)
S26	●	DePauw	13	6
O3		at Chicago	0	34
O10		at Illinois	0	51
O17	●	Northwestern	27	0
O31	●	Miami (Ohio)	48	3
N7		Ohio State	3	13
N21		at Purdue	13	23

1915　　　　3-3-1 (1-3-0)
O2	●	DePauw	7	0
O9	●	Miami (Ohio)	41	0
O16		at Chicago	7	13
O30	=	Wash. & Lee *IND*	7	7
N6		at Ohio State	9	10
N13	●	at Northwestern	14	6
N20		Purdue	0	7

EWALD O. STIEHM
1916-21 (.526)　　　　20-18-1

1916　　　　2-4-1 (0-3-1)
S30	●	DePauw	20	0
O14		at Chicago	0	22
O21		at Tufts	10	12
N4		Northwestern	0	7
N11		at Ohio State	7	46
N18	●	Florida	14	3
N25	=	at Purdue	0	0

1917　　　　5-2-0 (1-2-0)
S29	●	Franklin	50	0
O6	●	Wabash	51	0
O13	●	St. Louis	40	0
O27		at Minnesota	9	33
N3		Ohio State	3	26
N10	●	DePauw	35	0
N24	●	at Purdue	37	0

1918　　　　2-2-0 (0-0-0)
O5		Kentucky	7	24
N2		at Camp Taylor	3	7
N9	●	Fort Harrison	41	0
N16	●	DePauw	13	0

1919　　　　3-4-0 (0-2-0)
S27	●	Wabash	20	7
O4		Centre	3	12
O11	●	at Kentucky	24	0
O18		Minnesota	6	20
N1		Notre Dame *IND*	3	16
N15		at Northwestern	2	3
N22	●	Syracuse	12	6

1920　　　　5-2-0 (3-1-0)
S25		Franklin	47	0
O2		Iowa	7	14
O9		Mississippi State	24	0
O23		at Minnesota	21	7
O30	●	Northwestern *IND*	10	7
N13		Notre Dame *IND*	10	13
N20	●	at Purdue	10	7

1921 3-4-0 (1-2-0)
S24 ● Franklin 47 0
O1 ● Kalamazoo 29 0
O8 at Harvard 0 19
O22 | at Minnesota 0 6
O29 Notre Dame IND 7 28
N12 | at Iowa 0 41
N19 ● | Purdue 3 0

JAMES P. HERRON
1922 (.286) 1-4-2

1922 1-4-2 (0-2-1)
O7 = DePauw 0 0
O14 | Minnesota 0 20
O21 | at Wisconsin 0 20
O28 ● Michigan State 14 6
N4 at Notre Dame 0 27
N11 West Virginia 0 33
N25 = | at Purdue 7 7

WILLIAM A. INGRAM
1923-25 (.457) 10-12-1

1923 3-4-0 (2-2-0)
O6 DePauw 0 3
O13 ● | Northwestern IND 7 6
O20 | Wisconsin 0 52
O27 ● Hanover 32 0
N10 | at Chicago 0 27
N17 Wabash 6 29
N24 ● | Purdue 3 0

1924 4-4-0 (1-3-0)
S27 ● Rose Poly 65 0
O4 ● DePauw 21 0
O11 LSU IND 14 20
O18 | at Chicago 0 23
N1 | at Northwestern 7 17
N8 ● | at Ohio State 12 7
N15 ● Wabash 21 7
N22 | at Purdue 7 26

1925 3-4-1 (0-3-1)
O3 ● Indiana Normal 31 0
O10 | at Michigan 0 63
O17 Syracuse 0 14
O24 ● Miami (Ohio) 25 7
O31 | at Northwestern 14 17
N7 | at Ohio State 0 7
N14 ● Rose Poly 32 7
N21 = | Purdue 0 0

H.O. (PAT) PAGE
1926-30 (.378) 14-24-3

1926 3-5-0 (0-4-0)
O2 ● DePauw 31 7
O9 ● Kentucky 14 6
O16 | at Northwestern 0 20
O23 | at Wisconsin 2 27
O30 | Northwestern 0 21
N6 at Notre Dame 0 26
N13 ● Mississippi State 19 6
N20 | at Purdue 14 24

1927 3-4-1 (1-2-1)
O1 ● at Kentucky 21 0
O8 | at Chicago 0 13
O15 = | Minnesota 14 14
O22 Notre Dame 6 19
O29 at Harvard 6 26
N5 ● Michigan State 33 7
N12 ● | at Northwestern 18 7
N19 | Purdue 6 21

1928 4-4-0 (2-4-0)
S29 ● Wabash 14 0
O6 ● Oklahoma 10 7
O13 ● | at Michigan 6 0
O20 | at Illinois 7 13
O27 | Ohio State 0 13
N10 | at Minnesota 12 21
N17 ● | Northwestern 6 0
N24 | at Purdue 0 14

1929 2-6-1 (1-3-1)
S21 ● Wabash 19 2
S28 Ohio U. 0 18
O5 Notre Dame 0 14
O12 | at Chicago 7 13
O19 Colgate 6 21
O26 = | at Ohio State 0 0
N2 | at Minnesota 7 19
N16 ● | at Northwestern 19 14
N23 | Purdue 0 32

1930 2-5-1 (1-3-0)
S27 ● Miami (Ohio) 14 0
O4 | at Ohio State 0 23
O11 = Oklahoma State 7 7
O18 | at Minnesota 0 6
O25 at SMU 0 27
N1 at Notre Dame 0 27
N8 | Northwestern 0 25
N22 ● | at Purdue 7 6

BILLY HAYES
1931-33 (.340) 6-14-5

1931 2-5-2 (1-4-2)
S26 ● Ohio U. 7 6
O3 Notre Dame 0 25
O17 = | at Iowa 0 0
O24 ● | at Chicago 32 6
O31 | Ohio State 6 13
N7 | at Michigan 0 22
N14 | at Northwestern 6 7
N21 | Purdue 0 19
N26 = | Illinois CHI 0 0

1932 3-4-1 (1-4-1)
O1 ● Ohio U. 7 6
O8 = | at Ohio State 7 7
O15 ● | Iowa 12 0
O22 | at Chicago 7 13
O27 ● Mississippi State 19 0
N5 | Michigan 0 7
N12 | at Illinois 6 18
N19 | at Purdue 7 25

1933 1-5-2 (0-3-2)
S30 ● Miami (Ohio) 7 0
O7 = | at Minnesota 6 6
O14 Notre Dame 2 12
O21 | Northwestern CHI 0 25
N4 | at Ohio State 0 21
N11 = | at Chicago 7 7
N18 at Xavier 0 6
N25 | Purdue 3 19

A.N. (BO) MCMILLIN
1934-47 (.561) 63-48-11

1934 3-3-2 (1-3-1)
S29 ● Ohio U. 27 0
O6 | at Ohio State 0 33
O13 = at Temple 6 6
O20 | at Chicago 0 21
N3 = | Iowa 0 0
N10 | at Minnesota 0 30
N17 ● Maryland 17 14
N24 ● | at Purdue 17 6

1935 4-3-1 (2-2-1)
O5 ● Centre 14 0
O12 | at Michigan 0 7
O19 at Cincinnati 0 7
O26 | Ohio State 6 28
N2 = | at Iowa 6 6
N9 ● Maryland BALT 13 7
N16 ● | at Chicago 24 0
N23 ● | Purdue 7 0

1936 5-2-1 (3-1-1)
O3 ● Centre 38 0
O10 ● | at Michigan 14 3
O17 at Nebraska 9 13
O24 | at Ohio State 0 7
O31 ● | Iowa 13 6
N7 ● Syracuse 9 7
N14 ● | at Chicago 20 7
N21 = | at Purdue 20 20

1937 5-3-0 (3-2-0)
O2 ● Centre 12 0
O9 | at Minnesota 0 6
O16 ● | Illinois 13 6
O23 ● Cincinnati 27 0
O30 at Nebraska 0 7
N6 ● | at Ohio State 10 0
N13 ● | at Iowa 3 0
N20 | Purdue 7 13

1938 1-6-1 (1-4-0)
O1 | at Ohio State 0 6
O8 | at Illinois 2 12
O15 = at Nebraska 0 0
O22 Kansas State 6 13
O29 | at Wisconsin 0 6
N5 Boston College BOS 0 14
N12 ● | Iowa 7 3
N19 | at Purdue 6 13

1939 2-4-2 (2-3-0)
S30 = Nebraska 7 7
O7 | at Iowa 29 32
O14 ● | at Wisconsin 14 0
O21 ● | at Illinois 7 6
N4 | at Ohio State 0 24
N11 Fordham NYC 0 13
N18 = at Michigan State 7 7
N25 | Purdue 6 7

1940 3-5-0 (2-3-0)
O5 Texas 6 13
O12 at Nebraska 7 13
O19 ● | Iowa 10 6
O26 | at Northwestern 7 20
N2 | at Ohio State 6 21
N9 ● Michigan State 20 0
N16 | at Wisconsin 10 27
N23 ● | at Purdue 3 0

1941 2-6-0 (1-3-0)
S27 Detroit 7 14
O4 at Notre Dame 6 19
O11 TCU 14 20
O18 ● at Nebraska 21 13
O25 | at Wisconsin 25 27
N1 | at Iowa 7 13
N8 | at Northwestern 14 20
N22 ● | Purdue 7 0

1942 7-3-0 (2-2-0)
S26 ● Butler 53 0
O3 | at Ohio State 21 32
O10 ● at Nebraska 12 0
O17 ● at Pittsburgh 19 7
O24 | Iowa 13 14
O31 Iowa Pre-Flight 6 26
N7 ● | at Minnesota 7 0
N14 ● Kansas State 54 0
N21 ● | at Purdue 20 0
N28 ● at Fort Knox 51 0

1943 4-4-2 (2-3-1)
S18 = Miami (Ohio) 7 7
S25 | at Northwestern 6 14
O2 ● Wabash 52 0
O9 ● at Nebraska 54 13
O16 = | at Iowa 7 7
O23 ● | Wisconsin 34 0
O30 ● | at Ohio State 20 14
N6 | at Michigan 6 23
N13 Great Lakes NAS 7 21
N20 | Purdue 0 7

1944 7-3-0 (4-3-0)
S16 ● Fort Knox 72 0
S23 | at Illinois 18 26
S30 ● | at Michigan 20 0
O14 ● Nebraska 54 0
O21 ● | at Northwestern 14 7
O28 ● | Iowa 32 0
N4 | at Ohio State 7 21
N11 | at Minnesota 14 19
N18 ● Pittsburgh 47 0
N25 ● | at Purdue 14 6

1945 9-0-1 (5-0-1)
S22 ● | at Michigan 13 7
S29 = | at Northwestern 7 7
O6 ● | at Illinois 6 0
O13 ● Nebraska 54 14
O20 ● | at Iowa 52 20
O27 ● Tulsa 7 2
N3 ● Cornell Coll. 46 6
N10 ● | at Minnesota 49 0
N17 ● at Pittsburgh 19 0
N24 ● | Purdue 26 0

1946 6-3-0 (4-2-0)
S21 Cincinnati 6 15
S28 | at Michigan 0 21
O5 ● | at Minnesota 21 0
O12 ● | Illinois 14 7
O19 | Iowa 0 13
O26 ● at Nebraska 27 7
N2 ● Pittsburgh 20 6
N9 ● | at Northwestern 7 6
N23 ● | at Purdue 34 20

1947 5-3-1 (2-3-1)
S27 ● at Nebraska 17 0
O4 = | Wisconsin 7 7
O11 | at Iowa 14 27
O18 ● Pittsburgh 41 6
O25 | at Northwestern 6 7
N1 ● | at Ohio State 7 0
N8 | at Michigan 0 35
N15 ● Marquette 48 6
N22 ● | Purdue 16 14

CLYDE SMITH
1948-51 (.236) 8-27-1

1948 2-7-0 (2-4-0)
S25 ● | at Wisconsin 35 7
O2 ● | Iowa 7 0
O9 TCU 6 7
O16 | Ohio State 0 17
O23 at Pittsburgh 14 21
O30 | at Minnesota 7 30
N6 Notre Dame 6 42
N13 | at Michigan 0 54
N20 | at Purdue 0 39

1949 1-8-0 (0-6-0)
S24 at Notre Dame 6 49
O1 | at Ohio State 7 46
O8 TCU 6 13
O15 | at Iowa 9 35
O22 ● Pittsburgh 48 14
O29 | Wisconsin 14 30
N5 | at Illinois 14 33
N12 | at Michigan 7 20
N19 | Purdue 6 14

1950 3-5-1 (1-4-0)
S30 = at Nebraska 20 20
O7 ● | Iowa 20 7
O14 | Ohio State 14 26
O21 ● Notre Dame 20 7
O28 | at Illinois 0 20
N4 at Michigan State 0 35
N11 | at Michigan 7 20
N18 ● Marquette 18 7
N25 | at Purdue 0 13

1951 2-7-0 (1-5-0)
S29 at Notre Dame 6 48
O6 ● Pittsburgh 13 6
O13 | at Michigan 14 33
O20 ● | at Ohio State 32 10
O27 | Illinois 0 21
N3 | at Wisconsin 0 6
N10 | at Minnesota 14 16
N17 Michigan State 26 30
N24 | Purdue 13 21

BERNIE CRIMMINS
1952-56 (.289) 13-32

1952 2-7-0 (1-5-0)
S27 | at Ohio State 13 33
O4 ● | Iowa 20 13
O11 | at Michigan 13 28
O18 ● Temple 33 0
O25 | at Northwestern 13 23
N1 at Pittsburgh 7 28
N8 Michigan State 14 41
N15 | Wisconsin 14 37
N22 | at Purdue 16 21

1953 2-7-0 (1-5-0)
S26 | at Ohio State 12 36
O2 at USC 14 27
O10 ● Marquette 21 20
O17 | at Michigan State 18 47
O24 | at Iowa 13 19
O31 Missouri 7 14
N7 | at Minnesota 20 28
N14 ● | Northwestern 14 6
N21 | Purdue 0 30

1954 3-6-0 (2-4-0)
S25 | at Ohio State 0 28
O2 ● Pacific 34 6
O9 | Michigan State 14 21
O16 at Missouri 14 20
O23 | Iowa 14 27
O30 ● | at Michigan 13 9
N6 Miami (Ohio) 0 6
N13 ● | at Northwestern 14 13
N20 | at Purdue 7 13

1955 3-6-0 (1-5-0)
S24 | Michigan State 13 20
O1 at Notre Dame 0 19
O8 | at Iowa 6 20
O15 ● Villanova 14 7
O22 ● | at Northwestern 20 14
O29 ● Ohio U. 21 14
N5 | at Ohio State 13 20
N12 | at Michigan 0 30
N19 | Purdue 4 6

1956 3-6-0 (1-5-0)

S29	|	Iowa	0	27
O6		at Notre Dame	6	20
O13	|	at Michigan State	6	53
O20	●	at Nebraska	19	14
O27	● |	Northwestern	19	13
N3	●	Marquette	19	13
N10	|	at Ohio State	14	35
N17	|	at Michigan	26	49
N24	|	at Purdue	20	39

BOB HICKS
1957 (.111) 1-8

1957 1-8-0 (0-6-0)

S28	|	at Michigan State	0	54
O5		at Notre Dame	0	26
O12	|	Iowa	7	47
O19	|	at Ohio State	0	56
O26	●	Villanova	14	7
N2	|	at Minnesota	0	34
N9		Cincinnati	0	21
N16	|	at Michigan	13	27
N23	|	Purdue	13	35

PHIL DICKENS
1958-64 (.333) 20-41-2

1958 5-3-1 (3-2-1)

S27		at Notre Dame	0	18
O4	●	West Virginia	13	12
O11	|	at Iowa	13	34
O18	|	at Ohio State	8	49
O25	●	Miami (Ohio)	12	7
N1	● |	Minnesota	6	0
N8	● |	Michigan State	6	0
N15	● |	at Michigan	8	6
N22	= |	at Purdue	15	15

1959 4-4-1 (2-4-1)

S26	● |	Illinois	20	0
O3	|	at Minnesota	14	24
O10	●	Marquette	33	13
O17	●	at Nebraska	23	7
O24	|	at Michigan State	6	14
O31	|	at Northwestern	13	30
N7	= |	at Ohio State	0	0
N14	● |	Michigan	26	7
N21	|	Purdue	7	10

1960 1-8-0 (0-7-0)

S24	|	at Illinois	6	17
O1	|	at Minnesota	0	42
O8		Oregon State	6	20
O15	●	Marquette	34	8
O22	|	Michigan State	0	35
O29	|	Northwestern	3	21
N5	|	at Ohio State	7	36
N12	|	at Michigan	7	29
N19	|	at Purdue	6	35

1961 2-7-0 (0-6-0)

S23		at Kansas State	8	14
O7	|	Wisconsin	3	6
O14	|	at Iowa	8	27
O21	●	Washington State	33	7
O28	|	at Michigan State	0	35
N4	|	at Northwestern	8	14
N11	|	Ohio State	7	16
N18	●	at West Virginia	17	9
N25	|	Purdue	12	34

1962 3-6-0 (1-5-0)

S22	●	Kansas State	21	0
S29	●	at Cincinnati	26	6
O6	|	at Wisconsin	6	30
O13	|	Iowa	10	14
O20		Washington State Spo	15	21
O27	|	Michigan State	8	26
N3	|	Northwestern	21	26
N10	|	at Ohio State	7	10
N24	● |	at Purdue	12	7

1963 3-6-0 (1-5-0)

S28	|	at Northwestern	21	34
O5	|	Ohio State	0	21
O12	|	at Iowa	26	37
O19	|	at Michigan State	3	20
O26	●	Cincinnati	20	6
N2	● |	at Minnesota	24	6
N9	●	Oregon State	20	15
N16		Oregon Port	22	28
N30	|	Purdue	15	21

1964 2-7-0 (1-5-0)

S26	|	Northwestern	13	14
O3	|	at Ohio State	9	17
O10	|	Iowa	20	21
O17	● |	Michigan State	27	20
O23	●	at Miami, Fla.	28	14
O31	|	Minnesota	0	21
N7		at Oregon State	14	24
N14		Oregon	21	29
N21	|	at Purdue	22	28

JOHN PONT
1965-72 (.380) 31-51-1

1965 2-8-0 (1-6-0)

S18	●	Kansas State	19	7
S25	|	Northwestern	0	20
O2		at Texas	12	27
O9	|	at Minnesota	18	42
O16	|	at Illinois	13	34
O23		Washington State	7	8
O30	● |	Iowa	21	17
N6	|	at Ohio State	10	17
N13	|	at Michigan State	13	27
N20	|	Purdue	21	26

1966 1-8-1 (1-5-1)

S17		Miami (Ohio)	10	20
S24	● |	at Northwestern	26	14
O1		at Texas	0	35
O8	= |	Minnesota	7	7
O15	|	Illinois	10	24
O22		at Miami, Fla.	7	14
O29	|	at Iowa	19	20
N5	|	at Ohio State	0	7
N12	|	Michigan State	19	37
N19	|	at Purdue	6	51

1967 9-2-0 (6-1-0)

S23	●	Kentucky	12	10
S30	●	Kansas	18	15
O7	● |	at Illinois	20	7
O14	● |	Iowa	21	17
O21	● |	at Michigan	27	20
O28	●	at Arizona	42	7
N4	● |	Wisconsin	14	9
N11	● |	at Michigan State	14	13
N18	|	at Minnesota	7	33
N25	● |	Purdue	19	14
		ROSE BOWL		
J1		USC	3	14

1968 6-4-0 (4-3-0)

S21	●	Baylor	40	36
S28		at Kansas	20	38
O5	● |	Illinois	28	14
O12	● |	at Iowa	38	34
O19	|	Michigan	22	27
O26	●	Arizona	16	13
N2	● |	at Wisconsin	21	20
N9	● |	at Michigan State	24	22
N16	|	Minnesota	6	20
N23	|	at Purdue	35	38

1969 4-6-0 (3-4-0)

S20	●	at Kentucky	58	30
S27		California	14	17
O4		at Colorado	7	30
O11	● |	Minnesota	17	7
O18	● |	Illinois	41	20
O25	|	at Wisconsin	34	36
N1	● |	at Michigan State	16	0
N8	|	Iowa	17	28
N15	|	at Northwestern	27	30
N22	|	Purdue	21	44

1970 1-9-0 (1-6-0)

S19		Colorado	9	16
S26		at California	14	56
O3		West Virginia	10	16
O10	|	at Minnesota	0	23
O17	● |	at Illinois	30	24
O24	|	Wisconsin	12	30
O31	|	Michigan State	7	32
N7	|	at Iowa	13	42
N14	|	Northwestern	7	21
N21	|	at Purdue	0	40

1971 3-8-0 (2-6-0)

S11	|	at Minnesota	0	28
S18	●	Kentucky	26	8
S25		at Baylor	0	10
O2		Syracuse	0	7
O9	|	at Wisconsin	29	35
O16	|	Ohio State	7	27
O23	|	Northwestern	10	24
O30	|	at Michigan	7	61
N6	|	Illinois	21	22
N13	● |	at Iowa	14	7
N20	● |	Purdue	38	31

1972 5-6-0 (3-5-0)

S16	● |	Minnesota	27	23
S23		TCU	28	31
S30	●	at Kentucky	35	34
O7	●	at Syracuse	10	2
O14	● |	Wisconsin	33	7
O21	|	at Ohio State	7	44
O28	|	at Northwestern	14	23
N4	|	Michigan	7	21
N11	|	at Illinois	20	37
N18	● |	Iowa	16	8
N25	|	at Purdue	7	42

LEE CORSO
1973-82 (.378) 41-68-2

1973 2-9-0 (0-8-0)

S15	|	Illinois	14	28
S22		at Arizona	10	26
S29	●	Kentucky	17	3
O6	●	at West Virginia	28	14
O13	|	at Minnesota	3	24
O20	|	Ohio State	7	37
O27	|	at Wisconsin	7	31
N3	|	at Michigan	13	49
N10	|	Northwestern	20	21
N17	|	at Michigan State	9	10
N24	|	Purdue	23	28

1974 1-10-0 (1-7-0)

S14	|	at Illinois	0	16
S21		Arizona	20	35
S28		at Kentucky	22	28
O5		West Virginia	0	24
O12	● |	Minnesota	34	3
O19	|	at Ohio State	9	49
O26	|	Wisconsin	25	35
N2	|	Michigan	7	21
N9	|	at Northwestern	22	24
N16	|	Michigan State	10	19
N23	|	at Purdue	17	38

1975 2-8-1 (1-6-1)

S13	● |	Minnesota	20	14
S20		at Nebraska	0	45
S27	●	Utah	31	7
O4		at North Carolina St.	0	27
O11	|	at Northwestern	0	30
O18	|	Iowa	10	20
O25	|	at Michigan	7	55
N1	|	at Ohio State	14	24
N8	|	Michigan State	6	14
N15	= |	at Wisconsin	9	9
N22	|	Purdue	7	9

1976 5-6-0 (4-4-0)

S11	|	at Minnesota	13	32
S18		Nebraska	13	45
S25	●	at Washington	20	13
O2		North Carolina St.	21	24
O9	● |	Northwestern	7	0
O16	● |	at Iowa	14	7
O23	|	Michigan	0	35
O30	|	Ohio State	7	47
N6	|	at Michigan State	0	23
N13	● |	Wisconsin	15	14
N20	● |	at Purdue	20	14

1977 5-5-1 (4-3-1)

S10	|	Wisconsin	14	30
S17	●	LSU	24	21
S24		Miami (Ohio)	20	21
O1		at Nebraska	13	31
O8	● |	at Northwestern	28	3
O15	= |	Michigan State	13	13
O22	|	at Illinois	7	21
O29	● |	Minnesota	34	22
N5	● |	at Iowa	24	21
N12	|	at Ohio State	7	35
N19	● |	Purdue	21	10

1978 4-7-0 (3-5-0)

S16		at LSU	17	24
S23	●	Washington	14	7
S30		Nebraska	17	69
O7	|	at Wisconsin	7	34
O14	● |	Northwestern	38	10
O21	|	at Michigan State	14	49
O28	● |	Illinois	31	10
N4	|	at Minnesota	31	32
N11	● |	Iowa	34	14
N18	|	Ohio State	18	21
N25	|	at Purdue	7	20

1979 8-4-0 (5-3-0)

S8	● |	at Iowa	30	26
S15	●	Vanderbilt	44	13
S22	●	Kentucky	18	10
S29		Colorado	16	17
O6	● |	at Wisconsin	3	0
O13	|	at Ohio State	6	47
O20	● |	Northwestern	30	0
O27	|	at Michigan	21	27
N3	● |	Minnesota	42	24
N10	● |	at Illinois	45	14
N17	|	Purdue	21	37
		HOLIDAY BOWL		
D21	●	Brigham Young	38	37

1980 6-5-0 (3-5-0)

S13	|	Iowa	7	16
S20	●	at Kentucky	36	30
S27	●	at Colorado	49	7
O4	●	Duke	31	21
O11	● |	Wisconsin	24	0
O18	|	at Ohio State	17	27
O25	● |	at Northwestern	35	20
N1	|	Michigan	0	35
N8	|	at Minnesota	7	31
N15	● |	Illinois	26	24
N22	|	at Purdue	23	24

1981 3-8-0 (3-6-0)

S12	● |	at Northwestern	21	20
S19		USC	0	21
S26		at Syracuse	7	21
O3	|	Michigan	17	38
O10	|	at Iowa	28	42
O17	● |	Minnesota	17	16
O24	|	at Ohio State	10	29
O31	|	at Michigan State	3	26
N7	|	Wisconsin	7	28
N14	|	at Illinois	14	35
N21	● |	Purdue	20	17

1982 5-6-0 (4-5-0)

S11	● |	Northwestern	30	0
S18		at USC	7	28
S25	●	Syracuse	17	10
O2	|	at Michigan	10	24
O9	|	Iowa	20	24
O16	● |	at Minnesota	40	21
O23	|	Ohio State	25	49
O30	|	Michigan State	14	22
N6	● |	at Wisconsin	20	17
N13	|	Illinois	7	48
N20	● |	at Purdue	13	7

SAM WYCHE
1983 (.273) 3-8

1983 3-8-0 (2-7-0)

S10	●	Duke	15	10
S17		at Kentucky	13	24
S24	|	Northwestern	8	10
O1	|	at Michigan	18	43
O8	● |	Minnesota	38	31
O15	● |	Michigan State	24	12
O22	|	at Wisconsin	14	45
O29	|	at Iowa	3	49
N5	|	Ohio State	17	56
N12	|	at Illinois	21	49
N19	|	Purdue	30	31

BILL MALLORY
1984-96 (.466) 68-78-3

1984 0-11-0 (0-9-0)

S8		at Duke	24	31
S15		Kentucky	14	48
S22	|	at Northwestern	37	40
S29	|	Michigan	6	14
O6	|	at Minnesota	24	33
O13	|	at Michigan State	6	13
O20	|	Wisconsin	16	20
O27	|	Iowa	20	24
N3	|	at Ohio State	7	50
N10	|	Illinois Ind	7	34
N17	|	at Purdue	24	31

1985 4-7-0 (1-7-0)

S14	●	Louisville	41	28
S21	●	Navy	38	35
S28	●	at Missouri	36	17
O5	● |	Northwestern	26	7
O12	|	at Ohio State	7	48
O19	|	Minnesota	7	22
O26	|	at Michigan	15	42
N2	|	at Wisconsin	20	31
N9	|	Michigan State	16	35
N16	|	at Illinois	24	41
N23	|	Purdue	21	34

1986 — 6-6-0 (3-5-0)

Date		Opponent	IU	Opp
S13	●	Louisville	21	0
S20	●	Navy	52	29
S27	●	at Missouri	41	24
O4	●	at Northwestern	24	7
O11		Ohio State	22	24
O18		at Minnesota	17	19
O25		Michigan	14	38
N1	●	Wisconsin	21	7
N8	●	at Michigan State	17	14
N15		Illinois	16	21
N22	●	at Purdue	15	17
ALL-AMERICAN BOWL				
D31		Florida State	13	27

1987 — 8-4-0 (6-2-0)

Date		Opponent	IU	Opp
S12	●	Rice	35	13
S19		at Kentucky	15	34
S26	●	Missouri	20	17
O3	●	Northwestern	35	18
O10	●	at Ohio State	31	10
O16	●	at Minnesota	18	17
O24	●	Michigan	14	10
O31		at Iowa	21	29
N7		Illinois	34	22
N14		at Michigan State	3	27
N21	●	Purdue	35	14
PEACH BOWL				
J2		Tennessee	22	27

1988 — 8-3-1 (5-3-0)

Date		Opponent	IU	Opp
S10	●	at Rice	41	14
S17	●	Kentucky	36	15
S24	=	at Missouri	28	28
O1	●	at Northwestern	48	17
O8	●	Ohio State	41	7
O15	●	Minnesota	33	13
O22		at Michigan	6	31
O29	●	Iowa	45	34
N5		at Illinois	20	21
N12		Michigan State	12	38
N19	●	at Purdue	52	7
LIBERTY BOWL				
D28	●	South Carolina	34	10

1989 — 5-6-0 (3-5-0)

Date		Opponent	IU	Opp
S9		at Kentucky	14	17
S16	●	Missouri	24	7
S30	●	Toledo	32	12
O7	●	Northwestern	43	11
O14		at Ohio State	31	35
O21	●	Minnesota	28	18
O28		at Michigan	10	38
N4		Michigan State	20	51
N11	●	at Wisconsin	45	17
N18		at Illinois	28	41
N25		Purdue	14	15

1990 — 6-5-1 (3-4-1)

Date		Opponent	IU	Opp
S15	●	at Kentucky	45	24
S22	●	Missouri	58	7
S29	●	Eastern Michigan	37	6
O6	●	at Northwestern	42	0
O13	=	Ohio State	27	27
O20		at Minnesota	0	12
O27		Michigan	19	45
N3		at Michigan State	20	45
N10	●	Wisconsin	20	7
N17	●	Illinois	10	24
N24	●	at Purdue	28	14
PEACH BOWL				
D29	●	Auburn	23	27

1991 — 7-4-1 (5-3-0)

Date		Opponent	IU	Opp
S7		at Notre Dame	27	49
S21	●	Kentucky	13	10
S28	=	at Missouri	27	27
O5	●	Michigan State	31	0
O12	●	Northwestern	44	6
O19		at Michigan	16	24
O26	●	at Wisconsin	28	20
N2	●	Minnesota	34	8
N9		at Iowa	21	38
N16		at Ohio State	16	20
N23	●	Purdue	24	22
COPPER BOWL				
D31	●	Baylor	24	0

1992 — 5-6-0 (3-5-0)

Date		Opponent	IU	Opp
S12	●	Miami (Ohio)	16	0
S19	●	at Kentucky	25	37
S26		Missouri	20	10
O3		at Michigan State	31	42
O10	●	at Northwestern	28	3
O17		Michigan	3	31
O24	●	Wisconsin	10	3
O31	●	at Minnesota	24	17
N7		Iowa	0	14
N14		Ohio State	10	27
N21		at Purdue	10	13

1993 — 8-4-0 (5-3-0)

Date		Opponent	IU	Opp
S4	●	Toledo	27	0
S11	●	Northern Illinois	28	10
S18	●	Kentucky	24	8
S25		Wisconsin	15	27
O2	●	at Minnesota	23	19
O9	●	Iowa	16	10
O23	●	at Northwestern	24	0
O30	●	Michigan State	10	0
N6		at Penn State	31	38
N13		at Ohio State	17	23
N20	●	Purdue	24	17
INDEPENDENCE BOWL				
D31		Virginia Tech	20	45

1994 — 6-5-0 (3-5-0)

Date		Opponent	IU	Opp
S3	●	Cincinnati	28	3
S10	●	Miami (Ohio)	35	14
S17	●	at Kentucky	59	29
S24		at Wisconsin	13	62
O1	●	Minnesota	25	14
O8	●	at Iowa	27	20
O22		Northwestern	7	20
O29		at Michigan State	21	27 †
N5		Penn State	29	35
N12		Ohio State	17	32
N19	●	at Purdue	33	29

1995 — 2-9-0 (0-8-0)

Date		Opponent	IU	Opp
S9	●	Western Michigan	24	10
S16		Kentucky	10	17
S23	●	Southern Miss	27	26
S30		at Northwestern	7	31
O7		Illinois	10	17
O14	●	at Iowa	13	22
O21		Michigan	17	34
O28		at Penn State	21	45
N11		Michigan State	13	31
N18		at Ohio State	3	42
N24		Purdue	14	51

1996 — 3-8 (1-7)

Date		Opponent	IU	Opp
S7	●	at Toledo	40	6
S14	●	Miami (Ohio)	21	14
S21		at Kentucky	0	3
S28		Northwestern	17	35
O5		at Illinois	43	46
O12		Iowa	10	31
O19		at Michigan	20	27
O26		Penn State	26	48
N9		at Michigan State	15	38
N16		Ohio State	17	27
N23	●	at Purdue	33	16

CAM CAMERON
1997-2001 (.327)   18-37

1997 — 2-9 (1-7)

Date		Opponent	IU	Opp
S6	●	at North Carolina	6	23
S13	●	Ball State	33	6
S20		Kentucky	7	49
S27	●	at Wisconsin	26	27
O4		Michigan	0	37
O11		Michigan State	6	38
O18		at Ohio State	0	31
O25		at Iowa	0	62
N1	●	Illinois	23	6
N15		at Minnesota	12	24
N22		Purdue	7	56

1998 — 4-7 (2-6)

Date		Opponent	IU	Opp
S12	●	Western Michigan	45	30
S19		at Kentucky	27	31
S26	●	at Cincinnati	48	14
O3		Wisconsin	20	24
O10		at Michigan State	31	38
O17	●	Iowa	14	7
O24		at Michigan	10	21
O31		Ohio State	7	38
N7		at Illinois	16	31
N14	●	Minnesota	20	19
N21		at Purdue	7	52

1999 — 4-7 (3-5)

Date		Opponent	IU	Opp
S4	●	Ball State	21	9
S11	●	North Carolina	30	42
S18		Kentucky	35	44
S25		at Penn State	24	45
O2	●	Illinois	34	31
O9	●	Northwestern	34	17
O16		at Wisconsin	0	59
O23	●	at Iowa	38	31
O30		Michigan	31	34
N13		at Minnesota	20	44
N20		Purdue	24	30

2000 — 3-8 (2-6)

Date		Opponent	IU	Opp
S9		North Carolina St.	38	41
S16		at Kentucky	34	41
S23	●	Cincinnati	42	6
S30	●	Iowa	45	33
O7		at Northwestern	33	52
O14		at Michigan	0	58
O21	●	Minnesota	51	43
O28		Penn State IND	24	27
N4		at Illinois	35	42
N11		Wisconsin	22	43
N18		at Purdue	13	41

2001 — 5-6 (4-4)

Date		Opponent	IU	Opp
S6		at North Carolina St.	14	35
S22		Utah	26	28
S29		Ohio State	14	27
O6	●	at Wisconsin	63	32
O13		Illinois	14	35
O20		at Iowa	28	42
N3	●	Northwestern	56	21
N10	●	at Michigan State	37	28
N17		at Penn State	14	28
N24	●	Purdue	13	7
D1	●	Kentucky	26	15

GERRY DiNARDO
2002-04 (.229)   8-27

2002 — 3-9 (1-7)

Date		Opponent	IU	Opp
A31	●	William & Mary	25	17
S7		at Utah	13	40
S14		at Kentucky	17	27
S21	●	Central Michigan	39	29
S28		at Ohio State	17	45
O12	●	Wisconsin	32	29
O19		Iowa	8	24
O26		at Illinois	14	45
N2		at Northwestern	37	41
N9		Michigan State	21	56
N16		Penn State	25	58
N23		at Purdue	10	34

2003 — 2-10 (1-7)

Date		Opponent	IU	Opp
A30		at Connecticut	10	34
S6		at Washington	13	38
S13	●	Indiana St.	33	3
S20		Kentucky	17	34
S27		at Michigan	17	31
O4		at Michigan State	3	31
O11		Northwestern	31	37
O25		Ohio State	6	35
N1		at Minnesota	7	55
N8	●	Illinois	17	14
N15		at Penn State	7	52
N22		Purdue	16	24

2004 — 3-8 (1-7)

Date		Opponent	IU	Opp
S4	●	Central Michigan	41	10
S11	●	at Oregon	30	24
S18		at Kentucky	32	51
S25	●	Michigan State	20	30
O2		Michigan	14	35
O9		at Northwestern	24	31
O23		at Ohio State	7	30
O30	●	Minnesota	30	21
N6		at Illinois	22	26
N13		Penn State	18	22
N20		at Purdue	24	63

TERRY HOEPPNER
2005-06 (.391)   9-14

2005 — 4-7-0 (1-7-0)

Date		Opponent	IU	Opp
S2	●	at Central Michigan	20	13
S10	●	Nicholls St.	35	31
S17	●	Kentucky	38	14
O1		at Wisconsin	24	41
O8	●	Illinois	36	13
O15		at Iowa	21	38
O22		Ohio State	10	41
O29		at Michigan State	15	46
N5		Minnesota	21	42
N12		at Michigan	14	41
N19		Purdue	14	41

2006 — 5-7 (3-5)

Date		Opponent	IU	Opp
S2		Western Michigan	39	20
S9	●	at Ball State	24	23
S16		So. Illinois	28	35
S23		Connecticut	7	14
S30		Wisconsin	17	52
O7	●	at Illinois	34	32
O14	●	Iowa	31	28
O21		at Ohio State	3	44
O28	●	Michigan State	46	21
N4		at Minnesota	26	63
N11		Michigan	3	34
N18		at Purdue	19	28

Neutral Site key: *Balt* Baltimore, Md. / *Bos* Boston, Mass. / *Chi* Chicago, Ill. / *Ind* Indianapolis, Ind. / *NYC* New York, N.Y. / *Port* Portland, Ore. / *Spo* Spokane, Wash. / *Unk* Unknown
f Forfeit † Game Later Forfieted # Disputed Victor * Disputed Score || Designated Conference Game |2 Counted Twice in Conference Standings

INDIANA RECORD BOOK

SINGLE-GAME RECORDS

RUSHING YARDS

RANK	PLAYER	DATE	OPPONENT	ATT	AVG	YDS
1	Anthony Thompson	Nov. 11, 1989	Wisconsin	52	7.3	377
2	Levron Williams	Oct. 6, 2001	Wisconsin	20	14.0	280
3	Vaughn Dunbar	Sept. 28, 1991	Missouri	33	8.0	265
4	Levron Williams	Nov. 10, 2001	Michigan State	26	9.7	251
5	Alex Smith	Nov. 19, 1994	Purdue	31	7.9	245

PASSING YARDS

RANK	PLAYER	DATE	OPPONENT	ATT	COMP	YDS
1	Jay Rodgers	Sept. 13, 1997	Ball State	39	27	408
2	Babe Laufenberg	Oct. 9, 1982	Iowa	36	26	390
3	Antwaan Randle El	Sept. 12, 1998	Western Michigan	29	22	385
4	John Paci	Nov. 6, 1993	Penn State	37	20	379
5	Dave Schnell	Dec. 28, 1988	South Carolina	31	16	378

RECEIVING YARDS

RANK	PLAYER	DATE	OPPONENT	REC	AVG	YDS
1	Thomas Lewis	Nov. 6, 1993	Penn State	12	23.8	285
2	Tyrone Browning	Sept. 12, 1998	Western Michigan	13	19.8	258
3	Nate Lundy	Sept. 27, 1980	Colorado	5	51.2	256
4	James Hardy	Oct. 15, 2005	Iowa	12	16.9	203
5	Courtney Roby	Oct. 19, 2002	Iowa	11	18.0	198

POINTS

RANK	PLAYER	DATE	OPPONENT	TOT
1	Levron Williams	Oct. 6, 2001	Wisconsin	36
2	Anthony Thompson	Oct. 7, 1989	Northwestern	32
3	Anthony Thompson	Nov. 11, 1989	Wisconsin	24
	Anthony Thompson	Oct. 8, 1988	Ohio State	24
5	Tom Nowatzke	Nov. 14, 1964	Oregon	21

FIELD GOALS

RANK	PLAYER	DATE	OPPONENT	TOT
1	Andy Payne	Nov. 15, 1997	Minnesota	4
	Andy Payne	Nov. 27, 1997	Wisconsin	4
	Chris Gartner	Oct. 14, 1972	Wisconsin	4
	Chris Gartner	Sept. 18, 1971	Kentucky	4

TACKLES

RANK	PLAYER	DATE	OPPONENT	TOT
1	Joe Norman	Nov. 18, 1978	Ohio State	26
2	Donnie Thomas	Nov. 1, 1975	Ohio State	25
	Karl Pankratz	Oct. 29, 1969	Wisconsin	25
4	4 players tied at 24			

INTERCEPTIONS

RANK	PLAYER	DATE	OPPONENT	TOT
1	Greg Yeldell	Oct. 24, 1998	Michigan	3
	Tim Wilbur	Nov. 10, 1979	Illinois	3
	Ben Norman	Sept. 21, 1968	Baylor	3
	Milt Campbell	Oct. 29, 1955	Ohio	3
	Florian Helinski	Oct. 30, 1954	Michigan	3

RETIRED NUMBERS

11 Antwaan Randle El
14 Tim Clifford
32 Anthony Thompson

SINGLE-SEASON RECORDS

RUSHING YARDS

RANK	PLAYER	SEASON	G	ATT	YDS
1	Vaughn Dunbar	1991	12	364	1,805
2	Anthony Thompson	1989	11	358	1,793
3	Anthony Thompson	1988	12	355	1,686
4	Alex Smith	1994	11	265	1,475
5	Levron Williams	2001	10	212	1,401

PASSING YARDS

RANK	PLAYER	SEASON	G	ATT	COMP	PCT	YDS
1	Trent Green	1991	12	339	200	59	2,627
2	Steve Bradley	1984	11	402	208	52	2,544
3	Babe Laufenberg	1982	11	364	217	60	2,468
4	Blake Powers	2005	11	376	212	56	2,305
5	Steve Bradley	1983	11	355	182	51	2,298

RECEIVING YARDS

RANK	PLAYER	SEASON	G	REC	AVG	YDS
1	Ernie Jones	1987	11	66	19.2	1,265
2	Thomas Lewis	1993	12	55	19.2	1,058
3	Courtney Roby	2002	12	59	17.6	1,039
4	Kenny Allen	1985	10	61	15.2	929
5	James Hardy	2005	11	55	16.2	893

SCORING

RANK	PLAYER	SEASON	TD	FG	PAT	P2	TOT
1	Anthony Thompson	1988	26	0	0	0	156
2	Anthony Thompson	1989	25	0	0	2	154
3	Levron Williams	2001	19	0	0	0	114
4	Pete Stoyanovich	1988	0	17	45	0	96
5	5 players tied at 78						

TOUCHDOWNS

RANK	PLAYER	SEASON	G	TOT
1	Anthony Thompson	1988	12	26
2	Anthony Thompson	1989	11	25
3	Levron Williams	2001	10	19
4	5 players tied at 13			

TACKLES

RANK	PLAYER	SEASON	G	TOT
1	Joe Norman	1978	11	199
2	Steve Sanders	1976	11	165
3	Joe Fitzgerald	1984	11	155
4	Craig Brinkman	1974	11	141
5	Donnie Thomas	1975	11	137

INTERCEPTIONS

RANK	PLAYER	SEASON	G	YDS	TOT
1	Tim Wilbur	1979	12	167	8
2	Dave Abrams	1977	11	24	7
3	4 players tied at 6				

PUNTING

RANK	PLAYER	SEASON	PUNTS	YDS	AVG
1	Drew Hagan	1999	44	1,971	44.8
2	Jim DiGuilio	1992	53	2,347	44.3
3	Chuck Razmic	1984	57	2,505	43.9
4	Alan Sutkowski	1996	65	2,816	43.3
5	Tom Bolyard	1988	31	1,335	43.1

PUNT RETURNS/YARDS

RANK	PLAYER	SEASON	RET	YDS	AVG
1	Bob Hoernschemeyer	1943	NA	635	NA
2	Bill Hillenbrand	1941	NA	561	NA
3	Bill Hillenbrand	1942	NA	481	NA
4	Rob Turner	1990	28	376	13.4
5	Thomas Lewis	1993	45	342	7.6

KICKOFF RETURNS

RANK	PLAYER	SEASON	RET	YDS	AVG
1	Marcus Thigpen	2006	24	723	30.1
2	Lance Bennett	2004	20	599	30.0
3	Derin Graham	2000	38	897	23.6
4	Derin Graham	1998	30	643	21.4
5	A.C. Carter	2002	36	732	20.3

BIG TEN TEAMS

CAREER RECORDS

RUSHING YARDS

RANK	PLAYER	SEASONS	ATT	AVG	TD	YDS
1	Anthony Thompson	1986-89	1,161	4.6	67	5,299
2	Antwaan Randle El	1998-2001	857	4.5	44	3,895
3	Alex Smith	1994-96	723	4.8	21	3,492
4	Mike Harkrader	1976-80	718	4.5	15	3,257
5	Levron Williams	1998-2001	452	6.8	31	3,095
6	Vaughn Dunbar	1990-91	613	4.9	25	3,029
7	Courtney Snyder	1973-76	631	4.4	8	2,789
8	John Isenbarger	1967-69	487	5.0	14	2,453
9	Lonnie Johnson	1977-80	458	4.9	19	2,228
10	Ric Enis	1974-77	464	4.5	12	2,096

PASSING YARDS

RANK	PLAYER	SEASONS	ATT	COMP	PCT	INT	TD	YDS
1	Antwaan Randle El	1998-2001	1,060	528	49.8	37	42	7,469
2	Steve Bradley	1983-85	1,023	532	52.0	52	35	6,579
3	Dave Schnell	1986-89	722	406	56.2	31	27	5,470
4	Trent Green	1989-92	755	421	55.7	31	23	5,400
5	Tim Clifford	1977-80	631	333	52.7	22	31	4,338
6	Babe Laufenberg	1981-82	616	361	58.6	25	19	4,256
7	Matt LoVecchio	2003-04	562	308	54.8	16	16	3,729
8	Harry Gonso	1967-69	531	256	48.2	31	32	3,446
9	Chris Dittoe	1993-96	512	268	52.3	14	14	3,240
10	John Paci	1992-94	494	262	53.0	15	15	3,119

RECEIVING YARDS

RANK	PLAYER	SEASONS	REC	AVG	TD	YDS
1	Courtney Roby	2001-04	170	14.8	14	2,254
2	Ernie Jones	1984-87	133	17.8	20	2,361
3	Thomas Lewis	1991-93	148	15.7	18	2,324
4	Duane Gunn	1981-83	116	19.3	14	2,235
5	Jade Butcher	1967-69	117	15.5	30	1,810
6	Bill Malinchak	1963-65	115	14.7	14	1,686
7	Eddie Baety	1991-94	132	12.3	6	1,617
8	James Hardy	2005-	112	14.4	20	1,615
9	Rob Turner	1987-90	71	22.6	14	1,603
10	Keith Calvin	1974-77	122	13.0	4	1,590

SCORING

RANK	PLAYER	SEASONS	TD	FG	PAT	P2	TOT
1	Anthony Thompson	1986-89	68	0	0	2	412
2	Antwaan Randle El	1998-2001	45	0	0	0	270
3	Scott Bonnell	1989-92	0	48	117	0	261
4	Pete Stoyanovich	1985-88	0	47	107	0	248
5	Andy Payne	1997-2000	0	43	109	0	238

TOUCHDOWNS

RANK	PLAYER	SEASONS	TOT
1	Anthony Thompson	1986-89	68
2	Antwaan Randle El	1998-2001	45
3	Levron Williams	1998-2001	38
4	Jade Butcher	1967-69	30
5	Vaughn Dunbar	1990-91	25

TACKLES

RANK	PLAYER	SEASONS	TOT
1	Joe Norman	1975-78	444
2	Willie Bates	1985-88	384
3	Donnie Thomas	1973-75	369
4	Herana Daze-Jones	2001-04	342
5	2 players tied at 336		

INTERCEPTIONS

RANK	PLAYER	SEASONS	YDS	TOT
1	Tim Wilbur	1978-80, 82	360	19
2	John Cannady	1943-46	NA	11
	Dave Abrams	1977-78	43	11
	Lance Brown	1991-94	78	11
5	3 players tied at 10			

PUNTING

RANK	PLAYER	SEASONS	PUNTS	YDS	AVG
1	Alan Sutkowski	1995-97	198	8,419	42.5
2	Jim DiGuilio	1991-94	195	8,086	41.5
3	Macky Smith	1988-90	111	4,570	41.2
	Tyson Beattie	2003-05	208	8,581	41.2
5	Dan Stryzinski	1985-87	161	6,532	40.6

TEAM RECORDS

LONGEST WINNING STREAK
• 8 (tie), Oct. 6-Nov. 24, 1945
Streak broken vs. Cincinnati, 6-15, Sept. 21, 1946
Sept. 23-Nov. 11, 1967
Streak broken vs. Minnesota, 7-33, Nov. 18, 1967

LONGEST UNDEFEATED STREAK
• 12, Nov. 18, 1944-Nov. 24, 1945
Streak broken vs. Cincinnati, 6-15, Sept. 21, 1946

MOST CONSECUTIVE WINNING SEASONS
• 7, 1895-01

MOST CONSECUTIVE BOWL APPEARANCES
• 3, 1986-88

MOST POINTS IN A GAME
• 76, vs. Franklin, Oct. 19, 1901

MOST POINTS ALLOWED IN A GAME
• 69, vs. Nebraska, Sept. 30, 1978

LARGEST MARGIN OF VICTORY
• 76 (76-0), vs. Franklin, Oct. 19, 1901

LARGEST MARGIN OF DEFEAT
• 68 (0-68), vs. Purdue, Nov. 5, 1892

LONGEST RUN FROM SCRIMMAGE
• 98 yards, Mickey Erehar, vs. Iowa, Nov. 2, 1912

LONGEST PASS PLAY
• 99 yards, John Paci to Thomas Lewis, vs. Penn State, Nov. 6, 1993

LONGEST FIELD GOAL
• 55 yards, Scott Bonnell, vs. Michigan, Oct. 28, 1989

LONGEST PUNT
• 86 yards, Jim DiGuilio, vs. Wisconsin, Oct. 24, 1992

LONGEST INTERCEPTION RETURN
• 99 yards, Mike Dumas, vs. Purdue, Nov. 24, 1990

LONGEST PUNT RETURN
• 94 yards, Lance Bennett, vs. Michigan St., Nov. 25, 2004

PUNT RETURNS/YARDS

RANK	PLAYER	SEASON	RET	YDS	AVG
1	Bill Hillenbrand	1941-42	NA	1,402	NA
2	Bob Hoernschemeyer	1943-44	NA	817	NA
3	Tim Wilbur	1978-82	90	721	8.0
4	Tony Buford	1985-88	81	641	7.9
5	Steve Porter	1969-71	65	561	8.6

KICKOFF RETURNS

RANK	PLAYER	SEASON	RET	YDS	AVG
1	Lance Bennett	2003-05	62	1,566	25.3
2	Thomas Lewis	1991-93	52	1,183	22.8
3	Derin Graham	1998-2000	93	2,008	22.5
4	A.C. Carter	1999-2002	81	1,500	18.5
5	Keith Calvin	1974-77	70	1,271	18.2

INDIANA ANNUAL STATISTICAL LEADERS

YR	RUSHING	YDS	ATT	AVG	PASSING	ATT	CMP	PCT	YDS	RECEIVING	REC	YDS	AVG
1963	Tom Nowatzke	756	160	4.7	Richie Badar	94	55	.59	679	Bill Malinchak	25	353	14.1
1964	Tom Nowatzke	545	150	3.6	Richie Badar	245	121	.49	1,571	Bill Malinchak	46	634	13.8
1965	Terry Cole	286	91	3.1	Frank Stavroff	159	74	.47	1,045	Bill Malinchak	44	699	15.9
1966	Mike Krivoshia	675	179	3.8	Frank Stavroff	224	119	.53	1,406	Bill Couch	45	546	12.1
1967	John Isenbarger	579	120	4.8	Harry Gonso	143	67	.47	931	Jade Butcher	38	654	17.2
1968	John Isenbarger	669	130	5.1	Harry Gonso	163	76	.47	1,109	Jade Butcher	44	713	16.2
1969	John Isenbarger	1,217	233	5.2	Harry Gonso	207	107	.52	1,336	Jade Butcher	37	552	14.9
1970	John Motil	358	101	3.5	Ted McNulty	126	55	.44	488	John Andrews	29	268	9.2
1971	Ken St. Pierre	760	181	4.2	Ted McNulty	201	95	.47	1,140	Alan Dick	25	312	12.5
1972	Ken Starling	781	196	4.0	Ted McNulty	132	74	.56	906	Glenn Scolnick	53	727	13.7
1973	Ken Starling	676	180	3.8	Willie Jones	135	76	.56	881	Trent Smock	36	505	14.0
1974	Courtney Snyder	1,254	291	4.3	Terry Jones	220	129	.59	1,347	Trent Smock	31	549	17.7
1975	Courtney Snyder	1,103	248	4.4	Terry Jones	135	65	.48	787	Trent Smock	25	427	17.1
1976	Mike Harkrader	1,003	192	5.2	Scott Arnett	93	42	.45	398	Keith Calvin	26	319	12.3
1977	Ric Enis	978	199	4.9	Scott Arnett	151	73	.48	604	Keith Calvin	41	604	14.7
1978	Mike Harkrader	880	198	4.4	Tim Clifford	130	60	.46	726	Mike Friede	17	412	24.2
1979	Mike Harkrader	807	210	3.8	Tim Clifford	288	160	.56	2,078	Bob Stephenson	49	564	11.5
1980	Lonnie Johnson	1,075	200	5.4	Tim Clifford	198	105	.53	1,391	Bob Stephenson	26	337	13.0
1981	Tim Hines	271	67	4.0	Babe Laufenberg	252	144	.57	1,788	Bob Stephenson	32	230	7.2
1982	Orlando Brown	580	136	4.3	Babe Laufenberg	364	217	.60	2,468	Duane Gunn	35	764	21.8
1983	Orlando Brown	312	72	4.3	Steve Bradley	355	182	.51	2,298	Duane Gunn	50	815	16.3
1984	Bobby Howard	268	78	3.4	Steve Bradley	402	208	.52	2,544	Len Kenebrew	41	750	18.3
1985	Bobby Howard	967	194	5.0	Steve Bradley	266	142	.53	1,737	Kenny Allen	55	929	16.9
1986	Anthony Thompson	806	191	4.2	Dave Kramme	180	98	.54	1,334	Tony Buford	26	416	16.0
1987	Anthony Thompson	1,014	257	3.9	Dave Schnell	207	121	.58	1,707	Ernie Jones	66	1,265	19.2
1988	Anthony Thompson	1,686	355	4.7	Dave Schnell	225	119	.53	1,877	Rob Turner	36	814	22.6
1989	Anthony Thompson	1,793	358	5.0	Dave Schnell	258	146	.57	1,608	Eddie Thomas	38	559	14.7
1990	Vaughn Dunbar	1,224	250	4.9	Trent Green	128	60	.47	934	Rob Turner	33	717	21.7
1991	Vaughn Dunbar	1,805	364	5.0	Trent Green	339	200	.59	2,627	Eddie Thomas	54	687	12.7
1992	Brett Law	541	130	4.2	Trent Green	278	154	.55	1,780	Thomas Lewis	54	685	12.7
1993	Jermaine Chaney	716	186	3.8	John Paci	258	133	.52	1,796	Thomas Lewis	55	1,058	19.2
1994	Alex Smith	1,475	265	5.6	John Paci	176	96	.55	996	Eddie Baety	45	559	12.4
1995	Alex Smith	769	166	4.6	Chris Dittoe	196	102	.52	1,214	Sean Glover	33	239	7.2
1996	Alex Smith	1,248	292	4.3	Chris Dittoe	159	83	.52	1,035	Dorian Wilkerson	40	490	12.3
1997	De'Wayne Hogan	506	149	3.4	Jay Rodgers	330	192	.58	2,156	Chris Gall	54	422	7.8
1998	Antwaan Randle El	873	227	3.8	Antwaan Randle El	273	127	.47	1,745	Tyrone Browning	47	764	16.3
1999	Levron Williams	817	118	6.9	Antwaan Randle El	279	150	.54	2,277	Versie Gaddis	35	633	18.1
2000	Antwaan Randle El	1,270	218	5.8	Antwaan Randle El	277	133	.48	1,783	Versie Gaddis	29	554	19.1
2001	Levron Williams	1,401	212	6.6	Antwaan Randle El	231	118	.51	1,664	Levron Williams	26	289	11.1
2002	Yamar Washington	688	174	4.0	Gibran Hamdan	293	152	.52	2,115	Courtney Roby	59	1,039	17.6
2003	BenJarvus Green-Ellis	938	225	4.2	Matt LoVecchio	291	155	.53	1,778	Courtney Roby	45	504	11.2
2004	BenJarvus Green-Ellis	794	231	3.4	Matt LoVecchio	271	153	.57	1,951	Courtney Roby	55	810	14.7
2005	Chris Taylor	740	156	4.7	Blake Powers	376	212	.56	2,305	James Hardy	61	893	14.6
2006	Kellen Lewis	441	124	3.6	Kellen Lewis	346	190	.55	2,221	James Hardy	51	722	14.2

Receiving leaders by receptions
All statistics include postseason

IOWA

BY TODD JONES

THE HISTORY OF IOWA FOOTBALL reflects the agricultural nature of America's heartland. Some years have brought drought and minimal production, while others have been a bounty of excitement, awards, and championship glory. Memories of Aubrey Devine and Duke Slater starring for Howard Jones in the 1920s and Alex Karras and Randy Duncan starring for Forest Evashevski in the 1950s alleviate the pain of recent tough times. Hayden Fry showed in the 1980s that Iowa can reap as much success as any program. When his teams stumbled in his final years, in the 1990s, his successor, Kirk Ferentz, proved there's always a chance for new life. Through it all, good times and bad, there has never been any doubt about the passion of the Hawkeye fans and the sustenance of their teams. Iowa always pushes on, like its 1939 Heisman winner, Nile Kinnick.

TRADITION In 1935, Iowa governor Clyde Herring and Minnesota governor Floyd B. Olson wagered on the game between their state universities as a way to cool bad feelings and promote sportsmanship. Iowa lost to Minnesota, so Herring walked into Olson's office and presented him with Floyd of Rosedale—a full-blooded, award-winning pig named for Olson, raised by Iowa farmer Allen Loomis, and the brother of Blueboy from Will Rogers' movie *State Fair*. Olson, in turn, offered up Floyd as the grand prize in a statewide essay-writing contest. The winner, Robert Jones, then sold the hog to the University of Minnesota. Olson commissioned St. Paul artist Charles Brioschi to sculpt Floyd's image. The bronze pig, 21 inches long and 15 inches high, became the annual prize for the winner of the Iowa-Minnesota game. The Hawkeyes also play for the Cy-Hawk Trophy, awarded to the Iowa-Iowa State winner. Donated in 1977 by the Des Moines Athletic Club, the trophy features a running back and the school mascots, Herky the Hawkeye and Cy the Cardinal. Iowa hadn't played Iowa State in 43 years when the rivalry resumed in 1977.

BEST PLAYER The coins tossed by officials at the start of some Big Ten games bear Kinnick's face. He won the Heisman, Walter Camp, and Maxwell trophies in 1939 as a runner, passer, kicker, and defender on Iowa's legendary Ironmen team. The humble Iowa native was also Phi Beta Kappa with a 3.4 GPA. His play as a junior

> *Fry redesigned the uniforms for 1979 to change the mind-set of a losing program.*

was hampered by an ankle injury that Kinnick, a Christian Scientist, would not allow to be examined, much less treated. He returned healthy as a senior and led the Hawkeyes to a 6–1–1 record by rushing for 5 TDs and throwing for 11, drop-kicking 11 extra points and scoring 107 of the team's 130 points. He led the Hawkeyes to victory five times after facing fourth-quarter deficits. Kinnick, a stocky 5'9" and 175 pounds, played all 60 minutes in six games and 402 of a possible 420 minutes that season. He led the country in kickoff-return yardage (377) and tied for the lead in interceptions (8), an Iowa record he still shares with Lou King. The Associated Press named the "Cornbelt Comet" the nation's top male athlete of 1939, ahead of Joe DiMaggio and Joe Louis. His Heisman acceptance speech is renowned for its eloquence. For all the statistics and awards he chalked up, people were drawn to Kinnick as much for his aura, humbleness, compassion, and self-discipline. After a year of law school, Kinnick enlisted in the Naval Air Corps reserve instead of playing pro football. "I would be lacking in appreciation for all America has done for me did I not offer what little I had to her," he said. On June 2, 1943, above the Gulf of Paria in the Caribbean, west of Trinidad, his fighter plane's engine failed, and he crashed into the sea. Kinnick, 24, chose not to attempt to land on the U.S.S. *Lexington* because it would have endangered planes spotted for takeoff. His body was never found. Wrote Whitney Martin of the Associated Press: "Why does war have to take such really human humans? It doesn't seem fair."

BEST COACH Evashevski took Iowa to grand heights in the 1950s, but Fry is the man most identified with the program today. Previously at SMU (for 11 seasons) and North Texas State (for six), Fry didn't know the location of the state of Iowa when he inherited a struggling football program in December 1978. Everyone knew Iowa football when he retired as Hawkeyes coach in 1998. Fry led Iowa to three Big Ten titles, three Rose Bowl trips, and six other top-three league finishes. The ex-Marine from Eastland, Texas, altered Iowa's losing culture by immediately changing the team's logo and uniform design and by creating The Swarm, where players hold hands and walk slowly onto the field. Fry graduated from Baylor with a degree in psychology, and his creative tactics at Iowa included printing media guides an inch taller than those of other schools and painting the visitors locker room pink to pacify Iowa opponents. His folksy style, homespun humor, and endearing Texas drawl made him

FIGHT SONG

THE IOWA FIGHT SONG

The word is "Fight! Fight! Fight! for Iowa,"
Let every loyal Iowan sing
The word is "Fight! Fight! Fight! for Iowa";
Until the walls and rafters ring. (Rah! Rah!)

Come on and cheer, cheer, cheer for Iowa
We're gonna cheer until we hear the final gun.
The word is "Fight! Fight! Fight! for Iowa,"
Until the game is won.

FIRST-ROUND DRAFT CHOICES

1936	Dick Crayne, Dodgers (4)
1949	Bill Kay, Bills (6)[a]
1958	Alex Karras, Lions (10)
1959	Randy Duncan, Packers (1)
1966	John Niland, Cowboys (5)
1972	Craig Clemons, Bears (12)
1976	Rod Walters, Chiefs (14)
1982	Ron Hallstrom, Packers (22)
1984	John Alt, Chiefs (21)
1986	Chuck Long, Lions (12)
1986	Ronnie Harmon, Bills (16)
1986	Mike Haight, Jets (22)
1997	Tom Knight, Cardinals (9)
1997	Ross Verba, Packers (30)
2003	Dallas Clark, Colts (24)
2004	Robert Gallery, Raiders (2)
2006	Chad Greenway, Vikings (17)

[a] *Indicates All-America Football Conference*

CONSENSUS ALL-AMERICANS

1919	Lester Belding, E
1921	Aubrey Devine, B
1922	Gordon Locke, B
1939	Nile Kinnick, B
1954-55	Calvin Jones, G
1957	Alex Karras, T
1958	Randy Duncan, B
1981	Andre Tippett, DL
1981	Reggie Roby, P
1984-85	Larry Station, LB
1985	Chuck Long, QB
1988	Marv Cook, TE
1991	Leroy Smith, DL
1997	Tim Dwight, KR
1998	Jared DeVries, DL
2002	Dallas Clark, TE
2002	Eric Steinbach, OL
2003	Robert Gallery, OL
2003	Nate Kaeding, PK

popular. So did his wide-open passing attack, which featured ideas dating back to when Fry and friend Al Davis, later the Oakland Raiders owner, who coached six-man football against each other in the Marines. In 1981, Fry's third season, Iowa ended a streak of 19 nonwinning seasons, won its first Big Ten title in 21 years, and went to the Rose Bowl for the first time since 1959. Rose Bowl berths in the 1985 and 1990 seasons sealed Fry's reputation. His Iowa tenure ended with a school-record 143 wins and 14 bowl trips in 20 seasons. His coaching staff with the Hawkeyes included Bill Snyder, Dan McCarney, Barry Alvarez, Kirk Ferentz, Bob Stoops, Mike Stoops, Chuck Long, and Bret Bielema. The athletic department named all the football offices and facilities, except the stadium, the Hayden Fry Complex. He was inducted into the College Football Hall of Fame with a career record of 232–178–10 in 37 seasons.

BEST TEAM Evashevski constructed a wing-T offensive machine in 1958. Randy Duncan, All-America quarterback and Big Ten MVP, teamed with a strong line, a deep stable of backs, and a group of ends known as the Gluefingers Gang to lead the nation in total offense and the Big Ten in scoring, total yards, first downs, rushing, passing, and pass-completion percentage. Iowa went 8–1–1 while averaging 416.7 yards per game, second best in the nation. The Hawkeyes won the conference title for the second time in three seasons despite a 38-28 home loss to Ohio State in a November game in which the teams combined to gain 889 yards. Minnesota athletic director Ike Armstrong called the 1958 Hawkeyes "the best team I've ever seen in the Big Ten." Iowa rolled to a 20-0 halftime lead and a 38-12 victory over California in the Rose Bowl. Evashevski coached the game despite being bedridden the day before with the flu and a 101° fever. Bob Jeter ran for 194 yards on nine carries, and his 21.6 yards per carry and his 81-yard TD run were Rose Bowl records. The Hawkeyes set Rose Bowl records for total offense (516 yards) and rushing offense (429 yards), and they finished No. 2 behind LSU for the school's highest ever season-ending ranking. Randy Duncan won the Walter Camp Trophy and was runner-up for the Heisman. Evashevski's seniors finished a three-year run of 24–3–2 and took on the persona of their tough, temperamental coach, who had played for Michigan. Years later, at a Big Ten meeting, Ohio State's Woody Hayes got into an argument with Evashevski. Hayes tore off his jacket and stood over the sitting Evashevski, then Iowa's athletic director. "Woody, I'll never bother getting up for a one-punch fight," he said. "Now go sit down and shut up." That was Evashevski, and that was the spirit his Hawkeyes played with in 1958.

BEST BACKFIELD The Hawkeyes were difficult to defend against in 2005 when QB Drew Tate threw for

2,828 yards and 22 touchdowns, and Albert Young ran for 1,334 yards and eight scores. Ten years earlier, Hawkeye QB Matt Sherman had thrown for 2,546 yards and 14 TDs and Sedrick Shaw had run for 1,477 yards and 15 TDs. And in 2002, QB Brad Banks passed for 3,155 yards and 30 TDs while Fred Russell ran for 1,264 yards and nine scores. Iowa's most dynamic duo, however, was Chuck Long and Ronnie Harmon in 1985, when the Hawkeyes spent five weeks ranked No. 1 in the nation. Both players were selected by Iowa fans as members of the school's all-time team and were given the same honor by the Gannett News Service. The pair led Iowa to a 10–2 record, a Big Ten title, and a Rose Bowl berth. Long was a consensus All-America, MVP of the Big Ten, and runner-up for the Heisman Trophy to Bo Jackson in the closest vote in the award's history. He won the Maxwell Trophy, given to the nation's top college player, and the Davey O'Brien Award as the nation's top QB. Long completed 260 of 388 passes (67%) for a then-school record 3,297 yards and 27 TDs, an Iowa mark that still stands today. His best game that season came against Northwestern, when he completed 19 of 26 passes for 399 yards and six touchdowns. He also burned Michigan State for 380 yards passing and 4 TDs while completing 30 of 39, and he ended his career completing 29 of 37 for 319 and one score in a Rose Bowl loss to UCLA. Long became the first QB in NCAA history to pass for more than 10,000 career yards and was named All-Big Ten first team three times. He still holds many Iowa passing records, including those for career attempts (1,203), completions (782), completion percentage (.650), yards (10,461), and touchdowns (74). Long, a College Football Hall of Fame inductee, led Iowa to four consecutive bowl games and the Detroit Lions selected him 12th overall in the 1986 NFL draft. Four picks later, the Buffalo Bills took Harmon. The versatile running back averaged 5.2 yards per carry for Iowa in 1985, gaining 1,166 yards on 223 attempts and scoring nine touchdowns in 1985. He was named first-team All-Big Ten for also being dangerous on pass routes out of the backfield. Harmon, who originally came to Iowa as a wide receiver, led the Hawkeyes with 60 receptions for 699 yards and 1 TD. He finished his career as the second leading rusher in school history with 2,271 rushing yards and totaled 2,045 receiving yards.

BEST DEFENSE Iowa had suffered through 19 consecutive seasons without a winning record when its defense rose up to change everything in 1981. The Hawkeyes began that magical season by upsetting Nebraska 10-7, as defensive tackle Mark Bortz recovered two fumbles, one year after losing 57-0 to the Cornhuskers. Iowa went on to go 8–3 in the regular season while holding opponents to 11.7 points per game. Fry's squad posted one shut out and held six other teams

to seven points, including each of the final three regular-season opponents, while clinching the school's third bowl trip in history and first in 23 years. Defensive end Andre Tippett earned unanimous All-America honors. He is a member of Iowa's all-time team and the second-round pick later became an All-Pro for the New England Patriots. Besides Tippett, the Iowa defense had first-team All-Big Ten selections in Bortz, noseguard Pat Dean, linebacker Mel Cole, and cornerback Lou King, who tied Kinnick's school season record with eight interceptions. Bortz was drafted by the Chicago Bears, turned into an offensive lineman, and helped them win the 1986 Super Bowl. Bob Stoops, now coach of the Oklahoma Sooners, was a junior starter at defensive back for the Hawkeyes in 1981, and a year later he was named first-team All-Big Ten. Iowa's defense was helped by All-America punter Reggie Roby, who broke a 32-year-old NCAA record by averaging 49.8 yards per punt in 1981. Roby averaged 55.8 yards in the upset of Nebraska. During the regular season, Iowa's opponents averaged just 70 yards rushing and 2.1 yards per carry. However, against Washington in the Rose Bowl, the Hawkeyes gave up 186 yards on the ground and 328 total. Jacque Robinson ran for 142 yards and two scores in the Huskies' 28-0 win. Despite that Rose Bowl loss, the 1981 defense still holds Iowa records for fewest rushing yards per game (79.7) and average per rush (2.4). The Hawkeyes yielded 232.5 total yards per game, fourth fewest in school history, and the lowest average since 1957.

COLLEGE FOOTBALL HALL OF FAME INDUCTEES		
NAME	YEARS	INDUCTED
Duke Slater, T	1918-21	1951
Nile Kinnick, HB	1937-39	1951
Howard Jones, COACH	1916-23	1951
Gordon Locke, FB	1920-22	1960
Eddie Anderson, COACH	1939-42, 1946-49	1971
Aubrey Devine, QB	1919-21	1973
Slip Madigan, COACH	1943-44	1974
Calvin Jones, G	1953-55	1980
Alex Karras, T	1955-57	1991
Randy Duncan, QB	1956-58	1997
Chuck Long, QB	1981-85	1999
Forest Evashevski, COACH	1952-60	2000
Hayden Fry, COACH	1979-98	2003

BIGGEST GAME

Portable lights, used at Kinnick Stadium for the first time, cast an eerie, reflective glare on the artificial turf as No. 1 Iowa hosted No. 2 Michigan on Oct. 19, 1985. The nationally televised Poll Bowl between two 5–0 teams lived up to its hype as the lead changed hands three times. Iowa fans swarmed the field at game's end to celebrate the 12-10 victory after Hawkeye sophomore kicker Rob Houghtlin made a 29-yard field goal from the right hash mark as time expired. Michigan had taken a 10-9 lead on a Mike Gillette field goal with 10:55 remaining. The Wolverines were trying to run out the clock when Iowa's All-America linebacker Larry Station tackled Michigan's Jamie Morris for a two-yard loss on third and two, forcing a punt. Iowa took over on its own 22 with 5:27 remaining. Quarterback Chuck Long then engineered a 16-play drive capped by Houghtlin's taking center stage. The sophomore stood on the field, hunched over, hands on his knees, and prayed for 30

seconds as rain dripped off his helmet. Michigan coach Bo Schembechler called timeout to rattle the former walk-on who had missed three weeks of practice because of a sore leg. Houghtlin then looked at Schembechler and shook his hands up and down as if to say, "No problem." His kick was high, far, and split the uprights. "That rascal, he wanted to kick it," said Fry, whose team had outgained Michigan 422-182. Houghtlin, a native of Glenview, Ill., who had transferred from Miami of Ohio, went on to finish his Iowa career with the most field goals (54) and points (290) in school history to that point. He kicked five game-winning field goals for the Hawkeyes, none bigger than the one against Michigan that gave Iowa its first-ever unanimous No. 1 ranking.

BIGGEST UPSET

Evashevski's coaching tenure began with Iowa committing 22 turnovers while being outscored 129-54 in four losses. Ohio State, undefeated and ranked No. 16, then rolled into Iowa City on Oct. 25, 1952, as the homecoming opponent and a three-touchdown favorite. The Buckeyes had defeated Iowa the previous two seasons by a combined score of 130-42. Evashevski, however, surprised Ohio State by scrapping his traditional single-wing offense and installing an unbalanced split-T for the game, to spread the Buckeye defense and keep them off balance. The Hawkeyes scored first on a second-quarter safety when they tackled Ohio State's Doug Goodsell in the end zone after he had fumbled the ball trying to catch a punt. The Buckeye offense never got into gear, failing to cross Iowa's 28-yard line. The Hawkeyes held them to just 216 total yards, including 42 rushing. A one-yard TD run by Binkey Broeder with 2:17 left in the fourth quarter sealed the 8-0 win. Iowa's players carried Evashevski off the field. "It was like my 8-year-old granddaughter outboxing Sugar Ray Robinson," wrote *Des Moines Register* sports editor Sec Taylor.

HEARTBREAKER

The 1985 regular season played out like a Grimm's fairy tale, starring Fry and his consensus All-Americas, Long and linebacker Larry Station. Long finished runner-up in the Heisman race to Bo Jackson while leading the Hawkeyes to a school-record 10 wins. Iowa was ranked No. 1 for five weeks until losing 22-13 at No. 8 Ohio State on Nov. 2. The Hawkeyes rallied with three straight wins to earn the Big Ten championship. They were 10–1 heading into their second Rose Bowl in four years, but the giddiness ended

in Pasadena. Senior running back Ronnie Harmon lost four fumbles and dropped a certain TD pass as Iowa fell behind UCLA 24-10 at halftime. The Bruins cruised to a 45-28 win as freshman tailback Eric Ball came off the bench to run for 227 yards and 4 TDs. He scored on runs of 30, 40, 6, and 32 yards. Long completed 29 of 37 passes for 319 yards and one score, and Harmon caught a career-high 11 passes for 102 yards as the two teams combined for 889 yards of total offense and 54 first downs. But a season of Heisman dreams and national title hopes ended with Iowa settling for a No. 10 ranking in the final AP poll.

PRO FOOTBALL HALL OF FAME INDUCTEES		
NAME	YEARS	INDUCTED
Emlen Tunnell, DB	1948-61	1967
Paul Krause, S	1964-79	1998

WILDEST FINISH Less than five seconds remained in the Capital One Bowl on Jan. 1, 2005, when Iowa center Mike Elgin snapped the ball. The game seemed lost. LSU had taken a 25-24 lead with 46 seconds remaining on a three-yard touchdown pass from JaMarcus Russell to Skyler Green. And now here were the Hawkeyes, forgetting to call one of their final two timeouts, scrambling on their final play—but magic happened. Hawkeyes quarterback Drew Tate took the snap on his own 44 and dropped back to pass. He had called "All Up," a play sending four receivers toward the end zone. LSU slot defender Ronnie Prude was supposed to hit receiver Warren Holloway, but instead Prude gave chase for a few yards and turned to cover the flat. Holloway raced down the middle of the field untouched, wide open. He caught Tate's pass near the 17-yard line. "All I saw was the end zone," said Holloway, a fifth-year senior who had never scored a TD in his career. Tate said, "I was scared that I overthrew him." Holloway kept his balance after the reception and sprinted into the end zone as time expired for a 30-25 Iowa victory. Teammates mobbed Holloway after his game-ending score. "The hardest part was being underneath the pile," he said. "Scoring was the easiest part, believe it or not." Iowa's victory ended the five-year tenure of LSU coach Nick Saban, who had been named head coach of the Miami Dolphins one week earlier.

BEST GOAL-LINE STAND With QB Drew Tate out with a strained abdominal muscle, the No. 14-ranked Hawkeyes managed to take their game at Syracuse into overtime on Sept. 9, 2006. The Orange, losers of 10 consecutive games, traded field goals with Iowa to force a second overtime. Albert Young's one-yard TD run gave Iowa a 20-13 lead, but a third overtime seem to loom when Syracuse got a first down two yards from the end zone. The Hawkeyes then stopped the home team from scoring on seven consecutive plays from inside the 2. Syracuse fullback Tony Fiammetta was stopped for no gain up the middle on the first two plays. A pass

interference call then gave the Orange another first down at the 2. Iowa yielded just one yard on two more carries by Fiammetta. On third down, Syracuse QB Perry Patterson kept the ball on an option play but was stopped for no gain. Orange tailback Paul Chiara tried to run up the middle on fourth down, but defensive end Kenny Iwebema crunched him with a big hit, and the rest of the Hawkeyes wrapped him up to preserve a 20-13 win. "It might have been one of the greatest feelings ever, just knowing we gave them all the opportunities in the world to score," said Iowa defensive tackle Mitch King. "But we never gave up. It might have been the most exciting series I've ever been in."

BEST COMEBACK Iowa trailed 20-0 in the fourth quarter of the 1951 Minnesota game. Then fullback Bill Reichardt, known as The Bull, went wild. He rushed for two touchdowns, sandwiched around a "tackle eligible" scoring pass from Burt Britzmann to Hubert Johnson. Reichardt's final TD came on a 36-yard run with 1:47 remaining. He kicked the extra point, and the game ended in a 20-20 tie. Reichardt had rushed a school-record 31 times and gained a career-high 166 yards—a performance that helped him earn Big Ten MVP honors that season.

STADIUM Iowa Stadium opened in 1929 near the Iowa River at a cost of nearly $500,000, all financed by athletic event income. The Great Depression began nine days after Iowa tied Illinois 7-7 in the stadium's dedication game, and 10 years passed before the school could pay its debt on the facility. The stadium's brick facade and bleacher seats remain, but the original capacity of 53,000 has grown to 70,585 because of expansions, one of which enclosed the north end zone in 1983. The school changed the name to Kinnick Stadium in 1972. A two-year, $90 million renovation project completed before the 2006 season created new seating on the southern end zone side, and added 40 private suites, over 1,000 club seats, and new scoreboards.

RIVAL Iowa's most frequent opponent has been Minnesota. The Hawkeyes first played the Gophers in 1891, and the border-state schools have met almost every season since 1901. Minnesota became unpopular in Iowa by outscoring the Hawkeyes 463-30 while winning the first 12 games of the series. The Gophers had other long stretches of dominance before losing 21-16 in 1982. Iowa coach Fry celebrated that victory, his first over Minnesota, by meeting with reporters after the game dressed like a farmer and yelling, "Soo-eee." The Hawkeyes then won the Floyd of Rosedale 15 times in 22 meetings.

CONTROVERSY Iowa had a fit after being tied 14-14 by No. 1 Notre Dame in 1953. The visiting Hawkeyes, a two-touchdown underdog, led 7-0 when an official called timeout with one second left in the first half because Fighting Irish tackle Frank Varrichione was apparently injured. Rules at the time called for the clock to automatically stop if officials deemed a player hurt. Notre Dame QB Ralph Guglielmi then threw a 12-yard TD pass to Dan Shannon. Iowa led 14-7 with 37 seconds remaining when Notre Dame drove to within 10 yards of the end zone. With the clock ticking below 10 seconds, Irish captain Don Penza and tackle Art Hunter fell down with suspicious injuries. Officials called two timeouts. Guglielmi then hit Shannon for a nine-yard TD pass with six seconds remaining. Notre Dame was described as the "Fainting Irish" and dropped to No. 2 in the polls. At a campus pep rally the day after the tie, Evashevski said his team had been "gypped at Notre Dame." Three years earlier, Iowa had deliberately stalled in the game's final 25 seconds to preserve a 14-14 tie with Notre Dame.

DUBIOUS DISTINCTION The Roaring Twenties included scandal for the Iowa athletic program. Big Ten commissioner John Griffith announced in May 1929 that the Hawkeyes would be suspended from the conference on Jan. 1, 1930, because the school's alumni had created an illegal slush fund for athletes totaling $5,000. Students considered athletic director Paul Belting a traitor and marched on his house. The Big Ten readmitted Iowa as a member in February 1930 after the school banned 11 football players and three other athletes for having taken part in the fund. In 1931, the Hawkeyes scored only 1 TD and went 1–7 as the nation's lowest-scoring team. Burt Ingwersen resigned as coach after the season and was replaced by Ossie Solem. The scandal's damage led to Iowa's 18–40–6 record from 1931 through 1938.

NICKNAME James Fenimore Cooper named a character Hawkeye in his 1826 novel, *The Last of the Mohicans*. People living in the Iowa territory then began referring to themselves as Hawkeyes even though no such bird exists. Territorial officials formally approved usage of the name, and the school later adopted it for its teams.

MASCOT University of Iowa journalism instructor Richard Spencer III created a cartoon character of the Hawkeye in 1948. The athletic department later conducted a statewide contest to name the mascot and settled on Herky the Hawk, suggested by alumnus John Franklin. Herky became a mascot at Iowa games in the mid-1950s. His image was the insignia of the 124th Fighter Squadron during the Korean War.

UNIFORMS When Fry became Iowa coach before the 1979 season, he immediately redesigned the team's uniforms as a psychological ploy to change the mind-set of a program that hadn't had a winning season in 17 years. He was a fan of the Pittsburgh Steelers, who had just won the third of their four 1970s Super Bowl victories, and he received permission from the NFL team for Iowa to mimic its black-and-gold uniforms. Fry changed the school logo to a meaner-looking hawk and placed it on black helmets.

QUIRKS Fans were leaving the Metrodome in Minneapolis thinking that the 1986 edition of the Iowa-Minnesota rivalry would end in a tie. Iowa kicker Rob Houghtlin had just missed a 51-yard field goal attempt, and one second remained. The Gophers, however, were penalized 15 yards for having 12 men on the field. Houghtlin then made a 37-yard field goal for a 30-27 Iowa victory … Iowa coach Leonard Raffensperger of Victory, Iowa, and Notre Dame coach Frank Leahy of Winner, S.D., had to settle for ties when their teams played each other in 1950 and 1951.

LORE Near the end of his sophomore season, in 1955, an out-of-shape Alex Karras showed up late for practice. Evashevski told him to leave and never come back. After Karras apologized to his teammates a day later, they voted unanimously for his reinstatement. Karras played little in the season's final three games, then withdrew from school and returned home to Gary, Ind. His mother, Emiline Schofield, talked him into returning to Iowa. Karras was named All-America as an offensive and defensive tackle as a junior and led the Hawkeyes to the 1956 Big Ten title and a Rose Bowl win. He won the Outland Trophy, finished second in the Heisman Trophy voting, and became a two-time All-America his senior year. He went on to successful careers in the NFL and in Hollywood.

NUMBERS Calvin Jones was the first college football player and the first African-American to grace the cover of *Sports Illustrated*, in the fall of 1954. Jones was a three-time All-Big Ten selection and a two-time All-America offensive lineman, and he won the Outland Trophy as a senior, in 1955. He died on Dec. 9, 1956, in an airline crash in the Cascade mountains in Canada. Iowa retired his No. 62 jersey … There were 32 fumbles in the 1925 Iowa-Wisconsin game, played during a snowstorm. The Hawkeyes lost 10 of their 20 fumbles in a 6-0 defeat. They lost more yards on fumbles (95) than they gained on offense (79). Wisconsin won with 65 total yards of offense … The attendance for Iowa's 27-0 victory over Coe in 1918 was zero because the influenza epidemic caused the War Department to bar spectators … Thirteen Hawkeyes, known as The Ironmen played all 60 minutes of at least one

game in 1939 … Chuck Long set a then-NCAA record by completing 22 consecutive passes in a 24-20 win over Indiana on Oct. 27, 1984 … Carleton W. "Kinney" Holbrook was Iowa's first black player, in 1896. He scored 4 TDs in a season-opening win over Drake. He led Iowa to a 7–1–1 record. A game at Missouri had to be stopped eight minutes into the second half because fans wielding canes, clubs, and wagon spokes were yelling racial epithets at Holbrook. Iowa was awarded a 12-0 victory … The Hawkeyes won at least 10 games and finished ranked in the Top 10 in three consecutive seasons from 2002 through 2004 … Iowa scored 31 unanswered points in the third quarter of a 55-17 win over Texas in the 1984 Freedom Bowl. Long completed 12 of 14 passes for 241 yards and 4 TDs in that third quarter and finished the game with 461 yards passing and a bowl-game record 6 TD passes … Starting in 1983 with Chuck Long and continuing through Chuck Hartlieb and Matt Rodgers, an Iowa QB was named first-team All-Big Ten in seven of nine seasons … QB Brad Banks finished second in the Heisman Trophy voting in 2002. He joined Long in 1985, Randy Duncan in 1958, and Alex Karras in 1957 as Hawkeyes who finished runner-up for the Heisman … Kirk Ferentz lost 18 of his first 20 games as coach but has since gone 53-25 entering 2007 … The Hawkeyes' 31 turnovers in 2006 was their most since 1989 … A 37-17 win over Florida in the 2004 Outback Bowl was Iowa's first victory in a January game since 1959 … Iowa's 33-7 win over Ohio State in 2004 was its first over the Buckeyes in Kinnick Stadium since 1983 … The Hawkeyes didn't trail at home the entire 2004 season … Bill Reichardt won the Big Ten MVP in 1951 and is the only player to earn that honor for a team that failed to win a conference game … Iowa's 182 wins, including 124 in league games, made the Hawkeyes the third best Big Ten team behind Michigan and Ohio State from 1980 to 2005 … The 1946 defense allowed an Iowa record-low 200.7 yards per game … Iowa gave up just 1 TD and 11 points total while going 8–0–1 in 1899, then yielded just 12 points while going 7–0–1 in 1900 … Iowa lost four consecutive games to Michigan from 1953 through 1956 by a total of 17 points. The teams tied at 21 in 1957 … Iowa was No. 1 in 1985 when Ohio State pulled a 22-13 upset in Columbus. Two years later, the Hawkeyes won 29-27 at Ohio State when Chuck Hartlieb threw a 28-yard TD pass

to tight end Marv Cook on fourth down and 23 with 16 seconds left in the game and Iowa out of timeouts. It was Iowa's first win in Columbus in 28 years. Two days later, Ohio State fired Earle Bruce as coach … Fry's first Big Ten victory came in 1979 when the Hawkeyes kept Illinois from scoring on first and goal at the Iowa 5 in the final 30 seconds to hold on for a 13-7 victory … Hawkeyes QB Aubrey Devine intercepted three passes and drop-kicked a 30-yard field goal to defeat Notre Dame 10-7 in 1921 and end the Irish's 20-game winning streak … As a two-touchdown underdog, Iowa snapped a 12-game losing streak by upsetting No. 12 UCLA 21-10 in 1974 … Howard Jones coached Iowa to 7–0 records in 1921 and 1922 for the school's only undefeated seasons … The 2002 Hawkeyes, just three years removed from a 1–10 season, set a school record with 11 victories, including an 8–0 Big Ten mark … The Hawkeyes won 22 straight home games from 2002 through 2005 … Iowa reached No. 3 in 2002 for its highest ranking since being No. 1 in 1985 … A school-record 11 Hawkeyes earned first-team All-Big Ten honors in 2002 … From 2003 through 2006, Iowa played in four consecutive January bowl games for the first time in school history … The Oakland Raiders made offensive tackle Robert Gallery the No. 2 overall pick of the 2004 NFL draft after he won the Outland Trophy as a senior … Chuck Long, Ronnie Harmon, and offensive lineman Mike Haight were all first-round draft picks in 1986 … Receiver and kick returner Tim Dwight was All-America in two sports at Iowa, football and track and field … Tavian Banks scored on a 63-yard TD run on Iowa's first offensive play of the 1997 season. He ran for 314 yards that season against Tulsa … Leroy Smith made six tackles for loss, including five sacks, against Ohio State in 1991 … Dave Clement had a school-record 29 tackles against Oregon State in 1970 … Merton Hanks blocked seven kicks for the Hawkeyes from 1987 through 1990 … Quinn Early had 256 receiving yards on 10 catches against Northwestern in 1987 … The Hawkeyes gained 713 yards against Northwestern in 1983.

QUOTE "Scratch where it itches." —Hayden Fry, describing how Iowa's style of play was to do whatever it took to win

ALL-TIME TEAM

The Gannett News Service selected this team at the start of 2000.

OFFENSE

1918-21	Duke Slater,	OL
1956-57	Alex Karras,	OL
1963-65	John Niland,	OL
1980-83	John Alt,	OL
1951-53	Jerry Hilgenberg,	C
1985-88	Marv Cook,	TE
1994-97	Tim Dwight,	WR
1981-85	Chuck Long,	QB
1937-39	Nile Kinnick,	RB
1982-85	Ronnie Harmon,	RB
1949-51	Bill Reichardt,	FB

DEFENSE

1918-21	Lester Belding,	DL
1938-40	Mike Enich,	DL
1953-55	Calvin Jones,	DL
1983-85	Dave Haight,	DL
1995-98	Jared DeVries,	DL
1979-81	Andre Tippett,	LB
1982-85	Larry Station,	LB
1989-91	Leroy Smith,	LB
1920-22	Gordon Locke,	DB
1927-29	Willis Glassgow,	DB
1961-63	Paul Krause,	DB

IOWA ALL-TIME SCORES

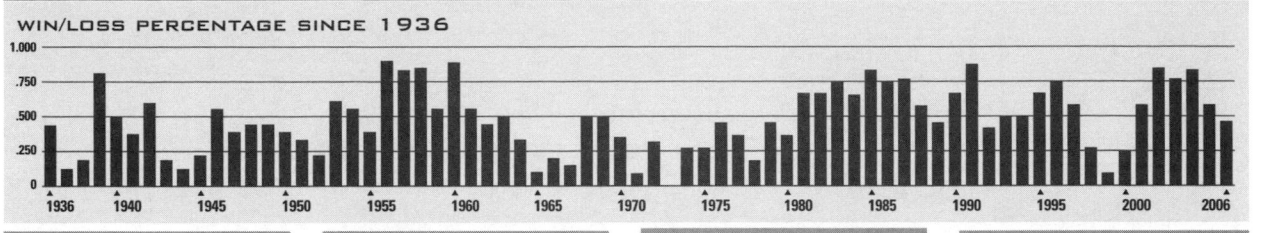

WIN/LOSS PERCENTAGE SINCE 1936

1.000 / .750 / .500 / .250 / 0

1936 1940 1945 1950 1955 1960 1965 1970 1975 1980 1985 1990 1995 2000 2006

NO HEAD COACH

1889 0-1-0
| N16 | at Grinnell | 0 | 24 |

1890 1-1-0
| O18 | Grinnell | 6 | 11 |
| N1 | at Iowa Wesleyan | 91 | 0 |

1891 2-3-0
O24 ●	Cornell Coll.	64	6
N2	Minnesota	4	42
N9	at Grinnell	4	6
N26 ●	Nebraska ᴼᴹᴬ	22	0
D5	Kansas ᴷᶜ	12	14#

E.A. DALTON
1892 (.583) 3-2-1

1892 3-2-1
O21 ●	Knox	44	0
O29 ●	at Coe	48	0
N5	Kansas ᴷᶜ	4	24
N12	at Missouri	0	22*
N16 ●	Grinnell	18	12
N24 =	Nebraskaᴼᴹᴬ	10	10

BEN DONNELLY
1893 (.429) 3-4

1893 3-4-0
O7 ●	at Coe	56	0
O14 ●	at Denver AC	0	58
O21 ●	Luther	32	0
N4 ●	Kansas ᴷᶜ	24	35
N11 ●	at Grinnell	14	36
N18 ●	Missouri	34	12*
N30 ●	Nebraska ᴼᴹᴬ	18	20

ROGER SHERMAN
1894 (.500) 4-4-1

1894 4-4-1
S29 ●	Iowa State	8	16
O13 ●	at Cornell Coll	60	0
O20 ●	at Augustana	34	0
O27 ●	at Chicago	18	18
O29 ●	at Wisconsin	0	44
N3 ●	Kansas	14	12
N10 ●	Grinnell	6	0
N17 ●	at Missouri	16	32*
N29 ●	Nebraska ᴼᴹᴬ	0	36

NO HEAD COACH

1895 2-5-0
O12 ●	Doane	0	10
O19 ●	at Parsons	28	0
O28 ●	Iowa State	0	24
N2 ●	at Kansas	0	52*
N18 ●	at Missouri	0	34
N19 ●	at Penn Coll.	14	12
N28 ●	Nebraska ᴼᴹᴬ	0	6

ALFRED BULL
1896 (.833) 7-1-1

1896 7-1-1
O3 ●	Drake	32	0
O10 ●	at Chicago	0	6
O25 ●	Kansas	6	0
N4 ●	Wilton	27	0
N9 ●	at Missouri	12	0
N14 ●	at Grinnell	15	6
N21 ●	at Des Moines YMCA	34	0
N26 =	Nebraska ᴼᴹᴬ	0	0
N28 ●	Nebraska ᴼᴹᴬ	6	0

OTTO WAGONHURST
1897 (.500) 4-4

1897 4-4-0
O2 ●	Wilton	22	4
O16 ●	at Northwestern	12	6
O23	Phys. & Surg.	0	14
O30 ●	at Kansas	0	56
N5 ●	Iowa State	0	6*
N13 ●	at Drake	16	0
N20 ●	Grinnell	16	12
N25 ●	Nebraska ᶜᴼᵁ	0	6

ALDEN KNIPE
1898-1902 (.705) 29-11-4

1898 3-4-2
O1 =	at Knox	0	0
O8 ●	at Chicago	0	38
O15 ●	Drake	5	18
O22 ●	Upper Iowa	23	5
O29 ●	at Rush	11	15
N5 ●	at No. Iowa	5	11
N12 =	at Grinnell	5	5
N17 ●	Simpson	12	0
N24 ●	Nebraska ᶜᴼᵁ	6	5

1899 8-0-1
S23 ●	No. Iowa	22	0
O7 =	at Chicago	5	5
O14 ●	William Penn	35	0
O21 ●	Rush	17	0
O28 ●	Iowa State	5	0
N4 ●	Nebraskaᴼᴹᴬ	30	0
N11 ●	Grinnell	16	0
N18 ●	at Knox	33	0
N30 ●	Illinois ᴿᴵ	58	0

1900-Present BIG 10

1900 7-0-1 (2-0-1)
S28 ●	Upper Iowa	57	0
O6 ●	No. Iowa	68	0
O12 ●	Simpson	47	0
O26 ●	Drake	26	0
N3 ●	at Chicago	17	0
N10 ●	Michigan ᴰᴱᵀ	28	5
N16 ●	Grinnell	63	2
N29 =	at Northwestern	5	5

1901 6-3-0 (0-3-0)
O5 ●	No. Iowa	16	0
O11 ●	at Drake	6	5
O18 ●	Iowa State	6	0*
O26 ●	at Minnesota	0	16
O30 ●	Coe	11	0
N2 ●	Knox	23	6
N9	Illinois	0	27
N16 ●	Grinnell	17	11
N28	Michigan ᶜᴴᴵ	0	50

1902 5-4-0 (0-3-0)
O4 ●	No. Iowa	26	5
O11 ●	at Drake	12	0
O18 ●	at Simpson	10	0
O25	Minnesota	0	34
N1 ●	Iowa State	12	6
N8	at Michigan	0	107
N15 ●	at Washington, Mo.	61	0
N20	Missouri	0	6
N27	at Illinois	0	80

JOHN CHALMERS
1903-05 (.750) 24-8

1903 9-2-0 (1-1-0)
S27 ●	Cornell Coll.	6	0
S29 ●	Coe	16	0
O3 ●	No. Iowa	29	0
O10 ●	Drake	22	6
O17	at Minnesota	0	75
O24 ●	at Grinnell	17	0
O31 ●	Nebraska	6	17
N6 ●	Simpson	35	2
N14 ●	at Missouri	16	0
N21 ●	Illinois	12	0
N26 ●	at Washington, Mo.	12	2

1904 7-4-0 (0-3-0)
S24 ●	Coe	17	0
S27 ●	Augustana	33	2
O1 ●	Cornell Coll.	88	0
O6 ●	at Drake	17	0
O15	at Chicago	0	39
O22 ●	No. Iowa	11	5
O29 ●	Iowa State	10	6
N5	at Nebraska	6	17
N12 ●	Grinnell	69	0
N19	at Illinois	0	29
N24	Minnesota	0	11

1905 8-2-0 (0-2-0)
S26 ●	Coe	27	0
S30 ●	Monmouth	40	0
O7	at Chicago	0	42
O21	at Minnesota	0	39
O28 ●	No. Iowa	41	5
N4 ●	Grinnell	46	0
N11 ●	Des Moines	72	0
N18 ●	Drake	44	0
N24 ●	at Iowa State	8	0
N30 ●	at St. Louis	31	0

MARK CATLIN
1906-08 (.412) 7 10

1906 2-3-0 (0-1-0)
O27 ●	Missouri	24	4
N3	at Wisconsin	4	18
N10	Coe	15	12
N24	Iowa State	0	2
N29	at St. Louis	0	39

1907 3-2-0 (1-1-0)
O19 ●	Missouri	21	6
O26 ●	at Drake	25	4
N2	Wisconsin	5	6
N9 ●	Illinois	25	12
N23	at Iowa State	14	20*

1908 2-5-0 (0-1-0)
O10 ●	Coe	92	0
O17 ●	at Missouri	5	10
O24 ●	at Morningside	16	0
O31 ●	Nebraska	8	11
N7	at Illinois	0	22
N14	Drake	6	12
N21	Kansas	5	10

JOHN GRIFFITH
1909 (.357) 2-4-1

1909 2-4-1 (0-1-0)
O2	at Minnesota	0	41
O9 ●	Cornell Coll.	3	0
O23 =	at Nebraska	6	6
O30	Missouri	12	13
N6	at Drake	14	17
N13 ●	Iowa State	13	0*
N20	at Kansas	7	20

JESSE HAWLEY
1910-15 (.571) 24-18

1910 5-2-0 (1-1-0)
O2 ●	Morningside	12	0
O8	at Northwestern	5	10
O15	at Missouri	0	5
O22 ●	Purdue	16	0
N5	at Iowa State	2	0
N12 ●	Drake	21	0
N19	at Washington, Mo.	38	0

1911 3-4-0 (2-2-0)
O14 ●	at Morningside	11	5
O21 ●	at Cornell Coll.	0	3
O28 ●	Minnesota	6	24
N4	at Wisconsin	0	12
N11 ●	at Purdue	11	0
N18	Iowa State	0	9
N25	Northwestern	6	0

1912 4-3-0 (1-3-0)
O7 ●	No. Iowa	35	7
O12 ●	Cornell Coll.	31	0
O19	at Chicago	14	34
O26	at Minnesota	7	56
N9 ●	at Indiana	13	6
N16 ●	at Iowa State	20	7
N23	Wisconsin	10	28

1913 5-2-0 (2-1-0)
O8 ●	No. Iowa	45	3
O15 ●	Cornell Coll.	76	0
O18	at Chicago	6	23
O25	at Northwestern	78	6
N8 ●	Indiana	60	0
N15 ●	Iowa State	45	7
N22	at Nebraska	0	12

1914 4-3-0 (1-2-0)
O3 ●	No. Iowa	95	0
O10 ●	Cornell Coll.	49	0
O17	at Chicago	0	7
O24	Minnesota	0	7
N7 ●	at Northwestern	27	0
N14 ●	at Iowa State	26	6
N21	Nebraska	7	16

1915 3-4-0 (1-2-0)
O2 ●	at Cornell Coll.	33	0
O9 ●	at Morningside	17	6
O16	Northwestern	9	6
O23	at Minnesota	13	51
N6	at Purdue	13	19
N13	Iowa State	0	16
N20	at Nebraska	7	52

HOWARD JONES
1916-23 (.708) 42-17-1

1916 4-3-0 (1-2-0)
O7 ●	Cornell Coll.	31	6
O14 ●	Grinnell	17	7
O21	Purdue	24	6
O28	at Minnesota	0	67
N10	at Northwestern	13	20
N18	at Iowa State	19	16
N25	Nebraska	17	34

1917 3-5-0 (0-2-0)
O6 ●	Cornell Coll.	22	13
O13	at Nebraska	0	47
O20	Grinnell	0	10
O27	at Wisconsin	0	20
N3	at Great Lakes NAS	14	23
N10	South Dakota	35	0
N17	at Northwestern	14	25
N24	Iowa State	6	3

1918 — 6-2-1 (2-1-0)

S28		Great Lakes NAS	0	10
O5	•	at Nebraska	12	0
O12	•	Coe	27	0
O19	•	Cornell Coll.	34	0
N2		Illinois	0	19
N9		Minnesota	6	0
N16	•	Iowa State	21	0
N23	•	Northwestern	23	7
N30	=	at Camp Dodge	0	0

1919 — 5-2-0 (2-2-0)

O4	•	Nebraska	18	0
O18		at Illinois	7	9
O25	•	at Minnesota	9	6
N1	•	South Dakota	26	13
N8	•	at Northwestern	14	7
N15		at Chicago	6	9
N22	•	Iowa State	10	0

1920 — 5-2-0 (3-2-0)

O2	•	at Indiana	14	7
O9	•	Cornell Coll.	63	0
O16	•	at Illinois	3	20
O23		at Chicago	0	10
N6	•	Northwestern	20	0
N13	•	Minnesota	28	7
N20	•	at Iowa State	14	10

1921 — 7-0-0 (5-0-0)

O1	•	Knox	52	14
O8	•	Notre Dame	10	7
O15	•	Illinois	14	2
O29	•	at Purdue	13	6
N5	•	at Minnesota	41	7
N12	•	Indiana	41	0
N19	•	at Northwestern	14	0

1922 — 7-0-0 (5-0-0)

O7	•	Knox	61	0
O14	•	at Yale	6	0
O21	•	at Illinois	8	7
O28	•	Purdue	56	0
N11	•	Minnesota	28	14
N18	•	at Ohio State	12	9
N25	•	Northwestern	37	3

1923 — 5-3-0 (3-3-0)

S29	•	Oklahoma State	20	0
O6	•	Knox	44	3
O13		Purdue	7	0
O20		at Illinois	6	9
O27		Ohio State	20	0
N3		at Michigan	3	9
N17		at Minnesota	7	20
N24		Northwestern	17	14

BURT INGWERSEN
1924-31 (.547) 33-27-4

1924 — 6-1-1 (3-1-1)

O4	•	S.E. Oklahoma	43	0
O11	=	Ohio State	0	0
O18	•	Lawrence	13	5
O25	•	Minnesota	13	0
N1		at Illinois	0	36
N8	•	Butler	7	0
N15	•	at Wisconsin	21	7
N22	•	at Michigan	9	2

1925 — 5-3-0 (2-2-0)

O3	•	Arkansas	25	0 *
O10	•	St. Louis	41	0
O17		Illinois	12	10
O24	•	at Ohio State	15	0
O31	•	Wabash	28	7
N7		Wisconsin	0	6
N14	•	at Minnesota	0	33
N21		at USC	0	18

1926 — 3-5-0 (0-5-0)

O2	•	Colorado Teachers	24	0
O9	•	North Dakota	40	7
O16	•	at Illinois	6	13
O23		at Ohio State	6	23
O30	•	Carroll	21	0
N6		Minnesota	0	41
N13	•	at Wisconsin	10	20
N20		Northwestern	6	13

1927 — 4-4-0 (1-4-0)

O1	•	Monmouth	32	6
O8		Ohio State	6	13
O15	•	Wabash	38	0
O22		at Minnesota	0	38
O29	•	Denver	15	0
N5		Illinois	0	14
N12	•	at Wisconsin	16	0
N19		at Northwestern	0	12

1928 — 6-2-0 (3-2-0)

O7	•	Monmouth	26	0
O13	•	at Chicago	13	0
O20		Ripon	61	6
O27		Minnesota	7	6
N3		South Dakota	19	0
N10	•	at Ohio State	14	7
N17		Wisconsin	0	13
N24		at Michigan	7	10

1929 — 4-2-2 (2-2-2)

S29	•	Carroll	46	0
O6	•	Monmouth	46	0
O12	•	at Ohio State	6	7
O20	=	Illinois	7	7
O26	•	at Wisconsin	14	0
N9	•	Minnesota	9	7
N16	•	at Purdue	0	7
N23		at Michigan	0	0

1930 — 4-4-0 (0-1-0)

S27	•	Bradley Tech	38	12
O4		Oklahoma State	0	6
O11	•	Centenary	12	19
O18		Purdue	0	20
N1	•	at Detroit	7	3
N8	•	at Marquette	0	7
N15	•	Penn State	19	0
N22	•	Nebraska	12	7

1931 — 1-6-1 (0-3-1)

O3		Pittsburgh	0	20
O10		Texas A&M DAL	0	29
O17	=	Indiana	0	0
O24		at Minnesota	0	34
O31	=	George Washington	7	0
N7		at Nebraska	0	7
N12		at Purdue	0	22
N21		Northwestern	0	19

OSSIE SOLEM
1932-36 (.425) 15-21-4

1932 — 1-7-0 (0-5-0)

O1	•	Bradley Tech	31	7
O8		at Wisconsin	0	34
O15		at Indiana	0	12
O22		Minnesota	6	21
O28		at George Washington	6	21
N5		Nebraska	13	14
N12		Purdue	0	18
N19		at Northwestern	6	44

1933 — 5-3-0 (3-2-0)

O7	•	Northwestern CHI	7	0
O14	•	Bradley Tech	38	0
O21	•	Wisconsin	26	7
O28		at Minnesota	7	19
N4	•	Iowa State	27	7
N11		at Michigan	6	10
N18	•	at Purdue	14	6
N25		at Nebraska	6	7

1934 — 2-5-1 (1-3-1)

S29	•	South Dakota	34	0
O6	=	at Northwestern	20	7
O13	•	at Nebraska	13	14
O20		at Iowa State	6	31
O28		Minnesota	12	48
N3	=	at Indiana	0	0
N10		Purdue	6	13
N24		at Ohio State	7	40

1935 — 4-2-2 (1-2-2)

S28	•	Bradley	26	0
O5	•	South Dakota	47	2
O12	•	Colgate	12	6
O26	•	at Illinois	19	0
N2		Indiana	6	6
N9		Minnesota	6	13
N16		at Purdue	6	12
N23		at Northwestern	0	0

1936 — 3-4-1 (0-4-1)

S26	•	Carleton	14	0
O3		at Northwestern	7	18
O10	•	South Dakota	33	7
O17	=	Illinois	0	0
O31		at Indiana	6	13
N7		at Minnesota	0	52
N14		Purdue	0	13
N21	•	at Temple	25	0

IRL TUBBS
1937-38 (.156) 2-13-1

1937 — 1-7-0 (0-5-0)

S25		at Washington	0	14
O9	•	Bradley Tech	14	7
O16		at Wisconsin	6	13
O23		Michigan	6	7
O30		at Purdue	0	13
N6		Minnesota	10	35
N13		Indiana	0	3
N20		at Nebraska	0	28

1938 — 1-6-1 (1-3-1)

S23		at UCLA	3	27
O8		Wisconsin	13	31
O15	•	at Chicago	27	14
O22		Colgate	0	14
O29		Purdue	0	0
N5		at Minnesota	0	28
N12		at Indiana	3	7
N19		Nebraska	0	14

EDDIE ANDERSON
1939-42 '46-49 (.514) 35-33-2

1939 — 6-1-1 (4-1-1)

S30	•	South Dakota	41	0
O7	•	Indiana	32	29
O14	•	at Michigan	7	27
O28	•	at Wisconsin	19	13
N4	•	at Purdue	4	0
N11	•	Notre Dame	7	6
N18	•	Minnesota	13	9
N25	=	at Northwestern	7	7

1940 — 4-4-0 (2-3-0)

O5	•	South Dakota	46	0
O12	•	Wisconsin	30	12
O19		at Indiana	6	10
O26		at Minnesota	6	34
N2		Purdue	6	21
N9	•	at Nebraska	6	14
N16	•	at Notre Dame	7	0
N23		Illinois	18	7

1941 — 3-5-0 (2-4-0)

S27	•	Drake	25	8
O4		at Michigan	0	6
O18		at Wisconsin	0	23
O25		at Purdue	6	7
N1	•	Indiana	13	7
N8	•	at Illinois	21	0
N15		Minnesota	13	34
N22	•	at Nebraska	13	14

1942 — 6-4-0 (3-3-0)

S19	•	Washington, Mo.	26	7
S26	•	Nebraska	27	0
O3		Great Lakes NAS	0	25
O10		Camp Grant	33	16
O17		Illinois	7	12
O24	•	at Indiana	14	13
O31	•	Purdue	13	7
N7	•	Wisconsin	6	0
N14		at Minnesota	7	27
N28		at Michigan	14	28

SLIP MADIGAN
1943-44 (.156) 2-13-1

1943 — 1-6-1 (0-4-1)

S25		at Great Lakes NAS	7	21
O2		Wisconsin	5	7
O9		Iowa Pre-Flight	0	25
O16	=	Indiana	7	7
O23		at Purdue	7	28
N6		Illinois	10	19
N13		at Minnesota	14	33
N20	•	at Nebraska	33	13

1944 — 1-7-0 (0-6-0)

O7		at Ohio State	0	34
O14		at Illinois	6	40
O21		Purdue	7	26
O28		at Indiana	0	32
N4	•	at Nebraska	27	6
N11		at Wisconsin	7	26
N18		Minnesota	0	46
N25		Iowa Pre-Flight	6	30

CLEM CROWE
1945 (.222) 2-7

1945 — 2-7-0 (1-5-0)

S29	•	Berg AAf	14	13
O6		at Ohio State	0	42
O13		at Purdue	0	40
O20		Indiana	20	52
O27		at Notre Dame	0	56
N3		Wisconsin	7	27
N10		at Illinois	7	48
N17	•	Minnesota	20	19
N24		at Nebraska	6	13

EDDIE ANDERSON

1946 — 5-4-0 (3-3-0)

S21	•	North Dakota St.	39	0
S28	•	Purdue	16	0
O5		at Michigan	7	14
O12	•	Nebraska	21	7
O19	•	at Indiana	13	0
O26		Notre Dame	6	41
N2		Illinois	0	7
N9	•	at Wisconsin	21	7
N16		at Minnesota	6	16

1947 — 3-5-1 (2-3-1)

S20	•	North Dakota St.	59	0
S26		at UCLA	7	22
O4		Illinois	12	35
O11	•	Indiana	27	14
O18	=	at Ohio State	13	13
O25		at Notre Dame	0	21
N1		at Purdue	0	21
N8		at Wisconsin	14	46
N15	•	Minnesota	13	7

1948 — 4-5-0 (2-4-0)

S25	•	Marquette	14	12
O2		at Indiana	0	7
O9	•	at Ohio State	14	7
O16		Purdue	13	20
O23		Notre Dame	12	27
O30	•	Wisconsin	19	13
N6		at Illinois	0	14
N13		Minnesota	21	28
N20	•	at Boston U.	34	14

1949 — 4-5-0 (3-3-0)

S24		UCLA	25	41
O1	•	at Purdue	21	7
O8		Illinois	14	20
O15	•	Indiana	35	9
O22	•	Northwestern	28	21
O29	•	Oregon	34	31
N5		at Minnesota	7	55
N12	•	at Wisconsin	13	35
N19		at Notre Dame	7	28

LEONARD RAFFENSPERGER
1950-51 (.361) 5-10-3

1950 — 3-5-1 (2-4-0)

S29		at USC	20	14
O7		at Indiana	7	20
O14		Wisconsin	0	14
O21	•	Purdue	33	21
O28		at Ohio State	21	83
N4	•	at Minnesota	13	0
N11		Illinois	7	21
N18	=	Notre Dame	14	14
N24		at Miami, Fla.	6	14

1951 — 2-5-2 (0-5-1)

S29	•	Kansas State	16	0
O6		at Purdue	30	34
O13	•	Pittsburgh	34	17
O20		Michigan	0	21
O27		at Ohio State	21	47
N3	=	Minnesota	20	20
N10		at Illinois	13	40
N17		at Wisconsin	7	34
N24	=	at Notre Dame	20	20

FOREST EVASHEVSKI
1952-60 (.651) 52-27-4

1952 — 2-7-0 (2-5-0)

S27		at Pittsburgh	14	26
O4		at Indiana	13	20
O11		at Purdue	14	41
O18		Wisconsin	13	42
O25	•	Ohio State	8	0
N1		at Minnesota	7	17
N8		Illinois	13	33
N15	•	at Northwestern	39	14
N22		Notre Dame	0	27

1953 5-3-1 (3-3-0)

S26	|	Michigan State	7	21
O3	●	Washington State	54	12
O10	|	at Michigan	13	14
O17	●	Wyoming	21	7
O24	● |	Indiana	19	13
O31	|	at Wisconsin	6	10
N7	● |	at Purdue	26	0
N14	● |	Minnesota	27	0
N21	=	at Notre Dame	14	14

1954 5-4-0 (4-3-0)

S25	● |	Michigan State	14	10
O2	●	Montana	48	6
O9	|	at Michigan	13	14
O16	|	at Ohio State	14	20
O23	● |	at Indiana	27	14
O30	● |	Wisconsin	13	7
N6	● |	Purdue	25	14
N13	|	at Minnesota	20	22
N20		Notre Dame	18	34

1955 3-5-1 (2-3-1)

S24	●	Kansas State	28	7
O1	|	at Wisconsin	14	37
O8	● |	Indiana	20	6
O15	= |	Purdue	20	20
O21		at UCLA	13	33
O29	|	at Michigan	21	33
N5	● |	Minnesota	26	0
N12	|	at Ohio State	10	20
N19		at Notre Dame	14	17

1956 9-1-0 (5-1-0)

S29	● |	at Indiana	27	0
O6	●	Oregon State	14	13
O13	● |	Wisconsin	13	7
O20	●	Hawaii	34	0
O27	● |	at Purdue	21	20
N3	|	Michigan	14	17
N10	● |	at Minnesota	7	0
N17	● |	Ohio State	6	0
N24	●	Notre Dame	48	8
ROSE BOWL				
J1	●	Oregon State	35	19

1957 7-1-1 (4-1-1)

S28	●	Utah State	70	14
O5	●	Washington State	20	13
O12	● |	at Indiana	47	7
O19	● |	Wisconsin	21	7
O26	● |	at Northwestern	6	0
N2	= |	at Michigan	21	21
N9	● |	Minnesota	44	20
N16	|	at Ohio State	13	17
N23	●	at Notre Dame	21	13

1958 8-1-1 (5-1-0)

S27	●	TCU	17	0
O4	=	Air Force	13	13
O11	● |	Indiana	34	13
O18	● |	at Wisconsin	20	9
O25	● |	Northwestern	26	20
N1	● |	at Michigan	37	14
N8	● |	at Minnesota	28	6
N15	|	Ohio State	28	38
N22	●	Notre Dame	31	21
ROSE BOWL				
J1	●	California	38	12

1959 5-4-0 (3-3-0)

S26	●	at California	42	12
O3	|	Northwestern	10	14
O10	● |	Michigan State	37	8
O17	|	at Wisconsin	16	25
O24	|	at Purdue	7	14
O31	●	Kansas State	53	0
N7	● |	Minnesota	33	0
N14	● |	at Ohio State	16	7
N21		Notre Dame	19	20

1960 8-1-0 (5-1-0)

S24	●	Oregon State	22	12
O1	● |	at Northwestern	42	0
O8	● |	at Michigan State	27	15
O15	● |	Wisconsin	28	21
O22	● |	Purdue	21	14
O29	●	Kansas	21	7
N5	|	at Minnesota	10	27
N12	● |	Ohio State	35	12
N19	●	at Notre Dame	28	0

JERRY BURNS
1961-65 (.378) 16-27-2

1961 5-4-0 (2-4-0)

S30	●	California	28	7
O7	●	at USC	35	34
O14	● |	Indiana	27	8
O21	● |	Wisconsin	47	15
O28	|	at Purdue	0	9
N4	|	at Ohio State	13	29
N11	|	Minnesota	9	16
N18	|	at Michigan	14	23
N25	●	Notre Dame	42	21

1962 4-5-0 (3-3-0)

S29	●	Oregon State	28	8
O6		USC	0	7
O13	● |	at Indiana	14	10
O20	|	at Wisconsin	14	42
O27	|	Purdue	3	26
N3	● |	Ohio State	28	14
N10	|	at Minnesota	0	10
N17	● |	Michigan	28	14
N24		at Notre Dame	12	35

1963 3-3-2 (2-3-1)

S28	=	Washington State	14	14
O5	●	at Washington	17	7
O12	● |	Indiana	37	26
O19	|	Wisconsin	7	10
O26	|	at Purdue	0	14
N2	|	at Ohio State	3	7
N9	● |	Minnesota	27	13
N16	= |	at Michigan	21	21

1964 3-6-0 (1-5-0)

S26	●	Idaho	34	24
O3	●	Washington	28	18
O10	● |	at Indiana	21	20
O17	|	at Wisconsin	21	31
O24	|	Purdue	14	19
O31	|	Ohio State	19	21
N7	|	at Minnesota	13	14
N14	|	Michigan	20	34
N21		at Notre Dame	0	28

1965 1-9-0 (0-7-0)

S18		Washington State	0	7
S25	●	Oregon State PORT	27	7
O2	|	at Wisconsin	13	16
O9	|	Purdue	14	17
O16	|	Minnesota	3	14
O23	|	at Northwestern	0	9
O30	|	at Indiana	17	21
N6	|	Michigan State	0	35
N13	|	at Ohio State	0	38
N20		North Carolina St.	20	28

RAY NAGEL
1966-70 (.340) 16-32-2

1966 2-8-0 (1-6-0)

S17	●	Arizona	31	20
S24		Oregon State	3	17
O1	|	Wisconsin	0	7
O8	|	at Purdue	0	35
O15	|	at Minnesota	0	17
O22	|	Northwestern	15	24
O29	● |	Indiana	20	19
N5	|	at Michigan State	7	56
N12	|	Ohio State	10	14
N18		at Miami, Fla.	0	44

1967 1-8-1 (0-6-1)

S23	●	TCU	24	9
S30		Oregon State	18	38
O7		at Notre Dame	6	56
O14	|	at Indiana	17	21
O21	= |	at Wisconsin	21	21
O28	|	Purdue	22	41
N4	|	Minnesota	0	10
N11	|	at Northwestern	24	39
N18	|	at Ohio State	10	21
N25	|	Illinois	19	21

1968 5-5-0 (4-3-0)

S21	●	Oregon State	21	20
S28		at TCU	17	28
O5		Notre Dame	28	51
O12	|	Indiana	34	38
O19	● |	Wisconsin	41	0
O26	|	at Purdue	14	44
N2	● |	at Minnesota	35	28
N9	● |	Northwestern	68	34
N16	|	Ohio State	27	33
N23	● |	at Illinois	37	13

1969 5-5-0 (3-4-0)

S20		Oregon State	14	42
S27	●	Washington State	61	35
O4	●	Arizona	31	19
O11	|	at Wisconsin	17	23
O18	|	at Purdue	31	35
O25	● |	Michigan State	19	18
N1	|	Minnesota	8	35
N8	● |	at Indiana	28	17
N15	|	Michigan	6	51
N22	● |	at Illinois	40	0

1970 3-6-1 (3-3-1)

S19		Oregon State PORT	14	21
S26		USC	0	48
O3		at Arizona	10	17
O10	● |	Wisconsin	24	14
O17	|	Purdue	3	24
O24	|	at Michigan State	0	37
O31	= |	at Minnesota	14	14
N7	● |	Indiana	42	13
N14	|	at Michigan	0	55
N21	● |	Illinois	22	16

FRANK LAUTERBUR
1971-73 (.136) 4-28-1

1971 1-10-0 (1-8-0)

S11	|	at Ohio State	21	52
S18		at Oregon State	19	33
S25		Penn State	14	44
O2	|	at Purdue	13	45
O9	|	Northwestern	3	28
O16	|	Minnesota	14	19
O23	|	at Michigan State	3	34
O30	● |	Wisconsin	20	16
N6	|	at Michigan	7	63
N13	|	Indiana	7	14
N20	|	at Illinois	0	31

1972 3-7-1 (2-6-1)

S16	|	at Ohio State	0	21
S23	●	Oregon State	19	11
S30		at Penn State	10	14
O7	|	Purdue	0	24
O14	● |	at Northwestern	23	12
O21	|	at Minnesota	14	43
O28	= |	Michigan State	6	6
N4	|	at Wisconsin	14	16
N11	|	Michigan	0	31
N18	|	at Indiana	8	16
N25	● |	Illinois	15	14

1973 0-11-0 (0-8-0)

S15	|	Michigan	7	31
S22		at UCLA	18	55
S29		at Penn State	8	27
O6		Arizona	20	23
O13	|	at Northwestern	15	31
O20	|	Minnesota	23	31
O27	|	at Illinois	0	50
N3	|	Purdue	23	48
N10	|	at Wisconsin	7	35
N17	|	at Ohio State	13	55
N24	|	Michigan State	6	15

BOB COMMINGS
1974-78 (.309) 17-38

1974 3-8-0 (2-6-0)

S14	|	at Michigan	7	24
S21	●	UCLA	21	10
S28		Penn State	0	27
O5		at USC	3	41
O12	● |	Northwestern	35	10
O19	|	at Minnesota	17	23
O26	● |	Illinois	14	12
N2	|	at Purdue	14	38
N9	|	Wisconsin	15	28
N16	|	Ohio State	10	35
N23	|	at Michigan State	21	60

1975 3-8-0 (3-5-0)

S13	|	Illinois	12	27
S20		at Syracuse	7	10
S27		Penn State	10	30
O4		USC	16	27
O11	|	at Ohio State	0	49
O18	● |	at Indiana	20	10
O25	|	Minnesota	7	31
N1	● |	at Northwestern	24	21
N8	● |	Wisconsin	45	28
N15	|	at Purdue	18	19
N22	|	Michigan State	23	27

1976 5-6-0 (3-5-0)

S11	|	at Illinois	6	24
S18	●	Syracuse	41	3
S25	●	at Penn State	7	6
O2		at USC	0	55
O9	|	Ohio State	14	34
O16	|	Indiana	7	14
O23	● |	at Minnesota	22	12
O30	● |	Northwestern	13	10
N6	|	at Wisconsin	21	38
N13	|	Purdue	0	21
N20	● |	at Michigan State	30	17

1977 4-7-0 (3-5-0)

S10	● |	Northwestern	24	0
S17	●	Iowa State	12	10
S24		Arizona	7	41
O1		at UCLA	16	34 †
O8	● |	Minnesota	18	6
O15	|	Ohio State	6	27
O22	|	at Purdue	21	34
O29	|	at Michigan	6	23
N5	|	Indiana	21	24
N12	● |	at Wisconsin	24	8
N19	|	Michigan State	16	22

1978 2-9-0 (2-6-0)

S16	● |	Northwestern	20	3
S23		Iowa State	0	31
S30		at Arizona	3	23
O7		Utah	9	13
O14	|	at Minnesota	20	22
O21	|	at Ohio State	7	31
O28	|	Purdue	7	34
N4	|	Michigan	0	34
N11	|	at Indiana	14	34
N18	● |	Wisconsin	38	24
N25	|	at Michigan State	7	42

HAYDEN FRY
1979-98 (.613) 143-89-6

1979 5-6-0 (4-4-0)

S8	|	Indiana	26	30
S15		at Oklahoma	6	21
S22		Nebraska	21	24
S29	●	Iowa State	30	14
O6	● |	at Illinois	13	7
O13	● |	at Northwestern	58	6
O20	|	Minnesota	7	24
O27	● |	at Wisconsin	24	13
N3	|	Purdue	14	20
N10	|	at Ohio State	7	34
N17	● |	Michigan State	33	23

1980 4-7-0 (4-4-0)

S13	● |	at Indiana	16	7
S20		at Nebraska	0	57
S27		Iowa State	7	10
O4		Arizona	3	5
O11	|	Illinois	14	20
O18	● |	Northwestern	25	3
O25	|	at Minnesota	6	24
N1	● |	Wisconsin	22	13
N8	|	at Purdue	13	58
N15	|	Ohio State	7	41
N22	● |	at Michigan State	41	0

1981 8-4-0 (6-2-0)

S12	●	Nebraska	10	7
S19		at Iowa State	12	23
S26	●	UCLA	20	7
O3	● |	at Northwestern	64	0
O10	● |	Indiana	42	28
O17	● |	at Michigan	9	7
O24	|	Minnesota	10	12
O31	|	at Illinois	7	24
N7	● |	Purdue	33	7
N14	● |	at Wisconsin	17	7
N21	● |	Michigan State	36	7
ROSE BOWL				
J1		Washington	0	28

1982 8-4-0 (6-2-0)

S11		at Nebraska	7	42
S18		Iowa State	7	19
S25	●	at Arizona	17	14
O2	● |	Northwestern	45	7
O9	● |	at Indiana	24	20
O16	|	Michigan	7	29
O23	● |	at Minnesota	21	16
O30	● |	Illinois	14	13
N6	|	at Purdue	7	16
N13	● |	Wisconsin	28	14
N20	● |	at Michigan State	24	18
PEACH BOWL				
D31	●	Tennessee	28	22

1983 9-3-0 (7-2-0)

S10	●	at Iowa State	51	10
S17	●	at Penn State	42	34
S24	● |	Ohio State	20	14
O1	|	at Illinois	0	33
O8	● |	Northwestern	61	21
O15	● |	Purdue	31	14
O22	|	at Michigan	13	16
O29	● |	Indiana	49	3
N5	● |	at Wisconsin	34	14
N12	● |	at Michigan State	12	6
N19	● |	Minnesota	61	10
		GATOR BOWL		
D30		Florida	6	14

1984 8-4-1 (5-3-1)

S8	●	Iowa State	59	21
S15		Penn State	17	20
S22	|	at Ohio State	26	45
S29	● |	Illinois	21	16
O6	● |	at Northwestern	31	3
O13	● |	at Purdue	40	3
O20	● |	Michigan	26	0
O27	● |	at Indiana	24	20
N3	= |	Wisconsin	10	10
N10	|	Michigan State	16	17
N17	|	at Minnesota	17	23
D1	●	at Hawaii	17	6
		FREEDOM BOWL		
D26	●	Texas	55	17

1985 10-2-0 (7-1-0)

S14	●	Drake	58	0
S21	●	Northern Illinois	48	20
S28	●	at Iowa State	57	3
O5	● |	Michigan State	35	31
O12	● |	at Wisconsin	23	13
O19	● |	Michigan	12	10
O26	● |	at Northwestern	49	10
N2	|	at Ohio State	13	22
N9	● |	Illinois	59	0
N16	● |	at Purdue	27	24
N23	● |	Minnesota	31	9
		ROSE BOWL		
J1		UCLA	28	45

1986 9-3-0 (5-3-0)

S13	●	Iowa State	43	7
S20	●	Northern Illinois	57	3
S27	●	Texas El Paso	69	7
O4	● |	at Michigan State	24	21
O11	● |	Wisconsin	17	6
O18	|	at Michigan	17	20
O25	● |	Northwestern	27	20
N1	|	Ohio State	10	31
N8	|	at Illinois	16	20
N15	● |	Purdue	42	14
N22	● |	at Minnesota	30	27
		HOLIDAY BOWL		
D30	●	San Diego State	39	38

1987 10-3-0 (6-2-0)

A30		Tennessee *ERut*	22	23
S12	●	at Arizona	15	14
S19	●	at Iowa State	48	9
S26	●	Kansas State	38	13
O3	|	Michigan State	14	19
O10	● |	at Wisconsin	31	10
O17	|	at Michigan	10	37
O24	● |	Purdue	38	14
O31	● |	Indiana	29	21
N7	● |	at Northwestern	52	24
N14	● |	at Ohio State	29	27
N21	● |	Minnesota	34	20
		HOLIDAY BOWL		
D30	●	Wyoming	20	19

1988 6-4-3 (4-1-3)

S3		at Hawaii	24	27
S10	●	at Kansas State	45	10
S17		Colorado	21	24
S24	●	Iowa State	10	3
O1	= |	at Michigan State	10	10
O8	● |	Wisconsin	31	6
O15	= |	Michigan	17	17
O22	● |	at Purdue	31	7
O29	|	at Indiana	34	45
N5	● |	Northwestern	35	10
N12	= |	Ohio State	24	24
N19	● |	at Minnesota	31	22
		PEACH BOWL		
D31		North Carolina St.	23	28

1989 5-6-0 (3-5-0)

S16		Oregon	6	44
S23	●	at Iowa State	31	21
S30	●	Tulsa	30	22
O7	|	Michigan State	14	17
O14	● |	at Wisconsin	31	24
O21	|	Michigan	12	26
O28	● |	at Northwestern	35	22
N4	|	Illinois	7	31
N11	|	at Ohio State	0	28
N18	● |	at Purdue	24	0
N25	|	Minnesota	7	43

1990 8-4-0 (6-2-0)

S15	●	Cincinnati	63	10
S22	●	Iowa State	45	35
S29		at Miami, Fla.	21	48
O6	● |	at Michigan State	12	7
O13	● |	Wisconsin	30	10
O20	● |	at Michigan	24	23
O27	● |	Northwestern	56	14
N3	● |	at Illinois	54	28
N10	|	Ohio State	26	27
N17	● |	Purdue	38	9
N24	|	at Minnesota	24	31
		ROSE BOWL		
J1		Washington	34	46

1991 10-1-1 (7-1-0)

S7	●	Hawaii	53	10
S14	●	at Iowa State	29	10
S28	●	Northern Illinois	58	7
O5	|	Michigan	24	43
O12	● |	at Wisconsin	10	6
O19	● |	Illinois	24	21
O26	● |	at Purdue	31	21
N2	● |	at Ohio State	16	9
N9	● |	Indiana	38	21
N16	● |	at Northwestern	24	10
N23	● |	Minnesota	23	8
		HOLIDAY BOWL		
D30	=	Brigham Young	13	13

1992 5-7-0 (4-4-0)

A29		North Carolina St. *ERut*	14	24
S5		Miami, Fla.	7	24
S12	●	Iowa State	21	7
S26		at Colorado	12	28
O3	|	at Michigan	28	52
O10	● |	Wisconsin	23	22
O17	● |	at Illinois	24	14
O24	|	Purdue	16	27
O31	|	Ohio State	15	38
N7	● |	at Indiana	14	0
N14	● |	Northwestern	56	14
N21	|	at Minnesota	13	28

1993 6-6-0 (3-5-0)

S4	●	Tulsa	26	25
S11	●	at Iowa State	31	28
S18	|	Penn State	0	31
O2	|	at Michigan	7	24
O9	|	at Indiana	10	16
O16	|	Illinois	3	49
O23	|	at Michigan State	10	24
O30	● |	Purdue	26	17
N6	●	Northern Illinois	54	20
N13	● |	at Northwestern	23	19
N20	● |	Minnesota	21	3
		ALAMO BOWL		
D31		California	3	37

1994 5-5-1 (3-4-1)

S3	●	Central Michigan	52	21
S10	●	Iowa State	37	9
S17	|	at Penn State	21	61
S24		at Oregon	18	40
O1	|	Michigan	14	29
O8	|	Indiana	20	27
O15	|	at Illinois	7	47
O22	● |	Michigan State	19	14
O29	= |	at Purdue	21	21
N12	● |	Northwestern	49	13
N19	● |	at Minnesota	49	42

1995 8-4-0 (4-4-0)

S9	●	No. Iowa	34	13
S16	●	at Iowa State	27	10
S30	●	New Mexico St.	59	21
O7	● |	at Michigan State	21	7
O14	● |	Indiana	22	13
O21	|	Penn State	27	41
O28	|	at Ohio State	35	56
N4	|	Illinois	7	26
N11	|	at Northwestern	20	31
N18	● |	at Wisconsin	33	20
N25	● |	Minnesota	45	3
		SUN BOWL		
D29	●	Washington	38	18

1996 9-3 (6-2)

S7	●	Arizona	21	20
S14	●	Iowa State	38	13
S21		at Tulsa	20	27
O5	● |	Michigan State	37	30
O12	● |	at Indiana	31	10
O19	● |	at Penn State	21	20
O26	|	Ohio State	26	38
N2	● |	at Illinois	31	21
N9	|	Northwestern	13	40
N16	● |	Wisconsin	31	0
N23	● |	at Minnesota	43	24
		ALAMO BOWL		
D29	●	Texas Tech	27	0

1997 7-5 (4-4)

S6	●	No. Iowa	66	0
S13	●	Tulsa	54	16
S20	●	at Iowa State	63	20
S27	● |	Illinois	38	10
O4	|	at Ohio State	7	23
O18	|	at Michigan	24	28
O25	● |	Indiana	62	0
N1	● |	Purdue	35	17
N8	|	at Wisconsin	10	13
N15	|	at Northwestern	14	15
N22	● |	Minnesota	31	0
		SUN BOWL		
D31		Arizona State	7	17

1998 3-8 (2-6)

S5	●	Central Michigan	38	0
S12		Iowa State	9	27
S19		at Arizona	11	35
S26	● |	at Illinois	37	14
O3	|	Michigan	9	12
O10	● |	Northwestern	26	24
O17	|	at Indiana	7	14
O24	|	Wisconsin	0	31
O31	|	at Purdue	14	36
N14	|	Ohio State	14	45
N21	|	at Minnesota	7	49

KIRK FERENTZ
1999-Present (.567) 55-43

1999 1-10 (0-8)

S4		Nebraska	7	42
S11		at Iowa State	10	17
S18	●	Northern Illinois	24	0
O2	|	at Michigan State	3	49
O9	|	Penn State	7	31
O16	|	at Northwestern	21	23
O23	|	Indiana	31	38
O30	|	at Ohio State	11	41
N6	|	Illinois	24	40
N13	|	at Wisconsin	3	41
N20	|	Minnesota	21	25

2000 3-9 (3-5)

A26		Kansas State *KC*	7	27
S9		Western Michigan	21	27
S16		Iowa State	14	24
S23		at Nebraska	13	42
S30		at Indiana	33	45
O7	● |	Michigan State	21	16
O14	|	at Illinois	0	31
O21	|	Ohio State	10	38
O28	|	Wisconsin	7	13
N4	● |	at Penn State	26	23
N11	● |	Northwestern	27	17
N18	|	at Minnesota	24	27

2001 7-5 (4-4)

S1	●	Kent	51	0
S8	●	Miami (Ohio)	44	19
S29	● |	Penn State	24	18
O6	|	at Purdue	14	23
O13	|	at Michigan State	28	31
O20	● |	Indiana	42	28
O27	|	Michigan	26	32
N3	|	at Wisconsin	28	34
N10	● |	at Northwestern	59	16
N17	● |	Minnesota	42	24
N24		at Iowa State	14	17
		ALAMO BOWL		
D29	●	Texas Tech	19	16

2002 11-2 (8-0)

A31	●	Akron	57	21
S7	●	at Miami (Ohio)	29	24
S14		Iowa State	31	36
S21	●	Utah State	48	7
S28	● |	at Penn State	42	35
O5	● |	Purdue	31	28
O12	● |	Michigan State	44	16
O19	● |	at Indiana	24	8
O26	● |	at Michigan	34	9
N2	● |	Wisconsin	20	3
N9	● |	Northwestern	62	10
N16	● |	at Minnesota	45	21
		ORANGE BOWL		
J2		USC	17	38

2003 10-3 (5-3)

A30	●	Miami (Ohio)	21	3
S6	●	Buffalo	56	7
S13	●	at Iowa State	40	21
S20	●	Arizona State	21	2
S27	|	at Michigan State	10	20
O4	● |	Michigan	30	27
O18	|	at Ohio State	10	19
O25	● |	Penn State	26	14
N1	● |	Illinois	41	10
N8	|	at Purdue	14	27
N15	● |	Minnesota	40	22
N22	● |	at Wisconsin	27	21
		OUTBACK BOWL		
J1	●	Florida	37	17

2004 10-2 (7-1)

S4	●	Kent State	39	7
S11	●	Iowa State	17	10
S18		at Arizona State	7	44
S25	|	at Michigan	17	30
O2	● |	Michigan State	38	16
O16	● |	Ohio State	33	7
O23	● |	at Penn State	6	4
O30	● |	at Illinois	23	13
N6	● |	Purdue	23	21
N13	● |	at Minnesota	29	27
N20	● |	Wisconsin	30	7
		CAPITAL ONE BOWL		
J1	●	LSU	30	25

2005 7-5 (5-3)

S3	●	Ball State	56	0
S10		at Iowa State	3	23
S17	●	Northern Iowa	45	21
S24	|	at Ohio State	6	31
O1	● |	Illinois	35	7
O8	● |	at Purdue	34	17
O15	● |	Indiana	38	21
O22	|	Michigan	20	23
N5	|	at Northwestern	27	28
N12	● |	at Wisconsin	20	10
N19	● |	Minnesota	52	28
		OUTBACK BOWL		
J2		Florida	24	31

2006 6-7 (2-6)

S2	●	Montana	41	7
S9	●	at Syracuse	20	13
S16	●	Iowa State	27	17
S23	● |	at Illinois	24	7
S30	|	Ohio State	17	38
O7	● |	Purdue	47	17
O14	|	at Indiana	28	31
O21	|	at Michigan	6	20
O28	●	Northern Illinois	24	14
N4	|	Northwestern	7	21
N11	|	Wisconsin	21	24
N18	|	at Minnesota	24	34
		ALAMO BOWL		
D30		Texas	24	26

Neutral Site key: *ERut* East Rutherford, N.J. / *KC* Kansas City, Mo. / *Dal* Dallas, Texas / *Cou* Council Bluffs, Neb. / *Oma* Omaha, Neb. / *RI* Rock Island, Ill. / *Det* Detroit, Mich. / *Chi* Chicago, Ill. / *Port* Portland, Ore.
f Forfeit † Game Later Forfeited # Disputed Victor * Disputed Score || Designated Conference Game |2 Counted Twice in Conference Standings

IOWA RECORD BOOK

SINGLE-GAME RECORDS

RUSHING YARDS

RANK	PLAYER	DATE	OPPONENT	ATT	AVG	YDS
1	Tavian Banks	Sept. 13, 1997	Tulsa	29	10.8	314
2	Ed Podolak	Nov. 9, 1968	Northwestern	17	16.8	286
3	Sedrick Shaw	Oct. 7, 1995	Michigan State	42	6.0	250
4	Phil Blatcher	Nov. 21, 1981	Michigan State	27	9.1	247
5	Dennis Mosley	Sept. 29, 1979	Iowa State	39	5.9	229

PASSING YARDS

RANK	PLAYER	DATE	OPPONENT	ATT	COMP	YDS
1	Chuck Hartlieb	Oct. 29, 1988	Indiana	60	44	558
2	Chuck Hartlieb	Nov. 7, 1987	Northwestern	32	25	471
3	Chuck Long	Dec. 26, 1984	Texas	39	29	461
4	Chuck Hartlieb	Dec. 31, 1988	North Carolina State	51	30	428
5	Scott Mullen	Oct. 23, 1999	Indiana	60	36	426

RECEIVING YARDS

RANK	PLAYER	DATE	OPPONENT	REC	AVG	YDS
1	Quinn Early	Nov. 7, 1987	Northwestern	10	25.6	256
2	Deven Harberts	Oct. 29, 1988	Indiana	11	21.2	233
3	Bill Happel	Sept. 21, 1985	Northern Illinois	9	23.0	207
4	Dave Moritz	Oct. 29, 1983	Indiana	11	17.5	192
5	Keith Chappelle	Oct. 11, 1980	Illinois	12	15.9	191

POINTS

RANK	PLAYER	DATE	OPPONENT	TOT
1	8 players tied at 24			

FIELD GOALS

RANK	PLAYER	DATE	OPPONENT	TOT
1	Kyle Schlicher	Nov. 13, 2004	Minnesota	5

TACKLES

RANK	PLAYER	DATE	OPPONENT	TOT
1	Dave Clement	Sept. 19, 1970	Oregon State	29
2	Bobby Diaco	Oct. 14, 1995	Indiana	26
	Dave Brooks	Nov. 21, 1970	Illinois	26
4	Bob Sanders	Oct. 20, 2001	Indiana	25
5	Dave Moreland	Oct. 15, 1966	Minnesota	23

INTERCEPTIONS

RANK	PLAYER	DATE	OPPONENT	TOT
1	Grant Steen	Oct. 19, 2002	Indiana	3

RETIRED NUMBERS

24 Nile Kinnick

62 Cal Jones

SINGLE-SEASON RECORDS

RUSHING YARDS

RANK	PLAYER	SEASON	G	ATT	YDS
1	Tavian Banks	1997	NA	260	1,691
2	Sedrick Shaw	1995	NA	316	1,477
3	Fred Russell	2003	13	282	1,355
4	Albert Young	2005	12	249	1,334
5	Dennis Mosley	1979	NA	270	1,267

PASSING YARDS

RANK	PLAYER	SEASON	G	ATT	COMP	PCT	YDS
1	Chuck Hartlieb	1988	NA	460	288	62.6	3,738
2	Chuck Long	1985	NA	388	260	67.0	3,297
3	Chuck Hartlieb	1987	NA	334	217	64.9	3,092
4	Chuck Long	1984	NA	322	216	67.0	2,871
5	Drew Tate	2005	12	352	219	62.2	2,828

RECEIVING YARDS

RANK	PLAYER	SEASON	REC	AVG	YDS
1	Keith Chappelle	1980	64	16.2	1,037
2	Kevin Kasper	2000	82	12.3	1,010
3	Quinn Early	1987	63	15.9	1,004
4	Maurice Brown	2002	48	20.1	966
5	Karl Noonan	1964	59	15.8	933

SCORING

RANK	PLAYER	SEASON	TD	FG	PAT	P2	TOT
1	Nate Kaeding	2002	0	21	57	0	120
2	Tavian Banks	1997	19	0	0	0	114
3	Nate Kaeding	2003	1	20	40	0	106
4	Rob Houghtlin	1985	0	19	48	0	105
5	Rob Houghtlin	1987	0	21	41	0	104

TOUCHDOWNS

RANK	PLAYER	SEASON	TOT
1	Tavian Banks	1997	19
2	Dennis Mosley	1979	16
3	Sedrick Shaw	1995	15
4	Nick Bell	1990	14
5	Mike Saunders	1991	13

TACKLES

RANK	PLAYER	SEASON	G	TOT
1	Andre Jackson	1972	NA	171
2	Abdul Hodge	2005	12	158
3	Chad Greenway	2005	12	156
4	Abdul Hodge	2003	13	141
5	Dave Clement	1970	NA	140

INTERCEPTIONS

RANK	PLAYER	SEASON	YDS	TOT
1	Lou King	1981	62	8
	Nile Kinnick	1939	52	8
3	Kerry Burt	1987	15	7
	Jay Norvell	1985	93	7
	Steve Wilson	1967	83	7

PUNTING

RANK	PLAYER	SEASON	PUNTS	YDS	AVG
1	Reggie Roby	1981	NA	NA	49.8

PUNT RETURNS

RANK	PLAYER	SEASON	RET	YDS	AVG
1	Roman Ochoa	2003	40	495	12.4

KICKOFF RETURNS

RANK	PLAYER	SEASON	RET	YDS	AVG
1	Earl Douthitt	1973	28	994	35.5

IOWA RECORD BOOK

CAREER RECORDS

RUSHING YARDS

RANK	PLAYER	SEASONS	ATT	AVG	TD	YDS
1	Sedrick Shaw	1993-96	837	5.0	33	4,156
2	Ladell Betts	1998-2001	831	4.4	25	3,686
3	Tavian Banks	1994-97	505	5.9	33	2,977
4	Fred Russell	2001-03	514	5.4	17	2,760
5	Tony Stewart	1987-90	532	4.8	17	2,562
6	Owen Gill	1981-84	489	5.2	22	2,556
7	Ronnie Harmon	1982-85	443	5.1	22	2,271
8	Albert Young	2004-06	454	4.9	17	2,205
9	Eddie Phillips	1980-83	465	4.7	19	2,177
10	Dennis Mosley	1976-79	458	4.6	14	2,133

PASSING YARDS

RANK	PLAYER	SEASONS	ATT	COMP	PCT	INT	TD	YDS
1	Chuck Long	1981-85	1,203	782	65.0	52	74	10,461
2	Drew Tate	2003-06	1,090	665	61.0	34	61	8,292
3	Chuck Hartlieb	1986-88	802	512	63.8	21	37	6,934
4	Matt Rodgers	1988-91	905	550	60.8	33	41	6,725
5	Matt Sherman	1994-97	776	448	57.7	33	43	6,399
6	Kyle McCann	1998-2001	603	357	59.2	21	23	4,349
7	Gary Snook	1963-65	631	280	44.3	42	20	3,738
8	Brad Banks	2001-02	362	213	58.8	7	30	3,155
9	Larry Lawrence	1968-69	395	201	50.9	20	17	2,987
10	Paul Burmeister	1990-93	419	242	57.8	15	16	2,943

RECEIVING YARDS

RANK	PLAYER	SEASONS	REC	AVG	TD	YDS
1	Tim Dwight	1994-97	139	16.3	21	2,271
2	Danan Hughes	1989-92	146	15.2	21	2,216
3	Ronnie Harmon	1982-85	146	14.0	10	2,045
4	Kevin Kasper	1997-2000	157	12.6	11	1,974
5	Dave Moritz	1980-83	109	17.5	9	1,912
6	Kahlil Hill	1998-2001	152	12.4	15	1,892
7	Clinton Solomon	2002, 04-05	118	15.8	14	1,864
8	Harold Jasper	1991-94	107	17.4	8	1,863
9	Quinn Early	1984-87	106	17.4	13	1,845
10	Marv Cook	1986-88	126	14.5	6	1,825

SCORING

RANK	PLAYER	SEASONS	TD	FG	PAT	P2	TOT
1	Nate Kaeding	2000-03	1	67	166	0	373
2	Rob Houghtlin	1985-87	0	54	128	0	290
3	Tom Nichol	1981-84	0	45	142	0	277
4	Kyle Schlecher	2004-06	36	0	51	107	260
5	Tavian Banks	1994-97	36	0	0	1	218
	Zach Bromert	1995-98	0	26	140	0	218

TOUCHDOWNS

RANK	PLAYER	SEASONS	TOT
1	Tavian Banks	1994-97	36
2	Sedrick Shaw	1993-96	35
3	Tim Dwight	1994-97	32
	Ronnee Harmon	1982-85	32
5	Ladell Betts	1998-2000	27

TACKLES

RANK	PLAYER	SEASONS	TOT
1	Larry Station	1982-85	492
2	Andre Jackson	1972-75	465
3	Abdul Hodge	2002-05	453
4	Brad Quast	1986-89	435
5	Chad Greenway	2002-05	416

INTERCEPTIONS

RANK	PLAYER	SEASONS	YDS	TOT
1	Devon Mitchell	2000-03	202	18
	Nile Kinnick	1985-87	91	18
3	Jovon Johnson	1981-84	183	17
4	Damien Robinson	1994-97	196	14
5	Steve Wilson	1995-98	118	12

PUNTING

RANK	PLAYER	SEASONS	PUNTS	YDS	AVG
1	Jason Baker	1997-2000	272	11,304	41.6

TEAM RECORDS

LONGEST WINNING STREAK
• 20, Nov. 6, 1920-Oct. 13, 1923
Streak broken vs. Illinois, 6-9, Oct. 20, 1923

LONGEST UNDEFEATED STREAK
• 23, Nov. 12, 1898 - Oct. 18, 1901
Streak broken vs. Minnesota, 0-16, Oct. 26, 1901

MOST CONSECUTIVE WINNING SEASONS
• 8 (tie), 1918-25; 1981-88

MOST CONSECUTIVE BOWL APPEARANCES
• 8, 1981-88

MOST POINTS IN A GAME
• 95, vs. Northern Iowa, Oct. 3, 1914

MOST POINTS ALLOWED IN A GAME
• 107, vs. Michigan, Nov. 8, 1902

LARGEST MARGIN OF VICTORY
• 95 (95-0), vs. Northern Iowa, Oct. 3, 1914

LARGEST MARGIN OF DEFEAT
• 107 (0-107), vs. Michigan, Nov. 8, 1902

LONGEST RUN FROM SCRIMMAGE
• 96 yards, Eddie Vincent, vs. Purdue, Nov. 6, 1954

LONGEST PASS PLAY
• 95 yards (tie), Chuck Hartlieb to Quinn Early, vs. Northwestern, Nov. 7, 1987; Brad Banks to Dallas Clark, vs. Purdue, Oct. 5, 2002

LONGEST FIELD GOAL
• 58 yards, Tim Douglas, vs. Illinois, Sept. 26, 1998

LONGEST PUNT
• 83 yards, Lonnie Rogers, vs. Oregon State, Sept. 26, 1962

LONGEST INTERCEPTION RETURN
• 98 yards, Adam Shada, vs. Purdue, Oct. 7, 2006

LONGEST PUNT RETURN
• 95 yards, Bill Happel, vs. Minnesota, Nov. 17, 1984

PUNT RETURNS

RANK	PLAYER	SEASON	RET	YDS	AVG
1	Tim Dwight	1994-97	76	1,102	14.5

KICKOFF RETURNS

RANK	PLAYER	SEASON	RET	YDS	AVG
1	Earl Douthitt	1972-74	43	1,762	41.0

IOWA ANNUAL STATISTICAL LEADERS

YR	RUSHING	YDS	ATT	AVG	PASSING	ATT	CMP	PCT	YDS	RECEIVING	REC	YDS	AVG
1940	Bill Green	483	115	4.2		NA	NA	NA	NA		NA	NA	NA
1941	Bill Green	420	114	3.7		NA	NA	NA	NA		NA	NA	NA
1942	Charles Uknes	445	84	5.3		NA	NA	NA	NA		NA	NA	NA
1943	Bill Gallagher	314	72	4.4	Roger Stephens		12		231	Bill Barbour	10	179	17.9
1944	Bill Kersten	301	106	2.8	Dick Woodard		11		128	John Stewart	7	46	6.6
1945	Arthur Johnson	290	65	4.5	Jerry Niles		63		889	Harold Loehlein	11	165	15.0
1946	Bob Smith	503	109	4.6	Emlen Tunnell	58	28	.48	228	Dick Hoerner	6	72	12.0
1947	Bob Smith	395	110	3.6	Al DiMarco	100	49	.49	644	Emlen Tunnell	12	262	21.8
1948	Jerry Faske	491	73	6.7	Al DiMarco	161	64	.40	1,105	Bob McKenzie	22	382	17.4
1949	Ralph Doran	342	53	6.5	Glenn Drahn	145	51	.35	735	Bob McKenzie	22	313	14.2
1950	Bill Reichardt	585	138	4.2	Glenn Drahn	168	55	.33	835	Bill Reichardt	11	95	8.6
1951	Bill Reichardt	737	178	4.1	Burt Britzmann	150	68	.45	942	Fred Ruck	25	274	11.0
1952	George Broeder	311	86	3.6	Burt Britzmann	94	37	.39	515	Dan McBride	29	448	15.4
1953	George Broeder	410	96	4.3	Lou Matykiewicz	44	18	.41	234	Frank Gilliam	12	71	5.9
1954	Eddie Vincent	618	95	6.5	Jerry Reichow	73	34	.47	386	Frank Gilliam	15	223	14.9
1955	Eddie Vincent	381	73	5.2	Jerry Reichow	88	48	.55	722	Jim Gibbons	16	257	16.1
1956	Ken Ploen	487	86	5.7	Ken Ploen	64	33	.52	386	Jim Gibbons	17	255	15.0
1957	Collins Hagler	456	67	6.8	Randy Duncan	119	70	.59	1,124	Jim Gibbons	36	587	16.3
1958	Ray Jauch	524	76	6.9	Randy Duncan	179	106	.59	1,397	Don Norton	25	374	15.0
1959	Bob Jeter	609	108	5.6	Olen Treadway	147	86	.59	1,014	Don Norton	30	428	14.3
1960	Larry Ferguson	665	90	7.4	Wilburn Hollis	62	22	.35	289	Felton Rogers	8	96	12.0
1961	Bill Perkins	380	62	6.1	Matt Szykowny	120	79	.66	1,078	Cloyd Webb	25	425	17.0
1962	Larry Ferguson	547	113	4.8	Matt Szykowny	115	59	.51	737	Paul Krause	16	214	13.4
1963	Bobby Grier	406	98	4.1	Gary Snook	90	34	.38	667	Cloyd Webb	24	424	18.0
1964	Dalton Kimble	284	68	4.2	Gary Snook	311	151	.49	2,062	Karl Noonan	59	933	15.8
1965	Silas McKinnie	286	89	3.2	Gary Snook	230	95	.41	1,009	Karl Noonan	43	545	12.7
1966	Silas McKinnie	516	124	4.2	Ed Podolak	191	77	.40	1,041	Al Bream	30	418	13.9
1967	Silas McKinnie	588	166	3.5	Ed Podolak	162	79	.49	1,014	Al Bream	55	703	12.8
1968	Ed Podolak	937	154	6.1	Larry Lawrence	156	88	.56	1,307	Ray Manning	35	426	12.2
1969	Steve Penney	484	102	4.7	Larry Lawrence	239	113	.47	1,680	Kerry Reardon	43	738	17.2
1970	Levi Mitchell	900	205	4.4	Roy Bash	70	32	.46	473	Kerry Reardon	27	438	16.2
1971	Levi Mitchell	623	149	4.2	Frank Sunderman	235	109	.46	1,297	Dave Triplett	28	426	15.2
1972	Dave Harris	621	136	4.6	Kyle Skogman	57	24	.42	356	Brian Rollins	29	378	13.0
1973	Jim Jensen	509	111	4.6	Butch Caldwell	99	36	.36	549	Brian Rollins	33	408	12.4
1974	Jim Jensen	659	163	4.0	Rob Fick	165	79	.48	1,059	Bill Schultz	25	432	17.3
1975	Dave Schick	482	90	5.4	Tom McLaughlin	87	23	.26	358	Bill Schultz	8	238	30.0
1976	Jon Lazar	392	95	4.1	Butch Caldwell	101	37	.37	616	Tom Grine	12	195	16.3
1977	Jon Lazar	411	100	4.1	Tom McLaughlin	152	78	.51	1,081	Mike Brady	26	357	13.7
1978	Jon Lazar	423	108	3.9	Jeff Green	103	41	.40	556	Jon Lazar	18	72	4.0
1979	Dennis Mosley	1,267	270	4.7	Phil Suess	159	88	.55	1,165	Brad Reid	25	290	11.6
1980	Jeff Brown	673	132	5.1	Phil Suess	166	87	.52	1,031	Keith Chappelle	64	1,037	16.2
1981	Phil Blatcher	708	145	4.9	Gordy Bohannon	142	72	.51	999	Jeff Brown	20	301	15.1
1982	Eddie Phillips	806	166	4.9	Chuck Long	227	148	.65	1,678	Dave Moritz	41	605	14.8
1983	Owen Gill	798	129	6.2	Chuck Long	265	157	.59	2,601	Dave Moritz	50	912	18.2
1984	Owen Gill	920	199	4.6	Chuck Long	322	216	.67	2,871	Bill Happel	47	632	13.4
1985	Ronnie Harmon	1,166	223	5.2	Chuck Long	388	260	.67	3,297	Ronnie Harmon	60	699	11.7
1986	Rick Bayless	1,150	216	5.3	Mark Vlasic	180	108	.60	1,456	Jim Mauro	30	600	20.0
1987	Kevin Harmon	715	151	4.7	Chuck Hartlieb	334	217	.65	3,092	Quinn Early	63	1,004	15.9
1988	Tony Stewart	1,036	215	4.8	Chuck Hartlieb	460	288	.63	3,738	Marv Cook	63	767	12.2
1989	Nick Bell	603	117	5.1	Matt Rodgers	312	178	.57	2,222	Travis Watkins	36	583	16.2
1990	Nick Bell	1,009	166	6.1	Matt Rodgers	310	187	.60	2,228	Danan Hughes	29	410	14.1
1991	Mike Saunders	1,022	216	4.7	Matt Rodgers	283	185	.65	2,275	Danan Hughes	43	757	17.6
1992	Marvin Lampkin	653	171	3.8	Jim Hartlieb	226	144	.64	1,579	Alan Cross	55	640	11.6
1993	Ryan Terry	664	157	4.2	Paul Burmeister	309	184	.60	2,152	Harold Jasper	38	641	16.9
1994	Sedrick Shaw	1,002	170	5.9	Ryan Driscoll	154	78	.51	1,018	Harold Jasper	33	621	18.8
1995	Sedrick Shaw	1,477	316	4.7	Matt Sherman	295	170	.58	2,546	Tim Dwight	46	816	17.7
1996	Sedrick Shaw	1,116	224	5.0	Matt Sherman	264	154	.58	1,918	Tim Dwight	51	751	14.7
1997	Tavian Banks	1,691	260	6.5	Matt Sherman	158	82	.52	1,199	Tim Dwight	42	704	16.8
1998	Ladell Betts	679	188	3.6	Kyle McCann	159	86	.54	1,179	Kahlil Hill	35	432	12.3
1999	Ladell Betts	857	189	4.5	Scott Mullen	226	126	.56	1,415	Kevin Kasper	60	664	11.1
2000	Ladell Betts	1,090	232	4.7	Scott Mullen	141	74	.52	877	Kevin Kasper	82	1,010	12.3
2001	Ladell Betts	1,060	222	4.7	Kyle McCann	252	167	.66	2,028	Kahlil Hill	59	841	14.3
2002	Fred Russell	1,264	220	5.7	Brad Banks	294	170	.58	2,573	Maurice Brown	48	966	20.1
2003	Fred Russell	1,355	282	4.8	Nathan Chandler	308	165	.54	2,040	Maurice Brown	33	507	15.4
2004	Sam Brownlee	227	94	2.4	Drew Tate	375	233	.62	2,786	Ed Hinkel	63	744	11.8
2005	Albert Young	1,334	249	5.4	Drew Tate	352	219	.62	2,828	Clinton Solomon	46	800	17.4
2006	Albert Young	779	178	4.4	Drew Tate	352	207	.59	2,623	Andy Brodell	39	724	18.6

Receiving leaders by receptions
All statistics include postseason

MICHIGAN

By Todd Jones

EVERYTHING ABOUT MICHIGAN football looms as large as the Great Lakes. The Wolverines have the most Division I-A victories (860 through 2006), the most conference championships (42 Big Ten titles), and the most winning seasons (109) of any school in the nation, as well as the largest stadium (107,501) in the land. The Wolverines have won nine national titles, carry a .745 all-time winning percentage (highest in Division I-A), the nation's longest current streak of nonlosing seasons (39 since 1967), the longest current bowl streak (32 seasons since 1975), and have played in more televised games (368) than any other school. But numbers speak only to the cold efficiency of the powerful football machine. Its heart has been warmed by the play of such stars as Bennie Oosterbaan, Benny Friedman, Tom Harmon, Rick Leach, Anthony Carter, Desmond Howard, and Charles Woodson, as well as by the coaching fire of Fielding Yost, Fritz Crisler, Bo Schembechler, and Lloyd Carr, men who have built a lasting legacy and a tradition matched by few other schools. "Tradition is something you can't bottle," Crisler once said. "You can't buy it at the corner store, but it is there to sustain you when you need it most. I've called upon it time and time again, and so have countless other Michigan athletes and coaches. There's nothing like it."

TRADITION Nothing sounds quite like "The Victors." Louis Elbel created one of college football's most recognizable fight songs—and the only one enshrined in the National Football Foundation College Hall of Fame—in 1899 after he watched Michigan upset Amos Alonzo Stagg's powerhouse Chicago team. Today, the University of Michigan Marching Band, a 225-member outfit, blasts the song when the Wolverines run out of the Michigan Stadium tunnel and touch the "Go Blue" banner as they take the field. It blares after every Michigan score, accompanied by cheerleaders doing backflips off the rail of the brick wall surrounding the homefield. Since 1953, the Wolverines and Michigan State have played annually for the Paul Bunyan Trophy—a four-foot wooden statue donated by then-governor G. Mennen Williams. The Little Brown Jug, however, is the oldest of college football's 57 trophy-game traditions. Yost, who feared his

---

PROFILE

University of Michigan
Ann Arbor, Mich.
Founded: 1817
Enrollment: 25,555
Colors: Maize and Blue
Nickname: Wolverines
Stadium: Michigan Stadium
　　Opened in 1927
　　FieldTurf; 107,501 capacity
First football game: 1879
All-time record: 860–282–36 (.745)
Bowl record: 18–20
Consensus national championships,
1936-present: 3 (1947, 1948, 1997)
Big Ten Conference championships:
42 (16 outright)
Heisman Trophy: Tom Harmon, 1940; Desmond Howard, 1991; Charles Woodson, 1997
First-round draft choices: 45
Website: www.mgoblue.com

THE BEST OF TIMES

Bo Schembechler's 50–4–1 record and four Big Ten championships from 1970 to 1974 are impressive, but they pale when compared with the "Point a Minute" Wolverines, who went 55–1–1 from 1901 to 1905. They outscored opponents 2,821-42 while winning four consecutive national championships.

THE WORST OF TIMES

Four years without a winning record as coach Harry G. Kipke went 10–22 (5–17 in the Big Ten) from 1934 to 1937. His 1934 and 1936 clubs each went 1–7.

CONFERENCE

The Wolverines were charter members of the Big Ten (then called the Western Conference) in 1896 but left to become an independent from 1907 to 1916. In 1917, they rejoined the conference, where they've remained since.

DISTINGUISHED ALUMNI

Clarence Darrow; Gerald Ford; Arthur Miller; Branch Rickey; Madonna; Mike Wallace; James Earl Jones; Nancy Kassebaum, U.S. senator; Lucy Liu, actress

FIGHT SONG

THE VICTORS
Now for a cheer they are here, triumphant!
Here they come with banners flying,
In stalwart step they're nighing,
With shouts of vict'ry crying,
We hurrah, hurrah, we greet you now, Hail!
Far we their praises sing
For the glory and fame they've brought us
Loud let the bells them ring
For here they come with banners flying
Here they come, Hurrah!
Hail! to the victors valiant
Hail! to the conqu'ring heroes
Hail! Hail! to Michigan
The leaders and best!
Hail! to the victors valiant
Hail! to the conqu'ring heroes
Hail! Hail! to Michigan
The champions of the West!

Wolverines might be served contaminated water at Minnesota in 1903, ordered team manager Tommy Roberts to buy a five-gallon jug from a Minneapolis store. Michigan drank from it during a 6-6 tie, then left the jug behind. When Yost asked for it back, Minnesota athletic director L.J. Cooke replied, "If you want it, you'll have to come up and win it." Michigan did so in 1909, and the two teams have played for the jug every year since 1929.

BEST PLAYER He was "Ol' 98," the needle-nosed, square-jawed, gregarious fellow who, as a child, learned how to play rough on the sandlots of Gary, Ind., and eventually ended up on a *Life* magazine cover under the headline, "Michigan's Great Harmon." That was November 1940, shortly before senior Tom Harmon won the Heisman Trophy and one year after he finished second in the voting. He was 6'1", 195 pounds, and played tailback, defensive back, kicker, and punter. Eight times in his career he played all 60 minutes in a game. Twice he led the nation in scoring, something no one had ever done before. His versatility was unstoppable on Sept. 28, 1940, at California. There, he ran the opening

The men in maize and blue have built a tradition matched by few other schools.

kickoff back 94 yards for a touchdown, returned a punt 72 yards for a TD, ran 86 and eight yards for two other scores and threw a TD pass in a 41-0 win over the Bears. Nothing could stop him, not even a drunken Cal fan named Bud Brennan, who ran out of the stands and tried to tackle Harmon during his 86-yard score. In his last game, a 40-0 win at Ohio State, Harmon was again as versatile as a Swiss Army knife. He scored three touchdowns—the second breaking Red Grange's career record of 31—threw 2 TD passes, rushed for 139 yards, passed for 151 (completing 11 of 12 attempts), kicked four extra points, averaged 50 yards on his punts, and intercepted three passes on defense, returning one for a score. The crowd of 73,000 gave him a standing ovation when he left the field for the final time near game's end. After he graduated, his life was depicted in the movie *Harmon of Michigan*. During World War II, he was shot down and listed as missing twice while serving as an Army Air Force pilot in the Pacific Theater. He won the Silver Star and the Purple Heart, then played briefly in the pro ranks with the Los Angeles Rams before becoming a nationally known sportscaster.

FIRST-ROUND DRAFT CHOICES

1941	Tom Harmon, Bears (1)
1941	Forest Evashevski, Redskins (10)
1942	Bob Westfall, Lions (5)
1944	Merv Pregulman, Packers (7)
1945	Elroy Hirsch, Rams (5)
1945	Don Lund, Bears (7)
1947	Elmer Madar, Seahawks (1)
1947	Bob Chappuis, Browns (8)
1949	Dan Dworsky, L.A. Dons
1949	Gene Derricotte, Browns
1957	Ron Kramer, Packers (4)
1958	Jim Pace, 49ers (8)
1966	Tom Mack, Rams (2)
1966	Bill Yearby, Jets
1967	James Detwiler, Colts (20)
1969	Ron Johnson, Browns (20)
1972	Thomas Darden, Browns (18)
1972	Mike Taylor, Jets (20)
1973	Paul Seymour, Bills (7)
1974	Dave Gallagher, Bears (20)
1975	Dave Brown, Steelers (26)
1978	Mike Kenn, Falcons (13)
1978	John Anderson, Packers (26)
1979	Jon Giesler, Dolphins (24)
1980	Curtis Greer, Cardinals (6)
1981	Mel Owens, Rams (9)
1982	Butch Woolfork, Giants (18)
1985	Kevin Brooks, Cowboys (17)
1987	Jim Harbaugh, Bears (26)
1991	Jarrod Bunch, Giants (27)
1992	Desmond Howard, Redskins (4)
1993	Steve Everitt, Browns (14)
1994	Derrick Alexander, Browns (29)
1995	Tyrone Wheatley, Giants (17)
1995	Ty Law, Patriots (23)
1995	Trezelle Jenkins, Chiefs (31)
1996	Tim Biakabutuka, Panthers (8)
1998	Charles Woodson, Raiders (4)
2001	David Terrell, Bears (8)
2001	Steve Hutchinson, Seahawks (17)
2001	Jeff Backus, Lions (18)
2004	Chris Perry, Bengals (26)
2005	Braylon Edwards Browns (3)
2005	Marlin Jackson Colts (29)
2007	Leon Hall, Bengals (18)

CONSENSUS ALL-AMERICANS

1898	William Cunningham, C
1901	Neil Snow, E
1903-04	Willie Heston, B
1907	Adolph Schulz, C
1909-10	Albert Benbrook, G
1910	Stanfield Wells, E
1913	Miller Pontius, T
1913	Jim Craig, B
1914	John Maulbetsch, B
1922	Harry Kipke, B
1923	Jack Blott, C
1925-27	Bennie Oosterbaan, E
1925-26	Benny Friedman, B
1928	Otto Pommerening, T
1932	Harry Newman, B
1933	Francis Wistert, T
1933	Chuck Bernard, C
1938	Ralph Heikkinen, G
1939-40	Tom Harmon, B
1941	Bob Westfall, B
1942	Albert Wistert, T
1942	Julie Franks, G
1943	Bill Daley, B
1947	Bob Chappuis, B

(Continued on next page)

BEST COACH "Meeshegan," as he pronounced it, might have been just another football school without the influence of Fielding H. Yost. It became a beast, however, when the man from West Virginia arrived in Michigan at the turn of the 20th century and told everyone to "hurry up." Yost was a lawyer, a nondrinker, a military historian, and a cigar-chompin' son of a Confederate soldier. He was also one of football's first giants—the creator of the linebacker position and the first to use offensive motion as a decoy. Some found his style of play—which frequently called for quick-kicking to achieve field position—boring and referred to his offense as "punt, pass, and pray." Yet Yost would embrace the forward pass and helped popularize its use. He was known for his ego, rarely praised opponents, showed no mercy in beating his alma mater, West Virginia, 130-0 in 1904, and was all business even in practice, during which he wore starched collars and ties. Yost coached the incredible "Point a Minute" Michigan teams that went 55–1–1 (with 50 shutouts) and outscored opponents 2,821-42 from 1901 to 1905. In all, he went 165–29–10, had eight undefeated teams, and won four national championships from 1901 to 1926 (he didn't coach in 1924). His seven Big Ten titles would have been more if the Wolverines had not dropped out of the league for 10 years because the school was upset with rules limiting a season to five games and with proposals to allow players only three seasons of varsity status. Yost later served as Michigan's athletic director, from 1921 to 1941.

BEST TEAM It's difficult to argue against Yost's "Point a Minute" machines, but "Michigan's Mad Magicians" in 1947 are still revered for their 10–0 record and national title. The Wolverines outscored their regular-season opponents 345-53 while leading the nation in total yards (412.7) and passing yards (173.9) per game. Michigan's defense—led by end Len Ford, tackle Alvin Wistert, and linebackers Dan Dworsky and Rick Kempthorn—shut out five opponents. Michigan was dangerous on special teams, too, with Gene

CONSENSUS ALL-AMERICANS (CONT.)	
1948	Dick Rifenburg, E
1948-49	Alvin Wistert, T
1955-56	Ron Kramer, E
1965	Bill Yearby, DT
1966	Jack Clancy, E
1969	Jim Mandich, E
1969	Tom Curtis, DB
1970	Dan Dierdorf, T
1971	Reggie McKenzie, G
1971	Mike Taylor, LB
1972	Paul Seymour, T
1972	Randy Logan, DB
1973	Dave Gallagher, DL
1973-74	Dave Brown, DB
1976	Rob Lytle, RB
1976-77	Mark Donahue, G
1979	Ron Simpkins, LB
1981-82	Anthony Carter, WR
1981	Ed Muransky, OL
1981	Kurt Becker, OL
1985	Mike Hammerstein, DL
1985	Brad Cochran, DB
1986	Garland Rivers, DB
1987	John "Jumbo" Elliott, OL
1988	John Vitale, C
1988	Mark Messner, DL
1989-90	Tripp Welborne, DB
1991	Greg Skrepenak, OL
1991	Desmond Howard, WR
1996	Jarrett Irons, LB
1997	Charles Woodson, DB
2000	Steve Hutchinson, OL
2003	Chris Perry, RB
2004	Braylon Edwards, WR
2004	David Baas, OL
2004	Marlin Jackson, DB
2004	Ernest Shazor, DB
2006	Leon Hall, DB
2006	Jake Long, OL
2006	Lamarr Woodley, DE

Derricotte returning punts. Crisler wore teams down with depth by using a two-platoon system he had introduced two years earlier against Army. All-America halfback Bob Chappuis, who appeared on the cover of *Time* magazine during the season, was the Heisman runner-up after leading the league in total offense for the second consecutive year. Chalmers "Bump" Elliott, a two-way player who later coached the Wolverines from 1959 to 1968, earned Big Ten MVP honors. Crisler forbade his players from saying "Rose Bowl" during the regular season, but that's where Michigan ended up on New Year's Day 1948. The Wolverines had something to prove in Pasadena because Notre Dame had been voted No. 1 after the regular season. Michigan, 15-point favorites, smashed USC 49-0. It was the Trojans' worst defeat in 60 years of football and remained so until 1966. Michigan set nine Rose Bowl records, including 491 total yards. Despite an injured hamstring, Chappuis set Rose Bowl marks for total offense (188 yards passing and 91 rushing) and pass completions (14). Wolverines fullback Jack Weisenburger scored 3 TDs. Michigan was so impressive, the Associated Press conducted a special poll after the game. The Wolverines were crowned national champs, receiving 226 votes to 119 for Notre Dame, which had beaten USC 38-7 earlier that season.

BEST BACKFIELD One newspaper account described them as a "backfield full of pervasive shadows that flit about like wraiths." Those 1947 Wolverines were powered by All-America halfbacks Bob Chappuis and Bump Elliott, more widely known as the "Dream Backfield." Crisler, called Gimlet Eye for his ability to stare through his players, devised an intricate single-wing offense that confounded defenses with passes, buck laterals, full spinners, and reverses. On some plays, seven players would touch the ball. QB Howard Yerges and fullback Jack Weisenburger started the spinner series. Chappuis, a triple threat at tailback, finished as runner-up to Notre Dame's Johnny Lujack for the Heisman that year. Chappuis was MVP of the Rose Bowl. Elliott was an All-

America, led the Big Ten in scoring with 54 points, and was named conference MVP.

BEST DEFENSE

Michigan's 1985 defense embodied the passion and toughness of its coach, Bo Schembechler. The Wolverines led the nation in scoring defense (6.8) that season while going 9–1–1 in the regular season. The Wolverines gave up just 75 points in those 11 games and never more than the 17 Ohio State scored in the regular-season finale. Michigan shut out Maryland, Michigan State, and Purdue, held South Carolina and Illinois to three points apiece, and yielded just six points to Wisconsin and only seven to Minnesota. Opponents totaled nine points in one four-game stretch. Tenacious defensive linemen Mike Hammerstein and Mark Messner anchored the unit. Hammerstein had nine sacks among his 23 tackles for losses of 120 yards. He ended the regular season as a finalist for the Lombardi Award and was named All-America and the Big Ten's Lineman of the Year. Messner had a team-high 11 sacks, and his tackles for losses totaled 120 yards. He was later voted to Michigan's All-Century Team by fans. Two of Michigan's three 1985 captains were defensive back Brad Cochran, an All-America selection, and inside linebacker Mike Mallory, a finalist for the Butkus Award. Mallory, Cochran, Hammerstein, and Messner were named All-Big Ten. Ivan Hicks led the Wolverines with six interceptions. Michigan capped its season with a 27-23 victory over Nebraska in the Fiesta Bowl. The Wolverines forced six fumbles and recovered three. Michigan finished No. 2 in the final polls. Only a 12-10 loss at then-No. 1 Iowa and a 3-3 tie at Illinois kept the Wolverines from being undefeated national champions.

BIGGEST GAME

The 1997 Wolverines rejuvenated a slumping program that was coming off four consecutive seasons of four defeats—something that hadn't happened at Michigan since 1934 through 1937. During their four-season tailspin in the 1990s, the Wolverines lost to seven different Big Ten opponents. Revenge came in abundance during 1997, much to the glee of surprised Michigan fans. The Wolverines—led by triple threat Charles Woodson, the first Heisman winner to primarily play defense—rolled to a perfect 11–0 regular season. They arrived in Pasadena for the Rose Bowl ranked No. 1 and one victory shy of their first national championship in half a century. Pac-10 champion Washington State and star QB Ryan Leaf showed quickly that they wouldn't be easy prey. Leaf threw a 15-yard TD pass to Kevin McKenzie, and the Cougars led 7-0 after one quarter. Michigan quarterback Brian Griese, son of former NFL QB and college football TV analyst Bob Griese, answered with a 53-yard TD pass to receiver Tai Streets in the second quarter, and the game was tied 7-7 at halftime. Washington State drove 99 yards in the third

quarter, ending the march with receiver Michael Tims scoring a TD on a 14-yard reverse. James Hall, however, blocked the point-after kick to keep Michigan's deficit at 13-7. Griese then earned his Rose Bowl MVP honors by throwing two more TD passes—58 yards to Streets and then 23 yards to All-America tight end Jerame Tuman—to put the Wolverines ahead 21-13. A field goal drew Washington State within five points, but Michigan's offense took seven minutes off the clock, leaving the Cougars without enough time to finish their comeback. Michigan held on for a 21-16 victory and its first national championship since the Mad Magicians' in 1947.

BIGGEST UPSET

Though it was Schembechler's first year as Michigan coach, he wasn't intimidated by his former boss, Ohio State coach Woody Hayes, when "the old man" brought his most powerful OSU team to Michigan Stadium on Nov. 22, 1969. The defending national champion Buckeyes were ranked No. 1 and were riding a 22-game winning streak. The Buckeyes had won a conference-record 17 consecutive Big Ten games, had outscored eight opponents 371-69, and had won each game that season by at least 27 points. Ohio State hadn't trailed in a game and was averaging 46 points and 512 yards of offense. The Buckeyes had walloped Michigan 50-14 the previous year, providing a rallying cry for Schembechler. He made every member of Michigan's scout team wear No. 50 during practices for the 1969 rematch. Before the game, Hayes had his Buckeyes warmup on Michigan's end of the field. Schembechler refused to back down, walked up to his former mentor, and ordered Ohio State to the stadium's other end. A national TV audience and a record crowd of 103,588 then saw the 17-point underdog Wolverines stun the Buckeyes. Michigan's defense recovered a fumble and intercepted six passes—three by Barry Pierson. The Wolverines outrushed Ohio State 266-22. Michigan won 24-12, with all scoring coming in the first half. Crisler watched the game on TV and wrote the new Michigan coach a letter telling him how he had shed tears of pride and joy over "the greatest upset I have ever witnessed." The "10-Year War" between Schembechler and Hayes was on.

HEARTBREAKER

A two-day period in 2006 will forever pain Michigan fans. On Nov. 17, the eve of the biggest game in Michigan's storied rivalry against Ohio State, Glenn "Bo" Schembechler died at age 77 of heart failure. He had more victories than any other coach in Michigan history while going 194–48–5 and winning 13 Big Ten titles in 21 seasons from 1969 to 1989. Although 17 years removed from last coaching the Wolverines, Schembechler had remained a dominant presence at the school and still had a campus office. The night before his death, he addressed the Michigan team at practice and

spoke about teamwork and pride. Schembechler had played a vital role in fueling the Ohio State rivalry, and a day after his death, the two teams met in the most hyped matchup in the 103-game series. For the first time, both teams were ranked in the Top 2—Ohio State No. 1 and Michigan No. 2—when they met. Only two other times since 1935 had both teams entered the game undefeated and untied. At stake was an outright Big Ten championship and a trip to the BCS national championship game. Both teams were 11–0 overall (7–0 in conference play) and standing atop the BCS ratings. An Ohio Stadium record crowd of 105,708 went respectfully silent during a pregame video tribute to Schembechler. Born a Buckeye in Barberton, Ohio, Schembechler received his master's degree from Ohio State in 1952 while serving as a graduate assistant coach for Woody Hayes, his future nemesis. The inspired Wolverines jumped quickly to a 7-0 lead, but twice they fell behind by 14 points in a wild scoring affair that looked nothing like the conservative games played in the Schembechler and Hayes era. Michigan pulled within three points with 2:16 remaining in the game, but Ohio State ran out the clock, extending its winning streak to 19 games with a 42-39 win, the second-highest scoring game in series history. The Buckeyes overcame three turnovers by churning out 503 yards against the nation's No. 3-ranked defense. Michigan had 397 yards of total offense and zero turnovers. Troy Smith, the eventual Heisman winner, became the first Ohio State player to throw 4 TD passes against Michigan. "I told our team we weren't going to use Bo and his passing away as a motivational deal," a choked-up Michigan coach Lloyd Carr said after the game. "That deal would have been to dishonor him. I simply told them that the way we could honor him is to coach and play in a way that would have made him proud."

WILDEST FINISH

The words "Rocket Left" still cut Michigan fans like a stiletto. That was the name of Colorado's final play in Michigan's 27-26 home loss on Sept. 24, 1994. The Wolverines led by five points with six seconds left and had the Buffaloes 64 yards from the end

COLLEGE FOOTBALL HALL OF FAME INDUCTEES

NAME	YEARS	INDUCTED
Benny Friedman, QB	1924-26	1951
Fielding Yost, COACH	1901-23, 1925-26	1951
Germany Schulz, C	1904-05, 1907-08	1951
Bennie Oosterbaan, E	1925-27	1954
Tom Harmon, HB	1938-40	1954
Willie Heston, HB	1901-04	1954
Fritz Crisler, COACH	1938-47	1954
George Little, COACH	1924	1955
Tad Wieman, FB	1927-28	1956
Harry Kipke, HB	1921-23	1958
Neil Snow, E/FB	1898-1901	1960
Francis Wistert, T	1931-33	1967
Albert Wistert, T	1940-42	1968
Albert Benbrook, G	1908-10	1971
Johnny Maulbetsch, FB	1914-16	1973
Elroy Hirsch, HB	1943	1974
Harry Newman, QB	1930-32	1975
Ron Kramer, E	1954-56	1978
Alvin Wistert, T	1947-49	1981
Merv Pregulman, T/C	1941-43	1982
Ernie Vick, C	1918-21	1983
Bob Westfall, FB	1939-41	1987
Bob Chappius, HB	1942, 1946-47	1988
Bump Elliott, HB	1946-47	1989
Ron Johnson, HB	1966-68	1992
Bo Schembechler, COACH	1969-89	1993
Pete Elliott, QB	1945-48	1994
Dan Dierdorf, T	1968-70	2000
Anthony Carter, WR	1979-82	2001
Reggie McKenzie, G	1969-71	2002
Jim Mandich, TE	1967-69	2004
Tom Curtis, S	1967-69	2005
Dave Brown, DB	1972-74	2007

zone. Colorado coach Bill McCartney, a former Michigan assistant, called for three Buffaloes receivers—Michael Westbrook, Blake Anderson, and Rae Carruth—to split wide left. James Kidd lined up wide right. They had tried the play at the end of the first half, and the pass had been intercepted by safety Chuck Winters. This time, quarterback Kordell Stewart threw the ball 73 yards into the wind. It came down at the goal line, where Anderson tipped it straight up over the Wolverines. Westbrook caught the ball in the end zone. More than 100,000 fans in Michigan Stadium fell silent as Colorado players jumped on each other in joy. The next day, the *Detroit News* had its Michigan beat reporter telephone Wolverines coach Gary Moeller to make certain he hadn't committed suicide. Asked about the game two years later, Moeller said: "Like the dark, it never goes away." A more satisfying wild finish for Michigan fans occurred in the 1995 Pigskin Classic. With Michigan trailing Virginia 17-0 entering the fourth quarter, freshman QB Scott Dreisbach produced 18 unanswered points for the Wolverines by passing for 236 yards. Michigan drove 80 yards in the final 2:35 and won Lloyd Carr's first game as coach when the redshirt freshman quarterback completed a 15-yard TD pass to Mercury Hayes in the right corner of the end zone.

BEST GOAL-LINE STAND

"Welcome to the Big Ten" was the message Michigan's defense sent to Penn State in the Nittany Lions' first season in the league. Penn State, ranked No. 7, was 5–0 and had won its first two conference games before meeting the Wolverines in 1993 at State College, Pa. Michigan, just 3–2 overall and 1–1 in the league, led 14-10 when it dished out a decisive heaping of physical Big Ten ball in the third quarter. Penn State had driven 79 yards for a first down inside the Wolverines' 1. Noseguard Tony Henderson stopped consecutive Kerry Collins QB sneaks for no gain. Nittany Lions tailback Ki-Jana Carter tried to leap the pile on third down but was stopped. Michigan linebacker Jarrett Irons then fought off a block by fullback Brian O'Neal and tackled Carter on a dive short of the end zone. Penn State drove to Michigan's 8-yard line on its next

possession but settled for a 25-yard field goal. The Wolverines won 21-13.

BEST COMEBACK What occurred in the final quarter at Minnesota on Oct. 10, 2003, confused even the No. 20 Wolverines. "We still don't know what happened," Michigan defensive end Larry Stevens said after the game. "How many points did we score in the fourth quarter? I don't even know." Michigan scored 31 fourth-quarter points to defeat the Gophers 38-35. The surprising Gophers, 6–0 and ranked No. 17, led 28-7 at the start of the fourth quarter. The Wolverines made it 28-14 when QB John Navarre hit Chris Perry with a 10-yard TD pass, and they sliced off another seven points from the deficit when safety Jacob Stewart intercepted Minnesota QB Asad Abdul-Khaliq and returned it 34 yards for a TD. Abdul-Khaliq answered with a 52-yard scoring run to push Minnesota's lead to 35-21. Navarre tossed a 52-yard TD to Braylon Edwards, and Perry added a 10-yard TD run to tie the game. Freshman Garrett Rivas completed the comeback by kicking a 33-yard field goal with 47 seconds left to give the Wolverines their first lead of the game.

STADIUM ABC-TV announcer Keith Jackson dubbed it the "Big House," but the nation's largest football facility is actually a deep crater. Nearly three-fourths of Michigan Stadium sits below ground, where a strawberry patch and a barn once sat above an underground spring. Fielding Yost fashioned the stadium after the Yale Bowl, and it opened in 1927 at a cost of $950,000. More than 40 million people have filed through the iron gates of the brick stadium to cheer from the wooden bleachers. All 200 home games since Oct. 25, 1975 (a 55-7 homecoming rout of Indiana), have drawn in excess of 100,000—the nation's longest such streak. An NCAA-record crowd of 112,118 jammed into the Big House for the 2003 Ohio State game. Originally designed for 84,401, the stadium at the corner of Main Street and Stadium Boulevard now holds 107,501. The capacity is always listed with a final digit of one, signifying an extra seat for Crisler. The location of that seat remains a secret. Michigan Stadium is undergoing a $226 million renovation that will add approximately 83 suites and 3,200 club seats. Work is due to be completed prior to the 2010 season and will push capacity to over 108,000.

HALLOWED GROUND A dark, concrete tunnel located at the 50-yard line on the east side of Michigan Stadium is the only way both teams can take the field.

PRO FOOTBALL HALL OF FAME INDUCTEES		
NAME	YEARS	INDUCTED
Elroy Hirsch, HB/E	1946-57	1968
Bill Hewitt, E	1932-39, 1943	1971
Len Ford, DE	1948-57	1976
Dan Dierdorf, T	1971-83	1996
Tom Mack, G	1966-78	1999
George Allen, COACH	1966-77	2002
Benny Friedman, QB	1927-34	2005

That field is where Oosterbaan, the first of only two Michigan players to win All-America honors three times (1925 to 1927), had his wish fulfilled. After he died, Michigan All-America Ron Kramer spread some of Oosterbaan's ashes near the stadium tunnel and all over the field.

RIVAL Gary Moeller, a former Ohio State player, caused a stir in the early 1990s when he suggested that the Michigan State Spartans—not the Buckeyes—were the Wolverines' biggest game because it was against an in-state opponent. But the Wolverines and Buckeyes have shared hatred since their first meeting, in 1897. ESPN named Michigan-Ohio State No. 1 in its list of 10 Greatest Sports Rivalries. Ohio State needed 16 games played over 22 years before it tasted victory in the series. The Wolverines outscored OSU 369-21 while going 14–0–1 through 1918. In 1902, Michigan led 45-0 at halftime and poured on 41 more unanswered points in the second half. A newspaper report of that 86-0 debacle said: "Lincoln, Ohio's big left guard, was ruled out for smearing his fist over Carter's nose." Hatred reached new heights as the series tightened over the decades. From 1928 through 1990, the annual grudge match was tied 30–30–3, with OSU scoring 909 points and Michigan 903. Then there were the exceedingly high stakes: the game's winner determined the Rose Bowl participant every year from 1972 to 1981. During that span, Michigan fans had rolls of toilet paper with Hayes' picture on them and a caption that read, "Put Woody where he belongs." In 1986, Wolverine QB Jim Harbaugh became a maize-and-blue hero when he predicted a win over Ohio State and then delivered a 26-24 victory by passing for 261 yards. Michigan dominated the 1990s, costing the Buckeyes possible national championships three times between 1993 and 1996. Tshimanga Biakabutuka burned Ohio State for 313 rushing yards—the second-highest single-game total in Michigan history—in a 31-23 upset of the Buckeyes in 1995. The Wolverines' 10–2–1 record against John Cooper got the OSU coach fired in 2000. Michigan, though, has had less luck against Buckeye coach Jim Tressel, losing five of six to Cooper's successor. Michigan leads the series 57–40–6 entering 2007. Since 1949, there have been three ties, 28 wins for Ohio State, and 27 for Michigan.

CONTROVERSY Michigan went 30–2–1 from 1972 to 1974 and didn't play in a bowl game. The tie was a 10-10 home game against Ohio State in the 1973 regular-season finale. The Wolverines entered the game 10–0 and

ranked No. 4; the Buckeyes were 9–0 and No. 1. Michigan's Mike Lantry, a veteran of the Vietnam War, missed field goal attempts of 58 and 48 yards in the final 1:06. The next day, Big Ten commissioner Wayne Duke took a poll of the league's athletic directors to decide whether the Wolverines or the Buckeyes should go to the Rose Bowl. The ADs chose Ohio State, 6-4. Michigan State's first-year AD, Burt Smith, voted against his in-state rival. Michigan QB Dennis Franklin had broken his collarbone in the Ohio State game, so some voted for the Buckeyes, reasoning they had a better chance to win the Rose Bowl. "This is the lowest day of my career as a player and a coach," Schembechler said. "I'm very resentful at the way this was handled. There were petty jealousies involved, and they used the injury to Dennis Franklin as a scapegoat." His complaints helped change the Big Ten's Rose Bowl selection rules before the next season, and beginning with the 1975 season, teams that hadn't won the conference title were allowed to accept bids to bowl games besides the Rose.

DUBIOUS DISTINCTION

Schembechler, for all his fire and accomplishments, never won a national championship, even during the 1970s when his 96–10–3 regular-season record was the nation's best. Michigan's best final ranking under Bo was No. 2, behind Oklahoma in 1985. Seven times, Schembechler's teams were one win or a tie from perfection. In 1976, his Wolverines were No. 1 but lost a November game to Purdue. A year later, No. 1 Michigan was shut out at Minnesota. "It's not a hole in my career as far as I'm concerned," Schembechler said about not winning a national title on the eve of his final game. Bo knew woes in postseason games, losing his first seven bowls and ending with a 5–12 bowl record, including 2–8 in the Rose Bowl. He had a heart attack at age 40 on the morning of his first Rose Bowl, at the end of the 1970 season, and was hospitalized during the 10-3 loss to USC. Schembechler lost his first five Rose Bowls before beating Washington in the 1981 game. That was the first time one of his Michigan teams finished a season with a victory. During Bo's 21 seasons, his Wolverines went 5–15–1 in their season finales, including nonbowl years.

ALL-CENTENNIAL TEAM	
Fans cast votes on the school's athletic website to determine Michigan's all-20th-century team.	
1969-89	Bo Schembechler, COACH
OFFENSE	
1968-70	Dan Dierdorf, OL
1969-71	Reggie McKenzie, OL
1984-87	John "Jumbo" Elliott, OL
1988-91	Greg Skrepenak, OL
1995-98	Jon Jansen, OL
1925-27	Bennie Oosterbaan, WR
1979-82	Anthony Carter, WR
1989-91	Desmond Howard, WR
1975-78	Rick Leach, QB
1938-40	Tom Harmon, RB
1991-94	Tyrone Wheatley, RB
1994-96	Remy Hamilton, PK
DEFENSE	
1985-88	Mark Messner, DL
1994-97	Glen Steele, DL
1989-92	Chris Hutchinson, DL
1988-91	Erick Anderson, LB
1993-96	Jarrett Irons, LB
1976-79	Ron Simpkins, LB
1995-98	Sam Sword, LB
1995-97	Charles Woodson, DB
1992-94	Ty Law, DB
1987-90	Tripp Welborne, DB
1967-69	Tom Curtis, DB
1984-87	Monte Robbins, P

Schembechler's final game as Michigan coach was the 1990 Rose Bowl. The Wolverines entered 10–1 and ranked No. 3 but lost 17-10 to No. 12 USC.

NICKNAME Michigan students and alumni have referred to themselves as Wolverines since the school's earliest history. Yost credited use of the name to the fur trading that took place at Sault St. Marie. The *Michigan Quarterly Review* said in 1952 that the moniker stemmed from the eating habits of the French who settled Michigan in the late 1700s. A third theory dates to the state's border dispute with Ohio in 1803.

MASCOT Wolverines don't live in Michigan, and the school doesn't use a furry mascot. In 1927, however, Alaska donated three wolverines to the Detroit Zoo. Two were taken to a game that year at Michigan Stadium, but they were so ferocious that the school decided not to bring them back.

UNIFORMS A committee of students from the school's literary department selected maize and blue as Michigan's colors in 1867. The school's athletic department decided on deep blue and bright yellow around the turn of the 20th century. The Wolverines wore plain black helmets until Fritz Crisler decided in 1938 that a new look would help end a streak of four consecutive losing seasons. He painted them blue and put gold on the wings and stripes on the Spalding FH5 leather helmets, which were the only helmets being used that had three straps running from front to back. Besides wanting to "dress it up a little," Crisler thought the helmet's new colored wings and stripes would help quarterbacks find receivers in pass patterns. The Michigan football uniform was voted the best in all sports in an ESPN.com poll in 2003, and its helmet was ranked the best in football, according to ESPN's "End of Century" special.

QUIRK Michigan tried to generate more revenue by scheduling a doubleheader to open the 1929 season. The Wolverines beat Albion 39-0 in the first game and Mount Union 16-6 in the second. However, only 16,412 fans attended. Undeterred, Michigan opened its next two

seasons with doubleheaders: Denison (33-0) and Eastern Michigan (7-0) were defeated on the same day in 1930, and Central Michigan (27-0) and Eastern Michigan (34-0) lost to the Wolverines in 1931.

LORE Michigan radio announcer Bob Ufer's screaming call of the final play of the 1979 homecoming game—"Oh, my god! Carter scored!"—still reverberates. Anthony Carter went on to become a three-time All-America, but he was just a 5'11", 160-pound freshman the day he sent Ufer and Michigan Stadium into a frenzy. The Wolverines were at the Indiana 45-yard line with six seconds remaining in a 21-21 game. Carter ran a post pattern through IU's wide-split defense, and QB John Wangler hit him with a pass at the 20. The skinny-legged flanker bounced off two defenders and then squirted free of Hoosier safety Tim Wilbur to dance into the end zone for a game-winning TD as the clock showed zeroes.

NUMBERS QB Rick Leach made 48 consecutive starts from 1975 to 1978 while being named All-Big Ten three times and earning All-America and Big Ten MVP honors as a senior … Gerald Ford, the 38th president of the United States, wore No. 48 while playing center on the Wolverines' national championship teams in 1932 and 1933. He was the team's MVP as a senior and graduated from Michigan in 1935 … The Wolverines have played in 19 Rose Bowls, more than any other Big Ten school … Desmond Howard carried only 176 pounds on a 5'9" frame, but he became the first receiver in Big Ten history to lead the league in scoring (90 points) and set a conference record with 19 TD receptions as he won the 1991 Heisman. His 640 first-place votes (85%) were the most ever for a Heisman winner … Ron Johnson set school records for rushing yards (347) and rushing TDs (five) in one game in 1968 against Wisconsin … Tom Brady, later a sixth-round NFL draft pick, threw for 369 yards and 4 TDs in a 35-34 overtime win over Alabama in the 2000 Orange Bowl … Brady set a school record with 56 pass attempts against Ohio State in 1998 … Bob Ufer called 363 consecutive games as Michigan's radio announcer from 1945 to 1981 … Michigan and Northwestern combined for 1,189 yards of offense on 171 plays when the Wolverines lost 54-51 on Nov. 4, 2000, at Evanston, Ill. QB Drew Henson threw for 312 yards and 4 TDs, with three of Michigan's scoring passes going to receiver David Terrell. He and teammate Marquis Walker each caught nine passes. Michigan tailback Anthony Thompson rushed for 199 yards and three scores … Walker caught a school-record 15 passes against Washington in 2001 and equaled that mark later the same season against Ohio State … Michigan's Steve Breaston set a Rose Bowl record with 316 all-purpose yards, and QB Chad Henne tied a record with 4 TD passes, but Texas beat the Wolverines 38-37 on a last-second field goal in the 2005 Rose Bowl … Willie Heston, a tailback on the famed "Point a Minute" teams at the beginning of the 20th century, scored 72 touchdowns in 36 games and averaged eight yards per carry while totaling over 5,000 rushing yards for the Wolverines … Michigan beat Stanford 49-0 on New Year's Day 1902 in what later became known as the first Rose Bowl, capping a 12–0 season in which the Wolverines outscored opponents 550-0 … Braylon Edwards' 39 career TD receptions are a Big Ten record … Michigan's 56-game undefeated streak came to an end on Thanksgiving Day 1905, when Amos Alonzo Stagg's Chicago team pulled a 2-0 upset in the first Game of the Century … From 1883 to 1901, Michigan played some games at the Detroit Athletic Club field in order to accommodate more fans … Entering the 2007 season, Michigan has lost four consecutive bowl games and five of its past six, dropping its all time bowl record to 18–20 … Tyrone Wheatley rushed for 235 yards, including a Rose Bowl-record 88-yard run, as the Wolverines beat Washington 38-31 on New Year's Day 1993 … In 2004, Michigan defeated Michigan State 45-37 in triple overtime after the Wolverines erased a 17-point deficit in the final 8:43 of the fourth quarter … Chris Perry had a school-record 51 rushing attempts against Michigan State in 2003 … *Michigan Replay*, entering its 33rd season, is the nation's longest-running coach's television show … Notre Dame's first three games of football were losses to Michigan, in 1887 and 1888 … Albert, Alvin, and Francis Wistert all were tackles who wore No. 11 and are the only threesome of brothers to be named first-team All-America … Michigan's 7–5 record in 2005 was its worst in 21 years, and for the first time in 22 years, the Wolverines finished a season out of the Top 25.

QUOTE "Who are they that they should beat a Michigan team?" —Fielding H. Yost

MICHIGAN ALL-TIME SCORES

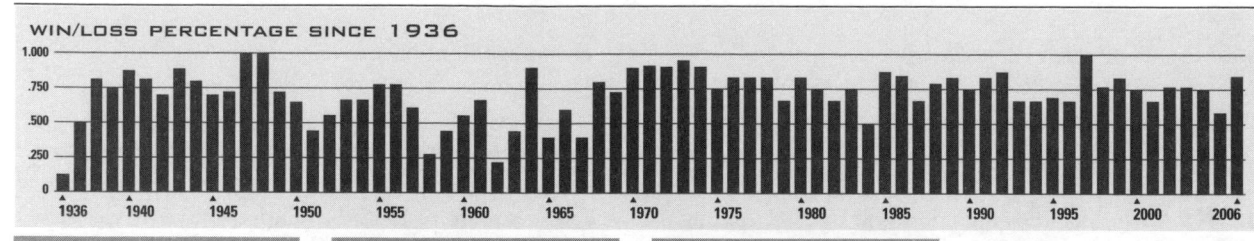

WIN/LOSS PERCENTAGE SINCE 1936

BIG TEN TEAMS

NO HEAD COACH

1879 1-0-1
M30	•	Racine CHI	1	0
N1	=	Toronto DET	0	0

1880 1-0-0
N5	•	at Toronto	13	6

1881 0-3-0
O31		Harvard Bos	0	1
N2		at Yale	0	2
N4		at Princeton	0	1

1882
NO TEAM

1883 1-4-0
M12	•	Detroit AC	40	5
N19		at Wesleyan	6	14
N21		at Yale	0	46
N22		at Harvard	0	3
N27		at Stevens	1	5

1884 2-0-0
N15	•	Albion	18	0
N22	•	U. Club Chicago	18	10

1885 3-0-0
N7	•	at Windsor Club	10	0
N14	•	Windsor Club	30	0
N26	•	at Peninsular Club DET	42	0

1886 2-0-0
O16	•	at Albion	50	0
O30	•	Albion	24	0

1887 3-0-0
N12	•	Albion	32	0
N23	•	at Notre Dame	8	0
N24	•	at Harvard Club	26	0

1888 4-1-0
P20	•	at Notre Dame	26	6
P21	•	at Notre Dame	10	4
N17	•	at Detroit AC	14	6
N24	•	Albion	76	4
N29	•	at U. Club Chicago	4	26

1889 1-2-0
N9	•	Albion	33	4
N23		Cornell Buf	0	56
N28		Chicago AA	0	20

1890 4-1-0
O11	•	Albion	56	10
O18	•	at Detroit A. C.	18	0
O25	•	Albion	16	0
N1	•	Purdue	34	6
N15	•	Cornell DET	5	20

M. MURPHY & F. CRAWFORD
1891 (.444) 4-5

1891 4-5-0
O10	•	Ann Arbor HS	62	0
O17	•	Albion	4	10
O19	•	at Olivet	18	6
O24	•	Oberlin	26	6
O31	•	Butler	42	6
N14		at Chicago AC	0	10
N21		Cornell CHI	12	58
N26		at Cleveland AA	4	8
N28		Cornell DET	0	10

FRANK E. BARBOUR
1892-93 (.636) 14-8

1892 7-5-0
O8	•	Michigan AA	74	0
O12	•	Michigan AA DET	68	0
O15	•	at Wisconsin	10	6
O17	•	at Minnesota	6	14
O22	•	DePauw IND	18	0
O24	•	at Purdue	0	24
O29	•	Northwestern CHI	8	10
N5	•	Albion	60	8
N8	•	at Cornell	0	44
N12	•	Chicago TOL	18	10
N19	•	Oberlin	26	24
N22	•	Cornell	10	30

1893 7-3-0
O7	•	Detroit AC	6	0
O14	•	at Detroit AC	26	0
O21	•	at Chicago	6	10
O28	•	Minnesota	20	34
N4	•	Wisconsin	18	34
N11	•	at Purdue	46	8
N13	•	at DePauw	34	0
N18	•	Northwestern	72	6
N25	•	Kansas KC	22	0
N30	•	at Chicago	28	0

WILLIAM L. MCCAULEY
1894-95 (.875) 17-2-1

1894 9-1-1
O6	=	Michigan M.A.	12	12
O13	•	Albion	26	10
O17	•	Olivet	48	0
O21	•	Michigan M.A.	40	6
O24	•	Adrian	46	0
O28	•	at Case	18	8
N3		at Cornell	0	22
N10	•	Kansas KC	22	12
N17	•	Oberlin	14	6
N24	•	Cornell	12	4
N29	•	at Chicago	6	4

1895 8-1-0
O5	•	Michigan M.A.	34	0
O12	•	Detroit AC	42	0
O19	•	Adelbert	64	0
O26	•	Rush Lake Forest	40	0
N2	•	Oberlin	42	0
N9		at Harvard	0	4
N16	•	Purdue	12	10
N23	•	Minnesota DET	20	0
N28	•	at Chicago	12	0

1896-1906
BIG TEN

WILLIAM D. WARD
1896 (.900) 9-1

1896 9-1-0 (2-1-0)
O3	•	Eastern Michigan	18	0
O10	•	Grand Rapids	44	0
O15	•	Phys & Surg.	28	0
O17	•	Lake Forest	66	0
O24	•		at Purdue	16	0
O31	•	Lehigh DET	40	0
N7	•		at Minnesota	6	4
N14	•	Oberlin	10	0
N21	•	Wittenberg	28	0
N26	•		Chicago CHI	6	7

GUSTAVE H. FERBERT
1897-99 (.875) 24-3-1

1897 6-1-1 (2-1-0)
O2	•	Eastern Michigan	24	0
O9	=	Ohio Wesleyan	0	0
O16	•	Ohio State	34	0 *
O23	•	Oberlin	16	6
N6	•		Purdue	34	4
N13	•	Minnesota DET	14	0
N20	•	Wittenberg	32	0
N25	•		Chicago CHI	12	21

1898 10-0-0 (3-0-0)
O1	•	Eastern Michigan	21	0 *
O8	•	Kenyon	29	0
O12	•	Michigan State	39	0
O17	•	Western Reserve	18	0
O19	•	Case	23	5
O23	•	Notre Dame	23	0
N5	•		Northwestern CHI	6	5
N12	•		Illinois DET	12	5
N19	•	Beloit	22	0
N24	•		at Chicago	12	11

1899 8-2-0 (1-1-0)
S30	•	Hillsdale	11	0
O7	•	Albion	26	0
O11	•	Western Reserve	17	0
O18	•	Notre Dame	12	0
O28	•		at Illinois	5	0
N4	•	Virginia DET	38	0
N11	•	at Pennsylvania	10	11
N18	•	Case	28	6
N25	•		Kalamazoo	24	9
N30	•		Wisconsin CHI	5	17

LANGDON "BIFF" LEA
1900 (.750) 7-2-1

1900 7-2-1 (3-2-0)
S29	•	Hillsdale	29	0
O6	•	Kalamazoo	11	0
O13	•	Case	24	6
O20	•	Purdue	11	6
O27	•		Illinois CHI	12	0
N3	•		Indiana	12	0
N10	•	Iowa DET	5	28
N17	•	Notre Dame	7	0
N24	=	Ohio State	0	0
N29	•		at Chicago	6	15

FIELDING H. YOST
1901-23, '25-26 (.833) 165-29-10

1901 11-0-0 (4-0-0)
S28	•	Albion	50	0
O5	•	Case	57	0
O12	•		Indiana	33	0
O19	•		Northwestern	29	0
O26	•	Buffalo	128	0
N2	•	Carlisle DET	22	0
N9	•	at Ohio State	21	0
N16	•		Chicago	22	0
N23	•	Beloit	89	0
N28	•		Iowa CHI	50	0

ROSE BOWL
J1	•	Stanford	49	0

1902 11-0-0 (5-0-0)
S27	•	Albion	88	0
O4	•	Case	48	6
O8	•	Michigan State	119	0
O11	•		Indiana	60	0
O18	•	Notre Dame TOL	23	0
O25	•	Ohio State	86	0
N1	•		Wisconsin CHI	6	0
N8	•		Iowa	107	0
N15	•		at Chicago	21	0
N22	•	Oberlin	63	0
N27	•		Minnesota	23	6

1903 11-0-1 (3-0-1)
O3	•	Case	31	0
O8	•	Albion	76	0
O10	•	Beloit	79	0
O14	•	Ohio Northern	65	0
O17	•		Indiana	51	0
O21	•	Ferris St.	88	0
O24	•	Drake	47	0
O31	=		at Minnesota	6	6
N7	•	Ohio State	36	0
N14	•		Wisconsin	16	0
N21	•	Oberlin	42	0
N26	•		at Chicago	28	0

1904 10-0-0 (2-0-0)
O1	•	Case	33	0
O5	•	Ohio Northern	48	0
O8	•	Kalamazoo	95	0
O12	•	P&S Chicago	72	0
O15	•	at Ohio State	31	6
O19	•	Am. Med. Chicago	72	0
O22	•	West Virginia	130	0
O29	•		at Wisconsin	28	0
N5	•	Drake	36	4
N12	•		Chicago	22	12

1905 12-1-0 (2-1-0)
S30	•	Ohio Wesleyan	65	0
O4	•	Kalamazoo	44	0
O7	•	Case	36	0
O11	•	Ohio Northern	23	0
O14	•	Vanderbilt	18	0
O21	•	Nebraska	31	0
O25	•	Albion	70	0
O28	•	Drake	48	0
N4	•		at Illinois	33	0
N11	•	Ohio State	40	0
N18	•		Wisconsin	12	0
N25	•	Oberlin	75	0
N30	•		at Chicago	0	2

1906 4-1-0 (1-0-0)
O6	•	Case	28	0
O20	•	at Ohio State	6	0
O27	•		Illinois	28	9
N3	•	Vanderbilt	10	4
N17	•	at Pennsylvania	0	17

1907-1916
INDEPENDENT

1907 5-1-0
O5	•	Case	9	0
O12	•	Michigan State	46	0
O19	•	Wabash IND	22	0
O26	•	Ohio State	22	0
N2	•	at Vanderbilt	8	0
N16	•	Pennsylvania	0	6

1908 5-2-1
O3	•	Case	16	6
O10	=	at Michigan State	0	0
O17	•	Notre Dame	12	6
O24	•	at Ohio State	10	6
O31	•	Vanderbilt	24	6
N7	•	Kentucky	62	0
N14	•	Pennsylvania	0	29
N21	•	at Syracuse	4	28

1909 6-1-0
O9	•	Case	3	0
O16	•	Ohio State	33	6
O23	•	at Marquette	6	5
O30	•	Syracuse	43	0
N6	•	Notre Dame	3	11
N13	•	at Pennsylvania	12	6
N20	•	at Minnesota	15	6

1910 3-0-3
O8	•	Case	3	3
O15	•	Michigan State	6	3
O22	=	at Ohio State	3	3
O29	•	at Syracuse	11	0
N12	=	at Pennsylvania	0	0
N19	•	Minnesota	6	0

1911 — 5-1-2

O7	●	Case	24	0
O14	●	at Michigan State	15	3
O21	●	Ohio State	19	0
O28	●	Vanderbilt	9	8
N4	=	Syracuse	6	6
N11		at Cornell	0	6
N18	●	Pennsylvania	11	9
N25	=	at Nebraska	6	6

1912 — 5-2-0

O5	●	Case	34	0
O12	●	Michigan State	55	7
O19	●	at Ohio State	14	0
O26		at Syracuse	7	18
N2	●	South Dakota	7	6
N9		at Pennsylvania	21	27
N16	●	Cornell	20	7

1913 — 6-1-0

O4	●	Case	48	0
O11	●	Mt. Union	14	0
O18		Michigan State	7	12
O25	●	at Vanderbilt	33	2
N1	●	Syracuse	43	7
N8	●	at Cornell	17	0
N15	●	Pennsylvania	13	0

1914 — 6-3-0

S30	●	DePauw	58	0
O3	●	Case	69	0
O7	●	Mt. Union	27	7
O10	●	Vanderbilt	23	3
O17	●	at Michigan State	3	0
O24		at Syracuse	6	20
O31		at Harvard	0	7
N7	●	Pennsylvania	34	3
N14		Cornell	13	28

1915 — 4-3-1

O6	●	Lawrence	39	0
O9	●	Mt. Union	35	0
O13	●	Marietta	28	6
O16	●	Case	14	3
O23		Michigan State	0	24
O30		Syracuse	7	14
N6		Cornell	7	34
N13	=	at Pennsylvania	0	0

1916 — 7-2-0

O4	●	Marietta	30	0
O7	●	Case	19	3
O11	●	Carroll	54	0
O14	●	Mt. Union	26	0
O21	●	Michigan State	9	0
O28	●	Syracuse	14	13
N4	●	Washington, Mo.	66	7
N11		at Cornell	20	23
N18		Pennsylvania	7	10

1917-Present
Big Ten

1917 — 8-2-0 (0-1-0)

O6	●	Case	41	0
O10	●	Western Michigan	17	13
O13	●	Mt. Union	69	0
O17	●	Detroit	14	3
O20	●	at Michigan State	27	0
O27	●	Nebraska	20	0
N3	●	Kalamazoo	62	0
N10	●	Cornell	42	0
N17		at Pennsylvania	0	16
N24	|	at Northwestern	12	21

1918 — 5-0-0 (2-0-0)

O5	●	Case	33	0
N9	● |	at Chicago	13	0
N16	●	Syracuse	15	0
N23	●	Michigan State	21	6
N30	● |	Ohio State	14	0

1919 — 3-4-0 (1-4-0)

O4	●	Case	34	0
O18	●	Michigan State	26	0
O25	|	Ohio State	3	13
N1	● |	Northwestern	16	13
N8	|	at Chicago	0	13
N15	|	at Illinois	7	29
N22	|	Minnesota	7	34

1920 — 5-2-0 (2-2-0)

O9	●	Case	35	0
O16	●	Michigan State	35	0
O23	|	Illinois	6	7
O30	●	Tulane	21	0
N6	|	at Ohio State	7	14
N13	● |	Chicago	14	0
N20	● |	at Minnesota	3	0

1921 — 5-1-1 (2-1-1)

O1	●	Mt. Union	44	0
O8	●	Case	65	0
O15	●	Michigan State	30	0
O22	|	Ohio State	0	14
O29	● |	at Illinois	3	0
N12	= |	at Wisconsin	7	7
N19	● |	Minnesota	38	0

1922 — 6-0-1 (4-0-0)

O7	●	Case	48	0
O14	=	at Vanderbilt	0	0
O21	● |	at Ohio State	19	0
O28	● |	Illinois	24	0
N4	●	Michigan State	63	0
N18	● |	Wisconsin	13	6
N25	● |	at Minnesota	16	7

1923 — 8-0-0 (4-0-0)

O6	●	Case	36	0
O13	●	Vanderbilt	3	0
O20	● |	Ohio State	23	0
O27	●	Michigan State	37	0
N3	● |	at Iowa	9	3
N10	●	Quantico Marines	26	6
N17	● |	at Wisconsin	6	3
N24	● |	Minnesota	10	0

GEORGE LITTLE
1924 (.750) 6-2

1924 — 6-2-0 (4-2-0)

O4	●	Miami (Ohio)	55	0
O11	●	at Michigan State	7	0
O18	|	at Illinois	14	39
O25	● |	Wisconsin	21	0
N1	● |	at Minnesota	13	0
N8	● |	Northwestern	27	0
N15	● |	at Ohio State	16	6
N22	|	Iowa	2	9

FIELDING H. YOST

1925 — 7-1-0 (5-1-0)

O3	●	Michigan State	39	0
O10	● |	Indiana	63	0
O17	● |	at Wisconsin	21	0
O24	● |	at Illinois	3	0
O31	●	Navy	54	0
N7	|	Northwestern CHI	2	3
N14	● |	Ohio State	10	0
N21	● |	Minnesota	35	0

1926 — 7-1-0 (5-0-0)

O2	●	Oklahoma State	42	3
O9	●	Michigan State	55	3
O16	● |	Minnesota	20	0
O23	● |	Illinois	13	0
O30		Navy BALT	0	10
N6	● |	Wisconsin	37	0
N13	● |	at Ohio State	17	16
N20	● |	at Minnesota	7	6

ELTON E. "TAD" WIEMAN
1927-28 (.594) 9-6-1

1927 — 6-2-0 (3-2-0)

O1	●	Ohio Wesleyan	33	0
O8	●	Michigan State	21	0
O15	● |	at Wisconsin	14	0
O22	● |	Ohio State	21	0
O29	|	at Illinois	0	14
N5	● |	at Chicago	14	0
N12	●	Navy	27	12
N19	|	Minnesota	7	13

1928 — 3-4-1 (2-3-0)

O6		Ohio Wesleyan	7	17
O13	|	Indiana	0	6
O20	|	at Ohio State	7	19
O27	|	Wisconsin	0	7
N3	● |	Illinois	3	0
N10	=	Navy BALT	6	6
N17	●	Michigan State	3	0
N24	● |	Iowa	10	7

HARRY G. KIPKE
1929-37 (.632) 46-26-4

1929 — 5-3-1 (1-3-1)

S28	●	Albion	39	0
S28	●	Mt. Union	16	6
O5	●	Michigan State	17	0
O12	|	at Purdue	16	30
O19	|	Ohio State	0	7
O26	|	at Illinois	0	14
N9	●	Harvard	14	12
N16	● |	at Minnesota	7	6
N23	= |	Iowa	0	0

1930 — 8-0-1 (5-0-0)

S27	●	Denison	33	0
S27	●	Eastern Michigan	7	0
O4	=	Michigan State	0	0
O11	● |	Purdue	14	13
O18	● |	at Ohio State	13	0
O25	● |	Illinois	15	7
N8	●	at Harvard	6	3
N15	● |	Minnesota	7	0
N22	● |	Chicago	16	0

1931 — 8-1-1 (5-1-0)

O3	●	Central St. Teachers	27	0
O3	●	Eastern Michigan	34	0
O10	● |	Chicago	13	7
O17	|	Ohio State	7	20
O24	● |	at Illinois	35	0
O31	●	at Princeton	21	0
N7	● |	Indiana	22	0
N14	=	Michigan State	0	0
N21	● |	Minnesota	6	0
N28	● |	Wisconsin	16	0

1932 — 8-0-0 (6-0-0)

O1	●	Michigan State	26	0
O8	● |	Northwestern	15	6
O15	● |	at Ohio State	14	0
O22	● |	Illinois	32	0
O29	●	Princeton	14	7
N5	● |	at Indiana	7	0
N12	● |	Chicago	12	0
N19	● |	at Minnesota	3	0

1933 — 7-0-1 (5-0-1)

O7	●	Michigan State	20	6
O14	●	Cornell	40	0
O21	● |	Ohio State	13	0
O28	● |	at Chicago	28	0
N4	● |	at Illinois	7	6
N11	● |	Iowa	10	6
N18	= |	Minnesota	0	0
N25	● |	at Northwestern	13	0

1934 — 1-7-0 (0-6-0)

O6		Michigan State	0	16
O13	|	at Chicago	0	27
O20	●	Georgia Tech	9	2
O27	|	Illinois	6	7
N3	|	at Minnesota	0	34
N10	|	Wisconsin	0	10
N17	|	at Ohio State	0	34
N24	|	Northwestern	6	13

1935 — 4-4-0 (2-3-0)

O5		Michigan State	6	25
O12	● |	Indiana	7	0
O19	● |	at Wisconsin	20	12
O26	●	at Columbia	19	7
N2	●	Pennsylvania	16	6
N9	|	at Illinois	0	3
N16	|	Minnesota	0	40
N23	|	Ohio State	0	38

1936 — 1-7-0 (0-5-0)

O3		Michigan State	7	21
O10	|	Indiana	3	14
O17	|	at Minnesota	0	26
O24	●	Columbia	13	0
O31	|	Illinois	6	9
N7		at Pennsylvania	7	27
N14	|	Northwestern	0	9
N21	|	at Ohio State	0	21

1937 — 4-4-0 (3-3-0)

O2		Michigan State	14	19
O9	|	at Northwestern	0	7
O16	|	Minnesota	6	39
O23	● |	at Iowa	7	6
O30	● |	at Illinois	7	6
N6	● |	Chicago	13	12
N13	●	at Pennsylvania	7	0
N20	|	Ohio State	0	21

HERBERT O. "FRITZ" CRISLER
1938-47 (.806) 71-16-3

1938 — 6-1-1 (3-1-1)

O1	●	Michigan State	14	0
O8	● |	Chicago	45	7
O15	|	at Minnesota	6	7
O22	●	at Yale	15	13
O29	● |	Illinois	14	0
N5	●	Pennsylvania	19	13
N12	= |	Northwestern	0	0
N19	● |	at Ohio State	18	0

1939 — 6-2-0 (3-2-0)

O7	●	Michigan State	26	13
O14	● |	Iowa	27	7
O21	● |	at Chicago	85	0
O28	●	Yale	27	7
N4	|	at Illinois	7	16
N11	|	Minnesota	7	20
N18	●	at Pennsylvania	19	17
N25	● |	Ohio State	21	14

1940 — 7-1-0 (3-1-0)

S28	●	at California	41	0
O5	●	Michigan State	21	14
O12	●	at Harvard	26	0
O19	● |	Illinois	28	0
O26	●	Pennsylvania	14	0
N9	|	at Minnesota	6	7
N16	● |	Northwestern	20	13
N23	● |	at Ohio State	40	0

1941 — 6-1-1 (3-1-1)

S27	●	Michigan State	19	7
O4	● |	Iowa	6	0
O11	●	Pittsburgh	40	0
O18	● |	at Northwestern	14	7
O25	|	Minnesota	0	7
N1	● |	at Illinois	20	0
N15	●	at Columbia	28	0
N22	= |	Ohio State	20	20

1942 — 7-3-0 (3-2-0)

S26	●	Great Lakes NAS	9	0
O3	●	Michigan State	20	0
O10		Iowa Pre-Flight	14	26
O17	● |	Northwestern	34	16
O24	|	at Minnesota	14	16
O31	● |	Illinois	28	14
N7	●	Harvard	35	7
N14	●	at Notre Dame	32	20
N21	|	at Ohio State	7	21
N28	● |	Iowa	28	14

1943 — 8-1-0 (6-0-0)

S18	●	at Camp Grant	26	0
S25	●	Western Michigan	57	6
O2	● |	at Northwestern	21	7
O9		Notre Dame	12	35
O23	● |	Minnesota	49	6
O30	● |	at Illinois	42	6
N6	● |	Indiana	23	6
N13	● |	Wisconsin	27	0
N20	● |	Ohio State	45	7

1944 — 8-2-0 (5-2-0)

S16	●	Iowa Pre-Flight	12	7
S23	●	at Marquette	14	0
S30	|	Indiana	0	20
O7	● |	at Minnesota	28	13
O14	● |	Northwestern	27	0
O28	● |	Purdue	40	14
N4	●	at Pennsylvania	41	19
N11	● |	Illinois	14	0
N18	● |	Wisconsin	14	0
N25	|	at Ohio State	14	18

1945 — 7-3-0 (5-1-0)

S15	●	Great Lakes NAS	27	2
S22	|	Indiana	7	13
S29	●	Michigan State	40	0
O6	● |	at Northwestern	20	7
O13		Army BRNX	7	28
O27	● |	at Illinois	19	0
N3	● |	Minnesota	26	0
N10		Navy BALT	7	33
N17	● |	Purdue	27	13
N24	● |	Ohio State	7	3

1946 — 6-2-1 (5-1-1)

S28	● |	Indiana	21	0
O5	● |	Iowa	14	7
O12		Army	13	20
O19	= |	Northwestern	14	14
O26	|	Illinois	9	13
N2	● |	at Minnesota	21	0
N9	●	Michigan State	55	7
N16	● |	Wisconsin	28	6
N23	● |	at Ohio State	58	6

1947 — 10-0-0 (6-0-0)

S27	●	Michigan State	55	0
O4	●	Stanford	49	13
O11	●	Pittsburgh	69	0
O18	● |	at Northwestern	49	21
O25	● |	Minnesota	13	6
N1	● |	at Illinois	14	7
N8	● |	Indiana	35	0
N15	● |	at Wisconsin	40	6
N22	● |	Ohio State	21	0
ROSE BOWL				
J1	●	USC	49	0

68 MICHIGAN

BIG TEN TEAMS

BENNIE G. OOSTERBAAN
1948-58 (.650) 63-33-4

1948 9-0-0 (6-0-0)

S25	●	at Michigan State	13	7
O2	●	Oregon	14	0
O9	● |	at Purdue	40	0
O16	● |	Northwestern	28	0
O23	● |	at Minnesota	27	14
O30	● |	Illinois	28	20
N6	●	Navy	35	0
N13	● |	Indiana	54	0
N20	● |	at Ohio State	13	3

1949 6-2-1 (4-1-1)

S24	●	Michigan State	7	3
O1	●	at Stanford	27	7
O8		Army	7	21
O15	|	at Northwestern	20	21
O22	● |	Minnesota	14	7
O29	● |	at Illinois	13	0
N5	● |	Purdue	20	12
N12	● |	Indiana	20	7
N19	= |	Ohio State	7	7

1950 6-3-1 (4-1-1)

S30		Michigan State	7	14
O7	●	Dartmouth	27	7
O14		Army BRNX	6	27
O21	● |	Wisconsin	26	13
O28	= |	at Minnesota	7	7
N4	|	Illinois	0	7
N11	● |	Indiana	20	7
N18	● |	Northwestern	34	23
N25	● |	at Ohio State	9	3
		ROSE BOWL		
J1	●	California	14	6

1951 4-5-0 (4-2-0)

S29		Michigan State	0	25
O6		Stanford	13	23
O13	● |	Indiana	33	14
O20	● |	at Iowa	21	0
O27	● |	Minnesota	54	27
N3	|	at Illinois	0	7
N10		at Cornell	7	20
N17	|	Northwestern	0	6
N24	● |	Ohio State	7	0

1952 5-4-0 (4-2-0)

S27		Michigan State	13	27
O4		at Stanford	7	14
O11	● |	Indiana	28	13
O18	● |	at Northwestern	48	14
O25	● |	Minnesota	21	0
N1	|	Illinois	13	22
N8	●	Cornell	49	7
N15	● |	Purdue	21	10
N22	|	at Ohio State	7	27

1953 6-3-0 (3-3-0)

S26	●	Washington	50	0
O3	●	Tulane	26	7
O10	● |	Iowa	14	13
O17	● |	Northwestern	20	12
O24	|	at Minnesota	0	22
O31	●	Pennsylvania	24	14
N7	|	at Illinois	3	19
N14	|	at Michigan State	6	14
N21	● |	Ohio State	20	0

1954 6-3-0 (5-2-0)

S25	●	at Washington	14	0
O2		Army	7	26
O9	● |	Iowa	14	13
O16	● |	at Northwestern	7	0
O23	● |	Minnesota	34	0
O30	|	Indiana	9	13
N6	● |	Illinois	14	7
N13	● |	Michigan State	33	7
N20	|	at Ohio State	7	21

1955 7-2-0 (5-2-0)

S24	●	Missouri	42	7
O1	● |	Michigan State	14	7
O8	●	Army	26	2
O15	● |	Northwestern	14	2
O22	● |	at Minnesota	14	13
O29	● |	Iowa	33	21
N5	|	at Illinois	6	25
N12	● |	Indiana	30	0
N19	|	Ohio State	0	17

1956 7-2-0 (5-2-0)

S29	●	UCLA	42	13
O6	|	Michigan State	0	9
O13	●	Army	48	14
O20	● |	Northwestern	34	20
O27	|	Minnesota	7	20
N3	● |	at Iowa	17	14
N10	● |	Illinois	17	7
N17	● |	Indiana	49	26
N24	● |	at Ohio State	19	0

1957 5-3-1 (3-3-1)

S28	●	at USC	16	6
O5	●	Georgia	26	0
O12	|	Michigan State	6	35
O19	● |	Northwestern	34	14
O26	● |	at Minnesota	24	7
N2	= |	Iowa	21	21
N9	|	at Illinois	19	20
N16	● |	Indiana	27	13
N23	|	Ohio State	14	31

1958 2-6-1 (1-5-1)

S27	●	USC	20	19
O4	= |	at Michigan State	12	12
O11		Navy	14	20
O18	|	at Northwestern	24	55
O25	● |	Minnesota	20	19
N1	|	Iowa	14	37
N8	|	Illinois	8	21
N15	|	Indiana	6	8
N22	|	at Ohio State	14	20

BUMP ELLIOTT
1959-68 (.547) 51-42-2

1959 4-5-0 (3-4-0)

S26		Missouri	15	20
O3	|	Michigan State	8	34
O10	●	Oregon State	18	7
O17	|	Northwestern	7	20
O24	● |	at Minnesota	14	6
O31	|	Wisconsin	10	19
N7	● |	at Illinois	20	15
N14	|	at Indiana	7	26
N21	● |	Ohio State	23	14

1960 5-4-0 (3-4-0)

S24	●	Oregon	21	0
O1	|	at Michigan State	17	24
O8	●	Duke	31	6
O15	● |	Northwestern	14	7
O22	|	Minnesota	0	10
O29	|	at Wisconsin	13	16
N5	● |	Illinois	8	7
N12	● |	Indiana	29	7
N19	|	at Ohio State	0	7

1961 6-3-0 (3-3-0)

S30	●	UCLA	29	6
O7	●	Army	38	8
O14	|	Michigan State	0	28
O21	● |	Purdue	16	14
O28	|	at Minnesota	20	23
N4	●	Duke	28	14
N11	● |	at Illinois	38	6
N18	● |	Iowa	23	14
N25	|	Ohio State	20	50

1962 2-7-0 (1-6-0)

S29		Nebraska	13	25
O6	●	Army	17	7
O13	|	at Michigan State	0	28
O20	|	at Purdue	0	37
O27	|	Minnesota	0	17
N3	|	Wisconsin	12	34
N10	● |	Illinois	14	10
N17	|	at Iowa	14	28
N24	|	at Ohio State	0	28

1963 3-4-2 (2-3-2)

S28	●	SMU	27	16
O5		Navy	13	26
O12	= |	Michigan State	7	7
O19	|	Purdue	12	23
O26	|	at Minnesota	0	6
N2	● |	Northwestern	27	6
N9	● |	at Illinois	14	8
N16	= |	Iowa	21	21
N23	|	Ohio State	10	14

1964 9-1-0 (6-1-0)

S26	●	Air Force	24	7
O3	●	Navy	21	0
O10	● |	at Michigan State	17	10
O17	|	Purdue	20	21
O24	● |	Minnesota	19	12
O31	● |	Northwestern	35	0
N7	● |	Illinois	21	6
N14	● |	at Iowa	34	20
N21	● |	at Ohio State	10	0
		ROSE BOWL		
J1	●	Oregon State	34	7

1965 4-6-0 (2-5-0)

S18	●	at North Carolina	31	24
S25	●	California	10	7
O2		Georgia	7	15
O9	|	Michigan State	7	24
O16	|	Purdue	15	17
O23	|	at Minnesota	13	14
O30	● |	Wisconsin	50	14
N6	● |	at Illinois	23	3
N13	|	at Northwestern	22	34
N20	|	Ohio State	7	9

1966 6-4-0 (4-3-0)

S17	●	Oregon State	41	0
S24	●	at California	17	7
O1		North Carolina	7	21
O8	|	at Michigan State	7	20
O15	|	Purdue	21	22
O22	● |	Minnesota	49	0
O29	● |	at Wisconsin	28	17
N5	|	Illinois	21	28
N12	● |	Northwestern	28	20
N19	● |	at Ohio State	17	3

1967 4-6-0 (3-4-0)

S23	●	Duke	10	7
S30		at California	9	10
O7		Navy	21	26
O14	|	Michigan State	0	34
O21	|	Indiana	20	27
O28	|	at Minnesota	15	20
N4	● |	Northwestern	7	3
N11	● |	at Illinois	21	14
N18	● |	at Wisconsin	27	14
N25	|	Ohio State	14	24

1968 8-2-0 (6-1-0)

S21		California	7	21
S28	●	at Duke	31	10
O5	●	Navy	32	9
O12	● |	Michigan State	28	14
O19	● |	at Indiana	27	22
O26	● |	Minnesota	33	20
N2	● |	at Northwestern	35	0
N9	● |	Illinois	36	0
N16	● |	Wisconsin	34	9
N23	|	at Ohio State	14	50

BO SCHEMBECHLER
1969-89 (.796) 194-48-5

1969 8-3-0 (6-1-0)

S20	●	Vanderbilt	42	14
S27	●	Washington	45	7
O4		Missouri	17	40
O11	● |	Purdue	31	20
O18	|	at Michigan State	12	23
O25	● |	at Minnesota	35	9
N1	● |	Wisconsin	35	7
N8	● |	at Illinois	57	0
N15	● |	at Iowa	51	6
N22	● |	Ohio State	24	12
		ROSE BOWL		
J1		USC	3	10

1970 9-1-0 (6-1-0)

S19	●	Arizona	20	9
S26	●	at Washington	17	3
O3	●	Texas A&M	14	10
O10	● |	at Purdue	29	0
O17	● |	Michigan State	34	20
O24	● |	Minnesota	39	13
O31	● |	at Wisconsin	29	15
N7	● |	Illinois	42	0
N14	● |	Iowa	55	0
N21	|	at Ohio State	9	20

1971 11-1-0 (8-0-0)

S11	● |	at Northwestern	21	6
S18	●	Virginia	56	0
S25	●	UCLA	38	0
O2	●	Navy	46	0
O9	● |	at Michigan State	24	13
O16	● |	Illinois	35	6
O23	● |	at Minnesota	35	7
O30	● |	Indiana	61	7
N6	● |	Iowa	63	7
N13	● |	at Purdue	20	17
N20	● |	Ohio State	10	7
		ROSE BOWL		
J1		Stanford	12	13

1972 10-1-0 (7-1-0)

S16	● |	Northwestern	7	0
S23	●	at UCLA	26	9
S30	●	Tulane	41	7
O7	●	Navy	35	7
O14	● |	Michigan State	10	0
O21	● |	at Illinois	31	7
O28	● |	Minnesota	42	0
N4	● |	at Indiana	21	7
N11	● |	at Iowa	31	0
N18	● |	Purdue	9	6
N25	|	at Ohio State	11	14

1973 10-0-1 (7-0-1)

S15	● |	at Iowa	31	7
S22	●	Stanford	47	10
S29	●	Navy	14	0
O6	●	Oregon	24	0
O13	● |	at Michigan State	31	0
O20	● |	Wisconsin	35	6
O27	● |	at Minnesota	34	7
N3	● |	Indiana	49	13
N10	● |	Illinois	21	6
N17	● |	at Purdue	34	9
N24	= |	Ohio State	10	10

1974 10-1-0 (7-1-0)

S14	● |	Iowa	24	7
S21	●	Colorado	31	0
S28	●	Navy	52	0
O5	●	at Stanford	27	16
O12	● |	Michigan State	21	7
O19	● |	at Wisconsin	24	20
O26	● |	Minnesota	49	0
N2	● |	at Indiana	21	7
N9	● |	at Illinois	14	6
N16	● |	Purdue	51	0
N23	|	at Ohio State	10	12

1975 8-2-2 (7-1-0)

S13	● |	at Wisconsin	23	6
S20	=	Stanford	19	19
S27	=	Baylor	14	14
O4	●	Missouri	31	7
O11	● |	at Michigan State	16	6
O18	● |	Northwestern	69	0
O25	● |	Indiana	55	7
N1	● |	at Minnesota	28	21
N8	● |	Purdue	28	0
N15	● |	at Illinois	21	15
N22	|	Ohio State	14	21
		ORANGE BOWL		
J1		Oklahoma	6	14

1976 10-2-0 (7-1-0)

S11	● |	Wisconsin	40	27
S18	●	Stanford	51	0
S25	●	Navy	70	14
O2	●	Wake Forest	31	0
O9	● |	Michigan State	42	10
O16	● |	at Northwestern	38	7
O23	● |	at Indiana	35	0
O30	● |	Minnesota	45	0
N6	|	at Purdue	14	16
N13	● |	Illinois	38	7
N20	● |	at Ohio State	22	0
		ROSE BOWL		
J1		USC	6	14

1977 10-2-0 (7-1-0)

S10	● |	at Illinois	37	9
S17	●	Duke	21	9
S24	●	Navy	14	7
O1	●	Texas A&M	41	3
O8	● |	at Michigan State	24	14
O15	● |	Wisconsin	56	0
O22	|	at Minnesota	0	16
O29	● |	Iowa	23	6
N5	●	Northwestern	63	20
N12	● |	at Purdue	40	7
N19	● |	Ohio State	14	6
		ROSE BOWL		
J2		Washington	20	27

1978
10-2-0 (7-1-0)

Date		Opponent		
S16	●	Illinois	31	0
S23	●	at Notre Dame	28	14
S30	●	Duke	52	0
O7	●	Arizona	21	17
O14	●	Michigan State	15	24
O21	●	at Wisconsin	42	0
O28	●	Minnesota	42	10
N4	●	at Iowa	34	0
N11	●	at Northwestern	59	14
N18	●	Purdue	24	6
N25	●	at Ohio State	14	3
ROSE BOWL				
J1		USC	10	17

1979
8-4-0 (6-2-0)

S8	●	Northwestern	49	7
S15	●	Notre Dame	10	12
S22	●	Kansas	28	7
S29	●	at California	14	10
O6	●	at Michigan State	21	7
O13	●	Minnesota	31	21
O20	●	at Illinois	27	7
O27	●	Indiana	27	21
N3	●	Wisconsin	54	0
N10	●	at Purdue	21	24
N17	●	Ohio State	15	18
GATOR BOWL				
D28		North Carolina	15	17

1980
10-2-0 (8-0-0)

S13	●	Northwestern	17	10
S20	●	at Notre Dame	27	29
S27	●	South Carolina	14	17
O4	●	California	38	13
O11	●	Michigan State	27	23
O18	●	at Minnesota	37	14
O25	●	Illinois	45	14
N1	●	at Indiana	35	0
N8	●	at Wisconsin	24	0
N15	●	Purdue	26	0
N22	●	at Ohio State	9	3
ROSE BOWL				
J1	●	Washington	23	6

1981
9-3-0 (6-3-0)

S12		at Wisconsin	14	21
S19		Notre Dame	25	7
S26	●	Navy	21	16
O3	●	at Indiana	38	17
O10	●	at Michigan State	38	20
O17	●	Iowa	7	9
O24	●	Northwestern	38	0
O31	●	at Minnesota	34	13
N7	●	Illinois	70	21
N14	●	at Purdue	28	10
N21		Ohio State	9	14
BLUEBONNET BOWL				
D31	●	UCLA	33	14

1982
8-4-0 (8-1-0)

S11		Wisconsin	20	9
S18		at Notre Dame	17	23
S25	●	UCLA	27	31
O2	●	Indiana	24	10
O9	●	Michigan State	31	17
O16	●	at Iowa	29	7
O23	●	at Northwestern	49	14
O30	●	Minnesota	52	14
N6	●	at Illinois	16	10
N13	●	Purdue	52	21
N20		at Ohio State	14	24
ROSE BOWL				
J1	●	UCLA	14	24

1983
9-3-0 (8-1-0)

S10	●	Washington State	20	17
S17		at Washington	24	25
S24	●	at Wisconsin	38	21
O1	●	Indiana	43	18
O8	●	at Michigan State	42	0
O15	●	Northwestern	35	0
O22	●	Iowa	16	13
O29	●	at Illinois	6	16
N5	●	Purdue	42	10
N12	●	at Minnesota	58	10
N19		Ohio State	24	21
SUGAR BOWL				
J2		Auburn	7	9

1984
6-6-0 (5-4-0)

S8	●	Miami, Fla.	22	14
S15	●	Washington	11	20
S22	●	Wisconsin	20	14
S29	●	at Indiana	14	6
O6	●	Michigan State	7	19
O13	●	Northwestern	31	0
O20		at Iowa	0	26
O27	●	Illinois	26	18
N3	●	at Purdue	29	31
N10	●	Minnesota	31	7
N17		at Ohio State	6	21
HOLIDAY BOWL				
D21	●	Brigham Young	17	24

1985
10-1-1 (6-1-1)

S14	●	Notre Dame	20	12
S21	●	at South Carolina	34	3
S28	●	Maryland	20	0
O5	●	Wisconsin	33	6
O12	●	at Michigan State	31	0
O19	●	at Iowa	10	12
O26	●	Indiana	42	15
N2	=	at Illinois	3	3
N9	●	Purdue	47	0
N16	●	at Minnesota	48	7
N23	●	Ohio State	27	17
FIESTA BOWL				
J1	●	Nebraska	27	23

1986
11-2-0 (7-1-0)

S13	●	at Notre Dame	24	23
S20	●	Oregon State	31	12
S27	●	Florida State	20	18
O4	●	at Wisconsin	34	17
O11	●	Michigan State	27	6
O18	●	Iowa	20	17
O25	●	at Indiana	38	14
N1	●	Illinois	69	13
N8	●	at Purdue	31	7
N15	●	Minnesota	17	20
N22	●	at Ohio State	26	24
D6	●	at Hawaii	27	10
ROSE BOWL				
J1	●	Arizona State	15	22

1987
8-4-0 (5-3-0)

S12		Notre Dame	7	26
S19	●	Washington State	44	18
S26	●	Long Beach St.	49	0
O3	●	Wisconsin	49	0
O10	●	at Michigan State	11	17
O17	●	Iowa	37	10
O24	●	at Indiana	10	14
O31	●	Northwestern	29	6
N7	●	at Minnesota	30	20
N14	●	at Illinois	17	14
N21		Ohio State	20	23
HALL OF FAME BOWL				
J2	●	Alabama	28	24

1988
9-2-1 (7-0-1)

S10	●	at Notre Dame	17	19
S17	●	Miami, Fla.	30	31
S24	●	Wake Forest	19	9
O1	●	at Wisconsin	62	14
O8	●	Michigan State	17	3
O15	=	at Iowa	17	17
O22	●	Indiana	31	6
O29	●	at Northwestern	52	7
N5	●	Minnesota	22	7
N12	●	Illinois	38	9
N19	●	at Ohio State	34	31
ROSE BOWL				
J2	●	USC	22	14

1989
10-2-0 (8-0-0)

S16	●	Notre Dame	19	24
S23	●	at UCLA	24	23
S30	●	Maryland	41	21
O7	●	Wisconsin	24	0
O14	●	at Michigan State	10	7
O21	●	at Iowa	26	12
O28	●	Indiana	38	10
N4	●	Purdue	42	27
N11	●	at Illinois	24	10
N18	●	at Minnesota	49	15
N25	●	Ohio State	28	18
ROSE BOWL				
J1	●	USC	10	17

GARY O. MOELLER
1990-94 (.758)   44-13-3

1990
9-3-0 (6-2-0)

S15		at Notre Dame	24	28
S22	●	UCLA	38	15
S29	●	Maryland	45	17
O6	●	at Wisconsin	41	3
O13	●	Michigan State	27	28
O20	●	Iowa	23	24
O27	●	at Indiana	45	19
N3	●	at Purdue	38	13
N10	●	Illinois	22	17
N17	●	Minnesota	35	18
N24	●	at Ohio State	16	13
GATOR BOWL				
J1	●	Mississippi	35	3

1991
10-2-0 (8-0-0)

S7	●	at Boston College	35	13
S14	●	Notre Dame	24	14
S28	●	Florida State	31	51
O5	●	at Iowa	43	24
O12	●	at Michigan State	45	28
O19	●	Indiana	24	16
O25	●	at Minnesota	52	6
N2	●	Purdue	42	0
N9	●	Northwestern	59	14
N16	●	at Illinois	20	0
N23	●	Ohio State	31	3
ROSE BOWL				
J1		Washington	14	34

1992
9-0-3 (6-0-2)

S12	=	at Notre Dame	17	17
S19	●	Oklahoma State	35	3
S26	●	Houston	61	7
O3	●	Iowa	52	28
O10	●	Michigan State	35	10
O17	●	at Indiana	31	3
O24	●	Minnesota	63	13
O31	●	at Purdue	24	17
N7	●	at Northwestern	40	7
N14	=	Illinois	22	22
N21	=	at Ohio State	13	13
ROSE BOWL				
J1	●	Washington	38	31

1993
8-4-0 (5-3-0)

S4	●	Washington State	41	14
S11		Notre Dame	23	27
S25	●	Houston	42	21
O2	●	Iowa	24	7
O9		at Michigan State	7	17
O16	●	at Penn State	21	13
O23	●	Illinois	21	24
O30	●	at Wisconsin	10	13
N6	●	Purdue	25	10
N13	●	at Minnesota	58	7
N20	●	Ohio State	28	0
HALL OF FAME BOWL				
J1	●	North Carolina St.	42	7

1994
8-4-0 (5-3-0)

S3	●	Boston College	34	26
S10	●	at Notre Dame	26	24
S24	●	Colorado	26	27
O1	●	at Iowa	29	14
O8	●	Michigan State	40	20
O15	●	Penn State	24	31
O22	●	at Illinois	19	14
O29	●	Wisconsin	19	31
N5	●	at Purdue	45	23
N12	●	Minnesota	38	22
N19		at Ohio State	6	22
HOLIDAY BOWL				
D30	●	Colorado State	24	14

LLOYD H. CARR
1995-PRESENT (.758)   113-36

1995
9-4-0 (5-3-0)

A26	●	Virginia	18	17
S2	●	at Illinois	38	14
S9	●	Memphis	24	7
S16	●	at Boston College	23	13
S30	●	Miami (Ohio)	38	19
O7		Northwestern	13	19
O21	●	at Indiana	34	17
O28	●	Minnesota	52	17
N4	●	at Michigan State	25	28
N11	●	Purdue	5	0
N18	●	at Penn State	17	27
N25	●	Ohio State	31	23
ALAMO BOWL				
D28	●	Texas A&M	20	22

1996
8-4 (5-3)

A31	●	Illinois	20	8
S14	●	at Colorado	20	13
S21	●	Boston College	20	14
S28	●	UCLA	38	9
O5	●	at Northwestern	16	17
O19	●	Indiana	27	20
O26	●	at Minnesota	44	10
N2	●	Michigan State	45	29
N9	●	at Purdue	3	9
N16	●	Penn State	17	29
N23	●	at Ohio State	13	9
OUTBACK BOWL				
J1	●	Alabama	14	17

1997
12-0 (9-0)

S13	●	Colorado	27	3
S20	●	Baylor	38	3
S27	●	Notre Dame	21	14
O4	●	at Indiana	37	0
O11	●	Northwestern	23	6
O18	●	Iowa	28	24
O25	●	at Michigan State	23	7
N1	●	Minnesota	24	3
N8	●	at Penn State	34	8
N15	●	at Wisconsin	26	16
N22	●	Ohio State	20	14
ROSE BOWL				
J1	●	Washington State	21	16

1998
10-3 (7-1)

S5	●	at Notre Dame	20	36
S12	●	Syracuse	28	38
S19	●	Eastern Michigan	59	20
S26	●	Michigan State	29	17
O3	●	at Iowa	12	9
O17	●	at Northwestern	12	6
O24	●	Indiana	21	10
O31	●	at Minnesota	15	10
N7	●	Penn State	27	0
N14	●	Wisconsin	27	10
N21	●	at Ohio State	16	31
N28	●	at Hawaii	48	17
CITRUS BOWL				
J1	●	Arkansas	45	31

1999
10-2 (6-2)

S4	●	Notre Dame	26	22
S11	●	Rice	37	3
S18	●	at Syracuse	18	13
S25	●	at Wisconsin	21	16
O2	●	Purdue	38	12
O9	●	at Michigan State	31	34
O23	●	Illinois	29	35
O30	●	at Indiana	34	31
N6	●	Northwestern	37	3
N13	●	at Penn State	31	27
N20	●	Ohio State	24	17
ORANGE BOWL				
J1	●	Alabama	35	34

2000
9-3 (6-2)

S2	●	Bowling Green	42	7
S9	●	Rice	38	7
S16	●	at UCLA	20	23
S23	●	at Illinois	35	31
S30	●	Wisconsin	13	10
O7	●	at Purdue	31	32
O14	●	Indiana	58	0
O21	●	at Michigan State	14	0
N4	●	at Northwestern	51	54
N11	●	Penn State	33	11
N18	●	at Ohio State	38	26
CITRUS BOWL				
J1	●	Auburn	31	28

2001
8-4 (6-2)

S1	●	Miami (Ohio)	31	13
S8	●	at Washington	18	23
S22	●	Western Michigan	38	21
S29	●	Illinois	45	20
O6	●	at Penn State	20	0
O13	●	Purdue	24	10
O27	●	at Iowa	32	26
N3	●	at Michigan State	24	26
N10	●	Minnesota	31	10
N17	●	at Wisconsin	20	17
N24		Ohio State	20	26
CITRUS BOWL				
J1		Tennessee	17	45

BIG TEN TEAMS

2002   10-3   (6-2)

A31	●	Washington	31	29
S7	●	Western Michigan	35	12
S14		at Notre Dame	23	25
S21	●	Utah	10	7
S28	● |	at Illinois	45	28
O12	● |	Penn State	27	24
O19	● |	at Purdue	23	21
O26	|	Iowa	9	34
N2	● |	Michigan State	49	3
N9	● |	at Minnesota	41	24
N16	● |	Wisconsin	21	14
N23	|	at Ohio State	9	14
		OUTBACK BOWL		
J1	●	Florida	38	30

2003   10-3   (7-1)

A30	●	Central Michigan	45	7
S6	●	Houston	50	3
S13	●	Notre Dame	38	0
S20		at Oregon	27	31
S27	● |	Indiana	31	17
O4	|	at Iowa	27	30
O10	● |	at Minnesota	38	35
O18	● |	Illinois	56	14
O25	● |	Purdue	31	3
N1	● |	at Michigan State	27	20
N15	● |	at Northwestern	41	10
N22	● |	Ohio State	35	21
		ROSE BOWL		
J1		USC	14	28

2004   9-3   (7-1)

S4	●	Miami (Ohio)	43	10
S11		at Notre Dame	20	28
S18	●	San Diego State	24	21
S25	● |	Iowa	30	17
O2	● |	at Indiana	35	14
O9	● |	Minnesota	27	24
O16	● |	at Illinois	30	19
O23	● |	at Purdue	16	14
O30	|	Michigan State	45	37
N13	● |	Northwestern	42	20
N20	|	at Ohio State	21	37
		ROSE BOWL		
J1		Texas	37	38

2005   7-5   (5-3)

S3	●	Northern Illinois	33	17
S10		Notre Dame	10	17
S17	●	Eastern Michigan	55	0
S24	|	at Wisconsin	20	23
O1	● |	at Michigan State	34	31
O8	|	Minnesota	20	23
O15	● |	Penn State	27	25
O22	● |	at Iowa	23	20
O29	● |	at Northwestern	33	17
N12	● |	Indiana	41	14
N19	|	Ohio State	21	25
		ALAMO BOWL		
D28		Nebraska	28	32

2006   11-2   (7-1)

S2	●	Vanderbilt	27	7
S9	●	Central Michigan	41	17
S16	●	at Notre Dame	47	21
S23	● |	Wisconsin	27	13
S30	● |	at Minnesota	28	14
O7	● |	Michigan State	31	13
O14	● |	at Penn State	17	10
O21	● |	Iowa	20	6
O28	● |	Northwestern	17	3
N4	●	Ball State	34	26
N11	● |	at Indiana	34	3
N18	|	at Ohio State	39	42
		ROSE BOWL		
J1		USC	18	32

MICHIGAN RECORD BOOK

SINGLE-GAME RECORDS

RUSHING YARDS

RANK	PLAYER	DATE	OPPONENT	ATT	AVG	YDS
1	Ron Johnson	Nov. 16, 1968	Wisconsin	31	11.2	347
2	Tshimanga Biakabutuka	Nov. 25, 1995	Ohio State	37	9.0	313
3	Jon Vaughn	Sept. 22, 1990	UCLA	32	9.0	288
4	Ron Johnson	Oct. 7, 1967	Navy	26	10.0	270
5	Butch Woolfolk	Oct. 10, 1981	Michigan State	39	7.0	253

PASSING YARDS

RANK	PLAYER	DATE	OPPONENT	ATT	COMP	YDS
1	John Navarre	Oct. 4, 2003	Iowa	49	26	389
2	Tom Brady	Nov. 21, 1998	Ohio State	56	31	375
3	Scott Dreisbach	Aug. 26, 1995	Virginia	52	27	372
4	Tom Brady	Jan. 1, 2000	Alabama	46	34	369
5	John Navarre	Sept. 20, 2003	Oregon	55	28	360

RECEIVING YARDS

RANK	PLAYER	DATE	OPPONENT	REC	AVG	YDS
1	Jack Clancy	Sept. 17, 1966	Oregon State	10	19.7	197
2	Tai Streets	Oct. 31, 1998	Minnesota	6	32.0	192
3	Braylon Edwards	Oct. 30, 2004	Michigan State	11	17.2	189
4	Derrick Alexander	Oct. 23, 1993	Illinois	7	26.9	188
5	Jim Smith	Nov. 8, 1975	Purdue	5	36.8	184

POINTS

RANK	PLAYER	DATE	OPPONENT	TOT
1	Ron Johnson	Nov. 16, 1968	Wisconsin	30
2	Tom Harmon	Sept. 28, 1940	California	28
3	Tom Harmon	Oct. 14, 1939	Iowa	27
4	9 players tied at 24			

FIELD GOALS

RANK	PLAYER	DATE	OPPONENT	TOT
1	Mike Gillette	Nov. 8, 1988	Minnesota	5
	John Carlson	Nov. 10, 1990	Illinois	5
3	8 players tied at 4			

TACKLES

RANK	PLAYER	DATE	OPPONENT	TOT
1	Garland Rivers	Dec. 21, 1984	Brigham Young	17
2	Erick Anderson	Nov. 23, 1991	Ohio State	16
	Mike Mallory	Nov. 3, 1984	Purdue	16
	Timothy Anderson	Nov. 3, 1984	Purdue	16
5	7 players tied at 15			

INTERCEPTIONS

RANK	PLAYER	DATE	OPPONENT	TOT
1	Tom Curtis	Nov. 11, 1967	Illinois	3
	Marty Huff	Oct. 11, 1969	Purdue	3
	Rodney Lyles	Sept. 8, 1984	Miami Fla.	3
	Andy Moeller	Oct. 4, 1986	Wisconsin	3
5	16 players tied at 2			

RETIRED NUMBERS

11 Francis, Albert, and Alvin Wistert

47 Bennie Oosterbaan

48 Gerald R. Ford

87 Ron Kramer

98 Tom Harmon

SINGLE-SEASON RECORDS

RUSHING YARDS

RANK	PLAYER	SEASON	G	ATT	YDS
1	Tshimanga Biakabutuka	1995	13	303	1,818
2	Anthony Thomas	2000	12	319	1,733
3	Jamie Morris	1987	12	282	1,703
4	Chris Perry	2003	13	338	1,674
5	Michael Hart	2006	13	318	1,562

PASSING YARDS

RANK	PLAYER	SEASON	G	ATT	COMP	PCT	YDS
1	John Navarre	2003	13	456	270	59.2	3,331
2	John Navarre	2002	13	448	248	55.3	2,905
3	Chad Henne	2004	12	399	240	60.1	2,743
4	Tom Brady	1998	13	350	214	61.1	2,636
5	Tom Brady	1999	12	341	214	62.7	2,586

RECEIVING YARDS

RANK	PLAYER	SEASON	G	REC	AVG	YDS
1	Braylon Edwards	2004	12	97	13.7	1,330
2	Marquise Walker	2001	12	86	13.3	1,143
3	Braylon Edwards	2003	13	85	13.4	1,138
4	David Terrell	2000	12	67	16.9	1,130
5	Amani Toomer	1994	12	54	20.3	1,096

SCORING

RANK	PLAYER	SEASON	TD	FG	PAT	P2	TOT
1	Desmond Howard	1991	23	0	0	0	138
2	Chris Perry	2003	20	0	0	0	120
3	Tom Harmon	1940	16	1	18	0	117
4	Ron Johnson	1968	19	0	0	1	116
5	Anthony Thomas	2000	19	0	0	0	114

TOUCHDOWNS

RANK	PLAYER	SEASON	G	TOT
1	Desmond Howard	1991	12	23
2	Chris Perry	2003	13	20
3	Ron Johnson	1968	10	19
	Anthony Thomas	2000	12	19
5	Tyrone Wheatley	1992	11	17

TACKLES

RANK	PLAYER	SEASON	G	TOT
1	Ron Simpkins	1977	12	144
	Ron Simpkins	1978	12	144
	Mike Boren	1981	12	144
4	Mike Boren	1982	12	142
5	Calvin O'Neal	1975	12	136

INTERCEPTIONS

RANK	PLAYER	SEASON	G	YDS	TOT
1	Tom Curtis	1968	10	182	10
2	Charles Woodson	1997	12	7	8
3	5 players tied at 6				

PUNTING

RANK	PLAYER	SEASON	PUNTS	YDS	AVG
1	Monte Robbins	1984	62	2,705	43.6
2	Monte Robbins	1986	39	1,701	43.6
3	Monte Robbins	1987	51	NA	43.5
4	Don Bracken	1981	50	NA	43.3
5	Adam Finley	2004	64	NA	43.0

PUNT RETURNS

RANK	PLAYER	SEASON	RET	YDS	AVG
1	Desmond Howard	1991	18	NA	15.7
2	Terry Barr	1955	15	NA	14.8
3	Tripp Welborne	1990	31	477	14.7
4	Derrick Alexander	1992	26	NA	14.3
5	Anthony Carter	1982	19	NA	14.2

KICKOFF RETURNS

RANK	PLAYER	SEASON	RET	YDS	AVG
1	Dave Raimey	1961	NA	NA	30.8
2	Desmond Howard	1990	17	504	29.6
3	Anthony Carter	1980	15	427	28.5
4	Tony Boles	1989	14	NA	28.2
5	Steve Breaston	2005	23	645	28.1

CAREER RECORDS

RUSHING YARDS

RANK	PLAYER	SEASONS	ATT	AVG	TD	YDS
1	Anthony Thomas	1997-2000	924	4.8	55	4,472
2	Jamie Morris	1984-87	806	5.5	25	4,392
3	Tyrone Wheatley	1991-94	688	6.1	47	4,178
4	Butch Woolfolk	1978-81	717	5.4	29	3,850
5	Chris Perry	2000-03	811	4.6	39	3,696
6	Michael Hart	2004-	750	4.9	27	3,679
7	Rob Lytle	1973-76	557	5.9	26	3,307
8	Bill Taylor	1969-71	587	5.2	30	3,072
9	Gordon Bell	1973-75	535	5.4	28	2,902
10	Tshimanga Biakabutuka	1993-95	472	6.0	24	2,810

PASSING YARDS

RANK	PLAYER	SEASONS	ATT	COMP	PCT	INT	TD	YDS
1	John Navarre	2000-03	1,366	765	56.0	31	72	9,254
2	Chad Henne	2004-	1,109	666	60.1	28	70	7,777
3	Elvis Grbac	1989-92	835	522	62.5	31	71	6,460
4	Todd Collins	1991-94	711	457	64.3	20	37	5,858
5	Jim Harbaugh	1983-86	620	387	62.4	22	77	5,449
6	Tom Brady	1996-99	711	443	62.3	19	35	5,351
7	Steve Smith	1980-83	648	324	50.6	32	42	4,860
8	Brian Griese	1995-97	606	355	58.6	18	33	4,383
9	Rick Leach	1975-78	537	250	46.6	35	48	4,284
10	John Wangler	1976-80	346	197	56.9	16	28	2,994

RECEIVING YARDS

RANK	PLAYER	SEASONS	REC	AVG	TD	YDS
1	Braylon Edwards	2001-04	252	14.1	39	3,541
2	Anthony Carter	1979-82	161	19.1	37	3,076
3	Amani Toomer	1992-95	143	18.6	18	2,657
4	David Terrell	1998-2000	152	15.2	23	2,317
5	Tai Streets	1995-98	144	15.9	19	2,284
6	Marquise Walker	1998-2001	176	12.9	17	2,269
7	Jason Avant	2002-05	169	13.3	13	2,247
8	Greg McMurtry	1986-89	111	19.5	15	2,163
9	Desmond Howard	1989-91	134	16.0	32	2,146
10	Mercury Hayes	1992-95	124	17.3	12	2,144

SCORING

RANK	PLAYER	SEASONS	TD	FG	PAT	P2	TOT
1	Garrett Rivas	2003-06	0	64	162	0	354
2	Anthony Thomas	1997-2000	56	0	0	0	336
3	Tyrone Wheatley	1991-94	54	0	0	0	324
4	Mike Gillette	1985-88	0	57	130	0	301
5	Remy Hamilton	1993-96	0	63	91	0	280

TOUCHDOWNS

RANK	PLAYER	SEASONS	G	TOT
1	Anthony Thomas	1997-2000	48	56
2	Tyrone Wheatley	1991-94	41	54
3	Chris Perry	2000-03	47	41
4	Anthony Carter	1979-82	47	40
5	Braylon Edwards	2001-04	44	39

TACKLES

RANK	PLAYER	SEASONS	G	TOT
1	Jarrett Irons	1993-96	49	429
2	Ron Simpkins	1976-79	42	415
3	Erick Anderson	1988-91	44	390
4	Sam Sword	1995-98	46	370
5	Steve Morrison	1990-94	39	315

INTERCEPTIONS

RANK	PLAYER	SEASONS	G	YDS	TOT
1	Tom Curtis	1967-69	28	351	22
2	Charles Woodson	1993-97	37	81	18
3	Leon Hall	2003-06	47	23	12
4	Vada Murray	1988-90	35	67	11
	Brad Cochran	1983-85	39	94	11
	DeWayne Patmon	1997-2000	41	58	11

PUNTING

RANK	PLAYER	SEASONS	PUNTS	YDS	AVG
1	Monte Robbins	1984-87	200	8,562	42.8
2	Adam Finley	2001-04	190	7,953	41.9
3	Don Bracken	1980-83	203	NA	40.8
4	Chris Stapleton	1989-93	132	NA	40.3
5	Hayden Epstein	1998-2001	167	NA	39.9

TEAM RECORDS

LONGEST WINNING STREAK
- 29, Sept. 28, 1901-Oct. 24, 1903
Streak broken vs. Minnesota, 6-6, Oct. 31, 1903

LONGEST UNDEFEATED STREAK
- 56, Sept. 28, 1901-Nov. 25, 1905
Streak broken vs. Chicago, 0-2, Nov. 30, 1905

MOST CONSECUTIVE WINNING SEASONS
- 27, 1892-1918

MOST CONSECUTIVE BOWL APPEARANCES
- 32, 1975-present

MOST POINTS IN A GAME
- 130, vs. West Virginia, Oct. 22, 1904

MOST POINTS ALLOWED IN A GAME
- 58, vs. Cornell, Nov. 21, 1891

LARGEST MARGIN OF VICTORY
- 130 (130-0), vs. West Virginia, Oct. 22, 1904

LARGEST MARGIN OF DEFEAT
- 56 (0-56), vs. Cornell, Nov. 23, 1889

LONGEST RUN FROM SCRIMMAGE
- 92 yards, Butch Woolfolk, vs. Wisconsin, Nov. 3, 1979

LONGEST PASS PLAY
- 90 yards, Todd Collins to Derrick Alexander, vs. Illinois, Oct. 23, 1993

LONGEST FIELD GOAL
- 57 yards, Hayden Epstein, vs. Michigan State, Nov. 3, 2001

LONGEST PUNT
- 82 yards, Monte Robbins, vs. Hawaii, Dec. 6, 1986

LONGEST INTERCEPTION RETURN
- 95 yards, John Harmon, vs. Hawaii, Oct. 14, 1939

PUNT RETURNS

RANK	PLAYER	SEASON	RET	YDS	AVG
1	George Hoey	1967-68	NA	NA	17.3
2	Gene Derricotte	1944-48	55	NA	13.7
3	Derrick Alexander	1989-93	NA	NA	12.7
4	Steve Breaston	2003-06	127	1,599	12.6
5	Wally Teninga	1945-49	43	NA	11.7

KICKOFF RETURNS

RANK	PLAYER	SEASON	RET	YDS	AVG
1	Desmond Howard	1989-91	45	1,211	26.9
2	Anthony Carter	1979-82	63	NA	26.3
3	Tony Boles	1987-89	NA	NA	25.6
4	Gil Chapman	1972-74	NA	NA	24.7
5	Steve Breaston	2003-06	81	1,993	24.6

MICHIGAN ANNUAL STATISTICAL LEADERS

YR	RUSHING	YDS	ATT	AVG	PASSING	ATT	CMP	PCT	YDS	RECEIVING	REC	YDS	AVG
1942	Bob Wiese	466	133	3.5	Bob Chappuis	64	28	.44	358	George Ceithaml	18	232	12.9
1943	Bill Daley	817	120	6.8	Elroy Hirsch	22	9	.41	213	Farnham Johnson	4	109	27.3
1944	Bob Nussbaumer	502	78	6.4	Bill Culligan	39	12	.31	245	Dick Rifenburg	8	232	29.0
1945	Wally Teninga	317	66	4.8	Pete Elliott	52	19	.37	393	Hank Fonde	11	148	13.5
1946	Bob Chappuis	502	116	4.3	Bob Chappuis	92	52	.57	734	Bobby Mann	14	285	20.4
1947	J. Weisenburger	773	121	6.4	Bob Chappuis	110	62	.56	1,164	Bump Elliott	18	318	19.9
1948	Tom Peterson	330	109	3.0	Chuck Ortmann	87	41	.47	856	Dick Rifenburg	22	508	23.1
1949	Don Dufek	392	122	3.2	Chuck Ortmann	126	45	.36	627	Harry Allis	23	338	14.7
1950	Don Dufek	702	174	4.0	Chuck Ortmann	120	56	.47	736	Lowell Perry	24	374	15.6
1951	Don Peterson	549	152	3.6	Bill Putich	77	32	.42	380	Lowell Perry	16	395	24.7
1952	Ted Kress	623	135	4.6	Ted Kress	85	45	.53	559	Lowell Perry	31	492	15.9
1953	Tony Branoff	501	101	5.0	Lou Baldacci	51	21	.41	302	Bob Topp	23	331	14.4
1954	Fred Baer	439	107	4.1	Jim Maddock	35	16	.46	293	Ron Kramer	23	303	13.2
1955	Tony Branoff	387	86	4.5	Jim Maddock	52	20	.39	343	Ron Kramer	12	253	21.1
1956	Jim Pace	498	103	4.8	Bob Ptacek	23	15	.65	245	Ron Kramer	18	353	19.6
1957	Jim Pace	664	123	5.4	Jim Van Pelt	80	42	.53	629	Gary Prahst	15	233	15.5
1958	Darrell Harper	309	55	5.6	Bob Ptacek	115	65	.57	763	Gary Prahst	22	313	14.2
1959	Fred Julian	289	72	4.0	Stan Noskin	115	61	.53	747	Bob Johnson	20	264	13.2
1960	Bennie McRae	352	80	4.4	Dave Glinka	124	54	.44	755	Bob Johnson	15	230	15.3
1961	Dave Raimey	496	99	5.0	Dave Glinka	96	46	.48	588	George Mans	15	149	9.9
1962	Dave Raimey	385	124	3.1	Bob Chandler	63	29	.46	401	Harvey Chapman	11	223	20.3
1963	Mel Anthony	394	103	3.8	Bob Timberlake	98	47	.48	593	John Henderson	27	330	12.2
1964	Mel Anthony	702	145	4.8	Bob Timberlake	137	70	.51	884	John Henderson	31	427	13.8
1965	Carl Ward	639	112	5.7	Wally Gabler	125	58	.46	825	Jack Clancy	52	762	14.7
1966	Dave Fisher	637	131	4.9	Dick Vidmer	226	117	.52	1,611	Jack Clancy	76	1,079	14.2
1967	Ron Johnson	1,005	220	4.6	Dennis Brown	156	82	.53	913	Jim Berline	54	624	11.6
1968	Ron Johnson	1,391	255	5.5	Dennis Brown	229	109	.48	1,562	Jim Mandich	43	576	13.4
1969	Bill Taylor	864	141	6.1	Don Moorhead	210	103	.49	1,261	Jim Mandich	50	662	13.2
1970	Bill Taylor	911	197	4.6	Don Moorhead	190	87	.46	1,167	Paul Staroba	35	519	14.8
1971	Bill Taylor	1,297	249	5.2	Tom Slade	63	27	.43	364	Glenn Doughty	16	203	12.7
1972	Ed Shuttlesworth	723	157	4.6	Dennis Franklin	123	59	.48	818	Paul Seal	18	243	13.5
1973	Ed Shuttlesworth	745	193	3.9	Dennis Franklin	67	36	.54	534	Paul Seal	14	254	18.1
1974	Gordon Bell	1,048	174	6.0	Dennis Franklin	104	58	.56	933	Gil Chapman	23	378	16.4
1975	Gordon Bell	1,388	273	5.1	Rick Leach	100	32	.32	680	Jim Smith	24	553	23.0
1976	Rob Lytle	1,469	221	6.6	Rick Leach	105	50	.48	973	Jim Smith	26	714	27.5
1977	Russell Davis	1,092	225	4.9	Rick Leach	174	90	.52	1,348	Ralph Clayton	24	477	19.9
1978	Harlan Huckleby	741	154	4.8	Rick Leach	158	78	.49	1,283	Ralph Clayton	25	546	21.8
1979	Butch Woolfolk	990	191	5.2	John Wangler	130	78	.60	1,431	Doug Marsh	33	612	18.5
1980	Butch Woolfolk	1,042	196	5.3	John Wangler	212	117	.55	1,522	Anthony Carter	51	818	16.0
1981	Butch Woolfolk	1,459	253	5.8	Steve Smith	210	97	.46	1,661	Anthony Carter	50	952	19.0
1982	Lawrence Ricks	1,388	266	5.2	Steve Smith	227	118	.52	1,735	Anthony Carter	43	844	19.6
1983	Rick Rogers	1,002	209	4.8	Steve Smith	205	106	.52	1,420	Sim Nelson	41	494	12.0
1984	Jamie Morris	574	118	4.9	Jim Harbaugh	111	60	.54	718	Sim Nelson	40	459	11.5
1985	Jamie Morris	1,030	197	5.2	Jim Harbaugh	227	145	.64	1,976	Eric Kattus	38	582	15.3
1986	Jamie Morris	1,086	212	5.1	Jim Harbaugh	277	180	.65	2,729	Gerald White	38	408	10.7
1987	Jamie Morris	1,703	282	6.0	Demetrius Brown	168	80	.48	1,251	Greg McMurtry	21	474	22.6
1988	Tony Boles	1,408	262	5.4	Michael Taylor	122	76	.62	957	Greg McMurtry	27	470	17.4
1989	Tony Boles	839	131	6.4	Michael Taylor	121	74	.61	1,081	Greg McMurtry	41	711	17.3
1990	Jon Vaughn	1,416	216	6.6	Elvis Grbac	266	155	.58	1,911	Desmond Howard	63	1,025	16.3
1991	Ricky Powers	1,364	240	5.7	Elvis Grbac	254	165	.65	2,085	Desmond Howard	62	985	15.9
1992	Tyrone Wheatley	1,357	185	7.3	Elvis Grbac	199	129	.65	1,640	Derrick Alexander	50	740	14.8
1993	Tyrone Wheatley	1,129	207	5.5	Todd Collins	296	189	.64	2,509	Derrick Alexander	35	621	17.7
1994	Tyrone Wheatley	1,144	210	5.4	Todd Collins	288	186	.65	2,518	Amani Toomer	54	1,096	20.3
1995	Tim Biakabutuka	1,818	303	6.0	Brian Griese	238	127	.53	1,577	Mercury Hayes	48	923	19.2
1996	Clarence Williams	837	202	4.1	Scott Dreisbach	269	149	.55	2,025	Tai Streets	44	730	16.6
1997	Chris Howard	938	199	4.7	Brian Griese	307	193	.63	2,293	Chris Howard	37	276	7.5
1998	Anthony Thomas	893	167	5.3	Tom Brady	350	214	.61	2,636	Tai Streets	67	1,035	15.4
1999	Anthony Thomas	1,297	301	4.3	Tom Brady	341	214	.63	2,586	David Terrell	71	1,038	14.6
2000	Anthony Thomas	1,733	319	5.4	Drew Henson	237	146	.62	2,146	David Terrell	67	1,130	16.9
2001	B.J. Askew	902	199	4.5	John Navarre	385	207	.54	2,435	Marquise Walker	86	1,143	13.3
2002	Chris Perry	1,110	267	4.2	John Navarre	448	248	.55	2,905	Braylon Edwards	67	1,035	15.4
2003	Chris Perry	1,674	338	5.0	John Navarre	456	270	.59	3,331	Braylon Edwards	85	1,138	13.4
2004	Mike Hart	1,455	282	5.2	Chad Henne	399	240	.60	2,743	Braylon Edwards	97	1,330	13.7
2005	Mike Hart	662	150	4.4	Chad Henne	382	223	.58	2,526	Jason Avant	82	1,007	12.3
2006	Mike Hart	1,562	318	4.9	Chad Henne	328	203	.62	2,508	Steve Breaston	58	670	11.6

Receiving leaders by receptions
All statistics include postseason

MICHIGAN STATE

By Todd Jones

THE STANDARD FOR MICHIGAN State was set in 1896, when the school was known as Michigan Agricultural College and its president, Jonathan L. Snyder, declared, "If we must have football, I want the kind that wins." Many great victories have since been part of Spartans lore, especially during the 1950s under coach Clarence "Biggie" Munn and his successor Hugh "Duffy" Daugherty. Michigan State has often been at or near the forefront of college football, whether by playing in a classic game such as the one against Notre Dame in 1966 or by producing a litany of top players. Some of those Spartans—such as Lynn Chandnois, Earl Morrall, Charles "Bubba" Smith, George Webster, Lorenzo White, Tony Mandarich, Jeff Smoker, and Charles Rogers—set a standard of achievement not only for their school, but for college football in general. Mark Dantonio, the school's fourth coach since 1999, plans to push the Spartans to live up to those high expectations as he enters his first season in 2007.

TRADITION Fans gather on campus at The Spartan, a 10'6" ceramic figure that weighs three tons and stands on a 5'4" brick-and-concrete base. The statue, also known as Sparty, was dedicated in 1945. Four years later, the Detroit alumni clubs of Michigan State and Notre Dame presented the first Megaphone Trophy, since awarded to the winner of that rivalry. Since 1950, the Spartans and Indiana Hoosiers have played for the Old Brass Spittoon. The Michigan-Michigan State game winner has earned the Paul Bunyan Trophy since 1953, when the governor, G. Mennen Williams, donated the four-foot wooden statue—which rests on a five-foot stand—to honor the Spartans' entry into the Big Ten. Michigan State and Penn State have played for the Land-Grant Trophy, first awarded when their series was renewed in 1993.

BEST PLAYER George Webster was fast and athletic at 6'4", 218 pounds, and his hard-hitting style epitomized two legendary Michigan State defenses. "George Webster is not only the finest football player I've ever seen, but he symbolizes our great '65 and '66 teams," said his coach, Duffy Daugherty, who created the roverback postion as a combination of safety and linebacker. Webster would revolutionize the position before he left Michigan State, adding an unprecedented blend of speed and power during his marauding, sideline-to-sideline play. "George

---

PROFILE

Michigan State University
East Lansing, Mich.
Founded: 1855
Enrollment: 45,520
Colors: Green and White
Nickname: Spartans
Stadium: Spartan Stadium
  Opened in 1923
  Grass; 75,005 capacity
First football game: 1896
All-time record: 599–403–44 (.594)
Bowl record: 7–10
Consensus national championships, 1936-present: 2 (1952, 1965)
Big Ten Conference championships: 6 (3 outright)
Outland Trophy: Ed Bagdon, 1949
First-round draft choices: 34
Website: www.msuspartans.com

THE BEST OF TIMES

The Spartans' national championship in 1965 and 9–0–1 record in 1966 brought back memories of the previous decade, when they won four national titles and went 62–12 from 1950 to 1957.

THE WORST OF TIMES

All Spartans fans want to forget the 2–9 debacle of 1982, part of a span of five straight losing seasons from 1979 to 1983 that yielded a cumulative record of 19–35–1.

CONFERENCE

Michigan State joined the Western Conference in 1953. The Western Conference had been popularly known as the Big Ten since 1917, but didn't officially change its name to the Big Ten Conference until 1987.

DISTINGUISHED ALUMNI

Magic Johnson; James Caan, actor; John Engler, Michigan governor; Jim Harrison, writer; James P. Hoffa, president of the teamsters; R. Drayton McClane Jr., Houston Astros owner; Sam Raimi, director and producer

FIGHT SONG

MSU FIGHT SONG
On the banks of the Red Cedar,
There's a school that's known to all;
Its specialty is winning,
And those Spartans play good ball;
Spartan teams are never beaten,
All through the game they'll fight;
Fight for the only colors,
Green and White.
Go right through for MSU,
Watch the points keep growing.
Spartan teams are bound to win,
They're fighting with a vim.
Rah! Rah! Rah!
See their team is weakening,
We're going to win this game.
Fight! Fight! Rah! Team, Fight!
Victory for MSU.

Webster played like a cobra striking its prey," said Hank Bullough, an assistant coach under Daugherty. Webster's play as a junior helped the Spartans set school records that still stand for total defense (169.9 yards allowed per game) and rushing defense (45.6 yards). As a senior, he had 93 tackles, including 10 for losses, on a unit that allowed 9.9 points and 51.4 yards rushing per game. The Spartans went 23–6–1 in Webster's career, and the school retired his No. 90 in 1967. Two years later, Michigan State fans voted the two-time All-America as the Spartans' greatest player ever.

The Houston Oilers selected Webster in the first round of the NFL's 1967 draft. He played 10 years in the pros, including NFL stints with the Pittsburgh Steelers and New England Patriots. In 1996, he was chosen for Michigan State's Centennial Super Squad. By then, he was struggling with postcareer injuries that caused him to lose most use of a hand, foot, knee, and ankle. Webster applied for benefits as totally and permanently disabled, arguing that his injuries were related to football, but the NFL ruled he didn't meet the definition of totally disabled. The U.S. Supreme Court agreed with the NFL that Webster's injuries weren't related to football and denied him a

Michigan State has often been at or near the forefront of college football.

pension increase from $750 a month to $4,000 a month. Circulation problems caused Webster to have his right leg amputated above the knee in 2002, and he battled throat cancer, prostate cancer, and congestive heart failure in recent years. He died at age 61 of heart failure on April 19, 2007, just two months after Michigan State had established the George Webster Scholarship Fund. His longtime friend and former teammate, Ernie Pasteur, described MSU's decision to establish the scholarship in Webster's name as "the biggest thrill of George's life."

BEST COACH Laughter always followed in the wake of Duffy Daugherty, the man Biggie Munn entrusted to maintain his national powerhouse. Hardship gave perspective to Duffy's humor. As a teenager, he worked in a Pennsylvania coal mine, just like his father. Daugherty later enlisted in the Army and spent three years fighting in the South Pacific, earning the Bronze Star during his rise from private to major. This experience helped him see the lighter side of Michigan State football while he was coach from 1954 to 1972. Daugherty invited fans to attend practice before the 1956 Rose Bowl and entertained the

FIRST-ROUND DRAFT CHOICES

1936	Sid Wagner, Lions (8)
1939	John Pingel, Lions (7)
1950	Lynn Chandnois, Steelers (8)
1952	Bob Carey, Rams (13)
1956	Earl Morrall, 49ers (2)
1957	Clarence Peaks, Eagles (7)
1958	Dan Currie, Packers (3)
1958	Walt Kowalczyk, Eagles (6)
1961	Herb Adderley, Packers (12)
1963	Ed Budde, Eagles (4) and Cowboys (8)*
1963	Dave Behrman, Bears (11) and Bills (4)*
1965	Jerry Rush, Patriots (1)
1967	Charles "Bubba" Smith, Colts (1)
1967	Clint Jones, Vikings (2)
1967	George Webster, Oilers (5)
1967	Gene Washington, Vikings (8)
1973	Billy Joe DuPree, Cowboys (20)
1973	Joe DeLamielleure, Bills (26)
1977	Mike Cobb, Bengals (22)
1978	Larry Bethea, Cowboys (28)
1984	Carl Banks, Giants (3)
1986	Anthony Bell, Cardinals (5)
1987	Mark Ingram, Giants (28)
1988	Lorenzo White, Oilers (22)
1989	Tony Mandarich, Packers (2)
1989	Andre Rison, Colts (22)
1990	Percy Snow, Chiefs (13)
1991	Bobby Wilson, Redskins (17)
1994	Rob Fredrickson, Raiders (22)
1999	Dimitrius Underwood, Vikings (29)
2000	Plaxico Burress, Steelers (8)
2000	Julian Peterson, 49ers (16)
2002	T.J. Duckett, Falcons (18)
2003	Charles Rogers, Lions (2)

From 1960-1966, the NFL and the AFL held separate, competing drafts

CONSENSUS ALL-AMERICANS

1915	Neno Jerry DaPrato, B
1935	Sidney Wagner, G
1949	Ed Bagdon, G
1951	Bob Carey, E
1951	Don Coleman, T
1953	Don Dohoney, E
1955	Norman Masters, T
1955	Earl Morrall, B
1957	Dan Currie, C
1957	Walt Kowalczyk, B
1958	Sam Williams, E
1962	George Saimes, B
1963	Sherman Lewis, B
1965-66	Bubba Smith, DE
1965-66	George Webster, DB
1966	Clint Jones, B
1972	Brad Van Pelt, DB
1985, 1987	Lorenzo White, RB
1988	Tony Mandarich, OL
1989	Bob Kula, OL
1989	Percy Snow, LB
2002	Charles Rogers, WR
2004	Brandon Fields, P

crowd of 3,500 by explaining the plays complete with team demonstrations through a public address microphone. Imagine that today. Daugherty not only enjoyed talking to sportswriters, he even wrote a column for the Associated Press for three years. All of the one-liners and great quotes, known as Duffyisms, masked a demanding perfectionism in Daugherty. There was nothing funny about his teams, which finished in the national Top 10 seven times, and included African-American players—Jimmy Raye was the starting quarter-back in 1966. The Spartans went 19–1–1 and won Big Ten titles in 1965 and 1966. The 1965 team finished No. 1 in the UPI poll. "We don't have any magic formula and neither does anyone else in the business," Daugherty once said. "The reason you win is because you've got more good players than the next guy. Most football games aren't won on the field. They are won from December to September, when recruiting is done. Eighty percent of a winning team is material." Daugherty was named national Coach of the Year in 1965 and 1966 and was later inducted into the College Football Hall of Fame.

BEST TEAM The high-water mark of Biggie Munn's successful tenure came in 1952, when the Spartans went 9–0 for the second consecutive year despite having to replace their quarterback and entire offensive line. Michigan State defeated three ranked opponents and finished No. 1 in both wire-service polls to earn the school's first national championship. The 1952 Spartans, one season from beginning Big Ten play, had All-Americas in guard Frank Kush, center and linebacker Richard Tamburo, and halfback Donald McAuliffe, the main threat in the "Light Brigade Backfield" that included QB Tom Yewcic, Billy "Menominee Meteor" Wells, Leroy Bolden, and Evan Slonac. Waves of other talent caused opponents to lose by an average score of 34.6 to 9.3. "It isn't so much what their first and second teams do to you, but the third, fourth, and fifth teams simply murder you," said Ray George after his Texas A&M team gave up 592 yards of offense in a 48-6 loss to Michigan State. That depth helped in the season's second game, at Oregon State, when reserve fullback Eugene Lekenta came off the bench to kick a 24-yard field goal with eight seconds remaining to give the Spartans a 17-14 victory. Michigan State concluded its season by rolling to 601 yards of offense in a 62-13 romp over Marquette. Munn was named 1952 national Coach of the Year, a fitting honor on a team deemed best in the land.

BEST BACKFIELD The Spartans have had some stellar duos of runners and passers in the same backfield. Among them, tailback Lorenzo White and quarterback Dave Yarema were dangerous in the mid-1980s, as were tailback Sedric Irvin and QB Bill Burke in the late 1990s.

For one season, however, no one-two combination can match the statistics put forth by tailback T.J. Duckett and QB Jeff Smoker in 2001.

Duckett ran for 1,420 yards on 263 carries and 12 touchdowns as a senior, bringing his career total to 3,379 rushing yards—fifth highest in school history. While Duckett provided the ground thunder, Smoker put up huge numbers in the air in 2001. The sophomore passed for 2,579 yards and 21 touchdowns that season. He completed 166 of 262 passes for 63.4%, and his passing efficiency mark of 166.4 still ranks as the Michigan State record. Smoker threw for 376 yards against Fresno State, 356 against Penn State, and had an 87-yard TD pass to Charles Rogers against Wisconsin. Rogers was his favorite target, catching 67 passes for 1,470 yards and 14 TDs. Although the Spartans averaged 447 yards of offense and 31.2 points per game, they finished the season 7–5 after a 5–2 start. A year later, Smoker was indefinitely suspended by Michigan State for a substance abuse problem. He came back and ended his career in 2003 as Michigan State's all-time leader in passing yards (8,932), attempts (1,150), completions (685), and touchdown passes (61).

BEST DEFENSE Few defenses in college football history can match those fielded by the Spartans when they went 19–1–1 and won two Big Ten championships in 1965 and 1966. Both ferocious units featured George Webster and defensive end Charles "Bubba" Smith, both two-time All-America selections, and members of the College Football Hall of Fame and Michigan State's Centennial Super Squad. Statistics give a razor-thin edge to the 1965 defense that helped the Spartans go 10–0 in the regular season before suffering an upset loss to UCLA in the Rose Bowl. Those 1965 Spartans led the nation in rushing defense and in scoring defense, and was No. 2 in allowing 169.9 yards, another school record. Defensive coordinator Hank Bullough had the luxury of having a player in Webster who was fast enough to cover receivers yet strong enough to stuff the run at a hybrid linebacker spot called roverback. Webster provided a unique match-up problem, but it was Smith who struck fear into the hearts of opponents. "Kill, Bubba, Kill," read the bumper stickers in East Lansing. The junior from Beaumont, Texas, stood 6'8" and weighed 280 pounds, size nearly unheard of in that era. Smith wasn't just big, he was athletic enough to ward off double- and triple-teams. Complementing Smith and Webster was a host of talent. Senior middle guard Harold Lucas was a load at 6'2", 286 pounds. At the time, he was the heaviest player to ever play for Michigan State. Like Smith and Webster, linebacker Ron Goovert was named first-team All-Big Ten. "I feel that Ron was the best college linebacker in the country," Daugherty said in 1965. "I wouldn't have traded him for anyone." Junior linebacker Charlie "Big Dog"

Thornhill, junior defensive back Jim Summers, and senior cornerback Don Japinga added to the mayhem inflicted on opponents. Big Ten teams averaged just 34.6 rushing yards per game, and Michigan State outscored opponents 115-7 in the fourth quarter. Two opponents were shut out by the Spartans, and five other's scored only seven points or less. Michigan had -39 yards rushing while losing 24-7. Ohio State had -22 yards rushing (the worst total ever under Woody Hayes) in a 32-7 defeat. The Buckeyes didn't convert a first down rushing and resorted to throwing passes on all 29 of their offensive plays in the second half. Northwestern lost 49-7 while totaling seven yards rushing. Iowa gained one yard rushing in a 35-0 loss. Notre Dame totaled 12 yards of offense (24 passing and −12 rushing) in a 12-3 loss in South Bend that concluded the 1965 regular season. United Press International crowned Michigan State national champion after the regular season and the Associated Press had the Spartans No. 1 heading into the Rose Bowl, but UCLA pulled off a 14-12 win.

COLLEGE FOOTBALL HALL OF FAME INDUCTEES		
NAME	YEARS	INDUCTED
Biggie Munn, COACH	1947-53	1959
John Pingel, HB	1936-38	1968
Don Coleman, T	1949-51	1975
Charlie Bachman, COACH	1933-46	1978
Duffy Daugherty, COACH	1954-72	1984
George Webster, LB	1964-66	1987
Charles "Bubba" Smith, DE	1964-66	1988
Muddy Waters, COACH	1980-82	2000
Brad Van Pelt, S	1970-72	2001

BIGGEST GAME The frenzy over Michigan State's showdown against Notre Dame on Nov. 19, 1966, crackled with unprecedented intensity. The Poll Bowl between the No. 1 Fighting Irish and No. 2 Spartans was scheduled for regional broadcast by ABC, until the network received one lawsuit and 50,000 letters asking it to be shown nationally. The NCAA finally told ABC it could show the game nationally if the telecast was delayed in some areas, and the network advertised the matchup as "the greatest battle since Hector fought Achilles." The Spartans had been No. 1 until the previous week when they had to overcome an 8-3 deficit in the fourth quarter to beat Ohio State 11-8 in Columbus. Notre Dame defeated North Carolina 32-0 at home the same day and took over the top spot in the next poll. Both were ranked in the top two for five weeks leading up to their clash. "We're No. 1 and Notre Dame is No.1-A," Daugherty said before the "Game of the Century." Michigan State fans lined the railroad track and held signs reading, "Hail Mary, full of grace, Notre Dame's in second place," as the train carrying the Fighting Irish headed to East Lansing. A crowd of 80,011—more than 4,000 over capacity—paid $5 face-value for tickets and crammed into Spartan Stadium on a cold, overcast afternoon, with the temperature in the low 30s. Michigan State had issued 745 media credentials, the most ever for a college football game. The city ran out of rental cars. Notre Dame fullback Rocky Bleier wrote in his book *Fighting Back*,

that he was "entranced" and "almost dizzy" by the sight and sound of the frenzied crowd. "Nothing I ever experienced on a football field, before or since, has equaled it," wrote Bleier, who later won four Super Bowls with the Pittsburgh Steelers. The ferocity of play on the field matched the pre-game buildup off it. Michigan State defenders Bubba Smith and Charley Thornhill knocked Notre Dame quarterback Terry Hanratty out of the game with a separated shoulder midway through the first quarter. The Spartans went up 10-0 but the Fighting Irish eventually tied the game at 10-10 on the first play of the fourth quarter. Both defenses ruled from that point as the teams combined for only three first downs the rest of the game. Notre Dame coach Ara Parseghian ordered his offense to run out the clock in the final minutes on six consecutive rushing plays instead of risking a turnover. "At that stage, your strategy is dictated by the fact that you don't want to lose the game," Parseghian later said. "Interceptions almost cost Michigan State the game. We weren't going to give it away cheaply." Michigan State's defenders taunted their counterparts on the field as the clock ticked away in the final minute. Dan Jenkins of *Sports Illustrated* wrote that Notre Dame "tied one for the Gipper." The next Associated Press poll had Notre Dame No. 1, but the United Press International poll had Michigan State No. 1. Notre Dame beat USC 51-0 a week later to finish No. 1 in both polls. With no games left (due to a Big Ten rule forbidding consecutive visits to the Rose Bowl), the Spartans finished No. 2. In 2006, both Michigan State and Notre Dame players wore "Game of the Century" commemorative patches on their jerseys when the teams met for the 70th time overall and the 40th anniversary of the 1966 game.

BIGGEST UPSET Ohio State, 8–0 and ranked No. 1 in the polls since the preseason, jumped all over a Michigan State team that limped into Ohio Stadium with a 4–4 record on Nov. 7, 1998. The Buckeyes led 17-3 after one quarter, and were up 24-9 at the 9:51 mark of the third quarter after Buckeye safety Damon Moore returned an interception 73 yards for a touchdown. "I told them it was going to be a 15-round fight and we needed to be Rocky in that 15th round," said Michigan State coach Nick Saban, a former Ohio State assistant coach. The Spartans kept slugging and scored the game's final 19 points. They led 28-24 when Ohio State drove down to the Michigan State 15-yard line with 1:29 remaining to play. With all 93,595 in Ohio Stadium standing, the Spartans forced three incomplete passes. On fourth down,

a blitz forced Buckeye, QB Joe Germaine to make a quick throw toward receiver Dee Miller, but Renaldo Hill intercepted the pass at the goal line and Michigan State had pulled off an improbable victory. The Spartans held an Ohio State offense that was leading the Big Ten with an average of more than 500 yards to just 353 despite star defensive end Robaire Smith breaking his leg in the first quarter. His replacement, Julian Peterson, forced two fumbles. Michigan State scored 19 second-half points against a Buckeye defense that had allowed just 16 points in the second half of its first eight games. "These are the kind of games you dream about," said Spartans QB Bill Burke, a Warren, Ohio, native.

PRO FOOTBALL HALL OF FAME INDUCTEES		
NAME	YEARS	INDUCTED
Herb Adderley, CB	1961-72	1980
Joe DeLamielleure, G	1973-85	2003

HEARTBREAKER Michigan State had defeated the Fighting Irish seven times in the previous nine years leading up to their Sept. 23, 2006, matchup in Spartan Stadium. After their 44-41 overtime win at South Bend in 2005, Michigan State players planted a school flag near midfield, and Notre Dame hadn't forgotten it. Still, it looked as if Michigan State would easily improve to 4–0 on the season when it jumped ahead of the Fighting Irish 17-0 after one quarter, and later took a 37-21 advantage into the fourth. But the Spartan's offense, which had gained 260 total yards in the first half, sputtered. That put too much pressure on the defense, as did Notre Dame's senior quarterback Brady Quinn. Unshaken by a slow start, Quinn threw TD passes of 43 yards to Jeff Samardzija and 14 yards to Rhema McKnight to draw to 37-33 with 4:57 left in the game. Fighting Irish cornerback Terrail Lambert then picked off a pass by Spartan's QB Drew Stanton and returned it 27 yards for a TD. Notre Dame led for the first time, 40-37, with 2:53 remaining. Lambert clinched the comeback win with another interception of Stanton in the closing seconds. Stanton committed three turnovers, including a fumble, in the game's final six minutes. "We just made too many mistakes when it counted," Michigan State coach John L. Smith said. The game brought back bad memories of 1990, when Michigan State led No. 1 Notre Dame 19-7 after three quarter only to see the visiting Irish pull out a 20-19 win. Notre Dame scored the winning TD with 34 seconds left in that game, three plays after the "Immaculate Deflection" of a pass off the shoulder pads of cornerback Todd Murray was caught by Notre Dame wide receiver Adrian Jarrell at the Michigan State 2-yard line. The 2006 loss to Notre Dame sent the Spartans into a free fall that cost Smith his job. They lost three of their next four games and stood 4–5 with three games remaining when the school announced on Nov. 1 that Smith would not return the next season despite having

two years remaining on a six-year contract. Mark Dantonio was hired as his replacement on Nov. 27, 2006, following a 4–8 season. Smith went 22–26 in four seasons.

WILDEST FINISH The Michigan Wolverines were ranked No. 1 when the Spartans went to Ann Arbor in 1990. The two teams combined for four touchdowns in the game's final 6:03. Hyland Hickson gave Michigan State a 21-14 lead with a 26-yard TD run, but Desmond Howard tied the score by taking the ensuing kickoff back 95 yards. A nine-yard TD run by Tico Duckett gave the Spartans a 28-21 lead with 1:59 remaining. Michigan quarterback Elvis Grbac hit Derrick Alexander with a seven-yard TD pass with six seconds left, but a pass to Howard for the two-point conversion attempt fell incomplete, giving Michigan State a 28-27 victory.

BEST GOAL-LINE STAND Notre Dame trailed 21-17 but had fourth down on the Michigan State 3-yard line with less than one minute to play in 1968. Al Brenner then saved the Spartans two ways on one play. The defensive back covered split end Jim Seymour so closely near the corner of the end zone that QB Terry Hanratty decided to run. Brenner left Seymour, sprinted toward the line, and hit Hanratty at the 2-yard line, jarring the ball loose on the tackle. Notre Dame recovered at the 5, but Michigan State took over on downs to preserve its upset victory.

BEST COMEBACK Michigan State's only victory in its final nine games of John L. Smith's reign of error was one for the ages. On Oct. 21, 2006, the Spartans trailed 38-3 in the third quarter of a game at Northwestern between two teams trying to break four-game losing streaks. The game ended with Michigan State somehow ahead 41-38. Down 35 points, Michigan State QB Drew Stanton started the biggest comeback in NCAA history by tossing an 18-yard TD pass to Jehuu Caulcrick. Teammate A.J. Jimmerson then scored on a four-yard run to cut the deficit to 38-17. Northwestern seemed poised to score again, but Spartans linebacker Kaleb Thornhill—the son of Charlie Thornhill from the 1965 and 1966 Michigan State defenses—intercepted a C.J. Bacher pass in the end zone. Stanton ran for a 12-yard TD with 7:54 left in the fourth quarter to cut Northwestern's lead to 38-31, and then tied the game on Michigan State's next possession with a 9-yard TD pass to T.J. Williams with 3:43 left. Defensive back Travis Key intercepted Bach at the Northwestern 30 with 2:59, setting up a 28-yard, game-winning field goal by Brett Swenson with 13 seconds remaining. The Spartans had

outscored Northwestern 24-0 in the fourth quarter. "They believed in each other," Smith said of his players. "They continued to fight, they pulled together and deserved everything they got today." The previous largest comeback in Division I-A was 31 points. Maryland beat Miami 42-40 in 1984 and Ohio State beat Minnesota 41-37 in 1989. The historic win made Michigan State 4–4, but it wasn't enough to save Smith's job.

STADIUM Spartan Stadium, a state-funded replacement for Old College Field, had no name when it opened on Oct. 6, 1923, with a win against Lake Forest. Fans called it College Field or College Stadium or Spartan Stadium until 1935, when it officially became Macklin Field in honor of former Spartans coach John Macklin. Four expansions in 22 years increased the original capacity of 14,000 to 76,000 by 1957, and that year the concrete stadium on the Grand River's south shore became known as Spartan Stadium. Capacity dropped to 72,027 in 1994 because of the first of two renovations that decade. In October of 2001, Spartan Stadium was the site of a world-record crowd for an outdoor hockey game when 74,544 turned out to watch Michigan State play Michigan on ice. A $64 million expansion project was completed before the 2005 season and added 3,000 seats and 24 suites, bringing capacity to 75,005.

RIVAL Michigan State has had a long, legendary rivalry with Notre Dame, but even that heated series doesn't generate the animosity the Spartans feel toward their neighbors in Ann Arbor. The Michigan Wolverines have been detested since the series began in 1898 because of their dominance and their depiction of land-grant Michigan State as Moo U. The Spartans went 2–23–3 and were outscored 726-64 in their first 28 games against the Wolverines. Michigan won 119-0 in 1902. The Spartans didn't score a TD against the Wolverines from 1919 through 1932. Michigan traveled to East Lansing in 1924 for the first time in 10 years and didn't see need to return for 24 years. Biggie Munn's first game as Michigan State coach was a 55-0 road loss to the Wolverines in 1947. Before the game, Michigan coach Fritz Crisler greeted Munn by saying, "And what are you doing back in the state of Michigan?" After the humiliating defeat, the Michigan band played "Old MacDonald Had a Farm" and the Spartans found their locker room inches deep with overflowed toilet water. Munn was so mad he cried, vowed he'd recruit the state better and get revenge. From 1950 through 1969, Munn and Daugherty combined to go 14–4–2 against the Wolverines. Bo Schembechler answered by ushering in another age of Michigan dominance that continues today. Only in the 1950s and 1960s did Michigan State hold an advantage in the series record, and some later victories haven't been altogether

sweet. The Spartans won the 1978 game and tied the Wolverines for a share of the Big Ten title, but Michigan went to the Rose Bowl because Michigan State was on NCAA probation. The Spartans, however, will always have 1973, when Michigan tied Ohio State for the Big Ten title. League athletic directors were asked to name the conference's Rose Bowl representative. Michigan State cast the deciding vote, sending the Buckeyes to Pasadena and Schembechler into a fit of anger.

CONTROVERSY Bitterness in the Michigan rivalry is summed up by one second of dispute in 2001. His team trailing 24-20 and out of timeouts, Spartan QB Jeff Smoker took a snap with 17 seconds left in the fourth quarter and scrambled to the Wolverine 2-yard line. Smoker then spiked the ball. Michigan thought the game had ended, but the Spartan Stadium clock showed one second remaining. Awarded a final play, Smoker avoided a rush and threw an off-balance lob pass that T.J. Duckett caught in a crowded end zone. Fans swarmed the field to celebrate the Spartans' 26-24 victory over the No. 6-ranked Wolverines in a game that had seven lead changes. Michigan thought it had the game won before the disputed finish when Smoker threw an incompletion on fourth and 16 from the 50-yard line with less than two minutes remaining. But the Spartans were given a first down on the play when Wolverine cornerback Jeremy LeSueur was called for a personal foul for making contact with receiver Charles Rogers' facemask. "Our players deserve better," Michigan coach Lloyd Carr complained after the loss. For the Wolverines, the ending was too reminiscent of 1990, when Michigan State won 28-27. After that game, Big Ten supervisor of officials Dave Parry said referee John Nealon's crew failed to make a pass interference call against the Spartans on Michigan's failed two-point conversion pass attempt with seconds left in the game.

DUBIOUS DISTINCTION Soon after joining the Big Ten in 1949 (they would not be full members until 1953), rumors spread that Michigan State athletes were being paid by a slush fund known as the Spartan Foundation of Lansing, Mich. The Big Ten investigated the outside organization, found that $3,800 had been given to Michigan State athletes, and on Feb. 22, 1953, placed the Spartans on one-year probation. The NCAA followed with its own investigation and probation. The scandal came after the undefeated seasons of 1951 and 1952. The Big Ten voided the punishment before a year had passed because Michigan State ordered the end of the Spartan Foundation. More trouble came in 1975 when Ohio State coach Woody Hayes accused the Spartans of cheating. A year later, the NCAA put Michigan State on three years probation for 34 recruiting violations. The

scandal cost Denny Stolz his job as head coach, caused the firing of assistant coach Howard Weyers, and led to the early retirement of athletic director Burt Smith.

NICKNAME Michigan State players proudly called themselves Farmers or Fighting Farmers in the school's early years, although Aggies was the official nickname. The school sponsored a contest in 1925 to replace Aggies. Voters selected the Michigan Staters as the name, but *Lansing State Journal* sports editor George S. Alderton decided it was too cumbersome. He picked out Spartans from the list of entries, and newspapers popularized the name.

MASCOT A Michigan State student wears a 40-pound Sparty costume that resembles a Spartan warrior. Several versions of the costume have been used since Theta Xi fraternity created Sparty in 1955. Sigma Phi Epsilon updated his current look in 1984. For one season in 1909, the school used a live brown bear named Brewer's Bruin as its mascot.

UNIFORMS On April 11, 1899, the Athletic Association of the Michigan Agricultural College adopted the green monogram "to be worn only by athletes who subsequently take part in intercollegiate events." Chester L. Brewer popularized the use of green and white as school colors when he became the school's first full-time athletic director in 1903. In 1939, the Spartans wore four different colored jerseys (green, white, black, and red) and the freshman team wore blue.

QUIRKS He was named the nation's Outstanding Offensive End after his senior season in 1978. He finished his career as the Spartans' leader in receptions (112), reception yardage (2,347), average yards per reception (21.0), and touchdown catches (24). He was named All-America in 1978. But Kirk Gibson will always be best remembered by sports fans for his walk-off—actually, limp-off—home run

against Dennis Eckersley in Game 1 of the 1988 World Series … On the 1963 squad, guard Dan Underwood used to occasionally turn from the huddle and somersault into his position.

ALL-CENTENNIAL TEAM	

Selected from an 850-ballot reader poll conducted by the Lansing State Journal *in 1996.*

1954-72	Duffy Daugherty, coach

OFFENSE

1953-55	Buck Nystrom, OL
1955-57	Dan Currie, OL
1960-62	Dave Behrman, OL
1970-72	Joe DeLamielleure, OL
1985-88	Tony Mandarich, OL
1964-66	Gene Washington, WR
1975-78	Kirk Gibson, WR
1953-55	Earl Morrall, QB
1964-66	Clinton Jones, RB
1969-71	Eric Allen, RB
1984-87	Lorenzo White, RB
1978-81	Morten Andersen, PK
1993-96	Derrick Mason, KR

DEFENSE

1956-58	Sam Williams, DE
1964-66	Charles "Bubba" Smith, DE
1974-77	Larry Bethea, DL
1964-66	George Webster, LB
1976-79	Dan Bass, LB
1980-83	Carl Banks, LB
1986-89	Percy Snow, LB
1958-60	Herb Adderley, DB
1966-68	Allen Brenner, DB
1970-72	Brad Van Pelt, DB
1971-73	Bill Simpson, DB
1985-87	Greg Montgomery, P

PRE-BIG TEN ERA	
1933-35	Sid Wagner, L
1946-49	Ed Bagdon, L
1950-52	Frank Kush, L
1949-51	Don Coleman, L
1950-52	Dick Tamburo, L
1949-51	Bob Carey, E
1951-53	Don Dohoney, E
1936-38	John Pingel, B
1946-49	Lynn Chandnois, B
1948-50	Sonny Grandelius, B
1950-52	Don McAuliffe, B

LORE He was called The Flea because he was 5'9" and 161 pounds, but Eric Allen's ability belied his stature. He rushed for a then-NCAA-record 350 yards on Oct. 30, 1971, in a 43-10 victory at Purdue. His 29 carries included 4 touchdown runs of 24, 59, 30, and 25 yards. Allen had totaled 325 yards when Daugherty removed him from the game early in the fourth quarter. The coach had a message for his little tailback: "They tell me in the press box that you need just 23 yards to break the collegiate rushing record. You're going back and you're going to carry the ball on every play until you get it." Two carries later, Allen ran for a 25-yard score to break the NCAA mark of 347 yards set by Michigan's Ron Johnson. Allen broke 11 Michigan State records, four Big Ten records, and two NCAA records that day. Daugherty called it, "the greatest individual performance I've personally witnessed" … Sportswriters struggled to spell Kajzerkowski so they referred to him as Dave Kaiser. After he beat UCLA in the 1956 Rose Bowl, he was called Golden Toe. Kaiser had made only two career field goals when he attempted a 41-yarder with seven seconds remaining in a 14-14 game. He was practicing his kicking motion when holder Earl Morrall received the snap. Kaiser somehow launched his attempt, but the farsighted kicker never saw the ball go through the uprights. He had removed his contact lenses because they were irritating his eyes.

NUMBERS Smith, Webster, and tackle Don Coleman (No. 98) are the only Michigan State players to have their jersey number retired. However, jersey No. 46 was retired in 1969 to honor former Michigan State president John Hannah, who was instrumental in getting the Spartans

into the Big Ten during his 46 years of school service … Michigan State won the 1987 Big Ten title under George Perles, played in its first Rose Bowl in 22 years, and won it (20-17 over USC) for the first time in 32 years … Sherman Lewis had TD receptions of 88 and 87 yards, a TD run of 87 yards, an 85-yard run and an 84-yard punt return in 1963 … Dan Bass was credited with a school-record 32 tackles against Ohio State in 1979 and also had 24 tackles against Notre Dame. He is Michigan State's all-time career leader with 541 stops … Lorenzo White rushed for over 200 yards in four games in 1985 while setting the all-time NCAA rushing record for sophomores with 2,066 yards. That total led the nation and set the single-season Big Ten record. As a senior, he ran for a personal-best 292 yards on 56 carries in his final home game and ended his final year with 1,572 rushing yards. White finished fourth in the Heisman voting in both 1985 and 1987 … Andre Rison had 252 receiving yards and 3 TDs on nine receptions against Georgia in the 1989 Gator Bowl. He had a 50-yard reception on a third-and-46 play … Derrick Mason returned a kickoff 100 yards against Penn State in 1994 and also did it against LSU in the 1995 Independence Bowl … Michigan State rushed for nine TDs against Hawaii in 1948 … Larry Bethea finished 1977 with 16 sacks in 11 games … Offensive lineman Tony Mandarich was 6'6", 310 pounds and ran the 40-yard dash in 4.65 seconds as a senior in 1989 … Chester Brewer served three stints as coach from 1903 to 1919, and his teams shut out 49 opponents in 88 games … Michigan State joined the Big Ten in May 1949 but didn't begin conference play in football until four years later … Plaxico Burress had a school-record 13 receptions for 185 yards and 3 TDs against Florida in 2000. Three times he caught three TD passes in a game … Eleven Spartans were named All-Big Ten in 1966 … The 1961 defense still holds the school record for scoring defense, allowing just 5.6 points per game … Michigan State was co-Big Ten champions in 1978 with an offense that averaged 481.3 yards and 37.4 points … Dick Panin ran 88 yards for a TD on the second play of a 35-0 win over Notre Dame in 1951 … The Spartans went 54–9–2 in seven seasons under Biggie Munn, culminating in a 1954 Rose Bowl win over UCLA … Jim Crowley was one of the Four Horsemen at Notre Dame. He became Michigan State's head coach in 1929 and led the Spartans to four consecutive winning seasons before becoming the head coach at Fordham, where he developed the Seven Blocks of Granite … Lynn Chandnois, a two-way star from 1946 to 1949, set five school records as a halfback, including 31 touchdowns, 186 career points, and 2,093 rushing yards—a record that stood until Eric Allen broke it in 1971. Chandnois also intercepted 20 passes in his career … The biggest player on the offensive line of the 1952 national champions was center Jim Neal at 215 pounds … Drew Stanton threw for a school-record five TD passes to five different receivers in the 2005 Big Ten opener vs. Illinois. The Spartans totaled 705 yards of offense that day … Morten Andersen's 63-yard field goal against Ohio State in 1981 still ranks as the Big Ten record … Blake Ezor rushed for six touchdowns against Northwestern in 1989 … Gene Washington averaged 25 yards per reception in 1966 … It took officials 46 minutes after the game ended to declare Michigan State a 16-13 winner over No. 1-ranked Ohio State on Nov. 9, 1974, since game officials differed on whether Ohio State had scored on the frantic final play, in which the ball rolled through Buckeyes quarterback Cornelius Greene's legs but was picked up and run into the end zone by running back Brian Baschnagel. A majority of officials, and Big Ten Commissioner Wayne Duke, finally ruled that the clock had expired before the play began, sealing Ohio State's first regular-season loss in two years … Danny Pobojewski, a transfer from Michigan State, scored the only touchdown in Purdue's 6-0 upset in 1953 that ended Michigan State's 28-game winning streak.

QUOTE "The alumni are always with you, win or tie."
—Duffy Daugherty

MICHIGAN STATE ALL-TIME SCORES

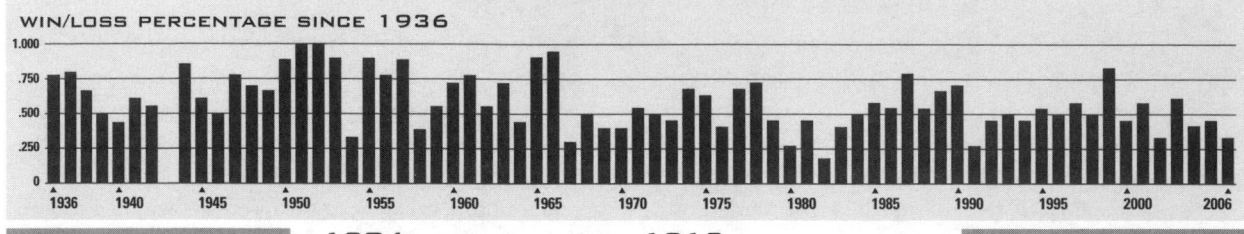

WIN/LOSS PERCENTAGE SINCE 1936

1936 1940 1945 1950 1955 1960 1965 1970 1975 1980 1985 1990 1995 2000 2006

NO HEAD COACH

1896 — 1-2-1

S26		Lansing High	10	0
O17		at Kalamazoo	0	24
O25	=	Alma	0	0
N11		Kalamazoo	16	18

HENRY KEEP
1897-1898 (.607)   8-5-1

1897 — 4-2-1

S25		Lansing High	28	0
O2	●	Olivet	26	6
O9		Kalamazoo	0	28
O16	=	at Olivet	18	18
O30	●	at Alma	30	16
N6	●	Alma	38	4
N25		at Notre Dame	6	34

1898 — 4-3-0

O8	●	Eastern Michigan	11	6
O12	●	at Michigan	0	39
O15		at Notre Dame	0	53
O20	●	Albion	62	6
O29	●	at Olivet	45	0
N19	●	Eastern Michigan	24	6
N24		at Kalamazoo	0	17

CHARLES O. BEMIES
1899-1900 (.318)   3-7-1

1899 — 2-4-1

S30		at Notre Dame	0	40
O7		at Detroit AC	6	16
O14		Kalamazoo	6	10
O21	=	at Alma	11	11
N11		at Ypsilanti	18	0
N25		at Olivet	17	18
N30		DePauw	23	6

1900 — 1-3-0

S29		Albion	0	23
O10	●	Adrian	45	0
O20		at Detroit AC	6	21
O27		Alma	0	23

GEORGE E. DENMAN
1901-02 (.441)   7-9-1

1901 — 3-4-1

S28		at Alma	5	6
O5	●	Hillsdale	22	0
O12	●	at Albion	11	0
O19		at Detroit AC	0	33
O26	●	Kalamazoo	42	0
N2	=	Albion	17	17
N16		at Kalamazoo	5	15
N28		Olivet	18	23

1902 — 4-5-0

S27		at Notre Dame	0	32
O4	●	Detroit	11	0
O8		at Michigan	0	119
O11	●	Hillsdale	35	0
O18	●	Michigan Freshmen	2	0
O25	●	DePauw	12	17
N1	●	at Olivet	6	11
N15		at Albion	22	11
N22		Alma	5	16

CHESTER L. BREWER
1903-10, '17, '19 (.699) 58-23-7

1903 — 6-1-1

O3		at Notre Dame	0	12
O10	●	at Alma	11	0
O14	●	Michigan JV	11	0
O17	●	Kalamazoo	11	0
O31	●	Detroit YMCA	51	6
N7	●	at Hillsdale	43	0
N14	=	Albion	6	6
N21	=	Olivet	45	0

1904 — 8-1-0

O1	●	Michigan Deaf School	47	0
O8	●	Ohio Northern	28	6
O15	●	Port Huron YMCA	29	0
O22		at Albion	0	4
O29	●	Hillsdale	104	0
N5	●	Michigan Freshmen	39	0
N12	●	at Olivet	35	6
N19		at Alma	40	0
N26		Kalamazoo	58	0

1905 — 9-2-0

S30	●	Michigan Deaf School	42	0
O3	●	Port Huron YMCA	43	0
O7		at Notre Dame	0	28
O14	●	Michigan Freshmen	24	0
O21	●	Olivet	30	0
O23	●	Hillsdale	18	0
O28	●	Armour Inst.	18	0
N4	●	at Kalamazoo	30	0
N11	●	Albion	46	10
N18		at Northwestern	11	37
N25	●	at Alma	18	0

1906 — 7-2-2

S29	●	Olivet	23	0
O6	●	Albion	37	0
O13	=	at Alma	0	0
O20	●	Kalamazoo	38	0
O27	●	DePauw	33	0
N3		at Notre Dame	0	5
N10	●	at Albion	5	0
N12	●	Alma	12	0
N17	●	at Hillsdale	35	9
N24		at Olivet	6	8
N29	=	at Detroit AC	6	6

1907 — 4-2-1

O3	●	Detroit	17	0
O5	●	Michigan Deaf School	40	0
O12		at Michigan	0	46
O26	●	Wabash	15	6
N16	●	Olivet	55	4
N23	=	at Alma	0	0
N28		at Detroit AC	0	4

1908 — 6-0-2

O10	=	Michigan	0	0
O10	●	Western Michigan	35	0
O17	●	Michigan Deaf School	51	0
O24	●	at DePaul	0	0
O31	●	Wabash	6	0
N7	●	at Olivet	46	2
N21	●	Saginaw Navy	30	6
N26	●	at Detroit AC	37	14

1909 — 8-1-0

O7	●	Detroit	27	0
O9	●	Alma	34	0
O16	●	Wabash	28	0
O23		at Notre Dame	0	17
O30	●	at Culver	29	0
N6	●	DePaul	51	0
N10	●	Marquette	10	0
N13	●	Olivet	20	0
N25	●	at Detroit AC	34	0

1910 — 6-1-0

O6	●	Detroit AC	35	0
O8	●	Alma	11	0
O15		at Michigan	3	6
O22	●	Lake Forest	37	0
O29	●	Notre Dame	17	0
N5	●	at Marquette	3	2
N19	●	Olivet	62	0

JOHN F. MACKLIN
1911-15 (.853)   29-5

1911 — 5-1-0

O7	●	Alma	12	0
O14		Michigan	3	15
O28	●	Olivet	29	3
N4	●	at DePauw	6	0
N11	●	Mt. Union	26	6
N30	●	Wabash	17	5

1912 — 7-1-0

O5	●	Alma	14	3
O12		at Michigan	7	55
O19	●	Olivet	52	0
O26	●	DePauw	58	0
N2	●	Ohio Wesleyan	46	0
N9	●	Mt. Union	61	20
N16	●	Wabash	24	0
N28		at Ohio State	35	20

1913 — 7-0-0

O4	●	Olivet	26	0
O11	●	Alma	57	0
O18	●	Michigan	12	7
O25	●	at Wisconsin	12	7
N1	●	Akron	41	0
N8	●	Mt. Union	13	7
N15	●	South Dakota	19	7

1914 — 5-2-0

O3	●	Olivet	26	7
O10	●	Alma	60	0
O17		Michigan	0	3
O24		at Nebraska	0	24
O31	●	Akron	75	6
N7	●	Mt. Union	21	14
N13		at Penn State	6	3

1915 — 5-1-0

O2	●	Olivet	34	0
O9	●	Alma	77	12
O16	●	Carroll	56	0
O23		at Michigan	24	0
O30		Oregon State	0	20
N6	●	Marquette	68	6

FRANK SOMMERS
1916 (.643)   4-2-1

1916 — 4-2-1

S30	●	Olivet	40	0
O7	●	Carroll	20	0
O14	●	at Alma	33	0
O21		at Michigan	0	9
O28	●	North Dakota St.	30	0
N4	=	at South Dakota	3	3
N18		Notre Dame	0	14

CHESTER L. BREWER

1917 — 0-9-0

O6		Alma	7	14
O13		Kalamazoo	3	7
O20		at Michigan	0	27
O27		Detroit	0	14
N3		Western Michigan	0	14
N10		at Northwestern	6	39
N17		at Notre Dame	0	23
N24		Syracuse	7	21
N29		Camp MacArthur	0	20

GEORGE E. GAUTHIER
1918 (.571)   4-3

1918 — 4-3-0

O5	●	Albion	21	6
O12	●	Hillsdale	66	6
N2	●	Western Michigan	16	7
N9		Purdue	6	14
N16	●	Notre Dame	13	7
N23		at Michigan	6	21
N28		at Wisconsin	6	7

CHESTER L. BREWER

1919 — 4-4-1

O4	●	Albion	14	13
O8	●	Alma	46	6
O11	●	Western Michigan	18	21
O18		at Michigan	0	26
O25	●	DePauw	27	0
N1		at Purdue	7	13
N8		South Dakota	13	0
N15		at Notre Dame	0	13
N27	=	Wabash	7	7

GEORGE "POTSY" CLARK
1920 (.400)   4-6

1920 — 4-6-0

S25		Kalamazoo	2	21
O2	●	Albion	16	0
O6	●	Alma	48	0
O9		at Wisconsin	0	27
O16		at Michigan	0	35
O23		Marietta	7	23
O30	●	Olivet	109	0
N13	●	Chicago YMCA	81	0
N20		at Nebraska	7	35
N25		Notre Dame	0	25

ALBERT M. BARRON
1921-22 (.389)   6-10-2

1921 — 3-5-0

O1	●	Alma	28	0
O8	●	Albion	7	24
O15		at Michigan	0	30
O22	●	Western Michigan	17	14
O27		at Marquette	0	7
N5	●	South Dakota	14	0
N12		at Butler	2	3
N24		at Notre Dame	0	48

1922 — 3-5-2

S30	●	Alma	33	0
O7	=	Albion	7	7
O14		at Wabash	0	26
O21	●	South Dakota	7	0
O28		at Indiana	6	14
N4		at Michigan	0	63
N11		Ohio Wesleyan	6	9
N18		at Creighton	0	9
N25	●	Massachusetts St.	45	0
N30	=	at St. Louis	7	7

RALPH H. YOUNG
1923-27 (.451)   18-22-1

1923 — 3-5-0

S29		at Chicago	0	34
O6	●	Lake Forest	21	6
O13		at Wisconsin	0	21
O20	●	Albion	13	0
O27		at Michigan	0	37
N3		Ohio Wesleyan	14	19
N10		Creighton	7	27
N17	●	at Detroit	2	0

1924 — 5-3-0

S26	●	North Central	59	0
O4	●	Olivet	54	3
O11		Michigan	0	7
O17	●	Chicago YMCA	34	3
O25		at Northwestern	9	13
N1	●	Lake Forest	42	13
N8		at St. Louis	3	9
N15	●	South Dakota St.	9	0

1925 3-5-0

S26	●	Adrian	16	0
O3		at Michigan	0	39
O10		Lake Forest	0	6
O17	●	Centre	15	13
O24		at Penn State	6	13
N1		Colgate	0	14
N7	●	Toledo	58	0
N14		at Wisconsin	10	21

1926 3-4-1

S26	●	Adrian	16	0
O2	●	Kalamazoo	9	0
O9		at Michigan	3	55
O16		at Cornell	14	24
O23	=	Lake Forest	0	0
O30		at Colgate	6	38
N6	●	Centre	42	14
N20		Haskell	7	40

1927 4-5-0

S24	●	Kalamazoo	12	6
O1	●	Ohio U.	27	0
O8		at Michigan	0	21
O15		at Cornell Coll.	13	19
O29		Detroit	7	24
N5		at Indiana	7	33
N11	●	Albion	20	6
N19	●	Butler	25	0
D3		at North Carolina St.	0	19

HARRY G. KIPKE
1928 (.438) 3-4-1

1928 3-4-1

S29	●	Kalamazoo	103	0
O6		Albion	0	2
O13	●	Chicago YMCA	37	0
O20		Colgate	0	16
N3	=	Mississippi State	6	6
N10		at Detroit	0	39
N17		at Michigan	0	3
N24	●	North Carolina St.	7	0

JAMES H. CROWLEY
1929-32 (.712) 22-8-3

1929 5-3-0

S28	●	Alma	59	6
O5		at Michigan	0	17
O12		at Colgate	0	31
O19	●	Adrian	74	0
O26	●	North Carolina St.	40	6
N2	●	Case	38	0
N9	●	Mississippi State [JAM]	33	19
N16		Detroit	0	25

1930 5-1-2

S27	●	Alma	28	0
O4	=	at Michigan	0	0
O11	●	Cincinnati	32	0
O18	●	Colgate	14	7
O25	●	Case	45	0
O31		at Georgetown	13	14
N8	●	North Dakota St.	19	11
N22	=	Detroit	0	0

1931 5-3-1

S26	●	Alma	74	0
O3	●	Cornell Coll.	47	0
O10		at Army	7	20
O17	●	Illinois Wesleyan	34	6
O24	●	Georgetown	6	0
O31		Syracuse	10	15
N7	●	Ripon	100	0
N14	=	at Michigan	0	0
N21		at Detroit	13	20

1932 7-1-0

S24	●	Alma	93	0
O1		at Michigan	0	26
O8	●	Grinnell	27	6
O15	●	Illinois Wesleyan	27	0
O22	●	Fordham [NYC]	19	13
O29	●	at Syracuse	27	13
N5	●	South Dakota	20	6
N19	●	Detroit	7	0

CHARLES W. BACHMAN
1933-46 (.658) 70-34-10

1933 4-2-2

S30	●	Grinnell	14	0
O7		at Michigan	6	20
O14	●	Illinois Wesleyan	20	12
O21	●	at Marquette	6	0
O28	●	Syracuse	27	3
N4	=	Kansas State	0	0
N11	=	Carnegie Tech	0	0
N25		at Detroit	0	14

1934 8-1-0

S29	●	Grinnell	33	20
O6	●	at Michigan	16	0
O13	●	Carnegie Tech	13	0
O20	●	at Manhattan	39	0
N3	●	Marquette	13	7
N10		at Syracuse	0	10
N17	●	Detroit	7	6
N24	●	at Kansas	6	0
D8	●	Texas A&M [SA]	26	13

1935 6-2-0

S28	●	Grinnell	41	0
O5	●	at Michigan	25	6
O12	●	Kansas	42	0
O19		at Boston College	6	18
O26	●	Washington, Mo.	47	13
N2	●	at Temple	12	7
N9		Marquette	7	13
N16	●	at Loyola Marymount	27	0

1936 6-1-2

S26	●	Wayne St.	27	0
O3	●	at Michigan	21	7
O10	●	at Carnegie Tech	7	0
O17	●	Missouri	13	0
O24		Marquette	7	13
O31	=	at Boston College	13	13
N7	=	at Temple	7	7
N14	●	at Kansas	41	0
N21	●	Arizona	7	0

1937 8-2-0

S25	●	Wayne St.	19	0
O2	●	at Michigan	19	14
O9		Manhattan [BKLN]	0	3
O16	●	at Missouri	2	0
O23	●	Marquette	21	7
O30	●	Kansas	16	0
N6	●	at Temple	13	6
N13	●	Carnegie Tech	13	6
N27	●	at San Francisco	14	0
		ORANGE BOWL		
J1		Auburn	0	6

1938 6-3-0

S24	●	Wayne St.	34	6
O1		at Michigan	0	14
O8	●	Illinois Wesleyan	18	0
O15	●	at West Virginia	26	0
O22	●	Syracuse	19	12
O29		Santa Clara	6	7
N5		at Missouri	0	6
N12	●	at Marquette	20	14
N19	●	Temple	10	0

1939 4-4-1

S30	●	Wayne St.	16	0
O7		at Michigan	13	26
O14		Marquette	14	17
O21		at Purdue	7	20
O28	●	Illinois Wesleyan	13	6
N4	●	at Syracuse	14	3
N11		at Santa Clara	0	6
N18	=	Indiana	7	7
N25	●	Temple	18	7

1940 3-4-1

O5		at Michigan	14	21
O12	●	Purdue	20	7
O18		at Temple	19	21
O25	=	Santa Clara	0	0
N2	●	Kansas State	32	0
N9		at Indiana	0	20
N16		at Marquette	6	7
N23	●	West Virginia	17	0

1941 5-3-1

S27		at Michigan	7	19
O11	●	Marquette	13	7
O18		at Santa Clara	0	7
O25	●	Wayne St.	39	6
N1		Missouri	0	19
N8	=	at Purdue	0	0
N15	●	Temple	46	0
N22	●	Ohio Wesleyan	31	7
N29	●	at West Virginia	14	12

1942 4-3-2

O3		at Michigan	0	20
O10	●	Waynes St.	46	6
O17		Marquette	7	28
O24	●	Great Lakes NAS	14	0
O31	=	at Temple	7	7
N7		Washington State [SPO]	13	25
N14	●	Purdue	19	6
N21	●	West Virginia	7	0
N28	=	Oregon State	7	7

1943

NO TEAM WWII

1944 6-1-0

S30	●	Scranton	40	12
O7	●	at Kentucky	2	0
O14	●	Kansas State	45	6
O21	●	at Maryland	8	0
O27	●	at Wayne St.	32	0
N4		at Missouri	7	13
N11	●	Maryland	33	0

1945 5-3-1

S29		at Michigan	0	40
O6	●	Kentucky	7	6
O13	●	at Pittsburgh	12	7
O20	●	Waynes St.	27	7
O27	=	Marquette	13	13
N3	●	Missouri	14	7
N10		Great Lakes NAS	7	27
N17	●	Penn State	33	0
N23		at Miami, Fla.	7	21

1946 5-5-0

S28	●	Wayne St.	42	0
O5		Boston College	20	34
O12		Mississippi State	0	6
O19	●	at Penn State	19	16
O26		Cincinnati	7	18
N2		at Kentucky	14	39
N9		at Michigan	7	55
N16	●	Marquette	20	0
N23	●	Maryland	26	14
N30	●	Washington State	26	20

CLARENCE "BIGGIE" MUNN
1947-53 (.846) 54-9-2

1947 7-2-0

S27		at Michigan	0	55
O4	●	Mississippi State	7	0
O11	●	at Washington State	21	7
O18	●	Iowa State	20	0
O25		Kentucky	6	7
N1	●	Marquette	13	7
N8	●	Santa Clara	28	0
N15	●	at Temple	14	6
N29	●	at Hawaii	58	19

1948 6-2-2

S25		Michigan	7	13
O2	●	Hawaii	68	21
O9		at Notre Dame	7	26
O16	●	Arizona	61	7
O23	=	at Penn State	14	14
O30	●	at Oregon State	46	21
N6	●	Marquette	47	0
N13	●	at Iowa State	48	7
N20	●	Washington State	40	0
N27	=	at Santa Clara	21	21

1949 6-3-0

S24		at Michigan	3	7
O1	●	Marquette	48	7
O8	●	Maryland	14	7
O15	●	William & Mary	42	13
O22	●	Penn State	24	0
O29	●	Temple	62	14
N5		Notre Dame	21	34
N12		Oregon State [PORT]	20	25
N19	●	at Arizona	75	0

1950 8-1-0

S23	●	Oregon State	38	13
S30	●	at Michigan	14	7
O7		Maryland	7	34
O14	●	William & Mary	33	14
O21	●	Marquette	34	6
O28	●	at Notre Dame	36	33
N4	●	Indiana	35	0
N11	●	Minnesota	27	0
N18	●	at Pittsburgh	19	0

1951 9-0-0

S22	●	Oregon State	6	0
S29	●	at Michigan	25	0
O6	●	at Ohio State	24	20
O13	●	Marquette	20	14
O20	●	at Penn State	32	21
O27	●	Pittsburgh	53	26
N10	●	Notre Dame	35	0
N17	●	at Indiana	30	26
N24	●	Colorado	45	7

1952 9-0-0

S27	●	at Michigan	27	13
O4	●	Oregon State [PORT]	17	14
O11	●	Texas A&M	48	6
O18	●	Syracuse	48	7
O25	●	Penn State	34	7
N1	●	at Purdue	14	7
N8	●	at Indiana	41	14
N15	●	Notre Dame	21	3
N22	●	Marquette	62	13

1953-PRESENT
BIG 10

1953 9-1-0 (5-1-0)

S26	● │	at Iowa	21	7
O3	● │	at Minnesota	21	0
O10	●	TCU	26	19
O17	● │	Indiana	47	18
O24	│	at Purdue	0	6
O31	●	Oregon State	34	6
N7	● │	at Ohio State	28	13
N14	● │	Michigan	14	6
N21	●	Marquette	21	15
		ROSE BOWL		
J1	●	UCLA	28	20

HUGH DUFFY DAUGHERTY
1954-72 (.609) 109-69-5

1954 3-6-0 (1-5-0)

S25	│	at Iowa	10	14
O2	│	Wisconsin	0	6
O9	● │	at Indiana	21	14
O16		at Notre Dame	19	20
O23	│	Purdue	13	27
O30	│	at Minnesota	13	19
N6	●	Washington State	54	6
N13	│	at Michigan	7	33
N20	●	Marquette	40	10

1955 9-1-0 (5-1-0)

S24	● │	at Indiana	20	13
O1	│	at Michigan	7	14
O8	●	Stanford	38	14
O15	●	Notre Dame	21	7
O22	● │	Illinois	21	7
O29	● │	at Wisconsin	27	0
N5	● │	at Purdue	27	0
N12	● │	Minnesota	42	14
N19	●	Marquette	33	0
		ROSE BOWL		
J2	●	UCLA	17	14

1956 7-2-0 (4-2-0)

S29	●	at Stanford	21	7
O6	● │	at Michigan	9	0
O13	● │	Indiana	53	6
O20	●	at Notre Dame	47	14
O27	│	at Illinois	13	20
N3	● │	Wisconsin	33	0
N10	● │	Purdue	12	9
N17	│	at Minnesota	13	14
N24	●	Kansas State	38	17

1957 8-1-0 (5-1-0)

S28	● │	Indiana	54	0
O5	●	at California	19	0
O12	● │	at Michigan	35	6
O19	│	Purdue	13	20
O26	● │	Illinois	19	14
N2	● │	at Wisconsin	21	7
N9	●	Notre Dame	34	6
N16	● │	Minnesota	42	13
N23	●	Kansas State	27	9

1958 3-5-1 (0-5-1)

S27	●	California	32	12
O4	= │	Michigan	12	12
O11	●	Pittsburgh	22	8
O18	│	at Purdue	6	14
O25	│	at Illinois	0	16
N1	│	Wisconsin	7	9
N8	│	at Indiana	0	6
N15	│	at Minnesota	12	39
N22	●	Kansas State	26	7

1959 5-4-0 (4-2-0)

S26		Texas A&M	7	9
O3	● │	at Michigan	34	8
O10	│	at Iowa	8	37
O17	●	Notre Dame	19	0
O24	● │	Indiana	14	6
O31	│	at Ohio State	24	30
N7	● │	Purdue	15	0
N14	● │	Northwestern	15	10
N20		at Miami, Fla.	13	18

1960 — 6-2-1 (4-2-0)

S24	=		at Pittsburgh	7	7
O1	●	│	Michigan	24	17
O8		│	Iowa	15	27
O15	●		at Notre Dame	21	0
O22	●	│	at Indiana	35	0
O29		│	Ohio State	10	21
N5	●	│	at Purdue	17	13
N12	●	│	at Northwestern	21	18
N19	●		Detroit	43	15

1961 — 7-2-0 (5-2-0)

S30	●	│	at Wisconsin	20	0
O7	●		Stanford	31	3
O14	●	│	at Michigan	28	0
O21	●		Notre Dame	17	7
O28	●	│	Indiana	35	0
N4		│	at Minnesota	0	13
N11		│	at Purdue	6	7
N18	●	│	Northwestern	21	13
N25	●	│	Illinois	34	7

1962 — 5-4-0 (3-3-0)

S29			at Stanford	13	16
O6	●		North Carolina	38	6
O13	●	│	Michigan	28	0
O20	●		at Notre Dame	31	7
O27	●	│	at Indiana	26	8
N3		│	Minnesota	7	28
N10		│	Purdue	9	17
N17	●	│	at Northwestern	31	7
N24		│	at Illinois	6	7

1963 — 6-2-1 (4-1-1)

S28	●		North Carolina	31	0
O4			at USC	10	13
O12	=	│	at Michigan	7	7
O19	●	│	Indiana	20	3
O26	●	│	at Northwestern	15	7
N2	●	│	Wisconsin	30	13
N9	●	│	at Purdue	23	0
N16	●		Notre Dame	12	7
N28		│	Illinois	0	13

1964 — 4-5-0 (3-3-0)

S26			at North Carolina	15	21
O3	●		USC	17	7
O10		│	Michigan	10	17
O17		│	at Indiana	20	27
O24	●	│	Northwestern	24	6
O31	●	│	at Wisconsin	22	6
N7	●	│	Purdue	21	7
N14			at Notre Dame	7	34
N21		│	at Illinois	0	16

1965 — 10-1-0 (7-0-0)

S18	●		UCLA	13	3
S25	●		at Penn State	23	0
O2	●	│	Illinois	22	12
O9	●	│	at Michigan	24	7
O16	●	│	Ohio State	32	7
O23	●	│	at Purdue	14	10
O30	●	│	Northwestern	49	7
N6	●	│	at Iowa	35	0
N13	●	│	Indiana	27	13
N20	●		at Notre Dame	12	3
			ROSE BOWL		
J1			UCLA	12	14

1966 — 9-0-1 (7-0-0)

S17	●		North Carolina St.	28	10
S24	●		Penn State	42	8
O1	●	│	at Illinois	26	10
O8	●	│	Michigan	20	7
O15	●	│	at Ohio State	11	8
O22	●	│	Purdue	41	20
O29	●	│	at Northwestern	22	0
N5	●	│	Iowa	56	7
N12	●	│	at Indiana	37	19
N19	=		Notre Dame	10	10

1967 — 3-7-0 (3-4-0)

S23			Houston	7	37
S30			USC	17	21
O7	●	│	Wisconsin	35	7
O14	●	│	at Michigan	34	0
O21		│	at Minnesota	0	21
O28			at Notre Dame	12	24
N4		│	Ohio State	7	21
N11		│	Indiana	13	14
N18		│	at Purdue	7	21
N25	●	│	Northwestern	41	27

1968 — 5-5-0 (2-5-0)

S21	●		Syracuse	14	10
S28	●		Baylor	28	10
O5	●	│	at Wisconsin	39	0
O12		│	at Michigan	14	28
O19		│	Minnesota	13	14
O26	●		Notre Dame	21	17
N2		│	at Ohio State	20	25
N9		│	Indiana	22	24
N16		│	Purdue	0	9
N23	●	│	at Northwestern	31	14

1969 — 4-6-0 (2-5-0)

S20	●		Washington	27	11
S27	●		SMU	23	15
O4			at Notre Dame	28	42
O11		│	at Ohio State	21	54
O18	●	│	Michigan	23	12
O25		│	at Iowa	18	19
N1		│	Indiana	0	16
N8		│	at Purdue	13	41
N15		│	Minnesota	10	14
N22	●	│	at Northwestern	39	7

1970 — 4-6-0 (3-4-0)

S19			at Washington	16	42
S26	●		Washington State	28	14
O3			Notre Dame	0	29
O10		│	Ohio State	0	29
O17		│	at Michigan	20	34
O24	●	│	Iowa	37	0
O31	●	│	at Indiana	32	7
N7	●	│	Purdue	24	14
N14		│	at Minnesota	13	23
N21		│	Northwestern	20	23

1971 — 6-5-0 (5-3-0)

S11	●	│	Illinois	10	0
S18			at Georgia Tech	0	10
S25	●		Oregon State	31	14
O2			at Notre Dame	2	14
O9		│	Michigan	13	24
O16		│	at Wisconsin	28	31
O23	●	│	Iowa	34	3
O30	●	│	at Purdue	43	10
N6	●	│	at Ohio State	17	10
N13	●	│	Minnesota	40	25
N20		│	at Northwestern	7	28

1972 — 5-5-1 (5-2-1)

S16	●	│	at Illinois	24	0
S23			Georgia Tech	16	21
S30			at USC	6	51
O7			Notre Dame	0	16
O14		│	at Michigan	0	10
O21	●	│	Wisconsin	31	0
O28	=	│	at Iowa	6	6
N4	●	│	Purdue	22	12
N11	●	│	Ohio State	19	12
N18		│	at Minnesota	10	14
N25	●	│	Northwestern	24	14

DENNIS E. STOLZ
1973-75 (.591) 19-13-1

1973 — 5-6-0 (4-4-0)

S15		│	at Northwestern	10	14
S22	●		at Syracuse	14	8
S29			UCLA	21	34
O6			at Notre Dame	10	14
O13		│	Michigan	0	31
O20		│	Illinois	3	6
O27	●	│	at Purdue	10	7
N3	●	│	Wisconsin	21	0
N10		│	at Ohio State	0	35
N17	●	│	Indiana	10	9
N24	●	│	at Iowa	15	6

1974 — 7-3-1 (6-1-1)

S14	●	│	Northwestern	41	7
S21	●		Syracuse	19	0
S28			at UCLA	14	56
O5			Notre Dame	14	19
O12		│	at Michigan	7	21
O19	=	│	at Illinois	21	21
O26	●	│	Purdue	31	7
N2	●	│	at Wisconsin	28	21
N9	●	│	Ohio State	16	13
N16	●	│	at Indiana	19	10
N23	●	│	Iowa	60	21

1975 — 7-4-0 (4-4-0)

S13		│	Ohio State	0	21
S20	●		Miami (Ohio)	14	13
S27	●		North Carolina St.	37	15
O4	●		at Notre Dame	10	3
O11		│	Michigan	6	16
O18	●	│	at Minnesota	38	15
O25		│	Illinois	19	21
N1		│	at Purdue	10	20
N8	●	│	at Indiana	14	6
N15	●	│	Northwestern	47	14
N22	●	│	at Iowa	27	23

DARRYL D. ROGERS
1976-79 (.568) 24-18-2

1976 — 4-6-1 (3-5-0)

S11		│	at Ohio State	21	49
S18	●		Wyoming	21	10
S25	=		at North Carolina St.	31	31
O2			Notre Dame	6	24
O9		│	at Michigan	10	42
O16		│	Minnesota	10	14
O23	●	│	at Illinois	31	23
O30	●	│	Purdue	45	13
N6	●	│	Indiana	23	0
N13		│	at Northwestern	21	42
N20		│	Iowa	17	30

1977 — 7-3-1 (6-1-1)

S10	●	│	Purdue	19	14
S17			Washington State	21	23
S24	●		Wyoming	34	16
O1			at Notre Dame	6	16
O8		│	Michigan	14	24
O15	=	│	at Indiana	13	13
O22	●	│	at Wisconsin	9	7
O29	●	│	Illinois	49	20
N5	●	│	at Minnesota	29	10
N11	●	│	Northwestern	44	3
N19	●	│	at Iowa	22	16

1978 — 8-3-0 (7-1-0)

S16		│	at Purdue	14	21
S23	●		Syracuse	49	21
S29			at USC	9	30
O7			Notre Dame	25	29
O14	●	│	at Michigan	24	15
O21	●	│	Indiana	49	14
O28	●	│	Wisconsin	55	2
N4	●	│	at Illinois	59	19
N11	●	│	Minnesota	33	9
N18	●	│	at Northwestern	52	3
N25	●	│	Iowa	42	7

1979 — 5-6-0 (3-5-0)

S8	●	│	Illinois	33	16
S15	●		Oregon	41	17
S22	●		Miami (Ohio)	24	21
S29			at Notre Dame	3	27
O6		│	Michigan	7	21
O13		│	at Wisconsin	29	38
O20		│	Purdue	7	14
O27		│	at Ohio State	0	42
N3	●	│	at Northwestern	42	7
N10	●	│	Minnesota	31	17
N17		│	at Iowa	23	33

FRANK "MUDDY" WATERS
1980-82 (.303) 10-23

1980 — 3-8-0 (2-6-0)

S13		│	at Illinois	17	20
S20			at Oregon	7	35
S27	●		Western Michigan	33	7
O4			Notre Dame	21	26
O11		│	at Michigan	23	27
O18		│	Wisconsin	7	17
O25		│	at Purdue	25	36
N1		│	Ohio State	16	48
N8	●	│	Northwestern	42	10
N15	●	│	at Minnesota	30	12
N22		│	Iowa	0	41

1981 — 5-6-0 (4-5-0)

S12		│	Illinois	17	27
S19		│	at Ohio State	13	27
S26	●		Bowling Green	10	7
O3			at Notre Dame	7	20
O10		│	Michigan	20	38
O17	●	│	Wisconsin	33	14
O24		│	at Purdue	26	27
O31	●	│	Indiana	26	3
N7	●	│	at Northwestern	61	14
N14	●	│	Minnesota	43	36
N21		│	at Iowa	7	36

1982 — 2-9-0 (2-7-0)

S11		│	at Illinois	16	23
S18		│	Ohio State	10	31
S25			at Miami, Fla.	22	25
O2			Notre Dame	3	11
O9		│	at Michigan	17	31
O16		│	at Wisconsin	23	24
O23		│	Purdue	21	24
O30	●	│	at Indiana	22	14
N6		│	Northwestern	24	28
N13	●	│	at Minnesota	26	7
N20		│	Iowa	18	24

GEORGE J. PERLES
1983-94 (.540) 73-62-4

1983 — 4-6-1 (2-6-1)

S10	●		Colorado	23	17
S17	●		at Notre Dame	28	23
S24		│	Illinois	10	20
O1	=	│	at Purdue	29	29
O8		│	Michigan	0	42
O15		│	at Indiana	12	24
O22		│	at Ohio State	11	21
O29	●	│	Minnesota	34	10
N5	●	│	at Northwestern	9	3
N12		│	Iowa	6	12
N19		│	at Wisconsin	0	32

1984 — 6-6-0 (5-4-0)

S8	●		at Colorado	24	21
S15			Notre Dame	20	24
S22		│	at Illinois	7	40
S29		│	Purdue	10	13
O6	●	│	at Michigan	19	7
O13	●	│	Indiana	13	6
O20		│	Ohio State	20	23
O27	●	│	at Minnesota	20	13
N3	●	│	Northwestern	27	10
N10	●	│	at Iowa	17	16
N17		│	Wisconsin	10	20
			CHERRY BOWL		
D22			Army	6	10

1985 — 7-5-0 (5-3-0)

S14	●		Arizona State	12	3
S21			at Notre Dame	10	27
S28	●		Western Michigan	7	3
O5		│	at Iowa	31	35
O12		│	Michigan	0	31
O19		│	Illinois	17	30
O26	●	│	at Purdue	28	24
N2	●	│	Minnesota	31	26
N9	●	│	at Indiana	35	16
N16	●	│	Northwestern	32	0
N23	●	│	at Wisconsin	41	7
			HALL OF FAME CLASSIC		
D31			Georgia Tech	14	17

1986 — 6-5-0 (4-4-0)

S13			at Arizona State	17	20
S20	●		Notre Dame	20	15
S27	●		Western Michigan	45	10
O4		│	Iowa	21	24
O11		│	at Michigan	6	27
O18	●	│	at Illinois	29	21
O25	●	│	Purdue	37	3
N1	●	│	at Minnesota	52	23
N8		│	Indiana	14	17
N15		│	at Northwestern	21	24
N22	●	│	Wisconsin	23	13

1987 — 9-2-1 (7-0-1)

S7	●		USC	27	13
S19			at Notre Dame	8	31
S26			Florida State	3	31
O3	●	│	at Iowa	19	14
O10	●	│	Michigan	17	11
O17	●	│	at Northwestern	38	0
O24	=	│	Illinois	14	14
O31	●	│	at Ohio State	13	7
N7	●	│	Purdue	45	3
N14	●	│	Indiana	27	3
N21	●	│	at Wisconsin	30	9
			ROSE BOWL		
J1	●		USC	20	17

1988 — 6-5-1 (6-1-1)

S10			Rutgers	13	17
S17			Notre Dame	3	20
S24			at Florida State	7	30
O1	=	│	Iowa	10	10
O8		│	at Michigan	3	17
O15	●	│	Northwestern	36	3
O22	●	│	at Illinois	28	21
O29	●	│	Ohio State	20	10
N5	●	│	at Purdue	48	3
N12	●	│	at Indiana	38	12
N19	●	│	Wisconsin	36	0
			GATOR BOWL		
J1			Georgia	27	34

1989 — 8-4-0 (6-2-0)

S16	•	Miami (Ohio)	49	0
S23		at Notre Dame	13	21
S30		Miami, Fla.	20	26
O7	•	at Iowa	17	14
O14		Michigan	7	10
O21	•	Illinois	10	14
O28	•	at Purdue	28	21
N4	•	at Indiana	51	20
N11	•	Minnesota	21	7
N18	•	Northwestern	76	14
N25	•	at Wisconsin	31	3
ALOHA BOWL				
D25	•	Hawaii	33	13

1990 — 8-3-1 (6-2-0)

S15	=	at Syracuse	23	23
S22		Notre Dame	19	20
S29	•	Rutgers *ERUT*	34	10
O6		Iowa	7	12
O13	•	at Michigan	28	27
O20		at Illinois	13	15
O27	•	Purdue	55	33
N3	•	Indiana	45	20
N10	•	at Minnesota	28	16
N17	•	at Northwestern	29	22
N24		Wisconsin	14	9
SUN BOWL				
D31	•	USC	17	16

1991 — 3-8-0 (3-5-0)

S14		Central Michigan	3	20
S21		at Notre Dame	10	49
S28		Rutgers	7	14
O5		at Indiana	0	31
O12		Michigan	28	45
O19	•	Minnesota	20	12
O26		at Ohio State	17	27
N2		Northwestern	13	16
N9	•	at Wisconsin	20	7
N16		at Purdue	17	27
N23	•	Illinois	27	24

1992 — 5-6-0 (5-3-0)

S12		Central Michigan	20	24
S19		Notre Dame	31	52
S26		at Boston College	0	14
O3	•	Indiana	42	31
O10		at Michigan	10	35
O17	•	at Minnesota	20	15
O24		Ohio State	17	27
O31	•	at Northwestern	27	26
N7	•	Wisconsin	26	10
N14	•	Purdue	35	13
N21		at Illinois	10	14

1993 — 6-6-0 (4-4-0)

S11	•	Kansas	31	14
S18		at Notre Dame	14	36
S25	•	Central Michigan	48	34
O9	•	Michigan	17	7
O16	•	at Ohio State	21	28
O23	•	Iowa	24	10
O30		at Indiana	0	10
N6		Northwestern	31	29
N13	•	at Purdue	27	24
N27		Penn State	37	38
D5		Wisconsin *Tok*	20	41
LIBERTY BOWL				
D28		Louisville	7	18

1994 — 5-6-0 (4-4-0)

S10		at Kansas	10	17	
S17		Notre Dame	20	21	
S24	•	Miami (Ohio)	45	10	
O1	•	Wisconsin	29	10	†
O8		at Michigan	20	40	
O15		Ohio State	7	23	
O22		at Iowa	14	19	
O29	•	Indiana	27	21	†
N5	•	at Northwestern	35	17	†
N12	•	Purdue	42	30	†
N26		at Penn State	31	59	

NICK SABAN — 1995-99 (.585) — 34-24-1

1995 — 6-5-1 (4-3-1)

S9		Nebraska	10	50
S16	•	at Louisville	30	7
S23	=	at Purdue	35	35
S30	•	Boston College	25	21
O7		Iowa	7	21
O14	•	at Illinois	27	21
O21	•	Minnesota	34	31
O28		at Wisconsin	14	45
N4	•	Michigan	28	25
N11	•	at Indiana	31	13
N25		Penn State	20	24
INDEPENDENCE BOWL				
D29		LSU	26	45

1996 — 6-6 (5-3)

A31	•	Purdue	52	14
S7		at Nebraska	14	55
S21		Louisville	20	30
S28	•	Eastern Michigan	47	0
O5		at Iowa	30	37
O12	•	Illinois	42	14
O19	•	at Minnesota	27	9
O26		Wisconsin	30	13
N2		at Michigan	29	45
N9	•	Indiana	38	15
N23		at Penn State	29	32
SUN BOWL				
D31		Stanford	0	38

1997 — 7-5 (4-4)

S6	•	Western Michigan	42	10
S13	•	Memphis	51	21
S20	•	at Notre Dame	23	7
O4	•	Minnesota	31	10
O11	•	at Indiana	38	6
O18		at Northwestern	17	19
O25		Michigan	7	23
N1		Ohio State	13	37
N8		at Purdue	21	22
N22	•	at Illinois	27	17
N29	•	Penn State	49	14
ALOHA BOWL				
D25		Washington	23	51

1998 — 6-6 (4-4)

A29		Colorado State	16	23
S5		at Oregon	14	48
S12	•	Notre Dame	45	23
S26		at Michigan	17	29
O3	•	Central Michigan	38	7
O10		Indiana	38	31
O24		at Minnesota	18	19
O31	•	Northwestern	29	5
N7	•	at Ohio State	28	24
N14	•	Purdue	24	25
N21	•	Illinois	41	9
N28		at Penn State	28	51

1999 — 10-2 (6-2)

S2	•	Oregon	27	20
S11	•	Eastern Michigan	51	7
S18	•	at Notre Dame	23	13
S25	•	at Illinois	27	10
O2	•	Iowa	49	3
O9	•	Michigan	34	31
O16	•	at Purdue	28	52
O23		at Wisconsin	10	40
N6	•	Ohio State	23	7
N13	•	at Northwestern	34	0
N20	•	Penn State	35	28
CITRUS BOWL				
J1	•	Florida	37	34

BOBBY WILLIAMS — 1999-2002 (.485) — 16-17

2000 — 5-6 (2-6)

S9	•	Marshall	34	24
S16	•	at Missouri	13	10
S23	•	Notre Dame	27	21
S30		Northwestern	17	37
O7		at Iowa	16	21
O14		Wisconsin	10	17
O21		at Michigan	0	14
O28	•	Illinois	14	10
N4		at Ohio State	13	27
N11	•	Purdue	30	10
N18		at Penn State	23	42

2001 — 7-5 (3-5)

S8	•	Central Michigan	35	21
S22		at Notre Dame	17	10
S29		at Northwestern	26	27
O13	•	Iowa	31	28
O20		at Minnesota	19	28
O27	•	at Wisconsin	42	28
N3	•	Michigan	26	24
N10		Indiana	28	37
N17		at Purdue	14	24
N24		Penn State	37	42
D1	•	Missouri	55	7
SILICON VALLEY CLASSIC				
D31		Fresno State	44	35

MORRIS WATTS — 2002 (.333) — 1-2-0

2002 — 4-8 (2-6)

A31	•	Eastern Michigan	56	7
S7	•	Rice	27	10
S14		California	22	46
S21		Notre Dame	17	21
S28	•	Northwestern	39	24
O12		at Iowa	16	44
O19		Minnesota	7	28
O26		Wisconsin	24	42
N2		at Michigan	3	49
N9	•	at Indiana	56	21
N16		Purdue	42	45
N23		at Penn State	7	61

JOHN L. SMITH — 2003-2006 (.458) — 22-26

2003 — 8-5 (5-3)

A30	•	Western Michigan	26	21
S6	•	Rutgers	44	28
S13		Louisiana Tech	19	20
S20	•	at Notre Dame	22	16
S27	•	Iowa	20	10
O4	•	Indiana	31	3
O11	•	at Illinois	49	14
O18	•	at Minnesota	44	38
N1		Michigan	20	27
N8		at Ohio State	23	33
N15		at Wisconsin	21	56
N22	•	Penn State	41	10
ALAMO BOWL				
D29		Nebraska	3	17

2004 — 5-7 (4-4)

S4		at Rutgers	14	19
S11	•	Central Michigan	24	7
S18		Notre Dame	24	31
S25	•	at Indiana	30	20
O2		at Iowa	16	38
O9	•	Illinois	38	25
O16	•	Minnesota	51	17
O30		at Michigan	37	45
N6		Ohio State	19	32
N13	•	Wisconsin	49	14
N20		at Penn State	13	37
D4		at Hawaii	38	41

2005 — 5-6 (2-6)

S3	•	Kent State	49	14
S10	•	Hawaii	42	14
S17	•	at Notre Dame	44	41
S24	•	at Illinois	61	14
O1		Michigan	31	34
O15		at Ohio State	24	35
O22		Northwestern	14	49
O29	•	Indiana	46	15
N5		at Purdue	21	28
N12		at Minnesota	18	41
N19		Penn State	22	31

2006 — 4-8 (1-7)

S2	•	Idaho	27	17
S9	•	Eastern Michigan	52	20
S16	•	at Pittsburgh	38	23
S23		Notre Dame	37	40
S30		Illinois	20	23
O7		at Michigan	13	37
O14		Ohio State	7	38
O21	•	at Northwestern	41	38
O28		at Indiana	21	46
N4		Purdue	15	17
N11		Minnesota	18	31
N18		at Penn State	13	17

Neutral Site key: *BKLN* Brooklyn, N.Y. / *ERUT* East Rutherford, N.J. / *JAM* Jackson, Miss. / *NYC* New York, N.Y. / *PORT* Portland, Ore. / *SA* San Antonio, Tx. / *TOK* Tokyo, Japan
ƒ Forfeit † Game Later Forfeited # Disputed Victor * Disputed Score || Designated Conference Game |2 Counted Twice in Conference Standings

MICHIGAN STATE RECORD BOOK

SINGLE-GAME RECORDS

RUSHING YARDS

RANK	PLAYER	DATE	OPPONENT	ATT	AVG	YDS
1	Eric Allen	Oct. 30, 1971	Purdue	29	12.1	350
2	Lorenzo White	Nov. 14, 1987	Indiana	56	5.2	292
3	Lorenzo White	Nov. 9, 1985	Indiana	25	11.4	286
4	Clinton Jones	Nov. 5, 1966	Iowa	21	12.8	268
5	Blake Ezor	Nov. 12, 1988	Indiana	44	5.7	250

PASSING YARDS

RANK	PLAYER	DATE	OPPONENT	ATT	COMP	YDS
1	Bill Burke	Oct. 9, 1999	Michigan	36	21	400
2	Jeff Smoker	Dec. 31, 2001	Fresno State	32	22	376
3	Ed Smith	Oct. 21, 1978	Indiana	30	20	369
4	Jim Miller	Oct. 16, 1993	Ohio State	42	31	360
5	Jeff Smoker	Nov. 22, 2003	Penn State	50	29	357

RECEIVING YARDS

RANK	PLAYER	DATE	OPPONENT	REC	AVG	YDS
1	Charles Rogers	Dec. 31, 2001	Fresno State	10	27.0	270
2	Plaxico Burress	Oct. 9, 1999	Michigan	10	25.5	255
3	Andre Rison	Jan. 1, 1989	Georgia	9	28.0	252
4	Charles Rogers	Oct. 27, 2001	Wisconsin	5	41.2	206
5	Courtney Hawkins	Nov. 11, 1989	Minnesota	9	21.9	197

POINTS

RANK	PLAYER	DATE	OPPONENT	TOT
1	Blake Ezor	Nov. 18, 1989	Northwestern	36
2	Scott Greene	Oct. 14, 1995	Illinois	26
3	14 players tied at 24			

FIELD GOALS

RANK	PLAYER	DATE	OPPONENT	TOT
1	Paul Edinger	Nov. 7, 1998	Ohio State	5
	Paul Edinger	Oct. 31, 1998	Northwestern	5
	John Langeloh	Nov. 19, 1988	Wisconsin	5
4	8 players tied at 4			

TACKLES

RANK	PLAYER	DATE	OPPONENT	TOT
1	Dan Bass	Oct. 27, 1979	Ohio State	32
2	Don Law	Oct. 11, 1969	Ohio State	28
3	Dan Bass	Sept. 29, 1979	Notre Dame	24
4	Percy Snow	Oct. 21, 1989	Illinois	23
5	5 players tied at 21			

INTERCEPTIONS

RANK	PLAYER	DATE	OPPONENT	TOT
1	John Miller	Oct. 10, 1987	Michigan	4
2	6 players tied at 3			

RETIRED NUMBERS

46 John Hannah (university president)

78 Don Coleman

90 George Webster

95 Charles "Bubba" Smith

SINGLE-SEASON RECORDS

RUSHING YARDS

RANK	PLAYER	SEASON	G	ATT	YDS
1	Lorenzo White	1985	12	419	2,066
2	Lorenzo White	1987	12	357	1,572
3	Blake Ezor	1988	12	322	1,496
4	Eric Allen	1971	11	259	1,494
5	T.J. Duckett	2001	12	263	1,420

PASSING YARDS

RANK	PLAYER	SEASON	G	ATT	COMP	PCT	YDS
1	Jeff Smoker	2003	13	488	302	61.9	3,395
2	Drew Stanton	2005	11	354	236	66.7	3,077
3	Bill Burke	1998	12	358	195	54.5	2,595
4	Dave Yarema	1986	11	297	202	67.3	2,581
5	Jeff Smoker	2001	11	202	186	63.4	2,579

RECEIVING YARDS

RANK	PLAYER	SEASON	G	REC	AVG	YDS
1	Charles Rogers	2001	12	67	21.9	1,470
2	Charles Rogers	2002	12	68	19.9	1,351
3	Plaxico Burress	1999	12	66	17.3	1,142
4	Courtney Hawkins	1989	12	60	18.0	1,080
5	Plaxico Burress	1998	12	65	15.6	1,013

SCORING

RANK	PLAYER	SEASON	TD	FG	PAT	P2	TOT
1	Blake Ezor	1989	19	0	0	0	114
2	Scott Greene	1995	18	0	0	2	112
3	Eric Allen	1971	18	0	0	1	110
4	Sedrick Irvin	1996	18	0	0	0	108
5	Dave Rayner	2004	0	22	39	0	105

TOUCHDOWNS

RANK	PLAYER	SEASON	G	TOT
1	Blake Ezor	1989	10	19
2	Sedrick Irvin	1996	12	18
	Scott Greene	1995	11	18
	Eric Allen	1971	11	18
5	Lorenzo White	1985	12	17

TACKLES

RANK	PLAYER	SEASON	G	TOT
1	Chuck Bullough	1991	11	175
2	Percy Snow	1989	12	172
3	Chuck Bullough	1990	12	164
	Percy Snow	1988	12	164
5	Dan Bass	1979	11	160

INTERCEPTIONS

RANK	PLAYER	SEASON	G	YDS	TOT
1	Todd Krumm	1987	12	129	9
2	Kurt Larson	1988	12	78	8
	John Miller	1987	12	44	8
	Jesse Thomas	1950	9	88	8
5	3 players tied at 7				

PUNTING

RANK	PLAYER	SEASON	PUNTS	YDS	AVG
1	Brandon Fields	2004	50	2,394	47.9
2	Greg Montgomery	1986	39	1,865	47.8
3	Brandon Fields	2003	62	2,878	46.4
4	Ray Stachowicz	1980	71	3,278	46.2
5	Greg Montgomery	1987	70	3,149	45.0

PUNT RETURNS

RANK	PLAYER	SEASON	RET	YDS	AVG
1	Jesse Thomas	1950	18	358	19.9
2	Gari Scott	1998	32	440	13.7
3	Bill Simpson	1972	21	286	13.6
4	Sedrick Irvin	1997	23	313	13.6
5	Gari Scott	1999	37	488	13.2

KICKOFF RETURNS

RANK	PLAYER	SEASON	RET	YDS	AVG
1	Eric Allen	1969	20	598	29.9
2	DeAndra Cobb	2003	28	763	27.2
3	Derrick Mason	1995	35	947	27.1
4	Derrick Mason	1994	36	966	26.8
5	Herb Haygood	2001	24	632	26.3

CAREER RECORDS

RUSHING YARDS

RANK	PLAYER	SEASONS	ATT	AVG	TD	YDS
1	Lorenzo White	1984-87	1,082	4.5	43	4,887
2	Tico Duckett	1989-92	836	5.0	26	4,212
3	Blake Ezor	1986-89	800	4.7	34	3,749
4	Sedrick Irvin	1996-98	755	4.6	35	3,504
5	T.J. Duckett	1999-2001	621	5.4	29	3,379
6	Duane Goulbourne	1992-94, 96	627	4.5	23	2,848
7	Steve Smith	1977-80	524	5.1	21	2,676
8	Eric Allen	1969-71	521	5.1	28	2,654
9	Marc Renaud	1994-95, 97	451	5.2	13	2,331
10	Levi Jackson	1973-76	474	4.8	10	2,287

PASSING YARDS

RANK	PLAYER	SEASONS	ATT	COMP	PCT	INT	TD	YDS
1	Jeff Smoker	2000-03	1,150	685	58.7	39	61	8,932
2	Drew Stanton	2003-06	846	543	64.2	28	42	6,524
3	Dave Yarema	1982-86	767	464	60.5	33	43	5,809
4	Ed Smith	1976-78	789	418	53.0	32	42	5,706
5	Bill Burke	1996-99	766	416	54.3	31	46	5,463
6	Jim Miller	1990-93	746	467	62.9	29	29	5,037
7	Drew Stanton	2003-05	846	543	64.2	28	42	4,717
8	Todd Schultz	1994-97	593	360	60.7	33	27	4,273
9	Tony Banks	1994-95	496	301	60.7	21	20	4,129
10	John Leister	1979-82	686	313	45.6	35	20	3,999

RECEIVING YARDS

RANK	PLAYER	SEASONS	REC	AVG	TD	YDS
1	Andre Rison	1985-88	146	20.5	20	2,992
2	Charles Rogers	2001-02	135	20.9	27	2,821
3	Kirk Gibson	1975-78	112	21.0	24	2,347
4	Courtney Hawkins	1988-91	138	16.0	12	2,210
5	Plaxico Burress	1998-99	131	16.5	20	2,155
6	Gari Scott	1996-99	134	15.6	18	2,095
7	Eugene Byrd	1975-79	114	18.3	15	2,082
8	Mark Ingram	1983-86	95	20.5	14	1,944
9	Derrick Mason	1993-96	120	16.0	20	1,914
10	Gene Washington	1964-66	112	18.2	16	1,857

SCORING

RANK	PLAYER	SEASONS	TD	FG	PAT	P2	TOT
1	Dave Rayner	2001-04	0	62	148	0	334
2	John Langeloh	1987-90	0	57	137	0	308
3	Chris Gardner	1994-97	0	52	125	0	281
4	Morten Andersen	1978-81	0	45	126	0	261
5	Lorenzo White	1984-87	43	0	0	0	258

TOUCHDOWNS

RANK	PLAYER	SEASONS	TOT
1	Lorenzo White	1984-87	43
2	Sedrick Irvin	1996-98	42
3	Blake Ezor	1986-89	34
4	Lynn Chandnois	1946-49	31
5	2 players tied at 30		

TACKLES

RANK	PLAYER	SEASONS	TOT
1	Dan Bass	1976-79	541
2	Percy Snow	1986-89	473
3	Ike Reese	1994-97	420
4	Josh Thornhill	1998-2001	395
5	Chuck Bullough	1988-91	391

INTERCEPTIONS

RANK	PLAYER	SEASONS	YDS	TOT
1	Lynn Chandnois	1946-49	384	20
2	Todd Krumm	1984-87	198	18
3	Phil Parker	1982-85	267	16
4	3 players tied at 14			

PUNTING

RANK	PLAYER	SEASONS	PUNTS	YDS	AVG
1	Greg Montgomery	1985-87	184	8,317	45.2
2	Brandon Fields	2003-06	209	9,405	45.0
3	Raif Mojsiejenko	1981-84	279	12,220	43.8
4	Ray Stachowicz	1977-80	230	9,959	43.3
5	Craig Jarrett	1998-2001	239	10,253	42.9

TEAM RECORDS

LONGEST WINNING STREAK
- 28, Oct. 14, 1950-Oct. 17, 1953

Streak broken vs. Purdue, 0-6, Oct. 24, 1953

LONGEST UNDEFEATED STREAK
- 28: Oct. 14, 1950-Oct. 17, 1953

Streak broken vs. Purdue, 0-6, Oct. 24, 1953

MOST CONSECUTIVE WINNING SEASONS
- 14, 1903-16

MOST CONSECUTIVE BOWL APPEARANCES
- 4, 1987-90

MOST POINTS IN A GAME
- 109, vs. Olivet, Oct. 30, 1920

MOST POINTS ALLOWED IN A GAME
- 119, vs. Michigan, Oct. 8, 1902

LARGEST MARGIN OF VICTORY
- 109 (109-0), vs. Olivet, Oct. 30, 1920

LARGEST MARGIN OF DEFEAT
- 119 (0-119), vs. Michigan, Oct. 8, 1902

LONGEST RUN FROM SCRIMMAGE
- 90 yards, Lynn Chandnois, vs. Arizona, Nov. 19, 1949

LONGEST PASS PLAY
- 93 yards, Tony Banks to Nigea Carter, vs. Indiana, Oct. 29, 1994

LONGEST FIELD GOAL
- 63 yards, Morten Anderson, vs. Ohio State, Sept. 19, 1981

LONGEST PUNT
- 86 yards, Greg Montgomery, vs. Michigan, Oct. 11, 1986

LONGEST INTERCEPTION RETURN
- 99 yards, Dan Bass, vs. Wisconsin, Oct. 28, 1978

PUNT RETURNS

RANK	PLAYER	SEASON	RET	YDS	AVG
1	Jesse Thomas	1948-50	27	490	18.1
2	George Guerre	1946-48	35	513	14.7
3	Gari Scott	1996-99	84	1,088	13.0
4	Jim Ellis	1951-53	55	619	11.3
5	Mill Coleman	1991-94	39	411	10.5

KICKOFF RETURNS

RANK	PLAYER	SEASON	RET	YDS	AVG
1	DeAndra Cobb	2001-04	64	1,632	25.5
2	Derek Hughes	1979-81	36	898	24.9
3	Derrick Mason	1993-96	106	2,575	24.2
	Courtney Hawkins	1988-91	65	1,571	24.2
5	Larry Jackson	1983-84	43	1,022	23.8

MICHIGAN STATE ANNUAL STATISTICAL LEADERS

YR	RUSHING	YDS	ATT	AVG	PASSING	ATT	CMP	PCT	YDS	RECEIVING	REC	YDS	AVG
1945	Jack Breslin	361	112	3.2	Russ Reader	90	53	.59	613	Steve Cantos	31	265	8.5
1946	George Guerre	337	46	7.3	George Guerre	60	25	.42	396	Warren Huey	11	214	19.5
1947	George Guerre	354	47	7.5	Gene Glick	26	8	.31	139	Warren Huey	7	60	8.6
1948	George Guerre	734	118	6.2	Gene Glick	56	26	.46	692	Ed Sobczak	20	465	23.3
1949	Lynn Chandnois	885	129	6.9	Gene Glick	71	38	.54	776	Robert Carey	26	523	20.1
1950	Sonny Grandelius	1,023	163	6.3	Al Dorow	105	45	.43	654	Robert Carey	19	268	14.1
1951	Don McAuliffe	566	124	4.6	Al Dorow	114	64	.56	842	Robert Carey	20	263	13.2
1952	Billy Wells	585	118	5.0	Tom Yewcic	95	41	.43	941	Ellis Duckett	10	323	32.3
1953	LeRoy Bolden	691	127	5.4	Tom Yewcic	80	34	.43	489	Ellis Duckett	10	169	16.9
1954	Clarence Peaks	321	45	7.1	Earl Morrall	99	39	.39	795	John Lewis	10	338	33.8
1955	Walt Kowalczyk	584	82	7.1	Earl Morrall	68	42	.62	941	David Kaiser	12	343	28.6
1956	Dennis Mendyk	495	85	5.8	Pat Wilson	39	20	.51	414	Tony Kolodziej	7	221	31.6
1957	Walt Kowalczyk	545	101	5.4	Jim Ninowski	79	45	.57	718	David Kaiser	19	267	14.1
1958	Dean Look	238	90	2.6	Mike Panitch	37	16	.43	250	Sam Williams	15	242	16.1
1959	Herb Adderly	419	93	4.5	Dean Look	100	49	.49	785	Herb Adderly	13	265	20.4
1960	Ron Hatcher	361	59	6.1	Tom Wilson	109	46	.42	761	Herb Adderly	9	154	17.1
1961	George Saimes	451	82	5.5	Pete Smith	94	42	.45	630	Lonnie Sanders	15	247	16.5
1962	George Saimes	642	122	5.3	Pete Smith	52	18	.35	241	Lonnie Sanders	7	109	15.6
1963	Roger Lopes	601	138	4.4	Steve Juday	68	30	.44	509	Sherman Lewis	11	303	27.5
1964	Dick Gordon	741	123	6.0	Steve Juday	148	79	.53	894	Gene Washington	35	542	15.5
1965	Clinton Jones	787	165	4.8	Steve Juday	168	89	.53	1,173	Gene Washington	40	638	16.0
1966	Clinton Jones	784	159	4.9	Jimmy Raye	123	62	.50	1,110	Gene Washington	27	677	25.1
1967	Dwight Lee	497	116	4.3	Jimmy Raye	107	42	.39	580	Allen Brenner	26	462	17.8
1968	Tommy Love	729	177	4.1	William Triplett	90	47	.52	714	Frank Foreman	29	456	15.7
1969	Don Highsmith	937	209	4.5	William Triplett	117	37	.32	715	Frank Foreman	22	537	24.4
1970	Eric Allen	811	186	4.4	Mike Rasmussen	199	91	.46	1,344	Gordon Bowdell	34	495	14.6
1971	Eric Allen	1,494	259	5.8	Mike Rasmussen	88	32	.36	642	Billy Joe DuPree	25	414	16.6
1972	David E. Brown	575	123	4.7	George Mihaiu	55	25	.45	367	Billy Joe DuPree	23	406	17.7
1973	Clarence Bullock	496	113	4.4	Charles Baggett	94	38	.40	516	Michael Hurd	11	163	14.8
1974	Levi Jackson	942	153	6.2	Charles Baggett	105	48	.46	965	Michael Hurd	18	373	20.7
1975	Levi Jackson	1,063	230	4.6	Charles Baggett	88	42	.48	854	Eugene Byrd	10	266	26.6
1976	Richard Baes	931	187	5.0	Ed Smith	257	132	.51	1,749	Kirk Gibson	39	748	19.2
1977	Leroy McGee	720	162	4.4	Ed Smith	240	117	.49	1,731	Kirk Gibson	22	531	24.1
1978	Steve Smith	772	115	6.7	Ed Smith	292	169	.58	2,226	Kirk Gibson	42	806	19.2
1979	Steve Smith	972	204	4.8	Bryan Clark	131	64	.49	800	Eugene Byrd	30	559	18.6
1980	Steve Smith	667	154	4.3	John Leister	247	103	.42	1,569	Ted Jones	40	568	14.2
1981	Aaron Roberts	461	94	4.9	Bryan Clark	294	109	.37	1,521	Ted Jones	44	624	14.2
1982	Tony Ellis	671	179	3.7	John Leister	251	119	.47	1,321	Otis Grant	36	547	15.2
1983	Carl Butler	549	126	4.4	Clark Brown	141	82	.58	837	Daryl Turner	26	549	21.1
1984	Lorenzo White	616	142	4.3	Dave Yarema	222	119	.54	1,477	Mark Ingram	22	499	22.7
1985	Lorenzo White	2,066	419	4.9	Dave Yarema	116	66	.57	840	Mark Ingram	34	745	21.9
1986	Lorenzo White	633	164	3.9	Dave Yarema	297	202	.68	2,581	Andre Rison	54	966	17.9
1987	Lorenzo White	1,572	357	4.4	Bobby McAllister	139	71	.51	1,171	Andre Rison	34	785	23.1
1988	Blake Ezor	1,496	322	4.6	Bobby McAllister	154	80	.52	1,406	Andre Rison	39	961	24.6
1989	Blake Ezor	1,299	267	4.9	Dan Enos	240	153	.64	2,066	Courtney Hawkins	60	1,080	18.0
1990	Tico Duckett	1,394	257	5.4	Dan Enos	220	137	.62	1,677	James Bradley	32	517	16.2
1991	Tico Duckett	1,204	272	4.4	Jim Miller	210	130	.62	1,368	Courtney Hawkins	47	656	14.0
1992	Tico Duckett	1,021	204	5.0	Jim Miller	191	122	.64	1,400	Mill Coleman	37	586	15.8
1993	Duane Goulbourne	973	196	5.0	Jim Miller	336	215	.64	2,269	Mill Coleman	48	671	14.0
1994	Duane Goulbourne	930	214	4.3	Tony Banks	238	145	.61	2,040	Scott Greene	42	452	10.8
1995	Marc Renaud	1,057	216	4.9	Tony Banks	258	156	.60	2,089	Derrick Mason	53	787	14.8
1996	Sedrick Irvin	1,067	237	4.5	Todd Schultz	209	130	.62	1,693	Derrick Mason	53	865	16.3
1997	Sedrick Irvin	1,270	246	5.2	Todd Schultz	299	177	.59	2,003	Gari Scott	41	680	16.6
1998	Sedrick Irvin	1,167	272	4.3	Bill Burke	358	195	.54	2,595	Plaxico Burress	65	1,013	15.6
1999	Lloyd Clemons	959	191	5.0	Bill Burke	312	173	.55	2,214	Plaxico Burress	66	1,142	17.3
2000	T.J. Duckett	1,353	240	5.6	Jeff Smoker	197	103	.52	1,365	Lavaile Richardson	40	459	11.5
2001	T.J. Duckett	1,420	263	5.4	Jeff Smoker	262	166	.63	2,579	Charles Rogers	67	1,470	21.9
2002	David Richard	654	133	4.9	Jeff Smoker	203	114	.56	1,593	Charles Rogers	68	1,351	20.4
2003	Jaren Hayes	609	145	4.2	Jeff Smoker	488	302	.62	3,395	Agim Shabaj	57	692	12.1
2004	DeAndra Cobb	728	96	7.6	Drew Stanton	220	141	.64	1,601	Jerramy Scott	39	444	11.4
2005	Javon Ringer	817	122	6.7	Drew Stanton	354	236	.67	3077	Jerramy Scott	49	722	14.7
2006	Javon Ringer	497	86	5.8	Drew Stanton	269	164	.61	1807	Kerry Reed	64	775	12.1

Receiving leaders by receptions
All statistics include postseason

MINNESOTA

By Todd Jones

RESEARCHERS AT THE UNIVERSITY of Minnesota invented the pacemaker. Good thing, since fans of the Golden Gophers have had their hearts broken many times since the school last won a Big Ten title in 1967. Passion for football dates to 1896, when Minnesota became an original member of the Big Ten. There's a famous photo from that early era showing fans climbing trees and telephone poles to watch the Gophers play. Minnesota's glory days were as good as any enjoyed by college football's powerhouses: The Gophers won six Big Ten championships between 1934 and 1941, and they won three national titles under Bernie Bierman in the final eight seasons of that magical span. At times the past can be both wonderful and a burden; the Gophers have tried (and failed) to live up to that tradition ever since. Minnesota never stops striving to make the present count too and enters 2007 with optimism thanks to a new coaching staff led by Tim Brewster.

TRADITION Cheerleading in college football originated at Minnesota in 1898. Some credit a student named Johnny Campbell for organizing cheers with fellow "yell leaders" at a home game against Northwestern. Others credit a professor for asking students to support the team before its game at Wisconsin with a rallying cry of "Go to Madison! Go to Madison! Apply the summation of stimuli!" Besides cheerleading, the trophy game also originated with the Golden Gophers. When Michigan left behind a five-gallon water jug after a 6-6 tie in 1903, Minnesota AD L.J. Cooke told the Wolverines that if they wanted their jug, they'd have to come back and win it. So now the two schools play for the Little Brown Jug. Since 1935, the Gophers have played Iowa for the rights to a bronze statue of a pig called Floyd of Rosedale. Minnesota and Wisconsin have played for the Paul Bunyan Axe since 1948. The first axe, with a six-foot handle, was donated to the College Football Hall of Fame in 2003 and replaced by a new one. Minnesota and Wisconsin originally competed for the Slab of Bacon trophy in 1930. The slab was lost during the 1940s but found in a Wisconsin storage room in 1994. Finally, the winner of the Gophers' game against Penn State receives the Governor's Victory Bell.

PROFILE

University of Minnesota, Twin Cities
Minneapolis, Minn.
Founded: 1851
Enrollment: 27,108
Colors: Maroon and Gold
Nickname: Golden Gophers
Stadium: Hubert H. Humphrey Metrodome
Opened in 1982
FieldTurf; 64,172 capacity
First football game: 1882
All-time record: 626–439–44 (.584)
Bowl record: 5–7
Consensus national championships, 1936-present: 4 (1936, 1940, 1941, 1960)
Big Ten Conference championships: 18 (7 outright)
Heisman Trophy: Bruce Smith, 1941
Outland Trophy: Tom Brown, 1960; Bobby Bell, 1962
First-round draft choices: 20
Website: www.gophersports.com

THE BEST OF TIMES

One of college football's great dynasties reigned in Minnesota from 1934 to 1941, when the Gophers won five national championships and went 8–0 in four of those seasons. Also don't forget 1900-05, when they went 65–4–5 and outscored opponents 2,702-121.

THE WORST OF TIMES

Minnesota's opponents enjoyed payback in the 1950s. The Gophers stumbled to six losing seasons and a 34–49–9 record. The 1990s, however, proved worse, with eight consecutive losing seasons and a 26–63 record from 1991 to 1998.

CONFERENCE

Minnesota was a charter member of the Western Conference in 1896 and has remained in the league since then. Popularly known as the Big Ten since 1917, the league didn't officially change its name to the Big Ten Conference until 1987.

DISTINGUISHED ALUMNI

Vice presidents Hubert H. Humphrey and Walter Mondale; Loni Anderson, actress; Dr. Christiaan Barnard, performed world's first human heart transplant; Herb Brooks, coach of 1980 gold medal-winning U.S. hockey team; Tom Lehman, pro golfer; Alford Pillsbury, founder of Pillsbury Corporation; Carl Rowan, syndicated newspaper columnist; Roy Wilkins, executive director, NAACP; Yanni (Chisomallis), new age pianist

> *Minnesota was the first major-college team to have a black All-America quarterback.*

BEST PLAYER Bruce Smith won the school's only Heisman Trophy in 1941, but Bronko Nagurski is more of a legend. As the story goes, Minnesota coach Clarence Spears asked a teenage farmhand how to find the home of a recruit. When the young man picked up a plow and pointed in the direction, Spears had his man: It was Nagurski, whose career began without a scholarship and ended with unprecedented acclaim. As a senior in 1929, Nagurski became the first player to be named All-America at two different positions (fullback and defensive tackle) in the same season. He also played end. The Gophers lost only four games, none by more than two points, in his three varsity seasons. At 6'2" and 228 pounds, Nagurski had a kindly nature and a high-pitched voice but a brutish style of play. He was first called Bronko while growing up in International Falls, Minn., when a teacher misunderstood his Ukrainian mother's pronunciation of Bronislaw. His name was spoken with awe after he cracked a transverse vertebra in his back during a 1928 game against Iowa but played the rest of that game. He played lineman in parts of the next three games while wearing a corset for protection. Still suffering from the injury, Nagurski demanded to play fullback in the season finale against Wisconsin. Wearing a special brace for his ribs and back, Nagurski caused a fumble that led to the only TD in a 6-0 Minnesota win that cost the Badgers the Big Ten title. Nagurski also knocked down a pass at the goal line and had three interceptions, the last of which ended the game. Such tales, including the three NFL titles he helped the Chicago Bears win, are recounted in an International Falls museum dedicated to Nagurski. Minnesota retired his No. 72 jersey in 1979.

BEST COACH The truest testament to Bernie Bierman's character doesn't involve football. The Minnesota native served as a Marine during World War I and World War II. This second stint in the service was a three-year interruption in a glorious coaching career at Minnesota that ran from 1932 to 1941 and 1945 to 1950. Bierman, who as a player captained the 1915 Gophers, created one of college football's great dynasties before going off to war a second time. Bierman never yelled at players but would inspect the practice grass to make certain their footsteps were where they should be on a play. The Golden Gophers flattened defenses with a single-wing backfield running behind an unbalanced line.

FIGHT SONG

MINNESOTA ROUSER
Minnesota, hats off to thee,
To thy colors true we shall ever be,
Firm and strong, united are we.
Rah! Rah! Rah! For Ski-U-Mah,
RAH! RAH! RAH! RAH!
Rah for the U. of M.
Minnesota, hats off to thee,
To thy colors true we shall ever be,
Firm and strong, united are we.
Rah! Rah! Rah! For Ski-U-Mah,
RAH! RAH! RAH! RAH!
Rah for the U. of M.
M-I-N-N-E-S-O-T-A!
Minnesota! Minnesota!
Yeaaaaaaaaaaaaaaaah GOPHERS!

FIRST-ROUND DRAFT CHOICES

1937	Ed Widseth, Giants (4)
1939	Larry Buhler, Packers (9)
1940	Hal Van Every, Packers (9)
1941	George Franck, Giants (6)
1942	Urban Odson, Packers (9)
1943	Bill Daley, Steelers (7)
1943	Dick Wildung, Packers (8)
1950	Clayton Tonnemaker, Packers (4)
1950	Leo Nomellini, 49ers (11)
1950	Harry "Bud" Grant, Eagles (14)
1961	Sandy Stephens, NY Titans
1962	Tom Brown, NY Titans
1964	Carl Eller, Vikings (6) and Bills (5)*
1966	Gale Gillingham, Packers (13)
1966	Aaron Brown, Chiefs
1968	John Williams, Colts (23)
1989	Brian Williams, Giants (18)
1990	Darrell Thompson, Packers (19)
2001	Willie Middlebrooks, Broncos (24)
2006	Laurence Maroney, Patriots (21)

From 1960 to 1966, the NFL and the AFL held separate, competing drafts

CONSENSUS ALL-AMERICANS

1903	Fred Schacht, T
1909	John McGovern, B
1910	James Walker, T
1916	Bert Baston, E
1917	George Hauser, T
1923	Ray Ecklund, E
1926-27	Herb Joesting, B
1929	Bronko Nagurski, T
1931	Biggie Munn, G
1934	Frank Larson, E
1934	Bill Bevan, G
1934	Pug Lund, B
1935-36	Ed Widseth, T
1940	Urban Odson, T
1940	George Franck, B
1941	Bruce Smith, B
1941-42	Dick Wildung, T
1948-49	Leo Nomellini, T
1949	Clayton Tonnemaker, C
1953	Paul Giel, B

(Continued on next page)

Their defense allowed only two opponents in 10 seasons to score 20 points or more in a game. Minnesota won five national championships and six Big Ten titles from 1934 to 1941 under the man known as the Grey Eagle or the Silver Fox for his prematurely gray hair. Minnesota, decked in all-gold uniforms, went undefeated in five of those seasons, shut out 23 opponents and had a 21-game winning streak.

BEST TEAM

"Bierman's Monsters" went 8–0 in 1934, were named national champions, and at the time were regarded as one of the greatest teams ever. Bierman used his roster's superior depth to grind opponents into sawdust. He played many players at one position, a decade before two-platoon football became popular. Eight different Gophers rushed for a TD during the season. Team captain Francis "Pug" Lund, Butch Larson, and Bill Bevan—the last Big Ten player not to wear a helmet—were named All-Americas. Guard Bud Wilkinson later went on to fame as a coach at Oklahoma. The Gophers ran for nearly 295 of their 325 yards of offense per game. They rushed for 514, all of their offensive yards, in a 48-12 win over Iowa. While quarterback Glenn Seidel led an offense that averaged 33.7 points, the Minnesota defense gave up just 4.8 points and 103 yards a game. Four opponents were shut out and two others scored just seven points. Indiana gained zero yards in a 30–0 loss. Minnesota's only scare of the season came in its third game, when it trailed at Pittsburgh 7-0 after three quarters before pulling out a 13-7 win. Each of the Gophers' seven other wins was by at least 20 points. They outscored their four final opponents 133-7.

BEST BACKFIELD

Glen Mason's powerful ground attack has defined the Gophers in the 21st century. Minnesota led the Big Ten in rushing three consecutive seasons and set a conference record with three straight years of at least 3,000 rushing yards from 2003 through 2005. Four Minnesota running backs have been drafted since 2000, including Laurence Maroney, a first-round pick of the New England Patriots after his stellar junior season in 2005. He ran for a Minnesota record 1,464 yards, averaging 5.2 on his 281 carries, with 10 touchdowns. That same year, Minnesota became the first school to have two players rush for more than 1,000 yards in three consecutive seasons. Gary Russell rushed for 1,130 yards and a school record 18 TDs. Maroney rushed for more than 100 yards in eight games, including six consecutive, and Russell did it four times. Maroney ran for 258 against Wisconsin—one of three times that season that he eclipsed 200 yards in a game—while Russell added 139. Maroney

CONSENSUS ALL-AMERICANS (CONT.)	
1960	Tom Brown, G
1961	Sandy Stephens, QB
1962	Bobby Bell, T
1963	Carl Eller, T
1965	Aaron Brown, DE
1999	Tyrone Carter, DB
1999-2000	Ben Hamilton, C/OL
2005	Greg Eslinger, C

had 129 and Russell 128 against Michigan. The Gophers, however, weren't one-dimensional. QB Bryan Cupito completed 176 of 297 passes (59.3%) for 2,530 yards and 19 TDs. His pass-efficiency rating was 145.87. He threw for 396 yards against Ohio State, 315 against Iowa, and tossed 4 TD passes against Virginia. Cupito threw a scoring pass in 11 of Minnesota's 12 games. Somehow, despite averaging 35.8 points and a school-record 494.8 yards of total offense, the Gophers finished seventh in the Big Ten and went 7–5.

BEST DEFENSE

Two of the greatest defensive players in football history anchored coach Murray Warmath's Minnesota team in 1962. Bobby Bell won the Outland Trophy while being named All-America at tackle and first-team all-Big Ten. Tackle Carl Eller, an All-America pick a year later as a senior tackle, was named second-team all-conference in 1962, along with defensive end Bob Prawdzik. Paul Ramseth led the team with four interceptions. Opponents averaged just 167.2 yards per game and scored 61 points during the season, an average of 6.8 per game. Navy totaled 48 yards. Teams rushed for a season total of 470 yards, an average of 52.2 per game. Michigan was held to -46 net rushing yards. The Gophers shut out their first two opponents and five in all, and two other teams scored seven points or less. Only Northwestern had offensive success in a 34-22 upset win. Wisconin, ranked No. 3, won the season's final game 14-9 over the No. 5 Gophers. Minnesota finished the season 6–2–1—the tie was 0-0 against Missouri in the season opener—and ranked No. 10. Bell and Eller are in both the College Football Hall of Fame and the Pro Football Hall of Fame. They played in six Super Bowls between them, with Bell winning one and losing one as a member of the Kansas City Chiefs and Eller losing four with the Minnesota Vikings.

BIGGEST GAME

Minnesota was 7–0 and had outscored opponents 236-38 when it went to Wisconsin on Nov. 24, 1934. The Badgers were 4–3 but had won two in a row. They also had split the previous four games of the Border Battle. Minnesota thwarted upset plans with a potent running attack. The Gophers scored 34 points against Wisconsin, which had yielded just 50 points in the season's first seven games while holding five opponents to a touchdown or less. Minnesota held the Badgers scoreless. The victory made the Gophers national champions for the first time.

BIGGEST UPSET

The 5–3 Golden Gophers trailed No. 2 Penn State 23-21 on Nov. 6, 1999. They faced fourth

and 16 at the Nittany Lions' 40-yard line late in the fourth quarter and seemed destined for a third consecutive defeat and fourth in five games. Minnesota QB Billy Cockerham, under a heavy blitz, tossed a desperation pass into the wind. The ball bounced off the hands of receiver Ron Johnson, ricocheted behind him, and was caught by Arland Bruce. The 27-yard gain silenced the Penn State crowd of 96,753. Dan Nystrom capped the last-minute drive by kicking a 32-yard field goal. The game-winning kick followed a Penn State possession that ended with the Nittany Lions punting from the Minnesota 33 instead of trying a 50-yard field goal in a gusting 20 mph wind. The 24–23 victory clinched the Gophers' first winning season since 1990. Penn State fell to 9–1, ending an 11-game winning streak and Joe Paterno's hopes for another national championship.

HEARTBREAKER No game in the Little Brown Jug series ended with as much disappointment for Minnesota as a 38-35 loss to Michigan in 2003. The Golden Gophers were 6–0, ranked No. 17, and primed for a breakout moment in Glen Mason's seventh season as coach. Minnesota led 14-0 at halftime and 28-7 after three quarters in a Friday night game televised nationally by ESPN. Michigan responded with its biggest comeback in school history. Minnesota's defense gave up 24 points in the fourth quarter, and the Wolverines added another seven when safety Jacob Stewart returned an interception 34 yards for a TD. Michigan completed its largest comeback ever by taking its only lead with 47 seconds remaining on freshman kicker Garrett Rivas' 33-yard field goal. "In the fourth quarter, we simply couldn't stop them," Mason said. The Gophers suffered their 15th consecutive loss in the series despite scoring their most points against Michigan since 1937 while rushing for 423 yards, including 197 by Marion Barber and 106 by QB Asad Abdul-Khaliq.

WILDEST FINISH The pigskin seemed greased late in Minnesota's 1952 game at Wisconsin as the teams combined for seven turnovers in the fourth quarter. The Golden Gophers came up with two interceptions by Gino Cappelletti and recovered a fumble by Badgers halfback Gerald Witt. Wisconsin had two interceptions by Paul Shwaiko and one by Burt Hable and recovered a fumble by Minnesota quarterback Paul Giel. Hable intercepted

Giel three times during the game, the final one coming in the Wisconsin end zone on the game's last play. The 21-21 tie sent the No. 13 Badgers to the Rose Bowl and ended Minnesota's season at 4–3–2.

COLLEGE FOOTBALL HALL OF FAME INDUCTEES

NAME	YEARS	INDUCTED
Bronko Nagurski, T/FB	1927-29	1951
Henry Williams, COACH	1900-21	1951
Bert Baston, E	1914-16	1954
Fritz Crisler, COACH	1930-31	1954
Herb Joesting, FB	1925-27	1954
Ed Widseth, T	1934-36	1954
Bernie Bierman, COACH	1932-41, 1945-50	1955
Dick Wildung, T	1940-42	1957
Pug Lund, HB	1932-34	1958
John McGovern, QB	1908-10	1966
Eddie Rogers, E	1900-03	1968
Bobby Marshall, E	1904-06	1971
Bruce Smith, HB	1939-41	1972
Paul Giel, HB	1951-53	1975
Leo Nomellini, T/G	1946-49	1977
Clayton Tonnemaker, C	1946-49	1980
Bobby Bell, T	1960-62	1991
George Franck, HB	1938-40	2002
Tom Brown, G	1958-60	2003
Carl Eller, T	1961-63	2006

BEST COMEBACK The entire 1960 season was a comeback. Minnesota was 2–7 the previous year, last in the Big Ten, and fans hung coach Murray Warmath in effigy after his third consecutive losing season. The Golden Gophers began 1960 unranked but opened the season with a 26-14 win at No. 12 Nebraska. They went on to win their next six games and rose to No. 1 after winning 27-10 at No. 1 Iowa on November 5. Minnesota lost to unranked Purdue 23-14 one week later but regained the No. 1 ranking by beating unranked Wisconsin 26-7 in the regular-season finale. The Gophers lost 17-7 to Washington in the Rose Bowl to finish 8–2, but the Associated Press had voted them national champions after the regular season.

STADIUM Attendance and revenue have been problematic for the Golden Gophers since 1982, when they moved their home games downtown to the 64,172-seat Hubert H. Humphrey Metrodome. Minnesota is the only Big Ten school to play its home games off campus. Fans have longed for the days when the Gophers played afternoons outdoors at Memorial Stadium, their campus home for 58 seasons before they moved to the dome. Memorial Stadium, built with more than one million bricks, was named in honor of the school's 3,527 World War I veterans . The Old Brickhouse opened in 1924 and in successful seasons would draw crowds of 66,000 despite having only 52,736 permanent seats. By 1975, average attendance had slipped to 31,000, and the old stadium was in need of $10 million in renovations. The Board of Regents instead decided to help Minneapolis build a downtown dome. The school's alumni band played "Taps" in 1992 as Memorial Stadium was torn down. Fans got their wish on March 24, 2005, when the school and TCF Bank, which contributed $35 million for naming rights, announced a deal on a new on-campus stadium. Construction on TCF Bank Stadium, on the northeast side of campus near the site of the soon-to-be former Memorial Stadium, began July 11, 2007, with the 50,000-seat horseshoe-style arena scheduled to open in 2009. The design will support future expansion to seat up to 80,000. The estimated cost is $288.5 million, with the

state of Minnesota paying approximately 52% of the cost and the school paying the rest.

RIVAL The emotions of Minnesota fans reach fever pitch for two rivalries with schools from bordering states. The Golden Gophers play Iowa and Wisconsin late each season for bragging rights and tradition-laden trophies. There was so much rancor in the Iowa series that, in order to cool heads, Iowa governor Clyde Herring and Minnesota governor Floyd Olson agreed in 1935 to wager on the game. The prize was a live pig: the legendary Floyd of Rosedale. The real Floyd was replaced by a bronze likeness the following year.

PRO FOOTBALL HALL OF FAME INDUCTEES		
NAME	YEARS	INDUCTED
Bronko Nagurski, FB	1930-37, 1943	1963
Leo Nomellini, DT	1950-63	1969
Bobby Bell, LB/D	1963-74	1983
Bud Grant, COACH	1967-83, 1985	1994
Carl Eller, DE	1964-78	2004
Charlie Sanders, TE	1968-77	2007

Minnesota has played Wisconsin 114 times, the most meetings between two major colleges. Such a long history makes it the premier rivalry for Gopher fans. Minnesota first met the Badgers in 1890, and bad blood quickly bubbled up. President Theodore Roosevelt canceled the 1906 game because there had been too many injuries and deaths on the field. The Wisconsin series resumed the next season and has been played annually ever since as the third-longest continuous series in college football. The Gophers and Badgers have met more times than any other NCAA Division I-A football rivals. Wisconsin was Minnesota's first homecoming opponent, in 1914, and the Gophers were the first homecoming opponents of the Badgers, in 1919.

CONTROVERSY About four minutes remained in the 1962 Border Battle at Wisconsin. Minnesota led 9-7 when Badger quarterback Ron Vander Kelen had a pass intercepted by Jack Perkovich. The Golden Gophers celebrated, but an official nullified the turnover by calling All-America tackle Bobby Bell for roughing Vander Kelen. Minnesota coach Murray Warmath protested and drew an unsportsmanlike-conduct penalty. Those 30 penalty yards gave Wisconsin a first down at the Gopher 13-yard line. Three plays later, Ralph Kurek ran five yards for a TD. Wisconsin's 14-9 victory sent the Badgers to the Rose Bowl.

DUBIOUS DISTINCTION Lou Holtz inherited a Minnesota team in 1984 that had gone 1–10 and lost 17 consecutive Big Ten games. He sugarcoated the mess with nonstop talk of a bright future. Fans were spellbound, and 42,000 showed up for Holtz's first spring game. The Golden Gophers went 4–7. They started 5–1 in Holtz's second season before finishing the regular season 6–5. The future ended on Nov. 27, 1985, when Holtz resigned to become Notre Dame coach. John Gutekunst took over as Minnesota coach before the Gophers beat Clemson

20-13 in the Independence Bowl. Holtz won a national championship at Notre Dame in 1988 as NCAA investigators showed up in Minneapolis. Three years later, the NCAA gave Minnesota a one-year bowl ban because a school administrator allegedly funneled unauthorized university funds to 23 players. Holtz allegedly gave $250 to one player and $25 and $40 to a visiting recruit.

NICKNAME The university adopted the name Gophers after Minnesota was called the Gopher State in an 1857 newspaper cartoon. The drawing was in response to legislative action for a $5 million railroad proposal and depicted nine Gophers with the heads of local politicians pulling a locomotive. During the 1930s, the football team wore gold jerseys and pants, so KSTP-AM radio announcer Halsey Hall began referring to the players as "Golden Gophers." The moniker stuck.

MASCOT Goldy the Gopher became the school's mascot during the 1940s. He resembles a chipmunk more than a gopher because his original designer had never seen a gopher and instead used a chipmunk as a model.

UNIFORMS In the spring of 1880, Minnesota president William Watts Folwell asked English instructor Augusta Norwood Smith—"a woman of excellent taste," Folwell said—to choose permanent school colors for graduation ribbons. She chose maroon and gold. The school's Board of Regents gave official approval to the use of those colors in March 1940. Minnesota has historically worn maroon jerseys at home games. The Gophers have had an M on their helmets since 1968, the year they switched the helmet color from white to gold. The Gophers wore gold helmets from 1968 to 1975 and again from 1992 to 1996. The helmets have been maroon since 1997, as they were from 1977 to 1991. The size, shape, and outline of the M on the helmets have changed over the last three-plus decades.

TRAGEDY Defensive lineman Brandon Hall of Detroit was fatally shot on a downtown Minneapolis street in the early morning hours of Sept. 1, 2002. His death came hours after the redshirt freshman had played his first college game, a 42-0 win over Southwest Texas State. At the time, Hall was downtown with some other players to help a teammate who had allegedly been robbed by three men.

QUIRK Glen Mason lost his job as Minnesota coach in part because his teams couldn't hold onto big leads. The

Gophers went to only three bowls in 21 years prior to his arrival in 1997, but under Mason, they made five consecutive bowl trips and seven in eight years. Still, Mason and his entire staff were fired on New Year's Eve 2006, exactly one year after the school gave him a four-year contract extension. Minnesota decided it could afford to pay $2.2 million to buy out his contract just two days after the Gophers blew a 31-point second-half lead and lost 44-41 to Texas Tech in overtime in the Insight Bowl. The defeat was the fourth time in seven years that Mason's Gophers blew a 21-point lead. Minnesota led Texas Tech 28-0, 35-7 at halftime, 38-7 with just over seven minutes left in the third quarter, and 38-14 heading into the fourth quarter. The Red Raider comeback was the largest in bowl history. Minnesota had trouble finishing things from the outset of Mason's tenure. During his second season, in 1998, the Gophers lost a bowl berth when Indiana beat them 20-19 in a game in which Minnesota missed four field goal attempts. The Gophers went 8–3 in 1999—the three losses by a total of 11 points—and rose to No. 12 in the polls before being upset by Oregon in the Sun Bowl. Minnesota lost to Michigan at home in 2003 despite leading 28-7 in the second half and by 20 points in the fourth quarter. The Gophers blew a 24-0 lead in the 2000 Micronpc.com Bowl and lost to North Carolina State 38-30. And they blew a 10-point lead with just over three minutes remaining to lose to Wisconsin in 2005 when punter Justin Kucek dropped a snap in the end zone and the Badgers recovered for a TD. Early in the 2006 season, Minnesota lost to Penn State 28-27 in overtime. The Gophers took a 27-21 lead in the extra period, but kicker Jason Gianinni missed the extra point. That allowed Penn State to win the game with a TD and conversion kick on its ensuing possession.

LORE Minnesota became the first major college team to have a black All-America quarterback when Sandy Stephens earned the honor in 1961, one year after he led the Golden Gophers to the national title. Minnesota coach Murray Warmath, a Tennessee native and former Mississippi State coach, began recruiting black players to Minneapolis in the late 1950s, before it was common practice. Besides Stephens, he gave scholarships over the

next decade to Judge Dickson, Bob NcNeil, Bobby Bell, Bill Munsey, Carl Eller, Aaron Brown, John Williams, Ezell Jones, Ed Duren, Charlie Sanders, and McKinley Boston. "The only people I discriminate against are people who can't play football," said Warmath, who coached the Gophers to the 1960 Big Ten and national titles, Rose Bowl trips in 1961 and 1962, and the school's last league title, in 1967. "Murray was more than just an autumn warrior," Jones said. "Everybody on the team knew Murray cared about them, and he cared about them as people." Bell went on to become an All-Pro with the Kansas City Chiefs. Boston became Minnesota's men's athletic director and later vice president for student affairs and athletics. Stephens' No. 15 was retired by Minnesota in 1990.

NUMBERS Minnesota went 65–4–5 from 1900 to 1905 and outscored opponents 2,702-121, including 618-12 in 1903. The Gophers beat Grinnell 146-0 in 1904 by scoring 73 points in each half ... All-America quarterback John McGovern played every minute of every game except one, in 1909 ... Alfred Pillsbury played at Minnesota for eight seasons from 1885 to 1892 because there were no governing bodies regulating collegiate eligibility ... Minnesota has retired four numbers: Bronko Nagurski (72), Bruce Smith (54), Paul Giel (10), and Sandy Stephens (15) ... The Gophers' 16-0 upset of No. 1 Michigan on Oct. 22, 1977, vaulted them into the national rankings at No. 19. They lost 34-22 at Indiana the next week, fell out of the polls, and were unranked for 15 years ... Minnesota trailed Indiana 24-0 in the second quarter on Nov. 4, 1978, before rallying to win its homecoming game 32-31 when Paul Rogind kicked a 31-yard field goal in the final seconds ... Indianapolis Colts coach Tony Dungy was a two-time Academic All-Big Ten selection while playing quarterback at Minnesota from 1974 to 1976 ... Ron Johnson holds the NCAA record catching a pass in 46 consecutive games from 1998 through 2001 ... Lamanzer Williams had a school-record 18.5 sacks in 1997 ... The Gophers scored nine points in the game's final 1:47 to end a 17-game losing streak against Michigan State and beat the Spartans 19-18 in 1998 ... When

---

ALL-TIME TEAM

Selected by sports information director Shane Sandersfeld in 2005

OFFENSE

1934-36	Ed Widseth	OL
1940-42	Richard Wildung	OL
1946-49	Clayton Tonnemaker	OL
1958-60	Tom Brown	OL
1997-2000	Ben Hamilton	OL
1998-2001	Ron Johnson	WR
1994-97	Chatarius Atwell	WR
1970-72	Doug Kingsriter	TE
1959-61	Sandy Stephens	QB
1939-41	Bruce Smith	RB
1951-53	Paul Giel	RB
1986-89	Darrell Thompson	RB
1999-2002	Dan Nystrom	K

DEFENSE

1927-29	Bronko Nagurski	DL
1946-49	Leo Nomellini	DL
1960-62	Bobby Bell	DL
1961-63	Carl Eller	DL
1966-68	Robert Stein	LB
1969-71	William Light	LB
1978-81	Jim Fahnhorst	LB
1968-70	Jeff Wright	DB
1988-91	Sean Lumpkin	DB
1996-99	Tyrone Carter	DB
1998-2000	Willie Middlebrooks	DB
1984-85	Adam Kelly	P

running back Bruce Smith won the Heisman in 1941, Bill Dailey led the Gophers in rushing with 726 yards as the Gophers went 8–0 and won the national title ... Tom Brown won the Outland Trophy in 1960 and also finished second for the Heisman, seven years after Paul Giel finished runner-up in the voting ... Minnesota and Michigan played twice in 1926, once at each other's stadium. When they played in Ann Arbor, fans in Minneapolis watched as two teams of scrubs acted out the plays that took place at Michigan and were reported back to Minnesota via telegraph ... Minnesota enters 2007 with the nation's longest streak, eight seasons, of rushing and passing for over 2,000 yards ... Bill Light had 32 tackles against Iowa in 1970 and 172 total for that season ... Rick Upchurch averaged 13.4 yards per punt return in 1973 and 1974 ... The Gophers upset No. 2 Penn State and No. 6 Ohio State in 1999 ... Minnesota scored the most points in a Big Ten game since 1916, when it defeated Indiana 63-26 in 2006 ... The Gophers went 58–9–5 and shut out 25 opponents from 1932 through 1941 but weren't invited to a bowl game during that span ... Bryan Cupito threw for a school-record 22 TD passes in 2006 ... Paul Giel handled the ball on 53 of 63 snaps when Minnesota upset Michigan in 1953. He rushed 35 times for 112 yards, completed 13 of 18 passes for 169 yards, returned four punts for 49 yards and one kickoff for 24 yards, and intercepted two passes ... Minnesota and Wisconsin combined to commit seven turnovers in the fourth quarter of a 21-21 tie in 1952 ... Minnesota started 6–0 in 2003, 5–0 in 2004, and 4–0 in 2002 and 2005 ... The offensive line allowed only nine sacks in 2004 and three in 2005. The Gophers averaged 5.4 yards per rush in each of those two seasons ... The Gophers won eight Big Ten championships between 1927 and 1941, their final outright title. Their last shared conference title came in

1967, and they've since had eight head coaches and only 15 winning seasons ... Four Gophers have been selected in the first round of the NFL draft since 1969 ... Minnesota hasn't had a QB drafted since Craig Curry in 1972 ... The Gophers' 7–1 start in 2002 was its best record after eight games since 1961 ... The 14 total wins in 1999 and 2000 were the most in a two-year span at Minnesota since winning 14 in 1967 and 1968 ... The Gophers' 8–4 record in 1999 was their most wins in a season since 1967 and ended a streak of eight consecutive losing seasons ... Minnesota set a Big Ten record with 6,430 yards of total offense in 2003. That season, Laurence Maroney averaged 6.92 yards per carry ... Darrell Thompson scored on a 98-yard run against Michigan in 1987 ... Maroney rushed for more than 100 yards in 16 games in 2004 and 2005 and 21 times in his three-year career. Thompson holds the school record with 23 games over 100 ... Wayne "Red" Williams averaged 6.25 yards per carry while rushing for 1,999 yards from 1942 to 1945 ... Jared Ellerson averaged a school-record 24.3 yards per reception in 2005 ... Adam Kelly averaged 46.2 yards per punt in 1984 ... Omar Douglas scored 5 TDs in a 1993 game against Purdue ... Chip Lohmiller kicked a 62-yard field goal against Iowa in 1986 that stands as the longest indoor field goal in college football history ... The Gophers lost to Nebraska by scores of 54-0 in 1974, 56-0 in 1990, and 84-13 in 1983 ... Minnesota gained 742 yards, including 489 rushing, against Ohio State in 1982 ... In 1903, the Gophers went 14–0–1 and outscored opponents 618-12.

QUOTE "I was going to be more than a Big Ten quarterback who was black. I was going to be a Big Ten quarterback who took his team to the Rose Bowl."
—Sandy Stephens, QB of Minnesota's 1961 and 1962 Rose Bowl teams

MINNESOTA ALL-TIME SCORES

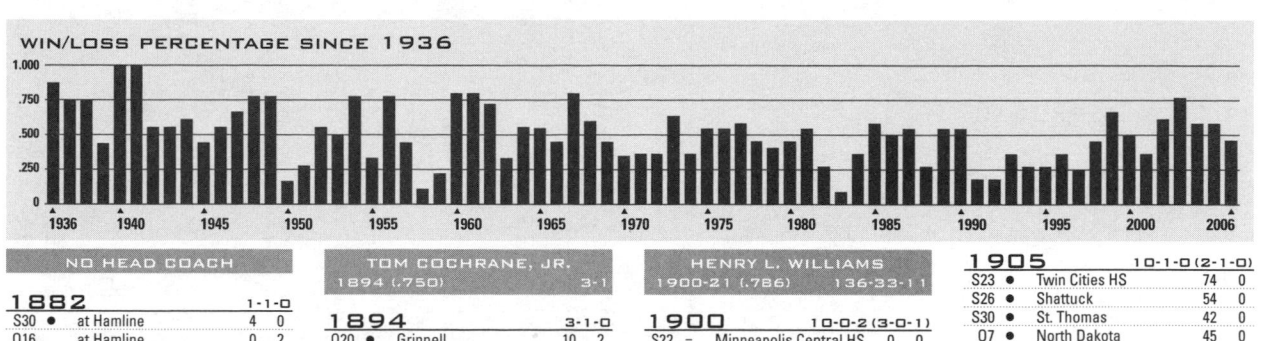

WIN/LOSS PERCENTAGE SINCE 1936

1936 1940 1945 1950 1955 1960 1965 1970 1975 1980 1985 1990 1995 2000 2006

NO HEAD COACH

1882   1-1-0
S30	●	at Hamline	4	0
O16	●	at Hamline	0	2

THOMAS PEEBLES   1883 (.333)   1-2

1883   1-2-0
U		at Carleton	2	4
N4	●	at Hamline	5	0
U		Alumni	2	4

1884-1885
NO TEAM

FREDERICK JONES   1886-88 (.500)   3-3

1886   0-2-0
U		at Shattuck	5	9
U		Shattuck	8	18

1887   2-0-0
U		Minneapolis HS	8	0
U		Alumni	14	0

1888   1-1-0
O28		at Shattuck	8	16
O31		Shattuck	14	0

NO HEAD COACH

1889   3-1-0
O5	●	Alumni	2	0
O26	●	Alumni	10	0
N11	●	at Shattuck	8	28
N20	●	Shattuck	26	0

TOM ECK   1890 (.786)   5-1-1

1890   5-1-1
O27	●	at Hamline	44	0
N3	●	at Shattuck	58	0
N5	=	Alumni	0	0
N8	●	Grinnell	18	13
N15	●	Wisconsin	63	0
N19	●	Alumni	11	14
N29	●	Alumni	14	6

ED "DAD" MOULTON   1891 (.700)   3-1-1

1891   3-1-1
O17	●	Alumni	0	4
O24	●	Wisconsin	26	12
O31	=	at Grinnell	12	12
N2	●	at Iowa	42	4
N14	●	Grinnell	22	14

NO HEAD COACH

1892   5-0-0
O8	●	Alumni	18	10
O17	●	Michigan	14	6
O22	●	Grinnell	40	24
O29	●	at Wisconsin	32	4
N8	●	Northwestern	18	12

WALLIE WINTER   1893 (1.000)   6-0

1893   6-0-0
O14	●	Kansas	12	6
O21	●	Grinnell	36	6
O25	●	at Hamline	10	6
O28	●	at Michigan	34	20
O30	●	at Northwestern	16	0
N11	●	Wisconsin	40	0

TOM COCHRANE, JR.   1894 (.750)   3-1

1894   3-1-0
O20	●	Grinnell	10	2
O27	●	Purdue	24	0
N10	●	Beloit	40	0
N17		at Wisconsin	0	6

WALT "PUDGE" HEFFELFINGER   1895 (.700)   7-3

1895   7-3-0
S28	●	at Minneapolis Central HS	20	0
O5	●	Grinnell	4	6
O12	●	at Boat Club	6	0
O19	●	Iowa State	24	0
O26	●	at Chicago	10	6
O29	●	at Purdue	4	16	*
N2	●	at Macalester	40	0
N16	●	Wisconsin	14	10
N23	●	Michigan *DET*	0	20
N28	●	Alumni	14	0

1896-Present
BIG 10

ALEXANDER JERREMS   1896-97 (.667)   12-6

1896   8-2-0 (1-2-0)
S19	●	at Minneapolis South HS	34	0
S26	●	at Minneapolis Central HS	50	0
O3	●	Carleton	16	6
O10	●	Grinnell	12	0
O17	●	Purdue	14	0
O24	●	Iowa State	18	6
O31	●	Alumni	8	0
N7		Michigan	4	6
N21		at Wisconsin	0	6
N28	●	Kansas *KC*	12	0

1897   4-4-0 (0-3-0)
S25	●	Minneapolis South HS	22	0
O2	●	Macalester	26	0
O9	●	Carleton	48	6
O16	●	Grinnell	6	0
O23	●	Iowa State	10	12
O30		Wisconsin	0	39
N13		Michigan *DET*	0	14
N20		at Purdue	0	6

JACK MINDS   1898 (.444)   4-5

1898   4-5-0 (1-2-0)
S24	●	Carleton	32	0
O1	●	Alumni	0	5
O8	●	Rush Medical	12	0
O15	●	Grinnell	6	16
O22	●	Iowa State	0	6
O29		at Wisconsin	0	28	*
N5	●	North Dakota St.	15	0
N12		Northwestern	17	6
N24		at Illinois	10	11

JOHN HARRISON, BILL LEARY   1899 (.636)   6-3-2

1899   6-3-2 (0-3-0)
S23	●	Minneapolis Central HS	20	0
S30	●	Macalester	29	0
O7	●	Shattuck	40	0
O14	●	Carleton	35	5
O21	●	Iowa State	6	0
O28	=	Grinnell	5	5
N4		Northwestern	5	11
N8	●	Alumni	6	5
N11	=	Beloit	5	5
N18		Wisconsin	0	19
N25		at Chicago	0	29

HENRY L. WILLIAMS   1900-21 (.786)   136-33-11

1900   10-0-2 (3-0-1)
S22	●	Minneapolis Central HS	0	0
S26	●	St. Paul Central HS	26	0
S29	●	Macalester	66	0
O3		Carleton	44	0
O6		Iowa State	27	0
O13	=	Chicago	6	6
O20	●	Grinnell	26	0
O27	●	North Dakota	34	0
N3		Wisconsin	6	5
N10	●	Illinois	23	0
N17	●	Northwestern	21	0
N29	●	at Nebraska	20	12

1901   9-1-1 (3-1-0)
S21	●	Minneapolis Central HS	0	0
S25	●	St. Paul Central HS	16	0
S28	●	Carleton	35	0
O5	●	Chicago Coll.	27	0
O12	●	Nebraska	19	0
O26	●	Iowa	16	0
N2	●	Haskell	28	0
N9	●	North Dakota St.	10	0
N16		Wisconsin	0	18
N23	●	Northwestern *CHI*	16	0
N28	●	at Illinois	16	0

1902   9-2-1 (3-1-0)
S20	●	St. Paul Central HS	0	0
S24	●	Minneapolis Central HS	28	0
S27	●	Carleton	33	0
O4	●	Iowa State	16	0
O8	●	Hamline	59	0
O11	●	Beloit	29	0
O18	●	Nebraska	0	6
O25	●	at Iowa	34	0
N1	●	Grinnell	102	0
N8	●	Illinois	17	5
N15	●	Wisconsin	11	0
N27		at Michigan	6	23

1903   14-0-1 (3-0-1)
S16	●	Minneapolis Central HS	21	6
S19	●	St. Paul Central HS	36	0
S23	●	Minneapolis Eastern HS	37	0
S26	●	Carleton	29	0
S30	●	Macalester	112	0
O3	●	Grinnell	39	0
O7	●	Hamline	65	0
O10	●	Iowa State	46	0
O17	=	Iowa	75	0
O24	●	Beloit	46	0
O31	=	Michigan	6	6
N7	●	at Lawrence	46	0
N14	●	at Illinois	32	0
N21	●	at North Dakota St.	11	0
N26	●	Wisconsin	17	0

1904   13-0-0 (3-0-0)
S17	●	Twin Cities HS	107	0
S24	●	South Dakota	77	0
O1	●	Carleton	65	0
O8	●	North Dakota	35	0
O15	●	Iowa State	32	0
O22	●	Grinnell	146	0
O29	●	Nebraska	16	12
N5	●	Lawrence	69	0
N12	●	Wisconsin	28	0
N19	●	Northwestern *CHI*	17	0
N24	●	at Iowa	11	0
N26	●	at Shattuck	75	0
D3	●	at St. Thomas	47	0

1905   10-1-0 (2-1-0)
S23	●	Twin Cities HS	74	0
S26	●	Shattuck	54	0
S30	●	St. Thomas	42	0
O7		North Dakota	45	0
O14	●	Iowa State	42	0
O21		Iowa	39	0
O28	●	Lawrence	46	0
N4		Wisconsin	12	16
N11	●	South Dakota	81	0
N18	●	Nebraska	35	0
N25	●	Northwestern	72	6

1906   4-1-0 (2-0-0)
O27	●	Iowa State	22	4
N3	●	Nebraska	13	0
N10	●	at Chicago	4	2
N17	●	Carlisle	0	17
N24	●	Indiana	8	6

1907   2-2-1 (0-1-1)
O12	●	Iowa State	8	0
O19	●	Nebraska	8	5
N2		Chicago	12	18
N16		Carlisle	10	12
N23	=	at Wisconsin	17	17

1908   3-2-1 (0-2-0)
O3	●	Lawrence	6	0
O10	●	Iowa State	15	10
O17	=	Nebraska	0	0
O31		at Chicago	0	29
N7		Wisconsin	0	5
N21	●	Carlisle	11	6

1909   6-1-0 (3-0-0)
S25	●	Lawrence	25	0
O2		Iowa	41	0
O9		Iowa State	18	0
O16	●	Nebraska *OMA*	14	0
O30		Chicago	20	6
N13	●	at Wisconsin	34	6
N20		Michigan	6	15

1910   6-1-0 (2-0-0)
S24	●	Lawrence	34	0
O1	●	South Dakota	17	0
O8	●	Iowa State	49	0
O15	●	Nebraska	27	0
O29		at Chicago	24	0
N12		Wisconsin	28	0
N19		at Michigan	0	6

1911   6-0-1 (3-0-1)
S30	●	Iowa State	5	0
O7		South Dakota	5	0
O21	●	Nebraska	21	3
O28	●	at Iowa	24	6
N4	●	Chicago	30	0
N18	●	at Wisconsin	6	6
N25	●	at Illinois	11	0

1912   4-3-0 (2-2-0)
S28	●	South Dakota	0	10
O5	●	Iowa State	5	0
O19	●	Nebraska	13	0
O26		Iowa	56	7
N2	●	Illinois	13	0
N16	●	Wisconsin	0	14
N23		at Chicago	0	7

1913   5-2-0 (2-1-0)
S27	●	South Dakota	14	0
O4	●	Iowa State	25	0
O18	●	at Nebraska	0	7
O25	●	North Dakota	30	0
N1		at Wisconsin	21	3
N15		Chicago	7	13
N22	●	at Illinois	19	9

1914 — 6-1-0 (3-1-0)

	Opp	PF	PA
O3 ●	North Dakota	28	6
O10 ●	Iowa State	26	0
O17 ●	South Dakota	29	7
O24 ●	at Iowa	7	0
O31 │	Illinois	6	21
N14 ●	Wisconsin	14	3
N21 ●	at Chicago	13	7

1915 — 6-0-1 (3-0-1)

	Opp	PF	PA
O2 ●	North Dakota	41	0
O9 ●	Iowa State	34	6
O16 ●	South Dakota	19	0
O23 ●	Iowa	51	13
N6 =	at Illinois	6	6
N13 ●	Chicago	20	7
N20 ●	at Wisconsin	20	3

1916 — 6-1-0 (3-1-0)

	Opp	PF	PA
O7 ●	South Dakota St.	41	7
O14 ●	North Dakota	47	7
O21 ●	South Dakota	81	0
O28 ●	Iowa	67	0
N4 │	Illinois	9	14
N18 ●	Wisconsin	54	0
N25 ●	at Chicago	49	0

1917 — 4-1-0 (3-1-0)

	Opp	PF	PA
O20 ●	South Dakota St.	64	0
O27 ●	Indiana	33	9
N3 │	at Wisconsin	7	10
N17 ●	Chicago	33	0
N24 ●	at Illinois	27	6

1918 — 5-2-1 (2-1-0)

	Opp	PF	PA
O5 =	All Stars	0	0
O12 ●	Overland Station	30	0
O19 ●	at St. Thomas	25	7
O26 ●	Carleton St. Olaf	59	6
N9 │	at Iowa	0	6
N16 ●	Wisconsin	6	0
N23 ●	Municipal Pier	6	20
N30 │	at Chicago	7	0

1919 — 4-2-1 (3-2-0)

	Opp	PF	PA
O4 ●	North Dakota	39	0
O11 =	Nebraska	6	6
O18 ●	at Indiana	20	6
O25 ●	Iowa	6	9
N1 ●	at Wisconsin	19	7
N8 ●	Illinois	6	10
N22 ●	at Michigan	34	7

1920 — 1-6-0 (0-6-0)

	Opp	PF	PA
O2 ●	North Dakota	41	3
O9 │	at Northwestern	0	17
O23 ●	Indiana	7	21
O30 │	at Illinois	7	17
N6 ●	Wisconsin	0	3
N13 │	at Iowa	7	28
N20 │	Michigan	0	3

1921 — 3-4-0 (2-4-0)

	Opp	PF	PA
O1 ●	North Dakota	19	0
O8 ●	Northwestern	28	0
O15 │	at Ohio State	0	27
O22 │	Indiana	6	0
O29 │	at Wisconsin	0	35
N5 │	Iowa	7	41
N19 │	at Michigan	0	38

1922 — 3-3-1 (2-3-1)

	Opp	PF	PA
O7 ●	North Dakota	22	0
O14 ●	at Indiana	20	0
O21 =	at Northwestern	7	7
O28 ●	Ohio State	9	0
N4 │	Wisconsin	0	14
N11 │	at Iowa	14	28
N25 │	Michigan	7	16

1923 — 5-1-1 (2-1-1)

	Opp	PF	PA
O6 ●	Iowa State	20	17
O13 ●	Haskell	13	12
O20 ●	North Dakota	27	0
O27 =	at Wisconsin	0	0
N3 ●	Northwestern	34	14
N17 ●	Iowa	20	7
N24 │	at Michigan	0	10

1924 — 3-3-2 (1-2-1)

	Opp	PF	PA
O4 ●	North Dakota	14	0
O11 ●	Haskell	20	0
O18 =	at Wisconsin	7	7
O25 │	at Iowa	0	13
N1 │	Michigan	0	13
N8 =	Iowa State	7	7
N15 ●	Illinois	20	7
N22 │	Vanderbilt	0	16

1925 — 5-2-1 (1-1-1)

	Opp	PF	PA
O3 ●	North Dakota	25	0
O10 ●	Grinnell	34	6
O17 ●	Wabash	32	6
O24 ●	Notre Dame	7	19
O31 = │	Wisconsin	12	12
N7 ●	Butler	33	7
N14 ●	Iowa	33	0
N21 │	at Michigan	0	35

1926 — 5-3-0 (2-2-0)

	Opp	PF	PA
O2 ●	North Dakota	51	0
O9 ●	Notre Dame	0	20
O16 │	at Michigan	0	20
O23 ●	Wabash	67	7
O30 ●	at Wisconsin	16	10
N6 ●	at Iowa	41	0
N13 ●	Butler	81	0
N20 │	Michigan	6	7

1927 — 6-0-2 (3-0-1)

	Opp	PF	PA
O1 ●	North Dakota	57	10
O8 ●	Oklahoma State	40	0
O15 = │	at Indiana	14	14
O22 ●	Iowa	38	0
O29 ●	Wisconsin	13	7
N5 ●	at Notre Dame	7	7
N12 ●	Drake	27	6
N19 │	at Michigan	13	7

1928 — 6-2-0 (4-2-0)

	Opp	PF	PA
O6 ●	Creighton	49	0
O13 ●	Purdue	15	0
O20 ●	Chicago	33	7
O27 ●	at Iowa	6	7
N3 │	at Northwestern	9	10
N10 ●	Indiana	21	12
N17 ●	Haskell	52	0
N24 │	at Wisconsin	6	0

1929 — 6-2-0 (3-2-0)

	Opp	PF	PA
O5 ●	Coe	39	0
O12 ●	Vanderbilt	15	6
O19 ●	at Northwestern	26	14
O26 ●	Ripon	54	0
N2 ●	Indiana	19	7
N9 ●	at Iowa	7	9
N16 ●	Michigan	6	7
N23 ●	Wisconsin	13	12

1930 — 3-4-1 (1-3-0)

	Opp	PF	PA
S27 ●	South Dakota St.	48	0
O4 ●	Vanderbilt	7	33
O11 =	Stanford	0	0
O18 ●	Indiana	6	0
N1 ●	Northwestern	6	27
N8 ●	South Dakota	59	0
N15 ●	at Michigan	0	7
N22 ●	at Wisconsin	0	14

1931 — 7-3-0 (3-2-0)

	Opp	PF	PA
S19 ●	Ripon	30	0
S26 ●	North Dakota St.	13	7
O3 ●	Oklahoma State	20	0
O10 │	at Stanford	0	13
O24 ●	Iowa	34	0
O31 ●	Wisconsin	14	0
N7 │	at Northwestern	14	32
N14 ●	Cornell Coll.	47	7
N21 │	at Michigan	0	6
N28 ●	Ohio State	19	7

1932 — 5-3-0 (2-3-0)

	Opp	PF	PA
O1 ●	South Dakota St.	12	0
O8 │	Purdue	0	7
O15 ●	Nebraska	7	6
O22 ●	at Iowa	21	6
O29 ●	Northwestern	7	0
N5 │	Mississippi	26	0
N12 ●	at Wisconsin	13	20
N19 │	Michigan	0	3

1933 — 4-0-4 (2-0-4)

	Opp	PF	PA
S30 ●	South Dakota St.	19	6
O7 = │	Indiana	6	6
O14 = │	Purdue	7	7
O21 ●	Pittsburgh	7	3
O28 ●	Iowa	19	7
N4 = │	at Northwestern	0	0
N18 = │	at Michigan	0	0
N25 ●	Wisconsin	6	3

1934 — 8-0-0 (5-0-0)

	Opp	PF	PA
S29 ●	North Dakota St.	56	12
O3 ●	Nebraska	20	0
O20 ●	at Pittsburgh	13	7
O28 │	at Iowa	48	12
N3 │	Michigan	34	0
N10 ●	Indiana	30	0
N17 ●	Chicago	35	7
N24 ●	at Wisconsin	34	0

1935 — 8-0-0 (5-0-0)

	Opp	PF	PA
O5 ●	North Dakota St.	26	6
O12 ●	at Nebraska	12	7
O19 ●	Tulane	20	0
O26 ●	Northwestern	21	13
N2 ●	Purdue	29	7
N9 ●	at Iowa	13	6
N16 ●	at Michigan	40	0
N23 ●	Wisconsin	33	7

1936 — 7-1-0 (4-1-0)

	Opp	PF	PA
S26 ●	at Washington	14	7
O10 ●	Nebraska	7	0
O17 ●	Michigan	26	0
O24 ●	Purdue	33	0
O31 │	at Northwestern	0	6
N7 ●	Iowa	52	0
N14 ●	Texas	47	19
N21 ●	at Wisconsin	24	0

1937 — 6-2-0 (5-0-0)

	Opp	PF	PA
S25 ●	North Dakota St.	69	7
O2 │	at Nebraska	9	14
O9 │	Indiana	6	0
O16 │	at Michigan	39	6
O30 │	Notre Dame	6	7
N6 ●	at Iowa	35	10
N13 ●	Northwestern	7	0
N20 ●	Wisconsin	13	6

1938 — 6-2-0 (4-1-0)

	Opp	PF	PA
S24 ●	Washington	15	0
O1 ●	Nebraska	16	7
O8 │	Purdue	7	0
O15 ●	Michigan	7	6
O29 ●	at Northwestern	3	6
N5 ●	Iowa	28	0
N12 ●	at Notre Dame	0	19
N19 │	at Wisconsin	21	0

1939 — 3-4-1 (2-3-1)

	Opp	PF	PA
S30 ●	Arizona	62	0
O7 ●	at Nebraska	0	6
O14 = │	Purdue	13	13
O21 ●	Ohio State	20	23
N4 ●	Northwestern	7	14
N11 ●	at Michigan	20	7
N18 ●	at Iowa	9	13
N25 ●	Wisconsin	23	6

1940 — 8-0-0 (6-0-0)

	Opp	PF	PA
S28 ●	Washington	19	14
O5 ●	Nebraska	13	7
O19 ●	at Ohio State	13	7
O26 ●	Iowa	34	6
N2 ●	at Northwestern	13	12
N9 ●	Michigan	7	6
N16 ●	Purdue	33	6
N23 ●	at Wisconsin	22	13

1941 — 8-0-0 (5-0-0)

	Opp	PF	PA
S27 ●	at Washington	14	6
O11 ●	Illinois	34	6
O18 ●	Pittsburgh	39	0
O25 ●	at Michigan	7	0
N1 ●	Northwestern	8	7
N8 ●	Nebraska	9	0
N15 ●	at Iowa	34	13
N22 ●	Wisconsin	41	6

1942 — 5-4-0 (3-3-0)

	Opp	PF	PA
S26 ●	Pittsburgh	50	7
O3 │	Iowa Pre-Flight	6	7
O10 │	at Illinois	13	20
O17 │	at Nebraska	15	2
O24 │	Michigan	16	14
O31 │	Northwestern	19	7
N7 │	Indiana	0	7
N14 │	Iowa	27	7
N21 │	at Wisconsin	6	20

1943 — 5-4-0 (2-3-0)

	Opp	PF	PA
S25 ●	Missouri	26	13
O2 ●	Nebraska	54	0
O16 ●	Camp Grant	13	7
O23 │	at Michigan	6	49
O30 │	at Northwestern	6	42
N6 │	Purdue	7	14
N13 ●	Iowa	33	14
N20 ●	Iowa	25	13
N27 │	Iowa Pre-Flight	0	32

1944 — 5-3-1 (3-2-1)

	Opp	PF	PA
S23 ●	Iowa Pre-Flight	13	19
S30 ●	Nebraska	39	0
O7 │	Michigan	13	28
O14 ●	Missouri	39	27
O28 │	at Ohio State	14	34
N4 = │	Northwestern	14	14
N11 ●	Indiana	19	14
N18 ●	at Iowa	46	0
N25 ●	at Wisconsin	28	26

1945 — 4-5-0 (1-5-0)

	Opp	PF	PA
S22 ●	Missouri	34	0
O6 ●	at Nebraska	61	7
O13 ●	Fort Warren	14	0
O20 ●	Northwestern	30	7
O27 │	Ohio State	7	20
N3 │	at Michigan	0	26
N10 ●	Indiana	0	49
N17 ●	at Iowa	19	20
N24 ●	Wisconsin	12	26

1946 — 5-4-0 (3-4-0)

	Opp	PF	PA
S28 ●	Nebraska	33	6
O5 │	Indiana	0	21
O12 │	at Northwestern	7	14
O19 ●	Wyoming	46	0
O26 │	at Ohio State	9	39
N2 │	Michigan	0	21
N9 ●	Purdue	13	7
N16 ●	Iowa	16	6
N23 ●	at Wisconsin	6	0

1947 — 6-3-0 (3-3-0)

	Opp	PF	PA
S27 ●	Washington	7	6
O4 ●	at Nebraska	28	13
O11 ●	Northwestern	37	21
O18 │	at Illinois	13	40
O25 ●	at Michigan	6	13
N1 ●	Pittsburgh	29	0
N8 │	Purdue	26	21
N15 ●	at Iowa	7	13
N22 ●	Wisconsin	21	0

1948 — 7-2-0 (5-2-0)

	Opp	PF	PA
S25 ●	at Washington	20	0
O2 ●	Nebraska	39	13
O9 │	at Northwestern	16	19
O16 ●	Illinois	6	0
O23 │	Michigan	14	27
O30 │	Indiana	30	7
N6 │	Purdue	34	7
N13 ●	at Iowa	28	21
N20 │	at Wisconsin	16	0

1949 — 7-2-0 (4-2-0)

	Opp	PF	PA
S24 ●	Washington	48	20
O1 ●	at Nebraska	28	6
O8 │	Northwestern	21	7
O15 ●	at Ohio State	27	0
O22 │	at Michigan	7	14
O29 │	Purdue	7	13
N5 │	Iowa	55	7
N12 ●	at Pittsburgh	24	7
N19 │	Wisconsin	14	6

1950 — 1-7-1 (1-4-1)

	Opp	PF	PA
S30 ●	at Washington	13	28
O7 ●	Nebraska	26	32
O14 │	at Northwestern	6	13
O21 │	Ohio State	0	48
O28 = │	Michigan	7	7
N4 │	Iowa	0	13
N11 │	at Michigan State	0	27
N18 ●	Purdue	27	14
N25 │	at Wisconsin	0	14

WES FESLER
1951-53 (.444) 10-13-4

1951 2-6-1 (1-4-1)

S29			Washington	20	25
O6			at California	14	55
O13		|	Northwestern	7	21
O20	●		Nebraska	39	20
O27		|	at Michigan	27	54
N3	=	|	at Iowa	20	20
N10	●	|	Indiana	16	14
N17		|	at Purdue	13	19
N24		|	Wisconsin	6	30

1952 4-3-2 (3-1-2)

S27			at Washington	13	19
O4			California	13	49
O11	●	|	Northwestern	27	26
O18	●	|	Illinois	13	7
O25		|	at Michigan	0	21
N1	●	|	Iowa	17	7
N8	=	|	Purdue	14	14
N15	●		at Nebraska	13	7
N22	=	|	at Wisconsin	21	21

1953 4-4-1 (3-3-1)

S26			at USC	7	17
O3		|	Michigan State	0	21
O10	●	|	at Northwestern	30	13
O17		|	at Illinois	7	27
O24	●	|	Michigan	22	0
O31	●		Pittsburgh	35	14
N7	●	|	Indiana	28	20
N14		|	at Iowa	0	27
N21	=	|	Wisconsin	21	21

MURRAY WARMATH
1954-71 (.526) 87-78-7

1954 7-2-0 (4-2-0)

S25	●		Nebraska	19	7
O2	●		at Pittsburgh	46	7
O9	●	|	Northwestern	26	7
O16	●	|	Illinois	19	6
O23		|	at Michigan	0	34
O30	●	|	Michigan State	19	13
N6	●		Oregon State	44	6
N13	●	|	Iowa	22	20
N20		|	at Wisconsin	0	27

1955 3-6-0 (2-5-0)

S24			Washington	0	30
O1		|	Purdue	6	7
O8	●	|	at Northwestern	18	7
O15		|	at Illinois	13	21
O22		|	Michigan	13	14
O29	●		USC	25	19
N5		|	at Iowa	0	26
N12		|	at Michigan State	14	42
N19	●	|	Wisconsin	21	6

1956 6-1-2 (4-1-2)

S29	●		at Washington	34	14
O6	●	|	Purdue	21	14
O13	=	|	Northwestern	0	0
O20	●	|	Illinois	16	13
O27	●	|	at Michigan	20	7
N3	●		Pittsburgh	9	6
N10		|	Iowa	0	7
N17	●	|	Michigan State	14	13
N24	=	|	at Wisconsin	13	13

1957 4-5-0 (3-5-0)

S28	●		Washington	46	7
O5	●	|	Purdue	21	17
O12	●	|	at Northwestern	41	6
O19		|	at Illinois	13	34
O26		|	Michigan	7	24
N2	●	|	Indiana	34	0
N9		|	at Iowa	20	44
N16		|	at Michigan State	13	42
N23		|	Wisconsin	6	14

1958 1-8-0 (1-6-0)

S27			at Washington	21	24
O4			Pittsburgh	7	13
O11		|	Northwestern	3	7
O18		|	Illinois	8	20
O25		|	at Michigan	19	20
N1		|	at Indiana	0	6
N8		|	Iowa	6	28
N15	●	|	Michigan State	39	12
N22		|	at Wisconsin	12	27

1959 2-7-0 (1-6-0)

S26			Nebraska	12	32
O3	●	|	Indiana	24	14
O10		|	at Northwestern	0	6
O17		|	at Illinois	6	14
O24		|	Michigan	6	14
O31	●		Vanderbilt	20	6
N7		|	at Iowa	0	33
N14		|	at Purdue	23	29
N21		|	Wisconsin	7	11

1960 8-2-0 (6-1-0)

S24	●		at Nebraska	26	14
O1	●	|	Indiana	42	0
O8	●	|	Northwestern	7	0
O15	●	|	Illinois	21	10
O22	●	|	at Michigan	10	0
O29	●		Kansas State	48	7
N5	●	|	Iowa	27	10
N12		|	Purdue	14	23
N19	●	|	at Wisconsin	26	7
			ROSE BOWL		
J2			Washington	7	17

1961 8-2-0 (6-1-0)

S30			Missouri	0	6
O7	●		Oregon	14	7
O14	●	|	at Northwestern	10	3
O21	●	|	at Illinois	33	0
O28	●	|	Michigan	23	20
N4	●	|	Michigan State	13	0
N11	●	|	at Iowa	16	9
N18	●	|	Purdue	10	7
N25		|	Wisconsin	21	23
			ROSE BOWL		
J1	●		UCLA	21	3

1962 6-2-1 (5-2-0)

S29	=		Missouri	0	0
O6	●		Navy	21	0
O13		|	Northwestern	22	34
O20	●	|	Illinois	17	0
O27	●	|	at Michigan	17	0
N3	●	|	at Michigan State	28	7
N10	●	|	Iowa	10	0
N17	●	|	Purdue	7	6
N24		|	at Wisconsin	9	14

1963 3-6-0 (2-5-0)

S28			Nebraska	7	14
O5	●		Army	24	8
O12		|	at Northwestern	8	15
O19		|	at Illinois	6	16
O26	●	|	Michigan	6	0
N2		|	Indiana	6	24
N9		|	at Iowa	13	27
N16		|	at Purdue	11	13
N28	●	|	Wisconsin	14	0

1964 5-4-0 (4-3-0)

S26			Nebraska	21	26
O3	●		at California	26	20
O10	●	|	Northwestern	21	18
O17		|	Illinois	0	14
O24		|	at Michigan	12	19
O31	●	|	at Indiana	21	0
N7	●	|	Iowa	14	13
N14	●	|	Purdue	14	7
N21		|	at Wisconsin	7	14

1965 5-4-1 (5-2-0)

S17	=		at USC	20	20
S25			Washington State	13	14
O2			Missouri	6	17
O9	●	|	Indiana	42	18
O16	●	|	at Iowa	14	3
O23	●	|	Michigan	14	13
O30		|	at Ohio State	10	11
N6	●	|	Northwestern	27	22
N13		|	at Purdue	0	35
N20	●	|	Wisconsin	42	7

1966 4-5-1 (3-3-1)

S17			at Missouri	0	24
S24	●		Stanford	35	21
O1			Kansas	14	16
O8	=	|	at Indiana	7	7
O15	●	|	Iowa	17	0
O22		|	at Michigan	0	49
O29	●	|	Ohio State	17	7
N5	●	|	at Northwestern	28	13
N12		|	Purdue	0	16
N19		|	at Wisconsin	6	7

1967 8-2-0 (6-1-0)

S23	●		Utah	13	12
S30			at Nebraska	0	7
O7	●		SMU	23	3
O14	●	|	at Illinois	10	7
O21	●	|	Michigan State	21	0
O28	●	|	Michigan	20	15
N4	●	|	Iowa	10	0
N11		|	at Purdue	12	41
N18	●	|	Indiana	33	7
N25	●	|	Wisconsin	21	14

1968 6-4-0 (5-2-0)

S21			USC	20	29
S28			Nebraska	14	17
O5	●		Wake Forest	24	19
O12	●	|	Illinois	17	10
O19	●	|	at Michigan State	14	13
O26		|	at Michigan	20	33
N2		|	Iowa	28	35
N9	●	|	Purdue	27	13
N16	●	|	at Indiana	20	6
N23	●	|	at Wisconsin	23	15

1969 4-5-1 (4-3-0)

S20			at Arizona State	26	48
S27	=		Ohio U.	35	35
O4			Nebraska	14	42
O11		|	at Indiana	7	17
O18		|	Ohio State	7	34
O25		|	Michigan	9	35
N1	●	|	at Iowa	35	8
N8	●	|	Northwestern	28	21
N15	●	|	at Michigan State	14	10
N22	●	|	Wisconsin	35	10

1970 3-6-1 (2-4-1)

S19			at Missouri	12	34
S26	●		Ohio U.	49	7
O3			Nebraska	10	35
O10	●	|	Indiana	23	0
O17		|	at Ohio State	8	28
O24		|	at Michigan	13	39
O31	=	|	Iowa	14	14
N7		|	at Northwestern	14	28
N14	●	|	Michigan State	23	13
N21		|	at Wisconsin	14	39

1971 4-7-0 (3-5-0)

S11	●	|	Indiana	28	0
S18			at Nebraska	7	35
S25			Washington State	20	31
O2	●		Kansas	38	20
O9		|	at Purdue	13	27
O16	●	|	at Iowa	19	14
O23		|	Michigan	7	35
O30		|	Ohio State	12	14
N6		|	at Northwestern	20	41
N13		|	at Michigan State	25	40
N20	●	|	Wisconsin	23	21

CAL STOLL
1972-78 (.500) 39-39

1972 4-7-0 (4-4-0)

S16		|	at Indiana	23	27
S23			Colorado	6	38
S30			at Nebraska	0	49
O7			Kansas	28	34
O14		|	Purdue	3	28
O21	●	|	Iowa	43	14
O28		|	at Michigan	0	42
N4		|	at Ohio State	19	27
N11	●	|	Northwestern	35	29
N18	●	|	Michigan State	14	10
N25	●	|	at Wisconsin	14	6

1973 7-4-0 (6-2-0)

S15		|	at Ohio State	7	56
S22	●		North Dakota	41	14
S29			at Kansas	19	34
O6			Nebraska	7	48
O13	●	|	Indiana	24	3
O20	●	|	at Iowa	31	23
O27		|	Michigan	7	34
N3	●	|	at Northwestern	52	43
N10	●	|	Purdue	34	7
N17	●	|	at Illinois	19	16
N24	●	|	Wisconsin	19	17

1974 4-7-0 (2-6-0)

S14		|	Ohio State	19	34
S21	●		North Dakota	42	30
S28	●		TCU	9	7
O5			at Nebraska	0	54
O12		|	at Indiana	3	34
O19	●	|	Iowa	23	17
O26		|	at Michigan	0	49
N2		|	Northwestern	13	21
N9	●	|	at Purdue	24	20
N16		|	Illinois	14	17
N23		|	at Wisconsin	14	49

1975 6-5-0 (3-5-0)

S13		|	at Indiana	14	20
S20	●		Western Michigan	38	0
S27	●		Oregon	10	7
O4	●		Ohio U.	21	0
O11		|	at Illinois	23	42
O18		|	Michigan State	15	38
O25	●	|	at Iowa	31	7
N1		|	Michigan	21	28
N8	●	|	Northwestern	33	9
N15		|	at Ohio State	6	38
N22	●	|	Wisconsin	24	3

1976 6-5-0 (4-4-0)

S11	●	|	Indiana	32	13
S18	●		Washington State	28	14
S25	●		Western Michigan	21	10
O2			at Washington	7	38
O9	●	|	Illinois	29	14
O16	●	|	at Michigan State	14	10
O23		|	Iowa	12	22
O30		|	at Michigan	0	45
N6	●	|	at Northwestern	38	10
N13		|	Ohio State	3	9
N20		|	at Wisconsin	17	26

1977 7-5-0 (4-4-0)

S10	●		Western Michigan	10	7
S17		|	at Ohio State	7	38
S24	●		UCLA	27	13
O1	●		Washington	19	17
O8		|	at Iowa	6	18
O15	●	|	Northwestern	13	7
O22	●	|	Michigan	16	0
O29		|	at Indiana	22	34
N5		|	Michigan State	10	29
N12	●	|	at Illinois	21	0
N19	●	|	Wisconsin	13	7
			HALL OF FAME CLASSIC		
D22			Maryland	7	17

1978 5-6-0 (4-4-0)

S16	●		Toledo	38	12
S23		|	Ohio State	10	27
S30			at UCLA	3	17
O7			Oregon State	14	17
O14	●	|	Iowa	22	20
O21	●	|	at Northwestern	38	14
O28		|	at Michigan	10	42
N4	●	|	Indiana	32	31
N11		|	at Michigan State	9	33
N18	●	|	Illinois	24	6
N25		|	at Wisconsin	10	48

JOE SALEM
1979-83 (.355) 19-35-1

1979 4-6-1 (3-5-1)

S8	●		Ohio U.	24	10
S15		|	Ohio State	17	21
S22			at USC	14	48
S29	●	|	Northwestern	38	8
O6	●	|	Purdue	31	14
O13		|	at Michigan	21	31
O20	●	|	at Iowa	24	7
O27	=	|	Illinois	17	17
N3		|	at Indiana	24	42
N10		|	at Michigan State	17	31
N17		|	Wisconsin	37	42

1980 5-6-0 (4-5-0)

S13	●		Ohio U.	38	14
S20		|	at Ohio State	0	47
S27			USC	7	24
O4	●	|	at Northwestern	49	21
O11		|	at Purdue	7	21
O18		|	Michigan	14	37
O25	●	|	Iowa	24	6
N1	●	|	at Illinois	21	18
N8	●	|	Indiana	31	7
N15		|	Michigan State	12	30
N22		|	at Wisconsin	7	25

100 MINNESOTA

BIG TEN TEAMS

1981 6-5-0 (4-5-0)

S12	●		Ohio U.	19	17
S19	●	|	Purdue	16	13
S26	●		Oregon State	42	12
O3		|	at Illinois	29	38
O10	●	|	Northwestern	35	23
O17		|	at Indiana	16	17
O24	●	|	at Iowa	12	10
O31		|	Michigan	13	34
N7	●	|	Ohio State	35	31
N14		|	at Michigan State	36	43
N21		|	Wisconsin	21	26

1982 3-8-0 (1-8-0)

S11	●		Ohio U.	57	3
S18	●	|	at Purdue	36	10
S25	●		Washington State	41	11
O2		|	Illinois	24	42
O9		|	at Northwestern	21	31
O16		|	Indiana	21	40
O23		|	Iowa	16	21
O30		|	at Michigan	14	52
N6		|	at Ohio State	10	35
N13		|	Michigan State	7	26
N20		|	at Wisconsin	0	24

1983 1-10-0 (0-9-0)

S10	●		at Rice	21	17
S17			Nebraska	13	84
S24		|	Purdue	20	32
O1		|	at Ohio State	18	69
O8		|	at Indiana	31	38
O15		|	Wisconsin	17	56
O22		|	at Northwestern	8	19
O29		|	at Michigan State	10	34
N5		|	Illinois	23	50
N12		|	Michigan	10	58
N19		|	at Iowa	10	61

LOU HOLTZ
1984-85 (.455) 10-12

1984 4-7-0 (3-6-0)

S8	●		Rice	31	24
S15			at Nebraska	7	38
S22		|	at Purdue	10	34
S29		|	Ohio State	22	35
O6	●	|	Indiana	33	24
O13	●	|	at Wisconsin	17	14
O20		|	Northwestern	28	31
O27		|	Michigan State	13	20
N3		|	at Illinois	3	48
N10		|	at Michigan	7	31
N17	●	|	Iowa	23	17

1985 7-5-0 (4-4-0)

S14	●		Wichita St.	28	14
S21	●		Montana	62	17
S28			Oklahoma	7	13
O5	●	|	Purdue	45	15
O12	●	|	at Northwestern	21	10
O19	●	|	at Indiana	22	7
O26		|	Ohio State	19	23
N2		|	at Michigan State	26	31
N9	●	|	Wisconsin	27	18
N16		|	Michigan	7	48
N23		|	at Iowa	9	31
			INDEPENDENCE BOWL		
D21	●		Clemson	20	13

JOHN GUTEKUNST
1985-91 (.441) 29-37-2

1986 6-6-0 (5-3-0)

S13	●		Bowling Green	31	7
S20			at Oklahoma	0	63
S27			Pacific	20	24
O4	●	|	at Purdue	36	9
O11	●	|	Northwestern	44	23
O18	●	|	Indiana	19	17
O25		|	at Ohio State	0	33
N1		|	Michigan State	23	52
N8	●	|	at Wisconsin	27	20
N15	●	|	at Michigan	20	17
N22		|	Iowa	27	30
			LIBERTY BOWL		
D29			Tennessee	14	21

1987 6-5-0 (3-5-0)

S12	●		No. Iowa	24	7
S19	●		California	32	23
S26	●		Central Michigan	30	10
O3	●	|	Purdue	21	19
O10	●	|	at Northwestern	45	33
O16		|	Indiana	17	18
O24		|	at Ohio State	9	42
O31		|	at Illinois	17	27
N7		|	Michigan	20	30
N14	●	|	Wisconsin	22	19
N21		|	at Iowa	20	34

1988 2-7-2 (0-6-2)

S10			Washington State	9	41
S17	●		Miami (Ohio)	35	3
S24	●		Northern Illinois	31	20
O1		|	at Purdue	10	14
O8	=	|	Northwestern	28	28
O15		|	at Indiana	13	33
O22		|	Ohio State	6	13
O29	=	|	Illinois	27	27
N5		|	at Michigan	7	22
N12		|	at Wisconsin	7	14
N19		|	Iowa	22	31

1989 6-5-0 (4-4-0)

S16	●		at Iowa State	30	20
S23			Nebraska	0	48
S30	●		Indiana St.	34	14
O7	●	|	Purdue	35	15
O14	●	|	at Northwestern	20	18
O21		|	at Indiana	18	28
O28		|	Ohio State	37	41
N4	●	|	Wisconsin	24	22
N11		|	at Michigan State	7	21
N18		|	Michigan	15	49
N25	●	|	at Iowa	43	7

1990 6-5-0 (5-3-0)

S8			Utah	29	35
S15	●		Iowa State	20	16
S22			at Nebraska	0	56
O6	●	|	at Purdue	19	7
O13	●	|	Northwestern	35	25
O20	●	|	Indiana	12	0
O27		|	at Ohio State	23	52
N3	●	|	at Wisconsin	21	3
N10		|	Michigan State	16	28
N17		|	at Michigan	18	35
N24	●	|	Iowa	31	24

1991 2-9-0 (1-7-0)

S14	●		San Jose State	26	20
S21			at Colorado	0	58
S28			Pittsburgh	13	14
O5		|	at Illinois	3	24
O12	●	|	Purdue	6	3
O19		|	at Michigan State	12	20
O25		|	Michigan	6	52
N2		|	at Indiana	8	34
N9		|	Ohio State	6	35
N16		|	Wisconsin	16	19
N23		|	at Iowa	8	23

JIM WACKER
1992-96 (.291) 16-39

1992 2-9-0 (2-6-0)

S12			San Jose State	30	39
S19			Colorado	20	21
S26			at Pittsburgh	33	41
O3	●	|	Illinois	18	17
O10		|	at Purdue	20	24
O17		|	Michigan State	15	20
O24		|	at Michigan	13	63
O31		|	Indiana	17	24
N7		|	at Ohio State	0	17
N14		|	at Wisconsin	6	34
N21	●	|	Iowa	28	13

1993 4-7-0 (3-5-0)

S4		|	at Penn State	20	38
S11	●		Indiana St.	27	10
S18			Kansas State	25	30
S25			at San Diego State	17	48
O2		|	Indiana	19	23
O9	●	|	Purdue	59	56
O16	●	|	at Northwestern	28	26
O23	●	|	Wisconsin	28	21
N6		|	at Illinois	20	23
N13		|	Michigan	7	58
N20		|	at Iowa	3	21

1994 3-8-0 (1-7-0)

S3		|	Penn State	3	56
S10	●		Pacific	33	7
S17	●		San Diego State	40	17
S24			at Kansas State	0	35
O1		|	at Indiana	14	25
O8		|	at Purdue	37	49
O15		|	Northwestern	31	37
O22	●	|	at Wisconsin	17	14
N5		|	Illinois	17	21
N12		|	at Michigan	22	38
N19		|	Iowa	42	49

1995 3-8-0 (1-7-0)

S16	●		Ball State	31	7
S23			at Syracuse	17	27
S30	●		Arkansas State	55	7
O7	●	|	Purdue	39	38
O14		|	Northwestern	17	27
O21		|	at Michigan State	31	34
O28		|	at Michigan	17	52
N4		|	Ohio State	21	49
N11		|	Wisconsin	27	34
N18		|	at Illinois	14	48
N25		|	at Iowa	3	45

1996 4-7 (1-7)

S7	●		at La. Monroe	30	3
S14	●		Ball State	26	23
S21	●		Syracuse	35	33
O5		|	at Purdue	27	30
O12		|	at Northwestern	24	26
O19		|	Michigan State	9	27
O26		|	Michigan	10	44
N2		|	at Ohio State	0	45
N9		|	at Wisconsin	28	45
N16	●	|	Illinois	23	21
N23		|	Iowa	24	43

GLEN MASON
1997-2006 (.529) 64-57

1997 3-9 (1-7)

A30			at Hawaii	3	17
S13	●		Iowa State	53	29
S20	●		at Memphis	20	17
S27			Houston	43	45
O4		|	at Michigan State	10	31
O11		|	Purdue	43	59
O18		|	at Penn State	15	16
O25		|	Wisconsin	21	22
N1		|	at Michigan	3	24
N8		|	Ohio State	3	31
N15	●	|	Indiana	24	12
N22		|	at Iowa	0	31

1998 5-6 (2-6)

S5	●		Arkansas State	17	14
S12	●		at Houston	14	7
S19	●		Memphis	41	14
O3		|	at Purdue	21	56
O10		|	Penn State	17	27
O17		|	at Ohio State	15	45
O24	●	|	Michigan State	19	18
O31		|	Michigan	10	15
N7		|	at Wisconsin	7	26
N14		|	at Indiana	19	20
N21	●	|	Iowa	49	7

1999 8-4 (5-3)

S4	●		Ohio U.	33	7
S11	●		La. Monroe	35	0
S18	●		Illinois St.	55	7
O2	●	|	at Northwestern	33	14
O9		|	Wisconsin	17	20
O16	●	|	at Illinois	37	7
O23		|	Ohio State	17	20
O30		|	Purdue	28	33
N6	●	|	at Penn State	24	23
N13	●	|	Indiana	44	20
N20	●	|	at Iowa	25	21
			SUN BOWL		
D31			Oregon	20	24

2000 6-6 (4-4)

S2	●		La. Monroe	47	10
S9			Ohio U.	17	23
S16	●		at Baylor	34	9
S23		|	at Purdue	24	38
S30	●	|	Illinois	44	10
O7	●	|	Penn State	25	16
O14	●	|	at Ohio State	29	17
O21		|	at Indiana	43	51
O28		|	Northwestern	35	41
N4		|	at Wisconsin	20	41
N18	●	|	Iowa	27	24
			MICRON PC.COM BOWL		
D28			North Carolina St.	30	38

2001 4-7 (2-6)

A30			at Toledo	7	38
S8	●		La. Lafayette	44	14
S29		|	Purdue	28	35
O6		|	at Illinois	14	25
O13		|	at Northwestern	17	23
O20	●	|	Michigan State	28	19
O27	●		Murray St.	66	10
N3		|	Ohio State	28	31
N10		|	at Michigan	10	31
N17		|	at Iowa	24	42
N24	●	|	Wisconsin	42	31

2002 8-5 (3-5)

A31	●		Texas St.	42	0
S7	●		at La. Lafayette	35	11
S14	●		Toledo	31	21
S21	●		Buffalo	41	17
S28		|	at Purdue	15	28
O3	●	|	Illinois	31	10
O10	●	|	Northwestern	45	42
O19	●	|	at Michigan State	28	7
N2		|	at Ohio State	3	34
N9		|	Michigan	24	41
N16		|	Iowa	21	45
N23		|	at Wisconsin	31	49
			MUSIC CITY BOWL		
D30	●		Arkansas	29	14

2003 10-3 (5-3)

A30	●		Tulsa	49	10
S6	●		Troy State	48	7
S13	●		at Ohio U.	42	20
S20	●		La. Lafayette	48	14
S27	●	|	at Penn State	20	14
O4	●	|	at Northwestern	42	17
O10		|	Michigan	35	38
O18		|	Michigan State	38	44
O25	●	|	at Illinois	36	10
N1	●	|	Indiana	55	7
N8	●	|	Wisconsin	37	34
N15		|	at Iowa	22	40
			SUN BOWL		
D31	●		Oregon	31	30

2004 7-5 (3-5)

S4	●		Toledo	63	21
S11	●		Illinois St.	37	21
S18	●		at Colorado State	34	16
S25	●	|	Northwestern	43	17
O2	●	|	Penn State	16	7
O9		|	at Michigan	24	27
O16		|	at Michigan State	17	51
O23	●	|	Illinois	45	0
O30		|	at Indiana	21	30
N6		|	at Wisconsin	14	38
N13		|	Iowa	27	29
			MUSIC CITY BOWL		
D31	●		Alabama	20	16

2005 7-5 (4-4)

S1	●		at Tulsa	41	10
S10	●		Colorado State	56	24
S17	●		Florida Atlantic	46	7
S24	●	|	Purdue	42	35
O1		|	at Penn State	14	44
O8	●	|	at Michigan	23	20
O15		|	Wisconsin	34	38
O29		|	Ohio State	31	45
N5	●	|	at Indiana	42	21
N12	●	|	Michigan State	41	18
N19		|	at Iowa	28	52
			MUSIC CITY BOWL		
D30			Virginia	31	34

2006 6-7 (3-5)

A31	●		at Kent State	44	0
S9			at California	17	42
S16	●		Temple	62	0
S23		|	at Purdue	21	27
S30		|	Michigan	14	28
O7		|	Penn State	27	28
O14		|	at Wisconsin	12	48
O21	●		N. Dakota St.	10	9
O28		|	at Ohio State	0	44
N4	●	|	Indiana	63	26
N11	●	|	at Michigan State	31	18
N18	●	|	Iowa	34	24
			INSIGHT BOWL		
D29			Texas Tech	41	44

Neutral Site key: *CHI* Chicago, Ill. / *DET* Detroit, Mich. / *KC* Kansas City, Mo. / *OMA* Omaha, Neb.
Forfeit Game Later Forfieted Disputed Victor Disputed Score ||Designated Conference Game |2Counted Twice in Conference Standings

MINNESOTA RECORD BOOK

SINGLE-GAME RECORDS

RUSHING YARDS

RANK	PLAYER	DATE	OPPONENT	ATT	AVG	YDS
1	Chris Darkins	Oct. 7, 1995	Purdue	38	7.7	294
2	Clarence Schutte	Nov. 15, 1924	Illinois	32	8.8	282
3	Kent Kitzmann	Nov. 12, 1977	Illinois	57	4.7	266
4	Laurence Maroney	Oct. 15, 2005	Wisconsin	43	6.0	258
5	Tellis Redmon	Dec. 27, 2000	N.C. State	42	5.9	246

PASSING YARDS

RANK	PLAYER	DATE	OPPONENT	ATT	COMP	YDS
1	Tim Schade	Sept. 4, 1993	Penn State	66	34	478
2	Mike Hohensee	Nov. 7, 1981	Ohio State	67	37	444
3	Cory Sauter	Oct. 21, 1995	Michigan State	37	24	404
4	Scott Eckers	Oct. 8, 1993	Purdue	36	24	402
5	Cory Sauter	Sept. 14, 1996	Ball State	35	23	397

RECEIVING YARDS

RANK	PLAYER	DATE	OPPONENT	REC	AVG	YDS
1	Ryan Thelwell	Sept. 14, 1996	Ball State	8	28.6	228
2	Omar Douglas	Sept. 4, 1993	Penn State	11	17.5	193
3	Jared Ellerson	Oct. 4, 2003	Northwestern	4	47.3	189
4	Aaron Osterman	Nov. 12, 1994	Michigan	13	14.4	187
5	Dwayne McMullen	Oct. 24, 1984	Northwestern	4	46.5	186

POINTS

RANK	PLAYER	DATE	OPPONENT	TOT
1	Omar Douglas	Oct. 9, 1993	Purdue	30
2	5 players tied at 24			

FIELD GOALS

RANK	PLAYER	DATE	OPPONENT	TOT
1	Dan Nystrom	Dec. 30, 2002	Arkansas	5
	Adam Bailey	Oct. 18, 1997	Penn State	5
3	9 players tied at 4			

TACKLES

RANK	PLAYER	DATE	OPPONENT	TOT
1	Bill Light	Oct. 31, 1970	Iowa	32
2	Bill Light	Oct. 11, 1969	Indiana	29
3	Pete Najarian	Sept. 22, 1984	Purdue	26
	Pete Najarian	Sept. 17, 1983	Nebraska	26
5	Wayne King	Oct. 25, 1969	Michigan	25

INTERCEPTIONS

RANK	PLAYER	DATE	OPPONENT	TOT
1	7 players tied at 3			

RETIRED NUMBERS

10 Paul Giel

15 Sandy Stephens

54 Bruce Smith

72 Bronko Nagurski

SINGLE-SEASON RECORDS

RUSHING YARDS

RANK	PLAYER	SEASON	G	ATT	YDS
1	Laurence Maroney	2005	11	281	1,464
2	Chris Darkins	1994	NA	277	1,443
3	Thomas Hamner	1999	12	308	1,426
4	Darrell Thompson	1986	NA	242	1,376
5	Tellis Redmon	2000	11	293	1,368

PASSING YARDS

RANK	PLAYER	SEASON	G	ATT	COMP	PCT	YDS
1	Bryan Cupito	2006	13	359	214	59.6	2,819
2	Cory Sauter	1995	11	352	204	58.0	2,600
3	Cory Sauter	1996	11	338	200	59.2	2,578
4	Bryan Cupito	2005	11	297	176	59.3	2,530
5	Mike Hohensee	1981	NA	362	182	50.3	2,412

RECEIVING YARDS

RANK	PLAYER	SEASON	G	REC	AVG	YDS
1	Ron Johnson	2000	11	61	18.4	1,125
2	Ryan Thelwell	1996	11	62	17.0	1,051
3	Chester Cooper	1981	11	58	17.4	1,012
4	Tutu Atwell	1997	12	58	15.9	924
5	Jard Ellerson	2003	12	44	20.7	909

SCORING

RANK	PLAYER	SEASON	TD	FG	PAT	P2	TOT
1	Gary Russell	2005	19	0	0	0	114
2	Dan Nystrom	2000	0	25	34	0	109
3	Marion Barber III	2003	17	0	0	0	102
	Dan Nystrom	2002	0	20	42	0	102
5	Rhys Lloyd	2003	0	14	59	0	101

TOUCHDOWNS

RANK	PLAYER	SEASON	G	TOT
1	Gary Russell	2005	12	19
2	Marion Barber III	2003	13	17
3	4 players tied at 13			

TACKLES

RANK	PLAYER	SEASON	G	TOT
1	Bill Light	1970	NA	172
2	Jon Leverenz	1987	NA	162
3	Tyrone Carter	1998	11	158
4	Jack Brewer	2001	11	155
5	George Washington	1975	NA	154

INTERCEPTIONS

RANK	PLAYER	SEASON	YDS	TOT
1	Jeff Wright	1970	65	7
2	Walter Bowser	1970	203	6
3	6 players tied at 5			

PUNTING

RANK	PLAYER	SEASON	PUNTS	YDS	AVG
1	Adam Kelly	1984	59	2,728	46.2
2	Preston Gruening	2000	50	2,222	44.4
3	Mike Perfetti	1971	60	2,496	41.6
4	Preston Gruening	2001	51	2,109	41.4
5	Adam Kelly	1985	54	2,229	41.3

PUNT RETURNS

RANK	PLAYER	SEASON	RET	YDS	AVG
1	Paul Giel	1953	17	288	16.9
2	Marion Barber III	2003	28	405	14.5
3	Rick Upchurch	1973	22	305	13.9
4	Tutu Atwell	1997	23	296	12.9

KICKOFF RETURNS

RANK	PLAYER	SEASON	RET	YDS	AVG
1	Bobby Weber	1977	13	356	27.4
2	Jakari Wallace	2005	20	540	27.0
3	Tyrone Carter	1999	17	300	26.7

CAREER RECORDS

RUSHING YARDS

RANK	PLAYER	SEASONS	ATT	AVG	TD	YDS
1	Darrell Thompson	1986-89	936	5.0	40	4,654
2	Laurence Maroney	2003-05	660	6.0	32	3,933
3	Thomas Hamner	1996-99	882	4.3	21	3,810
4	Marion Barber III	2001-04	575	5.7	35	3,276
5	Chris Darkins	1992-95	643	5.0	21	3,235
6	Marion Barber	1977-80	660	4.7	34	3,094
7	Tellis Redmon	1999-2001	486	5.1	15	2,481
8	Garry White	1977-80	444	5.3	16	2,353
9	Francis "Pug" Lund	1932-34	416	5.4	13	2,264
10	Paul Giel	1951-53	551	4.0	20	2,188

PASSING YARDS

RANK	PLAYER	SEASONS	ATT	COMP	PCT	INT	TD	YDS
1	Bryan Cupito	2003-06	918	513	55.9	25	55	7,446
2	Cory Sauter	1994-97	945	539	57.0	33	40	6,834
3	Asad Abdul-Khaliq	2000-03	847	481	56.8	26	55	6,660
4	Marquel Fleetwood	1989-92	876	465	53.1	44	18	5,279
5	Rickey Foggie	1984-87	628	311	49.5	32	34	5,162
6	Mike Hohensee	1981-82	722	392	54.3	31	33	4,792
7	Tim Schade	1993-94	627	322	51.4	23	22	3,986
8	Tony Dungy	1973-76	586	274	46.8	35	25	3,515
9	Billy Cockerham	1996-99	485	252	52.0	24	29	3,483
10	Scott Schaffner	1987-91	515	278	54.0	22	21	3,472

RECEIVING YARDS

RANK	PLAYER	SEASONS	REC	AVG	TD	YDS
1	Ron Johnson	1998-2001	198	15.1	31	2,989
2	Tutu Atwell	1994-97	171	15.4	17	2,640
3	Ryan Thelwell	1994-96	136	16.4	14	2,232
4	Jared Ellerson	2002-05	111	18.5	15	2,054
5	Luke Leverson	1996-99	132	14.0	10	1,843
6	Omar Douglas	1990-93	130	12.9	14	1,681
7	Ernie Wheelwright	2004-	93	17.8	17	1,659
8	Dwayne McMullen	1981-84	95	17.1	15	1,627
9	Aaron Osterman	1990-94	111	14.4	7	1,598
10	Aaron Hosack	2002-03	80	18.3	11	1,463

SCORING

RANK	PLAYER	SEASONS	TD	FG	PAT	P2	TOT
1	Dan Nystrom	1999-2002	0	71	154	0	367
2	Chip Lohmiller	1984-87	0	57	97	0	268
3	Darrell Thompson	1986-89	43	0	0	2	262
4	Marion Barber	1977-80	36	0	0	1	218
	Paul Rogind	1976-79	0	44	86	0	218

TOUCHDOWNS

RANK	PLAYER	SEASONS	G	TOT
1	Darrell Thompson	1986-89	NA	43
2	Marion Barber	1977-80	NA	36
3	Marion Barber III	2001-04	38	35
4	Laurence Maroney	2003-05	36	34
5	Ron Johnson	1998-2001	44	31

TACKLES

RANK	PLAYER	SEASONS	TOT
1	Tyrone Carter	1996-99	528
2	Pete Najarian	1982-85	482
3	Bill Light	1969-71	395
4	Parc Williams	1995-98	351
	Russ Heath	1990-93	329

INTERCEPTIONS

RANK	PLAYER	SEASONS	YDS	TOT
1	Sean Lumpkin	1988-91	283	12
	Jeff Wright	1968-70	100	12
3	Keith Edwards	1977-79	121	11
	Walter Bowser	1969-70	255	11
	Tom Sakal	1965-67	155	11

PUNTING

RANK	PLAYER	SEASONS	PUNTS	YDS	AVG
1	Adam Kelly	1983-85	136	5,883	43.3
2	Preston Gruening	1999-2002	158	6,613	41.9
3	Mike Perfetti	1970-71	68	2,795	41.1
4	Justin Kucek	2005-	93	3,713	39.9
5	Ryan Rindels	1997-99	217	8,620	39.7

TEAM RECORDS

LONGEST WINNING STREAK
- 24, Nov. 7, 1903-Oct. 28, 1905
Streak broken vs. Wisconsin, 12-16, Nov. 4, 1905

LONGEST UNDEFEATED STREAK
- 35, Sept. 16, 1903-Oct. 28, 1905
Streak broken vs. Wisconsin, 12-16, Nov. 4, 1905

MOST CONSECUTIVE WINNING SEASONS
- 12, 1908-1919

MOST CONSECUTIVE BOWL APPEARANCES
- 5, 2002-present

MOST POINTS IN A GAME
- 146, vs. Grinnell, Oct. 22, 1904

MOST POINTS ALLOWED IN A GAME
- 84, vs. Nebraska, Sept. 17, 1984

LARGEST MARGIN OF VICTORY
- 146 (146-0), vs. Grinnell, Oct. 22, 1904

LARGEST MARGIN OF DEFEAT
- 71 (13-84), vs. Nebraska, Sept. 17, 1984

LONGEST RUN
- 98 yards, Darrell Thompson, vs. Michigan, Nov. 7, 1987

LONGEST FIELD GOAL
- 62 yards, Chip Lohmiller, vs. Iowa, Nov. 22, 1986

LONGEST PUNT
- 88 yards, Dave Baldridge, vs. Utah, Sept. 23, 1967

LONGEST INTERCEPTION RETURN
- 99 yards, Gary Homan, vs. Nebraska, Oct. 4, 1969

LONGEST PASS
- 96 yards, Asad Abdul-Khaliq to Jared Ellerson, vs. Northwestern, Oct. 4, 1992

LONGEST PUNT RETURN
- 91 yards, Fred Houde, vs. Iowa, Oct. 27, 1928

PUNT RETURNS

RANK	PLAYER	SEASON	RET	YDS	AVG
1	Rick Upchurch	1973-74	33	430	13.4
2	Tellis Redmon	1999-2001	45	571	12.7
3	Dominic Jones	2005-06	31	338	10.9
4	Chris Gaiters	1987-89	51	541	10.6
5	Rodney Heath	1993-96	52	525	10.1

KICKOFF RETURNS

RANK	PLAYER	SEASON	RET	YDS	AVG
1	Jakari Wallace	2003-05	20	540	27.0
2	George Honza	1970-72	25	633	25.3
3	Bobby Weber	1974-77	NA	NA	24.9
4	Dominic Jones	2005-06	33	814	24.7
5	John Lewis	1990-92	38	930	24.5

MINNESOTA ANNUAL STATISTICAL LEADERS

YR	RUSHING	YDS	ATT	AVG	PASSING	ATT	CMP	PCT	YDS	RECEIVING	REC	YDS	AVG
1934	Francis Lund	667	100	6.7		NA	NA	NA	NA		NA	NA	NA
1935	George Roscoe	648	123	5.3		NA	NA	NA	NA		NA	NA	NA
1936	Andy Uram	456	64	7.1		NA	NA	NA	NA		NA	NA	NA
1937	Harold Van Every	526	91	5.8		NA	NA	NA	NA		NA	NA	NA
1938	Wilbur Moore	555	98	5.7		NA	NA	NA	NA		NA	NA	NA
1939	Harold Van Every	733	133	5.5		NA	NA	NA	NA		NA	NA	NA
1940	Bruce Smith	542	76	7.1		NA	NA	NA	NA		NA	NA	NA
1941	Bill Daley	726	157	4.6		NA	NA	NA	NA		NA	NA	NA
1942	Bill Daley	552	88	6.3		NA	NA	NA	NA		NA	NA	NA
1943	Red Williams	561	99	5.7		NA	NA	NA	NA		NA	NA	NA
1944	Red Williams	989	128	7.7		NA	NA	NA	NA		NA	NA	NA
1945	Vic Kulbitski	485	112	4.3		NA	NA	NA	NA		NA	NA	NA
1946	Billy Bye	467	70	6.7	Ev Faunce	36	31	.86	335		NA	NA	NA
1947	Billy Bye	433	87	5.0	Ev Faunce	44	15	.34	234		NA	NA	NA
1948	Ev Faunce	558	116	4.8	Ev Faunce	85	44	.52	567		NA	NA	NA
1949	Billy Bye	561	138	4.1	Billy Bye	77	41	.53	571		NA	NA	NA
1950	Dick Gregory	315	66	4.8	George Hudak	45	17	.38	131		NA	NA	NA
1951	Paul Giel	789	152	5.2	Paul Giel	124	57	.46	689		NA	NA	NA
1952	Paul Giel	650	201	3.2	Paul Giel	101	42	.42	643	Donald Swanson	16	169	10.6
1953	Paul Giel	749	198	3.8	Paul Giel	93	50	.54	590	Bob McNamara	15	204	13.6
1954	Bob McNamara	708	112	6.3	Gino Cappelletti	65	28	.43	434	Richard McNamara	12	107	8.9
1955	Dick Borstad	440	96	4.6	Dick Larson	27	12	.44	253	Thomas Juhl	11	172	15.6
1956	Bobby Cox	553	130	4.3	Bob Cox	53	18	.34	240	David Lindblom	12	156	13.0
1957	Bobby Blakely	324	65	5.0	Bob Cox	53	19	.36	268	Robert Schultz	7	94	13.4
1958	Bill Kauth	361	92	3.9	Larry Johnson	51	17	.33	406	Robert Soltis	11	172	15.6
1959	Tom Robbins	339	93	3.6	Larry Johnson	92	39	.42	497	Thomas Hall	22	322	14.6
1960	Roger Hagberg	443	101	4.4	Sandy Stephens	62	22	.35	326	Thomas Hall	11	150	13.6
1961	Sandy Stephens	534	122	4.4	Sandy Stephens	153	54	.35	869	Thomas Hall	10	207	20.7
1962	Jerry Jones	453	98	4.6	Duane Blaska	154	71	.46	862	Jim Cairns	14	221	15.8
1963	Mike Reid	392	102	3.8	Bob Sadek	128	58	.45	647	Gerald Pelletier	9	105	11.7
1964	Fred Farthing	433	113	3.8	John Hankinson	178	86	.48	1,084	Aaron Brown	27	207	7.7
1965	Joe Holmberg	352	106	3.3	John Hankinson	214	111	.52	1,477	Ken Last	31	463	14.9
1966	Curtis Wilson	546	138	4.0	Larry Carlson	108	56	.52	599	Ken Last	30	356	11.9
1967	Jim Carter	519	142	3.7	Curtis Wilson	76	33	.43	543	Charley Sanders	21	276	13.1
1968	Barry Mayer	662	130	5.1	Phil Hagen	157	75	.48	771	Ray Parson	30	333	11.1
1969	Barry Mayer	745	162	4.6	Phil Hagen	208	109	.52	1,266	Ray Parson	27	391	14.5
1970	Ernie Cook	495	107	4.6	Craig Curry	228	103	.45	1,315	Doug Kingsriter	26	362	13.9
1971	Ernie Cook	881	177	5.0	Craig Curry	266	118	.44	1,691	Doug Kingsriter	28	379	13.5
1972	John King	1,164	237	4.9	Bob Morgan	89	32	.36	475	Doug Kingsriter	16	178	11.1
1973	Rick Upchurch	841	141	6.0	John Lawing	48	23	.48	276	Keith Fahnhorst	10	102	10.2
1974	Rick Upchurch	942	153	6.2	Tony Dungy	94	39	.41	612	Rick Upchurch	14	209	14.9
1975	Bubby Holmes	573	132	4.3	Tony Dungy	225	123	.55	1,515	Ron Kullas	42	545	13.0
1976	Kent Kitzmann	696	168	4.1	Tony Dungy	234	104	.44	1,291	Ron Kullas	33	372	11.3
1977	Kent Kitzmann	723	175	4.1	Wendell Avery	99	45	.45	591	Jeff Anhorn	21	266	12.7
1978	Marion Barber	1,210	247	4.9	Mark Carlson	113	64	.57	736	Elmer Bailey	27	464	17.2
1979	Garry White	861	135	6.4	Mark Carlson	300	177	.59	2,188	Elmer Bailey	37	552	14.9
1980	Garry White	959	177	5.4	Tim Salem	170	81	.48	887	Chester Cooper	14	210	15.0
1981	Frank Jacobs	636	147	4.3	Mike Hohensee	362	182	.50	2,112	Chester Cooper	58	1,012	17.4
1982	Tony Hunter	395	69	5.7	Mike Hohensee	360	210	.58	2,380	Dwayne McMullen	41	640	15.6
1983	David Puk	287	73	3.9	Greg Murphy	242	115	.48	1,410	Jay Carroll	37	459	12.4
1984	Rickey Foggie	647	145	4.5	Rickey Foggie	121	57	.47	1,036	Dwayne McMullen	26	594	22.8
1985	Valdez Baylor	680	112	6.1	Rickey Foggie	162	74	.46	1,493	Melvin Anderson	26	554	21.3
1986	Darrell Thompson	1,376	242	5.7	Rickey Foggie	216	97	.45	1,401	Melvin Anderson	27	384	14.2
1987	Darrell Thompson	1,229	224	5.5	Rickey Foggie	175	83	.47	1,232	Craig Otto	22	309	14.0
1988	Darrell Thompson	910	210	4.3	Scott Schaffner	191	106	.55	1,234	Chris Gaithers	42	564	13.4
1989	Darrell Thompson	1,139	260	4.4	Scott Schaffner	190	101	.53	1,373	Chris Gaithers	31	366	11.8
1990	Mark Smith	700	196	3.6	Marquel Fleetwood	171	95	.56	1,199	Kevin Grant	28	413	14.8
1991	Antonio Carter	660	165	4.0	Marquel Fleetwood	264	155	.59	1,643	Patt Evans	35	454	13.0
1992	Antonio Carter	572	133	4.3	Marquel Fleetwood	385	192	.50	2,168	Omar Douglas	61	669	11.0
1993	Chris Darkins	610	124	4.9	Tim Schade	286	135	.47	1,648	Omar Douglas	60	880	14.7
1994	Chris Darkins	1,443	277	5.2	Tim Schade	341	187	.55	2,338	Chuck Rios	52	436	8.4
1995	Chris Darkins	825	164	5.0	Cory Sauter	338	204	.60	2,600	Ryan Thelwell	58	775	13.4
1996	Thomas Hamner	883	195	4.5	Cory Sauter	352	200	.57	2,578	Tutu Atwell	62	822	13.3
1997	Thomas Hamner	663	170	3.9	Cory Sauter	234	126	.54	1,576	Tutu Atwell	58	924	15.9
1998	Thomas Hamner	838	209	4.0	Billy Cockerham	180	92	.51	1,150	Luke Leverson	60	854	14.2
1999	Thomas Hamner	1,426	308	4.6	Billy Cockerham	276	147	.53	2,091	Ron Johnson	43	574	13.3
2000	Tellis Redmon	1,368	293	4.7	Travis Cole	252	147	.58	1,982	Ron Johnson	61	1,125	18.4
2001	Tellis Redmon	1,091	185	6.4	Asad Abdul-Khaliq	187	107	.57	1,393	Ron Johnson	56	895	16.0
2002	Terry Jackson II	1,317	239	5.5	Asad Abdul-Khaliq	314	164	.52	2,184	Antoine Burns	44	526	12.0
2003	Marion Barber	1,196	207	5.8	Asad Abdul-Khaliq	250	158	.64	2,401	Aaron Hosack	51	814	16.0
2004	Laurence Maroney	1,348	217	6.2	Bryan Cupito	261	123	.47	2,097	Jared Ellerson	37	521	14.1
2005	Laurence Maroney	1,464	281	5.2	Bryan Cupito	297	176	.59	2,530	Ernie Wheelwright	37	568	15.4
2006	Amir Pinnix	1,272	252	5.0	Bryan Cupito	359	214	.60	2,819	Logan Payne	59	804	13.6

Receiving leaders by receptions
All statistics include postseason

NORTHWESTERN

BY TODD JONES

As THE ONLY PRIVATE INSTITUTION in the conference, Northwestern has always seemed miscast in the Big Ten. Such a disadvantage has tested any optimism on the campus along Lake Michigan, just north of Chicago. The Wildcats, however, have persevered, even though their football history includes six seasons without a victory and 13 with only one win. They trudged through 23 consecutive losing seasons from 1972 to 1994, reaching their nadir with a record 34-game losing streak. Then, in 1995, like alum Charlton Heston playing Moses, coach Gary Barnett led the Wildcats out of the wilderness. That year of stunning successs—featuring NU's first conference title and Rose Bowl berth in more than four decades—harkened back to such joyous times as 1930 and 1931, when the Wildcats won consecutive Big Ten titles; the 1948 season, when they went to the Rose Bowl; and 1962, when they were briefly ranked No. 1. It's unlikely that Northwestern will ever consistently challenge perennial powers such as Michigan and Ohio State, but three Big Ten titles from 1995 to 2000 show that the Wildcats can do more than just hope to overcome.

TRADITION Northwestern's team crosses the Wisconsin border every August and gathers at the University of Wisconsin-Parkside, about 55 miles north of Evanston, Ill. There, the Wildcats hold two weeks of preseason workouts. Gary Barnett began the tradition of going to Camp Kenosha when he became Northwestern coach in 1992. Randy Walker, his successor, placed a 2-by-4 in the team's locker room in Evanston. The word "trust" is painted on it, and each player slaps the wood before taking the field and after leaving it. Touchdowns and significant plays are celebrated with the playing of a Wildcat "growl" on the Ryan Field PA system.

BEST PLAYER Northwestern coach Lynn "Pappy" Waldorf saw a freshman playing intramural football on campus in 1940. The kid, from Waukegan, Ill., was Otto Graham, attending Northwestern on a basketball scholarship. Waldorf convinced him to play varsity football in 1941. Good idea. Graham went on to break every Big Ten passing record, was named league MVP as a senior and twice earned All-America honors. The QB known as Automatic Otto threw for 2,072 yards and 15

PROFILE

Northwestern University
Evanston, Ill.
Founded: 1851
Enrollment: 7,800
Colors: Purple and White
Nickname: Wildcats
Stadium: Ryan Field
    Opened in 1926
    Grass; 47,130 capacity
First football game: 1876
All-time record: 451–605–44 (.430)
Bowl record: 1–5
Big Ten conference championships: 8
(2 outright)
First-round draft choices: 8
Website: www.nusports.com

THE BEST OF TIMES

A miracle seemed to happen in 1995 when the longtime Big Ten doormats went to the Rose Bowl. The Wildcats finished that magical season 10–2 overall, 8–0 in the league. The next season they went 9–3, earning a share of a Big Ten title with a 7–1 league mark.

THE WORST OF TIMES

Where to start? Okay, try 23 consecutive losing seasons from 1972-94. Everything bottomed out from 1976-81, when the Wildcats went 3–62–1.

CONFERENCE

Northwestern was a charter member of the Western Conference in 1896 and has remained in the league since then. Popularly known as the Big Ten since 1917, the league didn't officially change its name to the Big Ten Conference until 1987.

DISTINGUISHED ALUMNI

Kenesaw Mountain Landis; Charlton Heston; Julia Louis-Dreyfus, actress; Richard Gephardt, U.S. congressman; Garry Marshall, producer; John Paul Stevens, U.S. Supreme Court justice; Adlai Stevenson II, statesman; David Schwimmer, actor; Stephen Colbert, actor

TDs and rushed for 823 yards and 17 scores in his career. His 1,326 total yards in 1942 was a Northwestern record for 20 years, and his 61 points the next season stood as the school record for 43 years. Graham's 27 points in a 41-0 win over Wisconsin in 1943 is still a Northwestern record. He scored three TDs and kicked three extra points in that game's first 12 minutes, and later he returned a punt 55 yards for a TD and threw a TD pass. Graham was also All-America in basketball and earned two letters in baseball. During his freshman year, he suffered a knee injury that required surgery and nearly quit the game to concentrate on basketball, but friends talked him out of that. A music major who played the piano, violin, cornet, and French horn, he served in World War II for two years as an officer in the U.S. Navy Air Corps. After returning from the war, he signed with the Cleveland Browns of the new All-American Football Conference. Graham was the player around whom coach Paul Brown built his team, which won four straight AAFC titles then went to six consecutive NFL title games, winning three.

BEST COACH Ara Parseghian is best known as a Notre Dame coach, but he earned his spurs with a stint at Northwestern. The Wildcats went 11–40–3 from 1952 to

> *In 1995, NU embarked on one of the great storybook seasons in college football history.*

1957, including 0–9 in Parseghian's second season as coach, in '57. Five years later, he had Northwestern ranked No. 1 in the nation. Parseghian had had excellent tutors, playing for Sid Gillman at Miami of Ohio and for Paul Brown in the NFL before returning to Miami for his first coaching job, as a member of Woody Hayes' staff. The knowledge Parseghian acquired helped lead Northwestern to winning records in five of his final six seasons. The Wildcats had success throwing the ball, especially in 1962, when they started 6–0 and were ranked No. 1 for two weeks because of the passing combination of QB Tom Myers to flanker Paul Flatley. NU's 35-6 win over Notre Dame in 1962 was its fourth straight under Parseghian over the Fighting Irish. The Irish made Parseghian their coach before the 1964 season. After a three-year hiatus, the series resumed in 1965, and Parseghian then won nine consecutive games against Northwestern as Notre Dame coach. Parseghian went 95–17–4 in 11 seasons with the Fighting Irish. Northwestern went 17–41–1 in the six seasons after he left for South Bend. Parseghian, a member of the College Football Hall of Fame, is the last coach at Northwestern to have a career winning record with the Wildcats: 36–35–1.

FIGHT SONG

GO, U NORTHWESTERN

Go, U Northwestern,
Break right through that line,
With our colors flying, we will cheer you all the time,
U Rah, Rah,
Go, U Northwestern, fight for victory
Spread far the fame of our fair name,
Go, Northwestern, win that game! (whistle)
Go, Northwestern, go!
Go, Northwestern, go!
Hit 'em hard,
Hit 'em low,
Go, Northwestern, go!

FIRST-ROUND DRAFT CHOICES

1944	Otto Graham, Lions (4)	
1947	Vic Schwall, Giants (10)	
1960	Ron Burton, Eagles (9)	
1962	Fate Echols, Cardinals (6)	
1967	Cas Banaszek, 49ers (11)	
1983	Chris Hinton, Broncos (4)	
2002	Napoleon Harris, Raiders (23)	
2005	Luis Castillo, Chargers (28)	

CONSENSUS ALL-AMERICANS

1926	Ralph Baker,	B
1930	Frank Baker,	E
1931	Jack Riley,	T
1931	Dallas Marvil,	T
1931	Pug Rentner,	B
1936	Steve Reid,	G
1940	Alf Bauman,	T
1945	Max Morris,	E
1959	Ron Burton,	B
1962	Jack Cvercko,	G
1995-96	Pat Fitzgerald,	LB
2000	Damien Anderson,	RB

BEST TEAM The Wildcats were coming off a 3–7–1 year, their 23rd consecutive losing season, when they embarked on one of the great storybook seasons in college football history. In 1995, Gary Barnett's fourth NU squad produced the school's best regular-season record (10–1) and a Big Ten title as the Wildcats went to the Rose Bowl for the first time since 1948. Linebacker Pat Fitzgerald was the team's cornerstone, earning the first of his two National Defensive Player of the Year awards. Quarterback Steve Schnur threw for 1,792 yards, and Darnell Autry ran for 1,785. The team began to gel in the off-season, when players would run to the top of Evanston's "Mt. Trashmore," where a Rose Bowl flag was planted. Defensive back Marcel Price was killed in a shooting over the summer, and teammates put his nickname, Big Six, on patches on their jerseys. They also ended every preseason practice by singing the Frank Sinatra song "High Hopes." The unranked Wildcats opened the season by shocking 27½-point favorite Notre Dame 17-15 but then a week later lost 30-28 to Miami (Ohio). Nine consecutive victories followed, including their first over Michigan in 30 years (and their first at Ann Arbor since 1959), their first over Iowa in 22 years, and their first ever over Penn State. A 35-0 homecoming win over Wisconsin was Northwestern's first sellout in 12 years. That victory catapulted the Wildcats to No. 8 in the Associated Press poll, the first time they'd cracked the top 10 since 1963. Autry was pictured on the cover of *Sports Illustrated* after a 21-10 win over Penn State on Nov. 4, and when Ohio State was upset by Michigan two weeks later, NU was alone atop the Big Ten standings. "We're not any dumber now than when we stunk," said NU defensive tackle Matt Rice. The Wildcats, ranked No. 3, were the nation's darlings when they traveled to Pasadena for the Rose Bowl. They were on a Wheaties box. The team appeared on the Tonight Show, and actor and alum Charlton Heston greeted them at Universal Studios dressed as Moses. Despite leading in the fourth quarter, Northwestern lost 41-32 to Southern California. But the defeat couldn't dull the shine of 1995.

BEST BACKFIELD Randy Walker realized after one season at Northwestern that he needed to try something different on offense. The Wildcats had scored seven points or less in half their defeats while going 3-8 in 1999. They scored a total of 10 points in their final three games, all losses. So before the 2000 season Walker put in the spread offense, magic occurred. Quarterback Zak Kustok and

COLLEGE FOOTBALL HALL OF FAME INDUCTEES		
NAME	YEARS	INDUCTED
Otto Graham, HB	1941-43	1956
Lynn "Pappy" Waldorf, COACH	1935-46	1966
Jimmy Johnson, QB	1904-05	1969
Paddy Driscoll, HB	1915-16	1974
Charlie Bachman, COACH	1919	1978
Ernie Rentner, HB	1930-32	1979
Ara Parseghian, COACH	1956-63	1980
Ralph Baker, HB	1924-26	1981
Steve Reid, G	1934-36	1985
Jack Riley, T	1929-31	1988
Edgar Manske, E	1931-33	1989
Ron Burton, HB	1957-59	1990
Alex Sarkisian, C	1946-48	1998

running back Damien Anderson, both juniors, blossomed in the new attack and led Northwestern to a share of the Big Ten title. Walker, a former running back at Miami of Ohio, distinguished his spread attack by making certain it included a strong running game. Anderson carried the load, earning All-America honors that season while setting 10 Northwestern rushing records, including 2,063 yards and 23 touchdowns. He averaged 171.9 yards per game and 6.6 yards on his 311 carries. Anderson ran for 292 yards against Indiana, 268 against Michigan, and 230 against Minnesota. He rushed for four TDs against Indiana and Illinois, and scored a TD in nine consecutive games. Eight times he scored two or more touchdowns in a game. Anderson finished his career a year later as Northwestern's all-time leading rusher, with 4,485 yards, and the school's leader with 38 rushing TDs. Kustok hurt opponents with both his arm and his legs. He passed for 2,389 yards—1,648 more than the previous season—and rushed for 505. Kustok threw a TD pass in every game that season, 19 in all, and was intercepted just seven times. He also began a school-record streak of 277 passes without an interception that stretched into the following season. His pass-efficiency rating was 125.5 while completing 206 of 363 pass attempts for 60.1 percent.

The Wildcats scored a school-record 441 points, averaging 36.8 per game, with a school-record 58 TDs. They scored over 40 points in a game five times, over 50 twice, and over 60 once while going 8-3 overall, 6–2 in the Big Ten, during the regular season before losing 66-17 to Nebraska in the Alamo Bowl.

BEST DEFENSE Northwestern enjoyed a fairy tale season in 1995: Its defense seemingly wore a suit of armor. The Wildcats led the nation in scoring defense, giving up an average of 12.7 in 11 regular-season games and just 110 points in their 10 victories. They shut out Wisconsin, while forcing the Badgers into seven turnovers, and held five opponents to 10 points or less. Pat Fitzgerald, a junior linebacker from Orland Park, Ill., served as the unit's heart and soul. Despite breaking his leg in the second-to-last regular-season game against Iowa, he won both the Bronko Nagurski and Chuck Bednarik awards as the nation's top defensive player and was named Big Ten player of the year. A year later, he helped the Wildcats to a share of another Big Ten title, earning All-America for the second consecutive season and becoming the first two-time winner of the Nagurski

and Bednarik awards, as well as the Big Ten player of the year again. Besides Fitzgerald, senior cornerback Chris Martin made first-team all-Big Ten in 1995. He intercepted five passes and returned one 76 yards for a TD against Purdue, during a game in which he also blocked a punt for a safety. Martin recovered four fumbles, as did cornerback Hudhaifa Ismaeli, the team leader with seven sacks. Senior free safety William Bennett was the team's leading tackler, with 102, 57 of which were solo. Sophomore safety Eric Collier had 100 tackles, 53 solo, and clinched a 17-14 win over Illinois with a late interception. Casey Dailey led the team with 12 tackles for a loss of 76 yards, including six sacks. The sophomore defensive end finished his career in 1997 with school records for tackles for loss, 53, and sacks, 28.

BIGGEST GAME With the 1995 season opener approaching, Notre Dame coach Lou Holtz was asked about his team's opponent, Northwestern. "I have a great deal of respect for Leon Burtnett," he said. Of course, he meant Gary Barnett, coach of the Wildcats, and not Burtnett, the onetime Purdue coach. Northwestern hadn't had a winning season since 1971 and hadn't defeated Notre Dame in 33 years. Barnett, however, sensed an upset brewing. "I do not want you to carry me off the field after this game. I want you to act like you've been here before," he told his team before the game in South Bend, Ind. Northwestern took a 7-0 lead on a seven-yard TD pass from Steve Schnur to David Beazley, and led 10-9 at halftime. Schnur threw a TD pass to D'Wayne Bates early in the third quarter. Notre Dame scored with 6:16 left but failed on a two-point conversion. The Wildcats held on for a 17-15 victory. The *Chicago Tribune* ranked this game No. 13 on its list of the greatest moments in Chicago-area sports.

BIGGEST UPSET Bernie Bierman brought his Minnesota Golden Gophers and their 21-game winning streak to Evanston on Oct. 31, 1936. Minnesota was defending national champion, ranked No. 1 at 4–0, and hadn't lost in 28 games, since the final game of the 1932 season. Pappy Waldorf had his second Northwestern team ranked No. 3. Rain and wind made playing conditions treacherous, and the teams were scoreless after three quarters. In the fourth, Minnesota halfback Julius Alfonse mishandled a pitchout and fumbled. DeWitt Gibson recovered for Northwestern at the Gopher 13-yard line. Wildcat reserve fullback Don Geyer fumbled on the ensuing play, but Minnesota All-America tackle Ed Widseth was penalized for punching Geyer in the scramble for the loose ball. The penalty put the ball on the 1-yard line, and halfback Steve Toth scored from there on third down. Minnesota drove inside Northwestern's 20 on its next three possessions but couldn't score. The crowd of 48,347 rejoiced over a 6-0 victory that propelled the Wildcats toward the Big Ten championship.

HEARTBREAKER The Wildcats entered the top 10 of the 1962 polls after Week 3 when they went to Minneapolis and won 34-22 over Minnesota, the previous season's Rose Bowl participant. Northwestern then won at Ohio State, the defending Big Ten champion, which had elected not to go to the 1961 Rose Bowl. The Buckeyes began the 1962 season as No. 1 before falling in the polls prior to the NU game. Two more victories sent Northwestern to No. 1 in the polls with a 6–0 record. The Wildcats headed to Wisconsin, but couldn't stop the passing combination of Ron Vander Kelen to Pat Richter and lost to the Badgers 37-6. Northwestern also lost the next week, 31-7 at home to Michigan State. A 29-7 win over Miami (Ohio) ended the regular season and gave the school its best record in 14 years at 7–2 but couldn't assuage dashed Rose Bowl dreams.

WILDEST FINISH Northwestern's game against Michigan on Nov. 4, 2000, at Ryan Field played out like an amusement park ride. The two ranked teams combined for 105 points, 171 plays, and 1,189 total yards of offense. Michigan led 51-46 with less than two minutes remaining in the fourth quarter when Wildcat running back Damien Anderson dropped a fourth-down pass while alone in the end zone. "They'll have to kill us to beat us," Northwestern coach Randy Walker had said before the game. His team showed that fortitude 46 seconds later, when it recovered a fumble by Wolverine running back Anthony Thomas. Zak Kustok promptly completed three consecutive passes, the final one a 12-yard touchdown to Sam Simmons on a crossing pattern with 20 seconds left. Kustok made a two-point conversion pass to Teddy Johnson to give No. 21-ranked Northwestern a 54-51 lead. The No. 12 Wolverines answered with one final drive and set up for a 57-yard field goal attempt by Hayden Epstein, who earlier in the game had made a 52-yarder. This time he didn't get a chance, because the snap was mishandled. Fans stormed the field. ESPN dubbed the game an "instant classic." NU went on to earn a share of the Big Ten title with an 8–4 season under second-year coach Walker.

BEST GOAL-LINE STAND The Wildcats were in the final throes of the woeful Francis Peay era when Illinois came to Evanston ranked No. 17 on Oct. 26, 1991. Northwestern, wearing purple pants, pulled off a 17-11 upset, cemented late in the fourth quarter with a goal-line stand that stopped Illinois QB Jason Verduzco. Fans tore down the goal posts after the game, carried them to Lake Michigan, and threw them in. The Wildcats were 1–5 coming in and went on to finish 3–8 in Peay's sixth and final year. Gary Barnett was hired as coach after the season.

BEST COMEBACK Northwestern was always a strong finisher under Randy Walker. His Wildcats were 25–4 when leading after three quarters, and won six overtime games during his tenure. They displayed characteristic persistence and clutch play on Nov. 5, 2005, against Iowa. The Hawkeyes were in control most of the game. They led 14-0 after the first quarter, 24-7 at halftime, and seemed destined to win after Northwestern QB Brett Basanez threw his second interception, with 4:34 remaining and Iowa ahead 27-14. Northwestern's defense forced a punt, and the Wildcats then drove 77 yards on 12 plays. Tyrell Sutton's one-yard TD plunge cut Iowa's lead to 27-21. Place-kicker Joel Howells executed an onside kick, and Reggie McPherson recovered for the Wildcats. They marched again, aided by a late-hit penalty on Iowa during a 16-yard reception by Mark Philmore. Basanez threw a nine-yard TD pass to Ross Lane with 42 seconds remaining, and the Wildcats led for the first time, 28-27. Iowa rallied but was stopped on fourth down at the Northwestern 48-yard line. The Wildcats had pulled out a one-point win by scoring two touchdowns in an 88-second span in the game's final 2:10 to become bowl-eligible. "I'm very proud of them," Walker said. "As we were walking off the field, I caught myself almost breaking down. I'm just so overjoyed for them. The things they were able to overcome and do are a testament to their beliefs, confidence, and trust in each other."

STADIUM William Dyche was Northwestern's vice president and business manager in the early 1920s. He saw a need for the Wildcats to play in a larger place than their 10,000-seat wooden facility. His desire became reality in 1926, when 45,000-seat Dyche Stadium opened, at a cost of $1.4 million. After the 1948 Wildcats went to the Rose Bowl the south end was enclosed. Occasionally, capacity reached 55,000 when temporary bleachers were added in the north end. A $30 million fund-raising campaign produced major stadium renovations in 1996-97, adding a new sound system, locker rooms, and a press box, and dropping capacity to 47,130. Board of Trustees chairman Patrick Ryan donated $10 million, and Northwestern president Henry Bienen renamed the stadium Ryan Field in his honor.

RIVAL The University of Chicago, when it was a member of the Big Ten, served as Northwestern's main foil. The teams played 37 times between 1892 and 1926. Today the Wildcats call Illinois their top rival, in part because the schools battle for in-state recruits. Northwestern and Illinois first met in 1892 and have played for the Sweet Sioux Tomahawk since 1945. Originally designed as a wooden Indian, the trophy proved too difficult to take on road trips. A tomahawk replaced the Indian as the game's prize. The series has traditionally been close. Even during their worst era, the Wildcats beat the Illini 9–6 in 1973, won 21-7 in 1977,

and tied 0-0 in 1978. In 2006, the teams played one another for the 100th time. The Wildcats won 27-16 for their fourth consecutive victory over the Illini, but Illinois' lead in the series still stood at 51–44–5.

INSPIRATION When introduced before the 1999 season as the replacement for Gary Barnett as Northwestern coach, Randy Walker described himself as "not a 1-800 guy." He was indeed a people person and became beloved, as Coach Walk, as much for his loyalty, integrity, warmth, and generosity as for his high-scoring offenses. Walker died June 29, 2006, of a heart attack at age 52. The native of Troy, Ohio, had been hospitalized for two days in Oct. 2004 with inflammation of the heart muscle, but he'd seemed in good health two years later, having signed a contract extension running through the 2011 season just two months prior to his death. "Randy truly embraced Northwestern and its mission, and cared deeply for his student-athletes, both on and off the field," said Northwestern athletic director Mark Murphy. Walker came to Evanston from Miami University in Oxford, Ohio, where his record of 96 victories was better than those of other notable coaches at the Mid-American Conference school, including Sid Gillman, Woody Hayes, Bo Schembechler, Bill Mallory, and Ara Parseghian. His Miami of Ohio team was the only opponent to beat Northwestern in the 1995 regular season. Although his record with the Wildcats was just 37–46, Walker's win total was second at Northwestern only to Pappy Waldorf's. Walker was the first coach to lead Northwestern to three bowl games, the first to beat all 10 conference opponents, the first to win at Penn State, the first to beat Ohio State since 1971, and the first to defeat the Buckeyes in Evanston since 1958. The Wildcats were 14–10 in Big Ten play during his final three seasons marking the first time in school history that the team finished above .500 in conference play three consecutive years. Each of those Northwestern teams won at least six games, a feat that hadn't been accomplished in a three-season stretch in Evanston in 74 years. Walker was named Big Ten coach of the year in 2000 after the Wildcats won a share of the conference title. His spread offense produced many memorable shoot-out victories, including 54-51 over Michigan in 2000, 51-48 over Wisconsin in 2005, 47-44 over Wisconsin in two overtimes in 2000, 41-35 over Minnesota in 2000, 37-31 over Indiana in overtime in 2003, and a 33-27 overtime win against Ohio State in 2004. Statistics, however, don't measure his impact. Following his death, the school honored Walker throughout the 2006 season by wearing a "Walk" patch on its uniforms and coaching gear. The "Walk" logo was also painted on the grass at Ryan Field for all six home games. Northwestern memorialized him by creating a football scholarship in his name. The Wildcats named linebackers coach Pat Fitzgerald as his successor on July 7. Fitzgerald, star of Northwestern's 1995 and 1996 Big Ten champions, took over at age 31 with

only six years of coaching experience. The Wildcats went 3–8 in 2006 and tied for ninth in the Big Ten.

DISPUTES The Wildcats met their old coach Pappy Waldorf and his undefeated California Bears in the 1949 Rose Bowl. Controversy occurred twice during Northwestern's first bowl game. The game was tied 7-7 midway through the second quarter when fullback Art Murakowski scored for the Wildcats on a one-yard run. California argued that Murakowski fumbled before crossing the goal line. Field judge Jay Berwanger, who had won the first Heisman trophy for the University of Chicago, in 1935, ruled Murakowski had scored before losing the ball. More arguments occurred when the Wildcats took over the ball on their own 12-yard line, trailing 14-13 with 6:01 remaining. On first down, the Bears apparently recovered a fumble by Northwestern halfback Ed Tunnicliff. Referee Jimmy Cain ruled that Tunnicliff was down before fumbling. Northwestern drove to the California 43-yard line, where Tunnicliff took a direct snap and ran for a TD with 2:59 remaining. Northwestern won 20-14 to finish the season 8–2.

DUBIOUS DISTINCTION Northwestern was the first Division I-A school to be found guilty of point shaving in football. The scandal began during a 49-13 loss to Iowa on Nov. 12, 1994, when one of the Wildcats players, Rodney Ray, was heard on the sideline accusing running back Dennis Lundy of fumbling on purpose to win a bet. Investigations by the school and the FBI followed. Campus bookie Brian Ballarini, a former Northwestern player, was given three months, electronic home monitoring and three years probation for taking bets in a gambling ring that prosecutors said involved games in the 1993 and '94 seasons. Lundy admitted to fumbling on purpose in the Iowa game, pleaded guilty to perjury, was sentenced to a month in jail, and later had the charge dropped after two years of good behavior. Four of his Northwestern teammates—Chris Gamble, Greg Gill, Dwight Brown, and Michael Senters—were charged in the federal case. Gamble went to jail for two months for perjury. Gill received a fine and probation for perjury. Brown got 30 days in prison for perjury. Senters, who admitted to gambling, had his perjury charge dropped for good behavior. The investigation also turned up evidence that Northwestern basketball players Dion Lee and Dewey Williams were betting against their own team and then trying to make sure the Wildcats lost by more than the point spread. Each served a month in jail for point shaving. Northwestern president Henry Bienen said he had a "sense of dismay that the university's good name is besmirched."

NICKNAME Northwestern was known as the Purple until 1924, when the football team lost a hard-fought 3-0 game to the University of Chicago. The effort displayed by Northwestern prompted Chicago Tribune sportswriter Wallace Abbey to write that "football players had not come down from Evanston; Wildcats would be a name better suited." The school then adopted Wildcats as its nickname.

PRO FOOTBALL HALL OF FAME INDUCTEES		
NAME	YEARS	INDUCTED
John Driscoll, QB	1919-1929	1965
Otto Graham, QB	1946-55	1965

MASCOT In 1923, one year before adopting the Wildcats moniker, students at Northwestern brought a caged bear cub named Furpaw from the Lincoln Park Zoo to its home games. Northwestern went 2–6 that season. Furpaw was deemed to be bad luck and was never brought to another game. The current mascot, Willie the Wildcat, began as an advertising firm's caricature in 1933. Fourteen years later, four members of the Alpha Delta fraternity dressed up as Willie the Wildcat for their homecoming float.

UNIFORMS A special committee selected purple as the school's official color in 1894. The traditional purple used was a deep indigo blue, but the color was changed to royal purple in the mid 1970s. Silver was added to the purple-and-white uniforms in 1980. Black replaced silver in 1988 and has remained part of the uniform.

TRAGEDY Junior safety Rashidi Wheeler helped Northwestern tie for the Big Ten championship in 2000 by making 88 tackles, recovering a fumble, and breaking up three passes. He was preparing for his senior season, running in a conditioning drill with teammates on Aug. 3, 2001, when he collapsed. Wheeler suffered an asthma attack and was pronounced dead at Evanston Hospital. "I am beyond sorry," said a tearful Wildcat coach Randy Walker. Northwestern retired Wheeler's number, 30, and teammates wore patches with his initials, RAW, on them throughout the 2001 season. "I think his name and legacy will live on forever, beyond this season, on to the next level, and throughout our lives," said wide receiver Sam Simmons. The Wildcats were picked to win the Big Ten but struggled to a 4–7 record. They tied for 10th in the league at 2–6. In the fall of 2004, Wheeler's family reached a $100,000 settlement with three companies—NutraQuest, Phoenix Laboratories, and General Nutrition Corp.—that made and distributed one of the two performance-enhancing supplements the player had taken before he died. In 2006, a Cook County (Ill.) Circuit Court judge awarded an estimated $10.7 million to Linda Will, Wheeler's mother. The award was 70 percent of the $16 million settlement the university agreed to pay in 2005 to end a wrongful-death lawsuit filed by Wheeler's family four years earlier. After each season, Northwestern now

presents the Rashidi Wheeler award to a player who best embodies Wheeler's enthusiasm and spirit.

LORE College football has never seen an era of ineptitude quite like the one Northwestern suffered through from 1972-94. The Wildcats had 23 consecutive losing seasons under six different coaches. They went 46–203–4 in that span, with losing streaks of 34, 15, 14, and 11 (twice). Northwestern never lost fewer than seven games in any of those 23 seasons. Only twice did the Wildcats win as many as four. Four times they had winless seasons, and in three other years they won just one game. The Wildcats failed to score at least 10 points in 91 games, were shut out 31 times, and scored only three points in 16 games. Their defense gave up 40 or more points in 83 of those 253 games. Thirty-five opponents scored more than 50 points. Ohio State had nine wins over the Wildcats in which the average score was 57.0 to 6.7. Northwestern fans resorted to throwing marshmallows at each other during games and chanting, "That's all right, that's okay, you're going to work for us someday." The Wildcats went five years without a Big Ten victory. Rumors circulated about Northwestern's possibly being kicked out of the league, and some thought the school should drop football. Average attendance at home games fell below 20,000 when the Wildcats went 4–73–1 in a span from the third game of 1975 through the third game of '82. Rick Venturi coached three of those years and went 1–31–1. The Wildcats were a national punchline when they took the field against Northern Illinois on Sept. 25, 1982. Northwestern had lost 34 consecutive games, the longest such streak in Division I-A history, and in the process had been outscored 1,370 to 340. The Wildcats had been 0–11 and had been outscored 505–82 in 1981, and had began the '82 season with three losses in which they had minus 44 yards rushing. No wonder the Dyche Stadium crowd of 22,078 erupted with joy as senior running back Ricky Edwards ran through Northern Illinois for 177 rushing yards and four TDs. Fans tore down the goal post in the northern end zone with 34 seconds left and Northwestern ahead 31-6. Game officials let the clock run out. Northwestern had won for the first time since Sept. 15, 1979, when they'd beaten Wyoming. "Dream Come True" read the headline in the next day's *Chicago Tribune*.

NUMBERS The Wildcats upset undefeated Notre Dame 14–7 in 1935, for the first time in 34 years … Northwestern ended Minnesota's 21-game winning streak with a 6–0 win over the No. 1-ranked Golden Gophers in 1936 … Mike Adamle starred in 1969 and 1970 as a 5'9", 195-pound fullback. He set school records for rushing yards in a game

Starting in 1972, the Wildcats suffered 23 straight losing seasons.

(316 against Wisconsin in 1969), rushing yards in a season (1,255 in 1970), and career rushing yards (2,015) … In 1942, Northwestern's Charles Warren became the first African-American to play QB in the Big Ten … In 2000 the school clinched a share of its third Big Ten title in six years by beating Illinois 61-23 … LB Tim McGarigle finished his career in 2006 as the NCAA's all-time leading tackler with 549 … The Wildcats earned a No. 1 ranking in 1962 after a crowd of 55,752 at Dyche Stadium saw them defeat Notre Dame 35-6. Northwestern didn't defeat the Fighting Irish again until the 1995 season opener … The Wildcats converted on five fourth-down plays, four of them for scores, while wiping out a 35-21 deficit to defeat Minnesota 41-35 in 2000. Kunle Patrick threw a 45-yard TD pass to Sam Simmons on the game's final play … The Wildcats rushed for 444 yards in a 37-20 win over Illinois in 2003 … Northwestern produced a school-record 674 total yards of offense (313 rushing and 361 passing) during a 51-48 win over Wisconsin in 2005 … Noah Herron, wearing jersey numeral 33, gave Northwestern its first win over Ohio State in 33 years when he scored the game-winning TD on his 33rd carry in overtime for a 33-27 final … Five of the Wildcats' nine wins in 1996 were by a total of 13 points … Northwestern's football program has won the Academic Achievement award four times since 1998 … From 1968 through 2001, the Wildcats had only one player selected in the first round of the NFL draft: tackle Chris Hinton, selected fourth overall by the Denver Broncos in 1983 … QB Brett Basanez set a school record with 11,576 total yards from 2002 through 2005. He threw for 3,622 yards, a school record, and rushed for 423 as a senior and was named the Big Ten's Offensive Player of the Year. His 10,580 career passing yards are the most in Northwestern history. His 44 career TD passes tied Len Williams for the school mark … Lee Gissendaner's punt-return average of 21.8 yards led the nation in 1992 … Joel Howells made five field goals in a 34-29 loss to Penn State in 2005 … Brett Whitley intercepted a pass in four consecutive games in 1985 … The Wildcats haven't had four consecutive winning seasons since 1928 through 1931 … In 1977, the Wildcats lost 24 fumbles and threw 19 interceptions in 11 games … The 1996 co-Big Ten champions were known as the Cardiac Cats because six of their nine wins were by four points or less … The Wildcats scored eight rushing touchdowns against Illinois in 2000 and 37 rushing TDs for the season, both school records.

QUOTE "We're going to take the Purple to Pasadena." —Gary Barnett, when introduced to the student body as Northwestern's new coach on Jan. 11, 1992

NORTHWESTERN ALL-TIME SCORES

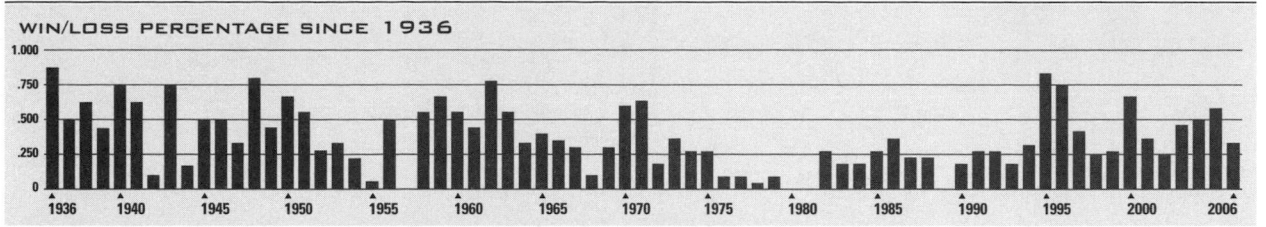

WIN/LOSS PERCENTAGE SINCE 1936

NO HEAD COACH

1876 — 0-1-0
F22	at Chicago Club	0	3

1877-1881
NO TEAM

1882 — 1-1-0
N11	at Lake Forest	0	1
N18 ●	Lake Forest	1	0

1883-1885
NO TEAM

1886 — 0-1-0
O30	Harvard Prep	4	32

1887
NO TEAM

1888 — 2-1-0
N20 ●	W. Division HS	16	6
N29 ●	at Lake Forest	4	18
D1 ●	Lake Forest	12	6

1889 — 2-2-0
N9 ●	Evanston H.S	18	4
N14 ●	Notre Dame	0	9
N23 ●	Alumni	0	25
D7 ●	at Chicago Wanderers	22	0

1890 — 4-1-1
O10 ●	Evanston HS	16	4
O22 ●	Evanston HS	18	0
O30 =	S. Division HS	0	0
N1 ●	Alumni	0	24
N15 ●	Beloit	22	6
N26 ●	at Wisconsin	22	10

KNOWLTON AMES
1891-92 (.559)   7-5-5

1891 — 2-2-3
S30 ●	Evanston HS	8	0
O17 =	Lake Forest	0	0
O31 =	at Wisconsin	0	0
N5 ●	Chicago YMCA	22	0
N14 =	at Beloit	12	12
N21 ●	Lake Forest	0	20
N29 ●	at Wisconsin	0	40

1892 — 5-3-2
O1 ●	Chicago YMCA	16	0
O12 =	at Illinois	16	16
O15 ●	Beloit	36	0
O22 =	at Chicago	0	0
O29 ●	Michigan *CHI*	10	8
N2 ●	Chicago	6	4
N8 ●	at Minnesota	12	18
N12 ●	at Lake Forest	18	0
N19 ●	Wisconsin	6	26
N24 ●	Wisconsin *MIL*	6	20

PAUL NOYES
1893 (.350)   2-5-3

1893 — 2-5-3
O4	Denver AC *CHI*	0	8
O18 ●	at Chicago	6	12
O21 =	Illinois	0	0
O27 =	Lake Forest	12	12
O30 ●	Minnesota	0	16
N4 ●	Beloit	10	6
N8 ●	Chicago	6	6
N11 ●	Lake Forest	38	22
N18 ●	at Michigan	6	72
D16 ●	at Chicago	14	22

AA EWING
1894 (.444)   4-5

1894 — 4-5-0
O6 ●	at Chicago	0	46
O11 ●	Evanston HS	14	0
O13 ●	at Lake Forest	6	24
O17 ●	Evanston HS	12	0
O20 ●	Beloit *Roc*	6	42
O24 ●	Evanston HS	22	6
O26 ●	Lake Forest	12	8
N3 ●	at Illinois	0	66
N24 ●	Chicago	0	36

ALVIN H. CULVER
1895-96 (.650)   12-6-2

1895 — 6-5-0
S21 ●	Wisconsin *MIL*	6	12
S28 ●	Iowa State	0	36
O3 ●	Evanston HS	16	0
O5 ●	Beloit	34	6
O12 ●	Armour	44	0
O19 ●	at Chicago	22	6
O31 ●	Lake Forest	24	0
N2 ●	at Purdue	24	6
N9 ●	Missouri *StL*	18	22
N16 ●	Chicago	0	6
N23 ●	at Illinois	4	38

1896-PRESENT
BIG 10

1896 — 6-1-2 (2-1-1)
O1 ●	Englewood HS	25	0
O3 ●	Chicago AC	4	0
O7 ●	Armour	42	0
O10 =	Beloit	6	6
O17 ●	Phys. & Surg.	16	6
O24 ●	Chicago *CHI*	46	6
N7 ●	at Illinois	10	4
N14	Chicago	6	18
N26 =	Wisconsin	6	6

JESSE VAN DOOZER
1897 (.625)   5-3

1897 — 5-3-0 (0-2-0)
S29 ●	Evanston HS	6	0
O9 ●	Beloit *Roc*	6	0
O16 ●	Iowa	6	12
O23	at Chicago	6	21
O30 ●	Phys & Surg	6	0
N6 ●	Rush	16	0
N13 ●	Alumni	25	0
N25	Wisconsin	0	22

W.H. BANNARD
1898 (.679)   9-4-1

1898 — 9-4-1 (0-4-0)
S21 ●	N.W. Division HS	34	0
S24 ●	Englewood HS	22	0
S28 ●	Hyde Park HS	18	0
O1 ●	Dixon	57	0
O8 ●	Beloit	17	11
O12 ●	Hahnemann Medical	22	6
O15 ●	Phys & Surg	11	2
O18 ●	Chicago AC	5	0
O22	at Chicago	5	34
O29 ●	Lake Forest	27	0
N5	Michigan *CHI*	5	6
N12	at Minnesota	6	17
N19	Armour	0	0
N24	Wisconsin	0	47

C.M. HOLLISTER
1899-1902 (.625)   28-16-4

1899 — 7-6-0 (2-2-0)
S21 ●	N.U. Dental	24	0
S23 ●	Englewood HS	29	0
S30 ●	Alumni	0	18
O4 ●	Lake Forest AC.	24	5
O7 ●	Rush Medical	0	6
O14	at Wisconsin	0	38
O21 ●	at Beloit	0	11
O25 ●	Lake Forest	16	0
O28 ●	at Notre Dame	0	12
N4 ●│	at Minnesota	11	5
N11 ●	at Chicago	0	76
N18 ●	Indiana	11	6
N25 ●│	Purdue	29	0

1900 — 7-2-3 (2-1-2)
S22 ●	North Central	26	0
S26 ●	North Division HS	18	6
S29 ●	Phys. & Surg.	0	6
O6 ●	Rush Medical	6	0
O13 ●│	Indiana	12	0
O17 ●	Lake Forest Academy	23	0
O20 =	Illinois	0	0
O27 =	Beloit	6	6
N3 =	Knox	11	5
N10 ●│	at Chicago	5	0
N17	at Minnesota	0	21
N29 │	Iowa	5	5

1901 — 8-2-1 (3-2-0)
S18 ●	Fort Sheridan	27	0
S21 ●	North Central	30	0
S28 ●	Lombard	47	0
O5 ●	Lake Forest	11	0
O12 ●	Notre Dame	2	0
O19 │	at Michigan	0	29
O26 ●│	Illinois	17	11
N9 ●	at Chicago	6	5
N16 =	Beloit	11	11
N23 │	Minnesota *CHI*	0	16
N28 ●│	at Purdue	10	5

1902 — 6-6-0 (0-4-0)
S20 ●	Fort Sheridan	15	0
S27 ●	North Central	10	5
O1 ●	Chicago Dental	11	0
O4 ●	Lake Forest	26	0
O11 ●	Rush Medical	11	0
O18 ●	Chicago *CHI*	0	12
O25 ●	Knox	0	15
N1 │	Purdue	0	5
N8 │	Wisconsin	0	51
N15 ●	Beloit	10	0
N22 │	Illinois	0	17
N27 │	at Nebraska	0	12

WALTER McCORNACK
1903-05 (.800)   26-5-4

1903 — 10-1-3 (1-0-2)
S19 ●	N.Division HS	22	5
S22 ●	Fort Sheridan	28	0
S23 ●	Englewood HS	35	0
S26 ●	North Central	22	6
S30 ●	Alumni	5	0
O3 ●	Lombard	23	0
O7 ●	Chicago Dental	18	11
O10 ●	at Washington, Mo.	23	0
O17 =	at Chicago	0	0
O24 ●	at Cincinnati	35	0
O31 ●	at Illinois	12	11
N14 =	Notre Dame *CHI*	0	0
N21 =	Wisconsin *CHI*	6	6
N26	Carlisle *CHI*	0	28

1904 — 8-2-0 (1-2-0)
S24 ●	Fort Sheridan	17	0
O1 ●	North Central	34	0
O5 ●	N. Division HS	18	0
O8 ●	Lombard	55	0
O15 ●	Beloit	34	0
O22 │	at Chicago	0	32
O29 │	DePauw	45	0
N5 ●	Oshkosh Normal	97	0
N12 ●	Illinois	12	6
N19 │	Minnesota *CHI*	0	17

1905 — 8-2-1 (0-2-0)
S20 ●	Evanston HS	32	0
S23 ●	at N. Division HS	11	0
S30 ●	St. Viator	41	0
O7 ●	Wabash	5	0
O14 ●	at Beloit	18	2
O21 =	Transylvania, Ky	0	0
O28 │	Chicago	0	32
N4 ●	Marquette	30	5
N11 ●	Ohio Northern	34	0
N18 ●	Michigan State	37	11
N25 │	at Minnesota	6	72

1906-1907
NO TEAM

ALTON JOHNSON
1908 (.500)   2-2

1908 — 2-2-0 (0-2-0)
O10 ●	Alumni	10	6
O24 ●	Beloit	44	4
N7 │	Purdue	10	16
N21 │	at Illinois	8	64

BILL HORR
1909 (.300)   1-3-1

1909 — 1-3-1 (1-3-0)
O2 =	Illinois Wesleyan	0	0
O9 ●│	at Purdue	14	5
O30 │	Wisconsin	11	21
N6 │	at Chicago	0	34
N13 │	Illinois	0	35

C.E. HAMMETT
1910-12 (.389)   6-10-2

1910 — 1-3-1 (1-2-1)
O1 │	Illinois Wesleyan	0	3
O8 ●	Iowa	10	5
O22 │	at Chicago	0	10
O29 = │	at Wisconsin	0	0
N12 │	Illinois	0	27

1911 — 3-4-0 (1-4-0)
O7 ●	Monmouth	26	0
O14 ●	Illinois Wesleyan	10	0
O21 ●	Indiana	5	0
O28 ●	Wisconsin	3	28
N11 ●	Chicago	3	9
N18 ●	at Illinois	13	27
N25 ●	at Iowa	0	6

1912 — 2-3-1 (2-3-0)
O5 =	Lake Forest	0	0
O12 │	at Wisconsin	0	56
O26 ●	at Indiana	20	7
N2 │	Purdue	6	21
N9 │	at Chicago	0	3
N23 ● │	Illinois	6	0

DENNIS GRADY
1913 (.143)   1-6

1913 — 1-6-0 (0-6-0)
O4 ●	Lake Forest	10	0
O11 │	at Purdue	0	34
O18 │	at Illinois	0	37
O25 │	Iowa	6	78
N8 │	Chicago	0	14
N15 │	Indiana	20	21
N22 │	at Ohio State	0	58

BIG TEN TEAMS

FRED MURPHY 1914-18 (.500)   16-16-1

1914   1-6-0 (0-6-0)
O3	•	Lake Forest	7	0
O10		at Chicago	0	28
O17		at Indiana	0	27
O24	•	Illinois	0	33
N7		Iowa	0	27
N14		Purdue	6	34
N21		at Ohio State	0	27

1915   2-5-0 (0-5-0)
O2	•	Lake Forest	27	6
O9		Chicago	0	7
O16		at Iowa	6	9
O23		at Illinois	6	36
N6	•	Missouri	24	6
N13		Indiana	6	14
N20		Ohio State	0	34

1916   6-1-0 (4-1-0)
O7	•	Lake Forest	26	7
O21	•	at Chicago	10	0
O28	•	Drake	40	6
N4	•	at Indiana	7	0
N10	•	Iowa	20	13
N18	•	Purdue	38	6
N25		at Ohio State	3	23

1917   5-2-0 (3-2-0)
O6	•	Lake Forest	48	0
O13		at Ohio State	0	40
O27		at Chicago	0	7
N3	•	at Purdue	12	6
N10	•	Michigan State	39	6
N17	•	Iowa	25	14
N24		Michigan	21	12

1918   2-2-1 (1-1-0)
O26	=	at Great Lakes NAS	0	0
N2		Chicago Navy	0	25
N9	•	Knox	47	7
N16		Chicago	21	6
N23		at Iowa	7	23

CHARLES BACHMAN 1919 (.286)   2-5

1919   2-5-0 (1-4-0)
O11	•	DePauw	20	0
O18		Wisconsin	6	10
O25		at Chicago	0	41
N1		at Michigan	13	16
N8		Iowa	7	14
N15	•	Indiana	3	2
N27		Rutgers Nwk	0	28

ELMER McDEVITT 1920-21 (.286)   4-10

1920   3-4-0 (2-3-0)
O2	•	Knox	14	0
O9	•	Minnesota	17	0
O16		at Wisconsin	7	27
O30		Indiana Ind	7	10
N6		at Iowa	0	20
N13	•	Purdue	14	0
N20		Notre Dame	7	33

1921   1-6-0 (0-5-0)
S24		Beloit	0	7
O1		at Chicago	0	41
O8		at Minnesota	0	28
O15		Wisconsin	0	27
O29	•	DePaul	34	0
N5		at Purdue	0	3
N19		Iowa	0	14

G. THISTLETHWAITE 1922-26 (.551)   21-17-1

1922   3-3-1 (1-3-1)
O7	•	Beloit	17	0
O14		at Chicago	7	15
O21	=	Minnesota	7	7
N4		at Illinois	3	6
N11	•	Purdue	24	13
N18	•	Monmouth	58	14
N25		at Iowa	3	37

1923   2-6-0 (0-6-0)
O6	•	Beloit	21	6
O13		Indiana Ind	6	7
O20		at Chicago	0	13
O27		Illinois Chi	0	29
N3		at Minnesota	14	34
N10	•	Lake Forest	32	0
N17		at Purdue	3	6
N24		Iowa	14	17

1924   4-4-0 (1-3-0)
O4	•	South Dakota	28	0
O11	•	Cincinnati	42	0
O18	•	Purdue	3	7
O25	•	Michigan State	13	9
N1	•	Indiana	17	7
N8		at Michigan	0	27
N15		at Chicago	0	3
N22		Notre Dame Chi	6	13

1925   5-3-0 (3-1-0)
O3	•	South Dakota	14	7
O10	•	Carleton	17	0
O17		at Chicago	0	6
O24	•	Tulane Chi	7	18
O31	•	Indiana	17	14
N7	•	Michigan Chi	3	2
N14	•	at Purdue	13	9
N21		at Notre Dame	10	13

1926   7-1-0 (5-0-0)
O2	•	South Dakota	34	0
O9	•	Carleton	31	3
O16	•	Indiana	20	0
O23		Notre Dame	0	6
O30	•	at Indiana	21	0
N6	•	Purdue	22	0
N13	•	Chicago	38	7
N20	•	at Iowa	13	6

DICK HANLEY 1927-34 (.576)   36-26-4

1927   4-4-0 (2-3-0)
O1	•	South Dakota	47	2
O8	•	Utah	13	6
O15	•	at Ohio State	19	13
O22		Illinois	6	7
O29		Missouri	19	34
N5		at Purdue	6	18
N12		Indiana	7	18
N19		Iowa	12	0

1928   5-3-0 (2-3-0)
O6	•	Butler	14	0
O13		Ohio State	0	10
O20	•	Kentucky	7	0
O27		at Illinois	0	6
N3	•	Minnesota	10	9
N10	•	Purdue	7	6
N17	•	at Indiana	0	6
N24	•	Dartmouth	27	6

1929   6-3-0 (3-2-0)
O5	•	Cornell Coll.	27	18
O5	•	Butler	13	0
O12	•	at Wisconsin	7	0
O19		Minnesota	14	26
O26	•	Wabash	66	0
N2	•	Illinois	7	0
N9	•	at Ohio State	18	6
N16		Indiana	14	19
N23		Notre Dame	6	26

1930   7-1-0 (5-0-0)
O4	•	Tulane	19	0
O11	•	Ohio State	19	2
O18	•	at Illinois	32	0
O25	•	Centre	45	7
N1	•	at Minnesota	27	6
N8	•	at Indiana	25	0
N15	•	Wisconsin	20	7
N22		Notre Dame	0	14

1931   7-1-1 (5-1-0)
O3	•	Nebraska	19	7
O10	=	Notre Dame Chi	0	0
O17	•	UCLA	19	0
O24	•	at Ohio State	10	0
O31	•	Illinois	32	6
N7	•	Minnesota	32	14
N14	•	Indiana	7	6
N21	•	at Iowa	19	0
N28		Purdue Chi	0	7

1932   3-4-1 (2-3-1)
O1	•	Missouri	27	0
O8		at Michigan	6	15
O15	•	at Illinois	26	0
O22	=	Purdue	7	7
O29		at Minnesota	0	7
N5		Ohio State	6	20
N12		Notre Dame Chi	0	21
N19	•	Iowa	44	6

1933   1-5-2 (1-4-1)
O7		Iowa Chi	0	7
O14	=	Stanford Chi	0	0
O21	•	Indiana Chi	25	0
O28		at Ohio State	0	12
N4		Minnesota	0	0
N11		Illinois	0	3
N18		Notre Dame	0	7
N25		Michigan	0	13

1934   3-5-0 (2-3-0)
S29	•	Marquette	21	12
O6		Iowa	7	20
O13		at Stanford	0	20
O27		Ohio State	6	28
N3	•	Wisconsin	7	0
N10		Illinois	3	14
N17		Notre Dame	7	20
N24	•	at Michigan	13	6

LYNN WALDORF 1935-46 (.520)   49-45-7

1935   4-3-1 (2-3-1)
S28	•	DePaul	14	0
O5		Purdue	0	7
O19		at Ohio State	7	28
O26	•	at Minnesota	13	21
N2	•	Illinois	10	3
N9	•	at Notre Dame	14	7
N16	•	Wisconsin	32	13
N23	=	Iowa	0	0

1936   7-1-0 (6-0-0)
O3	•	Iowa	18	7
O10	•	North Dakota St.	40	7
O17	•	Ohio State	14	13
O24	•	at Illinois	13	2
O31	•	Minnesota	6	0
N7	•	Wisconsin	26	18
N14	•	at Michigan	9	0
N21		at Notre Dame	6	26

1937   4-4-0 (3-3-0)
O2	•	Iowa State	33	0
O9	•	Michigan	7	0
O16	•	Purdue	14	7
O23	•	at Ohio State	0	7
O30	•	at Wisconsin	14	6
N6		Illinois	0	6
N13		at Minnesota	0	7
N20		Notre Dame	0	7

1938   4-2-2 (2-1-2)
O1	•	Kansas State	21	0
O8	•	Drake	33	0
O15	=	Ohio State	0	0
O22	•	at Illinois	13	0
O29	•	Minnesota	6	3
N5		Wisconsin	13	20
N12	=	at Michigan	0	0
N19		Notre Dame	7	9

1939   3-4-1 (3-2-1)
O7		Oklahoma	0	23
O14		at Ohio State	0	13
O21	•	Wisconsin	13	7
O28	•	Illinois	13	0
N4	•	at Minnesota	14	7
N11		Purdue	0	3
N18		at Notre Dame	0	7
N25	=	Iowa	7	7

1940   6-2-0 (4-2-0)
O5	•	at Syracuse	40	0
O12		Ohio State	6	3
O19	•	at Wisconsin	27	7
O26	•	Indiana	20	7
N2		Minnesota	12	13
N9	•	Illinois	32	14
N16		at Michigan	13	20
N23	•	Notre Dame	20	0

1941   5-3-0 (4-2-0)
O4	•	Kansas State	51	3
O11	•	Wisconsin	41	14
O18		Michigan	7	14
O25	•	at Ohio State	14	7
N1		at Minnesota	7	8
N8	•	Indiana	20	14
N15		Notre Dame	6	7
N22	•	Illinois	27	0

1942   1-9-0 (0-6-0)
S26		Iowa Pre-Flight	12	20
O3	•	Texas	3	0
O10		Purdue	6	7
O17		at Michigan	16	34
O24		Ohio State	6	20
O31		at Minnesota	7	19
N7		Illinois	7	14
N14		Wisconsin	19	20
N21		at Notre Dame	20	27
N26		Great Lakes NAS	0	48

1943   6-2-0 (5-1-0)
S25	•	Indiana	14	6
O2		Michigan	7	21
O16		Great Lakes NAS	13	0
O23	•	at Ohio State	13	0
O30		Minnesota	42	6
N6	•	at Wisconsin	41	0
N13		Notre Dame	6	25
N20	•	Illinois	53	6

1944   1-7-1 (0-5-1)
S23	•	DePauw	62	0
S30		Wisconsin	6	7
O7		Great Lakes NAS	0	25
O14		at Michigan	0	27
O21		Indiana	7	14
N4	=	at Minnesota	14	14
N11		Purdue	7	27
N18		at Notre Dame	0	21
N25		Illinois	6	25

1945   4-4-1 (3-3-1)
S22	•	Iowa State	18	6
S29	•	Indiana	7	7
O6		Michigan	7	20
O20		at Minnesota	7	30
O27	•	Purdue	26	14
N3		at Ohio State	14	16
N10	•	at Wisconsin	28	14
N17		Notre Dame	7	34
N24	•	Illinois	13	7

1946   4-4-1 (2-3-1)
S28	•	Iowa State	41	9
O5	•	Wisconsin	28	0
O12	•	Minnesota	14	7
O19	=	at Michigan	14	14
O26	•	Pacific	26	13
N2		Ohio State	27	39
N9	•	Indiana	6	7
N16		at Notre Dame	0	27
N23		Illinois	0	20

BOB VOIGTS 1947-54 (.459)   33-39-1

1947   3-6-0 (2-4-0)
S27		Vanderbilt	0	3
O4	•	UCLA	27	26
O11		at Minnesota	21	37
O18		Michigan	21	49
O25	•	Indiana	7	6
N1		Wisconsin	0	29
N8		at Ohio State	6	7
N15		Notre Dame	19	26
N22	•	at Illinois	28	13

1948   8-2-0 (5-1-0)
S25		at UCLA	19	0
O2	•	Purdue	21	0
O9		Minnesota	19	16
O16		at Michigan	0	28
O23	•	Syracuse	48	0
O30		Ohio State	21	7
N6	•	at Wisconsin	16	7
N13		at Notre Dame	7	12
N20	•	Illinois	20	7

ROSE BOWL
J1		California	20	14

1949   4-5-0 (3-4-0)
S24	•	Purdue	20	6
O1		Pittsburgh	7	16
O8		at Minnesota	7	21
O15	•	Michigan	21	20
O22		at Iowa	21	28
O29		at Ohio State	7	24
N5		Wisconsin	6	14
N12	•	Colgate	39	20
N19	•	at Illinois	9	7

1950 6-3-0 (3-3-0)

S30	●	Iowa State	23	13
O7	●	Navy BALT	22	0
O14	● |	Minnesota	13	6
O21	●	Pittsburgh	28	23
O28	|	at Wisconsin	13	14
N4	|	Ohio State	0	32
N11	● |	at Purdue	19	14
N18	|	at Michigan	23	34
N25	● |	Illinois	14	7

1951 5-4-0 (2-4-0)

S29	●	Colorado	35	14
O6	●	Army	20	14
O13	● |	at Minnesota	21	7
O20	●	Navy	16	7
O27	|	Wisconsin	0	41
N3	|	at Ohio State	0	3
N10	|	Purdue	14	35
N17	● |	at Michigan	6	0
N24	|	Illinois	0	3

1952 2-6-1 (2-5-0)

S26		at USC	0	31
O4	=	Vanderbilt	20	20
O11	|	at Minnesota	26	27
O18	|	Michigan	14	48
O25	● |	Indiana	23	13
N1	|	Ohio State	21	24
N8	|	at Wisconsin	20	24
N15	|	Iowa	14	39
N22	● |	at Illinois	28	26

1953 3-6-0 (0-6-0)

S26	●	Iowa State	35	0
O3	●	Army	33	20
O10	|	Minnesota	13	30
O17	|	at Michigan	12	20
O24	●	Pittsburgh	27	21
O31	|	at Ohio State	13	27
N7	|	Wisconsin	13	34
N14	|	at Indiana	6	14
N21	|	Illinois	14	39

1954 2-7-0 (1-5-0)

S25	●	Iowa State	27	14
O2		USC	7	12
O9	|	at Minnesota	7	26
O16	|	Michigan	0	7
O23		at Pittsburgh	7	14
O30	|	Ohio State	7	14
N6	|	at Wisconsin	13	34
N13	|	Indiana	13	14
N20	● |	at Illinois	20	7

LOU SABAN
1955 (.056) 0-8-1

1955 0-8-1 (0-6-1)

S24		Miami (Ohio)	14	25
O1		at Tulane	0	21
O8	|	Minnesota	7	18
O15	|	at Michigan	2	14
O22	|	Indiana	14	20
O29	|	at Ohio State	0	49
N5	|	Wisconsin	14	41
N12	|	at Purdue	8	46
N19	= |	Illinois	7	7

ARA PARSEGHIAN
1956-63 (.507) 36-35-1

1956 4-4-1 (3-3-1)

S29	●	Iowa State	14	13
O6		Tulane	13	20
O13	= |	at Minnesota	0	0
O20	|	at Michigan	20	34
O27	|	at Indiana	13	19
N3	|	Ohio State	2	6
N10	● |	at Wisconsin	17	7
N17	● |	Purdue	14	0
N24	● |	Illinois	14	13

1957 0-9-0 (0-7-0)

S28		at Stanford	6	26
O5		Oregon State	13	22
O12	|	Minnesota	6	41
O19	|	at Michigan	14	34
O26	|	Iowa	0	6
N2	|	at Ohio State	6	47
N9	|	Wisconsin	12	41
N16	|	at Purdue	0	27
N23	|	at Illinois	0	27

1958 5-4-0 (3-4-0)

S27	●	Washington State	29	28
O4	●	Stanford	28	0
O11	● |	at Minnesota	7	3
O18	● |	Michigan	55	24
O25	|	at Iowa	20	26
N1	● |	Ohio State	21	0
N8	|	at Wisconsin	13	17
N15	|	Purdue	6	23
N22	|	at Illinois	20	27

1959 6-3-0 (4-3-0)

S26	●	Oklahoma	45	13
O3	● |	at Iowa	14	10
O10	● |	Minnesota	6	0
O17	● |	at Michigan	20	7
O24	●	at Notre Dame	30	24
O31	● |	Indiana	30	13
N7	|	Wisconsin	19	24
N14	|	at Michigan State	10	15
N21	|	at Illinois	0	28

1960 5-4-0 (3-4-0)

S24	●	at Oklahoma	19	3
O1	|	Iowa	0	42
O8	|	at Minnesota	0	7
O15	|	at Michigan	7	14
O22	●	Notre Dame	7	6
O29	● |	at Indiana	21	3
N5	● |	at Wisconsin	21	0
N12	|	Michigan State	18	21
N19	● |	Illinois	14	7

1961 4-5-0 (2-4-0)

S30	●	Boston College	45	0
O7	● |	at Illinois	28	7
O14	|	Minnesota	3	10
O21	|	Ohio State	0	10
O28	●	at Notre Dame	12	10
N4	● |	Indiana	14	8
N11	|	Wisconsin	10	29
N18	|	at Michigan State	13	21
N24		at Miami, Fla.	6	10

1962 7-2-0 (4-2-0)

S22	●	South Carolina	37	20
O6	● |	Illinois	45	0
O13	● |	at Minnesota	34	22
O20	● |	at Ohio State	18	14
O27	●	Notre Dame	35	6
N3	● |	at Indiana	26	21
N10	|	at Wisconsin	6	37
N17	|	Michigan State	7	31
N23	●	at Miami, Fla.	29	7

1963 5-4-0 (3-4-0)

S21	●	at Missouri	23	12
S28	● |	Indiana	34	21
O5	|	at Illinois	9	10
O12	● |	Minnesota	15	8
O19	●	Miami (Ohio)	37	6
O26	|	Michigan State	7	15
N2	|	at Michigan	6	27
N9	|	at Wisconsin	14	17
N16	● |	at Ohio State	17	8

ALEX AGASE
1964-72 (.357) 32-58-1

1964 3-6-0 (2-5-0)

S19	●	Oregon State	7	3
S26	● |	at Indiana	14	13
O3	|	Illinois	6	17
O10	|	at Minnesota	18	21
O17		Miami (Ohio)	27	28
O24	|	at Michigan State	6	24
O31	|	at Michigan	0	35
N7	● |	Wisconsin	17	13
N14	|	at Ohio State	0	10

1965 4-6-0 (3-4-0)

S18		Florida	14	24
S25	● |	at Indiana	20	0
O2		at Notre Dame	7	38
O9	●	Oregon State	15	7
O16	|	Wisconsin	7	21
O23	● |	Iowa	9	0
O30	|	at Michigan State	7	49
N6	|	at Minnesota	22	27
N13	● |	Michigan	34	22
N20	|	Illinois	6	20

1966 3-6-1 (2-4-1)

S17		at Florida	7	43
S24	|	Indiana	14	26
O1		Notre Dame	7	35
O8	●	at Oregon State	14	6
O15	= |	at Wisconsin	3	3
O22	● |	at Iowa	24	15
O29	|	Michigan State	0	22
N5	|	Minnesota	13	28
N12	|	at Michigan	20	28
N19	● |	Illinois	35	7

1967 3-7-0 (2-5-0)

S23	●	Miami, Fla.	12	7
S30		Missouri	6	13
O7	|	at Purdue	16	25
O14		at Rice	6	50
O21	|	Ohio State	2	6
O28	● |	at Wisconsin	17	13
N4	|	at Michigan	3	7
N11	● |	Iowa	39	24
N18	|	Illinois	21	27
N25	|	at Michigan State	27	41

1968 1-9-0 (1-6-0)

S20		at Miami, Fla.	7	28
S28		USC	7	24
O5	|	Purdue	6	43
O12		at Notre Dame	7	27
O19	|	at Ohio State	21	45
O26	● |	Wisconsin	13	10
N2	|	Michigan	0	35
N9	|	at Iowa	34	68
N16	|	at Illinois	0	14
N23	|	Michigan State	14	31

1969 3-7-0 (3-4-0)

S20		at Notre Dame	10	35
S27		at USC	6	48
O4		UCLA	0	36
O11	● |	at Illinois	10	6
O18	● |	Wisconsin	27	7
O25	|	at Purdue	20	45
N1	|	Ohio State	6	35
N8	|	at Minnesota	21	28
N15	● |	Indiana	30	27
N22	|	Michigan State	7	39

1970 6-4-0 (6-1-0)

S19		Notre Dame	14	35
S26		at UCLA	7	12
O3		SMU	20	21
O10	● |	Illinois	48	0
O17	● |	at Wisconsin	24	14
O24	● |	Purdue	38	14
O31	|	at Ohio State	10	24
N7	● |	Minnesota	28	14
N14	● |	at Indiana	21	7
N21	● |	at Michigan State	23	20

1971 7-4-0 (6-3-0)

S11	|	Michigan	6	21
S18		at Notre Dame	7	50
S25	●	Syracuse	12	6
O2	● |	Wisconsin	24	11
O9	● |	at Iowa	28	3
O16	|	Purdue	20	21
O23	● |	at Indiana	24	10
O30	|	at Illinois	7	24
N6	● |	Minnesota	41	20
N13	● |	at Ohio State	14	10
N20	● |	Michigan State	28	7

1972 2-9-0 (1-8-0)

S16	|	at Michigan	0	7
S23		Notre Dame	0	37
S30	●	at Pittsburgh	27	22
O7	|	at Wisconsin	14	21
O14	|	Iowa	12	23
O21	|	at Purdue	0	37
O28	● |	Indiana	23	14
N4	|	Illinois	13	43
N11	|	at Minnesota	29	35
N18	|	Ohio State	14	27
N25	|	at Michigan State	14	24

JOHN PONT
1973-77 (.218) 12-43

1973 4-7-0 (4-4-0)

S15	● |	Michigan State	14	10
S22		at Notre Dame	0	44
S29		Pittsburgh	14	21
O6		Ohio U.	12	14
O13	● |	Iowa	31	15
O20	|	at Purdue	10	21
O27	|	at Ohio State	0	60
N3	|	Minnesota	43	52
N10	● |	at Indiana	21	20
N17	|	at Wisconsin	34	36
N24	● |	Illinois	9	6

1974 3-8-0 (2-6-0)

S14	|	at Michigan State	7	41
S21		Notre Dame	3	49
S28		at Nebraska	7	49
O5	●	Oregon	14	10
O12	|	at Iowa	10	35
O19	|	Purdue	26	31
O26	|	Ohio State	7	55
N2	● |	at Minnesota	21	13
N9	● |	Indiana	24	22
N16	|	Wisconsin	7	52
N23	|	at Illinois	14	28

1975 3-8-0 (2-6-0)

S13	● |	Purdue	31	25
S20	●	Northern Illinois	10	3
S27		at Notre Dame	7	31
O4		at Arizona	6	41
O11	● |	Indiana	30	0
O18	|	at Michigan	0	69
O25	|	at Wisconsin	14	17
N1	|	Iowa	21	24
N8	|	at Minnesota	9	33
N15	|	at Michigan State	14	47
N22	|	Illinois	7	28

1976 1-10-0 (1-7-0)

S11	|	at Purdue	19	31
S18		at North Carolina	0	12
S25		Notre Dame	0	48
O2		Arizona	15	27
O9	|	at Indiana	0	7
O16	|	Michigan	7	38
O23	|	Wisconsin	25	28
O30	|	at Iowa	10	13
N6	|	Minnesota	10	38
N13	● |	Michigan State	42	21
N20	|	at Illinois	6	48

1977 1-10-0 (1-8-0)

S10	|	at Iowa	0	24
S17		at Arizona State	3	35
S24		North Carolina	7	41
O1	|	at Wisconsin	7	19
O8	|	Indiana	3	28
O15	|	at Minnesota	7	13
O22	|	Ohio State	15	35
O29	|	Purdue	16	28
N5	|	at Michigan	20	63
N11	|	at Michigan State	3	44
N19	● |	Illinois	21	7

RICK VENTURI
1978-80 (.045) 1-31-1

1978 0-10-1 (0-8-1)

S9	= |	at Illinois	0	0
S16	|	at Iowa	3	20
S23	|	Wisconsin	7	28
S30		at Colorado	7	55
O7		Arizona State	14	56
O14	|	at Indiana	10	38
O21	|	Minnesota	14	38
O28	|	at Ohio State	20	63
N4	|	at Purdue	0	31
N11	|	Michigan	14	59
N18	|	Michigan State	3	52

1979 1-10-0 (0-9-0)

S8	|	at Michigan	7	49
S15	●	Wyoming	27	22
S22		Syracuse	21	54
S29	|	at Minnesota	8	38
O6	|	at Ohio State	7	16
O13	|	Iowa	6	58
O20	|	at Indiana	0	30
O27	|	at Purdue	16	20
N3	|	Michigan State	7	42
N10	|	at Wisconsin	3	28
N17	|	Illinois	13	29

1980 0-11-0 (0-9-0)

S6	|	at Illinois	9	35
S13	|	at Michigan	10	17
S20		at Washington	7	45
S27		at Syracuse	21	42
O4	|	Minnesota	21	49
O11	|	Ohio State	0	63
O18	|	at Iowa	3	25
O25	|	Indiana	20	35
N1	|	Purdue	31	52
N8	|	at Michigan State	10	42
N15	|	Wisconsin	19	39

DENNIS GREEN
1981-85 (.182)   10-45

1981   0-11-0 (0-9-0)

S12	Indiana	20	21
S19	Arkansas *LR*	7	38
S26	Utah	0	42
O3	Iowa	0	64
O10	at Minnesota	23	35
O17	Purdue	0	35
O24	at Michigan	0	38
O31	at Wisconsin	0	52
N7	Michigan State	14	61
N14	at Ohio State	6	70
N21	Illinois	12	49

1982   3-8-0 (2-7-0)

S4	at Illinois	13	49
S11	at Indiana	0	30
S18	Miami (Ohio)	13	27
S25 ●	Northern Illinois	31	6
O2	at Iowa	7	45
O9 ●	Minnesota	31	21
O16	at Purdue	21	34
O23	Michigan	14	49
O30	at Wisconsin	20	54
N6 ●	at Michigan State	28	24
N13	Ohio State	28	40

1983   2-9-0 (2-7-0)

S10	Washington	0	34
S17	at Syracuse	0	35
S24 ●	at Indiana	10	8
O1	Wisconsin	0	49
O8	at Iowa	21	61
O15	at Michigan	0	35
O22 ●	Minnesota	19	8
O29	at Purdue	17	48
N5	Michigan State	3	9
N12	at Ohio State	7	55
N19	Illinois	24	56

1984   2-9-0 (2-7-0)

S1	at Illinois	16	24
S8	at Washington	0	26
S15	Syracuse	12	13
S22 ●	Indiana	40	37
S29	at Wisconsin	16	31
O6	Iowa	3	31
O13	at Michigan	0	31
O20 ●	at Minnesota	31	28
O27	Purdue	7	49
N3	at Michigan State	10	27
N10	Ohio State	3	52

1985   3-8-0 (1-7-0)

S7	at Duke	17	40
S14 ●	at Missouri	27	23
S28 ●	Northern Illinois	38	16
O5	at Indiana	7	26
O12	Minnesota	10	21
O19 ●	at Wisconsin	17	14
O26	Iowa	10	49
N2	at Purdue	7	31
N9	Ohio State	17	35
N16	at Michigan State	0	32
N23	Illinois	20	45

FRANCIS PEAY
1986-91 (.212)   13-51-2

1986   4-7-0 (2-6-0)

S6	Duke	6	17
S20 ●	Army	25	18
S27 ●	at Princeton	37	0
O4	Indiana	7	24
O11	at Minnesota	23	44
O18	Wisconsin	27	35
O25	at Iowa	20	27
N1	Purdue	16	17
N8	at Ohio State	9	30
N15 ●	Michigan State	24	21
N22 ●	at Illinois	23	18

1987   2-8-1 (2-6-0)

S12	at Duke	16	31
S19	at Missouri	3	28
S26 =	Northern Illinois	16	16
O3	at Indiana	18	35
O10	Minnesota	33	45
O17	Michigan State	0	38
O24 ●	at Wisconsin	27	24
O31	at Michigan	6	29
N7	Iowa	24	52
N14	at Purdue	15	20
N21 ●	Illinois	28	10

1988   2-8-1 (2-5-1)

S3	Duke	21	31
S17	at Air Force	27	62
S24	at Army	7	23
O1	Indiana	17	48
O8	at Minnesota	28	28
O15	at Michigan State	3	36
O22 ●	Wisconsin	35	14
O29	Michigan	7	52
N5	at Iowa	10	35
N12 ●	Purdue	28	7
N19	at Illinois	9	14

1989   0-11-0 (0-8-0)

S9	at Duke	31	41
S16	Air Force	31	48
S23	Rutgers	27	38
O7	at Indiana	11	43
O14	Minnesota	18	20
O21	at Wisconsin	31	35
O28	Iowa	22	35
N4	Ohio State	27	52
N11	at Purdue	15	46
N18	at Michigan State	14	76
N25	Illinois	14	63

1990   2-9-0 (1-7-0)

S8	Duke	24	27
S22	at Rice	14	31
S29 ●	Northern Illinois	24	7
O6	Indiana	0	42
O13	at Minnesota	25	35
O20 ●	Wisconsin	44	34
O27	at Iowa	14	56
N3	at Ohio State	7	48
N10	Purdue	13	33
N17	Michigan State	22	29
N24	at Illinois	23	28

1991   3-8-0 (2-6-0)

S14	Rice	7	36
S21	at Rutgers	18	22
S28 ●	Wake Forest	41	14
O5	Purdue	14	17
O12	at Indiana	6	44
O19	Ohio State *CLEV*	3	34
O26 ●	Illinois	17	11
N2 ●	at Michigan State	16	13
N9	at Michigan	14	59
N16	Iowa	10	24
N23	at Wisconsin	14	32

GARY BARNETT
1992-98 (.438)   35-45-1

1992   3-8-0 (3-5-0)

S5	Notre Dame *CHI*	7	42
S12	at Boston College	0	49
S19	at Stanford	24	35
O3 ●	at Purdue	28	14
O10	Indiana	3	28
O17	at Ohio State	7	31
O24 ●	at Illinois	27	26
O31	Michigan State	26	27
N7	Michigan	7	40 *f*
N14	at Iowa	14	56
N21 ●	Wisconsin	27	25

1993   2-9-0 (0-8-0)

S4	at Notre Dame	12	27
S18 ●	Boston College	22	21
S25 ●	Wake Forest	26	14
O2	at Ohio State	3	51
O9	at Wisconsin	14	53
O16	Minnesota	26	28
O23	Indiana	0	24
O30	at Illinois	13	20
N6	at Michigan State	29	31
N13	Iowa	19	23
N20	Penn State	21	43

1994   3-7-1 (2-6-0)

S3	Notre Dame *CHI*	15	42
S10 =	Stanford	41	41
S17 ●	at Air Force	14	10
O1	Ohio State	15	17
O8	Wisconsin	14	46
O15 ●	at Minnesota	37	31
O22 ●	at Indiana	20	7
O29	Illinois	7	28
N5	Michigan State	17	35 †
N12	at Iowa	13	49
N19	at Penn State	17	45

1995   10-2-0 (8-0-0)

S2 ●	at Notre Dame	17	15
S16	Miami (Ohio)	28	30
S23	Air Force	30	6
S30 ●	Indiana	31	7
O7	at Michigan	19	13
O14	at Minnesota	27	17
O21 ●	Wisconsin	35	0
O28	at Illinois	17	14
N4 ●	Penn State	21	10
N11 ●	Iowa	31	20
N18	at Purdue	23	8

ROSE BOWL

J1	USC	32	41

1996   9-3 (7-1)

S7t	Wake Forest	27	28
S14 ●	at Duke	38	13
S21 ●	Ohio U.	28	7
S28 ●	at Indiana	35	17
O5 ●	Michigan	17	16
O12 ●	Minnesota	26	24
O19 ●	at Wisconsin	34	30
O26 ●	Illinois	27	24
N2	at Penn State	9	34
N9 ●	at Iowa	40	13
N16 ●	Purdue	27	24

CITRUS BOWL

J1	Tennessee	28	48

1997   5-7 (3-5)

A23 ●	Oklahoma *CHI*	24	0
S6	at Wake Forest	20	27
S13 ●	Duke	24	20
S20 ●	Rice	34	40
S27	at Purdue	9	21
O4	Wisconsin	25	26
O11	at Michigan	6	23
O18 ●	Michigan State	19	17
O25	at Ohio State	6	49
N1	Penn State	27	30
N8 ●	at Illinois	34	21
N15	Iowa	15	14

1998   3-9 (0-8)

S5 ●	Nevada-Las Vegas	41	7
S12 ●	Duke	10	44
S19 ●	at Rice	23	14
S26 ●	at Wisconsin	7	38
O3	Illinois	10	13
O10	at Iowa	24	26
O17	Michigan	6	12
O24	Ohio State	10	36
O31	at Michigan State	5	29
N7	Purdue	21	56
N14	at Penn State	10	41
N21 ●	at Hawaii	47	21

RANDY WALKER
1999-2005 (.446)   37-46

1999   3-8 (1-7)

S4	Miami (Ohio)	3	28
S11 ●	TCU	17	7
S18 ●	at Duke	15	12
S25 ●	at Purdue	23	31
O2	Minnesota	14	33
O9	at Indiana	17	34
O16 ●	Iowa	23	21
O30	Wisconsin	19	35
N6	at Michigan	3	37
N13	Michigan State	0	34
N20	at Illinois	7	29

2000   8-4 (6-2)

A31 ●	Northern Illinois	35	17
S9 ●	Duke	38	5
S16	at TCU	14	41
S23 ●	at Wisconsin	47	44
S30 ●	at Michigan State	37	17
O7 ●	Indiana	52	33
O14 ●	Purdue	28	41
O28 ●	at Minnesota	41	35
N4 ●	Michigan	54	51
N11 ●	at Iowa	17	27
N18 ●	Illinois	61	23

ALAMO BOWL

D30	Nebraska	17	66

2001   4-7 (2-6)

S7 ●	at Nevada-Las Vegas	37	28
S22 ●	at Duke	44	7
S29 ●	Michigan State	27	26
O6	at Ohio State	20	38
O13 ●	Minnesota	23	17
O20	Penn State	35	38
O27	at Purdue	27	32
N3	at Indiana	21	56
N10	Iowa	16	59
N17	Bowling Green	42	43
N22	at Illinois	28	34

2002   3-9 (1-7)

A31	at Air Force	3	52
S7	TCU	24	48
S14 ●	Duke	26	21
S21 ●	at Navy	49	40
S28	at Michigan State	24	39
O5	Ohio State	16	27
O10 ●	at Minnesota	42	45
O19	at Penn State	0	49
O26	Purdue	13	42
N2 ●	Indiana	41	37
N9	at Iowa	10	62
N23	Illinois	24	31

2003   6-7 (4-4)

A30	at Kansas	28	20
S6	Air Force	21	22
S13	Miami (Ohio)	14	44
S20 ●	at Duke	28	10
S27	at Ohio State	0	20
O4	Minnesota	17	42
O11 ●	at Indiana	37	31
O25 ●	Wisconsin	16	7
N1	at Purdue	14	34
N8 ●	Penn State	17	7
N15	Michigan	10	41
N22 ●	at Illinois	37	20

MOTOR CITY BOWL

D26	Bowling Green	24	28

2004   6-6 (5-3)

S2	at TCU	45	48
S11	Arizona State	21	30
S18 ●	Kansas	20	17
S25 ●	at Minnesota	17	43
O2 ●	Ohio State	33	27
O9 ●	Indiana	31	24
O23 ●	at Wisconsin	12	24
O30 ●	Purdue	13	10
N6 ●	at Penn State	14	7
N13 ●	at Michigan	20	42
N20 ●	Illinois	28	21
N27	at Hawaii	41	49

2005   7-5 (5-3)

S3 ●	Ohio U.	38	14
S10 ●	Northern Illinois	38	37
S17	at Arizona State	21	52
S24	Penn State	29	34
O8 ●	Wisconsin	51	48
O15 ●	at Purdue	34	29
O22 ●	at Michigan State	49	14
O29 ●	Michigan	17	33
N5 ●	Iowa	28	27
N12 ●	at Ohio State	7	48
N19 ●	at Illinois	38	21

SUN BOWL

D30	UCLA	38	50

PAT FITZGERALD
2006-PRESENT (.333)   4-8

2006   4-8 (2-6)

A31 ●	at Miami (Ohio)	21	3
S9	New Hampshire	17	34
S16 ●	Eastern Michigan	14	6
S22	at Nevada	21	31
S30 ●	at Penn State	7	33
O7	at Wisconsin	9	41
O14	Purdue	10	31
O21 ●	Michigan State	38	41
O28	at Michigan	3	17
N4 ●	at Iowa	21	7
N11	Ohio State	10	54
N18 ●	Illinois	27	16

NORTHWESTERN RECORD BOOK

SINGLE-GAME RECORDS

RUSHING YARDS

RANK	PLAYER	DATE	OPPONENT	ATT	AVG	YDS
1	Mike Adamle	Oct. 18, 1969	Wisconsin	40	7.9	316
2	Byron Sanders	Oct. 10, 1987	Minnesota	46	6.4	295
3	Damien Anderson	Oct. 7, 2000	Indiana	36	8.1	292
4	Damien Anderson	Nov. 4, 2000	Michigan	31	8.7	268
5	Jason Wright	Nov. 22, 2003	Illinois	42	6.0	251

PASSING YARDS

RANK	PLAYER	DATE	OPPONENT	ATT	COMP	YDS
1	Brett Basanez	Sept. 2, 2004	TCU	62	39	513
2	Brett Basanez	Oct. 15, 2005	Purdue	55	37	463
3	Mike Greenfield	Sept. 28, 1985	Northern Illinois	43	26	446
4	Sandy Schwab	Oct. 23, 1982	Michigan	71	45	436
5	Zak Kustok	Nov. 17, 2001	Bowling Green	39	26	421

RECEIVING YARDS

RANK	PLAYER	DATE	OPPONENT	REC	AVG	YDS
1	Jim Lash	Nov. 25, 1972	Michigan State	9	25.1	226
	Todd Sheets	Nov. 1, 1980	Purdue	11	20.5	226
3	Jon Harvey	Oct. 23, 1982	Michigan	17	12.2	208
4	Jonathan Fields	Sept. 2, 2004	TCU	8	25.3	202
5	Todd Jenkins	Oct. 16, 1982	Purdue	15	12.6	189

POINTS

RANK	PLAYER	DATE	OPPONENT	TOT
1	Otto Graham	Nov. 6, 1943	Wisconsin	27
2	12 players tied at 24			

FIELD GOALS

RANK	PLAYER	DATE	OPPONENT	TOT
1	John Howells	Sept. 25, 2005	Penn State	5

TACKLES

RANK	PLAYER	DATE	OPPONENT	TOT
1	Chuck Kern	Oct. 27, 1979	Purdue	31

INTERCEPTIONS

RANK	PLAYER	DATE	OPPONENT	TOT
1	Neil Little	Nov. 10, 1973	Indiana	3

RETIRED NUMBERS

Northwestern has no retired numbers

SINGLE-SEASON RECORDS

RUSHING YARDS

RANK	PLAYER	SEASON	G	ATT	YDS
1	Damien Anderson	2000	12	311	2,063
2	Darnell Autry	1995	NA	387	1,785
3	Tyrell Sutton	2005	12	250	1,474
4	Darnell Autry	1996	NA	280	1,452
5	Jason Wright	2003	13	267	1,388

PASSING YARDS

RANK	PLAYER	SEASON	G	ATT	COMP	PCT	YDS
1	Brett Basanez	2005	12	497	314	63.1	3,622
2	Brett Basanez	2004	12	460	247	53.6	2,838
3	Sandy Schwab	1982	NA	416	234	56.2	2,735
4	Zak Kustok	2001	11	404	231	57.1	2,692
5	Steve Schnur	1996	NA	368	221	60.0	2,632

RECEIVING YARDS

RANK	PLAYER	SEASON	REC	AVG	YDS
1	D'Wayne Bates	1998	83	15.0	1,245
2	D'Wayne Bates	1996	75	15.9	1,196
3	Richard Buchanan	1989	94	11.8	1,115
4	D'Wayne Bates	1995	49	18.1	889
5	Brian Musso	1997	58	14.9	865

SCORING

RANK	PLAYER	SEASON	TD	FG	PAT	P2	TOT
1	Damien Anderson	2000	23	0	0	0	138
2	Jason Wright	2003	21	0	0	0	126
3	Tyrell Sutton	2005	18	0	0	0	108
	Darnell Autry	1996	18	0	0	0	108
	Darnell Autry	1995	18	0	0	0	108

TOUCHDOWNS

RANK	PLAYER	SEASON	G	TOT
1	Damien Anderson	2000	12	23
2	Jason Wright	2003	13	21
3	Tyrell Sutton	2005	12	18
	Darnell Autry	1996	NA	18
	Darnell Autry	1995	NA	18

TACKLES

RANK	PLAYER	SEASON	TOT
1	Chuck Kern	1979	227
2	Chuck Kern	1978	218
3	John Voorhees	1971	192
4	Barry Gardner	1998	175
5	Barry Gardner	1997	174

INTERCEPTIONS

RANK	PLAYER	SEASON	YDS	TOT
1	Brett Whitley	1987	202	7
	Willie Lindsey	1991	52	7
3	Tom Worthington	1947	167	6
	Eric Hutchinson	1970	49	6

PUNTING

RANK	PLAYER	SEASON	PUNTS	YDS	AVG
1	John Kidd	1982	52	2,371	45.6
2	Paul Burton	1996	45	1,972	43.8
3	Ed Sutter	1989	33	1,436	43.5
4	J.J. Standring	2001	69	2,971	43.1
5	Paul Burton	1994	51	2,193	43.0

PUNT RETURNS

RANK	PLAYER	SEASON	RET	YDS	AVG
1	Lee Gissendaner	1992	15	327	21.8
2	Tom Worthington	1949	16	296	18.5
3	Vic Schwall	1946	10	159	15.9
4	Sam Simmons	1999	11	169	15.4
5	Ron Burton	1959	9	127	14.1

KICKOFF RETURNS

RANK	PLAYER	SEASON	RET	YDS	AVG
1	Jason Wright	2002	18	513	28.5
2	Willie Stinson	1963	13	369	28.3
3	Sam Simmons	1998	22	607	27.6
4	Ron Rector	1964	13	358	27.5
5	Curtis Duncan	1984	17	464	27.3

BIG TEN TEAMS

CAREER RECORDS

RUSHING YARDS

RANK	PLAYER	SEASONS	ATT	AVG	TD	YDS
1	Damien Anderson	1998-2001	953	4.7	38	4,485
2	Darnell Autry	1994-96	787	4.8	35	3,793
3	Bob Christian	1987-90	612	4.3	20	2,643
4	Jason Wright	2000-03	489	5.4	32	2,625
5	Noah Herron	2001-04	462	5.5	26	2,524
6	Tyrell Sutton	2005-06	439	5.6	21	2,474
7	Greg Boykin	1972-76	601	4.1	18	2,465
8	Mike Adamle	1968-70	483	4.2	15	2,015
9	Stanley Davenport	1984-87	522	3.7	NA	1,946
10	Byron Sanders	1987-88	451	4.1	NA	1,840

PASSING YARDS

RANK	PLAYER	SEASONS	ATT	COMP	PCT	INT	TD	YDS
1	Brett Basanez	2002-05	1,584	599	37.8	36	44	10,580
2	Len Williams	1990-93	1,076	644	59.8	37	44	7,487
3	Zak Kustok	1999-2001	767	507	66.1	23	42	5,822
4	Mike Greenfield	1984-87	784	497	63.3	39	21	5,803
5	Sandy Schwab	1982-85	948	533	56.2	49	23	5,679
6	Steve Schnur	1993-96	742	443	59.7	34	32	5,612
7	Maurie Daigneau	1969-71	659	298	45.2	53	23	4,237
8	Mike Kerrigan	1979-81	797	379	47.5	47	23	4,094
9	Mitch Anderson	1972-74	609	287	47.1	35	26	3,839
10	Tom Myers	1962-64	534	281	52.6	40	21	3,836

RECEIVING YARDS

RANK	PLAYER	SEASONS	REC	AVG	TD	YDS
1	D'Wayne Bates	1995-98	210	16.0	26	3,370
2	Richard Buchanan	1987-90	197	13.9	22	2,747
3	Shaun Herbert	2003-06	168	11.5	9	1,926
4	Lee Gissendaner	1990-93	156	12.0	13	1,878
5	Kunle Patrick	2000-03	171	11.0	8	1,873
6	Mark Philmore	2002-05	163	10.8	8	1,768
7	Scott Yelvington	1973-76	122	14.4	10	1,762
8	Brian Musso	1994-97	132	12.9	11	1,709
9	Sam Simmons	1998-2001	NA	NA	14	1,698
10	Jon Schweighardt	1999-2002	147	11.4	8	1,670

SCORING

RANK	PLAYER	SEASONS	TD	FG	PAT	P2	TOT
1	Brian Gowins	1995-98	0	58	88	0	262
2	Damien Anderson	1998-2001	38	0	0	0	228
3	Darnell Autry	1994-96	37	0	0	0	222
4	Jason Wright	2000-03	35	0	0	0	210
5	John Duvic	1983-86	0	46	62	0	200

TOUCHDOWNS

RANK	PLAYER	SEASONS	G	TOT
1	Damien Anderson	1998-2001	43	38
2	Darnell Autry	1994-96	NA	37
3	Jason Wright	2000-03	46	35
4	Noah Herron	2001-04	45	28
5	Bob Christian	1987-90	NA	27

TACKLES

RANK	PLAYER	SEASONS	G	TOT
1	Tim McGarigle	2002-05	48	545
2	Chuck Kern	1977-80	NA	503
3	Barry Gardner	1995-98	NA	468
4	Ed Sutter	1988-91	NA	429
5	William Bennett	1992-95	NA	418

INTERCEPTIONS

RANK	PLAYER	SEASONS	YDS	TOT
1	Brett Whitley	1984-87	NA	15
2	Tom Worthington	1946-49	319	14
3	Malcolm Hunter	1974-77	NA	11
4	Harold Blackmon	1997-2000	NA	10
	Eric Hutchinson	1969-71	NA	10

PUNTING

RANK	PLAYER	SEASONS	PUNTS	YDS	AVG
1	John Kidd	1980-83	261	10,916	41.8
2	J.J. Standring	1998-2001	305	12,639	41.4
3	Paul Burton	1993-96	216	8,948	41.4
4	Ed Sutter	1988-1991	218	8,803	40.4
	Brian Huffman	2000, 02-04	191	7,683	40.2

TEAM RECORDS

LONGEST WINNING STREAK
- 9, Sept. 23-Nov. 18, 1995

Streak broken vs. USC, 32-41, Jan. 1, 1996 (Rose Bowl)

LONGEST UNDEFEATED STREAK
- 13, Sept. 19-Nov. 21, 1903

Streak broken vs. Carlisle, 0-28, Nov. 26, 1903

MOST CONSECUTIVE WINNING SEASONS
- 4 (tie), 1895-98; 1928-31

MOST CONSECUTIVE BOWL APPEARANCES
- 2, 1995-96

MOST POINTS IN A GAME
- 97, vs. Oshkosh Normal, Nov. 5, 1904

MOST POINTS ALLOWED IN A GAME
- 78, vs. Iowa, Oct. 25, 1913

LARGEST MARGIN OF VICTORY
- 97 (97-0), vs. Oshkosh Normal, Nov. 5, 1904

LARGEST MARGIN OF DEFEAT
- 76 (0-76), vs. Chicago, Nov. 11, 1899

LONGEST RUN FROM SCRIMMAGE
- 95 yards, Bill Swingle, vs. Boston College, Sept. 30, 1961

LONGEST PASS PLAY
- 94 yards, Mitch Anderson to Jim Lash, vs. Michigan State, Nov. 25, 1972

LONGEST FIELD GOAL
- 54 yards, Nick Mirkopulos, vs. Arizona, Oct. 4, 1975

LONGEST PUNT
- 90 yards (tie), Steve Toth, vs. Wisconsin, Nov. 3, 1934; Paul Burton, vs. Indiana, Sept. 30, 1995

LONGEST INTERCEPTION RETURN
- 95 yards, E.P. Williams, vs. Purdue, Nov. 18, 1916

PUNT RETURNS

RANK	PLAYER	SEASON	RET	YDS	AVG
1	Lee Gissendaner	1990-93	41	606	14.8
2	Sam Simmons	1998-2001	40	511	12.8
3	Brian Musso	1993-97	96	1,075	11.2
4	Steve Tasker	1982-84	28	303	10.8
5	Roland Wahl	1962-63	20	194	9.7

KICKOFF RETURNS

RANK	PLAYER	SEASON	RET	YDS	AVG
1	Jeff Backes	2002-04	38	1,007	26.5
2	Curtis Duncan	1983-86	50	1,308	26.2
3	Willie Stinson	1961-63	28	718	25.6
4	Steve Tasker	1982-84	31	752	24.3
5	Lee Gissendaner	1990-93	34	750	22.1

NORTHWESTERN ANNUAL STATISTICAL LEADERS

YR	RUSHING	YDS	ATT	AVG	PASSING	ATT	CMP	PCT	YDS	RECEIVING	REC	YDS	AVG
1966	Bob McKelvey	459	128	3.6	Bill Melzer	176	94	.53	1,171	Roger Murphy	51	777	15.2
1967	Bob Olson	507	143	3.5	Bill Melzer	215	101	.47	1,146	Don Anderson	33	376	11.4
1968	Bob Olson	342	90	3.8	Dave Shelbourne	251	105	.42	1,358	Bruce Hubbard	33	551	16.7
1969	Mike Adamle	666	140	4.8	Maurie Daigneau	191	85	.45	1,276	Bruce Hubbard	25	384	15.4
1970	Mike Adamle	1,255	304	4.1	Maurie Daigneau	204	88	.43	1,228	Barry Pearson	33	552	16.7
1971	Al Robinson	881	277	3.2	Maurie Daigneau	264	125	.47	1,733	Barry Pearson	48	674	14.0
1972	Greg Boykin	625	159	3.9	Mitch Anderson	187	95	.51	1,333	Jim Lash	36	667	18.5
1973	Stan Key	894	197	4.5	Mitch Anderson	197	91	.46	1,224	Steve Craig	30	479	16.0
1974	Jim Pooler	949	216	4.4	Mitch Anderson	225	101	.45	1,282	Scott Yelvington	37	417	11.3
1975	Greg Boykin	1,105	239	4.6	Randy Dean	200	101	.51	1,315	Scott Yelvington	50	686	13.7
1976	Pat Geegan	537	154	3.5	Randy Dean	177	87	.49	1,384	Scott Yelvington	34	649	19.1
1977	Dave Mishler	520	115	4.5	Scott Stranski	95	37	.39	541	Mark Bailey	22	347	15.8
1978	Mike Cammon	322	73	4.4	Kevin Strasser	307	151	.49	1,526	Tim Hill	24	122	5.1
1979	Jeff Cohn	426	117	3.6	Mike Kerrigan	195	82	.42	961	Todd Sheets	43	614	14.3
1980	Jeff Cohn	503	137	3.7	Mike Kerrigan	337	173	.51	1,816	Todd Sheets	33	570	17.3
1981	Jim Browne	162	52	3.1	Mike Kerrigan	265	124	.47	1,317	Jim Browne	24	140	5.8
1982	Ricky Edwards	688	157	4.4	Sandy Schwab	416	234	.56	2,735	Jon Harvey	52	807	15.5
1983	Ricky Edwards	561	183	3.1	Sandy Schwab	334	188	.56	1,838	Ricky Edwards	83	570	6.9
1984	Casey Cummings	386	79	4.9	Sandy Schwab	198	93	.47	845	Casey Cummings	28	131	4.7
1985	Stanley Davenport	598	149	4.0	Mike Greenfield	335	199	.59	2,152	Brian Nuffer	40	328	8.2
1986	Stanley Davenport	703	181	3.9	Mike Greenfield	250	126	.50	1,653	Curtis Duncan	29	437	15.1
1987	Byron Sanders	778	187	4.2	Mike Greenfield	199	92	.46	1,265	George Jones	40	668	16.7
1988	Byron Sanders	1,062	264	4.0	Greg Bradshaw	257	129	.50	1,550	Richard Buchanan	41	514	12.5
1989	Bob Christian	1,291	277	4.7	Tim O'Brien	334	207	.62	2,218	Richard Buchanan	94	1,115	11.9
1990	Bob Christian	939	237	4.0	Len Williams	262	150	.57	1,700	Richard Buchanan	60	834	13.9
1991	Eric Dixon	227	64	3.5	Len Williams	212	131	.62	1,630	Mark Benson	45	831	18.5
1992	Len Williams	148	119	0.8	Len Williams	286	181	.63	2,110	Lee Gissendaner	68	846	12.4
1993	Robbie Glanton	159	36	4.4	Len Williams	316	182	.58	2,047	Lee Gissendaner	58	669	11.5
1994	Darnell Autry	556	120	4.6	Steve Schnur	117	61	.52	899	Michael Senters	28	385	13.8
1995	Darnell Autry	1,785	387	4.6	Steve Schnur	257	141	.55	1,792	D'Wayne Bates	49	889	18.1
1996	Darnell Autry	1,452	280	5.2	Steve Schnur	368	221	.60	2,632	D'Wayne Bates	75	1,196	15.9
1997	Adrian Autry	1,049	244	4.3	Tim Hughes	270	142	.53	1,862	Brian Musso	58	865	14.9
1998	Damien Anderson	537	164	3.3	Gavin Hoffman	323	176	.54	2,199	D'Wayne Bates	83	1,245	15.0
1999	Damien Anderson	1,128	306	3.7	Nick Kreinkbrink	158	60	.38	774	Teddy Johnson	23	354	15.4
2000	Damien Anderson	2,063	311	6.6	Zak Kustok	363	206	.57	2,389	Teddy Johnson	33	595	18.0
2001	Damien Anderson	757	172	4.4	Zak Kustok	404	231	.57	2,692	Sam Simmons	50	807	16.1
2002	Jason Wright	1,234	219	5.6	Brett Basanez	325	190	.58	2,204	Jon Schweighardt	58	719	12.4
2003	Jason Wright	1,388	267	5.2	Brett Basanez	302	162	.54	1,916	Roger Jordan	31	442	14.3
2004	Noah Herron	1,381	247	5.6	Brett Basanez	460	247	.54	2,838	Mark Philmore	54	633	11.7
2005	Tyrell Sutton	1,474	250	5.9	Brett Basanez	497	314	.63	3,622	Shaun Herbert	79	862	10.9
2006	Tyrell Sutton	1,000	189	5.3	C.J. Bacher	161	95	.59	1,172	Shaun Herbert	47	494	10.5

Receiving leaders by receptions
All statistics include postseason

OHIO STATE

BY TODD JONES

COLUMBUS IS A MYOPIC CITY where, nearly a quarter-century after Woody Hayes last coached Ohio State, men actually earn money by dressing up like the most beloved Buckeye and imitating him at parties and functions. Two weeks after Ohio State upset Miami in the 2003 Fiesta Bowl, a crowd of nearly 60,000 attended a ceremony at Ohio Stadium to honor the national champions. The people stood and cheered their 14-0 team during a 50-minute ceremony in 10° weather. Such is the love for the Buckeyes. Calendars for the 1.5 million residents in central Ohio are marked not just with birthdays and anniversaries but also with the annual Michigan grudge match. The state capital is a place where, as the nation struggled with a beef shortage in August 1973, locals were reassured by the front-page headline "OSU Gridders Will Get Meat." There is always something to chew on with the Buckeyes, and their performance determines many moods on fall weekends.

TRADITION Ceremonially dotting the "i" as the marching band performs its "Script Ohio" formation started in 1936 and is one of sport's more mesmerizing moments. The drum major of "The Best Damn Band in the Land" high-steps toward the "i" and points to a spot; the sousaphone player steps up, doffs his hat, and bows to each side of Ohio Stadium, with its 100,000 roaring fans. Bob Hope and Jack Nicklaus each dotted the "i." So did Woody Hayes. The 225-member band conducts a "Skull Session" 90 minutes before kickoff for fans in St. John Arena. The band then files due south, enters Ohio Stadium, and is greeted like a conquering army. Since 1954, wins are celebrated with the ringing of the 2,420-pound Victory Bell, which hangs in the stadium's southeast tower. Win or lose, the team gathers behind head coach Jim Tressel and sings "Carmen Ohio" to the band at game's end. The song concludes with everyone doing the "O-H-I-O" chant. "Senior Tackle" has been conducted since 1913, and it calls for senior players to hit the tackling sled once in the final practice prior to the Michigan game. Some years, Senior Tackle is a public event; in 1996, more than 20,000 came to Ohio Stadium to watch. Victories over Michigan have earned every player and coach a pair of miniature gold pants since 1934.

BEST PLAYER When Troy Smith won the 2006 Heisman Trophy, Ohio State tied Notre Dame and USC

PROFILE

Ohio State University
Columbus, Ohio
Founded: 1870
Enrollment: 52,320
Colors: Scarlet and Gray
Nickname: Buckeyes
Stadium: Ohio Stadium
　　Opened in 1922
　　FieldTurf; 102,329 capacity
First football game: 1890
All-time record: 787–301–53 (.713)
Bowl record: 18–20
Consensus national championships, 1936-present: 6 (1942, 1954, 1957, 1961, 1968, 2002)
Big Ten conference championships: 30 (16 outright)
Heisman Trophy: Les Horvath, 1944; Vic Janowicz, 1950; Howard Cassady, 1955; Archie Griffin, 1974-75; Eddie George, 1995; Troy Smith, 2006
Outland Trophy: Jim Parker, 1956; Jim Stillwagon, 1970; John Hicks, 1973; Orlando Pace, 1996
First-round draft choices: 65
Website: www.ohiostatebuckeyes.com

THE BEST OF TIMES

Woody Hayes' iconic powers peaked from 1968 to 1977, when he went 91–16–2, including a 68–8 Big Ten record that produced nine league titles (three outright) and a national championship in 1968.

THE WORST OF TIMES

Three consecutive losing seasons and a 12–14–5 record in a four-year span from 1922 to 1925 under coach John W. Wilce.

CONFERENCE

Ohio State joined the Western Conference in 1913 and has remained in the league since. The Western Conference was popularly known as the Big Ten since 1917, but didn't officially change its name to the Big Ten Conference until 1987.

DISTINGUISHED ALUMNI

Jesse Owens; Jack Nicklaus; Bobby Knight; Jack Buck, baseball announcer; John Havlicek, 13-time NBA All-Star; Richard Lewis, comedian; R.L. Stine, author; Leslie H. Wexner, founder and president, The Limited, Inc.; Mal Whitfield, Olympic track and field; Jerry Lucas, basketball.

FIGHT SONG

BUCKEYE BATTLE CRY
In old Ohio there's a team
That's known thru-out the land;
Eleven warriors, brave and bold,
Whose fame will ever stand.
And when the ball goes over,
Our cheers will reach the sky,
Ohio fields will hear again
The Buckeye Battle Cry—
Drive!
Drive on down the field,
Men of the scarlet and gray;
Don't let them thru that line,
We have to win this game today,
Come on, Ohio!
Smash through to Victory.
We cheer you as you go:
Our honor defend
We will fight to the end for O-hi-o.

Bob Hope and Jack Nicklaus have each dotted the "i."

for the most winners, with seven. One Buckeye, however, is the only player to win the award twice. Archie Griffin did so, despite playing at 5'9", 180 pounds. The Columbus native nearly went to Northwestern, but his parents wanted him to stay home so they could see him play, and he liked how Hayes didn't promise him anything during recruiting. Griffin gained 239 yards against North Carolina—an Ohio State single-game rushing record that stood for 27 years—in his second game as a freshman. Four Rose Bowl appearances later, he had a permanent place in the sport's history. "I was fortunate to be in the right place at the right time with the right people," Griffin once said. "I had the opportunity to play with guys who made me look good." He used his quickness to blast out of the Power-I formation and cut back against pursuing defenders. Griffin dashed and darted for 5,589 rushing yards during his career, including at least 100 in an NCAA-record 31 consecutive games. Teammates called him "Duckfoot" for his self-described running style.

Hayes called him "a better young man than he is a football player, and he's the best football player I've ever seen." As a senior in 1975, Griffin cast the deciding vote among teammates to name QB Cornelius Greene the team's MVP. In 1999, Ohio State retired Griffin's No. 45, an unprecedented honor at the school. The College Football Hall of Famer worked 18 years in OSU's athletic department before resigning as associate athletic director to become president and CEO of the Ohio State Alumni Association. The humble, easygoing Griffin remains the most in-demand speaker on Ohio State's banquet circuit, where he's introduced with "two-time Heisman winner" as a permanent part of his name.

BEST COACH Wayne Woodrow "Woody" Hayes is a caricature to many outside his native Ohio. He's the stompin', snortin', fire-breathin' bully who ran a caveman "three yards and a cloud of dust" offense, tormented game officials, tore up yard markers, smashed his wristwatches, and went down swinging. To Buckeyes fans, Hayes was the diabetic, sentimental, emotional, charming soul who quoted philosophers and generals, worked his entire career on one-year contracts, preached discipline to his players, and urged them to "pay forward" to others. Hayes last coached the Buckeyes in 1978 and died in 1987, but he remains a larger-than-life figure and a measuring stick for everything about Ohio State. He won 205 games, 13 Big

FIRST-ROUND DRAFT CHOICES

1938	Jim McDonald, Eagles (2)
1941	Don Scott, Bears (9)
1950	Fred "Curly" Morrison, Bears (10)
1956	Howard "Hopalong" Cassady, Lions (3)
1957	Jim Parker, Colts (8)
1959	Don Clark, Bears (7)
1959	Dan James, 49ers (8)
1960	Jim Houston, Browns (8)
1961	Tom Matte, Colts (7)
1962	Bob Ferguson, Steelers (5) and Chargers* (8)
1963	Bob Vogel, Colts (5)
1963	Daryl Sanders, Lions (12)
1964	Paul Warfield, Browns (11)
1964	Matt Snell, Jets (3)
1965	Jim Davidson, Bills
1969	Rufus Mayes, Bears (14)
1969	Dave Foley, Jets (26)
1971	John Brockington, Packers (9)
1971	Jack Tatum, Raiders (19)
1971	Tim Anderson, 49ers (23)
1971	Leo Hayden, Vikings (24)
1974	John Hicks, Giants (3)
1974	Rick Middleton, Saints (13)
1974	Randy Gradishar, Broncos (14)
1975	Kurt Schumacher, Saints (12)
1975	Doug France, Rams (20)
1975	Neil Colzi, Raiders (24)
1976	Tim Fox, Patriots (21)
1976	Archie Griffin, Bengals (24)
1977	Bob Brudzinski, Rams (23)
1978	Chris Ward, Jets (4)
1979	Tom Cousineau, Bills (1)
1982	Art Schlichter, Colts (4)
1984	William Roberts, Giants (27)
1985	Jim Lachey, Chargers (12)
1986	Keith Byars, Eagles (10)
1988	Eric Kumerow, Dolphins (16)
1991	Vinnie Clark, Packers (19)
1992	Alonzo Spellman, Bears (22)
1993	Robert Smith, Vikings (21)
1994	Dan Wilkinson, Bengals (1)
1995	Joey Galloway, Seahawks (8)
1995	Korey Stringer, Vikings (24)
1995	Craig Powell, Browns (30)
1996	Terry Glenn, Patriots (7)
1996	Rickey Dudley, Raiders (9)
1996	Eddie George, Oilers (14)
1997	Orlando Pace, Rams (1)
1997	Shawn Springs, Seahawks (3)
1999	David Boston, Cardinals (8)
1999	Antoine Winfield, Bills (23)
1999	Andy Katzenmoyer, Patriots (28)
2000	Ahmed Plummer, 49ers (24)
2001	Nate Clements, Bills (21)
2001	Ryan Pickett, Rams (29)
2004	Will Smith, Saints (18)
2004	Chris Gamble, Panthers (28)
2004	Michael Jenkins, Falcons (29)
2006	A.J. Hawk, Packers (5)
2006	Donte Whitner, Bills (8)
2006	Bobby Carpenter, Cowboys (18)
2006	Santonio Holmes, Steelers (25)
2006	Nick Mangold, Jets (29)
2007	Ted Ginn Jr., Dolphins (9)
2007	Anthony Gonzalez, Colts (32)

*From 1960 to 1966, the NFL and the AFL held separate, competing drafts.

Ten championships, and three national titles in 28 seasons. He did so with a complex combination—as a tough, irascible, colloquial, brilliant and polarizing autocrat who saw the world in black-and-white but had shades of gray to his personality. In practice, Hayes smashed his wristwatches and tore his caps for effect but didn't tell anyone the watches were cheap and that he had slit the seams of the hats with a razor blade so they would tear more easily. He cursed like a sailor and spoke with an endearing lisp. He was gregarious and yet difficult to quote. He wore white, short-sleeve shirts, even during snowy games. He demanded discipline from his teams yet had a volcanic temper. He'd pound his own players on their shoulder pads and helmets, but later would put a sympathetic arm around them and express compassion. The day before Hayes died, he had a friend drive him from Columbus to Dayton so he could rise out of his wheelchair and introduce his nemesis, Michigan coach Bo Schembechler, at a luncheon. "All good commanders want to die in the field," said Hayes, a former lieutenant commander in the Navy. In essence, he did so at the 1978 Gator Bowl. He punched Clemson noseguard Charlie Bauman after his interception sealed Ohio State's 17-15 loss. OSU president Harold Enarson fired Hayes the next day. Hayes cleaned out his office Monday morning, but he never really left Ohio State, even in death. His presence still hovers.

BEST TEAM While the nation seemed unhinged by social unrest in 1968, the conservative Hayes put together a monster team devoid of individualism and fueled by old-fashioned values. In search of his first Big Ten title in seven years, the Ohio State coach also went against his nature and started five sophomores on offense and six on defense. The Super Sophomores—including quarterback Rex Kern, defensive back Jack Tatum, and defensive lineman Jim Stillwagon—powered an offense that averaged 32 points and 440 yards per game and a defense that yielded an average of only 15 points and 292 yards. Kern replaced senior Bill Long, who had started at QB the previous two seasons, and established himself as the team's leader in the first game at home against Southern Methodist. Ignoring Hayes' instructions to punt, Kern ran 15 yards on fourth down and 10 at the SMU 41, sending the crowd into a

CONSENSUS ALL-AMERICANS	
1916-17, 1919	Charles "Chick" Harley, HB
1917	Charles Bolen, E
1920-21	Iolas Huffman, G/T
1920	Gaylord Stinchcomb, HB
1925	Ed Hess, G
1928-30	Wes Fesler, E
1935	Gomer Jones, C
1939	Esco Sarkkinen, E
1944	Jack Dugger, E
1944	Les Horvath, HB
1944	Bill Hackett, G
1945-46	Warren Amling, G/T
1950	Vic Janowicz, HB
1954-55	Howard Cassady, HB
1956	Jim Parker, G
1958	Bob White, HB
1960-61	Bob Ferguson, HB
1968	David Foley, T
1969	Jim Otis, RB
1969-70	Jack Tatum, DB
1969-70	Jim Stillwagon, MG
1972-73	Randy Gradishar, LB
1973	John Hicks, OT
1974	Steve Myers, C
1974	Kurt Schumacher, OT
1974-75	Archie Griffin, RB
1975	Ted Smith, G
1975	Tim Fox, DB
1976	Bob Brudzinski, DE

frenzy. The Buckeyes, spurred by an early-season upset of No. 1 Purdue, rolled 9–0 through the regular season and earned their first Rose Bowl in 10 years against USC. Hayes made trainers tape the players' ankles during the flight so they could practice as soon as the plane landed in California. "I'm looking forward to playing against O.J. Simpson, and I am also looking toward our victory party afterwards," Tatum said. After trailing 10-0 in the second quarter, the Buckeyes secured their national championship with a 27-16 win as Kern threw two TD passes in the fourth quarter. "I honestly thought we were a year away," said Hayes, who had gone 35–18–1 in the previous six seasons. Eleven players from that team, including seven of the sophomores, earned All-America honors during their careers. Six became first-round NFL draft picks. The Super Sophomores finished their careers with a 27-2 record. At their 20th reunion in 1988, members of the 1968 team presented Ohio State with a $1.2 million endowment in memory of Hayes.

BEST BACKFIELD Hayes had a heart attack in June of 1974 but was back on the sideline coaching when the season began 100 days later. He could be sure that Ohio State's offense wouldn't cause him any stress. The Buckeyes unit returned eight regulars, including QB Cornelius Greene, tailback Archie Griffin, wingback Brian Baschnagel, and fullbacks Pete Johnson and Champ Henson, who led the nation in scoring in 1972 before his knee injury sidelined him for all but two games in 1973. The amassed talent enabled Hayes to unleash his beloved brutal style of play. "It was popularly believed Woody's teams didn't even know a ball could be thrown," Jim Murray of the *Los Angeles Times* once wrote. "Getting beat on a pass by Ohio State is like getting mugged in church by a statue." Ohio State rushed for a school-record 4,199 yards behind All-America center Steve Myers and tackle Kurt Schumacher. Three times, Ohio State had two players rush for more than 100 yards in the same game. The Buckeyes rushed for 25 first downs while grinding out 517 yards on the ground, and 644 total, against Illinois. They had 33 first downs, 26 of them rushing, against Northwestern. Hayes used 13 different ballcarriers in that 55-7 rout. Johnson rushed for five TDs against North Carolina. Greene finished the season with 842 rushing yards to go with 939 passing. Griffin set the

Ohio State single-season record with 1,695 rushing yards, was named MVP of the Big Ten for a second time, and won the first of his two Heismans. The 1974 offense set school records for points (437), touchdowns (59), yards of total offense (5,252), and first downs (276).

BEST DEFENSE A trio of senior linebackers were the cornerstone of Ohio State's stonewall defense in 1973. With Randy Gradishar, Rick Middleton, and Vic Koegel wreaking havoc, the Buckeyes led the nation in scoring defense, allowing just 4.3 points per game—still the school's modern-day record. Ohio State shut out four opponents, held two others to just a field goal, and gave up just one TD in each of the other four regular-season games. The first eight opponents totaled 20 points against the Buckeyes. They yielded only seven points in one five-week stretch. Ohio State shut out Northwestern, Illinois, and Michigan State in three consecutive weeks, outscoring them 125-0, and that scoreless streak reached 15 quarters before Iowa, down 48-0, scored two TDs in the fourth quarter against Ohio State's reserves. The Buckeyes would have shut out Indiana, too, but Hoosiers coach Lee Corso, down 37-0 in the fourth quarter, ordered a pass off a reverse that produced a 51-yard TD. In a 30-0 win at Illinois, the Ohio State defense set up scoring drives of 41, 16, 31, and 31 yards. The Illini totaled 74 yards of offense. Michigan State was held to 94 yards, four first downs, and didn't cross midfield until midway through the fourth quarter. The Spartans didn't get within 32 yards of the end zone. Wisconsin never crossed the Ohio State 34 in a 24-0 loss. Gradishar, who led the team with 134 tackles, including 60 solo ones, and junior defensive end Van Ness DeCree were All-America selections. Middleton and Gradishar, both first-round NFL draft picks, were named All-Big Ten, as were DeCree, cornerback Neal Colzie, and tackle Pete Cusick. Colzie had a 55-yard interception return for a TD against Indiana and returned an interception 19 yards for a score against Northwestern. Ohio State went 10–0–1, beat USC 42-21 in the Rose Bowl, and finished No. 2 in the final poll behind 11–0 Notre Dame.

BIGGEST GAME ABC affiliate WSYX reported that 79% of the TVs turned on in Columbus on the night of the 2003 Fiesta Bowl were tuned in to the national championship game between Ohio State and Miami.

CONSENSUS ALL-AMERICANS (CONT.)	
1976-77	Chris Ward, T
1977-78	Tom Cousineau, LB
1979	Ken Fritz, G
1982	Marcus Marek, LB
1984	Keith Byars, RB
1984	Jim Lachey, G
1986	Cris Carter, WR
1986-87	Chris Spielman, LB
1987	Tom Tupa, P
1993	Dan Wilkinson, DL
1994	Korey Stringer, OL
1995	Eddie George, RB
1995	Terry Glenn, WR
1995-96	Orlando Pace, OL
1996	Mike Vrabel, DL
1996	Shawn Springs, DB
1997	Andy Katzenmoyer, LB
1998	Rob Murphy, OL
1998	Antoine Winfield, DB
2001	LeCharles Bentley, C
2002	Mike Nugent, PK
2002	Matt Wilhelm, LB
2002	Mike Doss, DB
2003	Will Allen, DB
2004	Mike Nugent, PK
2004-05	A.J. Hawk, LB
2006	Troy Smith, QB
2006	Quinn Pitcock, DL
2006	James Laurinaitis, LB

Viewers saw arguably the greatest college football game ever played—a long, jazzy riff of breathless moments, bone-jarring hits, controversy, and clutch performances. Ohio State's 31-24 double-overtime victory earned the school its first national championship since 1968. Freshman tailback Maurice Clarett ran five yards for the decisive TD in the second OT, then the Buckeyes defense held on four downs from inside its own 2 to complete the upset of a No. 1 Miami team which had won 34 consecutive games and was an 11½-point favorite. The Hurricanes forced the first OT when Todd Sievers made a 40-yard field goal on the final play of regulation, tying the game at 17. The clutch kick was set up by Roscoe Parrish's 50-yard punt return. Trailing 24-17 in the first OT, Ohio State QB Craig Krenzel converted a fourth-and-14 play with a pass to Michael Jenkins. The Buckeyes then faced fourth and three at the Miami 5. Krenzel threw incomplete to Chris Gamble in the right corner of the end zone. Fireworks went off. The Hurricanes celebrated—prematurely. Field judge Terry Porter, a Big 12 official, called pass interference on Miami's Glenn Sharpe, who was covering Gamble. Three plays later, Krenzel dove in from the 1 to force a second OT. "We've always had the best damn band in the land," Tressel said. "Now we've got the best damn team in the land."

BIGGEST UPSET Purdue was ranked No. 1 and was averaging 41.3 points when it entered Ohio Stadium on October 12, 1968, to face the No. 4-ranked Buckeyes. The Boilermakers were a 14-point favorite against an OSU team it had smashed 41-6 the previous year. Hayes thought Purdue coach Jack Mollenkopf showed up the Buckeyes by sitting on the bench with a hat over his eyes during that game's final two quarters, after the Boilermakers led 35-0 at halftime. A year later, a then-stadium-record crowd of 84,834 had revenge in mind when it filled the Horseshoe one hour before kickoff. Fans saw a 13-0 OSU victory on Columbus Day. "We just got clobbered," Mollenkopf said. Hayes' friend General Lewis Walt, commander of the Marine Corps, fired up the Buckeyes at halftime of the scoreless game with a speech about the Vietnam War. Ted Provost intercepted Purdue QB Mike Phipps on the fourth play of the second half and returned the ball 35 yards for a touchdown. Jim Stillwagon's interception later in the third

quarter set up the second Ohio State TD. Ohio State's ferocious defensive play allowed it to overcome its three missed field goals. The Buckeyes sacked Phipps four times and held him to 106 passing yards. Purdue star tailback Leroy Keyes gained just 18 yards—"Tatum is a monster," he said afterward—while fullback Jim Otis ground out 144 of Ohio State's 333 rushing yards. The victory catapulted the Buckeyes to No. 2 in the polls and sent them on their way to a perfect season and the national championship. "It was the greatest effort I've ever seen," Hayes said. "The coaches and the kids did a tremendous job. I can't remember a greater victory than this."

HEARTBREAKER Ohio State entered the 2007 BCS National Championship game in Glendale, Arizona, prepared for a coronation. The Buckeyes left bewildered and humiliated, 41-14 losers to Florida. Few saw the debacle in the desert coming. Ohio State was 12–0, the winners of 19 consecutive games, and seven-point favorites over SEC champion Florida. Led by Heisman-winning QB Troy Smith, the Buckeyes had been ranked No. 1 since the preseason and had twice defeated No. 2 teams: Texas in September and Michigan in the annual November grudge match. All season, Ohio State had trailed just once in the third quarter—by three points to Penn State—and never in the fourth. The Buckeyes' average margin of victory was 25.9 points. They had won nine of their 12 games by at least 21 points, including five by 30 or more and three by more than 40. Smith, flanker, and kick-returner Ted Ginn Jr., receiver Anthony Gonzalez, and tailback Antonio Pittman were part of an offense averaging 36.3 points. The defense gave up just 10.4 points per game. Ohio State coach Jim Tressel had been 4–0 in BCS games, including a national championship victory in the 2003 Fiesta Bowl. He had won four consecutive bowl games. He was coming off his fifth win in six tries against Michigan. He had been 8–2 against top 10 teams. All seemed well when Ginn took the opening kickoff against Florida and raced 93 yards for a TD. Then came a dark omen: Ginn injured his ankle celebrating the score and was on the field for one play from scrimmage the rest of the game. The Gators scored touchdowns the first three times they had the ball while building a 31-14 halftime lead. Florida defensive ends Derrick Harvey and Jarvis Moss tormented Smith, sacking him five times. Smith completed

COLLEGE FOOTBALL HALL OF FAME INDUCTEES		
NAME	YEARS	INDUCTED
Chic Harley, HB	1916-17, 1919	1951
Howard Jones, COACH	1910	1951
Wes Fesler, E	1928-30	1954
John Wilce, COACH	1913-28	1954
Les Horvath, HB/Q	1940-42, 1944	1969
Francis Schmidt, COACH	1934-40	1971
Bill Willis, T	1942-44	1971
Gaylord Stinchcomb, HB	1917, 1919-20	1973
Jim Parker, G	1954-56	1974
Gust Zarnas, G	1935-37	1975
Vic Janowicz, HB	1949-51	1976
Jim Daniell, T	1939-41	1977
Gomer Jones, C	1933-35	1978
Hopalong Cassady, HB	1952-55	1979
Woody Hayes, COACH	1951-78	1983
Warren Amling, G/T	1944-46	1984
Archie Griffin, HB	1972-75	1986
Aurealius Thomas, G	1955-57	1989
Jim Stillwagon, MG	1968-70	1991
Bob Ferguson, FB	1959-61	1996
Randy Gradishar, LB	1971-73	1998
John Hicks, T	1970, 1972-73	2001
Earle Bruce, COACH	1979-87	2002
Jack Tatum, S	1968-70	2004
Jim Houston, E	1957-59	2005
Rex Kern, QB	1968-70	2007

four of 14 passes for 35 yards and one interception. Ohio State had had 51 days to prepare for the game and finished with 82 total yards of offense. "Honestly, we've played a lot better teams than them," Moss said of the Buckeyes after the game. It was the ninth time since 1968 that the Buckeyes were ranked in the top three when they suffered a loss in either the final regular-season game or a bowl game. They were No. 1 six of those times.

WILDEST FINISH Scalpers were taking no less than $50, a princely sum during the Great Depression, when Notre Dame played at Ohio State on November 2, 1935, in a battle of unbeaten teams. A crowd of 81,018 saw the Buckeyes take a 13-0 lead after three quarters and 13-6 late in the game, before all heaven broke loose for the Fighting Irish. Notre Dame, which on its previous possession had been one yard from scoring until it lost a fumble in the end zone, now had to march 80 yards in three minutes. QB Andy Pilney, who had set up his team's first score with a 53-yard punt return, pushed the Irish forward again and capped the drive with a 15-yard TD pass to Mike Layden with 1:30 remaining to play. But for a second consecutive time, the Irish missed the extra point and Ohio State still led 13-12. The Buckeyes recovered the onside kick at their own 46, but on second down fumbled the ball out of bounds. Notre Dame's Henry Pojman last touched the ball, and under the rules at the time, that meant the Irish gained possession. Notre Dame was on its own 49 with 55 seconds left. Pilney drove the Irish to the Ohio State 19 but injured his knee and was carried off on a stretcher. With a name fitting the drama, Bill Shakespeare replaced him at QB and threw a TD pass to Wayne Millner on second down. The Irish missed their third consecutive PAT but still escaped with an improbable 18-13 victory. Notre Dame fans took the goalpost from Ohio Stadium's south end and carried it to downtown Columbus, where they celebrated with it at the Deshler Wallack Hotel.

The Buckeyes had better luck 12 years later against Northwestern. QB Pandel Savic had a pass from the Northwestern 12-yard line intercepted on the apparent final play of a 1947 game. The Ohio State band, figuring the home team had lost, took the field. Northwestern, however, was penalized for having 12 men on the field. The Buckeyes then tried a reverse, but Rodney Swinehart was tackled at

the 2-yard line. Northwestern was penalized for being offside. Savic then threw a TD pass to Jimmy Clark to tie the score. The Wildcats blocked Emil Moldea's point-after kick, but they were again caught offside. Head lineman E.C. Curtis called all three penalties with time expired. Moldea's second PAT was good for a 7-6 Ohio State win.

GOAL-LINE STAND

Ohio State had memorable defensive stands in the 1972 Michigan game and the 2003 Fiesta Bowl against Miami, but those didn't alter the program's history the way four plays in 1954 did. Woody Hayes had gone just 16–9–2 in his first three seasons at Ohio State and was picked to finish fifth in the Big Ten in 1954. Fans in Columbus, who had seen five Buckeyes coaches in the 1940s, were calling for Hayes' firing. Ohio State's defense went on to allow just 75 points in 10 games and might have saved Hayes' job when Michigan came to town for a nationally televised game to determine the Big Ten title and Rose Bowl berth. With the game tied 7-7 early in the fourth quarter, the Wolverines had first down on the Ohio State 4-yard line. The crowd of 82,438 rose up, and so did the Buckeyes. Michigan ran the ball up the middle four straight times, but Ohio State—led by linemen Jim Parker, the Outland Trophy winner two years later, Jim Reichenbach, Frank Machinsky, and linebacker Hubert Bobo—held the Wolverines scoreless, stopping them six inches from the goal line. At the time, Hayes said the goal-line stand was "the greatest thing that has happened in my coaching experience." The Buckeyes took over on downs, drove the length of the field for a touchdown on Dave Leggett's pass to end Dick Brubaker, and led for the first time, 14-7. They won 21-7, jumped to No. 1 in the polls, and were off to Pasadena for Hayes' first trip to the Rose Bowl. There, in a downpour, Ohio State defeated USC 20-7 to finish the season 10–0 and national champions.

BEST COMEBACK

Embattled coach John Cooper, 8–8–1 in his first 17 games at Ohio State, saw his 1989 team commit four turnovers while falling behind 31-0 at Minnesota with five minutes left in the second quarter. The visiting Buckeyes, however, scored 41 of the game's last 47 points to pull out a 41-37 victory that tied the previous mark for the biggest college comeback (by Maryland against Miami in 1984). QB Greg Frey capped a 73-yard drive by throwing a 15-yard touchdown pass to flanker Jeff Graham with 51 seconds remaining. Frey threw for 327 yards and three scores in the second half, and Ohio State overcame a 37-26 deficit in the game's final 5:15. Buckeyes tailback Carlos Snow finished the game with 278 all-purpose yards

and scored the team's first three TDs. "I've never been more proud of a football team," Cooper said.

PRO FOOTBALL HALL OF FAME INDUCTEES		
NAME	PRO YEARS	INDUCTED
Jim Parker, G/T	1957-67	1973
Lou Groza, T/K	1946-59, 1961-67	1974
Dante Lavelli, E	1946-56	1975
Bill Willis, MG	1946-53	1977
Sid Gillman, COACH	1955-69, 1971, 1973-74	1983
Paul Warfield, WR	1964-74, 1976-77	1983

STADIUM

When it opened in 1922 with a capacity of 66,210, Ohio Stadium was feared to be too large. Instead, so many fans consistently filled the concrete horseshoe that increasingly larger temporary bleachers were erected over the years in the open south end. Permanent seats now fill that area, but people still refer to it as the Horseshoe. The stadium, on the east bank of the Olentangy River, is also called "the house that Harley built" in honor of Chic Harley, who became Ohio State's first three-time All-America in 1919. He was such a popular player that Ohio Field became too small for the crowds, spurring a 1920 fund drive to build the $1.3 million Ohio Stadium, now listed on the National Register of Historic Places. Harley's name and retired No. 47 hangs in a place of honor on the northern end's façade, along with other those of Buckeyes whose jerseys have been retired: Howard Cassady (40), Eddie George (27), Archie Griffin (45), Les Horvath (22), and Vic Janowicz (31). Memories linger everywhere for the fans—who have numbered more than 100,000 for 34 consecutive games entering 2007—and tower above opponents like a scarlet wall of noise. Prior to the 2001 season, a three-year, $210 million renovation project added the permanent south-end seats, along with 81 private luxury suites and over 2,600 club seats. The project lowered the field and raised capacity to 102,329, in the process removing the track and field running lanes once dashed upon by Jesse Owens. During the 2006 season, Ohio State spent about $150,000 to resod the playing field twice. The natural grass was replaced with FieldTurf before the 2007 season.

HALLOWED GROUND

Buckeye Grove sits on the east side of Ohio Stadium, and since 1934, a buckeye tree has been planted in the spring to honor each Ohio State All-America from the previous season.

RIVAL

There are urinals throughout Columbus with a Michigan "M" painted on them, and auto insurance billboards in the city read, "In Case You Hit a Wolverine." "They brainwash you into hating those suckers, and then you really believe it," Ohio State linebacker Steve Tovar (1989-92) said. Some people won't refer to Michigan by name, instead calling it "that school up north." Hayes started that, and he's responsible for turning the annual season-ending game, first played in 1897, into the pigskin equivalent of Armageddon. Legend has it that Hayes once pushed his car across the state border rather than buy

gasoline in Michigan. In 1974, the Ohio State coach greeted then-president Gerald Ford, a Michigan alum, at the Columbus airport. A photo of the two ran in the next day's newspaper under the caption: "Woody Hayes and Friend." Hayes tried a two-point conversion with his team leading the Wolverines 50-14 in 1968. The play failed. Asked why he'd gone for two, Hayes said: "Because they wouldn't let me go for three." Four years later, Ohio State removed its steel goalposts and replaced them with wooden "tear-away" goalposts before the Michigan game. In 1985, a feeble Hayes left the hospital, visited the Ohio State team on the eve of the Michigan game, and told the players, "Take it against Bo and his smart alecks, and just kick the hell out of them." (Alas, the Wolverines did the kicking, topping Ohio State 27-17.)

There is no agreed-upon Fort Sumter moment between the two schools. The ill will doesn't stem from any single incident, and mutual respect has held the field from the start. In an account of the first Michigan game, in 1897, Ohio State's student newspaper, *The Lantern*, said, "The game was hard fought from start to finish and entirely free from slugging and objectionable features." Hayes' hatred and paranoia of Michigan, the final regular-season opponent every year since 1935, stemmed in part from Ohio State being known as "the graveyard of coaches" due to the Wolverines' dominance. The Buckeyes had 18 head coaches—including Pro Football Hall of Fame inductee Paul Brown—in the 60 years before Hayes' arrival in 1951. Cooper went 111–43–4 at Ohio State, but was fired after the 2000 season with a 2–10–1 record against the Wolverines. His successor, Tressel, has become a local legend for going 5–1 against Michigan, including a 42-39 win in a 2006 matchup considered to be the most highly anticipated in the 103-game series, with Ohio State ranked No. 1 and the Wolverines No. 2. That victory, before an Ohio Stadium-record crowd of 105,708, earned the Buckeyes their first outright Big Ten title since 1984 and sent them to the national championship game.

CONTROVERSY

Earle Bruce, Hayes' successor, was 81–26–1 when Ohio State president Edward H. Jennings announced thet Bruce was fired five days before the 1987 Michigan game. "Woody Hayes is probably rolling over

ALL-CENTURY TEAM

In February 2002, the Columbus Touchdown Club selected these players to the team.

OFFENSE

1954-56	Jim Parker, OL
1970, 1972-73	John Hicks, OL
1994-96	Orlando Pace, OL
1928-30	Wes Fesler, E
1984-86	Cris Carter, WR
1996-98	David Boston, WR
1968-70	Rex Kern, QB
1978-81	Art Schlichter, QB
1996-98	Joe Germaine, QB
1916-17, 1919	Chic Harley, RB
1940-42, 1944	Les Horvath, RB
1949-51	Vic Janowicz, RB
1952-55	Howard "Hopalong" Cassady, RB
1972-75	Archie Griffin, RB
1992-95	Eddie George, RB
1977-80	Vlade Janakievski, PK

DEFENSE

1942-44	Bill Willis, DL
1968-70	Jim Stillwagon, DL
1971-73	Randy Gradishar, LB
1984-87	Chris Spielman, LB
1996-98	Andy Katzenmoyer, LB
1968-70	Jack Tatum, DB
1972-74	Neal Colzie, DB
1995-98	Antoine Winfield, DB
1973-76	Tom Skladany, P

in his grave," said Iowa coach Hayden Fry, whose team had defeated the Buckeyes 29-27 two days earlier to drop them to 5-4. Ohio State athletic director Rick Bay made the announcement of Bruce's firing, reading Jennings' terse, 17-line statement, which contained no specific reason for the action. Bay then resigned in protest of Bruce's dismissal and was replaced by senior associate AD Jim Jones. A wave of national criticism crashed on Ohio State. Bruce had two years remaining on his contract and was permitted to coach the season's final game at Michigan. He cried when members of the school's marching band showed up at his house and played "Buckeye Battle Cry." Protestors showed him more support throughout the week's practices and at a pep rally. When Bruce, sporting a stylish suit and fedora, took the field in Ann Arbor for his final game, the Ohio State players were wearing white headbands with "EARLE" written on them. They carried him off after upsetting Michigan 23-20. "I always mind losing to Ohio State, but I didn't mind so much today," Bo Schembechler said. Bruce immediately filed a $7.44 million lawsuit against Ohio State and Jennings. He dropped the suit a week later after the school agreed to pay him the $471,000 remaining on his contract. Bruce went on to coach at Northern Iowa and Colorado State. He later made amends with Ohio State, does radio commentary about the Buckeyes, and has an office at the team's practice facility. Bruce was elected to the College Football Hall of Fame in 2002.

DISPUTES

Ohio State fans still insist that Brian Baschnagel scored from one yard out on the final play at Michigan State in 1974. The game officials ruled otherwise, and the Buckeyes suffered a 16-13 loss that cost them the No. 1 ranking. Ohio State entered the game 8–0 and the Spartans were 4–3–1. The frantic, final play occurred after Champ Henson had carried the ball five yards to within inches of the goal line with 29 seconds remaining. Ohio State was out of timeouts, and Michigan State's players were slow getting off the pile. The Buckeyes scrambled and snapped the ball, but it went through QB Cornelius Greene's legs. Baschnagel picked it up and ran into the end zone. Head linesman Ed Scheck signaled

touchdown, but field judge Robert Dagenhardt ruled that time had run out before the play began. Fans of each school climbed atop the goalposts, uncertain which team had won. Forty-six minutes later, with about 40,000 of the 78,533 fans still in the stadium, the public address announcer told the half-empty stadium that Big Ten commissioner Wayne Duke had decided the officials were correct in ruling that time had expired. Referee Gene Calhoun also said the Buckeyes would have been penalized if time had not run out because they didn't come to a one-second set before the snap of the ball.

DUBIOUS DISTINCTION Maurice Clarett helped the Buckeyes win one national championship and prompted two NCAA investigations of the program. The mercurial tailback from Youngstown, Ohio, ran for 1,237 yards and 16 touchdowns as a freshman in 2002. Clarett scored the winning touchdown, a five-yard run in the Fiesta Bowl's second overtime, as the Buckeyes upset Miami 31-24 in the BCS championship game to earn the school's first national title in 34 years. It was Clarett's last carry at Ohio State. He was suspended his sophomore season for violating 14 NCAA rules, 12 of them pertaining to receiving improper benefits and two for lying to investigators. Clarett left school and unsuccessfully sued the NFL, challenging the league's rules on early entry to the draft. In a November 2004 *ESPN The Magazine* story, Clarett accused Tressel, some members of his staff, and school boosters of a series of improprieties, including academic fraud and the arranging of loaner cars and no-show jobs. Tressel and Ohio State denied the charges, Clarett refused to cooperate with NCAA investigators, and the NCAA never proved his claims. Early in 2005, a "bone-weary" and "burned-out" Andy Geiger announced that he was retiring as Ohio State athletic director, a year prior to his contract's expiration. The Denver Broncos drafted Clarett in the third round but cut him during training camp. He never played in an NFL game. On January 1, 2006, he was accused of robbing two people at gunpoint in an alley behind a Columbus bar. With those two counts of aggravated robbery pending, Clarett was arrested again on August 9, 2006, and charged with carrying a concealed weapon after a highway chase ended with police finding four loaded guns in his sport-utility vehicle. A month later, he pleaded guilty in a plea bargain on charges in the two cases. Clarett is currently serving a 7½-year sentence, with release possible after 3½ years, in a single-person cell at the Toledo Correctional Institution.

NICKNAME For years, Ohio State athletic teams called themselves Buckeyes, after Ohio's state tree, the buckeye. The school made it the official moniker in 1950.

MASCOT Brutus Buckeye, a student dressed in a big head shaped like a buckeye nut, first appeared in 1965. He wears a scarlet-and-gray shirt with "BRUTUS" across the chest. On at least two occasions before Michigan games, the mascot's head has been stolen, later retrieved, and a kindof ransom paid.

UNIFORMS Three Ohio State students formed a selection committee in 1878 and chose orange and black as the school's colors. They later learned that Princeton already used those colors, so scarlet and gray was settled on for no significant reason. In 1968, Hayes began awarding buckeye leaf decals to players who made great plays in games. The decals are still placed on helmets today.

TRAGEDY Buckeyes center John Sigrist, a 27-year-old senior from Congress, Ohio, injured his neck during a 6-5 home win over Western Reserve on October 26, 1901, and died two days later at a Columbus hospital. Ohio State president William Oxley Thompson canceled the next game against Ohio Wesleyan, and the school's athletic board was persuaded by faculty and students to decide if Ohio State, in its 12th season of football, should drop the sport. The athletic board instead had the players vote on football's future at Ohio State. Sigrist's brother, Charlie, urged his teammates to vote in favor of continuing to play the game. Five days later, on November 4, the Ohio State faculty council took up the debate, but a resolution by professor N.W. Lord to drop football was defeated in a vote of 18 to 8. Ohio State's next game was a 21-0 loss to Michigan.

QUIRK The Buckeyes won the 1961 Big Ten championship with an 8–0–1 record, but the school's faculty committee voted 28 to 25 against accepting a Rose Bowl invitation. Their reasoning was that there was too much emphasis on football at Ohio State. Hayes and his supporters went berserk. More than 7,000 students staged a campus demonstration and marched downtown, where police chief George Scholar addressed the crowd over a cruiser's loudspeaker, saying, "I think the majority of Columbus is for you and the Rose Bowl." *Columbus Dispatch* sports editor Paul Hornung sarcastically wrote that the team should be called Woody Hayes' Buckeyes so its success wouldn't embarrass Ohio State and impair the school's academic prestige. More unrest followed the next day, but peace finally came when Hayes sent out co-captains Tom Perdue and Mike Ingram to tell protesting groups on campus to accept the school's decision. "The team did all the damn work," Ingram shouted. "If they can accept the decision, you certainly can."

LORE The game-time temperature was 10° for the Michigan game in Columbus on November 25, 1950.

Winds up to 40 mph blew snow horizontally. Before kickoff, Ohio State AD Dick Larkins and Michigan AD Fritz Crisler discussed the idea of postponing the game. "We're here, and we're not coming back down next week," Crisler said. No one could reach Big Ten commissioner Tug Wilson for advice. Some in the crowd of 50,535 helped the grounds crew remove the field's tarp and covered their heads with cardboard boxes for shelter. Officials used brooms to find yard lines. The teams combined for 68 total yards and booted 45 punts (some on first down) for 1,408 yards. Michigan, despite not making a first down or completing a pass, won 9-3, scoring a touchdown and a safety on blocked punts, to clinch a Big Ten championship. "It was a game played by heroes," said Buckeyes coach Wes Fesler, whose record against the Wolverines dropped to 0-3-1. "The conditions were the worst under which a game has been played. It should not have been played." A month later, Fesler resigned suddenly to go into private business, but he became Minnesota's coach in January 1951. Ohio State then hired Woody Hayes.

NUMBERS Eddie George ran for a school-record 1,927 yards and won the Heisman Trophy in 1995. He locked up the award with 313 rushing yards against Illinois ... The Buckeyes have had 65 players selected in the first round of the NFL draft, including 24 from 1995 through 2007. A school-record five Buckeyes were first-round picks in 2006 ... Chris Gamble was in 120 plays in the 2003 Fiesta Bowl at cornerback, wide receiver, and kick returner ... Troy Smith, the 2006 Heisman winner, became only the second Buckeyes QB to beat Michigan three times and the first since Tippy Dye, from 1934 to 1936. Smith passed for 857 yards, seven touchdowns, and one interception, and ran for 194 yards in three starts against the Wolverines. In 2006, he became the first Ohio State QB to throw four TD passes against them ... Defending national champion Ohio State, ranked No. 1 and riding a 22-game winning streak, had outscored opponents 371-69 and beaten all eight by at least 27 points before losing 24-12 at Michigan in 1969 ... The Buckeyes overcame a 13-point deficit in the game's final 4:24 to upset visiting LSU 36-33 in 1988 ... In 1973, offensive tackle John Hicks finished second in the Heisman voting, linebacker Randy Gradishar was third, and Archie Griffin was fifth ... Sophomore Tom Klaban kicked four field goals in a 12-10 win over Michigan in 1974 ... The 2006 Michigan game featured 81 points and 900 yards of total offense ... Uwe von Schamann's 41-yard field goal with three seconds left gave Oklahoma a 29-28 win at Ohio State in 1977 ... Michigan ran 12 plays from inside Ohio State's 5-yard line on three possessions but came away with only one TD while losing 14-11 in 1972 ... Keith Byars lost one of his shoes in 1984 while scoring on a 67-yard run, one

of his five TDs of the day, in a 45-38 win over Illinois. The Buckeyes trailed 24-0 early in the second quarter ... Woody Hayes tore up two yard markers and hurled them onto the field in protest of a noncall when he thought Michigan defender Thom Darden had committed pass interference in 1971 ... Senior fullback Bob Ferguson scored 4 TDs against Michigan in 1961, the year he finished runner-up to Ernie Davis in the Heisman voting. Fullback Jim Otis, with Ferguson's chinstrap taped under his shoulder pads for good luck, scored 4 TDs against the Wolverines in 1968 ... Paul Brown was just 32 years old when he became Ohio State coach in 1941 ... Fred Pagac was Ohio State's leading receiver in 1973 with 9 receptions for 159 yards ... Terry Glenn caught nine passes for 253 yards and four TDs against Pittsburgh in 1995 ... Hayes had 198 victories and Bear Bryant had 272 when the Buckeyes played Alabama in the 1978 Sugar Bowl ... Tim Spencer began the 1981 season with an 82-yard TD run against Duke on Ohio State's first play from scrimmage ... All-America split end Cris Carter did not play his senior season in 1987 because of his association with an agent ... Morris Bradshaw had an 88-yard TD run and an 88-yard kickoff return for a TD in a 1971 win over Wisconsin ... Two-time All-America end Mike Vrabel has won four Super Bowl rings with the New England Patriots ... From 1968 to 1980, the Ohio State-Michigan series was 6–6–1, and each team scored 176 points in the 13 games. During that span, the Buckeyes and Wolverines were a combined 83–5 against the rest of the Big Ten ... Archie Griffin is the only player to start in four Rose Bowls ... The Buckeyes have scored at least one TD in 215 consecutive games entering 2007 ... Joe Germaine's 3,330 passing yards in 1998 is 779 more than any Ohio State QB has thrown for in a season ... In three seasons, Ted Ginn returned six punts for TDs, two shy of the NCAA record, and returned two kickoffs for scores. He also scored by passing, receiving, and rushing ... As a junior in 1996, offensive tackle Orlando Pace was credited with 80 pancake blocks, knocking his defender to the ground and on his back. He was fourth in the Heisman voting that year and the winner of the Lombardi and Outland trophies ... Chris Spielman made a school-record 283 solo tackles from 1984 through 1987 ... Mike Nugent kicked eight field goals of 50 yards or more while setting a school record with 356 points from 2001 through 2004 ... Tressel is 55–9 in the past five seasons, with wins in 27 of the past 31 games ... The 1996 and 1998 Ohio State teams outscored 24 opponents by 610 points but didn't win a national title ... During the 2002 national championship season, the Buckeyes trailed in the second half or overtime in eight of 14 games, and six times they were tied or behind in the fourth quarter. Seven of their wins were by seven points or less.

QUOTE "You win with people." — Woody Hayes

OHIO STATE ALL-TIME SCORES

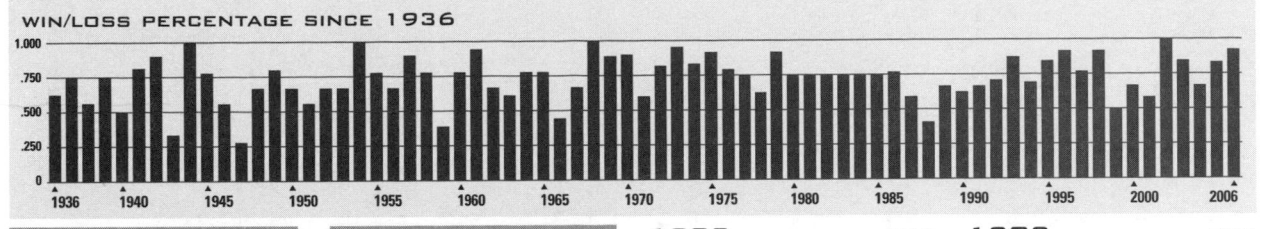

WIN/LOSS PERCENTAGE SINCE 1936

ALEXANDER S. LILLEY
1890-91 (.375)   3-5

1890   1-3-0
M3	●	at Ohio Wesleyan	20	14
N1		Wooster	0	64
N14		at Denison	0	14
N27		Kenyon	0	18

1891   2-2-0
N11		Western Reserve	6	50
N14		at Kenyon	0	26
N28	●	Denison	8	4
D5	●	at Akron	6	0

JACK RYDER
1892-95, '98 (.500)   22-22-2

1892   5-3-0
O15	●	at Oberlin	4	40
O22	●	at Akron	62	0
O29	●	Marietta	80	0
N5	●	at Denison	32	0
N7		Oberlin	0	50
N12	●	Dayton YMCA	42	4
N19		at Western Reserve	18	40
N24	●	Kenyon	26	10

1893   4-5-0
S30		at Otterbein	16	22
O14	●	Wittenberg	36	10
O21		Oberlin	10	38
O28		at Kenyon	6	42
N4		Western Reserve	16	30
N11	●	Akron	32	18
N18	●	Cincinnati	38	0
N25	●	Marietta	40	8
N30		Kenyon	8	10

1894   6-5-0
S15		at Akron	6	12
S17		at Wittenberg	0	6
O6	●	Antioch	32	0
O13		at Wittenberg	6	18
O20	●	at Columbus Barracks	30	0
O27		Western Reserve	4	24
N3	●	Marietta	10	4
N10		at Case	0	38
N17	●	at Cincinnati	6	4
N24	●	17th Regiment	46	4
N29	●	Kenyon	20	4

1895   4-4-2
O5	●	Akron	14	6
O12		at Otterbein	6	14
O19		Oberlin	0	12
O26	=	at Denison	4	4
N2	●	Ohio Wesleyan	8	8
N9		at Cincinnati	4	0
N15	●	at Kentucky	8	6
N16		at Central Kentucky	0	18
N23		at Marietta	0	24
N28	●	Kenyon	12	10

CHARLES A. HICKEY
1896 (.500)   5-5-1

1896   5-5-1
O3	●	Ohio Medical	24	0
O10		at Cincinnati	6	8
O17	●	at Otterbein	12	0
O23		at Oberlin	0	16
O30	●	Case	30	10
N5		Ohio Wesleyan	4	10
N7	●	Columbus Barracks	10	2
N11		Ohio Medical	0	0
N14		Wittenberg	6	24
N21	●	Ohio Medical	12	0
N26		Kenyon	18	34

DAVID F. EDWARDS
1897 (.167)   1-7-1

1897   1-7-1
O6	●	Ohio Medical	6	0
O9		Case	0	14
O16		at Michigan	0	34 *
O23	=	Otterbein	12	12
O26		Columbus Barracks	0	6
O30		Oberlin	0	44
N6		at West Virginia	0	24 *
N13		at Cincinnati	0	24 *
N25		Ohio Wesleyan	0	6

JACK RYDER

1898   3-5-0
O1	●	Heidelberg	17	0
O8		Ohio Medical	0	10
O15	●	Denison	34	0
O22		Marietta	0	10
N5		at Western Reserve	0	49
N12	●	Case	5	23
N19		Kenyon	0	29
N24	●	Ohio Wesleyan	24	0

JOHN B. ECKSTORM
1899-1901 (.810)   22-4-3

1899   9-0-1
S30	●	Otterbein	30	0
O7	●	Wittenberg	28	0
O14	=	at Case	5	5
O21	●	Ohio U.	41	0
O28	●	at Oberlin	6	0
N4	●	Western Reserve	6	0
N11	●	Marietta	17	0
N18	●	Ohio Medical	12	0
N25	●	at Muskingum	34	0
N30	●	Kenyon	5	0

1900   8-1-1
S29	●	Otterbein	20	0
O6	●	Ohio U.	20	0
O13	●	at Cincinnati	29	0
O20	●	Ohio Wesleyan	47	0
O27	●	Oberlin	17	0
N3	●	West Virginia	27	0
N10	●	Case	24	10
N17	●	Ohio Medical	6	11
N24	=	at Michigan	0	0
N29	●	Kenyon	23	5

1901   5-3-1
S28	=	Otterbein	0	0
O5	●	Wittenberg	30	0
O12	●	Ohio U.	17	0
O19	●	Marietta	24	0
O26	●	Western Reserve	6	5
N9		Michigan	0	21
N16		at Oberlin	0	6
N23		Indiana	6	18
N28	●	Kenyon	11	6

PERRY HALE
1902-03 (.714)   14-5-2

1902   6-2-2
S27	●	Otterbein	5	0
O4	●	Ohio U.	17	0
O11	●	West Virginia	30	0
O18	●	Marietta	34	0
O25		at Michigan	0	86
N1	●	Kenyon	51	5
N8		Case	12	23
N15	=	Illinois	0	0
N22	●	at Ohio Wesleyan	17	16
N27	=	Indiana	6	6

1903   8-3-0
S26	●	Otterbein	18	0
O3	●	Wittenberg	28	0
O10	●	Denison	24	5
O14	●	Muskingum	30	0
O17	●	Kenyon	59	0
O24		at Case	0	12
O31	●	West Virginia	34	6
N7		at Michigan	0	36
N14	●	Oberlin	27	5
N21	●	Ohio Wesleyan	29	6
N28		Indiana	16	17

E.R. SWEETLAND
1904-05 (.652)   14-7-2

1904   6-5-0
S24	●	Otterbein	34	0
O1	●	Miami (Ohio)	80	0
O5	●	Denison	24	0
O8	●	Muskingum	46	0
O15		Michigan	6	31
O22	●	Case	16	6
O29		at Indiana	0	8
N5		Illinois	0	46
N12		at Oberlin	2	4
N19	●	Kenyon	11	5
N24		Carlisle	0	23

1905   8-2-2
S23	=	Otterbein	6	6
S30	●	Heildelberg	28	0
O4	●	Muskingum	40	0
O7	●	Wittenberg	17	0
O14	●	Denison	2	0
O21	●	DePauw	32	6
O28	=	Case	0	0
N4	●	Kenyon	23	0
N11		at Michigan	0	40
N18	●	Oberlin	36	0
N25	●	Wooster	15	0
N30		Indiana	0	11

A.E. HERRNSTEIN
1906-09 (.731)   28-10-1

1906   8-1-0
S29	●	Otterbein	41	0
O6	●	Wittenberg	52	0
O10	●	Muskingum	16	0
O20		Michigan	0	6
N3	●	at Oberlin	6	0
N10	●	Kenyon	6	0
N17	●	at Case	9	0
N24	●	Wooster	12	0
N29	●	Ohio Medical	11	8

1907   7-2-1
S28	●	Otterbein	28	0
O5	●	Muskingum	16	0
O12	●	Denison	28	0
O19	=	Wooster	6	6
O26		at Michigan	0	22
N2	●	Kenyon	12	0
N9	●	Denison	22	10
N16		Case	9	11
N23	●	Heidleburg	23	0
N28	●	Ohio Wesleyan	16	0

1908   6-4-0
S26	●	Otterbein	18	0
O3		Wooster	0	8
O10	●	Denison	16	2
O17		Western Reserve	0	18
O24		Michigan	6	10
O31	●	Ohio Wesleyan	20	9
N7		at Case	8	18
N14	●	at Vanderbilt	17	6
N21	●	Oberlin	14	12
N26	●	Kenyon	19	9

1909   7-3-0
S25	●	Otterbein	14	0
O2	●	Wittenberg	39	0
O9	●	Wooster	74	0
O16		at Michigan	6	33
O23	●	Denison	29	0
O30	●	Ohio Wesleyan	21	6
N6		Case	3	11
N13	●	Vanderbilt	5	0
N20		at Oberlin	6	26
N25	●	Kenyon	22	0

HOWARD JONES
1910 (.750)   6-1-3

1910   6-1-3
S24	●	Otterbein	14	5
O1	●	Wittenberg	62	0
O8	●	Cinncinnati	23	0
O15	●	Western Reserve	6	0
O22	=	Michigan	3	3
O29	=	Denison	5	5
N5		at Case	10	14
N12	●	Ohio Wesleyan	6	0
N19	=	Oberlin	0	0
N24	●	Kenyon	53	0

HARRY VAUGHN
1911 (.600)   5-3-2

1911   5-3-2
S30	●	Otterbein	6	0
O7	●	Miami (Ohio)	3	0
O14	●	Western Reserve	0	0
O21		at Michigan	0	19
O28	●	Ohio Wesleyan	3	0
N4		Case	0	9
N11	●	Kenyon	24	0
N18	=	at Oberlin	0	0
N25		Syracuse	0	6
N30	●	at Cincinnati	11	6

JOHN R. RICHARDS
1912 (.667)   6-3

1912   6-3-0
O5	●	at Otterbein	55	0
O12	●	Denison	34	0
O19		Michigan	0	14
O26	●	Cincinnati	47	7 *
N2	●	at Case	31	6
N9	●	Oberlin	23	17
N16		Penn State	0	37
N23	●	at Ohio Wesleyan	36	6
N28		Michigan State	20	35

JOHN W. WILCE
1913-28 (.688)   78-33-9

1913-PRESENT
BIG 10

1913   4-2-1 (1-2-0)
O4	●	Ohio Wesleyan	58	0
O11	●	Western Reserve	14	8
O18	=	Oberlin	0	0
N1			Indiana	6	7
N8			at Wisconsin	0	12
N15			Case	18	0
N22	●		Northwestern	58	0

1914   5-2-0 (2-2-0)
O3	●	Ohio Wesleyan	16	2
O10	●	at Case	7	6
O17		at Illinois	0	37
O24		Wisconsin	6	7
N7	●	at Indiana	13	3
N14	●	Oberlin	39	0
N21	●		Northwestern	27	0

128 OHIO STATE

BIG TEN TEAMS

1915 — 5-1-1 (2-1-1)

O2	●	Ohio Wesleyan	19	6
O9	●	Case	14	0
O16	= |	Illinois	3	3
O23	|	at Wisconsin	0	21
N6	● |	Indiana	10	9
N13	●	Oberlin	25	0
N20	● |	at Northwestern	34	0

1916 — 7-0-0 (4-0-0)

O7	●	Ohio Wesleyan	12	0
O14	●	Oberlin	128	0
O21	● |	at Illinois	7	6
N4	● |	Wisconsin	14	13
N11	● |	Indiana	46	7
N18	●	at Case	28	0
N25	● |	Northwestern	23	3

1917 — 8-0-1 (4-0-0)

S29	●	Case	49	0
O6	●	Ohio Wesleyan	53	0
O13	● |	Northwestern	40	0
O27	●	Denison	67	0
N3	● |	at Indiana	26	3
N10	● |	at Wisconsin	16	3
N17	● |	Illinois	13	0
N24	=	Auburn MONT	0	0
N29	●	Camp Sherman	28	0

1918 — 3-3-0 (0-3-0)

O5	●	Ohio Wesleyan	41	0
O12	●	Denison	34	0
N9	●	Case	56	0
N16	|	at Illinois	0	13
N23	|	Wisconsin	3	14
N30	|	at Michigan	0	14

1919 — 6-1-0 (3-1-0)

O4	●	Ohio Wesleyan	38	0
O11	●	Cincinnati	46	0
O18	●	Kentucky	49	0
O25	● |	at Michigan	13	3
N8	● |	Purdue	20	0
N15	● |	at Wisconsin	3	0
N22	|	Illinois	7	9

1920 — 7-1-0 (5-0-0)

O2	●	Ohio Wesleyan	55	0
O9	●	Oberlin	37	0
O16	● |	Purdue	17	0
O23	● |	Wisconsin	13	7
O30	● |	at Chicago	7	6
N6	● |	Michigan	14	7
N20	● |	at Illinois	7	0
		ROSE BOWL		
J1		California	0	28

1921 — 5-2-0 (4-1-0)

O1	●	Ohio Wesleyan	28	0
O8		Oberlin	6	7
O15	● |	Minnesota	27	0
O22	● |	at Michigan	14	0
N5	● |	at Chicago	7	0
N12	● |	Purdue	28	0
N19	|	Illinois	0	7

1922 — 3-4-0 (1-4-0)

O7	●	Ohio Wesleyan	5	0
O14	●	Oberlin	14	0
O21	|	Michigan	0	19
O28	|	at Minnesota	0	9
N11	|	Chicago	9	14
N18	|	Iowa	9	12
N25	● |	at Illinois	6	3

1923 — 3-4-1 (1-4-0)

O6	●	Ohio Wesleyan	24	7
O13	=	Colgate	23	23
O20	|	at Michigan	0	23
O27	|	Iowa	0	20
N3	●	Denison	42	0
N10	● |	at Purdue	32	0
N17	|	at Chicago	3	17
N24	|	Illinois	0	9

1924 — 2-3-3 (1-3-2)

O4	● |	Purdue	7	0
O11	= |	at Iowa	0	0
O18	●	Ohio Wesleyan	10	0
O25	= |	Chicago	3	3
N1	=	Wooster	7	7
N8	|	Indiana	7	12
N15	|	Michigan	6	16
N22	|	at Illinois	0	7

1925 — 4-3-1 (1-3-1)

O3	●	Ohio Wesleyan	10	3
O10	●	Columbia	9	0
O17	= |	at Chicago	3	3
O24	|	Iowa	0	15
O31	●	Wooster	17	0
N7	● |	Indiana	7	0
N14	|	at Michigan	0	10
N21	|	Illinois	9	14

1926 — 7-1-0 (3-1-0)

O2	●	Wittenberg	40	0
O9	●	Ohio Wesleyan	47	0
O16	●	Columbia NYC	32	7
O23	● |	Iowa	23	6
O30	● |	at Chicago	18	0
N6	●	Wilmington	13	7
N13	|	Michigan	16	17
N20	● |	at Illinois	7	6

1927 — 4-4-0 (2-3-0)

O1	●	Wittenberg	31	0
O8	● |	at Iowa	13	6
O15	|	Northwestern	13	19
O22	|	at Michigan	0	21
O29	● |	Chicago	13	7
N5		at Princeton	0	20
N12	●	Denison	61	6
N19	|	Illinois	0	13

1928 — 5-2-1 (3-2-0)

O6	●	Wittenberg	41	0
O13	● |	at Northwestern	10	0
O20	● |	Michigan	19	7
O27	● |	at Indiana	13	0
N3	=	Princeton	6	6
N10	|	Iowa	7	14
N17	●	Muskingum	39	0
N24	|	at Illinois	0	8

SAM S. WILLAMAN
1929-33 (.695) 26-10-5

1929 — 4-3-1 (2-2-1)

O5	●	Wittenberg	19	0
O12	● |	Iowa	7	6
O19	● |	at Michigan	7	0
O26	= |	Indiana	0	0
N2		at Pittsburgh	2	18
N9	|	Northwestern	6	18
N16	●	Kenyon	54	0
N23	|	Illinois	0	27

1930 — 5-2-1 (2-2-1)

S27	●	Mt. Union	59	0
O4	● |	Indiana	23	0
O11	|	at Northwestern	2	19
O18	|	Michigan	0	13
N1	= |	Wisconsin	0	0
N8	●	Navy BALT	27	0
N15	●	Pittsburgh	16	7
N22	● |	at Illinois	12	9

1931 — 6-3-0 (4-2-0)

O3	●	Cincinnati	67	6
O10		Vanderbilt	21	26
O17	● |	at Michigan	20	7
O24	|	Northwestern	0	10
O31	● |	at Indiana	13	6 *
N7	●	Navy	20	0
N14	● |	at Wisconsin	6	0
N21	● |	Illinois	40	0
N28	|	at Minnesota	7	19

1932 — 4-1-3 (2-1-2)

O1	●	Ohio Wesleyan	34	7
O8	= |	Indiana	7	7
O15	|	Michigan	0	14
O22	=	at Pittsburgh	0	0
O29	= |	Wisconsin	7	7
N5	● |	at Northwestern	20	6
N12	●	Pennsylvania	19	0
N19	● |	at Illinois	3	0

1933 — 7-1-0 (4-1-0)

O7	●	Virginia	75	0
O14	●	Vanderbilt	20	0
O21	|	at Michigan	0	13
O28	● |	Northwestern	12	0
N4	● |	Indiana	21	0
N11	●	at Pennsylvania	20	7
N18	● |	at Wisconsin	6	0
N25	● |	Illinois	7	6

FRANCIS A. SCHMIDT
1934-40 (.705) 39-16-1

1934 — 7-1-0 (5-1-0)

O6	● |	Indiana	33	0
O13	|	at Illinois	13	14
O20	●	Colgate	10	7
O27	● |	at Northwestern	28	6
N3	●	at Western Reserve	76	0
N10	● |	Chicago	33	0
N17	● |	Michigan	34	0
N24	● |	Iowa	40	7

1935 — 7-1-0 (5-0-0)

O5	●	Kentucky	19	6
O12	●	Drake	85	7
O19	● |	Northwestern	28	7
O26	● |	at Indiana	28	6
N2		Notre Dame	13	18
N9	● |	at Chicago	20	13
N16	● |	Illinois	6	0
N23	● |	at Michigan	38	0

1936 — 5-3-0 (4-1-0)

O3	●	NYU	60	0
O10		Pittsburgh	0	6
O17	|	at Northwestern	13	14
O24	● |	Indiana	7	0
O31		at Notre Dame	2	7
N7	● |	Chicago	44	0
N14	● |	at Illinois	13	0
N21	● |	Michigan	21	0

1937 — 6-2-0 (5-1-0)

S25	●	TCU	14	0
O2	● |	Purdue	13	0
O9		at USC	12	13
O23	● |	Northwestern	7	0
O30	● |	at Chicago	39	0
N6	|	Indiana	0	10
N13	● |	Illinois	19	0
N20	● |	at Michigan	21	0

1938 — 4-3-1 (3-2-1)

O1	● |	Indiana	6	0
O8		USC	7	14
O15	= |	at Northwestern	0	0
O22	● |	Chicago	42	7
O29	●	NYU NYC	32	0
N5	|	Purdue	0	12
N12	● |	at Illinois	32	14
N19	|	Michigan	0	18

1939 — 6-2-0 (5-1-0)

O7	●	Missouri	19	0
O14	● |	Northwestern	13	0
O21	● |	at Minnesota	23	20
O28		Cornell	14	23
N4	● |	Indiana	24	0
N11	● |	at Chicago	61	0
N18	● |	Illinois	21	0
N25	|	at MIchigan	14	21

1940 — 4-4-0 (3-3-0)

S28	●	Pittsburgh	30	7
O5	● |	Purdue	17	14
O12	|	at Northwestern	3	6
O19	|	Minnesota	7	13
O26		at Cornell	7	21
N2	● |	Indiana	21	6
N16	● |	at Illinois	14	6
N23	|	Michigan	0	40

PAUL E. BROWN
1941-43 (.685) 18-8-1

1941 — 6-1-1 (3-1-1)

S27	●	Missouri	12	7
O4	●	at USC	33	0
O18	● |	Purdue	16	14
O25	|	Northwestern	7	14
N1	●	at Pittsburgh	21	14
N8	● |	Wisconsin	46	34
N15	● |	Illinois	12	7
N22	= |	at Michigan	20	20

1942 — 9-1-0 (5-1-0)

S26	●	Fort Knox	59	0
O3	● |	Indiana	32	21
O10	●	USC	28	12
O17	● |	Purdue	26	0
O24	● |	at Northwestern	20	6
O31	|	at Wisconsin	7	17
N7	●	Pittsburgh	59	19
N14	● |	Illinois CLEV	44	20
N21	● |	Michigan	21	7
N28	●	Iowa Pre-Flight	41	12

1943 — 3-6-0 (1-4-0)

S25		Iowa Pre-Flight	13	28
O2	●	Missouri	27	6
O9		at Great Lakes NAS	6	13
O16	|	Purdue CLEV	7	30
O23	|	Northwestern	0	13
O30	|	Indiana	14	20
N6	●	at Pittsburgh	46	6
N13	● |	Illinois	29	26
N20	|	at Michigan	7	45

CARROLL C. WIDDOES
1944-45 (.889) 16-2

1944 — 9-0-0 (6-0-0)

S30	●	Missouri	54	0
O7	● |	Iowa	34	0
O14	● |	at Wisconsin	20	7
O21	●	Great Lakes NAS	26	6
O28	● |	Minnesota	34	14
N4	● |	Indiana	21	7
N11	●	Pittsburgh	54	19
N18	● |	Illinois CLEV	26	12
N25	● |	Michigan	18	14

1945 — 7-2-0 (5-2-0)

S29	●	at Missouri	47	6
O6	● |	Iowa	42	0
O13	● |	Wisconsin	12	0
O20	|	Purdue	13	35
O27	● |	at Minnesota	20	7
N3	● |	Northwestern	16	14
N10	●	at Pittsburgh	14	0
N17	● |	Illinois	27	2
N24	|	at Michigan	3	7

PAUL O. BIXLER
1946 (.556) 4-3-2

1946 — 4-3-2 (2-3-1)

S28	=	Missouri	13	13
O5	●	at USC	21	0
O12	|	at Wisconsin	7	20
O19	= |	Purdue	14	14
O26	● |	Minnesota	39	9
N2	● |	at Northwestern	39	27
N9	●	Pittsburgh	20	13
N16	|	at Illinois	7	16
N23	|	Michigan	6	58

WESLEY E. FESLER
1947-50 (.608) 21-13-3

1947 — 2-6-1 (1-4-1)

S27	●	Missouri	13	7
O4	|	at Purdue	20	24
O11		USC	0	32
O18	= |	Iowa	13	13
O25		at Pittsburgh	0	12
N1	|	Indiana	0	7
N8	● |	Northwestern	7	6
N15	|	Illinois	7	28
N22	|	at Michigan	0	21

1948 — 6-3-0 (3-3-0)

S25	●	Missouri	21	7
O2	●	USC	20	0
O9	|	Iowa	7	14
O16	● |	at Indiana	17	0
O23	● |	Wisconsin	34	32
O30	|	at Northwestern	7	21
N6	●	Pittsburgh	41	0
N13	● |	at Illinois	34	7
N20	|	Michigan	3	13

1949 — 7-1-2 (4-1-1)

S24	●	Missouri	35	34
O1	● |	Indiana	46	7
O8	=	at USC	13	13
O15	|	Minnesota	0	27
O22	● |	at Wisconsin	21	0
O29	● |	Northwestern	24	7
N5	●	at Pittsburgh	14	10
N12	● |	Illinois	30	17
N19	= |	at Michigan	7	7
		ROSE BOWL		
J2	●	California	17	14

1950 6-3-0 (5-2-0)

S30			SMU	27	32
O7	●		Pittsburgh	41	7
O14	●	|	at Indiana	26	14
O21	●	|	at Minnesota	48	0
O28	●	|	Iowa	83	21
N4	●	|	at Northwestern	32	0
N11	●	|	Wisconsin	19	14
N18		|	at Illinois	7	14
N25		|	Michigan	3	9

W.W. "WOODY" HAYES
1951-78 (.761) 205-61-10

1951 4-3-2 (2-2-2)

S29	●		SMU	7	0
O6			Michigan State	20	24
O13	=	|	at Wisconsin	6	6
O20		|	Indiana	10	32
O27	●	|	Iowa	47	21
N3	●	|	Northwestern	3	0
N10	●		at Pittsburgh	16	14
N17	=	|	Illinois	0	0
N24		|	at Michigan	0	7

1952 6-3-0 (5-2-0)

S27	●	|	Indiana	33	13
O4		|	Purdue	14	21
O11	●	|	Wisconsin	23	14
O18	●		Washington State	35	7
O25		|	at Iowa	0	8
N1	●	|	at Northwestern	24	21
N8			Pittsburgh	14	21
N15	●	|	at Illinois	27	7
N22	●	|	Michigan	27	7

1953 6-3-0 (4-3-0)

S26	●	|	Indiana	36	12
O3	●		at California	33	19
O10		|	Illinois	20	41
O17	●		at Pennsylvania	12	6
O24	●	|	at Wisconsin	20	19
O31	●	|	Northwestern	27	13
N7		|	Michigan State	13	28
N14	●	|	Purdue	21	6
N21		|	at Michigan	0	20

1954 10-0-0 (7-0-0)

S25	●	|	Indiana	28	0
O2	●		California	21	13
O9	●	|	at Illinois	40	7
O16	●	|	Iowa	20	14
O23	●	|	Wisconsin	31	14
O30	●	|	at Northwestern	14	7
N6	●		Pittsburgh	26	0
N13	●	|	at Purdue	28	6
N20	●	|	Michigan	21	7
			ROSE BOWL		
J1	●		USC	20	7

1955 7-2-0 (6-0-0)

S24	●		Nebraska	28	20
O1			at Stanford	0	6
O8	●	|	Illinois	27	12
O15			Duke	14	20
O22	●	|	at Wisconsin	26	16
O29	●	|	Northwestern	49	0
N5	●	|	Indiana	20	13
N12	●	|	Iowa	20	10
N19	●	|	at Michigan	17	0

1956 6-3-0 (4-2-0)

S29	●		Nebraska	34	7
O6	●		Stanford	32	20
O13	●	|	at Illinois	26	6
O20			Penn State	6	7
O27	●	|	Wisconsin	21	0
N3	●	|	at Northwestern	6	2
N10	●	|	Indiana	35	14
N17		|	at Iowa	0	6
N24		|	Michigan	0	19

1957 9-1-0 (7-0-0)

S28			TCU	14	18
O5	●		at Washington	35	7
O12	●	|	Illinois	21	7
O19	●	|	Indiana	56	0
O26	●	|	at Wisconsin	16	13
N2	●	|	Northwestern	47	6
N9	●	|	Purdue	20	7
N16	●	|	Iowa	17	13
N23	●	|	at Michigan	31	14
			ROSE BOWL		
J1	●		Oregon	10	7

1958 6-1-2 (4-1-2)

S27	●		SMU	23	20
O4	●		Washington	12	7
O11	●	|	at Illinois	19	13
O18	●	|	Indiana	49	8
O25	=	|	Wisconsin	7	7
N1		|	at Northwestern	0	21
N8	=	|	Purdue	14	14
N15	●	|	at Iowa	38	28
N22	●	|	Michigan	20	14

1959 3-5-1 (2-4-1)

S26	●		Duke	14	13
O2			at USC	0	17
O10		|	Illinois	0	9
O17	●	|	Purdue	15	0
O24		|	at Wisconsin	3	12
O31	●	|	Michigan State	30	24
N7	=	|	Indiana	0	0
N14		|	Iowa	7	16
N21		|	at Michigan	14	23

1960 7-2-0 (5-2-0)

S24	●		SMU	24	0
O1	●		USC	20	0
O8	●	|	at Illinois	34	7
O15		|	at Purdue	21	24
O22	●	|	Wisconsin	34	7
O29	●	|	at Michigan State	21	10
N5	●	|	Indiana	36	7
N12		|	at Iowa	12	35
N19	●	|	Michigan	7	0

1961 8-0-1 (6-0-0)

S30	=		TCU	7	7
O7	●		UCLA	13	3
O14	●	|	Illinois	44	0
O21	●	|	at Northwestern	10	0
O28	●	|	at Wisconsin	30	21
N4	●	|	Iowa	29	13
N11	●	|	at Indiana	16	7
N18	●		Oregon	22	12
N25	●	|	at Michigan	50	20

1962 6-3-0 (4-2-0)

S29	●		North Carolina	41	7
O6			at UCLA	7	9
O13	●	|	at Illinois	51	15
O20		|	Northwestern	14	18
O27	●	|	Wisconsin	14	7
N3		|	at Iowa	14	28
N10	●	|	Indiana	10	7
N17	●		Oregon	26	7
N24	●	|	Michigan	28	0

1963 5-3-1 (4-1-1)

S28	●		Texas A&M	17	0
O5	●	|	at Indiana	21	0
O12	=	|	Illinois	20	20
O19			at USC	3	32
O26	●	|	at Wisconsin	13	10
N2	●	|	Iowa	7	3
N9			Penn State	7	10
N16		|	Northwestern	8	17
N23	●	|	at Michigan	14	10

1964 7-2-0 (5-1-0)

S26	●		SMU	27	8
O3	●	|	Indiana	17	9
O10	●	|	at Illinois	26	0
O17	●		USC	17	0
O24	●	|	Wisconsin	28	3
O31	●	|	at Iowa	21	19
N7			Penn State	0	27
N14	●	|	Northwestern	10	0
N21		|	Michigan	0	10

1965 7-2-0 (6-1-0)

S25			North Carolina	3	14
O2	●		at Washington	23	21
O9	●	|	Illinois	28	14
O16		|	at Michigan State	7	32
O23	●	|	at Wisconsin	20	10
O30	●	|	Minnesota	11	10
N6	●	|	Indiana	17	10
N13	●	|	Iowa	38	0
N20	●	|	at Michigan	9	7

1966 4-5-0 (3-4-0)

S24	●		TCU	14	7
O1			Washington	22	38
O8		|	at Illinois	9	10
O15		|	Michigan State	8	11
O22	●	|	Wisconsin	24	13
O29		|	at Minnesota	7	17
N5	●	|	Indiana	7	0
N12	●	|	at Iowa	14	10
N19		|	Michigan	3	17

1967 6-3-0 (5-2-0)

S30			Arizona	7	14
O7	●		at Oregon	30	0
O14		|	Purdue	6	41
O21	●	|	at Northwestern	6	2
O28		|	Illinois	13	17
N4	●	|	at Michigan State	21	7
N11	●	|	Wisconsin	17	15
N18	●	|	Iowa	21	10
N25	●	|	at Michigan	24	14

1968 10-0-0 (7-0-0)

S28	●		SMU	35	14
O5	●		Oregon	21	6
O12	●	|	Purdue	13	0
O19	●	|	Northwestern	45	21
O26	●	|	at Illinois	31	24
N2	●	|	Michigan State	25	20
N9	●	|	at Wisconsin	43	8
N16	●	|	at Iowa	33	27
N23	●	|	Michigan	50	14
			ROSE BOWL		
J1	●		USC	27	16

1969 8-1-0 (6-1-0)

S27	●		TCU	62	0
O4	●		at Washington	41	14
O11	●	|	Michigan State	54	21
O18	●	|	at Minnesota	34	7
O25	●	|	Illinois	41	0
N1	●	|	at Northwestern	35	6
N8	●	|	Wisconsin	62	7
N15	●	|	Purdue	42	14
N22		|	at Michigan	12	24

1970 9-1-0 (7-0-0)

S26	●		Texas A&M	56	13
O3	●		Duke	34	10
O10	●	|	at Michigan State	29	0
O17	●	|	Minnesota	28	8
O24	●	|	at Illinois	48	29
O31	●	|	Northwestern	24	10
N7	●	|	at Wisconsin	24	7
N14	●	|	at Purdue	10	7
N21	●	|	Michigan	20	9
			ROSE BOWL		
J1			Stanford	17	27

1971 6-4-0 (5-3-0)

S11	●	|	Iowa	52	21
S25			Colorado	14	20
O2	●		California	35	3
O9	●	|	at Illinois	24	10
O16	●	|	at Indiana	27	7
O23	●	|	Wisconsin	31	6
O30	●	|	at Minnesota	14	12
N6		|	Michigan State	10	17
N13		|	Northwestern	10	14
N20		|	at Michigan	7	10

1972 9-2-0 (7-1-0)

S16	●	|	Iowa	21	0
S30	●		North Carolina	29	14
O7	●		at California	35	18
O14	●	|	Illinois	26	7
O21	●	|	Indiana	44	7
O28	●	|	at Wisconsin	28	20
N4	●	|	Minnesota	27	19
N11		|	at Michigan State	12	19
N18	●	|	at Northwestern	27	14
N25	●	|	Michigan	14	11
			ROSE BOWL		
J1			USC	17	42

1973 10-0-1 (7-0-1)

S15	●	|	Minnesota	56	7
S29	●		TCU	37	3
O6	●		Washington State	27	3
O13	●	|	at Wisconsin	24	0
O20	●	|	at Indiana	37	7
O27	●	|	Northwestern	60	0
N3	●	|	at Illinois	30	0
N10	●	|	Michigan State	35	0
N17	●	|	Iowa	55	13
N24	=	|	at Michigan	10	10
			ROSE BOWL		
J1	●		USC	42	21

1974 10-2-0 (7-1-0)

S14	●	|	at Minnesota	34	19
S21	●		Oregon State	51	10
S28	●		SMU	28	9
O5	●		Washington State^SEA	42	7
O12	●	|	Wisconsin	52	7
O19	●	|	Indiana	49	9
O26	●	|	at Northwestern	55	7
N2	●	|	Illinois	49	7
N9		|	at Michigan State	13	16
N16	●	|	at Iowa	35	10
N23	●	|	Michigan	12	10
			ROSE BOWL		
J1			USC	17	18

1975 11-1-0 (8-0-0)

S13	●	|	at Michigan State	21	0
S20	●		Penn State	17	9
S27	●		North Carolina	32	7
O4	●		at UCLA	41	20
O11	●	|	Iowa	49	0
O18	●	|	Wisconsin	56	0
O25	●	|	at Purdue	35	6
N1	●	|	Indiana	24	14
N8	●	|	at Illinois	40	3
N15	●	|	Minnesota	38	6
N22	●	|	at Michigan	21	14
			ROSE BOWL		
J1			UCLA	10	23

1976 9-2-1 (7-1-0)

S11	●	|	Michigan State	49	21
S18	●		at Penn State	12	7
S25			Missouri	21	22
O2	=		UCLA	10	10
O9	●	|	at Iowa	34	14
O16	●	|	at Wisconsin	30	20
O23	●	|	Purdue	24	3
O30	●	|	at Indiana	47	7
N6	●	|	Illinois	42	10
N13	●	|	at Minnesota	9	3
N20		|	Michigan	0	22
			ORANGE BOWL		
J1	●		Colorado	27	10

1977 9-3-0 (7-1-0)

S10	●		Miami, Fla.	10	0
S17	●	|	Minnesota	38	7
S24			Oklahoma	28	29
O1	●		at SMU	35	7
O8	●	|	Purdue	46	0
O15	●	|	at Iowa	27	6
O22	●	|	at Northwestern	35	15
O29	●	|	Wisconsin	42	0
N5	●	|	at Illinois	35	0
N12	●	|	Indiana	35	7
N19		|	at Michigan	6	14
			SUGAR BOWL		
J1			Alabama	6	35

1978 7-4-1 (6-2-0)

S16			Penn State	0	19
S23	●	|	at Minnesota	27	10
S30	●		Baylor	34	28
O7	=		SMU	35	35
O14		|	at Purdue	16	27
O21	●	|	Iowa	31	7
O28	●	|	Northwestern	63	20
N4	●	|	at Wisconsin	49	14
N11	●	|	Illinois	45	7
N18	●	|	at Indiana	21	18
N25		|	Michigan	3	14
			GATOR BOWL		
D29			Clemson	15	17

EARLE BRUCE
1979-87 (.755) 81-26-1

1979 11-1-0 (8-0-0)

S8	●		Syracuse	31	8
S15	●	|	at Minnesota	21	17
S22	●		Washington State	45	29
S29	●		at UCLA	17	13
O6	●	|	Northwestern	16	7
O13	●	|	Indiana	47	6
O20	●	|	Wisconsin	59	0
O27	●	|	Michigan State	42	0
N3	●	|	at Illinois	44	7
N10	●	|	Iowa	34	7
N17	●	|	at Michigan	18	15
			ROSE BOWL		
J1			USC	16	17

1980 9-3-0 (7-1-0)

S13	●		Syracuse	31	21
S20	●	|	Minnesota	47	0
S27	●		Arizona State	38	21
O4			UCLA	0	17
O11	●	|	at Northwestern	63	0
O18	●	|	Indiana	27	17
O25	●	|	at Wisconsin	21	0
N1	●	|	at Michigan State	48	16
N8	●	|	Illinois	49	42
N15	●	|	at Iowa	41	7
N22		|	Michigan	3	9
			FIESTA BOWL		
D26			Penn State	19	31

1981 9-3-0 (6-2-0)

S12	●	Duke	34	13
S19	● |	Michigan State	27	13
S26	●	at Stanford	24	19
O3		Florida State	27	36
O10	|	at Wisconsin	21	24
O17	● |	Illinois	34	27
O24	● |	Indiana	29	10
O31	● |	at Purdue	45	33
N7	|	at Minnesota	31	35
N14	● |	Northwestern	70	6
N21	● |	at Michigan	14	9
		LIBERTY BOWL		
D30	●	Navy	31	28

1982 9-3-0 (7-1-0)

S11	●	Baylor	21	14
S18	● |	at Michigan State	31	10
S25		Stanford	20	23
O2		Florida State	17	34
O9	|	Wisconsin	0	6
O16	● |	at Illinois	26	21
O23	● |	at Indiana	49	25
O30	● |	Purdue	38	6
N6	● |	Minnesota	35	10
N13	● |	at Northwestern	40	28
N20	● |	Michigan	24	14
		HOLIDAY BOWL		
D17	●	Brigham Young	47	17

1983 9-3-0 (6-3-0)

S10	●	Oregon	31	6
S17	●	at Oklahoma	24	14
S24	|	at Iowa	14	20
O1	● |	Minnesota	69	18
O8	● |	Purdue	33	22
O15	|	at Illinois	13	17
O22	● |	Michigan State	21	11
O29	● |	Wisconsin	45	27
N5	● |	at Indiana	56	17
N12	● |	Northwestern	55	7
N19	|	at Michigan	21	24
		FIESTA BOWL		
J2	●	Pittsburgh	28	23

1984 9-3-0 (7-2-0)

S8	●	Oregon State	22	14
S15	●	Washington State	44	0
S22	● |	Iowa	45	26
S29	● |	at Minnesota	35	22
O6	|	at Purdue	23	28
O13	● |	Illinois	45	38
O20	● |	at Michigan State	23	20
O27	|	at Wisconsin	14	16
N3	● |	Indiana	50	7
N10	● |	at Northwestern	52	3
N17	● |	Michigan	21	6
		ROSE BOWL		
J1		USC	17	20

1985 9-3-0 (5-3-0)

S14	●	Pittsburgh	10	7
S21	●	at Colorado	36	13
S28	●	Washington State	48	32
O5	|	at Illinois	28	31
O12	● |	Indiana	48	7
O19	● |	Purdue	41	27
O26	● |	at Minnesota	23	19
N2	● |	Iowa	22	13
N9	● |	at Northwestern	35	17
N16	|	Wisconsin	7	12
N23	|	at Michigan	17	27
		CITRUS BOWL		
D28	●	Brigham Young	10	7

1986 10-3-0 (7-1-0)

A27		Alabama [ERUT]	10	16
S13		at Washington	7	40
S20	●	Colorado	13	10
S27	●	Utah	64	6
O4	● |	Illinois	14	0
O11	● |	at Indiana	24	22
O18	● |	at Purdue	39	11
O25	● |	Minnesota	33	0
N1	● |	at Iowa	31	10
N8	● |	Northwestern	30	9
N15	● |	at Wisconsin	30	17
N22	|	Michigan	24	26
		COTTON BOWL		
J1	●	Texas A&M	28	12

1987 6-4-1 (4-4-0)

S12	●	West Virginia	24	3
S19	●	Oregon	24	14
S26	=	at LSU	13	13
O3	● |	at Illinois	10	6
O10	|	Indiana	10	31
O17	● |	at Purdue	20	17
O24	● |	Minnesota	42	9
O31	|	Michigan State	7	13
N7	|	at Wisconsin	24	26
N14	|	Iowa	27	29
N21	● |	at Michigan	23	20

JOHN COOPER
1988-2000 (.715) 111-43-4

1988 4-6-1 (2-5-1)

S10	●	Syracuse	26	9
S17		at Pittsburgh	10	42
S24	●	LSU	36	33
O1	|	Illinois	12	31
O8	|	at Indiana	7	41
O15	|	Purdue	26	31
O22	● |	at Minnesota	13	6
O29	|	at Michigan State	10	20
N5	● |	Wisconsin	34	12
N12	= |	at Iowa	24	24
N19	|	Michigan	31	34

1989 8-4-0 (6-2-0)

S16	●	Oklahoma State	37	13
S23		at USC	3	42
S30	●	Boston College	34	29
O7	|	at Illinois	14	34
O14	● |	Indiana	35	31
O21	● |	Purdue	21	3
O28	● |	at Minnesota	41	37
N4	● |	at Northwestern	52	27
N11	● |	Iowa	28	0
N18	● |	Wisconsin	42	22
N25	|	at Michigan	18	28
		HALL OF FAME BOWL		
J1		Auburn	14	31

1990 7-4-1 (5-2-1)

S8	●	Texas Tech	17	10
S15	●	at Boston College	31	10
S29		USC	26	35
O6	|	Illinois	20	31
O13	= |	at Indiana	27	27
O20	● |	at Purdue	42	2
O27	● |	Minnesota	52	23
N3	● |	Northwestern	48	7
N10	● |	at Iowa	27	26
N17	● |	at Wisconsin	35	10
N24	|	Michigan	13	16
		LIBERTY BOWL		
D27		Air Force	11	23

1991 8-4-0 (5-3-0)

S7	●	Arizona	38	14
S14	●	Louisville	23	15
S21	●	Washington State	33	19
O5	● |	Wisconsin	31	16
O12	|	at Illinois	7	10
O19	● |	Northwestern [CLEV]	34	3
O26	● |	Michigan State	27	17
N2	|	Iowa	9	16
N9	● |	at Minnesota	35	6
N16	● |	Indiana	20	16
N23	|	at Michigan	3	31
		HALL OF FAME BOWL		
J1		Syracuse	17	24

1992 8-3-1 (5-2-1)

S5	●	Louisville	20	19
S12	●	Bowling Green	17	6
S19	●	at Syracuse	35	12
O3	|	at Wisconsin	16	20
O10	|	Illinois	16	18
O17	● |	Northwestern	31	7
O24	● |	at Michigan State	27	17
O31	● |	at Iowa	38	15
N7	● |	Minnesota	17	0
N14	● |	at Indiana	27	10
N21	= |	Michigan	13	13
		CITRUS BOWL		
J1		Georgia	14	21

1993 10-1-1 (6-1-1)

S4	●	Rice	34	7
S11	●	Washington	21	12
S18	●	at Pittsburgh	63	28
O2	● |	Northwestern	51	3
O9	● |	at Illinois	20	12
O16	● |	Michigan State	28	21
O23	● |	at Purdue	45	24
O30	● |	Penn State	24	6
N6	= |	at Wisconsin	14	14
N13	● |	Indiana	23	17
N20	|	at Michigan	0	28
		HOLIDAY BOWL		
D30	●	Brigham Young	28	21

1994 9-4-0 (6-2-0)

A29	●	Fresno State [ANA]	34	10
S10		at Washington	16	25
S17	●	Pittsburgh	27	3
S24	●	Houston	52	0
O1	● |	at Northwestern	17	15
O8	|	Illinois	10	24
O15	● |	at Michigan State	23	7
O22	● |	Purdue	48	14
O29	|	at Penn State	14	63
N5	● |	Wisconsin	24	3
N12	● |	at Indiana	32	17
N19	● |	Michigan	22	6
		CITRUS BOWL		
J2		Alabama	17	24

1995 11-2-0 (7-1-0)

A27	●	Boston College [ERUT]	38	6
S16	●	Washington	30	20
S23	●	at Pittsburgh	54	14
S30	●	Notre Dame	45	26
O7	● |	at Penn State	28	25
O14	● |	at Wisconsin	27	16
O21	● |	Purdue	28	0
O28	● |	Iowa	56	35
N4	● |	at Minnesota	49	21
N11	● |	Illinois	41	3
N18	● |	Indiana	42	3
N25	|	at Michigan	23	31
		CITRUS BOWL		
J1		Tennessee	14	20

1996 11-1 (7-1)

S7	●	Rice	70	7
S21	●	Pittsburgh	72	0
S28	●	at Notre Dame	29	16
O5	● |	Penn State	38	7
O12	● |	Wisconsin	17	14
O19	● |	at Purdue	42	14
O26	● |	at Iowa	38	26
N2	● |	Minnesota	45	0
N9	● |	at Illinois	48	0
N16	● |	at Indiana	27	17
N23	|	Michigan	9	13
		ROSE BOWL		
J1	●	Arizona State	20	17

1997 10-3 (6-2)

A28	●	Wyoming	24	10
S13	●	Bowling Green	44	13
S20	●	Arizona	28	20
S27	●	at Missouri	31	10
O4	● |	Iowa	23	7
O11	|	at Penn State	27	31
O18	● |	Indiana	31	0
O25	● |	Northwestern	49	6
N1	● |	at Michigan State	37	13
N8	● |	at Minnesota	31	3
N15	● |	Illinois	41	6
N22	|	at Michigan	14	20
		SUGAR BOWL		
J1		Florida State	14	31

1998 11-1 (7-1)

S5	●	at West Virginia	34	17
S12	●	Toledo	49	0
S19	●	Missouri	35	14
O3	● |	Penn State	28	9
O10	● |	at Illinois	41	0
O17	● |	Minnesota	45	15
O24	● |	at Northwestern	36	10
O31	● |	at Indiana	38	7
N7	|	Michigan State	24	28
N14	● |	at Iowa	45	14
N21	● |	Michigan	31	16
		SUGAR BOWL		
J1	●	Texas A&M	24	14

1999 6-6 (3-5)

A29		Miami, Fla. [ERUT]	12	23
S11	●	UCLA	42	20
S18	●	Ohio U.	40	16
S25	●	Cincinnati	34	20
O2	|	Wisconsin	17	42
O9	● |	Purdue	25	22
O16	|	at Penn State	10	23
O23	● |	at Minnesota	20	17
O30	● |	Iowa	41	11
N6	|	at Michigan State	7	23
N13	|	Illinois	20	46
N20	|	at Michigan	17	24

2000 8-4 (5-3)

S2	●	Fresno State	43	10
S9	●	at Arizona	27	17
S16	●	Miami (Ohio)	27	16
S23	● |	Penn State	45	6
O7	● |	at Wisconsin	23	7
O14	|	Minnesota	17	29
O21	● |	at Iowa	38	10
O28	|	at Purdue	27	31
N4	● |	Michigan State	27	13
N11	● |	at Illinois	24	21
N18	|	Michigan	26	38
		OUTBACK BOWL		
J1		South Carolina	7	24

JIM TRESSEL
2001-PRESENT (.816) 62-14

2001 7-5 (5-3)

S8	●	Akron	28	14
S22		at UCLA	6	13
S29	● |	at Indiana	27	14
O6	● |	Northwestern	38	20
O13	|	Wisconsin	17	20
O20	●	San Diego State	27	12
O27	|	at Penn State	27	29
N3	● |	at Minnesota	31	28
N10	● |	Purdue	35	9
N17	|	Illinois	22	34
N24	● |	at Michigan	26	20
		OUTBACK BOWL		
J1		South Carolina	28	31

2002 14-0 (8-0)

A24	●	Texas Tech	45	21
S7	●	Kent State	51	17
S14	●	Washington State	25	7
S21	●	at Cincinnati	23	19
S28	● |	Indiana	45	17
O5	● |	at Northwestern	27	16
O12	●	San Jose State	50	7
O19	● |	at Wisconsin	19	14
O26	● |	Penn State	13	7
N2	● |	Minnesota	34	3
N9	● |	at Purdue	10	6
N16	● |	at Illinois	23	16
N23	● |	Michigan	14	9
		FIESTA BOWL		
J3	●	Miami, Fla.	31	24

2003 11-2 (6-2)

A30	●	Washington	28	9
S6	●	San Diego State	16	13
S13	●	North Carolina St.	44	38
S20	●	Bowling Green	24	17
S27	● |	Northwestern	20	0
O11	|	at Wisconsin	10	17
O18	● |	Iowa	19	10
O25	● |	at Indiana	35	6
N1	● |	at Penn State	21	20
N8	● |	Michigan State	33	23
N15	● |	Purdue	16	13
N22	|	at Michigan	21	35
		FIESTA BOWL		
J2	●	Kansas State	35	28

2004 8-4 (4-4)

S4	●	Cincinnati	27	6
S11	●	Marshall	24	21
S18	●	at North Carolina St.	22	14
O2	|	at Northwestern	27	33
O9	|	Wisconsin	13	24
O16	|	at Iowa	7	33
O23	● |	Indiana	30	7
O30	● |	Penn State	21	10
N6	● |	at Michigan State	32	19
N13	|	at Purdue	17	24
N20	● |	Michigan	37	21
		ALAMO BOWL		
D29	●	Oklahoma State	33	7

2005   10-2 (7-1)

S3	●	Miami (Ohio)	34	14
S10		Texas	22	25
S17	●	San Diego State	27	6
S24	●	Iowa	31	6
O8	●	at Penn State	10	17
O15	●	Michigan State	35	24
O22	●	at Indiana	41	10
O29	●	at Minnesota	45	31
N5	●	Illinois	40	2
N12	●	Northwestern	48	7
N19	●	at Michigan	25	21
FIESTA BOWL				
J2	●	Notre Dame	34	20

2006   12-1 (8-0)

S2	●	Northern Illinois	35	12
S9	●	at Texas	24	7
S16	●	Cincinnati	37	7
S23	●	Penn State	28	6
S30	●	at Iowa	38	17
O7	●	Bowling Green	35	7
O14	●	at Michigan State	38	7
O21	●	Indiana	44	3
O28	●	Minnesota	44	0
N4	●	at Illinois	17	10
N11	●	at Northwestern	54	10
N18	●	Michigan	42	39
ROSE BOWL				
J8		Florida	14	41

OHIO STATE RECORD BOOK

SINGLE-GAME RECORDS

RUSHING YARDS

RANK	PLAYER	DATE	OPPONENT	ATT	AVG	YDS
1	Eddie George	Nov. 11, 1995	Illinois	36	8.7	314
2	Keith Byars	Oct. 13, 1984	Illinois	39	7.0	274
3	Archie Griffin	Nov. 17, 1973	Iowa	30	8.2	246
4	Archie Griffin	Sept. 30, 1972	North Carolina	27	8.9	239
5	Raymont Harris	Dec. 30, 1993	Brigham Young	39	6.0	235

PASSING YARDS

RANK	PLAYER	DATE	OPPONENT	ATT	COMP	YDS
1	Art Schlichter	Oct. 3, 1981	Florida State	52	31	458
2	Joe Germaine	Oct. 11, 1997	Penn State	43	29	378
3	Greg Frey	Oct. 28, 1989	Minnesota	31	20	362
4	Bobby Hoying	Oct. 7, 1995	Penn State	35	24	354
5	Joe Germaine	Oct. 31, 1998	Indiana	45	31	351

RECEIVING YARDS

RANK	PLAYER	DATE	OPPONENT	REC	AVG	YDS
1	Terry Glenn	Sept. 23, 1995	Pittsbugh	9	28.1	253
2	Santonio Holmes	Sept. 11, 2004	Marshall	10	22.4	224
3	Gary Williams	Oct. 3, 1981	Florida State	13	16.9	220
4	David Boston	Nov. 21, 1998	Michigan	10	21.7	217
5	Dimitrious Stanley	Oct. 12, 1996	Wisconsin	10	19.9	199

POINTS

RANK	PLAYER	DATE	OPPONENT	TOT
1	Keith Byars	Oct. 13, 1984	Illinois	30
	Pete Johnson	Sept. 27, 1975	North Carolina	30
3	Terry Glenn	Sept. 23, 1995	Pittsburgh	26
	Joel Payton	Oct. 8, 1977	Purdue	26
5	16 players tied at 24			

FIELD GOALS

RANK	PLAYER	DATE	OPPONENT	TOT
1	Josh Huston	Sept. 10, 2005	Texas	5
	Mike Nugent	Sept. 18, 2004	North Carollina St.	5
	Bob Atha	Oct. 24, 1981	Indiana	5
4	7 players tied at 4			

TACKLES

RANK	PLAYER	DATE	OPPONENT	TOT
1	Chris Spielman	Nov. 22, 1986	Michigan	29
	Tom Cousineau	Sept. 16, 1978	Penn State	29
3	Tom Cousineau	Oct. 7, 1978	Southern Methodist	28
4	David Adkins	Sept. 24, 1977	Oklahoma	24
	Arnie Jones	Nov. 25, 1972	Michigan	24

INTERCEPTIONS

RANK	PLAYER	DATE	OPPONENT	TOT
1	9 players tied at 3			

RETIRED NUMBERS

22 Les Horvath

27 Eddie George

31 Vic Janowicz

40 Howard "Hopalong" Cassady

45 Archie Griffin

47 Charles "Chic" Harley

SINGLE-SEASON RECORDS

RUSHING YARDS

RANK	PLAYER	SEASON	G	ATT	YDS
1	Eddie George	1995	13	328	1,927
2	Keith Byars	1984	12	336	1,764
3	Archie Griffin	1974	12	256	1,695
4	Archie Griffin	1973	11	247	1,577
5	Tim Spencer	1982	12	273	1,538

PASSING YARDS

RANK	PLAYER	SEASON	G	ATT	COMP	PCT	YDS
1	Joe Germaine	1998	12	384	230	59.9	3,330
2	Bobby Hoying	1995	13	341	211	61.9	3,269
3	Art Schlichter	1981	12	350	183	52.3	2,551
4	Troy Smith	2006	13	311	203	65.3	2,542
5	Bobby Hoying	1994	13	301	170	56.5	2,335

RECEIVING YARDS

RANK	PLAYER	SEASON	G	REC	AVG	YDS
1	David Boston	1998	12	85	23.5	1,435
2	Terry Glenn	1995	13	64	31.2	1,411
3	Cris Carter	1986	13	69	28.8	1,127
4	Michael Jenkins	2002	14	61	32.8	1,076
5	Dee Miller	1997	13	58	34.4	981

SCORING

RANK	PLAYER	SEASON	TD	FG	PAT	P2	TOT
1	Pete Johnson	1975	26	0	0	0	156
2	Eddie George	1995	25	0	0	1	152
3	Keith Byars	1984	24	0	0	0	144
4	Keith Byars	1983	22	0	0	0	132
5	Mike Nugent	2002	0	25	45	0	120
	Harold Henson	1972	20	0	0	0	120

TOUCHDOWNS

RANK	PLAYER	SEASON	G	TOT
1	Pete Johnson	1975	12	26
2	Eddie George	1995	13	25
3	Keith Byars	1984	12	24
4	Keith Byars	1983	12	22
5	"Champ" Henson	1972	11	20

TACKLES

RANK	PLAYER	SEASON	G	TOT
1	Tom Cousineau	1978	12	211
2	Chris Spielman	1986	13	205
3	Marcus Marek	1982	12	178
4	David Adkins	1977	12	172
5	Chris Spielman	1987	11	156
	Rowland Tatum	1983	12	156

INTERCEPTIONS

RANK	PLAYER	SEASON	G	YDS	TOT
1	Mike Sensibaugh	1969	9	125	9
	Craig Cassady	1975	12	105	9
3	Neal Colzie	1974	12	80	8
	Mike Sensibaugh	1970	9	40	8
5	Derek Ross	2001	11	194	7

PUNTING

RANK	PLAYER	SEASON	PUNTS	YDS	AVG
1	Tom Tupa	1984	45	2,118	47.1
2	Tom Tupa	1987	63	2,963	47.0
3	Tom Skladany	1975	41	1,918	46.8
4	Tom Skladany	1974	31	1,416	45.7
5	Brent Bartholomew	1997	72	3,252	45.0

PUNT RETURNS

RANK	PLAYER	SEASON	RET	YDS	AVG
1	Larry Zelina	1969	23	431	18.7
2	Neal Colzie	1973	40	679	17.0
3	Nate Clements	2000	39	513	13.2
4	Tom Campana	1971	37	447	12.1
5	Garcia Lane	1982	40	411	10.3

KICKOFF RETURNS

RANK	PLAYER	SEASON	RET	YDS	AVG
1	Tom Barrington	1965	14	480	34.3
2	Ted Ginn, Jr.	2005	18	532	29.6
3	Ken-Yon Rambo	2000	17	478	28.1
4	Carlos Snow	1988	19	513	27.0
5	Len Willis	1974	16	420	26.3

CAREER RECORDS

RUSHING YARDS

RANK	PLAYER	SEASONS	ATT	AVG	TD	YDS
1	Archie Griffin	1972-75	924	6.0	26	5,589
2	Eddie George	1992-95	683	5.5	44	3,768
3	Tim Spencer	1979-82	644	5.5	36	3,553
4	Keith Byars	1982-85	619	5.2	46	3,200
5	Pepe Pearson	1994-97	659	4.7	27	3,121
6	Carlos Snow	1987-89, 1991	610	4.9	30	2,974
7	Michael Wiley	1996-99	509	5.8	33	2,951
8	Antonio Pittman	2004-06	557	5.3	22	2,945
9	Raymont Harris	1990-93	574	4.6	27	2,649
10	Calvin Murray	1977-80	438	5.9	15	2,576

PASSING YARDS

RANK	PLAYER	SEASONS	ATT	COMP	PCT	INT	TD	YDS
1	Art Schlichter	1978-81	951	497	52.3	46	50	7,547
2	Bobby Hoying	1992-95	858	498	58.0	35	57	7,232
3	Joe Germaine	1996-98	741	439	59.2	20	56	6,370
4	Greg Frey	1987-90	835	443	53.1	39	37	6,316
5	Steve Bellisari	1998-2001	759	386	50.9	29	35	5,878
6	Troy Smith	2003-06	670	420	62.7	13	54	5,720
7	Mike Tomczak	1981-84	675	376	55.7	36	32	5,569
8	Jim Karsatos	1984-86	629	359	57.1	21	36	5,089
9	Craig Krenzel	2000-03	579	329	56.8	21	28	4,493
10	Stanley Jackson	1994-97	353	194	55.0	5	17	2,660

RECEIVING YARDS

RANK	PLAYER	SEASONS	REC	AVG	TD	YDS
1	Michael Jenkins	2000-03	165	17.6	16	2,898
2	David Boston	1996-98	191	14.9	34	2,855
3	Gary Williams	1979-82	154	18.1	16	2,792
4	Cris Carter	1984-86	168	16.2	27	2,725
5	Santonio Holmes	2003-05	140	16.4	25	2,295
6	Doug Donley	1977-80	106	21.2	16	2,252
7	Dee Miller	1995-98	132	15.8	8	2,090
8	Ted Ginn, Jr.	2004-06	135	14.4	15	1,943
9	Joey Galloway	1991-94	108	17.5	19	1,894
10	Ken-Yon Rambo	1997-2000	106	17.4	9	1,849

SCORING

RANK	PLAYER	SEASONS	TD	FG	PAT	P2	TOT
1	Mike Nugent	2001-04	0	72	140	0	356
2	Pete Johnson	1973-76	58	0	0	0	348
3	Dan Stultz	1997-2000	0	59	165	0	342
4	Keith Byars	1982-85	50	0	0	0	300
5	Vlade Janakievski	1977-80	0	41	172	0	295

TOUCHDOWNS

RANK	PLAYER	SEASONS	G	TOT
1	Pete Johnson	1973-76	43	58
2	Keith Byars	1982-85	37	50
3	Eddie George	1992-95	48	45
4	Tim Spencer	1979-82	47	37
	Howard Cassady	1952-55	37	37

TACKLES

RANK	PLAYER	SEASONS	G	TOT
1	Marcus Marek	1979-82	48	572
2	Tom Cousineau	1975-78	47	569
3	Chris Spielman	1984-87	42	546
4	Steve Tovar	1989-92	48	408
5	AJ Hawk	2002-05	51	394

INTERCEPTIONS

RANK	PLAYER	SEASONS	G	YDS	TOT
1	Mike Sensibaugh	1968-70	28	248	22
2	Fred Bruney	1950-52	27	212	17
3	William White	1984-87	46	153	16
	Ted Provost	1967-69	28	124	16
5	Neal Colzie	1972-74	34	205	15

PUNTING

RANK	PLAYER	SEASONS	PUNTS	YDS	AVG
1	Andy Groom	2001-02	109	4,901	45.0
2	Tom Tupa	1984-87	214	9,564	44.7
3	B.J. Sander	1999-2003	125	5,270	42.2
4	Kyle Turnao	2004	65	2,780	42.8
5	Tom Skladany	1973-76	160	6,838	42.7

TEAM RECORDS

LONGEST WINNING STREAK
- 22 games, Nov. 4, 1967-Nov. 15, 1969

Streak broken vs. Michigan, 12-24, Nov. 22, 1969

LONGEST UNDEFEATED STREAK
- 22 games, Nov. 6, 1915-Nov. 9, 1918

Streak broken vs. Illinois, 0-13, Nov. 16, 1918
- 22 games, Nov. 4, 1967-Nov. 15, 1969

Streak broken vs. Michigan, 12-24, Nov. 22, 1969

MOST CONSECUTIVE WINNING SEASONS
- 21, 1967-1987

MOST CONSECUTIVE BOWL APPEARANCES
- 15, 1972-1986

MOST POINTS IN A GAME
- 128, vs. Oberlin, Oct. 14, 1916

MOST POINTS ALLOWED IN A GAME
- 86, vs. Michigan, Oct. 25, 1902

LARGEST MARGIN OF VICTORY
- 128 (128-0), vs. Oberlin, Oct. 14, 1916

LARGEST MARGIN OF DEFEAT
- 86 (0-86), vs. Michigan, Oct. 25, 1902

LONGEST RUN FROM SCRIMMAGE
- 89 yards, Gene Fekete, vs. Pittsburgh, Nov. 7, 1942

LONGEST PASS PLAY
- 86 yards, Art Schlichter to Calvin Muray, vs. Washington State, Sept. 22, 1979

LONGEST FIELD GOAL
- 59 yards, Tom Skladany, vs. Illinois, Nov. 8, 1975

LONGEST PUNT
- 87, Karl Edwards, vs. Illinois, Oct. 15, 1983

LONGEST INTERCEPTION RETURN
- 100, Will Allen, vs. San Diego State, Sept. 6, 2003
- 100, Marlon Kerner, vs. Purdue, Oct. 23,1993
- 100, David Brown, vs. Purdue, Oct. 18, 1986

PUNT RETURNS

RANK	PLAYER	SEASON	RET	YDS	AVG
1	Neal Colzie	1972-74	60	855	14.3
2	Ted Ginn, Jr.	2004-06	64	900	14.1
3	Nate Clements	1998-2000	58	655	11.3
4	Mike Guess	1977-79	73	751	10.3
5	Garcia Lane	1981-83	89	895	10.1

KICKOFF RETURNS

RANK	PLAYER	SEASON	RET	YDS	AVG
1	Tom Barrington	1963-65	24	730	30.4
2	Ted Ginn, Jr.	2004-06	38	1,012	26.6
3	Paul Warfield	1961-63	29	702	24.2
4	Carlos Snow	1987-89, 1991	58	1,380	23.8
5	Howard Cassady	1952-55	42	981	23.4

OHIO STATE ANNUAL STATISTICAL LEADERS

YR	RUSHING	YDS	ATT	AVG	PASSING	ATT	CMP	PCT	YDS	RECEIVING	REC	YDS	AVG
1944	Les Horvath	924	163	5.7	Les Horvath	32	14	.44	344		NA	NA	NA
1945	Ollie Cline	936	181	5.2	Dick Fisher	28	9	.32	245		NA	NA	NA
1946	Joseph Whisler	544	129	4.2	George Spencer	51	25	.49	398	Cecil Soudere	9	157	17.4
1947	Ollie Cline	332	80	4.2	Dick Slager	69	19	.28	236	Fred Morrison	7	113	16.1
1948	Joseph Whisler	579	132	4.4	Pandel Savic	69	36	.52	486	Alex Verdova	12	117	9.8
1949	Gerald Krall	606	128	4.7	Pandel Savic	84	35	.42	581	Ray Hamilton	15	347	23.1
1950	Walt Klevay	520	66	7.9	Vic Janowicz	77	32	.42	561	Thomas Watson	23	461	20.0
1951	Vic Janowicz	376	106	3.5	Tony Curcillo	133	58	.44	912	Bob Joslin	18	281	15.6
1952	John Hlay	535	133	4.0	John Borton	196	115	.59	1,555	Bob Grimes	39	534	13.7
1953	Bob Watkins	875	153	5.7	John Borton	86	45	.52	522	Thomas Hague	19	275	14.5
1954	Howard Cassady	609	102	6.0	Bill Leggett	95	46	.48	578	Howard Cassady	12	137	11.4
1955	Howard Cassady	958	161	6.0	Frank Ellwood	23	9	.39	60	Paul Michael	4	50	12.5
1956	Don Clark	797	139	5.7	Don Clark	7	3	.43	88	Leo Brown	8	151	18.9
1957	Don Clark	737	132	5.6	Frank Kremblas	47	20	.43	337	Dick LeBeau	7	91	13.0
1958	Bob White	859	218	3.9	Frank Kremblas	42	16	.38	281	Dick LeBeau/Donald Clark	8	110	13.8
1959	Bob Ferguson	371	61	6.1	Tom Matte	51	28	.55	439	James Houston	11	214	19.5
1960	Bob Ferguson	853	160	5.3	Tom Matte	95	50	.53	737	Charles Bryant	17	336	19.8
1961	Bob Ferguson	938	202	4.6	Joe Sparma	38	16	.42	341	Charles Bryant	15	270	18.0
1962	David Francis	624	119	5.2	Joe Sparma	71	30	.42	288	Paul Warfield	8	139	17.4
1963	Matt Snell	491	134	3.7	Don Unverferth	117	48	.41	586	Paul Warfield	22	266	12.1
1964	Willard Sander	626	147	4.3	Don Unverferth	160	73	.46	871	Bo Rein	22	320	14.5
1965	Tom Barrington	554	139	4.0	Don Unverferth	191	91	.48	1,061	Bo Rein	29	328	11.3
1966	Bo Rein	456	139	3.3	Bill Long	192	106	.55	1,180	Billy Anders	55	671	12.2
1967	Jim Otis	530	103	5.1	Bill Long	102	44	.43	563	Billy Anders	28	403	14.4
1968	Jim Otis	985	141	7.0	Rex Kern	131	75	.57	972	Bruce Jankowski	31	328	10.6
1969	Jim Otis	1,027	219	4.7	Rex Kern	135	68	.50	1,002	Bruce Jankowski	23	404	17.6
1970	John Brockington	1,142	261	4.4	Rex Kern	98	45	.46	470	Jan White	17	171	10.1
1971	Rick Galbos	540	141	3.8	Don Lamka	107	54	.50	718	Dick Wakefield	31	432	13.9
1972	Archie Griffin	867	159	5.5	Greg Hare	111	55	.50	815	Rick Galbos	11	235	21.4
1973	Archie Griffin	1,577	247	6.4	Cornelius Greene	46	20	.43	343	Fred Pagac	9	159	17.7
1974	Archie Griffin	1,695	256	6.6	Cornelius Greene	97	58	.60	939	Brian Baschnagel	19	244	12.8
1975	Archie Griffin	1,450	262	5.5	Cornelius Greene	121	68	.56	1,066	Brian Baschnagel	24	362	15.1
1976	Jeff Logan	1,248	218	5.7	Jim Pacenta	54	28	.52	404	James Harrell	14	288	20.6
1977	Ron Springs	1,166	200	5.8	Rod Gerald	114	67	.59	1,016	Ron Springs	16	90	5.6
1978	Paul Campbell	591	142	4.2	Art Schlichter	175	87	.50	1,250	Doug Donley	24	510	21.3
1979	Calvin Murray	872	173	5.0	Art Schlichter	200	105	.53	1,816	Doug Donley	37	800	21.6
1980	Calvin Murray	1,267	195	6.5	Art Schlichter	226	122	.54	1,930	Doug Donley	43	887	20.6
1981	Tim Spencer	1,217	226	5.4	Art Schlichter	350	183	.52	2,551	Gary Williams	50	941	18.8
1982	Tim Spencer	1,538	273	5.6	Mike Tomczak	187	96	.51	1,602	Gary Williams	40	690	17.3
1983	Keith Byars	1,199	222	5.4	Mike Tomczak	237	131	.55	1,942	John Frank	45	641	14.2
1984	Keith Byars	1,764	336	5.3	Mike Tomczak	244	145	.59	1,952	Keith Byars	42	479	11.4
1985	John Wooldridge	820	174	4.7	Jim Karsatos	289	177	.61	2,311	Cris Carter	58	950	16.4
1986	Vince Workman	1,030	210	4.9	Jim Karsatos	272	145	.53	2,122	Cris Carter	69	1,127	16.3
1987	Vince Workman	470	118	4.0	Tom Tupa	242	134	.55	1,786	Everett Ross	29	585	20.2
1988	Carlos Snow	775	152	5.1	Greg Frey	293	152	.52	2,028	Jeff Ellis	40	492	12.3
1989	Carlos Snow	990	190	5.2	Greg Frey	246	144	.59	2,132	Jeff Graham	32	608	19.0
1990	Robert Smith	1,126	177	6.4	Greg Frey	276	139	.50	2,062	Bobby Olive	41	652	15.9
1991	Carlos Snow	828	169	4.9	Kent Graham	153	79	.52	1,018	Bernard Edwards	27	381	14.1
1992	Robert Smith	819	147	5.6	Kirk Herbstreit	264	155	.59	1,904	Brian Stablein	53	643	12.1
1993	Raymont Harris	1,344	273	4.9	Bobby Hoying	202	109	.54	1,570	Joey Galloway	47	946	20.1
1994	Eddie George	1,442	276	5.2	Bobby Hoying	301	170	.56	2,335	Joey Galloway	44	669	15.2
1995	Eddie George	1,927	328	5.9	Bobby Hoying	341	211	.62	3,269	Terry Glenn	64	1,411	22.0
1996	Pepe Pearson	1,484	299	5.0	Stanley Jackson	165	87	.53	1,298	Dimitrious Stanley	43	829	19.3
1997	Pepe Pearson	869	192	4.5	Joe Germaine	210	129	.61	1,847	David Boston	73	970	13.3
1998	Michael Wiley	1,235	198	6.2	Joe Germaine	384	230	.60	3,330	David Boston	85	1,435	16.9
1999	Michael Wiley	952	183	5.2	Steve Bellisari	224	101	.45	1,616	Reggie Germany	43	656	15.3
2000	Derek Combs	888	175	5.1	Steve Bellisari	310	163	.53	2,319	Ken-Yon Rambo	53	794	15.0
2001	Jonathan Wells	1,294	251	5.2	Steve Bellisari	220	119	.54	1,919	Michael Jenkins	49	988	20.2
2002	Maurice Clarett	1,237	222	5.6	Craig Krenzel	249	148	.59	2,110	Michael Jenkins	61	1,076	17.6
2003	Lydell Ross	826	193	4.3	Craig Krenzel	278	153	.55	2,040	Michael Jenkins	55	834	15.2
2004	Lydell Ross	475	117	4.1	Justin Zwick	187	93	.50	1,209	Santonio Holmes	55	769	14.0
2005	Antonio Pittman	1,331	243	5.5	Troy Smith	237	149	.63	2,282	Santonio Holmes	53	977	18.4
2006	Antonio Pittman	1,233	242	5.1	Troy Smith	311	203	.65	2,542	Ted Ginn Jr.	59	781	13.2

Receiving leaders by receptions
All statistics include postseason

PENN STATE

BY TODD JONES

LOCATING PENN STATE CAN BE A trying task for outsiders. In 1953, the TCU football team flew into Harrisburg, Pa. mistakenly thinking the school was there. But State College is 90 miles away, nestled in the state's central valley, in the shadow of Mount Nittany.

Though difficult to find on a map, Penn State is much easier to locate in the landscape of college-football history, where Happy Valley is a national landmark of gridiron stability and excellence. The Nittany Lions, who recorded 49 consecutive nonlosing seasons (from 1939 to 1987), have had just two coaches since 1950 and have enjoyed five undefeated seasons and two national championships since 1968. Penn State is where over 107,000 fans turn out to see old-fashioned football, with the home team in generic uniforms and its players helping opponents up, handing the ball to officials after scores, and providing pride for an entire region.

TRADITION Only one school is known as Linebacker U. Penn State has churned out top linebackers in assembly-line fashion. Eight of them—LaVar Arrington, Greg Buttle, Shane Conlan, Jack Ham, Dennis Onkotz, Brandon Short, John Skorupan and Paul Posluszny—have been named first-team All-America by the Associated Press. Many others have contributed to that position's legacy at Penn State. Since 1928, the team's exploits have been dissected and discussed every Wednesday during the season at the Nittany Lion Inn, rehashing the previous game and talk about the upcoming opponent. The gatherings became known as the State College Quarterback Club, and coach Joe Paterno still attends the weekly meetings. He also brings along players, providing fans a better connection to the men who inspire "We are Penn State" cheers during home games. That chant mixes with the sound of the Blue Band, blasts of a lion's roar from the public-address speakers, and the thunder from a student section of over 20,000 decked in a "whiteout" (most of the students wear white T-shirts sold by the Penn State alumni association to benefit its scholarship fund).

BEST PLAYER While Lydell Mitchell gained more yards in college and Franco Harris was among the career leading ground-gainers in the NFL, it was another Penn State back, Lenny Moore, whom Paterno would call the best player he ever coached. Moore, who played tailback

PROFILE

Pennsylvania State University
University Park, Pa.
Founded: 1855
Enrollment: 36,612
Colors: Blue and White
Nickname: Nittany Lions
Stadium: Beaver Stadium
    Opened in 1960
    FieldTurf; 107,282 capacity
First football game: 1887
All-time record: 780–343–42 (.688)
Bowl record: 25–12–2
Consensus national championships,
1936-present: 2 (1982, 1986)
Big Ten Conference championships:
2 (outright)
Heisman Trophy: John Cappelletti, 1973
Outland Trophy: Mike Reid, 1969
First -round draft choices: 34
Website: www.gopsusports.com

THE BEST OF TIMES

Two Joe Paterno eras stand out. Penn State went 76–19–1 from 1980 to 1987, including a two-season 23–1 mark ending with an undefeated national championship team in 1986. From 1967 to 1974, his teams went 80–10–1, including a 31-game unbeaten streak. The Nittany Lions were undefeated in 1968, 1969, and 1973 but were not national champions.

THE WORST OF TIMES

The Nittany Lions went seven straight seasons without a winning record while going 21–33–3 from 1930 to 1936 under Bob Higgins. Penn State was shut out 17 times during that span.

CONFERENCE

Penn State joined the Big Ten Conference in 1993, after playing as an independent for 106 seasons.

DISTINGUISHED ALUMNI

Guion Bluford, first African-American astronaut in space; Margaret Carlson, political commentator; Mary Ellen Clark, two-time Olympic bronze-medalist diver; Tom Ridge, politician; Rick Santorum, politician; Mike Reid, Grammy winner; Matt Millen, John Saraceno, Lisa Salters, Jimmy Cefalo

FIGHT SONG

FIGHT ON, STATE
Fight on, State, Fight on, State,
Strike your gait and win,
Victory we predict for thee,
We're ever true to you,
Dear old White and Blue.
Onward, State, Onward, State
Roar, Lions roar,
We'll hit that line, roll up the score,
Fight on to victory evermore,
Fight on, on,
On, on, on!
Fight on, on,
Penn State!

and defensive back, wasn't huge, at six feet and 185 pounds, and he never made first-team All-America (thanks to Syracuse's Jim Brown). But the Pennsylvania native could work magic on both sides of the ball. The Reading Rambler averaged 6.2 yards per rush from 1953 to 1955. He also intercepted 10 passes, six as a senior, and was a special-teams star. Moore still ranks fourth at Penn State in punt-return average (15.8 yards) and ninth in kickoff-return average (24.3). In 1954, a national-TV audience saw him run for 143 yards and 2 TDs, then clinch a 35-13 win at Pennsylvania by intercepting a fourth-quarter pass and returning it 53 yards for his third score. Moore went on to a Hall of Fame career in pro football, scoring 113 TDs and gaining more than 12,000 yards over 12 seasons with the Baltimore Colts.

Joe Pa, a brooding perfectionist decked out in trifocals, rolled-up trousers, white athletic socks, and black shoes, is synonymous with Penn State football.

BEST COACH Critics labeled him pious and self-righteous when he spoke in the late 1960s of a "grand experiment" to prove a school could win football games and educate players. But, Joe Paterno, a member of the National Football Foundation College Hall of Fame and recipient of the organization's Gold Medal, has done just

that. He's coached 73 first-team All-Americas and 26 first-team academic All-Americas. The 2006 NCAA Graduation Success Rate Report showed 83% of Penn State's football players who were freshmen in 1999-2000 went on to earn degrees, compared with the national Division I-A average of 50 percent. Paterno, 80, entered the 2007 season with the second-most Division I-A victories (363), two national championships, four other undefeated seasons, and 22 victories in 33 bowl games, all record totals. He's the only coach to win the Orange, Cotton, Sugar, Fiesta, and Rose bowls. Not bad for a Brown University English major who said he never wanted to coach football. Paterno, under contract through 2008, also spent 16 years as a Penn State assistant; 2007 marks his 42nd season as head coach. Since he became head coach, in 1966, there have been 798 head-coaching changes in Division I-A. His 58 seasons at Penn State is the longest tenure at one institution among major college coaches. Critics called for the legend's ouster after Penn State went 26-33 from 2000 through 2004, but Paterno held firm and rallied. In 2005, the Nittany Lions went 11–1, won the Big Ten, and finished the season ranked No. 3, and Paterno

FIRST-ROUND DRAFT CHOICES

1956	Lenny Moore, Colts (9)
1960	Richie Lucas, Redskins (4)* & Bills**
1963	Dave Robinson, Packers (4)
1969	Ted Kwalik, 49ers (7)
1970	Mike Reid, Bengals (7)
1972	Franco Harris, Steelers (13)
1974	Ed O'Neil, Lions (8)
1974	John Cappelletti, Rams (11)
1979	Keith Dorney, Lions (10)
1980	Bruce Clark, Packers (4)
1981	Booker Moore, Bills (28)
1982	Mike Munchak, Oilers (8)
1982	Sean Farrell, Buccaneers (17)
1983	Curt Warner, Seahawks (3)
1983	Todd Blackledge, Chiefs (7)
1984	Kenny Jackson, Eagles (4)
1987	Shane Conlan, Bills (8)
1987	D.J. Dozier, Vikings (14)
1990	Blair Thomas, Jets (2)
1993	O.J. McDuffie, Dolphins (25)
1995	Ki-Jana Carter, Bengals (1)
1995	Kerry Collins, Panthers (5)
1995	Kyle Brady, Jets (9)
1996	Jeff Hartings, Lions (23)
1996	Andre Johnson, Redskins (30)
1998	Curtis Enis, Bears (5)
2000	Courtney Brown, Browns (1)
2000	LaVar Arrington, Redskins (2)
2003	Jimmy Kennedy, Rams (12)
2003	Michael Haynes, Bears (14)
2003	Bryant Johnson, Cardinals (17)
2003	Larry Johnson, Chiefs (27)
2006	Tamba Hali, Chiefs (20)
2007	Levi Brown, Cardinals (5)

*From 1960-1966, the NFL and the AFL held separate, competing drafts
**First "territorial selection" by Buffalo in the inaugural AFL draft, held Nov. 22, 1959

CONSENSUS ALL-AMERICANS

1906	Mother Dunn, C
1919	Bob Higgins, E
1920	Charles Way, B
1921	Glenn Killinger, B
1923	Harry Wilson, B
1959	Rich Lucas, B
1964	Glenn Ressler, G
1968	Ted Kwalick, E
1968-69	Dennis Onkotz, LB
1969	Mike Reid, DT
1970	Jack Ham, LB
1971	Dave Joyner, T
1972	Bruce Bannon, DE
1972	John Skorupan, LB
1973	John Cappelletti, B
1974	Mike Hartenstine, DL
1975	Greg Buttle, LB
1978	Keith Dorney, OT
1978	Chuck Fusina, QB
1978-79	Bruce Clark, DL
1981	Sean Farrell, OL
1986	D.J. Dozier, RB
1986	Shane Conlan, LB
1992	O.J. McDuffie, WR
1994	Ki-Jana Carter, RB
1994	Kerry Collins, QB
1995	Jeff Hartings, OL
1997	Curtis Enis, RB
1999	LaVar Arrington, LB
1999	Brandon Short, LB
1999	Courtney Brown, DL
2002	Larry Johnson, RB
2005	Tamba Hali, DE
2005-06	Paul Posluszny, LB

earned numerous national coach-of-the-year honors, including an unprecedented fifth selection by the American Football Coaches Association. He was selected for induction into the College Football Hall of Fame in 2006, but his enshrinement ceremony was deferred until 2007 because he broke his left leg during a November game at Wisconsin. JoePa, a brooding perfectionist decked out in huge trifocals, rolled-up trousers, white athletic socks, and black shoes, is synonymous with Penn State football and a symbol of the entire college game.

BEST TEAM Paterno has coached in more than a third of the football games in Penn State's history, so he should know. He says his 1968 Nittany Lions, the school's first to win 10 games in a season, were his marquee team. They weren't big on defense, but they were quick, aggressive and tenacious. Junior tackles Mike Reid and Steve Smear set the tone up front as team captains, and linebackers Dennis Onkotz and Jack Ham, and the other "Rover Boys" cleaned up the rest. Much-maligned QB Chuck Burkart—"He can't run and he can't pass. All he does is think and win," Paterno said—and halfbacks Charlie Pittman and Bob Campbell and All-America tight end Ted Kwalick powered Penn State to a then school-record 4,025 total yards of offense, including a school-record 2,739 rushing yards. The Nittany Lions went 10–0 in the regular season and beat Kansas in the Orange Bowl, but finished No. 2 behind Ohio State in the final poll.

BEST BACKFIELD Franco Harris and Lydell Mitchell gave Penn State a dangerous duo while going 29–4 from 1969 through 1971, but the Nittany Lions have never had a backfield produce numbers like the one of 1994. The arm of quarterback Kerry Collins, the legs of tailback Ki-Jana Carter, and the body of fullback Brian Milne powered an offense that led the nation in yardage (520.2) and points per game (47.8). Carter finished second in the Heisman voting and Collins fourth. Both were named All-America—the first running back and QB from the same school to earn that consensus honor since 1949—along with receiver Bobby Engram, tight end Kyle Brady, and guard Jeff Hartings. The 1994 Nittany Lions scored 68 touchdowns, averaged 7.6 yards per play, and totaled 5,722 total yards while becoming the first Big Ten team to go 12–0. Collins, a senior, led the nation in passing efficiency with a rating of 172.9 that still stands as a Penn

State record. He also holds school records for passing yards in a season (2,679), completion percentage (66.7), yards per pass attempt (10.2), and TD passes in consecutive games (11). His 21 TD passes in 1994 was one shy of Todd Blackledge's school record, and Collins' 2,660 total yards of offense stood as the school record until eclipsed in 2005 by Michael Robinson. Carter, a junior, rushed for 1,539 yards, including nine games of 100-plus yards, scored 23 touchdowns, and averaged 7.8 yards per carry. He was second in the nation in scoring, fourth in rushing, and fifth in all-purpose yards. Carter ran for an 83-yard TD on the first play against Oregon in a Rose Bowl that Penn State won 38-20. The Cincinnati Bengals selected Carter with the No. 1 pick of the NFL draft, but injuries derailed his career. Collins, one of four other first-round draft picks from that offense, had a rocky pro career spotted with bouts of alcoholism and racial controversy.

COLLEGE FOOTBALL HALL OF FAME INDUCTEES		
NAME	YEARS	INDUCTED
Hugo Bezdek, COACH	1918-29	1954
Dick Harlow, COACH	1915-17	1954
Bob Higgins, COACH	1930-48	1954
Pete Mauthe, HB	1909-12	1957
Glenn Killinger, QB	1918-21	1971
Rip Engle, COACH	1950-65	1973
Harry Wilson, HB	1921-23	1973
Shorty Miller, QB	1910-13	1974
Dexter Very, E	1909-12	1976
Steve Suhey, G	1942, 1946-47	1985
Richie Lucas, QB	1957-59	1986
Mike Reid, DT	1966, 1968-69	1987
Ted Kwalick, QB	1968-70	1990
John Cappelletti, HB	1971-73	1993
Dennis Onkotz, LB	1967-69	1995
Dave Robinson, E	1960-62	1997
Glenn Ressler, C/G	1962-64	2001
Lydell Mitchell, RB	1969-71	2004
Keith Dorney, OT	1975-78	2005
Joe Paterno, COACH	1966-	2007

BEST DEFENSE In early 1969, Paterno rejected an offer to become coach of the Pittsburgh Steelers. Perhaps this was a factor in his decision: Penn State returned the bulk of a defense that had ranked No. 3 in the nation the previous season on a team that had gone 11–0 and finished No. 2. The Nittany Lions again went 11–0 in 1969 because of a defense that included All-Americas in defensive tackle Mike Reid, linebacker Dennis Onkotz and safety Neal Smith. Reid won the Maxwell Award, presented annually to "the outstanding player in collegiate football," won the Outland Trophy as the nation's best interior lineman, and finished fifth in the Heisman voting. Onkotz led the team, with 97 tackles. Smith had 10 interceptions in 1969 and still holds the school's career record with 19. Onkotz and Reid were later selected for the College Football Hall of Fame. So, too, was another linebacker on that Penn State team, Jack Ham. After Navy scored 22 in the season opener, the Nittany Lions gave up no more than 16 points in a game the rest of the year. They had two shutouts and two games in which they allowed only three points. Opponents totaled just 18 points in the last four games. Penn State, with defensive tackle Steve Smear serving as team captain along with Reid, capped the season by extending its undefeated streak to 30 games by intercepting seven passes in a 10-3 victory over Missouri in the Orange Bowl. When asked how long Penn State could have held Missouri, Onkotz said, "Forever." Afterward, Missouri coach Dan Devine said Penn State

had "the best defensive team I've seen in college football." For the second consecutive year, Penn State ended the season ranked No. 2, this time to Texas. Ham went on to be inducted into the Pro Football Hall of Fame after winning four Super Bowls with the Pittsburgh Steelers. After a short but successful stint in the NFL, Reid enjoyed a lengthier music career, in which he won a Grammy award for songwriting (the country hit "Stranger in the House") and also recorded two solo albums.

PRO FOOTBALL HALL OF FAME INDUCTEES		
NAME	YEARS	INDUCTED
Mike Michalske, G	1926-35, 1937	1964
Lenny Moore, F/RB	1956-67	1975
Jack Ham, LB	1971-82	1988
Franco Harris, RB	1972-84	1990
Mike Munchak, G	1982-93	2001

BIGGEST GAME Like a heavyweight title fight, the 1987 Fiesta Bowl was prepackaged as both a sports event and a battle of Good vs. Evil. Clean-cut Penn State (11–0) and rowdy Miami (11–0) staged a morality play in the Arizona desert to decide the national championship. Miami arrived in Tempe wearing combat fatigues, and the No. 1 Hurricanes walked out of a steak dinner they were sharing with No. 2 Penn State. "Did the Japanese sit down and eat with Pearl Harbor before they bombed them?" asked Miami defensive lineman Jerome Brown. The coat-and-tie-clad Nittany Lions kept their mouths shut and gained confidence in a defensive game plan designed to confuse Heisman-winning QB Vinny Testaverde. A college football-record 70 million people watching the game on NBC saw Penn State's defense intercept five Testaverde passes—two interceptions by linebackers Shane Conlan (playing with knee and ankle injuries) and Pete Giftopoulos—and sack him five times. The turnovers offset Miami's otherwise dominating performance; the Canes ran 93 offensive plays and held a 445-162 advantage in total offense, including 22 first downs to Penn State's eight. The Nittany Lions' 14-10 win gave them their second national championship in five years, and thousands of fans gathered along U.S. Route 322 and on campus in the early morning hours to greet the team buses upon their return.

BIGGEST UPSET Channels were being switched all over the country early in Penn State's nationally televised game against No. 1-ranked Pittsburgh on Nov. 28, 1981. Led by QB Dan Marino, Pitt was ahead 14-0 and threatening to score again with less than a minute remaining in the first quarter. Marino, who had completed nine of his first 10 passes, tried to hit Dwight Collins for a third TD, but Penn State DB Roger Jackson intercepted. The Nittany Lions promptly drove 80 yards and scored to make it a 14-7 game. And they kept scoring. Penn State rang up 48 consecutive points against the nation's No. 1 defense. The 48-14 upset cost the Panthers a chance for a national title.

HEARTBREAKER Alabama fans at the 1979 Sugar Bowl held up a sign reading "Remember Gettysburg." All Penn State could remember after the game was how a national championship was lost after a remarkable defensive stand. The Nittany Lions were top-ranked and had six first-team All-Americas. But Bear Bryant's Crimson Tide, ranked No. 2, pulled off a 14-7 upset. Penn State failed to score on first down from the Bama 8-yard line with about seven minutes left in the game. The final two plays began two feet from the end zone. Mike Guman tried to score over left tackle on fourth down, but was smashed short by Alabama linebacker Barry Krauss.

WILDEST FINISH Penn State trailed Kansas 14-7 and was out of timeouts late in the 1969 Orange Bowl, the first New Year's Day bowl for the Nittany Lions in 19 years. In Flushing, N.Y., Paterno's mother went into the bathroom, locked the door, and began saying the rosary. Neal Smith then partially blocked a Jayhawk punt to give the Nittany Lions the ball at the 50 with 1:16 remaining. QB Chuck Burkhart, as he was being hit by two linemen, threw a pass to Bob Campbell, who had split two defenders, made the catch at the 20, and got to the 3-yard line before being tackled. During the play, Kansas running back Donnie Shanklin was announced as the game's MVP. Three plays later, Burkhart rolled to his left and walked into the end zone untouched with 15 seconds remaining. His two-point conversion pass attempt fell incomplete to tight end Ted Kwalick. The pass was right in front of the Kansas band, which, along with some Jayhawk's fans, now took the field after the play and celebrated with the team. But Kansas was penalized for having 12 men on the field during the two-point conversion. (It was later noted that they had had 12 men on the field on every play of that goal-line stand.) Paterno sent in a play for Campbell to take a pitchout right, but the referees had to hold up the game because of the noise. Paterno then changed the play. Campbell took the handoff and scored two points by diving into the end zone with eight seconds remaining. "The last two minutes were pure, unadulterated insanity," wrote Roy McHugh in the *Pittsburgh Press*. Penn State's 15-14 win was its first in a major bowl and the first time an Eastern team had won the Orange Bowl since Duquesne in 1937. JoePa later said that the victory, which capped an 11–0 season, put Penn State on the national map.

BEST GOAL-LINE STAND The No. 2 Nittany Lions were clinging to a 14-10 lead as No. 1 Miami drove from its own 23-yard line to the Penn State 6 in the final

three minutes of the 1987 Fiesta Bowl. A similar situation had occurred in two of the Nittany Lions' previous three games. Penn State had forced an incompletion on a two-point conversion attempt by Maryland to preserve a 17-15 win. One week later, the Nittany Lions had held Notre Dame on downs in a 24-19 win after the Fighting Irish had driven to the Penn State 9 in the game's final minute. Now, with a national championship on the line, All-America defensive lineman Tim Johnson sacked Miami QB Vinny Testaverde for a seven-yard loss. The Heisman trophy winner threw an incompletion on third down. Needing eight yards for a first down and 13 for a TD, Testaverde tried to hit split end Brett Perriman in the end zone. "I had a gut feeling someone was going to make a big play," Conlan said. Testaverde's pass went to Pete Giftopoulos at the one. His interception secured JoePa's second national title.

BEST COMEBACK The defining moment of Penn State's 12–0 1994 season came on Nov. 12. Illinois led the Nittany Lions 31-28 with 6:07 left in the game. Penn State had trailed 21-0 after one quarter and needed to go 94 yards against an Illinois defense ranked No. 2 in the nation in scoring (11.3 points) and No. 4 in total defense (253.6 yards) to complete the biggest comeback of the Paterno era. Collins methodically drove the Nittany Lions downfield against a trio of All-America linebackers in Dana Howard, Simeon Rice, and Kevin Hardy. Milne completed the march by scoring from two yards out with 57 seconds remaining. Penn State preserved its 35-31 win by intercepting a Hail Mary pass in its own end zone with two seconds left to play.

STADIUM What began as a 30,000-seat horseshoe is now the nation's second-largest stadium, an intimidating 107,282-seat monstrosity distinguished by a hodgepodge of designs born out of repeated expansions. Beaver Stadium actually sat on the west side of campus for 50 years but was moved to the east side in 1960, when the school president wanted to make room for an academic building. The entire stadium was dismantled into 700 pieces and moved one mile to its new location. While reassembling the stadium, school officials added 16,000 seats, which kicked off five decades of sporadic growth in capacity. In 1978, the stadium was cut into sections, raised eight feet by hydraulic jacks, and precast concrete seating forms were placed within the inner circle of the stadium to expand its capacity. A $93 million expansion that included 12,000 new seats and 60 skyboxes was finished before the 2001 season. On game days, Beaver Stadium becomes the third-largest city in Pennsylvania. More than 20 million people have attended Penn State home games since 1960.

HALLOWED GROUND The Nittany Lion Shrine, a 13-ton block of Indiana limestone sculpted into the shape of a lion, sits amid trees near the campus recreation building. Heinz Warneke's sculpture was a gift to the school from the Class of 1940, and it was dedicated two years later. On graduation day a long line of students dressed in cap and gown wait with their families for a quick snapshot at the Shrine.

RIVAL Ohio State is probably Penn State's biggest current rival, but that series does not come close to matching the ferocity that defined the Nittany Lions' annual in-state grudge match with Pittsburgh. The Penn State-Pitt series began in 1893 and, from 1900, was played every season (except 1932-34) until 1993, when Penn State began playing in the Big Ten. It resumed in 1997 but ended in acrimony after the 2000 game. The rivalry between the schools, separated by 140 miles, reached a zenith in the late 1970s and early '80s, when Paterno's and Pitt coach Jackie Sherrill's teams met five times with the coaches squabbling as their teams battled with Eastern supremacy and national rankings on the line. Paterno went 3–2 against his nemesis. JoePa ended the series after Pitt refused a deal to play twice at State College and once at home. Critics say Paterno dropped Pitt as payback for the betrayal he still felt from the Panthers' joining the Big East in 1982 rather than helping Penn State form a proposed all-sports Eastern league. Paterno reiterated in 2007 that the series between Penn State and Pittsburgh won't be renewed.

INSPIRATION John Cappelletti won the 1973 Heisman trophy after running for more than 200 yards in three consecutive late-season games to finish the year with 1,522. The tailback is best remembered, however, for his Heisman acceptance speech, which stunned the crowd, including a mesmerized U.S. vice president Gerald Ford. Cappelletti spoke of how the rigors of football were nothing compared to the leukemia battle his 11-year-old brother Joey was fighting. "This trophy is more his than mine, because of the inspiration he has been to me," Cappelletti said. Joey Cappelletti died of leukemia on April 8, 1976. A year later, CBS aired a made-for-TV movie, called *Something for Joey*, based on the brothers.

On Sept. 23, 2000, Penn State cornerback Adam Taliaferro was lying on the soggy Ohio Stadium field without being able to move his fingers or legs. The freshman from Voorhees, N.J., had just attempted to tackle Ohio State running back Jerry Westbrooks. Taliaferro's C-5 vertebra was fractured and his spinal cord bruised. Two days later, doctors at the Ohio State Medical Center inserted a metal pin and grafted bone in place of broken vertebra piecesto stabilize Taliaferro's spine at the neck. Doctors said this type of spinal injury results in permanent paralysis of the legs in most cases, but in January 2001, Taliaferro left rehab on crutches. And on Sept. 1, 2001, Taliaferro led the Penn State team onto the field for its season-opening game against Miami. Although he couldn't play again, Taliaferro

smiled as he jogged out to midfield. The Beaver Stadium crowd erupted. "We believe" flashed on the scoreboard. Taliaferro earned a bachelor of science degree in labor and industrial relations from Penn State in 2005. He's currently enrolled in the Rutgers School of Law. The Adam Taliaferro Foundation raises more than $80,000 a year for spinal-cord injuries.

Sixteen years later, even McCloskey admitted that he was probably out of bounds.

CONTROVERSY Penn State's 6–0 start to the 2005 season ended Oct. 15, when Michigan won 27-25 on the game's final play after a fourth quarter in which the teams combined for 39 points and four lead changes. The Nittany Lions, ranked No. 8, drove 81 yards and took a 25-21 lead when QB Michael Robinson scored on a three-yard keeper with 53 seconds remaining. Chad Henne began Michigan's ensuing possession, set up by Steve Breaston's kickoff return to midfield, by throwing an interception. The Wolverines, however, maintained possession when officials checked the TV replays and ruled that the Penn State defender was out of bounds when he caught the ball. After a Henne completion, Michigan head coach Lloyd Carr called a timeout. There were 28 seconds on the Michigan Stadium scoreboard clock, but Carr argued with the officials that time should be added. A long conference between officials ended with them resetting the game clock at 0:30. Six plays later, Michigan won the game when Henne threw a 10-yard TD pass to Mario Manningham in the middle of the end zone. The play began with 1 second left on the clock … Nebraska fans still howl that Penn State's Mike McCloskey was out of bounds when he caught a crucial pass in no. 8-ranked Penn State's 27-24 upset over the No. 3 Cornhuskers at Beaver Stadium on Sept. 25, 1982. Both teams won the rest of their games, so this contest effectively decided the national championship. The winning score came two plays after McCloskey's controversial 15-yard reception put Penn State on the Nebraska 2. The Cornhuskers argued furiously that McCloskey failed to get a foot inbounds while making his catch, and TV replays seemed to support Nebraska's argument. In 1998, McCloskey appeared at a banquet in Omaha, Neb., where after viewing a video of the play, he admitted he appeared to be out-of-bounds.

CONFERENCE CALL Penn State spurred upheaval in conference lineups when it became a member of the Big Ten Conference, in June 1990. The move had seismic implications, indirectly leading the SEC to add new members and split into two divisions, prompting the Big Eight to follow suit (thereby contributing to the demise of the Southwest Conference), and creating jolts in almost every major conference in big-time college football. Paterno acknowledged that the challenge of joining the Big Ten had put an end to his thoughts of retiring. Not every school in the Midwestern conference was pleased to add an 11th member, especially one from the East. Michigan, Minnesota, and Indiana voted against adding Penn State, a 6-hour drive from Ohio State, its nearest Big Ten opponent. In 1993, the Nittany Lions played their first league game, ending 106 years of independence. They went 12–0 in 1994, claimed the Big Ten championship outright, and won the Rose Bowl. Success in the league fueled $55 million in construction and renovation projects for sports facilities at Penn State, and it led to increases in booster membership and alumni donations. The Nittany Lions, however, didn't win a second Big Ten title until 2005.

DUBIOUS DISTINCTION Harrisburg, Pa., TV-station WHTM reported on Dec. 19, 1996, that sports agent Jeff Nalley had bought a suit for Penn State's star running back Curtis Enis in violation of NCAA regulations. Both agent and player denied the story, but five days later, Enis told Paterno that the agent had indeed purchased a suit for him and other clothing worth $1,100. Paterno dropped Enis from the team, which really stung because it was just two days after top receiver Joe Jurevicius had been dropped for academic reasons. Enis had rushed for 3,256 yards in three seasons and was just 142 short of breaking Curt Warner's school career record. The junior tailback left Penn State and entered the subsequent NFL draft.

NICKNAME Legend has it that Mount Nittany, which overlooks Beaver Stadium, was named after Indian princess Nita-Nee by the Great Spirit. H.D. "Joe" Mason, a member of the Penn State Class of 1907, had seen the Princeton Tigers at a baseball game in 1906 and liked their moniker. With a Penn State publication asking people to select a mascot for the school, Mason pushed for the use of Lions. His campaign was so strong the students settled on Nittany Lions.

MASCOT The Nittany Lion made its first appearance when a student donned a lion suit and roamed the sideline at a 1922 Penn State game at the Polo Grounds in New York City. Today, the Lion remains a fixture on the road and at home. When he's not leading cheers or doing one-handed push-ups, he's being hoisted overhead by fans and passed to the top of Beaver Stadium.

UNIFORMS A three-member student committee decided in October 1887 that Penn State teams should wear dark pink and black. However, the pink in the baseball team's striped blazers and caps quickly faded to white. So the students instead picked blue and white. Those were named the school's official colors on March 18, 1890. Today, Penn State's uniforms are simple. Helmets are solid white with a single blue stripe in the middle. Players wear plain white pants and socks. Cleats are black. Jerseys have no names, only numerals—although the school was the first to allow Nike, in 1994, to move its swoosh from the sleeve to the chest, as part of a wide-ranging deal that included all of Penn State's athletic teams.

QUIRK Paterno broke Bear Bryant's Division I-A record for most wins, but JoePa went 0–4 against Bear's Alabama teams. The Crimson Tide beat Penn State 13-6 in the 1975 Sugar Bowl and 14-7 three years later in the same bowl. In 1981, Alabama won at Penn State 31-16. Penn State won the 1982 national title despite a 42-21 regular-season loss to Alabama at Birmingham's Legion Field.

LORE During a 31-6 win over Navy in 1968, the Nittany Lions not only intercepted five Navy passes and recovered four fumbles, they also found a lucky item. Penn State cheerleaders discovered a small bamboo horseshoe in the end zone after the game. The team took it everywhere for the rest of the season. The horseshoe hung on the goalpost crossbar during home games. On the road, it was placed near the bench. Clearly, it worked. Penn State finished the season 11–0 and ranked No. 2.

NUMBERS Penn State has won the Lambert-Meadowlands trophy, signifying Eastern football supremacy, 26 times … Charles A. "Rip" Engle, a member of the College Football Hall of Fame, served as Penn State's football coach for 16 years. He retired after the 1965 season with a 104–48–4 record … Defensive lineman Courtney Brown and linebacker LaVar Arrington were the top two picks, respectively, in the 2000 NFL

ALL-CENTURY TEAM	
Lou Prato, author of the Penn State Football Encyclopedia and director of the Penn State All-Sports Museum, selected the players from the 1900-1999 era.	
OFFENSE	
1921-23	Joe Bedenk, G
1962-64	Glenn Ressler, G
1979-81	Sean Farrell, G
1979, 1981	Mike Munchak, G
1914-17, 1919	Bob Higgins, TE
1966-68	Ted Kwalick, TE
1918-21	Glenn Killinger, QB
1992-94	Kerry Collins, QB
1980-83	Kenny Jackson, WR
1991, 1993-95	Bobby Engram, WR
1921-23	Harry Wilson, RB
1953-55	Lenny Moore, RB/KR
1979-82	Curt Warner, RB/KR
1976-79	Matt Suhey, FB
1909-12	Pete Mauthe, PK/FB
DEFENSE	
1945-48	Sam Tamburo, DE
1960-62	Dave Robinson, DE
1976-79	Bruce Clark, DT
1966, 1968-69	Mike Reid, DT
1903-06	Mother Dunn, LB
1967-69	Dennis Onkotz, LB
1967-69	Neal Smith, DB
1968-70	Jack Ham, LB
1997-99	LaVar Arrington, LB
1921-23	Harry Wilson, DB
1953-55	Lenny Moore, DB
1957-59	Rich Lucas, DB
1980-83	Mark Robinson, DB
1942, 1946-48	Joe Colone, P

draft, making Penn State the first school since Nebraska in 1984 to have players selected 1-2 … Jerry Sandusky, a former Penn State linebacker, served 32 years as an assistant coach on Paterno's staff, including 23 years as defensive coordinator … Paterno has missed just three of 642 Penn State games in his 57 seasons at the school … Entering 2007, Paterno has had 32 teams finish in the top 25 of a season's final Associated Press poll, including 21 in the top 10 and 13 in the top five … Penn State played against the eventual Heisman winner six times during the 1980s and won five of those games … At least one Penn State player has been an All-America selection in 36 of Paterno's 41 seasons. More than 300 of his players have signed NFL contracts, and 30 of them were first-round draft choices … Larry Johnson became just the ninth player to rush for 2,000 yards in a season in 2002, when he ran for a school-record 2,087, including 327 at Indiana. He ran for 200-plus yards in a game four times that season, a school record … Penn State defeated Florida State 26-23 in three overtimes in the 2006 Orange Bowl—a game that ended at 12:57 a.m. after 4 hours of play between teams coached by the two men with the most Division I-A wins of all-time, Paterno and Bobby Bowden… QB Michael Robinson scored six touchdowns against Illinois in 2005, tying a school record set by Harry Robb against Gettysburg in 1917. Robinson's 29 TDs and 3,156 total yards of offense that season are Penn State records … Don Jonas averaged 21.4 yards on his seven punt returns in 1960 … Curt Warner averaged 35.0 yards on 10 kickoff returns in 1980 … In 1991, the Nittany Lions beat visiting Cincinnati 81-0 with 706 total yards of offense … Penn State won 23 consecutive games from 1968 to 1970 … Boston College's Doug Flutie threw for 520 yards in a 1982 loss to Penn State.

QUOTE "How could Nixon know so little about Watergate and so much about football?"—Joe Paterno, three years after the president gave Texas a mythical national championship, despite Penn State's 30-game unbeaten streak after defeating Missouri in the 1970 Orange Bowl

PENN STATE ALL-TIME SCORES

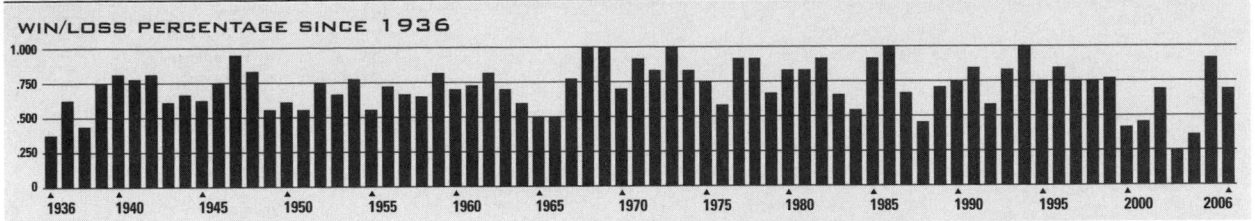

WIN/LOSS PERCENTAGE SINCE 1936

Chart with years: 1936, 1940, 1945, 1950, 1955, 1960, 1965, 1970, 1975, 1980, 1985, 1990, 1995, 2000, 2006

NO HEAD COACH

1887 — 2-0-0
N5	●	at Bucknell	54	0
N19	●	Bucknell	24	0

1888 — 0-2-1
N31	=	Dickinson	6	6
N7		at Dickinson	0	16
N10		Lehigh	0	30

1889 — 2-2-0
N2	●	Swarthmore	20	6
N9		at Lafayette	0	26
N11		at Lehigh	0	106
N25		Bucknell	12	0

1890 — 2-2-0
O10		at Pennsylvania	0	20
O12		at Franklin & Marshall	0	10
N15	●	Altoona	68	0
N22	●	at Bellefonte	23	0

1891 — 6-2-0
O2	●	at Lafayette	14	4
O3		at Lehigh	2	24
O17	●	at Swarthmore	44	0
O24	●	at Franklin & Marshall	26	6
O27	●	at Gettysburg	18	0
N7		at Bucknell	10	12
N26	●	Dickinson	1	0 f
D5	●	at Haverford	58	0

GEORGE HOSKINS
1892-95 (.760)   17-4-4

1892 — 5-1-0
O1		at Pennsylvania	0	20
O27	●	at Wyoming Seminary	40	0
N5	●	at Pittsburgh AC	16	0
N12	●	Bucknell	18	0
N23	●	Lafayette *WB*	18	0
N25	●	Dickinson *HARR*	16	0

1893 — 4-1-0
O14	●	at Virginia	6	0
O25		at Pennsylvania	6	18
N6	●	Pittsburgh	32	0
N11	●	at Bucknell	36	18
N30	●	at Pittsburgh AC	12	0

1894 — 6-0-1
O13	●	Gettysburg	60	0
O20	●	Lafayette	72	0
N10	=	at Navy	6	6
N17	●	Bucknell *WLM*	12	6
N23	●	at Wash. & Jeff	6	0
N24	=	at Oberlin	9	6
N29	●	at Pittsburg AC	14	0

1895 — 2-2-3
S25	●	Gettysburg	48	0
O5	=	at Cornell	0	0
O26	●	Bucknell *WLM*	16	0
N9		at Pennsylvania	4	35
N16		at Pittsburgh AC	10	11
N18	=	at Wash. & Jeff.	6	6
N28	=	at Western Reserve	8	8

DR. SAMUEL NEWTON
1896-98 (.462)   12-14

1896 — 3-4-0
S26	●	Gettysburg	40	0
O3	●	Pittsburgh	10	4
O10	●	Dickinson	8	0
O24		at Princeton	0	39
O31		Bucknell *WLM*	0	10
N14		at Pennsylvania	0	27
N28		Carlisle Indians *HARR*	5	48

1897 — 3-6-0
S25	●	Gettysburg	32	0
O2		at Lafayette	0	24
O13		at Princeton	0	34
O20		at Pennsylvania	0	24
O23		at Navy	0	4
O30		at Cornell	0	45
N13	●	Bucknell *WLM*	27	4
N20	●	Bloomsburg	10	0
N25		Dickinson *SUN*	0	6

1898 — 6-4-0
S24	●	Gettysburg	47	0
O1		at Pennsylvania	0	40
O8	●	at Lafayette	5	0
O15	●	Susquehanna	45	6
O22		at Navy	11	16
O26		at Princeton	0	5
O29	●	Duquesne AC *PIT*	5	18
N5	●	Bucknell *WLM*	16	0
N19	●	at Wash. & Jeff.	11	6
O28	●	Dickinson *WLM*	34	0

SAM BOYLE
1899 (.409)   4-6-1

1899 — 4-6-1
S23	●	Mansfield	38	0
S30	●	Gettysburg	40	0
O7	=	at Army	6	0
O13	=	Wash. & Jeff.	0	0
O18		at Princeton	0	12
O21		at Navy	0	6
O28	●	Dickinson	15	0
N4		Bucknell *WLM*	0	5
N11		at Yale	0	42
N17		at Pennsylvania	0	47
N25		Duquesne AC *PIT*	5	64

POP GOLDEN
1900-02 (.569)   16-12-1

1900 — 4-6-1
S23	●	Susquehanna	17	0
S30	●	Pittsburgh *BEL*	12	0
O6	=	at Army	0	0
O10		at Princeton	0	26
O17	●	at Pennsylvania	6	17 *
O20		at Dickinson	0	18
O27		Duquesne AC *PIT*	0	29
N3	●	Bucknell *WLM*	6	0
N10		at Navy	0	44
N17	●	at Gettysburg	44	0
N29		at Buffalo	0	10

1901 — 5-3-0
S22	●	Susquehanna	17	0
S29	●	Pittsburgh *BEL*	33	0 *
O5		at Pennsylvania	6	23
O19		at Yale	0	22
O26	●	at Navy	11	6
N2		Homestead AC *PIT*	0	39
N16	●	Lehigh *WLM*	38	0
N23	●	Dickinson	12	0

1902 — 7-3-0
S20	●	Dickinson Seminary	27	0
S27	●	Pittsburgh	27	0
O4		at Pennsylvania	0	17
O11	●	Villanova	32	0
O18		at Yale	0	11
O25	●	Susquehanna	55	0
N1	●	at Navy	6	0
N8	●	Gettysburg	37	0
N22	●	at Dickinson	23	0
N27		at Steelton YMCA	5	6

DAN REED
1903 (.625)   5-3

1903 — 5-3-0
S19	●	Dickinson Seminary	60	0
O3	●	Allegheny	24	5
O10		at Pennsylvania	0	39
O17		at Yale	0	27
O24	●	at Pittsburgh	59	0
O31	●	at Navy	17	0
N14		Dickinson *WLM*	0	6
N26	●	Wash. & Jeff. *PIT*	22	0

TOM FENNELL
1904-08 (.657)   33-17-1

1904 — 6-4-0
S24		at Pennsylvania	0	6
O1	●	Allegheny	50	0
O8		at Yale	0	24
O15	●	West Virginia	34	0
O22	●	Wash. & Jeff. *PIT*	12	0
O29	●	Jersey Shore	30	0
N5		at Navy	9	20
N12	●	Dickinson *WLM*	11	0
N19	●	Geneva	44	0
N24		at Pittsburgh	5	22 *

1905 — 8-3-0
S16	●	Lebanon Valley	23	0
S30	●	California St.	29	0
O7		Carlisle Indians *HARR*	0	11
O14	●	Gettysburg	18	0
O21		at Yale	0	12
O28	●	Villanova	29	0
N4		at Navy	5	11
N11	●	Geneva	73	0
N18	●	Dickinson *WLM*	6	0
N25	●	West Virginia	6	0
N30	●	at Pittsburgh	6	0

1906 — 8-1-1
S22	●	Lebanon Valley	24	0
S29	●	Allegheny	26	0
O6		Carlisle Indians *WLM*	4	0
O13	=	Gettysburg	0	0
O20		at Yale	0	10
N3	●	at Navy	5	0
N12	●	Bellefonte Aca.	12	0
N17	●	Dickinson *WLM*	6	0
N23	●	West Virginia	10	0 *
N29	●	at Pittsburgh	6	0

1907 — 6-4-0
S21	●	Altoona AA	27	0
S28	●	Geneva	34	0
O5		Carlisle Indians *WLM*	5	18
O12	●	Grove City	46	0
O19		at Cornell	8	6
O26	●	Lebanon Valley	75	0
N2	●	Dickinson *WLM*	52	0
N9		at Pennsylvania	0	28
N16		at Navy	4	6
N28		at Pittsburgh	0	6

1908 — 5-5-0
S19	●	Bellefonte Aca.	5	6
S26	●	Grove City	31	0
O3		Carlisle Indians *WB*	5	12
O10		at Pennsylvania	0	6
O17	●	Geneva	51	0
O24	●	West Virginia	12	0
O31		at Cornell	4	10
N7	●	Bucknell	33	6
N14		at Navy	0	5
N26	●	at Pittsburgh	12	6

BILL HOLLENBACK
1909, '11-14 (.732)   28-9-4

1909 — 5-0-2
O2	●	Grove City	31	0
O9	=	Carlisle Indians *WB*	8	8
O16	●	Geneva	46	0
O23	=	at Pennsylvania	3	3
N6	●	at Bucknell	33	0
N13	●	West Virginia	40	0
N25	●	at Pittsburgh	5	0

JACK HOLLENBACK
1910 (.688)   5-2-1

1910 — 5-2-1
O1	●	Harrisburg AC	58	0
O8	●	Carnegie Tech	61	0
O15	●	Sterling AC	45	0
O22		at Pennsylvania	0	10
O29	=	Villanova		
N5	●	St. Bonaventure	34	0
N12	●	Bucknell	45	3
N24		at Pittsburgh	0	11

BILL HOLLENBACK

1911 — 8-0-1
S30	●	Geneva	57	0
O7	●	Gettysburg	31	0
O14	●	at Cornell	5	0
O21	●	Villanova	18	0
O28	●	at Pennsylvania	22	6
N4	●	St. Bonaventure	46	0
N11	●	Colgate	17	9
N18	=	at Navy	0	0
N30	●	at Pittsburgh	3	0

1912 — 8-0-0
O5	●	Carnegie Tech	41	0
O12	●	Wash. & Jeff.	30	0
O19	●	at Cornell	29	6
O26	●	Gettysburg	25	0
N2	●	at Pennsylvania	14	0
N9	●	Villanova	71	0
N16	●	at Ohio State	37	0
N28	●	at Pittsburgh	38	0

1913 — 2-6-0
O4	●	Carnegie Tech	49	0
O11	●	Gettysburg	16	0
O18		at Wash. & Jeff.	0	17
O25		at Harvard	0	29
N1		at Pennsylvania	0	17
N7		Notre Dame	7	14
N15		at Navy	0	10
N27		at Pittsburgh	6	7

1914 — 5-3-1
S26	●	Westminster	13	0
O3	●	Muhlenberg	22	0
O10	●	Gettysburg	13	0
O17	●	Ursinus	30	0
O24	=	at Harvard	13	13
O31	●	at Lafayette	17	0
N7		at Lehigh	7	20
N13	●	Michigan State	3	6
N26		at Pittsburgh	3	13

DICK HARLOW
1915-17 (.714)   20-8

1915 — 7-2-0
S25	●	Westminster	26	0
O2	●	Lebanon Valley	13	0
O9	●	at Pennsylvania	13	3
O16	●	Gettysburg	27	12
O23	●	W. V. Wesleyan	28	0
O30		at Harvard	0	13
N5	●	Lehigh	7	0
N13	●	at Lafayette	33	3
N25		at Pittsburgh	0	20

144 PENN STATE

BIG TEN TEAMS

1916 8-2-0

S23	●	Susquehanna	27	0
S30	●	Westminster	55	0
O7	●	Bucknell	50	7
O14	●	W. V. Wesleyan	39	0
O21		at Pennsylvania	0	15
O28	●	Gettysburg	48	2
N4	●	Geneva	79	0
N11	●	at Lehigh	10	7
N17	●	Lafayette	40	0
N30		at Pittsburgh	0	31

1917 5-4-0

S29	●	Army Amb. Corp ALL	10	0
O6	●	Gettysburg	80	0
O13	●	St. Bonaventure	99	0
O20		at Wash. & Jeff.	0	7
O27	●	W. V. Wesleyan	8	7
N3		at Dartmouth	7	10
N10		Lehigh	0	9
N17	●	Maryland	57	0
N29		at Pittsburgh	6	28

HUGO BEZDEK
1918-29 (.665) 65-30-11

1918 1-2-1

N2	=	Wissahickon Barracks	6	6
N9		Rutgers	3	26
N16	●	at Lehigh	7	6
N28		at Pittsburgh	6	28

1919 7-1-0

O4	●	Gettysburg	33	0
O11	●	Bucknell	9	0
O18		at Dartmouth	13	19
O25	●	Ursinus	48	7
N1	●	at Pennsylvania	10	0
N8	●	Lehigh	20	7
N15	●	at Cornell	20	0
N27	●	at Pittsburgh	20	0

1920 7-0-2

S25	●	Muhlenburg	27	7
O2	●	Gettysburg	13	0
O9	●	Dartmouth	14	7
O16	●	North Carolina St.	41	0
O23	●	Lebanon Valley	109	7
O30	●	at Pennsylvania	28	7
N6	●	Nebraska	20	0
N13	=	at Lehigh	7	7
N25	=	at Pittsburgh	0	0

1921 8-0-2

S24	●	Lebanon Valley	53	0
O1	●	Gettysburg	24	0
O8	●	North Carolina St.	35	0
O15	●	Lehigh	28	7
O22	=	at Harvard	21	21
O29	●	Georgia Tech NYC	28	7
N5	●	Carnegie Tech	28	7
N12	●	Navy PHIL	13	7
N24	=	at Pittsburgh	0	0
D3	●	at Washington	21	7

1922 6-4-1

S23	●	St. Bonaventure	54	0
S30	●	William & Mary	27	7
O7	●	Gettysburg	20	0
O14	●	Lebanon Valley	32	6
O21	●	Middlebury	33	0
O28	=	Syracuse NYC	0	0
N3		Navy DC	0	14
N11	●	Carnegie Tech	10	0
N18		at Pennsylvania	6	7
N30		at Pittsburgh	0	14
		ROSE BOWL		
J1		USC	3	14

1923 6-2-1

S29	●	Lebanon Valley	58	0
O6	●	North Carolina St.	16	0
O13	●	Gettysburg	20	0
O20	●	Navy	21	3
O27	=	West Virginia BRNX	13	13
N3		at Syracuse	0	10
N10	●	Georgia Tech	7	0
N17	●	at Pennsylvania	21	0
N29		at Pittsburgh	3	20

1924 6-3-1

S27	●	Lebanon Valley	47	3
O4	●	North Carolina St.	51	6
O11	●	Gettysburg	26	0
O18		at Georgia Tech	13	15
O25		Syracuse	6	10
N1	●	at Navy	6	0
N8	●	Carnegie Tech	22	7
N15	=	at Pennsylvania	0	0
N22	●	Marietta	28	0
N27		at Pittsburgh	3	24

1925 4-4-1

S26	●	Lebanon Valley	14	0
O3	●	Franklin & Marshall	13	0
O10		Georgia Tech BRNX	7	16
O17	●	Marietta	13	0
O24	●	Michigan State	13	6
O31		at Syracuse	0	7
N7	=	Notre Dame	0	0
N14		at West Virginia	0	14
N26		at Pittsburgh	7	23

1926 5-4-0

S25	●	Susquehanna	82	0
O2	●	Lebanon Valley	35	0
O9	●	Marietta	48	6
O16		at Notre Dame	0	28
O23		Syracuse	0	10
O30	●	George Washington	20	12
N6		at Pennsylvania	0	3
N13	●	Bucknell	9	0
N25		at Pittsburgh	6	24

1927 6-2-1

S24	●	Lebanon Valley	27	0
O1	●	Gettysburg	34	13
O8		Bucknell	7	13
O15	●	at Pennsylvania	20	0
O22	●	at Syracuse	9	6
O29	●	Lafayette	40	6
N5	●	George Washington	13	0
N12	=	NYU	13	13
N24		at Pittsburgh	0	30

1928 3-5-1

S29	●	Lebanon Valley	25	0
O6	●	Gettysburg	12	0
O12		Bucknell	0	6
O20		at Pennsylvania	0	14
O26	=	Syracuse	6	6
N3		Notre Dame PHIL	0	9
N9	●	George Washington	50	0
N16		at Lafayette	0	7
N29		at Pittsburgh	0	26

1929 6-3-0

S28	●	Niagara	16	0
O5	●	Lebanon Valley	15	0
O12	●	Marshall	26	7
O19		NYU BRNX	0	7
O26	●	Lafayette	6	3
N2	●	at Syracuse	6	4
N9	●	at Pennsylvania	19	7
N16		Bucknell	6	27
N28		at Pittsburgh	7	20

BOB HIGGINS
1930-48 (.607) 91-57-11

1930 3-4-2

S27	●	Niagara	31	14
O4	●	Lebanon Valley	27	0
O11	●	Marshall	65	0
O18	=	at Lafayette	0	0
O25		Colgate	0	40
N1		at Bucknell	7	19
N8	=	Syracuse	0	0
N15		at Iowa	0	19
N26		at Pittsburgh	12	19

1931 2-8-0

S26		Waynesburg	0	7
O3	●	Lebanon Valley	19	6
O10		at Temple	0	12
O17		Dickinson	6	10
O24		at Syracuse	0	7
O31		Pittsburgh	6	41
N8		Colgate	7	32
N14		at Lafayette	0	33
N21		at West Virginia	0	19
N28	●	Lehigh PHIL	31	0

1932 2-5-0

O1	●	Lebanon Valley	27	0
O8		Waynesburg	6	7
O15		at Harvard	13	46
O22		Syracuse	6	12 *
O29		at Colgate	0	31
N3	●	Sewanee	18	6
N12		at Temple	12	13

1933 3-3-1

O7	●	Lebanon Valley	32	6
O14		Muhlenburg	0	3
O21	●	Lehigh	33	0
O28		at Columbia	0	33
N4		at Syracuse	6	12
N11	●	Johns Hopkins	40	6
N18	=	at Pennsylvania	6	6

1934 4-4-0

O6	●	Lebanon Valley	13	0
O13	●	Gettysburg	32	6
O20	●	at Lehigh	31	0
O27		at Columbia	7	14
N3		Syracuse	0	16
N10		at Pennsylvania	0	3
N17	●	Lafayette	25	6
N24		Bucknell	7	13

1935 4-4-0

O5	●	Lebanon Valley	12	6
O12	●	Western Maryland	2	0
O19	●	Lehigh	26	0
O26		at Pittsburgh	0	9
N2		at Syracuse	3	7
N9	●	Villanova	27	13
N16		at Pennsylvania	6	33
N23		at Bucknell	0	2

1936 3-5-0

O3	●	Muhlenburg	45	0
O10		Villanova	0	13
O17		at Lehigh	6	7
O24		at Cornell	7	13
O31	●	Syracuse	18	0
N7		at Pittsburgh	7	34
N14		at Pennsylvania	12	19
N21	●	Bucknell	14	0

1937 5-3-0

S25		at Cornell	19	26
O2	●	Gettysburg	32	6
O9	●	Bucknell	30	14
O16	●	Lehigh	14	7
O30		at Syracuse	13	19
N6	●	at Pennsylvania	7	0
N13	●	Maryland	21	14
N20		at Pittsburgh	7	28

1938 3-4-1

O1	●	Maryland	33	0
O8		Bucknell	0	14
O15	●	at Lehigh	59	6
O22		at Cornell	6	21
O29	●	Syracuse	33	6
N5		Lafayette	0	7
N12	=	at Pennsylvania	7	7
N19		at Pittsburgh	0	26

1939 5-1-2

O7	●	Bucknell	13	3
O14	●	Lehigh	49	7
O21		at Cornell	0	47
O28	=	at Syracuse	6	6
N4	●	Maryland	12	0
N11	●	at Pennsylvania	10	0
N18	=	at Army	14	14
N25	●	Pittsburgh	10	0

1940 6-1-1

O5	●	Bucknell	9	0
O12	●	West Virginia	17	13
O19	●	at Lehigh	34	0
O26	●	at Temple	18	0
N2	●	South Carolina	12	0
N9	=	at Syracuse	13	13
N16	●	NYU	25	0
N23		at Pittsburgh	7	20

1941 7-2-0

O4		Colgate BUF	0	7
O11	●	Bucknell	27	13
O18		at Temple	0	14
O25	●	Lehigh	40	6
O31	●	NYU NYC	42	0
N8	●	Syracuse	34	19
N15	●	West Virginia	7	0
N22	●	at Pittsburgh	31	7
N29	●	at South Carolina	19	12

1942 6-1-1

O3	●	Bucknell	14	7
O10	●	at Lehigh	19	3
O17	=	at Cornell	0	0
O24	●	Colgate	13	10
O31		at West Virginia	0	24
N7	●	Syracuse	18	13
N14	●	at Pennsylvania	13	7
N21	●	Pittsburgh	14	6

1943 5-3-1

S25	●	Bucknell	14	0
O2		at North Carolina	0	19
O9	=	Colgate	0	0
O16		at Navy	6	14
O23	●	at Maryland	45	0
O30	●	West Virginia	32	7
N6		at Cornell	0	13
N13	●	Temple	13	0
N20	●	at Pittsburgh	14	0

1944 6-3-0

S30	●	Muhlenburg	58	13
O7		at Navy	14	55
O14	●	Bucknell	20	6
O21	●	at Colgate	6	0
O28		West Virginia	27	28
N4	●	at Syracuse	41	0
N11	●	at Temple	7	6
N18	●	Maryland	34	19
N25		at Pittsburgh	0	14

1945 5-3-0

S29	●	Muhlenberg	47	7
O6	●	Colgate	27	7
O13		at Navy	0	28
O20	●	at Bucknell	46	7
N3	●	Syracuse	26	0
N10	●	Temple	27	0
N17		at Michigan State	0	33
N24		at Pittsburgh	0	7

1946 6-2-0

O5	●	Bucknell	48	6
O12	●	at Syracuse	9	0
O19		Michigan State	16	19
O26	●	at Colgate	6	2
N2	●	Fordham	68	0
N9	●	Temple	26	0
N16	●	at Navy	12	7
N23		at Pittsburgh	7	14

1947 9-0-1

S20	●	Washington State HER	27	6
O4	●	Bucknell	54	0
O11	●	Fordham NYC	75	0
O18	●	Syracuse	40	0
O25	●	West Virginia	21	14
N1	●	Colgate	46	0
N8	●	at Temple	7	0
N15	●	Navy BALT	20	7
N22	●	at Pittsburgh	29	0
		COTTON BOWL		
J1	=	SMU	13	13

1948 7-1-1

O2	●	Bucknell	35	0
O8	●	at Syracuse	34	14
O16	●	West Virginia	37	7
O23	=	Michigan State	14	14
O30	●	at Colgate	32	13
N6	●	at Pennsylvania	13	0
N13	●	Temple	47	0
N20		at Pittsburgh	0	7
N27	●	Washington State TAC	7	0

JOE BEDENK
1949 (.556) 5-4

1949 5-4-0

S24		Villanova	6	27
O1		at Army	7	42
O8	●	Boston College	32	14
O15	●	Nebraska	22	7
O22		at Michigan State	0	24
O29	●	Syracuse	33	21
N5	●	at West Virginia	34	14
N12	●	at Temple	28	7
N19		at Pittsburgh	0	19

RIP ENGLE
1950-65 (.679) 104-48-4

1950 5-3-1

S30	●	Georgetown	34	14
O7		at Army	7	41
O14		at Syracuse	7	27
O21		at Nebraska	0	19
O28	=	Temple	7	7
N4	●	at Boston College	20	13
N11	●	West Virginia	27	0
N18	●	Rutgers	18	14
N25	●	at Pittsburgh	21	20

1951 5-4-0

S29	●	Boston U.	40	34
O6		Villanova ALL	14	20
O13	●	at Nebraska	15	7
O20		Michigan State	21	32
O27	●	West Virginia	13	7
N3		at Purdue	0	28
N10	●	Syracuse	32	13
N17	●	at Rutgers	13	7
N24		at Pittsburgh	7	13

1952 7-2-1
S20	•	Temple	20	13
S27	=	Purdue	20	20
O4	•	William & Mary	35	23
O11	•	at West Virginia	35	21
O18	•	Nebraska	10	0
O25	•	at Michigan State	7	34
N1	•	at Pennsylvania	14	7
N8	•	at Syracuse	7	25
N15	•	Rutgers	7	6
N22	•	at Pittsburgh	17	0

1953 6-3-0
S26	•	at Wisconsin	0	20
O3	•	at Pennsylvania	7	13
O10	•	at Boston U.	35	13
O17	•	Syracuse	20	14
O24	•	TCU	27	21
O31	•	West Virginia	19	20
N7	•	Fordham	28	21
N14	•	at Rutgers	54	26
N21	•	at Pittsburgh	17	0

1954 7-2-0
S25	•	at Illinois	14	12
O2	•	at Syracuse	13	0
O9	•	Virginia	34	7
O16	•	West Virginia	14	19
O23	•	at TCU	7	20
O30	•	at Pennsylvania	35	13
N6	•	Holy Cross	39	7
N13	•	Rutgers	37	14
N20	•	at Pittsburgh	13	0

1955 5-4-0
S24	•	Boston U.	35	0
O1	•	at Army	6	35
O8	•	Virginia RICH	26	7
O15	•	Navy	14	34
O22	•	at West Virginia	7	21
O29	•	at Pennsylvania	20	0
N5	•	Syracuse	21	20
N12	•	at Rutgers	34	13
N19	•	Pittsburgh	0	20

1956 6-2-1
S29	•	at Pennsylvania	34	0
O6	•	at Army	7	14
O13	•	Holy Cross	43	0
O20	•	at Ohio State	7	6
O27	•	West Virginia	16	6
N3	•	at Syracuse	9	13
N10	•	Boston U.	40	7
N17	•	North Carolina St.	14	7
N24	=	at Pittsburgh	7	7

1957 6-3-0
S28	•	at Pennsylvania	19	14
O5	•	Army	13	27
O12	•	William & Mary	21	13
O19	•	Vanderbilt	20	32
O26	•	at Syracuse	20	12
N2	•	West Virginia	27	6
N9	•	at Marquette	20	7
N16	•	at Holy Cross	14	10
N23	•	at Pittsburgh	13	14

1958 6-3-1
S20	•	at Nebraska	7	14
S27	•	at Pennsylvania	43	0
O4	•	at Army	0	26
O11	•	Marquette	40	8
O18	•	at Boston U.	34	0
O25	•	Syracuse	6	14
N1	•	Furman	36	0
N8	=	at West Virginia	14	14
N15	•	Holy Cross	32	0
N27	•	at Pittsburgh	25	21

1959 9-2-0
S19	•	at Missouri	19	8
S26	•	VMI	21	0
O3	•	Colgate	58	20
O10	•	at Army	17	11
O17	•	Boston U.	21	12
O24	•	Illinois CLEV	20	9
O31	•	at West Virginia	28	10
N7	•	Syracuse	18	20
N14	•	Holy Cross	46	0
N21	•	at Pittsburgh	7	22
LIBERTY BOWL				
D19	•	Alabama	7	0

1960 7-3-0
S17	•	Boston U.	20	0
O1	•	Missouri	8	21
O8	•	at Army	27	16
O15	•	at Syracuse	15	21
O22	•	at Illinois	8	10
O29	•	West Virginia	34	13
N5	•	Maryland	28	9
N12	•	at Holy Cross	33	8
N19	•	at Pittsburgh	14	3
LIBERTY BOWL				
D17	•	Oregon	41	12

1961 8-3-0
S23	•	Navy	20	10
S29	•	at Miami, Fla.	8	25
O6	•	at Boston U.	32	0
O14	•	Army	6	10
O21	•	Syracuse	14	0
O28	•	California	33	16
N4	•	at Maryland	17	21
N11	•	at West Virginia	20	6
N18	•	Holy Cross	34	14
N25	•	at Pittsburgh	47	26
GATOR BOWL				
D30	•	Georgia Tech	30	15

1962 9-2-0
S22	•	Navy	41	7
S29	•	Air Force	20	6
O6	•	at Rice	18	7
O13	•	at Army	6	9
O20	•	Syracuse	20	19
O27	•	at California	23	21
N3	•	Maryland	23	7
N10	•	West Virginia	34	6
N17	•	at Holy Cross	48	20
N24	•	at Pittsburgh	16	0
GATOR BOWL				
D29	•	Florida	7	17

1963 7-3-0
S21	•	Oregon PORT	17	7
S28	•	UCLA	17	14
O5	•	Rice	28	7
O12	•	Army	7	10
O19	•	at Syracuse	0	9
O26	•	West Virginia	20	9
N2	•	at Maryland	17	15
N9	•	at Ohio State	10	7
N16	•	Holy Cross	28	14
D7	•	at Pittsburgh	21	22

1964 6-4-0
S19	•	Navy	8	21
S26	•	at UCLA	14	21
O3	•	Oregon	14	22
O10	•	at Army	6	2
O17	•	Syracuse	14	21
O24	•	at West Virginia	37	8
O31	•	Maryland	17	9
N7	•	at Ohio State	27	0
N14	•	at Houston	24	7
N21	•	at Pittsburgh	28	0

1965 5-5-0
S25	•	Michigan State	0	23
O2	•	UCLA	22	24
O9	•	at Boston College	17	0
O16	•	at Syracuse	21	28
O23	•	West Virginia	44	6
O30	•	at California	17	21
N6	•	Kent	21	6
N13	•	Navy	14	6
N20	•	at Pittsburgh	27	30
D4	•	at Maryland	19	7

JOE PATERNO
1966-Present (.750) 363-121-3

1966 5-5-0
S17	•	Maryland	15	7
S24	•	at Michigan State	8	42
O1	•	at Army	0	11
O8	•	Boston College	30	21
O15	•	at UCLA	11	49
O22	•	at West Virginia	38	6
O29	•	California	33	15
N5	•	Syracuse	10	12
N12	•	at Georgia Tech	0	21
N19	•	at Pittsburgh	48	24

1967 8-2-1
S23	•	at Navy	22	23
S29	•	at Miami, Fla.	17	8
O7	•	UCLA	15	17
O14	•	at Boston College	50	28
O21	•	West Virginia	21	14
O28	•	at Syracuse	29	20
N4	•	at Maryland	38	3
N11	•	North Carolina St.	13	8
N18	•	Ohio U.	35	14
N25	•	Pittsburgh	42	6
GATOR BOWL				
D30	=	Florida State	17	17

1968 11-0-0
S21	•	Navy	31	6
S28	•	Kansas State	25	9
O5	•	at West Virginia	31	20
O12	•	at UCLA	21	6
O26	•	at Boston College	29	0
N2	•	Army	28	24
N9	•	Miami, Fla.	22	7
N16	•	at Maryland	57	13
N23	•	at Pittsburgh	65	9
D7	•	Syracuse	30	12
ORANGE BOWL				
J1	•	Kansas	15	14

1969 11-0-0
S20	•	at Navy	45	22
S27	•	Colorado	27	3
O4	•	at Kansas State	17	14
O11	•	West Virginia	20	0
O18	•	at Syracuse	15	14
O25	•	Ohio U.	42	3
N1	•	Boston College	38	16
N15	•	Maryland	48	0
N22	•	at Pittsburgh	27	7
N29	•	at North Carolina St.	33	8
ORANGE BOWL				
J1	•	Missouri	10	3

1970 7-3-0
S19	•	Navy	55	7
S26	•	at Colorado	13	41
O3	•	at Wisconsin	16	29
O10	•	at Boston College	28	3
O17	•	Syracuse	7	24
O24	•	at Army	38	14
O31	•	West Virginia	42	8
N7	•	at Maryland	34	0
N14	•	Ohio U.	32	22
N21	•	Pittsburgh	35	15

1971 11-1-0
S18	•	at Navy	56	3
S25	•	at Iowa	44	14
O2	•	Air Force	16	14
O9	•	Army	42	0
O16	•	at Syracuse	31	0
O23	•	TCU	66	14
O30	•	at West Virginia	35	7
N6	•	Maryland	63	27
N13	•	North Carolina St.	35	3
N20	•	at Pittsburgh	55	18
D4	•	at Tennessee	11	31
COTTON BOWL				
J1	•	Texas	30	6

1972 10-2-0
S16	•	at Tennessee	21	28
S23	•	Navy	21	10
S30	•	Iowa	14	10
O7	•	at Illinois	35	17
O14	•	at Army	45	0
O21	•	Syracuse	17	0
O28	•	at West Virginia	28	19
N4	•	Maryland	46	16
N11	•	North Carolina St.	37	22
N18	•	at Boston College	45	26
N25	•	Pittsburgh	49	27
SUGAR BOWL				
D31	•	Oklahoma	0	14

1973 12-0-0
S15	•	at Stanford	20	6
S22	•	at Navy	39	0
S29	•	Iowa	27	8
O6	•	at Air Force	19	9
O13	•	Army	54	3
O20	•	at Syracuse	49	6
O27	•	West Virginia	62	14
N3	•	at Maryland	42	22
N10	•	North Carolina St.	35	29
N17	•	Ohio U.	49	10
N24	•	Pittsburgh	35	13
ORANGE BOWL				
J1	•	LSU	16	9

1974 10-2-0
S14	•	Stanford	24	20
S21	•	Navy	6	7
S28	•	at Iowa	27	0
O5	•	at Army	21	14
O12	•	Wake Forest	55	0
O19	•	Syracuse	30	14
O26	•	at West Virginia	21	12
N2	•	Maryland	24	17
N9	•	at North Carolina St.	7	12
N16	•	Ohio U.	35	16
N28	•	at Pittsburgh	31	10
COTTON BOWL				
J1	•	Baylor	41	20

1975 9-3-0
S6	•	Temple PHIL	26	25
S13	•	Stanford	34	14
S20	•	at Ohio State	9	17
S27	•	at Iowa	30	10
O4	•	Kentucky	10	3
O11	•	West Virginia	39	0
O18	•	at Syracuse	19	7
O25	•	Army	31	0
N1	•	at Maryland	15	13
N8	•	North Carolina St.	14	15
N22	•	at Pittsburgh	7	6
SUGAR BOWL				
D31	•	Alabama	6	13

1976 7-5-0
S11	•	Stanford	15	12
S18	•	Ohio State	7	12
S25	•	Iowa	6	7
O2	•	at Kentucky	6	22
O9	•	Army	38	16
O16	•	Syracuse	27	3
O23	•	at West Virginia	33	0
O30	•	at Temple	31	30
N6	•	North Carolina St.	41	20
N13	•	at Miami, Fla.	21	7
N26	•	at Pittsburgh	7	24
GATOR BOWL				
D27	•	Notre Dame	9	20

1977 11-1-0
S2	•	Rutgers ERUT	45	7
S17	•	Houston	31	14
S24	•	Maryland	27	9
O1	•	Kentucky	20	24
O8	•	Utah State	16	7
O15	•	at Syracuse	31	24
O22	•	West Virginia	49	28
O29	•	Miami, Fla.	49	7
N5	•	at North Carolina St.	21	17
N12	•	Temple	44	7
N19	•	at Pittsburgh	15	13
FIESTA BOWL				
D25	•	Arizona State	42	30

1978 11-1-0
S1	•	at Temple	10	7
S9	•	Rutgers	26	10
S16	•	at Ohio State	19	0
S23	•	SMU	26	21
S30	•	TCU	58	0
O7	•	at Kentucky	30	0
O21	•	Syracuse	45	15
O28	•	at West Virginia	49	21
N4	•	Maryland	27	3
N11	•	North Carolina St.	19	10
N25	•	Pittsburgh	17	10
SUGAR BOWL				
J1	•	Alabama	7	14

1979 8-4-0
S15	•	Rutgers	45	10
S22	•	Texas A&M	14	27
S29	•	at Nebraska	17	42
O6	•	at Maryland	27	7
O13	•	Army	24	3
O20	•	Syracuse ERUT	35	7
O27	•	West Virginia	31	6
N3	•	Miami, Fla.	10	26
N10	•	at North Carolina St.	9	7
N17	•	Temple	22	7
D1	•	at Pittsburgh	14	29
LIBERTY BOWL				
D22	•	Tulane	9	6

BIG TEN TEAMS

1980 — 10-2-0

S6	•	Colgate	54	10
S20	•	at Texas A&M	25	9
S27		Nebraska	7	21
O4	•	at Missouri	29	21
O11	•	at Maryland	24	10
O18	•	Syracuse	24	7
O25	•	at West Virginia	20	15
N1	•	Miami, Fla.	27	12
N8	•	North Carolina St.	21	13
N15	•	at Temple	50	7
N29		Pittsburgh	9	14
FIESTA BOWL				
D26	•	Ohio State	31	19

1981 — 10-2-0

S12	•	Cincinnati	52	0
S26	•	at Nebraska	30	24
O3	•	Temple	30	0
O10	•	Boston College	38	7
O17	•	at Syracuse	41	16
O24	•	West Virginia	30	7
O31	•	at Miami, Fla.	14	17
N7	•	at North Carolina St.	22	15
N14	•	Alabama	16	31
N21	•	Notre Dame	24	21
N28	•	at Pittsburgh	48	14
FIESTA BOWL				
J1	•	USC	26	10

1982 — 11-1-0

S4	•	Temple	31	14
S11	•	Maryland	39	31
S18	•	Rutgers	49	14
S25	•	Nebraska	27	24
O9	•	Alabama *Birm*	21	42
O16	•	Syracuse	28	7
O23	•	at West Virginia	24	0
O30	•	at Boston College	52	17
N6	•	North Carolina St.	54	0
N13	•	at Notre Dame	24	14
N27	•	Pittsburgh	19	10
SUGAR BOWL				
J1	•	Georgia	27	23

1983 — 8-4-1

A29	•	Nebraska *ERut*	6	44
S10	•	Cincinnati	3	14
S17	•	Iowa	34	42
S24	•	Temple *Phil*	23	18
O1	•	Rutgers *ERut*	36	25
O8	•	Alabama	34	28
O15	=	at Syracuse	17	6
O22	•	West Virginia	41	23
O29	•	Boston College *Fox*	17	27
N5	•	Brown	38	21
N12	•	Notre Dame	34	30
N19	=	at Pittsburgh	24	24
ALOHA BOWL				
D26	•	Washington	13	10

1984 — 6-5-0

S8	•	Rutgers	15	12
S15	•	at Iowa	20	17
S22	•	William & Mary	56	18
S29	•	Texas *ERut*	3	28
O6	•	Maryland	25	24
O13	•	at Alabama	0	6
O20	•	Syracuse	21	3
O27	•	at West Virginia	14	17
N3	•	Boston College	37	30
N17	•	at Notre Dame	7	44
N24	•	Pittsburgh	11	31

1985 — 11-1-0

S7	•	at Maryland	20	18
S14	•	Temple	27	25
S21	•	East Carolina	17	10
S28	•	Rutgers *ERut*	17	10
O12	•	Alabama	19	17
O19	•	at Syracuse	24	20
O26	•	West Virginia	27	0
N2	•	Boston College	16	12
N9	•	at Cincinnati	31	10
N16	•	Notre Dame	36	6
N23	•	at Pittsburgh	31	0
ORANGE BOWL				
J1	•	Oklahoma	10	25

1986 — 12-0-0

S6	•	Temple	45	15
S20	•	Boston College *Fox*	26	14
S27	•	East Carolina	42	17
O4	•	Rutgers	31	6
O11	•	Cincinnati	23	17
O18	•	Syracuse	42	3
O25	•	at Alabama	23	3
N1	•	at West Virginia	19	0
N8	•	Maryland	17	15
N15	•	at Notre Dame	24	19
N22	•	Pittsburgh	34	14
FIESTA BOWL				
J2	•	Miami, Fla.	14	10

1987 — 8-4-0

S5	•	Bowling Green	45	19
S12	•	Alabama	13	24
S19	•	Cincinnati	41	0
S26	•	Boston College *Fox*	27	17
O3	•	Temple	27	13
O10	•	Rutgers	35	21
O17	•	at Syracuse	21	48
O31	•	West Virginia	25	21
N7	•	Maryland *Balt*	21	16
N14	•	at Pittsburgh	0	10
N21	•	Notre Dame	21	20
CITRUS BOWL				
J1	•	Clemson	10	35

1988 — 5-6-0

S10	•	at Virginia	42	14
S17	•	Boston College	23	20
S24	•	Rutgers	16	21
O1	•	Temple *Phil*	45	9
O8	•	Cincinnati	35	9
O15	•	Syracuse	10	24
O22	•	Alabama *Birm*	3	8
O29	•	at West Virginia	30	51
N5	•	Maryland	17	10
N12	•	Pittsburgh	7	14
N19	•	at Notre Dame	3	21

1989 — 8-3-1

S9		Virginia	6	14
S16	•	Temple	42	3
S23	•	Boston College	7	3
S30	•	at Texas	16	12
O7	•	Rutgers *ERut*	17	0
O14	•	at Syracuse	34	12
O28	•	Alabama	16	17
N4	•	West Virginia	19	9
N11	=	Maryland *Balt*	13	13
N18	•	Notre Dame	23	34
N25	•	at Pittsburgh	16	13
HOLIDAY BOWL				
D29	•	Brigham Young	50	39

1990 — 9-3-0

S8		Texas	13	17
S15		at USC	14	19
S22	•	Rutgers	28	0
O6	•	Temple	48	10
O13	•	Syracuse	27	21
O20	•	at Boston College	40	21
O27	•	at Alabama	9	0
N3	•	at West Virginia	31	19
N10	•	Maryland	24	10
N17	•	at Notre Dame	24	21
N24	•	Pittsburgh	22	17
BLOCKBUSTER BOWL				
D28	•	Florida State	17	24

1991 — 11-2-0

A28	•	Georgia Tech *ERut*	34	22
S7	•	Cincinnati	81	0
S14	•	at USC	10	21
S21	•	Brigham Young	33	7
S28	•	Boston College	28	21
O5	•	Temple *Phil*	24	7
O12	•	at Miami, Fla.	20	26
O19	•	Rutgers	37	17
O26	•	West Virginia	51	6
N9	•	Maryland *Balt*	47	7
N16	•	Notre Dame	35	13
N30	•	at Pittsburgh	32	20
FIESTA BOWL				
J1	•	Tennessee	42	17

1992 — 7-5-0

S5	•	at Cincinnati	24	20
S12	•	Temple	49	8
S19	•	Eastern Michigan	52	7
S26	•	Maryland	49	13
O3	•	Rutgers *ERut*	38	24
O10	•	Miami, Fla.	14	17
O17	•	Boston College	32	35
O24	•	at West Virginia	40	26
O31	•	at Brigham Young	17	30
N14	•	at Notre Dame	16	17
N21	•	Pittsburgh	57	13
BLOCKBUSTER BOWL				
J1	•	Stanford	3	24

1993-Present
Big 10

1993 — 10-2-0 (6-2-0)

S4	•	Minnesota	38	20
S11	•	USC	21	20
S18	•	at Iowa	31	0
S25	•	Rutgers	31	7
O2	•	at Maryland	70	7
O16	•	Michigan	13	21
O30	•	at Ohio State	6	24
N6	•	Indiana	38	31
N13	•	Illinois	28	14
N20	•	at Northwestern	43	21
N27	•	at Michigan State	38	37
CITRUS BOWL				
J1	•	Tennessee	31	13

1994 — 12-0-0 (8-0-0)

S3	•	at Minnesota	56	3
S10	•	USC	38	14
S17	•	Iowa	61	21
S24	•	Rutgers	55	27
O1	•	at Temple	48	21
O15	•	at Michigan	31	24
O29	•	Ohio State	63	14
N5	•	at Indiana	35	29
N12	•	at Illinois	35	31
N19	•	Northwestern	45	17
N26	•	Michigan State	59	31
ROSE BOWL				
J2	•	Oregon	38	20

1995 — 9-3-0 (5-3-0)

S9	•	Texas Tech	24	23
S16	•	Temple	66	14
S23	•	Rutgers *ERut*	59	34
S30	•	Wisconsin	9	17
O7	•	Ohio State	25	28
O14	•	at Purdue	26	23
O21	•	at Iowa	41	27
O28	•	Indiana	45	21
N4	•	at Northwestern	10	21
N18	•	Michigan	27	17
N25	•	at Michigan State	24	20
HALL OF FAME BOWL				
J1	•	Auburn	43	14

1996 — 11-2 (6-2)

A25	•	USC *ERut*	24	7
S7	•	Louisville	24	7
S14	•	Northern Illinois	49	0
S21	•	Temple *ERut*	41	0
S28	•	at Wisconsin	23	20
O5	•	at Ohio State	7	38
O12	•	Purdue	31	14
O19	•	Iowa	20	21
O26	•	at Indiana	48	26
N2	•	Northwestern	34	9
N16	•	at Michigan	29	17
N23	•	Michigan State	32	29
FIESTA BOWL				
J1	•	Texas	38	15

1997 — 9-3 (6-2)

S6	•	Pittsburgh	34	17
S13	•	Temple	52	10
S20	•	at Louisville	57	21
O4	•	at Illinois	41	6
O11	•	Ohio State	31	27
O18	•	Minnesota	16	15
N1	•	at Northwestern	30	27
N8	•	Michigan	8	34
N15	•	at Purdue	42	17
N22	•	Wisconsin	35	10
N29	•	at Michigan State	14	49
CITRUS BOWL				
J1	•	Florida	6	21

1998 — 9-3 (5-3)

S5	•	So. Mississippi	34	6
S12	•	Bowling Green	48	3
S19	•	at Pittsburgh	20	13
O3	•	at Ohio State	9	28
O10	•	at Minnesota	27	17
O17	•	Purdue	31	13
O31	•	Illinois	27	0
N7	•	at Michigan	0	27
N14	•	Northwestern	41	10
N21	•	at Wisconsin	3	24
N28	•	Michigan State	51	28
OUTBACK BOWL				
J1	•	Kentucky	26	14

1999 — 10-3 (5-3)

A28	•	Arizona	41	7
S4	•	Akron	70	24
S11	•	Pittsburgh	20	17
S18	•	at Miami, Fla.	27	23
S25	•	Indiana	45	24
O9	•	at Iowa	31	7
O16	•	Ohio State	23	10
O23	•	at Purdue	31	25
O30	•	at Illinois	27	7
N6	•	Minnesota	23	24
N13	•	Michigan	27	31
N20	•	at Michigan State	28	35
ALAMO BOWL				
D28	•	Texas A&M	24	0

2000 — 5-7 (4-4)

A27	•	USC *ERut*	5	29
S2	•	Toledo	6	24
S9	•	Louisiana Tech	67	7
S16	•	at Pittsburgh	0	12
S23	•	at Ohio State	6	45
S30	•	Purdue	22	20
O7	•	at Minnesota	16	25
O21	•	Illinois	39	25
O28	•	Indiana *Ind*	27	24
N4	•	Iowa	23	26
N11	•	at Michigan	11	33
N18	•	Michigan State	42	23

2001 — 5-6 (4-4)

S1	•	Miami, Fla.	7	33
S22	•	Wisconsin	6	18
S29	•	at Iowa	18	24
O6	•	Michigan	0	20
O20	•	at Northwestern	38	35
O27	•	Ohio State	29	27
N3	•	So. Mississippi	38	20
N10	•	at Illinois	28	33
N17	•	Indiana	28	14
N24	•	at Michigan State	42	37
D1	•	at Virginia	14	20

2002 — 9-4 (5-3)

A31	•	Central Florida	27	24
S14	•	Nebraska	40	7
S21	•	Louisiana Tech	49	17
S28	•	Iowa	35	42
O5	•	at Wisconsin	34	31
O12	•	at Michigan	24	27
O19	•	Northwestern	49	0
O26	•	at Ohio State	7	13
N2	•	Illinois	18	7
N9	•	Virginia	35	14
N16	•	at Indiana	58	25
N23	•	Michigan State	61	7
CAPITAL ONE BOWL				
J1	•	Auburn	9	13

2003 — 3-9 (1-7)

A30	•	Temple	23	10
S6		Boston College	14	27
S13	•	at Nebraska	10	18
S20	•	Kent State	32	10
S27		Minnesota	14	20
O4		Wisconsin	23	30
O11	•	at Purdue	14	28
O25	•	at Iowa	14	26
N1		Ohio State	20	21
N8	•	at Northwestern	7	17
N15	•	Indiana	52	7
N22	•	at Michigan State	10	41

2004 — 4-7 (2-6)

S4	•	Akron	48	10
S11		at Boston College	7	21
S18	•	Central Florida	37	13
S25		at Wisconsin	3	16
O2		at Minnesota	7	16
O9		Purdue	13	20
O23		Iowa	4	6
O30		at Ohio State	10	21
N6		Northwestern	7	14
N13		at Indiana	22	18
N20		Michigan State	37	13

2005   11-1   (7-1)

S3	●	South Florida	23	13
S10	●	Cincinnati	42	24
S17	●	Central Michigan	40	3
S24	● |	at Northwestern	34	29
O1	● |	Minnesota	44	14
O8	● |	Ohio State	17	10
O15	|	at Michigan	25	27
O22	● |	at Illinois	63	10
O29	● |	Purdue	33	15
N5	● |	Wisconsin	35	14
N19	● |	at Michigan State	31	22
		ORANGE BOWL		
J3	●	Florida State	26	23

2006   9-4   (5-3)

S2	●	Akron	34	16
S9		at Notre Dame	17	41
S16	●	Youngstown St.	37	3
S23	|	at Ohio State	6	28
S30	● |	Northwestern	33	7
O7	● |	at Minnesota	28	27
O14	|	Michigan	10	17
O21	● |	Illinois	26	12
O28	● |	at Purdue	12	0
N4	|	at Wisconsin	3	13
N11	●	Temple	47	0
N18	● |	Michigan State	17	13
		OUTBACK BOWL		
J1	●	Tennessee	20	10

BIG TEN TEAMS

Neutral Site key: *ALL* Allentown, Pa. / *BALT* Baltimore, Md. / *BEL* Bellefonte, Pa. / *BIRM* Birmingham, Ala. / *BRNX* Bronx. N.Y. / *BUF* Buffalo, N.Y. / *CLEV* Cleveland, Ohio / *ERUT* East Rutherford, N.J. / *FOX* Foxboro, Mass. / *HARR* Harrisburg, Pa. / *HER* Hershey, Pa. / *IND* Indianapolis, Ind. / *NYC* New York, N.Y. / *PHIL* Philadelphia, Pa. / *PIT* Pittsburgh, Pa. / *PORT* Portland, Ore. / *RICH* Richmond, Va. / *SUN* Sunbury, Pa. / *TAC* Tacoma, Wash. / *DC* Washington, D.C. / *WLM* Williamsport, Pa. / *WB* Wilkes-Barre, Pa.

ƒ **Forfeit** † **Game Later Forfieted** # **Disputed Victor** * **Disputed Score** ‖ **Designated Conference Game** |2 **Counted Twice in Conference Standings**

PENN STATE RECORD BOOK

SINGLE-GAME RECORDS

RUSHING YARDS

RANK	PLAYER	DATE	OPPONENT	ATT	AVG	YDS
1	Larry Johnson	Nov. 16, 2002	Indiana	28	11.7	327
2	Larry Johnson	Nov. 2, 2002	Illinois	31	9.0	279
	Larry Johnson	Nov. 23, 2002	Michigan State	19	14.7	279
4	Larry Johnson	Oct. 19, 2002	Northwestern	23	11.2	257
5	Curt Warner	Oct. 17, 1981	Syracuse	26	9.8	256

PASSING YARDS

RANK	PLAYER	DATE	OPPONENT	ATT	COMP	YDS
1	Zach Mills	Sept. 28, 2002	Iowa	44	23	399
2	Michael Robinson	Oct. 4, 2003	Wisconsin	53	22	379
3	Mike McQueary	Sept. 6, 1997	Pittsburgh	36	21	366
4	Todd Blackledge	Oct. 31, 1981	Miami, Fla.	41	26	358
5	Kerry Collins	Nov. 27, 1993	Michigan State	42	23	352

RECEIVING YARDS

RANK	PLAYER	DATE	OPPONENT	REC	AVG	YDS
1	Dean Butler	Sept. 30, 2006	Northwestern	11	19.6	216
2	O.J.McDuffie	Oct. 17, 1992	Boston College	11	19.3	212
3	Bobby Engram	Oct. 14, 1995	Purdue	9	22.6	203
4	Bobby Engram	Sept. 24, 1994	Rutgers	8	26.0	200
5	Chafie Fields	Sept. 18, 1999	Miami, Fla.	5	35.4	177

POINTS

RANK	PLAYER	DATE	OPPONENT	TOT
1	Harry Robb	Oct. 6, 1917	Gettyburg	36
2	Carl Forkom	Oct. 24, 1903	Pittsburg	33
3	Charles Atherton	Oct. 13, 1894	Gettysburg	32
4 players tied at 30				

FIELD GOALS

RANK	PLAYER	DATE	OPPONENT	TOT
1	Brian Franco	Sept. 26, 1981	Nebraska	5
	Massimo Manca	Nov. 16, 1985	Notre Dame	5
	Travis Forney	Nov. 28, 1998	Michigan State	5
16 players tied at 4				

TACKLES

RANK	PLAYER	DATE	OPPONENT	TOT
1	Greg Buttle	Oct. 26, 1974	West Virginia	24
	Bill Banks	Nov. 5, 1977	N. Carolina State	24
3	Greg Buttle	Nov. 9, 1974	N. Carolina State	23
4	Ron Crosby	Nov. 16, 1974	Ohio U	22
	Paul Posluszny	Sept. 24, 2005	Northwestern	22

INTERCEPTIONS

RANK	PLAYER	DATE	OPPONENT	TOT
1	Mike Smith	Nov. 14, 1970	Ohio U	4

RETIRED NUMBERS

Penn State has no retired numbers

SINGLE-SEASON RECORDS

RUSHING YARDS

RANK	PLAYER	SEASON	G	ATT	YDS
1	Larry Johnson	2002	13	271	2,087
2	Lydell Mitchell	1971	NA	254	1,567
3	Ki-Jana Carter	1994	NA	198	1,539
4	John Cappelletti	1973	NA	286	1,522
5	Blair Thomas	1987	NA	268	1,414

PASSING YARDS

RANK	PLAYER	SEASON	G	ATT	COMP	PCT	YDS
1	Kerry Collins	1994	NA	264	176	66.7	2,679
2	Tony Sacca	1991	NA	292	169	57.9	2,488
3	Anthony Morelli	2006	13	386	208	53.9	2,424
4	Zach Mills	2002	13	333	188	56.5	2,417
5	Michael Robinson	2005	12	311	162	52.1	2,350

RECEIVING YARDS

RANK	PLAYER	SEASON	REC	AVG	YDS
1	Bobby Engram	1995	63	17.2	1,084
2	Bobby Engram	1994	52	19.8	1,029
3	O.J. McDuffie	1992	63	15.5	977
4	Freddie Scott	1994	47	20.7	973
5	Bobby Engram	1993	48	18.2	873

SCORING

RANK	PLAYER	SEASON	TD	FG	PAT	P2	TOT
1	Lydell Mitchell	1971	29	0	0	0	174
2	Larry Johnson	2002	23	0	0	1	140
3	Ki-Jana Carter	1994	23	0	0	0	138
4	Curtis Enis	1997	20	0	0	1	122

TOUCHDOWNS

RANK	PLAYER	SEASON	TOT
1	Lydell Mitchell	1971	29
2	Ki-Jana Carter	1994	23
	Larry Johnson	2002	23
4	Curtis Enis	1997	20

TACKLES

RANK	PLAYER	SEASON	TOT
1	Greg Buttle	1974	165
2	Shawn Mayer	2002	144
3	Greg Buttle	1975	140
4	Andre Collins	1989	130
5	Ed O'Neil	1972	126
	Brian Gelzheiser	1994	126

INTERCEPTIONS

RANK	PLAYER	SEASON	YDS	TOT
1	Neal Smith	1969	78	10
	Pete Harris	1978	155	10
3	Don Eyer	1952	67	8
	Jack Sherry	1952	101	8
	Neal Smith	1968	74	8

PUNTING

RANK	PLAYER	SEASON	PUNTS	YDS	AVG
1	Ralph Giacomarro	1981	55	2,395	43.6
2	Ralph Giacomarro	1980	52	2,252	43.3
3	John Bruno Jr.	1985	60	2,575	42.9
4	George Reynolds	1983	68	2,899	42.6
5	Pat Pidgeon	1997	55	2,391	42.6

PUNT RETURNS

RANK	PLAYER	SEASON	RET	YDS	AVG
1	Gary Hayman	1973	23	442	19.2
2	Lenny Moore	1953	13	228	17.5
3	Shorty Miller	1912	35	396	17.0
4	Ron Younker	1954	12	193	16.1

KICKOFF RETURNS

RANK	PLAYER	SEASON	RET	YDS	AVG
1	Curt Warner	1980	10	350	35.0
2	Blair Thomas	1986	12	383	31.9

CAREER RECORDS

RUSHING YARDS

RANK	PLAYER	SEASONS	ATT	AVG	TD	YDS
1	Curt Warner	1979-82	649	5.2	24	3,398
2	Tony Hunt	2003-06	654	5.1	25	3,320
3	Blair Thomas	1985-87, 89	606	5.4	21	3,301
4	Curtis Enis	1995-97	565	5.8	36	3,256
5	D.J. Dozier	1983-86	624	5.2	25	3,227
6	Larry Johnson	1999-2002	460	6.4	26	2,953
7	Lydell Mitchell	1969-71	501	5.9	38	2,934
8	Ki-Jana Carter	1992-94	395	7.2	34	2,829
9	Matt Suhey	1976-79	633	4.5	26	2,818
10	John Cappelletti	1972-73	519	5.1	29	2,639

PASSING YARDS

RANK	PLAYER	SEASONS	ATT	COMP	PCT	INT	TD	YDS
1	Zach Mills	2001-04	1,082	606	56.0	39	41	7,212
2	Tony Sacca	1988-91	824	401	48.7	24	41	5,869
3	Chuck Fusina	1975-78	665	371	55.8	32	37	5,382
4	Kerry Collins	1991-94	657	370	56.3	21	39	5,304
5	Todd Blackledge	1980-82	658	341	51.8	41	41	4,812
6	Wally Richardson	1992, 94-96	692	378	54.6	14	27	4,419
7	Kevin Thompson	1996-99	495	263	53.1	17	19	3,710
8	John Hufnagel	1970-72	408	225	55.1	17	26	3,545
9	Michael Robinson	2002-05	505	248	49.1	21	23	3,531
10	John Shaffer	1983-86	547	262	47.9	24	18	3,469

RECEIVING YARDS

RANK	PLAYER	SEASONS	REC	AVG	TD	YDS
1	Bobby Engram	1991, 93-95	167	18.1	31	3,026
2	Bryant Johnson	1999-2002	110	18.3	10	2,008
3	Kenny Jackson	1980-83	109	18.4	25	2,006
4	O.J. McDuffie	1988-92	125	15.9	16	1,988
5	Joe Jurevicius	1994-97	94	20.1	15	1,894
6	Jack Curry	1965-67	117	15.7	5	1,837
7	Terry Smith	1988-91	108	16.9	15	1,825
8	Tony Johnson	2000-03	107	15.9	11	1,702
9	Freddie Scott	1993-95	93	16.3	11	1,520
10	Chafie Fields	1996-99	88	16.3	8	1,437

SCORING

RANK	PLAYER	SEASONS	TD	FG	PAT	P2	TOT
1	Craig Fayak	1990-93	0	50	132	0	282
2	Brett Comsay	1993-96	0	45	141	0	276
3	Travis Forney	1996-99	0	47	117	0	258
4	Lydell Mitchell	1969-71	41	0	0	0	246
5	Robbie Gould	2001-04	0	39	115	0	232

TOUCHDOWNS

RANK	PLAYER	SEASONS	G	TOT
1	Lydell Mitchell	1969-71	NA	41
2	Curtis Enis	1995-97	NA	38
3	Larry Johnson	1999-2002	48	34
	Ki-Jana Carter	1992-94	NA	34
5	Curt Warner	1979-82	NA	33

TACKLES

RANK	PLAYER	SEASONS	G	TOT
1	Paul Posluszny	2003-06	44	372
2	Greg Buttle	1973-75	NA	343
3	Brian Gelzheiser	1991-94	NA	315
4	Dennis Onkotz	1967-69	NA	287
5	John Skorupan	1970-72	NA	274

INTERCEPTIONS

RANK	PLAYER	SEASONS	YDS	TOT
1	Neal Smith	1967-69	152	19
2	Pete Harris	1977-80	183	15
	Darren Perry	1988-91	299	15
4	Kim Herring	1994-96	106	13
4 players tied at 12				

PUNTING

RANK	PLAYER	SEASONS	PUNTS	YDS	AVG
1	George Reynolds	1981-83	72	3,096	43.0
2	Pat Pidgeon	1996-99	186	7,782	41.8
3	Ralph Giacomarro	1979-82	225	9,402	41.8
4	Jeremy Kapinos	2003-06	251	10,476	41.7
5	John Bruno Jr.	1934-36	204	8,508	41.7

PUNT RETURNS

RANK	PLAYER	SEASON	RET	YDS	AVG
1	Ron Younker	1953-54	16	281	17.6
2	Wally Triplett	1946-48	17	280	16.5
3	Don Jonas	1958-61	17	271	15.9
4	Lenny Moore	1953-55	24	378	15.8
5	Dick Hoak	1958-60	15	229	15.3

KICKOFF RETURNS

RANK	PLAYER	SEASON	RET	YDS	AVG
1	Larry Joe	1946-48	16	473	29.6
2	Curt Warner	1979-82	32	922	28.8
3	Charlie Pittman	1967-69	17	483	28.4
4	Gary Hayman	1972-73	18	484	26.9
5	Blair Thomas	1985-87, 89	25	658	26.3

TEAM RECORDS

LONGEST WINNING STREAK
• 23, Sept. 21, 1968-Sept. 19, 1970
Streak broken vs Colorado, 13-41, Sept. 26, 1970

LONGEST UNDEFEATED STREAK
• 31, Oct. 14, 1967-Sept. 19, 1970
Streak broekn vs Colorado, 13-41, Sept. 26, 1970

MOST CONSECUTIVE WINNING SEASONS
• 26, 1939-64

MOST CONSECUTIVE BOWL APPEARANCES
• 13, 1971-83

MOST POINTS IN A GAME
• 109, vs. Lebanon Valley, Oct. 23, 1920

MOST POINTS ALLOWED IN A GAME
• 106, vs. Lehigh, Nov. 13, 1889

LARGEST MARGIN OF VICTORY
• 102 (109-7), vs. Lebanon Valley, Oct. 23, 1920

LARGEST MARGIN OF DEFEAT
• 106 (0-106), vs. Lehigh, Nov. 13, 1889

LONGEST RUN FROM SCRIMMAGE
• 92 yards, Blair Thomas, vs. Syracuse, Oct. 18, 1986

LONGEST PASS PLAY
• 92 yards, Harold Hess to Bob Higgins, vs. Pittsburgh, Nov. 27, 1919

LONGEST FIELD GOAL
• 55 yards, (tie): Chris Bahr, vs. Temple, Sept. 6, 1975; Chris Bahr, vs. Ohio State, Sept. 20, 1975; Chris Bahr, vs. Syracuse, Oct. 18, 1975

LONGEST PUNT
• 89 yards, Coop French, vs. Iowa, Nov. 15, 1930

LONGEST INTERCEPTION RETURN
• 98 yards, Wayne Barfield, vs. Boston Unviversity, Oct. 18, 1958

PENN STATE ANNUAL STATISTICAL LEADERS

YR	RUSHING	YDS	ATT	AVG	PASSING	ATT	CMP	PCT	YDS	RECEIVING	REC	YDS	AVG
1946	Elwood Petchel	373	71	5.3	Elwood Petchel	37	16	.43	287	Sam Tamburo	7	126	18.0
1947	Fran Rogel	499	110	4.5	Elwood Petchel	38	18	.47	353	Jeff Durkota	6	110	18.3
1948	Fran Rogel	602	152	4.0	Elwood Petchel	100	48	.48	628	Sam Tamburo	17	301	17.7
1949	Fran Rogel	395	110	3.6	Owen Dougherty	28	12	.43	281	Robert Hicks	10	196	19.6
1950	Tony Orsini	563	146	3.9	Vince O'Bara	103	38	.37	640	John Smidansky	23	383	16.7
1951	Ted Shattuck	579	135	4.3	Bob Szajna	86	41	.48	528	Don Malinak	14	138	9.9
1952	Bob Pollard	341	110	3.1	Tony Rados	186	93	.50	937	Jesse Arnelle	33	291	8.8
1953	Lenny Moore	601	108	5.6	Tony Rados	171	81	.47	1,025	Jim Garrity	30	349	11.6
1954	Lenny Moore	1,082	136	8.0	Don Bailey	80	33	.41	393	Jack Sherry	11	160	14.5
1955	Lenny Moore	697	138	5.1	Bobby Hoffman	53	25	.47	355	Billy Kane	9	184	20.4
1956	Billy Kane	544	105	5.2	Milt Plum	75	40	.53	675	Billy Kane	16	232	14.5
1957	Dave Kasperian	469	122	3.8	Al Jacks	103	53	.51	673	Les Walters	24	440	18.3
1958	Dave Kasperian	381	98	3.9	Rich Lucas	80	36	.45	483	Maurice Schleicher	9	127	14.1
1959	Rich Lucas	325	99	3.3	Rich Lucas	117	58	.50	913	Dick Hoak	14	167	11.9
1960	Jim Kerr	389	93	4.2	Galen Hall	89	39	.44	448	Jim Kerr	13	163	12.5
1961	Roger Kochman	666	129	5.2	Galen Hall	97	50	.52	951	Jim Schwab	16	257	16.1
1962	Roger Kochman	652	120	5.4	Pete Liske	162	91	.56	1,037	Junior Powell	32	303	9.5
1963	Gary Klingensmith	450	102	4.4	Pete Liske	161	87	.54	1,117	Dick Anderson	21	229	10.9
1964	Tom Urbanik	625	134	4.7	Gary Wydman	149	70	.47	832	Bill Huber	25	347	13.9
1965	Dave McNaughton	884	193	4.6	Jack White	205	98	.48	1,275	Jack Curry	42	572	13.6
1966	Bob Campbell	482	79	6.1	Tom Sherman	135	58	.43	943	Jack Curry	34	584	17.2
1967	Charlie Pittman	580	119	4.9	Tom Sherman	205	104	.51	1,616	Jack Curry	41	681	16.6
1968	Charlie Pittman	950	186	5.1	Chuck Burkhart	177	87	.49	1,170	Ted Kwalick	31	403	13.0
1969	Charlie Pittman	706	149	4.7	Chuck Burkhart	114	59	.52	805	Greg Edmonds	20	246	12.3
1970	Lydell Mitchell	751	134	5.6	Mike Cooper	64	32	.50	429	Greg Edmonds	38	506	13.3
1971	Lydell Mitchell	1,567	254	6.2	John Hufnagel	136	86	.63	1,185	Bob Parsons	30	489	16.3
1972	John Cappelletti	1,117	233	4.8	John Hufnagel	216	115	.53	2,039	Dan Natale	30	460	15.3
1973	John Cappelletti	1,522	286	5.3	Tom Shuman	161	83	.52	1,375	Gary Hayman	30	525	17.5
1974	Tony Donchez	880	195	4.5	Tom Shuman	183	97	.53	1,355	Jerry Jeram	17	259	15.2
1975	Woody Petchel	621	148	4.2	John Andress	149	71	.48	991	Dick Barvinchak	17	327	19.2
1976	Steve Geise	560	116	4.8	Chuck Fusina	168	88	.52	1,260	Mickey Shuler	21	281	13.4
1977	Matt Suhey	638	139	4.6	Chuck Fusina	246	142	.58	2,221	Mickey Shuler	33	600	18.2
1978	Matt Suhey	720	184	3.9	Chuck Fusina	242	137	.57	1,859	Scott Fitzkee	37	630	17.0
1979	Matt Suhey	973	185	5.3	Dayle Tate	176	92	.52	1,179	Brad Scovill	26	331	12.7
1980	Curt Warner	922	196	4.7	Todd Blackledge	159	76	.48	1,037	Kenny Jackson	21	386	18.4
1981	Curt Warner	1,044	171	6.1	Todd Blackledge	207	104	.50	2,218	Gregg Garrity	23	415	18.0
1982	Curt Warner	1,041	198	5.3	Todd Blackledge	292	161	.55	1,557	Kenny Jackson	41	697	17.0
1983	D.J. Dozier	1,002	174	5.8	Doug Strang	259	134	.52	1,944	Kevin Baugh	36	547	15.2
1984	D.J. Dozier	691	125	5.5	Doug Strang	148	57	.39	840	Herb Bellamy	16	306	19.1
1985	D.J. Dozier	723	154	4.7	John Shaffer	228	103	.45	1,366	Ray Roundtree	15	285	19.0
1986	D.J. Dozier	811	171	4.7	John Shaffer	204	114	.56	1,510	D.J. Dozier	26	287	11.0
1987	Blair Thomas	1,414	268	5.3	Matt Knizner	223	113	.51	1,478	Blair Thomas	23	300	13.0
1988	Gary Brown	689	136	5.1	Tony Sacca	146	54	.37	821	Michael Timpson	22	342	15.5
1989	Blair Thomas	1,341	264	5.1	Tony Sacca	137	56	.41	694	David Daniels	22	362	16.5
1990	Leroy Thompson	573	152	3.8	Tony Sacca	249	122	.49	1,866	David Daniels	31	538	17.4
1991	Richie Anderson	779	152	5.1	Tony Sacca	292	169	.58	2,488	Terry Smith	55	846	15.4
1992	Richie Anderson	900	195	4.6	John Sacca	155	81	.52	1,118	O.J. McDuffie	63	977	15.5
1993	Ki-Jana Carter	1,026	155	6.6	Kerry Collins	250	127	.51	1,605	Bobby Engram	48	873	18.2
1994	Ki-Jana Carter	1,539	198	7.8	Kerry Collins	264	176	.67	2,679	Bobby Engram	52	1,029	19.8
1995	Curtis Enis	683	113	6.0	Wally Richardson	335	193	.58	2,198	Bobby Engram	63	1,084	17.2
1996	Curtis Enis	1,210	224	5.4	Wally Richardson	279	145	.52	1,732	Joe Jurevicius	41	869	21.2
1997	Curtis Enis	1,363	228	6.0	Mike McQueary	255	146	.57	2,211	Joe Jurevicius	39	817	20.9
1998	Eric McCoo	822	127	6.5	Kevin Thompson	226	121	.54	1,691	Corey Jones	27	368	13.6
1999	Eric McCoo	739	148	5.0	Kevin Thompson	242	133	.55	1,916	Chafie Fields	39	692	17.7
2000	Eric McCoo	692	140	4.9	Rashard Casey	309	163	.53	2,001	Tony Stewart	38	451	11.9
2001	Larry Johnson	337	71	4.7	Zack Mills	230	127	.55	1,669	Bryant Johnson	51	866	17.0
2002	Larry Johnson	2,087	271	7.7	Zack Mills	333	188	.56	2,417	Bryant Johnson	48	917	19.1
2003	Austin Scott	436	100	4.4	Zack Mills	251	136	.54	1,404	Tony Johnson	32	445	13.9
2004	Tony Hunt	777	169	4.6	Zack Mills	268	155	.58	1,722	Tony Hunt	39	334	8.6
2005	Tony Hunt	1,047	174	6.0	Michael Robinson	311	162	.52	2,350	Deon Butler	37	691	18.7
2006	Tony Hunt	1,386	277	5.0	Anthony Morelli	386	208	.54	2,424	Deon Butler	48	637	13.3

Receiving leaders by receptions
All statistics include postseason

PURDUE

BY TODD JONES

THERE MIGHT NEVER HAVE BEEN A Big Ten Conference without the Purdue Boilermakers. Purdue president James H. Smart invited six other university presidents to the Palmer House in Chicago on Jan. 11, 1895. He wanted to discuss possible solutions to the problems plaguing collegiate athletics. The meeting between Purdue, Michigan, Minnesota, Wisconsin, Illinois, Chicago, and Northwestern created the Intercollegiate Conference of Faculty Representatives and led to the affiliation that later became known as the Big Ten. Pride and passion for that league, and its football, have remained alive in western Indiana through various levels of success and failure at Purdue. Joe Tiller added to the spirit, and rekindled the glory days of Jack Mollenkopf, by coaching a wide-open offense and stout defense. The combination has again made every fall Saturday an event near the Wabash River in West Lafayette.

TRADITION A home game at Purdue doesn't begin until "I Am an American" is read over the public-address system. Throughout the game, the school's "All-American" Band, 340 members strong, entertains the crowd with the Big Bass Drum, built in 1921, and the Golden Girl twirling group. The Gimlets supporters group line the north end zone and, after every Purdue score, do push-ups for each of the team's points. If the Boilermakers win, the "W" flag is raised atop the stadium's south scoreboard. Big Ten wins at home are celebrated by the ringing of the Victory Bell, which hung in the school's bell tower in the 1870s and is now mounted on a four-wheel carriage near the north end zone. Purdue and Notre Dame play for The Shillelagh, donated in 1957 by merchant seaman Joe McLaughlin. Illinois plays the Boilermakers for ownership of The Cannon. Purdue students took the cannon to Champaign, Ill., in 1905 to fire it after an expected win, but Illinois fraternity brothers from Delta Upsilon confiscated the weapon until 1943, when Illinois fan Quincy A. Hall suggested the schools use it as a trophy. The oldest trophy Purdue plays for is the Old Oaken Bucket, which goes to the winner of the Indiana game. Chicago alumni groups from both schools decided in 1925 that the rivalry needed a trophy. Fritz Ernst of Purdue and Whiley J. Huddle of

PROFILE

Purdue University
West Lafayette, Ind.
Founded: 1869
Enrollment: 39,228
Colors: Old Gold and Black
Nickname: Boilermakers
Stadium: Ross-Ade Stadium
   Opened in 1924
   Bermuda grass; 62,500 capacity
First football game: 1887
All-time record: 556–475–48 (.538)
Bowl record: 7–7
Big Ten Conference championships: 8
(1 outright)
First-round draft choices: 21
Website: www.purduesports.com

THE BEST OF TIMES

The Boilermakers went 36–4–2 and won three Big Ten titles from 1929 to 1933. They went 40–10–1 from 1965 to 1969, with the 1966 season capped by a win in the school's first Rose Bowl trip.

THE WORST OF TIMES

Nearly a decade of suffering occurred from 1985 to 1993, with three head coaches enduring nine consecutive losing seasons and a 29–69–1 record. The 1993 squad went 1–10 and finished tied for 10th in the Big Ten.

CONFERENCE

Purdue was a charter member of the Western Conference in 1896, and has remained in the league since. Popularly known as the Big Ten since 1917, the league didn't officially change its name to the Big Ten Conference until 1987.

DISTINGUISHED ALUMNI

Neil Armstrong, astronaut; John Wooden; George Ade; Birch Bayh, U.S. senator; Brian Lamb, founder and chairman of C-SPAN; Orville Redenbacher, popcorn magnate

Indiana found an old bucket—supposedly used during the Civil War—on a southern Indiana farm, and the schools agreed to make it the game's trophy. A new link identifying the winner is added to a chain on the bucket made up of P's and I's.

BEST PLAYER Drew Brees arrived in West Lafayette as a tough Texan with a chip on his shoulder. The quarterback left Purdue as a legend. From 1997 to 2000, Brees set two NCAA records, 13 Big Ten records, and 19 Purdue records. No one in the Big Ten has ever thrown for more yards (11,792) or touchdowns (90), attempted more passes (1,678) or completed more (1,026), had a better completion percentage (61.1%), or produced more total offensive yards (12,693). Brees is the only quarterback in league history to twice pass for more than 500 yards in a game. He threw for more than 400 yards seven times, and more than 300 yards 16 times. More important, he was a winner. Brees was the quarterback on Purdue's only Big Ten championship team of the past 40 years. The senior led the Boilermakers to the 2001 Rose Bowl, their first in 34 years, and set that magical trip up in October by throwing a game-winning 64-yard TD pass to Seth Morales with 1:55 remaining to beat Ohio State. Brees won the Maxwell Award as the nation's outstanding player

His glasses made him look like a librarian, but foes knew Jack Mollenkopf as Jack the Ripper.

in 2000, and was third in the Heisman voting, a year after finishing fourth. As a sophomore in 1998, he led an 80-yard drive in 54 seconds to beat No. 4-ranked Kansas State with a 25-yard TD pass to Ike Jones with 45 seconds left in regulation. That year's offense set Purdue records for points (444), touchdowns (57), and first downs (315). As a senior, he was named Academic All-America Player of the Year, and received Purdue's Leonard Wilson Award for unselfishness and dedication, and seemed light years removed from the time when few schools showed interest in him as a high school senior in Austin, Texas. Brees tore an ACL in his knee during a playoff game in his junior season of high school, causing Texas and Texas A&M to back off from recruiting the native son. Tiller convinced Brees to turn down Kentucky in favor of Purdue. Critics said he was too small at six-feet and 210 pounds, and didn't have a strong enough arm. Brees proved doubters wrong with his smarts, tenacity, confidence, and ability to throw on the move. He was the last quarterback taken in the 2001 NFL draft and has since gone on to be a two-time Pro Bowl player, and was the league's 2004 Comeback Player of the Year. In 2006, he led the NFL with 4,418 passing yards and took the New Orleans Saints to their first NFC Championship game.

FIGHT SONG

HAIL PURDUE
To your call once more we rally,
Alma Mater, hear our praise;
Where the Wabash spreads its valley,
Filled with joy our voices raise.
From the skies in swelling echoes
Come the cheers that tell the tale
Of your vic't'ries and your heroes,
Hail Purdue! We sing all hail!

Hail, Hail to Old Purdue!
All hail to our old gold and black!
Hail, Hail to Old Purdue!
Our friendship may she never lack,
Ever grateful, ever true
Thus we raise our song anew,
Of the days we've spent with you,
All hail our own Purdue!

FIRST-ROUND DRAFT CHOICES

1937	Johnny Drake, Rams (10)
1938	Cecil Isbell, Packers (7)
1949	Abe Gibron, Bills[a]
1955	Tom Bettis, Packers (5)
1957	Len Dawson, Steelers (5)
1963	Don Brumm, Cardinals (13)
1966	Jerry Shay, Vikings (7) and Broncos*
1966	Karl Singer, Patriots
1967	Bob Griese, Dolphins (4)
1967	John Charles, Patriots (21)
1969	Leroy Keyes, Eagles (3)
1970	Mike Phipps, Browns (3)
1973	Dave Butz, Cardinals (5)
1973	Otis Armstrong, Broncos (9)
1973	Darryl Stingley, Patriots (19)
1975	Larry Burton, Saints (7)
1976	Mike Pruitt, Browns (7)
1976	Ken Novak, Colts (20)
1986	Jim Everett, Oilers (3)
1987	Rod Woodson, Steelers (10)
2007	Anthony Spencer, Cowboys (26)

[a] All-America Football Conference
*From 1960-1966, the NFL and the AFL held separate, competing drafts

CONSENSUS ALL-AMERICANS

1929	Elmer Sleight, T
1929	Ralph Welch, B
1932	Paul Moss, E
1933	Duane Purvis, B
1940	Dave Rankin, E
1943	Alex Agase, G
1952	Bernie Flowers, E
1965	Bob Griese, QB
1967-68	Leroy Keyes, B
1968	Chuck Kyle, MG
1969	Mike Phipps, QB
1972	Otis Armstrong, B
1972	Dave Butz, DT
1980	Dave Young, TE
1980	Mark Herrmann, QB
1986	Rod Woodson, DB
2001	Travis Dorsch, P
2004	Taylor Stubblefield, WR

BEST COACH His glasses made him look like a librarian, but opponents knew him as Jack the Ripper. Jack Mollenkopf earned a deadly reputation in big games by going 11–2–1 against Indiana and 10–4 against Notre Dame, and by leading Purdue to its only Rose Bowl victory, in its first appearance at the end of the 1966 season. The Ohio native was a football and baseball star at Bowling Green and later coached high school football in Toledo. He left the prep ranks to become one of Stuart Holcomb's assistant coaches at Purdue in 1947. Mollenkopf replaced the man who had hired him in 1956, and promptly suffered his only losing season as Purdue coach. That memory was buried by a slew of victories before Mollenkopf retired after the 1969 season. In the final six seasons of his 14-year tenure, the fundamentally sound Boilermakers went 46–13–1 and never finished below third in the Big Ten. He led them to a share of the 1967 Big Ten title with Indiana and Minnesota. The high-water mark of Mollenkopf's career came in 1968 when he had Purdue ranked No. 1 in October. He ended up with a school-record 84 wins, 39 defeats, and nine ties. "He was very intense, but in his intensity, he was also very honest and straightforward," said Leroy Keyes, the best Boilermaker to play for Mollenkopf. When he died, in 1975, The *Indianapolis Star* wrote: "What Purdue got from Mollenkopf was 24 hours of loyalty each and every day."

BEST TEAM Purdue went 9–0 in 1943, shared the Big Ten title with Michigan and ended the season ranked No. 5 in the nation. Those Boilermakers, however, can't quite match a team that had set Purdue's all-time standard for success 14 years earlier. Jimmy Phelan put together an undefeated (8–0) season in his final one as coach of the Boilermakers. A pair of All-Americas—halfback Ralph "Pest" Welch and tackle Elmer Sleight—anchored the 1929 team. Welch, quarterback John White, and running backs Glen Harmeson and Alex Yunevich served as the heart. Together, the Four Riveters, as they were called, averaged 4.5 yards per carry for an offense that outscored opponents 187-44. The season's highlight was a 30-16 win over Michigan, the school's first against the Wolverines since 1892. Michigan was the only Big Ten team to score against the Boilermakers that season. Only Iowa tested Purdue, in a game that was scoreless after three quarters. The Boilermakers pulled out a 7-0 victory when Harmeson threw an 18-yard TD pass to Bill Woerner. Purdue ended the year with a 32-0 win over Indiana that earned the Boilermakers their first Big Ten championship, still the school's only outright conference title. Phelan left after the season to become Washington's coach.

BEST BACKFIELD The only Purdue team to win a Rose Bowl was led by a precise and seasoned quarterback

and a pair of young running backs who made defenses quiver. In 1966, senior quarterback Bob Griese completed 60% of his passes (140 of 233), a school record that stood for 14 years, while earning first-team All-America and Big Ten MVP honors. He was runner-up in the Heisman voting. Sophomore fullback Perry Williams carried the ball 199 times for 750 yards and 10 touchdowns. Fellow sophomore Leroy Keyes spent most of the season at defensive back—he had four interceptions on the season and returned a fumble 95 yards for a TD against Notre Dame—and he averaged 26 yards on kickoff returns. But Keyes also played halfback during that 1966 season, averaging 7.7 yards on his 14 rushing attempts, when subbing in for juniors Bob Baltzell and Bob Hurst. Mollenkopf figured he had to get the football into Keyes' hands more often, so his talent was switched primarily to offense in 1967, although occasional defensive stints continued when necessity beckoned. As a junior, Keyes won MVP of the Big Ten and finished third in the Heisman Trophy balloting, rushing for 986 yards on a school-record 6.6 yards per carry, with 19 touchdowns, including 6 receiving TDs. His senior year in 1968 was even better, prompting Mollenkopf to refer to his beloved sweep play as "Leroy left and Leroy right." Keyes set Purdue records with 1,003 rushing yards and 14 rushing TDs. He capped his career in magnificent fashion, running for 140 yards, catching six passes for 149 yards, and scoring 4 TDs in a 38-35 win over Indiana. Keyes was runner-up for the 1968 Heisman. He ended his three seasons with numerous school records for scoring, rushing, and receiving and also completed 12 passes in his career, eight for touchdowns. Purdue fans named him the school's all-time greatest football player in 1987. Today, Keyes ranks ninth in career rushing yards at Purdue with 2,094, and Williams is 10th with 2,049. Williams' 30 career rushing TDs—including 4 against SMU in 1966—stood as a school record for 24 years, and Keyes' totaled 29 career TDs. Keyes went on to play in the NFL for the Eagles and Chiefs, and was later enshrined in the College Football Hall of Fame. Griese won two Super Bowls with the Miami Dolphins, and was inducted in both the College and Pro Football Hall of Fame. But he'll always be remembered at Purdue, along with backfield 'mates Williams and Keyes, for winning the 1966 Big Ten title and beating USC in the Rose Bowl.

BEST DEFENSE Purdue led the Big Ten in total defense in 2002 for the first time in 35 years, and only fifth time in school history, but the Boilermakers were even better on defense a year later, despite a drop to third in the conference's overall rankings. The 2003 defense allowed fewer yards and points a game than the previous season's league leaders and set a Purdue record with 41

sacks among its 105 tackles for loss, second-most in school history. The Boilermakers had the nation's No. 10 rushing defense (96.4 yards per game), No. 13 overall defense (302), and No. 14 scoring defense (17.4), holding four opponents to 10 points or less. Seven players from that defense finished their Purdue careers in the top 22 in school history for sacks. Seven went on to play in the NFL. After a season-opening loss to Bowling Green, the Boilermakers switched to black uniforms and took the field at home games to the AC/DC song "Back in Black." They left opposing offenses black and blue, holding Arizona to 174 total yards, Illinois to 191, and Penn State to 204. Senior linebackers Landon Johnson and Niko Koutouvides led Purdue in tackles with 102 and 101, respectively. Shaun Phillips had 23 tackles for loss in 2003 to give him 60.5 for his career. The senior linebacker had 14.5 sacks, including 3.5 at Wisconsin, and finished his career with a school-record 33.5. Senior defensive tackle Craig Terrill had 8.5 sacks to push his career total to 20.5. Five Boilermakers had at least two interceptions that season, led by junior safety Stuart Schweigert's four. He finished his career with a school-record 17 interceptions. Antwaun Rogers, another junior defensive back on that 2003 team, ended his career a year later with 30 pass breakups, tied for fourth all-time at Purdue. Senior linebacker Gilbert Gardner forced two fumbles at Wisconsin and recovered two against Northwestern. Gardner and Phillips each tied the school record with seven fumble recoveries in their careers. Purdue was stout up front, too. Defensive tackle Craig Terrill had 35.5 career tackles for loss and defensive tackle Brandon Villarreal had 35 career tackles for loss. Koutouvides, Phillips, and Schweigert were named All-Big Ten in 2003 as Purdue tied for second in the Big Ten and finished 9–4 with a 34-27 overtime loss to Georgia in the Capital One Bowl.

BIGGEST GAME Purdue's 41-20 loss to Michigan State on Oct. 22, 1966, ended up costing the Boilermakers the Big Ten championship. However, a Big Ten rule at the time kept league members from going to the Rose Bowl in consecutive years. So it was second-place Purdue—instead of repeat conference champ Michigan State—that headed to Pasadena. The Boilermakers were 8–2 and rolling, having ended the season with four consecutive victories, the final three by

COLLEGE FOOTBALL HALL OF FAME INDUCTEES		
NAME	YEARS	INDUCTED
Andy Smith, COACH	1913-15	1951
Elmer Oliphant, HB	1911-14	1955
Alex Agase, G	1946	1963
Cecil Isbell, HB	1935-37	1967
Jim Phelan, COACH	1922-29	1973
Bob Griese, QB	1964-66	1984
Jack Mollenkopf, COACH	1955-69	1988
Bump Elliott, HB	1943-44	1989
Leroy Keyes, HB	1966-68	1990
Jim Young, COACH	1977-81	1999
Mike Phipps, QB	1967-69	2007

PRO FOOTBALL HALL OF FAME INDUCTEES		
NAME	PRO YEARS	INDUCTED
Len Dawson, QB	1957-75	1987
Bob Griese, QB	1967-80	1990
Hank Stram, COACH	1960-74, 1976-77	2003

a total of 90-6. Purdue then found a way to win in its first Rose Bowl despite USC gaining more yards (323-244) and producing more first downs (18-11). Sophomore fullback Perry Williams scored on a 1-yard run in the second quarter and a 2-yard run in the third quarter to give the Boilermakers a 14-7 lead. USC dominated the fourth quarter, running 26 offensive plays to just eight for Purdue. The trailing Trojans scored their second TD with 2:28 remaining in the game on a 19-yard pass from Troy Winslow to Rod Sherman. Southern California coach John McKay ordered a two-point conversion attempt. Winslow tried to hit Jim Lawrence with a pass, but Purdue senior defensive back George Catavolos stepped in front for the interception. "I could almost feel the ball in my hands, it was so close," Lawrence said. Purdue senior defensive back John Charles was named Rose Bowl MVP, but the difference in the game was two extra-point conversions, both kicked by Boilermakers quarterback Bob Griese.

BIGGEST UPSET There really wasn't much reason for hope when Purdue traveled to South Bend, Ind., on Oct. 7, 1950. The 0–1 Boilermakers were facing defending national champion Notre Dame, a team that hadn't lost in 39 games. During that span, which stretched back to the 1946 season, the Irish only suffered two ties, to Army and USC. Notre Dame hadn't lost a home game in eight years and was 61–3–5 under coach Frank Leahy. Purdue entered the game a 20-point underdog but dominated play while building a 21-0 halftime lead. Fullback John Kerestes ran for TDs in the first and second quarters and QB Dale Samuels added a 30-yard scoring pass to halfback Neil Schmidt. In that first half, the Boilermakers had a fourth TD called back because of a penalty and had an 85-yard drive stall at Notre Dame's 1-yard line. The Fighting Irish rallied after Purdue lost a fumble on its own 10 in the third quarter. The turnover set up a 4-yard TD pass from Bob Williams to Jim Mutscheller. Notre Dame's John Petitbon added a six-yard scoring run early in the fourth to make the score 21-14. The Boilermakers immediately answered with a TD pass from Samuels to halfback Mike Maccioli. Coach Stu Holcomb's "Spoilermakers" won 28-14.

HEARTBREAKER Purdue never trailed while rolling to victories in its first five games of the 2004

season. The Boilermakers were ranked No. 5, their highest spot in the polls in a quarter century, and looked to be the favorite in the Big Ten. There was also conjecture about QB Kyle Orton possibly winning the Heisman. He was averaging 328 passing yards a game and had 18 TD passes and only two interceptions while Purdue was averaging more than 500 yards and 41.8 points on offense. The balloon popped when No. 10 Wisconsin came to West Lafayette on Oct. 16 for a nationally televised game, with the *ESPN GameDay* crew on site. Purdue led 17-13 late when Orton, running on a third-down naked bootleg, seemed to have picked up enough yardage for a first down that would clinch the victory. However, when the senior lunged forward, Wisconsin defender Robert Brooks forced a fumble. Scott Starks picked the loose ball up for the Badgers and returned it 40 yards for a touchdown with 2:36 left in the game. Officials reviewed the play but ruled the ball was out before Orton's arm hit the ground. The Boilermakers drove to the Wisconsin 25 on their ensuing possession, but Ben Jones' 42-yard field goal attempt was wide right. Wisconsin, which entered the game leading the nation in scoring defense (6.5 points per game), ran out the clock for the win. "It was a tough one to take, one of the [games] that could have put us on the top of the college football scene," linebacker George Hall said a year later. "That game was probably the worst game that I've ever had to deal with afterward." The bitter defeat began a four-game losing streak—by a total of 10 points—during which the Boilermakers had 12 turnovers. Purdue lost 11 of 15 games over two seasons and had a streak of eight consecutive bowl berths snapped. "Unfortunately, that's what more people remember about Kyle Orton than all the good things he did, because he did a lot of good things," Tiller said in 2006. "But I guess that's history for you. It'll be forever remembered as The Fumble."

WILDEST FINISH
The lead changed hands six times when Ohio State played at Purdue on Oct. 28, 2000. OSU led 20-10 after three quarters, and appeared to wrap up the victory when tailback Jerry Westbrooks ran two yards around right end for a touchdown to give it a 27-24 lead with 2:16 remaining in the game. That score was set up when Boilermaker quarterback Drew Brees was intercepted for the fourth time, with Buckeye Michael Doss returning the ball to the Purdue 2-yard line. Ohio State's lead lasted all of 21 seconds. Seth Morales got behind Doss on a deep pattern and Brees hit the wide receiver for a 64-yard touchdown with 1:55 left. Purdue clinched the victory when linebacker Landon Johnson recovered an Ohio State fumble on the ensuing possession. "I now have a greater belief in Lady Luck," said coach Joe Tiller. That year, the Boilermakers would win their first Big Ten championship in 34 years and go to their first Rose Bowl since 1967.

BEST GOAL-LINE STAND
Purdue had defeated Notre Dame only once in the previous 13 years when luck didn't shine on the Fighting Irish for a change in 1999. Travis Dorsch kicked two field goals in the fourth quarter to give No. 20 Purdue a 28-23 lead. Jarious Jackson drove visiting Notre Dame, ranked No. 16, to the Purdue 2-yard line with time running out. The Irish called timeout after Joey Goodspeed was stopped on second-and-goal at the 1. Notre Dame then lined up in a modified wishbone formation, and Jackson called a false check at the line of scrimmage. The Irish backs, however, were confused by Jackson's call. When the QB took the snap and headed left, a wave of Boilermakers pushed him back. Mike Rose tackled Jackson for a 9-yard loss, and time expired before Notre Dame could run another play.

BEST COMEBACK
On Nov. 8, 1997, Michigan State led 21-10 with less than three minutes to play when the Spartans attempted a 39-yard field goal. Purdue blocked the kick and returned it 62 yards for a touchdown. A failed two-point conversion left the Boilermakers trailing 21-16. Chris Daniels then recovered an onside kick for Purdue at its 45-yard line. Boilermaker QB Billy Dicken completed four passes and Edwin Watson capped the drive by carrying two Michigan State defenders into the end zone on a three-yard TD run. The extra point gave Purdue a 22-21 lead with 40 seconds remaining. The Spartans had one final chance to win, but Chris Gardner missed a 43-yard field goal attempt with three seconds left. "Divine intervention may have been on our side," Tiller said. One year later, Purdue erased an 11-point deficit in the fourth quarter and won 25-24 at Michigan State.

STADIUM
Purdue alum David E. Ross, president of the school's board of trustees, figured that new athletic facilities would create more successful teams, leading to more alumni donations. So he decided in the early 1920s that the Boilermakers needed to move out of dinky Stuart Field. Ross and George Ade—an alum, author, playwright, and humorist—paid $40,000 for a 65-acre dairy farm north of campus and donated it to Purdue. The Ross-Ade Foundation raised money for the construction of a stadium on that site. Purdue dedicated Ross-Ade Stadium on Nov. 22, 1924, with a 26-7 homecoming win over Indiana. Various expansions over the years took the original capacity of 13,500 to a high of 69,357 in 1970. A $70 million renovation program began after the 2000 season. A new press box, 34 luxury suites, and a brick-and-limestone façade were added to the stadium, which now seats 62,500.

RIVAL
Indiana has historically served as Purdue's main rival, with their first meeting dating back to 1891. The Boilermakers, however, have dominated the series, which

hasn't received much national buzz. Only once, in 1945, were Purdue and Indiana both ranked when they played. No wonder Purdue fans get more heated about a different in-state foe, tradition-laden Notre Dame. "The way you were measured around here is the way you fared against Notre Dame," said Brock Spack, a Purdue linebacker from 1980 to 1983, and the team's current defensive coordinator. The Boilermakers and Fighting Irish first played in 1896, and have met every year since 1946. Notre Dame leads the series 51–25–2, but Purdue has been an occasional thorn for the Irish. The Boilermakers actually even dominated the series from 1954 through 1969, winning 11 of 16 games. Since then, Notre Dame has given Purdue fans plenty of reason to scorn the Golden Dome. The Irish won 11 of 14 against the Boilermakers from 1970 to 1983 and enjoyed 11 consecutive victories over Purdue from 1986 to 1996.

NICKNAME

"Slaughter of Innocents," screamed the headline in the *Daily Argus News* in Crawfordsville, Ind., after Purdue beat Wabash College 44-0 in 1891. The smaller headline referred to the visiting team as "Burly Boiler Makers." The term Boilermakers was the latest in slurs aimed at Purdue, a land-grant university. Other nonflattering monikers were Pumpkin Shuckers, Rail Splitters, Cornfield Sailors, Foundry Hands, G Rangers, and Blacksmiths. Newspapers that liked Purdue, however, took the term "Boilermakers" and created a positive image, and the school adopted the name for its sports teams.

MASCOT

A Purdue student in 1930 decided to honor the school's engineering and agrarian heritage by creating a mascot using a replica Victorian-era locomotive. Ten years later, Purdue alumni provided the first Boilermaker Special mascot train. The Reamer Club, a spirit group, was picked by school president Edward Elliott to maintain and operate the train. There have been four versions of the Special, although the latest, debuted in 1993, was dubbed Special V. Since 1956, athletic mascot Purdue Pete has been played by a student outfitted with a huge head and a hammer. Purdue Pete actually began as a logo for

the university bookstore in 1940. Since 1997, Pete has been joined by a sidekick named Rowdy (a student inside a 10-foot inflatable costume), who often goes into the stands to rally the crowd.

ALL-TIME TEAM

As part of the celebration of the 100-year anniversary of Purdue football during the 1987 season, an all-time team was selected on the basis of ballots tabulated from game programs, the Purdue Alumnus and John Purdue Club mailings. Leroy Keyes was named the all-time greatest player.

OFFENSE

1943	Alex Agase,	OG
1951-54	Tom Bettis,	OG
1927-29	Elmer Sleight,	OT
1963-65	Karl Singer,	OT
1977-80	Pete Quinn,	C
1977-80	Dave Young,	TE
1965-67	Jim Beirne,	WR
1964-66	Bob Griese,	QB
1932-34	Duane Purvis,	RB
1966-68	Leroy Keyes,	RB
1970-72	Otis Armstrong,	RB
1976-78	Scott Sovereen,	PK

DEFENSE

1945-47	Ned Maloney,	DE
1954-56	Lamar Lundy,	DE
1966-68	Chuck Kyle,	MG
1970-72	Dave Butz,	DT
1973-75	Ken Novak,	DT
1970-72	Gregg Bingham,	LB
1976-79	Keena Turner,	LB
1964-66	John Charles,	DB
1966-68	Leroy Keyes,	DB
1967-69	Tim Foley,	DB
1983-86	Rod Woodson,	DB
1981-83	Matt Kinzer,	P

UNIFORMS

Purdue's first football team, in 1887, wanted to use Princeton's colors, but instead of that school's orange and black, the Boilermakers settled on gold and black. Boilermaker helmets have been gold since 1962, except for two seasons (1989 and 1990) when they were black. Purdue has had an elongated "P" on its helmet since 1971.

TRAGEDY

At about 9:45 in the morning on Oct. 31, 1903, a special 14-car train carrying the Purdue team, band, and fans to Indianapolis for the annual game with Indiana crashed into a 10-car section of coal cars being backed down the track inside the Indianapolis city limits. An assistant coach, a trainer, and 13 Purdue players were killed in the accident. Among the injured were coach Oliver Cutts and manager-player Harry Leslie, who later became governor of Indiana. Thirty-three years later, two players, Carl Dahlbeck and Tom McGannon, were killed on Sept. 12, when fire broke out in the team's locker room. Six others were injured.

QUIRK

The Boilermakers beat visiting Wisconsin 7-6 in 1930. Badger kicker Russ Rebholz missed the extra point after a touchdown. Wisconsin's radio announcer, Quinn Ryan, calling the game on Chicago's WGN, thought Rebholz had made the kick. He didn't realize his mistake until the game ended.

LORE

Purdue was known for throwing the football long before Joe Tiller brought his "Basketball on Grass" offense to West Lafayette in 1997. Bob DeMoss started the "Cradle of Quarterbacks" tradition by throwing for 2,790 yards and 20 touchdowns from 1945 to 1948. Dale Samuels and NFL Hall of Famers Len Dawson and Bob Griese added to Purdue's reputation for passing. Mike Phipps followed Griese and set numerous school records from 1967 to 1969, including passing yards (5,423) and passing TDs (37). Other top QBs kept up the tradition: Gary Danielson,

Mark Herrmann, Scott Campbell, Jim Everett, Eric Hunter, Rick Trefzger, Billy Dicken, and Kyle Orton. Drew Brees set the all-time standard at Purdue for prolific passing.

NUMBERS The 1943 Boilermakers, who went 9–0 and were Big Ten co-champs with Michigan, had a roster made up of 26 Marines, nine Navy men, and nine civilians … RB Otis Armstrong rushed for 3,315 yards from 1970 to 1972. He ran for 276 yards and 3 TDs in the final game of his career, a 42-7 win over Indiana … Mike Pruitt gained 179 yards on 10 carries in a 1974 game against Iowa in which the Boilermakers rushed for 501 yards … Although Purdue is known for QBs, Mike Alstott scored 39 touchdowns and ran for 3,635 yards from 1992 to 1995 … Purdue has not been ranked No. 1 since Oct. 7, 1968 … The Boilermakers upset No. 1 Michigan 16-14 on Nov. 6, 1976 … Purdue beat Minnesota 35-28 in overtime in 2001 despite trailing by three with 19 seconds remaining in regulation and having the ball on its own 3-yard line with no timeouts … Rod Woodson played cornerback, tailback, and wide receiver in a 17-15 win over Indiana in 1986. He played all 80 plays on defense, made 10 tackles, and broke up a pass. On offense, he rushed 15 times for 93 yards and caught three passes for 67 yards. Woodson also played special teams, returning three punts and two kickoffs … No Purdue player has ever won the Heisman Trophy, although eight have finished 11th or better in the balloting since 1965. Purdue had a player finish runner-up or third in the voting four times from 1966 through 1969. Griese was second to Steve Spurrier in 1966 by less than 200 points. Leroy Keyes was third in 1967 and second to O.J. Simpson in 1968. Mike Phipps was second to Oklahoma's Steve Owens by 154 points in 1969. Drew Brees twice finished in the top four: fourth in 1999 and third in 2000 … Purdue gained 692 yards against Minnesota in a 1998 game, and 604 of those were passing yards … Purdue went 9–1 and shared the Big Ten title in 1931 with a defense that shut out six opponents and allowed a total of only 39 points in 10 games … The Boilermakers went 26–1 against DePauw from 1889 to 1929 … Purdue averaged 250.5 yards rushing in 1972 … In 2004, the Boilermakers produced 763 yards of offense against Indiana, 599 against Ball State, and 571 against Syracuse … The 1891 Boilermakers shut out their four opponents 192-0 … Stan Brown returned two kickoffs for TDs in 1969 and three in 1970 … Orton threw for 385 yards and 4 TDs as Purde beat Notre Dame 41-16 for its first victory in South Bend in 30 years … Woodson is second in school history with 320 career tackles, and had 11 interceptions and 29 pass breakups from 1983 to 1986 … Purdue beat Michigan State, 6-0, in 1953 to end the Spartans' 28-game winning streak … In 2006, QB Mike Phipps became the seventh Purdue player inducted into the College Football Hall of Fame … The Boilermakers upset No. 4 Kansas State, 37-34, in the 1998 Alamo Bowl despite gaining just five net yards rushing … From 2001 through 2006, 20 of Purdue's 29 losses, were by seven points or less … Dorien Bryant caught 16 passes against Northwestern and 14 against Notre Dame in 2005 … Defending Big Ten champion Purdue was ranked No. 1 and a 14-point favorite when it lost 13-0 at Ohio State on Oct. 12, 1968 … Entering 2007, the Boilermakers have scored in 131 consecutive games dating to Sept. 14, 1996. They have scored 41-plus points in 28 games under Tiller.

QUOTE "Beat the little man." —Joe Tiller

PURDUE ALL-TIME SCORES

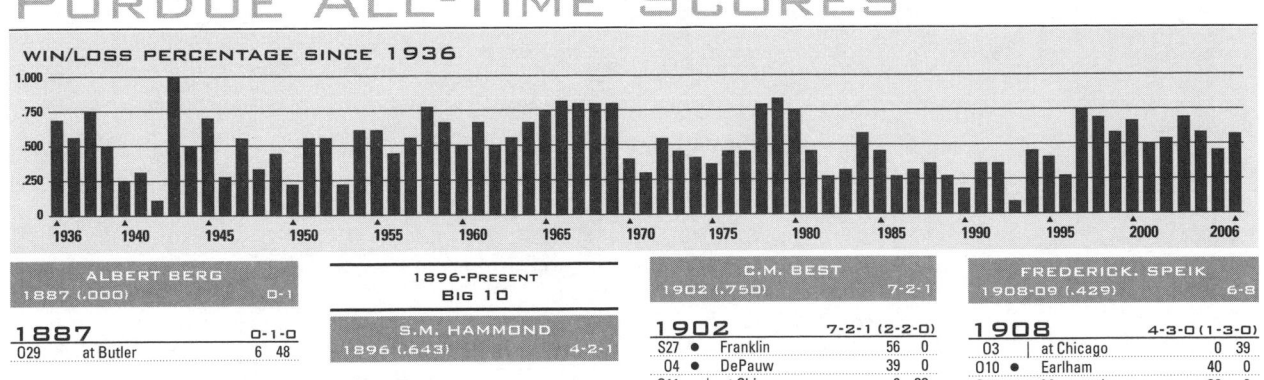

WIN/LOSS PERCENTAGE SINCE 1936

1.000 .750 .500 .250 0

1936 1940 1945 1950 1955 1960 1965 1970 1975 1980 1985 1990 1995 2000 2006

ALBERT BERG
1887 (.000)   0-1

1887   0-1-0
O29	at Butler	6	48

1888
NO TEAM

G.A. REISNER
1889 (.667)   2-1

1889   2-1-0
N16 ●	DePauw	34	10
N23	at Wabash	18	4
N29	at Butler	0	14

C.L. HARE
1890 (.500)   3-3

1890   3-3-0
O18	Chicago Stars	6	10
O25 ●	Wabash	54	0
N1	at Michigan	6	34
N15 ●	at DePauw	32	0
N22 ●	Illinois	62	0
N27	at Butler	10	12

KNOWLTON AMES
1891-92 (1.000)   12-0

1891   4-0-0
O24 ●	at Wabash	44	0
N9 ●	DePauw	30	0
N14 ●	Indiana	60	0
N26 ●	Butler	58	0

1892   8-0-0
O8 ●	at Illinois	12	6
O15 ●	at Wabash	72	0
O19 ●	Wisconsin	32	4 *
O24 ●	Michigan	24	0
O29 ●	Butler	40	6
N5 ●	Indiana	68	0
N19 ●	Chicago	38	0
N24 ●	at DePauw	32	6

D.M. BALLIET
1893-95,1901 (.667)   21-10-2

1893   5-2-1
O14 ●	Indiana	64	0
O21 ●	Butler	96	0
O25 ●	Chicago	20	10
N4 ●	Wabash	48	8
N11	Michigan	8	46
N18	at Wisconsin	30	36 †
N25 =	Illinois	26	26
N30 ●	DePauw IND	42	18

1894   9-1-0
O6 ●	Light Artillery	6	4
O13 ●	at Butler	30	0
O15 ●	at Wisconsin	1	0 f
O20 ●	Armour	36	0
O27	at Minnesota	0	24
N3 ●	at Chicago	10	6
N17 ●	at Illinois	22	2
N22 ●	at Wabash	44	0
N24 ●	at Indiana	1	0 f
N29 ●	at DePauw	28	0

1895   3-3-0
O12 ●	Kentucky	32	0
O19 ●	Missouri StL	6	16
O29 ●	Minnesota	16	4 *
N2 ●	Northwestern	6	24
N16 ●	at Michigan	10	12
N28 ●	Illinois	6	2

1896-PRESENT BIG 10

S.M. HAMMOND
1896 (.643)   4-2-1

1896   4-2-1 (0-2-1)
O3 ●	Greer	36	0
O10 ●	Rush Medical	32	4
O17	at Minnesota	0	14
O24	Michigan	0	16
N7 ●	at DePauw	22	0
N14 ●	at Notre Dame	28	22
N25 =	Illinois	4	4

WILLIAM S. CHURCH
1897 (.611)   5-3-1

1897   5-3-1 (1-2-0)
O2 ●	Illinois St.	28	0
O9 ●	Oberlin	6	22
O16 ●	at DePauw	8	0
O23	at Illinois	4	34
O30 ●	Indiana	20	6
N6	at Michigan	4	34
N13 ●	Missouri	30	12
N20 ●	Minnesota	6	0
N25 =	Alumni	0	0

ALPHA P. JAMISON
1898-1900 (.500)   11-11-1

1898   3-3-0 (0-1-0)
O8	Alumni	0	6
O18 ●	at Haskell	5	0
O22 ●	Haskell	15	0
N5	at Chicago	0	17
N12 ●	Indiana	14	0
N24	Oberlin	0	10

1899   4-4-1 (1-2-0)
S30 ●	Alumni	10	5
O7 ●	Earlham	30	5
O14	at Oberlin	0	12
O28 ●	DePauw	40	0
N4	at Chicago	0	44
N18 =	Notre Dame	10	10
N22	at Illinois	5	0
N25	at Northwestern	0	29
N30	Indiana	5	17

1900   4-4-0 (0-4-0)
S29	Illinois Wesleyan	39	0
O6	at Chicago	5	17
O13	DePauw	28	7
O20	at Michigan	6	11
O27 ●	Rose Poly	46	5
N3	at Illinois	5	17
N17 ●	Earlham	38	0
N29	Indiana	5	24

D.M. BALLIET

1901   4-4-1 (0-3-1)
S28	Franklin	24	0
O5 ●	Wabash	45	0
O12 =	at Chicago	5	5
O19 ●	DePauw	19	0
O26	at Indiana	6	11
N2 ●	Case	22	0
N9	at Notre Dame	6	12
N16	Illinois	6	28
N28	Northwestern	5	10

C.M. BEST
1902 (.750)   7-2-1

1902   7-2-1 (2-2-0)
S27 ●	Franklin	56	0
O4 ●	DePauw	39	0
O11	at Chicago	0	33
O18	at Illinois	5	29
O25 ●	Case	5	0
N1 ●	at Northwestern	5	0
N8 ●	at Greer	73	0
N15 ●	Indiana	39	0
N22 ●	Butler	87	0
N27 =	Notre Dame	6	6

OLIVER F. CUTTS
1903-04 (.722)   13-5

1903   4-2-0 (0-2-0)
S26 ●	Englewood HS	34	0
O1 ●	at Wabash	18	0
O3 ●	Beloit	17	0
O10	at Chicago	0	22
O17	Illinois	0	24
O24 ●	Oberlin	18	2

1904   9-3-0 (1-2-0)
S17	Alumni	2	6
S24	North Division HS	5	0
S28 ●	Beloit	11	0
O1 ●	at Earlham	28	11
O8	at Chicago	0	20
O15 ●	Wabash	6	0
O22	Illinois	6	24
O28 ●	Missouri StL	11	0
N5	Indiana Medical	34	5
N12 ●	Indiana IND	27	0
N19 ●	at Culver	10	0
N24 ●	Notre Dame	36	0

A.E. HERNSTEIN
1905 (.813)   6-1-1

1905   6-1-1 (1-1-1)
S23 ●	Wendell Phillips HS	33	0
S30 ●	Beloit	36	0
O14 ●	at Wabash	12	0
O21 ●	at Illinois	29	0
O28 =	Indiana IND	11	11
N4 ●	Missouri	24	0
N11	at Chicago	0	19
N24 ●	Notre Dame	32	0

M.E. WITHAM
1906 (.000)   0-5

1906   0-5-0 (0-3-0)
O20	at Chicago	0	39
O27	Wabash	0	11
N3	Notre Dame	0	2
N17	at Wisconsin	5	29
N25	Illinois	0	5

L.C. TURNER
1907 (.000)   0-5

1907   0-5-0 (0-3-0)
O12	Wabash	0	2
N2	at Illinois	4	21
N9	at Chicago	0	56
N16	Wisconsin	6	12
N23	Notre Dame	0	17

FREDERICK. SPEIK
1908-09 (.429)   6-8

1908   4-3-0 (1-3-0)
O3	at Chicago	0	39
O10 ●	Earlham	40	0
O17 ●	Monmouth	30	0
O31 ●	DePauw	28	4
N7 ●	at Northwestern	16	10
N14	Illinois	6	15
N21	Indiana	4	10

1909   2-5-0 (0-4-0)
O2	at Chicago	0	40
O9	Northwestern	5	14
O16 ●	DePauw	15	12
O30	at Illinois	6	24
N6	Wabash	17	18
N13 ●	Rose Poly	26	3
N20	Indiana	3	36

M.BILL. HORR
1910-12 (.425)   8-11-1

1910   1-5-0 (0-4-0)
O8	Wabash	0	3
O22	at Iowa	0	16
O29	Illinois	0	11
N5	at Chicago	5	14
N12 ●	DePauw	14	6
N19	Indiana	0	15

1911   3-4-0 (1-3-0)
O8	Wabash	0	3
O14	at Chicago	3	11
O28 ●	DePauw	5	0
N4	at Illinois	3	12
N11	Iowa	0	11
N18 ●	Rose Poly	35	6
N25	at Indiana	12	5

1912   4-2-1 (3-2-1)
O5 ●	DePauw	21	0
O19	at Wisconsin	0	41
O26	at Chicago	0	7
N2 ●	at Northwestern	21	6
N9 =	Illinois	9	9
N17 ●	Rose Poly	91	0
N24 ●	Indiana	34	7

ANDREW L. SMITH
1913-15 (.643)   12-6-3

1913   4-1-2 (2-1-2)
O4 ●	Wabash	26	0
O11 ●	Northwestern	34	0
O18 =	Wisconsin	7	7
O25	at Chicago	0	6
N8 ●	Rose Poly	62	0
N15 =	at Illinois	0	0
N23 ●	at Indiana	42	7

1914   5-2-0 (2-2-0)
O3 ●	Wabash	27	3
O10 ●	Western Reserve	26	0
O17	at Wisconsin	7	14
O24	at Chicago	0	21
N7 ●	Kentucky	40	6
N14 ●	at Northwestern	34	6
N21 ●	Indiana	23	13

1915   3-3-1 (2-2-0)
O2 =	Wabash	7	7
O9 ●	Beloit	26	0
O16	Wisconsin	3	28
O23	at Chicago	0	7
N6 ●	Iowa	19	13
N13	at Kentucky	0	7
N20 ●	at Indiana	7	0

CLEO O'DONNELL — 1916-17 (.393) — 5-8-1

1916 2-4-1 (0-4-1)
O7	•	DePauw	13	0
O14	•	Wabash	28	7
O21		at Iowa	6	24
O28		Illinois	7	14
N4		at Chicago	7	16
N18		at Northwestern	6	38
N25	=	Indiana	0	0

1917 3-4-0 (0-4-0)
O6	•	Franklin	54	0
O13	•	DePauw	7	6
O20		at Chicago	0	27
O27		at Illinois	0	27
N3		Northwestern	6	12
N17	•	Wabash	28	0
N24		Indiana	0	37

A. BUTCH SCANLON — 1918-20 (.375) — 7-12-1

1918 3-3-0 (1-0-0)
O26		DePauw	7	9
N2	•	Chicago	7	3
N9		at Michigan State	14	6
N16	•	Wabash IND	53	6
N23		Notre Dame	6	26
N30		at Great Lakes NAS Eva	0	28

1919 2-4-1 (0-3-0)
O4	=	Franklin	14	14
O11		Illinois	7	14
O18		at Chicago	0	16
N1		Michigan State	13	7
N8		at Ohio State	0	20
N17	•	DePauw	24	0
N22		Notre Dame	13	33

1920 2-5-0 (0-4-0)
O2	•	DePauw	10	0
O9		at Chicago	0	20
O16		at Ohio State	0	17
O30	•	Wabash	19	14
N6		at Notre Dame	0	28
N13		at Northwestern	0	14
N20		Indiana	7	10

WILLIAM H. DEITZ — 1921 (.143) — 1-6

1921 1-6-0 (1-4-0)
O1		Wabash	0	9
O8		at Chicago	0	9
O15		Notre Dame	0	33
O29		Iowa	6	13
N5	•	Northwestern	3	0
N12		at Ohio State	0	28
N19		at Indiana	0	3

JAMES PHELAN — 1922-29 (.605) — 35-22-5

1922 1-5-1 (0-3-1)
O7	•	James Milliken	10	0
O14		Notre Dame	0	20
O21		at Chicago	0	12
O28		at Iowa	0	56
N4		Wabash	6	7
N11		at Northwestern	13	24
N25	=	Indiana	7	7

1923 2-5-1 (1-4-0)
O6	•	Willmington	39	0
O13		at Iowa	0	7
O20	=	Wabash	7	7
O27		at Chicago	6	20
N3		at Notre Dame	7	34
N10		Ohio State	0	32
N17	•	Northwestern	6	3
N24		at Indiana	0	3

1924 5-2-0 (2-2-0)
S27	•	Wabash	21	7
O4		at Ohio State	0	7
O11	•	Rose Poly	41	3
O18	•	at Northwestern	7	3
N1		at Chicago	6	19
N8	•	DePauw	36	0
N22	•	Indiana	26	7

1925 3-4-1 (0-3-1)
O3		Wabash	7	13
O10	•	DePauw	39	0
O17	•	Rose Poly	44	0
O24		at Wisconsin	0	7
O31		at Chicago	0	6
N7		Franklin	20	0
N14		Northwestern	9	13
N21	=	at Indiana	0	0

1926 5-2-1 (2-1-1)
O2		at Navy	13	17
O9	•	Wabash	21	14
O16	=	Wisconsin	0	0
O23	•	at Chicago	0	0
O30	•	Indiana St.	38	0
N6		at Northwestern	0	22
N13	•	Franklin	44	0
N20	•	Indiana	24	14

1927 6-2-0 (2-2-0)
O1	•	DePauw	15	0
O8		at Harvard	19	0
O15		at Chicago	6	7
O22		at Wisconsin	6	12
O29	•	Montana St.	39	7
N5	•	Northwestern	18	6
N12	•	Franklin	46	0
N19	•	at Indiana	21	6

1928 5-2-1 (2-2-1)
O6	•	DePauw	31	0
O13	•	at Minnesota	0	15
O20	=	Wisconsin	19	19
O27	•	at Chicago	40	0
N3	•	Case	19	0
N10		at Northwestern	6	7
N17	•	Wabash	14	0
N24	•	Indiana	14	0

1929 8-0-0 (5-0-0)
O5	•	Kansas State	26	14
O12	•	Michigan	30	16
O19	•	DePauw	26	7
O26	•	at Chicago	26	0
N2	•	at Wisconsin	13	0
N9	•	Mississippi	27	7
N16	•	Iowa	7	0
N23	•	at Indiana	32	0

NOBLE KIZER — 1930-36 (.724) — 42-13-3

1930 6-2-0 (4-2-0)
O4	•	Baylor	20	7
O11	•	at Michigan	13	14
O18	•	at Iowa	20	0
O25	•	Wisconsin	7	6
N1	•	at Illinois	25	0
N8	•	at Chicago	27	7
N15	•	Butler	33	0
N22		Indiana	6	7

1931 9-1-0 (5-1-0)
O3	•	Western Reserve	28	0
O3	•	Coe	19	0
O10	•	Illinois	7	0
O17	•	Wisconsin	14	21
O24	•	at Carnegie Tech	13	6
O31	•	at Chicago	14	6
N7	•	Centenary	49	6
N14	•	Iowa	22	0
N21	•	at Indiana	7	0
N28	•	Northwestern CHI	7	0

1932 7-0-1 (5-0-1)
O1	•	Kansas State	29	13
O8	•	at Minnesota	7	0
O15	•	Wisconsin	7	0
O22	=	at Northwestern	7	7
O29	•	NYU Brnx	34	9
N5	•	at Chicago	37	0
N12	•	at Iowa	18	0
N19	•	Indiana	25	7

1933 6-1-1 3-1-1
O7	•	Ohio U.	13	6
O14	=	at Minnesota	7	7
O21	•	at Chicago	14	0
O28	•	at Wisconsin	14	0
N4	•	Carnegie Tech	17	7
N11	•	at Notre Dame	19	0
N18	•	Iowa	6	14
N25	•	at Indiana	19	3

1934 5-3-0 (3-1-0)
O6		Rice	0	14
O13		at Notre Dame	7	18
O20	•	Wisconsin	14	0
O27	•	at Carnegie Tech	20	0
N3	•	at Chicago	26	20
N10	•	at Iowa	13	6
N17	•	Fordham NYC	7	0
N24		Indiana	6	17

1935 4-4-0 (3-3-0)
O5	•	at Northwestern	7	0
O12	•	Fordham NYC	20	0
O19	•	at Chicago	19	0
O26		Carnegie Tech	0	7
N2		at Minnesota	7	29
N9		at Wisconsin	0	8
N16	•	Iowa	12	6
N23		at Indiana	0	7

1936 5-2-1 (3-1-1)
S26	•	Ohio U.	47	0
O10		Wisconsin	35	14
O17	•	at Chicago	35	7
O24		at Minnesota	0	33
O31	•	at Carnegie Tech	7	6
N7		Fordham NYC	0	15
N14	•	at Iowa	13	0
N21	=	Indiana	20	20

MAL ELWARD — 1937-41 (.475) — 16-18-6

1937 4-3-1 (2-2-1)
S25	•	Butler	33	7
O2		at Ohio State	0	13
O9		Carnegie Tech	7	0
O16		at Northwestern	7	14
O30	•	Iowa	13	0
N6		Fordham NYC	3	21
N13	=	at Wisconsin	7	7
N20	•	at Indiana	13	7

1938 5-1-2 (3-1-1)
S24	•	Detroit	19	6
O1		at Butler	21	6
O8		at Minnesota	0	7
O15		Fordham NYC	6	6
O22		Wisconsin	13	7
O29		at Iowa	0	0
N5		at Ohio State	12	0
N19		Indiana	13	6

1939 3-3-2 (2-1-2)
S30		at Notre Dame	3	3
O14	=	at Minnesota	13	13
O21	•	Michigan State	20	7
O28		at Santa Clara	6	13
N4		Iowa	0	4
N11	•	at Northwestern	3	0
N18		at Wisconsin	7	7
N25	•	at Indiana	7	6

1940 2-6-0 (1-4-0)
S28	•	Butler	28	0
O5		at Ohio State	14	17
O12		at Michigan State	7	20
O26	•	Wisconsin	13	14
N2	•	at Iowa	21	6
N9		Fordham NYC	7	13
N16		at Minnesota	6	33
N23		Indiana	0	3

1941 2-5-1 (1-3-0)
S27		Vanderbilt	0	3
O4	•	at Pittsburgh	6	0
O18		at Ohio State	14	16
O25	•	Iowa	7	6
N1		Fordham NYC	0	17
N8		Michigan State	0	0
N15		at Wisconsin	0	13
N22		at Indiana	0	7

ELMER BURNHAM — 1942-43 (.556) — 10-8

1942 1-8-0 (1-4-0)
S26		Fordham	7	14
O3		at Vanderbilt	0	26
O10	•	at Northwestern	7	6
O17		at Ohio State	0	26
O24		Wisconsin	0	13
O31		at Iowa	7	13
N7		Great Lakes NAS	0	42
N14		at Michigan State	6	19
N21		Indiana	0	20

1943 9-0-0 (6-0-0)
S18	•	at Great Lakes NAS	23	13
S25	•	at Marquette	21	0
O2	•	Illinois	40	21
O9	•	Camp Grant	19	0
O16	•	Ohio State CLEV	30	7
O23	•	Iowa	28	7
O30	•	at Wisconsin	32	0
N6	•	at Minnesota	14	7
N20	•	at Indiana	7	0

CECIL ISBELL — 1944-46 (.500) — 14-14-1

1944 5-5-0 (4-2-0)
S23		at Great Lakes NAS	18	27
S30	•	Marquette	40	7
O7	•	at Illinois	35	19
O14		Iowa Pre-Flight	6	13
O21	•	at Iowa	26	7
O28	•	at Michigan	14	40
N4	•	Wisconsin	35	0
N11	•	at Northwestern	27	7
N18	•	Navy BALT	0	32
N25	•	Indiana	6	14

1945 7-3-0 (3-3-0)
S22	•	Marquette	14	13
S29		at Great Lakes NAS	20	6
O6	•	at Wisconsin	13	7
O13	•	Iowa	40	0
O20	•	at Ohio State	35	13
O27	•	at Northwestern	14	26
N3	•	Pittsburgh	28	0
N10	•	Miami (Ohio)	21	7
N17	•	at Michigan	13	27
N24	•	at Indiana	0	26

1946 2-6-1 (0-5-1)
S21	•	Miami (Ohio)	13	7
S28		at Iowa	0	16
O5		at Illinois	7	43
O12		at Notre Dame	6	49
O19	=	at Ohio State	14	14
O26	•	at Pittsburgh	10	8
N2		Wisconsin	20	24
N9		at Minnesota	7	13
N23		Indiana	20	34

STUART HOLCOMB — 1947-55 (.457) — 35-42-4

1947 5-4-0 (3-3-0)
S27		at Wisconsin	14	32
O4	•	Ohio State	24	20
O11	•	Notre Dame	7	22
O18	•	Boston U. Bos	62	7
O25	•	Illinois	14	7
N1	•	Iowa	21	0
N8		at Minnesota	21	26
N15	•	Pittsburgh	28	0
N22		at Indiana	14	16

1948 3-6-0 (2-4-0)
S25		at Notre Dame	27	28
O2		at Northwestern	0	21
O9		Michigan	0	40
O16	•	at Iowa	20	13
O23		at Illinois	6	10
O30	•	Marquette	14	9
N6		at Minnesota	7	34
N13		Pittsburgh	13	20
N20	•	Indiana	39	0

1949 4-5-0 (2-4-0)
S24		at Northwestern	6	20
O1		Iowa	7	21
O8		Notre Dame	12	35
O14	•	at Miami, Fla.	14	0
O22		Illinois	0	19
O29	•	at Minnesota	13	7
N5		at Michigan	12	20
N12	•	Marquette	41	7
N19	•	at Indiana	14	6

1950 2-7-0 (1-4-0)
S30		at Texas	26	34
O7	•	at Notre Dame	28	14
O14		Miami, Fla.	14	20
O21		at Iowa	21	33
O28		UCLA	6	20
N4		at Wisconsin	7	33
N11		Northwestern	14	19
N18		at Minnesota	14	27
N25	•	Indiana	13	0

1951 5-4-0 (4-1-0)

S29		Texas	0	14
O6	● |	Iowa	34	30
O12		at Miami, Fla.	0	7
O20	|	Wisconsin	7	31
O27		at Notre Dame	9	30
N3	●	Penn State	28	0
N10	● |	at Northwestern	35	14
N17	● |	Minnesota	19	13
N24	● |	at Indiana	21	13

1952 4-3-2 (4-1-1)

S27	=	at Penn State	20	20
O4	● |	at Ohio State	21	14
O11	● |	Iowa	41	14
O18		Notre Dame	14	26
O25	● |	at Illinois	40	12
N1		Michigan State	7	14
N8	= |	at Minnesota	14	14
N15	|	at Michigan	10	21
N22	● |	Indiana	21	16

1953 2-7-0 (2-4-0)

S26		at Missouri	7	14
O3		Notre Dame	7	37
O10		at Duke	14	20
O17	|	Wisconsin	19	28
O24	● |	Michigan State	6	0
O31	|	at Illinois	0	21
N7	|	Iowa	0	26
N14	|	at Ohio State	6	21
N21	● |	at Indiana	30	0

1954 5-3-1 (3-3-0)

S25	●	Missouri	31	0
O2	●	at Notre Dame	27	14
O9	=	Duke	13	13
O16	|	at Wisconsin	6	20
O23	● |	at Michigan State	27	13
O30	● |	Illinois	28	14
N6	|	at Iowa	14	25
N13	|	Ohio State	6	28
N20	● |	Indiana	13	7

1955 5-3-1 (4-2-1)

S24	●	Pacific	14	7
O1	● |	at Minnesota	7	6
O8	|	Wisconsin	0	9
O15	= |	at Iowa	20	20
O22		Notre Dame	7	22
O29	● |	at Illinois	13	0
N5	|	Michigan State	0	27
N12	● |	Northwestern	46	8
N19	● |	at Indiana	6	4

JACK MOLLENKOPF
1956-69 (.670) 84-39-9

1956 3-4-2 (1-4-2)

S29	●	Missouri	16	7
O6	|	at Minnesota	14	21
O13	●	at Notre Dame	28	14
O20	= |	at Wisconsin	6	6
O27	|	Iowa	20	21
N3	= |	Illinois	7	7
N10	|	at Michigan State	9	12
N17	|	at Northwestern	0	14
N24	● |	Indiana	39	20

1957 5-4-0 (4-3-0)

S28		Notre Dame	0	12
O5	|	at Minnesota	17	21
O12	|	Wisconsin	14	23
O19	● |	at Michigan State	20	13
O26	●	Miami (Ohio)	37	6
N2	● |	at Illinois	21	6
N9	|	at Ohio State	7	20
N16	● |	Northwestern	27	0
N23	● |	at Indiana	35	13

1958 6-1-2 (3-1-2)

S27	●	Nebraska	28	0
O4	●	at Rice	24	0
O11	|	at Wisconsin	6	31
O18	● |	Michigan State	14	6
O25	●	at Notre Dame	29	22
N1	● |	Illinois	31	8
N8	= |	at Ohio State	14	14
N15	● |	at Northwestern	23	6
N22	= |	Indiana	15	15

1959 5-2-2 (4-2-1)

S18	=	at UCLA	0	0
O3	●	Notre Dame	28	7
O10	● |	Wisconsin	21	0
O17	|	at Ohio State	0	15
O24	● |	Iowa	14	7
O31	= |	at Illinois	7	7
N7	|	at Michigan State	0	15
N14	● |	Minnesota	29	23
N21	● |	at Indiana	10	7

1960 4-4-1 (3-4-0)

S24	=	UCLA	27	27
O1	●	at Notre Dame	51	19
O8	|	at Wisconsin	13	24
O15	● |	Ohio State	24	21
O22	|	at Iowa	14	21
O29	|	Illinois	12	14
N5	|	Michigan State	13	17
N12	● |	at Minnesota	23	14
N19	● |	Indiana	35	6

1961 6-3-0 (4-2-0)

S23	●	at Washington	13	6
O7		Notre Dame	20	22
O14	●	Miami (Ohio)	19	6
O21	|	at Michigan	14	16
O28	● |	Iowa	9	0
N4	● |	at Illinois	23	9
N11	● |	Michigan State	7	6
N18	|	at Minnesota	7	10
N25	● |	at Indiana	34	12

1962 4-4-1 (3-3-0)

S22	=	at Washington	7	7
O6	●	at Notre Dame	24	6
O13		Miami (Ohio)	7	10
O20	● |	Michigan	37	0
O27	● |	at Iowa	26	3
N3	|	Illinois	10	14
N10	● |	at Michigan State	17	9
N17	|	at Minnesota	6	7
N24	|	Indiana	7	12

1963 5-4-0 (4-3-0)

S28		at Miami, Fla.	0	3
O5	●	Notre Dame	7	6
O12	|	at Wisconsin	20	38
O19	● |	at Michigan	23	12
O26	● |	Iowa	14	0
N2	|	at Illinois	21	41
N9	|	Michigan State	0	23
N16	● |	Minnesota	13	11
N30	● |	at Indiana	21	15

1964 6-3-0 (5-2-0)

S26	●	Ohio U.	17	0
O3		at Notre Dame	15	34
O10	● |	Wisconsin	28	7
O17	● |	at Michigan	21	20
O24	● |	at Iowa	19	14
O31	● |	Illinois	26	14
N7	|	at Michigan State	7	21
N14	|	at Minnesota	7	14
N21	● |	Indiana	28	22

1965 7-2-1 (5-2-0)

S18	●	Miami (Ohio)	38	0
S25	●	Notre Dame	25	21
O2	=	SMU DAL	14	14
O9	● |	at Iowa	17	14
O16	● |	at Michigan	17	15
O23	|	Michigan State	10	14
O30	|	at Illinois	0	21
N6	● |	Wisconsin	45	7
N13	● |	Minnesota	35	0
N20	● |	at Indiana	26	21

1966 9-2-0 (6-1-0)

S17	●	Ohio U.	42	3
S24		at Notre Dame	14	26
O1	●	SMU	35	23
O8	● |	Iowa	35	0
O15	● |	at Michigan	22	21
O22	|	at Michigan State	20	41
O29	● |	Illinois	25	21
N5	● |	at Wisconsin	23	0
N12	● |	at Minnesota	16	0
N19	● |	Indiana	51	6
		ROSE BOWL		
J2	●	USC	14	13

1967 8-2-0 (6-1-0)

S23	●	Texas A&M DAL	24	20
S30	●	Notre Dame	28	21
O7	● |	Northwestern	25	16
O14	● |	at Ohio State	41	6
O21		Oregon State	14	22
O28	● |	at Iowa	41	22
N4	● |	at Illinois	42	9
N11	● |	Minnesota	41	12
N18	● |	Michigan State	21	7
N25	|	at Indiana	14	19

1968 8-2-0 (5-2-0)

S21	●	Virginia	44	6
S28	●	at Notre Dame	37	22
O5	● |	at Northwestern	43	6
O12	|	at Ohio State	0	13
O19	●	Wake Forest	28	27
O26	● |	Iowa	44	14
N2	● |	Illinois	35	17
N9	|	at Minnesota	13	27
N16	● |	at Michigan State	9	0
N23	● |	Indiana	38	35

1969 8-2-0 (5-2-0)

S20	●	at TCU	42	35
S27	●	Notre Dame	28	14
O4	●	Stanford	36	35
O11	|	at Michigan	20	31
O18	● |	Iowa	35	31
O25	● |	Northwestern	45	20
N1	● |	at Illinois	49	22
N8	● |	Michigan State	41	13
N15	|	at Ohio State	14	42
N22	● |	at Indiana	44	21

BOB DEMOSS
1970-72 (.419) 13-18

1970 4-6-0 (2-5-0)

S19	●	TCU	15	0
S26		at Notre Dame	0	48
O3	●	at Stanford	26	14
O10	|	Michigan	0	29
O17	● |	at Iowa	24	3
O24	|	at Northwestern	14	38
O31	|	Illinois	21	23
N7	|	at Michigan State	14	24
N14	|	Ohio State	7	10
N21	● |	Indiana	40	0

1971 3-7-0 (3-5-0)

S18		at Washington	35	38
S25		Notre Dame	7	8
O2	● |	Iowa	45	13
O9	● |	Minnesota	27	13
O16	● |	at Northwestern	21	20
O23	|	at Illinois	7	21
O30	|	Michigan State	10	43
N6	|	at Wisconsin	10	14
N13	|	Michigan	17	20
N20	|	at Indiana	31	38

1972 6-5-0 (6-2-0)

S16		Bowling Green	14	17
S23		Washington	21	22
S30		at Notre Dame	14	35
O7	● |	at Iowa	24	0
O14	● |	at Minnesota	28	3
O21	● |	Northwestern	37	0
O28	● |	Illinois	20	14
N4	|	at Michigan State	12	22
N11	● |	Wisconsin	27	6
N18	|	at Michigan	6	9
N25	● |	Indiana	42	7

ALEX AGASE
1973-76 (.420) 18-25-1

1973 5-6-0 (4-4-0)

S15	● |	at Wisconsin	14	13
S22		Miami (Ohio)	19	24
S29		Notre Dame	7	20
O6	●	Duke	27	7
O13	|	at Illinois	13	15
O20	● |	Northwestern	21	10
O27	|	Michigan State	7	10
N3	● |	at Iowa	48	23
N10	|	at Minnesota	7	34
N17	|	Michigan	9	34
N24	● |	at Indiana	28	23

1974 4-6-1 (3-5-0)

S14	|	Wisconsin	14	28
S21	=	Miami (Ohio)	7	7
S28	●	at Notre Dame	31	20
O5		at Duke	14	16
O12	|	Illinois	23	27
O19	● |	at Northwestern	31	26
O26	|	at Michigan State	7	31
N2	● |	Iowa	38	14
N9	|	Minnesota	20	24
N16	|	at Michigan	0	51
N23	● |	Indiana	38	17

1975 4-7-0 (4-4-0)

S13	|	at Northwestern	25	31
S20		Notre Dame	0	17
S27		at USC	6	19
O4		Miami (Ohio)	3	14
O11	|	Wisconsin	14	17
O18	● |	at Illinois	26	24
O25	|	Ohio State	6	35
N1	● |	Michigan State	20	10
N8	|	at Michigan	0	28
N15	● |	Iowa	19	18
N22	● |	at Indiana	9	7

1976 5-6-0 (4-4-0)

S11	● |	Northwestern	31	19
S18		at Notre Dame	0	23
S25		USC	13	31
O2	●	Miami (Ohio)	42	20
O9	● |	at Wisconsin	18	16
O16	|	Illinois	17	21
O23	|	at Ohio State	3	24
O30	|	at Michigan State	13	45
N6	● |	Michigan	16	14
N13	● |	at Iowa	21	0
N20	|	Indiana	14	20

JIM YOUNG
1977-81 (.664) 38-19-1

1977 5-6-0 (3-5-0)

S10	|	at Michigan State	14	19
S17	●	Ohio U.	44	7
S24		Notre Dame	24	31
O1	●	Wake Forest	26	17
O8	|	at Ohio State	0	46
O15	|	Illinois	22	29
O22	● |	Iowa	34	21
O29	● |	at Northwestern	28	16
N5	● |	at Wisconsin	22	0
N12	|	Michigan	7	40
N19	|	at Indiana	10	21

1978 9-2-1 (6-1-1)

S16	● |	Michigan State	21	14
S23	●	Ohio U.	24	0
S30		at Notre Dame	6	10
O7	●	Wake Forest	14	7
O14	● |	Ohio State	27	16
O21	● |	at Illinois	13	0
O28	● |	at Iowa	34	7
N4	● |	Northwestern	31	0
N11	= |	at Wisconsin	24	24
N18	|	at Michigan	6	24
N25	● |	Indiana	20	7
		PEACH BOWL		
D25	●	Georgia Tech	41	21

1979 10-2-0 (7-1-0)

S8	● |	Wisconsin	41	20
S15		at UCLA	21	31
S22	●	Notre Dame	28	22
S29	●	Oregon	13	7
O6	|	at Minnesota	14	31
O13	● |	Illinois	28	14
O20	● |	at Michigan State	14	7
O27	● |	Northwestern	20	16
N3	● |	at Iowa	20	14
N10	● |	Michigan	24	21
N17	● |	at Indiana	37	21
		BLUEBONNET BOWL		
D31	●	Tennessee	27	22

1980 9-3-0 (7-1-0)

S6		at Notre Dame	10	31
S13	● |	at Wisconsin	12	6
S20		UCLA	14	23
O4	●	Miami (Ohio)	28	3
O11	● |	Minnesota	21	7
O18	● |	at Illinois	45	20
O25	● |	Michigan State	36	25
N1	● |	at Northwestern	52	31
N8	● |	Iowa	58	13
N15	|	at Michigan	0	26
N22	● |	Indiana	24	23
		LIBERTY BOWL		
D27	●	Missouri	28	25

1981 5-6-0 (3-6-0)

S12	●	Stanford	27	19
S19	|	at Minnesota	13	16
S26	●	Notre Dame	15	14
O3	|	at Wisconsin	14	20
O10	● |	Illinois	44	20
O17	● |	at Northwestern	35	0
O24	● |	Michigan State	27	26
O31	|	Ohio State	33	45
N7	|	at Iowa	7	33
N14	|	Michigan	10	28
N21	|	at Indiana	17	20

LEON BURTNETT
1982-86 (.384)   21-34-1

1982   3-8-0 (3-6-0)
S11	Stanford	14	35
S18	Minnesota	10	36
S25	at Notre Dame	14	28
O2	Wisconsin	31	35
O9	at Illinois	34	38
O16 •	Northwestern	34	21
O23 •	at Michigan State	24	21
O30	at Ohio State	6	38
N6 •	Iowa	16	7
N13	at Michigan	21	52
N20	Indiana	7	13

1983   3-7-1 (3-5-1)
S10	Notre Dame	6	52
S17	at Miami, Fla.	0	35
S24 •	at Minnesota	32	20
O1 =	Michigan State	29	29
O8	at Ohio State	22	33
O15	at Iowa	14	31
O22	Illinois	21	35
O29 •	Northwestern	48	17
N5	at Michigan	10	42
N12	Wisconsin	38	42
N19 •	at Indiana	31	30

1984   7-5-0 (6-3-0)
S8 •	Notre Dame IND	23	21
S15	Miami, Fla.	17	28
S22 •	Minnesota	34	10
S29 •	at Michigan State	13	10
O6 •	Ohio State	28	23
O13	Iowa	3	40
O20	at Illinois	20	34
O27 •	at Northwestern	49	7
N3 •	Michigan	31	29
N10	at Wisconsin	13	30
N17	Indiana	31	24
PEACH BOWL			
D31	Virginia	24	27

1985   5-6-0 (3-5-0)
A31	at Pittsburgh	30	31
S21 •	Ball State	37	18
S28	Notre Dame	35	17
O5	at Minnesota	15	45
O12 •	Illinois	30	24
O19	at Ohio State	27	41
O26	Michigan State	24	28
N2 •	Northwestern	31	7
N9	at Michigan	0	47
N16 •	Iowa	24	27
N23 •	at Indiana	34	21

1986   3-8-0 (2-6-0)
S13 •	Ball State	20	3
S20	Pittsburgh	26	41
S27	at Notre Dame	9	41
O4	Minnesota	9	36
O11	at Illinois	27	34
O18	Ohio State	11	39
O25	at Michigan State	3	37
N1 •	at Northwestern	17	16
N8	Michigan	7	31
N15	at Iowa	14	42
N22 •	Indiana	17	15

FRED AKERS
1987-90 (.284)   12-31-1

1987   3-7-1 (3-5-0)
S12	at Washington	10	28
S19 =	Louisville	22	22
S26	Notre Dame	20	44
O3	at Minnesota	19	21
O10 •	Illinois	9	3
O17	Ohio State	17	20
O24	at Iowa	14	38
O31 •	Wisconsin	49	14
N7	at Michigan State	3	45
N14 •	Northwestern	20	15
N21	at Indiana	14	35

1988   4-7-0 (3-5-0)
S10	Washington	6	20
S17	Ohio U.	33	10
S24	at Notre Dame	7	52
O1 •	Minnesota	14	10
O8	at Illinois	0	20
O15 •	at Ohio State	31	26
O22	Iowa	7	31
O29 •	at Wisconsin	9	6
N5	Michigan State	3	48
N12	at Northwestern	7	28
N19	Indiana	7	52

1989   3-8-0 (2-6-0)
S9 •	Miami (Ohio)	27	10
S16	at Washington	9	38
S30	Notre Dame	7	40
O7	at Minnesota	15	35
O14	Illinois	2	14
O21	at Ohio State	3	21
O28	Michigan State	21	28
N4	at Michigan	27	42
N11 •	Northwestern	46	15
N18	Iowa	0	24
N25 •	at Indiana	15	14

1990   2-9-0 (1-7-0)
S15	Washington	14	20
S22	Indiana St.	41	13
S29	at Notre Dame	11	37
O6	Minnesota	7	19
O13	at Illinois	0	34
O20	Ohio State	2	42
O27	at Michigan State	33	55
N3	Michigan	13	38
N10 •	at Northwestern	33	13
N17	at Iowa	9	38
N24	Indiana	14	28

JIM COLLETTO
1991-96 (.326)   20-43-3

1991   4-7-0 (3-5-0)
S7 •	Eastern Michigan	49	3
S14	at California	18	42
S28	Notre Dame	20	45
O5 •	at Northwestern	17	14
O12	at Minnesota	3	6
O19 •	Wisconsin	28	7
O26	Iowa	21	31
N2	at Michigan	0	42
N9	Illinois	14	41
N16 •	Michigan State	27	17
N23	at Indiana	22	24

1992   4-7-0 (3-5-0)
S12 •	California	41	14
S19	Toledo	29	33
S26	at Notre Dame	0	48
O3	Northwestern	14	28
O10 •	Minnesota	24	20
O17	at Wisconsin	16	19
O24 •	at Iowa	27	16
O31	Michigan	17	24
N7	at Illinois	17	20
N14	at Michigan State	13	35
N21 •	Indiana	13	10

1993   1-10-0 (0-8-0)
S4	at North Carolina St.	7	20
S11 •	Western Michigan	28	13
S25	Notre Dame	0	17
O2	Illinois	10	28
O9	at Minnesota	56	59
O16	Wisconsin	28	42
O23	Ohio State	24	45
O30	at Iowa	17	26
N6	at Michigan	10	25
N13	Michigan State	24	27
N20	at Indiana	17	24

1994   4-5-2 (2-4-2)
S10 •	Toledo	51	17
S17 •	Ball State	49	21
S24	at Notre Dame	21	39
O1 •	at Illinois	22	16
O8	Minnesota	49	37
O15 =	at Wisconsin	27	27
O22	at Ohio State	14	48
O29 =	Iowa	21	21
N5	Michigan	23	45
N12 •	at Michigan State	30	42 †
N19	Indiana	29	33

1995   4-6-1 (2-5-1)
S2 •	at West Virginia	26	24
S9	Notre Dame	28	35
S23 =	Michigan State	35	35
S30 •	Ball State	35	13
O7	at Minnesota	38	39
O14	Penn State	23	26
O21	at Ohio State	0	28
N4 •	Wisconsin	38	27
N11	at Michigan	0	5
N18 •	Northwestern	8	23
N24 •	at Indiana	51	14

1996   3-8 (2-6)
A31	at Michigan State	14	52
S14	at Notre Dame	0	35
S21	West Virginia	6	20
S28	North Carolina St.	42	21
O5 •	Minnesota	30	27
O12	at Penn State	14	31
O19	Ohio State	14	42
N2	at Wisconsin	25	33
N9 •	Michigan	9	3
N16	at Northwestern	24	27
N23	Indiana	16	33

JOE TILLER
1997-Present (.605)   75-49

1997   9-3 (6-2)
S6	at Toledo	22	36
S13 •	Notre Dame	28	17
S20 •	Ball State	28	14
S27 •	Northwestern	21	9
O11 •	at Minnesota	59	43
O18 •	Wisconsin	45	20
O25 •	at Illinois	48	3
N1 •	at Iowa	17	35
N8 •	Michigan State	22	21
N15 •	Penn State	17	42
N22 •	at Indiana	56	7
ALAMO BOWL			
D30	Oklahoma State	33	20

1998   9-4 (6-2)
A30	at USC	17	27
S12 •	Rice	21	19
S19 •	Central Florida	35	7
S26 •	at Notre Dame	30	31
O3 •	Minnesota	56	21
O10 •	at Wisconsin	24	31
O17 •	at Penn State	13	31
O24 •	Illinois	42	9
O31 •	Iowa	36	14
N7 •	at Northwestern	56	21
N14 •	at Michigan State	25	24
N21 •	Indiana	52	7
ALAMO BOWL			
D29	Kansas Kansas State	37	34

1999   7-5 (4-4)
S4 •	at Central Florida	47	13
S11 •	Notre Dame	28	23
S18 •	Central Michigan	58	16
S25 •	Northwestern	31	23
O2 •	at Michigan	12	38
O9 •	at Ohio State	22	25
O16 •	Michigan State	52	28
O23 •	Penn State	25	31
O30 •	at Minnesota	33	28
N6 •	Wisconsin	21	28
N20 •	at Indiana	30	24
OUTBACK BOWL			
J1	Georgia	25	28

2000   8-4 (6-2)
S2 •	Central Michigan	48	0
S9 •	Kent	45	10
S16 •	at Notre Dame	21	23
S23 •	Minnesota	38	24
S30 •	at Penn State	20	22
O7 •	Michigan	32	31
O14 •	at Northwestern	41	28
O21 •	at Wisconsin	30	24
O28 •	Ohio State	31	27
N11 •	at Michigan State	10	30
N18 •	Indiana	41	13
ROSE BOWL			
J1	Washington	24	34

2001   6-6 (4-4)
S2 •	at Cincinnati	19	14
S22 •	Akron	33	14
S29 •	at Minnesota	35	28
O6 •	Iowa	23	14
O13 •	at Michigan	10	24
O27 •	Northwestern	32	27
N3 •	Illinois	13	38
N10 •	at Ohio State	9	35
N17 •	Michigan State	24	14
N24 •	at Indiana	7	13
D1	Notre Dame	18	24
SUN BOWL			
D31	Washington State	27	33

2002   7-6 (4-4)
A31 •	Illinois St.	51	10
S7	at Notre Dame	17	24
S14 •	Western Michigan	28	24
S21	Wake Forest	21	24
S28 •	Minnesota	28	15
O5 •	at Iowa	28	31
O12	at Illinois	31	38
O19	Michigan	21	23
O26 •	at Northwestern	42	13
N9	Ohio State	6	10
N16 •	at Michigan State	45	42
N23	Indiana	34	10
SUN BOWL			
D31 •	Washington	34	24

2003   9-4 (6-2)
S6 •	Bowling Green	26	27
S13 •	at Wake Forest	16	10
S20 •	Arizona	59	7
S27 •	Notre Dame	23	10
O4 •	Illinois	43	10
O11 •	Penn State	28	14
O18 •	at Wisconsin	26	23
O25 •	at Michigan	3	31
N1 •	Northwestern	34	14
N8 •	Iowa	27	14
N15 •	at Ohio State	13	16
N22 •	at Indiana	24	16
CAPITAL ONE BOWL			
J1	Georgia	27	34

2004   7-5 (4-4)
S5 •	Syracuse	51	0
S11 •	Ball State	59	7
S25 •	at Illinois	38	30
O2 •	at Notre Dame	41	16
O9 •	at Penn State	20	13
O16	Wisconsin	17	20
O23	Michigan	14	16
O30 •	at Northwestern	10	13
N6 •	at Iowa	21	23
N13 •	Ohio State	24	17
N20 •	Indiana	63	24
SUN BOWL			
D31	Arizona State	23	27

2005   5-6 (3-5)
S10 •	Akron	49	24
S17 •	at Arizona	31	24
S24 •	at Minnesota	35	42
O1	Notre Dame	28	49
O8	Iowa	17	34
O15	Northwestern	29	34
O22	at Wisconsin	20	31
O29	at Penn State	15	33
N5 •	Michigan State	28	21
N12 •	Illinois	37	3
N19 •	at Indiana	41	14

2006   8-6 (5-3)
S2 •	Indiana St.	60	35
S9 •	Miami (Ohio)	38	31
S16 •	Ball State	38	28
S23 •	Minnesota	27	21
S30 •	at Notre Dame	21	35
O7	at Iowa	17	47
O14 •	at Northwestern	31	10
O21	Wisconsin	3	24
O28	Penn State	0	12
N4 •	at Michigan State	17	15
N11 •	at Illinois	42	31
N18 •	Indiana	28	19
N25	at Hawaii		
CHAMPS SPORTS BOWL			
D29	Maryland	7	24

Neutral Site key: *BALT* Baltimore, Md. / *BOS* Boston, Mass. / *BRNX* Bronx, N.Y. / *CHI* Chicago, Ill. / *CLEV* Cleveland, Ohio / *DAL* Dallas, Texas / *EVA* Evanston, Ill. / *IND* Indianapolis, Ind. / *NYC* New York, N.Y. / *STL* St. Louis, Mo.
ƒ Forfeit † Game Later Forfeited # Disputed Victor * Disputed Score ‖ Designated Conference Game |2 Counted Twice in Conference Standings

PURDUE RECORD BOOK

SINGLE-GAME RECORDS

RUSHING YARDS

RANK	PLAYER	DATE	OPPONENT	ATT	AVG	YDS
1	Otis Armstrong	Nov. 25, 1972	Indiana	32	8.6	276
2	Mike Alstott	Nov. 24, 1995	Indiana	25	10.6	264
3	Otis Armstrong	Oct. 21, 1972	Northwestern	32	7.3	233
4	Edwin Watson	Sept. 28, 1996	North Carolina State	29	7.8	227
5	Leroy Keyes	Nov. 4, 1967	Illinois	21	10.7	225

PASSING YARDS

RANK	PLAYER	DATE	OPPONENT	ATT	COMP	YDS
1	Drew Brees	Oct. 3, 1998	Minnesota	36	31	522
	Kyle Orton	Nov. 20, 2004	Indiana	54	33	522
3	Scott Campbell	Oct. 31, 1981	Ohio State	52	31	516
4	Drew Brees	Oct. 16, 1999	Michigan State	57	40	509
5	Jim Everett	Oct. 19, 1985	Ohio State	55	35	497

RECEIVING YARDS

RANK	PLAYER	DATE	OPPONENT	REC	AVG	YDS
1	Chris Daniels	Oct. 16, 1999	Michigan State	21	14.3	301
2	Selwyn Lymon	Sept. 30, 2006	Notre Dame	8	29.8	238
3	Brian Alford	Oct. 11, 1997	Minnesota	4	53.8	215
4	Brian Alford	Sept. 6, 1997	Toledo	10	20.9	209
	Kyle Ingraham	Nov. 20, 2004	Indiana	11	19.0	209

POINTS

RANK	PLAYER	DATE	OPPONENT	TOT
1	Elmer Oliphant	Nov. 17, 1912	Rose Poly	43
2	Mike Northington	Nov. 3, 1973	Iowa	30
	Mike Alstott	Oct. 9, 1993	Minnesota	30
4	Cecil Isbell	Sept. 26, 1936	Ohio	25
5	8 players tied at 24			

FIELD GOALS

RANK	PLAYER	DATE	OPPONENT	TOT
1	E.C. Robertson	Oct. 27, 1900	Rose Poly	7
2	Rick Anderson	Oct. 25, 1980	Michigan State	5
3	5 players tied at 4			

TACKLES

RANK	PLAYER	DATE	OPPONENT	TOT
1	Chuck Kyle	Nov. 23, 1968	Indiana	27
2	Darrin Trieb	Nov. 3, 1990	Michigan	26
3	Rick Schavietello	Sept. 18, 1971	Washington	23
	Freddie Arrington	Nov. 19, 1977	Indiana	23
	James Looney	Nov. 15, 1980	Michigan	23

INTERCEPTIONS

RANK	PLAYER	DATE	OPPONENT	TOT
1	Paul Beery	Oct. 9, 1976	Wisconsin	4
2	9 players tied at 3			

RETIRED NUMBERS

Purdue has no retired numbers

SINGLE-SEASON RECORDS

RUSHING YARDS

RANK	PLAYER	SEASON	G	ATT	YDS
1	Mike Alstott	1995	NA	243	1,436
2	Otis Armstrong	1972	10	243	1,361
3	Mike Alstott	1994	NA	202	1,188
4	Joey Harris	2002	13	250	1,115
5	Otis Armstrong	1970	11	213	1,009

PASSING YARDS

RANK	PLAYER	SEASON	G	ATT	COMP	PCT	YDS
1	Curtis Painter	2006	14	530	315	59.4	3,985
2	Drew Brees	1998	13	569	361	63.4	3,983
3	Drew Brees	1999	12	554	337	60.8	3,909
4	Drew Brees	2000	12	512	309	60.3	3,668
5	Jim Everett	1985	11	450	285	63.3	3,651

RECEIVING YARDS

RANK	PLAYER	SEASON	G	REC	AVG	YDS
1	John Standeford	2002	13	75	17.4	1,307
2	Chris Daniels	1999	12	121	10.2	1,236
3	Brian Alford	1997	12	63	19.5	1,228
4	John Standeford	2003	13	77	14.9	1,150
5	Rodney Carter	1985	11	98	11.2	1,099

SCORING

RANK	PLAYER	SEASON	TD	FG	PAT	P2	TOT
1	Leroy Keyes	1967	19	0	0	0	114
2	Ben Jones	2003	0	25	36	0	111
3	Stan Brown	1969	18	0	0	0	108
4	3 players at 96						

TOUCHDOWNS

RANK	PLAYER	SEASON	G	TOT
1	Leroy Keyes	1967	10	19
2	Stan Brown	1969	NA	18
3	Tony Butkovich	1943	NA	16
	Taylor Stubblefield	2004	12	16
5	Leroy Keyes	1968	NA	15

TACKLES

RANK	PLAYER	SEASON	G	TOT
1	Mark Brown	1982	10	209
2	Fred Arrington	1977	11	182
3	James Looney	1980	12	180
4	Eric Beatty	1992	NA	175
5	Fred Strickland	1987	NA	168

INTERCEPTIONS

RANK	PLAYER	SEASON	G	YDS	TOT
1	Phil Mateja	1952	NA	62	7
	Bill Kay	1979	11	15	7
3	4 players tied at 6				

PUNTING

RANK	PLAYER	SEASON	PUNTS	YDS	AVG
1	Travis Dorsch	2001	53	2,547	48.1
2	Shawn McCarthy	1989	69	3,075	44.6
3	Eric Bruun	1991	59	2,548	43.2
4	Jared Armstrong	2006	50	2,154	43.1
5	Johnny Galvin	1946	NA	NA	42.9

PUNT RETURNS

RANK	PLAYER	SEASON	RET	YDS	AVG
1	Vinny Sutherland	1999	18	296	16.4
2	Phil Mateja	1951	12	190	15.8
3	Ken Gorgal	1948	17	252	14.8
4	Neil Schmidt	1950	11	148	13.5
5	Bill Canfield	1947	10	117	11.7

KICKOFF RETURNS

RANK	PLAYER	SEASON	RET	YDS	AVG
1	Stan Brown	1970	19	638	33.6
2	Otis Armstrong	1972	15	452	30.1
3	Stan Brown	1969	26	698	26.8
4	Rick Moss	1978	12	308	25.7
5	Jimmy Smith	1979	12	304	25.3

CAREER RECORDS

RUSHING YARDS

RANK	PLAYER	SEASONS	ATT	AVG	TD	YDS
1	Mike Alstott	1992-95	644	5.6	39	3,635
2	Otis Armstrong	1970-72	670	4.9	17	3,315
3	Scott Dierking	1973-76	578	5.0	25	2,863
4	Montrell Lowe	1999-2002	612	4.3	15	2,648
5	Edwin Watson	1994-97	530	4.8	25	2,520
6	Harry Szulborski	1946-49	478	5.2	NA	2,478
7	Corey Rogers	1991-95	489	5.0	27	2,436
8	Jerod Void	2002-05	569	4.3	36	2,429
9	Leroy Keyes	1966-68	356	5.9	29	2,094
10	Perry Williams	1966-68	514	4.0	30	2,049

PASSING YARDS

RANK	PLAYER	SEASONS	ATT	COMP	PCT	INT	TD	YDS
1	Drew Brees	1997-2000	1,678	1026	61.1	45	90	11,792
2	Mark Herrmann	1977-80	1,309	772	59.0	75	71	9,946
3	Kyle Orton	2001-04	1,336	786	58.8	28	63	9,337
4	Scott Campbell	1980-83	1,060	609	57.5	41	45	7,636
5	Jim Everett	1981-85	965	572	59.3	28	43	7,411
6	Eric Hunter	1989-92	818	422	51.6	32	33	5,598
7	Mike Phipps	1967-69	733	375	51.2	34	37	5,423
8	Rick Trefzger	1993-96	663	383	57.8	28	24	5,063
9	Curtis Painter	2005-	700	404	57.7	24	25	4,917
10	Bob Griese	1964-66	627	358	57.1	29	28	4,541

RECEIVING YARDS

RANK	PLAYER	SEASONS	REC	AVG	TD	YDS
1	John Standeford	2000-03	266	14.2	27	3,788
2	Taylor Stubblefield	2001-04	325	11.2	21	3,629
3	Brian Alford	1994-97	164	18.5	31	3,029
4	Dorien Bryant	2004-	205	12.7	13	2,612
5	Vinny Sutherland	1997-2000	176	13.5	25	2,370
6	Dave Young	1977-80	180	12.9	27	2,316
7	Steve Griffin	1982-85	146	15.3	12	2,234
8	Bart Burrell	1977-80	140	15.2	14	2,126
9	Tim Stratton	1998-2001	204	10.2	15	2,088
10	Jim Beirne	1965-67	142	13.1	17	1,864

SCORING

RANK	PLAYER	SEASONS	TD	FG	PAT	P2	TOT
1	Travis Dorsch	1998-2001	0	68	151	0	355
2	Mike Alstott	1992-95	42	0	0	2	256
3	Ben Jones	2003-05	0	43	125	0	254
4	Leroy Keyes	1966-68	37	0	0	0	222
5	Jerod Void	2002-05	36	0	0	0	216

TOUCHDOWNS

RANK	PLAYER	SEASONS	G	TOT
1	Mike Alstott	1992-95	NA	42
2	Leroy Keyes	1966-68	NA	37
3	Jerod Void	2002-05	47	36
4	Perry Williams	1966-68	NA	31
	Brian Alford	1994-97	NA	31

TACKLES

RANK	PLAYER	SEASONS	G	TOT
1	Kevin Motts	1976-79	NA	520
2	Fred Strickland	1984-87	NA	479
3	Eric Beatty	1989-92	NA	448
4	Rod Woodson	1983-86	45	445
5	Brock Spack	1980-83	NA	384

INTERCEPTIONS

RANK	PLAYER	SEASONS	G	YDS	TOT
1	Stuart Schweigert	2000-03	49	176	17
2	6 players tied at 11				

PUNTING

RANK	PLAYER	SEASONS	PUNTS	YDS	AVG
1	Travis Dorsch	1998-2001	66	3,199	48.5
2	Jared Armstrong	2006-	50	2,154	43.1
3	Eric Bruun	1990-91	120	5,091	42.4
4	Shawn McCarthy	1986-89	273	11,246	41.2
5	Brent Slaton	2002-03	141	5,788	41.0

TEAM RECORDS

LONGEST WINNING STREAK
• 16, Oct. 24, 1891-Nov. 4, 1893
Streak broken vs. Michigan, 8-46, Nov. 11, 1893

LONGEST UNDEFEATED STREAK
• 20, Oct. 24, 1931-Nov. 11, 1933
Streak broken vs. Iowa, 6-14, Nov. 18, 1933

MOST CONSECUTIVE WINNING SEASONS
• 9, 1926-1934

MOST CONSECUTIVE BOWL APPEARANCES
• 8, 1997-2004

MOST POINTS IN A GAME
• 96, vs. Butler, Oct. 21, 1893

MOST POINTS ALLOWED IN A GAME
• 59, vs. Minnesota, Oct. 9, 1993

LARGEST MARGIN OF VICTORY
• 96 (96-0), vs. Butler, Oct. 21, 1893

LARGEST MARGIN OF DEFEAT
• 56 (0-56) (tie), vs. Chicago, Nov. 9, 1907; vs. Iowa, Oct. 28, 1922

LONGEST RUN FROM SCRIMMAGE
• 94 yards, Mike Pruitt, vs. Iowa, Nov. 2, 1974

LONGEST PASS PLAY
• 99 yards, Drew Brees to Vinny Sutherland, vs. Northwestern, Sept. 25, 1999

LONGEST FIELD GOAL
• 51 yards, (tie), James Reichert, vs. Notre Dame, Oct. 27, 1951; Larry Sullivan, vs. Minnesota, Oct. 7, 1989; Travis Dorsch, vs. Washington State, in the Sun Bowl, Dec. 31, 2001

LONGEST PUNT
• 85 yards, Lou Brock, vs. Ohio State, Nov. 5, 1938

LONGEST INTERCEPTION RETURN
• 100 yards, (tie) Rod Woodson, vs. Iowa, Nov. 15, 1986; Michael Hawthorne and Billy Gustin, vs. Central Florida, Sept. 19, 1998

PUNT RETURNS

RANK	PLAYER	SEASON	RET	YDS	AVG
1	Phil Mateja	1951-52	25	300	12.0
2	Vinny Sutherland	1997-2000	59	684	11.6
3	Ken Gorgal	1947-49	37	417	11.3
4	Carl Capria	1971-73	24	252	10.5
5	Anthony Chambers	2002-03	75	780	10.4

KICKOFF RETURNS

RANK	PLAYER	SEASON	RET	YDS	AVG
1	Stan Brown	1968-70	49	1412	28.8
2	Gordon Teter	1963-65	26	650	25.0
3	Otis Armstrong	1970-72	36	897	24.9
4	Jimmy Smith	1979-81	35	848	24.2
5	Vinny Sutherland	1997-2000	24	567	23.6

PURDUE ANNUAL STATISTICAL LEADERS

YR	RUSHING	YDS	ATT	AVG	PASSING	ATT	CMP	PCT	YDS	RECEIVING	REC	YDS	AVG
1946	Ed Cody	378	80	4.7	Bob DeMoss	122	59	.48	814	Ned Maloney	22	269	12.2
1947	Harry Szulborski	851	136	6.3	Bob DeMoss	88	37	.42	509	Clyde Grimenstein	9	107	11.9
1948	Harry Szulborski	989	183	5.4	Bob DeMoss	105	40	.38	694	Bob Heck	12	119	9.9
1949	John Kerestes	647	146	4.4	Ken Gorgal	75	33	.44	503	Bob Whitmer	13	214	16.5
1950	John Kerestes	477	145	3.3	Dale Samuels	172	77	.45	1,076	Neil Schmidt	22	282	12.8
1951	Phil Klezek	441	72	6.1	Dale Samuels	160	79	.49	954	Bernie Flowers	24	222	9.3
1952	Max Schmaling	593	147	4.0	Dale Samuels	185	104	.56	1,131	Bernie Flowers	43	603	14.0
1953	Ed Neves	245	55	4.5	Roy Evans	76	30	.39	514	Rex Brock	9	187	20.8
1954	Bill Murakowski	404	93	4.3	Len Dawson	167	87	.52	1,464	John Kerr	20	337	16.9
1955	Bill Murakowski	493	125	3.9	Len Dawson	155	87	.56	1,005	Bob Khoenle	18	162	9.0
1956	Mel Dillard	873	193	4.5	Len Dawson	130	69	.53	856	Lamar Lundy	15	248	16.5
1957	Bob Jarus	278	72	3.9	Ross Fichtner	58	23	.40	355	Tom Franckhauser	12	228	19.0
1958	Bob Jarus	396	115	3.4	Ross Fichtner	67	25	.37	414	Tom Franckhauser	13	300	23.1
1959	Jack Laraway	281	65	4.3	Bernie Allen	86	33	.38	416	Len Wilson	8	75	9.4
1960	Willie Jones	575	124	4.6	Bernie Allen	103	61	.59	765	Jim Tiller	21	237	11.3
1961	Roy Walker	491	123	4.0	Ron DiGravio	100	52	.52	861	Jack Elwell	16	343	21.4
1962	Roy Walker	427	97	4.4	Ron DiGravio	92	34	.37	629	Tom Bloom	13	217	16.7
1963	John Kuzniewski	242	62	3.9	Ron DiGravio	161	88	.55	1,108	Bob Hadrick	29	388	13.4
1964	Gordon Teter	614	152	4.0	Bob Griese	156	76	.49	934	Bob Hadrick	37	441	11.9
1965	Gordon Teter	490	123	4.0	Bob Griese	238	142	.60	1,719	Bob Hadrick	47	562	12.0
1966	Perry Williams	750	199	3.8	Bob Griese	233	140	.60	1,888	Jim Beirne	68	837	12.3
1967	Leroy Keyes	986	149	6.6	Mike Phipps	243	118	.49	1,800	Leroy Keyes	45	758	16.8
1968	Leroy Keyes	1,003	193	5.2	Mike Phipps	169	88	.52	1,096	Bob Dillingham	35	456	13.0
1969	Randy Cooper	697	171	4.1	Mike Phipps	321	169	.53	2,527	Ashley Bell	49	669	13.7
1970	Otis Armstrong	1,009	213	4.7	Gary Danielson	98	39	.40	546	Darryl Stingley	23	286	12.4
1971	Otis Armstrong	945	214	4.4	Gary Danielson	154	89	.58	1,467	Rick Sayers	39	573	14.7
1972	Otis Armstrong	1,361	243	5.6	Gary Danielson	138	50	.36	735	Rick Sayers	16	196	12.3
1973	Pete Gross	560	133	4.2	Bo Bobrowski	135	57	.42	849	Larry Burton	15	271	18.1
1974	Scott Dierking	779	164	4.8	Mark Vitali	145	68	.47	1,006	Larry Burton	38	702	18.5
1975	Scott Dierking	914	180	5.1	Mark Vitali	127	46	.36	728	Paul Beery	27	454	16.8
1976	Scott Dierking	1,000	201	5.0	Mark Vitali	172	73	.42	1,184	Reggie Arnold	16	287	17.9
1977	John Skibinski	665	147	4.5	Mark Herrmann	319	175	.55	2,453	Reggie Arnold	44	840	19.1
1978	John Macon	913	225	4.1	Mark Herrmann	274	152	.55	1,904	Russell Pope	35	292	8.3
1979	Wally Jones	754	183	4.1	Mark Herrmann	348	203	.58	2,377	Dave Young	55	584	10.6
1980	Jimmy Smith	657	139	4.7	Mark Herrmann	368	242	.66	3,212	Bart Burrell	66	1,001	15.2
1981	Jimmy Smith	540	152	3.6	Scott Campbell	321	185	.58	2,686	Steve Bryant	60	971	16.2
1982	Mel Gray	916	195	4.7	Scott Campbell	399	218	.55	2,626	Cliff Benson	50	762	15.2
1983	Mel Gray	849	190	4.5	Scott Campbell	305	183	.60	2,031	Jeff Price	40	633	15.8
1984	Ray Wallace	587	145	4.0	Jim Everett	431	249	.58	3,256	Steve Griffin	64	1,060	16.6
1985	Ray Wallace	522	100	5.2	Jim Everett	450	285	.63	3,651	Rodney Carter	98	1,099	11.2
1986	James Medlock	488	137	3.6	Jeff George	227	122	.54	1,217	Jerry Chaney	46	257	5.6
1987	James Medlock	634	175	3.6	Shawn McCarthy	177	98	.55	1,088	Anthony Hardy	58	723	12.5
1988	Jarrett Scales	362	112	3.2	Brian Fox	235	121	.51	1,250	Calvin Williams	37	479	12.9
1989	Jerome Sparkman	451	118	3.8	Eric Hunter	178	91	.51	1,368	Calvin Williams	51	630	12.4
1990	Tony Vinson	198	49	4.0	Eric Hunter	366	200	.55	2,355	Ernest Calloway	47	541	11.5
1991	Jeff Hill	678	116	5.8	Eric Hunter	162	77	.48	1,018	Ernest Calloway	24	475	19.8
1992	Arlee Conners	676	154	4.4	Eric Hunter	112	54	.48	857	Jermaine Ross	26	579	22.3
1993	Mike Alstott	816	153	5.3	Rick Trefzger	154	90	.58	1,247	Jeff Hill	35	559	16.0
1994	Mike Alstott	1,188	202	5.9	Rick Trefzger	131	74	.56	1,137	Burt Thornton	45	726	16.1
1995	Mike Alstott	1,436	243	5.9	Rick Trefzger	208	123	.59	1,521	Brian Alford	34	686	20.2
1996	Edwin Watson	768	194	4.0	Rick Trefzger	170	96	.56	1,158	Brian Alford	63	1,057	16.8
1997	Edwin Watson	927	175	5.3	Billy Dicken	407	224	.55	3,136	Brian Alford	63	1,228	19.5
1998	J. Crabtree	648	152	4.3	Drew Brees	569	361	.63	3,983	Randall Lane	67	940	14.0
1999	Montrell Lowe	841	173	4.9	Drew Brees	554	337	.61	3,909	Chris Daniels	121	1,236	10.2
2000	Montrell Lowe	998	226	4.4	Drew Brees	512	309	.60	3,668	Vinny Sutherland	72	1,014	14.1
2001	Montrell Lowe	640	183	3.5	Brandon Hance	258	136	.53	1,529	Taylor Stubblefield	73	910	12.5
2002	Joey Harris	1,115	250	4.5	Kyle Orton	317	192	.61	2,257	Taylor Stubblefield	77	789	10.2
2003	Jerod Void	952	235	4.1	Kyle Orton	414	251	.61	2,885	Taylor Stubblefield	86	835	9.7
2004	Jerod Void	625	159	3.9	Kyle Orton	389	236	.61	3,090	Taylor Stubblefield	89	1,095	12.3
2005	Jerod Void	696	130	5.4	Brandon Kirsch	257	152	.59	1,727	Dorien Bryant	80	960	12.0
2006	Kory Sheets	780	158	4.9	Curtis Painter	530	315	.59	3,985	Dorien Bryant	87	1,068	12.3

Receiving leaders by receptions
All statistics include postseason

WISCONSIN

BY TODD JONES

WISCONSIN FOOTBALL IS AS subtle as cannon fire at dawn. The Badgers play a tough, physical game with few gimmicks and many bruises. Heisman Trophy winners Alan Ameche and Ron Dayne are exemplars of smashmouth Badgers football. Four decades apart, the two running backs hammered opponents with a power that resonated throughout this football-mad state. The head-banging style of play has linked Cheesehead-wearing Wisconsin fans through good times and bad in Camp Randall, a raucous relic of a stadium squeezed into a residential neighborhood on the southwestern edge of campus. While the Badgers touch a horseshoe for luck as they exit the stadium locker room, their fans can count on seeing a consistent blue-collar effort on fall afternoons in the eclectic state capital of Madison. Under Barry Alvarez and his successor, Bret Bielema, grinding, old-school football is celebrated through not just four quarters, but five. The more the merrier.

TRADITION Music has long been part of the Wisconsin football experience. William Purdy composed "On, Wisconsin" in 1909, and alumnus Carl Beck wrote the lyrics. About 2,500 high schools and colleges now use its melody as their fight song. Wisconsin has appropriated the Budweiser commercial jingle and made it its own with 79,500 fans singing "When you say Wisconsin, you've said it all." They lock arms, dance, and wave their arms when "Varsity" is played. The press box actually sways at the end of the third quarter, when thousands of fans jump up and down to House of Pain's rap anthem "Jump Around." Music defines pregame and postgame festivities, too. The Wisconsin marching band plays at Union South before kickoff and then takes part in the "run-on" into the stadium along with the Bucky Wagon, a restored fire engine carrying cheerleaders and the mascot, Bucky Badger. A postgame celebration called the fifth quarter is held, win or lose. The band marches in formation onto the field and then breaks into various songs with fans— and sometimes even players—singing and dancing along.

BEST PLAYER The names and jersey numbers of Ameche (35) and Dayne (33) are immortalized on the facade of Camp Randall Stadium's second deck. Each running back led Wisconsin to the Rose Bowl, and each won the Heisman Trophy. Ameche won his Heisman in

PROFILE

University of Wisconsin, Madison
Madison, Wis.
Founded: 1848
Enrollment: 28,462
Colors: Cardinal and White
Nickname: Badgers
Stadium: Camp Randall Stadium
    Opened in 1917
    FieldTurf; 80,321 capacity
First football game: 1889
All-time record: 586–453–53 (.561)
Bowl record: 10–8
Big Ten Conference championships: 11 (6 outright)
Heisman Trophy: Alan Ameche, 1954; Ron Dayne, 1999
Outland Trophy: Joe Thomas, 2006
First-round draft choices: 24
Website: www.uwbadgers.com

THE BEST OF TIMES

From 1896 to 1901, the Badgers went 51–6–1, including 9–0 in 1901. They outscored opponents 1,622-110 during those six seasons and posted 44 shutouts. Three Rose Bowl victories—1994, 1999, and 2000—and six other bowl trips (three of them wins) since 1995 have made modern-day heroes of coach Barry Alvarez and Heisman winner Ron Dayne.

THE WORST OF TIMES

The Badgers suffered through 10 consecutive losing seasons from 1964 to 1973, including 18 defeats in a row and a span of 1–27–2. They went 0–9–1 in 1967 and 0–10 in 1968.

CONFERENCE

Wisconsin was a charter member of the Western Conference in 1896, and has remained in the league since. The league has been popularly known as the Big Ten since 1917 but didn't officially change its name to the Big Ten Conference until 1987.

DISTINGUISHED ALUMNI

Charles Lindbergh; Bud Selig; Frank Lloyd Wright; Stephen E. Ambrose, historian; Jim Lovell, astronaut; D. Wayne Lukas, Thoroughbred trainer; John Muir, naturalist; Arthur Nielsen Sr., creator of Nielsen ratings; Dick Cheney

FIGHT SONG

ON, WISCONSIN
On, Wisconsin, on, Wisconsin
Plunge right through that line,
Run the ball clear down the field, boys
Touchdown sure this time
On, Wisconsin, on, Wisconsin
Fight on for her fame,
Fight, Fellows, Fight, Fight, Fight
We'll win this game!

*The head-banging
style of play has
linked Wisconsin
fans through good
times and bad.*

1954 after the "Horse from Kenosha, Wis.," ended his career with a then-NCAA-record 3,345 rushing yards. Although he also played linebacker, the bruising Ameche was surpassed for the title of the school's greatest player by Dayne four decades later. There was nothing fancy about Dayne. The tailback—254 pounds of muscle packed onto a 5'10" frame—took the ball, scattered defenders like bowling pins, got up, and did it again. His quiet, no-nonsense style matched his personality. Dayne arrived at Wisconsin as a shy kid from New Jersey hoping to start a new life after divorce and drugs had ravaged his family. He left Madison four years later still a man of few words, but with rushing records that screamed for attention. Dayne won the 1999 Heisman Trophy as a senior after rushing for 2,034 yards and 20 touchdowns. That year he became the first player to lead the Big Ten in rushing, scoring, and all-purpose yards. During his last game, fans at Camp Randall Stadium held up No. 33 commemorative towels in his honor. Dayne finished as college football's career rushing leader, with 6,397 yards, not counting bowl games. He was one of four players to run for 1,000 yards in each of four seasons, and he out-rushed the opposing team 29 times in 43 career starts. He averaged 148.8 yards per game, and the Badgers were 5–6 when he failed to gain 100 yards. "Ron really exemplified our program," Alvarez said. "I don't think there's a player that has ever meant more to a program. He's what our program is all about: blue-collar, tough, hard-nosed."

BEST COACH Nothing came easy to Barry Alvarez. He grew up in a working-class neighborhood in the western Pennsylvania mining town of Burgettstown and later played linebacker at Nebraska. Although he described himself as "short, slow, and fat," he was a member of the 1967 Cornhuskers who led the nation in total defense. His belief in toughness, discipline, and hard work was sorely needed at Wisconsin. The Badgers had endured five straight losing seasons and had gone 6–27 in the three years before Alvarez took over, in 1990. He came to an athletic department that had a $2.1 million deficit and inherited a football program that had averaged 41,734 fans—the school's lowest mark in 44 years—the previous season. His first Wisconsin team had 52 players quit and went 1–10. Alvarez kept working. Three years later, the Badgers went 10–1–1 and won the Rose Bowl. Alvarez learned how to maintain success as an assistant

FIRST-ROUND DRAFT CHOICES

1937	Eddie Jankowski, Packers (9)
1941	George Paskvan, Packers (7)
1944	Pat Harder, Cardinals (2)
1947	Don Kindt, Bears (11)
1948	Earl Girard, Packers (7)
1955	Alan Ameche, Colts (3)
1960	Dale Hackbart, Vikings**
1963	Pat Richter, Redskins (7)
1976	Dennis Lick, Bears (8)
1980	Ray Snell, Buccaneers (22)
1985	Al Toon, Jets (10)
1985	Richard Johnson, Oilers (11)
1985	Darryl Sims, Steelers (20)
1988	Paul Gruber, Buccaneers (4)
1992	Troy Vincent, Dolphins (7)
1999	Aaron Gibson, Lions (27)
2000	Ron Dayne, Giants (11)
2000	Chris McIntosh, Seahawks (22)
2001	Jamar Fletcher, Dolphins (26)
2001	Michael Bennett, Vikings (27)
2002	Wendell Bryant, Cardinals (12)
2004	Lee Evans, Bills (13)
2005	Erasmus James, Vikings (18)
2007	Joe Thomas, Browns (3)

** First "territorial selection" by Minneapolis franchise in the inaugural AFL draft, held Nov. 22, 1959. Minneapolis later withdrew from the AFL to join the NFL, and the negotiating rights to Hackbart were inherited by the Oakland Raiders, who replaced Minneapolis as the AFL's eighth franchise.

CONSENSUS ALL-AMERICANS

1912	Robert Butler, T
1913	Ray Keeler, G
1915	Howard Buck, T
1919	Charles Carpenter, C
1920	Ralph Scott, T
1923	Marty Below, T
1930	Milo Lubratovich, T
1942	Dave Schreiner, E
1954	Alan Ameche, B
1959	Dan Lanphear, T
1962	Pat Richter, E
1975	Dennis Lick, T
1981	Tim Krumrie, DL
1994	Cory Raymer, C
1998	Aaron Gibson, OL
1998	Tom Burke, DL
1999	Ron Dayne, RB
1999	Chris McIntosh, OL
2000	Jamar Fletcher, DB
2004	Erasmus James, DL
2006	Joe Thomas, OL

under Hayden Fry at Iowa and Lou Holtz at Notre Dame. His work ethic, and his ability to recruit in New York and New Jersey, ensured that Wisconsin remained a Big Ten force and perennial bowl game victor. Alvarez is the only Big Ten coach to win consecutive Rose Bowls, in 1999 and 2000, and the only conference coach beside Woody Hayes to win three Rose Bowls. In April 2004, he also became Wisconsin's athletic director, a job he retained after retiring from coaching at the end of the 2005 season. The Badgers upset No. 7 Auburn 24-10 in the 2006 Capital One Bowl, Alvarez's final game. His 118–73–4 record in 16 seasons as coach of the Badgers is the best in school history. Alvarez went 8–3 in bowl games, the best winning percentage (.727) ever for a coach with at least 11 bowl appearances. During his tenure, Wisconsin attendance nearly doubled, reaching 82,551 fans per home game in his final season. Alvarez appointed Bret Bielema, at age 36, as his successor for the 2006 season, and the new coach kept the Badgers pounding away at opponents. They finished the season 12–1, the best record in school history, and ranked No. 7.

BEST TEAM The 1998 Badgers epitomized the power football Alvarez loved. They weren't pretty, just a lunch-pail group that mashed opponents with hard-nosed defense, outstanding special teams, and a workmanlike, one-dimensional offense. Wisconsin overcame criticism of a soft schedule, won 11 games for the first time in school history, lost just once, and won its second Rose Bowl in five seasons. Dayne rumbled for 1,525 yards, an average of 5.2 per carry, and 15 TDs, and was a finalist for the Doak Walker Award. The junior ran behind a line anchored by behemoth tackle Aaron Gibson (6'7", 370 pounds), a finalist for the Lombardi Award and Outland Trophy. While the Badgers averaged 31.8 points per game, their defense allowed only 10.2, lowest in the nation. The Badgers began the season ranked No. 20, won their first nine games to tie a school record, and climbed to a No. 8 ranking before losing 27-10 at Michigan in mid-November. The Wolverines ended up helping out a week later; Michigan's 31-16 win over Ohio State, coupled with Wisconsin's 24-3 victory over Penn State, sent the Badgers to the Rose Bowl. Lingering distaste from the Michigan defeat was washed away by a Rose Bowl win over No. 6 UCLA. Before the game, CBS football analyst Craig James called the No. 9-ranked Badgers the worst team ever to play in a Rose Bowl. Dayne answered by running for 246 yards, one shy of Charles White's Rose Bowl record, and four touchdowns in the 38-31 victory. The Badgers ended the season ranked No. 6. Alvarez was named Big Ten coach of the year. Dayne, Gibson, and defensive end Tom Burke were selected All-America.

BEST BACKFIELD In 1993 Wisconsin followed Darrell Bevell, Brent Moss, and Terrell Fletcher as if they were pied pipers. The terrific trio led the Badgers to their first Big Ten title in 32 years, as co-champions with Ohio State, and to a 21-16 victory over UCLA in the Rose Bowl, en route to a final record of 10–1–1. Although just a sophomore at quarterback, Bevell set or tied school Wisconsin records in passing yards (2,390), completion percentage (.678), passing TDs (19), and pass efficiency (155.2). Bevell completed 177 of 256 passes in the regular season (.691) for 2,294 yards and 19 TDs. His 21-yard TD run was the key play in the Rose Bowl win. Bevell still holds the Wisconsin record for career passing yards with 7,686, a total that's nearly 2,000 more than the next Wisconsin passer, Brooks Bollinger. While Bevell kept defenses honest, juniors Moss and Fletcher wore opponents down with their one-two combination on the ground. Moss was named Big Ten MVP after rushing for 1,479 yards, on 5.4 yards per carry, and 14 TDs in the regular season. Fletcher averaged 5.9 yards per attempt while chipping in with 932 rushing yards and 10 scores. Overall the team averaged 5.0 yards per rushing attempt and totaled 2,759 on the ground in 11 regular-season games. In the regular-season finale, Moss ran for 149 yards and Fletcher for another 119 as the Badgers clinched their first Rose Bowl trip in 31 years with a 41-20 win over Michigan State in Tokyo, Japan. The Badgers then bashed UCLA for 250 rushing yards in the Rose Bowl, with Moss earning MVP honors with 158 yards on 36 carries and two TDs. Fletcher added 64 yards on seven carries. Good times didn't last for Moss. He was suspended from the team after being arrested for possession of crack cocaine on Nov. 4, 1994. He bounced around several professional football leagues but was arrested in 2006 for felonious possession of cocaine.

BEST DEFENSE Junior linebacker Donnell Thompson and senior linebacker Bob Adamov embodied the hardscrabble nature of Wisconsin's 1998 defense. Both were team captains that year after beginning their careers with the Badgers as walk-ons. Tom Burke, however, served as the heart and soul of a unit that led the nation in scoring defense (10.2) and turnover margin. The senior defensive end was named Big Ten defensive player of the year and All-America while leading the nation in sacks with a Wisconsin-record 22. Burke had nine other tackles for loss that season, and he still ranks second all-time at Wisconsin with 32 career sacks. Freshman cornerback Jamar Fletcher led the nation with seven interceptions—returning three for touchdowns against Illinois, Iowa, and UCLA in the Rose Bowl. Two years later, he was named Big Ten defensive player of the year. Fletcher finished his career as Wisconsin's all-time leader with 21 interceptions, having scored on five of them. Wisconsin allowed a school-record-low five rushing touchdowns. Opponents

averaged only 92.2 yards rushing. UNLV had 23 rushing yards on 29 attempts against Wisconsin. Ohio, one week after rushing for 361 yards against North Carolina State, gained 65 rushing yards on 38 carries. The Badger defense had not been scored on in 13 consecutive quarters before Northwestern scored late in a 38-7 loss. The Badgers held Illinois to 28 rushing yards. Wisconsin posted its first shutout in 15 years over Iowa, 31-0, as the Hawkeyes gained 30 rushing yards on 30 attempts. Minnesota gained 28 rushing yards on 24 carries, and QB Billy Cockerham was intercepted four times as Wisconsin improved to 9–0 for the first time in 97 years. The season's only blemish occurred a week later, when Michigan defeated the Badgers 27-10 while rushing for 257 yards. Despite that aberration, the Badgers finished the season third nationally in rushing defense, allowing just 89.6 yards per game.

BIGGEST GAME UCLA was playing in its hometown, but it didn't own the crowd at the 1994 Rose Bowl. More than 70,000 Wisconsin fans crammed into the stadium to see a Badger team that had won the school's first Big Ten title in 31 years. "When I saw that [inflatable] cow fly over the stadium, I knew right there that there's no way UCLA can beat us," said freshman linebacker Pete Monty. Wisconsin won 21-16 for the school's first New Year's Day bowl victory, and stadium vendors ran out of beer after three quarters. Badger tailback Brent Moss was named the game's MVP after running for 158 yards and two touchdowns on 36 carries. Wisconsin ran for 250 yards, and its defense forced six turnovers, including five fumbles. Clinging to a 14-10 lead in the fourth quarter, quarterback Darrell Bevell couldn't find an open receiver, tucked the ball under his arm, headed down the left sideline, and scored on a 21-yard keeper—the longest gain of his career and a play remembered by Wisconsin fans as "The Run." UCLA answered with a touchdown, then on the game's final possession drove to the Badger 18-yard line before time ran out. Wisconsin's first bowl game in 10 years, first bowl win in 12, and first Rose Bowl victory ever, legitimized the program's turnaround under Alvarez. "This is by far the hugest, the biggest win I've ever had in my life," Alvarez said.

BIGGEST UPSET Paul Brown brought the second, and best, of his three Ohio State teams to Madison in 1942. The Buckeyes were 5–0 and ranked No. 1 when they met the 5–0–1 and No. 6-ranked Badgers. Nearly 45,000 attended the homecoming game. Over 200 radio stations

COLLEGE FOOTBALL HALL OF FAME INDUCTEES		
NAME	YEARS	INDUCTED
George Little, COACH	1925-26	1955
Dave Schreiner, E	1940-42	1955
Pat O'Dea, FB	1896-99	1962
Bob Butler, T	1911-13	1972
Elroy Hirsch, HB	1942	1974
Alan Ameche, FB	1951-54	1975
Marty Below, T	1918-23	1988
Pat Harder, FB	1941-42	1993
Pat Richter, E	1960-62	1996

broadcast the action to U.S. servicemen in Alaska, Hawaii, Canada, and South America. The BBC carried the game to England, Ireland, Australia, Africa, and India. Wisconsin had its famed backfield of Elroy "Crazy Legs" Hirsch, Pat Harder, Mark Hoskins, and quarterbacks John Wink and Ashley Anderson. The coach was Harry Stuhldreher, of Four Horsemen fame, and he had taught the Badgers the Notre Dame "box" offense as well as the T formation. Wisconsin led 10-0 at halftime after a second quarter in which fullback Harder ran for an eight-yard TD—set up by a 59-yard run by Hirsch—and kicked a 37-yard field goal. The Buckeyes drew within 10-7 early in the fourth quarter with a 96-yard drive capped by a touchdown run by Paul Sarringhaus, but Hirsch tossed a 14-yard scoring pass to ensure the Badgers' 17-7 win, their first over a top-ranked team. Ohio State fans called the defeat "the bad water game" because half the OSU team got dysentery before the game from drinking rusty water while on the train from Columbus. The Buckeyes rebounded to finish 9–1 and were named national champions. Many of the 54 members of that Wisconsin team enlisted in the military and served in World War II, where some gave their lives. Two-time All-America end Dave Schreiner, the Big Ten player of the year in 1942, was killed on Okinawa three years later. Those Badgers are chronicled in the book *Third Down and a War to Go: The All-American 1942 Wisconsin Badgers,* by Terry Frei.

HEARTBREAKER One of the most beloved Wisconsin teams was the "Hard Rocks" of 1951. Those Badgers led the nation in defense, allowing only 154.8 yards and 6.6 points per game. The defense actually outscored opponents 58-53. Defensive stars Pat O'Donahue, Hal Faverty, and Ed Withers helped produce six straight victories to end the season, but a trip to Illinois in the season's second game cost Wisconsin a Rose Bowl berth. The Badgers led 10-7 at halftime, and on their first possession of the second half they drove 10 minutes to the Illini 1-yard line. Wisconsin failed to score on four plays. Rollie Strehlow lost three yards on a first-down run. The Badgers were penalized five yards for illegal motion on second down. John Coatta gained five on a run, but the freshman Alan Ameche was stopped for no gain on third down. Ameche was stopped for no gain again on fourth down from the 4. Illinois then drove 96 yards for a touchdown. Wisconsin lost 14-10, despite having more first downs (20-8) and more total yards (274-142). The Badgers finished the season 7–1–1, including a 6-6 tie with Ohio State, and finished third in the Big Ten. Wisconsin

sports information director Art Lentz wrote that year: "I don't know when a team so captured the interest of the state, alumni, and students as this one with its ability and tremendous spirit."

WILDEST FINISH

WILDEST FINISH Most of the 1963 Rose Bowl was an unforgettable mismatch, even though it was between the nation's top two ranked teams. The No. 1 USC Trojans jumped to a 21-7 halftime lead over Wisconsin and led 42-14 one play into the fourth quarter. At that point, USC fans were chanting, "We want the Packers." They were a bit premature in their celebration. Wisconsin, behind the duo of QB Ron Vander Kelen and All-America tight end Pat Richter, staged a comeback for the ages. The Badgers scored 23 unanswered points in the final 12 minutes but came up short in a 42-37 loss. Still, the passing display by Vander Kelen is part of Rose Bowl lore. He set Rose Bowl records for pass attempts (48), completions (33), passing yards (401), and total offense (406). Lou Richter finished with 11 receptions for 163 yards, and his 19-yard TD reception with 1:29 remaining drew the Badgers within five points. USC recovered the ensuing onside kick but lost 12 yards on three plays and punted from its own 29. Elmars Ezerins rushed in from the outside and barely missed blocking the kick, the ball appearing to sail through his outstretched arms. Wisconsin's Lou Holland caught the ball at midfield, ran straight ahead, and fumbled. Teammate Jim Schenk recovered at the Badger 40, but that was the final play of the game. Earlier, with four minutes left, the timer had rushed onto the field to tell the officials that the scoreboard clock was wrong, and Wisconsin later maintained that it had mistakenly lost 25 seconds. In the end, the Badgers out-gained USC 486-367 and had 32 first downs to the Trojans' 15. "We're still number one, and they're number two," said USC coach John McKay after his first Rose Bowl win. "They're a good team, but they'd finish about sixth in our league." Wisconsin finished No. 2 in the final AP and UPI polls behind the Trojans.

BEST COMEBACK

BEST COMEBACK The Badgers trailed Iowa 17-0 in the fourth quarter on Oct. 11, 1969. They were already 0–3 in John Coatta's third and final season. Wisconsin had gone 0–10 the previous year, and 0–9–1 in 1967. The Badgers were in the throes of an 18-game losing streak, dating to a 21-21 tie against Iowa on Oct. 21, 1967. They had not won since beating Minnesota 7-6 in the final game of the 1966 season. So another defeat seemed imminent even after Alan Thompson scored for Wisconsin on a two-yard run. He added a six-yard TD

PRO FOOTBALL HALL OF FAME INDUCTEES		
NAME	PRO YEARS	INDUCTED
Arnie Herber, QB	1930-40, 1944-45	1966
Elroy Hirsch, HB/E	1946-57	1968
Mike Webster, C	1974-90	1997

run to cut the deficit to 17-14. Badgers quarterback Neil Graff then threw a 17-yard TD pass to Randall Marks for a 21-17 lead with 2:08 remaining. Iowa's Dennis Green then fumbled the kickoff out of the end zone while trying to make a return. The safety closed the scoring on Wisconsin's 23-17 win. Hundreds of fans from the Camp Randall Stadium crowd of 53,1714 stormed the field with 1:10 remaining, which delayed the game's finish. The Badgers ended the season 3–7.

Brooks Bollinger twice led the Badgers from 17-0 deficits to win at Ohio State, in 1999 and in 2001. He was a redshirt freshman making his first start in 1999, when the Buckeyes took a 17-0 lead at 10:23 of the second quarter. After closing to within 17-6 at halftime, Bollinger converted seven of eight third downs in the second half and took the Badgers to six straight scores while running the option, scrambling, and hitting key passes. The North Dakota native completed 15 of 27 passes for 167 yards and rushed for 78 yards on 17 attempts. "I thought that was as fine an effort by a redshirt freshman—in a hostile environment, falling behind, to handle the crowd noise, to handle the OSU football tradition, and to make plays—as I've ever seen," Alvarez said. Ron Dayne rushed for 161 yards, 128 in the second half, on 32 carries and scored four TDs on runs as the Badgers won 42-17. Not since a 41-6 loss to Purdue in 1967 had an OSU team been beaten so badly in Ohio Stadium. Two years later, Ohio State again took a 17-0 lead over visiting Wisconsin with 10:27 left in the second quarter before the Badgers scored prior to halftime to cut the lead to 17-7. Bollinger produced another comeback, and Wisconsin won 20-17.

STADIUM

STADIUM It now boasts a classic horseshoe football structure, but previously the site of Camp Randall Stadium served as a military training center. Wisconsin's famous Iron Brigade drilled on the 53 acres of Camp Randall, and 1,400 Confederate soldiers were held prisoner there. Before and after the Civil War, the site was home to Wisconsin's state fair. In 1893, the state legislature fulfilled the desires of Civil War veterans and purchased the land and gave it to the school to serve as a memorial park for athletics. The football team began playing games at Camp Randall in 1913, but two years later, temporary wooden bleachers—rented from the circus—collapsed and 20 fans were injured. The state legislature responded by appropriating $15,000 to build concrete stands on the field's western side. The field was dedicated in 1917, and the stadium has grown in size over subsequent decades. A four-year, $109 million renovation was completed before the 2005 season, increasing capacity

to 80,321. Entering 2007, the Badgers have won 19 of their last 20 games at Camp Randall Stadium by an average margin of 19.2 points. "It's hard to hear yourself think [there]," said Penn State QB Michael Robinson. "And when they play 'Jump Around,' you can feel the place shake. It gets pretty loud and crazy."

RIVAL The most-played rivalry in Division I-A history took on special meaning long before the Paul Bunyan's Axe trophy was created. Minnesota became an immediate villain in 1890 by beating the Badgers 63-0 in the series' first game. Wisconsin was outscored 161-16 while losing the first four games before beating the Gophers 6-0 in 1894 when Ikey Karel scored on a 40-yard touchdown run. The *Milwaukee Journal* wrote: "When little Karel had done it, he sat down and wept. The excitement was too much for him." Wisconsin students celebrated with a campus bonfire that night and serenaded university president Charles Kendall Adams at his home. Such emotion still defines the game played every year since 1907 between schools from bordering states. Since 1948, the victors have gained possession of Paul Bunyan's Axe, created that year by the Wisconsin letterwinners' group, the National W Club. Wisconsin fans still take delight in their team's 23-21 upset of No. 3 Minnesota in 1961, which cost the Golden Gophers a share of the Big Ten title. A year later, the Badgers earned a Rose Bowl berth when Ralph Kurek scored the winning TD against the Gophers with 1:37 left for a 14-9 victory. An unranked Minnesota team, however, upset Wisconsin 28-21 in 1993. That was the Badgers' only defeat of the season, and might well have cost them a shot at the national championship.

CONTROVERSY The four-season coaching era of Dr. Clarence Spears ended in chaos. He was fired after a 1–7 record in 1935, but he didn't go down alone or without a fight. Team captain John Golemgeske told a university athletic council that Dr. Walter Meanwell, the athletic director and basketball coach, had instructed him at a season-ending party to circulate a petition calling for Spears' firing. Team trainer Bill Fallon and his assistant, Red Smith, told the council that Spears had ordered whiskey to be put in the coffee served to players at halftime of the Minnesota game. Smith also alleged the coach had given whiskey to two players after the Northwestern game. Spears denied the whiskey charges when the Board of Regents ordered an investigation. The Regents fired Spears anyway but also fired Fallon and Meanwell, despite 20 successful seasons as the school's basketball coach. Six members of the athletic council resigned in protest. The Big Ten threatened to expel Wisconsin from the league because the Badgers had run afoul of the league and its faculty reps in making the moves. Under the Big Ten system of the time, the faculty was the body that should have taken such action. When the Wisconsin faculty satisfied the other Big Ten members that it approved of the moves, the other nine league members withdrew their threat to suspend the Badgers. Harry Stuhldreher, one of the Notre Dame Four Horsemen, was hired as football coach and AD in 1936.

DUBIOUS DISTINCTION The Shoebox scandal, in which 157 athletes in 14 sports at Wisconsin accepted merchandise discounts, led to the university's being placed on NCAA probation in 2001 until October 2006. As part of the probation, scholarships were reduced in football and men's basketball because it was Wisconsin's third rules violation since the 1993-94 school year. The penalties exceeded those imposed by Wisconsin chancellor John Wiley. The NCAA did not ban Wisconsin teams from postseason play nor did it strip the school of any championships or records. The violations were uncovered by an investigation into Wisconsin's athlete discounts and interest-free credit lines at a Madison-area shoe store. Wisconsin was allowed to sign only 20 football players to scholarships in 2002-03 and 2004-05, five fewer than the maximum normally allowed each year. A total of 26 football players had to serve NCAA suspensions in 2000, ranging from one to three games.

NICKNAME In the 1820s, lead miners in Wisconsin burrowed tunnels into hillsides during the winter because they had no shelter. People said they "lived like badgers," and soon Wisconsin became known as the Badger State. The school adopted the name Badgers from those miners.

MASCOT Wisconsin used to use a real badger on a leash at games but stopped in 1940 when the animal proved too vicious; it was donated to the Madison zoo. Arthur Lentz, a PR man in the athletic department, came up with the idea of a cartoon badger and hired illustrator Art Evans, who drew one in a cardinal-and-white sweater. In 1949, art department student Connie Conrad was commissioned to mold a papier-mâché head of a badger. Bill Sagal, a cheerleader and gymnast, wore the outfit at that year's homecoming game. A school committee named the mascot Bucky Badger after deciding that Buckingham U. Badger, a name apparently taken from the lyrics of a song, encouraged the football team "to buck right through that line."

UNIFORMS The Badgers have always worn cardinal-red uniforms with the exception of one game in 1923. For an unknown reason, they wore all black that day against Indiana. Wisconsin won 52-0, but then went back to its traditional uniforms. A "W" has usually been on the Badgers' helmets, with the current design dating to 1991.

TRAGEDY The 1993 home game against Michigan unfortunately is known for more than Wisconsin's 13-10 win. At game's end, a stampede that took place in the student section ended with fans being pressed against a fence. Sixty-nine students were injured, seven critically. A Michigan player had his nose split open by a thrown object, and his teammates and coaches had beer and mustard dumped on them as they exited the lone ramp from the field. Wisconsin moved student seats further from the ramp prior to the 1994 season.

QUIRK Pat O'Dea came to Wisconsin from Melbourne, Australia, in 1896 as a rugby player and left two years later with the nickname the Kangaroo Kicker. He had a 110-yard punt (fields were that long then), drop-kicked field goals of 65 and 55 yards, and also place-kicked a 57-yard field goal while totaling 32 career field goals. Walter Camp wrote that O'Dea "put the foot in football as no man ever has or as no man probably ever will again." Many believed O'Dea died while serving Australia in World War I, but he actually disappeared into anonymity. He took a new name, Charles J. Mitchell, to avoid the attention he had gained as a football player. In 1934, a San Francisco newspaper made national news by revealing Mitchell's true identity while he was working at a California lumber company. That year, as Pat O'Dea once again, he was guest of honor at Wisconsin's homecoming game against Illinois.

LORE Michigan's 6-3 win at Wisconsin in 1923 ended with thousands of angry fans rushing the field and one of them being arrested for punching referee Walter Eckersall in the jaw. The crowd thought Eckersall should have ruled Michigan's Tod Rockwell down on his 50-yard punt return for a TD in the first half. After the game, Wisconsin players surrounded Eckersall to protect him from a mob that had gathered outside the officials' dressing room. The referee was supposed to take a train home to Chicago, but hundreds of fans were waiting for him at the Madison train station. Wisconsin coach Jack Ryan and some of his players drove Eckersall 85 miles, to Milwaukee, where he boarded a different train. Eckersall had charges dropped against the fan who had slugged him.

NUMBERS The Badgers were ranked No. 1 for the only time after a 20-6 win over Illinois on Oct. 4, 1952. They lost to Ohio State 23-14 the next week … Wisconsin upset No. 4 Nebraska 21-20 at Camp Randall in 1974

ALL-TIME TEAM	
In conjunction with the centennial celebration of college football in 1969, Wisconsin fans selected the school's all-time team. The 11-man unit features 1954 Heisman Trophy winner Alan Ameche, who was voted All-Time Greatest Player. The vote was conducted 30 years before running back Ron Dayne won the Heisman Trophy for the Badgers.	
1951-54	Alan Ameche, HB
1961-63	Ken Bowman, OL
1913-15	Howard Buck, OL
1941-42	Pat Harder, HB
1942	Elroy "Crazy Legs" Hirsch, WR
1957-59	Dan Lanphear, OL
1914	Arlie Mucks Sr., OL
1960-62	Pat Richter, WR
1940-42	Dave Schreiner, E
1962	Ron Vander Kelen, QB
1946-49	Robert "Red" Wilson, OL

when Gregg Bohlig completed a 77-yard TD pass to Jeff Mack with 3:29 remaining … Billy Marek ran for 3,709 yards and 44 TDs from 1972 to 1975. He averaged 5.2 yards per carry in his career. In 1974 he ran for 304 yards and 5 TDs against Minnesota … Five Badgers have their numbers retired: Elroy "Crazy Legs" Hirsch (40), Alan Ameche (35), Dave Schreiner (80), Allan Shafer (83), and Pat Richter (88). Shafer died from head injuries suffered during a 1944 home game against Iowa … Wisconsin upset No. 1-ranked Northwestern 37-6 in a homecoming game at Camp Randall on Nov. 10, 1962 … The 1901 Badgers went 9–0 with eight shutouts and outscored opponents 317-5. A year later, they held Michigan's "Point a Minute" team to six in a 6-0 loss … Pat Richter, one of seven Badgers inducted into the College Football Hall of Fame, was twice an All-America at tight end and led the nation in receiving as a junior. He lettered in football, basketball, and baseball at Wisconsin, and later served as athletic director … Wisconsin snapped Ohio State's 19-game winning streak with a 17-10 win over the visiting Buckeyes on Oct. 11, 2003 … Offensive tackle Joe Thomas won the 2006 Outland Trophy and was picked No. 3 overall in the NFL draft by the Cleveland Browns. Pat Harder, No. 2 in 1944, and Alan Ameche, No. 2 in 1955, are the only Badgers to go higher in the draft … The Badgers missed six field goal attempts in a 21-20 loss to Indiana in 1968 … Coming off a 4–7 season, the Badgers upset No. 1 Michigan in the 1981 season-opener 21-14 … Wisconsin beat Purdue 14-13 in 1940 after trailing 13-0 with less than five minutes remaining to play. John Tennant threw a 10-yard TD pass to Ray Kreick as time expired, and Kreick kicked the extra point … The Badgers had 705 total yards of offense against Indiana in 1999. They rushed for 461 and passed for 244 in a 59-0 win … Barry Alvarez coached eight games from the press box or hospital in 1999 because of midseason knee surgery … Jug Cirard had 85-yard and 65-yard punt returns for touchdowns in a 46-14 win over Iowa in 1947 … Dave Crossen had a school-record 28 tackles against Purdue in 1977 … The Badgers trailed Iowa 17-0 in the fourth quarter in 1969 but rallied for victory by scoring 23 consecutive points. They trailed Missouri 28-7 in the fourth quarter in 1984 but came back to win 35-34 … Al Toon set a then-Big Ten record with 252 receiving yards in a 1983 42-38 win over Purdue … In 2004, cornerback Scott Starks returned a fumble by Purdue QB Kyle Orton

40 yards for a touchdown with 2:36 left in the fourth quarter for the winning score in Wisconsin's 20-17 victory … George O'Brien returned a punt 96 yards to the Iowa 3-yard line in 1952 … Entering the 2007 season, the Badgers have won 9 of their last 12 bowl games. They have played in a bowl 12 times in the past 14 years, a total matched in the Big Ten only by Michigan and Ohio State … Richard Johnson set a school record by blocking six kicks in 1984 while being named All-America at defensive back … Rufus "Road Runner" Ferguson rushed for 2,814 yards and 26 TDs in the early 1970s … The 1959 Badgers won the school's first outright Big Ten championship in 47 years … Elroy Hirsch ran 60 yards for a TD that tied Notre Dame 7-7 in 1942, and because of that play, was named Crazy Legs … Former QB John Coatta went 3–26–1 as head coach from 1967 to 1969. He was hired over Bo Schembechler … Brian Calhoun rushed for 213 yards in Wisconsin's 24-10 win over Auburn in the 2006 Capital One Bowl … In a 46-34 loss at Ohio State in 1941, the Badgers' second TD was scored on a fifth down. Tom Farris had failed to score on fourth down, but confused referee Jim Masker gave Wisconsin another down from the 1-yard line. Bud Seelinger then passed to Farris for the score … The Badgers had a 1,000-yard rusher in 10 consecutive seasons from 1993 through 2002 … In 2006, P.J. Hill became just the seventh freshman in NCAA history to rush for more than 1,500 yards … The Badgers averaged just one Big Ten win per season from 1985 through 1990 … The 1994 defense allowed only 9.1 points per game in its first nine games but 34.3 in its final three … The 1999 Badgers won their first outright conference title in 37 years and became the first Big Ten team in history to win consecutive Rose Bowls. They finished No. 4 in the polls. Dayne, Fletcher, and Chris McIntosh were first-team All-Americas … Defensive end Erasmus James was a finalist for the Lombardi, Bednarik, Nagurski, and Hendricks awards in 2004 … The 1912 Badgers shut out four opponents and allowed only 29 points all season while going 7–0 … Wisconsin set school records for points in a season (446) and average points (34.3) in 2005 … The Badgers have defeated Ohio State three consecutive times in Columbus, heading into 2007 … Only Ron Dayne has rushed for more yards at Wisconsin than Anthony Davis' 4,676 … In 2001, Lee Evans broke the Big Ten record for most receiving yards with 1,545 on 75 catches and was the first Badger to lead the conference in receiving since 1963. He went on to set the all-time Wisconsin record for career receiving yards with 3,468 … Nine Badgers have been selected in the first round of the NFL draft since 1999 … Defensive back Jim Leonhard began his career as a walk-on and ended up a three-time All-America from 2001 through 2004. He tied Fletcher's school record with 21 career interceptions. He led the nation and tied the Big Ten record with 11 interceptions in 2002. Leonhard is the Big Ten's leader in career punt-return yardage, with 1,347.

QUOTE "Why not Wisconsin? Someone has to win the Big Ten Conference title. It might as well be us."
— Joe Panos, starting right offensive tackle and co-captain of the 1993 co-Big Ten champions

WISCONSIN ALL-TIME SCORES

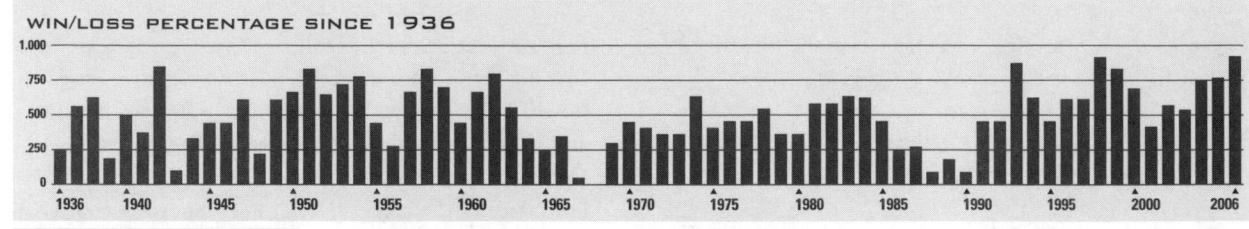

WIN/LOSS PERCENTAGE SINCE 1936

ALVIN KLETSCH
1889 (.000)   0-2

1889   0-2-0
N23		Calumet Club	0	27
D14		at Beloit	0	4

TED MESTRE
1890 (.250)   1-3

1890   1-3-0
N1	●	U.W. Whitewater	106	0
N15		at Minnesota	0	63
N22		Lake Forest	6	16
N26		Northwestern	10	22

HERB ALWARD
1891 (.700)   3-1-1

1891   3-1-1
O17	●	at Beloit	40	4
O24		at Minnesota	12	26
O31	=	Northwestern	0	0
N14		Lake Forest	6	4
N29		Northwestern	40	0

FRANK CRAWFORD
1892 (.571)   4-3

1892   4-3-0
O1	●	Beloit	32	4
O15		Michigan	6	10
O19		at Purdue	4	32 *
O22	●	Lake Forest *Mil*	10	6
O29		Minnesota	4	32
N19	●	at Northwestern	26	6
N24	●	Northwestern *Mil*	20	6

PARKE DAVIS
1893 (.667)   4-2

1893   4-2-0
O14		Chicago *Mil*	0	22
O21	●	Lake Forest	24	0
O28	●	Beloit	18	0
N4	●	at Michigan	34	18
N11	●	at Minnesota	0	40
N18	●	Purdue	36	30

H.O. STICKNEY
1894-95 (.700)   10-4-1

1894   5-2-0
O6	●	Chicago AC	22	4
O15	●	Purdue	0	1 f
O20	●	at Chicago	30	0
O27	●	at Chicago AC	4	16
O29	●	Iowa	44	0
N3	●	at Beloit	46	0
N17	●	Minnesota	6	0

1895   5-2-1
S21	●	Northwestern *Mil*	12	6
S30	●	Iowa State	28	6 *
O5	●	Armour	32	4
O12	●	Lake Forest	26	5
O19	●	Grinnell	14	4
O26	=	Illinois	10	10
N2		at Chicago	12	22
N16		at Minnesota	10	14

1896-PRESENT BIG 10

PHIL KING
1896-1902, '05 (.851) 65-11-1

1896   7-1-1 (2-0-1)
O10	●	Lake Forest	34	0
O14	●	Madison HS	18	0
O17	●	Rush Medical	50	0
O24	●	Grinnell	54	6
O31	●	at Beloit	6	0
N7	●		Chicago	24	0
N21	●		Minnesota	6	0
N26	=		at Northwestern	6	6
D19		Carlisle Indians *Chi*	8	18

1897   9-1-0 (3-0-0)
O2	●	Lake Forest	30	0
O6	●	Madison HS	8	0
O9	●	Rush Medical	28	0
O16	●	U.W. Platteville	20	0
O23	●	Madison HS	29	0
O30	●	at Minnesota	39	0
N6	●	Beloit	11	0
N13	●		at Chicago	25	8
N20		U.W. Alumni	0	6
N25	●		at Northwestern	22	0

1898   9-1-0 (2-1-0)
O1	●	Ripon	52	0
O5	●	Madison HS	21	0
O8	●	Dixon	76	0
O15	●	Rush Medical	42	0
O22	●	Beloit *Mil*	17	0
O29	●	Minnesota	28	0 *
N5	●	U.W. Alumni	12	11
N12			at Chicago	0	6
N19	●	U.W. WhiteWater	22	0
N24	●		at Northwestern	47	0

1899   9-2-0 (4-1-0)
S30	●	Lake Forest	45	0
O6	●	Beloit *Mil*	36	0
O14	●	Northwestern	38	0
O21	●	at Yale	0	6
O28	●	Rush Medical	17	0
N4	●	U.W. Alumni	17	5
N11	●		Illinois *Mil*	23	0
N18	●		at Minnesota	19	0
N25	●		Lawrence	58	0
N30	=		Michigan *Chi*	17	5
D9			Chicago	0	17

1900   8-1-0 (2-1-0)
S29	●	Ripon	50	0
O6	●	Chicago P&S	5	0
O13	●	Beloit *Mil*	11	0
O20	●	Upper Iowa	64	0
O27	●	Grinnell	45	0
N3			at Minnesota	5	6
N10	●	Notre Dame	54	0
N17	●		at Chicago	39	5
N24	●		Illinois	27	0

1901   9-0-0 (2-0-0)
S28	●	Milwaukee Medical	26	0
O5	●	Hyde Park HS	62	0
O12	●	Beloit *Mil*	40	0
O19	●	Knox	23	5
O26	●	Kansas	50	0
N2	●	Nebraska *Mil*	18	0
N9	●	Iowa State	45	0
N16	●		at Minnesota	18	0
N28	●		at Chicago	35	0

1902   6-3-0 (1-3-0)
S27	●	Lawrence	11	0
O4	●	Hyde Park HS	24	5
O11	●	Lawrence	52	0
O18	●	Beloit *Mil*	52	6
O25	●	Kansas	38	0
N1			Michigan *Chi*	0	6
N8	●		at Northwestern	51	0
N15			at Minnesota	0	11
N27			at Chicago	0	11

ART CURTIS
1903-04 (.639)   11-6-1

1903   6-3-1 (0-3-0)
O3	●	North Central	28	0
O10	●	Lawrence	40	7
O17	●	Beloit	87	0
O21	●	Osteopaths	32	0
O24	●	Knox	54	6
O31	●	Chicago	6	15
N7	●	U.W. Oshkosh	52	0
N14		at Michigan	0	16
N21	=	Northwestern *Chi*	6	6
N26		at Minnesota	0	17

1904   5-3-0 (0-3-0)
O1	●	Ft. Sheridan	45	0
O8	●	Marquette	33	0
O15	●	Notre Dame *Mil*	58	0
O22	●	Drake	82	0
O29		Michigan	0	28
N5	●	Beloit	36	0
N12		at Minnesota	0	28
N24		at Chicago	11	18

PHIL KING

1905   8-2-0 (1-2-0)
S23	●	at Company I.	16	0
S30	●	North Central	49	0
O4	●	Marquette	29	0
O7	●	Lawrence	34	0
O14	●	Notre Dame *Mil*	21	0
O21		Chicago	0	4
O28	●	U.W. Alumni	17	0
N4	●	at Minnesota	16	12
N11	●	Beloit	44	0
N18		at Michigan	0	12

CHARLES HUTCHINS
1906-07 (.850)   8-1-1

1906   5-0-0 (3-0-0)
O13	●	Lawrence	5	0
O20	●	North Dakota	10	0
N3	●		Iowa	18	4
N10	●		at Illinois	16	6
N17	●		Purdue	29	5

1907   3-1-1 (3-1-1)
O26		Illinois	4	15
N2	●		at Iowa	6	5
N9	●		Indiana	11	8
N16	●		at Purdue	12	6
N23	=		Minnesota	17	17

J.A. BARRY
1908-10 (.656)   9-4-3

1908   5-1-0 (2-1-0)
O10	●	Lawrence	35	0
O17	●		at Indiana	16	0
O24	●	U.W. JV	24	15
O31	●	Marquette	9	6
N7	●		at Minnesota	5	0
N21			Chicago	12	18

1909   3-1-1 (2-1-1)
O9	●	Lawrence	22	0
O23	●		Indiana	6	3
O30	●		at Northwestern	21	11
N13			Minnesota	6	34
N20	=		at Chicago	6	6

1910   1-2-2 (1-2-1)
O8	=	Lawrence	6	6
O22	●	Indiana *Ind*	3	12
O29	=	Northwestern	0	0
N12	●	at Minnesota	0	28
N19	●	Chicago	10	0

J.R. RICHARDS
1911, '17, '19-22 (.738) 29-9-4

1911   5-1-1 (2-1-1)
O7	●	Lawrence	15	0
O14	●	Ripon	24	0
O21	●	Colorado College	26	0
O28	●	at Northwestern	28	3
N4	●	Iowa	12	0
N18	●	Minnesota	6	6
N25		at Chicago	0	5

WILLIAM JUNEAU
1912-15 (.679)   18-8-2

1912   7-0-0 (5-0-0)
O5	●	Lawrence	13	0
O12	●	Northwestern	56	0
O19	●	Purdue	41	0
N2	●		Chicago	30	12
N9	●		Arkansas	64	7
N16	●		at Minnesota	14	0
N23	●		at Iowa	28	10

1913   3-3-1 (1-2-1)
O4	●	Lawrence	58	7
O11	●	Marquette	13	0
O18	=		at Purdue	7	7
O25	●	Michigan State	7	12
N1			Minnesota	3	21
N8	●		Ohio State	12	0
N22			at Chicago	0	19

1914   4-2-1 (2-2-1)
O3	●	Lawrence	21	0
O10	●	Marquette	48	0
O17	●	Purdue	14	7
O24	●	at Ohio State	7	6
O31	=		Chicago	0	0
N14	●		at Minnesota	3	14
N21			Illinois	9	24

1915   4-3-0 (2-3-0)
O2	●	Lawrence	82	0
O9	●	Marquette	85	0
O16	●	at Purdue	28	3
O23	●	Ohio State	21	0
O30	●	at Chicago	13	14
N13		at Illinois	3	17
N20		Minnesota	3	20

PAUL WITHINGTON
1916 (.643)   4-2-1

1916   4-2-1 (1-2-1)
O7	●	Lawrence	20	0
O14	●	South Dakota St.	28	3
O21	●	Haskell Indians	13	0
O28	●	Chicago	30	7
N4		at Ohio State	13	14
N18		at Minnesota	0	54
N25	=	Illinois	0	0

J.R. RICHARDS

1917 4-2-1 (3-2-0)

O6	●		Beloit	34	0
O13	=		Notre Dame	0	0
O20		|	at Illinois	0	7
O27	●	|	Iowa	20	0
N3	●	|	Minnesota	10	7
N10		|	Ohio State	3	16
N24	●	|	at Chicago	18	0

GUY LOWMAN
1918 (.500) 3-3

1918 3-3-0 (1-2-0)

O26			Camp Grant	0	7
N2	●		Beloit	21	0
N9		|	Illinois	0	22
N16		|	at Minnesota	0	6
N23	●	|	at Ohio State	14	3
N28	●		Michigan State	7	6

J.R. RICHARDS

1919 5-2-0 (3-2-0)

O4	●		Ripon	37	0
O11	●		Marquette	13	0
O18	●	|	at Northwestern	10	6
O25	●	|	at Illinois	14	10
N1		|	Minnesota	7	19
N15		|	Ohio State	0	3
N22	●	|	at Chicago	10	3

1920 6-1-0 (4-1-0)

O2	●		Lawrence	60	0
O9	●		Michigan State	27	0
O16	●	|	Northwestern	27	7
O23		|	at Ohio State	7	13
N6	●	|	at Minnesota	3	0
N13	●	|	Illinois	14	9
N20	●	|	at Chicago	3	0

1921 5-1-1 (3-1-1)

O1	●		Lawrence	28	0
O8	●		South Dakota St.	24	3
O15	●	|	at Northwestern	27	0
O22	●	|	at Illinois	20	0
O29	●	|	Minnesota	35	0
N12	=	|	Michigan	7	7
N19		|	at Chicago	0	3

1922 4-2-1 (2-2-1)

O7	●		Carleton	41	0
O14	●		South Dakota St.	20	6
O21	●	|	Indiana	20	0
N4	●	|	at Minnesota	14	0
N11		|	Illinois	0	3
N18		|	at Michigan	6	13
N25	=	|	at Chicago	0	0

JACK RYAN
1923-24 (.467) 5-6-4

1923 3-3-1 (1-3-1)

O6	●		Coe	7	3
O13	●		Michigan State	21	0
O20	●	|	at Indiana	52	0
O27	=	|	Minnesota	0	0
N10		|	at Illinois	0	10
N17		|	Michigan	3	6
N24		|	at Chicago	6	13

1924 2-3-3 (0-2-2)

S27	●		North Dakota St.	25	0
O4	●		Iowa State	17	0
O11	=		Coe	7	7
O18	=	|	Minnesota	7	7
O25		|	at Michigan	0	21
N8			Notre Dame	3	38
N15		|	Iowa	7	21
N22	=	|	at Chicago	0	0

GEORGE LITTLE
1925-26 (.750) 11-3-2

1925 6-1-1 (3-1-1)

O3	●		Iowa State	30	0
O10	●		Franklin	35	0
O17		|	Michigan	0	21
O24	●	|	Purdue	7	0
O31	=	|	at Minnesota	12	12
N7	●	|	at Iowa	6	0
N14	●		Michigan State	21	10
N21	●	|	at Chicago	20	7

1926 5-2-1 (3-2-1)

O2	●		Cornell Coll.	38	0
O9	●		Kansas	13	0
O16	=	|	at Purdue	0	0
O23	●	|	Indiana	27	2
O30		|	Minnesota	10	16
N6		|	at Michigan	0	37
N13	●	|	Iowa	20	10
N20	●	|	at Chicago	14	7

GLENN THISTLETHWAITE
1927-31 (.611) 26-16-3

1927 4-4-0 (1-4-0)

O1	●		Cornell Coll.	31	6
O8	●		at Kansas	26	6
O15		|	Michigan	0	14
O22	●	|	Purdue	12	6
O29		|	at Minnesota	7	13
N5	●		Grinnell	20	2
N12		|	Iowa	0	16
N19		|	at Chicago	0	6

1928 7-1-1 (3-1-1)

O6	●		Notre Dame	22	6
O13	●		Cornell Coll.	49	0
O13	●		North Dakota St.	13	7
O20	=	|	at Purdue	19	19
O27	●	|	at Michigan	7	0
N3	●		Alabama	15	0
N10	●	|	Chicago	25	0
N17	●	|	at Iowa	13	0
N24		|	Minnesota	0	6

1929 4-5-0 (1-4-0)

S28	●		Ripon	22	0
S28	●		South Dakota St.	21	0
O5	●		Colgate	13	6
O12		|	Northwestern	0	7
O19			Notre Dame CHI	0	19
O26		|	Iowa	0	14
N2		|	Purdue	0	13
N9	●	|	at Chicago	20	6
N23		|	at Minnesota	12	13

1930 6-2-1 (2-2-1)

O4	●		Lawrence	53	6
O4	●		Carleton	28	0
O11	●	|	Chicago	34	0
O18	●		Pennsylvania	27	0
O25		|	at Purdue	6	7
N1	=	|	at Ohio State	0	0
N8	●		South Dakota St.	58	7
N15		|	at Northwestern	7	20
N22	●	|	Minnesota	14	0

1931 5-4-1 (3-3-0)

O3	●		Bradley	33	6
O3	●		North Dakota St.	12	7
O10	=		Auburn	7	7
O17	●	|	Purdue	21	14
O24			at Pennsylvania	13	27
O31		|	at Minnesota	0	14
N7	●	|	at Illinois	7	6
N14		|	Ohio State	0	6
N21	●	|	at Chicago	12	7
N28		|	at Michigan	0	16

CLARENCE SPEARS
1932-35 (.438) 13-17-2

1932 6-1-1 (4-1-1)

O1	●		Marquette	7	2
O8	●	|	Iowa	34	0
O15		|	at Purdue	6	7
O22	●		Coe	39	0
O29	=	|	at Ohio State	7	7
N5	●	|	Illinois	20	12
N12	●	|	Minnesota	20	13
N19	●	|	at Chicago	18	7

1933 2-5-1 (0-5-1)

O7	●		Marquette	19	0
O14		|	at Illinois	0	21
O21		|	at Iowa	7	26
O28		|	Purdue	0	14
N4	=	|	at Chicago	0	0
N11	●		West Virginia	25	6
N18		|	Ohio State	0	6
N25		|	at Minnesota	3	6

1934 4-4-0 (2-3-0)

O6	●		Marquette	3	0
O13	●		South Dakota St.	28	7
O20		|	at Purdue	0	14
O27			at Notre Dame	0	19
N3		|	at Northwestern	0	7
N10	●	|	at Michigan	10	0
N17	●	|	Illinois	7	3
N24		|	Minnesota	0	34

1935 1-7-0 (1-4-0)

S28			South Dakota St.	6	13
O5			Marquette	0	33
O12			Notre Dame	0	27
O19		|	Michigan	12	20
O26		|	at Chicago	7	13
N9	●	|	Purdue	8	0
N16		|	at Northwestern	13	32
N23		|	at Minnesota	7	33

HARRY STUHLDREHER
1936-48 (.425) 45-62-6

1936 2-6-0 (0-4-0)

S26	●		South Dakota St.	24	7
O3			Marquette	6	12
O10		|	at Purdue	14	35
O17			at Notre Dame	0	27
O31		|	Chicago	6	7
N7		|	at Northwestern	18	26
N14	●		Cincinnati	27	6
N21		|	Minnesota	0	24

1937 4-3-1 (2-2-1)

S25	●		South Dakota St.	32	0
O2	●		Marquette	12	0
O9	●	|	at Chicago	27	0
O16	●	|	Iowa	13	6
O23			at Pittsburgh	0	21
O30		|	Northwestern	6	14
N13	=	|	Purdue	7	7
N20		|	at Minnesota	6	13

1938 5-3-0 (3-2-0)

O1	●		Marquette	27	0
O8	●	|	at Iowa	31	13
O15			Pittsburgh	6	26
O22		|	at Purdue	7	13
O29	●	|	Indiana	6	0
N5	●	|	at Northwestern	20	13
N12	●		at UCLA	14	7
N19		|	Minnesota	0	21

1939 1-6-1 (0-5-1)

S30	●		Marquette	14	13
O7			Texas	7	17
O14		|	Indiana	0	14
O21		|	at Northwestern	7	13
O28		|	Iowa	13	19
N11		|	at Illinois	0	7
N18	=	|	Purdue	7	7
N25		|	at Minnesota	6	23

1940 4-4-0 (3-3-0)

O5	●		Marquette	33	19
O12		|	at Iowa	12	30
O19		|	Northwestern	7	27
O26	●	|	at Purdue	14	13
N2	●	|	Illinois	13	6
N9			at Columbia	6	7
N16	●	|	Indiana	27	10
N23		|	Minnesota	13	22

1941 3-5-0 (3-3-0)

O4			Marquette	7	28
O11		|	at Northwestern	14	41
O18	●	|	Iowa	23	0
O25	●	|	Indiana	27	25
N1			Syracuse	20	27
N8		|	at Ohio State	34	46
N15	●	|	Purdue	13	0
N22		|	at Minnesota	6	41

1942 8-1-1 (4-1-0)

S19	●		Camp Grant	7	0
S26	=		Notre Dame	7	7
O3	●		Marquette	35	7
O10	●		Missouri	17	9
O17	●		Great Lakes NAS CHI	13	7
O24	●	|	at Purdue	13	0
O31	●	|	Ohio State	17	7
N7		|	at Iowa	0	6
N14	●	|	at Northwestern	20	19
N21	●	|	Minnesota	20	6

1943 1-9-0 (1-6-0)

S18			Marquette	7	33
S25			at Camp Grant	7	10
O2	●	|	at Iowa	7	5
O9		|	Illinois	7	25
O16			Notre Dame	0	50
O23		|	at Indiana	0	34
O30		|	Purdue	0	32
N6		|	Northwestern	0	41
N13		|	at Michigan	0	27
N20		|	at Minnesota	13	25

1944 3-6-0 (2-4-0)

S30	●	|	at Northwestern	7	6
O7	●		Marquette	21	2
O14		|	Ohio State	7	20
O21			at Notre Dame	13	28
O28			Great Lakes NAS	12	40
N4		|	at Purdue	0	35
N11	●	|	Iowa	26	7
N18		|	at Michigan	0	14
N25		|	Minnesota	26	28

1945 3-4-2 (2-3-1)

S22	=		at Great Lakes NAS	0	0
S29	●		Marquette	40	13
O6		|	Purdue	7	13
O13		|	at Ohio State	0	12
O20	=	|	Illinois	7	7
N3	●	|	at Iowa	27	7
N10		|	Northwestern	14	28
N17			Navy BALT	7	36
N24	●	|	at Minnesota	26	12

1946 4-5-0 (2-5-0)

S21	●		Marquette	34	0
S28	●		at California	28	7
O5		|	at Northwestern	0	28
O12	●	|	Ohio State	20	7
O19		|	at Illinois	21	27
N2	●	|	at Purdue	24	20
N9		|	Iowa	7	21
N16		|	at Michigan	6	28
N23		|	Minnesota	0	6

1947 5-3-1 (3-2-1)

S27	●	|	Purdue	32	14
O4	=	|	at Indiana	7	7
O11			California	7	48
O18	●		at Yale	9	0
O25	●		Marquette	35	12
N1	●	|	at Northwestern	29	0
N8	●	|	Iowa	46	14
N15		|	Michigan	6	40
N22		|	at Minnesota	0	21

1948 2-7-0 (1-5-0)

S25		|	Indiana	7	35
O2	●	|	Illinois	20	16
O9			at California	14	40
O16			Yale	7	17
O23		|	at Ohio State	32	34
O30		|	at Iowa	13	19
N6		|	Northwestern	7	16
N13	●		Marquette	26	0
N20		|	Minnesota	0	16

IVY WILLIAMSON
1949-55 (.672) 41-19-4

1949 5-3-1 (3-2-1)

S24	●		Marquette	41	0
O1	=	|	at Illinois	13	13
O8			California	20	35
O15	●		Navy	48	13
O22		|	Ohio State	0	21
O29	●	|	at Indiana	30	14
N5	●	|	at Northwestern	14	6
N12	●	|	Iowa	35	13
N19		|	at Minnesota	6	14

1950 6-3-0 (5-2-0)

S30	●		Marquette	28	6
O7	●	|	at Illinois	7	6
O14	●	|	at Iowa	14	0
O21		|	at Michigan	13	26
O28	●	|	Northwestern	14	13
N4	●	|	Purdue	33	7
N11		|	at Ohio State	14	19
N18			at Pennsylvania	0	20
N25	●	|	Minnesota	14	0

1951 7-1-1 (5-1-1)

S29	●		Marquette	22	6
O6		|	at Illinois	10	14
O13	=	|	Ohio State	6	6
O20	●	|	at Purdue	31	7
O27	●	|	at Northwestern	41	0
N3	●	|	Indiana	6	0
N10	●		Pennsylvania	16	7
N17	●	|	Iowa	34	7
N24	●	|	at Minnesota	30	6

1952 6-3-1 (4-1-1)

S27	●		Marquette	42	19
O4	●	|	Illinois	20	6
O11		|	at Ohio State	14	23
O18	●	|	at Iowa	42	13
O25			UCLA	7	20
N1	●		at Rice	21	7
N8	●	|	Northwestern	24	20
N15	●	|	at Indiana	37	14
N22	=	|	Minnesota	21	21
			ROSE BOWL		
J1			USC	0	7

176 WISCONSIN

BIG TEN TEAMS

1953 — 6-2-1 (4-1-1)

S26	●		Penn State	20	0
O3	●		Marquette	13	11
O9			at UCLA	0	13
O17	●	│	at Purdue	28	19
O24		│	Ohio State	19	20
O31	●	│	Iowa	10	6
N7	●	│	at Northwestern	34	13
N14	●	│	Illinois	34	7
N21	=	│	at Minnesota	21	21

1954 — 7-2-0 (5-2-0)

S25	●		Marquette	52	14
O2	●	│	at Michigan State	6	0
O9	●		Rice	13	7
O16	●	│	Purdue	20	6
O23		│	at Ohio State	14	31
O30		│	at Iowa	7	13
N6	●	│	Northwestern	34	13
N13	●	│	at Illinois	27	14
N20	●	│	Minnesota	27	0

1955 — 4-5-0 (3-4-0)

S24	●		Marquette	28	14
O1	●	│	Iowa	37	14
O8	●	│	at Purdue	9	0
O14			at USC	21	33
O22		│	Ohio State	16	26
O29		│	Michigan State	0	27
N5	●	│	at Northwestern	41	14
N12		│	Illinois	14	17
N19		│	at Minnesota	6	21

MILT BRUHN
1956-66 (.534) 52-45-6

1956 — 1-5-3 (0-4-3)

S29	●		Marquette	41	0
O6			USC	6	13
O13		│	at Iowa	7	13
O20	=	│	Purdue	6	6
O27		│	at Ohio State	0	21
N3		│	at Michigan State	0	33
N10		│	Northwestern	7	17
N17	=	│	at Illinois	13	13
N24	=	│	Minnesota	13	13

1957 — 6-3-0 (4-3-0)

S28	●		Marquette	60	6
O5	●		West Virginia	45	13
O12	●	│	at Purdue	23	14
O19		│	at Iowa	7	21
O26		│	Ohio State	13	16
N2		│	Michigan State	7	21
N9	●	│	at Northwestern	41	12
N16	●	│	Illinois	24	13
N23	●	│	at Minnesota	14	6

1958 — 7-1-1 (5-1-1)

S26	●		at Miami, Fla.	20	0
O4	●		Marquette	50	0
O11	●	│	Purdue	31	6
O18		│	Iowa	9	20
O25	=	│	at Ohio State	7	7
N1	●	│	at Michigan State	9	7
N8	●	│	Northwestern	17	13
N15	●	│	at Illinois	31	12
N22	●	│	Minnesota	27	12

1959 — 7-3-0 (5-2-0)

S26	●		Stanford	16	14
O3	●		Marquette	44	6
O10		│	at Purdue	0	21
O17	●	│	Iowa	25	16
O24	●	│	Ohio State	12	3
O31	●	│	at Michigan	19	10
N7	●	│	at Northwestern	24	19
N14		│	Illinois	6	9
N21	●	│	at Minnesota	11	7
ROSE BOWL					
J1			Washington	8	44

1960 — 4-5-0 (2-5-0)

S24	●		at Stanford	24	7
O1	●		Marquette	35	6
O8	●	│	Purdue	24	13
O15		│	at Iowa	21	28
O22		│	at Ohio State	7	34
O29	●	│	Michigan	16	13
N5		│	Northwestern	0	21
N12		│	at Illinois	14	35
N19		│	Minnesota	7	26

1961 — 6-3-0 (4-3-0)

S23	●		Utah	7	0
S30		│	Michigan State	0	20
O7	●	│	at Indiana	6	3
O14	●		Oregon State	23	20
O21		│	at Iowa	15	47
O28		│	Ohio State	21	30
N11	●	│	at Northwestern	29	10
N18	●	│	Illinois	55	7
N25	●	│	at Minnesota	23	21

1962 — 8-2-0 (6-1-0)

S29	●		New Mexico St.	69	13
O6	●	│	Indiana	30	6
O13	●		Notre Dame	17	8
O20	●	│	Iowa	42	14
O27		│	at Ohio State	7	14
N3	●	│	at Michigan	34	12
N10	●	│	Northwestern	37	6
N17	●	│	at Illinois	35	6
N24	●	│	Minnesota	14	9
ROSE BOWL					
J1			USC	37	42

1963 — 5-4-0 (3-4-0)

S21	●		Western Michigan	41	0
S28	●		at Notre Dame	14	9
O12	●	│	Purdue	38	20
O19	●	│	at Iowa	10	7
O26		│	Ohio State	10	13
N2		│	at Michigan State	13	30
N9	●	│	Northwestern	17	14
N16		│	Illinois	7	17
N28		│	at Minnesota	0	14

1964 — 3-6-0 (2-5-0)

S19	●		Kansas State	17	7
S26			Notre Dame	7	31
O10		│	at Purdue	7	28
O17	●	│	Iowa	31	21
O24		│	at Ohio State	3	28
O31		│	Michigan State	6	22
N7		│	at Northwestern	13	17
N14		│	at Illinois	0	29
N21	●	│	Minnesota	14	7

1965 — 2-7-1 (2-5-0)

S18	=		Colorado	0	0
S25			USC	6	26
O2	●	│	Iowa	16	13
O9			at Nebraska	0	37
O16	●	│	at Northwestern	21	7
O23		│	Ohio State	10	20
O30		│	at Michigan	14	50
N6		│	at Purdue	7	45
N13		│	Illinois	0	51
N20		│	at Minnesota	7	42

1966 — 3-6-1 (2-4-1)

S17	●		Iowa State	20	10
S24			at USC	3	38
O1	●	│	at Iowa	7	0
O8			Nebraska	3	31
O15	=	│	Northwestern	3	3
O22		│	at Ohio State	13	24
O29		│	Michigan	17	28
N5		│	Purdue	0	23
N12		│	at Illinois	14	49
N19	●	│	Minnesota	7	6

JOHN COATTA
1967-69 (.117) 3-26-1

1967 — 0-9-1 (0-6-1)

S23			at Washington	0	17
S30			Arizona State	16	42
O7		│	at Michigan State	7	35
O14			Pittsburgh	11	13
O21	=	│	Iowa	21	21
O28		│	Northwestern	13	17
N4		│	at Indiana	9	14
N11		│	at Ohio State	15	17
N18		│	Michigan	14	27
N25		│	at Minnesota	14	21

1968 — 0-10-0 (0-7-0)

S21			at Arizona State	7	55
S28			Washington	17	21
O5		│	Michigan State	0	39
O12			Utah State	0	20
O19		│	at Iowa	0	41
O26		│	at Northwestern	10	13
N2		│	Indiana	20	21
N9		│	Ohio State	8	43
N16		│	at Michigan	9	34
N23		│	Minnesota	15	23

1969 — 3-7-0 (3-4-0)

S20			Oklahoma	21	48
S27			UCLA	23	34
O4			Syracuse	7	43
O11	●	│	Iowa	23	17
O18		│	at Northwestern	7	27
O25	●	│	Indiana	36	34
N1		│	at Michigan	7	35
N8		│	at Ohio State	7	62
N15	●	│	Illinois	55	14
N22		│	at Minnesota	10	35

JOHN JARDINE
1970-77 (.443) 37-47-3

1970 — 4-5-1 (3-4-0)

S19			at Oklahoma	7	21
S26	=		TCU	14	14
O3	●		Penn State	29	16
O10		│	at Iowa	14	24
O17		│	Northwestern	14	24
O24	●	│	at Indiana	30	12
O31		│	Michigan	15	29
N7		│	Ohio State	7	24
N14	●	│	at Illinois	29	17
N21	●	│	Minnesota	39	14

1971 — 4-6-1 (3-5-0)

S11	●		Northern Illinois	31	0
S18	=		at Syracuse	20	20
S25			LSU	28	38
O2		│	at Northwestern	11	24
O9	●	│	Indiana	35	29
O16	●	│	Michigan State	31	28
O23		│	at Ohio State	6	31
O30		│	at Iowa	16	20
N6	●	│	Purdue	14	10
N13		│	Illinois	27	35
N20		│	at Minnesota	21	23

1972 — 4-7-0 (2-6-0)

S16	●		Northern Illinois	31	7
S23	●		Syracuse	31	7
S30			at LSU	7	27
O7	●	│	Northwestern	21	14
O14		│	at Indiana	7	33
O21		│	at Michigan State	0	31
O28		│	Ohio State	20	28
N4	●	│	Iowa	16	14
N11		│	at Purdue	6	27
N18		│	at Illinois	7	27
N25		│	Minnesota	6	14

1973 — 4-7-0 (3-5-0)

S15		│	Purdue	13	14
S22			Colorado	25	28
S29			at Nebraska	16	20
O6	●		Wyoming	37	28
O13		│	Ohio State	0	24
O20		│	at Michigan	6	35
O27	●	│	Indiana	31	7
N3		│	at Michigan State	0	21
N10	●	│	Iowa	35	7
N17	●	│	Northwestern	36	34
N24		│	at Minnesota	17	19

1974 — 7-4-0 (5-3-0)

S14	●	│	at Purdue	28	14
S21	●		Nebraska	21	20
S28			at Colorado	21	24
O5	●		Missouri	59	20
O12		│	at Ohio State	7	52
O19		│	Michigan	20	24
O26	●	│	at Indiana	35	25
N2		│	Michigan State	21	28
N9	●	│	at Iowa	28	15
N16	●	│	at Northwestern	52	7
N23	●	│	Minnesota	49	14

1975 — 4-6-1 (3-4-1)

S13		│	Michigan	6	23
S20	●		South Dakota	48	7
S27			at Missouri	21	27
O4			Kansas	7	41
O11	●	│	at Purdue	17	14
O18		│	at Ohio State	0	56
O25	●	│	Northwestern	17	14
N1	●	│	Illinois	18	9
N8		│	at Iowa	28	45
N15	=	│	Indiana	9	9
N22		│	at Minnesota	3	24

1976 — 5-6-0 (3-5-0)

S11		│	at Michigan	27	40
S18	●		North Dakota	45	9
S25	●		Washington State	35	26
O2			at Kansas	24	34
O9		│	Purdue	16	18
O16		│	Ohio State	20	30
O23	●	│	at Northwestern	28	25
O30		│	at Illinois	25	31
N6	●	│	Iowa	38	21
N13		│	at Indiana	14	15
N20	●	│	Minnesota	26	17

1977 — 5-6-0 (3-6-0)

S10	●	│	at Indiana	30	14
S17	●		Northern Illinois	14	3
S24	●		at Oregon	22	10
O1	●	│	Northwestern	19	7
O8	●	│	Illinois	26	0
O15		│	at Michigan	0	56
O22		│	Michigan State	7	9
O29		│	at Ohio State	0	42
N5		│	Purdue	0	22
N12		│	Iowa	8	24
N19		│	at Minnesota	7	13

DAVE McCLAIN
1978-85 (.522) 46-42-3

1978 — 5-4-2 (3-4-2)

S16	●		Richmond	7	6
S23	●	│	at Northwestern	28	7
S30	●		Oregon	22	19
O7	●	│	Indiana	34	7
O14	=	│	at Illinois	20	20
O21		│	Michigan	0	42
O28		│	at Michigan State	2	55
N4		│	Ohio State	14	49
N11	=	│	Purdue	24	24
N18		│	at Iowa	24	38
N25	●	│	Minnesota	48	10

1979 — 4-7-0 (3-5-0)

S8		│	at Purdue	20	41
S15	●		Air Force	38	0
S22			UCLA	12	37
S29			at San Diego State	17	24
O6		│	Indiana	0	3
O13	●	│	Michigan State	38	29
O20		│	at Ohio State	0	59
O27		│	Iowa	13	24
N3		│	at Michigan	0	54
N10	●	│	Northwestern	28	3
N17	●	│	at Minnesota	42	37

1980 — 4-7-0 (3-5-0)

S13		│	Purdue	6	12
S20			Brigham Young	3	28
S27			at UCLA	0	35
O4	●		San Diego State	35	12
O11		│	at Indiana	0	24
O18	●	│	at Michigan State	17	7
O25		│	Ohio State	0	21
N1		│	at Iowa	13	22
N8		│	Michigan	0	24
N15	●	│	at Northwestern	39	19
N22	●	│	Minnesota	25	7

1981 — 7-5-0 (6-3-0)

S12	●	│	Michigan	21	14
S19			UCLA	13	31
S26	●		Western Michigan	21	10
O3	●	│	Purdue	20	14
O10	●	│	Ohio State	24	21
O17		│	at Michigan State	14	33
O24		│	at Illinois	21	23
O31	●	│	Northwestern	52	0
N7	●	│	at Indiana	28	7
N14		│	Iowa	7	17
N21	●	│	at Minnesota	26	21
GARDEN STATE BOWL					
D13			Tennessee	21	28

1982 — 7-5-0 (5-4-0)

S11		│	at Michigan	9	20
S18			UCLA	26	51
S25	●		Toledo	36	27
O2	●	│	at Purdue	35	31
O9	●	│	at Ohio State	6	0
O16	●	│	Michigan State	24	23
O23		│	Illinois	28	29
O30	●	│	Northwestern	54	20
N6		│	Indiana	17	20
N13		│	at Iowa	14	28
N20	●	│	Minnesota	24	0
INDEPENDENCE BOWL					
D11	●		Kansas State	14	3

1983 — 7-4-0 (5-4-0)

S10	●	Northern Illinois	37 9
S17	●	Missouri	21 20
S24		Michigan	21 38
O1	●	at Northwestern	49 0
O8		Illinois	15 27
O15	●	at Minnesota	56 17
O22	●	Indiana	45 14
O29		at Ohio State	27 45
N5		Iowa	14 34
N12	●	at Purdue	42 38
N19		Michigan State	32 0

1984 — 7-4-1 (5-3-1)

S8	●	Northern Illinois	27 14
S15	●	at Missouri	35 34
S22		at Michigan	14 20
S29	●	Northwestern	31 16
O6		at Illinois	6 22
O13		Minnesota	14 17
O20	●	at Indiana	20 16
O27	●	Ohio State	16 14
N3	=	at Iowa	10 10
N10	●	Purdue	30 13
N17		at Michigan State	20 10

HALL OF FAME CLASSIC

D29		Kentucky	19 20

1985 — 5-6-0 (2-6-0)

S14	●	Northern Illinois	38 17
S21	●	Nevada-Las Vegas	26 23
S28	●	at Wyoming	41 17
O5		at Michigan	6 33
O12	●	Iowa	13 23
O19		Northwestern	14 17
O26	●	at Illinois	25 38
N2	●	Indiana	31 20
N9		at Minnesota	18 27
N16	●	at Ohio State	12 7
N23		Michigan State	7 41

JIM HILLES
1986 (.250)   3-9

1986 — 3-9-0 (2-6-0)

S6		at Hawaii	17 20
S13	●	Northern Illinois	35 20
S20	●	at Nevada-Las Vegas	7 17
S27		Wyoming	12 21
O4		Michigan	17 34
O11		at Iowa	6 17
O18	●	at Northwestern	35 27
O25	●	Illinois	15 9
N1		at Indiana	7 21
N8		Minnesota	20 27
N15		Ohio State	17 30
N22		at Michigan State	13 23

DON MORTON
1987-89 (.102)   G-27

1987 — 3-8-0 (1-7-0)

S12	●	Hawaii	28 7
S19	●	Utah	28 31
S26	●	Ball State	30 13
O3		at Michigan	0 49
O10		Iowa	10 31
O17		at Illinois	14 16
O24		Northwestern	24 27
O31		at Purdue	14 49
N7	●	Ohio State	26 24
N14		at Minnesota	19 22
N21		Michigan State	9 30

1988 — 1-10-0 (1-7-0)

S3		Western Michigan	14 24
S17		Northern Illinois	17 19
S24		at Miami, Fla.	3 23
O1		Michigan	14 62
O8		at Iowa	6 31
O15		Illinois	6 34
O22		at Northwestern	14 35
O29		Purdue	6 9
N5		at Ohio State	12 34
N12	●	Minnesota	14 7
N19		at Michigan State	0 36

1989 — 2-9-0 (1-7-0)

S9		Miami, Fla.	3 51
S16	●	Toledo	23 10
S23		at California	14 20
O7		at Michigan	0 24
O14		Iowa	24 31
O21	●	Northwestern	35 31
O28		at Illinois	9 32
N4		at Minnesota	22 24
N11		Indiana	17 45
N18		at Ohio State	22 42
N25		Michigan State	3 31

BARRY ALVAREZ
1990-2005 (.618)   118-73-4

1990 — 1-10-0 (0-8-0)

S8		California	12 28
S15	●	Ball State	24 7
S22		Temple	18 24
O6		Michigan	3 41
O13		at Iowa	10 30
O20		at Northwestern	34 44
O27		Illinois	3 21
N3		Minnesota	3 21
N10		at Indiana	7 20
N17		Ohio State	10 35
N24		at Michigan State	9 14

1991 — 5-6-0 (2-6-0)

S14	●	W. Illinois	31 13
S21	●	Iowa State	7 6
S28	●	Eastern Michigan	21 6
O5		at Ohio State	16 31
O12		Iowa	6 10
O19		at Purdue	7 28
O26		Indiana	20 28
N2		at Illinois	6 22
N9		Michigan State	7 20
N16	●	at Minnesota	19 16
N23	●	Northwestern	32 14

1992 — 5-6-0 (3-5-0)

S12		at Washington	10 27
S19	●	Bowling Green	39 18
S26	●	Northern Illinois	18 17
O3		Ohio State	20 16
O10		at Iowa	22 23
O17	●	Purdue	19 16
O24		at Indiana	3 10
O31		Illinois	12 13
N7		at Michigan State	10 26
N14	●	Minnesota	34 6
N21		at Northwestern	25 27

1993 — 10-1-1 (6-1-1)

S4	●	Nevada	35 17
S11	●	at SMU	24 16
S18	●	Iowa State	28 7
S25		at Indiana	27 15
O9		Northwestern	53 14
O16	●	at Purdue	42 28
O23		at Minnesota	21 28
O30	●	Michigan	13 10
N6		Ohio State	14 14
N20		at Illinois	35 10
D5	●	Michigan State [TOK]	41 20

ROSE BOWL

J1	●	UCLA	21 16

1994 — 7-4-1 (4-3-1)

S10	●	Eastern Michigan	56 0
S17		at Colorado	17 55
S24	●	Indiana	62 13
O1		at Michigan State	10 29 †
O8	●	at Northwestern	46 14
O15	=	Purdue	27 27
O22		Minnesota	14 17
O29	●	Michigan	31 19
N5		at Ohio State	3 24
N12		Cincinnati	38 7
N19		Illinois	19 13

HALL OF FAME BOWL

J2	●	Duke	34 20

1995 — 4-5-2 (3-4-1)

S2		Colorado	7 43
S16	=	at Stanford	24 24
S23	●	SMU	42 0
S30		at Penn State	17 9
O14		Ohio State	16 27
O21		at Northwestern	0 35
O28	●	Michigan State	45 14
N4		at Purdue	27 38
N11	●	at Minnesota	34 27
N18		Iowa	20 33
N25	=	Illinois	3 3

1996 — 8-5 (3-5)

S7	●	Eastern Michigan	24 3
S14	●	at Nevada-Las Vegas	52 17
S21		Stanford	14 0
S28		Penn State	20 23
O12		at Ohio State	14 17
O19		Northwestern	30 34
O26		at Michigan State	13 30
N2	●	Purdue	33 25
N9	●	Minnesota	45 28
N16		at Iowa	0 31
N23	●	at Illinois	35 15
N30	●	at Hawaii	59 10

COPPER BOWL

D27	●	Utah	38 10

1997 — 8-5 (5-3)

A24		Syracuse [ERUT]	0 34
S6	●	Boise State	28 24
S13		at San Jose State	56 10
S20	●	San Diego State	36 10
S27		Indiana	27 26
O4		at Northwestern	26 25
O11		Illinois	31 7
O18		at Purdue	20 45
O25		at Minnesota	22 21
N8	●	Iowa	13 10
N15		Michigan	16 26
N22		at Penn State	10 35

OUTBACK BOWL

J1		Georgia	6 33

1998 — 11-1 (7-1)

S5		at San Diego State	26 14
S12	●	Ohio U.	45 0
S19	●	Nevada-Las Vegas	52 7
S26	●	Northwestern	38 7
O3		at Indiana	24 20
O10	●	Purdue	31 24
O17	●	at Illinois	37 3
O24	●	at Iowa	31 0
N7	●	Minnesota	26 7
N14		at Michigan	10 27
N21	●	Penn State	24 3

ROSE BOWL

J1	●	UCLA	38 31

1999 — 10-2 (7-1)

S4	●	Murray St.	49 10
S11	●	Ball State	50 10
S18		at Cincinnati	12 17
S25		Michigan	16 21
O2	●	at Ohio State	42 17
O9	●	at Minnesota	20 17
O16		Indiana	59 0
O23	●	Michigan State	40 10
O30	●	at Northwestern	35 19
N6	●	at Purdue	28 21
N13	●	Iowa	41 3

ROSE BOWL

J1	●	Stanford	17 9

2000 — 9-4 (4-4)

A31	●	Western Michigan	19 7
S9	●	Oregon	27 23
S16	●	Cincinnati	28 25
S23	●	Northwestern	44 47
S30		at Michigan	10 13
O7		Ohio State	7 23
O14	●	at Michigan State	17 10
O21		Purdue	24 30
O28	●	at Iowa	13 7
N4	●	Minnesota	41 20
N11	●	at Indiana	43 22
N25	●	at Hawaii	34 18

SUN BOWL

D29	●	UCLA	21 20

2001 — 5-7 (3-5)

A25	●	Virginia	26 17
S1		at Oregon	28 31
S8		Fresno St.	20 32
S22	●	at Penn State	18 6
S29	●	Western Ky.	24 6
O6		Indiana	32 63
O13		at Ohio State	20 17
O20		at Illinois	35 42
O27		Michigan State	28 42
N3		Iowa	34 28
N17		Michigan	17 20
N24		at Minnesota	31 42

2002 — 8-6 (2-6)

A23	●	Fresno State	23 21
A31	●	at Nevada-Las Vegas	27 7
S7	●	West Virginia	34 17
S14	●	Northern Illinois	24 21
S21	●	Arizona	31 10
O5		Penn State	31 34
O12		at Indiana	29 32
O19		Ohio State	14 19
O26	●	at Michigan State	42 24
N2		at Iowa	3 20
N9		Illinois	20 37
N16		at Michigan	14 21
N23	●	Minnesota	49 31

ALAMO BOWL

D28	●	Colorado	31 28

2003 — 7-6 4-4

A30	●	at West Virginia	24 17
S6	●	Akron	48 31
S13		Nevada-Las Vegas	5 23
S20	●	North Carolina	38 27
S27	●	at Illinois	38 20
O4	●	at Penn State	30 23
O11	●	Ohio State	17 10
O18		Purdue	23 26
O25	●	at Northwestern	7 16
N8		at Minnesota	34 37
N15	●	Michigan State	56 21
N22		Iowa	21 27

MUSIC CITY BOWL

D31		Auburn	14 28

2004 — 9-3 (6-2)

S4	●	Central Florida	34 6
S11	●	Nevada-Las Vegas	18 3
S18	●	at Arizona	9 7
S25	●	Penn State	16 3
O2	●	Illinois	24 7
O9	●	at Ohio State	24 13
O16	●	at Purdue	20 17
O23	●	Northwestern	24 12
N6	●	Minnesota	38 14
N13		at Michigan State	14 49
N20	●	at Iowa	7 30

OUTBACK BOWL

J1		Georgia	21 24

2005 — 10-3 (5-3)

S3	●	Bowling Green	56 42
S10	●	Temple	65 0
S17		at North Carolina	14 5
S24	●	Michigan	23 20
O1		Indiana	41 24
O8	●	at Northwestern	48 51
O15		at Minnesota	38 34
O22	●	Purdue	31 20
O29	●	at Illinois	41 24
N5		at Penn State	14 35
N12		Iowa	10 20
N26	●	at Hawaii	41 24

CAPITOL ONE BOWL

J2	●	Auburn	24 10

BRET BIELEMA
2006-Present (.923)   12-1

2006 — 12-1 (7-1)

S2	●	Bowling Green [CLEV]	35 14
S9	●	Western Illinois	34 10
S16	●	San Diego State	14 0
S23		at Michigan	13 27
S30		at Indiana	52 17
O7		Northwestern	41 9
O14		Minnesota	48 12
O21		at Purdue	24 3
O28		Illinois	30 24
N4		Penn State	13 3
N11		at Iowa	24 21
N18	●	Buffalo	35 3

CAPITOL ONE BOWL

J1	●	Arkansas	17 14

WISCONSIN RECORD BOOK

SINGLE-GAME RECORDS

RUSHING YARDS

RANK	PLAYER	DATE	OPPONENT	ATT	AVG	YDS
1	Ron Dayne	Nov. 30, 1996	Hawaii	36	9.4	339
2	Billy Marek	Nov. 23, 1974	Minnesota	43	7.1	304
3	Anthony Davis	Nov. 23, 2002	Minnesota	45	6.7	301
4	Ron Dayne	Nov. 9, 1996	Minnesota	50	5.9	297
5	Michael Bennett	Sept. 23, 2000	Northwestern	48	6.1	293

PASSING YARDS

RANK	PLAYER	DATE	OPPONENT	ATT	COMP	YDS
1	Darrell Bevell	Oct. 13, 1993	Minnesota	48	31	423
2	Ron Vander Kelen	Jan. 1, 1963	USC	48	33	401
3	Jim Sorgi	Nov. 15, 2003	Michigan State	24	16	380
4	Tony Lowery	Oct. 20, 1990	Northwestern	31	21	355
5	Darrell Bevell	Nov. 18, 1995	Iowa	51	35	352

RECEIVING YARDS

RANK	PLAYER	DATE	OPPONENT	REC	AVG	YDS
1	Lee Evans	Dec. 4, 2003	Michigan State	10	25.8	258
2	Al Toon	Nov. 12, 1983	Purdue	8	31.5	252
3	Lee Evans	Oct. 27, 2001	Michigan State	9	25.3	228
4	Lee Evans	Sept. 6, 2003	Akron	9	23.8	214
5	Tim Ware	Oct. 20, 1990	Northwestern	7	27.6	193

POINTS

RANK	PLAYER	DATE	OPPONENT	TOT
1	Brian Calhoun	Sept. 3, 2005	Bowling Green	30
	Brian Calhoun	Oct. 29, 2005	Illinois	30
	Anthony Davis	Nov. 23, 2002	Minnesota	30
	Lee Evans	Nov. 15, 2003	Michigan State	30
	Billy Marek	Nov. 23, 1974	Minnesota	30

FIELD GOALS

RANK	PLAYER	DATE	OPPONENT	TOT
1	7 players tied at 4			

TACKLES

RANK	PLAYER	DATE	OPPONENT	TOT
1	Dave Crossen	Nov. 5, 1977	Purdue	28
2	Ken Criter	Nov. 9, 1968	Ohio State	27
	Dave Lokanc	Oct. 28, 1972	Ohio State	27
4	Mark Zakula	Nov. 17, 1973	Northwestern	25
5	3 players tied at 24			

INTERCEPTIONS

RANK	PLAYER	DATE	OPPONENT	TOT
1	Clarence Bratt	Nov. 19, 1954	at Minnesota	4
2	11 players tied at 3			

RETIRED NUMBERS

35	Alan Ameche
40	Elroy Hirsch
80	Dave Schreiner
83	Allan Schafer
88	Pat Richter

SINGLE-SEASON RECORDS

RUSHING YARDS

RANK	PLAYER	SEASON	ATT	YDS
1	Ron Dayne	1996	325	2,109
2	Ron Dayne	1999	337	2,034
3	Michael Bennett	2000	310	1,681
4	Brent Moss	1993	312	1,637
5	Brian Calhoun	2005	348	1,636

PASSING YARDS

RANK	PLAYER	SEASON	ATT	COMP	PCT	YDS
1	John Stocco	2005	328	197	.600	2,920
2	Darrell Bevell	1993	276	187	.677	2,390
3	Randy Wright	1983	323	173	.535	2,329
4	Randy Wright	1982	330	174	.527	2,292
5	Darrell Bevell	1995	300	195	.650	2,273

RECEIVING YARDS

RANK	PLAYER	SEASON	REC	AVG	YDS
1	Lee Evans	2001	75	20.6	1,545
2	Lee Evans	2003	64	19.0	1,213
3	Brandon Williams	2005	59	18.6	1,095
4	Lee DeRamus	1993	54	17.0	920
5	Al Toon	1983	45	19.6	881

SCORING

RANK	PLAYER	SEASON	TD	FG	PAT	P2	TOT
1	Brian Calhoun	2005	24	0	0	0	144
2	Ron Dayne	1996	21	0	0	0	126
3	Ron Dayne	1999	20	0	0	0	120
4	Billy Marek	1974	19	0	0	0	114
5	Matt Davenport	1998	0	19	42	0	99

TOUCHDOWNS

RANK	PLAYER	SEASON	TOT
1	Brian Calhoun	2005	24
2	Ron Dayne	1996	21
3	Ron Dayne	1999	20
4	Billy Marek	1974	19
5	Brent Moss	1993	16

TACKLES

RANK	PLAYER	SEASON	TOT
1	Dave Lokanc	1972	181
2	Pete Monty	1996	178
3	Dave Crossen	1977	175
4	Ken Criter	1967	169
5	Nick Greisen	2001	167
	Dave Lokanc	1971	167

INTERCEPTIONS

RANK	PLAYER	SEASON	YDS	TOT
1	Jim Leonhard	2002	115	11
2	Neovia Greyer	1970	116	9
3	8 players tied at 7			

PUNTING

RANK	PLAYER	SEASON	PUNTS	YDS	AVG
1	Ken DeBauche	2005	57	2,555	44.8
2	Kevin Stemke	2000	69	3,070	44.5
3	Kevin Stemke	1997	54	2,372	43.9
4	Kevin Stemke	1998	72	3,155	43.8
5	Scott Cepicky	1986	67	2,879	43.0

PUNT RETURNS

RANK	PLAYER	SEASON	RET	YDS	AVG
1	Ira Matthews	1978	16	270	16.9
2	Nick Davis	1998	28	427	15.2
3	Brandon Williams	2005	26	380	14.6
4	Troy Vincent	1989	17	235	13.8
	Jim Leonhard	2003	34	470	13.8

KICKOFF RETURNS

RANK	PLAYER	SEASON	RET	YDS	AVG
1	Ira Matthews	1976	14	415	29.6
2	Danny Crooks	1970	12	351	29.2
3	Greg Johnson	1971	19	540	28.4
4	Brandon Williams	2005	22	616	28.0
5	Michael Jones	1984	16	447	27.9

CAREER RECORDS

RUSHING YARDS

RANK	PLAYER	SEASONS	ATT	AVG	TD	YDS
1	Ron Dayne	1996-2000	1,220	5.8	71	7,125
2	Anthony Davis	2001-04	908	5.1	42	4,676
3	Billy Marek	1972-75	719	5.2	44	3,709
4	Brent Moss	1991-94	694	4.9	34	3,428
5	Terrell Fletcher	1991-94	614	5.6	25	3,414
6	Alan Ameche	1951-54	701	4.8	25	3,345
7	Larry Emery	1983-86	582	5.1	19	2,979
8	Rufus Ferguson	1970-72	594	4.7	26	2,814
9	Carl McCullough	1993-97	469	4.5	9	2,111
10	Alan Thompson	1969-71	462	4.3	19	2,005

PASSING YARDS

RANK	PLAYER	SEASONS	ATT	COMP	PCT	INT	TD	YDS
1	Darrell Bevell	1992-95	1,052	646	61.4	39	59	7,686
2	John Stocco	2003-06	934	534	57.2	22	47	7,227
3	Brooks Bollinger	1999-2002	771	414	53.6	17	38	5,627
4	Randy Wright	1981-83	714	377	52.8	32	38	5,003
5	Mike Samuel	1995-98	711	390	54.8	28	24	4,989
6	Jim Sorgi	2000-03	519	388	74.8	21	33	4,498
7	Tony Lowery	1987-91	648	355	54.7	32	14	4,006
8	Neil Graff	1969-71	551	273	49.5	23	22	3,699
9	Mike Howard	1983-86	547	307	56.1	30	20	3,402
10	Jim Haluska	1952-55	432	230	53.2	33	20	3,093

RECEIVING YARDS

RANK	PLAYER	SEASONS	REC	AVG	TD	YDS
1	Lee Evans	1999-2003	175	19.8	27	3,468
2	Brandon Williams	2002-05	202	14.5	10	2,924
3	Al Toon	1982-84	191	16.1	19	2,103
4	Chris Chambers	1997-2000	127	15.8	16	2,004
5	Tony Simmons	1994-97	99	20.1	23	1,991
6	Lee DeRamus	1991-93	119	16.6	15	1,974
7	Pat Richter	1960-62	121	15.5	15	1,873
8	Jonathan Orr	2002-05	107	17.0	19	1,824
9	Donald Hayes	1995-97	106	14.9	4	1,575
10	David Charles	1976-78	101	14.4	11	1,459

SCORING

RANK	PLAYER	SEASONS	TD	FG	PAT	P2	TOT
1	Ron Dayne	1998-99	71	0	0	0	426
2	Billy Marek	1996-99	44	0	0	7	278
	Todd Gregoire	1984-87	0	65	83	0	278
4	Anthony Davis	2001-04	42	0	0	0	252
5	Brent Moss	1991-94	34	0	0	0	204

TOUCHDOWNS

RANK	PLAYER	SEASONS	TOT
1	Ron Dayne	1996-99	71
2	Billy Marek	1972-74	44
3	Anthony Davis	2001-04	42
4	Brent Moss	1991-94	34
5	Lee Evans	1999-2003	28

TACKLES

RANK	PLAYER	SEASONS	TOT
1	Pete Monty	1993-96	451
2	Gary Casper	1989-92	447
3	Tim Krumrie	1979-82	444
4	Dave Lokanc	1970-72	427
	Dave Crossen	1975-78	427

INTERCEPTIONS

RANK	PLAYER	SEASONS	YDS	TOT
1	Jamar Fletcher	1998-2000	459	21
	Jim Leonhard	2001-04	251	21
3	Neovia Greyer	1969-71	285	18
	Jeff Messenger	1991-94	129	18
5	Scott Nelson	1990-93	261	14

PUNTING

RANK	PLAYER	SEASONS	PUNTS	YDS	AVG
1	Kevin Stemke	1997-2000	245	10,660	43.5
2	Ken DeBauche	2004-06	173	7,403	42.8
3	Scott Cepicky	1984-87	249	10,235	41.1
4	Dick Mileager	1975-77	112	4,881	40.7
5	Jim Bakken	1959-61	108	4,575	40.1

PUNT RETURNS

RANK	PLAYER	SEASON	RET	YDS	AVG
1	Jim Leonhard	2001-04	105	1,347	12.8
2	Nick Davis	1998-2001	83	1,007	12.1
3	Troy Vincent	1988-91	68	773	11.4
4	Thad McFadden	1980-81, 83-84	62	753	10.0
5	Ira Matthews	1975-78	45	443	9.8

KICKOFF RETURNS

RANK	PLAYER	SEASON	RET	YDS	AVG
1	Greg Johnson	1969-71	21	1,081	24.6
2	Chris Davis	1971-73	44	784	23.8
3	Ron Smith	1962-64	33	774	23.5
	Tom Schinke	1965-67	32	940	23.5
5	Nick Davis	1998-2001	77	1,778	23.1

TEAM RECORDS

LONGEST WINNING STREAK
• 17, Nov. 10, 1900-Oct. 25, 1902
Streak broken vs. Michigan, 0-6, Nov. 1, 1902

LONGEST UNDEFEATED STREAK
• 17, Nov. 10, 1900-Oct. 25, 1902
Streak broken vs. Michigan, 0-6, Nov. 1, 1902

MOST CONSECUTIVE WINNING SEASONS
• 19, 1891-1909

MOST CONSECUTIVE BOWL APPEARANCES
• 5 (tie), 1996-2000, 2002-present

MOST POINTS IN A GAME
• 106, vs. UW-Whitewater, Nov. 1, 1890

MOST POINTS ALLOWED IN A GAME
• 63, vs. Minnesota, Nov. 15, 1890 (the very next game!)

LARGEST MARGIN OF VICTORY
• 106 (106-0), vs. UW-Whitewater, Nov. 1, 1890

LARGEST MARGIN OF DEFEAT
• 63 (0-63), vs. Minnesota, Nov. 15, 1890

LONGEST RUN FROM SCRIMMAGE
• 91 yards, Tom Brigham, vs. Western Michigan, Sept. 21, 1963

LONGEST PASS PLAY
• 99 yards, Jim Sorgi to Lee Evans, vs. Akron, Sept. 6, 2003

LONGEST FIELD GOAL
• 60 yards, John Hall, vs. Minnesota, Nov. 11, 1995

LONGEST PUNT
• 96 yards, George O'Brien, vs. Iowa, Oct. 18, 1952

LONGEST INTERCEPTION RETURN
• 98 yards, Billy Lowe, vs. Purdue, Oct. 16, 1954

WISCONSIN ANNUAL STATISTICAL LEADERS

YR	RUSHING	YDS	ATT	AVG	PASSING	ATT	CMP	PCT	YDS	RECEIVING	REC	YDS	AVG
1946	Earl Maves	538	92	5.8	Lisle Blackbourne	26	10	.38	175	Tom Bennett	6	124	20.7
1947	Clarence Self	526	75	7.0	Earl Girard	55	25	.45	322	Tom Bennett	7	95	13.6
1948	Ben Bendrick	327	64	5.1	Bob Petruska	26	11	.42	125	Jim Embach	5	92	18.4
1949	Bob Teague	521	96	5.4	Bob Petruska	106	45	.42	620	Hal Haberman	17	194	11.4
1950	Rollie Strehlow	398	101	3.9	John Coatta	108	65	.60	727	Gene Felker	23	266	11.6
1951	Alan Ameche	824	157	5.2	John Coatta	185	91	.49	1,154	Jerry Witt	17	371	21.8
1952	Alan Ameche	1,079	233	4.6	Jim Haluska	225	123	.55	1,552	Jerry Witt	27	387	14.3
1953	Alan Ameche	801	165	4.9	Jim Miller	69	36	.52	683	Norbert Esser	19	238	12.5
1954	Alan Ameche	641	146	4.4	Jim Miller	88	46	.52	608	Ron Locklin	22	218	9.9
1955	Charles Thomas	477	98	4.9	Jim Haluska	132	71	.54	1,036	Dave Howard	15	273	18.2
1956	Danny Lewis	554	100	5.5	Sid Williams	19	10	.53	216	Dave Howard	16	247	15.4
1957	Danny Lewis	611	95	6.4	Sid Williams	54	25	.46	451	Earl Hill	11	197	17.9
1958	John Hobbs	401	117	3.4	Dale Hackbart	99	46	.46	641	Ron Steiner	11	171	15.5
1959	Dale Hackbart	387	103	3.8	Dale Hackbart	108	51	.47	734	Alan Schoonover	10	290	29.0
1960	Tom Wiesner	374	87	4.3	Ron Miller	188	97	.52	1,351	Pat Richter	25	362	14.5
1961	Jim Nettles	213	39	5.5	Ron Miller	198	104	.53	1,487	Pat Richter	47	817	17.4
1962	Ralph Kurek	367	67	5.5	Ron Vander Kelen	216	124	.57	1,582	Pat Richter	49	694	14.2
1963	Louis Holland	511	88	5.8	Harold Brandt	181	86	.48	1,006	Rick Reichardt	26	383	14.7
1964	Ronald Smith	438	101	4.3	Harold Brandt	176	85	.48	1,059	Jimmy Jones	34	529	15.6
1965	Tom Jankowski	271	86	3.2	Chuck Burt	235	121	.51	1,143	Dennis Lager	39	396	10.2
1966	Wayne Todd	480	128	3.8	John Boyajian	129	64	.50	863	Tom McCauley	46	689	15.0
1967	John Smith	362	96	3.8	John Boyajian	152	79	.52	966	Tom McCauley	37	525	14.2
1968	Wayne Todd	364	100	3.6	John Ryan	202	84	.42	855	Mel Reddick	34	375	11.0
1969	Alan Thompson	907	214	4.2	Neil Graff	191	93	.49	1,086	Stu Voigt	39	439	11.3
1970	Rufus Ferguson	588	130	4.5	Neil Graff	174	83	.48	1,313	Larry Mialik	33	702	21.3
1971	Rufus Ferguson	1,222	249	4.9	Neil Graff	186	97	.52	1,300	Albert Hannah	39	608	15.6
1972	Rufus Ferguson	1,004	215	4.7	Rudy Steiner	150	62	.41	1,080	Jeff Mack	27	528	19.6
1973	Billy Marek	1,207	241	5.0	Gregg Bohlig	172	78	.45	1,211	Jack Novak	13	282	21.7
1974	Billy Marek	1,215	205	5.9	Gregg Bohlig	143	79	.55	1,212	Jeff Mack	16	353	22.1
1975	Billy Marek	1,281	272	4.7	Mike Carroll	123	58	.47	708	Ray Bailey	18	223	12.4
1976	Larry Canada	993	221	4.5	Mike Carroll	262	132	.50	1,627	David Charles	34	449	13.2
1977	Mike Morgan	478	124	3.9	Anthony Dudley	127	64	.50	877	David Charles	29	437	15.1
1978	Ira Matthews	654	130	5.0	Mike Kalasmiki	231	107	.46	1,378	David Charles	38	573	15.1
1979	Dave Mohapp	603	117	5.2	Mike Kalasmiki	137	72	.53	1,082	Tom Stauss	38	660	17.4
1980	John Williams	526	119	4.4	John Josten	138	53	.38	622	Tim Stracka	28	462	16.5
1981	John Williams	634	116	5.5	Jess Cole	215	90	.42	1,269	Michael Jones	24	421	17.5
1982	Troy King	715	106	6.7	Randy Wright	330	174	.53	2,292	Tim Stracka	35	614	17.5
1983	Gary Ellerson	777	161	4.8	Randy Wright	323	173	.54	2,329	Al Toon	45	881	19.6
1984	Marck Harrison	848	179	4.7	Mike Howard	314	182	.58	2,127	Al Toon	54	750	13.9
1985	Larry Emery	1,113	224	5.0	Bud Keyes	147	60	.41	829	Tim Fullington	21	403	19.2
1986	Larry Emery	855	193	4.4	Bud Keyes	174	93	.53	1,002	Reggie Tompkins	32	443	13.8
1987	Marvin Artley	955	148	6.5	Tony Lowery	89	42	.47	572	Scott Bestor	18	257	14.3
1988	Marvin Artley	516	132	3.9	Tony Lowery	121	67	.55	712	Scott Bestor	26	327	12.6
1989	Jimmy Henderson	426	102	4.2	Sean Wilson	129	66	.51	667	Craig Hudson	24	206	8.6
1990	Robert Williams	541	139	3.9	Tony Lowery	280	159	.57	1,757	Tim Ware	24	473	19.7
1991	Terrell Fletcher	446	109	4.1	Tony Lowery	158	87	.55	965	Lee DeRamus	23	374	16.3
1992	Brent Moss	739	165	4.5	Darrell Bevell	245	125	.51	1,479	Lee DeRamus	42	680	16.2
1993	Brent Moss	1,637	312	5.2	Darrell Bevell	276	187	.68	2,390	Lee DeRamus	54	920	17.0
1994	Terrell Fletcher	1,476	244	6.0	Darrell Bevell	231	139	.60	1,544	Tony Simmons	22	588	26.7
1995	Carl McCullough	1,038	236	4.4	Darrell Bevell	300	195	.65	2,273	Michael London	41	587	14.3
1996	Ron Dayne	2,109	325	6.5	Mike Samuel	254	148	.58	1,752	Donald Hayes	44	629	14.3
1997	Ron Dayne	1,457	263	5.5	Mike Samuel	254	141	.56	1,896	Donald Hayes	45	618	13.7
1998	Ron Dayne	1,525	295	5.2	Mike Samuel	172	90	.52	1,175	Chris Chambers	28	563	20.1
1999	Ron Dayne	2,034	337	6.0	Brooks Bollinger	140	82	.59	1,133	Chris Chambers	41	578	14.1
2000	Michael Bennett	1,681	310	5.4	Brooks Bollinger	209	110	.53	1,479	Chris Chambers	52	813	15.6
2001	Anthony Davis	1,466	291	5.0	Brooks Bollinger	177	91	.51	1,257	Lee Evans	75	1,545	20.6
2002	Anthony Davis	1,555	300	5.2	Brooks Bollinger	245	131	.53	1,758	Brandon Williams	52	663	12.8
2003	Dwayne Smith	857	165	5.2	Jim Sorgi	248	140	.56	2,251	Lee Evans	64	1,213	19.0
2004	Anthony Davis	973	201	4.8	John Stocco	321	169	.53	1,999	Brandon Williams	42	517	12.3
2005	Brian Calhoun	1,636	348	4.7	John Stocco	328	197	.60	2,920	Brandon Williams	59	1,095	18.6
2006	P.J. Hill	1,569	311	5.0	John Stocco	268	158	.59	2,185	Travis Beckum	61	903	14.9

Receiving leaders by receptions
All statistics include postseason

BIG TEN ANNUAL REVIEW

What follows is a year-by-year rundown of 131 seasons of Big Ten college football, incorporating final poll rankings, All-American teams, bowl game results, all-conference teams, Heisman Trophy balloting, other award winners, and instances in which Big Ten teams and players ranked among NCAA team and individual statistical leaders.

Final Polls. From 1936 on, each season's review begins with the final writers and, eventually, coaches poll of the season, with the Big Ten teams in bold.

Consensus All-Americans. Beginning with Caspar Whitney's first All-America team of 1889, we also have an annual listing of Big Ten players who placed among each year's consensus All-Americas, along with the names of all of the other conference players who received first-team All-America mentions recognized by the NCAA.

Conference Standings. Beginning with 1896, when Wisconsin went undefeated with a 2–0–1 record to unofficially capture the first conference title, we run an annual review of the Big Ten standings throughout the years, assembled from NCAA records and Richard Billingsley's all-time scores database.

NCAA Statistical Leaders. Reliable statistics to determine top-10 category leaders in college football's first 60 seasons simply don't exist. It wasn't until Homer Cooke, founder of what would become the NCAA Statistics Service, began contacting every school in the country in 1937 that the NCAA began to tabulate national statistical rankings. Even in Cooke's early years, leaders were often determined with one or more games for a team going unreported. Those discrepancies as well as missing data for part of the '50s, makes the first few decades of the NCAA's record-keeping a somewhat rough guide to the era. Progress began in earnest in 1970, when the NCAA began to determine most categorical champions on a per-game basis rather than by accumulated totals. At any rate, we've isolated Big Ten performers who landed on the NCAA lists throughout.

We've also included information on conference members Michigan State (which joined the Big Ten in 1953) and Penn State (1993) from before they joined the conference, though when they're featured prior to their inclusion, the references carry asterisks (*) to note that the team was not yet a member of the Big Ten.

KEY TO ALL-AMERICA TEAMS

AA – All-America Board
AP – Associated Press
CF – Walter Camp Foundation
CM – *Collier's* magazine (selections by Grantland Rice, 1925 to '47; published American Football Coaches Association teams, 1948 to '56, listed under FC)
CN – CNN, SI.com
CP – Central Press
CW – Caspar Whitney (published in *The Week's Sport* in association with Walter Camp, 1889 to '90; published in *Harper's Weekly*, 1891 to '96, and in *Outing* magazine, which he owned, 1898 to 1908; Walter Camp substituted for Whitney, who was on a world sports tour, and selected *Harper's Weekly*'s team for 1897)

FC – American Football Coaches Association (published in *The Saturday Evening Post*, 1945 to '47; in *Collier's* magazine, 1948 to '56; sponsored by General Mills from 1957 to '59 and by Eastman Kodak from 1960 to '93)
FM – *Football World* magazine
FN – *Football News*
FW – Football Writers Association of America (published in *Look* magazine, 1946 to '70)
IN – International News Service (merged with United Press in 1958 to form UPI)
LK – *Look* magazine (published Football Writers Association of America teams, 1946 to '70, listed under FW)
LM – *Liberty* magazine
MS – Frank Menke Syndicate

NA – North American Newspaper Alliance
NE – Newspaper Enterprise Association
NW – *Newsweek*
PI – United Press International
SN – *The Sporting News*
UP – United Press (merged with International News Service in 1958 to form UPI)
WC – Walter Camp (published in *Harper's Weekly*, 1897; in *Collier's* magazine, 1898 to 1924)

BIG TEN ANNUAL REVIEW & BOWLS

1876

STANDINGS

	OVERALL		
	W	L	T
Northwestern*	0	1	0

1879

STANDINGS

	OVERALL		
	W	L	T
Michigan*	1	0	1

1880

STANDINGS

	OVERALL		
	W	L	T
Michigan*	1	0	0

1881

STANDINGS

	OVERALL		
	W	L	T
Michigan*	0	3	0

1882

STANDINGS

	OVERALL		
	W	L	T
Minnesota*	1	1	0
Northwestern*	1	1	0

1883

STANDINGS

	OVERALL		
	W	L	T
Minnesota*	1	2	0
Michigan*	1	4	0

1884

STANDINGS

	OVERALL		
	W	L	T
Michigan*	2	0	0

1885

STANDINGS

	OVERALL		
	W	L	T
Michigan*	3	0	0

1886

STANDINGS

	OVERALL		
	W	L	T
Michigan*	2	0	0
Northwestern*	0	1	0
Minnesota*	0	2	0

1887

STANDINGS

	OVERALL		
	W	L	T
Michigan*	3	0	0
Penn State*	2	0	0
Minnesota*	2	0	0
Purdue*	0	1	0
Indiana*	0	1	0

1888

STANDINGS

	OVERALL		
	W	L	T
Michigan*	4	1	0
Northwestern*	2	1	0
Minnesota*	1	1	0
Indiana*	0	0	1
Penn State*	0	2	1

1889

STANDINGS

	OVERALL		
	W	L	T
Northwestern*	4	1	1
Minnesota*	3	1	0
Purdue*	2	1	0
Penn State*	2	2	0
Michigan*	1	2	0
Iowa*	0	1	0
Indiana*	0	1	0
Wisconsin*	0	2	0

1890

STANDINGS

	OVERALL		
	W	L	T
Minnesota*	5	1	1
Michigan*	4	1	0
Northwestern*	4	1	1
Purdue*	3	3	0
Penn State*	2	2	0
Iowa*	1	1	0
Illinois*	1	2	0
Ohio State*	1	3	0
Wisconsin*	1	3	0

*Independent or other conference affiliation

1891

STANDINGS

	Overall W	L	T
Purdue*	4	0	0
Illinois*	5	1	0
Penn State*	6	2	0
Wisconsin*	3	1	1
Minnesota*	3	1	1
Ohio State*	2	2	0
Northwestern*	2	2	3
Michigan*	4	5	0
Iowa*	2	3	0
Indiana*	1	5	0

1892

STANDINGS

	Overall W	L	T
Purdue*	8	0	0
Minnesota*	5	0	0
Penn State*	5	1	0
Illinois*	7	4	1
Ohio State*	5	3	0
Northwestern*	5	3	2
Michigan*	7	5	0
Iowa*	3	2	1
Wisconsin*	4	3	0
Indiana*	2	2	0

1893

STANDINGS

	Overall W	L	T
Minnesota*	6	0	0
Penn State*	4	1	0
Michigan*	7	3	0
Purdue*	5	2	1
Wisconsin*	4	2	0
Illinois*	3	2	3
Ohio State*	4	5	0
Iowa*	3	4	0
Northwestern*	2	5	3
Indiana*	1	4	1

1894

STANDINGS

	Overall W	L	T
Penn State*	6	0	1
Purdue*	9	1	0
Michigan*	9	1	1
Minnesota*	3	1	0
Wisconsin*	5	2	0
Illinois*	4	3	0
Ohio State*	6	5	0
Iowa*	4	4	1
Northwestern*	4	5	0
Indiana*	0	4	0

1895

STANDINGS

	Overall W	L	T
Michigan*	8	1	0
Minnesota*	7	3	0
Wisconsin*	5	2	1
Illinois*	4	2	1
Northwestern*	6	5	0
Indiana*	4	3	1
Ohio State*	4	4	2
Purdue*	3	3	0
Penn State*	2	2	3
Iowa*	2	5	0

1896

CONFERENCE STANDINGS

	Conference W	L	T	Overall W	L	T
Wisconsin	2	0	1	7	1	1
Michigan	2	1	0	9	1	0
Northwestern	2	1	1	6	1	2
Chicago	3	2	0	11	2	1
Minnesota	1	2	0	8	2	0
Illinois	0	2	1	4	2	1
Purdue	0	2	1	4	2	1
Iowa*				7	1	1
Indiana*				6	2	0
Ohio State*				5	5	1
Penn State*				3	4	0
Michigan State*				1	2	1

1897

CONFERENCE STANDINGS

	Conference W	L	T	Overall W	L	T
Wisconsin	3	0	0	9	1	0
Chicago	3	1	0	8	1	0
Michigan	2	1	0	6	1	1
Illinois	1	1	0	6	2	0
Purdue	1	2	0	5	3	1
Northwestern	0	3	0	5	3	0
Minnesota	0	3	0	4	4	0
Indiana*				6	1	1
Michigan State*				4	2	1
Iowa*				4	4	0
Penn State*				3	6	0
Ohio State*				1	7	1

1898

CONFERENCE STANDINGS

	Conference W	L	T	Overall W	L	T
Michigan	3	0	0	10	0	0
Chicago	3	1	0	9	2	0
Wisconsin	2	1	0	9	1	0
Illinois	1	1	0	4	5	0
Minnesota	1	2	0	4	5	0
Northwestern	0	4	0	9	4	1
Purdue	0	1	0	3	3	0
Indiana*				4	1	2
Penn State*				6	4	0
Michigan State*				4	3	0
Iowa*				3	4	2
Ohio State*				3	5	0

CONSENSUS ALL-AMERICANS

POS	Name	School	CW	WC
B	Clarence Herschberger	Chicago		•
C	William Cunningham	Michigan	•	

1899

CONFERENCE STANDINGS

	Conference W	L	T	Overall W	L	T
Chicago	4	0	0	12	0	2
Wisconsin	4	1	0	9	2	0
Northwestern	2	2	0	7	6	0
Michigan	1	1	0	8	2	0
Purdue	1	2	0	4	4	1
Minnesota	0	3	0	6	3	2
Illinois	0	3	0	3	5	1
Ohio State*				9	0	1
Iowa*				8	0	1
Indiana*				6	2	0
Penn State*				4	6	1
Michigan State*				2	4	1

BIG TEN ANNUAL REVIEW & BOWLS

1900

CONFERENCE STANDINGS

	Conference			Overall		
	W	L	T	W	L	T
Minnesota	3	0	1	10	0	2
Iowa	2	0	1	7	0	1
Wisconsin	2	1	0	8	1	0
Michigan	3	2	0	7	2	1
Northwestern	2	1	2	7	2	3
Chicago	2	3	1	7	5	1
Indiana	1	2	1	4	2	2
Illinois	1	3	2	7	3	2
Purdue	0	4	0	4	4	0
Ohio State*				8	1	1
Penn State*				4	6	1
Michigan State*				1	3	0

1901

CONFERENCE STANDINGS

	Conference			Overall		
	W	L	T	W	L	T
Michigan	4	0	0	11	0	0
Wisconsin	2	0	0	9	0	0
Minnesota	3	1	0	9	1	1
Illinois	4	2	0	8	2	0
Northwestern	3	2	0	8	2	1
Indiana	1	2	0	6	3	0
Chicago	0	5	2	5	5	2
Purdue	0	3	1	4	4	1
Iowa	0	3	0	6	3	0
Penn State*				5	3	0
Ohio State*				5	3	1
Michigan State*				3	4	1

CONSENSUS ALL-AMERICANS

POS	Name	School	CW	WC
E	Neil Snow	Michigan	•	

BOWL GAMES

DATE	GAME	SCORE
J1	Rose	Michigan 49, Stanford 0

1902

CONFERENCE STANDINGS

	Conference			Overall		
	W	L	T	W	L	T
Michigan	5	0	0	11	0	0
Chicago	5	1	0	11	1	0
Minnesota	3	1	0	9	2	1
Illinois	4	2	0	10	2	1
Purdue	2	2	0	7	2	1
Wisconsin	1	3	0	6	3	0
Iowa	0	3	0	5	4	0
Northwestern	0	4	0	6	6	0
Indiana	0	4	0	3	5	1
Penn State*				7	3	0
Ohio State*				6	2	2
Michigan State*				4	5	0

ALL-CONFERENCE TEAM

POS	Name	School
FB	William Heston	Michigan
E	Curtis Redden	Michigan
T	Joseph Maddock	Michigan

1903

CONFERENCE STANDINGS

	Conference			Overall		
	W	L	T	W	L	T
Minnesota	3	0	1	14	0	1
Michigan	3	0	1	11	0	1
Chicago	4	1	1	10	2	1
Northwestern	1	0	2	10	1	3
Iowa	1	1	0	9	2	0
Indiana	1	2	0	4	4	0
Illinois	1	5	0	8	6	0
Wisconsin	0	3	1	6	3	1
Purdue	0	2	0	4	2	0
Michigan State*				6	1	1
Ohio State*				8	3	0
Penn State*				5	3	0

CONSENSUS ALL-AMERICANS

POS	Name	School	CW	WC
B	Willie Heston	Michigan	•	•
T	Fred Schacht	Minnesota	•	

1904

CONFERENCE STANDINGS

	Conference			Overall		
	W	L	T	W	L	T
Minnesota	3	0	0	13	0	0
Michigan	2	0	0	10	0	0
Chicago	5	1	1	8	1	1
Illinois	3	1	1	9	2	1
Northwestern	1	2	0	8	2	0
Purdue	1	2	0	9	3	0
Iowa	0	3	0	7	4	0
Wisconsin	0	3	0	5	3	0
Indiana	0	3	0	6	4	0
Michigan State*				8	1	0
Penn State*				6	4	0
Ohio State*				6	5	0

CONSENSUS ALL-AMERICANS

POS	Name	School	CW	WC
B	Walter Eckersall	Chicago	•	•
B	Willie Heston	Michigan		•
E	Fred Speik	Chicago	•	

*Independent or other conference affiliation

1905

CONFERENCE STANDINGS

	CONFERENCE			OVERALL		
	W	L	T	W	L	T
Chicago	7	0	0	10	0	0
Michigan	2	1	0	12	1	0
Minnesota	2	1	0	10	1	0
Purdue	1	1	1	6	1	1
Wisconsin	1	2	0	8	2	0
Indiana	0	1	1	8	1	1
Iowa	0	2	0	8	2	0
Northwestern	0	2	0	8	2	1
Illinois	0	3	0	5	4	0
Michigan State*				9	2	0
Ohio State*				8	2	2
Penn State*				8	3	0

CONSENSUS ALL-AMERICANS

POS	Name	School	CW	WC
B	Walter Eckersall	Chicago	•	•
E	Mark Catlin	Chicago	•	

1906

CONFERENCE STANDINGS

	CONFERENCE			OVERALL		
	W	L	T	W	L	T
Wisconsin	3	0	0	5	0	0
Minnesota	2	0	0	4	1	0
Michigan	1	0	0	4	1	0
Chicago	3	1	0	4	1	0
Illinois	1	3	0	1	3	1
Indiana	0	2	0	4	2	0
Iowa	0	1	0	2	3	0
Purdue	0	3	0	0	5	0
Northwestern	0	0	0	0	0	0
Ohio State*				8	1	0
Penn State*				8	1	1
Michigan State*				7	2	2

CONSENSUS ALL-AMERICANS

POS	Name	School	CW	WC
B	Walter Eckersall	Chicago	•	•
C	William Dunn	Penn State*		•

ALL-CONFERENCE TEAM

POS	Name	School
QB	Walter Eckersall	Chicago
HB-QB	Walter Steffen	Chicago
HB	Hezlep W. Clark	Indiana
FB	John Garrels	Michigan
C	Adolph "Germany" Schulz	Michigan
C	Ewald "Jumbo" Stiehm	Wisconsin
G	Forest Van Hook	Illinois
G	Theodore Vita	Minnesota
E	Robert "Bobby" Marshall	Minnesota
T	John "Joe" Curtis	Michigan
T	George Case	Minnesota

1907

CONFERENCE STANDINGS

	CONFERENCE			OVERALL		
	W	L	T	W	L	T
Chicago	4	0	0	4	1	0
Wisconsin	3	1	1	3	1	1
Illinois	3	2	0	3	2	0
Iowa	1	1	0	3	2	0
Minnesota	0	1	1	2	2	1
Indiana	0	3	0	2	3	1
Purdue	0	3	0	0	5	0
Northwestern	0	0	0	0	0	0
Michigan*				5	1	0
Ohio State*				7	2	1
Michigan State*				4	2	1

CONSENSUS ALL-AMERICANS

POS	Name	School	CW	WC
C	Adolph Schulz	Michigan*		•

ALL-CONFERENCE TEAM

POS	Name	School
HB-QB	Walter Steffen	Chicago
HB	Harry Iddings	Chicago
HB	Leo DeTray	Chicago
C	Adolph "Germany" Schulz	Michigan+
G	Forest Van Hook	Illinois
G	John Messmer	Wisconsin
E	Harry Hammond	Michigan+
E	Harry Capron	Minnesota
T	Walter Rheinschild	Michigan+
T	George Case	Minnesota

1908

CONFERENCE STANDINGS

	CONFERENCE			OVERALL		
	W	L	T	W	L	T
Chicago	5	0	0	5	0	1
Illinois	4	1	0	5	1	1
Wisconsin	2	1	0	5	1	0
Purdue	1	3	0	4	3	0
Indiana	1	3	0	3	4	0
Minnesota	0	2	0	3	2	1
Northwestern	0	2	0	2	2	0
Iowa	0	1	0	2	5	0
Michigan State*				6	0	2
Michigan*				5	2	1
Ohio State*				6	4	0
Penn State*				5	5	0

CONSENSUS ALL-AMERICANS

POS	Name	School	WC
B	Walter Steffen	Chicago	•

ALL-CONFERENCE TEAM

POS	Name	School
HB-QB	Walter Steffen	Chicago
HB	Harold "Hal" Iddings	Chicago
HB	Carrol "Chick" Kirk	Iowa
FB	Jack Wilce	Wisconsin
C	Orren Safford	Minnesota
G	Forest Van Hook	Illinois
G	John Messmer	Wisconsin
E	Harlan "Pat" Page	Chicago
E	Harlan Rogers	Wisconsin
T	Arthur Hoffman	Chicago
T	Oscar P. Ostoff	Wisconsin

+Michigan withdrew from the conference for the 1907 season, but players were named to the all-conference team that year

1909

CONFERENCE STANDINGS

	CONFERENCE			OVERALL		
	W	L	T	W	L	T
Minnesota	3	0	0	6	1	0
Chicago	4	1	1	4	1	2
Illinois	3	1	0	5	2	0
Wisconsin	2	1	1	3	1	1
Indiana	1	3	0	4	3	0
Northwestern	1	3	0	1	3	1
Iowa	0	1	0	2	4	1
Purdue	0	4	0	2	5	0
Michigan State*				8	1	0
Ohio State*				7	3	0
Michigan*				6	1	0
Penn State*				5	0	2

CONSENSUS ALL-AMERICANS

POS	Name	School	WC
B	John McGovern	Minnesota	•
G	Albert Benbrook	Michigan*	•

ALL-CONFERENCE TEAM

POS	Name	School
QB	John McGovern	Minnesota
HB	William Crawley	Chicago
HB	Reuben Rosenwald	Minnesota
FB	Earl Pickering	Minnesota
C	H.E. Farnam	Minnesota
G	Glenn Butzer	Illinois
G	William Mackmiller	Wisconsin
E	Harlan "Pat" Page	Chicago
E	James P. Dean	Wisconsin
T	Homer Dutter	Indiana
T	James Walker	Minnesota

1910

CONFERENCE STANDINGS

	CONFERENCE			OVERALL		
	W	L	T	W	L	T
Illinois	4	0	0	7	0	0
Minnesota	2	0	0	6	1	0
Indiana	3	1	0	6	1	0
Iowa	1	1	0	5	2	0
Wisconsin	1	2	1	1	2	2
Northwestern	1	2	1	1	3	1
Chicago	2	4	0	2	5	0
Purdue	0	4	0	1	5	0
Michigan State*				6	1	0
Ohio State*				6	1	3
Michigan*				3	0	3
Penn State*				5	2	1

CONSENSUS ALL-AMERICANS

POS	Name	School	WC
E	Stanfield Wells	Michigan*	•
T	James Walker	Minnesota	•
G	Albert Benbrook	Michigan*	•

ALL-CONFERENCE TEAM

POS	Name	School
QB	John McGovern	Minnesota
HB	Otto Seiler	Illinois
HB	Reuben Rosenwald	Minnesota
FB	Lisle Johnston	Minnesota
C	John "Heavy" Twist	Illinois
G	Glenn Butzer	Illinois
G	Allen Messick	Indiana
E	Arthur "Cotton" Berndt	Indiana
E	James P. Dean	Wisconsin
T	Homer Dutter	Indiana
T	James Walker	Minnesota

1911

CONFERENCE STANDINGS

	CONFERENCE			OVERALL		
	W	L	T	W	L	T
Minnesota	3	0	1	6	0	1
Chicago	5	1	0	6	1	0
Wisconsin	2	1	1	5	1	1
Illinois	2	2	1	4	2	1
Iowa	2	2	0	3	4	0
Purdue	1	3	0	3	4	0
Northwestern	1	4	0	3	4	0
Indiana	0	3	1	3	3	1
Penn State*				8	0	1
Michigan State*				5	1	0
Michigan*				5	1	2
Ohio State*				5	3	2

ALL-CONFERENCE TEAM

POS	Name	School
QB	John "Keckie" Moll	Wisconsin
HB	Clark Sauer	Chicago
FB	Reuben Rosenwald	Minnesota
FB	Al Tandberg	Wisconsin
C	Clifford Morrell	Minnesota
G	Horace Scruby	Chicago
G	Charles Rademacher	Chicago
E	H.S. "Hod" Ofstie	Wisconsin
E	Ed Hoeffel	Wisconsin
T	A.L. Buser	Wisconsin
T	R.E. Branstad	Wisconsin

1912

CONFERENCE STANDINGS

	CONFERENCE			OVERALL		
	W	L	T	W	L	T
Wisconsin	5	0	0	7	0	0
Chicago	6	1	0	6	1	0
Purdue	2	2	1	4	2	1
Minnesota	2	2	0	4	3	0
Northwestern	2	3	0	2	3	1
Illinois	1	3	1	3	3	1
Iowa	1	3	0	4	3	0
Indiana	0	5	0	2	5	0
Penn State*				8	0	0
Michigan State*				7	1	0
Michigan*				5	2	0
Ohio State*				6	3	0

CONSENSUS ALL-AMERICANS

POS	Name	School	WC
T	Robert Butler	Wisconsin	•

ALL-CONFERENCE TEAM

POS	Name	School
QB	Edmund Gillette	Wisconsin
HB	Elmer Oliphant	Purdue
HB	John VanRiper	Wisconsin
FB	Al Tandberg	Wisconsin
C	Paul "Shorty" DesJardien	Chicago
G	Ray "Tubby" Keeler	Wisconsin
G	Max Gelein	Wisconsin
E	H.S. "Hod" Ofstie	Wisconsin
E	Ed Hoeffel	Wisconsin
T	Edward Samp	Wisconsin
T	Robert "Butts" Butler	Wisconsin

*Independent or other conference affiliation

1913

Conference Standings

	Conference			Overall		
	W	L	T	W	L	T
Chicago	7	0	0	7	0	0
Minnesota	2	1	0	5	2	0
Iowa	2	1	0	5	2	0
Purdue	2	1	2	4	1	2
Illinois	2	2	1	4	2	1
Wisconsin	1	2	1	3	3	1
Indiana	2	4	0	3	4	0
Ohio State	1	2	0	4	2	1
Northwestern	0	6	0	1	6	0
Michigan State*				7	0	0
Michigan*				6	1	0
Penn State*				2	6	0

Consensus All-Americans

POS	Name	School	IN	WC
B	Jim Craig	Michigan*	•	•
T	Miller Pontius	Michigan*	•	
G	Ray Keeler	Wisconsin	•	
C	Paul Des Jardien	Chicago	•	•

All-Conference Team

POS	Name	School
QB	Paul "Pete" Russell	Chicago
HB	Nelson "Nels" Norgren	Chicago
HB	Elmer Oliphant	Purdue
FB	Clark Shaughnessy	Minnesota
C	Paul "Shorty" DesJardien	Chicago
G	H.B. Routh	Purdue
G	Ray "Tubby" Keeler	Wisconsin
E	Earl Huntington	Chicago
E-FB	Lorin Solon	Minnesota
T	Archie "Bunt" Kirk	Iowa
T	Robert "Butts" Butler	Wisconsin

1914

Conference Standings

	Conference			Overall		
	W	L	T	W	L	T
Illinois	6	0	0	7	0	0
Minnesota	3	1	0	6	1	0
Chicago	4	2	1	4	2	1
Purdue	2	2	0	5	2	0
Ohio State	2	2	0	5	2	0
Wisconsin	2	2	1	4	2	1
Iowa	1	2	0	4	3	0
Indiana	1	4	0	3	4	0
Northwestern	0	6	0	1	6	0
Michigan State*				5	2	0
Michigan*				6	3	0
Penn State*				5	3	1

Consensus All-Americans

POS	Name	School	MS	WC
B	John Maulbetsch	Michigan*	•	•
E	Perry Graves	Illinois	•	
G	Ralph Chapman	Illinois		•

Others receiving first-team honors

G	Arlie Mucks	Wisconsin	•	

All-Conference Team

POS	Name	School
QB	George "Potsy" Clark	Illinois
HB	Harold Pogue	Illinois
HB	Wilbur Hightower	Northwestern
C	Paul "Shorty" DesJardien	Chicago
G	Ralph "Slooie" Chapman	Illinois
G	H.B. Routh	Purdue
E	George Squier	Illinois
E	Boyd Cherry	Ohio State
E-FB	Lorin Solon	Minnesota
T	Laurens Shull	Chicago
T	Howard "Cub" Buck	Wisconsin

1915

CONFERENCE STANDINGS

	CONFERENCE			OVERALL		
	W	L	T	W	L	T
Minnesota	3	0	1	6	0	1
Illinois	3	0	2	5	0	2
Chicago	4	2	0	5	2	0
Ohio State	2	1	1	5	1	1
Purdue	2	2	0	3	3	1
Wisconsin	2	3	0	4	3	0
Iowa	1	2	0	3	4	0
Indiana	1	3	0	3	3	1
Northwestern	0	5	0	2	5	0
Michigan State*				5	1	0
Penn State*				7	2	0
Michigan*				4	3	1

CONSENSUS ALL-AMERICANS

POS	Name	School	MS	WC
B	Bart Macomber	Illinois		•
B	Neno Jerry DaPrato	Michigan State*	•	
T	Howard Buck	Wisconsin	•	

OTHERS RECEIVING FIRST-TEAM HONORS

E	Bob Higgins	Penn State*	•	
E	Bert Baston	Minnesota		•

ALL-CONFERENCE TEAM

POS	Name	School
QB	Paul "Pete" Russell	Chicago
HB-QB	Frank "Bart" Macomber	Illinois
HB	Dow Byers	Wisconsin
FB	Bernard "Bernie" Bierman	Minnesota
C	John Watson	Illinois
G	Merton Dunnigan	Minnesota
G	Frank Blocker	Purdue
E	George Squier	Illinois
E	Albert "Bert" Baston	Minnesota
T	Laurens Shull	Chicago
T	Howard "Cub" Buck	Wisconsin

1916

CONFERENCE STANDINGS

	CONFERENCE			OVERALL		
	W	L	T	W	L	T
Ohio State	4	0	0	7	0	0
Northwestern	4	1	0	6	1	0
Minnesota	3	1	0	6	1	0
Illinois	2	2	1	3	3	1
Wisconsin	1	2	1	4	2	1
Iowa	1	2	0	4	3	0
Indiana	0	3	1	2	4	1
Purdue	0	4	1	2	4	1
Penn State*				8	2	0
Michigan*				7	2	0
Michigan State*				4	2	1

CONSENSUS ALL-AMERICANS

POS	Name	School	IN	MS	WC
B	Charles Harley	Ohio State	•		•
E	Bert Baston	Minnesota	•	•	•

OTHERS RECEIVING FIRST-TEAM HONORS

B	Claire Long	Minnesota			•
T	Bob Karch	Ohio State		•	
T	George Hauser	Minnesota	•		

ALL-CONFERENCE TEAM

POS	Name	School
HB-QB	Frank "Bart" Macomber	Illinois
HB	John "Paddy" Driscoll	Northwestern
HB	Charles "Chic" Harley	Ohio State
FB	Arnold "Pudge" Wyman	Minnesota
C	Fred Becker	Iowa
G	Leonard Charpier	Illinois
G	Conrad L. Eklund	Minnesota
E	Albert "Bert" Baston	Minnesota
E	Paul Meyers	Wisconsin
T	Philbrick Jackson	Chicago
T	Frank Mayer	Minnesota

*Independent or other conference affiliation

1917

Conference Standings

	Conference			Overall		
	W	L	T	W	L	T
Ohio State	4	0	0	8	0	1
Minnesota	3	1	0	4	1	0
Northwestern	3	2	0	5	2	0
Wisconsin	3	2	0	4	2	1
Illinois	2	2	1	5	2	1
Chicago	2	2	1	3	2	1
Indiana	1	2	0	5	2	0
Michigan	0	1	0	8	2	0
Purdue	0	4	0	3	4	0
Iowa	0	2	0	3	5	0
Penn State*				5	4	0
Michigan State*				0	9	0

Consensus All-Americans

POS	Name	School	IN	MS	NE
B	Charles Harley	Ohio State	•		•
E	Charles Bolen	Ohio State		•	•
T	George Hauser	Minnesota	•		•

	Others receiving first-team honors				
G	C.G. Higgins	Chicago	•		
G	Frank Culver	Michigan			•

All-Conference Team

POS	Name	School
QB	Eber Simpson	Wisconsin
HB	Lloyd Ellingwood	Northwestern
HB	Charles "Chic" Harley	Ohio State
FB	Robert Koehler	Northwestern
C	Kelley VanDyne	Ohio State
G	John Ulrich	Northwestern
G-T	Charles Higgins	Chicago
E	Charles "Shifty" Bolen	Ohio State
E	W.M. Kelly	Wisconsin
T	George Hauser	Minnesota
T	Harold "Hap" Courtney	Ohio State

1918

Conference Standings

Converences played an abbreviated schedule due to World War I

	Conference			Overall		
	W	L	T	W	L	T
Illinois	4	0	0	5	2	0
Michigan	2	0	0	5	0	0
Purdue	1	0	0	3	3	0
Iowa	2	1	0	6	2	1
Minnesota	2	1	0	5	2	1
Northwestern	1	1	0	2	2	1
Wisconsin	1	2	0	3	3	0
Ohio State	0	3	0	3	3	0
Chicago	0	5	0	0	5	0
Indiana	0	0	0	2	2	0
Michigan State*				4	3	0
Penn State*				1	2	1

Consensus All-Americans

POS	Name	School	MS	WC
C	John Depler	Illinois	•	

	Others receiving first-team honors			
B	Frank Steketee	Michigan		•

All-Conference Team

POS	Name	School
QB	Eber Simpson	Wisconsin
QB	Marshall Underhill	Northwestern
HB	Jesse Kirkpatrick	Illinois
HB	Frank Steketee	Michigan
FB	Norman Kingsley	Minnesota
C	Henry "Ernie" Vick	Michigan
G	Albert Mohr	Illinois
G	Harry Hunzelman	Iowa
E	Ronald Reed	Iowa
E	Clarence MacDonald	Ohio State
T	Burt Ingwersen	Illinois
T	Angus Goetz	Michigan

1919

CONFERENCE STANDINGS

	CONFERENCE			OVERALL		
	W	L	T	W	L	T
Illinois	6	1	0	6	1	0
Ohio State	3	1	0	6	1	0
Chicago	4	2	0	5	2	0
Wisconsin	3	2	0	5	2	0
Minnesota	3	2	0	4	2	1
Iowa	2	2	0	5	2	0
Michigan	1	4	0	3	4	0
Northwestern	1	4	0	2	5	0
Indiana	0	2	0	3	4	0
Purdue	0	3	0	2	4	1
Penn State*				7	1	0
Michigan State*				4	4	1

CONSENSUS ALL-AMERICANS

POS	Name	School	MS	WC
B	Charles Harley	Ohio State	•	•
E	Bob Higgins	Penn State*	•	•
E	Lester Belding	Iowa	•	
C	Charles Carpenter	Wisconsin	•	

ALL-CONFERENCE TEAM

POS	Name	School
QB-HB	Gaylord "Pete" Stinchcomb	Ohio State
HB	Arnold Oss	Minnesota
HB	Charles "Chic" Harley	Ohio State
FB	Fred Lohman	Iowa
C	John Depler	Illinois
C	Henry "Ernie" Vick	Michigan
G	Clarence Applegran	Illinois
G	William McCaw	Indiana
G-T	Charles Higgins	Chicago
E	Lester Belding	Iowa
E	Paul Meyers	Wisconsin
T	Fred "Duke" Slater	Iowa

1920

CONFERENCE STANDINGS

	CONFERENCE			OVERALL		
	W	L	T	W	L	T
Ohio State	5	0	0	7	1	0
Wisconsin	4	1	0	6	1	0
Indiana	3	1	0	5	2	0
Illinois	4	2	0	5	2	0
Iowa	3	2	0	5	2	0
Michigan	2	2	0	5	2	0
Northwestern	2	3	0	3	4	0
Chicago	2	4	0	3	4	0
Purdue	0	4	0	2	5	0
Minnesota	0	6	0	1	6	0
Penn State*				7	0	2
Michigan State*				4	6	0

CONSENSUS ALL-AMERICANS

POS	Name	School	FM	IN	MS	WC
B	Gaylord Stinchcomb	Ohio State			•	•
B	Charles Way	Penn State*		•		•
E	Charles Carney	Illinois				•
T	Ralph Scott	Wisconsin				•
G	Iolas Huffman	Ohio State			•	
	OTHERS RECEIVING FIRST-TEAM HONORS					
E	Frank Weston	Wisconsin			•	
T	Charles McGuire	Chicago			•	
G	Paul Griffiths	Penn State*	•	•		

ALL-CONFERENCE TEAM

POS	Name	School
QB	Aubrey Devine	Iowa
QB-HB	Gaylord Stinchcomb	Ohio State
HB	Frank Steketee	Michigan
FB	Walter "Jack" Crangle	Illinois
C	John Depler	Illinois
C	Henry "Ernie" Vick	Michigan
G	Festus Tierney	Minnesota
G	Graham Penfield	Northwestern
E	Charles Carney	Illinois
E	Frank "Red" Weston	Wisconsin
T	Charles McGuire	Chicago
T	Fred "Duke" Slater	Iowa

BOWL GAMES

DATE	GAME	SCORE
J1	Rose	California 28, Ohio State 0

*Independent or other conference affiliation

1921

CONFERENCE STANDINGS

	Conference			Overall		
	W	L	T	W	L	T
Iowa	5	0	0	7	0	0
Chicago	4	1	0	6	1	0
Ohio State	4	1	0	5	2	0
Wisconsin	3	1	1	5	1	1
Michigan	2	1	1	5	1	1
Minnesota	2	4	0	3	4	0
Indiana	1	2	0	3	4	0
Illinois	1	4	0	3	4	0
Purdue	1	4	0	1	6	0
Northwestern	0	5	0	1	6	0
Penn State*				8	0	2
Michigan State*				3	5	0

CONSENSUS ALL-AMERICANS

POS	Name	School	WC
B	Aubrey Devine	Iowa	•
B	Glenn Killinger	Penn State*	•
T	Iolas Huffman	Ohio State	

	Others receiving first-team honors		
T	Charles McGuire	Chicago	•
C	Henry Vick	Michigan	•

ALL-CONFERENCE TEAM

POS	Name	School
QB	Aubrey Devine	Iowa
HB	Donald Peden	Illinois
HB	Alvah "Rowdy" Elliott	Wisconsin
FB	Gordon Locke	Iowa
C	Henry "Ernie" Vick	Michigan
G	Robert "Duke" Dunne	Michigan
G	Dean Trott	Ohio State
E	Herb "Fritz" Crisler	Chicago
E	Cyril "Truck" Myers	Ohio State
T	Charles McGuire	Chicago
T	Fred "Duke" Slater	Iowa

1922

CONFERENCE STANDINGS

	Conference			Overall		
	W	L	T	W	L	T
Iowa	5	0	0	7	0	0
Michigan	4	0	0	6	0	1
Chicago	4	0	1	5	1	1
Wisconsin	2	2	1	4	2	1
Minnesota	2	3	1	3	3	1
Illinois	2	4	0	2	5	0
Northwestern	1	3	1	3	3	1
Ohio State	1	4	0	3	4	0
Indiana	0	2	1	1	4	2
Purdue	0	3	1	1	5	1
Penn State*				6	4	1
Michigan State*				3	5	2

CONSENSUS ALL-AMERICANS

POS	Name	School	WC
B	Harry Kipke	Michigan	•
B	Gordon Locke	Iowa	•
B	John Thomas	Chicago	•

ALL-CONFERENCE TEAM

POS	Name	School
QB	Rollie Williams	Wisconsin
HB	Harry Kipke	Michigan
HB	Earl Martineau	Minnesota
FB	Gordon Locke	Iowa
C	Ralph King	Chicago
G	James McMillen	Illinois
G	Paul Minick	Iowa
E	Bernard "Bernie" Kirk	Michigan
E	Gustaf Tebell	Wisconsin
T	George Thompson	Iowa
T	Marty Below	Wisconsin

BOWL GAMES

DATE	GAME	SCORE
J1	Rose	USC 14, Penn State* 3

1923

CONFERENCE STANDINGS

	CONFERENCE			OVERALL		
	W	L	T	W	L	T
Illinois	5	0	0	8	0	0
Michigan	4	0	0	8	0	0
Chicago	5	1	0	7	1	0
Minnesota	2	1	1	5	1	1
Iowa	3	3	0	5	3	0
Indiana	2	2	0	3	4	0
Wisconsin	1	3	1	3	3	1
Ohio State	1	4	0	3	4	1
Purdue	1	4	0	2	5	1
Northwestern	0	6	0	2	6	0
Penn State*				6	2	1
Michigan State*				3	5	0

CONSENSUS ALL-AMERICANS

POS	Name	School	FW	WC
B	Red Grange	Illinois	•	•
B	Harry Wilson	Penn State*	•	
E	Ray Ecklund	Minnesota	•	
T	Marty Below	Wisconsin	•	
G	James McMillen	Illinois	•	
C	Jack Blott	Michigan	•	•

OTHERS RECEIVING FIRST-TEAM HONORS

B	Earl Martineau	Minnesota	•
G	Joe Bedenk	Penn State*	•

ALL-CONFERENCE TEAM

POS	Name	School
QB	Harry "Hoge" Workman	Ohio State
HB	Harold "Red" Grange	Illinois
HB	Harry Kipke	Michigan
FB	Merrill Taft	Wisconsin
C	Jack Blott	Michigan
G	Lloyd Rohrke	Chicago
G	James McMillen	Illinois
E	Frank Lowell Otte	Iowa
E	Ray Eklund	Minnesota
T	Stanley Muirhead	Michigan
T	Marty Below	Wisconsin

1924

CONFERENCE STANDINGS

	CONFERENCE			OVERALL		
	W	L	T	W	L	T
Chicago	3	0	3	4	1	3
Iowa	3	1	1	6	1	1
Illinois	3	1	1	6	1	1
Michigan	4	2	0	6	2	0
Purdue	2	2	0	5	2	0
Minnesota	1	2	1	3	3	2
Ohio State	1	3	2	2	3	3
Northwestern	1	3	0	4	4	0
Indiana	1	3	0	4	4	0
Wisconsin	0	2	2	2	3	3
Penn State*				6	3	1
Michigan State*				5	3	0

CONSENSUS ALL-AMERICANS

POS	Name	HT	WT	School	AA	FM	IN	LM	NE	WC
B	Red Grange	5-10	170	Illinois	•	•	•	•	•	•
G	Joe Pondelik	5-11	215	Chicago	•		•		•	

OTHERS RECEIVING FIRST-TEAM HONORS

T	Frank Gowdy	Chicago	•	•
G	Edliff Slaughter	Michigan		

ALL-CONFERENCE TEAM

POS	Name	School
QB	Leland Parkin	Iowa
HB	Harold "Red" Grange	Illinois
HB	Ralph "Moon" Baker	Northwestern
FB	Harry Thomas	Chicago
C	Ralph Claypool	Purdue
G	Joseph Pondelik	Chicago
G	George Abramson	Minnesota
E	Charles Kassell	Illinois
E	Frank Lowell Otte	Iowa
T	Franklin Gowdy	Chicago
T	Ted Cox	Minnesota

BIG TEN ANNUAL REVIEW & BOWLS

1925

CONFERENCE STANDINGS

	Conference W	L	T	Overall W	L	T
Michigan	5	1	0	7	1	0
Northwestern	3	1	0	5	3	0
Wisconsin	3	1	1	6	1	1
Iowa	2	2	0	5	3	0
Illinois	2	2	0	5	3	0
Chicago	2	2	0	3	5	1
Minnesota	1	1	1	5	2	1
Ohio State	1	3	1	4	3	1
Purdue	0	3	1	3	4	1
Indiana	0	3	1	3	4	1

	W	L	T
Penn State*	4	4	1
Michigan State*	3	5	0

CONSENSUS ALL-AMERICANS

POS	Name	HT	WT	School	AA	AP	CM	FW	IN	LM	NE	UP
B	**Red Grange**	5-10	170	Illinois	•	•	•	•	•	•	•	
B	**Benny Friedman**	5-8	170	Michigan	•					•		•
E	**Bennie Oosterbaan**	6-0	180	Michigan	•	•	•	•	•	•	•	
G	**Ed Hess**	6-1	190	Ohio State		•			•		•	•

OTHERS RECEIVING FIRST-TEAM HONORS

E	Dick Romney	Iowa	•
G	Harry Hawkins	Michigan	•
C	Tim Lowry	Northwestern	•
C	Robert Brown	Michigan	• • •

ALL-CONFERENCE TEAM

POS	Name	School
QB	Benny Friedman	Michigan
HB	Harold "Red" Grange	Illinois
HB	Wesley "Wes" Fry	Iowa
HB	Doyle Harmon	Wisconsin
FB	Austin "Five Yards" McCarty	Chicago
FB	Leland "Tiny" Lewis	Northwestern
C	Tim Lowry	Northwestern
G	Bernie Shively	Illinois
G	Bob Brown	Michigan
G	Len Walsh	Minnesota
G	Edwin Hess	Ohio State
E	Charles Kassell	Illinois
E	Bennie Oosterbaan	Michigan
T	Fred Henderson	Chicago
T	Harry Hawkins	Michigan
T	Thomas Edwards	Michigan

1926

CONFERENCE STANDINGS

	Conference W	L	T	Overall W	L	T
Northwestern	5	0	0	7	1	0
Michigan	5	0	0	7	1	0
Ohio State	3	1	0	7	1	0
Purdue	2	1	1	5	2	1
Wisconsin	3	2	1	5	2	1
Illinois	2	2	0	6	2	0
Minnesota	2	2	0	5	3	0
Indiana	0	4	0	3	5	0
Iowa	0	5	0	3	5	0
Chicago	0	5	0	2	6	0

	W	L	T
Penn State*	5	4	0
Michigan State*	3	4	1

CONSENSUS ALL-AMERICANS

POS	Name	HT	WT	School	AA	AP	CM	IN	NE	UP
B	**Benny Friedman**	5-8	172	Michigan	•	•	•		•	
B	**Ralph Baker**	5-10	172	Northwestern	•		•			
B	**Herb Joesting**	6-1	192	Minnesota	•	•	•	•	•	
E	**Bennie Oosterbaan**	6-0	186	Michigan	•	•		•		
G	**Bernie Shively**	6-4	208	Illinois	•	•	•	•	•	

OTHERS RECEIVING FIRST-TEAM HONORS

B	Marty Karow	Ohio State	•
T	Bob Johnson	Northwestern	•
G	Edwin Hayes	Ohio State	

ALL-CONFERENCE TEAM

POS	Name	School
QB	Benny Friedman	Michigan
HB	Ralph "Moon" Baker	Northwestern
HB	Marty Karow	Ohio State
FB	Herbert Joesting	Minnesota
C	Robert Reitsch	Illinois
G	Bernie Shively	Illinois
G	Justin Dart	Northwestern
G	Edwin Hess	Ohio State
E	William Flora	Michigan
E	Bennie Oosterbaan	Michigan
E	Roger Wheeler	Minnesota
T	Emerson Nelson	Iowa
T	Mitchell Gary	Minnesota
T	Robert Johnson	Northwestern
T	Leo Raskowski	Ohio State
I-G	Harold Hanson	Minnesota

1927

CONFERENCE STANDINGS

	CONFERENCE			OVERALL		
	W	L	T	W	L	T
Illinois	5	0	0	7	0	1
Minnesota	3	0	1	6	0	2
Michigan	3	2	0	6	2	0
Chicago	3	3	0	4	5	0
Purdue	2	2	0	6	2	0
Ohio State	2	3	0	4	4	0
Northwestern	2	3	0	4	4	0
Indiana	1	2	1	3	4	1
Wisconsin	1	4	0	4	4	0
Iowa	1	4	0	4	4	0
Penn State*				6	2	1
Michigan State*				4	5	0

CONSENSUS ALL-AMERICANS

POS	Name	HT	WT	School	AA	AP	CM	IN	NA	NE	UP
B	Herb Joesting	6-1	192	Minnesota	•	•	•	•		•	•
E	Bennie Oosterbaan	6-0	186	Michigan	•	•	•	•	•	•	•

OTHERS RECEIVING FIRST-TEAM HONORS

T	Leo Raskowski			Ohio State		•			•		
G	Russ Crane			Illinois		•					
G	Harold Hanson			Minnesota				•		•	
C	Bill Reitsch			Illinois				•			

ALL-CONFERENCE TEAM

POS	Name	School
QB	Harold "Shorty" Almquist	Minnesota
HB	Judson "Jud" Timm	Illinois
HB	Louis Gilbert	Michigan
HB	Edward "Toad" Crofoot	Wisconsin
FB	Herbert Joesting	Minnesota
C	Kenneth Rouse	Chicago
C	Robert Reitsch	Illinois
G	John Matthew	Indiana
G	Raymond Baer	Michigan
E	Bennie Oosterbaan	Michigan
E	Kenneth Haycraft	Minnesota
E	Waldo Fisher	Northwestern
T	Albert "Butch" Nowack	Illinois
T	Mitchell Gary	Minnesota
T	Leo Raskowski	Ohio State
T-G	Harold Hanson	Minnesota

1928

CONFERENCE STANDINGS

	CONFERENCE			OVERALL		
	W	L	T	W	L	T
Illinois	4	1	0	7	1	0
Wisconsin	3	1	1	7	1	1
Minnesota	4	2	0	6	2	0
Iowa	3	2	0	6	2	0
Ohio State	3	2	0	5	2	1
Purdue	2	2	1	5	2	1
Northwestern	2	3	0	5	3	0
Michigan	2	3	0	3	4	1
Indiana	2	4	0	4	4	0
Chicago	0	5	0	2	7	0
Michigan State*				3	4	1
Penn State*				3	5	1

CONSENSUS ALL-AMERICANS

POS	Name	HT	WT	School	AA	AP	CM	IN	NA	NE	UP
E	Wes Fesler	6-0	173	Ohio State	•		•	•		•	•
G	Otto Pommerening	6-0	178	Michigan			•	•	•	•	

OTHERS RECEIVING FIRST-TEAM HONORS

E	Kenneth Haycraft			Minnesota			•		•		
T	Albert Nowack			Illinois		•		•			
G	George Gibson			Minnesota		•				•	
G	Leroy Wietz			Illinois					•		
G	Peter Westra			Iowa					•		

ALL-CONFERENCE TEAM

POS	Name	School
QB	Fred Hovde	Minnesota
HB	Charles "Chuck" Bennett	Indiana
HB	Willis "Bill" Glassgow	Iowa
HB	Ralph "Pest" Welch	Purdue
FB	Walter Holmer	Northwestern
C	Clare Randolph	Indiana
C	Richard Brown	Iowa
G	Otto Pommerening	Michigan
G	George Gibson	Minnesota
E	Kenneth Haycraft	Minnesota
E	Wesley Fesler	Ohio State
T	Albert "Butch" Nowack	Illinois
T	Rube Wagner	Wisconsin

*Independent or other conference affiliation

1929

CONFERENCE STANDINGS

	CONFERENCE			OVERALL		
	W	L	T	W	L	T
Purdue	5	0	0	8	0	0
Illinois	3	1	1	6	1	1
Minnesota	3	2	0	6	2	0
Northwestern	3	2	0	6	3	0
Iowa	2	2	2	4	2	2
Ohio State	2	2	1	4	3	1
Michigan	1	3	1	5	3	1
Indiana	1	3	1	2	6	1
Chicago	1	3	0	7	3	0
Wisconsin	1	4	0	4	5	0

Penn State*				6	3	0
Michigan State*				5	3	0

CONSENSUS ALL-AMERICANS

POS	Name	HT	WT	School	AA	AP	CM	IN	NA	NE	UP
B	**Ralph Welch**	6-1	189	Purdue	•	•		•	•	•	
E	**Wes Fesler**	6-0	183	Ohio State		•					
T	**Bronko Nagurski**	6-2	217	Minnesota	•	•		•	•	•	
T	**Elmer Sleight**	6-2	193	Purdue	•	•	•	•			

	OTHERS RECEIVING FIRST-TEAM HONORS							
B	Willis Glassgow	Iowa		•			•	
E	Robert Tanner	Minnesota		•				
T	Lou Gordon	Illinois					•	
G	Harry Anderson	Northwestern					•	

ALL-CONFERENCE TEAM

POS	Name	School
QB	Glen Harmeson	Purdue
HB	Willis "Bill" Glassgow	Iowa
HB	Ralph "Pest" Welch	Purdue
FB	Russell Bergherm	Northwestern
C	Alan Bovard	Michigan
C	Milton Erickson	Northwestern
G	Russell Crane	Illinois
G	Fred Roberts	Iowa
G	Henry Anderson	Northwestern
G	John Parks	Wisconsin
E	Robert Tanner	Minnesota
E	Wesley Fesler	Ohio State
T	Bronko Nagurski	Minnesota
T	Elmer "Red" Sleight	Purdue

1930

CONFERENCE STANDINGS

	CONFERENCE			OVERALL		
	W	L	T	W	L	T
Michigan	5	0	0	8	0	1
Northwestern	5	0	0	7	1	0
Purdue	4	2	0	6	2	0
Wisconsin	2	2	1	6	2	1
Ohio State	2	2	1	5	2	1
Minnesota	1	3	0	3	4	1
Indiana	1	3	0	2	5	1
Illinois	1	4	0	3	5	0
Iowa	0	1	0	4	4	0
Chicago	0	4	0	2	5	2

Michigan State*				5	1	2
Penn State*				3	4	2

CONSENSUS ALL-AMERICANS

POS	Name	HT	WT	School	AA	AP	CM	IN	NA	NE	UP
E	**Wes Fesler**	6-0	185	Ohio State	•	•	•	•	•	•	•
E	**Frank Baker**	6-2	175	Northwestern		•		•		•	
T	**Milo Lubratovich**	6-2	216	Wisconsin						•	•

	OTHERS RECEIVING FIRST-TEAM HONORS						
B	Fayette Russell	Northwestern	•			•	
G	Wade Woodworth	Northwestern			•		

ALL-CONFERENCE TEAM

POS	Name	School
QB	Harry Newman	Michigan
HB	Lee Hanley	Northwestern
HB	Lew Hinchman	Ohio State
HB	John White	Purdue
HB	Eddie Risk	Purdue
FB	Fayette "Reb" Russell	Northwestern
FB-HB	Ernest "Pug" Rentner	Northwestern
C	Maynard Morrison	Michigan
G	Clarence Munn	Minnesota
G	Wade "Red" Woodworth	Northwestern
G	Gregory Kabat	Wisconsin
E	Wesley Fesler	Ohio State
E	Frank Baker	Northwestern
T	George VanBibber	Purdue
T	Milo Lubratovich	Wisconsin

1931

CONFERENCE STANDINGS

	CONFERENCE			OVERALL		
	W	L	T	W	L	T
Purdue	5	1	0	9	1	0
Michigan	5	1	0	8	1	1
Northwestern	5	1	0	7	1	1
Ohio State	4	2	0	6	3	0
Minnesota	3	2	0	7	3	0
Wisconsin	3	3	0	5	4	1
Indiana	1	4	2	2	5	2
Chicago	1	4	0	2	6	1
Iowa	0	3	1	1	6	1
Illinois	0	6	1	2	6	1
Michigan State*				5	3	1
Penn State*				2	8	0

CONSENSUS ALL-AMERICANS

POS	Name	HT	WT	School	AA	AP	CM	IN	LM	NE	UP
B	Pug Rentner	6-1	185	Northwestern	•	•	•	•		•	•
T	Jack Riley	6-2	218	Northwestern	•				•	•	
T	Dallas Marvil	6-3	227	Northwestern			•		•		
G	Biggie Munn	5-10	217	Minnesota	•	•	•	•		•	•

OTHERS RECEIVING FIRST-TEAM HONORS

POS	Name	School							
E	Paul Moss	Purdue					•		
C	Maynard Morrison	Michigan			•		•		
C	Charles Miller	Purdue							•

ALL-CONFERENCE TEAM

POS	Name	School
QB	Harry Newman	Michigan
QB	Carl Cramer	Ohio State
HB	Bill Hewitt	Michigan
HB	Lew Hinchman	Ohio State
FB	Jack Manders	Minnesota
FB-HB	Ernest "Pug" Rentner	Northwestern
C	Maynard Morrison	Michigan
C	Charles Miller	Purdue
G	Joe Zeller	Indiana
G	Clarence Munn	Minnesota
G	Gregory Kabat	Wisconsin
E	Ivan Williamson	Michigan
E	Paul Moss	Purdue
T	Jack Riley	Northwestern
T	Dallas Marvil	Northwestern

1932

CONFERENCE STANDINGS

	CONFERENCE			OVERALL		
	W	L	T	W	L	T
Michigan	6	0	0	8	0	0
Purdue	5	0	1	7	0	1
Wisconsin	4	1	1	6	1	1
Ohio State	2	1	2	4	1	3
Northwestern	2	3	1	3	4	1
Minnesota	2	3	0	5	3	0
Illinois	2	4	0	5	4	0
Indiana	1	4	1	3	4	1
Chicago	1	4	0	3	4	1
Iowa	0	5	0	1	7	0
Michigan State*				7	1	0
Penn State*				2	5	0

CONSENSUS ALL-AMERICANS

POS	Name	HT	WT	School	AA	AP	CM	FW	IN	LM	NE	UP
B	Harry Newman	5-7	175	Michigan	•	•	•	•	•	•	•	•
E	Paul Moss	6-2	185	Purdue	•	•	•	•	•	•	•	•

OTHERS RECEIVING FIRST-TEAM HONORS

POS	Name	School								
B	Roy Horstmann	Purdue	•				•			
E	Ted Petoskey	Michigan	•							
G	Joe Gailus	Ohio State					•			
C	Chuck Bernard	Michigan			•		•			

ALL-CONFERENCE TEAM

POS	Name	School
QB	Harry Newman	Michigan
HB	Gil Berry	Illinois
HB	Lew Hinchman	Ohio State
FB	Roy Horstmann	Purdue
C	Charles Bernard	Michigan
G	Joe Gailus	Ohio State
G	John Oehler	Purdue
G	Gregory Kabat	Wisconsin
E	Ivan Williamson	Michigan
E	Sid Gillman	Ohio State
E	Paul Moss	Purdue
T	Francis Wistert	Michigan
T	Marshall Wells	Minnesota
T	Ted Rosequist	Ohio State

*Independent or other conference affiliation

1933

CONFERENCE STANDINGS

	Conference W	L	T	Overall W	L	T
Michigan	5	0	1	7	0	1
Ohio State	4	1	0	7	1	0
Purdue	3	1	1	6	1	1
Minnesota	2	0	4	4	0	4
Illinois	3	2	0	5	3	0
Iowa	3	2	0	5	3	0
Northwestern	1	4	1	1	5	2
Chicago	0	3	2	3	3	2
Indiana	0	3	2	1	5	2
Wisconsin	0	5	1	2	5	1
Michigan State*				4	2	2
Penn State*				3	3	1

CONSENSUS ALL-AMERICANS

POS	Name	HT	WT	School	AA	AP	CM	FW	IN	LM	NE	UP
B	Duane Purvis	6-1	190	Purdue	•	•	•		•		•	•
T	Francis Wistert	6-3	212	Michigan	•		•	•	•			•
C	Chuck Bernard	6-2	215	Michigan	•	•	•	•	•	•	•	•

	OTHERS RECEIVING FIRST-TEAM HONORS											
B	Pug Lund			Minnesota		•		•				
E	Frank Larson			Minnesota			•			•		
E	Edgar Manske			Northwestern						•		
G	Francis Schammel			Iowa		•			•	•		•

ALL-CONFERENCE TEAM

POS	Name	School
QB	Joe Laws	Iowa
HB	Herman Everhardus	Michigan
HB-FB	Francis "Pug" Lund	Minnesota
FB-HB	Duane Purvis	Purdue
C	Charles Bernard	Michigan
G	Robert Jones	Indiana
G	Joe Gailus	Ohio State
E	Fred "Ted" Petoskey	Michigan
E	Frank "Butch" Larson	Minnesota
E	Edgar Manske	Northwestern
T	Francis Wistert	Michigan
T	Bill "Dutch" Fehring	Purdue
T-G	Francis Schammel	Iowa

1934

CONFERENCE STANDINGS

	Conference W	L	T	Overall W	L	T
Minnesota	5	0	0	8	0	0
Ohio State	5	1	0	7	1	0
Illinois	4	1	0	7	1	0
Purdue	3	1	0	5	3	0
Wisconsin	2	3	0	4	4	0
Northwestern	2	3	0	3	5	0
Chicago	2	4	0	4	4	0
Indiana	1	3	1	3	3	2
Iowa	1	3	1	2	5	1
Michigan	0	6	0	1	7	0
Michigan State*				8	1	0
Penn State*				4	4	0

CONSENSUS ALL-AMERICANS

POS	Name	HT	WT	School	AA	AP	CM	IN	LM	NA	NE	SN	UP
B	Pug Lund	5-11	185	Minnesota	•	•	•	•		•		•	•
E	Frank Larson	6-3	190	Minnesota		•	•			•	•	•	
G	Bill Bevan	5-11	194	Minnesota			•			•	•		•

	OTHERS RECEIVING FIRST-TEAM HONORS												
B	Jay Berwanger			Chicago		•							
B	Duane Purvis			Purdue									
E	Merle Wendt			Ohio State						•			
T	Ed Widseth			Minnesota						•			
G	Regis Monahan			Ohio State	•						•		
C	Ellmore Patterson			Chicago									

ALL-CONFERENCE TEAM

POS	Name	School
QB	Jack Beynon	Illinois
HB	Jay Berwanger	Chicago
HB-FB	Francis "Pug" Lund	Minnesota
FB-HB	Duane Purvis	Purdue
C	Ellmore Patterson	Chicago
G	Bill Bevan	Minnesota
G	Regis Monahan	Ohio State
E	Frank "Butch" Larson	Minnesota
E	Bob Tenner	Minnesota
E	Merle Wendt	Ohio State
T	Chuck Galbreath	Illlinois
T	Phil Bengtson	Minnesota
T	Edwin Widseth	Minnesota

BIG TEN ANNUAL REVIEW & BOWLS

1935

CONFERENCE STANDINGS

	CONFERENCE			OVERALL		
	W	L	T	W	L	T
Minnesota	5	0	0	8	0	0
Ohio State	5	0	0	7	1	0
Purdue	3	3	0	4	4	0
Indiana	2	2	1	4	3	1
Northwestern	2	3	1	4	3	1
Michigan	2	3	0	4	4	0
Chicago	2	3	0	4	4	0
Iowa	1	2	2	4	2	2
Illinois	1	4	0	3	5	0
Wisconsin	1	4	0	1	7	0
Michigan State*				6	2	0
Penn State*				4	4	0

CONSENSUS ALL-AMERICANS

POS	Name	HT	WT	School	AA	AP	CM	IN	LM	NA	NE	SN	UP
B	Jay Berwanger	6-0	195	Chicago	•	•	•	•	•		•	•	•
T	Ed Widseth	6-2	220	Minnesota	•			•	•	•		•	•
G	Sidney Wagner	5-11	186	Michigan St.*		•			•			•	
C	Gomer Jones	5-8	210	Ohio State	•			•	•			•	

	OTHERS RECEIVING FIRST-TEAM HONORS			
B	Sheldon Beise	Minnesota		
B	Ozzie Simmons	Iowa		•
E	Merle Wendt	Ohio State		
T	Dick Smith	Minnesota	• • •	•
G	Paul Tangora	Northwestern	•	•
G	Inwood Smith	Ohio State	•	

ALL-CONFERENCE TEAM

POS	Name	School
QB	Vernal "Babe" LeVoir	Minnesota
HB	Jay Berwanger	Chicago
HB	Ozzie Simmons	Iowa
FB	Sheldon Beise	Minnesota
C	Gomer Jones	Ohio State
G	Edward Gryboski	Illinois
G	Charles "Bud" Wilkinson	Minnesota
G	Paul Tangora	Northwestern
E	Matthew Patanelli	Michigan
E	Henry Longfellow	Northwestern
E	Merle Wendt	Ohio State
T	Dick Smith	Minnesota
T	Edwin Widseth	Minnesota

HEISMAN TROPHY VOTING

	PLAYER	POS	SCHOOL	TOTAL
1	Jay Berwanger	RB	Chicago	84

1936

FINAL POLL

AP	TEAM	RECORD
1	Minnesota	7-1-0
2	LSU	9-1-1
3	Pittsburgh	8-1-1
4	Alabama	8-0-1
5	Washington	7-2-1
6	Santa Clara	8-1-0
7	Northwestern	7-1-0
8	Notre Dame	6-2-1
9	Nebraska	7-2-0
10	Pennsylvania	7-1-0
11	Duke	9-1-0
12	Yale	7-1-1
13	Dartmouth	7-1-1
14	Duquesne	8-2-0
15	Fordham	5-1-2
16	TCU	9-2-2
17	Tennessee	6-2-2
18	Arkansas	7-3-0
19	Navy	6-3-0
20	Marquette	7-2-0

CONFERENCE STANDINGS

	CONFERENCE			OVERALL		
	W	L	T	W	L	T
Northwestern	6	0	0	7	1	0
Minnesota	4	1	0	7	1	0
Ohio State	4	1	0	5	3	0
Indiana	3	1	1	5	2	1
Purdue	3	1	1	5	2	1
Illinois	2	2	1	4	3	1
Chicago	1	4	0	2	5	1
Iowa	0	4	1	3	4	1
Wisconsin	0	4	0	2	6	0
Michigan	0	5	0	1	7	0
Michigan State*				6	1	2
Penn State*				3	5	0

CONSENSUS ALL-AMERICANS

POS	Name	HT	WT	School	AA	AP	CM	IN	LM	NA	NE	SN	UP
T	Ed Widseth	6-2	220	Minnesota	•	•	•	•	•	•	•	•	•
G	Steve Reid	5-9	192	Northwestern	•		•		•	•	•	•	

	OTHERS RECEIVING FIRST-TEAM HONORS		
B	Andy Uram	Minnesota	•

ALL-CONFERENCE TEAM

POS	Name	School
QB	Fred Vanzo	Northwestern
HB	Vernon Huffman	Indiana
HB	Andy Uram	Minnesota
HB	Don Heap	Northwestern
FB	Johnny Drake	Purdue
FB-HB	Cecil Isbell	Purdue
C	Elvin Sayre	Illinois
G	Lester Schreiber	Northwestern
G	Steve Reid	Northwestern
G	Inwood Smith	Ohio State
E	John Kovatch	Northwestern
E	Merle Wendt	Ohio State
T	Edwin Widseth	Minnesota
T	Charles Hamrick	Ohio State

HEISMAN TROPHY VOTING

	PLAYER	POS	SCHOOL	TOTAL
7	Ed Widseth	T	Minnesota	25

*Independent or other conference affiliation

1937

FINAL POLL

AP	TEAM	RECORD
1	Pittsburgh	9-0-1
2	California	10-0-1
3	Fordham	7-0-1
4	Alabama	9-1-0
5	**Minnesota**	6-2-0
6	Villanova	8-0-1
7	Dartmouth	7-0-2
8	LSU	9-2-0
9	Notre Dame	6-2-1
9	Santa Clara	9-0-0
11	Nebraska	6-1-2
12	Yale	6-1-1
13	**Ohio State**	6-2-0
14	Arkansas	6-2-2
14	Holy Cross	8-0-2
15	TCU	4-4-2
17	Colorado	8-1-0
18	Rice	6-3-2
19	North Carolina	7-1-1
20	Duke	7-2-1

CONFERENCE STANDINGS

	CONFERENCE			OVERALL		
	W	L	T	W	L	T
Minnesota	5	0	0	6	2	0
Ohio State	5	1	0	6	2	0
Indiana	3	2	0	5	3	0
Northwestern	3	3	0	4	4	0
Michigan	3	3	0	4	4	0
Wisconsin	2	2	1	4	3	1
Purdue	2	2	1	4	3	1
Illinois	2	3	0	3	3	2
Chicago	0	4	0	1	6	0
Iowa	0	5	0	1	7	0
Michigan State*				8	2	0
Penn State*				5	3	0

BOWL GAMES

DATE	GAME	SCORE
J1	**Orange**	Auburn 6, Michigan State* 0

CONSENSUS ALL-AMERICANS

POS	Name	School	HT WT	AA AP CM IN LM NA NE NW SN UP
	OTHERS RECEIVING FIRST-TEAM HONORS			
B	Corby Davis	Indiana		• • • •
E	Ray King	Minnesota		• • •
G	Gus Zarnas	Ohio State		•

ALL-CONFERENCE TEAM

POS	Name	School
QB	Jim McDonald	Ohio State
HB	Nile Kinnick	Iowa
HB	Rudy Gmitro	Minnesota
HB	Don Heap	Northwestern
FB	Corby Davis	Indiana
FB-HB	Cecil Isbell	Purdue
C	George Miller	Indiana
C	Ralph Wolf	Ohio State
G	Ralph Heikkinen	Michigan
G	Francis Twedell	Minnesota
G	Gust Zarnas	Ohio State
E	Bob Lannon	Iowa
E	Ray King	Minnesota
E	Jim Zachary	Purdue
T	Bob Haak	Indiana
T	Lou Midler	Minnesota
T	Carl Kaplanoff	Ohio State
T	Martin Schreyer	Purdue

NCAA STATISTICAL LEADERS

INDIVIDUAL

PASSING/COMPLETIONS

		G	ATT	COM	PCT	INT	I%	YDS	YPA	COM.PG
9	Frank Filchock, Indiana	8	92	45	48.9	10	10.9	585	6.4	5.6

RUSHING/YARDS PER CARRY

		G	ATT	YDS	YPC
5	Harold Van Every, Minnesota	8	88	526	6.0
10	Johnny Pingel, Michigan State*	9	116	590	5.1

Based on top 30 rushers

RECEIVING/RECEPTIONS

		G	REC	YDS	YPR	YPG	RPG
8	Walter Nelson, Michigan State*	9	18	388	21.6	43.1	2.0

PUNTING

		PUNT	YDS	AVG
1	Johnny Pingel, Michigan State*	49	2101	42.9
5	Ray King, Minnesota	21	883	42.1

TEAM

RUSHING OFFENSE

		G	YDS	YPG
5	Minnesota	8	1887	235.9

TOTAL OFFENSE

		G	YDS	YPG
3	Minnesota	8	2428	303.5

RUSHING DEFENSE

		G	YDS	YPG
6	Illinois	8	520	65.0
6	Ohio State	8	520	65.0
8	Michigan State*	9	588	65.3

PASSING DEFENSE

		G	ATT	COM	PCT	YPC	INT	I%	YDS	YPA	YPG
2	Chicago	5	49	13	26.5	13.2	11	22.4	171	3.5	34.2
3	Michigan State*	9	85	24	28.2	12.9	13	15.3	310	3.6	34.4

Based on 37 teams whose opponents had the lowest pass completion percentage.

TOTAL DEFENSE

		G	YDS	YPG
4	Michigan State*	9	898	99.8
8	Ohio State	8	924	115.5

BIG TEN ANNUAL REVIEW & BOWLS

1938

FINAL POLL

AP	TEAM	RECORD
1	TCU	11-0-0
2	Tennessee	11-0-0
3	Duke	9-1-0
4	Oklahoma	10-1-0
5	Notre Dame	8-1-0
6	Carnegie Tech	7-2-0
7	USC	9-2-0
8	Pittsburgh	8-2-0
9	Holy Cross	8-1-0
10	**Minnesota**	6-2-0
11	Texas Tech	10-1-0
12	Cornell	5-1-1
13	Alabama	7-1-1
14	California	10-1-0
15	Fordham	6-1-2
16	**Michigan**	6-1-1
17	**Northwestern**	4-2-2
18	Villanova	8-0-1
19	Tulane	7-2-1
20	Dartmouth	7-2-0

CONFERENCE STANDINGS

	CONFERENCE			OVERALL		
	W	L	T	W	L	T
Minnesota	4	1	0	6	2	0
Michigan	3	1	1	6	1	1
Purdue	3	1	1	5	1	2
Wisconsin	3	2	0	5	3	0
Northwestern	2	1	2	4	2	2
Ohio State	3	2	1	4	3	1
Illinois	2	3	0	3	5	0
Iowa	1	3	1	1	6	1
Indiana	1	4	0	1	6	1
Chicago	0	4	0	1	6	1
Michigan State*				6	3	0
Penn State*				3	4	1

CONSENSUS ALL-AMERICANS

POS	**Name**	HT	WT	**School**	AA	AP	CM	IN	LM	NE	NW	SN	UP
G	**Ralph Heikkinen**	5-10	185	Michigan	•	•	•	•	•	•	•	•	•

	OTHERS RECEIVING FIRST-TEAM HONORS										
B	Johnny Pingel	Michigan State*	•								
B	Howard Weiss	Wisconsin			•						
T	Bob Voigts	Northwestern	•								
G	Francis Twedell	Minnesota			•			•			

ALL-CONFERENCE TEAM

POS	**Name**	**School**
QB	Forest Evashevski	Michigan
QB	Wilbur Moore	Minnesota
HB	Tom Harmon	Michigan
HB	Lou Brock	Purdue
FB	Howard Weiss	Wisconsin
C	Jack Murray	Wisconsin
G	Ralph Heikkinen	Michigan
G	Francis Twedell	Minnesota
E	Frank Petrick	Indiana
E	Erwin Prasse	Iowa
E	Cleo Diehl	Northwestern
T	Bob Haak	Indiana
T	Bob Voigts	Northwestern
T	Joe Mihal	Purdue

HEISMAN TROPHY VOTING

PLAYER	POS	SCHOOL	TOTAL
6 **Howard Weiss**	FB	Wisconsin	60

NCAA STATISTICAL LEADERS

INDIVIDUAL

PASSING/COMPLETIONS

		G	ATT	COM	PCT	INT	I%	YDS	YPA	COM.PG
7	Johnny Pingel, Michigan State*	9	101	54	53.5	NA	NA	571	5.7	6.0

RUSHING/YARDS PER CARRY

		G	ATT	YDS	YPC
7	Johnny Pingel, Michigan State*	9	110	556	5.0

Based on top 20 rushers

PUNTING

		PUNT	YDS	AVG
2	Johnny Pingel, Michigan State*	99	4138	41.8
4	Nile Kinnick, Iowa	41	1686	41.1
9	Michael Kabealo, Ohio State	42	1692	40.3

INTERCEPTIONS

		INT	YDS
3	Russell Busk, Iowa	6	98
3	Nile Kinnick, Iowa	6	39

TEAM

RUSHING OFFENSE

		G	ATT	YDS	AVG	YPG
3	Penn State*	8	397	2012	5.1	251.5
9	Minnesota	8	452	1717	3.8	214.6

PASSING OFFENSE/YPG

		G	ATT	COM	INT	PCT	YDS	YPA	YPG	I%	YPC
8	Chicago	7	161	60	17	37.3	841	5.2	120.1	10.6	14.0

PASSING DEFENSE

		G	ATT	COM	PCT	YPC	INT	I%	YDS	YPA	YPG
1	Penn State*	8	59	10	16.9	10.5	14	23.7	105	1.8	13.1

*Independent or other conference affiliation

1939

FINAL POLL

AP	TEAM	RECORD
1	Texas A&M	11-0-0
2	Tennessee	10-1-0
3	USC	8-0-2
4	Cornell	8-0-0
5	Tulane	8-1-1
6	Missouri	8-2-0
7	UCLA	6-0-4
8	Duke	8-1-0
9	Iowa	6-1-1
10	Duquesne	8-0-1
11	Boston College	9-2-0
12	Clemson	9-1-0
13	Notre Dame	7-2-0
14	Santa Clara	5-1-3
15	Ohio State	6-2-0
16	Georgia Tech	8-2-0
17	Fordham	6-2-0
18	Nebraska	7-1-1
19	Oklahoma	6-2-1
20	Michigan	6-2-0

CONFERENCE STANDINGS

	CONFERENCE			OVERALL		
	W	L	T	W	L	T
Ohio State	5	1	0	6	2	0
Iowa	4	1	1	6	1	1
Michigan	3	2	0	6	2	0
Purdue	2	1	2	3	3	2
Northwestern	3	2	1	3	4	1
Illinois	3	3	0	3	4	1
Minnesota	2	3	1	3	4	1
Indiana	2	3	0	2	4	2
Wisconsin	0	5	1	1	6	1
Chicago	0	3	0	2	6	0
Penn State*				5	1	2
Michigan State*				4	4	1

CONSENSUS ALL-AMERICANS

POS	Name	HT	WT	School	AA	AP	CM	IN	LM	NE	NW	SN	UP
B	Nile Kinnick	5-8	167	Iowa	•	•	•	•		•	•	•	•
B	Tom Harmon	6-0	195	Michigan	•	•	•	•	•		•	•	•
E	Esco Sarkkinen	6-0	192	Ohio State	•		•		•			•	•

	Others receiving first-team honors			
B	Donald Scott	Ohio State		•
E	Dave Rankin	Purdue	•	
T	Jim Reeder	Illinois	•	
C	John Haman	Northwestern		•

ALL-CONFERENCE TEAM

POS	Name	School
QB	Forest Evashevski	Michigan
QB	Don Scott	Ohio State
HB	Tom Harmon	Michigan
HB	Nile Kinnick	Iowa
FB	George Paskvan	Wisconsin
C	John Haman	Northwestern
G	Hal Method	Northwestern
G	Vic Marino	Ohio State
G	Frank Bykowski	Purdue
E	Erwin Prasse	Iowa
E	Esco Sarkkinen	Ohio State
E	Dave Rankin	Purdue
T	Jim Reeder	Illinois
T	Mike Enich	Iowa
T	Win Pedersen	Minnesota

HEISMAN TROPHY VOTING

	PLAYER	POS	SCHOOL	TOTAL
1	Nile Kinnick	HB	Iowa	651
2	Tom Harmon	HB	Michigan	405

AWARD WINNERS

PLAYER	POS	SCHOOL	AWARD
Nile Kinnick	HB	Iowa	Maxwell

NCAA STATISTICAL LEADERS

INDIVIDUAL

PASSING/COMPLETIONS		G	ATT	COM	PCT	INT	I%	YDS	YPA	COM.PG
4	Harold Hursh, Indiana	8	125	59	47.2	11	8.8	913	7.3	7.4

ALL-PURPOSE		G	RUSH	REC	INT	PR	KR	YDS	YPG
1	Tom Harmon, Michigan	8	868	110	98	0	132	1208	151.0

RUSHING/YARDS		G	ATT	YDS	AVG	YPG
2	Tom Harmon, Michigan	8	129	868	6.7	108.5
6	Harold Van Every, Minnesota	8	132	676	5.1	84.5

RUSHING/YARDS PER CARRY		G	ATT	YDS	YPC
2	Jim Strausbaugh, Ohio State	8	71	526	7.4
5	Tom Harmon, Michigan	8	129	868	6.7

Based on top 20 rushers

SCORING		TDS	XP	FG	PTS
1	Tom Harmon, Michigan	14	15	1	102

INTERCEPTIONS		INT	YDS
1	Harold Van Every, Minnesota	8	59
1	Nile Kinnick, Iowa	8	52

KICKOFF RETURNS/YARDS		KR	YDS	AVG
1	Nile Kinnick, Iowa	15	377	25.1
6	R. H. Miller, Chicago	12	212	17.7
8	Harold Van Every, Minnesota	8	198	24.8

TEAM

RUSHING OFFENSE		G	ATT	YDS	AVG	YPG
4	Minnesota	8	470	1891	4.0	236.4
8	Ohio State	8	380	1711	4.5	213.9

PASSING OFFENSE		G	ATT	COM	INT	PCT	YDS	YPA	TD	I%	YPC
3	Indiana	8	142	69	14	48.6	1032	7.3	129.0	9.9	15.0

TOTAL DEFENSE		G	P	YDS	AVG	YPG
1	Ohio State	8	514	2474	4.8	309.3
10	Minnesota	8	544	2296	4.2	287.0

BIG TEN ANNUAL REVIEW & BOWLS

1940

FINAL POLL

AP	TEAM	RECORD
1	**Minnesota**	8-0-0
2	Stanford	10-0-0
3	**Michigan**	7-1-0
4	Tennessee	10-1-0
5	Boston College	11-0-0
6	Texas A&M	9-1-0
7	Nebraska	8-2-0
8	**Northwestern**	6-2-0
9	Mississippi State	10-0-1
10	Washington	7-2-0
11	Santa Clara	6-1-1
12	Fordham	7-2-0
13	Georgetown	8-2-0
14	Pennsylvania	6-1-1
15	Cornell	6-2-0
16	SMU	8-1-1
17	Hardin-Simmons	9-0-0
18	Duke	7-2-0
19	Lafayette	9-0-0

CONFERENCE STANDINGS

	CONFERENCE			OVERALL		
	W	L	T	W	L	T
Minnesota	6	0	0	8	0	0
Michigan	3	1	0	7	1	0
Northwestern	4	2	0	6	2	0
Wisconsin	3	3	0	4	4	0
Ohio State	3	3	0	4	4	0
Iowa	2	3	0	4	4	0
Indiana	2	3	0	3	5	0
Purdue	1	4	0	2	6	0
Illinois	0	5	0	1	7	0
Penn State*				6	1	1
Michigan State*				3	4	1

CONSENSUS ALL-AMERICANS

POS	Name	HT	WT	School	AA AP CM IN LM NE NW SN UP
B	**Tom Harmon**	6-0	195	Michigan	• • • • • • • • •
B	**George Franck**	6-0	175	Minnesota	• • • • • • •
E	**Dave Rankin**	6-1	190	Purdue	• • • •
T	**Alf Bauman**	6-1	210	Northwestern	• • •
T	**Urban Odson**	6-3	247	Minnesota	• • •

	OTHERS RECEIVING FIRST-TEAM HONORS		
E	Ed Frutig	Michigan	• •
T	Mike Enich	Iowa	•
G	Helge Pukema	Minnesota	•
C	Leon Gajecki	Penn State*	• •

ALL-CONFERENCE TEAM

POS	Name	School
QB	Forest Evashevski	Michigan
QB	Don Scott	Ohio State
HB	Tom Harmon	Michigan
HB	George Franck	Minnesota
FB	George Paskvan	Wisconsin
C	Paul Hiemenz	Northwestern
G	Ralph Fritz	Michigan
G	Joe Lokanc	Northwestern
E	Ed Frutig	Michigan
E	Dave Rankin	Purdue
T	Urban Odson	Minnesota
T	Alf Bauman	Northwestern

HEISMAN TROPHY VOTING

	PLAYER	POS	SCHOOL	TOTAL
1	**Tom Harmon**	HB	Michigan	1303
3	**George Franck**	HB	Minnesota	102

AWARD WINNERS

PLAYER	POS	SCHOOL	AWARD
Tom Harmon	HB	Michigan	Maxwell

NCAA STATISTICAL LEADERS

INDIVIDUAL

	PASSING/COMPLETIONS	G	ATT	COM	PCT	INT	I%	YDS	YPA	COM.PG
8	Harold Hursh, Indiana	8	111	53	47.7	10	9.0	699	6.3	6.6

	ALL-PURPOSE	G	RUSH	REC	INT	PR	KR	YDS	YPG
1	Tom Harmon, Michigan	8	844	0	20	244	204	1312	164.0

	RUSHING/YARDS	G	ATT	YDS	AVG	YPG
2	Tom Harmon, Michigan	8	186	844	4.5	105.5
4	Bob Westfall, Michigan	8	190	807	4.2	100.9

	RECEIVING/RECEPTIONS	G	REC	YDS	YPR	YPG	RPG
4	Lenny Krouse, Penn State*	8	25	420	16.8	52.5	3.1

	PUNTING		PUNT	YDS	AVG
7	Don Scott, Ohio State		39	1630	41.8

	KICKOFF RETURNS/YARDS		KR	YDS	AVG
5	George Franck, Minnesota		6	305	50.8
8	Chuck Peters, Penn State*		5	261	52.2

	SCORING		TDS	XP	FG	PTS
1	Tom Harmon, Michigan		16	18	1	117

TEAM

	RUSHING OFFENSE	G	ATT	YDS	AVG	YPG
4	Michigan	8	471	1921	4.1	240.1
7	Penn State*	8	423	1785	4.2	223.1
8	Minnesota	8	407	1782	4.4	222.8

	PASSING DEFENSE	G	ATT	COM	PCT	YPC	INT	I%	YDS	YPA	YPG
3	Indiana	8	67	22	32.8	15.8	11	16.4	347	5.2	43.4
7	Penn State*	8	86	24	27.9	15.6	16	18.6	374	4.3	46.8

	TOTAL DEFENSE	G	P	YDS	AVG	YPG
6	Penn State*	8	324	1073	3.3	134.1

	SCORING OFFENSE		G	PTS	AVG
5	Michigan		8	196	24.5

	SCORING DEFENSE		G	PTS	AVG
5	Michigan		8	34	4.3

*Independent or other conference affiliation

1941

FINAL POLL

AP	TEAM	RECORD
1	**Minnesota**	8-0-0
2	Duke	9-1-0
3	Notre Dame	8-0-1
4	Texas	8-1-1
5	**Michigan**	6-1-1
6	Fordham	8-1-0
7	Missouri	8-2-0
8	Duquesne	8-0-0
9	Texas A&M	9-2-0
10	Navy	7-1-1
11	**Northwestern**	5-3-0
12	Oregon State	8-2-0
13	**Ohio State**	6-1-1
14	Georgia	9-1-1
15	Pennsylvania	7-1-0
16	Mississippi State	8-1-1
17	Mississippi	6-2-1
18	Tennessee	8-2-0
19	Washington State	6-4-0
20	Alabama	9-2-0

CONFERENCE STANDINGS

	CONFERENCE			OVERALL		
	W	L	T	W	L	T
Minnesota	5	0	0	8	0	0
Ohio State	3	1	1	6	1	1
Michigan	3	1	1	6	1	1
Northwestern	4	2	0	5	3	0
Wisconsin	3	3	0	3	5	0
Iowa	2	4	0	3	5	0
Purdue	1	3	0	2	5	1
Indiana	1	3	0	2	6	0
Illinois	0	5	0	2	6	0
Penn State*				7	2	0
Michigan State*				5	3	1

CONSENSUS ALL-AMERICANS

POS	Name	HT	WT	School	AA	AP	CM	IN	LM	NE	NW	SN	UP
B	**Bob Westfall**	5-8	190	Michigan	•		•	•	•	•		•	•
B	**Bruce Smith**	6-0	193	Minnesota	•	•	•	•	•		•	•	•
T	**Dick Wildung**	6-0	210	Minnesota	•	•		•	•	•	•	•	•

OTHERS RECEIVING FIRST-TEAM HONORS									
E	Dave Schreiner	Wisconsin					•			
T	Alf Bauman	Northwestern	•					•		

ALL-CONFERENCE TEAM

POS	Name	School
QB-HB	Billy Hillenbrand	Indiana
HB	Bruce Smith	Minnesota
HB	Bill Daley	Minnesota
HB-FB	Marlin "Pat" Harder	Wisconsin
FB	Bob Westfall	Michigan
C	Bob Ingalls	Michigan
G	Len Levy	Minnesota
G	Tom Melton	Purdue
E	Bob Fitch	Minnesota
E	Bob Motl	Northwestern
E	Dave Schreiner	Wisconsin
T	Dick Wildung	Minnesota
T	Alf Bauman	Northwestern

HEISMAN TROPHY VOTING

PLAYER	POS	SCHOOL	TOTAL
1 **Bruce Smith**	HB	Minnesota	554
8 **Bob Westfall**	FB	Michigan	147

NCAA STATISTICAL LEADERS

INDIVIDUAL

RUSHING/YARDS		G	ATT	YDS	AVG	YPG
5	**Pat Harder, Wisconsin**	8	142	731	5.1	91.4
6	**Bob Westfall, Michigan**	8	156	688	4.4	86.0
7	**Bill Daley, Minnesota**	8	158	685	4.3	85.6
10	**Dick Fisher, Ohio State**	8	134	674	5.0	84.3

RUSHING/YARDS PER CARRY		G	ATT	YDS	YPC
8	**Pat Harder, Wisconsin**	8	142	731	5.1
9	**Dick Fisher, Ohio State**	8	134	674	5.0
Based on top 20 rushers					

RECEIVING/RECEPTIONS		G	REC	YDS	YPR	YPG	RPG
3	Lenny Krouse, Penn State*	9	32	536	16.8	59.6	3.6

PUNT RETURNS/YARDS		PR	YDS	AVG
3	Bill Hillenbrand, Indiana	41	524	12.8

SCORING		TDS	XP	FG	PTS
7	**Pat Harder, Wisconsin**	10	9	1	72
7	John Petrella, Penn State*	12	0	0	72

TEAM

RUSHING OFFENSE		G	ATT	YDS	AVG	YPG
3	**Minnesota**	8	476	2062	4.3	257.8
10	**Michigan**	8	420	1871	4.5	233.9

PASSING DEFENSE		G	ATT	COM	PCT	YPC	INT	I%	YDS	YPA	YPG
1	**Purdue**	8	74	21	28.4	10.3	11	14.9	217	2.9	27.1

SCORING DEFENSE		G	PTS	AVG
9	**Minnesota**	8	38	4.8

1942

FINAL POLL

AP	TEAM	RECORD
1	Ohio State	9-1-0
2	Georgia	11-1-0
3	Wisconsin	8-1-1
4	Tulsa	10-1-0
5	Georgia Tech	9-2-0
6	Notre Dame	7-2-2
7	Tennessee	9-1-1
8	Boston College	8-2-0
9	Michigan	7-3-0
10	Alabama	8-3-0
11	Texas	9-2-0
12	Stanford	6-4-0
13	UCLA	7-4-0
14	William & Mary	9-1-1
15	Santa Clara	7-2-0
16	Auburn	6-4-1
17	Washington State	6-2-2
18	Mississippi State	8-2-0
19	Holy Cross	5-4-1
19	Minnesota	5-4-0
19	Penn State*	6-1-1

CONFERENCE STANDINGS

	CONFERENCE			OVERALL		
	W	L	T	W	L	T
Ohio State	5	1	0	9	1	0
Wisconsin	4	1	0	8	1	1
Michigan	3	2	0	7	3	0
Illinois	3	2	0	6	4	0
Iowa	3	3	0	6	4	0
Minnesota	3	3	0	5	4	0
Indiana	2	2	0	7	3	0
Purdue	1	4	0	1	8	0
Northwestern	0	6	0	1	9	0
Penn State*				6	1	1
Michigan State*				4	3	2

CONSENSUS ALL-AMERICANS

POS	Name	HT	WT	School	AA	AP	CM	IN	LM	NE	NW	SN	UP
B	Bill Hillenbrand	6-0	195	Indiana	•								•
E	Dave Schreiner	6-2	198	Wisconsin	•	•	•	•		•	•	•	•
T	Dick Wildung	6-0	215	Minnesota	•	•	•			•	•	•	•
T	Albert Wistert	6-2	205	Michigan	•					•		•	•
G	Julie Franks	6-0	187	Michigan		•	•				•		

	OTHERS RECEIVING FIRST-TEAM HONORS							
B	Pat Harder	Wisconsin	•					
E	Bob Shaw	Ohio State		•				
T	Charles Csuri	Ohio State			•			
G	Lindell Houston	Ohio State	•	•				
G	Alex Agase	Illinois				•		• •
G	Merv Pregulman	Michigan			•			

ALL-CONFERENCE TEAM

POS	Name	School
QB	George Ceithaml	Michigan
QB-HB	Bill Hillenbrand	Indiana
HB	Paul Sarringhaus	Ohio State
HB	Elroy Hirsch	Wisconsin
HB-FB	Marlin "Pat" Harder	Wisconsin
C	Fred Negus	Wisconsin
G	Julius Franks	Michigan
G	Lindell Houston	Ohio State
E	Bob Shaw	Ohio State
E	Dave Schreiner	Wisconsin
T	Albert Wistert	Michigan
T	Dick Wildung	Minnesota

HEISMAN TROPHY VOTING

	PLAYER	POS	SCHOOL	TOTAL
5	Bill Hillenbrand	HB	Indiana	86
7	Dick Wildung	T	Minnesota	71
8	Gene Fekete	FB	Ohio State	65
10	Dave Schreiner	E	Wisconsin	60

NCAA STATISTICAL LEADERS

INDIVIDUAL

PASSING/COMPLETIONS	G	ATT	COM	PCT	INT	I%	YDS	YPA	COM.PG
2 Otto Graham, Northwestern	10	182	89	48.9	18	9.9	1092	6.0	8.9

RUSHING/YARDS	G	ATT	YDS	AVG	YPC
5 Gene Fekete, Ohio State	10	185	910	4.9	91.0
9 Elroy Hirsch, Wisconsin	10	141	767	5.4	76.7

RUSHING/YARDS PER CARRY	G	ATT	YDS	YPC
6 Elroy Hirsch, Wisconsin	10	141	767	5.4

PUNTING	PUNT	YDS	AVG
9 Joe Colone, Penn State*	46	1,845	40.1
10 Earl Dolaway, Indiana	30	1,202	40.1

PUNT RETURNS/YARDS	PR	YDS	AVG
1 Bill Hillenbrand, Indiana	23	481	20.9

SCORING	TDS	XPT	FG	PTS
4 Gene Fekete, Ohio State	10	29	1	92
5 Paul Sarringhaus, Ohio State	13	0	0	78

TEAM

RUSHING OFFENSE	G	ATT	YDS	AVG	YPG
3 Ohio State	10	571	2,833	5.0	283.3

TOTAL OFFENSE	G	P	YDS	AVG	PG
4 Ohio State	10	680	3,975	5.8	397.5
9 Indiana	10	620	3,301	5.3	330.1

RUSHING DEFENSE	G	ATT	YDS	AVG	YPG
9 Minnesota	9	320	762	2.4	84.7

PASSING DEFENSE	G	ATT	COM	PCT	YPC	INT	I%	YDS	YPA	YPG
4 Penn State*	8	93	32	34.4	12.2	11	11.8	389	4.2	48.6

TOTAL DEFENSE	G	P	YDS	AVG	PG
7 Minnesota	9	437	1,314	3.0	146.0

*Independent or other conference affiliation

1943

FINAL POLL

AP	TEAM	RECORD
1	Notre Dame	9-1-0
2	Iowa Pre-Flight	9-1-0
3	**Michigan**	8-1-0
4	Navy	8-1-0
5	**Purdue**	9-0-0
6	Great Lakes NAS	10-2-0
7	Duke	8-1-0
8	Del Monte Pre-Flight	7-1-0
9	**Northwestern**	6-2-0
10	March Field	9-1-0
11	Army	7-2-1
12	Washington	4-1-0
13	Georgia Tech	8-3-0
14	Texas	7-1-1
15	Tulsa	6-1-1
16	Dartmouth	6-1-0
17	Bainbridge NTS	7-0-0
18	Colorado College	7-0-0
19	College of Pacific	7-2-0
20	Pennsylvania	6-2-1

CONFERENCE STANDINGS

Conferences played an abbreviated schedule due to World War II

	CONFERENCE			OVERALL		
	W	L	T	W	L	T
Ohio State	5	1	0	9	1	0
Purdue	6	0	0	9	0	0
Michigan	6	0	0	8	1	0
Northwestern	5	1	0	6	2	0
Indiana	2	3	1	4	4	2
Minnesota	2	3	0	5	4	0
Illinois	2	4	0	3	7	0
Ohio State	1	4	0	3	6	0
Wisconsin	1	6	0	1	9	0
Iowa	0	4	1	1	6	1

Penn State*				5	3	1

Michigan State suspended play due to World War II

CONSENSUS ALL-AMERICANS

POS	Name	HT	WT	School	AA	AP	CM	FN	IN	LK	SN	UP
B	**Bill Daley**	6-2	206	Michigan	•	•	•	•	•	•	•	•
G	**Alex Agase**	5-10	190	Purdue			•	•	•	•	•	•

OTHERS RECEIVING FIRST-TEAM HONORS

POS	Name	School								
HB	Otto Graham	Northwestern	•	•						
B	Tony Butkovich	Purdue							•	•
E	Pete Pihos	Indiana	•		•		•			
E	Herb Hein	Northwestern								•
T	Merv Pregulman	Michigan			*	•		•	•	

ALL-CONFERENCE TEAM

POS	Name	School
QB	Bob Hoernschemeyer	Indiana
HB	Otto Graham	Northwestern
HB-FB	Bob Wiese	Michigan
HB-FB	Bill Daley	Michigan
FB	Tony Butkovich	Purdue
C	Fred Negus	Michigan
G	Dick Barwegan	Purdue
G	Alex Agase	Purdue
E-QB	Pete Pihos	Indiana
E	Herb Hein	Northwestern
T	Paul Mitchell	Minnesota
T	Bill Willis	Ohio State

HEISMAN TROPHY VOTING

	PLAYER	POS	SCHOOL	TOTAL
3	**Otto Graham**	HB	Northwestern	140
7	**Bill Dailey**	FB	Michigan	71
8	**Tony Butkovich**	FB	Purdue	65

NCAA STATISTICAL LEADERS

INDIVIDUAL

PASSING/COMPLETIONS	G	ATT	COM	PCT	INT	I%	YDS	YDA	COM.PG
2 Bob Hoernschemeyer, Indiana	10	154	69	44.8	15	9.7	1133	7.4	6.9

RUSHING/YARDS				G	ATT	YDS	AVG	YPC
3 Tony Butkovich, Purdue				9	142	833	5.9	92.6
4 Bill Daley, Michigan				9	120	817	6.8	90.8
6 Eddie Bray, Illinois				10	117	739	6.3	73.9
8 Ernie Parks, Ohio State				9	161	693	4.3	77.0
9 Dean Sensanbaugher, Ohio State				9	150	677	4.5	75.2

RUSHING/YARDS PER CARRY				G	ATT	YDS	YPC
1 Bill Daley, Michigan				9	120	817	6.8
3 Eddie Bray, Illinois				10	117	739	6.3
5 Tony Butkovich, Purdue				9	142	833	5.9
9 Dean Sensanbaugher, Ohio State				9	150	677	4.5
10 Ernie Parks, Ohio State				9	161	693	4.3

Based on top 10 rushers

RECEIVING/RECEPTIONS	G	REC	YDS	YPR	YPG	RPG
3 Pete Pihos, Indiana	10	20	241	12.1	24.1	2.0

SCORING	TDS	XPT	FG	PTS
2 Tony Butkovich, Purdue	16	0	0	96
7 Charles Avery, Minnesota	12	0	0	72
9 Elroy Hirsch, Michigan	11	2	0	68

TEAM

RUSHING OFFENSE				G	ATT	YDS	AVG	YPG
4 Michigan				9	508	2648	5.2	294.2
8 Minnesota				9	410	2202	5.4	244.7

PASSING OFFENSE/YPG	G	ATT	COM	INT	PCT	YDS	YPA	YPG	I%	YPC
6 Indiana	10	168	76	16	45.2	1241	7.4	124.1	9.5	16.3

TOTAL OFFENSE				G	P	YDS	AVG	PG
4 Michigan				9	582	3269	5.6	363.2

RUSHING DEFENSE				G	ATT	YDS	AVG	YPG
3 Penn State*				9	312	505	1.6	56.1

PASSING DEFENSE		G	ATT	COM	PCT	YPC	YDS	YPA	YPG
5 Northwestern		8	67	28	41.8	14.8	415	6.2	51.9
6 Indiana		10	103	39	37.9	14.2	555	5.4	55.5
7 Purdue		9	113	38	33.6	13.5	514	4.5	57.1
8 Wisconsin		9	72	29	40.3	18.0	523	7.3	58.1

TOTAL DEFENSE				G	P	YDS	AVG	PG
3 Penn State*				9	439	1176	2.7	130.7
10 Michigan				8	460	1313	2.9	164.1

1944

FINAL POLL

AP	TEAM	RECORD
1	Army	9-0-0
2	**Ohio State**	9-0-0
3	Randolph Field	12-0-0
4	Navy	6-3-0
5	Bainbridge NTS	9-0-0
6	Iowa Pre-Flight	10-1-0
7	USC	8-0-2
8	**Michigan**	8-2-0
9	Notre Dame	8-2-0
10	4th Air Force	7-0-2
11	Duke	6-4-0
12	Tennessee	7-1-1
13	Georgia Tech	8-3-0
14	Norman NAS	6-0-0
15	**Illinois**	5-4-1
16	El Toro, CA, Marines	7-1-0
17	Great Lakes NAS	9-2-1
18	Fort Pierce	9-0-0
19	St. Mary's Pre-Flight	4-4-0
20	2nd Air Force	10-4-1

CONFERENCE STANDINGS

	CONFERENCE			OVERALL		
	W	L	T	W	L	T
Ohio State	6	0	0	9	0	0
Michigan	5	2	0	8	2	0
Purdue	4	2	0	5	5	0
Minnesota	3	2	1	5	3	1
Indiana	4	3	0	7	3	0
Illinois	3	3	0	5	4	1
Wisconsin	2	4	0	3	6	0
Northwestern	0	5	1	1	7	1
Iowa	0	6	0	1	7	0
Michigan State*				6	1	0
Penn State*				6	3	0

CONSENSUS ALL-AMERICANS

POS	Name	HT	WT	School	AA	AP	CM	FN	FW	IN	LK	NE	SN	UP
B	Les Horvath	5-10	167	Ohio State	•	•	•	•	•	•	•	•	•	•
E	Jack Dugger	6-3	210	Ohio State	•				•	•			•	•
G	Bill Hackett	5-9	191	Ohio State	•	•	•	•	•					
C	John Tavener	6-0	220	Indiana					•	•	•	•	•	

	OTHERS RECEIVING FIRST-TEAM HONORS											
B	Boris Dimancheff	Purdue							•				
B	Buddy Young	Illinois								•			
B	Earl Girard	Wisconsin								•			
T	Bill Willis	Ohio State									•		•
G	Ralph Serpico	Illinois								•			

ALL-CONFERENCE TEAM

POS	Name	School
QB	Joe Ponsetto	Michigan
QB-HB	Les Horvath	Ohio State
HB	Claude "Buddy" Young	Illinois
HB-FB	Bob Wiese	Michigan
HB-FB	Boris Dimancheff	Purdue
C	John Tavener	Indiana
G	Ralph Serpico	Illinois
G	Bill Hackett	Ohio State
G	Dick Barwegan	Purdue
E	Jack Dugger	Ohio State
E	Frank Bauman	Purdue
T	Milan Lazetich	Michigan
T	Bill Willis	Ohio State

HEISMAN TROPHY VOTING

	PLAYER	POS	SCHOOL	TOTAL
1	**Les Horvath**	QB	Ohio State	412
5	**Buddy Young**	HB	Illinois	105

NCAA STATISTICAL LEADERS

INDIVIDUAL

	PASSING/COMPLETIONS	G	ATT	COM	PCT	INT	I%	YDS	YPA	COM.PG
9	John Yungwirth, Northwestern	9	99	48	48.5	11	11.1	613	6.2	5.3

	ALL-PURPOSE YARDS	G	RUSH	REC	INT	PR	KR	YDS	YPG
1	Wayne "Red" Williams, Minnesota	9	911	0	0	242	314	1,467	163.0

	RUSHING/YARDS			G	ATT	YDS	AVG	YPG
1	Wayne "Red" Williams, Minnesota			9	136	911	6.7	101.2
2	Les Horvath, Ohio State			9	163	905	5.6	100.6
5	Buddy Young, Illinois			10	94	840	8.9	84.0
6	Boris Dimancheff, Purdue			10	175	830	4.7	83.0
7	Paul Patterson, Illinois			10	131	790	6.0	79.0

	RUSHING/YARDS PER CARRY			G	ATT	YDS	YPC
2	Buddy Young, Illinois			10	94	840	8.9
4	Wayne "Red" Williams, Minnesota			9	136	911	6.7
7	Paul Patterson, Illinois			10	131	790	6.0

Based on top 20 rushers

	RECEIVING/RECEPTIONS	G	REC	YDS	YPR	YPG	RPG
5	Abe Addams, Indiana	9	21	332	15.8	36.9	2.3

	PUNTING	PUNT	YDS	AVG
2	Bob Wiese, Michigan	24	988	41.2
3	Jack Breslin, Michigan State*	20	816	40.8

	PUNT RETURNS/YARDS	PUNT	YDS	AVG
2	Elwood Petchel, Penn State*	22	328	14.9

	SCORING	TDS	XPT	FG	PTS
4	Buddy Young, Illinois	13	0	0	78
7	Boris Dimancheff, Purdue	12	0	0	72
7	Les Horvath, Ohio State	12	0	0	72

TEAM

	RUSHING OFFENSE	G	ATT	YDS	AVG	YPG
3	Illinois	10	449	2,940	6.5	294.0
5	Ohio State	9	542	2,506	4.6	278.4
7	Minnesota	9	452	2,381	5.3	264.6
9	Michigan	10	528	2,541	4.8	254.1

	TOTAL OFFENSE	G	P	YDS	AVG	YPG
5	Ohio State	9	635	3,264	5.1	362.7
6	Illinois	10	521	3,559	6.8	355.9

	RUSHING DEFENSE	G	ATT	YDS	AVG	YPG
10	Michigan State*	6	220	532	2.4	88.7

	PASSING DEFENSE	G	ATT	COM	PCT	YPC	INT	I%	YDS	YPA	YPG
1	Michigan State*	6	66	14	21.2	11.4	12	18.2	160	2.4	26.7
6	Northwestern	9	90	32	35.6	14.4	9	10.0	462	5.1	51.3

	TOTAL DEFENSE	G	P	YDS	AVG	YPG
3	Michigan State*	6	286	692	2.4	115.3

*Independent or other conference affiliation

1945

FINAL POLL

AP	TEAM	RECORD
1	Army	9-0-0
2	Navy	7-1-1
3	Alabama	10-0-0
4	Indiana	9-0-1
5	Oklahoma State	9-0-0
6	Michigan	7-3-0
7	Saint Mary's-Cal	6-2-0
8	Pennsylvania	6-2-0
9	Notre Dame	7-2-1
10	Texas	10-1-0
11	USC	7-4-0
12	Ohio State	7-2-0
13	Duke	6-2-0
14	Tennessee	8-1-0
15	LSU	7-2-0
16	Holy Cross	8-2-0
17	Tulsa	8-3-0
18	Georgia	9-2-0
19	Wake Forest	5-3-1
20	Columbia	8-1-0

CONFERENCE STANDINGS

Conferences played an abbreviated schedule due to World War II

	CONFERENCE			OVERALL		
	W	L	T	W	L	T
Indiana	5	0	1	9	0	1
Michigan	5	1	0	7	3	0
Ohio State	5	2	0	7	2	0
Purdue	3	3	0	7	3	0
Northwestern	3	3	1	4	4	1
Wisconsin	2	3	1	3	4	2
Illinois	1	4	1	2	6	1
Minnesota	1	5	0	4	5	0
Iowa	1	5	0	2	7	0
Penn State*				5	3	0
Michigan State*				5	3	1

CONSENSUS ALL-AMERICANS

POS	Name	HT	WT	School	AA	AP	CM	FC	FW	IN	LK	NE	SN	UP
E	Bob Ravensberg	6-1	180	Indiana				•		•		•		•
E	Max Morris	6-2	195	Northwestern	•			•		•				
G	Warren Amling	6-0	197	Ohio State	•	•	•	•	•	•	•		•	•

Others receiving first-team honors

T	Tom Hughes		Purdue		•

HEISMAN TROPHY VOTING

	PLAYER	POS	SCHOOL	TOTAL
7	Warren Amling	G	Ohio State	42
8	Pete Pihos	E-QB	Indiana	38

ALL-CONFERENCE TEAM

POS	Name	School
HB	George Taliaferro	Indiana
HB	Edward Cody	Purdue
FB	Ollie Cline	Ohio State
C	Harold Watts	Michigan
G	James Lecture	Northwestern
G	Dick Barwegan	Purdue
G-T	Warren Amling	Ohio State
E-QB	Pete Pihos	Indiana
E	Ted Kluszewski	Indiana
E	Max Morris	Northwestern
T	Russell Thomas	Ohio State
T	Tom Hughes	Purdue
T	Clarence Esser	Wisconsin

NCAA STATISTICAL LEADERS

INDIVIDUAL

PASSING/COMPLETIONS	G	ATT	COM	PCT	INT	I%	YDS	YPA	COM.PG
3 Jerry Niles, Iowa	9	179	63	35.2	15	8.4	872	4.9	7.0
8 Bob DeMoss, Purdue	10	117	55	47.0	12	10.3	742	6.3	5.5
9 Russell Reader, Michigan State*	9	90	53	58.9	5	5.6	613	6.8	5.9

RUSHING/YARDS				G	ATT	YDS	AVG	YPG
3 Ollie Cline, Ohio State				9	171	931	5.4	103.4
5 Ed Cody, Purdue				10	157	847	5.4	84.7
7 George Taliaferro, Indiana				10	156	728	4.7	72.8

RUSHING/YARDS PER CARRY			G	ATT	YDS	YPC
10 Dick Conners, Northwestern			9	116	671	5.8
Based on top 20 rushers						

RECEIVING/RECEPTIONS			G	REC	YDS	YPR	YPG	RPG
1 Steve Contos, Michigan State*			9	31	285	9.2	31.7	3.4
5 Bill Canfield, Purdue			10	23	314	13.7	31.4	2.3

PUNTING			PUNT	YDS	AVG
3 Floyd Lang, Penn State*			22	893	40.6

PUNT RETURNS/YARDS			PUNT	YDS	AVG
2 Elwood Petchel, Penn State*			22	328	14.9

SCORING			TDS	XPT	FG	PTS
6 Ed Cody, Purdue			12	0	0	72

TEAM

RUSHING OFFENSE			G	ATT	YDS	AVG	YPG
8 Ohio State			9	505	2,133	4.2	237.0
10 Indiana			10	484	2,331	4.8	233.1

TOTAL OFFENSE			G	P	YDS	AVG	YPG
9 Indiana			10	619	3,254	5.3	325.4

RUSHING DEFENSE			G	ATT	YDS	AVG	YPG
5 Penn State*			8	295	634	2.1	79.3

PASSING DEFENSE	G	ATT	COM	PCT	YPC	INT	I%	YDS	YPA	YPG
4 Iowa	9	83	32	38.6	13.5			433	5.2	48.1
7 Michigan State*	9	99	34	34.3	14.6			497	5.0	55.2
9 Illinois	9	118	34	28.8	15.2			518	4.4	57.6

TOTAL DEFENSE			G	P	YDS	AVG	YPG
9 Indiana			10	536	1641	3.1	164.1

1946

FINAL POLL

AP	TEAM	RECORD
1	Notre Dame	8-0-1
2	Army	9-0-1
3	Georgia	11-0-0
4	UCLA	10-1-0
5	Illinois	8-2-0
6	Michigan	6-2-1
7	Tennessee	9-2-0
8	LSU	9-1-1
9	North Carolina	8-2-1
10	Rice	9-2-0
11	Georgia Tech	9-2-0
12	Yale	7-1-1
13	Pennsylvania	6-2-0
14	Oklahoma	8-3-0
15	Texas	8-2-0
16	Arkansas	6-3-2
17	Tulsa	9-1-0
18	North Carolina St.	8-3-0
19	Delaware	10-0-0
20	Indiana	6-3-0

CONFERENCE STANDINGS

	CONFERENCE			OVERALL		
	W	L	T	W	L	T
Illinois	6	1	0	8	2	0
Michigan	5	1	1	6	2	1
Indiana	4	2	0	6	3	0
Iowa	3	3	0	5	4	0
Minnesota	3	4	0	5	4	0
Ohio State	2	3	1	4	3	2
Northwestern	2	3	1	4	4	1
Wisconsin	2	5	0	4	5	0
Purdue	0	5	1	2	6	1
Penn State*				6	2	0
Michigan State*				5	5	0

BOWL GAMES

DATE	GAME	SCORE
J1	Rose	Illinois 45, UCLA 14

CONSENSUS ALL-AMERICANS

POS	Name	HT	WT	School	AA	AP	CM	FC	FW	IN	NE	SN	UP
T	Warren Amling	6-0	197	Ohio State					*	•	•	•	•
G	Alex Agase	5-10	191	Illinois	•	•		•		•	•	•	•

OTHERS RECEIVING FIRST-TEAM HONORS

E	Elmer Madar			Michigan		•							

ALL-CONFERENCE TEAM

POS	Name	School
QB	Ben Raimondi	Indiana
HB	Bob Chappuis	Michigan
HB	Vic Schwall	Northwestern
FB	Lester "Dick" Hoerner	Iowa
C	John Cannady	Indiana
G	Alex Agase	Illinois
G	Dick Barwegan	Purdue
G-T	Warren Amling	Ohio State
E	Elmer Madar	Michigan
E	Cecil Souders	Ohio State
T	Russell Deal	Indiana

NCAA STATISTICAL LEADERS

INDIVIDUAL

PASSING/COMPLETIONS	G	ATT	COM	PCT	INT	I%	YDS	YPA	TD	TD%	COM.PG
3 Ben Raimondi, Indiana	9	138	74	53.6	8	5.8	956	6.9	7	5.1	8.2
9 Bob DeMoss, Purdue	8	122	59	48.4	9	7.4	814	6.7	6	4.9	7.4

RUSHING/YARDS PER CARRY								G	ATT	YDS	YPC
4 George Guerre, Michigan State*								10	90	633	7.0

Based on top 20 rushers

RECEIVING/RECEPTIONS			G	REC	YDS	YPR	YPG	RPG
9 Lou Mihajlovich, Indiana			9	25	300	12.0	33.3	2.8

PUNTING						PUNT	YDS	AVG
1 John Galvin, Purdue						30	1,286	42.9

TEAM

PASSING OFFENSE/YPG	G	ATT	COM	INT	PCT	YDS	YPA	TD	YPG	I%	YPC
5 Michigan	9	162	73	22	45.1	1,322	8.2	10	146.9	13.6	18.1
7 Indiana	9	185	95	15	51.4	1,264	6.8	8	140.4	8.1	13.3

TOTAL OFFENSE					G	P	YDS	AVG	YPG
6 Michigan					9	579	3166	5.5	351.8

PASSING DEFENSE			G	ATT	COM	PCT	YPC	YDS	YPA	YPG
4 Indiana			9	127	39	30.7	13.8	538	4.2	59.8
8 Penn State*			8	133	46	34.6	11.1	509	3.8	63.6

TOTAL DEFENSE					G	P	YDS	AVG	YPG
3 Penn State*					8	454	1,271	2.8	158.9

1947

FINAL POLL

AP	TEAM	RECORD
1	Notre Dame	9-0-0
2	**Michigan**	10-0-0
3	SMU	9-0-2
4	**Penn State***	9-0-1
5	Texas	10-1-0
6	Alabama	8-3-0
7	Pennsylvania	7-0-1
8	USC	7-2-1
9	North Carolina	8-2-0
10	Georgia Tech	10-1-0
11	Army	5-2-2
12	Kansas	8-1-2
13	Mississippi	9-2-0
14	William & Mary	9-2-0
15	California	9-1-0
16	Oklahoma	7-2-1
17	North Carolina St.	5-3-1
18	Rice	6-3-1
19	Duke	4-3-2
20	Columbia	7-2-0

BOWL GAMES

DATE	GAME	SCORE
J1	**Rose**	Michigan 49, USC 0
J1	**Cotton**	Penn State* 13, SMU 13

CONFERENCE STANDINGS

	CONFERENCE			OVERALL		
	W	L	T	W	L	T
Michigan	6	0	0	10	0	0
Wisconsin	3	2	1	5	3	1
Minnesota	3	3	0	6	3	0
Illinois	3	3	0	5	3	1
Purdue	3	3	0	5	4	0
Indiana	2	3	1	5	3	1
Iowa	2	3	1	3	5	1
Northwestern	2	4	0	3	6	0
Ohio State	1	4	1	2	6	1
Penn State*				9	0	1
Michigan State*				7	2	0

CONSENSUS ALL-AMERICANS

POS	Name	HT	WT	School	AP	CM	FC	FW	IN	NE	SN	UP
B	**Bob Chappuis**	6-0	180	Michigan	•	•	•	•	•	•	•	•

	OTHERS RECEIVING FIRST-TEAM HONORS		
B	Bump Elliott	Michigan	•
G	Steve Suhey	Penn State* • • •

ALL-CONFERENCE TEAM

POS	Name	School
HB	Bob Chappuis	Michigan
C-E	Bob "Red" Wilson	Wisconsin
G	Howard Brown	Indiana
G	Leo Nomellini	Minnesota
E	Ike Owens	Illinois
E	Bob Mann	Michigan
T	Lou Agase	Illinois
T	Phil O'Reilly	Purdue
B	Russ Steger	Illinois
B	Chalmers Elliott	Michigan
B	Howard Yerges	Michigan

HEISMAN TROPHY VOTING

PLAYER	POS	SCHOOL	TOTAL
2 **Bob Chappuis**	HB	Michigan	555

NCAA STATISTICAL LEADERS

INDIVIDUAL

PASSING/COMPLETIONS	G	ATT	COM	PCT	INT	I%	YDS	YPA	TD	TD%COM.PG
7 Perry Moss, Illinois	9	127	71	59.9	7	5.5	719	5.7	5	3.9 7.9

RUSHING/YARDS				G	ATT	YDS	AVG	YPG
4 Harry Szulborski, Purdue				9	136	851	6.3	94.6

RUSHING/YARDS PER CARRY				G	ATT	YDS	YPC
5 Jack Weisenburger, Michigan				9	101	682	6.8
7 Harry Szulborski, Purdue				9	136	851	6.3

Based on top 20 rushers

RECEIVING/RECEPTIONS	G	REC	YDS	TD	YPR	YPG	RPG
10 Lou Mihajlovich, Indiana	9	26	349	2	13.4	38.8	2.9

TEAM

RUSHING OFFENSE							G	ATT	YDS	AVG	YPG
2 Penn State*							9	527	2713	5.1	301.4
10 Michigan							9	429	2149	5.0	238.8

PASSING OFFENSE/YPG	G	ATT	COM	INT	PCT	YDS	YPA	TD	YPG	I%	YPC
1 Michigan	9	153	77	16	50.3	1565	10.2	15	173.9	10.5	20.3
3 Indiana	9	164	83	17	50.6	1393	8.5	10	154.8	10.4	16.8

TOTAL OFFENSE							G	P	YDS	AVG	YPG
1 Michigan							9	582	3714	6.4	412.7
4 Penn State*							9	606	3275	5.4	363.9

RUSHING DEFENSE							G	ATT	YDS	AVG	YPG
1 Penn State*							9	240	153	0.6	17.0

PASSING DEFENSE	G	ATT	COM	PCT	YPC	INT	I%	YDS	YPA	TD	YPG
7 Penn State*	9	147	40	27.2	13.5	22	15.0	538	3.7	2	59.8

TOTAL DEFENSE							G	P	YDS	AVG	YPG
1 Penn State*							9	387	691	1.8	76.8

SCORING OFFENSE								G	PTS	AVG
1 Michigan								9	345	38.3
2 Penn State*								9	319	35.4

SCORING DEFENSE								G	PTS	AVG
1 Penn State*								9	27	3.0
5 Michigan								9	53	5.9

1948

FINAL POLL

AP	TEAM	RECORD
1	**Michigan**	9-0-0
2	Notre Dame	9-0-1
3	North Carolina	9-1-1
4	California	10-1-0
5	Oklahoma	10-1-0
6	Army	8-0-1
7	**Northwestern**	8-2-0
8	Georgia	9-2-0
9	Oregon	9-2-0
10	SMU	9-1-1
11	Clemson	11-0-0
12	Vanderbilt	8-2-1
13	Tulane	9-1-0
14	**Michigan State***	6-2-2
15	Mississippi	8-1-0
16	**Minnesota**	7-2-0
17	William & Mary	7-2-2
18	**Penn State***	7-1-1
19	Cornell	8-1-0
20	Wake Forest	6-4-0

CONFERENCE STANDINGS

	CONFERENCE			OVERALL		
	W	L	T	W	L	T
Michigan	6	0	0	9	0	0
Northwestern	5	1	0	8	2	0
Minnesota	5	2	0	7	2	0
Ohio State	3	3	0	6	3	0
Iowa	2	4	0	4	5	0
Purdue	2	4	0	3	6	0
Indiana	2	4	0	2	7	0
Illinois	2	5	0	3	6	0
Wisconsin	1	5	0	2	7	0
Penn State*				7	1	1
Michigan State*				6	2	2

BOWL GAMES

DATE	GAME	SCORE
J1	**Rose**	Northwestern 20, California 14

CONSENSUS ALL-AMERICANS

POS	Name	HT	WT	School	AA	AP	FC	FW	IN	NE	SN	UP
E	**Dick Rifenburg**	6-3	197	Michigan	•	•	•		•	•	•	•
T	**Leo Nomellini**	6-2	248	Minnesota	•	•	•	•	•	•	•	•
T	**Alvin Wistert**	6-3	218	Michigan	•		•				•	•

	OTHERS RECEIVING FIRST-TEAM HONORS		
B	Art Murakowski	Northwestern	•
B	Pete Elliott	Michigan	•
B	George Taliaferro	Indiana	•
E	Sam Tamburo	Penn State*	• •
C	Alex Sarkisian	Northwestern	•

IN named Nomellini as a G

ALL-CONFERENCE TEAM

POS	Name	School
C	Alex Sarkisian	Northwestern
G	Dominic Tomasi	Michigan
G	Leo Nomellini	Minnesota
E	Rick Rifenburg	Michigan
E	Harry Grant	Minnesota
T	Bill Kay	Iowa
T	Alvin Wistert	Michigan
B	George Taliaferro	Indiana
B	Pete Elliott	Michigan
B	Art Murakowski	Northwestern
B	Harry Szulborski	Purdue

NCAA STATISTICAL LEADERS

INDIVIDUAL

RUSHING/YARDS		G	ATT	YDS	AVG	YPG
4	Harry Szulborski, Purdue	9	183	989	5.4	109.9

PUNTING		PUNT	YDS	AVG
3	Dike Eddleman, Illinois	59	2,531	42.9
7	George Taliaferro, Indiana	55	2,233	40.6

TEAM

RUSHING OFFENSE		G	ATT	YDS	AVG	YPG
4	Michigan State*	10	498	3,041	6.1	304.1

PASSING OFFENSE		G	ATT	COM	YPC	PCT	YDS	YPA	TD	YPG
6	Michigan	9	168	77	17.6	45.8	1,355	8.1	16	150.6
9	Minnesota	9	168	79	16.2	47.0	1,283	7.6	9	142.6

TOTAL OFFENSE		G	P	YDS	AVG	YPG
4	Michigan State*	10	627	4,027	6.4	402.7

RUSHING DEFENSE		G	ATT	YDS	AVG	YPG
2	Penn State*	9	311	750	2.4	83.3
3	Minnesota	9	312	786	2.5	87.3
4	Michigan	9	373	789	2.1	87.7

PASSING DEFENSE		G	ATT	COM	PCT	YPC	YDS	YPG	TD	YPG
1	Northwestern	9	129	42	32.6	11.6	487	3.8	2	54.1

TOTAL DEFENSE		G	P	YDS	AVG	YPG
2	Penn State*	9	454	1,424	3.1	158.2
7	Minnesota	9	481	1,674	3.5	186.0

SCORING OFFENSE		G	PTS	AVG
2	Michigan State*	10	359	35.9

SCORING DEFENSE		G	PTS	AVG
1	Michigan	9	44	4.9
4	Penn State*	9	55	6.1

*Independent or other conference affiliation

1949

FINAL POLL

AP	TEAM	RECORD
1	Notre Dame	10-0-0
2	Oklahoma	11-0-0
3	California	10-1-0
4	Army	9-0-0
5	Rice	10-1-0
6	**Ohio State**	7-1-2
7	**Michigan**	6-2-1
8	**Minnesota**	7-2-0
9	LSU	8-3-0
10	College of Pacific	10-0-0
11	Kentucky	9-3-0
12	Cornell	8-1-0
13	Villanova	8-1-0
14	Maryland	9-1-0
15	Santa Clara	8-2-1
16	North Carolina	7-4-0
17	Tennessee	7-2-1
18	Princeton	6-3-0
19	**Michigan State***	6-3-0
20	Baylor	8-2-0
20	Missouri	7-4-0

CONFERENCE STANDINGS

	CONFERENCE			OVERALL		
	W	L	T	W	L	T
Ohio State	4	1	1	7	1	2
Michigan	4	1	1	6	2	1
Minnesota	4	2	0	7	2	0
Wisconsin	3	2	1	5	3	1
Illinois	3	3	1	3	4	2
Iowa	3	3	0	4	5	0
Northwestern	3	4	0	4	5	0
Purdue	2	4	0	4	5	0
Indiana	0	6	0	1	8	0

Michigan State*				6	3	0
Penn State*				5	4	0

BOWL GAMES

DATE	GAME	SCORE
J2	**Rose**	Ohio State 17, California 14

CONSENSUS ALL-AMERICANS

POS	Name	HT	WT	School	AA	AP	FC	FW	IN	NE	SN	UP
T	**Leo Nomellini**	6-2	255	Minnesota	•	•			•		•	•
T	**Alvin Wistert**	6-3	223	Michigan	•				•		•	•
G	**Ed Bagdon**	5-10	200	Michigan State*			•			•	•	•
C	**Clayton Tonnemaker**	6-3	240	Minnesota	•	•	•	•		•	•	•

OTHERS RECEIVING FIRST-TEAM HONORS

POS	Name	School			
B	Lynn Chandnois	Michigan State*		•	•
T	Allen Wahl	Michigan		•	•

ALL-CONFERENCE TEAM

POS	Name	School
C	Clayton Tonnemaker	Minnesota
C-E	Bob "Red" Wilson	Wisconsin
G	Lloyd Heneveld	Michigan
G	Leo Nomellini	Minnesota
G	Jack Lininger	Ohio State
E	Harry Grant	Minnesota
T	Alvin Wistert	Michigan
B	Johnny Karras	Illinois
B	Charles Ortmann	Michigan
B	Don Burson	Northwestern
B	Gerry Krall	Ohio State

HEISMAN TROPHY VOTING

PLAYER	POS	SCHOOL	TOTAL
7 **Clayton Tonnemaker**	C	Minnesota	81

AWARD WINNERS

PLAYER	POS	SCHOOL	AWARD
Ed Bagdon	G	Michigan State*	Outland

NCAA STATISTICAL LEADERS

INDIVIDUAL

RUSHING/YARDS

		G	ATT	YDS	AVG	YPG
7	**Lynn Chandnois, Michigan State***	9	129	885	6.9	98.3

RUSHING/YARDS PER CARRY

		G	ATT	YDS	YPC
2	**Lynn Chandnois, Michigan State***	9	129	885	6.9
6	**John Karras, Illinois**	9	127	826	6.5

Based on top 20 rushers

INTERCEPTIONS

		INT	YDS
2	**Charles Lentz, Michigan**	9	NA

TEAM

RUSHING OFFENSE

		G	ATT	YDS	AVG	YPG
7	**Illinois**	9	484	2460	5.1	273.3

RUSHING DEFENSE

		G	ATT	YDS	AVG	YPG
3	**Minnesota**	9	349	742	2.1	82.4

PASSING DEFENSE

		G	ATT	COM	PCT	YPC	INT	I%	YDS	YPA	TD	YPG
4	**Purdue**	9	106	41	38.7	13.5	5	4.7	553	5.2	7	61.4

TOTAL DEFENSE

		G	P	YDS	AVG	YPG
8	**Minnesota**	9	570	1940	3.4	215.6

SCORING OFFENSE

		G	PTS	AVG
6	**Michigan State***	9	309	34.3

SCORING DEFENSE

		G	PTS	AVG
10	**Minnesota**	9	80	8.9

BIG TEN ANNUAL REVIEW & BOWLS

1950

FINAL POLL

UP	AP	TEAM	RECORD
1	1	Oklahoma	10-1-0
2	2	Army	8-1-0
4	3	Texas	9-2-0
5	4	Tennessee	11-1-0
3	5	California	9-1-1
6	6	Princeton	9-0-0
7	7	Kentucky	11-1-0
8	8	Michigan State*	8-1-0
9	9	Michigan	6-3-1
10	10	Clemson	9-0-1
13	11	Washington	8-2-0
14	12	Wyoming	10-0-0
12	13	Illinois	7-2-0
11	14	Ohio State	6-3-0
16	15	Miami, Fla.	9-1-1
16	16	Alabama	9-2-0
18	17	Nebraska	6-2-1
	18	Tulsa	9-1-1
	18	Washington & Lee	8-3-0
20	20	Tulane	6-2-1
15		SMU	6-4-0
19		Stanford	5-3-2

CONFERENCE STANDINGS

	CONFERENCE			OVERALL		
	W	L	T	W	L	T
Michigan	4	1	1	6	3	1
Ohio State	5	2	0	6	3	0
Wisconsin	5	2	0	6	3	0
Illinois	4	2	0	7	2	0
Northwestern	3	3	0	6	3	0
Iowa	2	4	0	3	5	1
Minnesota	1	4	1	1	7	1
Indiana	1	4	0	3	5	1
Purdue	1	4	0	2	7	0
Michigan State*				8	1	0
Penn State*				5	3	1

BOWL GAMES

DATE	GAME	SCORE
J1	Rose	Michigan 14, California 6

CONSENSUS ALL-AMERICANS

POS	Name	HT	WT	School	AA	AP	FC	FW	IN	NE	SN	UP
B	Vic Janowicz	5-9	189	Ohio State	•	•	•	•	•	•	•	•

Others receiving first-team honors

POS	Name	School	AA	AP	FC	FW	IN	NE	SN	UP
B	Everett Grandelius	Michigan State*		•			•			
B	Ed Withers	Wisconsin					•			
E	Don Stonesifer	Northwestern		•			•			
T	Allen Wahl	Michigan	•		•					
C	Bob McCullough	Ohio State		•						
C	Bill Vohaska	Illinois		•						

ALL-CONFERENCE TEAM

POS	Name	School
B	Dick Raklovits	Illinois
B	Bill Reichardt	Iowa
B	Don Dufek	Michigan
B	Charles Ortmann	Michigan
B	Vic Janowicz	Ohio State
C	Bill Vohaska	Illinois
G	Chuck Brown	Illinois
G	John Biltz	Ohio State
E	Tony Klimek	Illinois
E	Don Stonesifer	Northwestern
T	Al Wahl	Michigan
T	Bill Trautwein	Ohio State

HEISMAN TROPHY VOTING

	PLAYER	POS	SCHOOL	TOTAL
1	Vic Janowicz	HB	Ohio State	633

NCAA STATISTICAL LEADERS

INDIVIDUAL

RUSHING/YARDS		G	ATT	YDS	AVG	YPC
7	Everett Grandelius, Michigan State*	9	163	1,023	6.3	113.7

RECEIVING/RECEPTIONS		G	REC	YDS	TD	YPR	YPG	RPG
3	Don Stonesifer, Northwestern	9	42	560	5	13.3	62.2	4.7

PUNTING		PUNT	YDS	AVG
6	James Hammond, Wisconsin	26	1,079	41.5
10	Glenn Drahn, Iowa	56	2,296	41.0

PUNT RETURNS		PR	YDS	AVG
2	Jesse Thomas, Michigan State*	18	358	19.9

INTERCEPTIONS		INT	YDS
2	Al Brosky, Illinois	11	96

TEAM

RUSHING DEFENSE		G	ATT	YDS	AVG	YPG
1	Ohio State	9	341	576	1.7	64.0
8	Michigan State*	9	344	874	2.5	97.1

PASSING DEFENSE		G	ATT	COM	PCT	YPC	INT	I%	YDS	YPA	TD	YPG
2	Indiana	9	127	51	40.2	12.3	12	9.5	629	5.0	3	69.9
7	Penn State*	9	141	52	36.9	12.9	18	12.8	671	4.8	8	74.6

*Independent or other conference affiliation

1951

FINAL POLL

UP	AP	TEAM	RECORD
1	1	Tennessee	10-1-0
2	2	**Michigan State***	9-0-0
4	3	Maryland	10-0-0
3	4	**Illinois**	9-0-1
5	5	Georgia Tech	11-0-1
6	6	Princeton	9-0-0
7	7	Stanford	9-2-0
8	8	**Wisconsin**	7-1-1
9	9	Baylor	8-2-1
11	10	Oklahoma	8-2-0
10	11	TCU	6-5-0
12	12	California	8-2-0
	13	Virginia	8-1-0
14	14	San Francisco	9-0-0
17	15	Kentucky	8-4-0
	16	Boston U.	6-4-0
17	17	UCLA	5-3-1
14	18	Washington State	7-3-0
	19	Clemson	7-3-0
17	19	Holy Cross	8-2-0
13		Notre Dame	7-2-1
14		**Purdue**	5-4-0
20		Kansas	8-2-0

CONFERENCE STANDINGS

	CONFERENCE			OVERALL		
	W	L	T	W	L	T
Illinois	5	0	1	9	0	1
Purdue	4	1	0	5	4	0
Wisconsin	5	1	1	7	1	1
Michigan	4	2	0	4	5	0
Ohio State	2	2	2	4	3	2
Northwestern	2	4	0	5	4	0
Minnesota	1	4	1	2	6	1
Indiana	1	5	0	2	7	0
Iowa	0	5	1	2	5	2

Michigan State*				9	0	0
Penn State*				5	4	0

BOWL GAMES

DATE	GAME	SCORE
J1	**Rose**	Illinois 40, Stanford 7

CONSENSUS ALL-AMERICANS

POS	Name	HT	WT	School	AA	AP	FC	FW	IN	NE	SN	UP
B	**Johnny Karras**	5-11	171	Illinois	•	•	•	•			•	•
E	**Bob Carey**	6-5	215	Michigan St.*	•	•				•	•	•
T	**Don Coleman**	5-10	185	Michigan St.*	•	•	•	•	•	•	•	•

	OTHERS RECEIVING FIRST-TEAM HONORS											
B	Al Dorow			Michigan St.*			•					
E	Hal Faverty			Wisconsin				•				
E	Pat O'Donahue			Wisconsin					•			
T	Charles Ulrich			Illinois				•				
C	Charles Boerio			Illinois					•			

ALL-CONFERENCE TEAM

POS	Name	School
B	Johnny Karras	Illinois
B	Bill Reichardt	Iowa
B	Vic Janowicz	Ohio State
QB	John Coatta	Wisconsin
C	Chuck Boerio	Illinois
G	Charles Studley	Illinois
G	Don McRae	Northwestern
E	Lowell Perry	Michigan
E	Leo Sugar	Purdue
T	Chuck Ulrich	Illinois
T	Tom Johnson	Michigan

HEISMAN TROPHY VOTING

	PLAYER	POS	SCHOOL	1ST	2ND	3RD	TOTAL
6	**John Karras**	HB	Illinois	15	60	58	223
10	**Don Coleman**	T	Michigan State*	6	23	29	93

NCAA STATISTICAL LEADERS

INDIVIDUAL

INTERCEPTIONS		INT	YDS
3	**Alfred Brosky, Illinois**	10	183

TEAM

RUSHING OFFENSE		G	ATT	YDS	AVG	YPG
8	**Michigan State***	9	530	2,630	5.0	292.2

TOTAL OFFENSE		G	P	YDS	AVG	PG
8	**Michigan State***	9	667	3,627	5.4	403.0

RUSHING DEFENSE		G	ATT	YDS	AVG	YPG
2	**Wisconsin**	9	344	599	1.7	66.6
10	**Illinois**	9	422	1,020	2.4	113.3

PASSING DEFENSE		G	ATT	COM	PCT	YPC	INT	I%	YDS	YPA	TD	YPG
3	**Indiana**	9	128	53	41.4	13.2	14	10.9	702	5.5	8	78.0
6	**Purdue**	9	128	48	37.5	15.4	10	7.8	737	5.8	8	81.9

TOTAL DEFENSE		G	P	YDS	AVG	PG
1	**Wisconsin**	9	539	1,393	2.6	154.8
6	**Illinois**	9	552	1,954	3.5	217.1

SCORING DEFENSE		G	PTS	AVG
1	**Wisconsin**	9	53	5.9

1952

FINAL POLL

UP	AP	TEAM	RECORD
1	1	**Michigan State***	9-0-0
2	2	Georgia Tech	12-0-0
3	3	Notre Dame	7-2-1
4	4	Oklahoma	8-1-1
5	5	USC	10-1-0
6	6	UCLA	8-1-0
7	7	Mississippi	8-1-2
8	8	Tennessee	8-2-1
9	9	Alabama	10-2-0
11	10	Texas	9-2-0
10	11	**Wisconsin**	6-3-1
	12	Tulsa	8-2-1
13	11	Maryland	7-2-0
	14	Syracuse	7-3-0
	15	Florida	8-3-0
18	16	Duke	8-2-0
15	17	**Ohio State**	6-3-0
12	18	**Purdue**	4-3-2
14	19	Princeton	8-1-0
19	20	Kentucky	5-4-2
15		Pittsburgh	6-3-0
17		Navy	6-2-1
19		Houston	8-2-0

CONFERENCE STANDINGS

	CONFERENCE			OVERALL		
	W	L	T	W	L	T
Wisconsin	4	1	1	6	3	1
Purdue	4	1	1	4	3	2
Ohio State	5	2	0	6	3	0
Michigan	4	2	0	5	4	0
Minnesota	3	1	2	4	3	2
Illinois	2	5	0	4	5	0
Northwestern	2	5	0	2	6	0
Iowa	2	5	0	2	7	0
Indiana	1	5	0	2	7	0
Michigan State*				9	0	0
Penn State*				7	2	1

BOWL GAMES

DATE	GAME	SCORE
J1	**Rose**	USC 7, Wisconsin 0

CONSENSUS ALL-AMERICANS

POS	Name	HT	WT	School	AA	AP	FC	FW	IN	NE	SN	UP
E	**Bernie Flowers**	6-1	189	Purdue	•		•		•	•	•	•

OTHERS RECEIVING FIRST-TEAM HONORS

POS	Name	School								
B	Paul Giel	Minnesota		•	•					
B	Don McAuliffe	Michigan State*			•					
B	Lowell Perry	Michigan					•			
E	Joe Collier	Northwestern					•			
T	David Suminski	Wisconsin		•						
G	Mike Takacs	Ohio State					•			
C	Dick Tamburo	Michigan State*					•	•		

ALL-CONFERENCE TEAM

POS	Name	School
B	Alan Ameche	Wisconsin
B	Al Brosky	Illinois
B	Tom O'Connell	Illinois
B	Gene Gedman	Indiana
B	Bob McNamara	Minnesota
B	Fred Bruney	Ohio State
B	Paul Giel	Minnesota
C	Dick O'Shaughnessy	Michigan
C	Tony Curcillo	Ohio State
C	Walt Cudzik	Purdue
G	Bob Timm	Michigan
G	Percy Zachary	Minnesota
G	James Reichenbach	Ohio State
G	Bob Kennedy	Wisconsin
G	George O'Brien	Wisconsin
E	Frank Wodziak	Illinois
E	Bill Fenton	Iowa
E	Jot Collier	Northwestern
E	Bernie Flowers	Purdue
T	Roger Zatkoff	Michigan
T	Art Walker	Michigan
T	Ray Huzinga	Northwestern
T	George Jacoby	Ohio State
T	Fred Preziosio	Purdue
T	Dave Suminski	Wisconsin

HEISMAN TROPHY VOTING

	PLAYER	POS	SCHOOL	1ST	2ND	3RD	TOTAL
3	**Paul Giel**	TB	Minnesota	76	38	25	329
8	**Don McAuliffe**	HB	Michigan State*	26	29	28	164

NCAA STATISTICAL LEADERS

INDIVIDUAL

	PASSING/COMPLETIONS	G	ATT	COM	PCT	INT	I%	YDS	YPA	TD	TD%	COM.PG
2	Tommy O'Connell, Illinois	9	224	133	59.4	17	7.6	1,761	7.9	12	5.4	14.8
5	Johnny Borton, Ohio State	9	196	115	58.7	6	3.1	1,555	7.9	15	7.7	12.8
6	Jim Haluska, Wisconsin	9	199	112	56.3	18	9.0	1,410	7.1	12	6.0	12.4
8	Dale Samuels, Purdue	9	185	104	56.2	6	3.2	1,131	6.1	10	5.4	11.6

	RUSHING/YARDS				G	ATT	YDS	AVG	YPC
6	Alan Ameche, Wisconsin				9	205	946	4.6	105.1

	RECEIVING/RECEPTIONS			G	REC	YDS	TD	YPR	YPG	RPG
4	Rocky Ryan, Illinois			9	45	714	5	15.9	79.3	5.0
4	Rex Smith, Illinois			9	45	642	4	14.3	71.3	5.0
6	Bernie Flowers, Purdue			9	43	603	7	14.0	67.0	4.8

	INTERCEPTIONS	INT	YDS
4	Jack Sherry, Penn State*	8	101
4	Al Brosky, Illinois	8	77
4	Don Eyer, Penn State*	8	67

TEAM

	RUSHING DEFENSE	G	ATT	YDS	AVG	YPG
5	Michigan State*	9	508	2,452	4.8	272.4

	PASSING OFFENSE/YPG	G	ATT	COM	INT	PCT	YDS	YPA	TD	YPG	I%	YPC
2	Illinois	9	245	141	20	57.6	1,929	7.9	13	214.3	8.2	13.7
4	Ohio State	9	217	124	9	57.1	1,709	7.9	16	189.9	4.1	13.8
10	Wisconsin	9	211	117	19	55.5	1,476	7.0	13	164.0	9.0	12.6

	TOTAL OFFENSE	G	P	YDS	AVG	PG
3	Michigan State*	9	667	3858	5.8	428.7
6	Wisconsin	9	678	3497	5.2	388.6

	RUSHING DEFENSE	G	ATT	YDS	AVG	YPG
1	Michigan State*	9	342	755	2.2	83.9

Independent or other conference affiliation

1953

FINAL POLL

UP	AP	TEAM	RECORD
1	1	Maryland	10-1-0
2	2	Notre Dame	9-0-1
3	3	**Michigan State**	9-1-0
5	4	Oklahoma	9-1-1
4	5	UCLA	8-2-0
6	6	Rice	9-2-0
7	7	**Illinois**	7-1-1
9	8	Georgia Tech	9-2-1
10	9	**Iowa**	5-3-1
13	10	West Virginia	8-2-0
8	11	Texas	7-3-0
12	12	Texas Tech	11-1-0
11	13	Alabama	6-3-3
16	14	Army	7-1-1
14	15	**Wisconsin**	6-2-1
15	16	Kentucky	7-2-1
	17	Auburn	7-3-1
18	18	Duke	7-2-1
17	19	Stanford	6-3-1
19	20	**Michigan**	6-3-0
20		**Ohio State**	6-3-0

CONFERENCE STANDINGS

	CONFERENCE			OVERALL		
	W	L	T	W	L	T
Michigan State	5	1	0	9	1	0
Illinois	5	1	0	7	1	1
Wisconsin	4	1	1	6	2	1
Ohio State	4	3	0	6	3	0
Michigan	3	3	0	6	3	0
Iowa	3	3	0	5	3	1
Minnesota	3	3	1	4	4	1
Purdue	2	4	0	2	7	0
Indiana	1	5	0	2	7	0
Northwestern	0	6	0	3	6	0
Penn State*				6	3	0

BOWL GAMES

DATE	GAME	SCORE
J1	**Rose**	Michigan State 28, UCLA 20

CONSENSUS ALL-AMERICANS

POS	Name	HT	WT	School	AA	AP	FC	FW	IN	NE	SN	UP
B	**Paul Giel**	5-11	185	Minnesota	•	•	•	•	•	•	•	•
B	**J.C. Caroline**	6-0	184	Illinois		•	•				•	•
E	**Don Dohoney**	6-1	193	Michigan State	•	•	•		•			•

OTHERS RECEIVING FIRST-TEAM HONORS

B	Alan Ameche			Wisconsin		•		•				
E	Joe Collier			Northwestern		•						
C	Jerry Hilgenberg			Iowa		•						

ALL-CONFERENCE TEAM

POS	Name	School
B	J.C. Caroline	Illinois
B	Paul Giel	Minnesota
B	Alan Ameche	Wisconsin
C	Jerry Hilgenberg	Iowa
G	Jan Smid	Illinois
G	Calvin Jones	Iowa
G	Tom Bettis	Purdue
E	Ted Kress	Michigan
E	Bob Topp	Michigan
E	Don Dohoney	Michigan State
T	Stavros Canakes	Michigan
T	Leroy Bolden	Michigan State
T	George Jacoby	Ohio State
T	Art Walker	Michigan

HEISMAN TROPHY VOTING

	PLAYER	POS	SCHOOL	1ST	2ND	3RD	TOTAL
2	**Paul Giel**	TB	Minnesota	366	295	106	1,794
6	**Alan Ameche**	FB	Wisconsin	25	38	60	211
7	**J.C. Caroline**	HB	Illinois	15	37	74	193

NCAA STATISTICAL LEADERS

INDIVIDUAL

	PASSING/COMPLETIONS	G	ATT	COM	PCT	INT	I%	YDS	YPA	TD	TD%	COM.PG
5	Tony Rados, Penn State*	9	171	81	47.4	12	7.0	1,025	6.0	8	4.7	9.0
10	Dick Thomas, Northwestern	9	145	74	51.0	7	4.8	933	6.4	5	3.5	8.2

	ALL-PURPOSE/YARDS	CL	RUSH	REC	INT	PR	KR	YDS	YPG
1	J.C. Caroline, Illinois		9	1,256	52	0	129	33	1,470	163.3

	RUSHING/YARDS	G	ATT	YDS	AVG	YPG
1	J.C. Caroline, Illinois	9	194	1,256	6.5	139.6
4	Bob Watkins, Ohio State	9	153	875	5.7	97.2
7	Alan Ameche, Wisconsin	9	165	801	4.9	89.0

	RUSHING/YARDS PER CARRY	G	ATT	YDS	YPC
5	J.C. Caroline, Illinois	9	194	1,256	6.5
9	Bob Watkins, Ohio State	9	153	875	5.7
Based on top 20 rushers					

	RECEIVING/RECEPTIONS	G	REC	YDS	TD	YPR	YPG	RPG
6	Jim Garrity, Penn State*	9	30	349	3	11.6	38.8	3.3

	PUNTING	PUNT	YDS	AVG
8	Tom Yewcic, Michigan State	31	1,234	39.8

	PUNT RETURNS/YARDS	PR	YDS	AVG
1	Paul Giel, Minnesota	17	288	16.9
9	Lenny Moore, Penn State*	13	228	17.5

	KICKOFF RETURNS/YARDS	KR	YDS	AVG
2	Howard Cassady, Ohio State	15	343	22.9

TEAM

	RUSHING OFFENSE	G	ATT	YDS	AVG	YPG
6	Illinois	9	478	2,481	5.2	275.7

	TOTAL OFFENSE	G	P	YDS	AVG	PG
8	Illinois	9	575	3,205	5.6	356.1

	RUSHING DEFENSE	G	ATT	YDS	AVG	YPG
7	Iowa	9	367	1,051	2.9	116.8

1954

FINAL POLL

UP	AP	TEAM	RECORD
2	1	**Ohio State**	10-0-0
1	2	UCLA	9-0-0
3	3	Oklahoma	10-0-0
4	4	Notre Dame	9-1-0
5	5	Navy	8-2-0
6	6	Mississippi	9-2-0
7	7	Army	7-2-0
12	8	Maryland	7-2-1
10	9	**Wisconsin**	7-2-0
8	10	Arkansas	8-3-0
9	11	Miami, Fla.	8-1-0
	12	West Virginia	8-1-0
	13	Auburn	8-3-0
14	14	Duke	8-2-1
15	15	**Michigan**	6-3-0
	16	Virginia Tech	8-0-1
11	17	USC	8-4-0
	18	Baylor	7-4-0
18	19	Rice	7-3-0
15	20	**Penn State***	7-2-0
13		Georgia Tech	8-3-0
17		SMU	6-3-1
18		Denver	9-1-0
20		**Minnesota**	7-2-0

CONFERENCE STANDINGS

	CONFERENCE			OVERALL		
	W	L	T	W	L	T
Ohio State	7	0	0	10	0	0
Wisconsin	5	2	0	7	2	0
Michigan	5	2	0	6	3	0
Minnesota	4	2	0	7	2	0
Iowa	4	3	0	5	4	0
Purdue	3	3	0	5	3	1
Indiana	2	4	0	3	6	0
Michigan State	1	5	0	3	6	0
Northwestern	1	5	0	2	7	0
Illinois	0	6	0	1	8	0
Penn State*				7	2	0

BOWL GAMES

DATE	GAME	SCORE
J1	**Rose**	Ohio State 20, USC 7

CONSENSUS ALL-AMERICANS

POS	Name	HT	WT	School	AA	AP	FC	FW	IN	NE	SN	UP
B	**Howard Cassady**	5-10	177	Ohio State	•	•	•	•	•	•	•	•
B	**Alan Ameche**	6-0	215	Wisconsin	•	•	•	•	•	•	•	•
G	**Calvin Jones**	6-0	200	Iowa	•			•		•	•	•

OTHERS RECEIVING FIRST-TEAM HONORS

B	Bob McNamara	Minnesota	•
E	Dean Dugger	Ohio State	•
T	Art Walker	Michigan	•	•
G	Tom Bettis	Purdue	•	•

ALL-CONFERENCE TEAM

POS	Name	School
B	Bob McNamara	Minnesota
B	Howard Cassady	Ohio State
B	Alan Ameche	Wisconsin
QB	Len Dawson	Purdue
C	Gary Messner	Wisconsin
G	Calvin Jones	Iowa
G	Tom Bettis	Purdue
E	Ron Kramer	Michigan
E	Dean Dugger	Ohio State
T	Art Walker	Michigan
T	Dick Hilinski	Ohio State
T	Francis Machinsky	Ohio State

HEISMAN TROPHY VOTING

	PLAYER	POS	SCHOOL	1ST	2ND	3RD	TOTAL
1	**Alan Ameche**	FB	Wisconsin	214	157	112	1068
3	**Howard Cassady**	HB	Ohio State	137	139	121	810
10	**Bob McNamara**	FB	Minnesota	16	15	26	104

NCAA STATISTICAL LEADERS

INDIVIDUAL

PASSING/COMPLETIONS	G	ATT	COM	PCT	INT	I%	YDS	YPA	TD	TD%	COM.PG
3 Len Dawson, Purdue	9	167	87	52.1	8	4.8	1,464	8.8	15	9.0	9.7

RUSHING/YARDS				G	ATT	YDS	AVG	YPC
2 Lenny Moore, Penn State*				9	136	1,082	8.0	120.2

RUSHING/YARDS PER CARRY				G	ATT	YDS	YPC
3 Lenny Moore, Penn State*				9	136	1,082	8.0

Based on top 10 rushers

PUNT RETURNS/YARDS	PR	YDS	AVG
3 Earl Smith, Iowa	15	267	17.8
5 Bob McNamara, Minnesota	14	252	18.0
10 Ron Younker, Penn State*	12	193	16.1

SCORING	TDS	XP	FG	PTS
3 Lenny Moore, Penn State*	13	0	0	78

INTERCEPTIONS	INT	YDS
6 James Miller, Wisconsin	6	117
6 Lenny Moore, Penn State*	6	96

TEAM

RUSHING OFFENSE	G	ATT	YDS	AVG	YPG
8 Penn State*	9	421	2,415	5.7	268.3

PASSING OFFENSE/YPG	G	ATT	COM	INT	PCT	YDS	YPA	TD	YPG	I%	YPC
1 Purdue	9	195	99	11	50.8	1,596	8.2	15	177.3	5.6	16.1

RUSHING DEFENSE	G	ATT	YDS	AVG	YPG
8 Wisconsin	9	359	1,045	2.9	116.1

*Independent or other conference affiliation

1955

FINAL POLL

UP	AP	TEAM	RECORD
1	1	Oklahoma	11-0-0
2	2	**Michigan State**	9-1-0
3	3	Maryland	10-1-0
4	4	UCLA	9-2-0
6	5	**Ohio State**	7-2-0
5	6	TCU	9-2-0
7	7	Georgia Tech	9-1-1
10	8	Auburn	8-2-1
8	9	Notre Dame	8-2-0
9	10	Mississippi	10-1-0
11	11	Pittsburgh	7-4-0
13	12	**Michigan**	7-2-0
12	13	USC	6-4-0
18	14	Miami, Fla.	6-3-0
20	15	Miami (Ohio)	9-0-0
20	16	Stanford	6-3-1
14	17	Texas A&M	7-2-1
20	18	Navy	6-2-1
17	19	West Virginia	8-2-0
15	20	Army	6-3-0
15		Duke	7-2-1
19		Iowa	3-5-1

CONFERENCE STANDINGS

	CONFERENCE			OVERALL		
	W	L	T	W	L	T
Ohio State	6	0	0	7	2	0
Michigan State	5	1	0	9	1	0
Michigan	5	2	0	7	2	0
Purdue	4	2	1	5	3	1
Illinois	3	3	1	5	3	1
Wisconsin	3	4	0	4	5	0
Iowa	2	3	1	3	5	1
Minnesota	2	5	0	3	6	0
Indiana	1	5	0	3	6	0
Northwestern	0	6	1	0	8	1
Penn State*				5	4	0

BOWL GAMES

DATE	GAME	SCORE
J2	**Rose**	Michigan State 17, UCLA 14

CONSENSUS ALL-AMERICANS

POS	Name	HT	WT	School	AA	AP	FC	FW	IN	NE	SN	UP
B	**Howard Cassady**	5-10	172	Ohio State	•	•	•	•	•	•	•	•
B	**Earl Morrall**	6-1	180	Michigan State		•	•	•	•		•	•
E	**Ron Kramer**	6-3	218	Michigan	•	•		•	•			•
T	**Norman Masters**	6-2	225	Michigan State			•					•
G	**Calvin Jones**	6-0	220	Iowa	•		•		•			•

	OTHERS RECEIVING FIRST-TEAM HONORS		
G	Jim Parker	Ohio State	•

ALL-CONFERENCE TEAM

POS	Name	School
QB	Steve Juday	Michigan State
QB	Earl Morrall	Michigan State
B	Bobby Mitchell	Illinois
B	Howard Cassady	Ohio State
B	Bill Murkowski	Purdue
C	Ken Vargo	Ohio State
G	Calvin Jones	Iowa
G	Jim Parker	Ohio State
E	Brad Bomba	Indiana
E	Tom Maentz	Michigan
E	Ron Kramer	Michigan
T	Norm Masters	Michigan State
T	Joe Krupa	Purdue

HEISMAN TROPHY VOTING

	PLAYER	POS	SCHOOL	1ST	2ND	3RD	TOTAL
1	Howard Cassady	HB	Ohio State	594	179	79	2219
4	Earl Morrall	QB	Michigan State	23	97	60	323
8	Ron Kramer	E	Michigan	12	50	56	192
10	Calvin Jones	G	Iowa	14	40	16	138

AWARD WINNERS

PLAYER	POS	SCHOOL	AWARD
Howard Cassady	HB	Ohio State	Maxwell
Calvin Jones	G	Iowa	Outland

NCAA STATISTICAL LEADERS

INDIVIDUAL

PASSING/COMPLETIONS	G	ATT	COM	PCT	INT	I%	YDS	YPA	TD	TD%	COM.PG
3 Len Dawson, Purdue	9	155	87	56.1	14	9.0	1,005	6.5	7	4.5	9.7
7 James Haluska, Wisconsin	9	132	71	53.8	10	7.6	1,036	7.8	6	4.6	7.9

RUSHING/YARDS				G	ATT	YDS	AVG	YPC
3 Howard Cassady, Ohio State				9	161	958	6.0	106.4

RUSHING/YARDS PER CARRY				G	ATT	YDS	YPC
9 Howard Cassady, Ohio State				9	161	958	6.0

*-Based on top 20 rushers

PUNTING			PUNT	YDS	AVG
2 Earl Morrall, Michigan State			22	944	42.9
5 Kelvin Kleber, Minnesota			32	1,347	42.1

PUNT RETURNS/YARDS			PR	YDS	AVG
6 Terry Barr, Michigan			15	222	14.8
9 Howard Cassady, Ohio State			17	205	12.1

KICKOFF RETURNS			KR	YDS	AVG
10 Howard Cassady, Ohio State			10	313	31.3

SCORING			TD	XP	FG	PTS
6 Howard Cassady, Ohio State			15	0	0	90

INTERCEPTIONS				INT	YDS
2 Milton Campbell, Indiana				6	111

TEAM

PASSING OFFENSE/YPG	G	ATT	COM	INT	PCT	YDS	YPA	TD	YPG	I%	YPC
5 Wisconsin	9	171	84	13	49.1	1,309	7.7	11	145.4	7.6	15.6
7 Purdue	9	191	104	18	54.5	1,213	6.4	8	134.8	9.4	11.7
10 Michigan State	9	98	52	9	53.1	1,124	11.5	7	124.9	9.2	21.6

RUSHING OFFENSE			G	ATT	YDS	AVG	YPG
4 Ohio State			9	508	2,504	4.9	278.2

TOTAL OFFENSE			G	P	YDS	AVG	PG
4 Michigan State			9	521	3,280	6.3	364.4

PASSING DEFENSE	G	ATT	COM	PCT	YPC	INT	I%	YDS	YPA	TD	YPG
3 Michigan	9	86	28	32.6	14.4	10	11.6	402	4.7	4	44.7
9 Indiana	9	93	37	39.8	14.4	13	14.0	533	5.7	6	59.2

1956

FINAL POLL

UP	AP	TEAM	RECORD
1	1	Oklahoma	10-0-0
2	2	Tennessee	10-1-0
3	3	Iowa	9-1-0
4	4	Georgia Tech	10-1-0
5	5	Texas A&M	9-0-1
6	6	Miami, Fla.	8-1-1
7	7	**Michigan**	7-2-0
8	8	Syracuse	7-2-0
10	9	**Michigan State**	7-2-0
13	10	Oregon State	7-3-1
11	11	Baylor	9-2-0
9	12	**Minnesota**	6-1-2
12	13	Pittsburgh	7-3-1
14	14	TCU	8-3-0
	15	**Ohio State**	6-3-0
19	16	Navy	6-1-2
	17	George Washington	8-1-1
15	18	USC	8-2-0
	19	Clemson	7-2-2
18	20	Colorado	8-2-1
16		Wyoming	10-0-0
17		Yale	8-1-0
20		Duke	5-4-1

CONFERENCE STANDINGS

	CONFERENCE			OVERALL		
	W	L	T	W	L	T
Iowa	5	1	0	9	1	0
Michigan	5	2	0	7	2	0
Minnesota	4	1	2	6	1	2
Michigan State	4	2	0	7	2	0
Ohio State	4	2	0	6	3	0
Northwestern	3	3	1	4	4	1
Purdue	1	4	2	3	4	2
Illinois	1	4	2	2	5	2
Wisconsin	0	4	3	1	5	3
Indiana	1	5	0	3	6	0
Penn State*				6	2	1

BOWL GAMES

DATE	GAME	SCORE
J1	**Rose**	Iowa 35, Oregon State 19

CONSENSUS ALL-AMERICANS

POS	Name	HT	WT	School	AA AP FC FW IN NE SN
E	**Ron Kramer**	6-3	220	Michigan	• • • • • • • •
G	**Jim Parker**	6-2	251	Ohio State	• • • • • • •

OTHERS RECEIVING FIRST-TEAM HONORS

POS			
T	Bob Hobert	Minnesota	•
T	Alex Karras	Iowa	• •
G	Sam Valentine	Penn State*	•

ALL-CONFERENCE TEAM

POS	Name	School
B	Abe Woodson	Illinois
B	Ken Ploen	Iowa
B	Bob McKeiver	Northwestern
B	Mel Dillard	Purdue
C	Don Suchy	Iowa
G	Al Viola	Northwestern
G	Jim Parker	Ohio State
E	Ron Kramer	Michigan
E	Frank Gilliam	Iowa
T	Bob Hobert	Minnesota
T	Alex Karras	Iowa

HEISMAN TROPHY VOTING

PLAYER	POS	SCHOOL	1ST	2ND	3RD	TOTAL
6 Ron Kramer	E	Michigan	70	104	100	518
8 Jim Parker	G	Ohio State	34	51	44	248
9 Kenny Ploen	QB	Iowa	36	10	22	150

AWARD WINNERS

PLAYER	POS	SCHOOL	AWARD
Jim Parker	G	Ohio State	Outland

NCAA STATISTICAL LEADERS

INDIVIDUAL

RUSHING/YARDS

		G	ATT	YDS	AVG	YPC
6	Mel Dillard, Purdue	9	193	873	4.5	97.0
9	Don Clark, Ohio State	9	139	797	5.7	88.6

RUSHING/YARDS PER CARRY

		G	ATT	YDS	YPC
10	Don Clark, Ohio State	9	139	797	5.7

Based on top 20 rushers

RECEIVING/RECEPTIONS

		G	REC	YDS	TD	YPR	YPG	RPG
4	Brad Bomba, Indiana	9	31	407	1	13.1	45.2	3.4

KICKOFF RETURNS/YARDS

		KR	YDS	AVG
8	Robert Fee, Indiana	15	326	21.7

INTERCEPTIONS

		INT	YDS
1	Milt Plum, Penn State*	7	72

TEAM

RUSHING OFFENSE

		G	ATT	YDS	AVG	YPG
5	Ohio State	9	524	2,468	4.7	274.2
10	Michigan State	9	486	2,312	4.8	256.9

TOTAL OFFENSE

		G	P	YDS	AVG	PG
6	Michigan State	9	585	3,231	5.5	359.0

RUSHING DEFENSE

		G	ATT	YDS	AVG	YPG
9	Iowa	9	430	1,285	3.0	142.8

PASSING DEFENSE

		G	ATT	COM	PCT	YPC	INT	I%	YDS	YPA	TD	YPG
4	Penn State*	9	121	30	24.8	14.5	18	14.9	434	3.6	2	48.2

TOTAL DEFENSE

		G	P	YDS	AVG	YPG
9	Penn State*	9	534	1,903	3.6	211.4

*Independent or other conference affiliation

1957

Final Poll

UP	AP	TEAM	RECORD
2	1	Auburn	10-0-0
1	2	**Ohio State**	9-1-0
3	3	**Michigan State**	8-1-0
4	4	Oklahoma	10-1-0
6	5	Navy	9-1-1
5	6	Iowa	7-1-1
8	7	Mississippi	9-1-1
7	8	Rice	7-4-0
10	9	Texas A&M	8-3-0
9	10	Notre Dame	7-3-0
11	11	Texas	6-4-1
12	12	Arizona State	10-0-0
16	13	Tennessee	8-3-0
	14	Mississippi State	6-2-1
20	15	North Carolina St.	7-1-2
14	16	Duke	6-3-2
	17	Florida	6-2-1
13	18	Army	7-2-0
14	19	**Wisconsin**	6-3-0
	20	VMI	9-0-1
17		Oregon	7-4-0
18		Clemson	7-3-0
18		UCLA	8-2-0

Conference Standings

	CONFERENCE			OVERALL		
	W	L	T	W	L	T
Ohio State	7	0	0	9	1	0
Michigan State	5	1	0	8	1	0
Iowa	4	1	1	7	1	1
Wisconsin	4	3	0	6	3	0
Purdue	4	3	0	5	4	0
Michigan	3	3	1	5	3	1
Illinois	3	4	0	4	5	0
Minnesota	3	5	0	4	5	0
Indiana	0	6	0	1	8	0
Northwestern	0	7	0	0	9	0
Penn State*				6	3	0

Bowl Games

DATE	GAME	SCORE
J1	**Rose**	Ohio State 10, Oregon 7

Consensus All-Americans

POS	Name	HT	WT	School	AA	AP	FC	FW	IN	NE	SN	UP
B	**Walt Kowalczyk**	6-0	205	Michigan St.			•	•		•	•	•
T	**Alex Karras**	6-2	233	Iowa	•		•	•	•	•	•	•
C	**Dan Currie**	6-3	225	Michigan St.	•	•	•		•			

	Others receiving first-team honors		
B	Jim Pace	Michigan	•
E	Jim Gibbons	Iowa						•	•	•
G	Aurelius Thomas	Ohio State	•		•	•

All-Conference Team

POS	Name	School
B	Jim Pace	Michigan
B	Walt Kowalczyk	Michigan State
B	Don Clark	Ohio State
QB	Jim Ninowski	Michigan State
C	Dan Currie	Michigan State
G	Frank Bloomquist	Iowa
G	Ellison Kelly	Michigan State
G	Aurelius Thomas	Ohio State
E	Jim Gibbons	Iowa
E	Sam Williams	Michigan State
E	Leo Brown	Ohio State
T	Alex Karras	Iowa
T	Pat Burke	Michigan State

Heisman Trophy Voting

PLAYER	POS	SCHOOL	1ST	2ND	3RD	TOTAL
2 Alex Karras	DT	Iowa	128	109	91	693
3 Walt Kowalczyk	HB	Michigan State	116	93	96	630
8 Dan Currie	C	Michigan State	49	16	18	197

Award Winners

PLAYER	POS	SCHOOL	AWARD
Alex Karras	T	Iowa	Outland

NCAA Statistical Leaders

INDIVIDUAL

RUSHING/YARDS PER CARRY	G	ATT	YDS	YPC
8 Jim Pace, Michigan	9	123	664	5.4

Based on top 20 rushers

RECEIVING/RECEPTIONS	G	REC	YDS	TD	YPR	YPG	RPG
5 **Jim Gibbons, Iowa**	9	36	587	4	16.3	65.2	4.0

KICKOFF RETURNS/YARDS	KR	YDS	AVG
6 **Wilmer Fowler, Northwestern**	14	336	24.0

TEAM

RUSHING OFFENSE	G	ATT	YDS	AVG	YPG
3 **Ohio State**	9	555	2,681	4.8	297.9
7 **Wisconsin**	9	503	2,437	4.8	270.8
8 **Michigan State**	9	533	2,367	4.4	263.0

PASSING OFFENSE/YPG	G	ATT	COM	INT	PCT	YDS	YPA	TD	YPG	I%	YPC
9 **Iowa**	9	146	77	17	52.7	1,289	8.8	11	11.6	16.7	143.2
10 Penn State*	9	185	90	8	48.6	1,187	6.4	11	4.3	13.2	131.9

TOTAL OFFENSE	G	P	YDS	AVG	PG
4 **Iowa**	9	599	3,459	5.8	384.3
5 **Michigan State**	9	669	3,455	5.2	383.9

RUSHING DEFENSE	G	ATT	YDS	AVG	YPG
6 **Iowa**	9	372	1,014	2.7	112.7
8 **Michigan State**	9	422	1,055	2.5	117.2

TOTAL DEFENSE	G	P	YDS	AVG	YPG
5 **Michigan State**	9	556	1,724	3.1	191.6

1958

FINAL POLL

UP	AP	TEAM	RECORD
1	1	LSU	11-0-0
2	2	Iowa	8-1-1
3	3	Army	8-0-1
4	4	Auburn	9-0-1
5	5	Oklahoma	10-1-0
8	6	Air Force	9-0-2
6	7	Wisconsin	7-1-1
7	8	Ohio State	6-1-2
10	9	Syracuse	8-2-0
9	10	TCU	8-2-1
12	11	Mississippi	9-2-0
13	12	Clemson	8-3-0
11	13	Purdue	6-1-2
15	14	Florida	6-4-1
	15	South Carolina	7-3-0
16	16	California	7-4-0
14	17	Notre Dame	6-4-0
18	18	SMU	6-4-0
	19	Oklahoma State	8-3-0
	20	Rutgers	8-1-0
17		Northwestern	5-4-0

CONFERENCE STANDINGS

	CONFERENCE			OVERALL		
	W	L	T	W	L	T
Iowa	5	1	0	8	1	1
Wisconsin	5	1	1	7	1	1
Ohio State	4	1	2	6	1	2
Purdue	3	1	2	6	1	2
Indiana	3	2	1	5	3	1
Illinois	4	3	0	4	5	0
Northwestern	3	4	0	5	4	0
Michigan	1	5	1	2	6	1
Minnesota	1	6	0	1	8	0
Michigan State	0	5	1	3	5	1
Penn State*				6	3	1

BOWL GAMES

DATE	GAME	SCORE
J1	Rose	Iowa 38, California 12

CONSENSUS ALL-AMERICANS

POS	Name	HT	WT	School	AP	FC	FW	NE	SN	UP
B	Randy Duncan	6-0	180	Iowa	•	•	•	•	•	•
B	Bob White	6-2	212	Ohio State			•	•	•	•
E	Sam Williams	6-5	225	Michigan State		•			•	

	OTHERS RECEIVING FIRST-TEAM HONORS							
E	Jim Houston	Ohio State	•		•			
E	Curtis Merz	Iowa			•			
T	Andrew Cvercko	Northwestern			•			
T	Gene Selawski	Purdue			•			
T	Jim Marshall	Ohio State					•	

ALL-CONFERENCE TEAM

POS	Name	School
QB	Randy Duncan	Iowa
B	Willie Fleming	Iowa
B	Ron Burton	Northwestern
B	Don Clark	Ohio State
B	Bob White	Ohio State
C	Mike Wvendson	Minnesota
C	Dick Teteak	Wisconsin
G	Jerry Stalcup	Wisconsin
G	Bill Burrell	Illinois
G	Ellison Kelly	Michigan State
G	Ron Maltony	Purdue
E	Rich Kreitling	Illinois
E	Sam Williams	Michigan State
E	James Houston	Ohio State
T	Andy Cvercko	Northwestern
T	Jim Marshall	Ohio State
T	Gene Selawski	Purdue

HEISMAN TROPHY VOTING

	PLAYER	POS	SCHOOL	1ST	2ND	3RD	TOTAL
2	Randy Duncan	QB	Iowa	194	157	125	1021
4	Bob White	RB	Ohio State	40	88	69	365

NCAA STATISTICAL LEADERS

INDIVIDUAL

PASSING/COMPLETIONS		G	ATT	COM	PCT	INT	I%	YDS	YPA	TD	TD%	COM.PG
3	Randy Duncan, Iowa	9	172	101	58.7	9	5.2	1,347	7.8	11	6.4	11.2

RUSHING/YARDS		G	ATT	YDS	AVG	YPC
2	Bob White, Ohio State	9	218	859	3.9	95.4

RUSHING/YARDS PER CARRY		G	ATT	YDS	YPC
1	Ray Jauch, Iowa	9	72	506	7.0

Based on top 60 rushers

PUNTING		PUNT	YDS	AVG
9	Brad Myers, Michigan	24	989	41.2

PUNT RETURNS/YARDS		PR	YDS	AVG
5	Dale Hackbart, Wisconsin	7	193	27.6
8	Dean Look, Michigan State	5	179	35.8

SCORING		TDS	XP	FG	PTS
3	Ron Burton, Northwestern	12	4	0	76
7	Bob White, Ohio State	12	0	0	72

KICK SCORING		XPA	XP	FG	PTS
6	Bob Prescott, Iowa	24	18	1	21
8	David Kilgore, Ohio State	17	15	1	18

INTERCEPTIONS		INT	YDS
2	Dale Hackbart, Wisconsin	7	77
8	Jim Kerr, Penn State*	5	122

TEAM

RUSHING OFFENSE		G	ATT	YDS	AVG	YPG
6	Penn State*	10	597	2,429	4.1	242.9
9	Iowa	9	444	2,123	4.8	235.9
10	Purdue	9	550	2,094	3.8	232.7

PASSING OFFENSE		G	ATT	COM	INT	PCT	YDS	YPA	TD	YPG	I%	YPC
2	Iowa	9	205	115	11	56.1	1,530	7.5	11	5.4	13.3	170.0

TOTAL OFFENSE		G	P	YDS	AVG	YPG
1	Iowa	9	649	3,653	5.6	405.9

RUSHING DEFENSE		G	ATT	YDS	AVG	YPG
5	Purdue	9	372	849	2.3	94.3

TOTAL DEFENSE		G	P	YDS	AVG	YPG
2	Purdue	9	485	1,590	3.3	176.7

SCORING OFFENSE		G	PTS	AVG
9	Iowa	9	234	26.0

1959

FINAL POLL

UP	AP	TEAM	RECORD
1	1	Syracuse	11-0-0
2	2	Mississippi	10-1-0
3	3	LSU	9-2-0
4	4	Texas	9-2-0
5	5	Georgia	10-1-0
6	6	Wisconsin	7-3-0
8	7	TCU	8-3-0
7	8	Washington	10-1-0
9	9	Arkansas	9-2-0
13	10	Alabama	7-2-2
11	11	Clemson	9-2-0
10	12	Penn State*	9-2-0
12	13	Illinois	5-3-1
13	14	USC	8-2-0
17	15	Oklahoma	7-3-0
	16	Wyoming	9-1-0
18	17	Notre Dame	5-5-0
20	18	Missouri	6-5-0
20	19	Florida	5-4-1
19	20	Pittsburgh	6-4-0
15		Auburn	7-3-0
16		**Michigan State**	5-4-0

CONFERENCE STANDINGS

	CONFERENCE			OVERALL		
	W	L	T	W	L	T
Wisconsin	5	2	0	7	3	0
Michigan State	4	2	0	5	4	0
Purdue	4	2	1	5	2	2
Illinois	4	2	1	5	3	1
Northwestern	4	3	0	6	3	0
Iowa	3	3	0	5	4	0
Michigan	3	4	0	4	5	0
Indiana	2	4	1	4	4	1
Ohio State	2	4	1	3	5	1
Minnesota	1	6	0	2	7	0
Penn State*				9	2	0

BOWL GAMES

DATE	GAME	SCORE
D19	**Liberty**	Penn State* 7, Alabama 0
J1	**Rose**	Washington 44, Wisconsin 8

CONSENSUS ALL-AMERICANS

POS	Name	HT	WT	School	AP	FC	FW	NE	SN	PI
B	**Richie Lucas**	6-1	185	Penn State*	•	•	•	•	•	•
B	**Ron Burton**	5-9	185	Northwestern	•	•	•	•	•	•
T	**Dan Lanphear**	6-2	214	Wisconsin	•	•	•	•	•	•
G	**Bill Burrell**	6-0	210	Illinois	•		•			•

Others receiving first-team honors

POS	Name	School	
B	Dean Look	Michigan State	•
E	Don Norton	Iowa	•
C	Jim Andreotti	Northwestern	•

ALL-CONFERENCE TEAM

POS	Name	School
B	Bob Jeter	Iowa
B	Dale Hackbart	Wisconsin
B	Dean Look	Michigan State
B	Ron Burton	Northwestern
B	Mike Stock	Northwestern
C	Jim Andreotti	Northwestern
G	Jerry Stalcup	Wisconsin
G	Bill Burrell	Illinois
E	James Houston	Ohio State
E	Don Norton	Iowa
T	Gene Gossage	Northwestern
T	Don Lanphear	Wisconsin
T	Joe Rutgens	Illinois

HEISMAN TROPHY VOTING

	PLAYER	POS	SCHOOL	1ST	2ND	3RD	TOTAL
2	**Richie Lucas**	QB	Penn State*	97	109	104	613
4	**Bill Burrell**	G	Illinois	23	47	33	196
6	**Dean Look**	HB	Michigan State	23	41	25	176
7	**Dale Hackbart**	QB	Wisconsin	19	21	35	134
10	**Ron Burton**	RB	Northwestern	10	28	36	122

AWARD WINNERS

PLAYER	POS	SCHOOL	AWARD
Richie Lucas	QB	Penn State*	Maxwell

NCAA STATISTICAL LEADERS

INDIVIDUAL

RECEIVING/RECEPTIONS		G	REC	YDS	TD	YPR	YPG	RPG
9	Don Norton, Iowa	9	30	428	4	14.3	47.6	3.3

PUNT RETURNS/YARDS		PR	YDS	AVG
6	Gerald Mauren, Iowa	10	181	18.1

KICKOFF RETURNS/YARDS		KR	YDS	AVG
10	Sandy Stephens, Minnesota	11	299	27.2

KICK SCORING		XPA	XP	FG	PTS
5	Karl Holzwarth, Wisconsin	10	10	7	31
9	Sam Stellatella, Penn State*	23	20	2	26

INTERCEPTIONS		INT	YDS
6	Richie Lucas, Penn State*	5	114

TEAM

RUSHING OFFENSE		G	ATT	YDS	AVG	YPG
9	Iowa	9	440	2,151	4.9	239.0

TOTAL OFFENSE		G	P	YDS	AVG	PG
2	Iowa	9	632	3,399	5.4	377.7

TOTAL DEFENSE		G	P	YDS	AVG	YPG
8	Illinois	9	533	1,713	3.2	190.3

SCORING OFFENSE		G	PTS	AVG
8	Iowa	9	233	25.9
9	Penn State*	10	255	25.5

1960

FINAL POLL

UP	AP	TEAM	RECORD
1	1	**Minnesota**	8-2-0
3	2	Mississippi	10-0-1
2	3	Iowa	8-1-0
6	4	Navy	9-2-0
4	5	Missouri	10-1-0
5	6	Washington	10-1-0
7	7	Arkansas	8-3-0
8	8	**Ohio State**	7-2-0
9	9	Alabama	8-1-2
11	10	Duke	8-3-0
9	11	Kansas	7-2-1
12	12	Baylor	8-3-0
14	13	Auburn	8-2-0
18	14	Yale	9-0-0
13	15	**Michigan State**	6-2-1
	16	Penn State*	7-3-0
18	17	New Mexico State	11-0-0
16	18	Florida	9-2-0
15	19	**Purdue**	4-4-1
	19	Syracuse	7-2-0
17		Texas	7-3-1
18		Tennessee	6-2-2

CONFERENCE STANDINGS

	CONFERENCE			OVERALL		
	W	L	T	W	L	T
Minnesota	6	1	0	8	2	0
Iowa	5	1	0	8	1	0
Ohio State	5	2	0	7	2	0
Michigan State	4	2	0	6	2	1
Michigan	3	4	0	5	4	0
Illinois	3	4	0	5	4	0
Northwestern	3	4	0	5	4	0
Purdue	3	4	0	4	4	1
Wisconsin	2	5	0	4	5	0
Indiana	0	7	0	1	8	0
Penn State*				7	3	0

BOWL GAMES

DATE	GAME	SCORE
D17	**Liberty**	Penn State* 41, Oregon 12
J2	**Rose**	Washington 17, Minnesota 7

CONSENSUS ALL-AMERICANS

POS	Name	HT	WT	School	AP	FC	FW	NE	SN	PI
B	**Bob Ferguson**	6-0	217	Ohio State	•	•	•	•	•	•
G	**Tom Brown**	6-0	225	Minnesota	•	•	•	•	•	•

	Others receiving first-team honors									
B	Larry Ferguson			Iowa			•			
T	Jerry Beabout			Purdue						
G	Mark Manders			Iowa			•		•	

HEISMAN TROPHY VOTING

	PLAYER	POS	SCHOOL	1ST	2ND	3RD	TOTAL
2	**Tom Brown**	G	Minnesota	127	121	108	731
7	**Tom Matte**	QB	Ohio State	17	42	30	165

AWARD WINNERS

PLAYER	POS	SCHOOL	AWARD
Tom Brown	G	Minnesota	Outland

ALL-BIG TEN TEAM

POS	Offense
RB	Herb Adderley, Michigan State
RB	Bob Ferguson, Ohio State
RB	Larry Ferguson, Iowa
RB	Wilburn Hollis, Iowa
RB	Tom Matte, Ohio State
C	Greg Larson, Minnesota
G	Mark Manders, Iowa
G	Tom Brown, Minnesota
T	Joe Rutgens, Illinois
T	Jim Tryer, Ohio State
T	Jerry Beabout, Purdue
T	Don Lanphear, Wisconsin

POS	Defense
DE	Earl Faison, Indiana
DE	Elbert Kimbrough, Northwestern

NCAA STATISTICAL LEADERS

INDIVIDUAL

PASSING/COMPLETIONS	G	ATT	COM	PCT	INT	I%	YDS	YPA	TD	TD%	COM.PG
8 Ron Miller, Wisconsin	9	188	97	51.6	16	8.5	1351	7.2	8	4.3	10.8

RUSHING/YARDS					G	ATT	YDS	AVG	YPC
4 Bob Ferguson, Ohio State					9	160	853	5.3	94.8

RUSHING/YARDS PER CARRY				G	ATT	YDS	YPC
5 Larry Ferguson, Iowa				9	90	665	7.4
Based on top 40 rushers							

PUNTING	PR	YDS	AVG
7 Jim Bakken, Wisconsin	36	1508	41.9

SCORING	TDS	XP	FG	PTS
6 Bob Ferguson, Ohio State	13	0	0	78

INTERCEPTIONS	INT	YDS
9 Bill Munsey, Minnesota	5	130

TEAM

RUSHING OFFENSE					G	ATT	YDS	AVG	YPG
6 Iowa					9	439	2284	5.2	253.8

PASSING OFFENSE	G	ATT	COM	INT	PCT	YDS	YPA	TD	I%	YPC	YPG
2 Wisconsin	9	229	113	17	49.3	1526	6.7	8	7.4	13.5	169.6

SCORING OFFENSE			G	P	YDS	AVG	PG
7 Iowa			9		234		26.0

*Independent or other conference affiliation

1961

FINAL POLL

UP	AP	TEAM	RECORD
1	1	Alabama	11-0-0
2	2	**Ohio State**	8-0-1
4	3	Texas	10-1-0
3	4	LSU	10-1-0
5	5	Mississippi	9-2-0
6	6	**Minnesota**	8-2-0
7	7	Colorado	9-2-0
9	8	**Michigan State**	7-2-0
8	9	Arkansas	8-3-0
10	10	Utah State	9-1-1
11	11	Missouri	7-2-1
11	12	**Purdue**	6-3-0
13	13	Georgia Tech	7-4-0
16	14	Syracuse	8-3-0
	15	Rutgers	9-0-0
	16	UCLA	7-4-0
	17	Arizona	8-1-1
19	17	Penn State*	8-3-0
	17	Rice	7-4-0
14	20	Duke	7-3-0
15		Kansas	7-3-1
17		Wyoming	6-1-2
18		**Wisconsin**	6-3-0

CONFERENCE STANDINGS

	CONFERENCE			OVERALL		
	W	L	T	W	L	T
Ohio State	6	0	0	8	0	1
Minnesota	6	1	0	8	2	0
Michigan State	5	2	0	7	2	0
Purdue	4	2	0	6	3	0
Wisconsin	4	3	0	6	3	0
Michigan	3	3	0	6	3	0
Iowa	2	4	0	5	4	0
Northwestern	2	4	0	4	5	0
Indiana	0	6	0	2	7	0
Illinois	0	7	0	0	9	0
Penn State*				8	3	0

BOWL GAMES

DATE	GAME	SCORE
D30	**Gator**	Penn State* 30, Georgia Tech 15
J1	**Rose**	Minnesota 21, UCLA 3

CONSENSUS ALL-AMERICANS

POS	Name	HT	WT	School	AP	FC	FW	NE	SN	PI
B	**Bob Ferguson**	6-0	217	Ohio State	•	•	•	•	•	•
B	**Sandy Stephens**	6-0	215	Minnesota	•		•	•	•	•

	OTHERS RECEIVING FIRST-TEAM HONORS								
E	Bob Mitinger	Penn State			•				
E	Pat Richter	Wisconsin							•
T	Bobby Bell	Minnesota		•	•	•			
G	Dave Behrman	Michigan State	•		•				
C	Bill Van Buren	Iowa						•	

ALL-BIG TEN TEAM

POS	Offense
RB	Bob Ferguson, Ohio State
RB	Mike Ingram, Ohio State
RB	George Saimes, Michigan State
RB	Sandy Stephens, Minnesota
C	Larry Onesti, Northwestern
C	Dave Behrman, Michigan State
G	Tony Panilli, Illinois
G	Stan Sczurek, Purdue
T	Bobby Bell, Minnesota
T	Fate Echols, Northwestern

POS	Defense
DE	Tom Hall, Minnesota
DE	Jack Elwell, Purdue
DE	Pat Richter, Wiconsin
DB	Bennie McRae, Michigan

HEISMAN TROPHY VOTING

	PLAYER	POS	SCHOOL	1ST	2ND	3RD	TOTAL
2	**Bob Ferguson**	FB	Ohio State	122	156	93	771
4	**Sandy Stephens**	QB	Minnesota	104	78	68	543

AWARD WINNERS

PLAYER	POS	SCHOOL	AWARD
Bob Ferguson	FB	Ohio State	Maxwell

NCAA STATISTICAL LEADERS

INDIVIDUAL

	PASSING/COMPLETIONS	G	ATT	COM	PCT	INT	I%	YDS	YPA	TD	TD%	COM.PG
2	Ron Miller, Wisconsin	9	198	104	52.5	11	5.6	1487	7.5	11	5.6	11.6
7	Matthew Szykowny, Iowa	9	139	79	56.8	15	10.8	1078	7.8	7	5.0	8.8

	RUSHING/YARDS	G	ATT	YDS	AVG	YPC
3	Bob Ferguson, Ohio State	9	202	938	4.6	104.2

	RECEIVING/RECEPTIONS	G	REC	YDS	TD	YPR	YPG	RPG
2	Pat Richter, Wisconsin	9	47	817	8	17.4	90.8	5.2

	PUNTING	PUNT	YDS	AVG
4	Jim Bakken, Wisconsin	39	1583	40.6

	KICK SCORING	XPA	XP	FG	PTS
10	Dick Van Raaphorst, Ohio State	27	23	4	35
10	Don Jonas, Penn State*	22	17	6	35

TEAM

	RUSHING OFFENSE	G	ATT	YDS	AVG	YPG
4	**Ohio State**	9	522	2,447	4.7	271.9
7	**Michigan State**	9	463	2,135	4.6	237.2

	PASSING OFFENSE	G	ATT	COM	INT	PCT	YDS	YPA	TD	I%	YPC	YPG
1	**Wisconsin**	9	226	117	12	51.8	1696	7.5	13	5.3	14.5	188.4
8	**Iowa**	9	172	94	17	54.7	1319	7.7	9	9.9	14.0	146.6

	TOTAL OFFENSE	G	P	YDS	AVG	PG
6	**Penn State***	10	706	3691	5.2	369.1
8	**Ohio State**	9	612	3142	5.1	349.1

	SCORING OFFENSE	G	PTS	AVG
8	**Iowa**	9	233	25.9
9	**Penn State***	10	255	25.5

	RUSHING DEFENSE	G	ATT	YDS	AVG	YPG
6	**Minnesota**	9	364	759	2.1	84.3

	SCORING DEFENSE	G	PTS	AVG
6	**Michigan State**	9	50	5.6

BIG TEN ANNUAL REVIEW & BOWLS

1962

FINAL POLL

UP	AP	TEAM	RECORD
1	1	USC	11-0-0
2	2	Wisconsin	8-2-0
3	3	Mississippi	10-0-0
4	4	Texas	9-1-1
5	5	Alabama	10-1-0
6	6	Arkansas	9-2-0
8	7	LSU	9-1-1
7	8	Oklahoma	8-3-0
9	9	Penn State*	9-2-0
10	10	Minnesota	6-2-1

CONFERENCE STANDINGS

	CONFERENCE			OVERALL		
	W	L	T	W	L	T
Wisconsin	6	1	0	8	2	0
Minnesota	5	2	0	6	2	1
Northwestern	4	2	0	7	2	0
Ohio State	4	2	0	6	3	0
Michigan State	3	3	0	5	4	0
Purdue	3	3	0	4	4	1
Iowa	3	3	0	4	5	0
Illinois	2	5	0	2	7	0
Indiana	1	5	0	3	6	0
Michigan	1	6	0	2	7	0
Penn State				9	2	0

BOWL GAMES

DATE	GAME	SCORE
D29	Gator	Florida 17, Penn State* 7
J1	Rose	USC 42, Wisconsin 37

CONSENSUS ALL-AMERICANS

POS	Name	HT	WT	School	AP	FC	FW	NE	SN	PI
B	George Saimes	5-10	186	Michigan State	•	•	•		•	•
E	Pat Richter	6-5	229	Wisconsin	•	•	•		•	•
T	Bobby Bell	6-4	214	Minnesota	•	•	•	•	•	•
G	Jack Cvercko	6-0	230	Northwestern					•	•

	Others receiving first-team honors									
B	Tom Myers	Northwestern					•			
B	Roger Kochman	Penn State*				•				
E	Dave Robinson	Penn State*			•	•	•			
T	Don Brumm	Purdue			•		•			

HEISMAN TROPHY VOTING

	PLAYER	POS	SCHOOL	1ST	2ND	3RD	TOTAL
3	Bobby Bell	T	Minnesota	56	95	71	429
6	Pat Richter	E	Wisconsin	55	40	31	276
7	George Saimes	HB	Michigan State	48	36	38	254
9	Ron Vander Kelen	QB	Wisconsin	23	22	26	139

AWARD WINNERS

PLAYER	POS	SCHOOL	AWARD
Bobby Bell	T	Minnesota	Outland

ALL-BIG TEN TEAM

POS	Offense	POS	Defense
QB	Ron Vander Kelen, Wisconsin	DE	John Campbell, Minnesota
RB	Marv Woodson, Indiana	DE	Pat Richter, Wisconsin
RB	Larry Ferguson, Iowa	DT	Bobby Bell, Minnesota
C	Dave Behrman, Michigan State	DT	Don Brumm, Purdue
C	Bill Armstrong, Ohio State	DB	George Saimes, Michigan State
G	Julian Hook, Minnesota	DB	Paul Warfield, Ohio State
G	Jack Cvercko, Northwestern		

NCAA STATISTICAL LEADERS

INDIVIDUAL

PASSING/COMPLETIONS

		G	ATT	COM	PCT	INT	I%	YDS	YPA	TD	TD%	COM.PG
4	Tom Myers, Northwestern	9	195	116	59.5	14	7.2	1537	7.9	13	6.7	12.9

RUSHING/YARDS PER CARRY

		G	ATT	YDS	YPC
7	Sherman Lewis, Michigan State	9	98	590	6.0

Based on top 42 rushers

RECEIVING/RECEPTIONS

		G	REC	YDS	TD	YPR	YPG	RPG
6	Paul Flatley, Northwestern	9	45	632	5	14.0	70.2	5.0

PUNTING

		PR	YDS	AVG
6	Chuck Raisig, Penn State*	35	1439	41.1

KICKOFF RETURNS/YARDS

		KR	YDS	AVG
6	Marvin Woodson, Indiana	16	418	26.1

KICK SCORING

		XPA	XP	FG	PTS
9	Gary Kroner, Wisconsin	27	27	3	36

TEAM

RUSHING OFFENSE

		G	ATT	YDS	AVG	YPG
1	Ohio State	9	528	2510	4.8	278.9
3	Michigan State	9	498	2383	4.8	264.8

PASSING OFFENSE

		G	ATT	COM	INT	PCT	YDS	YPA	TD	I%	YPC	YPG
2	Northwestern	9	225	130	15	57.8	1758	7.8	13	6.7	13.5	195.3
7	Wisconsin	9	216	112	9	51.9	1444	6.7	14	4.2	12.9	160.4

TOTAL OFFENSE

		G	P	YDS	AVG	PG
6	Northwestern	9	674	3267	4.8	363.0
10	Wisconsin	9	600	3142	5.2	349.1

RUSHING DEFENSE

		G	ATT	YDS	AVG	YPG
1	Minnesota	9	362	470	1.3	52.2
9	Michigan State	9	368	851	2.3	94.6

TOTAL DEFENSE

		G	P	YDS	AVG	YPG
4	Minnesota	9	568	1,505	2.6	167.2
9	Michigan State	9	553	1,753	3.2	194.8

SCORING OFFENSE

		G	PTS	AVG
1	Wisconsin	9	285	31.7
10	Northwestern	9	237	26.3

SCORING DEFENSE

		G	PTS	AVG
9	Minnesota	9	61	6.8

*Independent or other conference affiliation

1963

FINAL POLL

UP	AP	TEAM	RECORD
1	1	Texas	11-0-0
2	2	Navy	9-2-0
4	3	**Illinois**	8-1-1
3	4	Pittsburgh	9-1-0
6	5	Auburn	9-2-0
5	6	Nebraska	10-1-0
7	7	Mississippi	7-1-2
9	8	Alabama	9-2-0
10	9	**Michigan State**	6-2-1
8	10	Oklahoma	8-2-0

CONFERENCE STANDINGS

	Conference			Overall		
	W	L	T	W	L	T
Illinois	5	1	1	8	1	1
Michigan State	4	1	1	6	2	1
Ohio State	4	1	1	5	3	1
Purdue	4	3	0	5	4	0
Wisconsin	3	4	0	5	4	0
Northwestern	3	4	0	5	4	0
Michigan	2	3	2	3	4	2
Iowa	2	3	1	3	3	2
Minnesota	2	5	0	3	6	0
Indiana	1	5	0	3	6	0
Penn State*				7	3	0

BOWL GAMES

DATE	GAME	SCORE
J1	**Rose**	Illinois 17, Washington 7

CONSENSUS ALL-AMERICANS

POS	Name	HT	WT	School	AP	FC	FW	NE	SN	PI
B	**Sherman Lewis**	5-8	154	Michigan State	•	•		•		
T	**Carl Eller**	6-6	241	Minnesota	•	•	•	•		•
C	**Dick Butkus**	6-3	234	Illinois	•	•	•	•	•	•

OTHERS RECEIVING FIRST-TEAM HONORS
| G | Mike Reilly | | | Iowa | | • | | | | |

ALL-BIG TEN TEAM

POS	Offense		POS	Defense
RB	Sherman Lewis, Michigan State		DE	Dan Underwood, Michigan State
RB	Tom Nowatzke, Indiana		DE	Chuck Logan, Northwestern
C	Dick Butkus, Illinois		DT	Carl Eller, Minnesota
G	Mike Reilly, Iowa		LB	Louis Holland, Wisconsin
G	Wally Hilgenberg, Iowa		DB	Paul Warfield, Ohio State
G	Joe O'Donnell, Michigan		DB	Ron DiGravio, Purdue
T	Archie Sutton, Illinois			
T	Tom Keating, Michigan			
TE	Bob Hadrick, Purdue			

HEISMAN TROPHY VOTING

	PLAYER	POS	SCHOOL	1ST	2ND	3RD	TOTAL
3	**Sherman Lewis**	RB	Michigan State	53	80	50	369
6	**Dick Butkus**	C	Illinois	10	49	44	172

NCAA STATISTICAL LEADERS

INDIVIDUAL

RUSHING/YARDS PER CARRY		G	ATT	YDS	YPC
6	Sherman Lewis, Michigan State	9	90	577	6.4

Based on top 42 rushers

PUNTING		PUNT	YDS	AVG
5	Merlin Norenberg, Northwestern	32	1325	41.4

PUNT RETURNS/YARDS		PR	YDS	AVG
4	Junior Powell, Penn State*	18	221	12.3

INTERCEPTIONS		INT	YDS
2	Mike Dundy, Illinois	6	82
6	Dick McCauley, Northwestern	5	36

TEAM

PASSING OFFENSE		G	ATT	COM	INT	PCT	YDS	YPA	TD	I%YPC	YPG
10	Northwestern	9	192	98	16	51.0	1473	7.7	7	8.3 15.0	163.7

RUSHING DEFENSE		G	ATT	YDS	AVG	YPG
4	Michigan State	9	343	738	2.2	82.0

TOTAL DEFENSE		G	P	YDS	AVG	YPG
4	Michigan State	9	516	1567	3.0	174.1

SCORING DEFENSE		G	PTS	AVG
4	Michigan State	9	63	7.0

1964

FINAL POLL

UP	AP	TEAM	RECORD
1	1	Alabama	10-1-0
2	2	Arkansas	11-0-0
3	3	Notre Dame	9-1-0
4	4	Michigan	9-1-0
5	5	Texas	10-1-0
6	6	Nebraska	9-2-0
7	7	LSU	8-2-1
8	8	Oregon State	8-3-0
9	9	Ohio State	7-2-0
10	10	USC	7-3-0

CONFERENCE STANDINGS

	CONFERENCE			OVERALL		
	W	L	T	W	L	T
Michigan	6	1	0	9	1	0
Ohio State	5	1	0	7	2	0
Purdue	5	2	0	6	3	0
Illinois	4	3	0	6	3	0
Minnesota	4	3	0	5	4	0
Michigan State	3	3	0	4	5	0
Wisconsin	2	5	0	3	6	0
Northwestern	2	5	0	3	6	0
Iowa	1	5	0	3	6	0
Indiana	1	5	0	2	7	0
Penn State*				6	4	0

BOWL GAMES

DATE	GAME	SCORE
J1	Rose	Michigan 34, Oregon State 7

CONSENSUS ALL-AMERICANS

POS	Name	HT	WT	School	AP	CP	FC	FW	NE	PI
G	Glenn Ressler	6-2	230	Penn State*	•	•	•	•		•
C	Dick Butkus	6-3	237	Illinois	•	•	•	•		•

	Others receiving first-team honors									
B	Bob Timberlake			Michigan		•				
B	Tom Nowatzke			Indiana			•			
B	Jim Grabowski			Illinois		•				•
B	Arnold Chonko			Ohio State					•	
E	Karl Noonan			Iowa					•	
T	Bill Yearby			Michigan		•			•	•
C	Dwight Kelley			Ohio State				•		

HEISMAN TROPHY VOTING

PLAYER	POS	SCHOOL	TOTAL
3 Dick Butkus	LB	Illinois	505
4 Bob Timberlake	QB	Michigan	361

AWARD WINNERS

PLAYER	POS	SCHOOL	AWARD
Glenn Ressler	C-G	Penn State*	Maxwell

ALL-BIG TEN TEAM

POS	Offense		POS	Defense
QB	Gary Snook, Iowa		DE	John Wright, Illinois
QB	Bob Timberlake, Michigan		DE	Bill Malinchak, Indiana
RB	Arnie Chonko, Ohio State		DE	Karl Nonan, Iowa
RB	Dick Gordon, Michigan State		DE	Bill Spahr, Ohio State
RB	Jim Grabowski, Illinois		DE	Harold Wells, Purdue
RB	Kraig Lofquist, Minnesota		DT	Archie Sutton, Illinois
RB	Charles Migvanka, Michigan State		DT	Jerry Rush, Michigan State
RB	Tom Nowatzke, Indiana		DT	Jim Garcia, Purdue
C	Dick Butkus, Illinois		LB	Tom Cecchini, Michigan
C	Joe Cerne, Northwestern		LB	Dwight Kelly, Ohio State
G	Don Croftcheck, Indiana		LB	Tom Bugel, Ohio State
G	Dan Poretta, Ohio State		DB	George Donnelly, Illinois
T	Bill Yearby, Michigan			
T	Jim Davidson, Ohio State			
TE	Aaron Brown, Minnesota			
TE	Jim Conley, Michigan			
TE	Bob Hadrick, Purdue			

NCAA STATISTICAL LEADERS

INDIVIDUAL

PASSING/COMPLETIONS	G	ATT	COM	PCT	INT	I%	YDS	YPA	TD	TD%	COM.PG
3 Gary Snook, Iowa	9	311	151	48.6	14	4.5	2062	6.6	11	3.5	16.8
6 Richie Badar, Indiana	9	245	121	49.4	15	6.1	1571	6.4	9	3.7	13.4

RUSHING/YARDS			G	ATT	YDS	AVG	YPC
2 Jim Grabowski, Illinois			9	186	1004	5.4	111.6

RUSHING/YARDS PER CARRY			G	ATT	YDS	YPC
1 Dick Gordon, Michigan State			9	123	741	6.0
6 Jim Grabowski, Illinois			9	186	1004	5.4
Based on top 42 rushers						

RECEIVING/RECEPTIONS	G	REC	YDS	TD	YPR	YPG	RPG
3 Karl Noonan, Iowa	9	59	933	4	15.8	103.7	6.6
10 Bill Malinchak, Indiana	9	46	634	5	13.8	70.4	5.1

PUNTING			PR	YDS	AVG
8 Lou Bobich, Michigan State			37	1536	41.5

PUNT RETURNS			PR	YDS	AVG
10 Joe Vargo, Penn State*			19	233	12.3

KICKOFF RETURNS/YARDS			KR	YDS	AVG
3 Ron Smith, Wisconsin			19	481	25.3

SCORING		TDS	XP	FG	PTS
4 Bob Timberlake, Michigan		8	20	4	80
7 Tom Nowatzke, Indiana		10	10	1	73

INTERCEPTIONS				INT	YDS
1 George Donnelly, Illinois				8	54
3 Arnie Chonko, Ohio State				7	72

TEAM

RUSHING OFFENSE			G	ATT	YDS	AVG	YPG
4 Michigan			9	516	2141	4.1	237.9

PASSING OFFENSE	G	ATT	COM	INT	PCT	YDS	YPA	TD	I%	YPC	YPG
3 Iowa	9	321	154	14	48.0	2125	6.6	11	4.4	13.8	236.1
9 Indiana	9	250	123	15	49.2	1597	6.4	9	6.0	13.0	177.4

TOTAL OFFENSE			G	P	YDS	AVG	PG
8 Michigan			9	659	3074	4.7	341.6

RUSHING DEFENSE			G	ATT	YDS	AVG	YPG
9 Michigan			9	326	781	2.4	86.8
10 Illinois			9	323	786	2.4	87.3

*Independent or other conference affiliation

1965

FINAL POLL

AP	TEAM	RECORD
1	Alabama	9-1-1
2	**Michigan State**	10-1-0
3	Arkansas	10-1-0
4	UCLA	8-2-1
5	Nebraska	10-1-0
6	Missouri	8-2-1
7	Tennessee	8-1-2
8	LSU	8-3-0
9	Notre Dame	7-2-1
10	USC	7-2-1

CONFERENCE STANDINGS

	CONFERENCE			OVERALL		
	W	L	T	W	L	T
Michigan State	7	0	0	10	1	0
Ohio State	6	1	0	7	2	0
Purdue	5	2	0	7	2	1
Minnesota	5	2	0	5	4	1
Illinois	4	3	0	6	4	0
Northwestern	3	4	0	4	6	0
Michigan	2	5	0	4	6	0
Wisconsin	2	5	0	2	7	1
Indiana	1	6	0	2	8	0
Iowa	0	7	0	1	9	0
Penn State*				5	5	0

BOWL GAMES

DATE	GAME	SCORE
J1	Rose	UCLA 14, Michigan State 12

CONSENSUS ALL-AMERICANS

POS	Offense	HT	WT	School	AP	CP	FC	FW	NE	PI
B	**Jim Grabowski**	6-2	211	Illinois	•	•	•	•	•	•
B	**Bob Griese**	6-1	185	Purdue		•	•		•	•

OTHERS RECEIVING FIRST-TEAM HONORS

POS				School	AP	CP	FC	FW	NE	PI
B	Clint Jones			Michigan State				•		
B	Steve Juday			Michigan State	•					
E	Gene Washington			Michigan State		•				
T	Ron Goovert			Michigan State				•		
T	Karl Singer			Purdue	•					
G	Doug Van Horn			Ohio State		•	•		•	
G	Harold Lucas			Michigan State		•		•		

CP and NE named Lucas as an MG; CP named Van Horn as a T

POS	Defense	HT	WT	School	AP	CP	FC	FW	NE	PI
E	**Aaron Brown**	6-4	230	Minnesota	•	•		•	•	•
E	**Bubba Smith**	6-7	268	Michigan State		•		•		
T	**Bill Yearby**	6-3	222	Michigan		•	•		•	
B	**George Webster**	6-4	204	Michigan State	•	•	•		•	•

OTHERS RECEIVING FIRST-TEAM HONORS

POS				School	AP	CP	FC	FW	NE	PI
DL	Jerry Shay			Purdue			•			
LB	Dwight Kelley			Ohio State		•			•	

FW picked one team and did not distinguish between offense and defense

ALL-BIG TEN TEAM

POS	Offense		POS	Defense
QB	Bob Griese, Purdue		DE	Dave Long, Iowa
RB	Jim Grabowski, Illinois		DE	Gene Washington, Michigan State
RB	Don Japinga, Michigan State		DE	Charles Smith, Michigan State
RB	Kraig Lofquist, Minnesota		DE	Aaron Brown, Minnesota
RB	Clint Jones, Michigan State		DT	Tom Mack, Michigan
RB	Charles King, Purdue		DT	Bill Yearby, Michigan
C	Ray Pryor, Ohio State		DT	Karl Singer, Purdue
C	Larry Kaminski, Purdue		DT	Jerry Shay, Purdue
G	John Niland, Iowa		LB	Don Hansen, Illinois
G	Harold Lucas, Michigan State		LB	Ron Goovert, Michigan State
G	Doug Van Horn, Ohio State		LB	John Fill, Ohio State
TE	Bob Hadrick, Purdue		LB	Dwight Kelly, Ohio State
			DB	Ron Acks, Illinois
			DB	Rick Volk, Michigan
			DB	Carl Ward, Michigan
			DB	George Webster, Michigan State

HEISMAN TROPHY VOTING

	PLAYER	POS	SCHOOL	1ST	2ND	3RD	TOTAL
3	Jim Grabowski	FB	Illinois	97	72	46	481
6	Steve Juday	QB	Michigan State	53	40	42	281
8	Bob Griese	QB	Purdue	32	36	25	193

NCAA STATISTICAL LEADERS

INDIVIDUAL

PASSING/COMPLETIONS	G	ATT	COM	PCT	INT	I%	YDS	YPA	TD	TD%	COM.PG
7 Bob Griese, Purdue	10	238	142	59.7	8	3.4	1719	7.2	11	4.6	14.2
10 Chuck Burt, Wisconsin	10	235	121	51.5	22	9.4	1143	4.9	5	2.1	12.1

RUSHING/YARDS				G	ATT	YDS	AVG	YPC
2 Jim Grabowski, Illinois				10	252	1,258	5.0	125.8

RUSHING/YARDS PER CARRY			G	ATT	YDS	YPC
8 Bob Apisa, Michigan State			10	121	666	5.5

Based on top 40 rushers

RECEIVING/RECEPTIONS		G	REC	YDS	TD	YPR	YPG	RPG
10 Jack Clancy, Michigan		10	52	762	5	14.7	76.2	5.2

KICKOFF RETURNS/YARDS			KR	YDS	AVG
7 Tom Barrington, Ohio State			14	480	34.3

KICK SCORING		XPA	XP	FGA	FG	PTS
4 Dick Kenney, Michigan State		23	20	18	11	53

INTERCEPTIONS			INT	YDS
4 Dick Gingrich, Penn State*			7	66
8 David Fronek, Wisconsin			6	115

TEAM

RUSHING OFFENSE		G	ATT	YDS	AVG	YPG
6 Michigan State		10	547	2375	4.3	237.5
9 Penn State*		10	525	2247	4.3	224.7

TOTAL OFFENSE		G	P	YDS	AVG	PG
10 Michigan State		10	717	3561	5.0	356.1

RUSHING DEFENSE		G	ATT	YDS	AVG	YPG
1 Michigan State		10	338	456	1.3	45.6

TOTAL DEFENSE		G	P	YDS	AVG	PG
2 Michigan State		10	572	1699	3.0	169.9

SCORING DEFENSE		G	PTS	AVG
1 Michigan State		10	62	6.2

1966

FINAL POLL

AP	TEAM	RECORD
1	Notre Dame	9-0-1
2	**Michigan State**	9-0-1
3	Alabama	11-0-0
4	Georgia	10-1-0
5	UCLA	9-1-0
6	Nebraska	9-2-0
7	**Purdue**	9-2-0
8	Georgia Tech	9-2-0
9	Miami, Fla.	8-2-1
10	SMU	8-3-0

CONFERENCE STANDINGS

	CONFERENCE			OVERALL		
	W	L	T	W	L	T
Michigan State	7	0	0	9	0	1
Purdue	6	1	0	9	2	0
Michigan	4	3	0	6	4	0
Illinois	4	3	0	4	6	0
Minnesota	3	3	1	4	5	1
Ohio State	3	4	0	4	5	0
Northwestern	2	4	1	3	6	1
Wisconsin	2	4	1	3	6	1
Indiana	1	5	1	1	8	1
Iowa	1	6	0	2	8	0
Penn State*				5	5	0

BOWL GAMES

DATE	GAME	SCORE
J2	**Rose**	Purdue 14, USC 13

CONSENSUS ALL-AMERICANS

POS	**Offense**	HT	WT	School	AP	CP	FC	FW	NE	PI
B	**Clint Jones**	6-0	206	Michigan State	•	•				•
E	**Jack Clancy**	6-1	192	Michigan	•	•	•	•	•	•

	OTHERS RECEIVING FIRST-TEAM HONORS									
B	Bob Griese			Purdue			•			
E	Gene Washington			Michigan State			•			•
E	Jim Bierne			Purdue			•			
T	Jerry West			Michigan State			•			•
C	Ray Pryor			Ohio State					•	

POS	**Defense**	HT	WT	School	AP	CP	FC	FW	NE	PI
E	**Bubba Smith**	6-7	283	Michigan State	•	•	•	•	•	•
B	**George Webster**	6-4	218	Michigan State	•	•	•	•	•	•

	OTHERS RECEIVING FIRST-TEAM HONORS									
B	Larry Wachholtz			Michigan State				•		

HEISMAN TROPHY VOTING

	PLAYER	POS	SCHOOL	1ST	2ND	3RD	TOTAL
2	**Bob Griese**	QB	Purdue	184	95	74	816
6	**Clint Jones**	RB	Michigan State	22	43	52	204

ALL-BIG TEN TEAM

POS	**Offense**	POS	**Defense**
QB	Bob Griese, Purdue	DE	Charles "Bubba" Smith, Michigan St.
RB	Phil Clark, Northwestern	DE	George Olion, Purdue
RB	Bruce Sullivan, Illinois	DG	Chuck Kyle, Purdue
RB	Ron Bess, Illinois	DT	Nick Jordan, Michigan State
RB	Rick Volk, Michigan	LB	Bob Richter, Wisconsin
RB	Jim Detwiler, Michigan	LB	Clinton Jones, Michigan State
RB	Clint Jones, Michigan State	LB	George Webster, Michigan State
FB	Bob Apisa, Michigan State	LB	Frank Nunley, Michigan
C	Ray Pryor, Ohio State	LB	Charles Thornhill, Michigan State
G	Tom Shuette, Indiana	LB	Dave Fisher, Michigan
G	Don Bailey, Michigan	DB	Ken Kmiec, Illinois
G	Tony Conti, Michigan State	DB	Bruce Sullivan, Illinois
G	Chuck Erlenbaugh, Purdue	DB	Jesse Phillips, Michigan State
T	Jerry West, Michigan State	DB	Carl Ward, Michigan
T	Dick Himes, Ohio State		
T	Jack Calcaterra, Purdue		
T	Lance Olssen, Purdue		
E	Jack Clancy, Michigan		
E	Gene Washington, Michigan State		

NCAA STATISTICAL LEADERS

INDIVIDUAL

RECEIVING/RECEPTIONS	G	REC	YDS	TD	YPR	YPG	RPG
2 Jack Clancy, Michigan	10	76	1079	4	14.2	107.9	7.6
6 Jim Beirne, Purdue	10	64	768	8	12.0	76.8	6.4
8 John Wright, Illinois	10	60	831	4	13.9	83.1	6.0

KICKOFF RETURNS/YARDS	KR	YDS	TD	AVG
2 John Ginter, Indiana	26	532	0	20.5
3 Tom Schinke, Wisconsin	21	527	0	25.1

SCORING	TDS	XP	FG	PTS
9 Bob Griese, Purdue	6	33	4	81

TEAM

RUSHING OFFENSE	G	ATT	YDS	AVG	TD	YPG
8 **Michigan State**	10	523	2305	4.4	29	230.5

RUSHING DEFENSE	G	ATT	YDS	AVG	TD	YPG
3 **Michigan State**	10	336	514	1.5	6	51.4

PASSING DEFENSE	G	ATT	COM	PCT	YPC	INT	I%	YDS	YPA	TD	YPG
7 **Michigan**	10	196	82	41.8	11.6	9	4.6	953	4.9	6	95.3

TOTAL OFFENSE	G	P	YDS	AVG	TD	YPG
8 **Michigan State**	10	596	2093	3.5	13	209.3

SCORING DEFENSE	G	PTS	AVG
7 **Michigan State**	10	293	29.3
9 **Purdue**	10	283	28.3

1967

FINAL POLL

UP	AP	TEAM	RECORD
1	1	USC	10-1-0
2	2	Tennessee	9-2-0
3	3	Oklahoma	10-1-0
6	4	**Indiana**	9-2-0
4	5	Notre Dame	8-2-0
5	6	Wyoming	10-1-0
8	7	Oregon State	7-2-1
7	8	Alabama	8-2-1
9	9	**Purdue**	8-2-0
	10	Penn State*	8-2-1
10		UCLA	7-2-1

CONFERENCE STANDINGS

	CONFERENCE			OVERALL		
	W	L	T	W	L	T
Indiana	6	1	0	9	2	0
Minnesota	6	1	0	8	2	0
Purdue	6	1	0	8	2	0
Ohio State	5	2	0	6	3	0
Illinois	3	4	0	4	6	0
Michigan	3	4	0	4	6	0
Michigan State	3	4	0	3	7	0
Northwestern	2	5	0	3	7	0
Iowa	0	6	1	1	8	1
Wisconsin	0	6	1	0	9	1
Penn State*				8	2	1

BOWL GAMES

DATE	GAME	SCORE
D30	**Gator**	Florida State 17, Penn State* 17
J1	**Rose**	USC 14, Indiana 3

CONSENSUS ALL-AMERICANS

POS	**Offense**	HT	WT	**School**	AP	CP	FC	FW	NE	PI
B	**Leroy Keyes**	6-3	199	Purdue	•	•	•	•	•	•

OTHERS RECEIVING FIRST-TEAM HONORS

POS					AP	CP	FC	FW	NE	PI
E	Ted Kwalick			Penn State*			•		•	
G	Garry Cassells			Indiana	•			•		

POS	**Defense**	HT	WT	**School**	AP	CP	FC	FW	NE	PI
None										

OTHERS RECEIVING FIRST-TEAM HONORS

POS								FW	NE	
E	Bob Stein			Minnesota				•	•	

HEISMAN TROPHY VOTING

	PLAYER	POS	SCHOOL	1ST	2ND	3RD	TOTAL
3	**Leroy Keyes**	HB	Purdue	278	142	248	1366

ALL-BIG TEN TEAM

POS	**Offense**	POS	**Defense**
QB	Harry Gonso, Indiana	DE	George Chatlos, Michigan State
QB	Mike Phipps, Purdue	DE	Bob Stein, Minnesota
RB	Ron Bess, Illinois	DE	Billy Anders, Ohio State
RB	Leroy Keyes, Purdue	DE	George Olion, Purdue
RB	Ron Johnson, Michigan	DT	John Williams, Minnesota
C	Joe Dayton, Michigan	DT	McKinley Boston, Minnesota
G	Gary Cassells, Indiana	DT	Tom Domres, Wisconsin
G	Bruce Gunstra, Northwestern	LB	Ken Kaczmarek, Indiana
G	Chuck Kyle, Purdue	LB	Jim Sniadecki, Indiana
T	Dick Himes, Ohio State	LB	Tom Stincic, Michigan
T	Lance Olssen, Purdue	LB	Ken Criter, Wisconsin
TE	Jim Beirne, Purdue	DB	Tom Sakal, Minnesota
		DB	Dick Marvel, Purdue
		DB	Perry Williams, Purdue
		K	Dick Emmerich, Northwestern

NCAA STATISTICAL LEADERS

INDIVIDUAL

	RUSHING/YARDS		G	ATT	YDS	TD	AVG	YPG
10	Ron Johnson, Michigan		10	220	1005	7	4.6	100.5

	RUSHING/YARDS PER CARRY			G	ATT	YDS	YPC
2	Leroy Keyes, Purdue			10	149	986	6.6

*-Based on top 34 rushers

	RECEIVING/RECEPTIONS	G	REC	YDS	TD	YPR	YPG	RPG
10	Allan Bream, Iowa	10	55	703	5	12.8	70.3	5.5

	KICKOFF RETURNS			KR	YDS	TD	AVG
5	Ron Johnson, Michigan			26	498	0	19.2
6	Jim Kirkpatrick, Purdue			20	487	0	24.4

	SCORING				TDS	XP	FG	PTS
1	Leroy Keyes, Purdue				19	0	0	114
5	Don Abbey, Penn State*				9	25	3	88

TEAM

	TOTAL OFFENSE	G	P	YDS	AVG	TD	YPG
2	Purdue	10	778	4236	5.4	41	423.6

	SCORING OFFENSE				G	PTS	AVG
9	Purdue				10	291	29.1

BIG TEN ANNUAL REVIEW & BOWLS

1968

FINAL POLL

AP	TEAM	RECORD
1	Notre Dame	9-0-1
1	Ohio State	10-0-0
2	Penn State*	11-0-0
3	Texas	9-1-1
4	USC	9-1-1
5	Notre Dame	7-2-1
6	Arkansas	10-1-0
7	Kansas	9-2-0
8	Georgia	8-1-2
9	Missouri	8-3-0
10	Purdue	8-2-0
11	Oklahoma	7-4-0
12	Michigan	8-2-0
13	Tennessee	8-2-1
14	SMU	8-3-0
15	Oregon State	7-3-0
16	Auburn	7-4-0
17	Alabama	8-3-0
18	Houston	6-2-2
19	LSU	8-3-0
20	Ohio U.	10-1-0

CONFERENCE STANDINGS

	CONFERENCE			OVERALL		
	W	L	T	W	L	T
Ohio State	7	0	0	10	0	0
Michigan	6	1	0	8	2	0
Purdue	5	2	0	8	2	0
Minnesota	5	2	0	6	4	0
Indiana	4	3	0	6	4	0
Iowa	4	3	0	5	5	0
Michigan State	2	5	0	5	5	0
Illinois	1	6	0	1	9	0
Northwestern	1	6	0	1	9	0
Wisconsin	0	7	0	0	10	0
Penn State*				11	0	0

BOWL GAMES

DATE	GAME	SCORE
J1	Rose	Ohio State 27, USC 16
J1	Orange	Penn State* 15, Kansas 14

CONSENSUS ALL-AMERICANS

POS	Offense	HT	WT	School	AP	CP	FC	FW	NE	PI
B	Leroy Keyes	6-3	205	Purdue	•	•	•	•	•	•
E	Ted Kwalick	6-4	230	Penn State*	•	•	•	•	•	•
T	Dave Foley	6-5	246	Ohio State	•	•	•	•	•	•

OTHERS RECEIVING FIRST-TEAM HONORS

B	Ron Johnson			Michigan				•		

POS	Defense	HT	WT	School	AP	CP	FC	FW	NE	PI
MG	Chuck Kyle	6-1	225	Purdue		•	•	•		•
LB	Dennis Onkotz	6-2	205	Penn State*	•		•			•

OTHERS RECEIVING FIRST-TEAM HONORS

B	Al Brenner			Michigan State		•		•		

HEISMAN TROPHY VOTING

	PLAYER	POS	SCHOOL	1ST	2ND	3RD	TOTAL
2	Leroy Keyes	HB	Purdue	49	358	240	1103
4	Ted Kwalick	TE	Penn State*	14	69	74	254
6	Ron Johnson	HB	Michigan	12	36	50	158

ALL-BIG TEN TEAM

POS	Offense		POS	Defense
QB	Dennis Brown, Michigan		DE	Jade Butcher, Indiana
RB	Ed Podolak, Iowa		DE	Jim Mandich, Michigan
RB	Ron Johnson, Michigan		DE	Bob Stein, Minnesota
FB	Leroy Keyes, Purdue		DE	Phil Seymour, Michigan
C	Jack Rudnay, Northwestern		DT	Tom Gross, Michigan
G	John Meskimen, Iowa		DT	Tom Curtis, Michigan
G	Dick Enderle, Minnesota		DT	Bill Yanchar, Purdue
G	Chuck Kyle, Purdue		DT	Rufus Mayers, Ohio State
G	Gary Roberts, Purdue		LB	Tom Stincic, Michigan
T	Tony Pleviak, Illinois		LB	Noel Jenke, Minnesota
T	Charles Bailey, Michigan State		LB	Ken Criter, Wisconsin
T	Paul DeNuccio, Purdue		LB	Al Brenner, Michigan State
T	Dave Foley, Ohio State		DB	Ted Provost, Ohio State
			DB	Jack Tatum, Ohio State
			DB	Nate Cunningham, Indiana
			DB	Perry Williams, Purdue

NCAA STATISTICAL LEADERS

INDIVIDUAL

RUSHING/YARDS	G	ATT	YDS	TD	AVG	YPG
6 Ron Johnson, Michigan	10	255	1391	19	5.5	139.1

RUSHING/YARDS PER CARRY	G	ATT	YDS	YPC
6 Ed Podolak, Iowa	10	154	937	6.1
9 Ron Johnson, Michigan	10	255	1391	5.5
Based on top 32 rushers				

KICKOFF RETURNS/YARDS	KR	YDS	TD	AVG
1 Mike Adamle, Northwestern	34	732	0	21.5

SCORING	TDS	XP	FG	PTS
4 Ron Johnson, Michigan	19	2	0	116
8 James Otis, Ohio State	16	0	0	96

INTERCEPTIONS	INT	YDS	TD
3 Tom Curtis, Michigan	10	182	0
8 Neal Smith, Penn State*	8	74	0

TEAM

RUSHING OFFENSE	G	ATT	YDS	AVG	TD	YPG
3 Ohio State	9	589	2758	4.7	33	306.4
10 Penn State*	10	614	2739	4.5	33	273.9

TOTAL OFFENSE	G	P	YDS	AVG	TD	YPG
5 Ohio State	9	762	4041	5.3	41	449.0
10 Iowa	10	759	4404	5.8	45	440.4

RUSHING DEFENSE	G	ATT	YDS	AVG	TD	YPG
6 Penn State*	10	404	831	2.1	6	83.1

SCORING OFFENSE	G	PTS	AVG
8 Penn State*	10	339	33.9
10 Ohio State	9	296	32.9

SCORING DEFENSE	G	PTS	AVG
6 Penn State*	10	106	10.6

1969

Final Poll

AP	TEAM	RECORD
1	Texas	11-0-0
2	Penn State*	11-0-0
3	USC	10-0-1
4	**Ohio State**	8-1-0
5	Notre Dame	8-2-1
6	Missouri	9-2-0
7	Arkansas	9-2-0
8	Mississippi	8-3-0
9	**Michigan**	8-3-0
10	LSU	9-1-0
11	Nebraska	9-2-0
12	Houston	9-2-0
13	UCLA	8-1-1
14	Florida	9-1-1
15	Tennessee	9-2-0
16	Colorado	8-3-0
17	West Virginia	10-1-0
18	**Purdue**	8-2-0
19	Stanford	7-2-1
20	Auburn	8-3-0

Conference Standings

	Conference			Overall		
	W	L	T	W	L	T
Ohio State	6	1	0	8	1	0
Michigan	6	1	0	8	3	0
Purdue	5	2	0	8	2	0
Minnesota	4	3	0	4	5	1
Iowa	3	4	0	5	5	0
Indiana	3	4	0	4	6	0
Wisconsin	3	4	0	3	7	0
Northwestern	3	4	0	3	7	0
Michigan State	2	5	0	4	6	0
Illinois	0	7	0	0	10	0
Penn State*				11	0	0

Bowl Games

DATE	GAME	SCORE
J1	**Orange**	Penn State* 10, Missouri 3
J1	**Rose**	USC 10, Michigan 3

Consensus All-Americans

POS	**Offense**	HT	WT	**School**	AP	CP	FC	FW	NE	PI
B	**Mike Phipps**	6-3	206	Purdue	•	•	•	•	•	•
B	**Jim Otis**	6-0	214	Ohio State	•		•		•	•
E	**Jim Mandich**	6-3	222	Michigan	•	•	•	•	•	•

	Others receiving first-team honors		
B	Charlie Pittman	Penn State*	•
B	Rex Kern	Ohio State	•
G	Ron Saul	Michigan State	•

POS	**Defense**	HT	WT	**School**	AP	CP	FC	FW	NE	PI
T	**Mike Reid**	6-3	240	Penn State*	•	•	•	•	•	•
MG	**Jim Stillwagon**	6-0	216	Ohio State	•	•	•	•	•	•
LB	**Dennis Onkotz**	6-2	212	Penn State*	•	•	•		•	•
B	**Jack Tatum**	6-0	204	Ohio State	•	•	•	•	•	•
B	**Tom Curtis**	6-1	190	Michigan	•	•				•

	Others receiving first-team honors		
B	Neal Smith	Penn State*	• •

Heisman Trophy Voting

	PLAYER	POS	SCHOOL	1ST	2ND	3RD	TOTAL
2	**Mike Phipps**	QB	Purdue	226	230	196	1334
3	**Rex Kern**	QB	Ohio State	154	134	126	856
5	**Mike Reid**	DT	Penn State*	61	39	36	297
7	**Jim Otis**	FB	Ohio State	12	27	31	121
10	**Jack Tatum**	DB	Ohio State	13	22	22	105

Award Winners

PLAYER	POS	SCHOOL	AWARD
Mike Reid	DT	Penn State*	Maxwell
Mike Reid	DT	Penn State*	Outland

All-Big Ten Team

POS	**Offense**
QB	Mike Phipps, Purdue
RB	John Isenbarger, Indiana
RB	John Isenbarger, Indiana
RB	Billy Taylor, Michigan
RB	Mike Sensibaugh, Ohio State
FB	Mike Adamle, Northwestern
C	Guy Murdock, Michigan
C	Brian Donovan, Ohio State
G	Don DeSalle, Indiana
G	John Meskimen, Iowa
G	Jim Stillwagon, Ohio State
G	Ron Saul, Michigan State
T	Dan Dierdorf, Michigan
T	Ron Curl, Michigan State
T	Rufus Mayers, Ohio State
T	Paul DeNuccio, Purdue
T	Paul Schmidlin, Ohio State
TE	Jim Mandich, Michigan
TE	Ray Parson, Minnesota

POS	**Defense**
DE	Jade Butcher, Indiana
DE	Dave Whitfield, Ohio State
DE	Mark Debevec, Ohio State
DE	Jim Seymour, Michigan
DE	Rich Saul, Michigan State
DT	Tom Curtis, Michigan
DT	Dave Foley, Ohio State
DT	Bill Yanchar, Purdue
DT	Charles Hutchinson, Ohio State
LB	Marty Huff, Michigan
LB	Doug Adams, Ohio State
LB	Veno Paraskevas, Purdue
DB	Jack Tatum, Ohio State
DB	Ted Provost, Ohio State

NCAA Statistical Leaders

INDIVIDUAL

	PASSING/COMPLETIONS	G	ATT	COM	PCT	INT	I%	YDS	YPA	TD	TD%	COM.PG
10	**Mike Phipps, Purdue**	10	321	169	52.6	18	5.6	2527	7.9	23	7.2	16.9

	RUSHING/YARDS	G	ATT	YDS	TD	AVG	YPG
6	**John Isenbarger, Indiana**	10	233	1,217	5	5.2	121.7

	RUSHING/YARDS PER CARRY	G	ATT	YDS	YPC
3	**Billy Taylor, Michigan**	10	123	808	6.6
10	**John Isenbarger, Indiana**	10	233	1217	5.2

Based on top 32 rushers

	PUNT RETURNS/YARDS	PR	YDS	TD	AVG
4	**Larry Zelina, Ohio State**	23	431	2	18.7

	KICKOFF RETURNS/YARDS	KR	YDS	TD	AVG
1	**Stan Brown, Purdue**	26	698	2	26.8
7	**Eric Allen, Michigan State**	29	598	0	20.6

	SCORING	TDS	XPT	FG	PTS
6	**Stan Brown, Purdue**	18	0	0	108
9	**Jim Otis, Ohio State**	16	0	0	96

	INTERCEPTIONS	INT	YDS	TD
2	**Neal Smith, Penn State***	10	78	1
3	**Mike Sensibaugh, Ohio State**	9	125	0
7	**Tom Curtis, Michigan**	8	165	0

TEAM

	RUSHING OFFENSE	G	ATT	YDS	AVG	TD	YPG
3	**Ohio State**	9	599	2774	4.6	36	308.2
7	**Michigan**	10	625	2776	4.4	37	277.6

	PASSING OFFENSE	G	ATT	COM	INT	PCT	YDS	YPA	TD	I%	YPC	YPG
7	**Purdue**	10	333	176	20	52.9	2679	8.0	23	6.0	15.2	267.9

	TOTAL OFFENSE	G	P	YDS	AVG	TD	YPG
4	**Ohio State**	9	829	4439	5.4	53	493.2
9	**Purdue**	10	794	4325	5.4	47	432.5

	PASSING DEFENSE	G	ATT	COM	PCT	INT	I%	YDS	YPA	TD	TD%	RATING
4	**Penn State***	10	221	86	38.9	11.3	24	10.9	972	4.4	3	97.2

	TOTAL DEFENSE	G	P	YDS	AVG	TD	YPG
3	**Penn State***	10	681	2,181	3.2	10	218.1

	SCORING OFFENSE	G	PTS	AVG
2	**Ohio State**	9	383	42.6
8	**Purdue**	10	354	35.4
9	**Michigan**	10	349	34.9

	SCORING DEFENSE	G	PTS	AVG
2	**Penn State***	10	87	8.7
8	**Ohio State**	9	93	10.3

BIG TEN ANNUAL REVIEW & BOWLS

1970

FINAL POLL

AP	TEAM	RECORD
1	Nebraska	11-0-1
2	Notre Dame	10-1-0
3	Texas	10-1-0
4	Tennessee	11-1-0
5	**Ohio State**	9-1-0
6	Arizona State	11-0-0
7	LSU	9-3-0
8	Stanford	9-3-0
9	**Michigan**	9-1-0
10	Auburn	9-2-0
11	Arkansas	9-2-0
12	Toledo	12-0-0
13	Georgia Tech	9-3-0
14	Dartmouth	9-0-0
15	USC	6-4-1
16	Air Force	9-3-0
17	Tulane	8-4-0
18	Penn State*	7-3-0
19	Houston	8-3-0
20	Mississippi	7-4-0
20	Oklahoma	7-4-1

CONFERENCE STANDINGS

	CONFERENCE			OVERALL		
	W	L	T	W	L	T
Ohio State	7	0	0	9	1	0
Michigan	6	1	0	9	1	0
Northwestern	6	1	0	6	4	0
Iowa	3	3	1	3	6	1
Wisconsin	3	4	0	4	5	1
Michigan State	3	4	0	4	6	0
Minnesota	2	4	1	3	6	1
Purdue	2	5	0	4	6	0
Illinois	1	6	0	3	7	0
Indiana	1	6	0	1	9	0
Penn State*				7	3	0

BOWL GAMES

DATE	GAME	SCORE
J1	**Rose**	Stanford 27, Ohio State 17

CONSENSUS ALL-AMERICANS

POS	Offense	HT	WT	School	AP	CP	FC	FW	NE	PI
T	**Dan Dierdorf**	6-4	250	Michigan	•		•	•	•	•

	OTHERS RECEIVING FIRST-TEAM HONORS									
RB	John Brockington			Ohio State		•				•
E	Jan White			Ohio State					•	

POS	Defense	HT	WT	School	AP	CP	FC	FW	NE	PI
MG	**Jim Stillwagon**	6-0	220	Ohio State	•	•	•	•	•	•
LB	**Jack Ham**	6-3	212	Penn State*	•	•		•	•	•
B	**Jack Tatum**	6-0	208	Ohio State	•	•	•	•	•	•

	OTHERS RECEIVING FIRST-TEAM HONORS									
T	Marty Huff			Michigan					•	
MG	Henry Hill			Michigan		•				
B	Mike Sensibaugh			Ohio State		•				•

HEISMAN TROPHY VOTING

	PLAYER	POS	SCHOOL	1ST	2ND	3RD	TOTAL
5	**Rex Kern**	QB	Ohio State	17	39	59	188
7	**Jack Tatum**	DB	Ohio State	8	48	53	173

AWARD WINNERS

PLAYER	POS	SCHOOL	AWARD
Jim Stillwagon	MG	Ohio State	Outland
Jim Stillwagon	MG	Ohio State	Lombardi

ALL-BIG TEN TEAM

POS	Offense	POS	Defense
QB	Don Moorhead, Michigan	DE	Doug Dieken, Illinois
RB	Billy Taylor, Michigan	DE	Paul Staroba, Michigan
RB	John Brockington, Ohio State	DE	Mark Devebec, Ohio State
FB	Mike Adamle, Northwestern	DE	Phil Seymour, Michigan
WR	Barry Peason, Northwestern	DT	Henry Hill, Michigan
C	Tom DeLeone, Ohio State	DT	Marty Huff, Michigan
C	Guy Murdock, Michigan	DT	John Rodman, Northwestern
C	Joe Zigulich, Northwestern	DT	Dave Cheney, Ohio State
C	Mick Sikich, Northwestern	LB	Chuck Winfrey, Wisconsin
G	Reggie McKenzie, Michigan	LB	Bill Light, Minnesota
G	Phil Strickland, Ohio State	DB	Thom Darden, Michigan
G	Jim Stillwagon, Ohio State	DB	Jeff Wright, Minnesota
T	Dan Dierdorf, Michigan	DB	Eric Hutchinson, Northwestern
I	Pete Newell, Michigan	DB	Mike Sensibaugh, Ohio State
T	Ron Curl, Michigan State	DB	Jack Tatum, Ohio State
TE	Bill Gregory, Wisconsin		

NCAA STATISTICAL LEADERS

INDIVIDUAL

ALL-PURPOSE	G	RUSH	REC	RET	YDS	YPG
6 **Eric Allen, Michigan State**	10	811	125	575	1,511	151.1

RUSHING/YARDS PER GAME	G	ATT	YDS	TD	AVG	YPG
6 **Mike Adamle, Northwestern**	10	304	1255	8	4.1	125.5
10 John Brockington, Ohio State	9	240	1041	15	4.3	115.7

PUNTING			PUNT	YDS	AVG
5 **Paul Staroba, Michigan**			54	2241	41.5

PUNT RETURNS			PR	YDS	TD	AVG
10 **Gary Windy, Illinois**			17	252	1	14.8

KICKOFF RETURNS/YARDS			KR	YDS	TD	AVG
1 **Stan Brown, Purdue**			19	638	3	33.6

SCORING		TDS	XP	FG	PTS	PTPG
6 **John Brockington, Ohio State**		15	0	0	90	10.0

INTERCEPTIONS			INT	YDS	TD	INT/GM
1 **Mike Sensibaugh, Ohio State**			8	40	0	1.00
3 Neovia Greyer, Wisconsin			9	116	0	0.90

TEAM

RUSHING OFFENSE	G	ATT	YDS	AVG	TD	YPG
3 **Ohio State**	9	564	2761	4.9	32	306.8
7 Penn State*	10	617	2768	4.5	31	276.8

RUSHING DEFENSE	G	ATT	YDS	AVG	TD	YPG
6 **Penn State***	10	442	1008	2.3	12	100.8
8 Michigan	10	416	1051	2.5	5	105.1
10 Ohio State	9	391	965	2.5	4	107.2

PASSING DEFENSE	G	ATT	COM	PCT	YPC	INT	I%	YDS	YPA	TD	YPG
2 **Northwestern**	10	191	61	31.9	13.0	18	9.4	793	4.2	4	79.3

TOTAL DEFENSE	G	P	YDS	AVG	TD	YPG
10 **Ohio State**	9	628	2224	3.5	11	247.1

SCORING DEFENSE	G	PTS	AVG
4 **Michigan**	10	90	9.0
8 Ohio State	9	93	10.3

*Independent or other conference affiliation

1971

FINAL POLL

UP	AP	TEAM	RECORD
1		Nebraska	13-0-0
2		Oklahoma	11-1-0
3		Colorado	10-2-0
4		Alabama	11-1-0
5		Penn State*	11-1-0
6		Michigan	11-1-0
7		Georgia	11-1-0
8		Arizona State	11-1-0
9		Tennessee	10-2-0
10		Stanford	9-3-0
11		LSU	9-3-0
12		Auburn	9-2-0
13		Notre Dame	8-2-0
14		Toledo	12-0-0
15		Mississippi	10-2-0
16		Arkansas	8-3-1
17		Houston	9-3-0
18		Texas	8-3-0
19		Washington	8-3-0
20		USC	6-4-1

CONFERENCE STANDINGS

	CONFERENCE			OVERALL		
	W	L	T	W	L	T
Michigan	8	0	0	11	1	0
Northwestern	6	3	0	7	4	0
Ohio State	5	3	0	6	4	0
Michigan State	5	3	0	6	5	0
Illinois	5	3	0	5	6	0
Wisconsin	3	5	0	4	6	1
Minnesota	3	5	0	4	7	0
Purdue	3	5	0	3	7	0
Indiana	2	6	0	3	8	0
Iowa	1	8	0	1	10	0
Penn State*				11	1	0

BOWL GAMES

DATE	GAME	SCORE
J1	Cotton	Penn State* 30, Texas 6
J1	Rose	Stanford 13, Michigan 12

CONSENSUS ALL-AMERICANS

POS	Offense	HT	WT	School	AP	FC	FW	NE	PI
G	Reggie McKenzie	6-4	232	Michigan	•		•	•	•
T	Dave Joyner	6-0	235	Penn State*	•		•	•	•

	Others receiving first-team honors								
RB	Eric Allen			Michigan State	•				
RB	Lydell Mitchell			Penn State*	•				
E	Doug Kingswriter			Minnesota	•				
C	Tom DeLeone			Ohio State				•	•

POS	Defense	HT	WT	School	AP	FC	FW	NE	PI
LB	Mike Taylor	6-2	224	Michigan	•	•	•	•	•

	Others receiving first-team honors								
T	Ron Curl			Michigan State			•		
LB	Charlie Zapiec			Penn State*				•	
B	Eric Hutchinson			Northwestern			•		
B	Tom Darden			Michigan			•		
B	Craig Clemons			Iowa				•	

HEISMAN TROPHY VOTING

	PLAYER	POS	SCHOOL	TOTAL
5	Lydell Mitchell	RB	Penn State*	251
10	Eric Allen	RB	Michigan State	109

ALL-BIG TEN TEAM

POS	Offense		POS	Defense
QB	Maurie Daigneau, Northwestern		DE	Tab Bennett, Illinois
RB	Eric Allen, Michigan Statet		DE	Mike Keller, Michigan
RB	Rufus Ferguson, Wisconsin		DE	Gary Hrivnak, Purdue
WR	Doug Kingsriter, Minnesota		DT	Ron Curl, Michigan State
WR	Barry Peason, Northwestern		LB	Mike Taylor, Michigan
C	Tom DeLeone, Ohio State		LB	Bill Light, Minnesota
G	Reggie McKenzie, Michigan		LB	Stan White, Ohio State
T	Tom McCreight, Northwestern		LB	Randy Gradishar, Ohio State
T	Rick Simon, Ohio State		LB	George Bingham, Purdue
T	George Hassenohrl, Ohio State		DB	Brad VanPelt, Michigan State
T	Tom Luken, Purdue		DB	Craig Clemons, Iowa
			DB	Thom Darden, Michigan
			DB	Eric Hutchinson, Northwestern

NCAA STATISTICAL LEADERS

INDIVIDUAL

ALL-PURPOSE	G	RUSH	REC	PR	KR	YDS	YPG
4 Eric Allen, Michigan State	11	1,494	275	0	193	1,962	178.4

RUSHING/YARDS	G	ATT	YDS	TD	AVG	YPG
5 Lydell Mitchell, Penn State*	11	254	1567	26	6.2	142.5
6 Eric Allen, Michigan State	11	259	1494	18	5.8	135.8

RUSHING/YARDS PER CARRY	G	ATT	YDS	YPC
7 Lydell Mitchell, Penn State*	11	254	1567	6.2
10 Eric Allen, Michigan State	11	259	1494	5.8
Based on top 24 rushers				

KICKOFF RETURNS/YARDS	KR	YDS	TD	AVG
3 Greg Johnson, Wisconsin	19	540	0	28.4

SCORING	TDS	XP	FG	PTS
4 Ron Johnson, Michigan	19	2	0	116
8 James Otis, Ohio State	16	0	0	96

SCORING	TDS	XP	FG	PTS	PTPG
2 Lydell Mitchell, Penn State*	29	0	0	174	15.8
3 Eric Allen, Michigan State	18	2	0	110	10.0

KICK SCORING	XPA	XP	FGA	FG	PTS	PTPG
3 Dana Coin, Michigan	54	54	12	7	75	6.8
6 Albert Vitiello, Penn State*	62	59	13	5	74	6.7

INTERCEPTIONS	INT	YDS	TD	INT/GM
8 Willie Osley, Illinois +	7	127	1	0.64

+-Six tied with seven

TEAM

RUSHING OFFENSE	G	ATT	YDS	AVG	TD	YPG
3 Michigan	11	768	3714	4.8	46	337.6
6 Penn State*	11	619	3347	5.4	42	304.3

TOTAL OFFENSE	G	P	YDS	AVG	TD	YPG
5 Penn State*	11	798	4995	6.3	60	454.1
10 Michigan	11	882	4397	5.0	51	399.7

RUSHING DEFENSE	G	ATT	YDS	AVG	TD	YPG
1 Michigan	11	418	696	1.7	3	63.3
10 Penn State*	11	483	1292	2.7	3	117.5

TOTAL DEFENSE	G	P	YDS	AVG	TD	YPG
2 Michigan	11	632	1977	3.1	9	179.7

SCORING OFFENSE	G	PTS	AVG
2 Penn State*	11	454	41.3
5 Michigan	11	409	37.2

SCORING DEFENSE	G	PTS	AVG
1 Michigan	11	70	6.4

1972

FINAL POLL

AP	TEAM	RECORD
1	USC	12-0-0
2	Oklahoma	11-1-0
3	Texas	10-1-0
4	Nebraska	9-2-1
5	Auburn	10-1-0
6	**Michigan**	10-1-0
7	Alabama	10-2-0
8	Tennessee	10-2-0
9	**Ohio State**	9-2-0
10	**Penn State***	10-2-0
11	LSU	9-2-1
12	North Carolina	11-1-0
13	Arizona State	10-2-0
14	Notre Dame	8-3-0
15	UCLA	8-3-0
16	Colorado	8-4-0
17	North Carolina St.	8-3-1
18	Louisville	9-1-0
19	Washington State	7-4-0
20	Georgia Tech	7-4-1

CONFERENCE STANDINGS

	CONFERENCE			OVERALL		
	W	L	T	W	L	T
Michigan	7	1	0	10	1	0
Ohio State	7	1	0	9	2	0
Purdue	6	2	0	6	5	0
Michigan State	5	2	1	5	5	1
Minnesota	4	4	0	4	7	0
Indiana	3	5	0	5	6	0
Illinois	3	5	0	3	8	0
Iowa	2	6	1	3	7	1
Wisconsin	2	6	0	4	7	0
Northwestern	1	8	0	2	9	0
Penn State*				10	2	0

BOWL GAMES

DATE	GAME	SCORE
D31	**Sugar**	Oklahoma 14, Penn State* 0
J1	**Rose**	USC 42, Ohio State 17

CONSENSUS ALL-AMERICANS

POS	Offense	HT	WT	School	AP	CF	FC	FW	NE	PI
RB	**Otis Armstrong**	5-11	197	Purdue	•	•		•	•	•
T	**Paul Seymour**	6-5	250	Michigan			•	•	•	

OTHERS RECEIVING FIRST-TEAM HONORS

POS				School	AP	CF				
QB	John Hufnagel			Penn State	•	•				
T	John Hicks			Ohio State	•	•				

POS	Defense	HT	WT	School	AP	CF	FC	FW	NE	PI
E	**Bruce Bannon**	6-3	224	Penn State		•	•	•	•	•
T	**Dave Butz**	6-7	279	Purdue		•	•	•	•	•
LB	**Randy Gradishar**	6-3	232	Ohio State	•	•		•	•	•
LB	**John Skorupan**	6-2	208	Penn State	•	•		•	•	•
B	**Brad VanPelt**	6-5	221	Michigan State	•	•	•	•	•	•
B	**Randy Logan**	6-2	192	Michigan	•	•		•		

HEISMAN TROPHY VOTING

	PLAYER	POS	SCHOOL	1ST	2ND	3RD	TOTAL
6	John Hufnagel	QB	Penn State	62	28	50	292
8	Otis Armstrong	HB	Purdue	44	24	28	208

AWARD WINNERS

PLAYER	POS	SCHOOL	AWARD
Brad VanPelt	DB	Michigan State	Maxwell

ALL-CONFERENCE TEAM

POS	Offense	POS	Defense
QB	Mike Wells, Illinois	DE	Clint Spearman, Michigan
RB	Ed Shuttlesworth, Michigan	DE	Steve Baumgartner, Purdue
RB	Rufus Ferguson, Wisconsin	DT	Fred Grambau, Michigan
RB	Otis Armstrong, Purdue	DT	Dave Butz, Purdue
WR	Glenn Scolnik, Indiana	LB	Gail Clark, Michigan State
WR	Jim Lash, Northwestern	LB	John King, Minnesota
WR	Steve Craig, Northwestern	LB	Bill Light, Minnesota
WR	Billy Joe DuPree, Michigan State	LB	Randy Gradishar, Ohio State
C	Larry McCarren, Illinois	LB	George Bingham, Purdue
G	Tom Coyle, Michigan	LB	Dave Lokanc, Wisconsin
G	Charles Bonica, Ohio State	DB	Randy Logan, Michigan
T	Paul Seymour, Michigan	DB	Dave Brown, Michigan
T	Ron Curl, Michigan State	DB	Bill Simpson, Michigan State
T	John Hicks, Ohio State	DB	Brad VanPelt, Michigan State
T	George Hassenohrl, Ohio State		
K	Chris Gartner, Indiana		

*Independent or other conference affiliation

1973

NCAA Statistical Leaders

INDIVIDUAL

ALL-PURPOSE

		G	RUSH	REC	PR	KR	YDS	YPG
5	Otis Armstrong, Purdue	11	1361	55	0	452	1868	169.8

RUSHING/Yards Per Game

		G	ATT	YDS	TD	AVG	YPG
5	Otis Armstrong, Purdue	11	243	1361	9	5.6	123.7

RUSHING/Yards Per Carry

		G	ATT	YDS	YPC
6	Otis Armstrong, Purdue	11	243	1361	5.6
	Based on top 26 rushers				

PUNT RETURNS

		PR	YDS	TD	AVG
8	Bill Simpson, Michigan State	21	286	2	13.6

KICKOFF RETURNS

		KR	YDS	TD	AVG
7	Earl Douthitt, Iowa	22	541	0	24.6

SCORING

		TDS	XP	FG	PTS	PTPG
1	Harold Henson, Ohio State	20	0	0	120	12.0

TEAM

PASSING DEFENSE

		G	ATT	COM	PCT	YPC	INT	I%	YDS	YPA	TD	YPG
2	Northwestern	11	129	57	44.2	15.6	7	5.4	889	6.9	8	80.8
4	Michigan	11	200	82	41.0	11.4	17	8.5	932	4.7	1	84.7
6	Iowa	11	172	78	45.3	12.7	11	6.4	989	5.8	6	89.9

TOTAL DEFENSE

		G	P	YDS	AVG	TD	YPG
3	Michigan	11	680	2372	3.5	7	215.6

SCORING OFFENSE

		G	PTS	AVG
8	Penn State*	11	358	32.5

SCORING DEFENSE

		G	PTS	AVG
1	Michigan	11	57	5.2

Final Poll

AP	Team	RECORD
1	Notre Dame	11-0-0
2	Ohio State	10-0-1
3	Oklahoma	10-0-1
4	Alabama	11-1-0
5	Penn State*	12-0-0
6	Michigan	10-0-1
7	Nebraska	9-2-1
8	USC	9-2-1
9	Arizona State	11-1-0
9	Houston	11-1-0
11	Texas Tech	11-1-0
12	UCLA	9-2-0
13	LSU	9-3-0
14	Texas	8-3-0
15	Miami, Ohio	11-0-0
16	North Carolina St.	9-3-0
17	Missouri	8-4-0
18	Kansas	7-4-1
19	Tennessee	8-4-0
20	Maryland	8-4-0
20	Tulane	9-3-0

Conference Standings

	CONFERENCE			OVERALL		
	W	L	T	W	L	T
Michigan	7	0	1	10	0	1
Ohio State	7	0	1	10	0	1
Minnesota	6	2	0	7	4	0
Illinois	4	4	0	5	6	0
Purdue	4	4	0	5	6	0
Michigan State	4	4	0	5	6	0
Northwestern	4	4	0	4	7	0
Wisconsin	3	5	0	4	7	0
Indiana	0	8	0	2	9	0
Iowa	0	8	0	0	11	0
Penn State*				12	0	0

Bowl Games

DATE	GAME	SCORE
J1	Rose	Ohio State 42, USC 21
J1	Orange	Penn State* 16, LSU 9

Consensus All-Americans

POS	Offense	HT	WT	School	AP	CP	FC	FW	NE	PI
RB	John Cappelletti	6-1	206	Penn State*	•	•	•	•	•	•
T	John Hicks	6-3	258	Ohio State	•	•	•	•	•	•

OTHERS RECEIVING FIRST-TEAM HONORS

POS				School						
RB	Archie Griffin			Ohio State						•

POS	Defense	HT	WT	School	AP	CP	FC	FW	NE	PI
L	Dave Gallagher	6-4	245	Michigan	•	•	•	•	•	
LB	Randy Gradishar	6-3	236	Ohio State	•	•	•	•	•	•
B	Dave Brown	6-1	188	Michigan			•	•		•

OTHERS RECEIVING FIRST-TEAM HONORS

POS				School						
L	Randy Crowder			Penn State*						•
L	Van DeCree			Ohio State						•
LB	Ed O'Neill			Penn State*				•		

1973, CONT.

ALL-CONFERENCE TEAMS

POS	Offense		POS	Defense
QB	Dennis Franklin, Michigan		DE	Octavus Morgan, Illinois
RB	Ed Shuttlesworth, Michigan		DE	Steve Neils, Minnesota
RB	Archie Griffin, Ohio State		DE	Van De Cree, Ohio State
RB	Clint Haslerig, Michigan		DT	Dave Gallagher, Michigan
RB	Billy Marek, Wisconsin		DT	Pete Cusick, Ohio State
WR	Garvin Roberson, Illinois		LB	Mike Varty, Northwestern
WR	Brian Rollins, Iowa		LB	Randy Gradishar, Ohio State
WR	Steve Craig, Northwestern		LB	Vic Koegel, Ohio State
C	Mike Webster, Wisconsin		LB	Rick Middleton, Ohio State
G	Mike Hoban, Michigan		DB	Mike Gow, Illinois
G	Jim Kregel, Ohio State		DB	Dave Brown, Michigan
T	Keith Fahnhorst, Minnesota		DB	Bill Simpson, Michigan State
T	John Hicks, Ohio State		DB	Neal Colzie, Ohio State
T	Kurt Schumacher, Ohio State			

HEISMAN TROPHY VOTING

	PLAYER	POS	SCHOOL	1ST	2ND	3RD	TOTAL
1	John Cappelletti	HB	Penn State*	229	142	86	1057
2	John Hicks	OT	Ohio State	114	64	54	524
5	Archie Griffin	TB	Ohio State	45	63	65	326
6	Randy Gradishar	LB	Ohio State	47	53	35	282

AWARD WINNERS

PLAYER	POS	SCHOOL	AWARD
John Cappelletti	RB	Penn State*	Maxwell
John Cappelletti	RB	Penn State*	Camp
John Hicks	OT	Ohio State	Outland
John Hicks	OT	Ohio State	Lombardi

NCAA STATISTICAL LEADERS

INDIVIDUAL

ALL-PURPOSE	G	RUSH	REC	PR	KR	YDS	YPG
4 Archie Griffin, Ohio State	10	1428	32	0	182	1642	164.2

RUSHING/YARDS PER GAME	G	ATT	YDS	TD	AVG	YPG
3 Archie Griffin, Ohio State	10	225	1428	6	6.3	142.8
5 John Cappelletti, Penn State*	11	286	1522	17	5.3	138.4

RUSHING/YARDS PER CARRY	G	ATT	YDS	YPC
5 Archie Griffin, Ohio State	10	225	1428	6.3
Based on top 25 rushers				

PUNT RETURNS	PR	YDS	TD	AVG
1 Gary Hayman, Penn State*	23	442	1	19.2
5 Neal Colzie, Ohio State	38	639	2	16.8

SCORING	TDS	XP	FG	PTS	PTPG
4 John Cappelletti, Penn State*	17	0	0	102	9.3

KICK SCORING	XPA	XP	FGA	FG	PTS	PTPG
3 Chris Bahr, Penn State*	42	37	19	11	70	7.0

INTERCEPTIONS	INT	YDS	TD	INT/GM
1 Mike Gow, Illinois	10	142	1	0.91

TEAM

RUSHING OFFENSE	G	ATT	YDS	AVG	TD	YPG
4 Ohio State	10	669	3588	5.4	41	358.8

RUSHING DEFENSE	G	ATT	YDS	AVG	TD	YPG
2 Penn State*	11	427	848	2.0	6	77.1
4 Michigan	11	444	1075	2.4	2	97.7

PASSING DEFENSE	G	ATT	COM	PCT	YPC	INT	I%	YDS	YPA	TD	YPG
2 Michigan State	11	139	54	38.8	11.4	14	10.1	613	4.4	4	55.7
3 Iowa	11	107	48	44.9	14.9	11	10.3	716	6.7	7	65.1
4 Ohio State	10	170	73	42.9	10.5	11	6.5	765	4.5	2	76.5
6 Indiana	11	142	67	47.2	13.5	9	6.3	905	6.4	2	82.3
7 Illinois	11	187	71	38.0	12.8	23	12.3	912	4.9	2	82.9

TOTAL DEFENSE	G	P	YDS	AVG	TD	YPG
3 Penn State*	11	689	2253	3.3	13	204.8
4 Ohio State	10	613	2056	3.4	5	205.6
5 Michigan	11	661	2396	3.6	7	217.8

SCORING OFFENSE	G	PTS	AVG
4 Penn State*	11	431	39.2
5 Ohio State	10	371	37.1

SCORING DEFENSE	G	PTS	AVG
1 Ohio State	10	43	4.3
2 Michigan	11	68	6.2
8 Penn State*	11	120	10.9

BIG TEN ANNUAL REVIEW & BOWLS

*Independent or other conference affiliation

1974

FINAL POLL

UP	AP	TEAM	RECORD
PB	1	Oklahoma	11-0-0
1	2	USC	10-1-1
5	3	**Michigan**	10-1-0
3	4	**Ohio State**	10-2-0
2	5	Alabama	11-1-0
4	6	Notre Dame	10-2-0
7	7	Penn State*	10-2-0
6	8	Auburn	10-2-0
8	9	Nebraska	9-3-0
10	10	Miami, Ohio	10-0-1
9	11	North Carolina St.	9-2-1
18	12	**Michigan State**	7-3-1
13	13	Maryland	8-4-0
14	14	Baylor	8-4-0
12	15	Florida	8-4-0
15	16	Texas A&M	8-3-0
17	17	Mississippi State	9-3-0
	17	Texas	8-4-0
11	19	Houston	8-3-1
15	20	Tennessee	7-3-2

CONFERENCE STANDINGS

	CONFERENCE			OVERALL		
	W	L	T	W	L	T
Michigan	7	1	0	10	1	0
Ohio State	7	1	0	10	2	0
Michigan State	6	1	1	7	3	1
Wisconsin	5	3	0	7	4	0
Illinois	4	3	1	6	4	1
Purdue	3	5	0	4	6	1
Minnesota	2	6	0	4	7	0
Iowa	2	6	0	3	8	0
Northwestern	2	6	0	3	8	0
Indiana	1	7	0	1	10	0
Penn State*				10	2	0

BOWL GAMES

DATE	GAME	SCORE
J1	**Cotton**	Penn State* 41, Baylor 20
J1	**Rose**	USC 18, Ohio State 17

CONSENSUS ALL-AMERICANS

POS	Offense	HT	WT	School	AP	CF	FC	FW	PI
RB	**Archie Griffin**	5-9	184	Ohio State	•	•	•	•	•
T	**Kurt Schumacher**	6-4	250	Ohio State	•		•	•	•
C	**Steve Myers**	6-2	244	Ohio State	•				•

OTHERS RECEIVING FIRST-TEAM HONORS

WR	Larry Burton			Purdue				•	
G	John Nessel			Penn State*		•			

POS	Defense	HT	WT	School	AP	CF	FC	FW	PI
L	**Mike Hartenstine**	6-4	233	Penn State*	•		•	•	•
B	**Dave Brown**	6-1	188	Michigan	•	•	•	•	•

OTHERS RECEIVING FIRST-TEAM HONORS

DL	Van DeCree			Ohio State					•
B	Neal Colzie			Ohio State					•
P	Tom Skladany			Ohio State				•	

HEISMAN TROPHY VOTING

	PLAYER	POS	SCHOOL	1ST	2ND	3RD	TOTAL
1	**Archie Griffin**	TB	Ohio State	483	198	75	1920
6	**Dennis Franklin**	DE	Michigan	6	30	22	100

AWARD WINNERS

PLAYER	POS	SCHOOL	AWARD
Archie Griffin	RB	Ohio State	Camp

ALL-CONFERENCE TEAMS

POS	Offense
QB	Cornelius Greene, Ohio State
RB	Archie Griffin, Ohio State
RB	Coutney Snyder, Indiana
RB	Levi Jackson, Michigan State
RB	Billy Marek, Wisconsin
WR	Doug France, Ohio State
WR	Larry Burton, Purdue
WR	Jack Novak, Wisconsin
C	Dennis Franks, Michigan
C	Steve Myers, Ohio State
G	Tim Davis, Michigan
G	Ralph Peretta, Purdue
G	Dick Mack, Ohio State
G	Terry Stieve, Wisconsin
T	Paul Hiemenz, Northwestern
T	Kurt Schumacher, Ohio State
T	Dennis Lick, Wisconsin

POS	Defense
DE	Dan Jilek, Michigan
DE	Otto Smith, Michigan State
DE	Van De Cree, Ohio State
DT	Pete Cusick, Ohio State
DT	Jeff Perlinger, Michigan
DT	Jim Taubert, Michigan State
DT	Ken Novak, Purdue
LB	Terry McClowry, Michigan State
LB	Steve Strinko, Michigan
LB	Tom Hicks, Illinois
DB	Earl Douthitt, Iowa
DB	Don Dufek, Michigan
DB	Dave Brown, Michigan
DB	Steve Luke, Ohio State
DB	Neal Colzie, Ohio State

BIG TEN ANNUAL REVIEW & BOWLS

1974, CONT.

NCAA STATISTICAL LEADERS

INDIVIDUAL

ALL-PURPOSE

		G	RUSH	REC	PR	KR	YDS	YPG
5	Jim Pooler, Northwestern	11	949	25	21	807	1802	163.8
6	Archie Griffin, Ohio State	11	1620	52	0	71	1743	158.5
7	Rick Upchurch, Minnesota	11	942	209	125	440	1716	156.0
10	Bill Marek, Wisconsin	9	1215	76	0	0	1291	143.4

RUSHING/YARDS PER GAME

		G	ATT	YDS	TD	AVG	YPG
2	Archie Griffin, Ohio State	11	236	1620	12	6.9	147.3
3	Bill Marek, Wisconsin	9	205	1215	18	5.9	135.0

RUSHING/YARDS PER CARRY

		G	ATT	YDS	YPC
1	Archie Griffin, Ohio State	11	236	1620	6.9
6	Gordon Bell, Michigan	11	174	1048	6.0
7	Bill Marek, Wisconsin	9	205	1215	5.9

Based on top 25 rushers

KICKOFF RETURNS

		KR	YDS	TD	AVG
4	Len Willis, Ohio State	14	401	2	28.6

SCORING

		TDS	XP	FG	PTS	PTPG
1	Bill Marek, Wisconsin	19	0	0	114	12.7

KICK SCORING

		XPA	XP	FGA	FG	PTS	PTPG
3	Tom Klaban, Ohio State	51	50	10	8	74	6.7

TEAM

RUSHING OFFENSE

		G	ATT	YDS	AVG	TD	YPG
2	Ohio State	11	685	4006	5.8	46	364.2
5	Michigan	11	686	3372	4.9	31	306.5
8	Wisconsin	11	612	3162	5.2	38	287.5

TOTAL OFFENSE

		G	P	YDS	AVG	TD	YPG
2	Ohio State	11	783	4966	6.3	55	451.5

RUSHING DEFENSE

		G	ATT	YDS	AVG	TD	YPG
2	Michigan	11	438	1163	2.7	3	105.7
7	Penn State*	11	499	1322	2.6	8	120.2

PASSING DEFENSE

	G	ATT	COM	PCT	IYPCNT	I%	YDS	YPA	TD	RATING
1 Iowa	11	130	50	38.5	14.5	6	4.6	723	5.6	7	65.7

TOTAL DEFENSE

		G	P	YDS	AVG	TD	YPG
3	Michigan	11	659	2353	3.6	7	213.9

SCORING OFFENSE

		G	PTS	AVG
2	Ohio State	11	420	38.2
8	Wisconsin	11	341	31.0
10	Michigan	11	324	29.5

SCORING DEFENSE

		G	PTS	AVG
1	Michigan	11	75	6.8
7	Ohio State	11	111	10.1
8	Penn State*	11	122	11.1

1975

FINAL POLL

UP	AP	Game	RECORD
1	1	Oklahoma	11-1-0
2	2	Arizona State	12-0-0
3	3	Alabama	11-1-0
4	4	Ohio State	11-1-0
5	5	UCLA	9-2-1
7	6	Texas	10-2-0
6	7	Arkansas	10-2-0
8	8	Michigan	8-2-2
9	9	Nebraska	10-2-0
10	10	Penn State*	9-3-0
12	11	Texas A&M	10-2-0
16	12	Miami, Ohio	11-1-0
11	13	Maryland	9-2-1
15	14	California	8-3-0
13	15	Pittsburgh	8-4-0
	16	Colorado	9-3-0
19	17	USC	8-4-0
13	18	Arizona	9-2-0
19	19	Georgia	9-3-0
17	20	West Virginia	9-3-0

CONFERENCE STANDINGS

	CONFERENCE			OVERALL		
	W	L	T	W	L	T
Ohio State	8	0	0	11	1	0
Michigan	7	1	0	8	2	2
Michigan State	4	4	0	7	4	0
Illinois	4	4	0	5	6	0
Purdue	4	4	0	4	7	0
Wisconsin	3	4	1	4	6	1
Minnesota	3	5	0	6	5	0
Iowa	3	5	0	3	8	0
Northwestern	2	6	0	3	8	0
Indiana	1	6	1	2	8	1
Penn State*				9	3	0

BOWL GAMES

DATE	GAME	SCORE
D31	Sugar	Alabama 13, Penn State* 6
J1	Orange	Oklahoma 14, Michigan 6
J1	Rose	UCLA 23, Ohio State 10

*Independent or other conference affiliation

BIG TEN ANNUAL REVIEW & BOWLS

CONSENSUS ALL-AMERICANS

POS	Offense	HT	WT	School	AP	FC	FW	PI
RB	Archie Griffin	5-9	182	Ohio State	•		•	•
T	Dennis Lick	6-3	262	Wisconsin			•	•
G	Ted Smith	6-1	242	Ohio State	•		•	

OTHERS RECEIVING FIRST-TEAM HONORS

| OL | Tom Rafferty | | | Penn State* | | | • | |

POS	Defense	HT	WT	School	AP	FC	FW	PI
LB	Greg Buttle	6-3	220	Penn State*	•		•	•
B	Tim Fox	6-0	186	Ohio State			•	•	•

OTHERS RECEIVING FIRST-TEAM HONORS

DL	Ken Novak			Purdue			•	
B	Don Dufek			Michigan		•	•	
P	Tom Skladany			Ohio State			•	

HEISMAN TROPHY VOTING

	PLAYER	POS	SCHOOL	1ST	2ND	3RD	TOTAL
1	Archie Griffin	TB	Ohio State	454	167	104	1800
8	Gordon Bell	TB	Michigan	2	27	24	84

AWARD WINNERS

PLAYER	POS	SCHOOL	AWARD
Archie Griffin	RB	Ohio State	Maxwell
Archie Griffin	RB	Ohio State	Camp

ALL-CONFERENCE TEAM

POS	Offense	POS	Defense
QB	Cornelius Greene, Ohio State	L	Joe Smalzer, Illinois
RB	Gordon Bell, Michigan	DT	Rod Walters, Iowa
RB	Pete Johnson, Ohio State	DT	Greg Morton, Michigan
RB	Archie Griffin, Ohio State	DT	Keith Simons, Minnesota
RB	Billy Marek, Wisconsin	DT	Nick Buonamici, Ohio State
WR	Joe Smalzer, Illinois	DE	Bob Brudzinski, Ohio State
WR	Jim Smith, Michigan	DE	Dan Jilek, Michigan
C	Jim Czirr, Michigan	DE	Blane Smith, Purdue
C	Paul Jasinskis, Northwestern	LB	Donnie Thomas, Indiana
G	Terry Stieve, Wisconsin	LB	Calvin O'Neal, Michigan
G	Joe Devlin, Iowa	LB	Ed Thompson, Ohio State
G	Tim Davis, Michigan	DB	Don Dufek, Michigan
G	Ted Smith, Ohio State	DB	Tom Hannon, Michigan State
T	Chris Ward, Ohio State	DB	Pete Shaw, Northwestern
T	Scott Dannelley, Ohio State	DB	Tim Fox, Ohio State
T	Dennis Lick, Wisconsin	P	Tom Skladany, Ohio State
TE	Michael Cobb, Michigan State		
K	Dan Beaver, Illinois		

NCAA STATISTICAL LEADERS

INDIVIDUAL

ALL-PURPOSE	G	RUSH	REC	PR	KR	YDS	YPG
9 Gordon Bell, Michigan	11	1335	67	18	207	1627	147.9
10 Archie Griffin, Ohio State	11	1357	158	0	91	1606	146.0

RUSHING/YARDS PER GAME	G	ATT	YDS	TD	AVG	YPG
7 Archie Griffin, Ohio State	11	245	1357	4	5.5	123.4
8 Gordon Bell, Michigan	11	255	1335	12	5.2	121.4

RUSHING/YARDS PER CARRY	G	ATT	YDS	YPC
10 Archie Griffin, Ohio State	11	245	1357	5.5
Based on top 27 rushers				

PUNTING	PUNT	YDS	AVG
1 Tom Skladany, Ohio State	36	1681	46.7

KICKOFF RETURNS	KR	YDS	TD	AVG
10 Dave Schick, Iowa	24	610	1	25.4

SCORING	TDS	XP	FG	PTS	PTPG
1 Pete Johnson, Ohio State	25	0	0	150	13.6

FIELD GOALS	FGA	FGM	PCT	FGG
2 Chris Bahr, Penn State*	33	18	.55	1.64

INTERCEPTIONS	INT	YDS	TD	INT/GM
3 Craig Cassady, Ohio State	8	78	0	0.73

TEAM

RUSHING OFFENSE	G	ATT	YDS	AVG	TD	YPG
2 Michigan	11	686	3679	5.4	34	334.5
8 Ohio State	11	678	3480	5.1	43	316.4

TOTAL OFFENSE	G	P	YDS	AVG	TD	YPG
10 Ohio State	11	785	4477	5.7	49	407.0

RUSHING DEFENSE	G	ATT	YDS	AVG	TD	YPG
9 Michigan	11	484	1323	2.7	7	120.3

PASSING DEFENSE	G	ATT	COM	PCT	YPC	INT	I%	YDS	YPA	TD	RATING
3 Wisconsin	11	129	51	39.5	14.1	22	17.1	717	5.6	8	65.2

SCORING OFFENSE	G	PTS	AVG
1 Ohio State	11	374	34.0

SCORING DEFENSE	G	PTS	AVG
2 Ohio State	11	79	7.2
9 Penn State*	11	110	10.0

BIG TEN ANNUAL REVIEW & BOWLS

1976

FINAL POLL

UP	AP	TEAM	RECORD
1	1	Pittsburgh	12-0-0
2	2	USC	11-1-0
3	3	**Michigan**	10-2-0
4	4	Houston	10-2-0
6	5	Oklahoma	9-2-1
5	6	**Ohio State**	9-2-1
8	7	Texas A&M	10-2-0
11	8	Maryland	11-1-0
7	9	Nebraska	9-3-1
10	10	Georgia	10-2-0
9	11	Alabama	9-3-0
12	12	Notre Dame	9-3-0
13	13	Texas Tech	10-2-0
14	14	Oklahoma State	9-3-0
15	15	UCLA	9-2-1
16	16	Colorado	8-4-0
17	17	Rutgers	11-0-0
19	18	Kentucky	8-4-0
18	19	Iowa State	8-3-0
	20	Mississippi State	9-2-0

CONFERENCE STANDINGS

	CONFERENCE			OVERALL		
	W	L	T	W	L	T
Michigan	7	1	0	10	2	0
Ohio State	7	1	0	9	2	1
Minnesota	4	4	0	6	5	0
Indiana	4	4	0	5	6	0
Illinois	4	4	0	5	6	0
Purdue	4	4	0	5	6	0
Wisconsin	3	5	0	5	6	0
Iowa	3	5	0	5	6	0
Michigan State	3	5	0	4	6	1
Northwestern	1	7	0	1	10	0
Penn State*				7	5	0

BOWL GAMES

DATE	GAME	SCORE
D27	**Gator**	Notre Dame 20, Penn State* 9
J1	**Orange**	Ohio State 27, Colorado 10
J1	**Rose**	USC 14, Michigan 6

CONSENSUS ALL-AMERICANS

POS	Offense	HT	WT	School	AP	FC	FW	PI
RB	**Rob Lytle**	6-1	195	Michigan	•	•		•
T	**Chris Ward**	6-4	274	Ohio State			•	
G	**Mark Donahue**	6-3	245	Michigan			•	•

OTHERS RECEIVING FIRST-TEAM HONORS

| KR | Jim Smith | | | Michigan | • | | • | |

AP named Smith as a SE

POS	Defense	HT	WT	School	AP	FC	FW	PI
E	**Bob Brudzinski**	6-4	228	Ohio State	•	•		•

OTHERS RECEIVING FIRST-TEAM HONORS

| LB | Calvin O'Neal | | | Michigan | | | | • |
| LB | Kurt Allerman | | | Penn State* | | | | • |

HEISMAN TROPHY VOTING

	PLAYER	POS	SCHOOL	1ST	2ND	3RD	TOTAL
3	**Rob Lytle**	RB	Michigan	35	85	138	413

ALL-CONFERENCE TEAM

POS	Offense	POS	Defense
QB	Rick Leach, Michigan	L	Greg Morton, Michigan
RB	Rob Lytle, Michigan	L	John Anderson, Michigan
RB	Scott Dierking, Purdue	L	Bob Brudzinski, Ohio State
RB	Paul Beery, Purdue	L	Nick Buonamici, Ohio State
WR	Scott Yelvington, Northwestern	L	Blane Smith, Purdue
WR	Jim Smith, Michigan	LB	Scott Studwell, Illinois
C	Walt Downing, Michigan	LB	Calvin O'Neal, Michigan
G	Mark Donahue, Michigan	LB	Tom Cousineau, Ohio State
G	Bill Lukens, Ohio State	DB	Tom Hannon, Michigan State
G	Aaron Brown, Ohio State	DB	George Adzick, Minnesota
G	Connie Zelencik, Purdue	DB	Pete Shaw, Northwestern
T	Bill Dufek, Michigan	P	Tom Skladany, Ohio State
T	Chris Ward, Ohio State		
TE	Mike Cobb, Michigan State		
K	Dan Beaver, Illinois		

*Independent or other conference affiliation

1977

NCAA Statistical Leaders

INDIVIDUAL

PASSING

		G	ATT	COM	PCT	INT	I%	YDS	YPA	TD	TD%	COM-PG
9	Ed Smith, Michigan State	10	257	132	51.4	10	3.9	1749	6.8	13	5.1	13.2

ALL-PURPOSE

		G	RUSH	EC	PR	KR	YDS	YPG
8	Rob Lytle, Michigan	11	1,402	81	0	26	1509	137.2

RUSHING/YARDS PER GAME

		G	ATT	YDS	AVG
7	Rob Lytle, Michigan	11	203	1,402	6.9
7	Jeff Logan, Ohio State	11	204	1,169	5.7

Based on top 38 rushers

RUSHING/YARDS PER CARRY

		G	ATT	YDS	YPC
2	Rob Lytle, Michigan	11	203	1,402	6.9
7	Jeff Logan, Ohio State	11	204	1,169	5.7

Based on top 38 rushers

PUNT RETURNS

		PR	YDS	TD	AVG
7	Jim Smith, Michigan	15	313	0	12.5
10	Rich Mauti, Penn State*	17	208	0	12.2

KICKOFF RETURNS

		KR	YDS	TD	AVG
1	Ira Matthews, Wisconsin	14	415	2	29.6

SCORING

		TDS	XP	FG	PTS	PTPG
6	Pete Johnson, Ohio State	18	0	0	108	9.8

INTERCEPTIONS

		INT	YDS	TD	INT/GM
7	Scott Erdmann, Wisconsin	7	143	1	0.64

TEAM

RUSHING OFFENSE

		G	ATT	YDS	AVG	TD	YPG
1	Michigan	11	661	3989	6.0	42	362.6

PASSING OFFENSE

		G	ATT	COM	INT	PCT	YDS	YPA	TD	I%	YPC	YPG
9	Michigan State	11	337	171	13	50.7	2322	6.9	17	3.9	13.6	211.1

TOTAL OFFENSE

		G	P	YDS	AVG	TD	YPG
1	Michigan	11	760	4929	6.5	55	448.1

RUSHING DEFENSE

		G	ATT	YDS	AVG	TD	YPG
5	Michigan	11	457	1254	2.7	6	114.0

PASSING DEFENSE

		G	ATT	COM	PCT	INT	I%	YDS	YPA	TD	TD%	RATING
1	Iowa	11	130	50	38.5	14.5	6	4.6	723	5.6	7		65.7

TOTAL DEFENSE

		G	P	YDS	AVG	TD	YPG
10	Michigan	11	721	2666	3.7	10	242.4

SCORING OFFENSE

		G	PTS	AVG
1	Michigan	11	426	38.7

SCORING DEFENSE

		G	PTS	AVG
1	Michigan	11	81	7.4

FINAL POLL

UP	AP	Game	RECORD
1	1	Notre Dame	11-1-0
2	2	Alabama	11-1-0
3	3	Arkansas	11-1-0
5	4	Texas	11-1-0
4	5	Penn State*	11-1-0
PB	6	Kentucky	10-1-0
6	7	Oklahoma	10-2-0
7	8	Pittsburgh	9-2-1
8	9	Michigan	10-2-0
9	10	Washington	8-4-0
12	11	Ohio State	9-3-0
10	12	Nebraska	9-3-0
11	13	USC	8-4-0
14	14	Florida State	10-2-0
15	15	Stanford	9-3-0
19	16	San Diego State	10-1-0
14	17	North Carolina	8-3-1
18	18	Arizona State	9-3-0
	19	Clemson	8-3-1
16	20	Brigham Young	9-2-0

CONFERENCE STANDINGS

	CONFERENCE			OVERALL		
	W	L	T	W	L	T
Michigan	7	1	0	10	2	0
Ohio State	7	1	0	9	3	0
Michigan State	6	1	1	7	3	1
Indiana	4	3	1	5	5	1
Minnesota	4	4	0	7	5	0
Purdue	3	5	0	5	6	0
Iowa	3	5	0	4	7	0
Wisconsin	3	6	0	5	6	0
Illinois	2	6	0	3	8	0
Northwestern	1	8	0	1	10	0
Penn State				11	1	0

BOWL GAMES

DATE	GAME	SCORE
D22	**All-American**	Maryland 17, Minnesota 7
D25	**Fiesta**	Penn State* 42, Arizona State 30
J2	**Sugar**	Alabama 35, Ohio State 6
J2	**Rose**	Washington 27, Michigan 20

CONSENSUS ALL-AMERICANS

POS	Offense	HT	WT	School	AP	FC	FW	PI
T	**Chris Ward**	6-4	272	Ohio State	•	•	•	•
G	**Mark Donahue**	6-3	245	Michigan	•	•	•	•

OTHERS RECEIVING FIRST-TEAM HONORS

POS				School	AP	FC	FW	PI
T	Keith Dorney			Penn State*			•	
C	Walt Downing			Michigan		•		•

POS	Defense	HT	WT	School	AP	FC	FW	PI
LB	**Tom Cousineau**	6-3	228	Ohio State			•	•

OTHERS RECEIVING FIRST-TEAM HONORS

POS		School	AP	FC	FW	PI
MG	Aaron Brown	Ohio State		•		
MG	Randy Sidler	Penn State*	•			
LB	John Anderson	Michigan			•	

HEISMAN TROPHY VOTING

	PLAYER	POS	SCHOOL	1ST	2ND	3RD	TOTAL
8	**Rick Leach**	QB	Michigan	6	9	23	59

1977, CONT.

ALL-CONFERENCE TEAM

POS	Offense	POS	Defense
QB	Rick Leach, Michigan	L	John Anderson, Michigan
QB	Ron Gerald, Ohio State	L	Larry Bethea, Michigan State
RB	Ric Enis, Indiana	L	Kelton Dansler, Ohio State
RB	Ron Springs, Ohio State	L	Reggie Arnold, Purdue
RB	Jeff Logan, Ohio State	L	Dennis Stejskal, Wisconsin
WR	Keith Calvin, Indiana	LB	John Sullivan, Illinois
C	Walt Downing, Michigan	LB	Tom Rusk, Iowa
C	Al Pitts, Michigan State	LB	Tom Cousineau, Ohio State
G	Kevin Pancratz, Illinois	DB	Dwight Hicks, Michigan
G	Mark Donahue, Michigan	DB	Jim Pickens, Michigan
G	Aaron Brown, Ohio State	DB	Steve Midboe, Minnesota
T	Charles Peal, Indiana	DB	Ray Griffin, Ohio State
T	Chris Ward, Ohio State	DB	Mike Guess, Ohio State
T	Mike Kenn, Michigan	P	Ray Stachowitz, Michigan State
TE	Jimmy Moore, Ohio State		
K	Hans Nielsen, Michigan State		
K	Paul Rogind, Minnesota		

NCAA STATISTICAL LEADERS

INDIVIDUAL

PASSING

		G	ATT	COM	PCT	INT	I%	YDS	YPA	TD	TD%	COM.PG
5	Mark Herrmann, Purdue	11	319	175	54.9	27	8.5	2453	7.7	18	5.6	15.9

RUSHING/YARDS PER CARRY

		G	ATT	YDS	YPC
10	Ron Springs, Ohio State	11	190	1092	5.7

PUNT RETURNS

		PR	YDS	TD	AVG
2	Jimmy Cefalo, Penn State*	18	247	2	13.7

SCORING

		TDS	XP	FG	PTS	PTPG
7	Joel Payton, Ohio State	13	2	0	80	8.9

FIELD GOALS

		FGA	FGM	PCT	FGG
3	Paul Rogind, Minnesota	26	18	0.69	1.64
6	Hans Nielsen, Michigan State	28	17	0.61	1.55

INTERCEPTIONS

		INT	YDS	TD	INT/GM
4	Dave Abrams, Indiana	7	24	0	0.64

TEAM

RUSHING OFFENSE

		G	ATT	YDS	AVG	TD	YPG
2	Ohio State	11	731	3534	4.8	39	321.3

PASSING OFFENSE

		G	ATT	COM	INT	PCT	YDS	YPA	TD	I%	YPC	YPG
6	Purdue	11	350	190	30	54.3	2631	7.5	18	8.6	13.8	239.2

TOTAL OFFENSE

		G	P	YDS	AVG	TD	YPG
9	Penn State*	11	865	4646	5.4	39	422.4

RUSHING DEFENSE

		G	ATT	YDS	AVG	TD	YPG
10	Michigan	11	488	1287	2.6	6	117.0

PASSING DEFENSE

		G	ATT	COM	PCT	YPC	INT	I%	YDS	YPA	TD	YPG
4	Indiana	11	178	74	41.6	13.3	13	7.3	984	5.5	5	89.5
6	Wisconsin	11	149	58	38.9	17.3	7	4.7	1002	6.7	4	91.1

TOTAL DEFENSE

		G	P	YDS	AVG	TD	YPG
7	Ohio State	11	694	2539	3.7	10	230.8

SCORING DEFENSE

		G	PTS	AVG
2	Ohio State	11	85	7.7
4	Michigan	11	97	8.8

1978

FINAL POLL

UP	AP	Game	RECORD
2	1	Alabama	11-1-0
1	2	USC	12-1-0
3	3	Oklahoma	11-1-0
4	4	Penn State*	11-1-0
5	5	**Michigan**	10-2-0
6	6	Clemson	11-1-0
6	7	Notre Dame	9-3-0
8	8	Nebraska	9-3-0
9	9	Texas	9-3-0
11	10	Houston	9-3-0
10	11	Arkansas	9-2-1
PB	12	**Michigan State**	8-3-0
13	13	**Purdue**	9-2-1
	14	UCLA	8-3-1
14	15	Missouri	8-4-0
15	16	Georgia	9-2-1
16	17	Stanford	8-4-0
19	18	North Carolina St.	9-3-0
18	19	Texas A&M	8-4-0
	20	Maryland	9-3-0

CONFERENCE STANDINGS

	Conf.			Overall		
	W	L	T	W	L	T
Michigan	7	1	0	10	2	0
Michigan State	7	1	0	8	3	0
Purdue	6	1	1	9	2	1
Ohio State	6	2	0	7	4	1
Minnesota	4	4	0	5	6	0
Wisconsin	3	4	2	5	4	2
Indiana	3	5	0	4	7	0
Iowa	2	6	0	2	9	0
Illinois	0	6	2	1	8	2
Northwestern	0	8	1	0	10	1
Penn State*				11	1	0

BOWL GAMES

DATE	GAME	SCORE
D25	**Peach**	Purdue 41, Georgia Tech 21
D29	**Gator**	Clemson 17, Ohio State 15
J1	**Sugar**	Alabama 14, Penn State* 7
J1	**Rose**	USC 17, Michigan 10

*Independent or other conference affiliation

CONSENSUS ALL-AMERICANS

POS	Offense	HT	WT	School	AP	FC	FW	PI
QB	Chuck Fusina	6-1	195	Penn State*	•	•	•	•
T	Keith Dorney	6-5	257	Penn State*	•	•	•	•

OTHERS RECEIVING FIRST-TEAM HONORS

POS				School	AP	FC	FW	PI
QB	Rick Leach			Michigan			•	
WR	Kirk Gibson			Michigan State				•
TE	Mark Brammer			Michigan State				•

POS	Defense	HT	WT	School	AP	FC	FW	PI
L	Bruce Clark	6-3	246	Penn State*	•	•	•	•
LB	Tom Cousineau	6-3	227	Ohio State	•	•		

OTHERS RECEIVING FIRST-TEAM HONORS

POS				School	AP	FC	FW	PI
DL	Matt Millen			Penn State*				•
B	Pete Harris			Penn State*				•

HEISMAN TROPHY VOTING

	PLAYER	POS	SCHOOL	1ST	2ND	3RD	TOTAL
2	Chuck Fusina	QB	Penn State*	163	89	83	750
3	Rick Leach	QB	Michigan	89	58	52	435

AWARD WINNERS

PLAYER	POS	SCHOOL	AWARD
Chuck Fusina	QB	Penn State*	Maxwell
Bruce Clark	D	Penn State*	Lombardi

ALL-CONFERENCE TEAMS

POS	Offense		POS	Defense
QB	Rick Leach, Michigan		L	Curtis Greer, Michigan
RB	Russell Davis, Michigan		L	Melvin Land, Michigan State
RB	Marion Barber, Minnesota		L	Stan Sytsma, Minnesota
WR	Kirk Gibson, Michigan State		L	Kelton Dansler, Ohio State
WR	Eugene Byrd, Michigan State		L	Keena Turner, Purdue
C	Mark Heidel, Indiana		LB	Joe Norman, Indiana
G	John Arbeznik, Michigan		LB	Ron Simpkins, Michigan
G	Ken Fritz, Ohio State		LB	Tom Cousineau, Ohio State
G	Ken Loushin, Purdue		DB	Mike Jolly, Michigan
T	Jon Giesler, Michigan		DB	Mike Harden, Michigan
T	Joe Robinson, Ohio State		DB	Tom Graves, Michigan State
T	Jim Hinesly, Michigan State		DB	Vince Skillings, Ohio State
TE	Mark Brammer, Michigan State		DB	Keith Brown, Minnesota
K	Paul Rogind, Minnesota		DB	Mike Guess, Ohio State
			P	Ray Stachowitz, Michigan State
			P	Tom Orosz, Ohio State

NCAA STATISTICAL LEADERS

INDIVIDUAL

PASSING		G	ATT	COM	PCT	INT	I%	YDS	YPA	TD	TD%	COM.PG
5	Ed Smith, Michigan State	10	292	169	57.9	8	2.7	2226	7.6	20	6.8	16.9

PUNTING		PUNT	YDS	AVG
2	Tom Orosz, Ohio State	43	2464	43.9
8	Ray Stachowicz, Michigan State	39	1681	43.1

PUNT RETURNS		PUNT	YDS	TD	AVG
1	Ira Matthews, Wisconsin	16	270	3	16.9

SCORING		TDS	XP	FG	PTS	PTPG
5	Matt Bahr, Penn State*	0	31	22	97	8.8

FIELD GOALS		FGA	FGM	PCT	FGG
1	Matt Bahr, Penn State*	27	22	0.82	2.00
10	Scott Sovereen, Purdue	21	15	0.71	1.40

INTERCEPTIONS		INT	YDS	TD	INT/GM
1	Pete Harris, Penn State*	10	155	0	0.91

TEAM

RUSHING OFFENSE		G	ATT	YDS	AVG	TD	YPG
7	Ohio State	11	688	3160	4.6	35	287.3
9	Michigan	11	694	3152	4.5	31	286.5

PASSING OFFENSE		G	ATT	COM	INT	PCT	YDS	YPA	TD	I%	YPC	YPG
7	Michigan State	11	340	194	10	57.1	2631	7.7	22	2.9	13.7	239.2

TOTAL OFFENSE		G	P	YDS	AVG	TTD	YPG
3	Michigan State	11	838	5294	6.3	54	481.3

RUSHING DEFENSE		G	ATT	YDS	AVG	TD	PG
1	Penn State*	11	408	599	1.5	4	54.5
8	Michigan	11	426	1240	2.9	6	112.7

TOTAL DEFENSE		G	P	YDS	AVG	TTD	YPG
1	Penn State*	11	729	2243	3.1	10	203.9
4	Michigan	11	665	2372	3.6	10	215.6

SCORING OFFENSE		G	PTS	AVG
3	Michigan State	11	411	37.4
4	Michigan	11	362	32.9

SCORING DEFENSE		G	PTS	AVG
2	Michigan	11	88	8.0
3	Michigan State	11	97	8.8
4	Purdue	11	109	9.9

TURNOVER MARGIN		G	FR	INT	TOT	FL	INTL	TOT	MAR
1	Penn State*	11	14	28	42	6	14	20	2.0

1979

FINAL POLL

UP	AP	TEAM	RECORD
1	1	Alabama	12-0-0
2	2	USC	11-0-1
3	3	Oklahoma	11-1-0
4	4	**Ohio State**	11-1-0
5	5	Houston	11-1-0
8	6	Florida State	11-1-0
6	7	Pittsburgh	11-1-0
9	8	Arkansas	10-2-0
7	9	Nebraska	10-2-0
10	10	**Purdue**	10-2-0
11	11	Washington	9-3-0
13	12	Texas	9-3-0
12	13	Brigham Young	11-1-0
15	14	Baylor	8-4-0
14	15	North Carolina	8-3-1
PB	16	Auburn	8-3-0
17	17	Temple	10-2-0
19	18	**Michigan**	8-4-0
16	19	Indiana	8-4-0
18	20	**Penn State***	8-4-0

CONFERENCE STANDINGS

	CONFERENCE			OVERALL		
	W	L	T	W	L	T
Ohio State	8	0	0	11	1	0
Purdue	7	1	0	10	2	0
Michigan	6	2	0	8	4	0
Indiana	5	3	0	8	4	0
Iowa	4	4	0	5	6	0
Minnesota	3	5	1	4	6	1
Michigan State	3	5	0	5	6	0
Wisconsin	3	5	0	4	7	0
Illinois	1	6	1	2	8	1
Northwestern	0	9	0	1	10	0
Penn State*				8	4	0

BOWL GAMES

DATE	GAME	SCORE
D21	**Holiday**	Indiana 38, Brigham Young 37
D22	**Liberty**	Penn State* 9, Tulane 6
D28	**Gator**	North Carolina 17, Michigan 15
D31	**Bluebonnet**	Purdue 27, Tennessee 22
J1	**Rose**	USC 17, Ohio State 16

CONSENSUS ALL-AMERICANS

POS	Offense	HT	WT	School	AP	FC	FW	PI
G	Ken Fritz	6-3	238	Ohio State	•		•	•

POS	Defense	HT	WT	School	AP	CF	FC	FW	PI
L	Bruce Clark	6-3	255	Penn State*			•	•	•
LB	Ron Simpkins	6-2	220	Michigan	•		•		•

OTHERS RECEIVING FIRST-TEAM HONORS
| DL | Curtis Greer | Michigan | | • | • |

| TE | Mark Brammer, Michigan State |
| K | Vlade Janakievski, Ohio State |

HEISMAN TROPHY VOTING

POS	PLAYER	POS	SCHOOL	1ST	2ND	3RD	TOTAL
4	**Art Schlichter**	QB	Ohio State	19	54	86	251
8	**Mark Herrmann**	QB	Purdue	5	12	15	54

ALL-CONFERENCE TEAM

POS	Offense	POS	Defense
QB	Art Schlichter, Ohio State	L	Curtis Greer, Michigan
RB	Dennis Mosely, Iowa	L	Elmer Bailey, Minnesota
RB	Marion Barber, Minnesota	L	Luther Henson, Ohio State
RB	Butch Woolfolk, Michigan	L	Keena Turner, Purdue
RB	Dave Mohapp, Wisconsin	L	Calvin Clark, Purdue
WR	Elmer Bailey, Minnesota	L	Doug Donley, Ohio State
C	Tom Waugh, Ohio State	LB	Jim Laughlin, Ohio State
C	Jay Hilgenberg, Iowa	LB	Ron Simpkins, Michigan
G	Mike Trgovac, Michigan	LB	Leven Weiss, Iowa
G	John Arbeznik, Michigan	DB	Tim Wilbur, Indiana
G	Ken Fritz, Ohio State	DB	Mike Jolly, Michigan
G	Ken Loushin, Purdue	DB	Dan Bass, Michigan State
G	Dale Schwann, Purdue	DB	Vince Skillings, Ohio State
T	Steve McKenzie, Purdue	DB	Mike Guess, Ohio State
T	Ray Snell, Wisconsin	DB	Todd Bell, Ohio State
TE	Dave Young, Purdue	P	Ray Stachowitz, Michigan State
TE	Mark Brammer, Michigan State		
K	Vlade Janakievski, Ohio State		

BIG TEN ANNUAL REVIEW & BOWLS

1980

NCAA Statistical Leaders

INDIVIDUAL

PASSING

	G	ATT	COM	PCT	INT	I%	YDS	YPA	TD	TD%	RATING
5 Art Schlichter, Ohio State	11	179	94	52.5	5	2.8	1519	8.5	13	7.3	142.28

RUSHING/YARDS PER GAME

	G	ATT	YDS	TD	AVG	YPG
9 Dennis Mosley, Iowa	11	270	1267	12	4.7	115.2

PUNTING

	PUNT	YDS	AVG
5 Ray Stachowicz, Michigan State	62	2749	44.3

PUNT RETURNS

	PUNT	YDS	TD	AVG
4 Anthony Carter, Michigan	20	265	1	13.2
9 Mike Guess, Ohio State	22	273	0	12.4

KICKOFF RETURNS

	KR	YDS	TD	AVG
2 Derek Hughes, Michigan State	16	497	2	31.1

SCORING

	TDS	XP	FG	PTS	PTPG
5 Dennis Mosley, Iowa	16	0	0	96	8.7
8 Vlade Janakievski, Ohio State	0	42	15	87	7.9
10 Butch Woolfolk, Michigan	13	0	0	78	7.8

FIELD GOALS

	FGA	FGM	PCT	FGG
5 Vlade Janakievski. Ohio State	18	15	0.83	1.36

INTERCEPTIONS

	INT	YDS	TD	INT/GM
5 Bill Kay, Purdue	7	15	0	0.70
6 Tim Wilbur, Indiana	7	165	2	0.64

TEAM

RUSHING DEFENSE

	G	ATT	YDS	AVG	YPG
4 Michigan	11	443	1092	2.5	8	99.3

SCORING OFFENSE

	G	PTS	AVG
4 Ohio State	11	374	34.0

SCORING DEFENSE

	G	PTS	AVG
8 Ohio State	11	109	9.9

TURNOVER MARGIN

	G	FR	INT	TOT	FL	INTL	TOT	MAR
5 Ohio State	11	14	17	31	10	5	15	1.5

Final Poll

UP	AP	TEAM	RECORD
1	1	Georgia	12-0-0
2	2	Pittsburgh	11-1-0
3	3	Oklahoma	10-2-0
4	4	**Michigan**	10-2-0
5	5	Florida State	10-2-0
6	6	Alabama	10-2-0
7	7	Nebraska	10-2-0
8	8	Penn State*	10-2-0
10	9	Notre Dame	9-2-1
9	10	North Carolina	11-1-0
12	11	USC	8-2-1
11	12	Brigham Young	12-1-0
14	13	UCLA	9-2-0
13	14	Baylor	10-2-0
15	15	**Ohio State**	9-3-0
17	16	Washington	9-3-0
16	17	**Purdue**	9-3-0
18	18	Miami, Fla.	9-3-0
	19	Mississippi State	9-3-0
20	20	SMU	8-4-0

Conference Standings

	Conf.			Overall		
	W	L	T	W	L	T
Michigan	8	0	0	10	2	0
Purdue	7	1	0	9	3	0
Ohio State	7	1	0	9	3	0
Iowa	4	4	0	4	7	0
Minnesota	4	5	0	5	6	0
Indiana	3	5	0	6	5	0
Wisconsin	3	5	0	4	7	0
Illinois	3	5	0	3	7	1
Michigan State	2	6	0	3	8	0
Northwestern	0	9	0	0	11	0
Penn State*				10	2	0

Bowl Games

DATE	GAME	SCORE
D26	Fiesta	Penn State* 31, Ohio State 19
D27	Liberty	Purdue 28, Missouri 25
J1	Rose	Michigan 23, Washington 6

Consensus All-Americans

POS	Offense	HT	WT	School	AP	FC	FW	PI
QB	**Mark Herrmann**	6-4	187	Purdue	•	•	•	•
TE	**Dave Young**	6-6	242	Purdue	•	•	•	•

	OTHERS RECEIVING FIRST-TEAM HONORS		
WR	Anthony Carter	Michigan	•
L	Bill Dugan	Penn State*	•

Heisman Trophy Voting

	PLAYER	POS	SCHOOL	1ST	2ND	3RD	TOTAL
4	**Mark Herrmann**	QB	Purdue	58	71	89	405
6	**Art Schlichter**	QB	Ohio State	18	34	36	158
10	**Anthony Carter**	WR	Michigan	4	6	10	34

1980, CONT.

ALL-CONFERENCE TEAM

POS	Offense	POS	Defense
QB	Art Schlichter, Ohio State	L	John Harty, Iowa
QB	Mark Herrmann, Purdue	L	Jeff Schuh, Minnesota
RB	Butch Woolfolk, Michigan	L	Doug Donley, Ohio State
RB	Marion Barber, Minnesota	L	Calvin Clark, Purdue
RB	Calvin Murray, Ohio State	L	Jerome Foster, Ohio State
FB	Dave Mohapp, Wisconsin	LB	Andy Cannavino, Michigan
FB	Garry White, Minnesota	LB	Mel Owens, Michigan
WR	Anthony Carter, Michigan	LB	Marcus Marek, Ohio State
C	George Lilja, Michigan	LB	James Looney, Purdue
G	John Powers, Michigan	DB	Tim Wilbur, Indiana
G	Mike Trgovac, Michigan	DB	Todd Bell, Ohio State
G	Joe Lukens, Ohio State	DB	Ray Ellis, Ohio State
G	Tim Krumrie, Wisconsin	DB	Bill Kay, Purdue
G	Kurt Becker, Michigan	DB	Vince Skillings, Ohio State
T	Bubba Paris, Michigan	P	Ray Stachowitz, Michigan State
T	Ed Muransky, Michigan		
TE	Dave Young, Purdue		
K	Vlade Janakievski, Ohio State		

NCAA STATISTICAL LEADERS

INDIVIDUAL

PASSING

		CL	G	ATT	COM	PCT	INT	I%	YDS	YPA	TD	TD%	RATING
5	Mark Herrmann, Purdue	SR	10	340	220	64.7	17	5.0	2923	8.6	19	5.6	145.4
7	Art Schlichter, Ohio State	JR	11	191	102	53.4	8	4.2	1628	8.5	12	6.3	137.4

ALL-PURPOSE

		CL	G	RUSH	REC	PR	KR	YDS	YPG
9	Calvin Murray, Ohio State	SR	11	1192	197	0	236	1625	147.7

RUSHING/Yards Per Carry

		CL	G	ATT	YDS	YPC
2	Calvin Murray, Ohio State	SR	11	185	1192	6.4
10	Garry White, Minnesota	SR	11	177	959	5.4

Based on top 38 rushers

RECEIVING

		CL	G	REC	YDS	TD	YPR	YPG	RPG
1	Dave Young, Purdue	SR	11	67	917	8	13.7	83.4	6.1
3	Keith Chappelle, Iowa	SR	11	64	1037	6	16.2	94.3	5.8
7	Bart Burrell, Purdue	SR	11	58	888	6	15.3	80.7	5.3

PUNTING

		CL	PUNT	YDS	AVG
2	Ray Stachowicz, Michigan State	SR	71	3278	46.2

KICKOFF RETURNS

		CL	KR	YDS	TD	AVG
2	Anthony Carter, Michigan	SO	14	411	0	29.4

SCORING

		CL	TDS	XP	FG	PTS	PTPG
4	Vlade Janakievski, Ohio State	SR	0	45	15	90	9.0

FIELD GOALS

		CL	FGA	FGM	PCT	FGG
6	Herb Menhardt, Penn State*	SR	21	15	.71	1.50
6	Vlade Janakievski, Ohio State	SR	22	15	.68	1.50
8	Rick Anderson, Purdue	JR	23	16	.70	1.45

TEAM

PASSING OFFENSE

		G	ATT	COM	INT	PCT	YDS	YPA	TD	I%	YPC	YPG
2	Illinois	11	471	250	15	53.1	3227	6.9	20	3.2	12.9	293.4
3	Purdue	11	375	243	17	64.8	3216	8.6	20	4.5	13.2	292.4

TOTAL OFFENSE

		G	P	YDS	AVG	TD	YPG
5	Purdue	11	845	4856	5.7	35	441.5
8	Ohio State	11	812	4703	5.8	45	427.5

SCORING OFFENSE

		G	PTS	AVG
5	Ohio State	11	368	33.5

SCORING DEFENSE

		G	PTS	AVG
8	Michigan	11	123	11.2

TURNOVER MARGIN

		G	FR	INT	TOT	FL	INTL	TOT	MAR
1	Ohio State	11	16	25	41	9	9	18	2.1

1981

FINAL POLL

UP	AP	TEAM	RECORD
1	1	Clemson	12-0-0
4	2	Texas	10-1-1
3	3	Penn State*	10-2-0
2	4	Pittsburgh	11-1-0
PB	5	SMU	10-1-0
5	6	Georgia	10-2-0
6	7	Alabama	9-2-1
PB	8	Miami, Fla.	9-2-0
8	9	North Carolina	10-2-0
7	10	Washington	10-2-0
9	11	Nebraska	9-3-0
10	12	Michigan	9-3-0
11	13	Brigham Young	11-2-0
13	14	USC	9-3-0
12	15	Ohio State	9-3-0
PB	16	Arizona State	9-2-0
18	17	West Virginia	9-3-0
15	18	Iowa	8-4-0
20	19	Missouri	8-4-0
14	20	Oklahoma	7-4-1

CONFERENCE STANDINGS

	CONFERENCE			OVERALL		
	W	L	T	W	L	T
Ohio State	6	2	0	9	3	0
Iowa	6	2	0	8	4	0
Michigan	6	3	0	9	3	0
Illinois	6	3	0	7	4	0
Wisconsin	6	3	0	7	5	0
Minnesota	4	5	0	6	5	0
Michigan State	4	5	0	5	6	0
Purdue	3	6	0	5	6	0
Indiana	3	6	0	3	8	0
Northwestern	0	9	0	0	11	0
Penn State*				10	2	0

BOWL GAMES

DATE	GAME	SCORE
D13	Garden State	Tennessee 28, Wisconsin 21
D30	Liberty	Ohio State 31, Navy 28
D31	Bluebonnet	Michigan 33, UCLA 14
J1	Fiesta	Penn State* 26, USC 10
J1	Rose	Washington 28, Iowa 0

*Independent or other conference affiliation

CONSENSUS ALL-AMERICANS

POS	Offense	HT	WT	School	AP	FC	FW	PI
WR	Anthony Carter	5-11	161	Michigan	•	•	•	•
L	Sean Farrell	6-3	266	Penn State*	•	•	•	•
L	Ed Muransky	6-7	275	Michigan	•		•	
L	Kurt Becker	6-6	260	Michigan	•	•		

OTHERS RECEIVING FIRST-TEAM HONORS

| RB | Curt Warner | | | Penn State* | | | | • |

POS	Defense	HT	WT	School	AP	FC	FW	PI
L	Andre Tippett	6-4	235	Iowa	•		•	•
L	Tim Krumrie	6-3	237	Wisconsin	•			•
P	Reggie Roby	6-3	215	Iowa				

OTHERS RECEIVING FIRST-TEAM HONORS

| DB | Matt Vanden Boom | | | Wisconsin | | | | • |

HEISMAN TROPHY VOTING

	PLAYER	POS	SCHOOL	1ST	2ND	3RD	TOTAL
5	Art Schlichter	QB	Ohio State	21	15	56	149
7	Anthony Carter	WR	Michigan	2	11	14	42

ALL-CONFERENCE TEAM

POS	Offense	POS	Defense
QB	Tony Eason, Illinois	L	Mark Bortz, Iowa
QB	Art Schlichter, Ohio State	L	Pat Dean, Iowa
RB	Butch Woolfolk, Michigan	L	Andre Tippett, Iowa
RB	Dave Mohapp, Wisconsin	L	Jerome Foster, Ohio State
RB	Tim Spencer, Ohio State	L	Darryl Sims, Wisconsin
WR	Anthony Carter, Michigan	LB	Mel Cole, Iowa
WR	Steve Bryant, Purdue	LB	Carl Banks, Michigan State
C	Greg Boeke, Illinois	LB	Jim Fahnhorst, Minnesota
C	Tom Piette, Michigan State	LB	Marcus Marek, Ohio State
G	Ron Hallstrom, Iowa	LB	Brock Spack, Purdue
G	Kurt Becker, Michigan	DB	Lou King, Iowa
G	Joe Lukens, Ohio State	DB	James Burroughs, Michigan State
G	Tim Krumrie, Wisconsin	DB	David Greenwood, Wisconsin
T	Bubba Paris, Michigan	DB	Matt Vanden Boom, Wisconsin
T	Ed Muransky, Michigan	P	Reggie Roby, Iowa
T	Ken Dallafior, Minnesota		
TE	Bob Stephenson, Indiana		
K	Morten Anderson, Michigan State		

NCAA STATISTICAL LEADERS

INDIVIDUAL

PASSING	CL	G	ATT	COM	PCT	INT	I%	YDS	YPA	TD	TD%	RATING
4 Tony Eason, Illinois	JR	11	406	248	61.1	14	3.5	3360	8.3	20	4.9	140.0
6 Scott Campbell, Purdue	SO	11	321	185	57.6	13	4.1	2686	8.4	18	5.6	138.3

ALL-PURPOSE	CL	G	RUSH	REC	PR	KR	YDS	YPG
9 Tim Spencer, Ohio State	JR	11	1121	205	0	307	1633	148.5

RUSHING/YARDS PER CARRY	CL	G	ATT	YDS	YPC
5 Curt Warner, Penn State*	JR	9	171	1044	6.1
9 Butch Woolfolk, Michigan	SR	11	226	1273	5.6
Based on top 30 rushers					

RECEIVING	CL	G	REC	YDS	TD	RPG	YPR	YPG
10 Steve Bryant, Purdue	SR	11	60	971	11	16.2	88.3	5.5

PUNTING	CL	PUNT	YDS	AVG
1 Reggie Roby, Iowa	JR	44	2193	49.8

KICKOFF RETURNS	CL	KR	YDS	TD	AVG
3 Anthony Carter, Michigan	JR	15	406	0	27.1

INTERCEPTIONS	CL	INT	YDS	TD	INT/GM
2 Lou King, Iowa	SR	8	62	0	0.73

TEAM

RUSHING OFFENSE						G	ATT	YDS	AVG	TD	YPG
9 Michigan						11	572	2973	5.2	28	270.3

PASSING OFFENSE	G	ATT	COM	INT	PCT	YDS	YPA	TD	I%	YPC	YPG
3 Illinois	11	409	250	14	61.1	3398	8.3	20	3.4	13.6	308.9

TOTAL OFFENSE	G	P	YDS	AVG	TD	YPG
8 Ohio State	11	865	4677	5.4	45	425.2

RUSHING DEFENSE	G	ATT	YDS	AVG	TD	YPG
5 Iowa	11	421	956	2.3	7	86.9
9 Ohio State	11	380	1060	2.8	5	96.4

TOTAL DEFENSE	G	P	YDS	AVG	TD	YPG
10 Iowa	11	736	2790	3.8	14	253.6

SCORING OFFENSE	G	PTS	AVG
5 Ohio State	11	356	32.4
9 Penn State*	11	345	31.4

SCORING DEFENSE	G	PTS	AVG
7 Iowa	11	129	11.7

TURNOVER MARGIN	G	FR	INT	TOT	FL	INTL	TOT	MAR
7 Penn State*	11	22	20	42	10	16	26	1.5

BIG TEN ANNUAL REVIEW & BOWLS

1982

FINAL POLL

UP	AP	TEAM	RECORD
1	1	**Penn State***	11-1-0
2	2	SMU	11-0-1
3	3	Nebraska	12-1-0
4	4	Georgia	11-1-0
5	5	UCLA	10-1-1
6	6	Arizona State	10-2-0
7	7	Washington	10-2-0
PB	8	Clemson	9-1-1
8	9	Arkansas	9-2-1
9	10	Pittsburgh	9-3-0
11	11	LSU	8-3-1
12	12	**Ohio State**	9-3-0
10	13	Florida State	9-3-0
14	14	Auburn	9-3-0
PB	15	USC	8-3-0
16	16	Oklahoma	8-4-0
18	17	Texas	9-3-0
13	18	North Carolina	8-4-0
19	19	West Virginia	9-3-0
20	20	Maryland	8-4-0

CONFERENCE STANDINGS

	CONFERENCE			OVERALL		
	W	L	T	W	L	T
Michigan	8	1	0	8	4	0
Ohio State	7	1	0	9	3	0
Iowa	6	2	0	8	4	0
Illinois	6	3	0	7	5	0
Wisconsin	5	4	0	7	5	0
Indiana	4	5	0	5	6	0
Purdue	3	6	0	3	8	0
Northwestern	2	7	0	3	8	0
Michigan State	2	7	0	2	9	0
Minnesota	1	8	0	3	8	0
Penn State*				11	1	0

BOWL GAMES

DATE	GAME	SCORE
D11	**Independence**	Wisconsin 14, Kansas State 3
D17	**Holiday**	Ohio State 47, Brigham Young 17
D29	**Liberty**	Alabama 21, Illinois 15
D31	**Peach**	Iowa 28, Tennessee 22
J1	**Sugar**	Penn State* 27, Georgia 23
J1	**Rose**	UCLA 24, Michigan 14

CONSENSUS ALL-AMERICANS

POS	**Offense**	HT	WT	**School**	AP	FC	FW	PI
WR	**Anthony Carter**	5-11	161	Michigan	•	•	•	•

	OTHERS RECEIVING FIRST-TEAM HONORS							
WR	Kenny Jackson			Penn State*		•		

POS	**Defense**	HT	WT	**School**	AP	FC	FW	PI
LB	**Marcus Marek**	6-2	224	Ohio State		•		•

	OTHERS RECEIVING FIRST-TEAM HONORS							
DB	Mark Robinson			Penn State*			•	

HEISMAN TROPHY VOTING

	PLAYER	POS	SCHOOL	1ST	2ND	3RD	TOTAL
4	**Anthony Carter**	WR	Michigan	11	27	55	142
6	**Todd Blackledge**	QB	Penn State*	4	26	44	108
8	**Tony Eason**	QB	Illinois	5	6	33	60
11	**Curt Warner**	TB	Penn State*	2	8	18	40

AWARD WINNERS

PLAYER	POS	SCHOOL	AWARD
Todd Blackledge	QB	Penn State*	O'Brien

ALL-CONFERENCE TEAM

POS	**Offense**
QB	Tony Eason, Illinois
RB	Lawrence Ricks, Michigan
RB	Tim Spencer, Ohio State
WR	Mike Martin, Illinois
WR	Duane Gunn, Indiana
WR	Anthony Carter, Michigan
C	Tom Dixon, Michigan
G	Joe Lukens, Ohio State
G	Tim Krumrie, Wisconsin
T	Stefan Humphries, Michigan
T	Rich Strenger, Michigan
T	Bob Winckler, Wisconsin
T	Chris Hinton, Northwestern
TE	John Frank, Ohio State
TE	Cliff Benson, Purdue
K	Mike Bass, Illinois

POS	**Defense**
L	Mark Bortz, Iowa
L	Jerome Foster, Ohio State
L	Darryl Sims, Wisconsin
LB	Robert Thompson, Michigan
LB	Paul Girgash, Michigan
LB	Carl Banks, Michigan State
LB	Marcus Marek, Ohio State
DB	Bobby Stoops, Iowa
DB	Keith Bostic, Michigan
DB	David Greenwood, Wisconsin
DB	Matt Vanden Boom, Wisconsin
P	Reggie Roby, Iowa

*Independent or other conference affiliation

1983

NCAA Statistical Leaders

INDIVIDUAL

PASSING

	CL	G	ATT	COM	PCT	INT	I%	YDS	YPA	TD	TD%	RAT
10 Todd Blackledge, Penn State*	JR	11	292	161	.551	14	4.8	2218	7.6	22	7.5	134.2

ALL-PURPOSE

	CL	G	RUSH	REC	PR	KR	YDS	YPG
9 Tim Spencer, Ohio State	SR	11	1371	115	0	117	1603	145.7

RUSHING/YARDS PER GAME

	CL	G	ATT	YDS	TD	AVG	YPG
8 Tim Spencer, Ohio State	SR	11	252	1371	12	5.4	124.6
9 Lawrence Ricks, Michigan	SR	11	243	1300	8	5.3	118.2

RECEIVING

	CL	G	REC	YDS	TD	RPG	YPR	YPG
2 Mike Martin, Illinois	SR	11	69	941	5	13.6	85.5	6.3

PUNTING

	CL	PUNT	YDS	AVG
1 Reggie Roby, Iowa	SR	52	2501	48.1
6 John Kidd, Northwestern	JR	52	2371	45.6
8 Ralf Mojsiejenko, Michigan State	SO	77	3434	44.6

PUNT RETURNS

	CL	PR	YDS	TD	AVG
2 Anthony Carter, Michigan	SR	17	265	1	15.6

SCORING

	CL	TDS	XP	FG	PTS	PTPG
8 Mike Bass, Illinois	SR	0	32	23	101	9.2

FIELD GOALS

	CL	FGA	FGM	PCT	FGG
4 Mike Bass, Illinois	SR	26	23	.89	2.09

TEAM

PASSING OFFENSE

	G	ATT	COM	INT	PCT	YDS	YPA	TD	I%	YPC	YPG
4 Illinois	11	453	279	15	61.6	3254	7.2	17	3.3	11.7	295.8

TOTAL OFFENSE

	G	P	YDS	AVG	TD	YPG
10 Penn State*	11	812	4652	5.7	43	422.9

SCORING OFFENSE

	G	PTS	AVG
5 Penn State*	11	368	33.5

Final Poll

UP	AP	TEAM	RECORD
1	1	Miami, Fla.	11-1-0
2	2	Nebraska	12-1-0
3	3	Auburn	11-1-0
4	4	Georgia	10-1-1
5	5	Texas	11-1-0
6	6	Florida	9-2-1
7	7	Brigham Young	11-1-0
9	8	Michigan	9-3-0
8	9	Ohio State	9-3-0
10	10	Illinois	10-2-0
PB	11	Clemson	9-1-1
11	12	SMU	10-2-0
15	13	Air Force	10-2-0
14	14	Iowa	9-3-0
12	15	Alabama	8-4-0
16	16	West Virginia	9-3-0
13	17	UCLA	7-4-1
19	18	Pittsburgh	8-3-1
20	19	Boston College	9-3-0
	20	East Carolina	8-3-0

Conference Standings

	CONFERENCE			OVERALL		
	W	L	T	W	L	T
Ohio State	7	2	0	9	3	0
Illinois	6	3	0	7	4	0
Purdue	6	3	0	7	5	0
Iowa	5	3	1	8	4	1
Wisconsin	5	3	1	7	4	1
Michigan State	5	4	0	6	6	0
Michigan	5	4	0	6	6	0
Minnesota	3	6	0	4	7	0
Northwestern	2	7	0	2	9	0
Indiana	0	9	0	0	11	0
Penn State*				6	5	0

Bowl Games

DATE	GAME	SCORE
D26	Aloha	Penn State* 13, Washington 10
D30	Gator	Florida 14, Iowa 6
J2	Sugar	Auburn 9, Michigan 7
J2	Fiesta	Ohio State 28, Pittsburgh 23
J2	Rose	UCLA 45, Illinois 9

Consensus All-Americans

POS	**Offense**	HT	WT	**School**		AP	CF	FC	FW	PI
None										

OTHERS RECEIVING FIRST-TEAM HONORS

| L | Stefan Humphries | | | Michigan | | | | | • | • |
| C | Tom Dixon | | | Michigan | | • | | • | | |

POS	**Defense**	HT	WT	**School**		AP	CF	FC	FW	PI
None										

OTHERS RECEIVING FIRST-TEAM HONORS

| L | Don Thorp | | | Illinois | | | | | • | |

BIG TEN ANNUAL REVIEW & BOWLS

1983, CONT.

ALL-CONFERENCE TEAM

POS	Offense	POS	Defense
QB	Chuck Long, Iowa	L	Don Thorp, Illinois
RB	Dwight Beverly, Illinois	L	Mark Butkus, Illinois
RB	Keith Byars, Ohio State	L	Paul Hufford, Iowa
WR	Duane Gunn, Indiana	L	Kevin Brooks, Michigan
WR	Dave Moritz, Iowa	LB	Larry Station, Iowa
WR	Al Toon, Wisconsin	LB	Carl Banks, Michigan State
C	Tom Dixon, Michigan	LB	Rowland Tatum, Ohio State
G	Chris Babyar, Illinois	LB	Jim Melka, Wisconsin
G	Al Sincich, Michigan	DB	Craig Swoope, Illinois
T	Jim Juriga, Illinois	DB	Mike Stoops, Iowa
T	John Alt, Iowa	DB	Evan Cooper, Michigan
T	Stefan Humphries, Michigan	DB	Phil Parker, Michigan State
TE	John Frank, Ohio State	DB	Garcia Lane, Ohio State
K	Chris White, Illinois	P	John Kidd, Northwestern
K	Bob Bergeron, Michigan		

NCAA STATISTICAL LEADERS

INDIVIDUAL

PASSING

		CL	G	ATT	COM	PCT	INT	I%	YDS	YPA	TD	TD%	RATING
2	Chuck Long, Iowa	JR	10	236	144	61.0	8	3.4	2434	10.3	14	5.9	160.4
9	Jack Trudeau, Illinois	SO	11	324	203	62.7	13	4.0	2446	7.6	18	5.6	136.4

ALL-PURPOSE

		CL	G	RUSH	REC	PR	KR	YDS	YPG
7	Ricky Edwards, Northwestern	SR	11	561	570	0	523	1654	150.4
9	Keith Byars, Ohio State	SO	11	1126	338	0	37	1501	136.5

RUSHING/YARDS PER CARRY

		CL	G	ATT	YDS	YPC
9	D.J. Dozier, Penn State*	FR	12	174	1002	5.8

Based on top 30 rushers

RECEIVING

		CL	G	REC	YDS	TD	RPG	YPR	YPG
2	Ricky Edwards, Northwestern	SR	11	83	570	0	6.9	51.8	7.5

PUNTING

		CL	PUNT	YDS	AVG
5	Ralf Mojsiejenko, Michigan State	JR	74	3249	43.9

SCORING

		CL	TDS	XP	FG	PTS	PTPG
2	Keith Byars, Ohio State	SO	20	0	0	120	10.9
10	Bob Bergeron, Michigan	SR	0	30	15	75	8.3

FIELD GOALS

		CL	FGA	FGM	PCT	FGG
9	Bob Bergeron, Michigan	SR	17	15	.88	1.67

INTERCEPTIONS

		CL	INT	YDS	TD	INT/GM
7	Phil Parker, Michigan State	JR	7	203	1	0.64

TEAM

RUSHING OFFENSE

		G	ATT	YDS	AVG	TD	YPG
8	Michigan	11	614	3042	5.0	28	276.5

PASSING OFFENSE

		G	ATT	COM	INT	PCT	YDS	YPA	TD	I%	YPC	YPG
7	Iowa	11	315	181	10	57.5	3072	9.8	20	3.2	17.0	279.3

TOTAL OFFENSE

		G	P	YDS	AVG	TD	YPG
3	Iowa	11	807	5366	6.6	48	487.8

RUSHING DEFENSE

		G	ATT	YDS	AVG	TD	YPG
2	Illinois	11	422	1034	2.5	5	94.0
3	Michigan	11	360	1051	2.9	5	95.5

PASSING DEFENSE

		G	ATT	COM	PCT	YPC	INT	I%	YDS	YPA	TD	RATING
10	Wisconsin	11	290	140	48.3	11.8	21	7.2	1656	5.7	13	150.5

TOTAL DEFENSE

		G	P	YDS	AVG	TD	YPG
5	Michigan	11	683	2937	4.3	17	267.0

SCORING OFFENSE

		G	PTS	AVG
3	Ohio State	11	382	34.7
4	Iowa	11	374	34.0
5	Wisconsin	11	359	32.6
9	Michigan	11	348	31.6
10	Illinois	11	338	30.7

1984

FINAL POLL

UP	AP	TEAM	RECORD
1	1	Brigham Young	13-0-0
2	2	Washington	11-1-0
7	3	Florida	9-1-1
3	4	Nebraska	10-2-0
4	5	Boston College	10-2-0
6	6	Oklahoma	9-2-1
5	7	Oklahoma State	10-2-0
8	8	SMU	10-2-0
10	9	UCLA	9-3-0
9	10	USC	9-3-0
13	11	South Carolina	10-2-0
11	12	Maryland	9-3-0
12	13	Ohio State	9-3-0
14	14	Auburn	9-4-0
16	15	LSU	8-3-1
15	16	Iowa	8-4-1
19	17	Florida State	7-3-2
	18	Miami, Fla.	8-5-0
19	19	Kentucky	9-3-0
17	20	Virginia	8-2-2

CONFERENCE STANDINGS

	CONFERENCE			OVERALL		
	W	L	T	W	L	T
Ohio State	7	2	0	9	3	0
Illinois	6	3	0	7	4	0
Purdue	6	3	0	7	5	0
Iowa	5	3	1	8	4	1
Wisconsin	5	3	1	7	4	1
Michigan State	5	4	0	6	6	0
Michigan	5	4	0	6	6	0
Minnesota	3	6	0	4	7	0
Northwestern	2	7	0	2	9	0
Indiana	0	9	0	0	11	0
Penn State				6	5	0

BOWL GAMES

DATE	GAME	SCORE
D21	Holiday	Brigham Young 24, Michigan 17
D22	Cherry	Army 10, Michigan State 6
D26	Freedom	Iowa 55, Texas 17
D29	All-American	Kentucky 20, Wisconsin 19
D31	Peach	Virginia 27, Purdue 24
J1	Rose	USC 20, Ohio State 17

*Independent or other conference affiliation

CONSENSUS ALL-AMERICANS

POS	Offense	HT	WT	School	AP	CF	FC	FW	PI
RB	Keith Byars	6-2	233	Ohio State	•	•	•	•	•
WR	David Williams	6-3	195	Illinois	•	•	•	•	•
G	Jim Lachey	6-6	274	Ohio State				•	•

POS	Defense	HT	WT	School	AP	CF	FC	FW	PI
LB	Larry Station		5-11 233	Iowa	•	•	•		•

OTHERS RECEIVING FIRST-TEAM HONORS

DB	Richard Johnson	Wisconsin	•

HEISMAN TROPHY VOTING

	PLAYER	POS	SCHOOL	1ST	2ND	3RD	TOTAL
2	Keith Byars	TB	Ohio State	87	427	136	1251
7	Chuck Long	QB	Iowa	2	6	19	37

ALL-CONFERENCE TEAM

POS	Offense
QB	Chuck Long, Iowa
RB	Thomas Rooks, Illinois
RB	Ronnie Harmon, Iowa
RB	Keith Byars, Ohio State
WR	David Williams, Illinois
WR	Al Toon, Wisconsin
C	Kirk Lowdermilk, Ohio State
G	Chris Babyar, Illinois
G	Jim Lachey, Ohio State
T	Jim Juriga, Illinois
T	Mark Krerowicz, Ohio State
T	Jeff Dellenbach, Wisconsin
TE	Cap Boso, Illinois
K	Chris White, Illinois

POS	Defense
L	Paul Hufford, Iowa
L	George Little, Iowa
L	Kevin Brooks, Michigan
L	Keith Cruise, Northwestern
L	Darryl Sims, Wisconsin
LB	Joe Fitzgerald, Indiana
LB	Larry Station, Iowa
LB	Jim Morrissey, Michigan State
LB	Thomas Johnson, Ohio State
LB	Mike Mallory, Michigan
DB	Mike Stoops, Iowa
DB	Devon Mitchell, Iowa
DB	Phil Parker, Michigan State
DB	Rod Woodson, Purdue
DB	Richard Johnson, Wisconsin
P	Tom Tupa, Ohio State

NCAA STATISTICAL LEADERS

INDIVIDUAL

PASSING	CL	G	ATT	COM	PCT	INT	I%	YDS	YPA	TD	TD%	RATING
7 Chuck Long, Iowa	JR	12	283	187	66.1	13	4.6	2410	8.5	16	5.7	147.1

ALL-PURPOSE	CL	G	RUSH	REC	PR	KR	YDS	YPG
1 Keith Byars, Ohio State	JR	11	1655	453	0	176	2284	207.6
2 Ronnie Harmon, Iowa	JR	9	907	318	0	262	1487	165.2

RUSHING/YARDS PER GAME	CL	G	ATT	YDS	TD	AVG	YPG
1 Keith Byars, Ohio State	JR	11	313	1655	22	5.3	150.5

RUSHING/YARDS PER CARRY	CL	G	ATT	YDS	YPC
8 Keith Byars, Ohio State	JR	11	313	1655	5.3

Based on top 23 rushers

RECEIVING	CL	G	REC	YDS	TD	RPG	YPR	YPG
1 David Williams, Illinois	JR	11	101	1278	8	12.7	116.2	9.2
7 Steve Griffin, Purdue	JR	11	60	991	4	16.5	90.1	5.5

PUNTING	CL	PUNT	YDS	AVG
5 Tom Tupa, Ohio State	FR	41	1927	47.0
6 Adam Kelly, Minnesota	JR	59	2726	46.2

PUNT RETURNS	CL	PR	YDS	TD	AVG
6 Bob Morse, Michigan State	SO	17	204	1	12.0

KICKOFF RETURNS	CL	KR	YDS	TD	AVG
4 Curt Duncan, Northwestern	SO	17	464	1	27.3
5 Larry Jackson, Michigan State	SR	20	522	1	26.1
10 Ronnie Harmon, Iowa	JR	11	262	0	23.8

SCORING	CL	TDS	XP	FG	PTS	PTPG
1 Keith Byars, Ohio State	JR	24	0	0	144	13.1
4 Chris White, Illinois	JR	0	31	24	103	9.4

FIELD GOALS	CL	FGA	FGM	PCT	FGG
2 Chris White, Illinois	JR	28	24	.86	2.18

TEAM

RUSHING OFFENSE	G	ATT	YDS	AVG	TD	YPG
10 Ohio State	11	574	2772	4.8	35	252.0

PASSING OFFENSE	G	ATT	COM	INT	PCT	YDS	YPA	TD	I%	YPC	YPG
5 Illinois	11	423	276	10	65.2	3130	7.4	22	2.4	11.3	284.5
7 Purdue	11	398	229	14	57.5	3019	7.6	15	3.5	13.2	274.5

TOTAL OFFENSE	G	P	YDS	AVG	TD	YPG
7 Illinois	11	875	4860	5.6	35	441.8
8 Ohio State	11	820	4803	5.9	47	436.6

RUSHING DEFENSE	G	ATT	YDS	AVG	TD	YPG
6 Iowa	12	439	1193	2.7	7	99.4

TOTAL DEFENSE	G	P	YDS	AVG	TD	YPG
7 Iowa	12	790	3239	4.1	20	269.9

SCORING OFFENSE	G	PTS	AVG
4 Ohio State	11	374	34.0

BIG TEN ANNUAL REVIEW & BOWLS

1985

FINAL POLL

UP	AP	TEAM	RECORD
1	1	Oklahoma	11-1-0
2	2	Michigan	10-1-1
3	3	Penn State*	11-1-0
4	4	Tennessee	9-1-2
PB	5	Florida	9-1-1
7	6	Texas A&M	10-2-0
6	7	UCLA	9-2-1
5	8	Air Force	12-1-0
8	9	Miami, Fla.	10-2-0
9	10	Iowa	10-2-0
10	11	Nebraska	9-3-0
12	12	Arkansas	10-2-0
14	13	Alabama	9-2-1
11	14	Ohio State	9-3-0
13	15	Florida State	9-3-0
17	16	Brigham Young	11-3-0
15	17	Baylor	9-3-0
19	18	Maryland	9-3-0
18	19	Georgia Tech	9-2-1
20	20	LSU	9-2-1

CONFERENCE STANDINGS

	CONFERENCE			OVERALL		
	W	L	T	W	L	T
Iowa	7	1	0	10	2	0
Michigan	6	1	1	10	1	1
Illinois	5	2	1	6	5	1
Ohio State	5	3	0	9	3	0
Michigan State	5	3	0	7	5	0
Minnesota	4	4	0	7	5	0
Purdue	3	5	0	5	6	0
Wisconsin	2	6	0	5	6	0
Indiana	1	7	0	4	7	0
Northwestern	1	7	0	3	8	0
Penn State*				11	1	0

BOWL GAMES

DATE	GAME	SCORE
D21	Independence	Minnesota 20, Clemson 13
D28	Florida Citrus	Ohio State 10, Brigham Young 7
D31	Peach	Army 31, Illinois 29
D31	All-American	Georgia Tech 17, Michigan State 14
J1	Fiesta	Michigan 27, Nebraska 23
J1	Orange	Oklahoma 25, Penn State* 10
J1	Rose	UCLA 45, Iowa 28

CONSENSUS ALL-AMERICANS

POS	Offense	HT	WT	School	AP	CF	FC	FW	PI
QB	Chuck Long	6-4	213	Iowa	•	•	•	•	•
RB	Lorenzo White	5-11	205	Michigan State	•	•	•	•	•
WR	David Williams	6-3	195	Illinois	•	•	•	•	•

POS	Defense	HT	WT	School	AP	CF	FC	FW	PI
L	Mike Hammerstein	6-4	240	Michigan	•		•		•
LB	Larry Station	5-11	227	Iowa	•	•	•	•	•
DB	Brad Cochran	6-3	219	Michigan		•	•	•	•

	OTHERS RECEIVING FIRST-TEAM HONORS								
LB	Thomas Johnson			Ohio State					•
DB	Michael Zordich			Penn State*				•	

HEISMAN TROPHY VOTING

	PLAYER	POS	SCHOOL	1ST	2ND	3RD	TOTAL
2	Chuck Long	QB	Iowa	286	254	98	1464
4	Lorenzo White	TB	Michigan State	50	63	115	391
6	Jim Everett	QB	Purdue	12	11	19	77

AWARD WINNERS

PLAYER	POS	SCHOOL	AWARD
Chuck Long	QB	Iowa	Maxwell
Chuck Long	QB	Iowa	O'Brien

ALL-CONFERENCE TEAM

POS	Offense	POS	Defense
QB	Chuck Long, Iowa	L	Guy Teafatiller, Illinois
RB	Ronnie Harmon, Iowa	L	Hap Peterson, Iowa
RB	Lorenzo White, Michigan State	L	Jeff Drost, Iowa
RB	Rodney Carter, Purdue	L	Mike Hammerstein, Michigan
WR	David Williams, Illinois	LB	Mark Messner, Michigan
WR	Chris Carter, Ohio State	LB	Mike Mallory, Michigan
C	Bob Maggs, Ohio State	LB	Thomas Johnson, Ohio State
G	John Wojciechowski, Michigan State	LB	Chris Spielman, Ohio State
G	Bob Landsee, Wisconsin	LB	Larry Station, Iowa
T	Jim Juriga, Illinois	DB	Jay Norvell, Iowa
T	Mike Haight, Iowa	DB	Brad Cochran, Michigan
T	Clay Miller, Michigan	DB	Phil Parker, Michigan State
T	Rory Graves, Ohio State	DB	Rod Woodson, Purdue
TE	Eric Kattus, Michigan	P	Greg Montgomery, Michigan State
K	Chris White, Illinois	P	Tom Tupa, Ohio State
K	Rob Houghtlin, Iowa		

*Independent or other conference affiliation

1986

NCAA STATISTICAL LEADERS

INDIVIDUAL

PASSING

		CL	G	ATT	COM	PCT	INT	I%	YDS	YPA	TD	TD%	RATING
1	Jim Harbaugh, Michigan	JR	11	212	139	65.6	6	2.8	1913	9.0	18	8.5	163.7
3	Chuck Long, Iowa	SR	11	351	231	65.8	15	4.3	2978	8.5	26	7.4	153.0
4	Jim Karsatos, Ohio State	JR	11	254	158	62.2	8	3.2	2115	8.3	19	7.5	150.5
9	Jim Everett, Purdue	SR	11	450	285	63.3	11	2.4	3651	8.1	23	5.1	143.5

ALL-PURPOSE

		CL	G	RUSH	REC	PR	KR	YDS	YPG
4	Lorenzo White, Michigan State	SO	11	1908	28	0	0	1936	176.0
6	Ronnie Harmon, Iowa	SR	11	1111	597	0	147	1855	168.6

RUSHING/YARDS PER GAME

		CL	G	ATT	YDS	TD	AVG	YPG
1	Lorenzo White, Michigan State	SO	11	386	1908	17	4.9	173.5

RECEIVING

		CL	G	REC	YDS	TD	RPG	YPR	YPG
1	Rodney Carter, Purdue	SR	11	98	1099	4	11.2	99.9	8.9
3	David Williams, Illinois	SR	11	85	1047	8	12.3	95.2	7.7

PUNTING

		CL	PUNT	YDS	AVG
10	Greg Montgomery, Michigan State	SO	69	3084	44.7

PUNT RETURNS

		CL	PR	YDS	TD	AVG
5	Gilvanni Johnson, Michigan	SR	12	169	1	14.1
10	Nate Odomes, Wisconsin	JR	14	160	0	11.4

KICKOFF RETURNS

		CL	KR	YDS	TD	AVG
3	Curtis Duncan, Northwestern	JR	11	299	0	27.2

SCORING

		CL	TDS	XP	FG	PTS	PTPG
2	Lorenzo White, Michigan State	SO	17	0	0	102	9.3
8	Rob Houghtlin, Iowa	SO	0	46	17	97	8.8

FIELD GOALS

		CL	FGA	FGM	PCT	FGG
4	Massimo Manca, Penn State*	SR	26	21	0.81	1.91

INTERCEPTIONS

		CL	INT	YDS	TD	INT/GM
5	Jay Norvell, Iowa	SR	7	93	0	0.64

TEAM

PASSING OFFENSE

		G	ATT	COM	INT	PCT	YDS	YPA	TD	I%	YPC	YPG
2	Purdue	11	471	292	13	62.0	3760	8.0	23	2.8	12.9	341.8
4	Iowa	11	382	247	15	64.7	3292	8.6	29	3.9	13.3	299.3
8	Illinois	11	462	290	17	62.8	2992	6.5	16	3.7	10.3	272.0

TOTAL OFFENSE

		G	P	YDS	AVG	TD	YPG
4	Iowa	11	815	5106	6.3	52	464.2
9	Purdue	11	822	4801	5.8	36	436.5

RUSHING DEFENSE

		G	ATT	YDS	AVG	TD	YPG
5	Iowa	11	434	1117	2.6	8	101.5
6	Michigan	11	385	1135	2.9	2	103.2

TOTAL DEFENSE

		G	P	YDS	AVG	TD	YPG
2	Michigan	11	689	2790	4.0	5	253.6
5	Iowa	11	755	3044	4.0	16	276.7

SCORING OFFENSE

		G	PTS	AVG
2	Iowa	11	412	37.5

SCORING DEFENSE

		G	PTS	AVG
1	Michigan	11	75	6.8
5	Penn State*	11	128	11.6
10	Iowa	11	142	12.9

FINAL POLL

UP	AP	TEAM	RECORD
1	1	Penn State*	12-0-0
2	2	Miami, Fla.	11-1-0
3	3	Oklahoma	11-1-0
5	4	Arizona State	10-1-1
4	5	Nebraska	10-2-0
6	6	Auburn	10-2-0
6	7	**Ohio State**	10-3-0
7	8	**Michigan**	11-2-0
9	9	Alabama	10-3-0
11	10	LSU	9-3-0
10	11	Arizona	9-3-0
13	12	Baylor	9-3-0
12	13	Texas A&M	9-3-0
14	14	UCLA	8-3-1
16	15	Arkansas	9-3-0
15	16	Iowa	9-3-0
19	17	Clemson	8-2-2
17	18	Washington	8-3-1
18	19	Boston College	9-3-0
	20	Virginia Tech	9-2-1

CONFERENCE STANDINGS

	Conf.			Overall		
	W	L	T	W	L	T
Michigan	7	1	0	11	2	0
Ohio State	7	1	0	10	3	0
Iowa	5	3	0	9	3	0
Minnesota	5	3	0	6	6	0
Michigan State	4	4	0	6	5	0
Indiana	3	5	0	6	6	0
Illinois	3	5	0	4	7	0
Northwestern	2	6	0	4	7	0
Purdue	2	6	0	3	8	0
Wisconsin	2	6	0	3	9	0

Penn State*				12	0	0

BOWL GAMES

DATE	GAME	SCORE
D29	**Liberty**	Tennessee 21, Minnesota 14
D30	**Holiday**	Iowa 39, San Diego State 38
D31	**All-American**	Florida State 27, Indiana 13
J1	**Rose**	Arizona State 22, Michigan 15
J1	**Cotton**	Ohio State 28, Texas A&M 12
J2	**Fiesta**	Penn State* 14, Miami, Fla. 10

CONSENSUS ALL-AMERICANS

POS	**Offense**	HT	WT	**School**	AP	CF	FC	FW	PI
RB	**D.J. Dozier**	6-1	204	Penn State*		•			
WR	**Cris Carter**	6-3	194	Ohio State	•	•	•		•

	OTHERS RECEIVING FIRST-TEAM HONORS								
L	Chris Conlin			Penn State*				•	
L	Dave Croston			Iowa					
L	John Elliott			Michigan					

POS	**Defense**	HT	WT	**School**	AP	CF	FC	FW	PI
LB	**Shane Conlan**	6-3	225	Penn State*	•	•	•	•	
LB	**Chris Spielman**	6-2	227	Ohio State	•	•	•	•	
DB	**Rod Woodson**	6-0	195	Purdue	•	•			
DB	**Garland Rivers**	6-1	187	Michigan		•	•		

	OTHERS RECEIVING FIRST-TEAM HONORS								
DL	Tim Johnson			Penn State*		•			
P	Greg Montgomery			Michigan State				•	

HEISMAN TROPHY VOTING

	PLAYER	POS	SCHOOL	1ST	2ND	3RD	TOTAL
3	**Jim Harbaugh**	QB	Michigan	25	136	111	458
8	**D.J. Dozier**	TB	Penn State*	0	23	31	77
10	**Chris Spielman**	LB	Ohio State	5	9	27	60

BIG TEN ANNUAL REVIEW & BOWLS

1986, CONT.

ALL-CONFERENCE TEAM

POS	Offense		POS	Defense
QB	Jim Harbaugh, Michigan		L	Dave Haight, Iowa
RB	Rick Bayless, Iowa		L	Jeff Drost, Iowa
RB	Jamie Morris, Michigan		L	Mark Messner, Michigan
RB	Lorenzo White, Michigan State		LB	Van Waiters, Indiana
RB	Darrell Thompson, Minnesota		LB	Andy Moeller, Michigan
WR	Andre Rison, Michigan State		LB	Shane Bullough, Michigan State
WR	Chris Carter, Ohio State		LB	Bruce Holmes, Minnesota
C	Bob Maggs, Ohio State		LB	Eric Kumerow, Ohio State
G	Bob Kratch, Iowa		LB	Michael Reid, Wisconsin
G	Mark Hammerstein, Michigan		LB	Chris Spielman, Ohio State
G	Jeff Uhlenhake, Ohio State		DB	Garland Rivers, Michigan
T	Dave Croston, Iowa		DB	Sonny Gordon, Ohio State
T	John Elliott, Michigan		DB	Rod Woodson, Purdue
TE	Rich Borresen, Northwestern		DB	Nate Odomes, Wisconsin
TE	Ed Taggart, Ohio State		P	Greg Montgomery, Michigan State
K	Rob Houghtlin, Iowa			
K	Chip Lohmiller, Minnesota			
K	John Duvic, Northwestern			

NCAA STATISTICAL LEADERS

INDIVIDUAL

PASSING	CL	G	ATT	COM	PCT	INT	I%	YDS	YPA	TD	TD%	RATING
2 Jim Harbaugh, Michigan	SR	12	254	167	65.8	8	3.2	2557	10.1	10	3.9	157.0
3 Dave Yarema, Michigan State	SR	11	297	200	67.3	11	3.7	2581	8.7	16	5.4	150.7
5 Mark Vlasic, Iowa	SR	9	152	93	61.2	4	2.6	1234	8.1	9	5.9	143.7

RUSHING/Yards Per Carry	CL	G	ATT	YDS	YPC
7 Darrell Thompson, Minnesota	FR	11	217	1240	5.7

PUNTING	CL	PUNT	YDS	AVG
10 Tom Tupa, Ohio State	JR	50	2180	43.6

KICKOFF RETURNS	CL	KR	YDS	TD	AVG
2 Blair Thomas, Penn State*	SO	12	383	1	31.9
5 Keith Jones, Illinois	SO	15	398	0	26.5

FIELD GOALS	CL	FGA	FGM	PCT	FGG
6 John Duvic, Northwestern	SR	23	19	0.83	1.73

TEAM

TOTAL OFFENSE	G	P	YDS	AVG	TD	YPG
7 Michigan	12	870	5175	5.9	44	431.3
9 Iowa	11	772	4628	6.0	42	420.7

RUSHING DEFENSE	G	ATT	YDS	AVG	TD	YPG
3 Penn State*	11	383	767	2.0	5	69.7

TOTAL DEFENSE	G	P	YDS	AVG	TD	YPG
8 Iowa	11	717	3031	4.2	18	275.5

SCORING DEFENSE	G	PTS	AVG
3 Penn State*	11	123	11.2

1987

FINAL POLL

UP	AP	TEAM	RECORD
1	1	Miami, Fla.	12-0-0
2	2	Florida State	11-1-0
3	3	Oklahoma	11-1-0
4	4	Syracuse	11-0-1
5	5	LSU	10-1-1
6	6	Nebraska	10-2-0
7	7	Auburn	9-1-2
8	8	**Michigan State**	9-2-1
11	9	UCLA	10-2-0
9	10	Texas A&M	10-2-0
12	11	Oklahoma State	10-2-0
10	12	Clemson	10-2-0
14	13	Georgia	9-3-0
13	14	Tennessee	10-2-1
15	15	South Carolina	8-4-0
15	16	**Iowa**	10-3-0
	17	Notre Dame	8-4-0
17	18	USC	8-4-0
18	19	**Michigan**	8-4-0
	20	Arizona State	7-4-1
19		Texas	7-5-1
20		Indiana	8-4-0

CONFERENCE STANDINGS

	CONFERENCE			OVERALL		
	W	L	T	W	L	T
Michigan State	7	0	1	9	2	1
Iowa	6	2	0	10	3	0
Indiana	6	2	0	8	4	0
Michigan	5	3	0	8	4	0
Ohio State	4	4	0	6	4	1
Minnesota	3	5	0	6	5	0
Purdue	3	5	0	3	7	1
Illinois	2	5	1	3	7	1
Northwestern	2	6	0	2	8	1
Wisconsin	1	7	0	3	8	0
Penn State*				8	4	0

BOWL GAMES

DATE	GAME	SCORE
D30	**Holiday**	Iowa 20, Wyoming 19
J1	**Citrus**	Clemson 35, Penn State* 10
J1	**Rose**	Michigan State 20, USC 17
J2	**Hall of Fame**	Michigan 28, Alabama 24
J2	**Peach**	Tennessee 27, Indiana 22

*Independent or other conference affiliation

CONSENSUS ALL-AMERICANS

POS	Offense	HT	WT	School	AP	CF	FC	FW	PI
RB	Lorenzo White	5-11	211	Michigan State	•	•	•	•	
L	John Elliott	6-7	306	Michigan	•	•	•	•	

OTHERS RECEIVING FIRST-TEAM HONORS

WR	Ernie Jones			Indiana	•				

POS	Defense	HT	WT	School	AP	CF	FC	FW	PI
LB	Chris Spielman	6-2	236	Ohio State	•	•	•	•	
P	Tom Tupa	6-5	215	Ohio State	•	•	•	•	

HEISMAN TROPHY VOTING

PLAYER	POS	SCHOOL	1ST	2ND	3RD	TOTAL
4 Lorenzo White	TB	Michigan State	89	121	123	632
6 Chris Spielman	LB	Ohio State	15	20	25	110

AWARD WINNERS

PLAYER	POS	SCHOOL	AWARD
Chris Spielman	LB	Ohio State	Lombardi

ALL-CONFERENCE TEAM

POS	Offense	POS	Defense
QB	Chuck Hartlieb, Iowa	L	Scott Davis, Illinois
RB	Jamie Morris, Michigan	L	Dave Haight, Iowa
RB	Lorenzo White, Michigan State	L	Mark Messner, Michigan
WR	Ernie Jones, Indiana	LB	Van Waiters, Indiana
WR	Quinn Early, Iowa	LB	Percy Snow, Michigan State
C	John Vitale, Michigan	LB	Jon Leverenz, Minnesota
C	Pat Shurmur, Michigan State	LB	Eric Kumerow, Ohio State
G	Don Shrader, Indiana	LB	Chris Spielman, Ohio State
G	Bob Kratch, Iowa	LB	Fred Strickland, Purdue
G	Mike Husar, Michigan	DB	Kerry Burt, Iowa
G	Troy Wolkow, Minnesota	DB	John Miller, Michigan State
T	John Elliott, Michigan	DB	Todd Krumm, Michigan State
T	Tony Mandarich, Michigan State	DB	William White, Ohio State
T	Paul Gruber, Wisconsin	DB	Marc Foster, Purdue
TE	Marv Cook, Iowa	P	Greg Montgomery, Michigan State
K	Rob Houghtlin, Iowa	P	Tom Tupa, Ohio State

NCAA STATISTICAL LEADERS

INDIVIDUAL

PASSING	CL	G	ATT	COM	PCT	INT	I%	YDS	YPA	TD	TD%	RATING
3 Chuck Hartlieb, Iowa	SR	12	299	196	65.6	8	2.7	2855	9.6	19	6.4	161.4

ALL-PURPOSE	CL	G	RUSH	REC	PR	KR	YDS	YPG
8 Blair Thomas, Penn State*	JR	11	1414	300	0	58	1772	161.1
10 Jamie Morris, Michigan	SR	11	1469	126	0	147	1742	158.4

RUSHING/YARDS PER GAME	CL	G	ATT	YDS	TD	AVG	YPG
5 Jamie Morris, Michigan	SR	11	259	1469	11	5.7	133.6
6 Lorenzo White, Michigan State	SR	11	322	1459	14	4.5	132.6
7 Blair Thomas, Penn State*	JR	11	268	1414	11	5.3	128.6

RUSHING/YARDS PER CARRY	CL	G	ATT	YDS	YPC
9 Jamie Morris, Michigan	SR	11	259	1469	5.7
10 Darrell Thompson, Minnesota	SO	11	224	1229	5.5

Based on top 23 rushers

PUNTING	CL	PUNT	YDS	AVG
1 Tom Tupa, Ohio State	SR	63	2963	47.0
5 Greg Montgomery, Michigan State	SR	62	2772	44.7
9 Monte Robbins, Michigan	SR	45	1964	43.6

KICKOFF RETURNS	CL	KR	YDS	TD	AVG
2 Darryl Usher, Illinois	SR	15	445	0	29.7

FIELD GOALS	CL	FGA	FGM	PCT	FGG
6 Rob Houghtlin, Iowa	SR	29	21	.72	1.75

INTERCEPTIONS	CL	INT	YDS	TD	INT/GM
2 Todd Krumm, Michigan State	SR	9	129	0	0.82
10 Brett Whitley, Northwestern	SR	7	202	0	0.64

TEAM

PASSING OFFENSE	G	ATT	COM	INT	PCT	YDS	YPA	TD	I%	YPC	YPG
7 Iowa	12	413	255	13	61.7	3559	8.6	23	3.2	14.0	296.6

RUSHING DEFENSE	G	ATT	YDS	AVG	TD	YPG
1 Michigan State	11	360	676	1.9	5	61.5

PASSING DEFENSE	G	ATT	COM	PCT	YPC	INT	I%	YDS	YPA	TD	RATING
2 Illinois	11	185	83	44.9	13.9	9	4.9	1152	6.2	5	104.7

TOTAL DEFENSE	G	P	YDS	AVG	TD	YPG
2 Michigan State	11	676	2482	3.7	13	225.6

SCORING DEFENSE	G	PTS	AVG
8 Michigan State	11	136	12.4
9 Michigan	11	148	13.5

1988

Final Poll

UP	AP	TEAM	RECORD
1	1	Notre Dame	12-0-0
2	2	Miami, Fla.	11-1-0
3	3	Florida State	11-1-0
4	4	**Michigan**	9-2-1
5	5	West Virginia	11-1-0
6	6	UCLA	10-2-0
9	7	USC	10-2-0
7	8	Auburn	10-2-0
8	9	Clemson	10-2-0
10	10	Nebraska	11-2-0
11	11	Oklahoma State	10-2-0
13	12	Arkansas	10-2-0
12	13	Syracuse	10-2-0
14	14	Oklahoma	9-3-0
15	15	Georgia	9-3-0
16	16	Washington State	9-3-0
17	17	Alabama	9-3-0
	18	Houston	9-3-0
	19	LSU	8-4-0
19	20	**Indiana**	8-3-1

Conference Standings

	Conference			Overall		
	W	L	T	W	L	T
Michigan	7	0	1	9	2	1
Michigan State	6	1	1	6	5	1
Illinois	5	2	1	6	5	1
Iowa	4	1	3	6	4	3
Indiana	5	3	0	8	3	1
Purdue	3	5	0	4	7	0
Ohio State	2	5	1	4	6	1
Northwestern	2	5	1	2	8	1
Wisconsin	1	7	0	1	10	0
Minnesota	0	6	2	2	7	2
Penn State*				5	6	0

Bowl Games

DATE	GAME	SCORE
D28	**Liberty**	Indiana 34, South Carolina 10
D29	**All-American**	Florida 14, Illinois 10
D31	**Peach**	North Carolina St. 28, Iowa 23
J1	**Gator**	Georgia 34, Michigan State 27
J2	**Rose**	Michigan 22, USC 14

Consensus All-Americans

POS	Offense	HT	WT	School	AP	CF	FC	FW	PI
RB	**Anthony Thompson**	6-0	205	Indiana		•		•	•
TE	**Marv Cook**	6-4	243	Iowa			•		•
L	**Tony Mandarich**	6-6	315	Michigan State	•	•	•	•	•
C	**John Vitale**	6-1	273	Michigan		•			•

	OTHERS RECEIVING FIRST-TEAM HONORS								
L	Steve Wisniewski			Penn State*			•		

POS	Defense	HT	WT	School	AP	CF	FC	FW	PI
L	**Mark Messner**	6-3	244	Michigan	•	•	•	•	•

	OTHERS RECEIVING FIRST-TEAM HONORS								
L	Dave Haight			Iowa		•			

Heisman Trophy Voting

	PLAYER	POS	SCHOOL	1ST	2ND	3RD	TOTAL
6	**Tony Mandarich**	OT	Michigan State	3	9	25	52
9	**Anthony Thompson**	TB	Indiana	0	4	13	21

All-Conference Team

POS	Offense	POS	Defense
QB	Chuck Hartlieb, Iowa	L	Moe Gardner, Illinois
RB	Anthony Thompson, Indiana	L	Joe Huff, Indiana
RB	Tony Boles, Michigan	L	Dave Haight, Iowa
WR	Devon Harberts, Iowa	L	Joe Mott, Iowa
WR	John Kolesar, Michigan	L	Mark Messner, Michigan
C	John Vitale, Michigan	LB	Darrick Brownlow, Illinois
G	Don Shrader, Indiana	LB	Willie Bates, Indiana
G	Bob Kratch, Iowa	LB	Brad Quast, Iowa
G	Mike Husar, Michigan	LB	Percy Snow, Michigan State
T	Tony Mandarich, Michigan State	DB	Glen Cobb, Illinois
TE	Marv Cook, Iowa	DB	David Arnold, Michigan
K	Pete Stoyanovich, Indiana	DB	John Miller, Michigan State
K	Mike Gillette, Michigan	DB	Marc Foster, Purdue
		P	Mike Gillette, Michigan

*Independent or other conference affiliation

1989

NCAA Statistical Leaders

INDIVIDUAL

ALL-PURPOSE

		CL	G	RUSH	REC	PR	KR	YDS	YPG
4	Tony Boles, Michigan	JR	10	1359	64	0	302	1725	172.5
8	Anthony Thompson, Indiana	JR	11	1546	219	0	0	1765	160.5

RUSHING/YARDS PER GAME

		CL	G	ATT	YDS	TD	AVG	YPG
3	Anthony Thompson, Indiana	JR	11	329	1546	24	4.7	140.6
4	Tony Boles, Michigan	JR	10	248	1359	9	5.5	135.9
7	Blake Ezor, Michigan State	JR	11	290	1358	10	4.7	123.5

RECEIVING

		CL	G	REC	YDS	TD	RPG	YPR	YPG
9	Marv Cook, Iowa	SR	9	55	645	3	11.7	71.7	6.1

PUNT RETURNS

		CL	PR	YDS	TD	AVG
10	John Miller, Michigan State	SR	15	179	0	11.9

KICKOFF RETURNS

		CL	KR	YDS	TD	AVG
4	Carlos Snow, Ohio State	SO	19	513	1	27.0
10	Tony Boles, Michigan	JR	12	302	0	25.2

SCORING

		CL	TDS	XP	FG	PTS	PTPG
2	Anthony Thompson, Indiana	JR	24	0	0	144	13.1

FIELD GOALS

		CL	FGA	FGM	PCT	FGG
9	Pat O'Morrow, Ohio State	JR	23	18	0.78	1.64
9	John Langeloh, Michigan State	SO	26	18	0.69	1.64

INTERCEPTIONS

		CL	INT	YDS	TD	INT/GM
1	Kurt Larson, Michigan State	SR	8	78	1	0.73

TEAM

PASSING OFFENSE

		G	ATT	COM	INT	PCT	YDS	YPA	TD	I%	YPC	YPG
7	Iowa	12	419	260	10	62.1	3324	7.9	15	2.4	12.8	277.0

PASSING DEFENSE

		G	ATT	COM	PCT	YPC	INT	I%	YDS	YPA	TD	RATING
4	Purdue	11	232	93	40.1	15.4	16	6.9	1430	6.2	10	130.0

SCORING DEFENSE

		G	PTS	AVG
6	Michigan State	11	143	13.0
9	Michigan	11	153	13.9

FINAL POLL

UP	AP	TEAM	RECORD
1	1	Miami, Fla.	11-1-0
3	2	Notre Dame	12-1-0
2	3	Florida State	10-2-0
4	4	Colorado	11-1-0
5	5	Tennessee	11-1-0
6	6	Auburn	10-2-0
8	7	**Michigan**	10-2-0
9	8	USC	9-2-1
7	9	Alabama	10-2-0
10	10	**Illinois**	10-2-0
12	11	Nebraska	10-2-0
11	12	Clemson	10-2-0
13	13	Arkansas	10-2-0
PB	14	Houston	9-2-0
14	15	Penn State*	8-3-1
16	16	**Michigan State**	8-4-0
19	17	Pittsburgh	8-3-1
15	18	Virginia	10-3-0
16	19	Texas Tech	9-3-0
	20	Texas A&M	8-4-0
	21	West Virginia	8-3-1
18	22	Brigham Young	10-3-0
20	23	Washington	8-4-0
	24	**Ohio State**	8-4-0
	25	Arizona	8-4-0

CONFERENCE STANDINGS

	Conf.			Overall		
	W	L	T	W	L	T
Michigan	8	0	0	10	2	0
Illinois	7	1	0	10	2	0
Michigan State	6	2	0	8	4	0
Ohio State	6	2	0	8	4	0
Minnesota	4	4	0	6	5	0
Indiana	3	5	0	5	6	0
Iowa	3	5	0	5	6	0
Purdue	2	6	0	3	8	0
Wisconsin	1	7	0	2	9	0
Northwestern	0	8	0	0	11	0
Penn State*				8	3	1

BOWL GAMES

DATE	GAME	SCORE
D25	**Aloha**	Michigan State 33, Hawaii 13
D29	**Holiday**	Penn State* 50, Brigham Young 39
J1	**Hall of Fame**	Auburn 31, Ohio State 14
J1	**Citrus**	Illinois 31, Virginia 21
J1	**Rose**	USC 17, Michigan 10

CONSENSUS ALL-AMERICANS

POS	**Offense**	HT	WT	**School**	AP	CF	FC	FW	PI
RB	**Anthony Thompson**	6-0	209	Indiana	•	•	•	•	•
L	**Bob Kula**	6-4	282	Michigan State	•		•		

OTHERS RECEIVING FIRST-TEAM HONORS

POS				School	AP	CF	FC	FW	PI
RB	Blair Thomas			Penn State*			•		

POS	**Defense**	HT	WT	**School**	AP	CF	FC	FW	PI
L	**Moe Gardner**	6-2	250	Illinois	•	•	•	•	•
LB	**Percy Snow**	6-3	240	Michigan State	•	•	•	•	•
DB	**Tripp Welborne**	6-1	193	Michigan	•	•	•	•	•

OTHERS RECEIVING FIRST-TEAM HONORS

POS				School	AP	CF	FC	FW	PI
LB	Andre Collins			Penn State*			•		

HEISMAN TROPHY VOTING

	PLAYER	POS	SCHOOL	1ST	2ND	3RD	TOTAL
2	**Anthony Thompson**	TB	Indiana	185	170	108	1003
8	**Percy Snow**	LB	Michigan State	7	15	19	70
10	**Blair Thomas**	TB	Penn State*	4	12	12	48

BIG TEN ANNUAL REVIEW & BOWLS

1989, CONT.

AWARD WINNERS

PLAYER	POS	SCHOOL	AWARD
Anthony Thompson	RB	Indiana	Maxwell
Anthony Thompson	RB	Indiana	Camp
Percy Snow	LB	Michigan State	Lombardi
Percy Snow	LB	Michigan State	Butkus

ALL-CONFERENCE TEAM†

POS	Offense	POS	Defense
QB	Jeff George, Illinois	L	Moe Gardner, Illinois
RB	Anthony Thompson, Indiana	L	Mel Agee, Illinois
RB	Tony Boles, Michigan	L	Jim Johnson, Iowa
WR	Courtney Hawkins, Michigan State	L	Travis Davis, Michigan State
WR	Richard Buchanan, Northwestern	LB	Darrick Brownlow, Illinois
C	Curt Lovelace, Illinois	LB	Brad Quast, Iowa
G	Dean Dingman, Michigan	LB	Percy Snow, Michigan State
G	Jeff Davidson, Ohio State	DB	Henry Jones, Illinois
T	Bob Kula, Michigan State	DB	Mike Dumas, Indiana
T	Joe Staysniak, Ohio State	DB	Tripp Welborne, Michigan
TE	Derrick Walker, Michigan	DB	Harlon Barnett, Michigan State
K	J.D. Carlson, Michigan	P	Shawn McCarthy, Purdue

NCAA STATISTICAL LEADERS

INDIVIDUAL

PASSING

		CL	G	ATT	COM	PCT	INT	I%	YDS	YPA	TD	TD%	RATING
9	Greg Frey, Ohio State	JR	11	215	128	59.5	7	3.3	1900	8.8	12	5.6	145.7

ALL-PURPOSE

		CL	G	RUSH	REC	PR	KR	YDS	YPG
4	Anthony Thompson, Indiana	SR	11	1793	201	0	394	2388	217.1

RUSHING/YARDS PER GAME

		CL	G	ATT	YDS	TD	AVG	YPG
1	Anthony Thompson, Indiana	SR	11	358	1793	24	5.0	163.0
7	Blake Ezor, Michigan State	SR	9	226	1120	16	5.0	124.4
10	Blair Thomas, Penn State*	SR	11	264	1341	5	5.1	121.9

RECEIVING

		CL	G	REC	YDS	TD	RPG	YPR	YPG
2	Richard Buchanan, Northwestern	JR	11	94	1115	9	11.9	101.4	8.6

PUNTING

		CL	PUNT	YDS	AVG
4	Shawn McCarthy, Purdue	SR	69	3075	44.6

PUNT RETURNS

		CL	PR	YDS	TD	AVG
7	O.J. McDuffie, Penn State*	SO	19	278	1	14.6
10	Troy Vincent, Wisconsin	SO	17	235	1	13.8

KICKOFF RETURNS

		CL	KR	YDS	TD	AVG
2	Mike Bellamy, Illinois	SR	14	432	0	30.9

SCORING

		CL	TDS	XP	FG	PTS	PTPG
1	Anthony Thompson, Indiana	SR	25	4	0	154	14.0
6	Blake Ezor, Michigan State	SR	16	0	0	96	10.7

TEAM

PASSING DEFENSE

		G	ATT	COM	PCT	YPC	INT	I%	YDS	YPA	TD	RATING
2	Illinois	11	259	127	49.0	12.2	18	7.0	1545	6.0	3	140.5
7	Indiana	11	217	123	56.7	13.4	9	4.2	1654	7.6	15	150.4

TOTAL DEFENSE

		G	P	YDS	AVG	TD	YPG
10	Illinois	11	721	3136	4.3	15	285.1

SCORING DEFENSE

		G	PTS	AVG
4	Penn State*	11	130	11.8
6	Michigan State	11	150	13.6
9	Illinois	11	161	14.6

1990

FINAL POLL

UP	AP	Team	RECORD
2	1	Colorado	11-1-1
1	2	Georgia Tech	11-0-1
3	3	Miami, Fla.	10-2-0
4	4	Florida State	10-2-0
5	5	Washington	10-2-0
6	6	Notre Dame	9-3-0
8	7	**Michigan**	9-3-0
7	8	Tennessee	9-2-2
9	9	Clemson	10-2-0
PB	10	Houston	10-1-0
10	11	Penn State*	9-3-0
11	12	Texas	10-2-0
PB	13	Florida	9-2-0
12	14	Louisville	10-1-1
13	15	Texas A&M	9-3-1
14	16	**Michigan State**	8-3-1
PB	17	Oklahoma	8-3-0
16	18	**Iowa**	8-4-0
19	19	Auburn	8-3-1
22	20	USC	8-4-1
23	21	Mississippi	9-3-0
17	22	Brigham Young	10-3-0
15	23	Virginia	8-4-0
17	24	Nebraska	9-3-0
24	25	**Illinois**	8-4-0

CONFERENCE STANDINGS

	CONFERENCE			OVERALL		
	W	L	T	W	L	T
Michigan	6	2	0	9	3	0
Michigan State	6	2	0	8	3	1
Illinois	6	2	0	8	4	0
Iowa	6	2	0	8	4	0
Ohio State	5	2	1	7	4	1
Minnesota	5	3	0	6	5	0
Indiana	3	4	1	6	5	1
Purdue	1	7	0	2	9	0
Northwestern	1	7	0	2	9	0
Wisconsin	0	8	0	1	10	0
Penn State*				9	3	0

BOWL GAMES

DATE	GAME	SCORE
D27	**Liberty**	Air Force 23, Ohio State 11
D28	**Blockbuster**	Florida State 24, Penn State* 17
D29	**Peach**	Auburn 27, Indiana 23
J1	**Hall of Fame**	Clemson 30, Illinois 0
J1	**Gator**	Michigan 35, Mississippi 3
J1	**Rose**	Washington 46, Iowa 34

*Independent or other conference affiliation
† From 1989 to 1996, the Big Ten recognized all-conference teams selected both by the conference coaches and members of the media

CONSENSUS ALL-AMERICANS

POS	Offense	HT	WT	School	AP	CF	FC	FW	PI
None									

OTHERS RECEIVING FIRST-TEAM HONORS

OL	Greg Skrepenak			Michigan		•			
OL	Dean Dingman			Michigan			•		

POS	Defense	HT	WT	School	AP	CF	FC	FW	PI
DL	Moe Gardner	6-2	258	Illinois		•	•		•
DB	Tripp Welborne	6-1	201	Michigan	•	•	•	•	•

ALL-CONFERENCE TEAM†

POS	Offense
QB	Matt Rodgers, Iowa
RB	Nick Bell, Iowa
RB	Tico Duckett, Michigan State
WR	Shawn Wax, Illinois
WR	Desmond Howard, Michigan
WR	Courtney Hawkins, Michigan State
WR	Richard Buchanan, Northwestern
WR	Jeff Graham, Ohio State
C	Curt Lovelace, Illinois
C	Chris Thoe, Minnesota
C	Dan Beatty, Ohio State
G	Dean Dingman, Michigan
T	Greg Skrepenak, Michigan
T	Tom Dohring, Michigan
T	Jim Johnson, Michigan State
T	Eric Moten, Michigan State
TE	Mike Titley, Iowa
TE	Duane Young, Michigan State
K	J.D. Carlson, Michigan
K	John Langeloh, Michigan State

POS	Defense
L	Mel Agee, Illinois
L	Moe Gardner, Illinois
L	Matt Ruhland, Iowa
L	Jim Johnson, Iowa
L	Don Davey, Wisconsin
LB	Darrick Brownlow, Illinois
LB	Melvin Foster, Iowa
LB	Erick Anderson, Michigan
LB	Carlos Jenkins, Michigan State
LB	Steve Tovar, Ohio State
DB	Mike Dumas, Indiana
DB	Merton Hanks, Iowa
DB	Tripp Welborne, Michigan
DB	Jon Vaughn, Michigan
P	Macky Smith, Indiana

NCAA STATISTICAL LEADERS

INDIVIDUAL

	RUSHING/YARDS PER GAME	CL	G	ATT	YDS	TD	AVG	YPG
5	Tico Duckett, Michigan State	SO	11	249	1376	10	5.5	125.1

	RUSHING/YARDS PER CARRY	CL	G	ATT	YDS	YPC
2	Robert Smith, Ohio State	FR	11	164	1064	6.5
5	Jon Vaughn, Michigan	SO	11	201	1236	6.1
9	Howard Griffith, Illinois	SR	11	186	1056	5.7

Based on top 22 rushers

	PUNT RETURNS	CL	PR	YDS	TD	AVG
3	Jeff Graham, Ohio State	SR	22	327	2	14.9
5	Tripp Welborne, Michigan	SR	31	455	0	14.7
8	Rob Turner, Indiana	JR	27	373	2	13.8

	KICKOFF RETURNS	CL	KR	YDS	TD	AVG
2	Desmond Howard, Michigan	JR	16	472	1	29.5

	INTERCEPTIONS	CL	INT	YDS	TD	INT/GM
3	Darren Perry, Penn State*	SR	7	125	1	0.64

TEAM

	RUSHING OFFENSE	G	ATT	YDS	AVG	TD	YPG
10	Michigan State	11	590	2793	4.7	34	253.9

	RUSHING DEFENSE	G	ATT	YDS	AVG	TD	YPG
7	Penn State*	11	401	1040	2.6	8	94.5
8	Iowa	11	392	1095	2.8	14	99.5

	PASSING DEFENSE	G	ATT	COM	PCT	INT	I%	YDS	YPA	TD	TD%	RATING
10	Penn State*	11	361	178	49.3	23	6.4	2023	5.6	9	2.5	91.9

	SCORING DEFENSE	G	PTS	AVG
9	Penn State*	11	155	14.1

1991

FINAL POLL

UP	AP	TEAM	RECORD
2	1	Miami, Fla.	12-0-0
1	2	Washington	12-0-0
3	3	Penn State*	11-2-0
4	4	Florida State	11-2-0
5	5	Alabama	11-1-0
6	6	Michigan	10-2-0
7	7	Florida	10-2-0
8	8	California	10-2-0
9	9	East Carolina	11-1-0
10	10	Iowa	10-1-1
11	11	Syracuse	10-2-0
13	12	Texas A&M	10-2-0
12	13	Notre Dame	10-3-0
14	14	Tennessee	9-3-0
15	15	Nebraska	9-2-1
16	16	Oklahoma	9-3-0
20	17	Georgia	9-3-0
17	18	Clemson	9-2-1
19	19	UCLA	9-3-0
18	20	Colorado	8-3-1
21	21	Tulsa	10-2-0
22	22	Stanford	8-4-0
24	23	Brigham Young	8-3-2
23	24	North Carolina St.	9-3-0
	25	Air Force	10-3-0
25		Ohio State	8-4-0

CONFERENCE STANDINGS

	CONFERENCE			OVERALL		
	W	L	T	W	L	T
Michigan	8	0	0	10	2	0
Iowa	7	1	0	10	1	1
Ohio State	5	3	0	8	4	0
Indiana	5	3	0	7	4	1
Illinois	4	4	0	6	6	0
Purdue	3	5	0	4	7	0
Michigan State	3	5	0	3	8	0
Wisconsin	2	6	0	5	6	0
Northwestern	2	6	0	3	8	0
Minnesota	1	7	0	2	9	0
Penn State*				11	2	0

BOWL GAMES

DATE	GAME	SCORE
D30	Holiday	Brigham Young 13, Iowa 13
D31	Copper	Indiana 24, Baylor 0
D31	Sun	UCLA 6, Illinois 3
J1	Fiesta	Penn State* 42, Tennessee 17
J1	Hall of Fame	Syracuse 24, Ohio State 17
J1	Rose	Washington 34, Michigan 14

CONSENSUS ALL-AMERICANS

POS	Offense	HT	WT	School	AP	CF	FC	FW	PI
RB	Vaughn Dunbar	6-0	207	Indiana	•	•	•	•	•
WR	Desmond Howard	5-9	176	Michigan	•	•	•	•	•
OL	Greg Skrepenak	6-8	322	Michigan	•	•	•	•	•

OTHERS RECEIVING FIRST-TEAM HONORS

POS		School	AP	CF	FC	FW	PI
OL	Tim Simpson	Illinois				•	

POS	Defense	HT	WT	School	AP	CF	FC	FW	PI
DL	Leroy Smith	6-2	214	Iowa	•				

OTHERS RECEIVING FIRST-TEAM HONORS

POS		School	AP	CF	FC	FW	PI
LB	Steve Tovar	Ohio State				•	
LB	Erick Anderson	Michigan					•
DB	Darren Perry	Penn State*					•
DB	Troy Vincent	Wisconsin				•	•

HEISMAN TROPHY VOTING

	PLAYER	POS	SCHOOL	1ST	2ND	3RD	TOTAL
1	Desmond Howard	WR	Michigan	640	68	21	2077
6	Vaughn Dunbar	TB	Indiana	6	51	53	173

AWARD WINNERS

PLAYER	POS	SCHOOL	AWARD
Desmond Howard	WR	Michigan	Maxwell
Desmond Howard	WR	Michigan	Camp
Erick Anderson	LB	Michigan	Butkus

ALL-CONFERENCE TEAMS†

POS	Offense		POS	Defense
QB	Elvis Grbac, Michigan		L	Leroy Smith, Iowa
QB	Matt Rodgers, Iowa		L	Ron Geater, Iowa
RB	Vaughn Dunbar, Indiana		L	Mike Evans, Michigan
RB	Mike Saunders, Iowa		L	Jason Simmons, Ohio State
RB	Ricky Powers, Michigan		L	Chris Hutchinson, Michigan
WR	Danan Hughes, Iowa		LB	Mike Poloskey, Illinois
WR	Desmond Howard, Michigan		LB	John Derby, Iowa
WR	Courtney Hawkins, Michigan State		LB	Erick Anderson, Michigan
C	Mike Devlin, Iowa		LB	Chuck Bullough, Michigan State
G	Tim Simpson, Illinois		LB	Steve Tovar, Ohio State
G	Matt Elliott, Michigan		LB	Alonzo Spellman, Ohio State
T	Rob Baxley, Iowa		DB	Sean Lumpkin, Minnesota
T	Greg Skrepenak, Michigan		DB	Jimmy Young, Purdue
T	Alan Kline, Ohio State		DB	Troy Vincent, Wisconsin
TE	Rod Coleman, Indiana		P	Eric Bruun, Purdue
TE	Patt Evans, Minnesota			
K	J.D. Carlson, Michigan			
K	Scott Bonnell, Indiana			

*Independent or other conference affiliation
† From 1989 to 1996, the Big Ten recognized all-conference teams selected both by the conference coaches and members of the media

1992

NCAA Statistical Leaders

INDIVIDUAL

PASSING

		CL	G	ATT	COM	PCT	INT	I%	YDS	YPA	TD	TD%	RATING
1	Elvis Grbac, Michigan	JR	11	228	152	66.7	5	2.2	1955	8.6	24	10.5	169.0
7	Tony Sacca, Penn State*	SR	12	292	169	57.9	5	1.7	2488	8.5	21	7.2	149.8

ALL-PURPOSE

		CL	G	RUSH	REC	PR	KR	YDS	YPG
2	Vaughn Dunbar, Indiana	SR	11	1699	252	0	262	2213	201.2
7	Desmond Howard, Michigan	JR	11	165	950	261	373	1749	159.0

RUSHING/Yards Per Game

		CL	G	ATT	YDS	TD	AVG	YPG
2	Vaughn Dunbar, Indiana	SR	11	336	1699	11	5.1	154.5

RECEIVING

		CL	G	REC	YDS	TD	RPG	YPR	YPG
10	Desmond Howard, Michigan	JR	11	61	950	19	5.5	15.6	86.4

PUNTING

		CL	PUNT	YDS	AVG
6	Eric Bruun, Purdue	SR	59	2548	43.2

PUNT RETURNS

		CL	PR	YDS	TD	AVG
2	Desmond Howard, Michigan	JR	15	261	1	17.4

KICKOFF RETURNS

		CL	KR	YDS	TD	AVG
4	Courtney Hawkins, Michigan State	SR	20	548	0	27.4

SCORING

		CL	TDS	XP	FG	PTS	PTPG
2	Desmond Howard, Michigan	JR	23	0	0	138	12.6

FIELD GOALS

		CL	FGA	FGM	PCT	FGG
9	Craig Fayak, Penn State*	SO	26	17	0.65	1.42

INTERCEPTIONS

		CL	INT	YDS	TD	INT/GM
6	Willie Lindsey, Northwestern	JR	7	52	0	0.64

TEAM

RUSHING DEFENSE

		G	ATT	YDS	AVG	TD	YPG
5	Penn State*	12	408	1120	2.7	9	93.3
10	Michigan	11	397	1142	2.9	7	103.8

PASSING DEFENSE

		G	ATT	COM	PCT	INT	I%	YDS	YPA	TD	TD%	RATING
5	Penn State*	12	397	172	43.3	26	6.6	2246	5.7	13	3.3	88.6

TOTAL DEFENSE

		G	P	YDS	AVG	TD	YPG
6	Iowa	11	712	2987	4.2	20	271.5
9	Penn State*	12	805	3366	4.2	22	280.5

SCORING OFFENSE

		G	PTS	AVG
4	Michigan	11	406	36.9
9	Penn State*	12	432	36.0

Final Poll

UP	AP	TEAM	RECORD
1	1	Alabama	13-0-0
2	2	Florida State	11-1-0
3	3	Miami, Fla.	11-1-0
4	4	Notre Dame	10-1-1
5	5	Michigan	9-0-3
7	6	Syracuse	10-2-0
6	7	Texas A&M	12-1-0
8	8	Georgia	10-2-0
9	9	Stanford	10-3-0
11	10	Florida	9-4-0
10	11	Washington	9-3-0
12	12	Tennessee	9-3-0
13	13	Colorado	9-2-1
14	14	Nebraska	9-3-0
17	15	Washington State	9-3-0
16	16	Mississippi	9-3-0
15	17	North Carolina St.	9-3-1
19	18	Ohio State	8-3-1
18	19	North Carolina	9-3-0
20	20	Hawaii	11-2-0
21	21	Boston College	8-3-1
23	22	Kansas	8-4-0
	23	Mississippi State	7-5-0
22	24	Fresno State	9-4-0
25	25	Wake Forest	8-4-0
24		Penn State*	7-5-0

Conference Standings

	CONFERENCE			OVERALL		
	W	L	T	W	L	T
Michigan	6	0	2	9	0	3
Ohio State	5	2	1	8	3	1
Michigan State	5	3	0	5	6	0
Illinois	4	3	1	6	5	1
Iowa	4	4	0	5	7	0
Indiana	3	5	0	5	6	0
Wisconsin	3	5	0	5	6	0
Purdue	3	5	0	4	7	0
Northwestern	3	5	0	3	8	0
Minnesota	2	6	0	2	9	0
Penn State*				7	5	0

Bowl Games

DATE	GAME	SCORE
D30	**Holiday**	Hawaii 27, Illinois 17
J1	**Citrus**	Georgia 21, Ohio State 14
J1	**Rose**	Michigan 38, Washington 31
J1	**Blockbuster**	Stanford 24, Penn State* 3

Consensus All-Americans

POS	**Offense**	HT	WT	**School**	AP	CF	FC	FW	PI
WR	O.J. McDuffie	5-11	185	Penn State*	•	•	•		•

Others receiving first-team honors

| C | Mike Devlin | | | Iowa | | | • | • | |

POS	**Defense**	HT	WT	**School**	AP	CF	FC	FW	PI
None									

Others receiving first-team honors

| DL | Chris Hutchinson | | | Michigan | | | • | • | |
| LB | Steve Tovar | | | Ohio State | | | • | | |

BIG TEN ANNUAL REVIEW & BOWLS

1992, CONT.

ALL-CONFERENCE TEAM[†]

POS	Offense	POS	Defense
QB	Elvis Grbac, Michigan	L	Mike Wells, Iowa
RB	Tyrone Wheatley, Michigan	L	Dan Wilkinson, Ohio State
RB	Tico Duckett, Michigan State	L	Jeff Zgonia, Purdue
WR	Derrick Alexander, Michigan	L	Lamark Shackerford, Wisconsin
WR	Lee Gissendaner, Northwestern	L	Chris Hutchinson, Michigan
C	Mike Devlin, Iowa	LB	Dana Howard, Illinois
C	Steve Everitt, Michigan	LB	Matt Dyson, Michigan
G	Joe Cocozzo, Michigan	LB	Steve Tovar, Ohio State
G	Doug Skene, Michigan	LB	Eric Beatty, Purdue
G	Chuck Belin, Wisconsin	LB	Gary Casper, Wisconsin
T	Brad Hopkins, Illinois	DB	Carlos James, Iowa
T	Scott Davis, Iowa	DB	Corwin Brown, Michigan
T	Rob Doherty, Michigan	DB	Shonte Peoples, Michigan
TE	Alan Cross, Iowa	DB	Roger Harper, Ohio State
TE	Tony McGee, Michigan	P	Jim DiGuilio, Indiana
K	Rich Thompson, Wisconsin		
K	Scott Bonnell, Indiana		

NCAA STATISTICAL LEADERS

INDIVIDUAL

PASSING

		CL	G	ATT	COM	PCT	INT	I%	YDS	YPA	TD	TD%	RATING
1	Elvis Grbac, Michigan	SR	9	169	112	66.3	12	7.1	1465	8.7	15	8.9	154.2

ALL-PURPOSE

		CL	G	RUSH	REC	PR	KR	YDS	YPG
6	O.J. McDuffie, Penn State*	SR	11	133	977	398	323	1831	166.5
9	Tyrone Wheatley, Michigan	SO	10	1122	141	0	260	1523	152.3

RUSHING/YARDS PER CARRY

		CL	G	ATT	YDS	YPC
5	Tyrone Wheatley, Michigan	SO	10	170	1122	6.6

Based on top 25 rushers

PUNTING

		CL	PUNT	YDS	AVG
8	Jim DiGuilio, Indiana	SO	53	2347	44.3

PUNT RETURNS

		CL	PR	YDS	TD	AVG
1	Lee Gissendaner, Northwestern	JR	15	327	1	21.8
9	Derrick Alexander, Michigan	SR	25	343	2	13.7
10	O.J. McDuffie, Penn State*	SR	30	398	0	13.3

KICKOFF RETURNS

		CL	KR	YDS	TD	AVG
8	John Lewis, Minnesota	SR	29	755	1	26.0

SCORING

		CL	TDS	XP	FG	PTS	PTPG
2	Richie Anderson, Penn State*	SR	19	2	0	116	10.6
6	Tyrone Wheatley, Michigan	SO	14	0	0	84	8.4
8	Craig Thomas, Michigan State	JR	15	0	0	90	8.2

FIELD GOALS

		CL	FGA	FGM	PCT	FGG
2	Rich Thompson, Wisconsin	SR	32	22	.69	2.00

TEAM

RUSHING OFFENSE

		G	ATT	YDS	AVG	TD	YPG
5	Michigan	11	531	2909	5.5	28	264.5

TOTAL OFFENSE

		G	P	YDS	AVG	TD	YPG
5	Michigan	11	806	5120	6.4	51	465.5

RUSHING DEFENSE

		G	ATT	YDS	AVG	TD	YPG
4	Michigan	11	369	985	2.7	6	89.5

SCORING OFFENSE

		G	PTS	AVG
5	Michigan	11	393	35.7
6	Penn State*	11	388	35.3

SCORING DEFENSE

		G	PTS	AVG
4	Ohio State	11	137	12.5
5	Michigan	11	140	12.7

1993

FINAL POLL

CNN	AP	Team	RECORD
1	1	Florida State	12-1-0
2	2	Notre Dame	11-1-0
3	3	Nebraska	11-1-0
PB	4	Auburn	11-0-0
4	5	Florida	11-2-0
5	6	Wisconsin	10-1-1
6	7	West Virginia	11-1-0
7	8	Penn State	10-2-0
8	9	Texas A&M	10-2-0
9	10	Arizona	10-2-0
10	11	Ohio State	10-1-1
11	12	Tennessee	9-2-1
12	13	Boston College	9-3-0
13	14	Alabama	9-3-1
15	15	Miami, Fla.	9-3-0
16	16	Colorado	8-3-1
14	17	Oklahoma	9-3-0
17	18	UCLA	8-4-0
21	19	North Carolina	10-3-0
18	20	Kansas State	9-2-1
19	21	Michigan	8-4-0
20	22	Virginia Tech	9-3-0
22	23	Clemson	9-3-0
23	24	Louisville	9-3-0
24	25	California	9-4-0

CONFERENCE STANDINGS

	CONFERENCE			OVERALL		
	W	L	T	W	L	T
Ohio State	6	1	1	10	1	1
Wisconsin	6	1	1	10	1	1
Penn State	6	2	0	10	2	0
Indiana	5	3	0	8	4	0
Michigan	5	3	0	8	4	0
Illinois	5	3	0	5	6	0
Michigan State	4	4	0	6	6	0
Iowa	3	5	0	6	6	0
Minnesota	3	5	0	4	7	0
Northwestern	0	8	0	2	9	0
Purdue	0	8	0	1	10	0

BOWL GAMES

DATE	GAME	SCORE
D28	Liberty	Louisville 18, Michigan State 7
D30	Holiday	Ohio State 28, Brigham Young 21
D31	Alamo	California 37, Iowa 3
D31	Independence	Virginia Tech 45, Indiana 20
J1	Hall of Fame	Michigan 42, North Carolina St. 7
J1	Citrus	Penn State 31, Tennessee 13
J1	Rose	Wisconsin 21, UCLA 16

*Independent or other conference affiliation
[†] From 1989 to 1996, the Big Ten recognized all-conference teams selected both by the conference coaches and members of the media

CONSENSUS ALL-AMERICANS

POS	Offense	HT	WT	School	AP	CF	FC	FN	FW	PI	SN
None

OTHERS RECEIVING FIRST-TEAM HONORS

POS					AP	CF	FC	FN	FW	PI	SN
OL	Korey Stringer			Ohio State		•	•				

POS	Defense	HT	WT	School	AP	CF	FC	FN	FW	PI	SN
DL	Dan Wilkinson	6-5	300	Ohio State	•	•		•	•	•	•

OTHERS RECEIVING FIRST-TEAM HONORS

POS					AP	CF	FC	FN	FW	PI	SN
DL	Lou Benfatti			Penn State		•					
LB	Dana Howard			Illinois		•	•				

HEISMAN TROPHY VOTING

PLAYER	POS	SCHOOL	1ST	2ND	3RD	TOTAL
8 Tyrone Wheatley	RB	Michigan	2	31	32	100

ALL-CONFERENCE TEAM†

POS	Offense		POS	Defense
QB	Darrell Bevell, Wisconsin		L	Hurvin McCormack, Indiana
RB	Tyrone Wheatley, Michigan		L	Mike Wells, Iowa
RB	Brent Moss, Wisconsin		L	Buster Stanley, Michigan
WR	Joey Galloway, Ohio State		L	Dan Wilkinson, Ohio State
WR	Bobby Engram, Penn State		L	Tyoka Jackson, Penn State
C	Cory Raymer, Wisconsin		L	Lamark Shackerford, Wisconsin
G	Jason Winrow, Ohio State		LB	Simeon Rice, Illinois
G	Jeff Hartings, Penn State		LB	John Holecek, Illinois
G	Joe Rudolph, Wisconsin		LB	Dana Howard, Illinois
T	Korey Stringer, Ohio State		LB	Lorenzo Styles, Ohio State
T	Joe Panos, Wisconsin		DB	Ty Law, Michigan
TE	Kyle Brady, Penn State		DB	Chico Nelson, Ohio State
TE	Michael Roan, Wisconsin		DB	Jimmy Young, Purdue
K	Bill Manolopolous, Indiana		DB	Jeff Messenger, Wisconsin
K	Tim Williams, Ohio State		P	Jim DiGuilio, Indiana

NCAA STATISTICAL LEADERS

INDIVIDUAL

PASSING		CL	G	ATT	COM	PCT	INT	I%	YDS	YPA	TD	TD%	RATING
3	Darrell Bevell, Wisconsin	SO	11	256	177	69.1	10	3.9	2294	9.0	19	7.4	161.1

ALL-PURPOSE		CL	G	RUSH	REC	PR	KR	YDS	YPG
8	Tyrone Wheatley, Michigan	JR	9	1005	152	0	246	1403	155.9

RUSHING/YARDS PER GAME		CL	G	ATT	YDS	TD	AVG	YPG
3	Brent Moss, Wisconsin	JR	11	276	1479	14	5.4	134.5

RUSHING/YARDS PER CARRY		CL	G	ATT	YDS	YPC
3	Ki-Jana Carter, Penn State	SO	9	155	1026	6.6

Based on top 21 rushers

PUNT RETURNS		CL	PR	YDS	TD	AVG
3	Lee Gissendaner, Northwestern	SR	16	223	0	13.9
9	Bobby Engram, Penn State	SO	33	402	0	12.2

INTERCEPTIONS		CL	INT	YDS	TD	INT/GM
7	Jeff Messenger, Wisconsin	JR	6	41	0	0.55

TEAM

RUSHING OFFENSE		G	ATT	YDS	AVG	TD	YPG
8	Wisconsin	11	557	2759	5.0	26	250.8

RUSHING DEFENSE		G	ATT	YDS	AVG	TD	YPG
8	Michigan	11	379	1179	3.1	6	107.2
10	Illinois	11	444	1265	2.8	10	115.0

PASSING DEFENSE		G	ATT	COM	PCT	INT	I%	YDS	YPA	TD	TD%	RATING
6	Iowa	11	291	143	49.1	18	6.2	1798	6.2	6	2.1	95.5

TOTAL DEFENSE		G	P	YDS	AVG	TD	YPG
9	Ohio State	11	744	3293	4.4	19	299.4
10	Indiana	11	747	3336	4.5	18	303.3

SCORING OFFENSE		G	PTS	AVG
2	Michigan	11	406	36.9
9	Penn State	12	432	36.0

SCORING DEFENSE		G	PTS	AVG
7	Indiana	11	152	13.8
8	Michigan	11	153	13.9

TURNOVER MARGIN		G	FR	INT	TOT	FL	INTL	TOT	MAR
4	Penn State	11	11	21	32	6	13	19	1.2

1994

FINAL POLL

CNN	AP	TEAM	RECORD
1	1	Nebraska	13-0-0
2	2	**Penn State**	12-0-0
3	3	Colorado	11-1-0
5	4	Florida State	10-1-1
4	5	Alabama	12-1-0
6	6	Miami, Fla.	10-2-0
7	7	Florida	10-2-1
PB	8	Texas A&M	10-0-1
PB	9	Auburn	9-1-1
8	10	Utah	10-2-0
11	11	Oregon	9-4-0
12	12	**Michigan**	8-4-0
15	13	USC	8-3-1
9	14	**Ohio State**	9-4-0
13	15	Virginia	9-3-0
14	16	Colorado State	10-2-0
17	17	North Carolina St.	9-3-0
10	18	Brigham Young	10-3-0
16	19	Kansas State	9-3-0
20	20	Arizona	8-4-0
19	21	Washington State	8-4-0
18	22	Tennessee	8-4-0
22	23	Boston College	7-4-1
25	24	Mississippi State	8-4-0
23	25	Texas	8-4-0

CONFERENCE STANDINGS

	CONFERENCE			OVERALL		
	W	L	T	W	L	T
Penn State	8	0	0	12	0	0
Ohio State	6	2	0	9	4	0
Michigan	5	3	0	8	4	0
Wisconsin	4	3	1	7	4	1
Illinois	4	4	0	7	5	0
Michigan State	4	4	0	5	6	0
Iowa	3	4	1	5	5	1
Indiana	3	5	0	6	5	0
Purdue	2	4	2	4	5	2
Northwestern	2	6	0	3	7	1
Minnesota	1	7	0	3	8	0

BOWL GAMES

DATE	GAME	SCORE
D30	**Holiday**	Michigan 24, Colorado State 14
D31	**Liberty**	Illinois 30, East Carolina 0
J2	**Citrus**	Alabama 24, Ohio State 17
J2	**Rose**	Penn State 38, Oregon 20
J2	**Hall of Fame**	Wisconsin 34, Duke 20

CONSENSUS ALL-AMERICANS

POS	**Offense**	HT	WT	School	AP	CF	FC	FN	FW	PI	SN
QB	**Kerry Collins**	6-5	235	Penn State	•	•		•	•	•	
RB	**Ki-Jana Carter**	5-10	212	Penn State	•	•	•	•	•	•	•
OL	**Korey Stringer**	6-5	315	Ohio State	•	•	•	•		•	•
C	**Cory Raymer**	6-4	290	Wisconsin	•	•		•	•	•	

	OTHERS RECEIVING FIRST-TEAM HONORS		
WR	Bobby Engram	Penn State	•
TE	Kyle Brady	Penn State	•
OL	Jeff Hartings	Penn State	• •
PK	Remy Hamilton	Michigan	•

POS	**Defense**	HT	WT	School	AP	CF	FC	FN	FW	PI	SN
LB	**Dana Howard**	6-0	235	Illinois	•	•	•	•	•	•	•

	OTHERS RECEIVING FIRST-TEAM HONORS		
DL	Simeon Rice	Illinois	• •
DB	Ty Law	Michigan	•

FN named Rice as a LB

HEISMAN TROPHY VOTING

	PLAYER	POS	SCHOOL	1ST	2ND	3RD	TOTAL
2	**Ki-Jana Carter**	RB	Penn State	115	205	146	901
4	**Kerry Collins**	QB	Penn State	101	117	102	639

AWARD WINNERS

PLAYER	POS	SCHOOL	AWARD
Kerry Collins	QB	Penn State	Maxwell
Kerry Collins	QB	Penn State	O'Brien
Dana Howard	LB	Illinois	Butkus
Bobby Engram	WR	Penn State	Biletnikoff

ALL-CONFERENCE TEAM[†]

POS	**Offense**	POS	**Defense**
QB	Kerry Collins, Penn State	L	Jason Horn, Michigan
RB	Tyrone Wheatley, Michigan	L	Ed Hawthorne, Minnesota
RB	Chris Darkins, Minnesota	L	Matt Finkes, Ohio State
RB	Ki-Jana Carter, Penn State	L	Mike Vrabel, Ohio State
WR	Amani Toomer, Michigan	L	Mike Thompson, Wisconsin
WR	Bobby Engram, Penn State	LB	Kevin Hardy, Illinois
C	Cory Raymer, Wisconsin	LB	Simeon Rice, Illinois
G	Matt O'Dwyer, Northwestern	LB	Dana Howard, Illinois
G	Jeff Hartings, Penn State	LB	Steve Morrison, Michigan
G	Joe Rudolph, Wisconsin	LB	Lorenzo Styles, Ohio State
T	Brian DeMarco, Michigan State	LB	Brian Gelzheiser, Penn State
T	Korey Stringer, Ohio State	DB	Ty Law, Michigan
T	Mike Verstegen, Wisconsin	DB	Demetrice Martin, Michigan State
TE	Kyle Brady, Penn State	DB	Brian Miller, Penn State
K	Remy Hamilton, Michigan	DB	Jeff Messenger, Wisconsin
		P	Paul Burton, Northwestern

BIG TEN ANNUAL REVIEW & BOWLS

[†] From 1989 to 1996 the Big Ten recognized all-conference teams selected both by the conference coaches and members of the media

1995

NCAA Statistical Leaders

INDIVIDUAL

PASSING

		CL	G	ATT	COM	PCT	INT	I%	YDS	YPA	TD	TD%	RATING
1	Kerry Collins, Penn State	SR	11	264	176	66.7	7	2.7	2679	10.2	21	8.0	172.9
9	Todd Collins, Michigan	SR	11	264	172	65.2	7	2.7	2356	8.9	11	4.2	148.6

ALL-PURPOSE

		CL	G	RUSH	REC	PR	KR	YDS	YPG
5	Ki-Jana Carter, Penn State	JR	11	1539	123	0	81	1743	158.5
6	Chris Darkins, Minnesota	JR	11	1443	299	0	0	1742	158.4
8	Terrell Fletcher, Wisconsin	SR	11	1235	172	0	314	1721	156.5

RUSHING/YARDS PER GAME

		CL	G	ATT	YDS	TD	AVG	YPG
4	Ki-Jana Carter, Penn State	JR	11	198	1539	23	7.8	139.9
6	Alex Smith, Indiana	FR	11	265	1475	10	5.6	134.1
7	Chris Darkins, Minnesota	JR	11	277	1443	11	5.2	131.2

RUSHING/YARDS PER CARRY

		CL	G	ATT	YDS	YPC
1	Ki-Jana Carter, Penn State	JR	11	198	1539	7.8
4	Terrell Fletcher, Wisconsin	SR	11	205	1235	6.0
6	Mike Alstott, Purdue	JR	11	202	1188	5.9

Based on top 30 rushers

RECEIVING

		CL	G	REC	YDS	TD	RPG	YPR	YPG
8	Amani Toomer, Michigan	JR	11	49	1033	5	4.5	21.1	93.9
9	Bobby Engram, Penn State	JR	11	52	1029	7	4.7	19.8	93.6

KICKOFF RETURNS

		CL	KR	YDS	TD	AVG
5	Derrick Mason, Michigan State	SO	36	966	1	26.8
6	Joey Galloway, Ohio State	SR	15	401	1	26.7
9	Seth Smith, Michigan	FR	18	468	1	26.0

SCORING

		CL	TDS	XP	FG	PTS	PTPG
2	Ki-Jana Carter, Penn State	JR	23	0	0	138	12.6
7	Tyrone Wheatley, Michigan	SR	13	0	0	78	8.7
8	Remy Hamilton, Michigan	SO	0	23	24	95	8.6
10	Brett Conway, Penn State	SO	0	62	10	92	8.4

FIELD GOALS

		CL	FGA	FGM	PCT	FGG
1	Remy Hamilton, Michigan	SO	29	24	.83	2.18
5	Mike Chalberg, Minnesota	JR	23	17	.74	1.70

INTERCEPTIONS

		CL	INT	YDS	TD	INT/GM
4	Demetrice Martin, Michigan State	JR	7	41	0	0.64

TEAM

RUSHING OFFENSE

		G	ATT	YDS	AVG	TD	YPG
6	Penn State	11	450	2760	6.1	45	250.9
10	Wisconsin	11	497	2649	5.3	23	240.8

TOTAL OFFENSE

		G	P	YDS	AVG	TD	YPG
1	Penn State	11	749	5722	7.6	68	520.2

TOTAL DEFENSE

		G	P	YDS	AVG	TD	YPG
9	Illinois	11	700	3138	4.5	16	285.3

SCORING OFFENSE

		G	PTS	AVG
1	Penn State	11	526	47.8

SCORING DEFENSE

		G	PTS	AVG
5	Illinois	11	156	14.2
10	Ohio State	12	187	15.6

TURNOVER MARGIN

		G	FR	INT	TOT	FL	INTL	TOT	MAR
7	Penn State	11	12	11	23	4	7	11	1.1

FINAL POLL

CNN	AP	TEAM	RECORD
1	1	Nebraska	12-0-0
3	2	Florida	12-1-0
2	3	Tennessee	11-1-0
5	4	Florida State	10-2-0
4	5	Colorado	10-2-0
8	6	**Ohio State**	11-2-0
6	7	Kansas State	10-2-0
7	8	**Northwestern**	10-2-0
10	9	Kansas	10-2-0
9	10	Virginia Tech	10-2-0
13	11	Notre Dame	9-3-0
11	12	USC	9-2-1
12	13	**Penn State**	9-3-0
14	14	Texas	10-2-1
15	15	Texas A&M	9-3-0
17	16	Virginia	9-4-0
19	17	**Michigan**	9-4-0
18	18	Oregon	9-3-0
16	19	Syracuse	9-3-0
PB	20	Miami, Fla.	8-3-0
PB	21	Alabama	8-3-0
21	22	Auburn	8-4-0
20	23	Texas Tech	9-3-0
24	24	Toledo	11-0-1
22	25	**Iowa**	8-4-0

CONFERENCE STANDINGS

	CONFERENCE			OVERALL		
	W	L	T	W	L	T
Northwestern	8	0	0	10	2	0
Ohio State	7	1	0	11	2	0
Penn State	5	3	0	9	3	0
Michigan	5	3	0	9	4	0
Michigan State	4	3	1	6	5	1
Iowa	4	4	0	8	4	0
Illinois	3	4	1	5	5	1
Wisconsin	3	4	1	4	5	2
Purdue	2	5	1	4	6	1
Minnesota	1	7	0	3	8	0
Indiana	0	8	0	2	9	0

BOWL GAMES

DATE	GAME	SCORE
D28	**Alamo**	Texas A&M 22, Michigan 20
D29	**Sun**	Iowa 38, Washington 18
D29	**Independence**	LSU 45, Michigan State 26
J1	**Outback**	Penn State 43, Auburn 14
J1	**Rose**	USC 41, Northwestern 32
J1	**Citrus**	Tennessee 20, Ohio State 14

CONSENSUS ALL-AMERICANS

POS	**Offense**	HT	WT	**School**	AP	CF	FC	FN	FW	PI	SN
RB	**Eddie George**	6-3	230	Ohio State	•	•	•	•	•	•	•
WR	**Terry Glenn**	5-11	185	Ohio State	•	•	•	•	•	•	•
OL	**Orlando Pace**	6-6	320	Ohio State	•	•	•	•	•		•
OL	**Jeff Hartings**	6-3	278	Penn State		•	•	•		•	

OTHERS RECEIVING FIRST-TEAM HONORS

PK	Sam Valenzisi	Northwestern	•

POS	**Defense**	HT	WT	**School**	AP	CF	FC	FN	FW	PI	SN
LB	**Kevin Hardy**	6-4	243	Illinois	•	•		•	•	•	•
LB	**Pat Fitzgerald**	6-4	228	Northwestern	•		•	•		•	•

OTHERS RECEIVING FIRST-TEAM HONORS

DL	Jason Horn	Michigan	•
DL	Mike Vrabel	Ohio State	•
LB	Simeon Rice	Illinois	• •

HEISMAN TROPHY VOTING

	PLAYER	POS	SCHOOL	1ST	2ND	3RD	TOTAL
1	**Eddie George**	RB	Ohio State	268	248	160	1460
4	**Darnell Autry**	RB	Northwestern	87	78	118	535
8	**Tim Biakabutuka**	RB	Michigan	1	11	6	31
10	**Bobby Hoying**	QB	Ohio State	0	9	10	28

1995, CONT.

AWARD WINNERS

PLAYER	POS	SCHOOL	AWARD
Eddie George	RB	Ohio State	Maxwell
Eddie George	RB	Ohio State	Camp
Orlando Pace	OT	Ohio State	Lombardi
Kevin Hardy	LB	Illinois	Butkus
Eddie George	RB	Ohio State	Walker
Pat Fitzgerald	LB	Northwestern	Nagurski
Pat Fitzgerald	LB	Northwestern	Bednarik
Terry Glenn	WR	Ohio State	Biletnikoff

ALL-CONFERENCE TEAM[†]

POS	Offense		POS	Defense
QB	Bobby Hoying, Ohio State		L	Jason Horn, Michigan
RB	Darnell Autry, Northwestern		L	Mike Vrabel, Ohio State
RB	Eddie George, Ohio State		L	Tarek Saleh, Wisconsin
WR	Terry Glenn, Ohio State		LB	Kevin Hardy, Illinois
WR	Bobby Engram, Penn State		LB	Simeon Rice, Illinois
C	Rod Payne, Michigan		LB	Jarrett Irons, Michigan
C	Rob Johnson, Northwestern		LB	Pat Fitzgerald, Northwestern
G	Jon Runyan, Michigan		DB	Clarence Thompson, Michigan
G	Ryan Padgett, Northwestern		DB	Charles Woodson, Michigan
G	Jeff Hartings, Penn State		DB	Chris Martin, Northwestern
T	Orlando Pace, Ohio State		DB	Shawn Springs, Ohio State
TE	Rickey Dudley, Ohio State		DB	Brian Miller, Penn State
K	Sam Valenzisi, Northwestern		P	Nick Gallery, Iowa

NCAA STATISTICAL LEADERS

INDIVIDUAL

PASSING	CL	G	ATT	COM	PCT	INT	I%	YDS	YPA	TD	TD%	RATING
2 Bobby Hoying, Ohio State	SR	12	303	192	63.4	11	3.6	3023	10.0	28	9.2	170.4

ALL-PURPOSE	CL	G	RUSH	REC	PR	KR	YDS	YPG
4 Eddie George, Ohio State	SR	12	1826	399	0	0	2225	185.4
9 Darnell Autry, Northwestern	SO	11	1675	130	0	45	1850	168.2

RUSHING/YARDS PER GAME	CL	G	ATT	YDS	TD	AVG	YPG
4 Darnell Autry, Northwestern	SO	11	355	1675	14	4.7	152.3
5 Eddie George, Ohio State	SR	12	303	1826	23	6.0	152.2
8 Tim Biakabutuka, Michigan	JR	12	279	1724	12	6.2	143.7

RUSHING/YARDS PER CARRY	CL	G	ATT	YDS	YPC
3 Tim Biakabutuka, Michigan	JR	12	279	1724	6.2
6 Eddie George, Ohio State	SR	12	303	1826	6.0
7 Mike Alstott, Purdue	SR	11	243	1436	5.9
Based on top 30 rushers					

RECEIVING	CL	G	REC	YDS	TD	RPG	YPR	YPG
4 Terry Glenn, Ohio State	JR	11	57	1316	17	5.2	23.1	119.6
10 Bobby Engram, Penn State	SR	11	63	1084	11	5.7	17.2	98.6

PUNT RETURNS	CL	PR	YDS	TD	AVG
9 Brian Musso, Northwestern	JR	28	393	1	14.0

KICKOFF RETURNS	CL	KR	YDS	TD	AVG
10 Derrick Mason, Michigan State	JR	31	815	1	26.3

SCORING	CL	TDS	XP	FG	PTS	PTPG
1 Eddie George, Ohio State	SR	24	0	0	144	12.0
4 Scott Greene, Michigan State	SR	17	2	0	104	10.4
8 Terry Glenn, Ohio State	JR	17	2	0	104	9.5

FIELD GOALS	CL	FGA	FGM	PCT	FGG
4 Brett Conway, Penn State	JR	24	16	.67	1.45
8 Remy Hamilton, Michigan	JR	25	17	.68	1.42

INTERCEPTIONS	CL	INT	YDS	TD	INT/GM
5 Plez Atkins, Iowa	SO	6	97	2	0.60

TEAM

RUSHING OFFENSE	G	ATT	YDS	AVG	TD	YPG
8 Purdue	11	522	2567	4.9	25	233.4

TOTAL OFFENSE	G	P	YDS	AVG	TD	YPG
5 Ohio State	12	865	5887	6.8	60	490.6

RUSHING DEFENSE	G	ATT	YDS	AVG	TD	YPG
3 Michigan	12	419	1081	2.6	12	90.1

SCORING OFFENSE	G	PTS	AVG
6 Ohio State	12	461	38.4

SCORING DEFENSE	G	PTS	AVG
1 Northwestern	11	140	12.7

TURNOVER MARGIN	G	FR	INT	TOT	FL	INTL	TOT	MAR
3 Northwestern	11	16	16	32	6	6	12	1.8

BIG TEN ANNUAL REVIEW & BOWLS

[†] *From 1989 to 1996 the Big Ten recognized all-conference teams selected both by the conference coaches and members of the media*

1996

FINAL POLL

CNN	AP	TEAM	RECORD
1	1	Florida	12-1
2	2	**Ohio State**	11-1
3	3	Florida State	11-1
4	4	Arizona State	11-1
5	5	Brigham Young	14-1
6	6	Nebraska	11-2
7	7	**Penn State**	11-2
8	8	Colorado	10-2
9	9	Tennessee	10-2
10	10	North Carolina	10-2
11	11	Alabama	10-3
13	12	LSU	10-2
12	13	Virginia Tech	10-2
14	14	Miami, Fla.	9-3
16	15	**Northwestern**	9-3
15	16	Washington	9-3
17	17	Kansas State	9-3
18	18	**Iowa**	9-3
21	19	Notre Dame	8-3
20	20	**Michigan**	8-4
19	21	Syracuse	9-3
22	22	Wyoming	10-2
23	23	Texas	8-5
24	24	Auburn	8-4
25	25	Army	10-2

CONFERENCE STANDINGS

	CONFERENCE		OVERALL	
	W	L	W	L
Ohio State	7	1	11	1
Northwestern	7	1	9	3
Penn State	6	2	11	2
Iowa	6	2	9	3
Michigan	5	3	8	4
Michigan State	5	3	6	6
Wisconsin	3	5	8	5
Purdue	2	6	3	8
Minnesota	1	7	4	7
Indiana	1	7	3	8
Illinois	1	7	2	9

BOWL GAMES

DATE	GAME	SCORE
D27	**Copper**	Wisconsin 38, Utah 10
D29	**Alamo**	Iowa 27, Texas Tech 0
D31	**Sun**	Stanford 38, Michigan State 0
J1	**Outback**	Alabama 17, Michigan 14
J1	**Rose**	Ohio State 20, Arizona State 17
J1	**Fiesta**	Penn State 38, Texas 15
J1	**Florida Citrus**	Tennessee 48, Northwestern 28

CONSENSUS ALL-AMERICANS

POS	**Offense**	HT	WT	CL	**School**	AP	CF	FC	FN	FW	SN
OL	**Orlando Pace**	6-6	330	Jr.	Ohio State	•	•	•	•	•	•

OTHERS RECEIVING FIRST-TEAM HONORS

POS						AP	CF	FC	FN	FW	SN
RB	Darnell Autry				Northwestern			•			
C	Rod Payne				Michigan			•			
KR	Tim Dwight				Iowa					•	

POS	**Defense**	HT	WT	CL	**School**	AP	CF	FC	FN	FW	SN
DL	**Mike Vrabel**	6-4	260	Sr.	Ohio State		•	•			
LB	**Pat Fitzgerald**	6-2	243	Sr.	Northwestern	•	•	•	•	•	
LB	**Jarrett Irons**	6-2	234	Sr.	Michigan		•	•	•		
DB	**Shawn Springs**	6-0	188	Jr.	Ohio State		•	•			

OTHERS RECEIVING FIRST-TEAM HONORS

POS						AP	CF	FC	FN	FW	SN
DL	Tarek Saleh				Wisconsin			•			
DB	Charles Woodson				Michigan	•			•		
DB	Kim Herring				Penn State						•

HEISMAN TROPHY VOTING

PLAYER	POS	SCHOOL	1ST	2ND	3RD	TOTAL
4 **Orlando Pace**	OT	Ohio State	87	101	136	599
7 **Darnell Autry**	RB	Northwestern	9	19	20	85

AWARD WINNERS

PLAYER	POS	SCHOOL	AWARD
Orlando Pace	OT	Ohio State	Outland, Lombardi,
Pat Fitzgerald	LB	Northwestern	Nagurski, Bednarik

ALL-CONFERENCE TEAM†

POS	Offense	POS	Defense
QB	Steve Schnur, Northwestern	L	Jared DeVries, Iowa
RB	Sedrick Shaw, Iowa	L	William Carr, Michigan
RB	Curtis Enis, Penn State	L	Matt Finkes, Ohio State
RB	Ron Dayne, Wisconsin	L	Mike Vrabel, Ohio State
RB	Darnell Autry, Northwestern	L	Tarek Saleh, Wisconsin
WR	D'Wayne Bates, Northwestern	LB	Pete Monty, Wisconsin
WR	Brian Alford, Purdue	LB	Andy Katzenmoyer, Ohio State
C	Rod Payne, Michigan	LB	Jarrett Irons, Michigan
G	Jamie Vandervelt, Wisconsin	LB	Pat Fitzgerald, Northwestern
G	Damon Denson, Michigan	DB	Damien Robinson, Iowa
G	Justin Chabot, Northwestern	DB	Charles Woodson, Michigan
T	Ross Verba, Iowa	DB	Shawn Springs, Ohio State
T	Orlando Pace, Ohio State	DB	Brian Miller, Penn State
TE	Jerame Tuman, Michigan	DB	Kim Herring, Penn State
K	Brett Conway, Penn State	P	Nick Gallery, Iowa

1996, CONT.

NCAA STATISTICAL LEADERS

INDIVIDUAL

ALL-PURPOSE

		CL	G	RUSH	REC	PR	KR	YDS	YPG
10	Ron Dayne, Wisconsin	FR	12	1863	133	0	0	1996	166.3

RUSHING/YARDS PER GAME

		CL	G	ATT	YDS	TD	AVG	YPG
4	Ron Dayne, Wisconsin	FR	12	295	1863	18	6.3	155.3
7	Darnell Autry, Northwestern	JR	10	263	1386	15	5.3	138.6

RUSHING/YARDS PER CARRY

		CL	G	ATT	YDS	YPC
6	Ron Dayne, Wisconsin	FR	12	295	1863	6.3

*-Based on top 50 rushers

PUNT RETURNS

		CL	PR	YDS	TD	AVG
2	Tim Dwight, Iowa	JR	22	417	2	19.0

SCORING

		CL	TDS	XP	FG	PTS	PTPG
8	Sedrick Irvin, Michigan State	FR	18	0	0	108	9.8

FIELD GOALS

		CL	FGA	FGM	PCT	FGG
9	Chris Gardner, Michigan State	JR	22	17	0.77	1.55
10	Brett Conway, Penn State	SR	24	18	0.75	1.50

INTERCEPTIONS

		CL	INT	YDS	TD	INT/GM
3	Kim Herring, Penn State	SR	7	64	0	0.58
5	Damien Robinson, Iowa	SR	6	99	0	0.55

TEAM

RUSHING OFFENSE

		G	ATT	YDS	AVG	TD	YPG
6	Ohio	12	685	3286	4.8	29	273.8

RUSHING DEFENSE

		G	ATT	YDS	AVG	TD	YPG
9	Ohio State	11	398	1074	2.7	7	97.6

PASSING DEFENSE

		G	ATT	COM	PCT	INT	I%	YDS	YPA	TD	TD%	RATING
1	Ohio State	11	309	140	45.3	20	6.5	1602	5.2	5	1.6	81.3

TOTAL DEFENSE

		G	P	YDS	AVG	TD	YPG
6	Ohio State	11	707	2676	3.8	12	243.3

SCORING OFFENSE

		G	PTS	AVG
6	Ohio State	11	435	39.5

SCORING DEFENSE

		G	PTS	AVG
2	Ohio State	11	114	10.4
8	Michigan	11	167	15.2

TURNOVER MARGIN

		G	FR	INT	TOT	FL	INTL	TOT	MAR
2	Ohio State	11	10	20	30	7	9	16	1.3

1997

FINAL POLL

ESPN	AP	TEAM	RECORD
2	1	**Michigan**	12-0
1	2	Nebraska	13-0
3	3	Florida State	11-1
6	4	Florida	10-2
5	5	UCLA	10-2
4	6	North Carolina	11-1
8	7	Tennessee	11-2
7	8	Kansas State	11-1
9	9	Washington State	10-2
10	10	Georgia	10-2
11	11	Auburn	10-3
12	12	**Ohio State**	10-3
13	13	LSU	9-3
14	14	Arizona State	9-3
15	15	**Purdue**	9-3
17	16	**Penn State**	9-3
16	17	Colorado State	11-2
18	18	Washington	8-4
19	19	Southern Miss	9-3
21	20	Texas A&M	9-4
20	21	Syracuse	9-4
22	22	Mississippi	8-4
23	23	Missouri	7-5
24	24	Oklahoma State	8-4
	25	Georgia Tech	7-5
25		Air Force	10-3

CONFERENCE STANDINGS

	CONFERENCE		OVERALL	
	W	L	W	L
Michigan	8	0	12	0
Ohio State	6	2	10	3
Purdue	6	2	9	3
Penn State	6	2	9	3
Wisconsin	5	3	8	5
Iowa	4	4	7	5
Michigan State	4	4	7	5
Northwestern	3	5	5	7
Minnesota	1	7	3	9
Indiana	1	7	2	9
Illinois	0	8	0	11

BOWL GAMES

DATE	GAME	SCORE
D25	**Aloha**	Washington 51, Michigan State 23
D30	**Alamo**	Purdue 33, Oklahoma State 20
D31	**Sun**	Arizona State 17, Iowa 7
D31	**Florida Citrus**	Florida 21, Penn State 6
J1	**Outback**	Georgia 33, Wisconsin 6
J1	**Rose**	Michigan 21, Washington State 16
J1	**Sugar**	Florida State 31, Ohio State 14

CONSENSUS ALL-AMERICANS

POS	Offense	HT	WT	CL	School	AP	CF	FC	FN	FW	SN
RB	Curtis Enis	6-1	233	Jr.	Penn State	•	•	•			
KR	Tim Dwight	5-9	185	Sr.	Iowa	•		•		•	•

	OTHERS RECEIVING FIRST-TEAM HONORS										
RB	Ron Dayne				Wisconsin				•		
WR	Brian Alford				Purdue				•		
TE	Jerame Tuman				Michigan				•		
OL	Flozell Adams				Michigan State			•			
OL	Rob Murphy				Ohio State				•		

POS	Defense	HT	WT	CL	School	AP	CF	FC	FN	FW	SN
LB	Andy Katzenmoyer	6-4	260	So.	Ohio State	•	•	•	•	•	
DB	Charles Woodson	6-1	198	Jr.	Michigan	•	•	•	•	•	•

	OTHERS RECEIVING FIRST-TEAM HONORS										
DL	Lamanzer Williams				Minnesota				•		
DL	Glen Steele				Michigan						
DB	Antoine Winfield				Ohio State			•		•	

HEISMAN TROPHY VOTING

	PLAYER	POS	SCHOOL	1ST	2ND	3RD	TOTAL
1	Charles Woodson	CB	Michigan	433	209	98	1815
6	Curtis Enis	RB	Penn State	3	18	20	65
7	Tim Dwight	WR	Iowa	5	3	11	32

AWARD WINNERS

PLAYER	POS	SCHOOL	AWARD
Charles Woodson	DB	Michigan	Camp, Nagurski, Bednarik, Thorpe
Andy Katzenmoyer	LB	Ohio State	Butkus

ALL-CONFERENCE TEAM

POS	Offense	MEDIA	COACHES
QB	Brian Griese, Michigan	•	
QB	Billy Dicken, Purdue		•
RB	Curtis Enis, Penn State	•	•
RB	Tavian Banks, Iowa	•	•
WR	Brian Alford, Purdue	•	•
WR	David Boston, Ohio State	•	•
WR	Tim Dwight, Iowa	•	•
C	Zach Adami, Michigan	•	•
G	Phil Ostrowski, Penn State	•	•
G	Steve Hutchinson, Michigan	•	
G	Mike Goff, Iowa		•
T	Flozell Adams, Michigan State	•	
T	Eric Gohlstin, Ohio State	•	
T	Jon Jansen, Michigan		•
TE	Jerame Tuman, Michigan	•	•
K	Brian Gowins, Northwestern	•	
K	Matt Davenport, Wisconsin		•

POS	Defense	MEDIA	COACHES
L	Jared De Vries, Iowa	•	•
L	Lamanzer Williams, Minnesota	•	•
L	Glen Steele, Michigan	•	•
L	Casey Dailey, Northwestern	•	
L	Adewale Ogunleye, Indiana		•
LB	Andy Katzenmoyer, Ohio State	•	•
LB	Barry Gardner, Northwestern	•	•
LB	Sam Sword, Michigan	•	
LB	Ike Reese, Michigan State		•
DB	Charles Woodson, Michigan	•	•
DB	Antoine Winfield, Ohio State	•	•
DB	Marcus Ray, Michigan	•	•
DB	Damon Moore, Ohio State	•	
DB	Andre Weathers, Michigan		•
P	Brent Bartholomew, Ohio State	•	•

NCAA STATISTICAL LEADERS

INDIVIDUAL

	PASSING	CL	G	ATT	COM	PCT	INT	I%	YDS	YPA	TD	TD%	RATING
3	Joe Germaine, Ohio State	SR	12	184	119	64.7	7	3.8	1674	9.1	15	8.2	160.4

	ALL-PURPOSE	CL	G	RUSH	REC	PR	KR	YDS	YPG
6	Tutu Atwell, Minnesota	SR	12	77	924	296	776	2073	172.8
8	Tavian Banks, Iowa	SR	11	1639	200	0	0	1839	167.2
10	Sedrick Irvin, Michigan State	SO	11	1211	339	263	0	1813	164.8

	RUSHING/YARDS PER GAME	CL	G	ATT	YDS	TD	AVG	YPG
4	Tavian Banks, Iowa	SR	11	246	1639	17	6.7	149.0
5	Ron Dayne, Wisconsin	SO	10	249	1421	15	5.7	142.1

	RUSHING/YARDS PER CARRY	CL	G	ATT	YDS	YPC
4	Tavian Banks, Iowa	SR	11	246	1639	6.7

*-Based on top 50 rushers

	RECEIVING	CL	G	REC	YDS	TD	RPG	YPR	YPG
7	Brian Alford, Purdue	SR	11	59	1167	9	5.4	19.8	106.1

	PUNTING	CL	PUNT	YDS	AVG
9	Brent Bartholomew, Ohio State	JR	65	2934	45.1

	PUNT RETURNS	CL	PR	YDS	TD	AVG
1	Tim Dwight, Iowa	SR	19	367	3	19.3
9	Steve Neal, Western Michigan	SO	14	204	1	14.6

	KICKOFF RETURNS	CL	KR	YDS	TD	AVG
10	Tyrone Carter, Minnesota	SO	17	455	0	26.8

	SCORING	CL	TDS	XP	FG	PTS	PTPG
5	Curtis Enis, Penn State	JR	20	2	0	122	11.1
8	Tavian Banks, Iowa	SR	19	0	0	114	10.4

	FIELD GOALS	CL	FGA	FGM	PCT	FGG
6	Brian Gowins, Northwestern	SR	27	20	.74	1.67

	INTERCEPTIONS	CL	INT	YDS	TD	INT/GM
2	Tevell Jones, Ohio	SR	7	36	0	0.64
2	Charles Woodson, Michigan	JR	7	7	0	0.64

TEAM

	RUSHING OFFENSE	G	ATT	YDS	AVG	TD	YPG
4	Ohio	11	649	3321	5.1	32	301.9
8	Iowa	11	492	2505	5.3	25	235.0

	TOTAL OFFENSE	G	P	YDS	AVG	TD	YPG
7	Purdue	11	794	5056	6.4	42	459.6

	RUSHING DEFENSE	G	ATT	YDS	AVG	TD	YPG
7	Michigan	11	368	1001	2.7	6	91.0

	PASSING DEFENSE	G	ATT	COM	PCT	INT	I%	YDS	YPA	TD	TD%	RATING
1	Michigan	11	292	145	49.7	22	7.5	1275	4.4	4	1.4	75.8
2	Ohio State	12	360	160	44.4	19	5.3	1724	4.8	6	1.7	79.6
4	Iowa	11	325	146	44.9	22	6.8	1766	5.4	12	3.7	89.2

	TOTAL DEFENSE	G	P	YDS	AVG	TD	YPG
1	Michigan	11	660	2276	3.4	10	206.9
7	Iowa	11	733	2927	4.0	18	266.1
8	Ohio State	12	820	3215	3.9	13	267.9

	SCORING OFFENSE	G	PTS	AVG
9	Iowa	11	404	36.7

	SCORING DEFENSE	G	PTS	AVG
1	Michigan	11	98	8.9
2	Ohio State	12	139	11.6
4	Iowa	11	142	12.9

	TURNOVER MARGIN	G	FR	INT	TOT	FL	INTL	TOT	MAR
9	Purdue	11	11	20	31	5	14	19	1.1

1998

FINAL POLL

ESPN	AP	TEAM	RECORD
1	1	Tennessee	13-0
2	2	**Ohio State**	11-1
3	3	Florida State	11-2
4	4	Arizona	12-1
6	5	Florida	10-2
5	6	**Wisconsin**	11-1
7	7	Tulane	12-0
8	8	UCLA	10-2
11	9	Georgia Tech	10-2
9	10	Kansas State	11-2
13	11	Texas A&M	11-3
12	12	**Michigan**	10-3
10	13	Air Force	12-1
14	14	Georgia	9-3
16	15	Texas	9-3
17	16	Arkansas	9-3
15	17	**Penn State**	9-3
18	18	Virginia	9-3
20	19	Nebraska	9-4
21	20	Miami, Fla.	9-3
25	21	Missouri	8-4
22	22	Notre Dame	9-3
19	23	Virginia Tech	9-3
23	24	**Purdue**	9-4
24	25	Syracuse	8-4

CONFERENCE STANDINGS

	CONFERENCE		OVERALL	
	W	L	W	L
Ohio State	7	1	11	1
Wisconsin	7	1	11	1
Michigan	7	1	10	3
Purdue	6	2	9	4
Penn State	5	3	9	3
Michigan State	4	4	6	6
Minnesota	2	6	5	6
Indiana	2	6	4	7
Iowa	2	6	3	8
Illinois	2	6	3	8
Northwestern	0	8	3	9

BOWL GAMES

DATE	GAME	SCORE
D29	**Alamo**	Purdue 37, Kansas State 34
J1	**Florida Citrus**	Michigan 45, Arkansas 31
J1	**Outback**	Penn State 26, Kentucky 14
J1	**Rose**	Wisconsin 38, UCLA 31
J1	**Sugar**	Ohio State 24, Texas A&M 14

CONSENSUS ALL-AMERICANS

POS	**Offense**	HT	WT	CL	**School**	AP	CF	FC	FN	FW	SN
OL	**Aaron Gibson**	6-7	372	Sr.	Wisconsin	•	•	•	•	•	
OL	**Rob Murphy**	6-5	300	Jr.	Ohio State	•			•		•

	OTHERS RECEIVING FIRST-TEAM HONORS										
RB	Ron Dayne				Wisconsin			•			
WR	David Boston				Ohio State				•	•	
OL	Jon Jansen				Michigan				•		

POS	**Defense**	HT	WT	CL	**School**	AP	CF	FC	FN	FW	SN
DL	**Tom Burke**	6-4	249	Sr.	Wisconsin	•	•	•	•	•	
DL	**Jared DeVries**	6-4	284	Sr.	Iowa		•	•			•
DB	**Antoine Winfield**	5-9	180	Sr.	Ohio State	•	•	•	•	•	•

	OTHERS RECEIVING FIRST-TEAM HONORS										
DL	Robaire Smith				Michigan State			•			
LB	LaVar Arrington				Penn State						•
DB	Tyrone Carter				Minnesota						
DB	Damon Moore				Ohio State						•

HEISMAN TROPHY VOTING

	PLAYER	POS	SCHOOL	1ST	2ND	3RD	TOTAL
9	**Joe Germaine**	QB	Ohio State	2	11	15	43

AWARD WINNERS

PLAYER	POS	SCHOOL	AWARD
Antoine Winfield	DB	Ohio State	Thorpe

ALL-CONFERENCE TEAM

POS	**Offense**	MEDIA	COACHES
QB	Joe Germaine, Ohio State	•	•
RB	Ron Dayne, Wisconsin	•	•
RB	Michael Wiley, Ohio State	•	•
WR	David Boston, Ohio State	•	•
WR	D'Wayne Bates, Northwestern	•	•
C	Jason Strayhorn, Michigan State	•	•
G	Steve Hutchinson, Michigan	•	•
G	Rob Murphy, Ohio State	•	•
T	Jon Jansen, Michigan	•	•
T	Aaron Gibson, Wisconsin	•	
T	Floyd Wedderburn, Penn State	•	
TE	Jerame Tuman, Michigan	•	•
K	Matt Davenport, Wisconsin	•	•

POS	**Defense**	MEDIA	COACHES
L	Tom Burke, Wisconsin	•	•
L	Rosevelt Colvin, Purdue	•	•
L	Jared DeVries, Iowa	•	•
L	Courtney Brown, Penn State	•	
L	Brad Scioli, Penn State	•	
LB	LaVar Arrington, Penn State	•	•
LB	Barry Gardner, Northwestern	•	
LB	Andy Katzenmoyer, Ohio State	•	•
LB	Na'il Diggs, Ohio State	•	
LB	Brandon Short, Penn	•	
DB	Tyrone Carter, Minnesota	•	•
DB	Antoine Winfield, Ohio State	•	•
DB	Damon Moore, Ohio State	•	•
DB	Jamar Fletcher, Wisconsin	•	
DB	David Macklin, Penn State		
P	Kevin Stemke, Wisconsin	•	•

1999

NCAA STATISTICAL LEADERS

INDIVIDUAL

PASSING

		CL	G	ATT	COM	PCT	INT	I%	YDS	YPA	TD	TD%	RATING
10	Joe Germaine, Ohio State	SR	11	346	209	60.4	7	2.0	3108	9.0	24	6.9	154.7

RUSHING/YARDS PER GAME

		CL	G	ATT	YDS	TD	AVG	YPG
9	Ron Dayne, Wisconsin	JR	10	268	1279	11	4.8	127.9

RUSHING/YARDS PER CARRY

		CL	G	ATT	YDS	YPC
3	Michael Wiley, Ohio State	JR	11	182	1147	6.3

*-Based on top 50 rushers

RECEIVING

		CL	G	REC	YDS	TD	RPG	YPR	YPG
5	David Boston, Ohio State	JR	11	74	1330	13	6.8	18.0	120.9

PUNTING

		CL	PUNT	YDS	AVG
10	Kevin Stemke, Wisconsin	SO	67	2949	44.0

PUNT RETURNS

		CL	PR	YDS	TD	AVG
3	Nick Davis, Wisconsin	FR	27	424	2	15.7
4	David Boston, Ohio State	JR	18	268	1	14.9
9	Gari Scott, Michigan State	JR	32	440	0	13.8

KICKOFF RETURNS

		CL	KR	YDS	TD	AVG
8	Sam Simmons, Northwestern	FR	22	607	0	27.6
9	Russell Harvey, Illinois	FR	15	406	0	27.1

FIELD GOALS

		CL	FGA	FGM	PCT	FGG
3	Paul Edinger, Michigan State	JR	26	22	0.85	2.00
7	Travis Forney, Penn State	JR	29	20	0.69	1.82
10	Matt Davenport, Wisconsin	SR	20	18	0.90	1.64

INTERCEPTIONS

		CL	INT	YDS	TD	INT/GM
1	Jamar Fletcher, Wisconsin	FR	6	99	2	0.67
5	David Macklin, Penn State	JR	6	120	1	0.55

TEAM

PASSING OFFENSE

		G	ATT	COM	INT	PCT	YDS	YPA	TD	I%	YPC	YPG
7	Purdue	12	541	352	17	65.1	3978	7.4	40	3.1	11.3	331.5

TOTAL OFFENSE

		G	P	YDS	AVG	TD	YPG
6	Ohio State	11	853	5539	6.5	46	503.6

RUSHING DEFENSE

		G	ATT	YDS	AVG	TD	YPG
1	Ohio State	11	348	741	2.1	5	67.4
3	Wisconsin	11	377	986	2.6	4	89.6
8	Penn State	11	407	1070	2.6	7	97.3

PASSING DEFENSE

		G	ATT	COM	PCT	INT	I%	YDS	YPA	TD	TD%	RATING
2	Ohio State	11	414	197	47.6	17	4.1	2094	5.1	7	1.7	87.4
6	Wisconsin	11	337	182	54.0	18	5.3	1987	5.9	5	1.5	97.8
8	Penn State	11	362	188	51.9	17	4.7	2170	6.0	9	2.5	101.1
10	Michigan State	12	385	188	48.8	13	3.4	2298	6.0	11	2.9	101.6

TOTAL DEFENSE

		G	P	YDS	AVG	TD	YPG
2	Ohio State	11	762	2835	3.7	12	257.7
4	Wisconsin	11	714	2973	4.2	9	270.3

SCORING OFFENSE

		G	PTS	AVG
9	Ohio State	11	406	36.9

SCORING DEFENSE

		G	PTS	AVG
1	Wisconsin	11	112	10.2
3	Ohio State	11	130	11.8

TURNOVER MARGIN

		G	FR	INT	TOT	FL	INTL	TOT	MAR
1	Wisconsin	11	13	18	31	4	5	9	2.00

FINAL POLL

ESPN	AP	TEAM	RECORD
1	1	Florida State	12-0
3	2	Virginia Tech	11-1
2	3	Nebraska	12-1
4	4	Wisconsin	10-2
5	5	Michigan	10-2
6	6	Kansas State	11-1
7	7	Michigan State	10-2
8	8	Alabama	10-3
9	9	Tennessee	9-3
10	10	Marshall	13-0
11	11	Penn State	10-3
14	12	Florida	9-4
12	13	Mississippi State	10-2
13	14	Southern Miss	9-3
15	15	Miami, Fla.	9-4
16	16	Georgia	8-4
19	17	Arkansas	8-4
17	18	Minnesota	8-4
18	19	Oregon	9-3
21	20	Georgia Tech	8-4
23	21	Texas	9-5
22	22	Mississippi	8-4
20	23	Texas A&M	8-4
25	24	Illinois	8-4
	25	Purdue	7-5
24		Stanford	8-4

CONFERENCE STANDINGS

	CONFERENCE		OVERALL	
	W	L	W	L
Wisconsin	7	1	10	2
Michigan State	6	2	10	2
Michigan	6	2	10	2
Penn State	5	3	10	3
Minnesota	5	3	8	4
Illinois	4	4	8	4
Purdue	4	4	7	5
Ohio State	3	5	6	6
Indiana	3	5	4	7
Northwestern	1	7	3	8
Iowa	0	8	1	10

BOWL GAMES

DATE	GAME	SCORE
D28	Alamo	Penn State 24, Texas A&M 0
D30	Micron PC	Illinois 63, Virginia 21
D31	Sun	Oregon 24, Minnesota 20
J1	Outback	Georgia 28, Purdue 25, OT
J1	Orange	Michigan 35, Alabama 34, OT
J1	Florida Citrus	Michigan State 37, Florida 34
J1	Rose	Wisconsin 17, Stanford 9

CONSENSUS ALL-AMERICANS

POS	Offense	HT	WT	CL	School	AP	CF	FC	FN	FW	SN
RB	Ron Dayne	5-10	254	Sr.	Wisconsin	•	•	•	•	•	•
OL	Chris McIntosh	6-7	310	Sr.	Wisconsin	•	•	•	•	•	
C	Ben Hamilton	6-5	271	Jr.	Minnesota	•					•

POS	Defense	HT	WT	CL	School	AP	CF	FC	FN	FW	SN
DL	Courtney Brown	6-5	270	Sr.	Penn State	•	•	•	•	•	•
LB	LaVar Arrington	6-3	242	Jr.	Penn State	•	•	•	•	•	•
LB	Brandon Short	6-3	252	Sr.	Penn State	•	•			•	
DB	Tyrone Carter	5-9	184	Sr.	Minnesota	•	•	•		•	•

OTHERS RECEIVING FIRST-TEAM HONORS

DL	Rob Renes	Michigan			•			•
LB	Julian Peterson	Michigan State					•	
LB	Na'il Diggs	Ohio State					•	
DB	Jamar Fletcher	Wisconsin					•	

1999, cont.

Heisman Trophy Voting

	PLAYER	POS	SCHOOL	1ST	2ND	3RD	TOTAL
1	Ron Dayne	RB	Wisconsin	586	121	42	2042
4	Drew Brees	QB	Purdue	3	89	121	308
9	LaVar Arrington	LB	Penn State	3	14	17	54

Award Winners

PLAYER	POS	SCHOOL	AWARD
Ron Dayne	RB	Wisconsin	Maxwell, Camp, Walker
LaVar Arrington	LB	Penn State	Butkus, Bednarik
Tyrone Carter	DB	Minnesota	Thorpe

All-Conference Team

POS	**Offense**	MEDIA	COACHES
QB	Drew Brees, Purdue	•	•
RB	Ron Dayne, Wisconsin	•	•
RB	Thomas Hammer, Minnesota	•	•
WR	Plaxico Burress, Michigan State	•	•
WR	Chris Daniels, Purdue	•	
WR	David Terrell, Michigan		•
C	Casey Rabach, Wisconsin	•	•
C	Ben Hamilton, Minnesota	•	•
G	Bill Ferrario, Wisconsin	•	•
G	Steve Hutchinson, Michigan	•	•
T	Chris McIntosh, Wisconsin	•	•
T	Jeff Backus, Michigan	•	
T	Kareem McKenzie, Penn State		•
TE	Tim Stratton, Purdue	•	•
K	Vitaly Pisetsky, Wisconsin	•	•

POS	**Defense**	MEDIA	COACHES
L	Courtney Brown, Penn State	•	•
L	Rob Renes, Michigan	•	•
L	Robaire Smith, Michigan St.	•	•
L	Karon Riley, Minnesota	•	•
L	Wendell Bryant, Wisconsin		•
LB	LaVar Arrington, Penn St.	•	•
LB	Brandon Short, Penn St.	•	•
LB	Julian Peterson, Michigan St.	•	
LB	Ian Gold, Michigan		•
DB	Amp Campbell, Michigan St.	•	•
DB	Tyrone Carter, Minnesota	•	•
DB	Jamar Fletcher, Wisconsin	•	•
DB	Ahmed Plummer, Ohio State	•	
DB	Tommy Hendricks, Michigan		•
P	Drew Hagan, Indiana	•	
P	Craig Jarrett, Michigan St.		•

NCAA Statistical Leaders

INDIVIDUAL

ALL-PURPOSE

		CL	G	RUSH	REC	PR	KR	YDS	YPG
8	Ron Dayne, Wisconsin	SR	11	1834	9	0	0	1843	167.6

RUSHING/YARDS PER GAME

		CL	G	ATT	YDS	TD	AVG	YPG
2	Ron Dayne, Wisconsin	SR	11	303	1834	19	6.1	166.7

RUSHING/YARDS PER CARRY

		CL	G	ATT	YDS	YPC
5	Ron Dayne, Wisconsin	SR	11	303	1834	6.1

Based on top 50 rushers

RECEIVING

		CL	G	REC	YDS	TD	RPG	YPR	YPG
9	Chris Daniels, Purdue	SR	11	109	1133	5	9.9	10.4	103.0

PUNTING

		CL	PUNT	YDS	AVG
6	Drew Hagan, Indiana	SR	44	1971	44.8

PUNT RETURNS

		CL	PR	YDS	TD	AVG
3	Vinny Sutherland, Purdue	JR	17	295	2	17.4

SCORING

		CL	TDS	XP	FG	PTS	PTPG
4	Ron Dayne, Wisconsin	SR	19	0	0	114	10.4

FIELD GOALS

		CL	FGA	FGM	PCT	FGG
2	Neil Rackers, Illinois	SR	25	20	.80	1.82
4	Travis Forney, Penn State	SR	26	21	.81	1.75
6	Paul Edinger, Michigan State	SR	22	18	.82	1.64
6	Travis Dorsch, Purdue	SO	28	18	.64	1.64

INTERCEPTIONS

		CL	INT	YDS	TD	INT/GM
5	Jamar Fletcher, Wisconsin	SO	7	135	2	0.64

TEAM

RUSHING OFFENSE

		G	ATT	YDS	AVG	TD	YPG
3	Wisconsin	11	583	3075	5.3	34	279.5

PASSING OFFENSE

		G	ATT	COM	INT	PCT	YDS	YPA	TD	I%	YPC	YPG
4	Purdue	11	508	306	12	60.2	3608	7.1	23	2.4	11.8	328.0

TOTAL OFFENSE

		G	P	YDS	AVG	TD	YPG
8	Purdue	11	859	5016	5.8	38	456.0

RUSHING DEFENSE

		G	ATT	YDS	AVG	TD	YPG
5	Michigan State	11	376	847	2.3	7	77.0

PASSING DEFENSE

		G	ATT	COM	PCT	INT	I%	YDS	YPA	TD	TD%	RATING
5	Wisconsin	11	351	176	50.1	16	4.6	1994	5.7	8	2.3	96.3
8	Minnesota	11	340	159	46.8	8	2.4	1921	5.7	9	2.7	98.3

SCORING OFFENSE

		G	PTS	AVG
9	Wisconsin	11	392	35.6

SCORING DEFENSE

		G	PTS	AVG
5	Wisconsin	11	145	13.2
8	Minnesota	11	172	15.6

TURNOVER MARGIN

		G	FR	INT	TOT	FL	INTL	TOT	MAR
2	Illinois	11	11	14	25	7	5	12	1.2
5	Wisconsin	11	6	16	22	8	3	11	1.0
6	Michigan	11	12	10	22	4	8	12	0.9

2000

FINAL POLL

ESPN	AP	TEAM	RECORD
1	1	Oklahoma	13-0
2	2	Miami, Fla.	11-1
3	3	Washington	11-1
5	4	Oregon State	11-1
4	5	Florida State	11-2
6	6	Virginia Tech	11-1
9	7	Oregon	10-2
7	8	Nebraska	10-2
8	9	Kansas State	11-3
11	10	Florida	10-3
10	11	**Michigan**	9-3
12	12	Texas	9-3
13	13	**Purdue**	8-4
15	14	Colorado State	10-2
16	15	Notre Dame	9-3
14	16	Clemson	9-3
19	17	Georgia Tech	9-3
20	18	Auburn	9-4
21	19	South Carolina	8-4
17	20	Georgia	8-4
18	21	TCU	10-2
	22	LSU	8-4
24	23	**Wisconsin**	9-4
22	24	Mississippi State	8-4
23	25	Iowa State	9-3
25		Tennessee	8-4

CONFERENCE STANDINGS

	CONFERENCE		OVERALL	
	W	L	W	L
Michigan	6	2	9	3
Northwestern	6	2	8	4
Purdue	6	2	8	4
Ohio State	5	3	8	4
Wisconsin	4	4	9	4
Minnesota	4	4	6	6
Penn State	4	4	5	7
Iowa	3	5	3	9
Michigan State	2	6	5	6
Illinois	2	6	5	6
Indiana	2	6	3	8

BOWL GAMES

DATE	GAME	SCORE
D30	**Holiday**	Brigham Young 13, Iowa 13
D28	**Micron PC**	North Carolina St. 38, Minnesota 30
D29	**Sun**	Wisconsin 21, UCLA 20
D30	**Alamo**	Nebraska 66, Northwestern 17
J1	**Florida Citrus**	Michigan 31, Auburn 28
J1	**Outback**	South Carolina 24, Ohio State 7
J1	**Rose**	Washington 34, Purdue 24

CONSENSUS ALL-AMERICANS

POS	**Offense**	HT	WT	CL	**School**	AP	CF	FC	FN	FW	SN
RB	**Damien Anderson**	5-11	202	Jr.	Northwestern	•	•		•	•	•
OL	**Steve Hutchinson**	6-5	299	Sr.	Michigan	•	•	•	•	•	•
OL	**Ben Hamilton**	6-5	285	Sr.	Minnesota		•	•	•		•

POS	**Defense**	HT	WT	CL	**School**	AP	CF	FC	FN	FW	SN
DB	**Jamar Fletcher**	5-10	175	Jr.	Wisconsin	•	•	•		•	•

	OTHERS RECEIVING FIRST-TEAM HONORS		
DB	Mike Doss	Ohio State	•

HEISMAN TROPHY VOTING

	PLAYER	POS	SCHOOL	1ST	2ND	3RD	TOTAL
3	Drew Brees	QB	Purdue	69	107	198	619
5	Damien Anderson	RB	Northwestern	6	20	43	101

AWARD WINNERS

PLAYER	POS	SCHOOL	AWARD
Drew Brees	QB	Purdue	Maxwell
Jamar Fletcher	DB	Wisconsin	Thorpe
Kevin Stemke	P	Wisconsin	Guy
Tim Stratton	TE	Purdue	Mackey

ALL-CONFERENCE TEAM

POS	**Offense**	MEDIA	COACHES
QB	Drew Brees, Purdue	•	
RB	Damien Anderson, Northwestern	•	
RB	Anthony Thomas, Michigan	•	•
WR	David Terrell, Michigan	•	•
WR	Ron Johnson, Minnesota	•	
WR	Vinny Sutherland, Purdue		•
C	Ben Hamilton, Minnesota	•	•
G	Steve Hutchinson, Michigan	•	•
G	Casey Rabach, Wisconsin	•	•
T	Jeff Backus, Michigan	•	•
T	Matt Light, Purdue	•	•
TE	Tim Stratton, Purdue	•	•
K	Dan Stultz, Ohio State	•	•

POS	**Defense**	MEDIA	COACHES
L	Dwayne Missouri, Northwestern	•	•
L	Karon Riley, Minnesota	•	•
L	Fred Wakefield, Illinois	•	
L	Justin Kurpeikis, Penn State	•	
L	Wendell Bryant, Wisconsin		•
LB	Josh Thornhill, Michigan State	•	•
LB	Nick Greisen, Wisconsin	•	
LB	Billy Silva, Northwestern	•	
LB	Joe Cooper, Ohio State		•
LB	Larry Foote, Michigan		•
DB	Nate Clements, Ohio State	•	•
DB	Jamar Fletcher, Wisconsin	•	•
DB	James Boyd, Penn State	•	•
DB	Mike Doss, Ohio State	•	
DB	Renaldo Hill, Michigan State		•
DB	Willie Middlebrooks, Minnesota		•
P	Kevin Stemke, Wisconsin	•	•

2000, CONT.

NCAA STATISTICAL LEADERS

INDIVIDUAL

ALL-PURPOSE

		POS	CL	G	RUSH	REC	PR	KR	YDS	YPG
4	Damien Anderson, Northwestern	RB	SR	11	1914	120	0	0	2034	184.9
9	Michael Bennett, Wisconsin	TB	JR	10	1598	23	0	94	1715	171.5

RUSHING/YARDS PER GAME

		POS	CL	G	ATT	YDS	TD	AVG	YPG
2	Damien Anderson, Northwestern	RB	SR	11	293	1914	22	6.5	174.0
3	Michael Bennett, Wisconsin	TB	JR	10	294	1598	10	5.4	159.8
5	Anthony Thomas, Michigan	HB	SR	11	287	1551	16	5.4	141.0

RUSHING/YARDS PER CARRY

		POS	CL	G	ATT	YDS	YPC
2	Levron Williams, Indiana	RB	SR	10	116	821	7.1
8	Damien Anderson, Northwestern	RB	SR	11	293	1914	6.5

*-Based on top 50 rushers

PUNTING

		POS	CL	PUNT	YDS	AVG
1	Preston Gruening, Minnesota	P	SO	46	2080	45.2
3	Kevin Stemke, Wisconsin	P	SR	65	2915	44.9

KICKOFF RETURNS

		POS	CL	KR	YDS	TD	AVG
5	Ken-Yon Rambo, Ohio State	FL	SR	17	478	0	28.1
6	Kahlil Hill, Iowa	WR	JR	25	680	1	27.2

SCORING

		POS	CL	TDS	XP	FG	PTS	PTPG
2	Damien Anderson, Northwestern	RB	SR	22	0	0	132	12.0

FIELD GOALS

		POS	CL	FGA	FGM	PCT	FGG
2	Dan Nystrom, Minnesota	K	SO	34	22	0.65	2.00
4	Dan Stultz, Ohio State	K	SR	23	19	0.83	1.73

INTERCEPTIONS

		POS	CL	INT	YDS	TD	INT/GM
4	Jamar Fletcher, Wisconsin	DB	JR	6	159	0	0.67
8	Todd Howard, Michigan	DB	JR	6	1	0	0.55

TEAM

RUSHING OFFENSE

		G	ATT	YDS	AVG	TD	YPG
7	Indiana	11	505	2930	5.8	34	266.4
8	Northwestern	11	565	2830	5.0	36	257.3

PASSING OFFENSE

		G	ATT	COM	INT	PCT	YDS	YPA	TD	I%	YPC	YPG
6	Purdue	11	489	292	12	59.7	3438	7.0	26	2.5	11.8	312.5

TOTAL OFFENSE

		G	P	YDS	AVG	TD	YPG
3	Northwestern	11	911	5232	5.7	56	475.6
4	Purdue	11	904	5183	5.7	47	471.2

RUSHING DEFENSE

		G	ATT	YDS	AVG	TD	YPG
9	Ohio State	11	396	1008	2.6	10	91.6

SCORING OFFENSE

		G	PTS	AVG
9	Northwestern	11	424	38.6

TURNOVER MARGIN

		G	FR	INT	TOT	FL	INTL	TOT	MAR
6	Northwestern	11	13	12	25	6	7	13	1.09
10	Michigan	11	12	14	26	10	5	15	1.00

2001

FINAL POLL

ESPN	AP	TEAM	RECORD
1	1	Miami, Fla.	12-0
2	2	Oregon	11-1
3	3	Florida	10-2
4	4	Tennessee	11-2
5	5	Texas	11-2
6	6	Oklahoma	11-2
8	7	LSU	10-3
7	8	Nebraska	11-2
9	9	Colorado	10-3
11	10	Washington State	10-2
10	11	Maryland	10-2
12	12	Illinois	10-2
13	13	South Carolina	9-3
14	14	Syracuse	10-3
15	15	Florida State	8-4
17	16	Stanford	9-3
16	17	Louisville	11-2
18	18	Virginia Tech	8-4
19	19	Washington	8-4
20	20	Michigan	8-4
23	21	Boston College	8-4
25	22	Georgia	8-4
22	23	Toledo	10-2
	24	Georgia Tech	8-5
24	25	Brigham Young	12-2
21		Marshall	11-2

CONFERENCE STANDINGS

	Conference		Overall	
	W	L	W	L
Illinois	7	1	10	2
Michigan	6	2	8	4
Ohio State	5	3	7	5
Iowa	4	4	7	5
Purdue	4	4	6	6
Penn State	4	4	5	6
Indiana	4	4	5	6
Michigan State	3	5	7	5
Wisconsin	3	5	5	7
Minnesota	2	6	4	7
Northwestern	2	6	4	7

BOWL GAMES

DATE	GAME	SCORE
D29	**Alamo**	Iowa 19, Texas Tech 16
D31	**Sun**	Washington State 33, Purdue 27
D31	**Silicon Valley Classic**	Michigan State 44, Fresno State 35
J1	**Outback**	South Carolina 31, Ohio State 28
J1	**Florida Citrus**	Tennessee 45, Michigan 17
J1	**Sugar**	LSU 47, Illinois 34

CONSENSUS ALL-AMERICANS

POS	Offense	HT	WT	CL	School	AP	CF	CN	FC	FN	FWSN
C	LeCharles Bentley	6-2	300	Sr.	Ohio State	•	•		•		• •

	OTHERS RECEIVING FIRST-TEAM HONORS						
QB	Antwaan Randle El		Indiana				•
WR	Marquise Walker		Michigan		•		
WR	Lee Evans		Wisconsin				
KR	Herb Haygood		Michigan State	•	•		

POS	Defense	HT	WT	CL	School	AP	CF	CN	FC	FN	FWSN
P	Travis Dorsch	6-6	222	Jr.	Purdue	•	•		•		

	OTHERS RECEIVING FIRST-TEAM HONORS						
DL	Wendell Bryant		Wisconsin	•	•	•	•
LB	Larry Foote		Michigan		•		
DB	Mike Doss		Ohio State		•		

HEISMAN TROPHY VOTING

	PLAYER	POS	SCHOOL	1ST	2ND	3RD	TOTAL
6	Antwaan Randel El	QB	Indiana	46	39	51	267

AWARD WINNERS

PLAYER	POS	SCHOOL	AWARD
Kahlil Hill	WR	Iowa	Tatupu
Travis Dorsch	P	Purdue	Guy
LeCharles Bentley	C	Ohio State	Rimington

ALL-CONFERENCE TEAM

POS	Offense	MEDIA	COACHES
QB	Antwaan Randle El, Indiana	•	•
RB	Anthony Davis, Wisconsin	•	•
RB	Levron Williams, Indiana	•	•
WR	Lee Evans, Wisconsin	•	•
WR	Marquise Walker, Michigan	•	•
C	LeCharles Bentley, Ohio State	•	•
G	Jay Kulaga, Illinois	•	
G	Jonathan Goodwin, Michigan	•	
G	Eric Steinbach, Iowa		•
T	Tony Pashos, Illinois	•	
T	Tyson Walter, Ohio State	•	•
TE	Tim Stratton, Purdue	•	
TE	Mark Anelli, Wisconsin		•
K	Travis Dorsch, Purdue	•	•

POS	Defense	MEDIA	COACHES
L	Akin Ayodele, Purdue	•	•
L	Wendell Bryant, Wisconsin	•	•
L	Aaron Kampman, Iowa	•	
L	Dan Rumishek, Michigan	•	
L	Jimmy Kennedy, Penn State		•
L	Matt Mitrione, Purdue		•
LB	Larry Foote, Michigan	•	•
LB	Nick Greisen, Wisconsin	•	•
LB	Josh Thornhill, Michigan State	•	•
DB	Mike Doss, Ohio State	•	•
DB	Eugene Wilson, Illinois	•	•
DB	Jack Brewer, Minnesota	•	
DB	Stuart Schweigert, Purdue	•	
DB	Bob Sanders, Iowa		•
DB	Mike Echols, Wisconsin		•
P	Travis Dorsch, Purdue	•	•

NCAA STATISTICAL LEADERS

INDIVIDUAL

	PASSING	POS	CL	G	ATT	COM	PCT	INT	I%	YDS	YPA	TD	TD%	RATING
6	Jeff Smoker, Mich. St	QB	SO	10	230	144	62.6	7	3.0	2203	9.58	18	7.8	162.8

	ALL-PURPOSE	POS	CL	G	RUSH	REC	PR	KR	YDS	YPG
1	Levron Williams, Indiana	RB	SR	11	1401	289	0	511	2201	200.1

	RUSHING/YARDS PER GAME	POS	CL	G	ATT	YDS	TD	AVG	YPG
5	Anthony Davis, Wisconsin	RB	FR	11	291	1466	11	5.0	133.3
8	Levron Williams, Indiana	RB	SR	11	212	1401	17	6.6	127.4

	RUSHING/YARDS PER CARRY	POS	CL	G	ATT	YDS	YPC
5	Levron Williams, Indiana	RB	SR	11	212	1401	6.6
7	Marion Barber, Minnesota	RB	FR	11	118	742	6.3

	RECEIVING	POS	CL	G	REC	YDS	TD	RPG	YPR	YPG
4	Lee Evans, Wisconsin	WR	JR	12	75	1545	9	6.3	20.6	128.8
7	Charles Rogers, Michigan State	WR	SO	11	57	1200	12	5.2	21.1	109.1

	PUNTING	POS	CL	PUNT	YDS	AVG
1	Travis Dorsch, Purdue	K	SR	49	2370	48.4
3	Andy Groom, Ohio State	DT	SR	44	1981	45.0

	KICKOFF RETURNS	POS	CL	KR	YDS	TD	AVG
9	Herb Haygood, Michigan State	WR	SR	19	524	2	27.6

	SCORING	POS	CL	TDS	XP	FG	PTS	PTPG
5	Levron Williams, Indiana	RB	SR	19	0	0	114	10.4

	FIELD GOALS	POS	CL	FGA	FGM	FGT	FGG
3	Travis Dorsch, Purdue	K	SR	25	20	.80	1.82

	INTERCEPTIONS	POS	CL	INT	YDS	TD	INT/GM
3	Derek Ross, Ohio State	DB	SR	7	194	1	0.64
7	Stuart Schweigert, Purdue	DB	SO	6	110	0	0.55
7	Eugene Wilson, Illinois	CB	JR	6	29	0	0.55

TEAM

	RUSHING OFFENSE	G	ATT	YDS	AVG	TD	YPG
4	Indiana	11	541	2964	5.5	33	269.5

	RUSHING DEFENSE	G	ATT	YDS	AVG	TD	YPG
8	Michigan	11	391	996	2.6	9	90.5

	SCORING DEFENSE	G	PTS	AVG
9	Michigan	11	192	17.5

	TURNOVER MARGIN	G	FR	INT	TOT	FL	INTL	TOT	MAR
8	Purdue	11	18	18	36	11	13	24	1.1
10	Ohio State	11	10	19	29	8	10	18	1.0

BIG TEN ANNUAL REVIEW & BOWLS

2002

FINAL POLL

ESPN	AP	TEAM	RECORD
1	1	**Ohio State**	14-0
2	2	Miami, Fla.	12-1
3	3	Georgia	13-1
4	4	USC	11-2
5	5	Oklahoma	12-2
7	6	Texas	11-2
6	7	Kansas State	11-2
8	8	**Iowa**	11-2
9	9	**Michigan**	10-3
10	10	Washington State	10-3
PB	11	Alabama	10-3
11	12	North Carolina St.	11-3
13	13	Maryland	11-3
16	14	Auburn	9-4
12	15	Boise State	12-1
15	16	**Penn State**	9-4
17	17	Notre Dame	10-3
14	18	Virginia Tech	10-4
18	19	Pittsburgh	9-4
21	20	Colorado	9-5
23	21	Florida State	9-5
25	22	Virginia	9-5
22	23	TCU	10-2
19	24	Marshall	11-2
20	25	West Virginia	9-4
24		Florida	8-4

CONFERENCE STANDINGS

	CONFERENCE W	L	OVERALL W	L
Ohio State	8	0	14	0
Iowa	8	0	11	2
Michigan	6	2	10	3
Penn State	5	3	9	4
Purdue	4	4	7	6
Illinois	4	4	5	7
Minnesota	3	5	8	5
Wisconsin	2	6	8	6
Michigan State	2	6	4	8
Northwestern	1	7	3	9
Indiana	1	7	3	9

BOWL GAMES

DATE	GAME	SCORE
D28	**Alamo**	Wisconsin 31, Colorado 28, OT
D30	**Music City**	Minnesota 29, Arkansas 14
D31	**Sun**	Purdue 34, Washington 24
J1	**Outback**	Michigan 38, Florida 30
J1	**Capital One**	Auburn 13, Penn State 9
J2	**Orange**	USC 38, Iowa 17
J3	**Fiesta**	Ohio State 31, Miami, Fla. 24, 2 OT

CONSENSUS ALL-AMERICANS

POS	Offense	HT	WT	CL	School	AP	CF	FC	FW	SN
RB	**Larry Johnson**	6-2	222	Sr.	Penn State	•	•	•	•	•
WR	**Charles Rogers**	6-4	205	Jr.	Michigan State	•	•	•	•	•
TE	**Dallas Clark**	6-4	244	Jr.	Iowa		•	•	•	•
OL	**Eric Steinbach**	6-7	284	Sr.	Iowa		•	•		•
PK	**Mike Nugent**	5-10	170	So.	Ohio State	•	•	•		

	OTHERS RECEIVING FIRST-TEAM HONORS									
QB	Brad Banks				Iowa		•			
OL	Bruce Nelson				Iowa				•	
PK	Nate Kaeding				Iowa				•	•

POS	Defense	HT	WT	CL	School	AP	CF	FC	FW	SN
LB	**Matt Wilhelm**	6-5	245	Sr.	Ohio State	•		•		•
DB	**Mike Doss**	5-11	204	Sr.	Ohio State	•	•	•	•	•

	OTHERS RECEIVING FIRST-TEAM HONORS							
DL	Michael Haynes	Penn State				•		
DL	Jimmy Kennedy	Penn State		•			•	
P	Andy Groom	Ohio State				•		

HEISMAN TROPHY VOTING

	PLAYER	POS	SCHOOL	1ST	2ND	3RD	TOTAL
2	**Brad Banks**	QB	Iowa	199	173	152	1095
3	**Larry Johnson**	RB	Penn State	108	130	142	726

AWARD WINNERS

PLAYER	POS	SCHOOL	AWARD
Larry Johnson	RB	Penn State	Maxwell, Camp, Walker
Brad Banks	QB	Iowa	O'Brien
Nate Kaeding	K	Iowa	Groza
Charles Rogers	WR	Michigan State	Biletnikoff
Dallas Clark	TE	Iowa	Mackey

ALL-CONFERENCE TEAM

POS	Offense	MEDIA	COACHES
QB	Brad Banks, Iowa	•	•
RB	Larry Johnson, Penn State	•	•
RB	Maurice Clarett, Ohio State	•	
RB	Fred Russell, Iowa		•
WR	Charles Rogers, Michigan State	•	•
WR	John Standeford, Purdue	•	
WR	Bryant Johnson, Penn State		•
C	Bruce Nelson, Iowa	•	•
G	David Baas, Michigan	•	•
G	Eric Steinbach, Iowa	•	•
T	Robert Gallery, Iowa	•	•
T	Tony Pashos, Illinois	•	
T	Tony Pape, Michigan		•
TE	Dallas Clark, Iowa	•	•
K	Mike Nugent, Ohio State	•	
K	Nate Kaeding, Iowa		•

POS	Defense	MEDIA	COACHES
L	Jared De Vries, Iowa	•	•
L	Colin Cole, Iowa	•	•
L	Michael Haynes, Penn State	•	•
L	Jimmy Kennedy, Penn State	•	•
L	Howard Hodges, Iowa	•	
L	Darrion Scott, Ohio State		•
LB	Victor Hobson, Michigan	•	•
LB	Matt Wilhelm, Ohio State	•	•
LB	Niko Koutouvides, Purdue	•	
LB	Fred Barr, Iowa		•
DB	Bob Sanders, Iowa	•	•
DB	Marlin Jackson, Michigan	•	•
DB	Mike Doss, Ohio State	•	•
DB	Jim Leonhard, Wisconsin	•	
DB	Chris Gamble, Ohio State		•
P	Andy Groom, Ohio State	•	•

2003

NCAA Statistical Leaders

INDIVIDUAL

PASSING

		POS	CL	G	ATT	COM	PCT	INT	I%	YDS	YPA	TD	TD%	RATING
1	Brad Banks, Iowa	QB	SR	13	294	170	57.8	5	1.7	2573	8.8	26	8.8	157.1

ALL-PURPOSE

		POS	CL	G	RUSH	REC	PR	KR	YDS	YPG
1	Larry Johnson, Penn State	TB	SR	13	2087	349	0	219	2655	204.2
4	Jason Wright, Northwestern	WR	JR	12	1234	266	0	513	2013	167.8

RUSHING/YARDS PER GAME

		POS	CL	G	ATT	YDS	TD	AVG	YPG
1	Larry Johnson, Penn State	TB	SR	13	271	2087	20	7.7	160.5

RUSHING/YARDS PER CARRY

		POS	CL	G	ATT	YDS	YPC
2	Larry Johnson, Penn State	TB	SR	13	271	2087	7.7

RECEIVING

		POS	CL	G	REC	YDS	TD	RPG	YPR	YPG
8	Charles Rogers, Michigan State	WR	JR	12	68	1351	13	5.7	19.9	112.6

PUNTING

		POS	CL	PUNT	YDS	AVG
4	Andy Groom, Ohio State	P	SR	60	2697	45.0

PUNT RETURNS

		CL	PR	YDS	TD	AVG
2	Desmond Howard, Michigan	JR	15	261	1	17.4

KICKOFF RETURNS

		POS	CL	KR	YDS	TD	AVG
4	Jason Wright, Northwestern	WR	JR	18	513	1	28.5

SCORING

		POS	CL	TDS	XP	FG	PTS	PTPG
4	Larry Johnson, Penn State	TB	SR	23	0	0	140	10.8
9	Maurice Clarett, Ohio State	RB	FR	18	0	0	108	9.8

FIELD GOALS

		POS	CL	FGA	FGM	PCT	FGG
3	Mike Nugent, Ohio State	K	SO	28	25	0.89	1.79

INTERCEPTIONS

		POS	CL	INT	YDS	TD	INT/GM
1	Jim Leonhard, Wisconsin	DB	SO	11	115	0	0.79

TEAM

RUSHING OFFENSE

		G	ATT	YDS	AVG	TD	YPG
10	Penn State	13	526	2972	5.7	36	228.6

TOTAL OFFENSE

		G	P	YDS	AVG	TD	YPG
7	Purdue	13	1034	5879	5.7	51	452.2
10	Illinois	12	915	5356	5.9	43	446.3

RUSHING DEFENSE

		G	ATT	YDS	AVG	TD	YPG
3	Ohio State	14	418	1088	2.6	5	77.7
5	Iowa	13	416	1065	2.6	17	81.9

SCORING OFFENSE

		G	PTS	AVG
7	Iowa	13	484	37.2

SCORING DEFENSE

		G	PTS	AVG
2	Ohio State	14	183	13.1

TURNOVER MARGIN

		G	FR	INT	TOT	FL	INTL	TOT	MAR
9	Wisconsin	14	13	22	35	9	8	17	1.3

Final Poll

ESPN	AP	TEAM	RECORD
2	1	USC	12-1
1	2	LSU	13-1
3	3	Oklahoma	12-2
4	4	Ohio State	11-2
5	5	Miami, Fla.	11-2
7	6	Michigan	10-3
6	7	Georgia	11-3
8	8	Iowa	10-3
9	9	Washington State	10-3
12	10	Miami, Ohio	13-1
10	11	Florida State	10-3
11	12	Texas	10-3
14	13	Mississippi	10-3
13	14	Kansas State	11-4
16	15	Tennessee	10-3
15	16	Boise State	13-1
20	17	Maryland	10-3
19	18	Purdue	9-4
18	19	Nebraska	10-3
17	20	Minnesota	10-3
21	21	Utah	10-2
22	22	Clemson	9-4
23	23	Bowling Green	11-3
25	24	Florida	8-5
24	25	TCU	11-2

Conference Standings

	Conference		Overall	
	W	L	W	L
Michigan	7	1	10	3
Ohio State	6	2	11	2
Purdue	6	2	9	4
Iowa	5	3	10	3
Minnesota	5	3	10	3
Michigan State	5	3	8	5
Wisconsin	4	4	7	6
Northwestern	4	4	6	7
Penn State	1	7	3	9
Indiana	1	7	2	10
Illinois	0	8	1	11

Bowl Games

DATE	GAME	SCORE
D26	Motor City	Bowling Green 28, Northwestern 24
D29	Alamo	Nebraska 17, Michigan State 3
D31	Music City	Auburn 28, Wisconsin 14
D31	Sun	Minnesota 31, Oregon 30
J1	Outback	Iowa 37, Florida 17
J1	Capital One	Georgia 34, Purdue 27, OT
J1	Rose	USC 28, Michigan 14
J2	Fiesta	Ohio State 35, Kansas State 28

2003, CONT.

CONSENSUS ALL-AMERICANS

POS	Offense	HT	WT	CL	School		AP	CF	FC	FW	SN
RB	Chris Perry	6-1	218	Jr.	Michigan		•	•	•		
OL	Robert Gallery	6-7	321	Sr.	Iowa		•		•	•	•
PK	Nate Kaeding	6-0	180	Sr.	Iowa		•		•		

POS	Defense	HT	WT	CL	School		AP	CF	FC	FW	SN
DB	Will Allen	6-2	190	Sr.	Ohio State		•	•		•	

	OTHERS RECEIVING FIRST-TEAM HONORS					
DL	Will Smith	Ohio State		•	•	

HEISMAN TROPHY VOTING

	PLAYER	POS	SCHOOL	1ST	2ND	3RD	TOTAL
4	Chris Perry	RB	Michigan	27	66	128	341

AWARD WINNERS

PLAYER	POS	SCHOOL	AWARD
Robert Gallery	OL	Iowa	Outland
Chris Perry	RB	Michigan	Walker
B.J. Sander	P	Ohio State	Guy

ALL-CONFERENCE TEAM

POS	Offense	MEDIA	COACHES
QB	John Navarre, Michigan	•	•
RB	Chris Perry, Michigan	•	•
RB	Marion Barber III, Minnesota	•	•
WR	Braylon Edwards, Michigan	•	•
WR	Lee Evans, Wisconsin	•	•
C	Greg Eslinger, Minnesota	•	•
G	David Baas, Michigan	•	•
G	Alex Stepanovich, Ohio State	•	•
T	Robert Gallery, Iowa	•	•
T	Tony Pape, Michigan	•	•
TE	Ben Hartsock, Ohio State	•	
TE	Ben Utecht, Minnesota		•
K	Nate Kaeding, Iowa	•	•

POS	Defense	MEDIA	COACHES
L	Matt Roth, Iowa	•	•
L	Will Smith, Ohio State	•	•
L	Shaun Phillips, Purdue	•	•
L	Anttaj Hawthorne, Wisconsin	•	
L	Tim Anderson, Ohio State		•
LB	A.J. Hawk, Ohio State	•	•
LB	Niko Koutouvides, Purdue	•	•
LB	Abdul Hodge, Iowa	•	
LB	Alex Lewis, Wisconsin		•
DB	Bob Sanders, Iowa	•	•
DB	Stuart Schweigert, Purdue	•	•
DB	Jim Leonhard, Wisconsin	•	•
DB	Chris Gamble, Ohio State	•	
DB	Will Allen, Ohio State		•
P	Brandon Fields, Michigan State	•	
P	B.J. Sander, Ohio State		•

NCAA STATISTICAL LEADERS

INDIVIDUAL

	PASSING	POS	CL	G	ATT	COM	PCT	INT	I%	YDS	YPA	TD	TD%	RATING
5	Asad Abdul-Khaliq, Minn.	QB	SR	13	250	158	63.2	5	2.0	2401	9.6	17	6.8	162.3

	ALL-PURPOSE	POS	CL	G	RUSH	REC	PR	KR	YDS	YPG
8	Chris Perry, Michigan	RB	SR	13	1674	367	0	0	2041	157.0

	RUSHING/YARDS PER GAME	POS	CL	G	ATT	YDS	TD	AVG	YPG
6	Chris Perry, Michigan	RB	SR	13	338	1674	18	5.0	128.8

	RUSHING/YARDS PER CARRY	POS	CL	G	ATT	YDS	YPC
3	Laurence Maroney, Minnesota	RB	FR	13	162	1121	6.9

	PUNTING	POS	CL	PUNT	YDS	AVG
2	Brandon Fields, Michigan State	P	SO	62	2878	46.4
10	Steve Weatherford, Illinois	P	SO	46	2045	44.5

	PUNT RETURNS	POS	CL	PR	YDS	TD	AVG
7	Marion Barber III, Minnesota	RB	SO	28	405	0	14.5
8	Jim Leonhard, Wisconsin	DB	JR	34	470	2	13.8
9	Steve Breaston, Michigan	WR	SO	45	619	2	13.8

	SCORING	POS	CL	TDS	XP	FG	PTS	PTPG
6	Jason Wright, Northwestern	RB	SR	21	0	0	126	9.7

	FIELD GOALS	POS	CL	FGA	FGM	PCT	FGG
4	Ben Jones, Purdue	K	SO	30	25	.83	1.92
10	David Rayner, Michigan State	K	JR	29	22	.76	1.69

	INTERCEPTIONS	POS	CL	INT	YDS	TD	INT/GM
8	Jim Leonhard, Wisconsin	DB	JR	7	98	0	0.54

TEAM

	RUSHING OFFENSE	G	ATT	YDS	AVG	TD	YPG
3	Minnesota	13	683	3759	5.5	46	289.2

	TOTAL OFFENSE	G	P	YDS	AVG	TD	YPG
4	Minnesota	13	970	6430	6.6	66	494.6

	RUSHING DEFENSE	G	ATT	YDS	AVG	TD	YPG
2	Ohio State	13	415	810	2.0	12	62.3
8	Iowa	13	480	1205	2.5	10	92.7
10	Purdue	13	467	1260	2.7	9	96.9

	PASSING DEFENSE	G	ATT	COM	PCT	INT	I%	YDS	YPA	TD	TD%	RATING
9	Michigan	13	411	221	53.8	14	3.4	2347	5.71	9	2.2	102.2

	TOTAL DEFENSE	G	P	YDS	AVG	TD	YPG
10	Ohio State	13	930	3859	4.2	28	296.9

	SCORING OFFENSE	G	PTS	AVG
7	Minnesota	13	503	38.7

	SCORING DEFENSE	G	PTS	AVG
7	Iowa	13	210	16.2

	TURNOVER MARGIN	G	FR	INT	TOT	FL	INTL	TOT	MAR
8	Purdue	13	14	14	28	9	7	16	0.9
10	Michigan State	13	14	15	29	3	15	18	0.9

2004

FINAL POLL

ESPN	AP	TEAM	RECORD
1	1	USC	13-0
2	2	Auburn	13-0
3	3	Oklahoma	12-1
5	4	Utah	12-0
4	5	Texas	11-1
7	6	Louisville	11-1
6	7	Georgia	10-2
8	8	Iowa	10-2
9	9	California	10-2
10	10	Virginia Tech	10-3
11	11	Miami, Fla.	9-3
13	12	Boise State	11-1
15	13	Tennessee	10-3
12	14	Michigan	9-3
14	15	Florida State	9-3
16	16	LSU	9-3
18	17	Wisconsin	9-3
17	18	Texas Tech	8-4
20	19	Arizona State	9-3
19	20	Ohio State	8-4
21	21	Boston College	9-3
22	22	Fresno State	9-3
23	23	Virginia	8-4
24	24	Navy	10-2
	25	Pittsburgh	8-4
25		Florida	7-5

CONFERENCE STANDINGS

	Conference W	Conference L	Overall W	Overall L
Michigan	7	1	9	3
Iowa	7	1	10	2
Wisconsin	6	2	9	3
Northwestern	5	3	6	6
Purdue	4	4	7	5
Ohio State	4	4	8	4
Michigan State	4	4	5	7
Minnesota	3	5	7	5
Penn State	2	6	4	7
Illinois	1	7	3	8
Indiana	1	7	3	8

BOWL GAMES

DATE	GAME	SCORE
D29	**Alamo**	Ohio State 33, Oklahoma State 7
D31	**Sun**	Arizona State 27, Purdue 23
D31	**Music City**	Minnesota 20, Alabama 16
J1	**Outback**	Georgia 24, Wisconsin 21
J1	**Capital One**	Iowa 30, Louisiana State 25
J1	**Rose**	Texas 38, Michigan 37

CONSENSUS ALL-AMERICANS

POS	**Offense**	HT	WT	CL	School	AP	CF	FC	FN	FW
WR	**Braylon Edwards**	6-3	208	Sr.	Michigan	•	•	•	•	•
WR	**Taylor Stubblefield**	6-1	182	Sr.	Purdue	•		•		•
OL	**David Baas**	6-5	323	Sr.	Michigan	•	•		•	
PK	**Mike Nugent**	5-10	180	Sr.	Ohio State	•	•	•	•	

OTHERS RECEIVING FIRST-TEAM HONORS

OL	Greg Eslinger				Minnesota			•		

POS	**Defense**	HT	WT	CL	School	AP	CF	FC	FN	FW
DL	**Erasmus James**	6-4	263	Sr.	Wisconsin	•	•	•	•	
LB	**A.J. Hawk**	6-1	238	Jr.	Ohio State	•	•		•	
DB	**Marlin Jackson**	6-1	196	Sr.	Michigan	•		•	•	•
DB	**Ernest Shazor**	6-4	229	Sr.	Michigan	•	•		•	•
P	**Brandon Fields**	6-6	234	So.	Michigan State	•	•		•	

HEISMAN TROPHY VOTING

	PLAYER	POS	SCHOOL	1ST	2ND	3RD	TOTAL
10	**Braylon Edwards**	WR	Michigan	3	13	27	62

AWARD WINNERS

PLAYER	POS	SCHOOL	AWARD
Mike Nugent	K	Ohio State	Groza
Braylon Edwards	WR	Michigan	Biletnikoff
David Baas	OL	Michigan	Rimington

ALL-CONFERENCE TEAM

POS	**Offense**	MEDIA	COACHES
QB	Kyle Orton, Purdue	•	
QB	Drew Tate, Iowa		•
RB	Michael Hart, Michigan	•	•
RB	Laurence Maroney, Minnesota	•	•
WR	Braylon Edwards, Michigan	•	•
WR	Taylor Stubblefield, Purdue	•	•
C	Greg Eslinger, Minnesota	•	•
C	David Baas, Michigan	•	•
G	Dan Buenning, Wisconsin	•	•
G	Mark Setterstrom, Minnesota	•	•
G	Matt Lentz, Michigan		•
T	Rian Melander, Minnesota	•	
T	Sean Poole, Michigan State	•	•
T	Adam Stenavich, Michigan		•
TE	Tim Massaquoi, Michigan	•	
K	Mike Nugent, Ohio State	•	•

POS	**Defense**	MEDIA	COACHES
L	Matt Roth, Iowa	•	•
L	Anttaj Hawthorne, Wisconsin	•	•
L	Erasmus James, Wisconsin	•	•
L	Jonathan Babineaux, Iowa	•	
L	Gabe Watson, Michigan		•
LB	Chad Greenway, Iowa	•	•
LB	A.J. Hawk, Ohio State	•	•
LB	Tim McGarigle, Northwestern	•	
LB	Abdul Hodge, Iowa		•
DB	Marlin Jackson, Michigan	•	•
DB	Ernest Shazor, Michigan	•	•
DB	Jim Leonhard, Wisconsin	•	•
DB	Ukee Dozier, Minnesota	•	
DB	Scott Starks, Wisconsin		•
P	Brandon Fields, Michigan State	•	
P	Steve Weatherford, Illinois		•

2004, CONT.

NCAA STATISTICAL LEADERS

INDIVIDUAL

PASSING

		POS	CL	G	ATT	COM	PCT	INT	I%	YDS	YPA	TD	TD%	RATING
10	Kyle Orton, Purdue	QB	SR	11	389	236	60.7	5	1.3	3090	7.9	31	8.0	151.1

RUSHING/YARDS PER GAME

		POS	CL	G	ATT	YDS	TD	AVG	YPG
10	Michael Hart, Michigan	RB	FR	12	282	1455	9	5.2	121.3

RUSHING/YARDS PER CARRY

		POS	CL	G	ATT	YDS	YPC
1	Drew Stanton, Michigan State	QB	JR	10	96	687	7.2

RECEIVING

		POS	CL	G	REC	YDS	TD	RPG	YPR	YPG
5	Braylon Edwards, Michigan	WR	SR	12	97	1330	15	8.1	13.7	110.8

PUNTING

		POS	CL	PUNT	YDS	AVG
1	Brandon Fields, Michigan State	P	JR	50	2394	47.9
4	Steve Weatherford, Illinois	P	JR	57	2589	45.4

PUNT RETURNS

		POS	CL	PR	YDS	TD	AVG
1	Ted Ginn Jr., Ohio State	DB	FR	15	384	4	25.6

KICKOFF RETURNS

		POS	CL	KR	YDS	TD	AVG
4	Lance Bennett, Indiana	RB	SO	20	599	1	30.0
10	Pierre Thomas, Illinois	RB	SO	25	677	1	27.1

FIELD GOALS

		POS	CL	FGA	FGM	PCT	FGG
1	Mike Nugent, Ohio State	K	SR	27	24	.89	2.00
4	David Rayner, Michigan State	K	SR	31	22	.71	1.83
7	Kyle Schlicher, Iowa	K	SO	26	21	.81	1.75

TEAM

RUSHING OFFENSE

		G	ATT	YDS	AVG	TD	YPG
5	Minnesota	12	572	3082	5.4	29	256.8
10	Michigan State	12	500	2862	5.7	22	238.5

PASSING OFFENSE

		G	ATT	COM	INT	PCT	YDS	YPA	TD	I%	YPC	YPG
4	Purdue	12	486	297	8	61.1	3854	7.9	38	1.7	13.0	321.1

TOTAL OFFENSE

		G	P	YDS	AVG	TD	YPG
10	Michigan State	12	899	5520	6.1	41	460.0

RUSHING DEFENSE

		G	ATT	YDS	AVG	TD	YPG
5	Iowa	12	392	1110	2.8	8	92.5

PASSING DEFENSE

		G	ATT	COM	PCT	INT	I%	YDS	YPA	TD	TD%	RATING
4	Penn State	11	310	175	56.5	16	5.2	1785	5.8	5	1.6	99.9
5	Wisconsin	12	369	180	48.8	11	3.0	2007	5.4	13	3.5	100.2

TOTAL DEFENSE

		G	P	YDS	AVG	TD	YPG
9	Wisconsin	12	756	3495	4.6	22	291.3
10	Penn State	11	753	3207	4.3	18	291.6

SCORING DEFENSE

		G	PTS	AVG
5	Penn State	11	168	15.3
6	Wisconsin	12	185	15.4

TURNOVER MARGIN

		G	FR	INT	TOT	FL	INTL	TOT	MAR
6	Iowa	12	15	17	32	5	14	19	1.1

2005

FINAL POLL

ESPN	AP	TEAM	RECORD
1	1	Texas	13-0
2	2	USC	12-1
3	3	Penn State	11-1
4	4	Ohio State	10-2
6	5	West Virginia	11-1
5	6	LSU	11-2
7	7	Virginia Tech	11-2
8	8	Alabama	10-2
11	9	Notre Dame	9-3
10	10	Georgia	10-3
9	11	TCU	11-1
16	12	Florida	9-3
12	13	Oregon	10-2
14	14	Auburn	9-3
15	15	Wisconsin	10-3
13	16	UCLA	10-2
18	17	Miami, Fla.	9-3
17	18	Boston College	9-3
20	19	Louisville	9-3
19	20	Texas Tech	9-3
21	21	Clemson	8-4
22	22	Oklahoma	8-4
23	23	Florida State	8-5
24	24	Nebraska	8-4
25	25	California	8-4

CONFERENCE STANDINGS

	CONFERENCE		OVERALL	
	W	L	W	L
Penn State	7	1	11	1
Ohio State	7	1	10	2
Wisconsin	5	3	10	3
Michigan	5	3	7	5
Northwestern	5	3	7	5
Iowa	5	3	7	5
Minnesota	4	4	7	5
Purdue	3	5	5	6
Michigan State	2	6	5	6
Indiana	1	7	4	7
Illinois	0	8	2	9

BOWL GAMES

DATE	GAME	SCORE
D28	Alamo	Nebraska 32, Michigan 28
D30	Music City	Virginia 34, Minnesota 31
D30	Sun	UCLA 50, Northwestern 38
J2	Outback	Florida 31, Iowa 24
J2	Capital One	Wisconsin 24, Auburn 10
J2	Fiesta	Ohio State 34, Notre Dame 20
J3	Orange	Penn State 26, Florida State 23 (3OT)

CONSENSUS ALL-AMERICANS

POS	Offense	HT	WT	CL	School	AP	CF	FC	SN	FW
OL	Greg Eslinger	6-3	285	Sr.	Minnesota	•	•	•	•	•

OTHERS RECEIVING FIRST-TEAM HONORS

POS					School	AP	CF	FC	SN	FW
OL	Zach Strief				Northwestern					•

POS	Defense	HT	WT	CL	School	AP	CF	FC	SN	FW
DL	Tamba Hali	6-3	258	Sr.	Penn State	•	•	•	•	•
LB	Paul Posluszny	6-2	230	Jr.	Penn State	•	•		•	•
LB	A.J. Hawk	6-1	238	Sr.	Ohio State	•	•	•	•	•

HEISMAN TROPHY VOTING

	PLAYER	POS	SCHOOL	1ST	2ND	3RD	TOTAL
5	Michael Robinson	QB	Penn State	2	7	29	49
6	A.J. Hawk	LB	Ohio State	0	3	23	29

AWARD WINNERS

PLAYER	POS	SCHOOL	AWARD
Paul Posluszny	LB	Penn State	Bednarik, Butkus
Greg Eslinger	C	Minnesota	Outland, Rimington
A.J. Hawk	LB	Ohio State	Lombardi

ALL-CONFERENCE TEAM

POS	Offense	MEDIA	COACHES
QB	Brett Basanez, Northwestern	•	•
RB	Laurence Maroney, Minnesota	•	•
RB	Brian Calhoun, Wisconsin	•	•
WR	Jason Avant, Michigan	•	•
WR	Santonio Holmes, Ohio State	•	•
C	Greg Eslinger, Minnesota	•	•
G	Mark Setterstrom, Minnesota	•	•
G	Matt Lentz, Michigan	•	
G	Rob Sims, Ohio State		•
T	Joe Thomas, Wisconsin	•	•
T	Adam Stenavich, Michigan	•	•
T	Levi Brown, Penn State		•
TE	Matt Spaeth, Minnesota	•	•
K	John Huston, Ohio State	•	•

POS	Defense	MEDIA	COACHES
L	Gabe Watson, Michigan	•	•
L	Tamba Hali, Penn State	•	•
L	Mike Kudla, Ohio State	•	•
L	Scott Paxson, Penn State		•
L	Kenny Iwebema, Iowa	•	
LB	Chad Greenway, Iowa	•	•
LB	A.J. Hawk, Ohio State	•	•
LB	Paul Posluszny, Penn State	•	•
DB	Nate Salley, Ohio State	•	•
DB	Ashton Youboty, Ohio State	•	•
DB	Alan Zemaitis, Penn State	•	•
DB	Jovon Johnson, Iowa	•	
DB	Donte Whitner, Ohio State		•
DB	Calvin Lowry, Penn State		•
P	Kenneth Debauche, Wisconsin	•	•

NCAA STATISTICAL LEADERS

INDIVIDUAL

	PASSING	POS	CL	G	ATT	COM	PCT	INT	I%	YDS	YPA	TD	TD%	RAT
4	Troy Smith, Ohio State	QB	SR	11	237	149	62.9	4	1.7	2282	9.6	16	6.8	162.7
10	Drew Stanton, Mich. St.	QB	JR	11	354	236	66.7	12	3.4	3077	8.7	22	6.2	153.4

	ALL-PURPOSE	POS	CL	G	RUSH	REC	PR	KR	YDS	YPG
6	Brian Calhoun, Wisconsin	RB	JR	13	1636	571	0	0	2207	169.8
8	Brandon Williams, Wisconsin	WR	SR	13	47	1095	380	616	2138	164.5

	RUSHING/YARDS PER GAME	POS	CL	G	ATT	YDS	TD	AVG	YPG
5	Laurence Maroney, Minnesota	RB	JR	11	281	1464	10	5.2	133.1
6	Brian Calhoun, Wisconsin	RB	JR	13	348	1636	22	4.7	125.9
8	Tyrell Sutton, Northwestern	RB	FR	12	250	1474	16	5.9	122.8

	RUSHING/YARDS PER CARRY	POS	CL	G	ATT	YDS	YPC
8	Javon Ringer, Michigan State	RB	FR	11	122	817	6.7

	PUNTING	POS	CL	PUNT	YDS	AVG
8	Kenneth DeBauche, Wisconsin	P	SR	57	2555	44.8

	KICKOFF RETURNS	POS	CL	KR	YDS	TD	AVG
4	Ted Ginn Jr., Ohio State	WR	SO	18	532	1	29.6
8	Steve Breaston, Michigan	WR	SR	23	646	1	28.1
9	Brandon Williams, Wisconsin	WR	SR	22	616	0	28.0

	SCORING	POS	CL	TDS	XP	FG	PTS	PTPG
5	Brian Calhoun, Wisconsin	RB	JR	24	0	0	144	11.1
9	Gary Russell, Minnesota	RB	SO	19	0	0	116	9.7

	FIELD GOALS	POS	CL	FGA	FGM	PCT	FGG
5	Josh Huston, Ohio State	K	SR	28	22	.79	1.83

	INTERCEPTIONS	POS	CL	INT	YDS	TD	INT/GM
5	Alan Zemaitis, Penn State	CB	SR	6	35	0	.50

TEAM

	RUSHING OFFENSE	G	ATT	YDS	AVG	TD	YPG
3	Minnesota	12	610	3277	5.4	34	273.1

	PASSING OFFENSE	G	ATT	COM	INT	PCT	YDS	YPA	TD	I%	YPC	YPG
7	Northwestern	12	512	320	9	62.5	3681	7.2	22	1.8	11.5	306.8

	TOTAL OFFENSE	G	P	YDS	AVG	TD	YPG
4	Northwestern	12	974	6004	6.2	51	500.3
5	Michigan State	11	834	5470	6.6	50	497.3
7	Minnesota	12	933	5937	6.4	56	494.8

	RUSHING DEFENSE	G	ATT	YDS	AVG	TD	YPG
1	Ohio State	12	375	881	2.4	12	73.4
7	Penn State	12	442	1116	2.5	12	93.0

	TOTAL DEFENSE	G	P	YDS	AVG	TD	YPG
5	Ohio State	12	780	3376	4.3	21	281.3

	SCORING OFFENSE	G	PTS	AVG
10	Minnesota	12	429	35.8

	SCORING DEFENSE	G	PTS	AVG
5	Ohio State	12	183	15.3
10	Penn State	12	204	17.0

BIG TEN ANNUAL REVIEW & BOWLS

2006

FINAL POLL

ESPN	AP	TEAM	RECORD
1	1	Florida	13-1
2	2	**Ohio State**	12-1
3	3	LSU	11-2
4	4	USC	11-2
6	5	Boise State	13-0
7	6	Louisville	12-1
5	7	**Wisconsin**	12-1
9	8	**Michigan**	11-2
8	9	Auburn	11-2
10	10	West Virginia	11-2
11	11	Oklahoma	11-3
12	12	Rutgers	11-2
13	13	Texas	10-3
14	14	California	10-3
16	15	Arkansas	10-4
15	16	Brigham Young	11-2
19	17	Notre Dame	10-3
17	18	Wake Forest	11-3
18	19	Virginia Tech	10-3
20	20	Boston College	10-3
22	21	Oregon State	10-4
21	22	TCU	11-2
	23	Georgia	9-4
25	24	**Penn State**	9-4
23	25	Tennessee	9-4
24		Hawaii	11-3

CONFERENCE STANDINGS

	CONFERENCE		OVERALL	
	W	L	W	L
Ohio State	8	0	12	1
Wisconsin	7	1	12	1
Michigan	7	1	11	2
Penn State	5	3	9	4
Purdue	5	3	8	6
Minnesota	3	5	6	7
Indiana	3	5	5	7
Iowa	2	6	6	7
Northwestern	2	6	4	8
Michigan State	1	7	4	8

BOWL GAMES

DATE	GAME	SCORE
D29	**Champs Sports**	Maryland 24, Purdue 7
D29	**Insight**	Texas Tech 44, Minnesota 41 (OT)
D30	**Alamo**	Texas 26, Iowa 24;
J1	**Outback**	Penn State 20, Tennessee 10
J1	**Capital One**	Wisconsin 17, Arkansas 14
J1	**Rose**	USC 32, Michigan 18
J8	**BCS Championship**	Florida 41, Ohio State 14

CONSENSUS ALL-AMERICANS

POS	**Offense**	HT	WT	CL	**School**	AP	CF	FC	SN	FW
QB	**Troy Smith**	6-1	215	Sr.	Ohio State	•	•	•	•	•
OL	**Jake Long**	6-7	313	Sr.	Michigan	•	•	•		•
OL	**Joe Thomas**	6-8	313	Sr.	Wisconsin	•	•	•	•	

OTHERS RECEIVING FIRST-TEAM HONORS

			AP	CF	FC	SN	FW
TE	Matt Spaeth	Minnesota		•			
KR	Marcus Thigpen	Indiana				•	

POS	**Defense**	HT	WT	CL	**School**	AP	CF	FC	SN	FW
DL	**LaMarr Woodley**	6-2	269	Sr.	Michigan	•	•	•	•	•
DL	**Quinn Pitcock**	6-3	295	Sr.	Ohio State	•	•	•	•	
LB	**Paul Posluszny**	6-2	238	Sr.	Penn State	•	•			
LB	**James Laurinaitis**	6-3	244	So.	Ohio State	•			•	•
DB	**Leon Hall**	5-11	193	Sr.	Michigan	•	•	•		•

OTHERS RECEIVING FIRST-TEAM HONORS

			AP	CF	FC	SN	FW
LB	Dan Connor	Penn State					•

HEISMAN TROPHY VOTING

	PLAYER	POS	SCHOOL	1ST	2ND	3RD	TOTAL
1	Troy Smith	QB	Ohio State	801	62	13	2540
5	Mike Hart	RB	Michigan	5	58	79	210

AWARD WINNERS

PLAYER	POS	SCHOOL	AWARD
Troy Smith	QB	Ohio State	O'Brien
Paul Posluszny	LB	Penn State	Bednarik
LaMarr Woodley	LB	Michigan	Lombardi, Hendricks
James Laurinaitis	LB	Ohio State	Nagurski
Matt Spaeth	TE	Minnesota	Mackey
Joe Thomas	OL	Wisconsin	Outland

ALL-CONFERENCE TEAM

POS	Offense	MEDIA	COACHES
QB	Troy Smith, Ohio State	•	•
RB	Mike Hart, Michigan	•	•
RB	P.J. Hill, Wisconsin	•	
RB	Antonio Pittman, Ohio State		•
WR	Ted Ginn Jr., Ohio State		•
WR	Dorien Bryant, Purdue	•	
WR	Mario Manningham, Michigan		•
WR	Anthony Gonzalez, Ohio State		•
C	Doug Datish, Ohio State	•	•
G	T.J. Downing, Ohio State	•	•
G	Adam Kraus, Michigan	•	•
G	Mike Jones, Iowa	•	
T	Jake Long, Michigan	•	•
T	Joe Thomas, Wisconsin	•	•
TE	Matt Spaeth, Minnesota	•	•
K	Garrett Rivas, Michigan	•	•

POS	Defense	MEDIA	COACHES
L	Alan Branch, Michigan	•	•
L	LaMarr Woodley, Michigan	•	•
L	Quinn Pitcock, Ohio State	•	•
L	Anthony Spencer, Purdue	•	•
LB	James Laurinaitis, Ohio State	•	•
LB	Paul Posluszny, Penn State	•	•
LB	J Leman, Illinois	•	
LB	David Harris, Michigan		•
DB	Leon Hall, Michigan	•	•
DB	Malcolm Jenkins, Ohio State	•	•
DB	Antonio Smith, Ohio State	•	
DB	Jack Ikegwuonu, Wisconsin		•
DB	Anthony Scirrotto, Penn State		•
P	Brandon Fields, Michigan State	•	•

NCAA STATISTICAL LEADERS

INDIVIDUAL

PASSING

		POS	CL	G	ATT	COM	PCT	INT	I%	YDS	YPA	TD	TD%	RATING
7	Troy Smith, Ohio State	QB	SR	13	311	203	65.3	6	1.9	2542	8.2	30	9.7	161.9

RUSHING/YARDS PER GAME

		POS	CL	G	ATT	YDS	TD	AVG	YPG
8	P.J. Hill, Wisconsin	RB	FR	13	311	1569	15	5.1	120.7
9	Michael Hart, Michigan	RB	JR	13	318	1562	14	4.9	120.2

KICKOFF RETURNS

		POS	CL	KR	YDS	TD	AVG
1	Marcus Thigpen, Indiana	RB	So.	24	723	3	30.1

FIELD GOALS

		POS	CL	FGA	FGM	PCT	FGG
2	Kevin Kelly, Penn State	K	SO	34	22	.65	1.69

TEAM

RUSHING OFFENSE

		G	ATT	YDS	AVG	TD	YPG
10	Illinois	12	434	2266	5.2	15	188.8

PASSING OFFENSE

		G	ATT	COM	INT	PCT	YDS	YPA	TD	I%	YPC	YPG
6	Purdue	14	541	322	20	59.5	4082	7.6	24	3.7	12.7	291.6

RUSHING DEFENSE

		G	ATT	YDS	AVG	TD	YPG
1	Michigan	13	301	564	1.9	5	43.4
7	Penn State	13	400	1137	2.8	8	87.5

PASSING DEFENSE

		G	ATT	COM	PCT	INT	I%	YDS	YPA	TD	TD%	RATING
1	Wisconsin	13	387	185	47.8	15	3.9	1798	4.7	6	1.6	84.2
10	Ohio State	13	415	242	58.3	21	5.1	2368	5.7	10	2.4	104.1

TOTAL DEFENSE

		G	P	YDS	AVG	TD	YPG
5	Wisconsin	13	775	3290	4.3	18	253.1
10	Michigan	13	789	3488	4.4	25	268.3

SCORING OFFENSE

		G	PTS	AVG
8	Ohio State	13	450	34.6

SCORING DEFENSE

		G	PTS	AVG
2	Wisconsin	13	157	12.1
5	Ohio State	13	166	12.8
8	Penn State	13	187	14.4

TURNOVER MARGIN

		G	FR	INT	TOT	FL	INTL	TOT	MAR
1	Minnesota	13	15	17	32	3	11	14	1.38
4	Michigan	13	14	12	26	4	8	12	1.08

BIG TEN ANNUAL REVIEW & BOWLS

Big Ten Bowls

Considering that for much of its first 80 years, the Big Ten Conference forbid its schools from going anywhere but Pasadena, the league has compiled an impressive postseason travelogue. Though the conference hasn't made its mark everywhere, its schools have grown comfortable in the state of Florida, as well as certain parts of Texas.

What follows is a compendium of every bowl game in which a Big Ten team ever played, along with a record of the pre- and (when recorded) postgame national rankings for each team. When possible, we have also included the MVPs cited in media guides, on the bowls' websites, or in reported accounts of the game.

The summaries were assembled from a variety of sources, including bowl records, local libraries, newspapers, media guides, books, and the Pro Football Hall of Fame (for the College All-Star Game). If a scoring summary does not appear, we were unable to piece one together through published accounts of the game.

Following the Rose Bowl, bowl games currently certified by the NCAA are listed in alphabetical order. Defunct bowls—excluding unsanctioned games involving lesser quality opponents or squads of servicemen—appear in alphabetical order after that.

A Bed of Roses

An open letter from the oldest bowl game to its longtime, occasionally estranged companion, the Big Ten Conference

BY MARK WANGRIN

YOU'VE HEARD IT FOREVER: "GIVE TRADITION ITS DUE," came the clamor when the Bowl Alliance wanted me—the Rose Bowl—to join for the 1998 season. Forget money, forget national title shots, forget television exposure and income and big-dollar college sports, the crowd implored. Don't sell out. Do the right thing.

After all, Big Ten versus Pac-10 was history. It was special. It was the heartbeat of the Granddaddy of Them All, the bowl that hadn't kowtowed to sponsors or the lure of the Bowl Alliance or anybody else.

We paid handsomely, more than any other bowl, but we also represented an old-school way of thinking, an adherence to the aforementioned tradition. For more than five decades we had featured you, the Big Ten, against the Pac-10. Midwest brawn against West Coast flight. There were streaks, lopsided eras, but it was tradition. And, came the cries when the Bowl Alliance tried to spin us into its web, for all that is good in college football, don't abandon tradition.

And to think there were times we just wanted you to go away. Again … and again … and again.

I say "we" only out of a sense of modesty. Okay, and to diffuse any hard feelings over our sometimes fractious relationship. I'm the Rose Bowl. I've got a cadre of flacks who speak for me, presidents and tournament directors and the like who say the right thing when they're supposed to say it, but nobody ever asked me how I felt. Nobody's asking still, but I'm telling anyway.

These days they call me The Grandaddy of Them All. Pretty ironic, really, because that's what I felt like in the early days of the 1890s: Grandpa at the family reunion picnic, marshalling the sack races and horseshoe pitching and watermelon-eating contests. That's what I was back then. We had sack races. We had camel vs. elephant races (quaint in those days; today that's the Michael Jackson family picnic). We didn't have football until 1902. Boy, would things change.

Against Stanford in the inaugural bowl game, the invited guests from Michigan were unstoppable.

> *In 1916, we brought back football, thank goodness. Over the next 31 years, we were the Ellis Island of bowl games.*

Now, more than a century later, we can look back at what we built—you, me, and the Pac-10—and with the lessons learned and perspective gained, wonder why we ever doubted you.

Our game set the trend. We were the first bowl game, by 33 years, and we even trademarked that Granddaddy of Them All moniker. We've crammed more than 90,000 butts into our seats for all but two games since 1947—a sellout every year. We were the first college football game broadcast on national television (1952), and when they went color a decade later, we were the first to do that, too. Our TV ratings were boffo—since the BCS was formed, we've had five of their top-10-rated games—and our payout (more than $30 million total) was sweeter than anybody else's. And while others trotted out Nokia and FedEx and Poulan/Weed Eater as courtesy titles, we just stayed the Rose Bowl. Sure, since 1999 we've been "presented by" AT&T, PlayStation 2, or Citi, but when do you ever hear anybody really call us that? We get the money and the last laugh.

Most of all, we love the way TV makes us look even bigger. We love the way the tall pines creeping over the back row, backed by mountains and a sun-streaked blue sky turning to dusk, show up on TV. Too bad we didn't have high-def a lot sooner.

Of course, we were pretty happy there wasn't TV or even radio coverage on New Year's Day in 1902, when we had our first game. We invited one of your teams, the first of Fielding Yost's "Point a Minute" Michigan powerhouses, and in front of 8,000 once-curious souls, you beat the dog out of Stanford 49-0.

That's when you gave us the first reason not to have you around. We had our first traffic jam, sure, but the worst of it was that nobody wanted to see a slaughter like that. Our intent behind this whole shindig was to showcase beauty, not brutality.

It started in the early 1890s when Charles Holder, the naturalist and globe-trotter who had moved from Massachusetts to Pasadena because of the natural beauty that surrounds us, wanted to draw more Eastern tourists westward.

Holder made his pitch to the Valley Hunt Club, noting that New York was at the time digging out from a blizzard. "I came from the East … and discovered happiness and beauty. In New York people are buried in snow. Here our flowers are blooming, and our oranges are about to bear. Let's have a festival and tell the world about our paradise."

Intrigued, Dr. Francis F. Rowland suggested they copy a festival of roses his wife had just visited in Nice, France. "Let's call our festival the Battle of Roses," he offered.

But we had more than roses. We had tugs-of-war, chariot races, and an offbeat game of Spanish origin called the tourney of the rings, a combination of jousting and ring toss. That's where we'd get our new name—the Tournament of Roses—in 1890, in case you were curious.

Then came football. In 1901, we called a former Stanford coach, Fielding Yost, who was then at Michigan. Yost had led Stanford to a 7–2–1 season in 1900, but his counterparts, perhaps jealous of his success, passed a rule that only graduate students could coach football. Yost left for the Wolverines, where his first team was 10–0 and hung 128 points on Buffalo. We gave him a shot at Cal, but the Bears turned down the bid. Who accepted? Stanford. Perfect, we thought.

Yost accepted too, as we figured he would, but he didn't come cheap. We offered $2 a day in meal money; he demanded $3 and threatened a boycott. We caved, then so did Stanford. With eight minutes left in the game, Stanford captain R.S. Fisher reportedly turned to his Michigan counterpart, Hugh White, and said, "If you are willing, we are ready to quit."

It wasn't quite the way we'd wanted to gin up interest in our little festival. So we dumped football and went back to chariot races—and we nearly lost our president in 1907 during one crash. We had fortune-telling birds and magic fish ponds and tent-pegging competitions and a 25-foot whale made of geraniums and carnations. One event had motorcar drivers negotiate a set course. Whoever came closest to averaging four miles an hour won a pair of women's gloves. Now, that's drama.

In 1916, we brought back football, thank goodness. Over the next 31 years, we were the Ellis Island of bowl games. The East sent us Harvard, Penn State, Navy, Pitt, and Columbia. The South came rarin' to go in the form of Washington & Jefferson, Alabama, Georgia Tech. The Midwest kicked in Notre Dame and Nebraska.

It wasn't until 1921 that we got around to inviting another one of your schools, Ohio State. The Buckeyes lost to Cal 28 to zip, and six months later, the conference leaders ruled that bowl games were too much of a distraction from academics and banned them.

Kenneth "Tug" Wilson, who became Big Ten commissioner in 1944, wanted to have it both ways. In the Pacific Coast, he saw a conference that approached academics and scholarship regulations with similar earnestness. The Big Ten would again play in the postseason, and they would play the PCC.

And for the second time, we didn't want you.

Buddy Young led an army of Illini to the 1947 Rose Bowl.

We wanted mighty Army. We only wanted you to do the right thing: abdicate. We asked. The public asked. Army, in its own double-secret, read-between-the-lines way, asked. Hell, everybody asked.

Forget the vote of conference members to join, you were begged. Forget the five-year contract binding you to the Rose Bowl and the PCC beginning with the 1947 game—word of which started coming out in late October of 1946, to the dismay of many. The team you were sending didn't even want to come. Illinois, your champion, voted it down. So why send a malcontent? Let top-ranked Army fill the spot against UCLA. Give the fans, media, bowl officials, and most of the college football world what they want. Please. For the sake, future, and tradition of all that is dear about college football just do one thing: Go away.

The chorus grew. In early November the Southern California chapter of the Football Writers Association voted to implore the PCC-Rose Bowl Committee to invite Army at the "earliest possible date." As in yesterday. Wrote Paul Zimmerman, the *Los Angeles Times* sports editor and chapter president, "The presence of the Cadets here would add greatly to the prestige of the annual grid battle of the roses and would serve to temper the criticism of the New York press that likes to take an opportunity to look down its nose at this, the first of all bowl games."

A hastily organized group of 563 fans signed a letter and sent it to Cal and PCC president Dr. Stanley B. Freeborn, stating, "The five-year pact has begun with a dud." USC alums publicly announced that they would consider leaving the PCC. The Los Angeles City Council unanimously voted to invite Army and Notre Dame to come out to the Coliseum for a Christmastime rematch of their scoreless tie in November. Five days before the 1947 Rose Bowl, still aching that Army had turned down all bids rather than be a second choice, the City Council voted again, this time to create a new bowl game to go head-to-head with us in the future. Luckily, it was quickly shot down. You almost ruined everything.

And still you scoffed. You came anyway, pasty-faced but full of speed in the form of Illinois, in most minds a poor but contractually bound substitute for the powerful Cadet team that featured Glenn Davis of nearby Claremont.

Nobody, and I mean nobody, wanted the Illini. Pat Harmon, then covering the team for the *Champaign News-Gazette* and later the historian with the College Football Hall of Fame, recalled an LA reporter sidling up to him and asking, with unabashed sincerity, if any Illinois players had volunteered to drop out to let Army come in. "Can you imagine that?" Harmon said 60 years later. "That's how bad

the feelings were."

Sure, Illinois, had had a very nice year. The Illini were 7–2, fresh off their conference title, and that Buddy Young sure was a heckuva scatback. But … Army. Now, Army had had a great *decade*. From 1944 to '46, the Cadets went 27–0–1 and won three consensus national titles. They had back-to-back Heisman Trophy winners in Doc Blanchard and Davis, Mr. Inside and Mr. Outside. And we won't even mention those two big come-from-behind routs of Tojo and Hitler, which still register more clearly than any 4.1 Richter scale wake-me-up we feel out here on random mornings.

In Pasadena, Woody Hayes passed on Disneyland and steak and quelled a player insurrection.

We knew that deep down you wanted to come out here, see what blue skies and grass looked like again, maybe regain the feeling in your extremities after that last tangle with the snow shovel. We got it. You wanted to be here, watching the shadows lengthen over the field, the sun creep down past the large pine trees in Arroyo Seco, feel that dusky chill. Reading about it in the morning paper while watching three inches of fresh snow cover your driveway just didn't cut it. We knew. Sorry about that. But look on the bright side: We never had the chance to make snow angels.

We can admit now that we were wrong. Time provides that allowance. No shame in that. We wanted Army. That would have been a helluva game. But the Illini, like good soldiers, took the bid. Then they took the bait, running for a then-game-record 320 yards and embarrassing UCLA 45-14. When the Bruin tacklers got close enough, which wasn't often, the Illini taunted them, "We know we're not Army, but you'll wish it was Army before this game's over."

Over the coming years, you gave us another reason not to want you, a happier one from your point of view: You dominated. Listen to that. Savor that. It actually happened. From 1947 to '59, you won 12 of 13. You were operating under more names than Sean Combs—the Intercollegiate Conference of Faculty Representatives, the Western Conference, the Big Nine, the Big Ten—but the PCC was the one that needed an alias or three. You embarrassed our West Coast boys. You twisted their arms

behind their backs and they cried uncle.

You even humbled them with your runners-up. You didn't want one team to hog all the sunshine, so you instituted a no-repeat rule (which lasted until 1971). Some of your best teams stayed home. Michigan was national champion in 1948. Defending national champ Michigan State went undefeated in 1966. Neither could play in the Rose Bowl.

Of course, you had some bluster with that high-mindedness. After the 1949 game, when you sent your second-place team, Northwestern, and the Wildcats beat Cal, Minnesota president James Lewis Morrill vowed to vote against the pact when it came up for renewal, saying he didn't like the pressure it placed on the schools. But in 1953, the Gophers were the deciding vote in a new deal. In '61 they accepted their first bid. Way to dig in your heels, James Lewis.

After Illinois beat Stanford 40-7 in 1952, the vultures came out. The pact had one year remaining and now the media again wanted the Big Ten outta there. "After six defeats in a row, it appears, the West is a sucker who has not yet learned the old frontier adage: Never play a man at his own game," wrote Al Santoro of the *Los Angeles Examiner*.

Others provided hope, albeit resting it on divine intervention. "The only hope for the future is that, having fulfilled the biblical prophecy of a seven-year famine, the Pacific Coast [Conference] should have seven good years to come," wrote L.H. Gregory of Portland's *Oregonian*.

Funny thing. USC beat Wisconsin 7-0 the next year and the pact was renewed. But the PCC, dogs that they were at the time, lived in dog years—those seven years became one. The next year, Michigan State beat UCLA 28-20.

And then we got Woody. Wayne Woodrow Hayes, how we loved him. The guy who as a teen charted plays of the 1928 Rose Bowl, who eventually married a woman who had done the same, who made extra money as a teen boxing for $5 a bout, who knew no compromise. We hid a grin when he came. Old Woody, he always made it interesting.

The first year he came, in 1955, he dispatched USC 20-7—publicly relishing that his assistants told him that if

it had been a dry field, the Buckeyes would have beaten the Trojans worse—and then shoved this at his Western counterparts: "There are about four, possibly five teams in the Big Ten that could beat USC … Big Ten teams are better in the bowl because they are raised on tougher competition."

The Big Ten would keep proving it, with Woody winning again in 1958. But now the pact was once more in danger. The PCC, filled with internal strife, was near being disbanded. The Big Ten—which had added Michigan State in 1953—voted 5-5 to renew. League officials left it up to the individual schools to decide if they wanted to keep playing.

Iowa took the bid and then took Cal apart 38-12. *Los Angeles Mirror* columnist Maxwell Stiles dryly noted, "Maybe it is just as well the Pacific Coast Conference is dying. That's one way to end the pain. Until we signed the pact with the Big Ten, I always thought Vassar was located in the East. Now I'm not so sure."

Yeah, that hurt. The local boys spent too much time at the beach. Your guys pulled plows. We got it. That's what everybody thought. It was your time. You were physical. You dominated, but if you look at the scores, only six of those 12 losses were by more than a touchdown. The West Coast boys hadn't yet mastered the forward pass or gotten

Et tu, Bo? Until 1981, at the Rose Bowl Schembechler was Sisyphus with a football.

over their own petty bickering, but they would learn.

The PCC disbanded and reformed as the Athletic Association of Western Universities—with Cal, Washington, Stanford, UCLA, and USC, but apparently without any of the Vassars of the West, because the tide turned. In the 1960 game, Washington stunned Wisconsin 44-8—the parade theme that year was "Tall Tales and True"—prompting AAWU commissioner Tom Hamilton to caution, "The belief existing here, called Big Tenitis, that the Big Ten is always superior, has been disproved … From now on the Big Ten had better be ready when New Year's Day comes around."

Minnesota was the top-ranked team in 1961 when, without a contract in place between the leagues and the bowl, the Gophers voted to come anyway. Washington gave the Westerners their first winning streak with a 17-7 victory. The next year we would have had Woody and the Buckeyes again, but OSU faculty voted to keep the Big Ten champs at home. They held a protest sit-in on High Street in Columbus. Minnesota, aching for revenge, stepped in and beat UCLA 21-3.

Through that controversy came peace. Meetings between league officials led to a new pact under which the league champions would again meet, although the Big Ten would continue to send its runner-up in years when the champion would be making a repeat performance.

Then 1963 gave us one of your greatest performances, with Ron Vander Kelen's record-setting passing rallying Wisconsin back from a 42-14 deficit early in the fourth quarter, only to fall 42-37 to John McKay's No. 1-ranked USC squad. And in 1965 we finally brought in an army— Arnie's Army—when we invited Arnold Palmer to be our grand marshal.

By then you were still holding your own, mixing the good with the bad. In 1966, unbeaten Michigan State was stunned 14-12 by lightly regarded UCLA. In 1969, Woody came in and beat USC 27-16.

Woody came back in 1971, unbeaten and ready to run his record to 4–0. Maybe too ready. Woody never did cotton much to all the hoopla out here, passing on Disneyland and the Beef Bowl—where teams try to put down more cow carcass than their opponents—saying, "We are not pigs at Ohio State." Palm trees, sun, and Hollywood were rumors. "Woody had a saying," running back John Brockington said. "'We're going out there to kick their ass and go home.'"

His Buckeyes rebelled. Facing a steady diet of two-a-days and full-contact drills, they voted to go home before the game. The seniors delivered the message to Hayes. "Everyone was scared to death," Brockington said. "We were

going up against Woody Hayes, for God's sake, and we were talking about what we wanted."

Hayes loved military history, and one of his role models was General George Patton, who was from Pasadena. Like ol' Blood and Guts, Hayes stared down the seniors. The insurgency dissolved.

Even as Hayes was ruling Columbus with an iron fist, his hegemony was being threatened by one of his former players and assistants. *Et tu*, Bo? In 1970, that traitor, Bo Schembechler, had led rival Michigan back to its first Rose Bowl since 1965. Bo. We loved Bo too. God bless him. He was Sisyphus without the boulder. Dutifully, he'd bring the Maize and Blue to Pasadena only to find a different way to lose. That first year he missed the game because of a heart attack. That should have been a sign. He lost eight of 10, including his first five. When he arrived in 1978 for his fourth game, he looked up at the rainy, overcast skies descending on LA and quipped, "There's that black cloud again."

Bo lost even when he didn't play. In the 1973 season, the Buckeyes and Wolverines—both undefeated—played to a 10-10 tie. Big Ten officials, having recently discarded the no-repeat role, picked OSU over Michigan, which had lost quarterback Dennis Franklin to injury. It only made Bo feel worse when the Buckeyes beat USC 42-21, though he didn't know at the time that it would be Woody's last Rose Bowl victory.

The Buckeyes lost in 1975 and again in '76, when Dick Vermeil's UCLA squad handed unbeaten OSU and back-to-back Heisman Trophy winner Archie Griffin a 23-10 loss. After that one, Woody locked himself in the locker room for a full hour and barred his players from talking to reporters.

Bo finally broke through in 1981, though it took an NCAA probation that had made five Pac-10 schools—USC, UCLA, Oregon, Oregon State, and Arizona State—ineligible for postseason games. Led by wideout Anthony Carter, the Wolverines fulfilled Bo's promise that "this is a team that knows how to win" by beating Washington 23-6.

Still, the Pac-10 was getting the best of you, and some blamed Bo and Woody. *Sports Illustrated* writer Robert Creamer noted that before 1969, every team in the league had played in the game and the Big Ten was 16–6. Over the next nine years, only "over-inflated" Michigan and Ohio

The only way you could tell your quarterbacks from your halfbacks was that they wore smaller shoulder pads.

State went to Pasadena. "The obvious conclusion," Creamer wrote, "seems to be that the Big Ten was far more effective when it was a competitive conference, when playing talent was more evenly distributed, when its eventual champion had to win more than a two-team race."

Jabbed Jim Murray of the *Los Angeles Times* after Michigan lost in '77, "Whatever happened to the Big Ten teams that could scratch matches on their beards … Aren't the coal mines working anymore? The steel mills shut down, are they? Who's doing the plowing back there? Surely not these nice little fellows they keep sending out. These guys belong in the Ivy League, not the Big Ten."

Critics charged that the Big Ten's ground-based attacks were no match for the West's passing games—or their underrated defenses. Bo's 1977 quarterback, Rick Leach, gave the critics ammo, saying, "I think if I had thrown more during the year, I could have been more effective. But all year long, our offensive line did such a great job that we never needed to pass."

Woody's guys saw it too. Decades later, noseguard Jim Stillwagon would say, "Woody Hayes was a great horse-and-plow coach. When we became a John Deere team, he didn't want to read the instructions."

After Washington blanked Iowa 28-0 in 1982, your 11th loss in 13 games, reporters tried to give Hawkeye coach Hayden Fry an out. "People kept asking me about distractions, things like Disneyland and Universal Studios," Fry said. "They aren't distractions, they are positive things."

Positively depressing, at least from your point of view. Why did you guys struggle? How much time do you have?

There was the long layoff between the regular season and the game, nearly a month and a half. There was integration, after which Southern schools finally started opening up to the talented black athlete. Bubba Smith had come from southeast Texas all the way to Michigan State. Now many studs like him were staying closer to home.

Heck, everybody knows that in the playoffs, pitching holds sway in the major leagues and defense is the bedrock of the NBA. In college football? You need to run, but you gotta heave the rock, and we're not talking about an option pitch. You'd better go downtown. The Pac-10 had Jim Plunkett, Pat Haden, Vince Evans, and Warren Moon behind

center in our game. You had Cornelius Greene, Rex Kern, and Tom Slade. The only way you could tell your quarterbacks from your halfbacks was that they wore smaller shoulder pads. Heck, you didn't even have any team pass for more than 2,000 yards in conference play until Illinois, with Tony Eason, did it in 1980. You weren't used to seeing the ball in the air, and it showed.

And by your own holier-than-thou rules, you made just getting here the be-all, end-all. Until the 1975 season, only one team could go to any bowl. So when Michigan and Ohio State met in the Horseshoe or the Big House, winning was everything. Pasadena was gravy. When you have a steady diet of steak and potatoes, you understand gravy.

And yeah, for the longest time you were a guest in our game, not a true partner. We shorted you on tickets and revenue, until you threw your TV ratings in our face when you added Penn State for the 1993 season.

We understood that long-resting chip on your shoulder. What we didn't understand was how, with such great intrinsic motivation, you underachieved.

In 1985, the Buckeyes were presupposed to run all over USC. Instead, the Trojans tap-danced across the Scarlet and Gray. Quoth Jim Murray in the *Times*, "It was like Marilyn Monroe playing a nun—the Pac-10 beating you with a hard-nosed football is like Babe Ruth out-bunting you." When Arizona State rallied from a 15-3 deficit in 1987 to send Bo to his seventh loss in eight appearances, the headline writers worked every angle of your misery, dwelling on jeers and curses and bedevilment. In the *Pasadena Star-News,* writer Jim Gordon celebrated the obvious: "In this uncertain age, it's comforting to know there are still some things in the universe one can depend upon. The moon circles the earth, the earth circles the sun, the Big Ten champion circled the wagons after losing another Rose Bowl game." Ouch.

We felt your pain. Really, we did.

You tried everything. Heck, for the 1996 game, you pulled out all the stops and sent Northwestern, which in most years was like getting Paris Hilton nominated for the Oscars opposite some Brit who'd played a royal. The Wildcats were legit, won the old-fashioned Big Ten way with a strong

> *When the BCS was formed, even we had to see how tradition was a weak consolation prize for being denied a shot at the new title game.*

running game featuring Hollywood wannabe Darnell Autry and a stifling defense spearheaded by future Northwestern coach Pat Fitzgerald, at least until the Hawkeyes broke his leg in the regular season's penultimate game. The Purple showed up in Pasadena, Charlton Heston parted the waters at the *Jaws* exhibit at Universal Studios, and the team even hung with Jay Leno. They hung with the Trojans, too, coming back from a 24-7 deficit to take a one-point fourth-quarter lead, but in the end it was too much of that other Hollywood wannabe, USC receiver Keyshawn Johnson, who shredded the Wildcat secondary for 216 yards on 12 catches in a 41-32 Trojan victory. NU had Charlton, Ann-Margret, Julia Louis-Dreyfus, Warren Beatty. Heck, half of Hollywood matriculated at NU (yeah, we know the other half went to USC), but you couldn't even get that Cinderella angle working for you.

Northwestern in the Rose Bowl was one sign that the world was changing. First came the Bowl Coalition (1992-94) and then the Bowl Alliance (1995-97), as college football and TV tried to work a No. 1 vs. No. 2 game into the existing bowl system. Conferences were realigning and making their own TV deals.

We tried to resist, pointing to our tradition. When the Bowl Championship Series was formed for the 1998 season, even we had to see how tradition was a weak consolation prize for being denied a shot at the new title game. We were the Grandaddy, but even old dogs need to learn new tricks. We joined up, though we reserved the right, when not hosting the BCS title game, to get a Big Ten–Pac-10 matchup if there were eligible teams from those leagues not headed to the title game.

It backfired in the 2002 game, big time. That was our first shot to host the BCS title game and it looked like one of our boys, Oregon, would fill a spot against Miami. But the infernal selection process bypassed the Ducks in favor of Nebraska, which didn't even play in its conference title game and was coming off a 62-36 beat-down by Colorado in the final regular-season game. Nebraska bowed up, dug in ... and got beat by 23.

What had we wrought?

It got better in the 2004 game. We got USC and Michigan, just like the old times, and the Trojans beat the

Wolverines, just like the old times, and they even got a share of the national title, just like the old times. Sweet, too, because the Associated Press voters refused to recognize LSU, the BCS victor over Oklahoma, as the champion.

Still …

Heck, we're friends here; we can be honest. We can tell you that maybe the Big Ten–Pac-10 thing isn't the be-all, end-all after all.

In late 1946, Cal coach Frank Wickhorst lauded the original agreement, saying it would go a long way toward limiting teams "proselytizing" for bowl berths. Fifty-eight years later, the Bears got a kick in the karma when Texas' Mack Brown politicked Cal right out of a spot in the 2005 Rose Bowl. When it rained the whole week leading up to the game and it looked as if the Rose Parade would be washed out for the first time in recent memory, nobody hesitated to blame Texas.

"'Dismay' is a very polite word," said Dave Davis, the Tournament of Roses Association president and CEO. "There's been considerable consternation, and confusion and dismay."

Dave was speaking for the committee, not me. I saw Vince Young and knew he could light things up. And he did. Young, the Longhorns' phenomenally gifted quarterback, ran for 192 yards and a Rose Bowl-record four touchdowns, and Dusty Mangum kicked a field goal on the game's final play—the first time the Rose Bowl had been decided at the gun—for a 38-37 victory over Michigan. We got a dandy. Oh yeah, sorry you lost.

The next year we got Young again, and he pretty much single-handedly engineered a 41-38 upset of USC for the national title. Let me tell you a secret: We'd scouted Texas back in 1947, when we coveted Army over you guys. It didn't happen then, but I don't feel bad telling you it was worth the wait.

Many things are. Like us. Now, with our hair-pulling and eye-gouging behind us, we're like a couple of old men sitting on a porch, tossing back a few cold ones, recalling old lies and making up new ones. Can we go back to the way it was? Sure, it would be nice, just not very practical. So it tickles us when we can do what we did in January 2007, the last time we were able to put together an old-fashioned Big Ten–Pac-10 matchup. For old time's sake, it was Michigan against USC, a timely booster shot of nostalgia.

That game didn't decide a national title, didn't make or break a championship run, didn't tip a streak one way or another. It was your shot to edge back ahead in a series that, since the 1947 marriage, had been tied 28–28. A chance for you to feel young again, to howl at the moon.

The Trojans won. It figures. But you and I know you'll get another chance, and then another, and maybe someday you will regain the upper hand. Runs come and go, feelings change. Traditions hold. For all the incessant playoff talk, all the annual tweaks in the bowl configurations and computer selection programs, all that money talks and college football listens, we'll always have Pasadena. That's one thing nobody will ever be able to take away from us.

ROSE BOWL

PROFILE

Site: Pasadena, Calif.
Stadium: Rose Bowl
Capacity: 92,542
Surface: Grass

PLAYING SITES

Tournament Park, Pasadena, 1902, 1916-22
Rose Bowl Stadium, 1923-41
Duke Stadium, Durham, N.C., 1942
Rose Bowl Stadium, since 1943

NAME CHANGES

Rose Bowl, 1902-1998
Rose Bowl Presented by AT&T, 1999-2002
Rose Bowl Presented by PlayStation 2, 2003
Rose Bowl Presented by Citi, since 2004

SEASON	DATE	PRE-GAME RANK	TEAMS	SCORE	FINAL RANK	MOST VALUABLE PLAYER(S)	ATT.
1901	Jan. 1, 1902		Michigan	49		Neil Snow, Michigan, FB	8,000
			Stanford	0			
1920	Jan. 1, 1921		California	28		Harold "Brick" Muller, California, E	42,000
			Ohio State	0			
1922	Jan. 1, 1923		USC	14		Leo Calland, USC, G	43,000
			Penn State*	3			
1946	Jan. 1, 1947	5	Illinois	45		Claude "Buddy" Young, Illinois, HB	90,000
		4	UCLA	14		Julius Rykovich, Illinois, HB	
1947	Jan. 1, 1948	2	Michigan	49		Robert Chappuis, Michigan, HB	93,000
		8	USC	0			
1948	Jan. 1, 1949	7	Northwestern	20		Frank Aschenbrenner, Northwestern, HB	93,000
		4	California	14			
1949	Jan. 2, 1950	6	Ohio State	17		Fred Morrison, Ohio State, FB	100,963
		3	California	14			
1950	Jan. 1, 1951	9	Michigan	14		Donald Dufek, Michigan, FB	98,939
		5	California	6			
1951	Jan. 1, 1952	7	Illinois	40		William Tate, Illinois, HB	96,825
		4	Stanford	7			
1952	Jan. 1, 1953	5	USC	7		Rudy Bukich, USC, QB	101,500
		11	Wisconsin	0			
1953	Jan. 1, 1954	3	Michigan State	28		Billy Wells, Michigan State, HB	101,000
		5	UCLA	20			
1954	Jan. 1, 1955	1	Ohio State	20		Dave Leggett, Ohio State, QB	89,191
		17	USC	7			
1955	Jan. 2, 1956	2	Michigan State	17		Walter Kowalczyk, Michigan State, HB	100,809
		4	UCLA	14			
1956	Jan. 1, 1957	3	Iowa	35		Kenneth Ploen, Iowa, QB	97,126
		10	Oregon State	19			
1957	Jan. 1, 1958	2	Ohio State	10		Jack Crabtree, Oregon, QB	98,202
			Oregon	7			
1958	Jan. 1, 1959	2	Iowa	38		Bob Jeter, Iowa, HB	98,297
		16	California	12			
1959	Jan. 1, 1960	8	Washington	44		Bob Schloredt, Washington, QB	100,809
		6	Wisconsin	8		George Fleming, Washington, HB	
1960	Jan. 2, 1961	6	Washington	17		Bob Schloredt, Washington, QB	97,314
		1	Minnesota	7			
1961	Jan. 1, 1962	6	Minnesota	21		Sandy Stephens, Minnesota, QB	98,214
		16	UCLA	3			
1962	Jan. 1, 1963	1	USC	42		Pete Beathard, USC, QB	98,698
		2	Wisconsin	37		Ron Vander Kelen, Wisconsin, QB	
1963	Jan. 1, 1964	3	Illinois	17		Jim Grabowski, Illinois, FB	96,957
			Washington	7			
1964	Jan. 1, 1965	4	Michigan	34		Mel Anthony, Michigan, FB	100,423
		8	Oregon State	7			
1965	Jan. 1, 1966	5	UCLA	14	4	Bob Stiles, UCLA, DB	100,087
		1	Michigan State	12	2		
1966	Jan. 2, 1967	7	Purdue	14		John Charles, Purdue, DB	100,807
			USC	13			
1967	Jan. 1, 1968	1	USC	14		O.J. Simpson, USC, TB	102,946
		4	Indiana	3			
1968	Jan. 1, 1969	1	Ohio State	27	1	Rex Kern, Ohio State, QB	102,063
		2	USC	16	4		
1969	Jan. 1, 1970	5	USC	10	3	Bob Chandler, USC, FL	103,878
		7	Michigan	3	9		
1970	Jan. 1, 1971	12	Stanford	27	8	Jim Plunkett, Stanford, QB	103,839
		2	Ohio State	17	5		
1971	Jan. 1, 1972	16	Stanford	13	10	Don Bunce, Stanford, QB	103,154
		4	Michigan	12	6		
1972	Jan. 1, 1973	1	USC	42	1	Sam Cunningham, USC, FB	106,869
		3	Ohio State	17	9		
1973	Jan. 1, 1974	4	Ohio State	42	2	Cornelius Greene, Ohio State, QB	105,267
		7	USC	21	8		
1974	Jan. 1, 1975	5	USC	18	2	Pat Haden, USC, QB	106,721
		3	Ohio State	17	4	John McKay Jr., USC, SE	
1975	Jan. 1, 1976	11	UCLA	23	5	John Sciarra, UCLA, QB	105,464
		1	Ohio State	10	4		
1976	Jan. 1, 1977	3	USC	14	2	Vince Evans, USC, QB	106,182
		2	Michigan	6	3		
1977	Jan. 2, 1978	13	Washington	27	10	Warren Moon, Washington, QB	105,312
		4	Michigan	20	9		
1978	Jan. 1, 1979	3	USC	17	2	Charles White, USC, TB	105,629
		5	Michigan	10	5	Rick Leach, Michigan, QB	
1979	Jan. 1, 1980	3	USC	17	2	Charles White, USC, TB	105,526
		1	Ohio State	16	4		
1980	Jan. 1, 1981	5	Michigan	23	4	Butch Woolfolk, Michigan, RB	104,863
		16	Washington	6	16		
1981	Jan. 1, 1982	12	Washington	28	10	Jacque Robinson, Washington, RB	105,611
		13	Iowa	0	18		
1982	Jan. 1, 1983	5	UCLA	24	5	Don Rogers, UCLA, FS	104,991
		19	Michigan	14		Tom Ramsey, UCLA, QB	
1983	Jan. 2, 1984		UCLA	45	17	Rick Neuheisel, UCLA, QB	103,217
		4	Illinois	9	10		
1984	Jan. 1, 1985	18	USC	20	10	Tim Green, USC, QB	102,594
		6	Ohio State	17	13	Jack Del Rio, USC, LB	
1985	Jan. 1, 1986	13	UCLA	45	7	Eric Ball, UCLA, TB	103,292
		4	Iowa	28	10		
1986	Jan. 1, 1987	7	Arizona State	22	4	Jeff Van Raaphorst, Arizona State, QB	103,168
		4	Michigan	15	8		
1987	Jan. 1, 1988	8	Michigan State	20	8	Percy Snow, Michigan State, LB	103,847
		16	USC	17	18		
1988	Jan. 2, 1989	11	Michigan	22	4	Leroy Hoard, Michigan, FB	101,688
		5	USC	14	7		
1989	Jan. 1, 1990	12	USC	17	8	Ricky Ervins, USC, TB	103,450
		3	Michigan	10	7		
1990	Jan. 1, 1991	8	Washington	46	2	Mark Brunell, Washington, QB	101,273
		17	Iowa	34	18		

SEASON	DATE	PRE-GAME RANK	TEAMS	SCORE	FINAL RANK	MOST VALUABLE PLAYER(S)	ATT.
1991	Jan. 1, 1992	2	Washington	34	2	Steve Emtman, Washington, DT	103,566
		4	Michigan	14	6	Billy Joe Hobert, Washington, QB	
1992	Jan. 1, 1993	7	Michigan	38	5	Tyrone Wheatley, Michigan, RB	94,236
		9	Washington	31	11		
1993	Jan. 1, 1994	9	Wisconsin	21	6	Brent Moss, Wisconsin, TB	101,237
		14	UCLA	16	18		
1994	Jan. 2, 1995	2	Penn State	38	2	Danny O'Neil, Oregon, QB	102,247
		12	Oregon	20	11	Ki-Jana Carter, Penn State, RB	
1995	Jan. 1, 1996	17	USC	41	12	Keyshawn Johnson, USC, WR	100,102
		3	Northwestern	32	8		
1996	Jan. 1, 1997	4	Ohio State	20	2	Joe Germaine, Ohio State, QB	100,635
		2	Arizona State	17	4		
1997	Jan. 1, 1998	1	Michigan	21	1	Brian Griese, Michigan, QB	101,219
		8	Washington State	16	9		
1998	Jan. 1, 1999	9	Wisconsin	38	6	Ron Dayne, Wisconsin, RB	93,872
		6	UCLA	31	8		
1999	Jan. 1, 2000	4	Wisconsin	17	4	Ron Dayne, Wisconsin, RB	93,731
		22	Stanford	9			
2000	Jan. 1, 2001	4	Washington	34	3	Marques Tuiasosopo, Washington, QB	94,392
		14	Purdue	24	13		
2003	Jan. 1, 2004	1	USC	28	1	Matt Leinart, USC, QB	93,849
		4	Michigan	14	6		
2004	Jan. 1, 2005	6	Texas	38	5	Vince Young, Texas, QB	93,465
		13	Michigan	37	14		
2006	Jan. 1, 2007	8	USC	32	4	Dwayne Jarrett, USC, WR	93,852
		3	Michigan	18	8	Brian Cushing, USC, LB	

JANUARY 1, 1902
MICHIGAN 49, STANFORD 0

	1ST	2ND	3RD	4TH	FINAL
MICH	0	17	0	32	49
STAN	0	0	0	0	0

SCORING SUMMARY
MICH	FG Sweely 20
MICH	Redden 25 punt return (Short kick)
MICH	Snow 2 run (kick failed)
MICH	Redden 25 fumble return (Short kick)
MICH	Snow 8 run (kick failed)
MICH	Snow 17 run (kick failed)
MICH	Snow 4 run (Short kick)
MICH	Herrenstein 21 run (kick failed)

MICH	TEAM STATISTICS	STAN
27	First Downs	5
527	Rushing Yards	67
21-38.9	Punts - Average	16-34.9
1	Fumbles Lost	9
10	Penalty Yards	15

JANUARY 1, 1921
CALIFORNIA 28, OHIO STATE 0

	1ST	2ND	3RD	4TH	FINAL
CAL	7	14	0	7	28
OSU	0	0	0	0	0

SCORING SUMMARY
CAL	Sprott 1 run (Toomey kick)
CAL	Stephens 37 pass from Muller (Toomey kick)
CAL	Sprott 5 run (Erb kick)
CAL	Deeds 1 run (Toomey kick)

CAL	TEAM STATISTICS	OSU
17	First Downs	11
244	Rushing Yards	105
6-9-1	Passing	11-24-4
102	Passing Yards	133
346	Total Yards	238
10-37.6	Punts - Average	7-43.3
52	Penalty Yards	0

INDIVIDUAL LEADERS
RUSHING
CAL: Sprott 20-94, 2 TD; Toomey 7-61.
OSU: Stinchcomb 11-82; Blair 6-11.

JANUARY 1, 1923
USC 14, PENN STATE 3

	1ST	2ND	3RD	4TH	FINAL
USC	0	7	7	0	14
PSU	3	0	0	0	3

SCORING SUMMARY
PSU	FG Palm 20
USC	Campbell 1 run (Hawkins kick)
USC	Baker 1 run (Hawkins kick)

USC	TEAM STATISTICS	PSU
13	First Downs	5
254	Rushing Yards	98
6-12-1	Passing	5-11-3
39	Passing Yards	6
293	Total Yards	104
6-1	Fumbles - Lost	2-1
3-35	Penalties - Yards	2-10

INDIVIDUAL LEADERS
RUSHING
USC: Baker 29-123, 1 TD; Campbell 17-52, 1 TD.
PSU: Wilson 20-55; Palm 16-25.
PASSING
USC: Galloway 1-3-1, 23 yards.
PSU: Wilson 2-5-0, 5 yards.
RECEIVING
USC: Pythian 1-23; Campbell 2-8.
PSU: Palm 2-5; Wilson 3-1.

JANUARY 1, 1947
ILLINOIS 45, UCLA 14

	1ST	2ND	3RD	4TH	FINAL
ILL	6	19	0	20	45
UCLA	7	7	0	0	14

SCORING SUMMARY
ILL	Rykovich 1 run (kick failed)
UCLA	Case 1 run (Case kick)
ILL	Young 2 run (Maechtle kick)
ILL	Patterson 4 run (kick failed)
ILL	Moss 1 run (kick blocked)
UCLA	Hoisch 100 kick return (Case kick)
ILL	Young 1 run (Maechtle kick)
ILL	Steger 68 interception return (kick failed)
ILL	Green 81 interception return (Maechtle kick)

ILL	TEAM STATISTICS	UCLA
23	First Downs	12
320	Rushing Yards	62
4-15-2	Passing	13-29-4
78	Passing Yards	176
398	Total Yards	238

INDIVIDUAL LEADERS
RUSHING
ILL: Young 20-103, 2 TD; Rykovich 18-103, 1 TD.
UCLA: Hoisch 4-27; Rossi 10-25.
PASSING
ILL: Moss 3-8-0, 85 yards.
UCLA: Case 11-24-2, 165 yards.
RECEIVING
ILL: Rykovich 1-44; Huber 2-21.
UCLA: Baldwin 3-57; Dobrow 2-28.

JANUARY 1, 1948
MICHIGAN 49, USC 0

	1ST	2ND	3RD	4TH	FINAL
MICH	7	14	7	21	49
USC	0	0	0	0	0

SCORING SUMMARY
MICH	Weisenburger 1 run (Brieske kick)
MICH	Weisenburger 1 run (Brieske kick)
MICH	Elliott 11 pass from Chappuis (Brieske kick)
MICH	Yerges 18 pass from Chappuis (Brieske kick)
MICH	Weisenburger 1 run (Brieske kick)
MICH	Derricotte 45 pass from Fonde (Brieske kick)
MICH	Rifenburg 29 pass from Yerges (Brieske kick)

MICH	TEAM STATISTICS	USC
21	First Downs	10
268	Rushing Yards	91
17-27-1	Passing	6-11-1
223	Passing Yards	42
491	Total Yards	133
4-38.3	Punts - Average	8-43.8
2-1	Fumbles - Lost	4-2
4-40	Penalties - Yards	1-10

INDIVIDUAL LEADERS
RUSHING
MICH: Weisenburger 20-91, 3 TD; Chappuis 13-91.
USC: Garlin 5-25.
PASSING
MICH: Chappuis 14-24-0, 139 yards, 2 TD.
USC: Powers 4-5-0, 22 yards.

JANUARY 1, 1949
NORTHWESTERN 20, CALIFORNIA 14

	1ST	2ND	3RD	4TH	FINAL
NU	7	6	0	7	20
CAL	7	0	7	0	14

SCORING SUMMARY
NU	Aschenbrenner 73 run (Farrar kick)
CAL	Jensen 67 run (Cullom kick)
NU	Marakowski 1 run (kick failed)
CAL	Swaner run (Cullom kick)
NU	Tunnicliff 43 run (Farrar kick)

NU	TEAM STATISTICS	CAL
6	First Downs	12
273	Rushing Yards	173
1-4-0	Passing	6-16-4
17	Passing Yards	83
290	Total Yards	256
6-43.0	Punts - Average	4-33.0
3-2	Fumbles - Lost	3-1
3-15	Penalties - Yards	2-5

INDIVIDUAL LEADERS
RUSHING
NU: Aschenbrenner 11-119, 1 TD.
CAL: Swaner 17-79, 1 TD.
PASSING
NU: Aschenbrenner 1-1-0, 17 yards.
CAL: Celeri 3-8-2, 50 yards.

*Played as an independent or with other conference affiliation

JANUARY 2, 1950
Ohio State 17, California 14

	1st	2nd	3rd	4th	FINAL
CAL	0	7	7	0	14
OSU	0	0	14	3	17

CAL	TEAM STATISTICS	OSU
11	First Downs	19
133	Rushing Yards	221
3-13-4	Passing	4-13-1
106	Passing Yards	34
239	Total Yards	255
5-25.4	Punts - Average	4-39.8
0-0	Fumbles - Lost	4-1
9-45	Penalties - Yards	7-50

INDIVIDUAL LEADERS
RUSHING
CAL: Monachino 14-90; Brunk 9-38.
OSU: Morrison 24-127; Krall 24-50.
PASSING
CAL: Celeri 3-11-3, 106 yards.
OSU: Krall 3-8-0, 20 yards.

JANUARY 1, 1951
Michigan 14, California 6

	1st	2nd	3rd	4th	FINAL
MICH	0	0	0	14	14
CAL	0	6	0	0	6

SCORING SUMMARY
CAL Cummings 39 pass from Marinos (kick failed)
MICH Dufek 1 run (Allis kick)
MICH Dufek 7 run (Allis kick)

MICH	TEAM STATISTICS	CAL
17	First Downs	12
145	Rushing Yards	175
15-21-2	Passing	4-8-0
146	Passing Yards	69
291	Total Yards	244
2-32.5	Punts - Average	4-35.7
2-2	Fumbles - Lost	2-2
2-20	Penalties - Yards	6-50

INDIVIDUAL LEADERS
RUSHING
MICH: Dufek 23-113, 2 TD; Koceski 7-19.
CAL: Olszewski 16-58; Schabarum 15-57.
PASSING
MICH: Ortmann 15-19-1, 146 yards.
CAL: Marinos 4-7-0, 69 yards, 1 TD.

JANUARY 1, 1952
Illinois 40, Stanford 7

	1st	2nd	3rd	4th	FINAL
ILL	6	0	7	27	40
STAN	7	0	0	0	7

SCORING SUMMARY
ILL Bachourus 6 run (kick failed)
STAN Hugasian 1 run (Kerkorian kick)
ILL Tate 5 run (Rebecca kick)
ILL Karras 8 run (Rebecca kick)
ILL Tate 8 run (Rebecca kick)
ILL Stevens 7 run (kick blocked)
ILL Ryan 6 pass from Engels (Rebecca kick)

ILL	TEAM STATISTICS	STAN
19	First Downs	16
361	Rushing Yards	53
7-15-1	Passing	14-29-3
73	Passing Yards	180
434	Total Yards	233
2-10	Punt Returns - Yards	0-0
2-28	Kickoff Returns - Yards	7-88
2-50.1	Punts - Average	6-30.3
0-0	Fumbles - Lost	2-0
4-43	Penalties - Yards	6-50

INDIVIDUAL LEADERS
RUSHING
ILL: Tate 20-150, 2 TD; Bachouros 15-86.
STAN: Hugasian 14-41, 1 TD.
PASSING
ILL: O'Connell 6-14-1, 67yards.
STAN: Kerkorian 11-22-2, 166 yards.
RECEIVING
ILL: Bachouros 3-36.
STAN: McColl 4-62; Hugasian 4-49.

JANUARY 1, 1953
USC 7, Wisconsin 0

	1st	2nd	3rd	4th	FINAL
WISC	0	0	0	0	0
USC	0	0	7	0	7

SCORING SUMMARY
USC Carmichael 22 pass from Bukich (Tsagalakis kick)

WISC	TEAM STATISTICS	USC
19	First Downs	16
211	Rushing Yards	48
11-26-2	Passing	18-27-2
142	Passing Yards	185
353	Total Yards	233
5-39.2	Punts - Average	8-51.4
2-1	Fumbles - Lost	1-0
2-20	Penalties - Yards	6-62

INDIVIDUAL LEADERS
RUSHING
WISC: Ameche 28-133; Witt 10-47.
USC: Haw 6-28; Dandoy 5-18.
PASSING
WISC: Haluska 11-26-2, 142 yards.
USC: Bukich 12-20-2, 137, yards, 1 TD.
RECEIVING
WISC: Witt 2-46; Andrykowski 3-32.
USC: Nickoloff 7-73; Stillwell 3-35.

JANUARY 1, 1954
Michigan State 28, UCLA 20

	1st	2nd	3rd	4th	FINAL
MSU	0	7	14	7	28
UCLA	7	7	0	6	20

SCORING SUMMARY
UCLA Stits 13 pass from Cameron (Hermann kick)
UCLA Cameron 2 run (Hermann kick)
MSU Duckett 6 blocked punt return (Slonac kick)
MSU Bolden 1 run (Slonac kick)
MSU Wells 2 run (Slonac kick)
UCLA Loudd 28 pass from Cameron (kick failed)
MSU Wells 62 punt return (Slonac kick)

MSU	TEAM STATISTICS	UCLA
14	First Downs	16
195	Rushing Yards	90
2-10-1	Passing	9-24-2
11	Passing Yards	152
206	Total Yards	242
5-80	Punt Returns - Yards	3-31
4-60	Kickoff Returns - Yards	4-100
5-35.4	Punts - Average	6-38.7
4-4	Fumbles - Lost	4-3
2-15	Penalties - Yards	4-30

INDIVIDUAL LEADERS
RUSHING
MSU: Wells 14-80-1; Bolden 14-52, 1 TD.
UCLA: Stits 5-25; Davenport 8-22.
PASSING
MSU: Yewcic 2-8-1, 11 yards.
UCLA: Cameron 9-22-1, 152 yards, 2 TD.
RECEIVING
MSU: Bolden 1-18.
UCLA: Stits 2-46, 1 TD; Heydenfeldt 1-33.

JANUARY 1, 1955
Ohio State 20, USC 7

	1st	2nd	3rd	4th	FINAL
USC	0	7	0	0	7
OSU	0	14	0	6	20

SCORING SUMMARY
OSU Leggett 3 run (Weed kick)
OSU Watkins 21 pass from Leggett (Watkins good)
USC Dandoy 86 punt return
OSU Harkrader 9 run

USC	TEAM STATISTICS	OSU
6	First Downs	22
177	Rushing Yards	295
3-8-0	Passing	6-11-1
29	Passing Yards	63
206	Total Yards	358
5-46.4	Punts - Average	4-38.2
3	Fumbles Lost	3
60	Penalty Yards	40

INDIVIDUAL LEADERS
RUSHING
USC: Arnett 9-123; Duvall 5-23.
OSU: Cassady 21-92; Leggett 16-67, 1 TD.
PASSING
USC: Hall 1-4-0, 23 yards.
OSU: Leggett 6-11-1, 63 yards, 1 TD.
RECEIVING
USC: Bordier 1-23.
OSU: Watkins 3-43.

JANUARY 2, 1956
Michigan State 17, UCLA 14

	1st	2nd	3rd	4th	FINAL
MSU	0	7	0	10	17
UCLA	7	0	0	7	14

SCORING SUMMARY
UCLA Davenport 2 run (Decker kick)
MSU Peaks 13 pass from Morrall (Planutis kick)
MSU Lewis 67 yard pass from Peaks (Planutis kick)
UCLA Peters 1 run (Decker kick)
MSU FG Kaiser 41

MSU	TEAM STATISTICS	UCLA
18	First Downs	13
251	Rushing Yards	136
6-18-2	Passing	2-10-2
130	Passing Yards	61
381	Total Yards	197
6-8	Punt Returns - Yards	2-12
3-61	Kickoff Returns - Yards	2-58
2-40.0	Punts - Average	7-39.6
4-1	Fumbles - Lost	2-0
10-98	Penalties - Yards	8-60

INDIVIDUAL LEADERS
RUSHING
MSU: Kowalczyk 13-88; Planutis 12-66.
UCLA: Brown 14-63; Davenport 10-26, 1 TD.
PASSING
MSU: Morrall 4-15-2, 38 yards, 1 TD.
UCLA: Knox 2-8-1, 61 yards.
RECEIVING
MSU: Lewis 1-67, 1 TD; Peaks 3-40, 1 TD.
UCLA: Decker 1-47; Loudd 1-14.

JANUARY 1, 1957
Iowa 35, Oregon State 19

	1st	2nd	3rd	4th	FINAL
IA	14	7	7	7	35
OSU	0	6	6	7	19

SCORING SUMMARY
IA Ploen 49 run (Prescott kick)
IA Hagler 9 run (Prescott kick)
OSU Berry 3 run (kick failed)
IA Happel 5 run (Prescott kick)
IA Hagler 66 run (Prescott kick)
OSU Beamer 1 run (kick failed)
IA Gibbons 16 pass from Ploen (Prescott kick)
OSU Hammack 35 pass from Francis (Beamer run)

IA	TEAM STATISTICS	OSU
16	First Downs	16
301	Rushing Yards	166
11-15-1	Passing	10-14-0
107	Passing Yards	130
408	Total Yards	296
2-36.0	Punts - Average	3-35.0
3-3	Fumbles - Lost	4-3
5-50	Penalties - Yards	6-60

INDIVIDUAL LEADERS
RUSHING
IA: Hagler 10-85, 2 TD; Dobrino 4-64.
OSU: Francis 15-73; Beamer 7-31, 1 TD.
PASSING
IA: Ploen 9-10-0, 83 yards, 1 TD.
OSU: Francis 10-12-0, 130 yards, 1 TD.
RECEIVING
IA: Gibbons 5-61, 1 TD; Harris 2-21.
OSU: Hammack 4-65, 1 TD; Beamer 2-31.

JANUARY 1, 1958
Ohio State 10, Oregon 7

	1st	2nd	3rd	4th	FINAL
ORE	0	7	0	0	7
OSU	7	0	0	3	10

SCORING SUMMARY
OSU Kremblas 1 run (Kremblas kick)
ORE Shanley 5 run (Morris kick)
OSU FG Sutherlin 34

ORE	TEAM STATISTICS	OSU
21	First Downs	19
160	Rushing Yards	245
14-21-2	Passing	2-6-0
191	Passing Yards	59
351	Total Yards	304
0-0	Punts - Average	2-19.0
3-2	Fumbles - Lost	0-0
3-25	Penalties - Yards	3-15

INDIVIDUAL LEADERS
RUSHING
ORE: Morris 11-60; Shanley 11-59, 1 TD.
OSU: White 25-93; Clark 14-82.
PASSING
ORE: Crabtree 10-17-2, 135 yards.
OSU: Kremblas 2-6-0, 59 yards.
RECEIVING
ORE: Stover 10-144; Tourville 2-27.
OSU: Houston 2-59.

JANUARY 1, 1959
Iowa 38, California 12

	1ST	2ND	3RD	4TH	FINAL
IA	7	13	12	6	38
CAL	0	0	6	6	12

SCORING SUMMARY

IA	Duncan 2 run (Prescott kick)
IA	Langston 7 pass from Duncan (Prescott kick)
IA	Horn 4 run (kick failed)
CAL	Hart 1 run (pass failed)
IA	Fleming 37 run (pass failed)
IA	Jeter 81 run (pass failed)
IA	Fleming 7 run (pass failed)
CAL	Hart 17 pass from Kapp (run failed)

IA	TEAM STATISTICS	CAL
24	First Downs	20
429	Rushing Yards	214
9-14-0	Passing	9-20-2
87	Passing Yards	130
516	Total Yards	344
3-41.0	Punts - Average	5-37.0
3-1	Fumbles - Lost	2-2
5-55	Penalties - Yards	5-35

INDIVIDUAL LEADERS

RUSHING
IA: Jeter 9-194, 1 TD; Fleming 9-85, 2 TD.
CAL: Olguin 9-62; Patton 9-45.

PASSING
IA: Ogiego 4-5-0, 37 yards.
CAL: Kapp 8-17-1, 126 yards, 1 TD.

RECEIVING
IA: Prescott 3-31.
CAL: Hart 4-61, 1TD; Garvin 1-31.

JANUARY 1, 1960
Washington 44, Wisconsin 8

	1ST	2ND	3RD	4TH	FINAL
WISC	0	8	0	0	8
WASH	17	7	7	13	44

SCORING SUMMARY

WASH	McKeta 6 run (Fleming kick)
WASH	FG Fleming 36
WASH	Fleming 53 punt return (Fleming kick)
WISC	Wiesner 4 run (Schoonover pass from Hackbart)
WASH	Folkins 23 pass from Schloredt (Fleming kick)
WASH	Jackson 2 run (Fleming kick)
WASH	Schloredt 3 run (Fleming kick)
WASH	Millich 1 pass from Hivner (pass failed)

WISC	TEAM STATISTICS	WASH
13	First Downs	16
123	Rushing Yards	215
14-32-0	Passing	7-13-0
153	Passing Yards	137
276	Total Yards	352
6-36.8	Punts - Average	6-36.0
4-4	Fumbles - Lost	2-0
3-18	Penalties - Yards	7-85

INDIVIDUAL LEADERS

RUSHING
WISC: Hobbs 7-32.
WASH: Schloredt 21-81, 1 TD; Jackson 12-61, 1 TD.

PASSING
WISC: Hackbart 11-25-0, 145 yards.
WASH: Schloredt 4-7-0, 102 yards, 1 TD.

RECEIVING
WISC: Schoonover 3-57.
WASH: Fleming 1-65.

JANUARY 2, 1961
Washington 17, Minnesota 7

	1ST	2ND	3RD	4TH	FINAL
WASH	3	14	0	0	17
MINN	0	0	7	0	7

SCORING SUMMARY

WASH	FG Fleming 34
WASH	Wooten 4 pass from Schloredt (Fleming kick)
WASH	Schloredt 1 run (Fleming kick)
MINN	Munsey 18 run (Rogers kick)

WASH	TEAM STATISTICS	MINN
11	First Downs	14
177	Rushing Yards	202
2-5-0	Passing	5-18-3
16	Passing Yards	51
193	Total Yards	253
3-2	Fumbles - Lost	0-0
6-50	Penalties - Yards	3-35

INDIVIDUAL LEADERS

RUSHING
WASH: Schloredt 5-68, 1 TD; Jackson 13-60.
MINN: Stephens 10-51; Hagberg 11-44.

PASSING
WASH: Schloredt 2-4-0, 16 yards, 1 TD.
MINN: Stephens 2-10-3, 21 yards.

RECEIVING
WASH: Jackson 1-12; Wooten 1-4, 1 TD.
MINN: Hagberg 1-18; Hall 1-15.

JANUARY 1, 1962
Minnesota 21, UCLA 3

	1ST	2ND	3RD	4TH	FINAL
MINN	7	7	0	7	21
UCLA	3	0	0	0	3

SCORING SUMMARY

UCLA	FG Smith 28
MINN	Stephens 1 run (Loechler kick)
MINN	Munsey 3 run (Loechler kick)
MINN	Stephens 2 run (Loechler kick)

MINN	TEAM STATISTICS	UCLA
21	First Downs	8
222	Rushing Yards	55
7-11-0	Passing	5-8-0
75	Passing Yards	52
297	Total Yards	107
3-2	Fumbles - Lost	2-2
6-70	Penalties - Yards	1-5

INDIVIDUAL LEADERS

RUSHING
MINN: Stephens 12-46, 2 TD; Dickson 12-45.
UCLA: Alexander 10-48.

PASSING
MINN: Stephens 7-11-0, 75 yards.
UCLA: Smith 2-5-0, 22 yards.

RECEIVING
MINN: Cairns 2-24.
UCLA: Alexander 3-26.

JANUARY 1, 1963
USC 42, Wisconsin 37

	1ST	2ND	3RD	4TH	FINAL
WISC	7	0	7	23	37
USC	7	14	14	7	42

SCORING SUMMARY

USC	Butcher 13 pass from Beathard (Lupo kick)
WISC	Kurek 1 run (Kroner kick)
USC	Wilson 1 run (Lupo kick)
USC	Heller 25 run (Lupo kick)
USC	Bedsole 57 pass from Beathard (Lupo kick)
WISC	Vander Kelen 17 run (Kroner kick)
USC	Bedsole 23 pass from Beathard (Lupo kick)
USC	Hill 13 pass from Beathard (Lupo Kick)
WISC	Holland 13 run (Kroner kick)
WISC	Kroner 4 pass from Vander Kelen (Kroner kick)
WISC	Safety
WISC	Richter 18 pass from Vander Kelen (Kroner kick)

WISC	TEAM STATISTICS	USC
32	First Downs	15
67	Rushing Yards	114
34-49-3	Passing	10-20-0
419	Passing Yards	253
486	Total Yards	367
4-40.3	Punts - Average	5-40.4
6-0	Fumbles - Lost	2-2
7-77	Penalties - Yards	12-93

INDIVIDUAL LEADERS

RUSHING
WISC: Vander Kelen 9-30, 1 TD; Holland 4-27, 1 TD.
USC: Wilson 17-57, 1 TD; Heller 4-32, 1 TD.

PASSING
WISC: Vander Kelen 33-48-3, 401 yards, 2 TD.
USC: Beathard 8-12-0, 190 yards, 4 TD.

RECEIVING
WISC: Richter 11-163, 1 TD; Holland 8-72.
USC: Brown 3-108; Bedsole 4-101, 2 TD.

JANUARY 1, 1964
Illinois 17, Washington 7

	1ST	2ND	3RD	4TH	FINAL
ILL	0	3	7	7	17
WASH	0	7	0	0	7

SCORING SUMMARY

WASH	Kopay 7 run (Medved kick)
ILL	FG Plankenhorn 32
ILL	Warren 2 run (Plankenhorn kick)
ILL	Grabowski 10 run (Plankenhorn kick)

ILL	TEAM STATISTICS	WASH
22	First Downs	12
291	Rushing Yards	114
6-15-0	Passing	8-19-3
59	Passing Yards	69
350	Total Yards	183
5-3	Fumbles - Lost	5-3
6-64	Penalties - Yards	5-25

INDIVIDUAL LEADERS

RUSHING
ILL : Grabowski 23-125, 1 TD; Price 10-55.
WASH: Kopay 4-29, 1TD.

PASSING
ILL : Custardo 4-7-0, 43 yards.
WASH: Siler 6-17-3, 46 yards.

RECEIVING
ILL: Fearn 3-24.
WASH: Libke 3-19.

JANUARY 1, 1965
Michigan 34, Oregon State 7

	1ST	2ND	3RD	4TH	FINAL
MICH	0	12	15	7	34
OSU	0	7	0	0	7

SCORING SUMMARY

OSU	McDougal 5 pass from Brothers (Clark kick)
MICH	Anthony 84 run (kick failed)
MICH	Ward 43 run (pass failed)
MICH	Anthony 1 run (Timberlake run)
MICH	Anthony 7 run (Timberlake kick)
MICH	Timberlake 24 run (Timberlake kick)

MICH	TEAM STATISTICS	OSU
18	First Downs	14
332	Rushing Yards	64
8-11-0	Passing	19-33-0
83	Passing Yards	179
415	Total Yards	243
5-33.6	Punts - Average	9-43.5
2-1	Fumbles - Lost	1-1
6-55	Penalties - Yards	5-57

INDIVIDUAL LEADERS

RUSHING
MICH: Anthony 13-123, 3 TD; Ward 10-88, 1 TD.
OSU: Shaw 4-28; Watkins 8-24.

PASSING
MICH: Timberlake 7-10-0, 77 yards.
OSU: Brothers 9-17-0, 89 yards, 1 TD; Queen 10-16-0, 90 yards.

RECEIVING
MICH: Henderson 4-34; Defuller 1-30.
OSU: Watkins 3-43; Grim 3-42.

JANUARY 1, 1966
UCLA 14, Michigan State 12

	1ST	2ND	3RD	4TH	FINAL
MSU	0	0	0	12	12
UCLA	0	14	0	0	14

SCORING SUMMARY

UCLA	Beban 1 run (Zimmerman kick)
UCLA	Beban 1 run (Zimmerman kick)
MSU	Apisa 38 run (pass failed)
MSU	Juday 1 run (run failed)

MSU	TEAM STATISTICS	UCLA
13	First Downs	10
204	Rushing Yards	65
8-22-3	Passing	8-20-0
110	Passing Yards	147
314	Total Yards	212
4-3	Punt Returns - Yards	2-2
2-23	Kickoff Returns - Yards	3-49
5-42.4	Punts - Average	11-39.9
3-2	Fumbles - Lost	3-2
1-14	Penalties - Yards	9-06

INDIVIDUAL LEADERS

RUSHING
MSU: Jones 20-113; Apisa 4-49, 1 TD.
UCLA: Farr 10-36; Beban 25-14, 2 TD.

PASSING
MSU: Steve Juday 6-18-3, 80 yards.
UCLA: Gary Beban 8-20-0, 147 yards.

RECEIVING
MSU: Washington 4-81; Lee 3-23.
UCLA: Altenberg 3-55; Nelson 2-29.

JANUARY 2, 1967
Purdue 14, USC 13

	1ST	2ND	3RD	4TH	FINAL
PU	0	7	7	0	14
USC	0	7	0	6	13

SCORING SUMMARY

PU	Williams 1 run (Griese kick)
USC	McCall 1 run (Russovich kick)
PU	Williams 2 run (Griese kick)
USC	Sherman 19 pass from Winslow (pass failed)

PU	TEAM STATISTICS	USC
11	First Downs	18
105	Rushing Yards	149
10-18-0	Passing	12-17-0
139	Passing Yards	174
244	Total Yards	323
4-38.75	Punts - Average	3-34.00
1-1	Fumbles - Lost	2-2
2-10	Penalties - Yards	2-16

INDIVIDUAL LEADERS

RUSHING
PU: Williams 20-61, 2 TD; Baltzell 11-25.
USC: McCall 22-92, 1 TD; Hull 7-53.

PASSING
PU: Griese 10-18-0, 139 yards.
USC: Winslow 12-17-0, 174 yards, 1 TD.

RECEIVING
PU: Beirne 4-69; Hurst 2-27.
USC: Sherman 7-102, 1 TD; Lawrence 3-52.

USC 14, Indiana 3
JANUARY 1, 1968

	1ST	2ND	3RD	4TH	FINAL
IND	0	3	0	0	3
USC	7	0	7	0	14

SCORING SUMMARY
USC Simpson 2 run (Aldridge kick)
IND FG Koronwa 17
USC Simpson 3 run (Aldridge kick)

IND	TEAM STATISTICS	USC
13	First Downs	20
79	Rushing Yards	248
9-25-1	Passing	5-9-1
110	Passing Yards	69
189	Total Yards	317
4-41.0	Punts - Average	4-41.3
2-1	Fumbles - Lost	3-1
4-29	Penalties - Yards	8-65

INDIVIDUAL LEADERS
RUSHING
IND: Isenbarger 12-38; Cole 10-21.
USC: Simpson 25-128, 2 TD; Scott 18-85.
PASSING
IND: Gonso 9-25-1, 110 yards.
USC: Sogge 4-7-1, 57 yards.
RECEIVING
IND: Gage 6-67; Butcher 3-43.
USC: Rake 3-46.

Ohio State 27, USC 16
JANUARY 1, 1969

	1ST	2ND	3RD	4TH	FINAL
OSU	0	10	3	14	27
USC	0	10	0	6	16

SCORING SUMMARY
USC FG Ayala 21
USC Simpson 80 run (Ayala kick)
OSU Otis 1 run (Roman kick)
OSU FG Roman 26
OSU FG Roman 25
OSU Hayden 4 pass from Kern (Roman kick)
OSU Gillian 16 pass from Kern (Roman kick)
USC Dickerson 19 pass from Sogge (pass failed)

OSU	TEAM STATISTICS	USC
21	First Downs	19
260	Rushing Yards	177
9-15-0	Passing	19-32-2
101	Passing Yards	189
361	Total Yards	366
7-45.6	Punts - Average	6-36.9
1-0	Fumbles - Lost	3-3
6-53	Penalties - Yards	3-51

INDIVIDUAL LEADERS
RUSHING
OSU: Otis 30-101, 1 TD; Hayden 15-90.
USC: Simpson 28-171, 1 TD.
PASSING
OSU: Kern 9-15-0, 101 yards, 2 TD.
USC: Sogge 19-30-1, 189 yards, 1 TD.
RECEIVING
OSU: Gillian 4-69, 1 TD; White 1-17.
USC: Simpson 8-85; Dickerson 3-50, 1 TD.

USC 10, Michigan 3
JANUARY 1, 1970

	1ST	2ND	3RD	4TH	FINAL
USC	3	0	7	0	10
MICH	0	3	0	0	3

SCORING SUMMARY
USC FG Ayala 25
MICH FG Killian 20
USC Chandler 33 pass from Jones (Ayala kick)

USC	TEAM STATISTICS	MICH
16	First Downs	20
195	Rushing Yards	162
10-17-0	Passing	14-32-1
128	Passing Yards	127
323	Total Yards	289
5-40.6	Punts - Average	6-36.2
2-0	Fumbles - Lost	1-0
6-38	Penalties - Yards	2-20

INDIVIDUAL LEADERS
RUSHING
USC: Davis 15-76; Berry 23-65.
MICH: Moorhead 18-60; Taylor 18-56.
PASSING
USC: Jones 10-17-0, 128 yards, 1 TD.
MICH: Moorhead 14-32-1, 127 yards.
RECEIVING
USC: Chandler 3-78, 1 TD; Debrah 3-27.
MICH: Mandich 8-79; Oldham 2-19.

Stanford 27, Ohio State 17
JANUARY 1, 1971

	1ST	2ND	3RD	4TH	FINAL
STAN	10	0	3	14	27
OSU	7	7	3	0	17

SCORING SUMMARY
STAN Brown 4 run (Horowitz kick)
STAN FG Horowitz 37
OSU Brockington 1 run (Schram kick)
OSU Brockington 1 run (Schram kick)
STAN FG Horowitz 48
OSU FG Schram 32
STAN Brown 1 run (Horowitz kick)
STAN Vataha 10 pass from Plunkett (Horowitz kick)

STAN	TEAM STATISTICS	OSU
21	First Downs	22
143	Rushing Yards	380
20-30-1	Passing	7-20-1
265	Passing Yards	75
408	Total Yards	455
3-33	Punts - Average	2-28
3-2	Fumbles - Lost	2-0
3-46	Penalties - Yards	6-64

INDIVIDUAL LEADERS
RUSHING
STAN: Brown 10-41, 2 TD; Cross 1-41.
OSU: Kern 20-129; Brockington 21-101, 2 TD.
PASSING
STAN: Plunkett 20-30-1, 265 yards, 1 TD.
OSU: Kern 4-13-1, 40 yards.
RECEIVING
STAN: Moore 5-113; Washington 6-80.
OSU: White 4-28; Zelina 2-27.

Stanford 13, Michigan 12
JANUARY 1, 1972

	1ST	2ND	3RD	4TH	FINAL
STAN	0	0	3	10	13
MICH	0	3	0	9	12

SCORING SUMMARY
MICH FG Coin 30
STAN FG Garcia 42
MICH Seyferth 1 run (Coin kick)
STAN Brown 24 run (Garcia kick)
MICH Safety
STAN FG Garcia 31

STAN	TEAM STATISTICS	MICH
22	First Downs	16
93	Rushing Yards	264
24-44-0	Passing	3-11-1
290	Passing Yards	26
383	Total Yards	290
4-30	Punt Returns - Yards	2-14
3-35	Kickoff Returns - Yards	5-108
4-41.5	Punts - Average	7-38.9
4-4	Fumbles - Lost	2-1
3-14	Penalties - Yards	2-23

INDIVIDUAL LEADERS
RUSHING
STAN: Brown 6-60, 1 TD; Sanderson 5-16.
MICH: Taylor 32-82; Shuttlesworth 13-62.
PASSING
STAN: Bunce 24-44-0, 290 yards.
MICH: Slade 3-10-1, 26 yards.
RECEIVING
STAN: Winesberry 8-112; Scott 5-55.
MICH: Doughty 2-13; Seymour 1-13.

USC 42, Ohio State 17
JANUARY 1, 1973

	1ST	2ND	3RD	4TH	FINAL
OSU	0	7	3	7	17
USC	7	0	21	14	42

SCORING SUMMARY
USC Swann 10 pass from Rae (Roe kick)
OSU Keith 1 run (Conway kick)
USC Cunningham 2 run (Roe kick)
OSU FG Conway 21
USC Davis 20 run (Roe kick)
USC Cunningham 1 run (Roe kick)
USC Cunningham 1 run (Roe kick)
USC Cunningham 1 run (Roe kick)
OSU Bledsoe 5 run (Conway kick)

OSU	TEAM STATISTICS	USC
21	First Downs	24
285	Rushing Yards	207
5-11-2	Passing	19-27-0
81	Passing Yards	244
366	Total Yards	451
5-36.2	Punts - Average	4-41.3
2-1	Fumbles - Lost	2-1
2-7	Penalties - Yards	6-48

INDIVIDUAL LEADERS
RUSHING
OSU: Griffin 20-95; Keith 15-59, 1 TD.
USC: Davis 23-157, 1 TD; Cunningham 11-38, 4 TD.
PASSING
OSU: Hare 4-8-1, 64 yards.
USC: Rae 18-25-0, 229 yards, 1 TD.
RECEIVING
OSU: Holycross 2-37; Griffin 2-27.
USC: Swann 6-108, 1 TD; Young 6-82.

Ohio State 42, USC 21
JANUARY 1, 1974

	1ST	2ND	3RD	4TH	FINAL
OSU	7	7	13	15	42
USC	3	11	7	0	21

SCORING SUMMARY
USC FG Limahelu 47
OSU Johnson 1 run (Conway kick)
USC FG Limahelu 42
USC McKay 10 pass from Davis (McKay pass from Haden)
OSU Johnson 1 run (Conway kick)
USC Davis 1 run (Limahelu kick)
OSU Johnson 4 run (kick failed)
OSU Greene 1 run (Conway kick)
OSU Elia 2 run (Greene run)
OSU Griffin 47 run (Conway kick)

OSU	TEAM STATISTICS	USC
20	First Downs	27
320	Rushing Yards	167
6-8-1	Passing	22-40-0
129	Passing Yards	239
449	Total Yards	406
2-41.0	Punts - Average	3-36.0
2-1	Fumbles - Lost	2-1
7-59	Penalties - Yards	6-40

INDIVIDUAL LEADERS
RUSHING
OSU: Griffin 22-149, 1 TD; Johnson 21-94, 3 TD.
USC: Davis 16-74, 1 TD; McNeill 8-46.
PASSING
OSU: Greene 6-8-1, 129 yards.
USC: Haden 21-39-0, 229 yards.
RECEIVING
OSU: Pagac 4-89; Bashnagel 1-25.
USC: McKay 6-83, 1 TD; Swann 5-47.

BIG TEN ANNUAL REVIEW & BOWLS

JANUARY 1, 1975
USC 18, OHIO STATE 17

	1ST	2ND	3RD	4TH	FINAL
OSU	0	7	0	10	17
USC	3	0	0	15	18

SCORING SUMMARY
USC   FG Limahelu 30
OSU   Henson 2 run (Klaban kick)
USC   Obradovich 8 pass from Haden (Limahelu kick)
OSU   Greene 3 run (Klaban kick)
OSU   FG Klaban 32
USC   McKay 38 pass from Haden (Diggs pass from Haden)

OSU	TEAM STATISTICS	USC
14	First Downs	24
193	Rushing Yards	280
8-14-1	Passing	12-22-2
93	Passing Yards	181
286	Total Yards	461
3-47.6	Punts - Average	2-14.5
4-2	Fumbles - Lost	2-2
3-25	Penalties - Yards	2-21

INDIVIDUAL LEADERS
RUSHING
OSU: Griffin 20-75; Greene 11-52, 1 TD.
USC: Carter 18-75; Davis 13-67; Farmer 7-67.
PASSING
OSU: Greene 8-14-1, 93 yards.
USC: Haden 12-22-2, 181 yards, 2 TD.
RECEIVING
OSU: France 2-28; Griffin 2-25.
USC: McKay 5-104, 1 TD; Obradovich 4-75, 1 TD.

JANUARY 1, 1976
UCLA 23, OHIO STATE 10

	1ST	2ND	3RD	4TH	FINAL
OSU	3	0	0	7	10
UCLA	0	0	16	7	23

SCORING SUMMARY
OSU   FG Klaban 42
UCLA   FG White 33
UCLA   Henry 16 pass from Sciarra (kick failed)
UCLA   Henry 67 pass from Sciarra (White kick)
OSU   Johnson 3 run (Klaban kick)
UCLA   Tyler 54 run (White kick)

OSU	TEAM STATISTICS	UCLA
20	First Downs	19
208	Rushing Yards	202
7-18-2	Passing	13-19-2
90	Passing Yards	212
298	Total Yards	414
5-47.2	Punts - Average	5-39.4
3-1	Fumbles - Lost	2-1
3-25	Penalties - Yards	4-30

INDIVIDUAL LEADERS
RUSHING
OSU: Griffin 17-93; Johnson 19-70, 1 TD.
UCLA: Tyler 21-172, 1 TD; Ayers 12-36.
PASSING
OSU: Greene 7-18-2, 90 yards.
UCLA: Sciarra 13-19-2, 212 yards, 2 TD.
RECEIVING
OSU: Baschnagel 3-26; Kain 1-19.
UCLA: Henry 5-113, 2 TD; Anderson 3-39.

JANUARY 1, 1977
USC 14, MICHIGAN 6

	1ST	2ND	3RD	4TH	FINAL
MICH	0	6	0	0	6
USC	0	7	0	7	14

SCORING SUMMARY
MICH   Lytle 1 run (kick failed)
USC   Evans 1 run (Walker kick)
USC   White 7 run (Walker kick)

MICH	TEAM STATISTICS	USC
12	First Downs	19
155	Rushing Yards	200
4-12-0	Passing	14-20-1
76	Passing Yards	181
231	Total Yards	381
5-45.0	Punts - Average	3-29.7
4-2	Fumbles - Lost	2-1
24:03	Possession Time	35:57

INDIVIDUAL LEADERS
RUSHING
MICH: Lytle 18-67, 1 TD; Davis 10-39.
USC: White 32-114, 1 TD; Tatupu 7-60.
PASSING
MICH: Leach 4-12-0, 76 yards.
USC: Evans 14-20-1, 181 yards.
RECEIVING
MICH: Smith 2-52; Johnson 2-24.
USC: Diggs 8-98; Robinson 2-42.

JANUARY 2, 1978
WASHINGTON 27, MICHIGAN 20

	1ST	2ND	3RD	4TH	FINAL
MICH	0	0	7	13	20
WASH	7	10	10	0	27

SCORING SUMMARY
WASH   Moon 2 run (Robbins kick)
WASH   FG Robbins 30
WASH   Moon 1 run (Robbins kick)
WASH   Gaines 28 pass from Moon (Robbins kick)
MICH   Stephenson 76 pass from Leach (Willner kick)
WASH   FG Robbins 18
MICH   Davis 2 run (Willner kick)
MICH   Edwards 32 pass from Leach (kick failed)

MICH	TEAM STATISTICS	WASH
22	First Downs	17
149	Rushing Yards	164
14-27-2	Passing	13-24-2
239	Passing Yards	234
388	Total Yards	398
4-42.5	Punts - Average	5-39.0
2-1	Fumbles - Lost	0-0
3-11	Penalties - Yards	6-47

INDIVIDUAL LEADERS
RUSHING
MICH: Davis 18-79, 1 TD; Edwards 15-74.
WASH: Steele 13-77; Gipson 15-48.
PASSING
MICH: Leach 14-27-2, 239 yards, 2 TD.
WASH: Moon 12-23-2, 188 yards, 1 TD.
RECEIVING
MICH: Clayton 5-84; Stephenson 1-76, 1 TD.
WASH: Gaines 4-122, 1 TD; Stevens 1-46.

JANUARY 1, 1979
USC 17, MICHIGAN 10

	1ST	2ND	3RD	4TH	FINAL
MICH	0	3	7	0	10
USC	7	10	0	0	17

SCORING SUMMARY
USC   Brenner 9 pass from McDonald (Jordan kick)
MICH   FG Willner 36
USC   White 3 run (Jordan kick)
USC   FG Jordan 35
MICH   Smith 44 pass from Leach (Willner kick)

MICH	TEAM STATISTICS	USC
12	First Downs	14
99	Rushing Yards	134
10-22-2	Passing	4-9-0
137	Passing Yards	23
236	Total Yards	157
8-29.5	Punts - Average	9-38.6
2-0	Fumbles - Lost	2-1
4-30	Penalties - Yards	2-21

INDIVIDUAL LEADERS
RUSHING
MICH: Huckleby 9-28; Davis 8-28.
USC: White 32-99, 1; Cain 14-90.
PASSING
MICH: Leach 10-21-2, 137 yards, 1 TD.
USC: McDonald 4-9-0, 23 yards, 1 TD.
RECEIVING
MICH: Smith 4-58, 1 TD; Clayton 2-40.
USC: Garcia 1-12; Brenner 1-9, 1 TD.

JANUARY 1, 1980
USC 17, OHIO STATE 16

	1ST	2ND	3RD	4TH	FINAL
OSU	0	10	3	3	16
USC	3	7	0	7	17

SCORING SUMMARY
USC   FG Hipp 41
USC   Williams 53 pass from McDonald (Hipp kick)
OSU   FG Janakievski 35
OSU   Williams 53 pass from Schlichter (Janakievski kick)
OSU   FG Janakievski 37
OSU   FG Janakievski 24
USC   White 1 run (Hipp kick)

OSU	TEAM STATISTICS	USC
16	First Downs	23
115	Rushing Yards	285
11-21-1	Passing	11-24-1
297	Passing Yards	234
412	Total Yards	519
3-43.3	Punts - Average	1-52
1-1	Fumbles - Lost	2-1
2-18	Penalties - Yards	3-33
28:13	Possession Time	31:47

INDIVIDUAL LEADERS
RUSHING
OSU: Murray 18-73.
USC: White 39-242-1 TD; Pillen 9-43.
PASSING
OSU: Schlichter 11-21-1, 297 yards, 1 TD.
USC: McDonald 11-24-1, 234 yards, 1 TD.
RECEIVING
OSU: Williams 3-131, 1 TD; Donley 4-110.
USC: Williams 2-70, 1 TD; Garcia 2-57.

JANUARY 1, 1981
MICHIGAN 23, WASHINGTON 6

	1ST	2ND	3RD	4TH	FINAL
MICH	0	7	10	6	23
WASH	0	6	0	0	6

SCORING SUMMARY
WASH   FG Nelson 35
MICH   Woolfolk 6 run (Haji-Sheikh kick)
WASH   FG Nelson 26
MICH   FG Haji-Sheikh 25
MICH   Carter 7 pass from Wangler (Haji-Sheikh kick)
MICH   Edwards 1 run (kick failed)

MICH	TEAM STATISTICS	WASH
23	First Downs	20
292	Rushing Yards	92
12-20-0	Passing	23-39-2
145	Passing Yards	282
437	Total Yards	374
6-47.3	Punts - Average	5-39.2
0-0	Fumbles - Lost	2-1
3-37	Penalties - Yards	5-32

INDIVIDUAL LEADERS
RUSHING
MICH: Woolfolk 26-182, 1 TD; Edwards 19-68, 1 TD.
WASH: Stevens 17-59; Tyler 10-45.
PASSING
MICH: Wangler 12-20-0, 145 yards, 1 TD.
WASH: Flick 23-39-2, 282 yards.
RECEIVING
MICH: Carter 5-68, 1 TD; B. Mitchell 2-36.
WASH: Allen 6-101; Bayle 6-45.

JANUARY 1, 1982
WASHINGTON 28, IOWA 0

	1ST	2ND	3RD	4TH	FINAL
WASH	0	13	0	15	28
IA	0	0	0	0	0

SCORING SUMMARY
WASH   Robinson 1 run (Nelson kick)
WASH   Coby 1 run (pass failed)
WASH   Robinson 34 run (Skansi pass from Pelluer)
WASH   Cowan 3 run (Nelson kick)

WASH	TEAM STATISTICS	IA
22	First Downs	14
186	Rushing Yards	180
15-29-1	Passing	10-21-3
142	Passing Yards	84
328	Total Yards	264
7-35.6	Punts - Average	5-47.0
0-0	Fumbles - Lost	2-2
3-28	Penalties - Yards	6-73

INDIVIDUAL LEADERS
RUSHING
WASH: Robinson 20-142, 2 TD.
IA: Granger 13-80; Bohannon 10-44.
PASSING
WASH: Pulluer 15-29-1, 142 yards.
IA: Bohannon 6-14-2, 33 yards.
RECEIVING
WASH: Skansi 4-69; Allen 5-68.
IA: Brown 6-52.

JANUARY 1, 1983
UCLA 24, MICHIGAN 14

	1ST	2ND	3RD	4TH	FINAL
MICH	0	0	7	7	14
UCLA	7	3	7	7	24

SCORING SUMMARY
UCLA   Ramsey 1 run (Lee kick)
UCLA   FG Lee 39
MICH   Garrett 1 pass from Hall (Haji-Sheikh kick)
UCLA   Andrews 9 run (Lee kick)
UCLA   Montgomery 11 interception return (Lee kick)
MICH   Rice 4 pass from Hall (Haji-Sheikh kick)

MICH	TEAM STATISTICS	UCLA
19	First Downs	19
110	Rushing Yards	181
19-34-3	Passing	18-25-0
209	Passing Yards	162
319	Total Yards	343
6-40.3	Punts - Average	6-32.2
1-1	Fumbles - Lost	1-0
3-17	Penalties - Yards	2-10

INDIVIDUAL LEADERS
RUSHING
MICH: Ricks 23-88; Smith 3-15.
UCLA: Nelson 11-48; Cephous 8-46.
PASSING
MICH: Hall 13-24-2, 155 yards, 2 TD.
UCLA: Ramsey 18-25-0, 162 yards.
RECEIVING
MICH: Dunaway 5-110, 1 TD; Carter 5-59.
UCLA: Bergmann 6-48; Townsell 4-45.

JANUARY 2, 1984
UCLA 45, ILLINOIS 9

	1ST	2ND	3RD	4TH	FINAL
ILL	0	3	0	6	9
UCLA	7	21	10	7	45

SCORING SUMMARY
UCLA   Bergmann 3 pass from Neuheisel (Lee kick)
ILL   FG White 41
UCLA   Nelson 28 run (Lee kick)
UCLA   Dorrell 16 pass from Neuheisel (Lee kick)
UCLA   Young 53 pass from Neuheisel (Lee kick)
UCLA   Dorrell 15 pass from Neuheisel (Lee kick)
UCLA   FG Lee 29
ILL   Rooks 5 pass from Trudeau (pass failed)
UCLA   Wiley 8 run (Lee kick)

ILL	TEAM STATISTICS	UCLA
16	First Downs	27
0	Rushing Yards	213
25-47-4	Passing	22-31-0
205	Passing Yards	298
205	Total Yards	511

INDIVIDUAL LEADERS
RUSHING
ILL: Beverly 4-22; Rooks 8-21.
UCLA: Cephous 12-86; Nelson 18-69, 1 TD.
PASSING
ILL: Trudeau 23-39-3, 178 yards, 1 TD.
UCLA: Neuheisel 22-31-0, 298 yards, 4 TD.
RECEIVING
ILL: Williams 10-88; Brewster 5-60.
UCLA: Young 5-129, 1 TD; Dorrell 5-61, 2 TD.

JANUARY 1, 1985
USC 20, OHIO STATE 17

	1ST	2ND	3RD	4TH	FINAL
OSU	3	3	3	8	17
USC	10	7	3	0	20

SCORING SUMMARY
OSU   FG Spangler 21
USC   FG Jordan 51
USC   Cormier 3 pass from Green (Jordan kick)
USC   Ware 19 pass from Green (Jordan kick)
OSU   FG Spangler 46
OSU   FG Spangler 52
USC   FG Jordan 51
OSU   Carter 18 pass from Tomczak (Tomczak run)

OSU	TEAM STATISTICS	USC
19	First Downs	16
113	Rushing Yards	133
24-37-3	Passing	13-25-0
290	Passing Yards	128
403	Total Yards	261
4-47.8	Punts - Average	7-42.1
4-1	Fumbles - Lost	2-1
4-46	Penalties - Yards	4-38
28:49	Possession Time	31:11

INDIVIDUAL LEADERS
RUSHING
OSU: Byars 23-109.
USC: Crutcher 21-72; Pola 9-52.
PASSING
OSU: Tomczak 24-37-3, 290 yards, 1 TD.
USC: Green 13-24-0, 128 yards, 2 TD.
RECEIVING
OSU: Carter 9-172, 1 TD; Lanese 3-33.
USC: Ware 3-56, 1 TD; Cormier 3-19, 1 TD.

JANUARY 1, 1986
UCLA 45, IOWA 28

	1ST	2ND	3RD	4TH	FINAL
IA	7	3	7	11	28
UCLA	10	14	7	14	45

SCORING SUMMARY
IA   Hudson 1 run (Houghtlin kick)
UCLA   Ball 30 run (Lee kick)
UCLA   FG Lee 42
IA   FG Houghtlin 24
UCLA   Ball 40 run (Lee kick)
UCLA   Ball 6 run (Lee kick)
IA   Long 4 run (Houghtlin kick)
UCLA   Sherrard 6 pass from Stevens (Lee kick)
UCLA   Ball 32 run (Lee kick)
IA   FG Houghtlin 52 field goal
UCLA   Stevens 1 run (Lee kick)
IA   Happel 11 pass from Long (Harmon run)

IA	TEAM STATISTICS	UCLA
25	First Downs	29
82	Rushing Yards	299
29-38-1	Passing	16-26-1
319	Passing Yards	189
401	Total Yards	488
2-32.0	Punts - Average	2-38.0
4-4	Fumbles - Lost	3-2
5-40	Penalties - Yards	6-36

INDIVIDUAL LEADERS
RUSHING
IA: Harmon 14-55; Hudson 13-53, 1 TD.
UCLA: Ball 22-227, 4 TD; Green 13-46.
PASSING
IA: Long 29-37-1, 319 yards, 1 TD.
UCLA: Stevens 16-26-1, 189 yards, 1 TD.
RECEIVING
IA: Harmon 11-102; Happel 6-89, 1 TD.
UCLA: Dorrell 3-59; Sherrard 4-48, 1 TD.

JANUARY 1, 1987
ARIZONA STATE 22, MICHIGAN 15

	1ST	2ND	3RD	4TH	FINAL
MICH	8	7	0	0	15
ASU	0	13	6	3	22

SCORING SUMMARY
MICH   Morris 18 run (White pass from Gillette)
ASU   FG Bostrom 37
MICH   Harbaugh 2 run (Gillette kick)
ASU   FG Bostrom 27
ASU   Hill 4 pass from Van Raaphorst (Bostrom kick)
ASU   Hill 1 pass from Van Raaphorst (pass failed)
ASU   FG Bostrom 25

MICH	TEAM STATISTICS	ASU
13	First Downs	22
59	Rushing Yards	188
13-23-3	Passing	16-30-0
172	Passing Yards	193
231	Total Yards	381
6-40.8	Punts - Average	4-39.0
3-0	Fumbles - Lost	1-0
6-42	Penalties - Yards	6-26

INDIVIDUAL LEADERS
RUSHING
MICH: Morris 16-47, 1 TD.
ASU: Harris 23-109; Williams 18-69.
PASSING
MICH: Harbaugh 13-23-3, 172 yards.
ASU: Van Raaphorst 16-30-0, 193 yards, 2 TD.
RECEIVING
MICH: McMurtry 3-59; Morris 4-47.
ASU: Cox 6-104; Harris 3-34.

JANUARY 1, 1988
MICHIGAN STATE 20, USC 17

	1ST	2ND	3RD	4TH	FINAL
USC	3	0	7	7	17
MSU	7	7	0	6	20

SCORING SUMMARY
USC   FG Rodriguez 34
MSU   White 5 run (Langeloh kick)
MSU   White 3 run (Langeloh kick)
USC   Henry 33 pass from Peete (Rodriguez kick)
MSU   FG Langeloh 40
USC   Henry 22 pass from Peete (Rodriguez kick)
MSU   FG Langeloh 36

USC	TEAM STATISTICS	MSU
21	First Downs	11
161	Rushing Yards	148
22-42-4	Passing	4-7-0
249	Passing Yards	128
410	Total Yards	276
4-45.0	Punts - Average	8-47.1
4-1	Fumbles - Lost	0-0
4-20	Penalties - Yards	5-32
27:13	Possession Time	32:47

INDIVIDUAL LEADERS
RUSHING
USC: Peete 11-54; Holt 10-44.
MSU: White 35-113, 2 TD.
PASSING
USC: Peete 22-41-3, 249 yards, 2 TD.
MSU: McAllister 4-7-0, 128 yards.
RECEIVING
USC: Henry 3-66, 2 TD; Green 7-58.
MSU: Rison 2-91; Bouyer 1-29.

MICHIGAN 22, USC 14

	1ST	2ND	3RD	4TH	FINAL
MICH	3	0	6	13	22
USC	0	14	0	0	14

SCORING SUMMARY
MICH	FG Gillette 49
USC	Peete 1 run (Rodriguez kick)
USC	Peete 4 run (Rodriguez kick)
MICH	Calloway 6 pass from Brown (run failed)
MICH	Hoard 1 run (pass failed)
MICH	Hoard 1 run (Gillette kick)

MICH	TEAM STATISTICS	USC
19	First Downs	15
208	Rushing Yards	138
11-24-0	Passing	15-21-2
144	Passing Yards	158
352	Total Yards	296
4-34.8	Punts - Average	4-50.3
1-1	Fumbles - Lost	3-3
4-20	Penalties - Yards	11-83
31:01	Possession Time	28:59

INDIVIDUAL LEADERS
RUSHING
MICH: Hoard 19-142, 2 TD; Boles 14-49.
USC: Emanuel 16-55; Peete 9-42, 2 TD.
PASSING
MICH: Brown 11-24-0, 144 yards, 1 TD.
USC: Peete 15-21-2, 158 yards.
RECEIVING
MICH: Walker 3-54; Kolesar 3-49.
USC: Affholter 5-56; Wellman 2-47.

USC 17, MICHIGAN 10

	1ST	2ND	3RD	4TH	FINAL
MICH	0	3	7	0	10
USC	0	10	0	7	17

SCORING SUMMARY
USC	Marinovich 1 run (Rodriguez kick)
MICH	FG Carlson 19
USC	FG Rodriguez 34
MICH	Jefferson 2 run (Carlson kick)
USC	Ervins 14 run (Rodriguez kick)

MICH	TEAM STATISTICS	USC
11	First Downs	23
119	Rushing Yards	181
10-20-0	Passing	22-31-1
115	Passing Yards	178
234	Total Yards	359
7-35.9	Punts - Average	4-39.3
2-0	Fumbles - Lost	0-0
8-62	Penalties - Yards	8 87
27:20	Possession Time	32:40

INDIVIDUAL LEADERS
RUSHING
MICH: Hoard 17-108.
USC: Ervins 30-126, 1 TD; Holt 8-35.
PASSING
MICH: Taylor 10-19-0, 116 yards.
USC: Marinovich 22-31-1, 178 yards.
RECEIVING
MICH: McMurty 4-56; Calloway 2-33.
USC: Jackson 5-56; Ervins 5-44.

WASHINGTON 46, IOWA 34

	1ST	2ND	3RD	4TH	FINAL
IA	0	7	7	20	34
WASH	10	23	6	7	46

SCORING SUMMARY
WASH	FG Hanson 23
WASH	Hall 27 blocked punt return (Hanson kick)
IA	Bell 15 run (Skillet kick)
WASH	FG Hanson 38
WASH	Mincy 37 interception return (pass failed)
WASH	Brunell 5 run (Hanson kick)
WASH	M. Bailey 22 pass from Brunell (Hanson kick)
IA	Rodgers 7 run (Skillett kick)
WASH	Brunell 20 run (run failed)
IA	Rodgers 9 run (run failed)
IA	Bell 20 run (pass failed)
WASH	M. Bailey 31 pass from Brunell (Hanson kick)
IA	Saunders 12 pass from Rodgers (Velicer pass from Rodgers)

IA	TEAM STATISTICS	WASH
19	First Downs	19
139	Rushing Yards	222
17-37-4	Passing	14-25-2
315	Passing Yards	163
454	Total Yards	385
6-33.3	Punts - Average	4-41.8
4-1	Fumbles - Lost	3-1
8-55	Penalties - Yards	5-45
29:30	Possession Time	30:30

INDIVIDUAL LEADERS
RUSHING
IA: Bell 11-64, 2 TD; Montgomery 4-26.
WASH: Lewis 19-128; Bryant 3-47.
PASSING
IA: Rodgers 15-34-3, 196 yards, 1 TD.
WASH: Brunell 14-22-1, 163 yards, 2 TD.
RECEIVING
IA: Saunders 5-99, 1 TD; Bell 3-85.
WASH: Bailey 2-53, 2 TD; Turner 3-36.

WASHINGTON 34, MICHIGAN 14

	1ST	2ND	3RD	4TH	FINAL
WASH	0	13	8	13	34
MICH	0	7	0	7	14

SCORING SUMMARY
WASH	Hobert 2 run (Hanson kick)
MICH	Smith 9 pass from Grbac (Carlson kick)
WASH	FG Hanson 24
WASH	FG Handon 23
WASH	Bruener 5 pass from Hobert (Pierce from Hobert)
WASH	Pierce 2 pass from Hobert (kick failed)
WASH	Bailey 38 pass from Brunell (Hanson kick)
MICH	Wheatley 53 run (Carlson kick)

WASH	TEAM STATISTICS	MICH
19	First Downs	10
123	Rushing Yards	72
25-42-2	Passing	14-28-1
281	Passing Yards	133
404	Total Yards	205
6-41.8	Punts - Average	10-37.8
0-0	Fumbles - Lost	3-0
6-50	Penalties - Yards	8-62

INDIVIDUAL LEADERS
RUSHING
WASH: Bryant 15-38; Barry 13-37.
MICH: Wheatley 9-68, 1 TD; Johnson 4-30.
PASSING
WASH: Hobert 18-34-2, 192 yards, 2 TD; Brunell 7-8-0, 89 yards, 1 TD.
MICH: Grbac 13-26-1, 130 yards, 1 TD.
RECEIVING
WASH: M. Bailey 6-126, 1 TD; Pierce 7-86, 1 TD.
MICH: Howard 1-35; Wheatley 3-30.

MICHIGAN 38, WASHINGTON 31

	1ST	2ND	3RD	4TH	FINAL
MICH	10	7	14	7	38
WASH	7	14	10	0	31

SCORING SUMMARY
MICH	FG Elezovic 41
WASH	Turner 1 run (Hanson kick)
MICH	McGee 49 pass from Grbac (Elezovic kick)
MICH	Wheatley 56 run (Elezovic kick)
WASH	Shelley 64 pass from Brunell (Hanson kick)
WASH	Bruener 18 pass from Brunell (Hanson kick)
MICH	Wheatley 88 run (Elezovic kick)
WASH	Kaufman 1 run (Hanson kick)
WASH	FG Hanson 44
MICH	Wheatley 24 run (Elezovic kick)
MICH	McGee 15 pass from Grbac (Elezovic kick)

MICH	TEAM STATISTICS	WASH
16	First Downs	19
308	Rushing Yards	105
17-30-0	Passing	18-31-0
175	Passing Yards	308
483	Total Yards	413
6-37.0	Punts - Average	5-39.2
1-0	Fumbles - Lost	1-1
8-72	Penalties - Yards	5-43
28:12	Possession Time	31:48

INDIVIDUAL LEADERS
RUSHING
MICH: Wheatley 15-235, 3 TD; Davis 9-35.
WASH: Kaufman 20-39, 1 TD.
PASSING
MICH: Grbac 17-30-0, 175 yards, 2 TD.
WASH: Brunell 18-30-0, 308 yards, 2 TD.
RECEIVING
MICH: McGee 6-117, 2 TD.
WASH: Shelley 3-100, 1 TD; Bruener 4-85, 1 TD.

WISCONSIN 21, UCLA 16

	1ST	2ND	3RD	4TH	FINAL
UCLA	3	0	0	13	16
WISC	7	7	0	7	21

SCORING SUMMARY
UCLA	FG Merten 27
WISC	Moss 3 run (Schnetzky kick)
WISC	Moss 1 run (Schnetzky kick)
UCLA	Davis 12 run (Merten kick)
WISC	Bevell 21 run (Schnetzky kick)
UCLA	Nguyen five pass from Cook (pass failed)

UCLA	TEAM STATISTICS	WISC
31	First Downs	21
212	Rushing Yards	250
28-43-1	Passing	10-20-1
288	Passing Yards	96
500	Total Yards	346
2-35.0	Punts - Average	6-38.0
5-5	Fumbles - Lost	2-0
9-95	Penalties - Yards	12-89

INDIVIDUAL LEADERS
RUSHING
UCLA: Davis 13-88, 1 TD; Hicks 8-67.
WISC: Moss 36-158, 2 TD; Fletcher 7-64.
PASSING
UCLA: Bevell 10-20-1, 96 yards.
WISC: Cook 28-43-1, 288 yards, 1 TD.
RECEIVING
UCLA: Stokes 14-176; Allen 4-32.
WISC: Dawkins 4-33.

JANUARY 2, 1995
PENN STATE 38, OREGON 20

	1ST	2ND	3RD	4TH	FINAL
ORE	7	0	7	6	20
PSU	7	7	14	10	38

SCORING SUMMARY

PSU	Carter 83 run (Conway kick)
ORE	Wilcox 1 pass from O'Neil (Belden kick)
PSU	Milne 1 run (Conway kick)
ORE	McLemore 17 pass from O'Neil (Belden kick)
PSU	Carter 17 run (Conway kick)
PSU	Carter 3 run (Conway kick)
PSU	FG Conway 43
PSU	Witman 9 run (Baminger kick)
ORE	Whittle 3 run (pass failed)

ORE	TEAM STATISTICS	PSU
27	First Downs	22
45	Rushing Yards	228
41-61-2	Passing	20-31-1
456	Passing Yards	202
501	Total Yards	430
6-42.8	Punts - Average	6-41.7
1-0	Fumbles - Lost	1-1
6-52	Penalties - Yards	5-37

INDIVIDUAL LEADERS

RUSHING
ORE: Whittle 12-45, 1 TD; Philyaw 4-14.
PSU: Carter 21-156, 3 TD; Milne 9-36, 1 TD.

PASSING
ORE: O'Neil 41-61-2, 456 yards, 2 TD.
PSU: K. Collins 19-30-1, 200 yards.

RECEIVING
ORE: Wilcox 11-135, 1 TD; McLemore 10-90, 1 TD.
PSU: Engram 5-52; Scott 4-41

JANUARY 1, 1996
USC 41, NORTHWESTERN 32

	1ST	2ND	3RD	4TH	FINAL
USC	7	17	7	10	41
NU	7	3	16	6	32

SCORING SUMMARY

USC	L. Woods 1 run (Abrams kick)
NU	D. Autry 3 run (Gowins kick)
USC	Barnum 21 pass from Otton (Abrams kick)
USC	FG Abrams 30
USC	McCutcheon 53 fumble return (Abrams kick)
NU	FG Gowins 29
NU	FG Gowins 28
NU	D. Autry 9 run (pass failed)
USC	K. Johnson 56 pass from Otton (Abrams kick)
NU	Schnur 1 run (Gowins kick)
NU	D. Autry 2 run (pass failed)
USC	FG Abrams 46
USC	Washington 2 run (Abrams kick)

USC	TEAM STATISTICS	NU
22	First Downs	23
29	Rushing Yards	139
29-44-0	Passing	23-39-1
391	Passing Yards	336
420	Total Yards	475
2-18	Punt Returns - Yards	0-0
3-31	Kickoff Returns - Yards	8-225
2-44.5	Punts - Average	2-38.5
1-1	Fumbles - Lost	1-1
11-86	Penalties - Yards	7-72
29:47	Possession Time	30:13

INDIVIDUAL LEADERS

RUSHING
USC: Washington 16-51, 1 TD.
NU: D. Autry 32-110, 3 TD; Schnur 3-13, 1 TD.

PASSING
USC: Otton 29-44-0, 391 yards, 2 TD.
NU: Schnur 23-39-1, 336 yards.

RECEIVING
USC: Johnson 12-216, 1 TD; C Miller 3-50, Barnum 4-42, 1 TD.
NU: Bates 7-145; Musso 5-91.

JANUARY 1, 1997
OHIO STATE 20, ARIZONA STATE 17

	1ST	2ND	3RD	4TH	FINAL
ASU	0	7	3	7	17
OSU	7	0	7	6	20

SCORING SUMMARY

OSU	Boston 9 pass from S. Jackson (J. Jackson kick)
ASU	Boyer 25 pass from Plummer (Nycz kick)
ASU	FG Nycz 37
OSU	Stanley 72 pass from Germaine (J. Jackson kick)
ASU	Plummer 11 run (Nycz kick)
OSU	Boston 5 pass from Germaine (kick failed)

ASU	TEAM STATISTICS	OSU
18	First Downs	18
75	Rushing Yards	133
19-35-1	Passing	15-31-0
201	Passing Yards	190
276	Total Yards	323
1-0	Fumbles - Lost	1-0
9-85	Penalties - Yards	10-75
33:17	Possession Time	26:43

INDIVIDUAL LEADERS

RUSHING
ASU: Battle 18-34; Redmond 8-26.
OSU: Pearson 13-114; Wiley 7-32.

PASSING
ASU: Plummer 19-35-1, 201 yards, 1 TD.
OSU: Germaine 9-17-0, 131 yards, 2 TD.

RECEIVING
ASU: L. Jackson 5-71; Bush 3-41.
OSU: Stanley 5-124, 1 TD; Keller 3-24.

JANUARY 1, 1998
MICHIGAN 21, WASHINGTON STATE 16

	1ST	2ND	3RD	4TH	FINAL
WSU	7	0	6	3	16
MICH	0	7	7	7	21

SCORING SUMMARY

WSU	McKenzie 15 pass from Leaf (Lindell kick)
MICH	Streets 53 pass from Griese (Baker kick)
WSU	Tims 14 reverse (kick blocked)
MICH	Streets 58 pass from Griese (Baker kick)
MICH	Tuman 23 pass from Griese (Baker kick)
WSU	FG Lindell 48

WSU	TEAM STATISTICS	MICH
18	First Downs	22
67	Rushing Yards	128
17-35-1	Passing	18-30-1
331	Passing Yards	251
398	Total Yards	379
6-40.3	Punts - Average	6-30.5
2-0	Fumbles - Lost	0-0
4-43	Penalties - Yards	4-40
27:46	Possession Time	32:14

INDIVIDUAL LEADERS

RUSHING
WSU: Black 7-24; Gilmore 8-20.
MICH: Howard 19-70; Thomas 7-20.

PASSING
WSU: Leaf 17-35-1, 331 yards, 1 TD.
MICH: Griese 18-30-1, 251 yards, 3 TD.

RECEIVING
WSU: Jackson 5-89; McKenzie 5-78, 1 TD.
MICH: Streets 4-127, 2 TD; Shaw 6-49.

JANUARY 1, 1999
WISCONSIN 38, UCLA 31

	1ST	2ND	3RD	4TH	FINAL
WISC	7	17	7	7	38
UCLA	7	14	7	3	31

SCORING SUMMARY

WISC	Dayne 54 run (Davenport kick)
UCLA	Lewis 38 pass from McNown (Sailer kick)
WISC	Dayne 7 run (Davenport kick)
UCLA	Price 61 pass from Mitchell (Sailer kick)
UCLA	Farmer 41 pass from McNown (Sailer kick)
WISC	Dayne 10 run (Davenport kick)
WISC	FG Davenport 40
WISC	Dayne 22 run (Davenport kick)
UCLA	Lewis 10 run (Sailer kick)
WISC	Fletcher 46 interception return (Davenport kick)
UCLA	FG Sailer 30

WISC	TEAM STATISTICS	UCLA
22	First Downs	25
343	Rushing Yards	120
9-17-0	Passing	21-36-1
154	Passing Yards	418
497	Total Yards	538
5-41.0	Punts - Average	3-47.0
2-1	Fumbles - Lost	1-1
7-45	Penalties - Yards	9-94
29:15	Possession Time	30:45

INDIVIDUAL LEADERS

RUSHING
WISC: Dayne 27-246, 4 TD; Samuel 13-65.
UCLA: Lewis 10-50, 1 TD; Foster 10-38.

PASSING
WISC: Samuel 9-17-0, 154 yards.
UCLA: McNown 19-34-1, 340 yards, 2 TD.

RECEIVING
WISC: Davis 3-57.
UCLA: Farmer 7-142, 1 TD; Price 3-102, 1 TD.

JANUARY 1, 2000
WISCONSIN 17, STANFORD 9

	1ST	2ND	3RD	4TH	FINAL
STAN	0	9	0	0	9
WISC	0	3	7	7	17

SCORING SUMMARY

STAN	FG Biselli 28
WISC	FG Pisetsky 31
STAN	K. Carter 1 run (run failed)
WISC	Dayne 4 run (Pisetsky kick)
WISC	Bollinger 1 run (Pisetsky kick)

STAN	TEAM STATISTICS	WISC
14	First Downs	16
-5	Rushing Yards	226
18-35-0	Passing	7-14-0
264	Passing Yards	105
259	Total Yards	331
8-38.3	Punts - Average	8-43.4
2-0	Fumbles - Lost	0-0
7-50	Penalties - Yards	8-72
26:32	Possession Time	33:28

INDIVIDUAL LEADERS

RUSHING
STAN: Wire 5-6; Allen 6-4; K.Carter 6-3, 1 TD.
WISC: Dayne 34-200, 1 TD.

PASSING
STAN: Husak 17-34-0, 258 yards.
WISC: Bollinger 7-14-0, 105 yards.

RECEIVING
STAN: Pitts 6-81; Uso 3-60.
WISC: Chambers 5-76; Sigmund 2-29.

JANUARY 1, 2001
WASHINGTON 34, PURDUE 24

	1ST	2ND	3RD	4TH	FINAL
PU	0	10	7	7	24
WASH	14	0	6	14	34

SCORING SUMMARY
WASH	Cleman 1 run (Anderson kick)
WASH	Tuiasosopo 5 run (Anderson Kick)
PU	Sutherland 5 pass from Brees (Dorsch kick)
PU	FG Dorsch 26
WASH	FG Anderson 47
PU	Sutherland 24 pass from Brees (Dorsch kick)
WASH	FG Anderson 42
WASH	Elstrom 8 pass from Tuiasosopo (Anderson kick)
WASH	Hurst 8 run (Anderson kick)
PU	Brown 42 run (Dorsch kick)

PU	TEAM STATISTICS	WASH
19	First Downs	23
76	Rushing Yards	268
23-39-0	Passing	18-24-0
275	Passing Yards	149
351	Total Yards	417
4-41.0	Punts - Average	3-37.7
3-1	Fumbles - Lost	2-1
11-69	Penalties - Yards	6-48
24:07	Possession Time	35:53

INDIVIDUAL LEADERS
RUSHING
PU: Lowe 20-79; Brown 3-52, 1 TD.
WASH: Alexis 10-78; Tuiasosopo 15-75, 1 TD.

PASSING
PU: Brees 23-39-0, 275 yards, 2 TD.
WASH: Tuiasosopo 16-22-0, 138 yards, 1 TD.

RECEIVING
PU: Sutherland 7-88, 2 TD; Standeford 5-67.
WASH: Stevens 5-51; Elstrom 4-24, 1 TD.

JANUARY 1, 2004
USC 28, MICHIGAN 14

	1ST	2ND	3RD	4TH	FINAL
USC	7	7	14	0	28
MICH	0	0	7	7	14

SCORING SUMMARY
USC	Colbert 25 pass from Leinart (Killeen kick)
USC	White 6 pass from Leinart (Killeen kick)
USC	Colbert 47 pass from Leinart (Killeen kick)
MICH	Massaquoi 5 pass from Navarre (Rivas kick)
USC	Leinart 15 pass from Williams (Killeen kick)
MICH	Perry 2 run (Rivas kick)

USC	TEAM STATISTICS	MICH
19	First Downs	25
68	Rushing Yards	49
24-35-0	Passing	27-46-1
342	Passing Yards	271
410	Total Yards	320
2-4	Punt Returns - Yards	2-45
1-0	Kickoff Returns - Yards	2-48
3-46.7	Punts - Average	4-44.0
2-1	Fumbles - Lost	3-0
3-22	Penalties - Yards	2-10
25:34	Possession Time	34:26

INDIVIDUAL LEADERS
RUSHING
USC: Bush 8-41; White 8-26.
MICH: Perry 23-85, 1 TD.

PASSING
USC: Leinart 23-34-0, 327 yards, 3 TD.
MICH: Navarre 27-46-1, 271 yards, 1 TD.

RECEIVING
USC: Colbert 6-149, 2 TD; Williams 8-88.
MICH: Edwards 10-107; Breaston 6-61; Avant 4-61.

JANUARY 1, 2005
TEXAS 38, MICHIGAN 37

	1ST	2ND	3RD	4TH	FINAL
TEX	7	7	7	17	38
MICH	0	14	17	6	37

SCORING SUMMARY
TEX	Young 20 run (Mangum kick)
MICH	Edwards 39 pass from Henne (Rivas kick)
TEX	Thomas 11 pass from Young (Mangum kick)
MICH	Edwards 8 pass from Henne (Rivas kick)
TEX	Young 60 run (Mangum kick)
MICH	Breaston 50 pass from Henne (Rivas kick)
MICH	Edwards 9 pass from Henne (Rivas kick)
MICH	FG Rivas 44
TEX	Young 10 run (Mangum kick)
MICH	FG Rivas 32
TEX	Young 23 run (Mangum kick)
MICH	FG Rivas 42
TEX	FG Mangum 37

TEX	TEAM STATISTICS	MICH
25	First Downs	17
264	Rushing Yards	125
16-28-1	Passing	18-34-0
180	Passing Yards	227
444	Total Yards	352
4-9	Punt Returns - Yards	1-2
8-214	Kickoff Returns - Yards	6-221
4-39.8	Punts - Average	5-42
1-1	Fumbles - Lost	1-0
5-40	Penalties - Yards	9-67
32:40	Possession Time	27:20

INDIVIDUAL LEADERS
RUSHING
TEX: Young 21-192, 4 TD.
MICH: Hart 21-83.

PASSING
TEX: Young 16-28-1, 180 yards, 1 TD.
MICH: Henne 18-34-0, 227 yards, 4 TD.

RECEIVING
TEX: Scaife 5-68; Thomas 4-54, 1 TD.
MICH: Edwards 10-109, 3 TD.

JANUARY 1, 2007
USC 32, MICHIGAN 18

	1ST	2ND	3RD	4TH	FINAL
USC	3	0	16	13	32
MICH	0	3	0	15	18

SCORING SUMMARY
USC	FG Danelo 26
MICH	FG Rivas 43
USC	McFoy 2 pass from Booty (Danelo kick)
USC	Jarrett 22 pass from Booty (kick failed)
USC	FG Danelo 26
MICH	Arrington 11 pass from Henne (Hart rush)
USC	Jarrett 62 pass from Booty (kick failed)
USC	Smith 7 pass from Booty (Danelo kick)
MICH	Breaston 41 pass from Henne (Rivas kick)

USC	TEAM STATISTICS	MICH
21	First Downs	19
48	Rushing Yards	12
27-45-0	Passing	26-41-1
391	Passing Yards	309
439	Total Yards	321
4-14	Punt Returns - Yards	0-0
2-49	Kickoff Returns - Yards	4-52
4-35.2	Punts - Average	6-41.8
1-1	Fumbles - Lost	1-1
3-27	Penalties - Yards	2-20
30:02	Possession Time	29:58

INDIVIDUAL LEADERS
RUSHING
USC: Gable 13-25; Bradford 4-19.
MICH: Hart 17-47; Minor 2-3.

PASSING
USC: Booty 27-45-0, 391 yards, 4 TD.
MICH: Henne 26-41-1, 309 yards, 2 TD.

RECEIVING
USC: Jarrett 11-205, 2 TD; Smith 7-108, 1 TD.
MICH: Breaston 7-115, 1 TD; Manningham 6-79.

BIG TEN ANNUAL REVIEW & BOWLS

ALAMO BOWL

PROFILE

Site: San Antonio, Texas
Stadium: Alamodome
Capacity: 65,000
Surface: SportField

PLAYING SITES

Alamodome, since 1993

NAME CHANGES

Builders Square Alamo Bowl,
　1993-98
Sylvania Alamo Bowl, 1999-2001
Alamo Bowl Presented by
　MasterCard, 2002
MasterCard Alamo Bowl, 2003-05
Alamo Bowl, 2006
Valero Alamo Bowl, since 2007

SEASON	DATE	PRE-GAME RANK	TEAMS	SCORE	FINAL RANK	MOST VALUABLE PLAYER(S)	ATT.
1993	Dec. 31, 1993		**California**	37	25	Dave Barr, California, QB	45,716
			Iowa	3		Jerrott Willard, California, LB	
1995	Dec. 28, 1995	19	**Texas A&M**	22	15	Kyle Bryant, Texas A&M, K	64,597
		14	Michigan	20	17	Keith Mitchell, Texas A&M, LB	
1996	Dec. 29, 1996	21	**Iowa**	27	18	Sedrick Shaw, Iowa, RB	55,677
			Texas Tech	0		Jared DeVries, Iowa, DL	
1997	Dec. 30, 1997	17	**Purdue**	33	15	Billy Dicken, Purdue, QB	55,552
		24	Oklahoma State	20		Adrian Beasley, Purdue, S	
1998	Dec. 29, 1998		**Purdue**	37	24	Drew Brees, Purdue, QB	60,780
		4	Kansas State	34	10	Rosevelt Colvin, Purdue, DE	
1999	Dec. 28, 1999	13	**Penn State**	24	11	Rashard Casey, Penn State, QB	65,380
		18	Texas A&M	0	23	LaVar Arrington, Penn State, LB	
2000	Dec. 30, 2000	9	**Nebraska**	66	8	Dan Alexander, Nebraska, RB	60,028
		18	Northwestern	17		Kyle Vanden Bosch, Nebraska, DL	
2001	Dec. 29, 2001		**Iowa**	19		Aaron Greving, Iowa, RB	65,232
			Texas Tech	16		Derrick Pickens, Iowa, DL	
2002	Dec. 28, 2002		**Wisconsin**	31	OT	Brooks Bollinger, Wisconsin, QB	50,690
		14	Colorado	28		Jeff Mack, Wisconsin, LB	
2003	Dec. 29, 2003		**Nebraska**	17		Jammal Lord, Nebraska, QB	56,229
			Michigan State	3		Trevor Johnson, Nebraska, DL	
2004	Dec. 29, 2004	24	**Ohio State**	33	20	Ted Ginn Jr., Ohio State, FL	65,265
			Oklahoma State	7		Simon Fraser, Ohio State, DE	
2005	Dec. 28, 2005		**Nebraska**	32		Cory Ross, Nebraska, RB	62,016
			Michigan	28		Leon Hall, Michigan, CB	
2006	Dec. 30, 2006	18	**Texas**	26	13	Colt McCoy, Texas, QB	65,875
			Iowa	24		Aaron Ross, Texas, DB	

DECEMBER 31, 1993
CALIFORNIA 37, IOWA 3

	1ST	2ND	3RD	4TH	FINAL
CAL	6	17	7	7	37
IOWA	0	0	3	0	3

SCORING SUMMARY
CAL　FG Brien 37
CAL　FG Brien 20
CAL　FG Brien 30
CAL　Caldwell 6 pass from Barr (Brien kick)
CAL　Willard 61 interception return (Brien kick)
IOWA　FG Hurley 42
CAL　Uwaezuoke 34 pass from Barr (Brien kick)
CAL　Remington 12 pass from Barr (Brien kick)

CAL	TEAM STATISTICS	IOWA
28	First Downs	5
179	Rushing Yards	20
21-28-0	Passing	6-17-1
266	Passing Yards	70
445	Total Yards	90
2-42.0	Punts - Average	8-43.0
3-1	Fumbles - Lost	1-0
5-35	Penalties - Yards	10-74
43:14	Possession Time	16:46

INDIVIDUAL LEADERS
RUSHING
CAL: Chapman 24-89; Edwards 6-42.
IOWA: Kahl 5-27; King 5-19.
PASSING
CAL: Barr 21-28-0, 266 yards, 3 TD.
IOWA: Burmeister 6-17-1, 70 yards.
RECEIVING
CAL: Caldwell 5-80, 1 TD; Uwaezuoke 2-55, 1 TD.
IOWA: Jasper 4-55; Dean 2-15.

DECEMBER 28, 1995
TEXAS A&M 22, MICHIGAN 20

	1ST	2ND	3RD	4TH	FINAL
A&M	10	3	3	6	22
MICH	7	3	3	7	20

SCORING SUMMARY
A&M　Bernard 9 run (Bryant kick)
MICH　Toomer 41 pass from Griese (Hamilton kick)
A&M　FG Bryant 27
MICH　FG Hamilton 28
A&M　FG Bryant 49
A&M　FG Bryant 47
MICH　FG Hamilton 26
A&M　FG Bryant 31
A&M　FG Bryant 37
MICH　Toomer 44 pass from Griese (Hamilton kick)

A&M	TEAM STATISTICS	MICH
17	First Downs	19
130	Rushing Yards	129
12-22-0	Passing	9-23-1
136	Passing Yards	182
266	Total Yards	311
5-43.0	Punts - Average	7-36.0
2-1	Fumbles - Lost	2-1
11-110	Penalties - Yards	6-60
31:07	Possession Time	28:53

INDIVIDUAL LEADERS
RUSHING
A&M: Parker 21-56; Hardeman 6-41; Bernard 15-40, 1 TD.
MICH: Biakabutuka 24-94; Wlliams 7-36.
PASSING
A&M: Pullig 12-22-0, 136 yards.
MICH: Griese 9-23-1, 182 yards, 2 TD.
RECEIVING
A&M: Hardeman 3-41; Connell 3-36.
MICH: Toomer 5-135, 2 TD; Hayes 2-35.

DECEMBER 29, 1996
IOWA 27, TEXAS TECH 0

	1ST	2ND	3RD	4TH	FINAL
IOWA	6	11	0	10	27
TT	0	0	0	0	0

SCORING SUMMARY
IOWA　Sherman 1 run (run failed)
IOWA　Shaw 20 run (Knipper pass from Sherman)
IOWA　FG Bromert 36
IOWA　FG Bromert 26
IOWA　Filer 14 run (Bromert kick)

IOWA	TEAM STATISTICS	TT
23	First Downs	13
217	Rushing Yards	61
10-17-1	Passing	14-32-1
139	Passing Yards	145
356	Total Yards	206
5-52.0	Punts - Average	4-45.8
8-78	Penalties - Yards	7-68
34:56	Possession Time	25:04

INDIVIDUAL LEADERS
RUSHING
IOWA: Shaw 20-113, 1 TD; Filer 4-41, 1 TD.
TT: Hanspard 18-64.
PASSING
IOWA: Sherman 9-16-0, 126 yards.
TT: Lethridge 13-28-1, 139 yards.
RECEIVING
IOWA: Dwight 6-105; Knipper 1-17.
TT: Hart 4-46; McKenzie 3-38.

DECEMBER 30, 1997
PURDUE 33, OKLAHOMA STATE 20

	1ST	2ND	3RD	4TH	FINAL
PUR	7	3	20	3	33
OKST	3	3	7	7	20

SCORING SUMMARY
OKST　FG Sydnes 34
PUR　Alford 18 pass from Dicken (Ryan kick)
OKST　FG Sydnes 22
PUR　FG Ryan 42
PUR　Dicken 1 run (kick failed)
OKST　Fobbs 21 run (Sydnes kick)
PUR　Sutherland 16 run (Ryan kick)
PUR　Daniels 69 pass from Dicken (Ryan kick)
PUR　FG Ryan 37
OKST　McQuarters 17 pass from Lindsay (Sydnes kick)

PUR	TEAM STATISTICS	OKST
20	First Downs	24
129	Rushing Yards	162
18-36-3	Passing	17-35-3
325	Passing Yards	206
454	Total Yards	368
2-45.0	Punts - Average	4-45.0
1-0	Fumbles - Lost	2-1
9-81	Penalties - Yards	8-70
25:35	Possession Time	34:25

INDIVIDUAL LEADERS
RUSHING
PUR: Watson 13-45; Dicken 8-43, 1 TD; Sutherland 2-38, 1 TD.
OKST: Fobbs 11-82, 1 TD; Lindsay 12-61.
PASSING
PUR: Dicken 18-34-3, 325 yards, 2 TD.
OKST: Lindsay 9-18-2, 111 yards, 1 TD; Chaloupka 8-17-1, 95 yards.
RECEIVING
PUR: Watson 5-102; Daniels 1-69, 1 TD; Alford 4-61, 1 TD.
OKST: G. Brown 4-52; McQuarters 4-43, 1 TD.

December 29, 1998
Purdue 37, Kansas State 34

	1ST	2ND	3RD	4TH	FINAL
PUR	0	17	10	10	37
KSU	0	7	6	21	34

SCORING SUMMARY
PUR	Daniels 5 pass from Brees (Dorsch kick)
PUR	FG Dorsch 25
KSU	McDonald 1 pass from Bishop (Gramatica kick)
PUR	Jones 30 pass from Brees (Dorsch kick)
KSU	Havick recovered fumble in end zone (kick failed)
PUR	Nugent recovered fumble in end zone (Dorsch kick)
PUR	FG Dorsch 26
KSU	Allen 3 run (Gramatica kick)
PUR	FG Dorsch 37
KSU	McDonald 88 pass from Bishop (Gramatica kick)
KSU	Swift 2 pass from Bishop (Gramatica kick)
PUR	Jones 24 pass from Brees (Dorsch kick)

PUR	TEAM STATISTICS	KSU
19	First Downs	12
5	Rushing Yards	126
25-53-3	Passing	9-24-4
230	Passing Yards	182
235	Total Yards	308
7-38.3	Punts - Average	7-44.1
2-1	Fumbles - Lost	3-3
7-35	Penalties - Yards	14-125
28:58	Possession Time	31:02

INDIVIDUAL LEADERS
RUSHING
PUR: Crabtree 12-46; Brees 10-25.
KSU: Allen 13-83, 1 TD; Hickson 7-35.

PASSING
PUR: Brees 25-53-3, 230 yards, 3 TD.
KSU: Bishop 9-24-4, 182 yards, 3 TD.

RECEIVING
PUR: Jones 11-98, 2 TD; Daniels 6-47, 1 TD.
KSU: McDonald 5-124, 2 TD; Peries 1-52.

December 28, 1999
Penn State 24, Texas A&M 0

	1ST	2ND	3RD	4TH	FINAL
PSU	7	7	0	10	24
A&M	0	0	0	0	0

SCORING SUMMARY
PSU	Fox 34 interception return (Forney kick)
PSU	Drummond 45 pass from Casey (Forney kick)
PSU	Casey 4 run (Forney kick)
PSU	FG Forney 39

PSU	TEAM STATISTICS	A&M
17	First Downs	16
175	Rushing Yards	80
8-17-1	Passing	15-28-4
146	Passing Yards	122
321	Total Yards	202
2-35	Punt Returns - Yards	2-9
0-0	Kickoff Returns - Yards	4-70
4-45.5	Punts - Average	3-52.0
0-0	Fumbles - Lost	2-1
7-74	Penalties - Yards	2-27
29:23	Possession Time	30:37

INDIVIDUAL LEADERS
RUSHING
PSU: McCoo 6-43; Johnson 6-30; Casey 7-27, 1 TD.
A&M: Toombs 19-70; Hardeman 10-41.

PASSING
PSU: Casey 8-16-1, 146 yards, 1 TD.
A&M: McCown 13-22-4, 105 yards.

RECEIVING
PSU: Drummond 1-45, 1 TD; Stewart 2-27.
A&M: Bumgardner 5-59; Taylor 6-38.

December 30, 2000
Nebraska 66, Northwestern 17

	1ST	2ND	3RD	4TH	FINAL
NEB	7	31	21	7	66
NU	3	14	0	0	17

SCORING SUMMARY
NEB	Alexander 15 run (Brown kick)
NU	FG Long 44
NU	Johnson 10 pass from Kustok (Long kick)
NEB	Crouch 50 run (Brown kick)
NEB	Alexander 2 run (Brown kick)
NEB	Buckhalter 2 run (Brown kick)
NEB	FG Brown 51
NU	Anderson 69 run (Long kick)
NEB	Newcombe 58 pass from Crouch (Brown kick)
NEB	Davison 11 pass from Crouch (Brown kick)
NEB	Crouch 2 run (Brown kick)
NEB	Davison 69 pass from Newcombe (Brown kick)
NEB	Diedrick 9 run (Brown kick)

NEB	TEAM STATISTICS	NU
28	First Downs	14
476	Rushing Yards	232
6-14-1	Passing	17-43-1
160	Passing Yards	151
636	Total Yards	383
3-44.3	Punts - Average	10-35.7
2-1	Fumbles - Lost	1-0
4-67	Penalties - Yards	7-46
33:37	Possession Time	26:23

INDIVIDUAL LEADERS
RUSHING
NEB: Alexander 20-240, 2 TD; Crouch 15-90, 2 TD; Buckhalter 12-58, 1 TD.
NU: Anderson 18-149, 1 TD; Kustok 14-55.

PASSING
NEB: Crouch 5-13-1, 91 yards, 2 TD; Newcombe 1-1-0, 69 yards, 1 TD.
NU: Kustok 15-35-0, 138 yards, 1 TD.

RECEIVING
NEB: Davison 3-85, 2 TD; Newcombe 1-58, 1 TD.
NU: Johnson 4-53, 1 TD; Anderson 4-12.

December 29, 2001
Iowa 19, Texas Tech 16

	1ST	2ND	3RD	4TH	FINAL
IOWA	3	7	3	6	19
TT	0	3	7	6	16

SCORING SUMMARY
IOWA	FG Kaeding 36
IOWA	Greving 1 run (Kaeding kick)
TT	FG Greathouse 50
TT	Welker 20 pass from Kingsbury (Treece kick)
IOWA	FG Kaeding 31
IOWA	FG Kaeding 46
TT	FG Treece 23
TT	FG Treece 37
IOWA	FG Kaeding 47

IOWA	TEAM STATISTICS	TT
20	First Downs	20
178	Rushing Yards	80
19-26-0	Passing	29-49-3
161	Passing Yards	309
339	Total Yards	389
0-0	Punt Returns - Yards	4-13
4-82	Kickoff Returns - Yards	5-76
5-36.0	Punts - Average	5-37.2
1-0	Fumbles - Lost	0-0
5-26	Penalties - Yards	5-35
35:03	Possession Time	24:57

INDIVIDUAL LEADERS
RUSHING
IOWA: Greving 25-115, 1 TD; Allen 7-36.
TT: Kingsbury 9-42; Williams 9-30.

PASSING
IOWA: McCann 19-26-0, 161 yards.
TT: Kingsbury 29-49-3, 309 yards, 1 TD.

RECEIVING
IOWA: Hill 6-49; Clark 4-30.
TT: Glover 6-77; Welker 6-62, 1 TD; Peters 8-60.

December 28, 2002
Wisconsin 31, Colorado 28

	1ST	2ND	3RD	4TH	OT	FINAL
WISC	7	14	0	7	3	31
COLO	14	0	14	0	0	28

SCORING SUMMARY
COLO	Strickland 91 interception return (Brougham kick)
WISC	A. Davis 4 run (Allen kick)
COLO	Hackett 10 pass from Hodge (Brougham kick)
WISC	Williams 10 pass from Bollinger (Allen kick)
WISC	Charles 7 pass from Bollinger (Allen kick)
COLO	Brown 4 run (Brougham kick)
COLO	Hackett 11 pass from Colvin (Brougham kick)
WISC	Bollinger 1 run (Allen kick)
WISC	FG Allen 37

WISC	TEAM STATISTICS	COLO
21	First Downs	13
193	Rushing Yards	123
12-24-1	Passing	9-18-3
163	Passing Yards	77
356	Total Yards	200
3-30	Punt Returns - Yards	3-8
4-84	Kickoff Returns - Yards	3-49
5-36.0	Punts - Average	6-40.8
3-3	Fumbles - Lost	1-0
6-64	Penalties - Yards	9-71
30:37	Possession Time	29:23

INDIVIDUAL LEADERS
RUSHING
WISC: A. Davis 25-99, 1 TD; Bollinger 20-82, 1 TD.
COLO: Brown 28-97, 1 TD; Calhoun 9-16.

PASSING
WISC: Bollinger 12-24-1, 163 yards, 2 TD.
COLO: Hodge 6-13-3, 62 yards, 1 TD; Colvin 3-5-0, 15 yards, 1 TD.

RECEIVING
WISC: Williams 5-83, 1 TD; Charles 5-67, 1 TD.
COLO: Hackett 3-30, 2 TD; Monteilh 1-20.

December 29, 2003
Nebraska 17, Michigan State 3

	1ST	2ND	3RD	4TH	FINAL
NEB	3	14	0	0	17
MSU	3	0	0	0	3

SCORING SUMMARY
NEB	FG Dyches 29
MSU	FG Rayner 46
NEB	Ross 2 run (Dyches kick)
NEB	Ross 6 run (Dyches kick)

NEB	TEAM STATISTICS	MSU
20	First Downs	13
229	Rushing Yards	18
8-17-0	Passing	21-39-3
160	Passing Yards	156
389	Total Yards	174
4-28	Punt Returns - Yards	2-3
0-0	Kickoff Returns - Yards	3-47
7-42.9	Punts - Average	8-46.4
1-0	Fumbles - Lost	0-0
8-69	Penalties - Yards	5-53
30:29	Possession Time	29:31

INDIVIDUAL LEADERS
RUSHING
NEB: Ross 37-138, 2 TD; Lord 10-79.
MSU: Dortch 9-31; Hayes 6-13.

PASSING
NEB: Lord 8-17-0, 160 yards.
MSU: Smoker 21-39-3, 156 yards.

RECEIVING
NEB: Fluellen 4-84; Pilkington 3-70.
MSU: Alexander 8-63; Brown 4-41.

DECEMBER 29, 2004
OHIO STATE 33, OKLAHOMA STATE 7

	1ST	2ND	3RD	4TH	FINAL
OSU	13	10	7	3	33
OKST	0	0	0	7	7

SCORING SUMMARY

OSU	Gonzalez 23 pass from Zwick (Nugent kick)
OSU	FG Nugent 37
OSU	FG Nugent 35
OSU	Ross 1 run (Nugent kick)
OSU	FG Nugent 41
OSU	Ginn Jr. 5 run (Nugent kick)
OSU	FG Nugent 37
OKST	Willis 4 run (Ricks kick)

OSU	TEAM STATISTICS	OKST
19	First Downs	15
214	Rushing Yards	149
17-27-0	Passing	15-35-1
189	Passing Yards	137
403	Total Yards	286
3-17	Punt Returns - Yards	2-1
1-26	Kickoff Returns - Yards	1-15
4-42.3	Punts - Average	7-41.9
1-1	Fumbles - Lost	1-1
2-25	Penalties - Yards	6-45
34:51	Possession Time	25:09

INDIVIDUAL LEADERS

RUSHING
OSU: Ross 12-99, 1 TD; Branden 13-57.
OKST: Woods 12-72; Elliott 3-39.

PASSING
OSU: Zwick 17-27-0, 189 yards, 1 TD.
OKST: Woods 15-34-1, 137 yards.

RECEIVING
OSU: Ginn Jr. 6-78; Holmes 5-47.
OKST: Woods 4-40; Bajema 2-29.

DECEMBER 28, 2005
NEBRASKA 32, MICHIGAN 28

	1ST	2ND	3RD	4TH	FINAL
NEB	7	7	3	15	32
MICH	7	7	7	7	28

SCORING SUMMARY

NEB	Nunn 52 pass from Taylor (Congdon kick)
MICH	Ecker 13 pass from Henne (Rivas kick)
MICH	Massey 16 pass from Henne (Rivas kick)
NEB	Swift 14 pass from Taylor (Congdon kick)
NEB	FG Congdon 20
MICH	Manningham 21 pass from Henne (Rivas kick)
MICH	Henne 7 run (Rivas kick)
NEB	Ross 31 run (Peterson pass from Taylor)
NEB	Nunn 13 pass from Taylor (Congdon kick)

NEB	TEAM STATISTICS	MICH
16	First Downs	23
151	Rushing Yards	130
14-31-2	Passing	21-43-1
167	Passing Yards	270
318	Total Yards	400
3-32	Punt Returns - Yards	7-72
2-43	Kickoff Returns - Yards	6-186
8-51.5	Punts - Average	7-34.9
0-0	Fumbles - Lost	4-2
9-76	Penalties - Yards	6-49
28:39	Possession Time	31:21

INDIVIDUAL LEADERS

RUSHING
NEB: Ross 28-161, 1 TD; Lucky 1-3.
MICH: Hart 19-74; Henne 13-38, 1 TD.

PASSING
NEB: Taylor 14-31-2, 167 yards, 3 TD.
MICH: Henne 21-43-1, 270 yards, 3 TD.

RECEIVING
NEB: Nunn 4-91, 2 TD; Swift 3-31, 1 TD.
MICH: Ecker 1-71, 1 TD; Avant 8-71.

DECEMBER 30, 2006
TEXAS 26, IOWA 24

	1ST	2ND	3RD	4TH	FINAL
TEX	3	7	10	6	26
IA	14	0	7	3	24

SCORING SUMMARY

IA	A. Young 1 run (Schlicher kick)
IA	Brodell 63 pass from Tate (Schlicher kick)
TEX	FG Bailey 27
TEX	Sweed 20 pass from McCoy (Bailey kick)
TEX	FG Bailey 43
TEX	Charles 72 pass from McCoy (Bailey kick)
IA	Brodell 23 pass from Tate (Schlicher kick)
TEX	S. Young 2 run (Pass failed)
IA	FG Schlicher 38

TEX	TEAM STATISTICS	IA
17	First Downs	17
70	Rushing Yards	89
26-40-0	Passing	15-25-1
308	Passing Yards	274
378	Total Yards	363
2-1	Punt Returns - Yards	2-4
5-139	Kickoff Returns - Yards	3-56
6-37.8	Punts - Average	5-42.4
2-1	Fumbles - Lost	2-1
6-60	Penalties - Yards	8-53
29:04	Possession Time	30:56

INDIVIDUAL LEADERS

RUSHING
TEX: Charles 4-26; Shipley 1-14.
IA: A. Young 13-64, 1 TD; Sims 12-26.

PASSING
TEX: McCoy 26-40-0, 308 yards, 2 TD.
IA: Tate 15-25-1, 274 yards, 2 TD.

RECEIVING
TEX: Finley 8-46; Cosby 7-59.
IA: Brodell 6-159, 2 TD; Douglas 3-40.

BCS National Championship Game

ORIGIN

Between 1992 and 1996, conference alignments with bowl games started to break down, increasing the likelihood that the two top teams in the country would meet. The Bowl Championship Series was created in 1998, with the national championship game rotating among the Fiesta, Sugar, Orange, and Rose bowls. To decide which teams would compete, the BCS standings—a mathematical formula based on polls, computer rankings, results, and strength of schedule—was devised.

For the 2006 season, the BCS created a fifth bowl, the BCS National Championship, in which the top two teams would compete. The national championship game is played the week after the four original BCS bowls, and rotates among those venues.

SEASON	DATE	PRE-GAME RANK	TEAMS	SCORE	FINAL RANK	MOST VALUABLE PLAYER(S)	ATT.
2006	Jan. 8, 2007	2	**Florida**	**41**	1	Chris Leak, Florida, QB	74,628
		1	**Ohio State**	**14**	2		

JANUARY 8, 2007

FLORIDA 41, OHIO STATE 14
at Glendale, Ariz. (University of Phoenix Stadium)

	1ST	2ND	3RD	4TH	FINAL
UF	14	20	0	7	41
OSU	7	7	0	0	14

SCORING SUMMARY

OSU	Ginn Jr. 93 kickoff return (Pettrey kick)
UF	Baker 14 pass from Leak (Hetland kick)
UF	Harvin 4 run (Hetland kick)
UF	Wynn 2 run (Hetland kick)
OSU	Pittman 18 run (Pettrey kick)
UF	FG Hetland 42
UF	FG Hetland 40
UF	Caldwell 1 pass from Tebow (Hetland kick)
UF	Tebow 1 run (Hetland kick)

UF	TEAM STATISTICS	OSU
21	First Downs	8
156	Rushing Yards	47
26-37-0	Passing	4-14-1
214	Passing Yards	35
370	Total Yards	82
4-28	Punt Returns - Yards	1-13
1-33	Kickoff Returns - Yards	6-193
4-44.2	Punts - Average	6-37.8
0-0	Fumbles - Lost	1-1
6-50	Penalties - Yards	5-50
40:48	Possession Time	19:12

INDIVIDUAL LEADERS

RUSHING
UF: Wynn 19-69, 1 TD; Tebow 10-39, 1 TD; Harvin 5-22, 1 TD.
OSU: Pittman 10-62, 1 TD; Wells 2-9.

PASSING
UF: Leak 25-36-0, 213 yards, 1 TD; Tebow 1-1-0, 1 yard, 1 TD.
OSU: Smith 4-14-1, 35 yards.

RECEIVING
UF: Harvin 9-60; Cornelius 5-50
OSU: Gonzalez 2-11; Hartline 1-13.

CAPITAL ONE BOWL

PROFILE

Site: Orlando, Fla.
Stadium: Florida Citrus Bowl
Capacity: 70,000
Surface: Grass

PLAYING SITES

Tangerine Bowl, 1947-72
Florida Field, 1973
Tangerine Bowl, now Florida Citrus Bowl, 1974-82
Orlando Stadium, now Florida Citrus Bowl, 1983-85
Florida Citrus Bowl, since 1986

NAME CHANGES

Tangerine Bowl, 1947-82
Florida Citrus Bowl, 1983-93
CompUSA Florida Citrus Bowl, 1994-99
OurHouse.com Florida Citrus Bowl, 2000
Capital One/Florida Citrus Bowl, 2001-02
Capital One Bowl, since 2003

SEASON	DATE	PRE-GAME RANK	TEAMS	SCORE	FINAL RANK	MOST VALUABLE PLAYER(S)	ATT.
1985	Dec. 28, 1985	17	Ohio State	10	14	Larry Kolic, Ohio State, LB	50,920
		19	BYU	7	16		
1987	Jan. 1, 1988	14	Clemson	35	12	Rodney Williams, Clemson, QB	53,152
		20	Penn State*	10			
1989	Jan. 1, 1990	11	Illinois	31	10	Jeff George, Illinois, QB	60,016
		15	Virginia	21	18		
1992	Jan. 1, 1993	8	Georgia	21	8	Garrison Hearst, Georgia, RB	65,861
		15	Ohio State	14	18		
1993	Jan. 1, 1994	13	Penn State	31	8	Bobby Engram, Penn State, WR	72,456
		6	Tennessee	13	12		
1994	Jan. 2, 1995	6	Alabama	24	5	Sherman Williams, Alabama, RB	71,195
		13	Ohio State	17	14		
1995	Jan. 1, 1996	4T	Tennessee	20	3	Jay Graham, Tennessee, RB	70,797
		4T	Ohio State	14	6		
1996	Jan. 1, 1997	9	Tennessee	48	9	Peyton Manning, Tennessee, QB	63,467
		11	Northwestern	28	15		
1997	Jan. 1, 1998	6	Florida	21	4	Fred Taylor, Florida, TB	72,940
		11	Penn State	6	16		
1998	Jan. 1, 1999	15	Michigan	45	12	Anthony Thomas, Michigan, RB	63,584
		11	Arkansas	31	16		
1999	Jan. 1, 2000	9	Michigan State	37	7	Plaxico Burress, Michigan State, WR	62,011
		10	Florida	34	12		
2000	Jan. 1, 2001	17	Michigan	31	11	Anthony Thomas, Michigan, RB	66,928
		20	Auburn	28	18		
2001	Jan. 1, 2002	8	Tennessee	45	4	Casey Clausen, Tennessee, QB	59,693
		17	Michigan	17	20		
2002	Jan. 1, 2003	19	Auburn	13	14	Ronnie Brown, Auburn, TB	66,334
		10	Penn State	9	16		
2003	Jan. 1, 2004	11	Georgia	34 OT	7	David Greene, Georgia, QB	64,565
		12	Purdue	27	18		
2004	Jan. 1, 2005	11	Iowa	30	8	JaMarcus Russell, LSU, QB	70,227
		12	LSU	25	16		
2005	Jan. 2, 2006	21	Wisconsin	24	15	Brian Calhoun, Wisconsin, RB	57,221
		7	Auburn	10	14		
2006	Jan. 1, 2007	6	Arkansas	14	7	John Stocco, Wisconsin, QB	60,774
		12	Wisconsin	17	15		

DECEMBER 28, 1985
OHIO STATE 10, BYU 7

	1ST	2ND	3RD	4TH	FINAL
OSU	0	3	7	0	10
BYU	0	7	0	0	7

SCORING SUMMARY
OSU — FG Spangler 47
BYU — Miles 38 pass from Bosco (Webster kick)
OSU — Kolic 14 interception return (Spangler kick)

OSU	TEAM STATISTICS	BYU
20	First Downs	19
133	Rushing Yards	88
19-36-0	Passing	26-50-4
196	Passing Yards	261
329	Total Yards	349
8-38.6	Punts - Average	7-45.3
2-2	Fumbles - Lost	3-2
10-61	Penalties - Yards	6-54

INDIVIDUAL LEADERS
RUSHING
OSU: Woolridge 25-92; Workman 5-23.
BYU: Tuipulotu 9-43; Sikahema 5-23.
PASSING
OSU: Karsatos 19-35-0, 196 yards.
BYU: Bosco 26-50-4, 261 yards, 1 TD.
RECEIVING
OSU: Carter 5-71; Cooper 5-48.
BYU: Bellini 5-87; Heimuli 10-77.

JANUARY 1, 1988
CLEMSON 35, PENN STATE 10

	1ST	2ND	3RD	4TH	FINAL
CLEM	7	7	7	14	35
PSU	7	0	3	0	10

SCORING SUMMARY
CLEM — Johnson 7 run (Treadwell kick)
PSU — Alexander 39 pass from Knizner (Etze kick)
CLEM — Johnson 6 run (Treadwell kick)
PSU — FG Etze 27
CLEM — Johnson 1 run (Treadwell kick)
CLEM — Allen 25 run (Treadwell kick)
CLEM — Henderson 4 run (Treadwell kick)

CLEM	TEAM STATISTICS	PSU
25	First Downs	12
285	Rushing Yards	111
15-24-0	Passing	14-23-2
214	Passing Yards	194
499	Total Yards	305
5-39.0	Punts - Average	5-51.0
0-0	Fumbles - Lost	2-1
8-44	Penalties - Yards	4-26

INDIVIDUAL LEADERS
RUSHING
CLEM: Allen 11-105, 1 TD; Johnson 18-88, 3 TD.
PSU: Thompson 6-55; Brown 13-51.
PASSING
CLEM: Williams 15-24-0, 214 yards.
PSU: Knizner 13-22-2, 148 yards, 1 TD.
RECEIVING
CLEM: Jennings 7-110; Cooper 4-56.
PSU: Timpson 4-81; Thompson 3-19.

JANUARY 1, 1990
ILLINOIS 31, VIRGINIA 21

	1ST	2ND	3RD	4TH	FINAL
ILL	7	10	7	7	31
UVA	0	7	7	7	21

SCORING SUMMARY
ILL — Williams 35 pass from George (Higgins kick)
UVA — Finkelston 30 pass from S. Moore (McInerney kick)
ILL — Donovan 1 pass from George (Higgins kick)
ILL — FG Higgins 34
ILL — Griffith 3 run (Higgins kick)
UVA — Wilson 2 run (McInerney kick)
ILL — Bellamy 24 pass from George (Higgins kick)
UVA — H. Moore 3 pass from S. Moore (McInerney kick)

ILL	TEAM STATISTICS	UVA
29	First Downs	18
176	Rushing Yards	110
26-38-1	Passing	19-30-2
321	Passing Yards	212
497	Total Yards	322
3-38.0	Punts - Average	6-41.3
3-3	Fumbles - Lost	2-1
4-35	Penalties - Yards	6-40

INDIVIDUAL LEADERS
RUSHING
ILL: Griffith 18-93, 1 TD; Feagin 10-54.
UVA: Kirby 8-64; S. Moore 15-34.
PASSING
ILL: George 26-38-1, 321 yards, 3 TD.
UVA: S. Moore 17-27-2, 191 yards, 2 TD.
RECEIVING
ILL: Bellamy 8-166, 1 TD; Williams 4-45, 1 TD.
UVA: Finkelston 3-69, 1 TD; H. Moore 5-56, 1 TD.

---

*Played as an independent or with other conference affiliation

JANUARY 1, 1993
GEORGIA 21, OHIO STATE 14

	1ST	2ND	3RD	4TH	FINAL
UGA	7	0	7	7	21
OSU	0	7	7	0	14

SCORING SUMMARY
UGA Hearst 1 run (Peterson kick)
OSU Smith 1 run (Williams kick)
UGA Hearst 5 run (Peterson kick)
OSU Smith 5 run (Williams kick)
UGA Harvey 1 run (Peterson kick)

UGA	TEAM STATISTICS	OSU
26	First Downs	18
202	Rushing Yards	179
21-31-0	Passing	8-24-1
242	Passing Yards	110
444	Total Yards	289
6-39.0	Punts - Average	8-37.1
2-2	Fumbles - Lost	1-1
3-30	Penalties - Yards	5-35

INDIVIDUAL LEADERS
RUSHING
UGA: Hearst 28-163, 2 TD; Davis 7-42.
OSU: Smith 25-112, 2 TD; Harris 7-38.
PASSING
UGA: Zeier 21-31-0, 242 yards.
OSU: Herbstreit 8-24-1, 110 yards.
RECEIVING
UGA: Hastings 8-113; Mitchell 2-39.
OSU: Smith 2-49; Stablein 2-31.

JANUARY 1, 1994
PENN STATE 31, TENNESSEE 13

	1ST	2ND	3RD	4TH	FINAL
PSU	7	10	7	7	31
TENN	10	3	0	0	13

SCORING SUMMARY
TENN FG Becksvoort 46
TENN Fleming 19 pass from Shuler (Becksvoort kick)
PSU   Carter 3 run (Fayak kick)
PSU   FG Fayak 19
TENN FG Becksvoort 50
PSU   Carter 14 run (Fayak kick)
PSU   Brady 7 pass from Collins (Fayak kick)
PSU   Engram 15 pass from Collins (Fayak kick)

PSU	TEAM STATISTICS	TENN
20	First Downs	16
209	Rushing Yards	135
15-24-1	Passing	23-44-1
162	Passing Yards	213
371	Total Yards	348
6-32.0	Punts - Average	6-44.2
0-0	Fumbles - Lost	0-0
4-30	Penalties - Yards	10-79

INDIVIDUAL LEADERS
RUSHING
PSU: Carter 19-93, 2 TD; Archie 13-69.
TENN: Garner 16-89; Williams 1-38.
PASSING
PSU: Collins 15-24-1, 162 yards, 2 TD.
TENN: Shuler 22-42-1, 205 yards, 1 TD.
RECEIVING
PSU: Engram 7-107, 1 TD; O'Neal 2-19.
TENN: Fleming 7-101, 1 TD; Phillips 3-23.

JANUARY 2, 1995
ALABAMA 24, OHIO STATE 17

	1ST	2ND	3RD	4TH	FINAL
ALA	0	14	0	10	24
OSU	0	14	0	3	17

SCORING SUMMARY
ALA Lynch 9 run (Proctor kick)
OSU Galloway 69 pass from Hoying (Jackson kick)
OSU Galloway 11 pass from Hoying (Jackson kick)
ALA Williams 7 run (Proctor kick)
OSU FG Jackson 34
ALA FG Proctor 27
ALA Williams 50 pass from Barker (Proctor kick)

ALA	TEAM STATISTICS	OSU
28	First Downs	15
204	Rushing Yards	96
18-37-0	Passing	11-27-1
317	Passing Yards	180
521	Total Yards	276
4-24.0	Punts - Average	7-36.1
3-3	Fumbles - Lost	4-1
4-45	Penalties - Yards	6-43

INDIVIDUAL LEADERS
RUSHING
ALA: Williams 27-166, 1 TD; Lynch 13-35.
OSU: George 15-89; Sualua 6-44.
PASSING
ALA: Barker 18-37-0, 317 yards, 1 TD.
OSU: Hoying 11-27-1, 180 yards, 2 TD.
RECEIVING
ALA: Williams 8-155, 1 TD; Malone 3-70.
OSU: Galloway 8-146, 2 TD; Dudley 2-26.

JANUARY 1, 1996
TENNESSEE 20, OHIO STATE 14

	1ST	2ND	3RD	4TH	FINAL
TENN	0	7	7	6	20
OSU	7	0	0	7	14

SCORING SUMMARY
OSU   George 2 run (Jackson kick)
TENN Graham 69 run (Hall kick)
TENN Kent 47 pass from Manning (Hall kick)
OSU   Dudley 32 pass from Hoying (Jackson kick)
TENN FG Hall 29
TENN FG Hall 25

TENN	TEAM STATISTICS	OSU
15	First Downs	17
145	Rushing Yards	89
20-35-0	Passing	19-38-1
182	Passing Yards	246
327	Total Yards	335
9-34.2	Punts-Average	7-48.1
1-1	Fumbles-Lost	5-3
8-43	Penalties-Yards	6-57
30:39	Possession Time	29:21

INDIVIDUAL LEADERS
RUSHING
TENN: Graham 26-168, 1 TD.
OSU: George 25-107, 1 TD.
PASSING
TENN: Manning 20-35-0, 182 yards, 1 TD.
OSU: Hoying 19-38-1, 246 yards, 1 TD.
RECEIVING
TENN: Kent 7-109, 1 TD.
OSU: Glenn 7-95; Dudley 5-106, 1 TD.

JANUARY 1, 1997
TENNESSEE 48, NORTHWESTERN 28

	1ST	2ND	3RD	4TH	FINAL
TENN	21	10	7	10	48
NU	0	21	0	7	28

SCORING SUMMARY
TENN Price 43 pass from Manning (Hall kick)
TENN Manning 10 run (Hall kick)
TENN Kent 11 pass from Manning (Hall kick)
NU   D. Autry 2 run (Gowins kick)
NU   Musso 20 pass from Schnur (Gowins kick)
NU   D. Autry 28 run (Gowins kick)
TENN Kent 67 pass from Manning (Hall kick)
TENN FG Hall 19
TENN Hines 30 interception return (Hall kick)
TENN FG Hall 28
NU   Bates 22 pass from Schnur (Gowins kick)
TENN Moore 6 pass from Manning (Hall kick)

TENN	TEAM STATISTICS	NU
29	First Downs	22
115	Rushing Yards	43
27-39-0	Passing	27-51-4
408	Passing Yards	242
523	Total Yards	285
4-35.8	Punts - Average	6-37.3
4-2	Fumbles - Lost	1-1
13-112	Penalties - Yards	5-40

INDIVIDUAL LEADERS
RUSHING
TENN: Graham 14-79; Levine 7-33.
NU: D. Autry 17-66, 2 TD; Gooch 2-10.
PASSING
TENN: Manning 27-39-0, 408 yards, 4 TD.
NU: Schnur 25-45-3, 228 yards, 2 TD.
RECEIVING
TENN: Kent 5-122, 2 TD; Price 6-110, 1 TD.
NU: Bates 10-97, 1 TD; Musso 10-91, 1 TD.

JANUARY 1, 1998
FLORIDA 21, PENN STATE 6

	1ST	2ND	3RD	4TH	FINAL
UF	14	0	0	7	21
PSU	0	3	3	0	6

SCORING SUMMARY
UF   Brindise 1 run (Cooper kick)
UF   Green 35 pass from Johnson (Cooper kick)
PSU FG Forney 42
PSU FG Jackson 30
UF   Green 37 pass from Palmer (Cooper kick)

UF	TEAM STATISTICS	PSU
23	First Downs	9
254	Rushing Yards	47
9-19-2	Passing	10-32-3
143	Passing Yards	92
397	Total Yards	139
5-36.4	Punts - Average	7-42.1
2-1	Fumbles - Lost	0-0
5-46	Penalties - Yards	1-5

INDIVIDUAL LEADERS
RUSHING
UF: Taylor 43-234; Carroll 9-28.
PSU: Eberly 14-53; Watson 4-5.
PASSING
UF: Johnson 5-12-1, 77 yards, 1 TD; Brindise 3-6-1, 29 yards.
PSU: McQuery 10-32-3, 92 yards.
RECEIVING
UF: Green 2-72, 2 TD; Taylor 1-19.
PSU: Brown 3-25; Natasi 2-26.

JANUARY 1, 1999
MICHIGAN 45, ARKANSAS 31

	1ST	2ND	3RD	4TH	FINAL
MICH	3	21	0	21	45
ARK	0	10	14	7	31

SCORING SUMMARY
MICH	FG Feely 43
ARK	Williams 35 pass from Stoerner (Latourette kick)
MICH	Thomas 2 run (Feely kick)
MICH	Gold 46 interception return (Feely kick)
ARK	FG Latourette 42
MICH	Thomas 5 run (Feely kick)
ARK	Chukwuma 2 run (Latourette kick)
ARK	Chukwuma 1 run (Latourette kick)
ARK	Davenport 9 pass from Stoerner (Latourette kick)
MICH	Thomas 1 run (Feely kick)
MICH	Johnson 21 pass from Brady (Feely kick)
MICH	Whitley 26 interception return (Feely kick)

MICH	TEAM STATISTICS	ARK
21	First Downs	20
204	Rushing Yards	116
16-30-2	Passing	17-42-2
230	Passing Yards	232
434	Total Yards	348
5-40.0	Punts - Average	7-33.9
78	Return Yards	81
1-1	Fumbles - Lost	0-0
12-104	Penalties - Yards	4-31
31:17	Possession Time	28:43

INDIVIDUAL LEADERS
RUSHING
MICH: Thomas 21-132, 3 TD; Williams 19-72.
ARK: Chukwuma 17-56, 2 TD; Hill 13-35.
PASSING
MICH: Brady 14-27-2, 209 yards, 1 TD.
ARK: Stoerner 17-42-2, 232 yards, 2 TD.
RECEIVING
MICH: Streets 7-129; Williams 2-15.
ARK: Williams 7-90, 1 TD; Lucas 3-63.

JANUARY 1, 2000
MICHIGAN STATE 37, FLORIDA 34

	1ST	2ND	3RD	4TH	FINAL
MSU	3	17	6	11	37
UF	7	14	6	7	34

SCORING SUMMARY
MSU	FG Edinger 46
UF	Taylor 12 pass from Johnson (Chandler kick)
MSU	Burress 37 pass from Burke (Edinger kick)
MSU	Turner 24 fumble return (Edinger kick)
UF	Taylor 8 pass from Johnson (Chandler kick)
MSU	FG Edinger 20
UF	Johnson 1 run (Chandler kick)
MSU	Burress 21 pass from Burke (pass failed)
UF	Taylor 39 pass from Johnson (pass failed)
UF	Gillespie 2 run (Chandler kick)
MSU	Burress 30 pass from Burke (Scott pass from Burke)
MSU	FG Edinger 39

MSU	TEAM STATISTICS	UF
25	First Downs	27
143	Rushing Yards	67
21-35-2	Passing	25-51-0
257	Passing Yards	300
400	Total Yards	367
3-43.3	Punts - Average	6-35.5
3-1	Fumbles - Lost	4-2
7-80	Penalties - Yards	10-100
32:49	Possession Time	27:11

INDIVIDUAL LEADERS
RUSHING
MSU: Clemons 20-105; Duckett 14-77.
UF: Gilespie 15-74, 1 TD; Carroll 5-14.
PASSING
MSU: Burke 21-35-2, 257 yards, 3 TD.
UF: Johnson 24-50-0, 288 yards, 3 TD.
RECEIVING
MSU: Burress 13-185, 3 TD; Baker 2-21.
UF: Taylor 11-156, 3 TD; Jackson 5-61.

JANUARY 1, 2001
MICHIGAN 31, AUBURN 28

	1ST	2ND	3RD	4TH	FINAL
MICH	7	14	10	0	31
AU	0	14	7	7	28

SCORING SUMMARY
MICH	Terrell 31 pass from Henson (Epstein kick)
AU	Daniels 19 pass from Leard (Duval kick)
AU	Robinson 20 pass from Leard (Duval kick)
MICH	Askew 4 pass from Henson (Epstein kick)
MICH	Thomas 11 run (Epstein kick)
MICH	Thomas 25 run (Epstein kick)
AU	Johnson 12 run (Duval kick)
MICH	FG Epstein 41
AU	Green 21 pass from Leard (Duval kick)

MICH	TEAM STATISTICS	AU
21	First Downs	23
159	Rushing Yards	92
15-21-0	Passing	28-37-2
294	Passing Yards	394
453	Total Yards	486
4-43.5	Punts - Average	3-42.7
2-1	Fumbles - Lost	2-1
2-20	Penalties - Yards	7-60
29:57	Possession Time	30:03

INDIVIDUAL LEADERS
RUSHING
MICH: Thomas 32-182, 2 TD; Bellamy 3-13.
AU: Johnson 25-85, 1 TD; Evans 3-16.
PASSING
MICH: Henson 15-20-0, 294 yards, 2 TD.
AU: Leard 28-37-2, 394 yards, 3 TD.
RECEIVING
MICH: Terrell 4-136, 1 TD; Walker 4-100.
AU: Daniels 7-98, 1 TD; Willis 5-69.

JANUARY 1, 2002
TENNESSEE 45, MICHIGAN 17

	1ST	2ND	3RD	4TH	FINAL
TENN	10	14	7	14	45
MICH	0	10	0	7	17

SCORING SUMMARY
TENN	FG Walls 32
TENN	Washington 3 pass from Clausen (Walls kick)
TENN	Clausen 1 run (Walls kick)
MICH	Askew 14 pass from Navarre (Epstein kick)
TENN	Clausen 1 run (Walls kick)
MICH	FG Epstein 28
TENN	Witten 64 pass from Clausen (Walls kick)
TENN	Washington 37 pass from Clausen (Walls kick)
TENN	Stephens 3 run (Walls kick)
MICH	Bell 24 pass from Navarre (Epstein kick)

TENN	TEAM STATISTICS	MICH
22	First Downs	20
97	Rushing Yards	103
27-35-0	Passing	21-39-1
406	Passing Yards	240
503	Total Yards	343
4-36	Punt Returns - Yards	3-14
3-67	Kickoff Returns - Yards	8-125
5-31.8	Punts - Average	7-39.6
3-32	Penalties - Yards	6-42
34:13	Possession Time	25:47

INDIVIDUAL LEADERS
RUSHING
TENN: Stallworth 2-44; Stephens 16-38, 1 TD.
MICH: Askew 9-76; Perry 17-41.
PASSING
TENN: Clausen 26-34-0, 393 yards, 3 TD.
MICH: Navarre 21-39-1, 240 yards, 2 TD.
RECEIVING
TENN: Witten 6-125, 1 TD; Stallworth 8-119; Washington 6-70, 2 TD.
MICH: Walker 5-100; Joppru 5-45.

JANUARY 1, 2003
AUBURN 13, PENN STATE 9

	1ST	2ND	3RD	4TH	FINAL
AU	0	0	7	6	13
PSU	3	3	0	3	9

SCORING SUMMARY
PSU	FG Gould 21
PSU	FG Gould 27
AU	Brown 1 run (Duval kick)
PSU	FG Gould 31
AU	Brown 17 run (pass failed)

AU	TEAM STATISTICS	PSU
15	First Downs	15
200	Rushing Yards	170
10-17-1	Passing	10-27-1
78	Passing Yards	98
278	Total Yards	268
4-48.2	Punts - Average	5-38.2
1-1	Fumbles - Lost	3-0
9-84	Penalties - Yards	7-68

INDIVIDUAL LEADERS
RUSHING
AU: Brown 37-184, 2 TD; Smith 5-10.
PSU: L. Johnson 20-72; Mills 9-56.
PASSING
AU: Campbell 10-17-1, 78 yards.
PSU: Mills 8-24-1, 67 yards.
RECEIVING
AU: Aromashodu 2-18; Johnson 2-17.
PSU: T. Johnson 2-54; Kranchick 2-15.

JANUARY 1, 2004
GEORGIA 34, PURDUE 27

	1ST	2ND	3RD	4TH	OT	FINAL
GEO	14	10	0	3	7	34
PUR	0	10	0	17	0	27

SCORING SUMMARY
GEO	Gibson 6 pass from Greene (Bennett kick)
GEO	Gibson 4 pass from Greene (Bennett kick)
GEO	FG Bennett 28
GEO	Brown 11 pass from Greene (Bennett kick)
PUR	Orton 17 run (Jones kick)
PUR	FG Jones 27
PUR	Orton 2 run (Jones kick)
GEO	FG Bennett 40
PUR	Chambers 3 pass from Orton (Jones kick)
PUR	FG Jones 44
GEO	Lumpkin 1 run (Bennett kick)

GEO	TEAM STATISTICS	PUR
23	First Downs	15
113	Rushing Yards	59
27-37-0	Passing	20-35-1
327	Passing Yards	230
440	Total Yards	289
4-34	Punt Returns - Yards	5-53
2-48	Kickoff Returns - Yards	6-163
6-44.7	Punts - Average	9-44.4
34	Return Yards	53
2-2	Fumbles - Lost	1-0
10-90	Penalties - Yards	10-69
35:29	Possession Time	24:31

INDIVIDUAL LEADERS
RUSHING
GEO: Lumpkin 27-90, 1 TD.
PUR: Void 15-63.
PASSING
GEO: Greene 27-37-0, 327 yards, 3 TD.
PUR: Orton 20-34-1, 230 yards, 1 TD.
RECEIVING
GEO: Brown 5-99, 1 TD; Gary 2-53; Browning 2-48.
PUR: Standeford 7-102; Stubblefield 8-99.

JANUARY 1, 2005
IOWA 30, LSU 25

	1ST	2ND	3RD	4TH	FINAL
IA	7	7	3	13	30
LSU	0	12	0	13	25

SCORING SUMMARY

IA	Solomon 57 pass from Tate (Schlicher kick)
LSU	FG Jackson 29
LSU	FG Jackson 47
IA	Considine 7 blocked punt return (Schlicher kick)
LSU	Broussard 74 run (kick failed)
IA	FG Schlicher 19
IA	Simmons 4 run (Schlicher kick)
LSU	Green 22 pass from Russell (Jackson kick)
LSU	Green 3 pass from Russell (kick failed)
IA	Holloway 56 pass from Tate

IA	TEAM STATISTICS	LSU
16	First Downs	19
47	Rushing Yards	118
20-32-2	Passing	23-35-1
287	Passing Yards	228
334	Total Yards	346
5-45	Punt Returns - Yards	4-42
5-76	Kickoff Returns - Yards	5-134
6-49.2	Punts - Average	6-30.2
1-0	Fumbles - Lost	1-0
9-50	Penalties - Yards	5-42
25:48	Possession Time	34:12

INDIVIDUAL LEADERS

RUSHING
IA: Simmons 13-35, 1 TD.
LSU: Broussard 13-109, 1 TD.

PASSING
IA: Tate 20-32-2, 287 yards, 2 TD.
LSU: Russell 12-15-0, 128 yards, 2 TD.

RECEIVING
IA: Hinkel 10-93; Solomon 4-81, 1 TD.
LSU: Bowe 8-122; Green 6-59, 2 TD.

JANUARY 2, 2006
WISCONSIN 24, AUBURN 10

	1ST	2ND	3RD	4TH	FINAL
WISC	10	7	0	7	24
AUB	0	0	3	7	10

SCORING SUMMARY

WISC	Williams 30 pass from Stocco (Mehlhaff kick)
WISC	FG Mehlhaff 19
WISC	Daniels 13 pass from Stocco (Mehlhaff kick)
AUB	FG Vaughn 19
AUB	Taylor 9 pass from Cox (Vaughn kick)
WISC	Calhoun 33 run (Mehlhaff kick)

WISC	TEAM STATISTICS	AUB
24	First Downs	19
247	Rushing Yards	99
15-27-0	Passing	15-33-1
301	Passing Yards	137
548	Total Yards	236
2-5	Punt Returns - Yards	1-10
0-0	Kickoff Returns - Yards	3-58
3-45.3	Punts - Average	6-45.7
0-0	Fumbles - Lost	0-0
7-56	Penalties - Yards	5-35
30:48	Possession Time	29:12

INDIVIDUAL LEADERS

RUSHING
WISC: Calhoun 30-213, 1 TD; Williams 4-35.
AUB: Irons 22-88; Lester 7-31.

PASSING
WISC: Stocco 15-27-0, 301 yards, 2 TD.
AUB: Cox 15-33-1, 137 yards, 1 TD.

RECEIVING
WISC: Williams 6-173, 1 TD; Orr 4-74.
AUB: Obomanu 5-62; Irons 1-21.

JANUARY 1, 2007
WISCONSIN 17, ARKANSAS 14

	1ST	2ND	3RD	4TH	FINAL
ARK	7	0	0	7	14
WISC	10	7	0	0	17

SCORING SUMMARY

WISC	FG Mehlhaff 52
ARK	Jones 76 run (Davis kick)
WISC	Hubbard 22 pass from Stocco (Mehlhaff kick)
WISC	Beckum 13 pass from Stocco (Mehlhaff kick)
ARK	Jones 12 run (Davis kick)

ARK	TEAM STATISTICS	WISC
18	First Downs	15
232	Rushing Yards	-5
15-32-2	Passing	14-34-2
136	Passing Yards	206
368	Total Yards	201
5-15	Punt Returns - Yards	2-19
3-54	Kickoff Returns - Yards	2-27
8-33.6	Punts - Average	7-42.7
1-0	Fumbles - Lost	1-1
12-123	Penalties - Yards	4-35
30:29	Possession Time	29:31

INDIVIDUAL LEADERS

RUSHING
ARK: Jones 14-150, 2 TD; McFadden 19-89.
WISC: Hill 19-36; Stocco 9--41.

PASSING
ARK: Dick 9-21-1, 98 yards; Mustain 5-10-1, 41 yards.
WISC: Stocco 14-34-2, 206 yards, 2 TD.

RECEIVING
ARK: Johnson 4-46; Jones 4-2.
WISC: Beckum 5-82, 1 TD; Hubbard 4-73, 1 TD.

CHAMPS SPORTS BOWL

PROFILE

Site: Orlando, Fla.
Stadium: Florida Citrus Bowl
Capacity: 70,000
Surface: Grass

PLAYING SITES

Joe Robbie Stadium, renamed Pro Player Stadium in 1996, 1990-2000

Florida Citrus Bowl Stadium, since 2001

NAME CHANGES

Blockbuster Bowl, 1990-93
Carquest Bowl, 1994-97
Micron PC Bowl, 1998-99
MicronPC.com Bowl, 2000
Visit Florida Tangerine Bowl, 2001
Mazda Tangerine Bowl, 2002-03
Champs Sports Bowl, since 2004

SEASON	DATE	PRE-GAME RANK	TEAMS	SCORE	FINAL RANK	MOST VALUABLE PLAYER(S)	ATT.
1990	Dec. 28, 1990	6	Florida State	24	4	Amp Lee, Florida State, RB	74,021
		7	Penn State*	17	11		
1992	Jan. 1, 1993	13	Stanford	24	9	Darrien Gordon, Stanford, CB	45,554
		21	Penn State*	3			
1999	Dec. 30, 1999		Illinois	63	24	Kurt Kittner, Illinois, QB	31,089
			Virginia	21			
2000	Dec. 28, 2000		North Carolina State	38		Philip Rivers, North Carolina St., QB	28,359
			Minnesota	30			
2006	Dec. 29, 2006		Maryland	24		Sam Hollenbach, Maryland, QB	40,168
			Purdue	7			

DECEMBER 28, 1990
FLORIDA STATE 24, PENN STATE 17

	1ST	2ND	3RD	4TH	FINAL
FSU	10	7	7	0	24
PSU	7	0	3	7	17

SCORING SUMMARY
FSU FG Andrews 41
FSU Lee 1 run (Andrews kick)
PSU Daniels 56 pass from Sacca (Fayak kick)
FSU Lee 7 run (Andrews Kick)
PSU FG Fayak 32
FSU Weldon 5 run (Andrews kick)
PSU T. Smith 37 pass from Bill (Fayak kick)

FSU	TEAM STATISTICS	PSU
19	First Downs	17
152	Rushing Yards	122
22-36-2	Passing	15-32-3
248	Passing Yards	278
400	Total Yards	400
43	Punt Returns - Yards	72
7-37.6	Punts - Average	6-36.3
0-0	Fumbles - Lost	2-0
4-35	Penalties - Yards	6-46
33:47	Possession Time	26:13

INDIVIDUAL LEADERS
RUSHING
FSU: Lee 21-86, 2 TD; Bennett 7-30.
PSU: Brown 14-46; Thompson 8-33.
PASSING
FSU: Weldon 22-36-2, 248 yards.
PSU: Sacca 12-25-2, 194 yards, 1 TD; Bill 3-7-1, 84 yards, 1 TD.
RECEIVING
FSU: Dawsey 8-107; Bennett 4-49.
PSU: Daniels 7-154, 1TD; T. Smith 5-100, 1 TD.

JANUARY 1, 1993
STANFORD 24, PENN STATE 3

	1ST	2ND	3RD	4TH	FINAL
STAN	7	7	10	0	24
PSU	3	0	0	0	3

SCORING SUMMARY
STAN Wetnight 2 pass from Stenstrom (Abrams kick)
PSU FG Muscillo 33
STAN Lasley 5 run (Abrams kick)
STAN FG Abrams 28
STAN Milburn 40 pass from Stenstrom (Abrams kick)

STAN	TEAM STATISTICS	PSU
16	First Downs	12
155	Rushing Yards	107
17-29-2	Passing	13-40-2
210	Passing Yards	156
365	Total Yards	263
7-42.4	Punts - Average	11-38.4
2-1	Fumbles - Lost	0-0
5-41	Penalties - Yards	3-25

INDIVIDUAL LEADERS
RUSHING
STAN: Roberts 17-98; Lasley 4-19, 1 TD.
PSU: Anderson 13-40; O'Neal 11-38.
PASSING
STAN: Stenstrom 17-28-1, 210 yards, 2 TD.
PSU: Collins 12-30-1, 145 yards.
RECEIVING
STAN: Wetnight 5-71, 1 TD; Cook 4-55.
PSU: McDuffie 6-111; Drayton 3-21.

DECEMBER 30, 1999
ILLINOIS 63, VIRGINIA 21

	1ST	2ND	3RD	4TH	FINAL
ILL	14	28	7	14	63
VIR	7	0	7	7	21

SCORING SUMMARY
ILL Kittner 1 run (Rackers kick)
VIR Jones 7 run (Braverman kick)
ILL Harvey 47 run (Rackers kick)
ILL Kittner 30 pass from Lloyd (Rackers kick)
ILL Cook 61 pass from Kittner (Rackers kick)
ILL Cook 1 pass from Kittner (Rackers kick)
VIR Coffey 5 pass from Ellis (Braverman kick)
ILL Havard 2 run (Rackers kick)
ILL Harvey 9 run (Rackers kick)
ILL Johnson 1 run (Rackers kick)
VIR Thompson 55 pass from Rivers (Braverman kick)

ILL	TEAM STATISTICS	VIR
26	First Downs	20
325	Rushing Yards	172
16-26-1	Passing	17-35-1
286	Passing Yards	208
611	Total Yards	380
0-0	Punts - Average	6-36.7
2-1	Fumbles - Lost	1-1
5-39	Penalties - Yards	5-25
33:23	Possession Time	26:37

INDIVIDUAL LEADERS
RUSHING
ILL: Harvey 10-122, 2 TD; Havard 15-75, 2 TD.
VIR: Jones 23-110, 1 TD.
PASSING
ILL: Kittner 14-24-1, 254 yards, 2 TD.
VIR: Ellis 15-32-1, 146 yards, 1 TD.
RECEIVING
ILL: Cook 4-88, 2 TD; Lloyd 3-57.
VIR: Jones 5-31; McMullen 3-31.

DECEMBER 28, 2000
NC STATE 38, MINNESOTA 30

	1ST	2ND	3RD	4TH	FINAL
NCST	0	8	17	13	38
MINN	21	3	0	6	30

SCORING SUMMARY
MINN Redmon 12 run (Nystrom kick)
MINN Redmon 3 run (Nystrom kick)
MINN Cole 2 run (Nystrom kick)
MINN FG Nystrom 27
NCST Vanderveer 2 pass from Rivers (Robinson pass from Cole)
NCST K. Robinson 19 run (Leak pass from Cole)
NCST FG Passingham 37
NCST R. Robinson 3 run (pass failed)
MINN FG Nystrom 23
NCST K. Robinson 23 pass from Rivers (conversion failed)
MINN FG Nystrom 29
NCST R. Robinson 8 run (Passingham kick)

NCST	TEAM STATISTICS	MINN
22	First Downs	31
109	Rushing Yards	300
24-39-2	Passing	16-30-1
310	Passing Yards	202
419	Total Yards	502
5-44.6	Punts - Average	5-28.4
2-0	Fumbles - Lost	2-1
7-75	Penalties - Yards	14-107
24:27	Possession Time	35:33

INDIVIDUAL LEADERS
RUSHING
NCST: R. Robinson 15-74, 2 TD; K. Robinson 1-19, 1 TD.
MINN: Redmon 42-246, 2 TD.
PASSING
NCST: Rivers 24-39-2, 310 yards, 2 TD.
MINN: Cole 16-29-0, 202 yards.
RECEIVING
NCST: K. Robinson 7-157, 1 TD; Leak 4-76.
MINN: Keller 5-51; Patterson 4-30.

DECEMBER 29, 2006
MARYLAND 24, PURDUE 7

	1ST	2ND	3RD	4TH	FINAL
PU	0	7	0	0	7
MD	7	14	3	0	24

SCORING SUMMARY
MD Haynos 4 pass from Hollenbach (Ennis kick)
MD Jackson 1 run (Ennis kick)
MD Heyward-Bey 46 pass from Hollenbach (Ennis kick)
PU Orton 12 pass from Painter (Summers kick)
MD FG Ennis 22

PU	TEAM STATISTICS	MD
12	First Downs	20
21	Rushing Yards	206
23-36-1	Passing	15-24-0
264	Passing Yards	223
285	Total Yards	429
0-0	Punt Returns - Yards	1-4
5-75	Kickoff Returns - Yards	2-9
6-42.2	Punts - Average	4-39.2
1-1	Fumbles - Lost	1-0
4-33	Penalties - Yards	5-31
20:12	Possession Time	39:48

INDIVIDUAL LEADERS
RUSHING
PU: Taylor 6-19; Sheets 2-11.
MD: Ball 18-98; Lattimore 20-85.
PASSING
PU: Painter 23-36-1, 264 yards, 1 TD.
MD: Hollenbach 15-24-0, 223 yards, 2 TD.
RECEIVING
PU: Bryant 8-101; Orton 8-95, 1 TD.
MD: Heyward-Bey 4-81, 1 TD; Oquendo 3-60.

---

*Played as an independent or with other conference affiliation

COTTON BOWL

PROFILE

Site: Dallas, Texas
Stadium: Cotton Bowl
Capacity: 68,252
Surface: Grass

PLAYING SITES

Fair Park Stadium, 1937
Cotton Bowl, since 1938

NAME CHANGES

Cotton Bowl Classic, 1937-88
Mobil Cotton Bowl Classic,
  1989-95
Cotton Bowl Classic, 1996
Southwestern Bell Cotton Bowl
  Classic, 1997-2000
SBC Cotton Bowl Classic, 2001-05
AT&T Cotton Bowl, since 2006

SEASON	DATE	PRE-GAME RANK	TEAMS	SCORE	FINAL RANK	MOST VALUABLE PLAYER(S)	ATT.
1947	Jan. 1, 1948	4	**Penn State***	13		Steve Suhey, Penn State, G	43,000
		3	**SMU**	13		Doak Walker, SMU, RB	
1971	Jan. 1, 1972	10	**Penn State***	30	5	Bruce Bannon, Penn State, DE	72,000
		12	**Texas**	6	18	Lydell Mitchell, Penn State, RB	
1974	Jan. 1, 1975	7	**Penn State***	41	7	Tom Shuman, Penn State, QB	67,500
		12	**Baylor**	20	14	Ken Quesenberry, Baylor, S	
1986	Jan. 1, 1987	11	**Ohio State**	28	7	Chris Spielman, Ohio State, LB	74,188
		8	**Texas A&M**	12	13	Roger Vick, Texas A&M, FB	

JANUARY 1, 1948
PENN STATE 13, SMU 13

	1ST	2ND	3RD	4TH	FINAL
PSU	0	7	6	0	13
SMU	7	6	0	0	13

SCORING SUMMARY
SMU   Page 53 pass from Walker (Walker kick)
SMU   Walker 2 run (kick failed)
PSU   Larry Cooney 38 pass from Petchel (Czekaj kick)
PSU   Triplett 6 pass from Petchel (kick failed)

PSU	TEAM STATISTICS	SMU
12	First Downs	12
165	Rushing Yards	92
7-15-1	Passing	11-25-1
93	Passing Yards	114
258	Total Yards	206
2	Fumbles Lost	1
3-15	Penalties - Yards	1-5

INDIVIDUAL LEADERS
RUSHING
PSU: Rogel 25-95.
SMU: Walker 18-56, 1 TD.

PASSING
PSU: Petchel 7-16, 91 yards, 2 TD.
SMU: Walker 5-9, 69 yards, 1 TD.

JANUARY 1, 1972
PENN STATE 30, TEXAS 6

	1ST	2ND	3RD	4TH	FINAL
PSU	0	3	17	10	30
TEX	3	3	0	0	6

SCORING SUMMARY
TEX   FG Valek 29
PSU   FG Vitiello 21
TEX   FG Valek 40
PSU   Mitchell 1 run (Vitiello kick)
PSU   Skarzynski 65 pass from Hufnagel (Vitiello kick)
PSU   FG Vitiello 37
PSU   FG Vitiello 22
PSU   Hufnagel 4 run (Vitiello kick)

PSU	TEAM STATISTICS	TEX
18	First Downs	15
239	Rushing Yards	159
7-13-1	Passing	5-14-0
137	Passing Yards	83
376	Total Yards	242
5-36.0	Punts - Average	5-33.0
1-0	Fumbles - Lost	5-3
2-30	Penalties - Yards	1-5

INDIVIDUAL LEADERS
RUSHING
PSU: Mitchell 27-146, 1 TD; Harris 11-47.
TEX: Bertelsen 14-58; Ladd 8-45.

PASSING
PSU: Hufnagel 7-12-1, 137 yards, 1 TD.
TEX: Phillips 3-8-0, 59 yards.

RECEIVING
PSU: Skarzynski 2-81, 1 TD; Parson 3-48.
TEX: Burrisk 3-45; Kelly 2-38.

JANUARY 1, 1975
PENN STATE 41, BAYLOR 20

	1ST	2ND	3RD	4TH	FINAL
PSU	0	3	14	24	41
BU	7	0	7	6	20

SCORING SUMMARY
BU   Beaird 4 run (Hicks kick)
PSU   FG Bahr 25
PSU   Donchez 1 run (Reihner kick)
BU   Thompson 35 pass from Jeffrey (Hicks kick)
PSU   Cefalo 49 pass from Shuman (Reihner kick)
PSU   Cefalo 3 run (Reihner kick)
PSU   FG Bahr 33
PSU   Shuman 2 run (Reihner kick)
BU   Thompson 11 pass from Jackson (pass failed)
PSU   Jackson 50 kickoff return (Reihner kick)

PSU	TEAM STATISTICS	BU
23	First Downs	20
265	Rushing Yards	138
10-20-0	Passing	10-23-2
226	Passing Yards	175
491	Total Yards	313
2-36.5	Punts - Average	6-34.0
3-2	Fumbles - Lost	4-0
8-70	Penalties - Yards	7-45

INDIVIDUAL LEADERS
RUSHING
PSU: Donchez 25-116, 1 TD; Hutton 12-79.
BU: Beaird 21-84, 1 TD; McNeil 8-36.

PASSING
PSU: Shuman 10-20-0, 226 yards, 1 TD.
BU: Jeffrey 7-19-2, 135 yards, 1 TD.

RECEIVING
PSU: Cefalo 3-102, 1 TD; Natale 3-74.
BU: Thompson 3-62, 2 TD; Harper 3-45.

JANUARY 1, 1987
OHIO STATE 28, TEXAS A&M 12

	1ST	2ND	3RD	4TH	FINAL
OSU	0	7	14	7	28
A&M	3	3	0	6	12

SCORING SUMMARY
A&M   FG Slater 30
OSU   Karsatos 3 run (Frantz kick)
A&M   FG Slater 44
OSU   Spielman 24 interception return (Frantz kick)
OSU   Workman 8 run (Frantz kick)
A&M   Vick 2 run (pass failed)
OSU   Kee 49 interception return (Frantz kick)

OSU	TEAM STATISTICS	A&M
16	First Downs	18
85	Rushing Yards	160
13-29-3	Passing	13-33-5
218	Passing Yards	136
303	Total Yards	296
6-35.2	Punts - Average	6-42.2
1-0	Fumbles - Lost	1-0
11-70	Penalties - Yards	3-15

INDIVIDUAL LEADERS
RUSHING
OSU: Cooper 13-55; Workman 13-45, 1 TD.
A&M: Vick 24-113, 1 TD; Woodside 11-32.

PASSING
OSU: Karsatos 10-21-2, 195 yards.
A&M: Murray 12-31-5, 143 yards.

RECEIVING
OSU: Harris 6-105; Carter 4-61.
A&M: Bernstine 4-59; Walker 3-35.

BIG TEN ANNUAL REVIEW & BOWLS

*Played as an independent or with other conference affiliation

FIESTA BOWL

PROFILE

Site: Glendale, Ariz.
Stadium: University of Phoenix Stadium
Capacity: 73,000
Surface: Grass

PLAYING SITES

Sun Devil Stadium, 1971-2006
University of Phoenix Stadium, 2007

NAME CHANGES

Fiesta Bowl, 1971-85
Sunkist Fiesta Bowl, 1986-90
Fiesta Bowl, 1991-92
IBM OS/2 Fiesta Bowl, 1993-95
Tostitos Fiesta Bowl, since 1996

SEASON	DATE	PRE-GAME RANK	TEAMS	SCORE	FINAL RANK	MOST VALUABLE PLAYER(S)	ATT.
1977	Dec. 25, 1977	8	Penn State*	42	5	Matt Millen, Penn State, LB	57,727
		15	Arizona State	30	18	Dennis Sproul, Arizona State, QB	
1980	Dec. 26, 1980	10	Penn State*	31	8	Curt Warner, Penn State, RB	66,738
		11	Ohio State	19	15	Frank Case, Penn State, DE	
1981	Jan. 1, 1982	7	Penn State*	26	3	Curt Warner, Penn State, RB	71,053
		8	USC	10	14	Leo Wisniewski, Penn State, NT	
1983	Jan. 2, 1984	14	Ohio State	28	9	John Congemi, Pittsburgh, QB	66,484
		15	Pittsburgh	23	18	Rowland Tatum, Ohio State, LB	
1985	Jan. 1, 1986	5	Michigan	27	8	Jamie Morris, Michigan, RB	72,454
		7	Nebraska	23	11	Mark Messner, Michigan, DT	
1986	Jan. 2, 1987	2	Penn State*	14	1	D.J. Dozier, Penn State, RB	73,098
		1	Miami (Fla.)	10	2	Shane Conlan, Penn State, LB	
1991	Jan. 1, 1992	6	Penn State*	42	3	O.J. McDuffie, Penn State, WR	71,133
		10	Tennessee	17	14	Reggie Givens, Penn State, OLB	
1996	Jan. 1, 1997	7	Penn State	38	7	Curtis Enis, Penn State, TB	65,106
		20	Texas	15	23	Brandon Noble, Penn State, DT	
2002	Jan. 3, 2003	2	Ohio State	31 2OT	1	Craig Krenzel, Ohio State, QB	77,502
		1	Miami (Fla.)	24	2	Mike Doss, Ohio State, DB	
2003	Jan. 2, 2004	7	Ohio State	35	4	Craig Krenzel, Ohio State, QB	73,425
		8	Kansas State	28	14	A.J. Hawk, Ohio State, CB	
2005	Jan. 2, 2006	4	Ohio State	34	4	Troy Smith, Ohio State, QB	76,196
		5	Notre Dame	20	9	A.J. Hawk, Ohio State, LB	

DECEMBER 25, 1977
PENN STATE 42, ARIZONA STATE 30

	1ST	2ND	3RD	4TH	FINAL
PSU	14	3	7	18	42
ASU	0	14	0	16	30

SCORING SUMMARY
PSU	Lally 21 blocked punt return (Bahr kick)
PSU	Torrey 3 pass from Fusina (Bahr kick)
ASU	Lane 11 pass from Sproul (Hicks kick)
PSU	FG Bahr 23
ASU	Washington 13 pass from Sproul (Hicks kick)
PSU	Geise 18 run (Bahr kick)
PSU	Suhey 3 run (Bahr kick)
ASU	Washington 30 pass from Sproul (Hicks kick)
PSU	FG Bahr 32
ASU	Perry 1 run (Hicks kick)
PSU	Suhey 3 run (Geise run)
ASU	Safety (Fitzkee tackled in end zone)

PSU	TEAM STATISTICS	ASU
18	First Downs	29
268	Rushing Yards	90
9-23-0	Passing	23-47-2
83	Passing Yards	336
351	Total Yards	426
7-40.0	Punts - Average	5-34.8
1-0	Fumbles - Lost	1-1
12-126	Penalties - Yards	5-33

INDIVIDUAL LEADERS
RUSHING
PSU: Geise 26-111, 1 TD; Torrey 9-107; Suhey 13-76, 2 TD.
ASU: Harris 20-56; Sproul 15-16.
PASSING
PSU: Fusina 9-23-0, 83 yards, 1 TD.
ASU: Sproul 23-47-2, 336 yards, 3 TD.
RECEIVING
PSU: Cefalo 3-39; Fitzkee 1-24.
ASU: DeFrance 7-123; Washington 4-76, 2 TD.

DECEMBER 26, 1980
PENN STATE 31, OHIO STATE 19

	1ST	2ND	3RD	4TH	FINAL
PSU	7	3	7	14	31
OSU	6	13	0	0	19

SCORING SUMMARY
PSU	Warner 64 run (Menhardt kick)
OSU	Donley 23 pass from Schlichter (kick failed)
OSU	Williams 33 pass from Schlichter (run failed)
OSU	Donley 19 pass from Schlichter (Atha kick)
PSU	FG Menhardt 38
PSU	Blackledge 3 run (Menhardt kick)
PSU	Williams 4 run (Menhardt kick)
PSU	Moore 37 run (Menhardt kick)

PSU	TEAM STATISTICS	OSU
22	First Downs	23
351	Rushing Yards	110
8-22-0	Passing	20-35-1
117	Passing Yards	302
468	Total Yards	412
5-40.8	Punts - Average	7-38.7
1-1	Fumbles - Lost	1-0
1-10	Penalties - Yards	2-30

INDIVIDUAL LEADERS
RUSHING
PSU: Warner 18-155, 1 TD; Moore 10-76, 1 TD.
OSU: Murray 10-75; Gayle 11-39.
PASSING
PSU: Blackledge 8-22-0, 117 yards.
OSU: Schlichter 20-35-1, 302 yards, 3 TD.
RECEIVING
PSU: Baugh 3-53; Scovill 3-42.
OSU: Donley 5-112, 2 TD; Williams 7-112, 1 TD.

JANUARY 1, 1982
PENN STATE 26, USC 10

	1ST	2ND	3RD	4TH	FINAL
PSU	7	10	9	0	26
USC	7	0	3	0	10

SCORING SUMMARY
PSU	Warner 17 run (Franco kick)
USC	Banks 20 interception return (Jordan kick)
PSU	Garrity 52 pass from Blackledge (Franco kick)
PSU	FG Franco 21
PSU	Warner 21 run (Franco kick)
USC	FG Jordan 37
PSU	Safety

PSU	TEAM STATISTICS	USC
20	First Downs	19
218	Rushing Yards	60
11-24-2	Passing	16-32-3
175	Passing Yards	202
393	Total Yards	262
4-50.8	Punts - Average	5-40.2
3-2	Fumbles - Lost	3-2
7-70	Penalties - Yards	7-49

INDIVIDUAL LEADERS
RUSHING
PSU: Warner 26-145, 2 TD; Meade 9-60.
USC: Allen 30-85; Spencer 3-16.
PASSING
PSU: Blackledge 11-24-2, 175 yards, 1 TD.
USC: Mazur 11-23-2, 123 yards.
RECEIVING
PSU: Jackson 3-55; Garrity 1-52, 1 TD.
USC: Ware 4-75; Simmons 3-51

JANUARY 2, 1984
OHIO STATE 28, PITTSBURGH 23

	1ST	2ND	3RD	4TH	FINAL
OSU	7	7	0	14	28
PITT	0	7	0	16	23

SCORING SUMMARY
OSU	Tomczak 3 run (Spangler kick)
PITT	Wilson 6 pass from Congemi (Everett kick)
OSU	Byars 11 run (Spangler kick)
PITT	Wilson fumble recovery in end zone (Everett kick)
OSU	Byars 99 kickoff return (Spangler kick)
PITT	Collins 11 pass from Congemi (pass failed)
PITT	FG Everett 37
OSU	Jemison 39 pass from Tomczak (Spangler kick)

OSU	TEAM STATISTICS	PITT
27	First Downs	27
184	Rushing Yards	146
15-32-1	Passing	31-46-2
226	Passing Yards	341
410	Total Yards	487
4-37.3	Punts - Average	3-39.0
3-1	Fumbles - Lost	2-1
8-70	Penalties - Yards	8-60

INDIVIDUAL LEADERS
RUSHING
OSU: Byars 15-73, 1 TD; Broadnax 6-38.
PITT: McCall 26-115; Congemi 6-20.
PASSING
OSU: Tomczak 15-32-1, 226 yards, 1 TD.
PITT: Congemi 31-44-2, 341 yards, 2 TD.
RECEIVING
OSU: Jemison 8-131, 1 TD; Frank 4-57.
PITT: Wallace 8-97; McCall 6-75; Collins 7-72, 1 TD.

JANUARY 1, 1986
MICHIGAN 27, NEBRASKA 23

	1ST	2ND	3RD	4TH	FINAL
MICH	3	0	24	0	27
NEB	0	14	0	9	23

SCORING SUMMARY
MICH	FG Moons 42
NEB	DuBose 5 pass from Clayton (Klein kick)
NEB	DuBose 3 run (Klein kick)
MICH	White 1 run (Moons kick)
MICH	Harbaugh 1 run (Moons kick)
MICH	FG Moons 19
MICH	Harbaugh 2 run (Moons kick)
NEB	Taylor 1 run (Klein kick)
NEB	Safety

MICH	TEAM STATISTICS	NEB
16	First Downs	20
171	Rushing Yards	304
6-16-0	Passing	6-15-1
63	Passing Yards	66
234	Total Yards	370
5-43.8	Punts - Average	3-40.3
2-0	Fumbles - Lost	6-3
8-43	Penalties - Yards	7-46

INDIVIDUAL LEADERS
RUSHING
MICH: Morris 22-156; White 13-38, 1 TD.
NEB: Dubose 17-99, 1 TD; Taylor 10-76, 1 TD; Clayton 14-68.
PASSING
MICH: Harbaugh 6-15-0, 63 yards.
NEB: Clayton 4-6-0, 51 yards, 1 TD.
RECEIVING
MICH: Kattus 3-38; Morris 2-10.
NEB: Frain 3-46; Smith 1-8.

Played as an independent or with other conference affiliation

January 2, 1987
Penn State 14, Miami (Fla.) 10

	1ST	2ND	3RD	4TH	FINAL
PSU	0	7	0	7	14
MIA	0	7	0	3	10

SCORING SUMMARY
MIA	Bratton 1 run (Cox kick)
PSU	Shaffer 4 run (Manca kick)
MIA	FG Seelig 38
PSU	Dozier 6 run (Manca kick)

PSU	TEAM STATISTICS	MIA
8	First Downs	22
109	Rushing Yards	160
5-16-1	Passing	26-50-5
53	Passing Yards	285
162	Total Yards	445
9-43.4	Punts - Average	4-46.0
5-2	Fumbles - Lost	4-2
4-39	Penalties - Yards	9-62

INDIVIDUAL LEADERS
RUSHING
PSU: Dozier 20-99, 1 TD; Manoa 8-36.
MIA: Highsmith 18-119; Bratton 11-31, 1 TD.

PASSING
PSU: Shaffer 5-16-1, 53 yards.
MIA: Testaverde 26-50-5, 285 yards.

RECEIVING
PSU: Dozier 2-12; Hamilton 1-23.
MIA: Blades 5-81; Irvin 5-55.

January 1, 1992
Penn State 42, Tennessee 17

	1ST	2ND	3RD	4TH	FINAL
PSU	7	0	14	21	42
TENN	10	0	7	0	17

SCORING SUMMARY
PSU	Gash 10 pass from Sacca (Fayak kick)
TENN	Stewart 1 run (Becksvoort kick)
TENN	FG Becksvoort 24
TENN	Fleming 44 pass from Kelly (Becksvoort kick)
PSU	LaBarca 3 pass from Sacca (Fayak kick)
PSU	Brady 13 pass from Sacca (Fayak kick)
PSU	Anderson 2 run (Fayak kick)
PSU	Givens 23 fumble return (Fayak kick)
PSU	McDuffie 37 pass from Sacca (Fayak kick)

PSU	TEAM STATISTICS	TENN
12	First Downs	25
76	Rushing Yards	171
11-28-0	Passing	21-43-1
150	Passing Yards	270
226	Total Yards	441
9-47.9	Punts - Average	6-36.3
0-0	Fumbles - Lost	5 3
3-36	Penalties - Yards	3-34

INDIVIDUAL LEADERS
RUSHING
PSU: Anderson 17-57, 1 TD; Gash 7-15.
TENN: Stewart 15-84, 1 TD; Hayden 13-56.

PASSING
PSU: Sacca 11-28-0, 150 yards, 4 TD.
TENN: Kelly 20-40-1, 273 yards, 1 TD.

RECEIVING
PSU: McDuffie 4-78, 1 TD; Drayton 3-35.
TENN: Pickens 8-100; Fleming 2- 68, 1 TD.

January 1, 1997
Penn State 38, Texas 15

	1ST	2ND	3RD	4TH	FINAL
PSU	7	0	21	10	38
TEX	3	9	3	0	15

SCORING SUMMARY
PSU	Enis 4 pass from Richardson (Conway kick)
TEX	FG Dawson 28
TEX	FG Dawson 28
TEX	Williams 7 run (pass failed)
PSU	Harris 5 run (Enis pass from Richardson)
TEX	FG Dawson 48
PSU	Enis 2 run (Conway kick)
PSU	Cleary 1 run (kick failed)
PSU	FG Conway 23
PSU	Enis 12 run (Conway kick)

PSU	TEAM STATISTICS	TEX
19	First Downs	19
330	Rushing Yards	73
12-20-0	Passing	27-43-1
95	Passing Yards	287
425	Total Yards	360
5-35.6	Punts - Average	6-37.7
0-0	Fumbles - Lost	2-1
4-49	Penalties - Yards	8-57

INDIVIDUAL LEADERS
RUSHING
PSU: Enis 16-95, 2 TD; Fields 1-84.
TEX: Williams 11-48, 1 TD; Mitchell 7-24.

PASSING
PSU: Richardson 12-20-0, 95 yards, 1 TD.
TEX: Brown 26-42-1, 254 yards.

RECEIVING
PSU: Brown 3-32; Jurevicius 2-22.
TEX: Adams 4-73; Davis 5-72.

January 3, 2003
Ohio State 31, Miami (Fla.) 24

	1ST	2ND	3RD	4TH	OT	2OT	FINAL
OSU	0	14	3	0	7	7	31
MIA	7	0	7	3	7	0	24

SCORING SUMMARY
MIA	Parrish 25 pass from Dorsey (Sievers kick)
OSU	Krenzel 1 run (Nugent kick)
OSU	Clarett 7 run (Nugent kick)
OSU	FG Nugent 44
MIA	McGahee 9 run (Sievers kick)
MIA	FG Sievers 40
MIA	Winslow 7 pass from Dorsey (Sievers kick)
OSU	Krenzel 1 run (Nugent kick)
OSU	Clarett 5 run (Nugent kick)

OSU	TEAM STATISTICS	MIA
14	First Downs	19
145	Rushing Yards	65
7-21-2	Passing	29-44-2
122	Passing Yards	304
267	Total Yards	369
1-1	Punt Returns - Yards	2-56
1-15	Kickoff Returns - Yards	1-39
6-47.7	Punts - Average	4-43.2
0-0	Fumbles - Lost	3-3
9-49	Penalties - Yards	6-30
31:27	Possession Time	28:33

INDIVIDUAL LEADERS
RUSHING
OSU: Krenzel 19-81, 2 TD; Clarett 23-47, 2 TD.
MIA: McGahee 20-67, 1 TD; Payton 8-17.

PASSING
OSU: Krenzel 7-21-2, 122 yards.
MIA: Dorsey 28-43-2, 296 yards, 2 TD.

RECEIVING
OSU: Gamble 2-69; Jenkins 4-45.
MIA: Winslow 11-122, 1 TD; Parrish 5-70, 1 TD; Johnson 4-54.

January 2, 2004
Ohio State 35, Kansas State 28

	1ST	2ND	3RD	4TH	FINAL
OSU	14	0	14	7	35
KSU	0	7	7	14	28

SCORING SUMMARY
OSU	Hollins 7 blocked punt return (Nugent kick)
OSU	Holmes 6 pass from Krenzel (Nugent kick)
OSU	Jenkins 17 pass from Krenzel (Nugent kick)
KSU	Sproles 6 run (Rheem kick)
KSU	Roberson 14 run (Rheem kick)
OSU	Jenkins 8 pass from Krenzel (Nugent kick)
OSU	Holmes 31 pass from Krenzel (Nugent kick)
KSU	Saba 3 run (Rheem kick)
KSU	Roberson 1 run (Rheem kick)

OSU	TEAM STATISTICS	KSU
15	First Downs	25
148	Rushing Yards	84
11-24-2	Passing	20-52-1
189	Passing Yards	294
337	Total Yards	378
5-48	Punt Returns - Yards	4-10
3-60	Kickoff Returns - Yards	5-79
7-40.1	Punts - Average	8-40.0
0-0	Fumbles - Lost	0-0
9-63	Penalties - Yards	8-51
31:28	Possession Time	28:32

INDIVIDUAL LEADERS
RUSHING
OSU: Ross 20-82; Joe 11-46.
KSU: Sproles 13-38, 1 TD; Roberson 16-32, 2 TD.

PASSING
OSU: Krenzel 11-24-2, 189 yards, 4 TD.
KSU: Roberson 20-51-1, 294 yards.

RECEIVING
OSU: Jenkins 5-96, 2 TD; Childress 2-44.
KSU: Dennis 7-113; Moreira 3-59.

January 2, 2006
Ohio State 34, Notre Dame 20

	1ST	2ND	3RD	4TH	FINAL
OSU	7	14	3	10	34
ND	7	0	6	7	20

SCORING SUMMARY
ND	Walker 20 run (Fitzpatrick kick)
OSU	Ginn Jr. 56 pass from Smith (Huston kick)
OSU	Ginn Jr. 68 pass from Smith (Huston kick)
OSU	Holmes 85 pass from Smith (Huston kick)
ND	Walker 18 run (kick failed)
OSU	FG Huston 40
OSU	FG Huston 26
ND	Walker 3 run (Fitzpatrick kick)
OSU	Pittman 60 run (Huston kick)

OSU	TEAM STATISTICS	ND
27	First Downs	22
275	Rushing Yards	62
19-28-0	Passing	29-45-0
342	Passing Yards	286
617	Total Yards	348
2-20	Punt Returns - Yards	1-0
3-51	Kickoff Returns - Yards	2-23
1-40.0	Punts - Average	6-42.3
2-2	Fumbles - Lost	1-0
7-53	Penalties - Yards	6-48
29:16	Possession Time	30:44

INDIVIDUAL LEADERS
RUSHING
OSU: Pittman 21-136, 1 TD; Ginn Jr. 2-73, 1 TD.
ND: Walker 16-90, 3 TD; Schwapp 2-4.

PASSING
OSU: Smith 19-28-0, 342 yards, 2 TD.
ND: Quinn 29-45-0, 286 yards.

RECEIVING
OSU: Ginn Jr. 8-167, 1 TD; Holmes 5-124, 1 TD.
ND: Stovall 9-126; Samardzija 6-59.

BIG TEN ANNUAL REVIEW & BOWLS

GATOR BOWL

PROFILE

Site: Jacksonville, Fla.
Stadium: Jacksonville Municipal Stadium
Capacity: 76,976
Surface: Grass

PLAYING SITES

Gator Bowl, 1946-93
Florida Field, 1994
Jacksonville Municipal Stadium, renamed Alltel Stadium in 1997, renamed back to Jacksonville Municipal Stadium in 2007, since 1995

NAME CHANGES

Gator Bowl, 1946-85
Mazda Gator Bowl, 1986-90
Gator Bowl, 1991
Outback Steakhouse Gator Bowl, 1992-94
Toyota Gator Bowl, since 1995

SEASON	DATE	PRE-GAME RANK	TEAMS	SCORE	FINAL RANK	MOST VALUABLE PLAYER(S)	ATT.
1961	Dec. 30, 1961	17	Penn State*	30		Galen Hall, Penn State, QB	50,202
		13	Georgia Tech	15		Joe Auer, Georgia Tech, HB	
1962	Dec. 29, 1962		Florida	17		Tom Shannon, Florida, QB	50,026
		9	Penn State*	7		Dave Robinson, Penn State, E	
1967	Dec. 30, 1967		Florida State	17		Kim Hammond, Florida State, QB	68,019
		10	Penn State*	17		Tom Sherman, Penn State, QB	
1976	Dec. 27, 1976	15	Notre Dame	20	12	Al Hunter, Notre Dame, HB	67,827
		20	Penn State*	9		Jim Cefalo, Penn State, WR	
1978	Dec. 29, 1978	7	Clemson	17	6	Steve Fuller, Clemson, QB	72,011
		20	Ohio State	15		Art Schlichter, Ohio State, QB	
1979	Dec. 28, 1979		North Carolina	17	15	Matt Kupec, QB, Amos Lawrence, RB, North Carolina	70,407
		14	Michigan	15	18	John Wangler QB, Anthony Carter, WR, Michigan	
1983	Dec. 30, 1983	11	Florida	14	6	Tony Lilly, Florida, S	81,293
		10	Iowa	6	14	Owen Gill, Iowa, FB	
1988	Jan. 1, 1989	19	Georgia	34	15	Wayne Johnson, Georgia, QB	76,236
			Michigan State	27		Andre Rison, Michigan State, WR	
1990	Jan. 1, 1991	12	Michigan	35	7	Michigan offensive line	68,927
		15	Mississippi	3	21	Tyrone Ashley, Mississippi, DB	

DECEMBER 30, 1961
PENN STATE 30, GEORGIA TECH 15

	1ST	2ND	3RD	4TH	FINAL
PSU	0	14	6	10	30
GT	2	7	0	6	15

SCORING SUMMARY
GT Safety (Hall intentional grounding in end zone)
GT Auer 68 run (Lothridge kick)
PSU Gursky 13 pass from Hall (Jonas kick)
PSU Kochman 27 pass from Hall (Jonas kick)
PSU Powell 35 pass from Hall (kick failed)
GT Auer 14 run (run failed)
PSU FG Jonas 23
PSU Torris 1 run (Jonas kick)

PSU	TEAM STATISTICS	GT
13	First Downs	19
138	Rushing Yards	211
12-22-0	Passing	12-24-2
175	Passing Yards	201
313	Total Yards	412
8-41.0	Punts - Average	5-27.6
1-1	Fumbles - Lost	6-3
6-63	Penalties - Yards	2-14

INDIVIDUAL LEADERS
RUSHING
PSU: Kochman 13-76; Torris 12-27, 1 TD.
GT: Auer 10-98, 2 TD; Williamson 11-44.
RECEIVING
PSU: Robinson 4-40; Anderson 3-40.
GT: Williamson 4-102; Martin 3-36.

DECEMBER 29, 1962
FLORIDA 17, PENN STATE 7

	1ST	2ND	3RD	4TH	FINAL
UF	3	7	0	7	17
PSU	0	7	0	0	7

SCORING SUMMARY
UF FG Hall 43
UF Dupree 7 pass from Shannon (Hall kick)
PSU Liske 1 run (Coates kick)
UF Clarke 19 pass from Shannon (Hall kick)

UF	TEAM STATISTICS	PSU
14	First Downs	8
162	Rushing Yards	89
8-13-1	Passing	5-21-2
86	Passing Yards	58
248	Total Yards	147
6-23.8	Punts - Average	6-40.8
4-1	Fumbles - Lost	4-3
5-42	Penalties - Yards	2-10

INDIVIDUAL LEADERS
RUSHING
UF: Dupree 25-66; Mack 10-33.
PSU: Kochman 6-51; Hayes 10-25.
PASSING
UF: Shannon 7-9-1, 79 yards, 2 TD.
PSU: Liske 5-18-1, 58 yards.
RECEIVING
UF: Clarke 2-27, 1 TD; Brown 3-25.
PSU: Powell 4-40; Yost 1-18.

DECEMBER 30, 1967
FLORIDA STATE 17, PENN STATE 17

	1ST	2ND	3RD	4TH	FINAL
FSU	0	0	14	3	17
PSU	3	14	0	0	17

SCORING SUMMARY
PSU FG Sherman 27
PSU Curry 9 pass from Sherman (Sherman kick)
PSU Kwalick 12 pass from Sherman (Sherman kick)
FSU Sellers 20 pass from Hammond (Guthrie kick)
FSU Hammond 1 run (Guthrie kick)
FSU FG Guthrie 26

FSU	TEAM STATISTICS	PSU
23	First Downs	12
55	Rushing Yards	175
38-55-4	Passing	7-19-2
363	Passing Yards	69
418	Total Yards	244
4-29.8	Punts - Average	7-39.9
1-0	Fumbles - Lost	3-2
4-40	Penalties - Yards	1-5

INDIVIDUAL LEADERS
RUSHING
FSU: Green 12-34; Hammond 9-28, 1 TD.
PSU: Pittman 19-128; Sherman 6-27.
PASSING
FSU: Hammond 37-53-4, 362 yards, 1 TD.
PSU: Sherman 9-17-2, 69 yards, 2 TD.
RECEIVING
FSU: Sellers 14-145, 1 TD; Moremen 12-106.
PSU: Kwalick 2-25, 1 TD; Curry 2-22, 1 TD.

*Played as an independent or with other conference affiliation

NOTRE DAME 20, PENN STATE 9
DECEMBER 27, 1976

	1ST	2ND	3RD	4TH	FINAL
ND	7	13	0	0	20
PSU	3	0	0	6	9

SCORING SUMMARY
PSU	FG Capozzolli 26
ND	Hunter 1 run (Reeve kick)
ND	FG Reeve 23
ND	Hunter 1 run (Reeve kick)
ND	FG Reeve 23
PSU	Suhey 8 pass from Fusina (run failed)

ND	TEAM STATISTICS	PSU
17	First Downs	16
132	Rushing Yards	156
10-20-0	Passing	14-33-2
141	Passing Yards	118
273	Total Yards	274
5-33.2	Punts - Average	5-29.2
2-0	Fumbles - Lost	4-1
5-62	Penalties - Yards	6-55

INDIVIDUAL LEADERS
RUSHING
ND: Hunter 26-102, 2 TD; Ferguson 10-22.
PSU: Torrey 12-63; Suhey 9-40.

PASSING
ND: Slager 10-19-0, 141 yards.
PSU: Fusina 14-33-2, 118 yards, 1 TD.

RECEIVING
ND: MacAfee 5-78; Kelleher 3-46.
PSU: Cefalo 5-60; Mauti 1-21; Suhey 2-17, 1 TD.

CLEMSON 17, OHIO STATE 15
DECEMBER 29, 1978

	1ST	2ND	3RD	4TH	FINAL
CLEM	0	10	7	0	17
OSU	0	9	0	6	15

SCORING SUMMARY
OSU	FG Atha 27
CLEM	Fuller 4 run (Ariri kick)
OSU	Schlichter 4 run (kick failed)
CLEM	FG Ariri 47
CLEM	Austin 1 run (Ariri kick)
OSU	Schlichter 1 run (run failed)

CLEM	TEAM STATISTICS	OSU
20	First Downs	16
207	Rushing Yards	150
9-20-0	Passing	16-20-1
123	Passing Yards	205
330	Total Yards	355
6-38.3	Punts - Average	4-41.5
5-1	Fumbles - Lost	1-0
7-65	Penalties - Yards	7-83

INDIVIDUAL LEADERS
RUSHING
CLEM: Perry 14-54; Ratchford 10-54; Fuller 17-38, 1 TD.
OSU: Schlichter 18-70, 2 TD; Springs 10-42.

PASSING
CLEM: Fuller 9-20-0, 123 yards.
OSU: Schlichter 16-20-1, 205 yards.

RECEIVING
CLEM: Butler 4-44; Tuttle 3-41.
OSU: Barwig 2-51; Hunter 2-49.

NORTH CAROLINA 17, MICHIGAN 15
DECEMBER 28, 1979

	1ST	2ND	3RD	4TH	FINAL
UNC	0	7	7	3	17
MICH	0	9	0	6	15

SCORING SUMMARY
MICH	FG Virgil 20
MICH	Carter 53 pass from Wangler (kick failed)
UNC	Paschal 1 run (Hayes kick)
UNC	Farris 12 pass from Kupec (Hayes kick)
UNC	FG Hayes 32
MICH	Carter 30 pass from Dickey (pass failed)

UNC	TEAM STATISTICS	MICH
20	First Downs	18
169	Rushing Yards	152
19-28-0	Passing	17-26-2
161	Passing Yards	328
330	Total Yards	480
6-45.4	Punts - Average	6-35.1
3-2	Fumbles - Lost	2-2
6-74	Penalties - Yards	8-87

INDIVIDUAL LEADERS
RUSHING
UNC: Lawrence 23-118; Paschal 14-49, 1 TD.
MICH: Woolfolk 16-63; Smith 8-51.

PASSING
UNC: Kupec 18-28-0, 161 yards, 1 TD.
MICH: Wangler 6-8-0, 203 yards, 1 TD; Dickey 11-18-2, 125 yards, 1 TD.

RECEIVING
UNC: Lawrence 5-38; Chatham 5-37; Farris 2-34, 1 TD.
MICH: Carter 4-141, 2 TD; Clayton 1-50.

FLORIDA 14, IOWA 6
DECEMBER 30, 1983

	1ST	2ND	3RD	4TH	FINAL
UF	7	7	0	0	14
IA	0	3	3	0	6

SCORING SUMMARY
UF	Anderson 1 run (Raymond kick)
IA	FG Nichol 32
UF	Drew fumble recovery in end zone (Raymond kick)
IA	FG Nichol 31

UF	TEAM STATISTICS	IA
14	First Downs	16
168	Rushing Yards	114
9-23-2	Passing	13-30-4
92	Passing Yards	167
260	Total Yards	281
7-37.5	Punts - Average	2-40.0
0-0	Fumbles - Lost	2-1
12-105	Penalties - Yards	7-44

INDIVIDUAL LEADERS
RUSHING
UF : Anderson 17-84, 1 TD; Williams 10-68.
IA: Gill 10-83; Granger 9-37.

PASSING
UF : Peace 9-22-2, 92 yards.
IA: Long 13-29-4, 167 yards.

RECEIVING
UF : Dixon 5-55.
IA: Harmon 6-90.

GEORGIA 34, MICHIGAN STATE 27
JANUARY 1, 1989

	1ST	2ND	3RD	4TH	FINAL
UGA	7	10	10	7	34
MSU	0	7	6	14	27

SCORING SUMMARY
UGA	Hampton 6 pass from Johnson (Kasay kick)
UGA	FG Crumley 39
UGA	Hampton 30 pass from Johnson (Kasay kick)
MSU	Rison 4 pass from McAllister (Langeloh kick)
UGA	Warner 18 pass from Johnson (Kasay kick)
MSU	Rison 55 pass from McAllister (kick failed)
UGA	FG Crumley 36
MSU	Ezor 3 run (Langeloh kick)
UGA	Hampton 32 run (Kasay kick)
MSU	Rison 50 pass from McAllister (Langeloh kick)

UGA	TEAM STATISTICS	MSU
22	First Downs	22
182	Rushing Yards	158
15-27-0	Passing	14-24-0
227	Passing Yards	288
409	Total Yards	446
4-34.0	Punts - Average	6-42.8
0-0	Fumbles - Lost	1-0
5-25	Penalties - Yards	8-102

INDIVIDUAL LEADERS
RUSHING
UGA: Hampton 10-109, 1 TD; Johnson 14-30.
MSU: Ezor 33-146, 1 TD; Selzer 5-13.

PASSING
UGA: Johnson 15-27-0, 227 yards, 3 TD.
MSU: McAllister 14-24-0, 228, 3 TD.

RECEIVING
UGA: Hampton 4-71, 2 TD; Worley 3-36.
MSU: Rison 9-252, 3 TD; Montgomery 4-21.

MICHIGAN 35, MISSISSIPPI 3
JANUARY 1, 1991

	1ST	2ND	3RD	4TH	FINAL
MICH	7	7	21	0	35
MISS	0	3	0	0	3

SCORING SUMMARY
MICH	Howard 63 pass from Grbac (Carlson kick)
MISS	FG Lee 51
MICH	Bunch 7 pass from Grbac (Carlson kick)
MICH	Howard 50 pass from Grbac (Carlson kick)
MICH	Bunch 5 run (Carlson kick)
MICH	Alexander 33 pass from Grbac (Carlson kick)

MICH	TEAM STATISTICS	MISS
35	First Downs	20
391	Rushing Yards	93
20-32-1	Passing	18-32-4
324	Passing Yards	240
715	Total Yards	333
2-24.5	Punts - Average	5-38.0
2-1	Fumbles - Lost	4-2
6-69	Penalties - Yards	4-49

INDIVIDUAL LEADERS
RUSHING
MICH: Vaughn 15-128; Powers 14-112; Bunch 11-54, 1 TD.
MISS: Baldwin 8-53; Thigpen 6-32.

PASSING
MICH: Grbac 16-25-1, 296 yards, 4 TD.
MISS: Shows 13-21-3, 175 yards.

RECEIVING
MICH: Howard 6-167, 2 TD; Alexander 2-50, 1 TD.
MISS: Brownlee 5-71; Roberts 4-67.

BIG TEN ANNUAL REVIEW & BOWLS

HOLIDAY BOWL

PROFILE

Site: San Diego, Calif.
Stadium: Qualcomm Stadium
Capacity: 71,400
Surface: Grass

PLAYING SITES

San Diego Jack Murphy Stadium, renamed Qualcomm Stadium in 1997, since 1978

NAME CHANGES

Holiday Bowl, 1978-85
Sea World Holiday Bowl, 1986-91
Thrifty Car Rental Holiday Bowl, 1992-94
Plymouth Holiday Bowl, 1995-97
Culligan Holiday Bowl, 1998-2001
Holiday Bowl, 2002
Pacific Life Holiday Bowl, since 2002

SEASON	DATE	PRE-GAME RANK	TEAMS	SCORE	FINAL RANK	MOST VALUABLE PLAYER(S)	ATT.
1979	Dec. 21, 1979		Indiana	38	19	Marc Wilson, BYU, QB	52,200
		9	BYU	37	13	Tim Wilbur, Indiana, CB	
1982	Dec. 17, 1982		Ohio State	47		Tim Spencer, Ohio State, RB	52,533
			BYU	17		Garcia Lane, Ohio State, CB	
1984	Dec. 21, 1984	1	BYU	24	1	Robbie Bosco, BYU, QB	61,243
			Michigan	17		Leon White, BYU, LB	
1986	Dec. 30, 1986	19	Iowa	39	16	Mark Vlasic, Iowa, QB, Todd Santos, San Diego State, QB	59,473
			San Diego State	38		Richard Brown, San Diego State, LB	
1987	Dec. 30, 1987	18	Iowa	20	16	Craig Burnett, Wyoming, QB	61,892
			Wyoming	19		Anthony Wright, Iowa, CB	
1989	Dec. 29, 1989	18	Penn State*	50	15	Blair Thomas, Penn State, RB	61,113
		19	BYU	39	22	Ty Detmer, BYU, QB	
1991	Dec. 30, 1991		BYU	13	23	Ty Detmer, QB, Josh Arnold, DB, BYU	60,646
		7	Iowa	13	10	Carlos James, Iowa, DB	
1992	Dec. 30, 1992		Hawaii	27	20	Michael Carter, Hawaii, QB	44,457
			Illinois	17		Junior Tagoai, Hawaii, DT	
1993	Dec. 30, 1993	11	Ohio State	28	11	Raymont Harris, Lorenzo Styles, Ohio State	52,108
			BYU	21		John Walsh, BYU, QB	
1994	Dec. 30, 1994	20	Michigan	24	12	Todd Collins, QB, Matt Dyson, LB, Michigan	59,453
		10	Colorado State	14	16	Anthoney Hill, Colorado State, QB	

DECEMBER 21, 1979
INDIANA 38, BYU 37

	1ST	2ND	3RD	4TH	FINAL
IND	14	7	10	7	38
BYU	14	3	17	3	37

SCORING SUMMARY
BYU   Lane 1 run (Johnson kick)
IND   Stephenson 38 pass from Clifford (Kellogg kick)
IND   Clifford 1 run (Kellogg kick)
BYU   M. Wilson 3 run (Johnson kick)
BYU   FG Johnson 40
IND   Clifford 1 run (Kellogg kick)
BYU   H. Jones 13 pass from M. Wilson (Johnson kick)
IND   Harkrader 1 run (Kellogg kick)
IND   FG Kellogg 26
BYU   FG Johnson 29
BYU   Lane 15 pass from M. Wilson (Johnson kick)
BYU   FG Johnson 28
IND   Wilbur 62 punt return (Kellogg kick)

IND	TEAM STATISTICS	BYU
21	First Downs	31
183	Rushing Yards	140
11-30-1	Passing	28-43-3
171	Passing Yards	380
354	Total Yards	520
2-66	Punt Returns - Yards	5-30
6-114	Kickoff Returns - Yards	7-126
6-41.3	Punts - Average	2-38.0
1-0	Fumbles - Lost	1-1
7-70	Penalties - Yards	1-15
35:07	Possession Time	24:53

INDIVIDUAL LEADERS
RUSHING
IND: Johnson 21-76; Harkrader 24-71, 1 TD.
BYU: H. Jones 8-55, 1 TD; Phillips 4-31.
PASSING
IND: Clifford 11-29-1, 171 yards, 1 TD.
BYU: M. Wilson 28-3-3, 380 yards, 2 TD.
RECEIVING
IND: Stephenson 5-91, 1 TD; Friede 2-43.
BYU: C. Brown 9-142; Lane 9-79, 1 TD.

DECEMBER 17, 1982
OHIO STATE 47, BYU 17

	1ST	2ND	3RD	4TH	FINAL
OSU	3	14	17	13	47
BYU	0	10	0	7	17

SCORING SUMMARY
OSU   FG Spangler 47
BYU   Balholm 7 pass from Young (Gunther kick)
OSU   Spencer 61 run (Spangler kick)
OSU   Tomczak 3 run (Spangler kick)
BYU   FG Gunther 39
OSU   Broadnax 1 run (Spangler kick)
OSU   Spencer 18 run (Spangler kick)
OSU   FG Spangler 37
OSU   Gayle 1 run (Spangler kick)
BYU   Hudson 13 pass from Young (Gunther kick)
OSU   Gayle 5 run (kick failed)

OSU	TEAM STATISTICS	BYU
24	First Downs	21
329	Rushing Yards	19
11-19-0	Passing	28-46-1
132	Passing Yards	352
461	Total Yards	371
4-41	Punt Returns - Yards	0-0
4-55	Kickoff Returns - Yards	7-124
3-37.7	Punts - Average	5-34.8
1-1	Fumbles - Lost	1-1
12-109	Penalties - Yards	9-75
34:33	Possession Time	25:27

INDIVIDUAL LEADERS
RUSHING
OSU: Spencer 21-167, 2 TD; Gayle 17-80, 2 TD; Broadnax 15-58, 1 TD.
BYU: Hamilton 3-14; Tiumalu 3-13.
PASSING
OSU: Tomczak 11-19-0, 132 yards.
BYU: Young 27-45-1, 341 yards, 2 TD.
RECEIVING
OSU: Williams 5-63; Spencer 1-23.
BYU: Hudson 7-81, 1 TD; Balholm 3-58, 1 TD.

DECEMBER 21, 1984
BYU 24, MICHIGAN 17

	1ST	2ND	3RD	4TH	FINAL
BYU	0	10	0	14	24
MICH	0	7	7	3	17

SCORING SUMMARY
BYU   Smith 5 run (Johnson kick)
MICH   Rogers 5 run (Bergeron kick)
BYU   FG Johnson 31
MICH   Perryman 10 pass from Zurbrugg (Bergeron kick)
MICH   FG Bergeron 32
BYU   Kozlowski 7 pass from Bosco (Johnson kick)
BYU   Smith 13 pass from Bosco (Johnson kick)

BYU	TEAM STATISTICS	MICH
32	First Downs	13
112	Rushing Yards	120
35-49-3	Passing	7-15-1
371	Passing Yards	82
483	Total Yards	202
2-(-6)	Punt Returns - Yards	0-0
3-24	Kickoff Returns - Yards	2-23
1-45.0	Punts - Average	7-39.1
4-3	Fumbles - Lost	2-0
9-82	Penalties - Yards	11-112
28:59	Possession Time	31:01

INDIVIDUAL LEADERS
RUSHING
BYU: Heimuli 16-82; Bosco 6-16.
MICH: Perryman 13-110; Rogers 19-60, 1 TD.
PASSING
BYU: Bosco 30-42-3, 343 yards, 2 TD.
MICH: Zurbrugg 7-15-1, 82 yards, 1 TD.
RECEIVING
BYU: Mills 11-103; Smith 10-88, 1 TD.
MICH: Bean 3-46; Perryman 2-15, 1 TD.

---

*Played as an independent or with other conference affiliation

DECEMBER 30, 1986
IOWA 39, SAN DIEGO STATE 38

	1ST	2ND	3RD	4TH	FINAL
IOWA	7	6	8	18	39
SDSU	6	15	7	10	38

SCORING SUMMARY
IOWA	Bayless 5 run (Houghtlin kick)
SDSU	Hardy 6 pass from Santos (kick failed)
SDSU	Jackson 44 pass from Santos (Hardy run)
IOWA	Vlasic 1 run (kick failed)
SDSU	Gilbreath 28 pass from Santos (Rahill kick)
SDSU	Gilmore 1 run (Rahill kick)
IOWA	Hudson 1 run (Smith pass from Vlasic)
SDSU	Hardy 6 run (Rahill kick)
IOWA	Cook 29 pass from Vlasic (Flagg pass from Vlasic)
IOWA	Flagg 4 pass from Vlasic (Houghtlin kick)
SDSU	FG Rahill 21
IOWA	FG Houghtlin 41

IOWA	TEAM STATISTICS	SDSU
21	First Downs	17
141	Rushing Yards	117
15-29-1	Passing	21-33-2
222	Passing Yards	298
363	Total Yards	415
3-6	Punt Returns - Yards	3-12
7-161	Kickoff Returns - Yards	6-98
4-42.5	Punts - Average	5-47.0
2-1	Fumbles - Lost	0-0
4-17	Penalties - Yards	7-70

INDIVIDUAL LEADERS
RUSHING
IOWA: Bayless 19-110, 1 TD; Hudson 9-43, 1 TD.
SDSU: Hardy 26-83, 1 TD; Gilmore 7-35, 1 TD.
PASSING
IOWA: Vlasic 15-28-1, 222 yards, 2 TD.
SDSU: Santos 21-33-2, 298 yards, 3 TD.
RECEIVING
IOWA: Flagg 4-66, 1 TD; Early 3-57; Cook 2-51, 1 TD.
SDSU: Jackson 2-89, 1 TD; Gilbreath 5-87, 1 TD; Gilmore 9-70.

DECEMBER 30, 1987
IOWA 20, WYOMING 19

	1ST	2ND	3RD	4TH	FINAL
IOWA	0	7	0	13	20
WYO	12	7	0	0	19

SCORING SUMMARY
WYO	FG Worker 43
WYO	FG Worker 38
WYO	Loving 15 pass from Burnett (pass failed)
IOWA	Hess 10 blocked punt return (Houghtlin kick)
WYO	Abraham 3 run (Worker kick)
IOWA	Wright 33 interception return (Houghtlin kick)
IOWA	Hudson 1 run (pass failed)

IOWA	TEAM STATISTICS	WYO
17	First Downs	19
94	Rushing Yards	43
21-35-0	Passing	28-51-1
237	Passing Yards	332
331	Total Yards	375
4-19	Punt Returns - Yards	5-27
5-92	Kickoff Returns - Yards	4-63
8-42.0	Punts - Average	6-30.0
1-1	Fumbles - Lost	0-0
6-57	Penalties - Yards	7-61
30:34	Possession Time	29:26

INDIVIDUAL LEADERS
RUSHING
IOWA: Harmon 12-47; Hudson 10-43, 1 TD.
WYO: Abraham 14-39, 1 TD; Bena 4-14.
PASSING
IOWA: Hartlieb 21-35-0, 237 yards.
WYO: Burnett 28-51-1, 332 yards, 1 TD.
RECEIVING
IOWA: Flagg 6-93; Watkins 4-72.
WYO: Sargent 8-106; Loving 5-63, 1 TD.

DECEMBER 29, 1989
PENN STATE 50, BYU 39

	1ST	2ND	3RD	4TH	FINAL
PSU	3	9	17	21	50
BYU	3	10	13	13	39

SCORING SUMMARY
PSU	FG Tarasi 30
BYU	FG Chaffetz 20
PSU	Smith 24 pass from Sacca (kick failed)
BYU	Detmer 1 run (Chaffetz kick)
PSU	FG Tarasi 36
BYU	FG Chaffetz 22
PSU	FG Tarasi 51
PSU	Thompson 16 run (Tarasi kick)
BYU	Detmer 1 run (kick failed)
PSU	Thompson 14 run (Tarasi kick)
BYU	Boyce 12 pass from Detmer (Chaffetz kick)
PSU	Thomas 7 run (run failed)
PSU	Daniels 52 pass from Sacca (pass failed)
BYU	Whittingham 10 run (Chaffetz kick)
BYU	Nyberg 3 pass from Detmer (pass failed)
PSU	Collins 2 point conversion interception return
PSU	Brown 53 fumble return (Tarasi kick)

PSU	TEAM STATISTICS	BYU
26	First Downs	35
249	Rushing Yards	75
11-21-1	Passing	42-59-2
215	Passing Yards	576
464	Total Yards	651
1-7	Punt Returns - Yards	1-3
7-167	Kickoff Returns - Yards	9-117
2-38.0	Punts - Average	1-39.0
0-0	Fumbles - Lost	3-1
10-93	Penalties - Yards	10-88
31:04	Possession Time	28:56

INDIVIDUAL LEADERS
RUSHING
PSU: Thomas 35-186, 1 TD; Thompson 14-68, 2 TD.
BYU: Whittingham 9-39, 1 TD; Detmer 8-18, 2 TD.
PASSING
PSU: Sacca 10-19-1, 206 yards, 2 TD.
BYU: Detmer 42-59-2, 576 yards, 2 TD.
RECEIVING
PSU: Thomas 2-46; McDuffie 2-36.
BYU: Boyce 8-127, 1 TD; Bellini 10-124; Nyberg 8-117, 1 TD.

DECEMBER 30, 1991
BYU 13, IOWA 13

	1ST	2ND	3RD	4TH	FINAL
BYU	0	6	0	7	13
IOWA	6	7	0	0	13

SCORING SUMMARY
IOWA	Saunders 13 run (kick failed)
IOWA	Saunders 5 run (Skillett kick)
BYU	Tulpulotu 9 pass from Detmer (kick failed)
BYU	Anderson 26 pass from Detmer (Kauffman kick)

BYU	TEAM STATISTICS	IOWA
26	First Downs	20
80	Rushing Yards	125
29-44-1	Passing	19-28-1
350	Passing Yards	221
430	Total Yards	346
1-14	Punt Returns - Yards	0-0
3-50	Kickoff Returns - Yards	3-38
2-44.0	Punts - Average	4-34.8
1-1	Fumbles - Lost	0-0
7-60	Penalties - Yards	7-61
32:23	Possession Time	27:37

INDIVIDUAL LEADERS
RUSHING
BYU: Willis 13-61; Tuipulotu 12-44.
IOWA: Saunders 19-103, 2 TD; Montgomery 7-35.
PASSING
BYU: Detmer 29-44-1, 350 yards, 2 TD.
IOWA: Rodgers 19-28-1, 221 yards.
RECEIVING
BYU: Tuipulotu 8-85, 1 TD; Rex 6-71; Drage 5-62.
IOWA: Filloon 7-107; Hughes 5-48.

DECEMBER 30, 1992
HAWAII 27, ILLINOIS 17

	1ST	2ND	3RD	4TH	FINAL
HAW	0	7	10	10	27
ILL	7	3	0	7	17

SCORING SUMMARY
ILL	Wright 14 pass from Verduzco (Richardson kick)
HAW	Sims 6 run (Elam kick)
ILL	FG Richardson 19
HAW	Sims 1 run (Elam kick)
HAW	FG Elam 45
HAW	FG Elam 37
HAW	Branch 53 pass from Carter (Elam kick)
ILL	Wright 18 pass from Verduzco (Richardson kick)

HAW	TEAM STATISTICS	ILL
23	First Downs	23
287	Rushing Yards	108
6-17-2	Passing	26-34-1
115	Passing Yards	239
402	Total Yards	347
1-11	Punt Returns - Yards	1-5
3-45	Kickoff Returns - Yards	5-82
2-41.0	Punts - Average	3-46.0
2-0	Fumbles - Lost	2-1
3-26	Penalties - Yards	3-25
32:33	Possession Time	27:27

INDIVIDUAL LEADERS
RUSHING
HAW: Sims 29-113, 2 TD; Carter 21-105.
ILL: Boyer 11-39; Feagin 7-31.
PASSING
HAW: Carter 6-16-2, 115 yards, 1 TD.
ILL: Verduzco 26-34-1, 248 yards, 2 TD.
RECEIVING
HAW: Branch 1-53, 1 TD; Gordon 2-23.
ILL: Wright 7-82, 2 TD; Klein 3-59; Strong 5-55.

DECEMBER 30, 1993
OHIO STATE 28, BYU 21

	1ST	2ND	3RD	4TH	FINAL
OSU	14	7	7	0	28
BYU	7	14	0	0	21

SCORING SUMMARY
OSU	Patillo 4 punt return (Williams kick)
BYU	Willis 27 pass from Walsh (Herrick kick)
OSU	Harris 2 run (Williams kick)
OSU	Harris 2 run (Williams kick)
BYU	Lewis 8 pass from Walsh (Herrick kick)
BYU	Doman 27 pass from Walsh (Herrick kick)
OSU	Harris 1 run (Williams kick)

OSU	TEAM STATISTICS	BYU
21	First Downs	24
330	Rushing Yards	50
6-13-0	Passing	25-44-1
61	Passing Yards	389
391	Total Yards	439
1-4	Punt Returns - Yards	2-24
2-24	Kickoff Returns - Yards	5-139
6-36.3	Punts - Average	2-20.5
0-0	Fumbles - Lost	2-1
7-45	Penalties - Yards	5-25
32:23	Possession Time	27:37

INDIVIDUAL LEADERS
RUSHING
OSU: Harris 39-235, 3 TD; By'not'e 9-61.
BYU: Hall 11-42; Heimuli 6-21.
PASSING
OSU: Hoying 5-11-0, 55 yards.
BYU: Walsh 25-44-1, 389 yards, 3 TD.
RECEIVING
OSU: Galloway 2-19; Tillman 1-17.
BYU: Doman 3-82, 1 TD; Willis 2-72, 1 TD.

DECEMBER 30, 1994
MICHIGAN 24, COLORADO STATE 14

	1ST	2ND	3RD	4TH	FINAL
MICH	10	7	7	0	24
CSU	7	0	0	7	14

SCORING SUMMARY
MICH	Toomer 4 pass from Collins (Hamilton kick)
CSU	Turner 32 pass from Hill (McDougal kick)
MICH	FG Hamilton 34
MICH	Hayes 16 pass from Collins (Hamilton kick)
MICH	Wheatley 3 run (Hamilton kick)
CSU	Burkett 18 pass from Hill (McDougal kick)

MICH	TEAM STATISTICS	CSU
18	First Downs	20
179	Rushing Yards	51
14-24-3	Passing	22-40-2
162	Passing Yards	289
341	Total Yards	340
0-0	Punt Returns - Yards	2-15
2-61	Kickoff Returns - Yards	5-102
5-28.0	Punts - Average	4-35.5
0-0	Fumbles - Lost	2-2
11-97	Penalties - Yards	8-72
27:40	Possession Time	32:20

INDIVIDUAL LEADERS
RUSHING
MICH: Wheatley 16-80, 1 TD; Biakabutuka 9-70.
CSU: Watson 17-47; Ward 1-8.
PASSING
MICH: Collins 14-24-3, 162 yards, 2 TD.
CSU: Hill 22-40-2, 289 yards, 2 TD.
RECEIVING
MICH: Toomer 5-63, 1 TD; Hayes 3-41, 1 TD.
CSU: Shull 3-101; Burkett 5-62, 1 TD; Turner 4-62, 1 TD.

BIG TEN ANNUAL REVIEW & BOWLS

INDEPENDENCE BOWL

PROFILE

Site: Shreveport, La.
Stadium: Independence Stadium
Capacity: 50,459
Surface: Grass

PLAYING SITES

Independence Stadium, since 1976

NAME CHANGES

Independence Bowl, 1976-90
Poulan/Weed Eater Independence Bowl, 1991-97
Sanford Independence Bowl, 1998-2000
MainStay Independence Bowl, 2001-03
Independence Bowl, 2004-05
PetroSun Independence Bowl, since 2006

SEASON	DATE	PRE-GAME RANK	TEAMS	SCORE	FINAL RANK	MOST VALUABLE PLAYER(S)	ATT.
1982	Dec. 11, 1982		Wisconsin	14		Randy Wright, Wisconsin, QB	49,503
		3	Kansas State			Tim Krumrie, Wisconsin, NG	
1985	Dec. 21, 1985		Minnesota	20		Rickey Foggie, Minnesota, QB	42,800
			Clemson	13		Bruce Holmes, Minnesota, LB	
1993	Dec. 31, 1993	22	Virginia Tech	45	22	Maurice DeShazo, Virginia Tech, QB	33,819
		21	Indiana	20		Antonio Banks, Virginia Tech, S	
1995	Dec. 29, 1995		LSU	45		Kevin Faulk, LSU, RB	48,835
			Michigan State	26		Gabe Northern, LSU, DE	

DECEMBER 11, 1982
WISCONSIN 14, KANSAS STATE 3

	1ST	2ND	3RD	4TH	FINAL
WISC	0	7	7	0	14
KSU	0	3	0	0	3

SCORING SUMMARY
KSU   FG Willis 29
WISC   Jones 16 pass from Wright (Rohde kick)
WISC   Stracka 87 pass from Wright (Rohde kick)

WISC	TEAM STATISTICS	KSU
14	First Downs	12
131	Rushing Yards	65
9-24-0	Passing	13-35-1
183	Passing Yards	127
314	Total Yards	192
6-40.7	Punts - Average	8-36.8
4-3	Fumbles - Lost	2-1
5-40	Penalties - Yards	9-75

INDIVIDUAL LEADERS
RUSHING
WISC: Williams 11-57; Ellerson 13-47.
KSU: Taluao 10-31; Fergimo 11-25.
PASSING
WISC: Wright 9-24-0, 183 yards, 2 TD.
KSU: Dickey 13-35-1, 127 yards.
RECEIVING
WISC: Stracka 187, 1 TD; Keeling 4-64.
KSU: Wallace 3-51; Dageforde 4-30.

DECEMBER 21, 1985
MINNESOTA 20, CLEMSON 13

	1ST	2ND	3RD	4TH	FINAL
MINN	3	7	0	10	20
CLEM	0	6	7	0	13

SCORING SUMMARY
MINN   FG Lohmiller 22
MINN   Anderson 9 pass from Foggie (Lohmiller kick)
CLEM   FG Treadwell 39
CLEM   FG Treadwell 21
CLEM   Jennings 3 pass from Driver (Treadwell kick)
MINN   FG Lohmiller 19
MINN   Baylor 1 run (Lohmiller kick)

MINN	TEAM STATISTICS	CLEM
20	First Downs	18
257	Rushing Yards	211
9-22-0	Passing	10-29-1
123	Passing Yards	162
380	Total Yards	373
6-37.5	Punts - Average	4-41.5
1-1	Fumbles - Lost	5-3
7-55	Penalties - Yards	5-51
28:22	Possession Time	31:38

INDIVIDUAL LEADERS
RUSHING
MINN: Baylor 13-98, 1 TD; Puk 15-69.
CLEM: Flowers 27-148; Driver 13-37.
PASSING
MINN: Foggie 9-22-0, 123 yards, 1 TD.
CLEM: Rodney Williams 9-23-1, 159 yards.
RECEIVING
MINN: Anderson 4-34, 1 TD.
CLEM: Ray Williams 5-58.

DECEMBER 31, 1993
VIRGINIA TECH 45, INDIANA 20

	1ST	2ND	3RD	4TH	FINAL
VT	7	21	0	17	45
IND	7	6	0	7	20

SCORING SUMMARY
IND   Lewis 75 pass from Paci (Manolopoulos kick)
VT   Thomas 13 pass from DeShazo (Williams kick)
VT   Swarm 6 run (Williams kick)
VT   Lewis 20 fumble return (Williams kick)
VT   Banks 80 blocked FG return (Williams kick)
IND   FG Manolopoulos 26
IND   FG Manolopoulos 40
VT   Freeman 42 pass from DeShazo (Williams kick)
VT   Edwards 5 run (Williams kick)
VT   FG Williams 42
IND   Lewis 42 pass from Dittoe (Manolopoulos kick)

VT	TEAM STATISTICS	IND
17	First Downs	11
125	Rushing Yards	20
19-33-2	Passing	17-37-2
193	Passing Yards	276
318	Total Yards	296
8-39.1	Punts - Average	7-38.4
2-1	Fumbles - Lost	2-2
8-84	Penalties - Yards	7-55
32:48	Possession Time	27:12

INDIVIDUAL LEADERS
RUSHING
VT: Thomas 24-65.
IND: Thurman 1-37.
PASSING
VT: DeShazo 19-33-2, 193 yards, 2 TD.
IND: Paci 10-22-1, 171 yards, 1 TD; Dittoe 7-14-1, 105 yards, 1 TD.
RECEIVING
VT: Freeman 5-66, 1 TD.
IND: Lewis 6-177, 2 TD.

DECEMBER 29, 1995
LSU 45, MICHIGAN STATE 26

	1ST	2ND	3RD	4TH	FINAL
LSU	7	14	21	3	45
MSU	7	17	0	2	26

SCORING SUMMARY
MSU   Muhammed 78 pass from Banks (Gardner kick)
LSU   Cleveland 6 run (LaFleur kick)
MSU   Greene 3 run (kick blocked)
MSU   Mason 100 kick return (Greene run)
MSU   FG Gardner 37
LSU   Kennison 92 kick return (LaFleur kick)
LSU   Faulk 51 run (LaFleur kick)
LSU   Faulk 5 run (LaFleur kick)
LSU   Northern 37 fumble return (LaFleur kick)
LSU   Kennison 27 pass from Tyler (LaFleur kick)
LSU   FG Richey 48
MSU   Safety

LSU	TEAM STATISTICS	MSU
17	First Downs	23
272	Rushing Yards	100
10-20-1	Passing	22-44-3
164	Passing Yards	348
436	Total Yards	448
4-150	Kickoff Returns - Yards	7-158
4-44.5	Punts - Average	6-37.5
2-1	Fumbles - Lost	4-3
5-42	Penalties - Yards	9-80

INDIVIDUAL LEADERS
RUSHING
LSU: Faulk 25-234, 2 TD.
MSU: Renaud 16-79.
PASSING
LSU: Tyler 10-20-1, 164 yards, 1 TD.
MSU: Banks 22-44-3, 348 yards, 1 TD.
RECEIVING
LSU: Kennison 5-124, 1 TD.
MSU: Muhammed 9-171, 1 TD.

INSIGHT BOWL

PROFILE

Site: Tempe, Ariz.
Stadium: Sun Devil Stadium
Capacity: 73,752
Surface: Grass

PLAYING SITES

Arizona Stadium, 1989-99
Bank One Ballpark, renamed
Chase Field in 2005, 2000-05
Sun Devil Stadium, since 2006

NAME CHANGES

Copper Bowl, 1989
Domino's Pizza Copper Bowl,
1990-91
Weiser Lock Copper Bowl,
1992-95
Copper Bowl, 1996
Insight.com Bowl, 1997-2001
Insight Bowl, since 2002

SEASON	DATE	PRE-GAME RANK	TEAMS	SCORE	FINAL RANK	MOST VALUABLE PLAYER(S)	ATT.
1991	Dec. 31, 1991		**Indiana**	24		Vaughn Dunbar, Indiana, TB	35,752
			Baylor	0		Mark Hagen, Indiana, LB	
1996	Dec. 27, 1996		**Wisconsin**	38		Ron Dayne, Wisconsin, RB	42,122
			Utah	10		Tarek Saleh, Wisconsin, LB	
2006	Dec. 29, 2006		**Texas Tech**	44	OT	Graham Harrell, Texas Tech, QB	48,391
			Minnesota	41		Antonio Hoffman, Texas Tech, CB	

DECEMBER 31, 1991
INDIANA 24, BAYLOR 0

	1ST	2ND	3RD	4TH	FINAL
IND	7	10	0	7	24
BU	0	0	0	0	0

SCORING SUMMARY
IND   Green 1 run (Bonnell kick)
IND   FG Bonnell 27
IND   Dunbar 5 run (Bonnell kick)
IND   Green 4 run (Bonnell kick)

IND	TEAM STATISTICS	BU
20	First Downs	17
147	Rushing Yards	138
12-22-0	Passing	10-27-1
176	Passing Yards	131
323	Total Yards	269
6-49.0	Punts - Average	6-34.8
2-0	Fumbles - Lost	4-1
6-59	Penalties - Yards	4-29
32:55	Possession Time	27:05

INDIVIDUAL LEADERS
RUSHING
IND: Dunbar 28-106, 1 TD; Law 6-38.
BU: Strait 15-72, Mims 9-49.
PASSING
IND: Green 11-21-0, 165 yards.
BU: Joe 10-26-1, 131 yards.
RECEIVING
IND: McGowan 3-63; Thomas 4-58.
BU: Miles 2-41; Pierce 3-32; Bonner 3-32.

DECEMBER 27, 1996
WISCONSIN 38, UTAH 10

	1ST	2ND	3RD	4TH	FINAL
WISC	14	17	0	7	38
UTAH	3	0	7	0	10

SCORING SUMMARY
WISC   Samuel 38 run (Hall kick)
UTAH   FG Pulsipher 24
WISC   Dayne 40 run (Hall kick)
WISC   Weems 82 interception return (Hall kick)
WISC   FG Hall 38
WISC   Dayne 3 run (Hall kick)
UTAH   Johnson 1 run (Pulsipher kick)
WISC   Dayne 1 run (Hall kick)

WISC	TEAM STATISTICS	UTAH
16	First Downs	26
349	Rushing Yards	103
2-6-0	Passing	27-49-4
16	Passing Yards	327
365	Total Yards	430
0-0	Punt Returns - Yards	1-8
3-59	Kickoff Returns - Yards	2-46
2-41.0	Punts - Average	2-31.0
2-1	Fumbles - Lost	1-0
3-31	Penalties - Yards	2-11
25:42	Possession Time	34:18

INDIVIDUAL LEADERS
RUSHING
WISC: Dayne 30-246, 3 TD; Samuel 5-44, 1 TD.
UTAH: Johnson 20-88, 1 TD; Bacon 4-9.
PASSING
WISC: Samuel 2-6-0, 16 yards.
UTAH: Fouts 27-49-4, 327 yards.
RECEIVING
WISC: Hayes 1-9; Brown 1-7.
UTAH: Keehan 6-100; Dyson 6-95.

DECEMBER 29, 2006
TEXAS TECH 44, MINNESOTA 41

	1ST	2ND	3RD	4TH	OT	FINAL
TT	0	7	7	24	6	44
MINN	14	21	3	0	3	41

SCORING SUMMARY
MINN   Simmons 2 pass from Cupito (Monroe kick)
MINN   Pinnix 2 run (Monroe kick)
MINN   Valentine 1 run (Monroe kick)
MINN   Wheelwright 14 pass from Cupito (Monroe kick)
TT   Woods 1 run (Trlica kick)
MINN   Payne 3 pass from Cupito (Monroe kick)
MINN   FG Monroe 20
TT   Filani 43 pass from Harrell (Trlica kick)
TT   Johnson 8 pass from Harrell (Trlica kick)
TT   Harrell 1 run (Trlica kick)
TT   Woods 1 run (Trlica kick)
TT   FG Trlica 52
MINN   FG Monroe 32
TT   Woods 3 run

TT	TEAM STATISTICS	MINN
29	First Downs	25
103	Rushing Yards	195
36-55-1	Passing	19-31-1
445	Passing Yards	263
548	Total Yards	458
3-37	Punt Returns - Yards	0-0
5-56	Kickoff Returns - Yards	4-103
1-46.0	Punts - Average	3-43.7
2-2	Fumbles - Lost	1-0
4-30	Penalties - Yards	5-23
24:11	Possession Time	35:49

INDIVIDUAL LEADERS
RUSHING
TT: Woods 19-109, 3 TD; Harrell 5-6, 1 TD.
MINN: Pinnix 34-179, 1 TD; Thomas 6-21.
PASSING
TT: Harrell 36-55-1, 445 yards, 2 TD.
MINN: Cupito 19-31-1, 263 yards, 3 TD.
RECEIVING
TT: Filani 11-162, 1 TD; Johnson 9-97, 1 TD.
MINN: Simmons 7-134, 1 TD; Wheelwright 4-45, 1 TD.

LIBERTY BOWL

PROFILE

Site: Memphis, Tenn.
Stadium: Liberty Bowl Memorial Stadium
Capacity: 62,338
Surface: FieldTurf

PLAYING SITES

Municipal Stadium, 1959-1963
Atlantic City Convention Hall, 1964
Liberty Bowl Memorial Stadium, since 1965

NAME CHANGES

Liberty Bowl Classic, 1959-92
St. Jude Liberty Bowl, 1993-96
AXA Liberty Bowl, 1997-2003
AutoZone Liberty Bowl, since 2004

SEASON	DATE	PRE-GAME RANK	TEAMS	SCORE	FINAL RANK	MOST VALUABLE PLAYER(S)	ATT.
1959	Dec. 19, 1959	12	Penn State*	7		Jay Huffman, Penn State, C	36,211
		10	Alabama	0			
1960	Dec. 17, 1960	16	Penn State*	41		Dick Hoak, Penn State, RB	16,624
			Oregon	12			
1979	Dec. 22, 1979		Penn State*	9		Roch Hontas, Tulane, QB	50,021
		15	Tulane	6			
1980	Dec. 27, 1980		Purdue	28	17	Mark Herrmann, Purdue, QB	53,667
			Missouri	25			
1981	Dec. 30, 1981	15	Ohio State	31	15	Eddie Meyers, Navy, TB	43,216
			Navy	28			
1982	Dec. 29, 1982		Alabama	21		Jeremiah Castille, Alabama, DB	54,123
			Illinois	15			
1986	Dec. 29, 1986		Tennessee	21		Jeff Francis, Tennessee, QB	51,327
			Minnesota	14			
1988	Dec. 28, 1988		Indiana	34	20	Dave Schnell, Indiana, QB	39,210
			South Carolina	10			
1990	Dec. 27, 1990		Air Force	23		Rob Perez, Air Force, QB	13,144
		24	Ohio State	11			
1993	Dec. 28, 1993	25	Louisville	18	24	Jeff Brohm, Louisville, QB	21,097
			Michigan State	7			
1994	Dec. 31, 1994		Illinois	30		Johnny Johnson, Illinois, QB	33,280
			East Carolina	0			

DECEMBER 19, 1959
PENN STATE 7, ALABAMA 0

	1ST	2ND	3RD	4TH	FINAL
PSU	0	7	0	0	7
ALA	0	0	0	0	0

SCORING SUMMARY
PSU   Kochman 18 pass from Hall (Stellatella kick)

PSU	TEAM STATISTICS	ALA
18	First Downs	8
278	Rushing Yards	104
2-10-0	Passing	2-8-0
41	Passing Yards	27
319	Total Yards	131
6-29.0	Punts - Average	8-34.4
4-4	Fumbles - Lost	7-4
4-45	Penalties - Yards	3-45

INDIVIDUAL LEADERS
RUSHING
PSU: Lucas 9-54.
ALA: Trammel 13-37.
PASSING
PSU: Lucas 1-4-0, 23 yards; Hall 1-6-0, 18 yards, 1 TD.
ALA: Trammel 1-4-0, 20 yards.

DECEMBER 17, 1960
PENN STATE 41, OREGON 12

	1ST	2ND	3RD	4TH	FINAL
PSU	0	21	0	20	41
ORE	6	0	6	0	12

SCORING SUMMARY
ORE   Grosz 1 run (kick failed)
PSU   Jonas 1 run (Opperman kick)
PSU   Gursky 2 run (Opperman kick)
PSU   Hoak 6 run (Opperman kick)
ORE   Grayson 10 run (pass failed)
PSU   Caye 1 run (Opperman kick)
PSU   Hoak 11 run (kick failed)
PSU   Pae 33 pass from Hoak (Jonas kick)

PSU	TEAM STATISTICS	ORE
25	First Downs	17
301	Rushing Yards	187
8-14-0	Passing	10-16-2
119	Passing Yards	173
420	Total Yards	360
4-25.0	Punts - Average	4-34.0
2-1	Fumbles - Lost	4-2
6-40	Penalties - Yards	2-12

INDIVIDUAL LEADERS
RUSHING
PSU: Hoak 9-61, 2 TD; Jonas 13-40, 1 TD.
ORE: Grayson 10-93, 1 TD.
PASSING
PSU: Hall 4-7-0, 47 yards.
ORE: Grosz 9-15-2, 178 yards.
RECEIVING
PSU: Opperman 4-49.
ORE: Bruce 4-90.

DECEMBER 22, 1979
PENN STATE 9, TULANE 6

	1ST	2ND	3RD	4TH	FINAL
PSU	0	6	0	3	9
TUL	0	0	0	6	6

SCORING SUMMARY
PSU   FG Menhardt 33
PSU   FG Menhardt 27
TUL   FG Murray 26
TUL   FG Murray 26
PSU   FG Menhardt 20

PSU	TEAM STATISTICS	TUL
27	First Downs	10
242	Rushing Yards	-8
6-11-2	Passing	21-39-0
95	Passing Yards	210
337	Total Yards	202
2-2	Fumbles - Lost	1-0
1-5	Penalties - Yards	5-40

INDIVIDUAL LEADERS
RUSHING
PSU: Suhey 19-112; Warner 14-57.
TUL: Christian 6-12.
PASSING
PSU: Rocco 5-10-2, 56 yards.
TUL: Hontas 21-39-0, 210 yards.
RECEIVING
PSU: Donovan 2-53.
TUL: Alexis 7-77; Griffin 3-50.

DECEMBER 27, 1980
PURDUE 28, MISSOURI 25

	1ST	2ND	3RD	4TH	FINAL
PUR	7	14	7	0	28
MO	0	12	3	10	25

SCORING SUMMARY
PUR   Burrell 8 pass from Herrmann (Anderson kick)
PUR   Bryant 43 pass from Herrmann (Anderson kick)
MO   Fellows 92 kickoff return (kick failed)
MO   Wilder 1 run (pass failed)
PUR   Young 5 pass from Herrmann (Anderson kick)
PUR   Burrell 27 pass from Herrmann (Anderson kick)
MO   FG Verrelli 45
MO   Safety (Herrmann tackled in end zone)
MO   Hill 1 run (Hornof pass from Bradley)

PUR	TEAM STATISTICS	MO
18	First Downs	17
124	Rushing Yards	103
22-28-0	Passing	16-29-1
289	Passing Yards	210
413	Total Yards	313
6-34.0	Punts - Average	6-43.8
1-1	Fumbles - Lost	2-1
5-31	Penalties - Yards	1-5

INDIVIDUAL LEADERS
RUSHING
PUR: McCall 17-85; Macon 16-69.
MO: Hill 9-54, 1 TD; Wilder 16-49, 1 TD.
PASSING
PUR: Herrmann 22-28-0, 289 yards, 4 TD.
MO: Bradley 16-29-1, 210 yards.
RECEIVING
PUR: Burrell 8-113, 2 TD.
MO: Blair 3-62.

DECEMBER 30, 1981
OHIO STATE 31, NAVY 28

	1ST	2ND	3RD	4TH	FINAL
OSU	10	7	7	7	31
NAVY	7	6	7	8	28

SCORING SUMMARY
OSU   FG Atha 35
OSU   Williams 50 pass from Schlichter (Atha kick)
NAVY   Papajohn 1 pass from Pagnanelli (Fehr kick)
NAVY   FG Fehr 23
OSU   Gayle 1 run (Atha kick)
NAVY   FG Fehr 23
NAVY   Olson 20 blocked kick return (Fehr kick)
OSU   Gayle 2 run (Atha kick)
OSU   Anderson 9 pass from Schlichter (Atha kick)
NAVY   Papajohn 1 pass from Pagnanelli (Papajohn pass from Pagnanelli)

OSU	TEAM STATISTICS	NAVY
19	First Downs	19
173	Rushing Yards	75
11-26-1	Passing	15-29-1
159	Passing Yards	240
332	Total Yards	315
6-32.6	Punts - Average	5-22.8
3-2	Fumbles - Lost	2-1
9-76	Penalties - Yards	2-20

INDIVIDUAL LEADERS
RUSHING
OSU: Spencer 22-96; Gayle 15-88, 2 TD.
NAVY: Meyers 30-117.
PASSING
OSU: Schlichter 11-26-1, 159 yards, 2 TD.
NAVY: Pagnanelli 14-27-1, 201 yards, 2 TD.
RECEIVING
OSU: Williams 2-61; Anderson 5-57.
NAVY: Weller 2-50; Papajohn 4-41, 2 TD.

DECEMBER 29, 1982
ALABAMA 21, ILLINOIS 15

	1ST	2ND	3RD	4TH	FINAL
ALA	7	0	7	7	21
ILL	0	6	0	9	15

SCORING SUMMARY
ALA   Moore 4 run (Kim kick)
ILL   Curtis 1 run (kick failed)
ALA   Bendross 8 run (Kim kick)
ILL   Williams 2 pass from Eason (pass failed)
ILL   FG Bass 23
ALA   Turner 1 run (Kim kick)

ALA	TEAM STATISTICS	ILL
19	First Downs	21
217	Rushing Yards	21
7-13-2	Passing	35-58-4
130	Passing Yards	423
347	Total Yards	444

INDIVIDUAL LEADERS
RUSHING
ALA: Moore 13-65, 1 TD; Turner 11-36, 1 TD.
ILL: Curtis 7-13, 1 TD.
PASSING
ALA: Lewis 7-13-2, 130 yards.
ILL: Eason 35-55-4, 423 yards, 1 TD.
RECEIVING
ALA: Jones 2-60; Bendross 3-51.
ILL: Martin 8-127; Williams 7-84, 1 TD.

*Played as an independent or with other conference affiliation

DECEMBER 29, 1986
TENNESSEE 21, MINNESOTA 14

	1ST	2ND	3RD	4TH	FINAL
TENN	7	7	0	7	21
MINN	0	3	8	3	14

SCORING SUMMARY

TENN	Clinkscales 18 pass from Francis (Reveiz kick)
TENN	Howard 23 pass from Francis (Reveiz kick)
MINN	FG Lohmiller 27
MINN	Foggie 11 run (Thompson run)
MINN	FG Lohmiller 25
TENN	Clinkscales 15 pass from Francis (Reveiz kick)

TENN	TEAM STATISTICS	MINN
17	First Downs	20
81	Rushing Yards	238
22-31-0	Passing	10-25-0
243	Passing Yards	136
324	Total Yards	374
5-38.4	Punts - Average	3-39.7
4-1	Fumbles - Lost	2-2
5-49	Penalties - Yards	5-30
28:40	Possession Time	31:20

INDIVIDUAL LEADERS

RUSHING
TENN: Howard 16-63.
MINN: Thompson 25-136.

PASSING
TENN: Francis 22-31-0, 243 yards, 3 TD.
MINN: Foggie 10-25-0, 136 yards.

RECEIVING
TENN: Clinkscales 7-72, 2 TD; Miller 6-72.
MINN: Anderson 3-31.

DECEMBER 28, 1988
INDIANA 34, SOUTH CAROLINA 10

	1ST	2ND	3RD	4TH	FINAL
IND	7	10	3	14	34
SC	0	0	10	0	10

SCORING SUMMARY

IND	Thompson 7 run (Stoyanovich kick)
IND	Miller 10 pass from Schnell (Stoyanovich kick)
IND	FG Stoyanovich 28
SC	Tolbert 34 block punt return (Mackie kick)
IND	FG Stoyanovich 19
SC	FG Mackie 43
IND	Turner 88 pass from Schnell (Stoyanovich kick)
IND	Thompson 8 run (Stoyanovich kick)

IND	TEAM STATISTICS	SC
23	First Downs	12
185	Rushing Yards	23
17-32-1	Passing	15-37-3
390	Passing Yards	130
575	Total Yards	153
6-26.0	Punts - Average	9-38.0
1-0	Fumbles - Lost	1-1
6-40	Penalties - Yards	2-15

INDIVIDUAL LEADERS

RUSHING
IND: Thompson 26-140, 2 TD.
SC: Green 11-41.

PASSING
IND: Schnell 16-31-1, 378 yards, 2 TD.
SC: Ellis 15-37-3, 130 yards.

RECEIVING
IND: Turner 5-182, 1 TD; Thompson 2-14, 2 TD.
SC: Brooks 2-35.

DECEMBER 27, 1990
AIR FORCE 23, OHIO STATE 11

	1ST	2ND	3RD	4TH	FINAL
AFA	0	6	7	10	23
OSU	5	0	0	6	11

SCORING SUMMARY

OSU	Safety (punter tackled in end zone)
OSU	FG Williams 28
AFA	Perez 1 run (run failed)
AFA	Perez 1 run (Wood kick)
OSU	Smith 29 run (pass failed)
AFA	FG Wood 46
AFA	McDonald 40 interception return (Wood kick)

AFA	TEAM STATISTICS	OSU
16	First Downs	14
254	Rushing Yards	80
1-3-1	Passing	12-32-2
11	Passing Yards	134
265	Total Yards	214
6-60.0	Punts - Average	6-42.0
3-2	Fumbles - Lost	1-0
6-60	Penalties - Yards	6-42
33:23	Possession Time	26:37

INDIVIDUAL LEADERS

RUSHING
AFA: Perez 26-93, 2 TD; Lewis 12-74.
OSU: Smith 13-62, 1 TD.

PASSING
AFA: Perez 1-3-1, 11 yards.
OSU: Frey 10-27-3, 110 yards.

RECEIVING
AFA: Mott 1-11.
OSU: Olive 4-63.

DECEMBER 28, 1993
LOUISVILLE 18, MICHIGAN STATE 7

	1ST	2ND	3RD	4TH	FINAL
LOU	3	0	0	15	18
MSU	7	0	0	0	7

SCORING SUMMARY

MSU	Goulborne 1 run (Stoyanovich kick)
LOU	FG Akers 31
LOU	Ferguson 25 pass from Brohm (Akers kick)
LOU	Safety (Thomas tackled in end zone)
LOU	Dawkins 11 run (kick failed)

LOU	TEAM STATISTICS	MSU
20	First Downs	18
172	Rushing Yards	114
19-31-0	Passing	15-28-1
197	Passing Yards	193
369	Total Yards	307
1-25	Punt Returns - Yards	1-3
2-48	Kickoff Returns - Yards	4-59
5-36.2	Punts - Average	5-29.0
1-0	Fumbles - Lost	0-0
6-45	Penalties - Yards	5-60

INDIVIDUAL LEADERS

RUSHING
LOU: Dawkins 14-88, 1 TD; Shelman 17-59.
MSU: Goulborne 19-63, 1 TD; Thomas 10-57.

PASSING
LOU: Brohm 19-29-0, 197 yards, 1 TD.
MSU: Miller 15-28-1, 193 yards.

RECEIVING
LOU: Dawkins 8-68; Ferguson 3-68.
MSU: Coleman 6-100; Greene 4-49.

DECEMBER 31, 1994
ILLINOIS 30, EAST CAROLINA 0

	1ST	2ND	3RD	4TH	FINAL
ILL	14	10	6	0	30
ECU	0	0	0	0	0

SCORING SUMMARY

ILL	Dilger 17 pass from Johnson (Richardson kick)
ILL	Strong 73 pass from Johnson (Richardson kick)
ILL	FG Richardson 21
ILL	Dulick 5 pass from Johnson (Richardson kick)
ILL	Douthard 9 pass from Johnson (Richardson kick)

ILL	TEAM STATISTICS	ECU
18	First Downs	17
134	Rushing Yards	92
20-34-0	Passing	20-41-4
255	Passing Yards	179
389	Total Yards	271
15-164	Penalties - Yards	6-40

INDIVIDUAL LEADERS

RUSHING
ILL: Douthard 13-52; Holcome 12-46.
ECU: Smith 15-46.

PASSING
ILL: Johnson 18-30-0, 250 yards, 4 TD.
ECU: Crandell 20-41-4, 179 yards.

RECEIVING
ILL: Strong 3-96, 1 TD; Dilger 7-60, 1 TD.
ECU: Nichols 6-55; Richards 4-25.

MOTOR CITY BOWL

PROFILE

Site: Detroit, Mich.
Stadium: Ford Field
Capacity: 65,000
Surface: FieldTurf

PLAYING SITES

Pontiac Silverdome, 1997-2001
Ford Field, since 2002

NAME CHANGES

Motor City Bowl, since 1997

SEASON	DATE	PRE-GAME RANK	TEAMS	SCORE	FINAL RANK	MOST VALUABLE PLAYER(S)	ATT.
2003	Dec. 26, 2003		**Bowling Green**	**28**	23	Josh Harris, Bowling Green, QB	51,286
			Northwestern	**24**		Jason Wright, Northwestern, RB	

DECEMBER 26, 2003
BOWLING GREEN 28, NORTHWESTERN 24

	1ST	2ND	3RD	4TH	FINAL
BG	0	7	7	14	28
NU	7	3	7	7	24

SCORING SUMMARY

NU	Herron 40 run (Huffman kick)
NU	FG Huffman 31
BG	Harris 4 run (Suisham kick)
NU	Wright 77 run (Huffman kick)
BG	Magner 7 pass from Harris (Suisham kick)
BG	Sanders 11 pass from Harris (Suisham kick)
NU	Herron 2 run (Huffman kick)
BG	Magner 3 pass from Harris (Suisham kick)

BG	TEAM STATISTICS	NU
30	First Downs	16
88	Rushing Yards	357
38-51-3	Passing	7-15-0
386	Passing Yards	58
474	Total Yards	415
2-21	Punt Returns - Yards	2-3
3-46.0	Punts - Average	5-34.4
0-0	Fumbles - Lost	2-2
1-15	Penalties - Yards	3-40
34:08	Possession Time	25:52

INDIVIDUAL LEADERS

RUSHING
BG: Harris 21-68, 1 TD; Pope 11-23.
NU: Wright 21-237, 1 TD; Herron 12-80, 2 TD.

PASSING
BG: Harris 38-50-2, 386 yards, 3 TD.
NU: Basanez 7-15-0, 58 yards.

RECEIVING
BG: Magner 12-97, 2 TD; Sharon 7-93; Sanders 5-74, 1 TD.
NU: Philmore 3-43; Wright 2-11.

MUSIC CITY BOWL

BIG TEN ANNUAL REVIEW & BOWLS

PROFILE

Site: Nashville, Tenn.
Stadium: The Coliseum
Capacity: 67,000
Surface: Grass

PLAYING SITES

Vanderbilt Stadium, 1998
Adelphia Coliseum, renamed The Coliseum in 2002, renamed LP Field in 2006, since 1999

NAME CHANGES

Music City Bowl, 1998
HomePoint.com Music City Bowl, 1999
Music City Bowl, 2000-01
Gaylord Hotels Music City Bowl, 2002-03
Gaylord Hotels Music City Bowl Presented by Bridgestone, since 2004

SEASON	DATE	PRE-GAME RANK	TEAMS	SCORE	FINAL RANK	MOST VALUABLE PLAYER(S)	ATT.
2002	Dec. 30, 2002		Minnesota	29		Dan Nystrom, Minnesota, K	39,183
		25	Arkansas	14			
2003	Dec. 31 2003		Auburn	28		Jason Campbell, Auburn, QB	55,109
			Wisconsin	14			
2004	Dec. 31, 2004		Minnesota	20		Marion Barber, Minnesota, RB	66,089
			Alabama	16			
2005	Dec. 30, 2005		Virginia	34		Marques Hagans, Virginia, QB	40,519
			Minnesota	31			

DECEMBER 30, 2002
MINNESOTA 29, ARKANSAS 14

	1ST	2ND	3RD	4TH	FINAL
ARK	7	0	0	7	14
MINN	6	6	7	10	29

SCORING SUMMARY
ARK Wilson 2 pass from Jones (Carlton kick)
MINN FG Nystrom 24
MINN FG Nystrom 45
MINN FG Nystrom 21
MINN FG Nystrom 22
MINN Utecht 19 pass from Abdul-Khaliq (Nystrom kick)
MINN FG Nystrom 29
MINN Tapeh 33 run (Nystrom kick)
ARK Smith 10 pass from Sorahan (Carlton kick)

ARK	TEAM STATISTICS	MINN
19	First Downs	21
80	Rushing Yards	168
18-40-3	Passing	17-32-0
208	Passing Yards	266
288	Total Yards	434
2-15	Punt Returns - Yards	4-3
8-128	Kickoff Returns - Yards	2-42
5-34.2	Punts - Average	2-32.5
2-1	Fumbles - Lost	0-0
6-44	Penalties - Yards	9-71
21:45	Possession Time	38:15

INDIVIDUAL LEADERS
RUSHING
ARK: Talley 14-33; Jones 7-14.
MINN: Tapeh 19-99, 1 TD; Jackson II 16-37.
PASSING
ARK: Jones 12-24-2, 119 yards, 1 TD; Sorahan 6-15-1, 89 yards, 1 TD.
MINN: Abdul-Khaliq 16-31-0, 216 yards, 1 TD.
RECEIVING
ARK: Wilson 8-111, 1 TD; Smith 5-65, 1 TD.
MINN: Burns 4-88; Utecht 5-77, 1 TD.

DECEMBER 31, 2003
AUBURN 28, WISCONSIN 14

	1ST	2ND	3RD	4TH	FINAL
AUB	0	7	7	14	28
WIS	0	6	0	8	14

SCORING SUMMARY
WIS FG Allen 20
AUB Brown 1 run (Vaughn kick)
WIS FG Allen 35
AUB Williams 1 run (Vaughn kick)
WIS Evans 12 pass from Sorgi (Daniels pass from Sorgi)
AUB Brown 2 run (Vaughn kick)
AUB Williams 1 run (Vaughn kick)

AUB	TEAM STATISTICS	WIS
15	First Downs	18
197	Rushing Yards	58
11-23-1	Passing	17-29-1
157	Passing Yards	203
354	Total Yards	261
5-99	Punt Returns - Yards	3-35
4-64	Kickoff Returns - Yards	2-6
5-45.2	Punts - Average	4-38.5
0-0	Fumbles - Lost	2-1
8-66	Penalties - Yards	4-25
29:00	Possession Time	31:00

INDIVIDUAL LEADERS
RUSHING
AUB: Williams 18-68, 2 TD; Campbell 9-67; Brown 13-62, 2 TD.
WIS: Davis 17-77; Evans 3-19.
PASSING
AUB: Campbell 10-22-1, 138 yards.
WIS: Sorgi 13-22-1, 169 yards, 1 TD.
RECEIVING
AUB: McIntyre 3-74, Daniels 3-40.
WIS: Williams 6-57; Evans 4-51, 1 TD.

DECEMBER 31, 2004
MINNESOTA 20, ALABAMA 16

	1ST	2ND	3RD	4TH	FINAL
MINN	7	10	3	0	20
ALA	7	7	0	2	16

SCORING SUMMARY
ALA McClain 2 pass from Pennington (Bostick kick)
MINN Lipka 1 fumble return (Lloyd kick)
MINN Barber 5 run (Lloyd kick)
MINN FG Lloyd 27
ALA McClain 1 run (Bostick kick)
MINN FG Lloyd 24
ALA Saftey

MINN	TEAM STATISTICS	ALA
23	First Downs	13
276	Rushing Yards	21
5-13-2	Passing	22-36-0
75	Passing Yards	243
351	Total Yards	264
4-10	Punt Returns - Yards	2-10
1-18	Kickoff Returns - Yards	5-76
4-37.8	Punts - Average	7-37.1
2-1	Fumbles - Lost	2-2
11-84	Penalties - Yards	4-35
37:54	Possession Time	22:06

INDIVIDUAL LEADERS
RUSHING
MINN: Barber 37-187, 1 TD; Maroney 29-105.
ALA: Brown 1-17.
PASSING
MINN: Cupito 5-12-1, 75 yards.
ALA: Pennington 22-36-0, 243 yards, 1 TD.
RECEIVING
MINN: Ellerson 3-51.
ALA: Prothro 4-82; Brown 3-56.

DECEMBER 30, 2005
VIRGINIA 34, MINNESOTA 31

	1ST	2ND	3RD	4TH	FINAL
UVA	7	3	14	10	34
MINN	14	7	3	7	31

SCORING SUMMARY
MINN Valentine 7 pass from Cupito (Monroe kick)
MINN Wheelwright 44 pass from Cupito (Monroe kick)
UVA Williams 6 pass from Hagans (Hughes kick)
MINN Ellerson 57 pass from Cupito (Monroe kick)
UVA FG Hughes 32
UVA Lundy 7 run (Hughes kick)
MINN FG Monroe 39
UVA Mines 2 pass from Hagans (Hughes kick)
MINN Ellerson 23 pass from Cupito (Monroe kick)
UVA Lundy 2 run (Hughes kick)
UVA FG Hughes 39

UVA	TEAM STATISTICS	MINN
20	First Downs	48
103	Rushing Yards	198
26-33-1	Passing	18-28-1
365	Passing Yards	263
468	Total Yards	461
2-8	Punt Returns - Yards	2-13
5-75	Kickoff Returns - Yards	4-87
3-42.3	Punts - Average	4-37.3
2-1	Fumbles - Lost	1-0
4-30	Penalties - Yards	6-52
25:59	Possession Time	34:01

INDIVIDUAL LEADERS
RUSHING
UVA: Lundy 16-59, 2 TD; Hagans 10-26.
MINN: Maroney 26-109; Russell 22-85.
PASSING
UVA: Hagans 25-32-1, 358 yards, 2 TD.
MINN: Cupito 18-28-1, 263 yards, 4 TD.
RECEIVING
UVA: Santi 5-128; Williams 6-88, 1 TD.
MINN: Wheelwright 7-120, 1 TD; Ellerson 3-80, 2 TD.

ORANGE BOWL

PROFILE

Site: Miami, Fla.
Stadium: Dolphins Stadium
Capacity: 72,319
Surface: Prescription Athletic Turf

PLAYING SITES

Miami Field Stadium, 1935-37
Orange Bowl, 1938-95, 1999
Pro Player Stadium, renamed
Dolphins Stadium in 2005,
1996-98, since 2000

NAME CHANGES

Orange Bowl, 1935-88
Federal Express Orange Bowl,
1989-94
FedEx Orange Bowl, since 1995

SEASON	DATE	PRE-GAME RANK	TEAMS	SCORE	FINAL RANK	MOST VALUABLE PLAYER(S)	ATT.
1937	Jan. 1, 1938		**Auburn**	6			18,972
			Michigan State*	0			
1968	Jan. 1, 1969	3	**Penn State***	15	2	Donnie Shanklin, Kansas, HB	77,719
		6	**Kansas**	14	7		
1969	Jan. 1, 1970	2	**Penn State***	10	2	Chuck Burkhart, Penn State, QB	77,282
		6	**Missouri**	3	6	Mike Reid, Penn State, DT	
1973	Jan. 1, 1974	6	**Penn State***	16	5	Tom Shuman, Penn State, QB	60,477
		13	**LSU**	9	13	Randy Crowder, Penn State, DT	
1975	Jan. 1, 1976	3	**Oklahoma**	14	1	Steve Davis, Oklahoma, QB	80,307
		5	**Michigan**	6	8	Lee Roy Selmon, Oklahoma, DT	
1976	Jan. 1, 1977	11	**Ohio State**	27	6	Rod Gerald, Ohio State, QB	65,537
		12	**Colorado**	10	16	Tom Cousineau, Ohio State, LB	
1985	Jan. 1, 1986	3	**Oklahoma**	25	1	Sonny Brown, Oklahoma, DB	74,178
		1	**Penn State***	10	3	Tim Lashar, Oklahoma, K	
1999	Jan. 1, 2000	8	**Michigan**	35 OT	5	David Terrell, Michigan, WR	70,461
		5	**Alabama**	34	8		
2002	Jan. 2, 2003	5	**USC**	38	4	Carson Palmer, USC, QB	75,971
		3	**Iowa**	17	8		
2005	Jan. 3, 2006	3	**Penn State**	26 3OT	3	Willie Reid, Florida State, WR	77,773
		22	**Florida State**	23	23		

JANUARY 1, 1938
AUBURN 6, MICHIGAN STATE 0

	1ST	2ND	3RD	4TH	FINAL
AUB	0	6	0	0	6
MSU	0	0	0	0	0

SCORING SUMMARY
AUB   O'Gwynne 2 run (kick failed)

AUB	TEAM STATISTICS	MSU
12	First Downs	2
197	Rushing Yards	40
4-12-2	Passing	2-9-3
81	Passing Yards	25
278	Total Yards	65
10-33.7	Punts - Average	12-35.2
0-0	Fumbles - Lost	0-0
50	Penalty Yards	35

JANUARY 1, 1969
PENN STATE 15, KANSAS 14

	1ST	2ND	3RD	4TH	FINAL
PSU	0	7	0	8	15
KU	7	0	0	7	14

SCORING SUMMARY
KU   Reeves 2 run (Bell kick)
PSU   Pittman 13 run (Garthwaite kick)
KU   Riggins 1 run (Bell kick)
PSU   Burkhart 3 run (Campbell run)

PSU	TEAM STATISTICS	KU
17	First Downs	16
207	Rushing Yards	76
12-23-1	Passing	9-18-2
154	Passing Yards	165
361	Total Yards	241
9-38.0	Punts - Average	10-38.3
2-2	Fumbles - Lost	2-0
1-15	Penalties - Yards	2-11

INDIVIDUAL LEADERS
RUSHING
PSU: Campbell 18-101; Pittman 14-58, 1 TD.
KU: Riggins 18-47, 1 TD.
PASSING
PSU: Burkhart 12-23-2, 154 yards.
KU: Douglass 9-17-1, 165 yards.
RECEIVING
PSU: Kwalick 6-74; Campbell 2-55.
KU: Mosier 5-77; Shanklin 1-42.

JANUARY 1, 1970
PENN STATE 10, MISSOURI 3

	1ST	2ND	3RD	4TH	FINAL
PSU	10	0	0	0	10
MO	0	3	0	0	3

SCORING SUMMARY
PSU   FG Reitz 29
PSU   Mitchell 28 pass from Burkhart (Rietz kick)
MO   FG Brown 33

PSU	TEAM STATISTICS	MO
12	First Downs	13
57	Rushing Yards	189
11-26-1	Passing	6-26-7
187	Passing Yards	117
244	Total Yards	306
12-43.1	Punts - Average	6-44.7
0-0	Fumbles - Lost	4-2
5-40	Penalties - Yards	3-25

INDIVIDUAL LEADERS
RUSHING
PSU: Harris 17-46.
MO: Staggers 9-69; Moore 19-62.
PASSING
PSU: Burkhart 11-26-1, 187 yards, 1 TD.
MO: McMillan 4-17-5, 73 yards; Roper 2-9-2, 44 yards.
RECEIVING
PSU: Mitchell 5-81, 1 TD.
MO: Henley 2-44; Shryock 3-33.

JANUARY 1, 1974
PENN STATE 16, LSU 9

	1ST	2ND	3RD	4TH	FINAL
PSU	3	13	0	0	16
LSU	7	0	2	0	9

SCORING SUMMARY
LSU   Rogers 3 run (Jackson kick)
PSU   FG Bahr 44
PSU   Herd 72 pass from Shuman (Bahr kick)
PSU   Cappelletti 1 run (kick failed)
LSU   Safety (Shuman fumbled snap in end zone)

PSU	TEAM STATISTICS	LSU
9	First Downs	19
28	Rushing Yards	205
6-17-1	Passing	8-20-1
157	Passing Yards	69
185	Total Yards	274
7-34.7	Punts - Average	8-46.8
1-0	Fumbles - Lost	3-1
3-37	Penalties - Yards	3-30

INDIVIDUAL LEADERS
RUSHING
PSU: Cappelletti 26-50, 1 TD.
LSU: Davis 19-70; Robiskie 10-58.
PASSING
PSU: Shuman 6-17-1, 157 yards, 1 TD.
LSU: Miley 8-18-1, 69 yards.
RECEIVING
PSU: Herd 1-72, 1 TD; Hayman 3-35.
LSU: Davis 6-20.

JANUARY 1, 1976
OKLAHOMA 14, MICHIGAN 6

	1ST	2ND	3RD	4TH	FINAL
OKLA	0	7	0	7	14
MICH	0	0	0	6	6

SCORING SUMMARY
OKLA   Brooks 39 run (DiRienzo kick)
OKLA   Davis 9 run (DiRienzo kick)
MICH   G. Bell 2 run (run failed)

OKLA	TEAM STATISTICS	MICH
16	First Downs	12
282	Rushing Yards	169
3-5-0	Passing	2-20-3
63	Passing Yards	33
345	Total Yards	202
9-34.9	Punts - Average	10-38.6
4-3	Fumbles - Lost	1-0
9-90	Penalties - Yards	5-24

INDIVIDUAL LEADERS
RUSHING
OKLA: Washington 17-73; Culbreath 11-63.
MICH: Leach 13-62; G. Bell 18-53, 1 TD.
PASSING
OKLA: Davis 3-5-0, 63 yards.
MICH: Leach 2-15-3, 30 yards.
RECEIVING
OKLA: Owens 3-63.
MICH: Bell 1-17.

JANUARY 1, 1977
OHIO STATE 27, COLORADO 10

	1ST	2ND	3RD	4TH	FINAL
OSU	7	10	3	7	27
COLO	10	0	0	0	10

SCORING SUMMARY
COLO   FG Zetterberg 26
COLO   Moorehead 11 pass from Knapple (Zetterberg kick)
OSU   Logan 36 run (Skladany kick)
OSU   FG Skladany 28
OSU   Johnson 3 run (Skladany kick)
OSU   FG Skladany 20
OSU   Gerald 4 run (Skladany kick)

OSU	TEAM STATISTICS	COLO
21	First Downs	12
271	Rushing Yards	134
2-7-0	Passing	8-23-2
59	Passing Yards	137
330	Total Yards	271
3-42.2	Punts - Average	7-35.2
4-4	Fumbles - Lost	1-0
4-37	Penalties - Yards	8-60
34:29	Possession Time	25:31

INDIVIDUAL LEADERS
RUSHING
OSU: Springs 23-98; Gerald 14-81, 1 TD; Logan 14-79, 1 TD.
COLO: Reed 22-58.
PASSING
OSU: Gerald 2-6-0, 59 yards.
COLO: Knapple 8-22-2, 137 yards, 1 TD.
RECEIVING
OSU: Harrell 2-59.
COLO: Moorehead 4-68, 1 TD; Reed 2-51.

JANUARY 1, 1986
OKLAHOMA 25, PENN STATE 10

	1ST	2ND	3RD	4TH	FINAL
OKLA	0	16	3	6	25
PSU	7	3	0	0	10

SCORING SUMMARY
PSU	Manoa 1 run (Manca kick)
OKLA	FG Lashar 21
OKLA	K. Jackson 71 pass from Holieway (Lashar kick)
OKLA	FG Lashar 31
OKLA	FG Lashar 26
PSU	FG Manca 27
OKLA	FG Lashar 22
OKLA	Carr 61 run (kick failed)

OKLA	TEAM STATISTICS	PSU
12	First Downs	14
228	Rushing Yards	103
3-6-0	Passing	18-34-4
91	Passing Yards	164
319	Total Yards	267
5-42.6	Punts - Average	6-46.3
5-1	Fumbles - Lost	2-1
7-45	Penalties - Yards	6-49
28:37	Possession Time	31:23

INDIVIDUAL LEADERS
RUSHING
OKLA: Carr 19-148, 1 TD.
PSU: Dozier 12-39.
PASSING
OKLA: Holieway 3-6-0, 91 yards, 1 TD.
PSU: Knizer 8-11-1, 90 yards; Shaffer 10-22-3, 74 yards.
RECEIVING
OKLA: K. Jackson 2-83, 1 TD.
PSU: Dimidio 6-50.

JANUARY 1, 2000
MICHIGAN 35, ALABAMA 34

	1ST	2ND	3RD	4TH	OT	FINAL
MICH	0	7	21	0	7	35
ALA	0	14	14	0	6	34

SCORING SUMMARY
ALA	Alexander 5 run (Pflugner kick)
ALA	Alexander 6 run (Pflugner kick)
MICH	Terrell 27 pass from Brady (Epstein kick)
MICH	Terrell 57 pass from Brady (Epstein kick)
ALA	Alexander 50 run (Pflugner kick)
ALA	Milons 62 punt return (Pflugner kick)
MICH	Terrell 20 pass from Brady (Epstein kick)
MICH	A. Thomas 3 run (Epstein kick)
MICH	Thompson 25 pass from Brady (Epstein kick)
ALA	Carter 21 pass from Zow (kick failed)

MICH	TEAM STATISTICS	ALA
18	First Downs	12
37	Rushing Yards	184
35-47-0	Passing	13-20-1
369	Passing Yards	111
406	Total Yards	295
8-43.4	Punts - Average	9-34.4
2-1	Fumbles - Lost	1-0
10-115	Penalties - Yards	18-132
32:08	Possession Time	27:52

INDIVIDUAL LEADERS
RUSHING
MICH: A. Thomas 18-40, 1 TD.
ALA: Alexander 25-161, 3 TD, Watts 4-15.
PASSING
MICH: Brady 34-46-0, 369 yards, 4 TD.
ALA: Zow 7-14-0, 86 yards, 1 TD.
RECEIVING
MICH: Terrell 10-150, 3 TD; Shea 7-50; Thompson 3-47, 1 TD.
ALA: Carter 4-38, 1 TD; Alexander 2-21.

JANUARY 2, 2003
USC 38, IOWA 17

	1ST	2ND	3RD	4TH	FINAL
USC	7	3	14	14	38
IOWA	10	0	0	7	17

SCORING SUMMARY
IOWA	Jones 100 kick return (Kaeding kick)
USC	Fargas 4 run (Killeen kick)
IOWA	FG Kaeding 35
USC	FG Killeen 35
USC	Williams 18 pass from Palmer (Killeen kick)
USC	Fargas 50 run (Killeen kick)
USC	McCullough 5 run (Killeen kick)
USC	Byrd 6 run (Killeen kick)
IOWA	Brown 18 pass from Banks (Kaeding kick)

USC	TEAM STATISTICS	IOWA
30	First Downs	18
247	Rushing Yards	119
21-31-0	Passing	15-36-1
303	Passing Yards	204
550	Total Yards	323
4-49	Punt Returns - Yards	0-0
2-33	Kickoff Returns - Yards	7-224
2-37.5	Punts - Average	5-42.6
2-0	Fumbles - Lost	2-1
6-45	Penalties - Yards	13-85
38:06	Possession Time	21:54

INDIVIDUAL LEADERS
RUSHING
USC: Fargas 20-122, 2 TD; McCullough 12-77, 1 TD.
IOWA: Russell 9-45; Banks 8-36.
PASSING
USC: Palmer 21-31-0, 303 yards, 1 TD.
IOWA: Banks 15-36-1, 204 yards, 1 TD.
RECEIVING
USC: Williams 6-99, 1 TD; Colbert 6-81; Kelly 3-74.
IOWA: Clark 4-97; Brown 6-63, 1 TD.

JANUARY 3, 2006
PENN STATE 26, FLORIDA STATE 23

	1ST	2ND	3RD	4TH	OT	FINAL
PSU	7	7	0	2	10	26
FSU	0	13	0	3	7	23

SCORING SUMMARY
PSU	Scott 2 run (Kelly kick)
FSU	Reid 87 punt return (Cismesia kick)
FSU	Booker 57 pass from Weatherford (kick failed)
PSU	Kilmer 24 pass from Robinson (Kelly kick)
PSU	Safety
FSU	FG Cismesia 48
PSU	Scott 2 run (Kelly kick)
FSU	Dean 1 run (Cismesia kick)
PSU	FG Kelly 29

PSU	TEAM STATISTICS	FSU
23	First Downs	12
138	Rushing Yards	26
21-39-1	Passing	24-43-1
253	Passing Yards	258
391	Total Yards	284
0-0	Punt Returns - Yards	7-180
5-52	Kickoff Returns - Yards	2-71
11-43.4	Punts - Average	9-39.2
1-1	Fumbles - Lost	0-0
8-55	Penalties - Yards	11-115
34:16	Possession Time	25:44

INDIVIDUAL LEADERS
RUSHING
PSU: Scott 26-110, 2 TD; Robinson 17-21.
FSU: Washington 6-30; Booker 7-2.
PASSING
PSU: Robinson 21-39-1, 253 yards, 1 TD.
FSU: Weatherford 24-43-1, 258 yards, 1 TD.
RECEIVING
PSU: Norwood 6-110; Kilmer 6-79, 1 TD.
FSU: Booker 3-69, 1 TD; Reid 4-55.

OUTBACK BOWL

BIG TEN ANNUAL REVIEW & BOWLS

PROFILE

Site: Tampa, Fla.
Stadium: Raymond James Stadium
Capacity: 65,657
Surface: Grass

PLAYING SITES

Tampa Stadium, renamed Houlihan's Stadium in 1997, 1986-98
Raymond James Stadium, since 1999

NAME CHANGES

Hall of Fame Bowl, 1986-95
Outback Bowl, since 1996

SEASON	DATE	PRE-GAME RANK	TEAMS	SCORE	FINAL RANK	MOST VALUABLE PLAYER(S)	ATT.
1987	Jan. 2, 1988		**Michigan**	28	19	Jamie Morris, Michigan, TB	60,156
			Alabama	24		Bobby Humphrey, Alabama, TB	
1989	Jan. 1, 1990	9	**Auburn**	31	6	Reggie Slack, Auburn, QB	52,535
		21	Ohio State	14	24		
1990	Jan. 1, 1991	14	**Clemson**	30	9	DeChane Cameron, Clemson, QB	63,154
		16	Illinois	0	25		
1991	Jan. 1, 1992	16	**Syracuse**	24	11	Marvin Graves, Syracuse, QB	57,789
		25	Ohio State	17			
1993	Jan. 1, 1994	23	**Michigan**	42	21	Tyrone Wheatley, Michigan, RB	52,649
			North Carolina State	7			
1994	Jan. 2, 1995		**Wisconsin**	34		Terrell Fletcher, Wisconsin, RB	61,384
		25	Duke	20			
1995	Jan. 1, 1996	15	**Penn State**	43	13	Bobby Engram, Penn State, WR	65,313
		16	Auburn	14	22		
1996	Jan. 1, 1997	16	**Alabama**	17	11	Dwayne Rudd, Alabama, LB	53,161
		15	Michigan	14	20		
1997	Jan. 1, 1998	12	**Georgia**	33	10	Mike Bobo, Georgia, QB	56,186
			Wisconsin	6			
1998	Jan. 1, 1999	22	**Penn State**	26	17	Courtney Brown, Penn State, DE	66,005
			Kentucky	14			
1999	Jan. 1, 2000	21	**Georgia**	28 OT	16	Drew Brees, Purdue, QB	54,059
		19	Purdue	25	25		
2000	Jan. 1, 2001		**South Carolina**	24	19	Ryan Brewer, South Carolina, WR	65,229
		19	Ohio State	7			
2001	Jan. 1, 2002	14	**South Carolina**	31	13	Phil Petty, South Carolina, QB	66,249
		22	Ohio State	28			
2002	Jan. 1, 2003	12	**Michigan**	38	9	Chris Perry, Michigan, TB	65,101
		22	Florida	30			
2003	Jan. 1, 2004	13	**Iowa**	37	8	Fred Russell, Iowa, RB	65,657
		17	Florida	17	24		
2004	Jan. 1, 2005	8	**Georgia**	24	7	David Pollack, Georgia, DE	62,414
		16	Wisconsin	21	17		
2005	Jan. 2, 2006	22	**Florida**	31	23	Dallas Baker, Florida, WR	65,881
			Iowa	24			
2006	Jan. 1, 2007		**Tennessee**	10	24	Tony Hunt, Penn State, RB	65,601
		17	Penn State	20	25		

JANUARY 2, 1988
MICHIGAN 28, ALABAMA 24

	1ST	2ND	3RD	4TH	FINAL
MICH	0	14	7	7	28
ALA	3	0	6	15	24

SCORING SUMMARY
ALA FG Doyle 51
MICH Morris 25 run (Gillette kick)
MICH Morris 14 run (Gillette kick)
MICH Morris 77 run (Gillette kick)
ALA Cross 16 pass from Dunn (run failed)
ALA Humphrey 1 run (Doyle kick)
ALA Humphrey 17 run (Whitehurst pass from Dunn)
MICH Kolesar 20 pass from Brown (Gillette kick)

MICH	TEAM STATISTICS	ALA
12	First Downs	28
278	Rushing Yards	191
6-17-0	Passing	23-40-1
68	Passing Yards	269
346	Total Yards	460
6-42.5	Punts - Average	4-42.5
0-0	Fumbles - Lost	1-1
4-30	Penalties - Yards	1-5
21:42	Possession Time	38:18

INDIVIDUAL LEADERS
RUSHING
MICH: Morris 23-234, 3 TD; Bunch 3-16.
ALA: Humphrey 27-149, 2 TD; Goode 6-14.
PASSING
MICH: Brown 4-13-0, 72 yards, 1 TD.
ALA: Dunn 23-40-1, 269 yards, 1 TD.
RECEIVING
MICH: McMurtry 1-31; Kolesar 1-20, 1 TD.
ALA: Whitehurst 6-85; Cross 6-81, 1 TD.

JANUARY 1, 1990
AUBURN 31, OHIO STATE 14

	1ST	2ND	3RD	4TH	FINAL
AU	3	7	7	14	31
OSU	7	7	0	0	14

SCORING SUMMARY
OSU Snow 1 run (O'Morrow kick)
AU FG Lyle 19
OSU Stablein 9 pass from Frey (O'Morrow kick)
AU Taylor 11 pass from Slack (Lyle kick)
AU Taylor 4 pass from Slack (Lyle kick)
AU Slack 5 run (Lyle kick)
AU Casey 2 pass from Slack (Lyle kick)

AU	TEAM STATISTICS	OSU
21	First Downs	18
171	Rushing Yards	66
16-23-2	Passing	16-31-1
141	Passing Yards	232
312	Total Yards	298
3-72	Punt Returns - Yards	4-25
2-57	Kickoff Returns - Yards	6-121
5-40.8	Punts - Average	7-41.1
1-0	Fumbles - Lost	1-0
2-15	Penalties - Yards	5-33
31:47	Possession Time	28:13

INDIVIDUAL LEADERS
RUSHING
AU: Danley 20-85; Williams 10-46.
OSU: S. Graham 12-53; Snow 13-42, 1 TD.
PASSING
AU: Slack 16-22-2, 141 yards, 3 TD.
OSU: Frey 16-31-1, 232 yards, 1 TD.
RECEIVING
AU: Wright 4-59; Taylor 4-33, 2 TD.
OSU: J. Graham 5-103; Snow 3-30.

JANUARY 1, 1991
CLEMSON 30, ILLINOIS 0

	1ST	2ND	3RD	4TH	FINAL
CLEM	10	14	3	3	30
ILL	0	0	0	0	0

SCORING SUMMARY
CLEM FG Gardocki 18
CLEM Thomas 14 pass from Cameron (Gardocki kick)
CLEM Hall 17 pass from Cameron (Gardocki kick)
CLEM Nunn 34 interception return (Gardocki kick)
CLEM FG Gardocki 26
CLEM FG Gardocki 43

CLEM	TEAM STATISTICS	ILL
18	First Downs	14
148	Rushing Yards	62
16-24-0	Passing	18-36-2
157	Passing Yards	185
305	Total Yards	247
6-72	Punt Returns - Yards	3-18
1-26	Kickoff Returns - Yards	4-77
5-46.0	Punts - Average	7-34.6
1-0	Fumbles - Lost	2-2
10-75	Penalties - Yards	2-28

INDIVIDUAL LEADERS
RUSHING
CLEM: Cameron 17-76; Williams 14-27.
ILL: Griffith 15-59; Feagin 5-28.
PASSING
CLEM: Cameron 14-19-0, 141 yards, 2 TD.
ILL: Verduzco 13-25-2, 121 yards.
RECEIVING
CLEM: Thomas 5-57, 1 TD; Smith 3-43.
ILL: Wax 6-77; Mueller 3-76.

JANUARY 1, 1992
SYRACUSE 24, OHIO STATE 17

	1ST	2ND	3RD	4TH	FINAL
SYR	14	0	3	7	24
OSU	0	3	7	7	17

SCORING SUMMARY
SYR Hill 50 pass from Graves (Biskup kick)
SYR Graves 3 run (Biskup kick)
OSU FG Williams 34
SYR FG Biskup 32
OSU Snow 2 run (Williams kick)
OSU Paul blocked punt recovery in end zone (Williams kick)
SYR Johnson 60 pass from Graves (Biskup kick)

SYR	TEAM STATISTICS	OSU
16	First Downs	17
99	Rushing Yards	93
18-31-1	Passing	14-33-0
309	Passing Yards	174
408	Total Yards	267
4-13	Punt Returns - Yards	3-23
3-65	Kickoff Returns - Yards	4-147
7-40.0	Punts - Average	7-40.9
3-0	Fumbles - Lost	0-0
9-49	Penalties - Yards	5-45
32:01	Possession Time	27:59

INDIVIDUAL LEADERS
RUSHING
SYR: Walker 14-60; Ferrell 1-24.
OSU: Snow 10-56, 1 TD; Harris 7-28.
PASSING
SYR: Graves 18-31-1, 309 yards, 2 TD.
OSU: Herbstreit 14-32-0, 174 yards.
RECEIVING
SYR: Johnson 4-85, 1 TD; Hill 3-62, 1 TD.
OSU: Galloway 6-88, Saunders 1-28.

JANUARY 1, 1994
MICHIGAN 42, NC STATE 7

	1ST	2ND	3RD	4TH	FINAL
MICH	0	21	21	0	42
NCST	0	0	7	0	7

SCORING SUMMARY
MICH Wheatley 26 run (Elezovic kick)
MICH Alexander 79 punt return (Elezovic kick)
MICH Toomer 31 pass from Collins (Elezovic kick)
MICH Thompson 43 interception return (Elezovic kick)
MICH Wheatley 18 run (Elezovic kick)
NCST Fitzgerald 12 pass from Bender (Videtich kick)
MICH Powers 16 run (Elezovic kick)

MICH	TEAM STATISTICS	NCST
21	First Downs	18
265	Rushing Yards	117
12-23-0	Passing	19-38-4
201	Passing Yards	195
466	Total Yards	312
3-92	Punt Returns - Yards	1-5
2-48	Kickoff Returns - Yards	6-110
6-47.0	Punts - Average	6-42.0
1-0	Fumbles - Lost	4-2
5-35	Penalties - Yards	3-15
27:29	Possession Time	32:31

INDIVIDUAL LEADERS
RUSHING
MICH: Wheatley 18-124, 2 TD; Davis 7-36.
NCST: Downs 13-102; George 3-21.
PASSING
MICH: Collins 11-22-0, 189 yards, 1 TD.
NCST: Harvey 13-27-2, 108 yards; Bender 6-10-2, 87 yards, 1 TD.
RECEIVING
MICH: Jones 2-65; Smith 3-48.
NCST: Goines 7-72; Downs 4-34.

JANUARY 2, 1995
WISCONSIN 34, DUKE 20

	1ST	2ND	3RD	4TH	FINAL
WISC	13	0	7	14	34
DUKE	0	10	3	7	20

SCORING SUMMARY
WISC Messenger 19 interception return (Schnetzky kick)
WISC FG Hall 48
WISC FG Hall 43
DUKE Baldwin 7 run (Cochran kick)
DUKE FG Cochran 30
DUKE FG Cochran 30
WISC Fletcher 1 run (Schnetzky kick)
WISC Burns 11 pass from Bevell (Fletcher pass from Bevell)
DUKE Baldwin 2 run (Cochran kick)
WISC Fletcher 49 run (Schnetzky kick)

WISC	TEAM STATISTICS	DUKE
19	First Downs	23
278	Rushing Yards	68
11-20-1	Passing	28-46-4
161	Passing Yards	314
439	Total Yards	382
4-49	Punt Returns - Yards	0-0
5-75	Kickoff Returns - Yards	4-61
1-38.0	Punts - Average	4-42.5
2-2	Fumbles - Lost	0-0
12-86	Penalties - Yards	5-40
30:46	Possession Time	29:14

INDIVIDUAL LEADERS
RUSHING
WISC: Fletcher 39-241, 2 TD; Burns 6-45.
DUKE: Baldwin 21-70, 2 TD; Fischer 6-15.
PASSING
WISC: Bevell 11-20-1, 161 yards 1 TD.
DUKE: Fischer 28-46-4, 314 yards.
RECEIVING
WISC: Simmons 1-52; Dawkins 3-29.
DUKE: Khayat 11-109; Jensen 6-97.

JANUARY 1, 1996
PENN STATE 43, AUBURN 14

	1ST	2ND	3RD	4TH	FINAL
PSU	3	13	27	0	43
AU	0	7	0	7	14

SCORING SUMMARY
PSU FG Conway 19
AU Baker 25 pass from Nix (Hawkins kick)
PSU FG Conway 22
PSU FG Conway 38
PSU Archie 8 pass from Richardson (Conway kick)
PSU Engram 9 pass from Richardson (Conway kick)
PSU Pitts 4 pass from Richardson (pass failed)
PSU Enis 1 run (Conway kick)
PSU Engram 20 pass from Richardson (Conway kick)
AU McLeod 12 run (Hawkins kick)

PSU	TEAM STATISTICS	AU
22	First Downs	19
266	Rushing Yards	220
14-29-2	Passing	8-33-2
221	Passing Yards	94
487	Total Yards	314
4-33	Punt Returns - Yards	2-10
1-37	Kickoff Returns - Yards	5-101
4-35.7	Punts - Average	8-39.1
2-1	Fumbles - Lost	5-2
6-35	Penalties - Yards	5-59
32:11	Possession Time	27:49

INDIVIDUAL LEADERS
RUSHING
PSU: Pitts 15-115; Milne 12-82.
AU: Davis 12-119; Morrow 10-39.
PASSING
PSU: Richardson 13-24-1, 217 yards, 4 TD.
AU: Nix 5-25-2, 48 yards, 1 TD.
RECEIVING
PSU: Engram 4-113, 2 TD; Jurevicius 1-43.
AU: Bailey 1-32; Baker 1-25, 1 TD.

JANUARY 1, 1997
ALABAMA 17, MICHIGAN 14

	1ST	2ND	3RD	4TH	FINAL
ALA	3	0	7	7	17
MICH	0	6	0	8	14

SCORING SUMMARY
ALA FG Brock 43
MICH FG Hamilton 44
MICH FG Hamilton 22
ALA Rudd 88 interception return (Brock kick)
ALA Alexander 46 run (Brock kick)
MICH Shaw 9 pass from Griese (Floyd run)

ALA	TEAM STATISTICS	MICH
13	First Downs	22
182	Rushing Yards	124
9-18-1	Passing	22-38-1
65	Passing Yards	291
247	Total Yards	415
0-0	Punt Returns - Yards	4-17
1-9	Kickoff Returns - Yards	1-22
6-46.5	Punts - Average	7-26.1
2-1	Fumbles - Lost	3-0
8-42	Penalties - Yards	6-47
25:28	Possession Time	34:32

INDIVIDUAL LEADERS
RUSHING
ALA: Alexander 9-99, 1 TD; Riddle 13-58.
MICH: Williams 12-58; Floyd 6-35.
PASSING
ALA: Kitchens 9-18-1, 65 yards.
MICH: Griese 21-37-1, 287 yards, 1 TD.
RECEIVING
ALA: Vaughn 2-27; Rutledge 1-13.
MICH: Williams 5-113; Shaw 6-84, 1 TD.

JANUARY 1, 1998
GEORGIA 33, WISCONSIN 6

	1ST	2ND	3RD	4TH	FINAL
UGA	12	7	7	7	33
WISC	0	0	0	6	6

SCORING SUMMARY
UGA Edwards 2 run (kick blocked)
UGA Edwards 40 run (pass failed)
UGA Gary 3 run (Hines kick)
UGA Edwards 13 run (Hines kick)
UGA Allen 7 pass from Bobo (Hines kick)
WISC Retzlaff 12 pass from Kavanagh (kick failed)

UGA	TEAM STATISTICS	WISC
25	First Downs	18
207	Rushing Yards	74
26-29-0	Passing	14-36-2
235	Passing Yards	160
442	Total Yards	234
1-0	Punt Returns - Yards	2-0
1-16	Kickoff Returns - Yards	5-104
3-35.7	Punts - Average	5-43.6
2-1	Fumbles - Lost	0-0
5-59	Penalties - Yards	7-71
34:05	Possession Time	25:55

INDIVIDUAL LEADERS
RUSHING
UGA: Edwards 22-110, 3 TD; Gary 4-61, 1 TD.
WISC: McCullough 4-37; Dayne 14-36.
PASSING
UGA: Bobo 26-28-0, 235 yards, 1 TD.
WISC: Samuel 8-27-2, 84 yards; Kavanagh 6-9-0, 76 yards, 1 TD.
RECEIVING
UGA: Ward 12-122; Allen 3-22, 1 TD.
WISC: Chambers 4-46; Hayes 5-44.

JANUARY 1, 1999
PENN STATE 26, KENTUCKY 14

	1ST	2ND	3RD	4TH	FINAL
PSU	3	10	6	7	26
UK	14	0	0	0	14

SCORING SUMMARY

UK	Mickelsen 36 pass from Couch (Hanson kick)
PSU	FG Forney 43
UK	White 16 pass from Couch (Hanson kick)
PSU	Nastasi 56 pass from Thompson (Forney kick)
PSU	FG Forney 26
PSU	FG Forney 21
PSU	FG Forney 25
PSU	Fields 19 run (Forney kick)

PSU	TEAM STATISTICS	UK
24	First Downs	24
233	Rushing Yards	105
14-27-0	Passing	30-48-2
187	Passing Yards	336
420	Total Yards	441
2-25	Punt Returns - Yards	0-0
3-64	Kickoff Returns - Yards	4-126
3-30.3	Punts - Average	3-17.0
1-1	Fumbles - Lost	1-1
8-58	Penalties - Yards	14-103
27:07	Possession Time	32:53

INDIVIDUAL LEADERS

RUSHING
PSU: McCoo 21-105; Harris 13-54.
UK: White 8-61; Homer 12-26.

PASSING
PSU: Thompson 14-27-0, 187 yards, 1 TD.
UK: Couch 30-48-2, 336 yards, 2 TD.

RECEIVING
PSU: Stewart 7-71; Nastasi 2-70, 1 TD.
UK: Mickelsen 3-65, 1 TD; Homer 7-64.

JANUARY 1, 2000
GEORGIA 28, PURDUE 25

	1ST	2ND	3RD	4TH	OT	FINAL
UGA	0	10	8	7	3	28
PU	19	6	0	0	0	25

SCORING SUMMARY

PU	Daniels 3 pass from Brees (Dorsch kick)
PU	Daniels 11 pass from Brees (kick failed)
PU	Sutherland 21 pass from Brees (pass failed)
PU	James 32 pass from Brees (pass failed)
UGA	Edwards 74 run (Hines kick)
UGA	FG Hines 32
UGA	Carter 8 run (Pass run)
UGA	McMichael 8 pass from Carter (Hines kick)
UGA	FG Hines 21

UGA	TEAM STATISTICS	PU
21	First Downs	30
154	Rushing Yards	150
20-33-0	Passing	36-60-1
243	Passing Yards	378
397	Total Yards	528
2-24	Punt Returns - Yards	1-1
3-63	Kickoff Returns - Yards	2-31
3-48.0	Punts - Average	3-45.3
2-2	Fumbles - Lost	2-1
10-55	Penalties - Yards	14-153
25:11	Possession Time	34:49

INDIVIDUAL LEADERS

RUSHING
UGA: Edwards 2-70, 1 TD; Carter 16-41, 1 TD.
PU: Lowe 15-87; Sutherland 2-65.

PASSING
UGA: Carter 20-33-0, 243 yards, 1 TD.
PU: Brees 36-60-1, 378 yards, 4 TD.

RECEIVING
UGA: Edwards 8-97; Greer 5-86.
PU: Daniels 12-103, 2 TD; James 4-65, 1 TD.

JANUARY 1, 2001
SOUTH CAROLINA 24, OHIO STATE 7

	1ST	2ND	3RD	4TH	FINAL
SC	0	3	7	14	24
OSU	0	0	7	0	7

SCORING SUMMARY

SC	FG Corse 23
SC	Brewer 7 run (Corse kick)
OSU	Gurr fumble recovery in end zone (Stultz kick)
SC	Brewer 28 pass from Petty (Corse kick)
SC	Brewer 2 run (Corse kick)

SC	TEAM STATISTICS	OSU
18	First Downs	16
218	Rushing Yards	85
9-19-1	Passing	16-28-2
175	Passing Yards	173
393	Total Yards	258
2-18	Punt Returns - Yards	3-43
2-33	Kickoff Returns - Yards	5-100
4-46.8	Punts - Average	6-37.5
1-0	Fumbles - Lost	3-1
7-50	Penalties - Yards	9-65
33:33	Possession Time	26:27

INDIVIDUAL LEADERS

RUSHING
SC: Brewer 19-109, 2 TD; Pinnock 11-33.
OSU: Wells 14-52; Combs 8-25.

PASSING
SC: Petty 9-19-1, 175 yards, 1 TD.
OSU: Bellisari 14-25-1, 157 yards.

RECEIVING
SC: Brewer 3-92, 1 TD; Kelly 3-43.
OSU: Rambo 2-65; Sanders 5-47.

JANUARY 1, 2002
SOUTH CAROLINA 31, OHIO STATE 28

	1ST	2ND	3RD	4TH	FINAL
SC	0	14	14	3	31
OSU	0	0	7	21	28

SCORING SUMMARY

SC	Pinnock 1 run (Weaver kick)
SC	Scott 7 pass from Petty (Weaver kick)
SC	Gause 50 pass from Petty (kick failed)
SC	Pinnock 10 run (Watson pass from Petty)
OSU	Bellisari 2 run (Nugent kick)
OSU	Sanders 16 pass from Bellisari (Nugent kick)
OSU	Wells 1 run (Nugent kick)
OSU	Sanders 9 pass from Bellisari (Nugent kick)
SC	FG Weaver 42

SC	TEAM STATISTICS	OSU
17	First Downs	21
120	Rushing Yards	64
19-37-1	Passing	22-37-1
227	Passing Yards	324
347	Total Yards	388
2-16	Punt Returns - Yards	4-20
4-66	Kickoff Returns - Yards	4-101
6-47.7	Punts - Average	5-44.6
2-1	Fumbles - Lost	2-2
8-43	Penalties - Yards	6-40
31:23	Possession Time	28:37

INDIVIDUAL LEADERS

RUSHING
SC: Brewer 5-61; Pinnock 12-49, 2 TD.
OSU: Wells 19-37, 1 TD; Ross 1-13.

PASSING
SC: Petty 19-37-1, 227 yards, 2 TD.
OSU: Bellisari 21-35-1, 320 yards, 2 TD.

RECEIVING
SC: Scott 7-83, 1 TD; Gause 3-72, 1 TD.
OSU: Jenkins 8-152; Vance 5-61; Sanders 5-56, 2 TD.

JANUARY 1, 2003
MICHIGAN 38, FLORIDA 30

	1ST	2ND	3RD	4TH	FINAL
MICH	7	14	14	3	38
UF	0	16	7	7	30

SCORING SUMMARY

MICH	Perry 4 run (Finley kick)
UF	Graham 2 run (Leach kick)
UF	Graham `1 run (run failed)
MICH	Perry 1 run (Finley kick)
UF	FG Leach 29
MICH	Bellamy 8 pass from Navarre (Finley kick)
UF	Ratliff 33 pass from Grossman (Leach kick)
MICH	Perry 7 run (Finley kick)
MICH	Perry 12 run (Finley kick)
UF	Walker 3 pass from Grossman (Leach kick)
MICH	FG Finley 33

MICH	TEAM STATISTICS	UF
17	First Downs	28
104	Rushing Yards	183
21-37-0	Passing	21-42-1
319	Passing Yards	323
423	Total Yards	506
3-29	Punt Returns - Yards	3-10
2-45	Kickoff Returns - Yards	5-101
9-38.6	Punts - Average	8-32.1
1-0	Fumbles - Lost	2-2
3-23	Penalties - Yards	6-38
32:39	Possession Time	27:21

INDIVIDUAL LEADERS

RUSHING
MICH: Perry 28-85, 4 TD; Bellamy 2-20.
UF: Graham 22-120, 2 TD; Carthon 6-56.

PASSING
MICH: Navarre 21-36-0, 319 yards, 1 TD.
UF : Grossman 21-41-0, 323 yards, 2 TD.

RECEIVING
MICH: Perry 6-108; Edwards 4-110.
UF : Jacobs 7-88; Carthon 3-65.

JANUARY 1, 2004
IOWA 37, FLORIDA 17

	1ST	2ND	3RD	4TH	FINAL
UI	7	13	14	3	37
UF	7	0	3	7	17

SCORING SUMMARY

UF	Kight 70 pass from Leak (Leach kick)
UI	Brown 3 pass from Chandler (Kaeding kick)
UI	FG Kaeding 47
UI	Chandler 5 run (Kaeding kick)
UI	Melloy recovered blocked punt (Kaeding kick)
UF	FG Leach 48
UI	Russell 34 run (Kaeding kick)
UI	FG Kaeding 38
UF	Baker 25 pass from Leak (Leach kick)

UI	TEAM STATISTICS	UF
22	First Downs	16
238	Rushing Yards	57
13-26-0	Passing	22-41-1
170	Passing Yards	268
408	Total Yards	325
5-71	Punt Returns - Yards	3-26
3-54	Kickoff Returns - Yards	5-66
7-42.6	Punts - Average	10-40.1
1-0	Fumbles - Lost	1-0
3-15	Penalties - Yards	4-43
34:10	Possession Time	25:50

INDIVIDUAL LEADERS

RUSHING
UI: Russell 21-150, 1 TD; Lewis 12-45.
UF: Carthon 10-44; Fason 4-23.

PASSING
UI : Chandler 13-25-0, 170 yards, 1 TD.
UF : Leak 22-41-1, 268 yards, 1 TD.

RECEIVING
UI : Brown 6-96, 1 TD; Hinkel 3-44.
UF : Kight 2-75, 1 TD; Perez 7-70.

JANUARY 1, 2005
GEORGIA 24, WISCONSIN 21

	1ST	2ND	3RD	4TH	FINAL
UGA	3	7	14	0	24
WISC	3	3	7	8	21

SCORING SUMMARY

UGA	FG Coutu 20
WISC	FG Allen 46
WISC	FG Allen 44
UGA	Gibson 19 pass from Greene (Coutu kick)
UGA	Thomas 24 pass from Greene (Coutu kick)
UGA	Brown 29 run (Coutu kick)
WISC	Charles 19 pass from Stocco (Allen kick)
WISC	Crooks 11 Interception return (Orr pass from Stocco)

UGA	TEAM STATISTICS	WISC
21	First Downs	14
196	Rushing Yards	60
19-41-2	Passing	12-27-0
264	Passing Yards	170
460	Total Yards	230
5-45	Punt Returns - Yards	3-34
4-49	Kickoff Returns - Yards	5-49
6-33.2	Punts - Average	7-44.3
1-1	Fumbles - Lost	2-2
8-85	Penalties - Yards	7-45
29:05	Possession Time	30:55

INDIVIDUAL LEADERS

RUSHING
UGA: Brown 16-111, 1 TD; Ware 12-61.
WISC: Davis 21-79; Donovan 2-15.

PASSING
UGA: Greene 19-38-2, 264 yards, 2 TD.
WISC: Stocco 12-27-0, 170 yards, 1 TD.

RECEIVING
UGA: Pope 3-65; Brown 4-44.
WISC: Williams 3-56; Charles 3-52, 1 TD.

JANUARY 2, 2006
FLORIDA 31, IOWA 24

	1ST	2ND	3RD	4TH	FINAL
UF	7	17	7	0	31
IA	0	7	0	17	24

SCORING SUMMARY

UF	McCollum 6 blocked punt return (Hetland kick)
UF	FG Hetland 21
UF	Brown 60 interception return (Hetland kick)
IA	Solomon 20 pass from Tate (Schlicher kick)
UF	Baker 24 pass from Leak (Hetland kick)
UF	Baker 38 pass from Leak (Hetland kick)
IA	Hinkel 4 pass from Tate (Schlicher kick)
IA	Hinkel 14 pass from Tate (Schlicher kick)
IA	FG Schlicher 45

UF	TEAM STATISTICS	IA
26	First Downs	23
169	Rushing Yards	64
25-40-0	Passing	32-55-1
278	Passing Yards	346
447	Total Yards	410
3-32	Punt Returns - Yards	1-2
4-35	Kickoff Returns - Yards	6-113
3-46.3	Punts - Average	6-30.7
1-1	Fumbles - Lost	0-0
5-30	Penalties - Yards	8-60
35:25	Possession Time	24:35

INDIVIDUAL LEADERS

RUSHING
UF: Moore 13-88; Wynn 8-34.
IA: Young 13-34; Tate 3-24.

PASSING
UF: Leak 25-40-0, 278 yards, 2 TD.
IA: Tate 32-55-1, 346 yards, 3 TD.

RECEIVING
UF: Baker 10-147, 2 TD; Jackson 7-76.
IA: Solomon 7-96, 1 TD; Chandler 7-89.

JANUARY 1, 2007
PENN STATE 20, TENNESSEE 10

	1ST	2ND	3RD	4TH	FINAL
TENN	3	7	0	0	10
PSU	0	10	0	10	20

SCORING SUMMARY

TENN	FG Wilhoit 44
PSU	FG Kelly 34
PSU	Quarless 2 pass from Morelli (Kelly kick)
TENN	Coker 42 run (Wilhoit kick)
PSU	Davis 88 fumble return (Kelly kick)
PSU	FG Kelly 22

TENN	TEAM STATISTICS	PSU
17	First Downs	19
83	Rushing Yards	183
25-37-1	Passing	14-25-0
267	Passing Yards	197
350	Total Yards	380
1-2	Punt Returns - Yards	2-29
1-21	Kickoff Returns - Yards	2-34
5-44.0	Punts - Average	4-37.5
2-2	Fumbles - Lost	0-0
7-55	Penalties - Yards	6-45
26:58	Possession Time	33:02

INDIVIDUAL LEADERS

RUSHING
TENN: Foster 12-65; Coker 5-36, 1 TD.
PSU: Hunt 31-158; Wallace 1-11.

PASSING
TENN: Ainge 25-37-1, 267 yards.
PSU: Morelli 14-25-0, 197 yards, 1 TD

RECEIVING
TENN: Swain 7-84; Brown 7-66.
PSU: Norwood 4-35; Butler 3-73.

PEACH BOWL

PROFILE

Site: Atlanta, Ga.
Stadium: Georgia Dome
Capacity: 71,500
Surface: FieldTurf

PLAYING SITES

Grant Field, 1968-70
Atlanta-Fulton County Stadium,
1971-92
Georgia Dome, since 1993

NAME CHANGES

Peach Bowl, 1968-96
Chick-fil-A Peach Bowl, since
1997

SEASON	DATE	PRE-GAME RANK	TEAMS	SCORE	FINAL RANK	MOST VALUABLE PLAYER(S)	ATT.
1978	Dec. 25, 1978	17	**Purdue**	**41**	13	Mark Herrmann, Purdue, QB	20,277
			Georgia Tech	21		Calvin Clark, Purdue, DT	
1982	Dec. 31, 1982		**Iowa**	**28**		Chuck Long, Iowa, QB	50,134
			Tennessee	22		Clay Uhlenhake, Iowa, DT	
1984	Dec. 31, 1984		**Virginia**	**27**	20	Howard Petty, Virginia, TB	41,107
			Purdue	24		Ray Daly, Virginia, DB	
1985	Dec. 31, 1985		**Army**	**31**		Rob Healy, Army, QB	29,857
			Illinois	29		Peel Chronister, Army, S	
1987	Jan. 2, 1988	17	**Tennessee**	**27**	14	Reggie Cobb, Tennessee, TB	58,737
			Indiana	22		Van Waiters, Indiana, LB	
1988	Dec. 31, 1988		**North Carolina State**	**28**		Shane Montgomery, North Carolina State, QB	44,635
			Iowa	23		Michael Brooks, North Carolina St., FS	
1990	Dec. 29, 1990		**Auburn**	**27**	19	Stan White, QB Darrel Crawford,LB, Auburn	38,962
			Indiana	23		Vaughn Dunbar, RB, Mike Dumas, FS, Indiana	

DECEMBER 25, 1978
PURDUE 41, GEORGIA TECH 21

	1ST	2ND	3RD	4TH	FINAL
PUR	21	13	0	7	41
GT	0	7	0	14	21

SCORING SUMMARY
PUR Jones 3 run (Savereen kick)
PUR Jones 8 run (Savereen kick)
PUR Smith 10 pass from Herrmann (Savereen kick)
PUR Herrmann 2 run (Savereen kick)
GT Lee 1 run (Smith kick)
PUR Macon 1 run (kick failed)
PUR Burrell 12 pass from Herrmann (Savereen kick)
GT Moore 3 pass from Kelley (Hill run)
GT Hill 31 pass from Kelley (pass failed)

PUR	TEAM STATISTICS	GT
24	First Downs	14
157	Rushing Yards	12
12-27-2	Passing	17-38-2
166	Passing Yards	168
323	Total Yards	180
5-36.6	Punts - Average	7-36.7
3-1	Fumbles - Lost	2-2
9-78	Penalties - Yards	5-48

INDIVIDUAL LEADERS
RUSHING
PUR: Macon 19-66, 1 TD; Jones 13-50, 2 TD.
GT: Lee 6-24, 1 TD.
PASSING
PUR: Herrmann 12-24-2, 166 yards, 2 TD.
GT: Kelley 17-38-2, 168 yards, 2 TD.
RECEIVING
PUR: Burrell 4-55, 1 TD; Harris 2-38.
GT: Hill 5-77, 1 TD; Hardie 4-40.

DECEMBER 31, 1982
IOWA 28, TENNESSEE 22

	1ST	2ND	3RD	4TH	FINAL
IA	0	21	7	0	28
TENN	7	0	12	3	22

SCORING SUMMARY
TENN Cockrell 6 run (Reveiz kick)
IA Moritz 57 pass from Long (Nichol kick)
IA Harmon 18 pass from Long (Nichol kick)
IA Harmon 8 pass from Long (Nichol kick)
TENN Coleman 10 run (kick failed)
IA Phillips 2 run (Nichol kick)
TENN Gault 19 pass from Cockrell (pass failed)
TENN FG Reveiz 27

IA	TEAM STATISTICS	TENN
24	First Downs	23
110	Rushing Yards	154
19-26-1	Passing	22-41-0
304	Passing Yards	221
414	Total Yards	375
5-35.0	Punts - Average	5-45.0
1-1	Fumbles - Lost	2-1
3-30	Penalties - Yards	7-47

INDIVIDUAL LEADERS
RUSHING
IA: Gill 16-70; Phillips 10-34, 1 TD.
TENN: Coleman 11-103, 1 TD; Fumas 12-52.
PASSING
IA: Long 19-26-1, 304 yards, 3 TD.
TENN: Cockrell 22-41-0, 221 yards, 1 TD.
RECEIVING
IA: Moritz 8-168, 1 TD; Harmon 3-44, 2 TD.
TENN: Wilson 7-62; Duncan 3-52.

DECEMBER 31, 1984
VIRGINIA 27, PURDUE 24

	1ST	2ND	3RD	4TH	FINAL
UVA	7	7	7	6	27
PUR	10	14	0	0	24

SCORING SUMMARY
UVA Petty 11 run (Stadlin kick)
PUR FG Rendina 24
PUR Griffin 23 pass from Everett (Rendina kick)
UVA Zimmerlink 3 pass from Majkowski (Stadlin kick)
PUR Price 17 pass from Everett (Rendina kick)
PUR Scott 12 pass from Everett (Rendina kick)
UVA Majkowski 1 run (Stadlin kick)
UVA FG Stadlin 19
UVA FG Stadlin 22

UVA	TEAM STATISTICS	PUR
24	First Downs	20
274	Rushing Yards	75
8-17-2	Passing	22-42-3
118	Passing Yards	253
392	Total Yards	328
3-34.0	Punts - Average	4-43.0
1-0	Fumbles - Lost	1-1
3-20	Penalties - Yards	5-45
36:34	Possession Time	23:26

INDIVIDUAL LEADERS
RUSHING
UVA: Petty 21-114, 1 TD; Word 17-86.
PUR: Carter 8-33; King 6-29.
PASSING
UVA: Majkowski 8-17-2, 118 yards, 1 TD.
PUR: Everett 22-42-3, 253 yards, 3 TD.
RECEIVING
UVA: Zimmerlink 3-35, 1 TD; Merrick 2-32.
PUR: Griffin 4-69, 1 TD; Scott 4-50, 1 TD.

ARMY 31, ILLINOIS 29

	1ST	2ND	3RD	4TH	FINAL
ARMY	7	14	7	3	31
ILL	3	13	7	6	29

SCORING SUMMARY
ARMY	Healy 22 run (Stopa kick)
ILL	FG White 45
ILL	Boso 1 pass from Trudeau (White kick)
ARMY	Black 1 run (Stopa kick)
ARMY	White 33 pass from Lampley (Stopa kick)
ILL	Williams 15 pass from Trudeau (pass failed)
ILL	Wilson 1 run (White kick)
ARMY	Spellmon 26 pass from Jones (Stopa kick)
ARMY	FG Stopa 39
ILL	Williams 54 pass from Trudeau (pass failed)

ARMY	TEAM STATISTICS	ILL
20	First Downs	26
291	Rushing Yards	77
5-7-1	Passing	38-55-2
94	Passing Yards	401
385	Total Yards	478
5-36.0	Punts - Average	3-45.0
0-0	Fumbles - Lost	2-2
3-35	Penalties - Yards	8-67
30:14	Possession Time	29:46

INDIVIDUAL LEADERS
RUSHING
ARMY: Healy 23-107, 1 TD; Lampley 16-76.
ILL: Rooks 10-35; Wilson 8-31, 1 TD.
PASSING
ARMY: Healy 3-6-1, 35 yards.
ILL: Trudeau 38-55-2, 401 yards, 3 TD.
RECEIVING
ARMY: Spellmon 2-43, 1 TD.
ILL: Williams 7-109, 2 TD; Pierce 6-92.

TENNESSEE 27, INDIANA 22

	1ST	2ND	3RD	4TH	FINAL
TENN	14	7	0	6	27
IU	3	7	6	6	22

SCORING SUMMARY
TENN	Cobb 6 run (Reich kick)
IU	FG Stoyanovich 52
TENN	Miller 45 pass from Francis (Reich kick)
TENN	Cleveland 15 pass from Francis (Reich kick)
IU	Jones 43 pass from Schnell (Stoyanovich kick)
IU	Thompson 12 run (pass failed)
IU	Jorden 12 run (pass failed)
TENN	Cobb 9 run (pass failed)

TENN	TEAM STATISTICS	IU
26	First Downs	16
244	Rushing Yards	96
21-27-0	Passing	18-33-2
230	Passing Yards	218
474	Total Yards	314
2-36.0	Punts - Average	6-30.0
2-2	Fumbles - Lost	0-0
5-35	Penalties - Yards	4-37
33:19	Possession Time	26:41

INDIVIDUAL LEADERS
RUSHING
TENN: Cobb 21-146, 2 TD; Davis 9-51.
IU: Thompson 18-67, 1 TD.
PASSING
TENN: Francis 20-26-0, 225 yards, 2 TD.
IU: Schnell 18-33-2, 218 yards, 1 TD.
RECEIVING
TENN: Miller 5-78, 1 TD; Woods 4-43.
IU: Jones 7-150, 1 TD; Thompson 6-28.

NC STATE 28, IOWA 23

	1ST	2ND	3RD	4TH	FINAL
NCST	7	21	0	0	28
IA	3	7	7	6	23

SCORING SUMMARY
NCST	Davenport 1 run (Hartman kick)
IA	FG Murphy 30
NCST	Peebles 75 pass from Montgomery (Hartman kick)
NCST	Jackson 2 run (Hartman kick)
NCST	Jackson 30 run (Hartman kick)
IA	Harberts 8 pass from Hartlieb (Murphy kick)
IA	Harberts 22 pass from Hartlieb (Murphy kick)
IA	S. Smith 7 pass from Hartlieb (pass failed)

NCST	TEAM STATISTICS	IA
24	First Downs	21
236	Rushing Yards	19
11-23-2	Passing	30-51-4
195	Passing Yards	428
431	Total Yards	447
8-5	Fumbles - Lost	4-3
4-40	Penalties - Yards	4-44
5-36.0	Possession Time	6-36.3

INDIVIDUAL LEADERS
RUSHING
NCST: Jackson 17-86, 2 TD.
IA: Saunders 6-22.
PASSING
NCST: Montgomery 7-10-1, 152 yards, 1 TD.
IA: Hartlieb 30-51-4, 428 yards, 3 TD.
RECEIVING
NCST: Peebles 2-91, 1 TD.
IA: Cook 8-122; Harberts 6-101, 2 TD.

AUBURN 27, INDIANA 23

	1ST	2ND	3RD	4TH	FINAL
AUB	7	10	3	7	27
IND	7	3	0	13	23

SCORING SUMMARY
AUB	White 6 run (Von Wyl kick)
IND	Green 3 run (Bonnell kick)
AUB	Smith 11 pass from White (Von Wyl kick)
IND	FG Bonnell 42
AUB	FG Von Wyl 26
AUB	FG Von Wyl 43
IND	Green 2 run (run failed)
IND	Green 11 run (Bonnell kick)
AUB	White 1 run (Von Wyl kick)

AUB	TEAM STATISTICS	IND
24	First Downs	15
89	Rushing Yards	121
31-48-0	Passing	10-19-0
351	Passing Yards	99
440	Total Yards	220
3-23.0	Punts - Average	5-41.4
2-2	Fumbles - Lost	1-1
12-75	Penalties - Yards	6-55
28:09	Possession Time	31:51

INDIVIDUAL LEADERS
RUSHING
AUB: Williams 12-52; Smith 5-24.
IND: Dunbar 21-81.
PASSING
AUB: White 31-48-0, 351 yards, 1 TD.
IND: Green 10-19-0, 99 yards.
RECEIVING
AUB: Casey 7-159; Hall 9-74.
IND: Thomas 3-43; Turner 3-26.

SUGAR BOWL

PROFILE

Site: New Orleans
Stadium: Louisiana Superdome
Capacity: 72,003
Surface: Momentum Turf

PLAYING SITES

Tulane Stadium, 1935-74
Louisiana Superdome, 1975-2005
Georgia Dome, 2006
Louisiana Superdome, 2007

NAME CHANGES

Sugar Bowl Football Classic, 1935-87
USF&G Sugar Bowl, 1988-95
Nokia Sugar Bowl, 1996-2006
Allstate Sugar Bowl, since 2007

SEASON	DATE	PRE-GAME RANK	TEAMS	SCORE	FINAL RANK	MOST VALUABLE PLAYER(S)	ATT.
1972	Dec. 31, 1972	2	**Oklahoma**	14	2	Tinker Owens, Oklahoma, FL	80,123
		5	Penn State*	0	10		
1975	Dec. 31, 1975	4	**Alabama**	13	3	Richard Todd, Alabama, QB	74,331
		8	Penn State*	6	10		
1977	Jan. 2, 1978	3	**Alabama**	35	2	Jeff Rutledge, Alabama, QB	76,811
		9	Ohio State	6	11		
1978	Jan. 1, 1979	2	**Alabama**	14	1	Barry Krauss, Alabama, LB	76,824
		1	Penn State*	7	4		
1982	Jan. 1, 1983	2	**Penn State***	27	1	Todd Blackledge, Penn State, QB	78,124
		1	Georgia	23	4		
1983	Jan. 2, 1984	3	**Auburn**	9	3	Bo Jackson, Auburn, RB	77,893
		8	Michigan	7	8		
1997	Jan. 1, 1998	4	**Florida State**	31	3	E.G. Green, Florida State, WR	67,289
		9	Ohio State	14	12		
1998	Jan. 1, 1999	3	**Ohio State**	24	2	David Boston, Ohio State, WR	76,503
		8	Texas A&M	14	11		
2001	Jan. 1, 2002	12	**LSU**	47	7	Rohan Davey, LSU, QB	77,688
		7	Illinois	34	12		

DECEMBER 31, 1972
OKLAHOMA 14, PENN STATE 0

	1ST	2ND	3RD	4TH	FINAL
OKLA	0	7	0	7	14
PSU	0	0	0	0	0

SCORING SUMMARY
OKLA   Owens 27 pass from Robertson (Fulcher kick)
OKLA   Crosswhite 1 run (Fulcher kick)

OKLA	TEAM STATISTICS	PSU
20	First Downs	11
278	Rushing Yards	49
7-12-0	Passing	12-31-1
175	Passing Yards	147
453	Total Yards	196
8-32.8	Punts - Average	10-42.9
8-5	Fumbles - Lost	6-4
3-55	Penalties - Yards	3-15

INDIVIDUAL LEADERS
RUSHING
OKLA: Pruitt 21-86; Crosswhite 22-82, 1 TD.
PSU: Nagle 10-22; Addie 7-18.
PASSING
OKLA: Robertson 3-6-0, 88 yards, 1 TD.
PSU: Hufnagel 12-31-1, 147 yards.
RECEIVING
OKLA: Owens 5-132, 1 TD; Pruitt 2-43.
PSU: Scott 3-59; Bland 3-39.

DECEMBER 31, 1975
ALABAMA 13, PENN STATE 6

	1ST	2ND	3RD	4TH	FINAL
ALA	3	0	7	3	13
PSU	0	0	3	3	6

SCORING SUMMARY
ALA   FG Ridgeway 25
PSU   FG Bahr 42
ALA   Stock 14 run (Ridgeway kick)
PSU   FG Bahr 37
ALA   FG Ridgeway 28

ALA	TEAM STATISTICS	PSU
14	First Downs	12
106	Rushing Yards	157
10-12-0	Passing	8-14-1
210	Passing Yards	57
316	Total Yards	214
5-40.8	Punts - Average	4-48.5
1-0	Fumbles - Lost	1-0
3-22	Penalties - Yards	0

INDIVIDUAL LEADERS
RUSHING
ALA: Shelby 8-45; Davis 12-32.
PSU: Geise 8-46; Taylor 12-36.
PASSING
ALA: Todd 10-12-0, 210 yards.
PSU: Andress 8-14-1, 57 yards.
RECEIVING
ALA: Newsome 4-97; Harris 2-69.
PSU: Cefalo 2-18; Petchel 2-13.

JANUARY 2, 1978
ALABAMA 35, OHIO STATE 6

	1ST	2ND	3RD	4TH	FINAL
ALA	0	13	8	14	35
OSU	0	0	0	6	6

SCORING SUMMARY
ALA   Nathan 1 run (Chapman kick)
ALA   Bolton 27 pass from Rutledge (kick failed)
ALA   Neal 3 pass from Rutledge
              (Nathan pass from Rutledge)
OSU   Harrell 38 pass from Gerald (run failed)
ALA   Ogilvie 1 run (Chapman kick)
ALA   Davis 5 run (Chapman kick)

ALA	TEAM STATISTICS	OSU
25	First Downs	13
286	Rushing Yards	179
8-11-0	Passing	7-17-3
109	Passing Yards	103
395	Total Yards	282
1-33.0	Punts - Average	4-37.5
1-5	Penalties - Yards	4-40

INDIVIDUAL LEADERS
RUSHING
ALA: Davis 24-95, 1 TD; Crow 5-46.
OSU: Springs 10-74; Logan 13-57.
PASSING
ALA: Rutledge 8-11-0, 109 yards, 2 TD.
OSU: Gerald 7-17-3, 103 yards, 1 TD.
RECEIVING
ALA: Newsom 2-45; Ferguson 2-28.
OSU: Hunter 2-25; Springs 2-6.

JANUARY 1, 1979
ALABAMA 14, PENN STATE 7

	1ST	2ND	3RD	4TH	FINAL
ALA	0	7	7	0	14
PSU	0	0	7	0	7

SCORING SUMMARY
ALA   Bolton 30 pass from Rutledge (McElroy kick)
PSU   Fitzkee 17 pass from Fusina (Bahr kick)
ALA   Ogilvie 8 run (McElroy kick)

ALA	TEAM STATISTICS	PSU
12	First Downs	12
208	Rushing Yards	19
8-15-2	Passing	15-30-4
91	Passing Yards	163
299	Total Yards	182
10-38.8	Punts - Average	10-38.7
2-1	Fumbles - Lost	2-0
11-75	Penalties - Yards	8-51

INDIVIDUAL LEADERS
RUSHING
ALA: Nathan 21-127; Whitman 11-51.
PSU: Suhey 10-48; Guman 9-22.
PASSING
ALA: Rutledge 8-15-2, 91 yards, 1 TD.
PSU: Fusina 15-30-4, 163 yards, 1 TD.
RECEIVING
ALA: Bolton 2-46, 1 TD; Whitman 2-27.
PSU: Guman 5-59; Fitzkee 3-38, 1 TD.

JANUARY 1, 1983
PENN STATE 27, GEORGIA 23

	1ST	2ND	3RD	4TH	FINAL
PSU	7	13	0	7	27
UGA	3	7	7	6	23

SCORING SUMMARY
PSU   Warner 2 run (Gancitano kick)
UGA   FG Butler 27
PSU   FG Gancitano 38
PSU   Warner 9 run (Gancitano kick)
PSU   FG Grancitano 45
UGA   Archie 10 pass from Lastinger (Butler kick)
UGA   Walker 1 run (Butler kick)
PSU   Garrity 47 pass from Blackledge (Gancitano kick)
UGA   Kay 9 pass from Lastinger (run failed)

PSU	TEAM STATISTICS	UGA
19	First Downs	19
139	Rushing Yards	160
13-23-0	Passing	12-28-2
228	Passing Yards	166
367	Total Yards	326
7-42.5	Punts - Average	8-41.7
2-1	Fumbles - Lost	3-0
7-39	Penalties - Yards	7-42

INDIVIDUAL LEADERS
RUSHING
PSU: Warner 18-117, 2 TD.
UGA: Walker 28-103, 1 TD.
PASSING
PSU: Blackledge 13-23-0, 228 yards, 1 TD.
UGA: Lastinger 12-27-2, 166 yards, 2 TD.
RECEIVING
PSU: Garrity 4-116, 1 TD.
UGA: Kay 5-61, 1 TD.

JANUARY 2, 1984
AUBURN 9, MICHIGAN 7

	1ST	2ND	3RD	4TH	FINAL
AUB	0	0	3	6	9
MICH	7	0	0	0	7

SCORING SUMMARY
MICH   Smith 4 run (Bergeron kick)
AUB   FG Del Greco 31
AUB   FG Del Greco 32
AUB   FG Del Greco 19

AUB	TEAM STATISTICS	MICH
21	First Downs	12
301	Rushing Yards	118
2-6-1	Passing	9-25-1
21	Passing Yards	125
322	Total Yards	243
4-42.0	Punts - Average	8-38.3
4-3	Fumbles - Lost	2-1
3-15	Penalties - Yards	6-49

INDIVIDUAL LEADERS
RUSHING
AUB: Jackson 22-130; Agee 16-93.
MICH: Rogers 17-86; Garrett 5-18.
PASSING
AUB: Campbell 2-6-1, 21 yards.
MICH: Smith 9-25-1, 125 yards.
RECEIVING
AUB: James 1-15.
MICH: Markray 3-68; Bean 3-37.

---

*Played as an independent or with other conference affiliation

JANUARY 1, 1998
FLORIDA STATE 31, OHIO STATE 14

	1ST	2ND	3RD	4TH	FINAL
FSU	7	14	0	10	31
OSU	3	0	5	6	14

SCORING SUMMARY

OSU	FG Stultz 40
FSU	Green 27 pass from Busby (Janikowski kick)
FSU	Busby 9 run (Janikowski kick)
FSU	McCray 1 run (Janikowski kick)
OSU	FG Stultz 34
OSU	Safety
FSU	FG Janikowski 35
OSU	Lumpkin 50 pass from Germaine (pass failed)
FSU	McCray 1 run (Janikowski kick)

FSU	TEAM STATISTICS	OSU
18	First Downs	21
60	Rushing Yards	118
22-33-2	Passing	16-36-3
334	Passing Yards	207
394	Total Yards	325
0-0	Fumbles - Lost	1-0
9-74	Penalties - Yards	10-70
24:56	Possession Time	35:04

INDIVIDUAL LEADERS

RUSHING
FSU: Minor 12-53; Feaster 2-10.
OSU: Pearson 22-60; Keller 6-20.

PASSING
FSU: Busby 22-33-2, 334 yards, 1 TD.
OSU: Germaine 10-26-2, 173 yards, 1 TD.

RECEIVING
FSU: Green 7-176, 1 TD; Warrick 3-82.
OSU: Miller 6-79; Lumpkin 2-61, 1 TD.

JANUARY 1, 1999
OHIO STATE 24, TEXAS A&M 14

	1ST	2ND	3RD	4TH	FINAL
OSU	21	3	0	0	24
A&M	7	0	7	0	14

SCORING SUMMARY

A&M	Hall 9 run (Bynum kick)
OSU	Germany 18 pass from Germaine (Stultz kick)
OSU	Montgomery 10 run (Stultz kick)
OSU	Griffin 16 blocked punt return (Stultz kick)
OSU	FG Stultz 31
A&M	Hodge 7 pass from Stewart (Bynum kick)

OSU	TEAM STATISTICS	A&M
25	First Downs	17
210	Rushing Yards	96
21-38-0	Passing	22-39-0
222	Passing Yards	187
432	Total Yards	283
6-38.3	Punts - Average	10-39.8
3-0	Fumbles - Lost	1-1
6-61	Penalties - Yards	6-43
31:42	Possession Time	28:18

INDIVIDUAL LEADERS

RUSHING
OSU: Montgomery 9-96, 1 TD; Wiley 16-88.
A&M: Toombs 10-62; Hall 11-53, 1 TD.

PASSING
OSU: Germaine 21-38-0, 222 yards, 1 TD.
A&M: Stewart 22-39-0, 187 yards, 1 TD.

RECEIVING
OSU: Boston 11-105; Wiley 5-40.
A&M: Taylor 5-52; Spiller 5-43.

JANUARY 1, 2002
LSU 47, ILLINOIS 34

	1ST	2ND	3RD	4TH	FINAL
LSU	7	27	7	6	47
ILL	0	7	14	13	34

SCORING SUMMARY

LSU	Davis 4 run (Corbello kick)
LSU	Davis 25 run (Corbello kick)
LSU	Davis 16 run (Corbello kick)
LSU	Reed 5 pass from Davey (Corbello kick)
ILL	Hodges 2 pas from Kittner (Christofilakos kick)
LSU	Royal 7 pass from Davey (Corbello kick)
ILL	Lloyd 17 pass from Kittner (Christofilakos kick)
LSU	Reed 32 pass from Davey (Corbello kick)
ILL	Lloyd 10 pass from Kittner (Christofilakos kick)
ILL	Young 17 pass from Kittner (Christofilakos kick)
LSU	Davis 4 run (pass failed)
ILL	Young 40 pass from Lloyd (pass failed)

LSU	TEAM STATISTICS	ILL
32	First Downs	14
151	Rushing Yards	61
31-53-0	Passing	15-36-1
444	Passing Yards	302
595	Total Yards	363
3-36	Punt Returns - Yards	2-9
6-147	Kickoff Returns - Yards	5-89
8-39.4	Punts - Average	9-40.4
2-1	Fumbles - Lost	1-1
13-113	Penalties - Yards	4-39
39:16	Possession Time	20:44

INDIVIDUAL LEADERS

RUSHING
LSU: Davis 28-129, 4 TD; Henderson 13-55.
ILL: Harvey 9-42.

PASSING
LSU: Davey 31-53-0, 444 yards, 3 TD.
ILL: Kittner 14-35-1, 262 yards, 4 TD.

RECEIVING
LSU: Reed 14-239, 2 TD; Clayton 8-120.
ILL: Young 6-178, 2 TD; Lloyd 5-56, 2 TD.

SUN BOWL

PROFILE

Site: El Paso, Texas
Stadium: Sun Bowl Stadium
Capacity: 50,426
Surface: AstroPlay

PLAYING SITES

El Paso High School Stadium, 1935-37
Kidd Field, 1938-62
Sun Bowl Stadium, since 1963

NAME CHANGES

Sun Bowl, 1935-85
John Hancock Sun Bowl, 1986-89
John Hancock Bowl, 1990-93
Sun Bowl, 1994-95
Norwest Sun Bowl, 1996-98
Wells Fargo Sun Bowl, 1999-2003
Vitalis Sun Bowl, 2004-05
Brut Sun Bowl, since 2006

SEASON	DATE	PRE-GAME RANK	TEAMS	SCORE	FINAL RANK	MOST VALUABLE PLAYER(S)	ATT.
1990	Dec. 31, 1990	22	Michigan State	17	16	Courtney Hawkins, Michigan State, WR	50,562
		21	USC	16	20	Craig Hartsuyker, USC, LB	
1991	Dec. 31, 1991	22	UCLA	6	19	Arnold Ale, UCLA, LB	42,281
			Illinois	3		Mike Poloskey, Illinois, LB	
1995	Dec. 29, 1995		Iowa	38	25	Sedrick Shaw, Iowa, RB	49,116
		20	Washington	18		Jared DeVries, DT, Brion Hurley, K, Iowa	
1996	Dec. 31, 1996		Stanford	38		Troy Walters, WR , Chad Hutchinson, QB, Stanford	42,721
			Michigan State	0		Kailee Wong, Stanford, DE	
1997	Dec. 31, 1997	16	Arizona State	17	14	Mike Martin, Arizona State, RB	49,104
			Iowa	7			
1999	Dec. 31, 1999		Oregon	24	19	Billy Cockerham, Minnesota, QB	48,757
		12	Minnesota	20	18	Dyron Russ, T, Ryan Rindels, P, Minnesota	
2000	Dec. 29, 2000		Wisconsin	21	23	Freddie Mitchell, WR, Oscar Cabrera, OL, UCLA	49,093
			UCLA	20		Michael Bennett, Wisconsin, RB	
2001	Dec. 31, 2001	13	Washington State	33	10	Lamont Thompson, S, Drew Dunning, K, Washington State	47,812
			Purdue	27		Akin Ayodele, Purdue, DE	
2002	Dec. 31, 2002		Purdue	34		Kyle Orton, Purdue, QB	48,917
			Washington	24		Shaun Phillips, DE, Anthony Chambers, WR, Purdue	
2003	Dec. 31, 2003	24	Minnesota	31		Samie Parker, Oregon, WR	49,894
			Oregon	30		Junior Siavii, DT, Jared Siegel, K, Oregon	
2004	Dec. 31, 2004	21	Arizona State	27	19	Sam Keller, Arizona State, QB	51,288
			Purdue	23			
2005	Dec. 30, 2005	17	UCLA	50	16	Chris Markey, UCLA, RB	50,426
			Northwestern	38		Kahlil Bell, UCLA, RB	

DECEMBER 31, 1990
MICHIGAN STATE 17, USC 16

	1ST	2ND	3RD	4TH	FINAL
MSU	0	7	10	0	17
USC	7	0	3	6	16

SCORING SUMMARY
USC — Wellman 7 pass from Marinovich (Rodriguez kick)
MSU — Hickson 18 run (Langeloh kick)
USC — FG Rodriguez 20
MSU — Hawkins 21 pass from Enos (Rodriguez kick)
MSU — FG Langeloh 52
USC — FG Rodriguez 54
USC — FG Rodriguez 43

MSU	TEAM STATISTICS	USC
12	First Downs	21
84	Rushing Yards	156
9-17-1	Passing	19-32-3
131	Passing Yards	180
215	Total Yards	336
1-7	Punt Returns - Yards	2-27
5-38.0	Punts - Average	1-50.0
1-1	Fumbles - Lost	2-1

INDIVIDUAL LEADERS
RUSHING
MSU: Hickson 14-68, 1 TD; Duckett 8-18.
USC: Royster 32-125; Lockwood 5-18.
PASSING
MSU: Enos 9-17-1, 131 yards, 1 TD.
USC: Marinovich 18-30-3, 174 yards, 1 TD.
RECEIVING
MSU: Hawkins 6-106, 1 TD; Roy 2-14.
USC: Lockwood 5-41; Morton 3-36.

DECEMBER 31, 1991
UCLA 6, ILLINOIS 3

	1ST	2ND	3RD	4TH	FINAL
UCLA	3	0	0	3	6
ILL	0	0	3	0	3

SCORING SUMMARY
UCLA — FG Perez 32
ILL — FG Richardson 27
UCLA — FG Perez 19

UCLA	TEAM STATISTICS	ILL
14	First Downs	19
92	Rushing Yards	119
17-28-1	Passing	17-38-3
176	Passing Yards	189
268	Total Yards	308
4-58	Punt Returns - Yards	2-2
6-40.0	Punts - Average	7-34.0
1-1	Fumbles - Lost	2-1

INDIVIDUAL LEADERS
RUSHING
UCLA: Williams 23-52; Carter 6-22.
ILL: Feagin 12-71; Bell 6-22.
PASSING
UCLA: Maddox 17-28-1, 176 yards.
ILL: Verduzco 17-38-3, 189 yards.
RECEIVING
UCLA: LaChapelle 5-69; Davis 4-41.
ILL: Wright 9-94; Turner 1-53.

DECEMBER 29, 1995
IOWA 38, WASHINGTON 18

	1ST	2ND	3RD	4TH	FINAL
IOWA	10	11	10	7	38
WASH	0	0	6	12	18

SCORING SUMMARY
IOWA — Shaw 58 run (Bromert kick)
IOWA — FG Hurley 49
IOWA — Safety (Washington punt snap out of end zone)
IOWA — FG Bromert 33
IOWA — FG Bromert 34
IOWA — FG Hurley 47
IOWA — FG Hurley 50
WASH — Pathon 30 pass from Fortney (pass failed)
IOWA — Burger 8 run (Bromert kick)
IOWA — Burger 1 run (Bromert kick)
WASH — Coleman 3 pass from Huard (pass failed)
WASH — Conwell 20 pass from Huard (run failed)

IOWA	TEAM STATISTICS	WASH
18	First Downs	14
286	Rushing Yards	96
11-26-2	Passing	19-37-0
135	Passing Yards	250
421	Total Yards	346
7-22	Punt Returns - Yards	5-3
5-39.0	Punts - Average	7-27.0
1-0	Fumbles - Lost	3-3

INDIVIDUAL LEADERS
RUSHING
IOWA: Shaw 21-135, 1 TD; Banks 13-122.
WASH: Neal 9-65; Shehee 8-38.
PASSING
IOWA: Sherman 11-24 -1, 135 yards.
WASH: Huard 14 -26-0, 194 yards, 2 TD.
RECEIVING
IOWA: Slutzker 4-66; Dwight 3-40.
WASH: Conwell 4 -71, 1 TD; Pathon 4-62, 1 TD.

DECEMBER 31, 1996
STANFORD 38, MICHIGAN STATE 0

	1ST	2ND	3RD	4TH	FINAL
STAN	7	14	10	7	38
MSU	0	0	0	0	0

SCORING SUMMARY
STAN — Pruitt 50 lateral return of an interception by Madsen (Miller kick)
STAN — Ritchie 8 pass from Hutchinson (Miller kick)
STAN — Salina 1 run (Miller kick)
STAN — FG Miller 25
STAN — Dunn 27 run (Miller kick)
STAN — Allen 9 run of blocked punt (Miller kick)

STAN	TEAM STATISTICS	MSU
25	First Downs	13
257	Rushing Yards	68
23-30-1	Passing	13-33-3
238	Passing Yards	151
495	Total Yards	219
7-94	Punt Returns - Yards	2-19
2-52.5	Punts - Average	9-41.9
3-1	Fumbles - Lost	3-2

INDIVIDUAL LEADERS
RUSHING
STAN: Bookman 11-103; Mitchell 16-74.
MSU: Goldbourne 12-51; Irvin 9-31.
PASSING
STAN: Hutchinson 22-28-1, 135 yards, 1 TD.
MSU: Schultz 8-21-2, 68 yards; Burke 4-7-0, 71 yards.
RECEIVING
STAN: Dunn 4 -63; Manning 3-42.
MSU: Long 2-46; Mason 4-43.

DECEMBER 31, 1997
ARIZONA STATE 17, IOWA 7

	1ST	2ND	3RD	4TH	FINAL
ASU	0	10	7	0	17
IOWA	0	0	0	7	7

SCORING SUMMARY
ASU — Jackson 35 pass from Campbell (Nycz kick)
ASU — FG Nycz 20
ASU — Martin 1 run (Nycz kick)
IOWA — Carter 26 pass from Reiners (Bromert kick)

ASU	TEAM STATISTICS	IOWA
18	First Downs	10
268	Rushing Yards	19
5-11-0	Passing	12-27-0
109	Passing Yards	190
377	Total Yards	209
4-26	Punt Returns - Yards	4-16
9-36.1	Punts - Average	8-48.9
2-0	Fumbles - Lost	2-1

INDIVIDUAL LEADERS
RUSHING
ASU: Martin 27-169, 1 TD; Redmond 13-50.
IOWA: Banks 14-52; Thein 3-5.
PASSING
ASU: Campbell 5-11-0, 109 yards, 1 TD.
IOWA: Sherman 8-22-0, 120 yards; Reiners 4 -5-0, 70 yards, 1 TD.
RECEIVING
ASU: Jackson 2-44, 1 TD; Mitchell 1-41.
IOWA: Gibson 3-79; Dwight 3-51.

DECEMBER 31, 1999
OREGON 24, MINNESOTA 20

	1ST	2ND	3RD	4TH	FINAL
ORE	0	7	10	7	24
MINN	7	0	6	7	20

SCORING SUMMARY
MINN — Johnson 1 pass from Cockerham (Nystrom kick)
ORE — Harrington 5 run (Villegas kick)
MINN — Bruce 38 pass from Cockerham (kick failed)
ORE — Harrington 1 run (Villegas kick)
ORE — FG Villegas 37
MINN — Johnson 7 pass from Cockerham (Nystrom kick)
ORE — Howry 10 pass from Harrington (Villegas kick)

ORE	TEAM STATISTICS	MINN
22	First Downs	19
156	Rushing Yards	96
20-43-0	Passing	19-37-2
232	Passing Yards	257
388	Total Yards	353
4-40	Punt Returns - Yards	3-20
8-40.6	Punts - Average	7-46.1
2-1	Fumbles - Lost	1-1
35:25	Possession Time	24:35

INDIVIDUAL LEADERS
RUSHING
ORE: Droughns 21-95; Ho-Ching 9-56.
MINN: Hamner 20-64; Cockerham 12-26.
PASSING
ORE: Harrington 20-43-0, 232 yards, 1 TD.
MINN: Cockerham 19-37-2, 257 yards, 3 TD.
RECEIVING
ORE: Hartley 7-113; Howry 3-54, 1 TD.
MINN: Leverson 6-126; Johnson 7-54, 2 TD.

December 29, 2000
Wisconsin 21, UCLA 20

	1ST	2ND	3RD	4TH	FINAL
WISC	7	0	7	7	21
UCLA	10	7	3	0	20

SCORING SUMMARY
WISC   Evans 54 pass from Bollinger (Pisetsky kick)
UCLA   Mitchell 64 pass from Paus (Griffith kick)
UCLA   FG Griffith 31
UCLA   Foster 7 run (Griffith kick)
UCLA   FG Griffith 25
WISC   Chambers 3 pass from Bollinger (Pisetsky kick)
WISC   Bennett 6 run (Pisetsky kick)

WISC	TEAM STATISTICS	UCLA
18	First Downs	20
177	Rushing Yards	114
9-18-1	Passing	20-33-1
130	Passing Yards	282
307	Total Yards	396
2-12	Punt Returns - Yards	0-0
5-37.2	Punts - Average	3-45.7
0-0	Fumbles - Lost	0-0
29:38	Possession Time	30:22

INDIVIDUAL LEADERS
RUSHING
WISC: Bennett 16-83, 1 TD; Bollinger 16-55.
UCLA: Foster 26-107, 1 TD; Lewis 4 -8.
PASSING
WISC: Bollinger 8-16-0, 107 yards, 2 TD.
UCLA: McEwan 12-18-1, 135 yards; Paus 8-15-0, 147 yards, 1 TD.
RECEIVING
WISC: Evans 3-86, 1 TD; Chambers 4 -30, 1 TD.
UCLA: Mitchell 9-180, 1 TD; Poli-Dixon 7-50.

December 31, 2001
Washington State 33, Purdue 27

	1ST	2ND	3RD	4TH	FINAL
WSU	14	3	13	3	33
PU	0	20	0	7	27

SCORING SUMMARY
WSU   David 45 interception return (Dunning kick)
WSU   Bush 46 pass from Gesser (Dunning kick)
PU   Lowe 1 run (Dorsch kick)
PU   FG Dorsch 28
WSU   FG Dunning 47
PU   Stubblefield 3 pass from Orton (Dorsch kick)
PU   FG Dorsch 51
WSU   FG Dunning 34
WSU   Gesser 1 run (Dunning kick)
WSU   FG Dunning 30
WSU   FG Dunning 37
PU   Stubblefield 51 pass from Orton (Dorsch kick)

WSU	TEAM STATISTICS	PU
15	First Downs	28
81	Rushing Yards	55
15-41-3	Passing	38-75-4
281	Passing Yards	419
362	Total Yards	474
5-29	Punt Returns - Yards	4-31
6-44.3	Punts - Average	6-38.8
2-1	Fumbles - Lost	2-1
26:08	Possession Time	33:52

INDIVIDUAL LEADERS
RUSHING
WSU: Minnich 17-51; Cox 1-20.
PU: Lowe 17-45, 1 TD; Harris 5-27.
PASSING
WSU: Gesser 15-40-3, 281 yards, 1 TD.
PU: Orton 38-74 -4, 419 yards, 2 TD.
RECEIVING
WSU: McElrath 5-116; Riley 6-65.
PU: Stubblefield 9-196, 2 TD; Standeford 12-103.

December 31, 2002
Purdue 34, Washington 24

	1ST	2ND	3RD	4TH	FINAL
PU	0	14	17	3	34
WASH	17	0	0	7	24

SCORING SUMMARY
WASH   Reddick 7 pass from Pickett (Anderson kick)
WASH   Cooper 31 fumble recovery (Anderson kick)
WASH   FG Anderson 38
PU   Standeford 7 pass from Orton (Lacevic kick)
PU   Williams fumble recovery in end zone (Lacevic kick)
PU   FG Lacevic 22
PU   Harris 10 run (Lacevic kick)
PU   Gardner 19 fumble recovery (Lacevic kick)
PU   FG Lacevic 29
WASH   Reddick 12 pass from Pickett (Anderson kick)

PU	TEAM STATISTICS	WASH
24	First Downs	23
117	Rushing Yards	44
25-37-0	Passing	25-54-1
283	Passing Yards	272
400	Total Yards	316
4-39.2	Punts - Average	5-36.4
13-118	Penalties - Yards	5-44

INDIVIDUAL LEADERS
RUSHING
PU: Harris 23-93, 1 TD; Jones 9-28.
WASH: Alexis 7-18; Cleman 7-13.
PASSING
PU: Orton 25-37-0, 283 yards, 2 TD.
WASH: Pickett 25-54-1, 272 yards, 2 TD.
RECEIVING
PU: Standeford 10-105, 1 TD; Stubblefield 7-92.
WASH: Williams 5-64; Reddick 6-63, 2 TD.

December 31, 2003
Minnesota 31, Oregon 30

	1ST	2ND	3RD	4TH	FINAL
MINN	0	14	14	3	31
ORE	0	17	7	6	30

SCORING SUMMARY
ORE   Rosario 9 pass from Clemens (Siegel kick)
MINN   Tapeh 1 run (Lloyd kick)
ORE   Parker 18 pass from Clemens (Siegel kick)
MINN   Tapeh 1 run (Lloyd kick)
ORE   FG Siegel 30
MINN   Tapeh 6 run (Lloyd kick)
ORE   Parker 40 pass from Clemens (Siegel kick)
MINN   Maroney 22 run (Lloyd kick)
ORE   FG Siegel 32
ORE   FG Siegel 47
MINN   FG Lloyd 42

MINN	TEAM STATISTICS	ORE
23	First Downs	25
241	Rushing Yards	77
12-21-0	Passing	33-44-1
172	Passing Yards	376
413	Total Yards	453
1-4	Punt Returns - Yards	2-47
2-47	Kickoff Returns - Yards	5-97
3-38.7	Punts - Average	4-29.0
2-1	Fumbles - Lost	0-0
3-19	Penalties - Yards	5-40
31:33	Possession Time	28:27

INDIVIDUAL LEADERS
RUSHING
MINN: Maroney 15-131, 1 TD; Tapeh 13-40, 3 TD.
ORE: Whitehead 6-35; Washington 6-28.
PASSING
MINN: Abdul-Khaliq 12-21-0, 172 yards.
ORE: Clemens 32-42-1, 363 yards, 3 TD.
RECEIVING
MINN: Hosack 6-107; Patterson 3-33.
ORE: Parker 16-200, 2 TD; Williams 4-49.

December 31, 2004
Arizona State 27, Purdue 23

	1ST	2ND	3RD	4TH	FINAL
ASU	3	0	7	17	27
PU	0	2	7	14	23

SCORING SUMMARY
ASU   FG Ainsworth 22
PU   Saftey
PU   Hare 80 pass from Orton (Jones kick)
ASU   Hagan 27 pass from Keller (Ainsworth kick)
PU   Stubblefield 5 pass from Orton (Jones kick)
ASU   FG Ainsworth 34
ASU   Burgess 41 pass from Keller (Ainsworth kick)
PU   Davis 6 pass from Orton (Jones kick)
ASU   Burgess 19 pass from Keller (Ainsworth kick)

ASU	TEAM STATISTICS	PU
26	First Downs	15
158	Rushing Yards	66
25-45-0	Passing	23-47-0
370	Passing Yards	281
528	Total Yards	347
2-1	Fumbles - Lost	2-2
9-66	Penalties - Yards	6-55
32:19	Possession Time	27:41

INDIVIDUAL LEADERS
RUSHING
ASU: Burgess 20-125; Jones 9-35.
PU: Jones 5-30.
PASSING
ASU: Keller 25-45-0, 370 yards, 3 TD.
PU: Orton 23-47-0, 281 yards, 3 TD.
RECEIVING
ASU: Hagan 9-182, 1 TD; Burgess 3-64, 2 TD.
PU: Hare 3-97, 1 TD; Stubblefield 7-81, 1 TD.

December 30, 2005
UCLA 50, Northwestern 38

	1ST	2ND	3RD	4TH	FINAL
UCLA	7	22	7	14	50
NU	22	0	3	13	38

SCORING SUMMARY
NU   FG Howells 33
NU   Mims 30 interception return (kick failed)
NU   Philmore 19 run (kick failed)
NU   Roach 35 interception return (Howells kick)
UCLA   Bell 5 run (Rotstein kick)
UCLA   Moya 58 pass from Olson (Rotstein kick)
UCLA   Bell 6 run (Lewis pass from Olson)
UCLA   Everett 8 pass from Olson (Rotstein kick)
UCLA   Pitre 5 pass from Olson (Rotstein kick)
NU   FG Villarreal 31
NU   Philmore 8 pass from Basanez (Pass failed)
UCLA   Breazell 42 kickoff return (Rotstein kick)
NU   Herbert 5 pass from Basanez (Howells kick)
UCLA   Breazell 45 kickoff return (Rotstein kick)

UCLA	TEAM STATISTICS	NU
24	First Downs	33
310	Rushing Yards	168
10-24-3	Passing	38-70-2
143	Passing Yards	416
453	Total Yards	584
1-20	Punt Returns - Yards	5-12
6-156	Kickoff Returns - Yards	6-74
5-40.4	Punts - Average	5-31.0
2-1	Fumbles - Lost	4-1
8-69	Penalties - Yards	6-49
29:10	Possession Time	30:50

INDIVIDUAL LEADERS
RUSHING
UCLA: Markey 23-150; Bell 19-136, 2 TD.
NU: Sutton 18-84; Basanez 8-32.
PASSING
UCLA: Olson 10-24-3, 143 yards, 3 TD.
NU: Basanez 38-70-2, 416 yards, 2 TD.
RECEIVING
UCLA: Moya 1-58, 1 TD; Drew 2-29.
NU: Lane 7-136; Sutton 7-67.

DEFUNCT BOWLS
ALL-AMERICAN BOWL

PROFILE

Site: Birmingham, Ala.
Stadium: Legion Field
Capacity: 75,952
Surface: AstroTurf

PLAYING SITES

Legion Field, 1977-90

NAME CHANGES

Hall of Fame Classic, 1977-85
All-American Bowl, 1986-90

SEASON	DATE	PRE-GAME RANK	TEAMS	SCORE	FINAL RANK	MOST VALUABLE PLAYER(S)	ATT.
1977	Dec. 22, 1977		**Maryland**	17		Chuck White, Maryland, SE	47,000
			Minnesota	7		Charles Johnson, Maryland, DT	
1984	Dec. 29, 1984		**Kentucky**	20	19	Mark Logan, Kentucky, RB	47,300
		20	Wisconsin	19		Todd Gregoire, Wisconsin, K	
1985	Dec. 31, 1985		**Georgia Tech**	17	19	Mark Ingram, Michigan State, WR	45,000
			Michigan State	14			
1986	Dec. 31, 1986		**Florida State**	27		Sammie Smith, Florida State, RB	30,000
			Indiana	13			
1988	Dec. 29, 1988		**Florida**	14		Emmitt Smith, Florida, RB	48,218
			Illinois	10			

DECEMBER 22, 1977
MARYLAND 17, MINNESOTA 7

	1ST	2ND	3RD	4TH	FINAL
MARY	3	14	0	0	17
MINN	7	0	0	0	7

SCORING SUMMARY
MINN   Barber 1 run (Rogind kick)
MARY   FG Sochko 32
MARY   Scott 2 run (Sochko kick)
MARY   Scott 1 run (Sochko kick)

MARY	TEAM STATISTICS	MINN
15	First Downs	17
120	Rushing Yards	113
12-23-1	Passing	13-26-0
211	Passing Yards	155
331	Total Yards	268
2-3	Punt Returns - Yards	2-6
2-34	Kickoff Returns - Yards	4-70
5-36.8	Punts - Average	9-27.7
3-2	Fumbles - Lost	3-2
12-80	Penalties - Yards	6-54

INDIVIDUAL LEADERS
RUSHING
MARY: Scott 24-75, 2 TD; Maddox 2-17.
MINN: Kitzmann 24-76; Thompson 4-11.
PASSING
MARY: Dick 12-20-0, 211 yards.
MINN: Avery 12-23-0, 130 yards.
RECEIVING
MARY: White 8-126; Sievers 1-57.
MINN: Barber 4-58; Anhorn 5-49.

DECEMBER 29, 1984
KENTUCKY 20, WISCONSIN 19

	1ST	2ND	3RD	4TH	FINAL
UK	0	7	10	3	20
WISC	10	6	3	0	19

SCORING SUMMARY
WISC   FG Gregoire 40
WISC   McFadden 3 pass from Howard (Gregoire kick)
WISC   FG Gregoire 27
UK   Logan 9 run (Worley kick)
WISC   FG Gregoire 20
UK   FG Worley 22
WISC   FG Gregoire 40
UK   Logan 27 pass from Ransdell (Worley kick)
UK   FG Worley 52

UK	TEAM STATISTICS	WISC
19	First Downs	17
124	Rushing Yards	181
18-34-0	Passing	19-30-2
188	Passing Yards	203
312	Total Yards	384
3-(-1)	Punt Returns - Yards	3-78
4-133	Kickoff Returns - Yards	5-100
6-37.5	Punts - Average	5-41.4
1-0	Fumbles - Lost	0-0
6-49	Penalties - Yards	13-133
28:57	Possession Time	31:03

INDIVIDUAL LEADERS
RUSHING
UK: Adams 18-62; Higgs 9-39.
WISC: Armentrout 15-105; Harrison 14-52.
PASSING
UK: Ransdell 18-34-0, 188 yards, 1 TD.
WISC: Howard 19-29-1, 203 yards, 1 TD.
RECEIVING
UK: Phillips 6-55; Adams 5-34.
WISC: Pearson 5-55; Toon 4-48.

DECEMBER 31, 1985
GEORGIA TECH 17, MICHIGAN STATE 14

	1ST	2ND	3RD	4TH	FINAL
GT	0	0	7	10	17
MSU	0	7	7	0	14

SCORING SUMMARY
MSU   Ingram 6 pass from Yarema (Caudell kick)
GT   Rampley 1 run (Bell kick)
MSU   Ingram 27 pass from Yarema (Caudell kick)
GT   FG Bell 40
GT   King 5 run (Bell kick)

GT	TEAM STATISTICS	MSU
16	First Downs	14
182	Rushing Yards	148
12-23-1	Passing	6-15-1
99	Passing Yards	85
281	Total Yards	233
1-11	Punt Returns - Yards	2-14
2-30	Kickoff Returns - Yards	4-47
6-37.8	Punts - Average	6-36.7
2-0	Fumbles - Lost	2-1
5-47	Penalties - Yards	3-28
35:03	Possession Time	24:57

INDIVIDUAL LEADERS
RUSHING
GT: King 16-122, 1 TD; Kelsey 8-30.
MSU: White 33-158; Morse 2-8.
PASSING
GT: Rampley 12-23-1, 99 yards.
MSU: Yarema 6-15-1, 85 yards, 2 TD.
RECEIVING
GT: Massey 2-23; Mayes 3-22.
MSU: Ingram 3-70, 2 TD; Rison 1-18.

DECEMBER 31, 1986
FLORIDA STATE 27, INDIANA 13

	1ST	2ND	3RD	4TH	FINAL
FSU	6	7	7	7	27
IU	3	0	7	3	13

SCORING SUMMARY
IU   FG Stoyanovich 35
FSU   Smith 4 run (kick failed)
FSU   Smith 9 run (Schmidt kick)
FSU   Holloman 8 run (Schmidt kick)
IU   Powell 2 run (Stoyanovich kick)
IU   FG Stoyanovich 30
FSU   Holloman 10 run (Schmidt kick)

FSU	TEAM STATISTICS	IU
20	First Downs	23
288	Rushing Yards	215
6-14-1	Passing	11-25-1
54	Passing Yards	168
342	Total Yards	383
1-12	Punt Returns - Yards	1-7
4-97	Kickoff Returns - Yards	5-70
2-35.0	Punts - Average	2-35.0
2-1	Fumbles - Lost	1-0
6-50	Penalties - Yards	10-88
22:41	Possession Time	37:19

INDIVIDUAL LEADERS
RUSHING
FSU: Smith 25-205, 2 TD; Holloman 6-36, 2 TD.
IU: Thompson 28-127; Powell 6-38, 1 TD.
PASSING
FSU: McManus 6-14-1, 54 yards.
IU: Kramme 11-25-1, 168 yards.
RECEIVING
FSU: O'Malley 2-20; Gainer 1-19.
IU: Dawsey 5-74; Lilja 2-44.

DECEMBER 29, 1988
FLORIDA 14, ILLINOIS 10

	1ST	2ND	3RD	4TH	FINAL
FLA	7	0	7	0	14
ILL	0	7	0	3	10

SCORING SUMMARY
FLA   Smith 55 run (Francis kick)
ILL   Jones 30 run (Higgins kick)
ILL   FG Higgins 44
FLA   Smith 2 run (Francis kick)

FLA	TEAM STATISTICS	ILL
12	First Downs	17
187	Rushing Yards	55
8-16-2	Passing	20-38-2
69	Passing Yards	194
256	Total Yards	249
3-10	Punt Returns - Yards	0-0
3-90	Kickoff Returns - Yards	3-60
4-29.8	Punts - Average	7-35.3
1-1	Fumbles - Lost	1-1
5-36	Penalties - Yards	8-59
26:38	Possession Time	33:22

INDIVIDUAL LEADERS
RUSHING
FLA: Smith 28-159, 2 TD; McClendon 9-34.
ILL: Jones 18-88, 1 TD; Griffith 5-8.
PASSING
FLA: Morris 6-12-2, 50 yards.
ILL: George 20-37-2, 194 yards.
RECEIVING
FLA: Barber 4-29; Smith 2-19.
ILL: Bellamy 5-49; Williams 5-49.

ALOHA BOWL

PROFILE

Site: Honolulu, Hawaii
Stadium: Aloha Stadium
Capacity: 50,000
Surface: AstroTurf

PLAYING SITES

Aloha Stadium, 1982-2000

NAME CHANGES

Aloha Bowl, 1982-84
Eagle Aloha Bowl, 1985-88
Jeep Eagle Aloha Bowl, 1989-96
Eagle Aloha Bowl Football Classic, 1997
Jeep Aloha Christmas Football Classic, 1998-2000

SEASON	DATE	PRE-GAME RANK	TEAMS	SCORE	FINAL RANK	MOST VALUABLE PLAYER(S)	ATT.
1983	Dec. 26, 1983		**Penn State***	**13**		George Reynolds, Penn State, P	37,212
			Washington	**10**		Danny Greene, Washington, WR	
1989	Dec. 25, 1989	22	**Michigan State**	**33**	16	Blake Ezor, Michigan State, TB	50,000
		23	**Hawaii**	**13**		Chris Roscoe, Hawaii, WR	
1997	Dec. 25, 1997	21	**Washington**	**51**	18	Rashaan Shehee, Washington, RB	44,598
		25	**Michigan State**	**23**			

DECEMBER 26, 1983
PENN STATE 13, WASHINGTON 10

	1ST	2ND	3RD	4TH	FINAL
PSU	3	0	0	10	13
WASH	0	10	0	0	10

SCORING SUMMARY
PSU FG Gancitano 23
WASH Greene 57 punt return (Jaeger kick)
WASH FG Jaeger 39
PSU FG Gancitano 49
PSU Dozier 2 run (Gancitano kick)

PSU	TEAM STATISTICS	WASH
15	First Downs	18
95	Rushing Yards	126
14-34-1	Passing	19-40-0
118	Passing Yards	153
213	Total Yards	279
8-46.6	Punts - Average	9-39.6
0-0	Fumbles - Lost	0-0
7-6	Penalties - Yards	6-50

INDIVIDUAL LEADERS
RUSHING
PSU: Williams 12-48; Dozier 15-37, 1 TD.
WASH: Jackson 7-34.
PASSING
PSU: Strang 14-34-1, 118 yards.
WASH: Pelluer 19-40-0, 153 yards.
RECEIVING
PSU: DiMidio 4-35.
WASH: Pattison 6-55; Wroten 4-25.

DECEMBER 25, 1989
MICHIGAN STATE 33, HAWAII 13

	1ST	2ND	3RD	4TH	FINAL
MSU	6	13	0	14	33
HAW	0	0	6	7	13

SCORING SUMMARY
MSU Ezor 3 run (kick blocked)
MSU Ezor 2 run (Langeloh kick)
MSU FG Langeloh 30
MSU FG Langeloh 34
HAW Roscoe 11 pass from Gabriel (kick blocked)
MSU Hickson 1 run (Langeloh kick)
HAW McArthur 23 pass from Gabriel (Khan kick)
MSU Ezor 26 run (Langeloh kick)

MSU	TEAM STATISTICS	HAW
21	First Downs	19
225	Rushing Yards	82
7-12-2	Passing	20-33-4
116	Passing Yards	198
341	Total Yards	280
0-0	Punt Returns - Yards	2-31
1-2	Kickoff Returns - Yards	7-174
3-50.7	Punts - Average	1-27.0
0-0	Fumbles - Lost	7-4
9-85	Penalties - Yards	3-30

INDIVIDUAL LEADERS
RUSHING
MSU: Ezor 41-179, 3 TD; Hawkins 1-31.
HAW: McArthur 2-34, Ahuna 3-21.
PASSING
MSU: Enos 7-12-2, 116 yards.
HAW: Gabriel 19-31-3, 197 yards, 2 TD.
RECEIVING
MSU: Bradley 4-85; Hickson 1-13.
HAW: Roscoe 6-71, 1 TD; Lau 2-34.

DECEMBER 25, 1997
WASHINGTON 51, MICHIGAN STATE 23

	1ST	2ND	3RD	4TH	FINAL
WASH	14	17	13	7	51
MSU	7	3	7	6	23

SCORING SUMMARY
WASH Shehee 33 run (Lentz kick)
WASH Coleman 15 pass from Huard (Lentz kick)
MSU Scott 12 pass from Schultz (Edinger kick)
WASH Coleman 22 pass from Huard (Lentz kick)
WASH FG Lentz 41
MSU FG Edinger 43
WASH Parrish 56 interception return (Lentz kick)
WASH Shehee 15 run (Lentz kick)
MSU Scott 28 pass from Schultz (Edinger kick)
WASH Reed 64 run (kick failed)
WASH Towns 66 interception return (Lentz kick)
MSU Richardson 21 pass from Burke (kick failed)

WASH	TEAM STATISTICS	MSU
23	First Downs	15
298	Rushing Yards	47
18-30-0	Passing	20-35-3
179	Passing Yards	296
477	Total Yards	343
2-7	Punt Returns - Yards	4-70
1-25	Kickoff Returns - Yards	8-217
6-39.8	Punts - Average	3-30.0
2-1	Fumbles - Lost	6-2
13-126	Penalties - Yards	4-28

INDIVIDUAL LEADERS
RUSHING
WASH: Shehee 29-193, 2 TD; Reed 2-70, 1 TD.
MSU: Irvin 15-59; McFadden 2-10.
PASSING
WASH: Huard 18-30-0, 179 yards, 2 TD.
MSU: Schultz 14-24-3, 220 yards, 2 TD; Burke 6-10-0, 76 yards, 1 TD.
RECEIVING
WASH: Coleman 5-68, 2 TD; Pathon 4-54.
MSU: Scott 5-114, 2 TD; Richardson 3-42, 1 TD.

Played as an independent or with other conference affiliation

BLUEBONNET BOWL

PROFILE

Site: Houston, Texas
Stadium: Astrodome
Capacity: 60,000
Surface: AstroTurf

PLAYING SITES

Rice Stadium, 1959-67 and 1985
Astrodome, 1964-84 and 1986-87

NAME CHANGES

Bluebonnet Bowl, 1959-67 and 1977-87
Astro-Bluebonnet Bowl, 1968-76

SEASON	DATE	PRE-GAME RANK	TEAMS	SCORE	FINAL RANK	MOST VALUABLE PLAYER(S)	ATT.
1979	Dec. 31, 1979	12	**Purdue**	**27**	10	Mark Herrmann, Purdue, QB	40,542
			Tennessee	22		Roland James, Tennessee, DB	
1981	Dec. 31, 1981	16	**Michigan**	**33**	12	Butch Woolfolk, Michigan, RB	40,309
		19	UCLA	14		Ben Needham, Michigan, LB	

DECEMBER 31, 1979
PURDUE 27, TENNESSEE 22

	1ST	2ND	3RD	4TH	FINAL
PUR	0	14	7	6	27
TENN	0	0	6	16	22

SCORING SUMMARY
PUR   McCall 6 run (Seibel kick)
PUR   Burrell 12 pass from Herrmann (Seibel kick)
PUR   Young 12 pass from Herrmann (Seibel kick)
TENN   Ford 8 pass from Streater (pass failed)
TENN   Berry 15 pass from Ingram (Simpson run)
TENN   Simpson 1 run (Simpson pass from Streater)
PUR   Young 17 pass from Herrmann (pass failed)

PUR	TEAM STATISTICS	TENN
31	First Downs	19
180	Rushing Yards	146
21-39-0	Passing	17-36-3
303	Passing Yards	234
483	Total Yards	380
7-43.6	Punts - Average	6-38.0
2-1	Fumbles - Lost	3-2
3-25	Penalties - Yards	7-56

INDIVIDUAL LEADERS
RUSHING
PUR: McCall 18-91, 1 TD.
TENN: Simpson 16-47, 1 TD.
PASSING
PUR: Herrmann 21-39-0, 303 yards, 3 TD.
TENN: Streater 16-34-3, 219 yards, 1 TD.
RECEIVING
PUR: Burrell 8-144, 1 TD.
TENN: Gault 4-22.

DECEMBER 31, 1981
MICHIGAN 33, UCLA 14

	1ST	2ND	3RD	4TH	FINAL
MICH	10	0	3	20	33
UCLA	0	0	7	7	14

SCORING SUMMARY
MICH   FG Haji-Sheikh 24
MICH   Carter 50 pass from Smith (Haji-Sheikh kick)
UCLA   Townsell 17 pass from Ramsey (Johnson kick)
MICH   FG Haji-Sheikh 47
MICH   Woolfolk 1 run (run failed)
UCLA   Wrightman 9 pass from Ramsey (Johnson kick)
MICH   Smith 9 run (Haji-Sheikh kick)
MICH   Dickey 5 run (Haji-Sheikh kick)

MICH	TEAM STATISTICS	UCLA
25	First Downs	14
320	Rushing Yards	33
10-16-0	Passing	12-26-2
168	Passing Yards	162
488	Total Yards	195
5-39.6	Punts - Average	8-47.8
1-1	Fumbles - Lost	1-0
14-148	Penalties - Yards	9-94

INDIVIDUAL LEADERS
RUSHING
MICH: Woolfolk 27-186, 1 TD; Smith 10-64, 1 TD.
UCLA: Nelson 18-33.
PASSING
MICH: Smith 9-15-0, 152 yards, 1 TD.
UCLA: Ramsey 12-25-1, 162 yards, 2 TD.
RECEIVING
MICH: Carter 6-127, 1 TD; Bean 2-33.
UCLA: Carney 5-89; Townsell 3-37, 1 TD.

CHERRY BOWL

PROFILE

Site: Pontiac, Mich.
Stadium: Pontiac Silverdome
Capacity: 80,311
Surface: AstroTurf

YEAR	DATE	GAME RANK	TEAMS	SCORE	FINAL RANK	MOST VALUABLE PLAYER(S)	ATT.
1984	Dec. 22, 1984		**Army**	**10**		Nate Sassaman, Army, QB	70,332
			Michigan State	6			

DECEMBER 22, 1984
ARMY 10, MICHIGAN STATE 6

	1ST	2ND	3RD	4TH	FINAL
ARMY	0	7	0	3	10
MSU	0	0	0	6	6

SCORING SUMMARY
ARMY   Jones 4 run (Stopa kick)
ARMY   FG Stopa 38
MSU   Wasczenski 36 pass from Yarema (pass failed)

ARMY	TEAM STATISTICS	MSU
15	First Downs	13
256	Rushing Yards	89
1-2-1	Passing	11-25-3
10	Passing Yards	155
266	Total Yards	244
2-18	Punt Returns - Yards	6-23
0-0	Kickoff Returns - Yards	2-29
7-36.7	Punts - Average	4-55.8
2-1	Fumbles - Lost	3-2
1-7	Penalties - Yards	4-26

INDIVIDUAL LEADERS
RUSHING
ARMY: Sassaman 28-136; Black 22-57; Jones 10-41, 1 TD.
MSU: White 23-103.
PASSING
ARMY: Sassaman 1-2-1, 10 yards.
MSU: Yarema 11-25-3, 155 yards, 1 TD.
RECEIVING
ARMY: Hollingsworth 1-10.
MSU: Rolle 5-65; Wasczenski 2-54, 1 TD.

FREEDOM BOWL

Site: Anaheim, Calif.
Stadium: Anaheim Stadium
Capacity: 69,008
Surface: Grass

SEASON	DATE	PRE-GAME RANK	TEAMS	SCORE	FINAL RANK	MOST VALUABLE PLAYER(S)	ATT.
1984	Dec. 26, 1984		Iowa	55	16	Chuck Long, Iowa, QB	24,093
		19	Texas	17		William Harris, Texas, TE	

DECEMBER 26, 1984
IOWA 55, TEXAS 17

	1ST	2ND	3RD	4TH	FINAL
IOWA	14	10	31	0	55
TEX	0	17	0	0	17

SCORING SUMMARY
IOWA   Hayes 6 pass from Long (Nichol kick)
IOWA   Flagg 11 pass from Long (Nichol kick)
TEX   Bryant 11 pass from Dodge (Ward kick)
IOWA   Bush 1 run (Nichol kick)
TEX   Harris 1 pass from Dodge (Ward kick)
TEX   FG Ward 46
IOWA   FG Nichol 27
IOWA   FG Nichol 35
IOWA   Happel 33 pass from Long (Nichol kick)
IOWA   Smith 49 pass from Long (Nichol kick)
IOWA   Helverson 4 pass from Long (Nichol kick)
IOWA   Hayes 15 pass from Long (Nichol kick)

IOWA	TEAM STATISTICS	TEX
28	First Downs	15
91	Rushing Yards	115
30-40-0	Passing	17-34-2
469	Passing Yards	185
560	Total Yards	300
4-42.0	Punts - Average	5-43.0
5-2	Fumbles - Lost	3-3
4-27	Penalties - Yards	6-50
33:32	Possession Time	26:28

INDIVIDUAL LEADERS
RUSHING
IOWA: Gill 17-61; Long 7-20.
TEX: Orr 12-67; Johnson 8-56.
PASSING
IOWA: Long 29-39-0, 461 yards, 6 TD.
TEX: Dodge 16-32-2, 180, 2 TD.
RECEIVING
IOWA: Smith 4-115, 1 TD; Happel 8-104, 1 TD.
TEX: Bryant 3-50, 1 TD; Duhon 1-47.

GARDEN STATE BOWL

Site: East Rutherford, N.J.
Stadium: Giants Stadium
Capacity: 77,716
Surface: AstroTurf

SEASON	DATE	PRE-GAME RANK	TEAMS	SCORE	FINAL RANK	MOST VALUABLE PLAYER(S)	ATT.
1981	Dec. 13, 1981		Tennessee	28		Steve Alatorre, QB and Anthony Hancock, Tennessee, WR	38,782
			Wisconsin	21		Randy Wright, Wisconsin, QB	

DECEMBER 13, 1981
TENNESSEE 28, WISCONSIN 21

	1ST	2ND	3RD	4TH	FINAL
TENN	13	8	0	7	28
WISC	7	0	0	14	21

SCORING SUMMARY
TENN   FG Reveiz 22
WISC   Cole 3 run (Doran kick)
TENN   Gault 87 kickoff return (Reveiz kick)
TENN   FG Reveiz 44
TENN   Hancock 43 pass from Alatorre (Cofer pass from Alatorre)
WISC   Nault 6 pass from Wright (Doran kick)
TENN   Alatorre 6 run (Reveiz kick)
WISC   McFadden 11 pass from Wright (Doran kick)

TENN	TEAM STATISTICS	WISC
27	First Downs	22
89	Rushing Yards	177
24-42-0	Passing	14-37-3
315	Passing Yards	212
404	Total Yards	389
6-45.2	Punts - Average	6-36.7
4-0	Fumbles - Lost	1-1
8-84	Penalties - Yards	6-73

INDIVIDUAL LEADERS
RUSHING
TENN: Berry 10-44; Morris 10-39.
WISC: Davis 6-44; Cole 9-39, 1 TD.
PASSING
TENN: Alatorre 24-42-0, 315 yards, 1 TD.
WISC: Wright 9-21-1, 123 yards, 2 TD.
RECEIVING
TENN: Hancock 11-196, 1 TD; Miller 4-42.
WISC: Nault 5-85, 1 TD; McFadden 3-74, 1 TD.

SILICON VALLEY CLASSIC

PROFILE

Site: San Jose, Calif.
Stadium: Spartan Stadium
Capacity: 31,500
Surface: Grass

PLAYING SITES

Spartan Stadium, since 2000

NAME CHANGES

Silicon Valley Football Classic,
   since 2000

SEASON	DATE	PRE-GAME RANK	TEAMS	SCORE	FINAL RANK	MOST VALUABLE PLAYER(S)	ATT.
2001	Dec. 31, 2001		**Michigan State**	44		Nick Myers and Charles Rogers, Michigan State	30,456
		20	**Fresno State**	35		Bryce McGill, Fresno State	

DECEMBER 31, 2001
MICHIGAN STATE 44, FRESNO STATE 35

	1ST	2ND	3RD	4TH	FINAL
MSU	17	20	0	7	44
FRES	14	7	7	7	35

SCORING SUMMARY

FRES	Spach 5 pass from Carr (Asparuhov kick)
MSU	Rogers 72 pass from Smoker (Rayner kick)
MSU	Wedlow fumble recovery in end zone (Rayner kick)
FRES	Wright 36 pass from Carr (Asparuhov kick)
MSU	FG Rayner 41
MSU	Duckett 5 run (Rayner kick)
FRES	Wright 79 pass from Carr (Asparuhov kick)
MSU	Duckett 39 run (Rayner kick)
MSU	Rogers 69 pass from Smoker (kick failed)
FRES	Gaines 2 run (Asparuhov kick)
FRES	Gaines 15 pass from Carr (Asparuhov kick)
MSU	McCoy 5 pass from Smoker (Rayner kick)

MSU	TEAM STATISTICS	FRES
23	First Downs	25
210	Rushing Yards	29
22-32-1	Passing	35-58-2
376	Passing Yards	531
586	Total Yards	560
2-3	Punt Returns - Yards	3-27
5-108	Kickoff Returns - Yards	6-115
6-38.7	Punts - Average	5-39.6
0-0	Fumbles - Lost	0-0
8-64	Penalties - Yards	6-30
34:43	Possession Time	25:17

INDIVIDUAL LEADERS

RUSHING
MSU: Duckett 27-184, 2 TD; Smoker 9-17.
FRES: Gaines 10-26, 1 TD; Wright 2-19.

PASSING
MSU: Smoker 22-32-1, 376 yards, 3 TD.
FRES: Carr 35-56-2, 531 yards, 4 TD.

RECEIVING
MSU: Rogers 10-270, 2 TD; Haygood 5-49.
FRES: Wright 13-299, 2 TD; Berrian 9-94.

MAC TEAMS

This section contains historical essays and statistical data on each of the Mid-American Conference's 13 universities, including its newest addition, Temple, which joined in 2007.

Here's what you should know about information that appears in these pages:

- **Enrollment.** Undergraduate enrollment only.
- **National championships.** According to the NCAA's recognized list of consensus national champions since 1936 (the first year of the Associated Press poll).
- **Conference championships.** Overall and outright titles in the conference.
- **First-round draftees.** Updated through the 2007 NFL draft.
- **Consensus All-Americans.** As designated by the NCAA. Because the NCAA recognizes multiple lists, it's quite common for a player to receive first-team All-America honors from one or more selectors and not be acknowledged as a consensus All-American.
- **All-time team.** Whenever a team recently selected by a respected authority was available, we included it.
- **All-time scores.** Compiled by BCS pollster Richard Billingsley, this section offers a bar chart for each school showing yearly winning percentage since 1936. (In calculating this percentage, a tie is treated as a half-win and a half-loss.) In the year-by-year summaries, the vertical lines beside opponents indicate a conference game. A bullet indicates a win, a blank indicates a loss, an equal sign indicates a tie. Conference affiliations are noted throughout.

In the early years, forfeits were not uncommon, frequently because of difficult travel arrangements. There were, however, instances where opponents did not agree on which team had forfeited. Since it's impossible to judge who did what 100 years after the fact, only the instances where *both* schools agreed are included.

American football evolved from rugby, and for over a decade shared many of its predecessor's characteristics. Not until Walter Camp, the father of American football, established a point value system and basic rules of play (1878-82) did the sport assume the basic form we love today. Only games that were played by American football rules resulting in American point values are listed in this encyclopedia.

Billingsley and the ESPN research staff went to heroic lengths to determine, once and for all, the definitive final score for every disputed game. All games with disputed scores are footnoted, but we had to decide which outcome to record. If there was overwhelming evidence one way or another, through multiple reports or consensus, we selected the majority decision. Otherwise, we granted the losing team the smallest margin of defeat.

- **Team record books.** Among the new features in *The ESPN Big Ten Football Encyclopedia* is this three-page section that includes significant single-game, single-season, and career records for each school. This section also incorporates the annual leaders in rushing, passing, and receiving, which now appear in an easier-to-read format. Due to recent changes in the NCAA's official record-keeping methodology, there is a great deal of disparity here. Before 2002, bowl game performances were not included in a school's rushing, passing, and receiving statistics. Some schools have yet to revise their numbers. Until all schools update their stats according to the NCAA model, records will skew to more recent performances, because today's players will be credited with stats from an extra game or two (in the case of conference championship games).

Another complication: Some schools identify as their receiving leader the player who gained the most yards in receptions, while others prefer the player who caught the most passes. When two players caught the same number of passes, we've listed the player who gained the most yards.

AKRON

BY ED KRZEMIENSKI

AFTER SPENDING 40 YEARS AT the small-college level, the Zips jumped to Division I-AA in 1980, then to Division I-A in 1987. Led by former Notre Dame coach Gerry Faust, Akron hit its peak in 1992 with a 7-3-1 record. Since then, Akron has sent nine players to the NFL. Coach J.D. Brookhart and the growing band of Akron supporters have the right to be optimistic about the future of Zips football. They won the 2005 MAC championship, have a solid recruiting base, and an annual schedule that includes games against nationally-ranked opponents.

TRADITION Legend has it that in 1870, while scouting real estate for a proposed college, Akron industrialist John R. Buchtel lost a wagon wheel in a muddy bog at what is now the site of Kent State University. Buchtel returned to Akron and, along with the Ohio Universalist Convention, created Buchtel College, which in 1913 was renamed the University of Akron. Thirty-two years later, one of the original wagon wheels was discovered, and in 1946, the two schools began competing annually for the blue-and-gold Wagon Wheel. Kent State won the initial meeting and the schools vied for the Wagon Wheel until 1954. In 1972,

when the rivalry resumed, 25,000 fans turned out at the Rubber Bowl.

BEST PLAYER Before he helped the Tampa Bay Buccaneers to a Super Bowl victory in January of 2003, Dwight Smith led the nation with 10 interceptions, including two for touchdowns, as a cornerback for the Zips in 2000. In the third round of the NFL draft the Bucs selected Smith, Akron's only consensus Division I-A All-America selection. In Super Bowl XXXVII, he returned two interceptions for touchdowns, helping the Bucs to a 48-21 win over the Oakland Raiders.

BEST COACH From 1973 to 1985, Jim Dennison guided the Zips to 80 wins and nine winning seasons, and oversaw the transition from Division II to 1-AA status in 1980. In 1976, after the 10–3 Zips ended the season second overall in Division II, the American Football Coaches Association named Dennison the College Division II Coach of the Year. Five years later, he had the Zips ranked in the 1-AA Top 10. Despite his success, in December 1985, Akron removed Dennison as coach (he was named an associate athletic director) and replaced him with the high-profile Faust.

BEST TEAM Larson's 1968 Zips won seven games and earned the school its first bowl berth. That Zips team packed an offensive wallop. Sophomore Jack Beidleman ran for 799 yards, classmate Dan Ruff caught 52 passes and accounted for more than 1,300 yards of total offense, and senior quarterback Don Zwisler passed for 2,012 yards, the

PROFILE

University of Akron
Akron, Ohio
Founded: 1870
Enrollment: 23,539
Colors: Akron Blue and Gold
Nickname: Zips
Stadium: Rubber Bowl
    Opened in 1940
    AstroPlay; 31,000 capacity
First football game: 1891
All-time record: 473–449–36 (.513)
Bowl record: 0–1
MAC championships: 1
First-round draft choices: 0
Website: www.gozips.com

THE BEST OF TIMES

Before joining Division I, the Zips regularly appeared and won in the Division II playoffs. Akron finished No. 3 in the AP College Division poll in 1969. In 1976, Akron lost to Montana State in the Pioneer Bowl (the Division II title game).

THE WORST OF TIMES

From 1993 to 1998, the Zips endured six losing seasons, including two 2–9 marks and a 1–10 finish.

CONFERENCE

Akron became a member of the Mid-American Conference in 1992, and has remained there since. Prior to joining the MAC, the Zips played independently (1891-1914, 1937-42, 1966-77 and 1987-91), in the Ohio Athletic Conference (1915-36 and 1946-65), in the Mid-Continent Conference (1978-79), and in the Ohio Valley Conference (1980-86).

DISTINGUISHED ALUMNI

Dan Moldea, author; Jim Tressel, Ohio State football coach; George Wallace, comedian; Karen Ziemba, actress

fourth most in the nation. In the Grantland Rice Bowl, Zwisler and the Zips met their match against Louisiana Tech, losing 33-13. No shame for Akron, though, since Tech had a pretty good QB of its own—a junior named Terry Bradshaw.

The nickname was shortened to Zips when zippers became affiliated with fastening pants.

BEST BACKFIELD Luke Getsy just missed Akron's single-season passing record in 2005, when he threw for 3,455 yards and 23 touchdowns. Still, it was a great season for the junior quarterback who threw for more than 400 yards in three separate games. Sharing the backfield with Getsy was Brett Biggs, who ran for 1,230 yards and 10 TDs. Most importantly, the two led Akron to its first MAC championship. They also showcased their abilities in the Motor City Bowl. In a 38-31 loss to Memphis, Getsy threw for 455 yards and four TDs. Biggs gained only 44 yards on the ground, but caught a 72-yard TD pass.

BEST DEFENSE Akron coach Gordon Larson could probably forgive his 1961 defense for having some animosity toward its offense. The '61 Zips lost only two games: both of them by scores of 7-0. Otherwise, the defense, led by All-Ohio Athletic Conference defensive end Ray Greene, chalked up three shutouts and gave up a total of only 57 points.

BIGGEST GAME In the 2005 MAC championship, Akron faced Northern Illinois and the possibility of its first league title in school history. At the end of the third quarter, the Zips trailed 24-10 and were being shredded by NIU's star running back, Garrett Wolfe, who ended up with 270 yards rushing. Losing by six and with no timeouts, Luke Getsy led the Zips to the NIU 36-yard line. With ten seconds left, Getsy hit Dominick Hixon in the back of the end zone. With the extra point, Akron ended its 90-season quest for a conference title, and earned its first bowl berth—the Motor City Bowl against Memphis.

BIGGEST UPSET John W. Heisman coached and quarterbacked Buchtel College (the predecessor to the University of Akron) to a 1894 victory in its only game of the year, a 12-6 win over Ohio State. Interestingly, Heisman did not technically work for the college.

HEARTBREAKER Akron needed a win in the last game of the 1986 season in order to gain a Division I-AA playoff berth. They needed a win over the 1–9 Youngstown State squad and a loss by Ohio Valley Conference rival Murray State. With under a minute left in the game, YSU threw a Hail Mary that two Akron defenders tipped into the hands of a Youngstown receiver. Then, with 27 seconds left, YSU cashed in with a touchdown pass to Lorenzo Davis. Akron's 40-39 loss, coupled with a Murray State win, scuttled the Zips' playoff hopes.

STADIUM In 1940, the University of Akron moved its home from Buchtel Field to the municipally owned

MAC TEAMS

HIGHEST DRAFT CHOICES

1997	Jason Taylor, Dolphins (3rd/73)
2001	Dwight Smith, Buccaneers (3rd/84)
2005	Charlie Frye, Browns (3rd/67)
2007	Andy Alleman, Saints (3rd/88)

CONSENSUS ALL-AMERICANS

1969	John Travis, OG
1971	Michael Hatch, DB
1976	Mark Van Horn, OG
1976-77	Steve Cockerham, LB
1980-81	Brad Reece, LB
1985	Wayne Grant, DL
1986	Mike Clark, RB
2000	Dwight Smith, DB

COLLEGE FOOTBALL HALL OF FAME INDUCTEES

NAME	YEARS	INDUCTED
John Heisman, COACH	1893	1954

Rubber Bowl, built in conjunction with the Civil Works Authority. In 1971, the school took over ownership of the Rubber Bowl and refurbished the stadium, adding lights and artificial turf. Located off-campus, the stadium trails only Ohio State's Ohio Stadium as the state's largest college football venue. The Cleveland Browns regularly played preseason games in the Rubber Bowl until 1973. In more than six decades playing at the Rubber Bowl, Akron has won 59% of its home games.

RIVAL The Zips consider Kent State their biggest rival, and the feeling is mutual. Though located just 10 miles apart, the schools' respective campuses appear vastly different, with Akron's urban milieu contrasting sharply with the bucolic, rural Kent State. However, that is the singular difference; the schools share identical colors and a similar student body. Inevitably, many of each team's players have competed against and beside each other in high school, adding familiarity to the rivalry. The Zips and Flashes first met in 1923 and played off and on until beginning their Wagon Wheel series in 1946, but the rivalry reached new heights in 1992, when Akron joined Kent State in the MAC. Akron leads the series 26–19–2.

NICKNAME In 1927, student Margaret Hamlin suggested that Akron take its nickname from a popular pair of rubber overshoes produced by the local B.F. Goodrich Company called Zippers. The school received permission from the company to use the name. (Today a company would have to pay for advertising like that.) Eventually the nickname was shortened to Zips when zippers came to be known primarily for fastening pants. But as long as there are Golden Flashes up the road, Akron isn't alone in the least menacing nicknames category.

> *After one year and a $900 payment, the faculty and board of trustees voted Heisman's job out of existence.*

MASCOT While the original Zip was an overshoe, the Akron Zip is a kangaroo. Zippy, originally known as Mr. Zip, was born in 1953 when Dick Hansford, the UA Student Council adviser, got the idea for the mascot from a popular comic strip called "Kicky the Kangaroo." Despite a less-than-enthusiastic response from local newspapers, Mr. Zip debuted in 1955 and was upgraded a decade later to Zippy. Zippy now roams the sideline of the Rubber Bowl as a fluffy representation of a kangaroo in an Akron sweater and matching beanie.

UNIFORMS The official colors are metallic gold and Akron Blue, and the Zips' uniforms have always involved these colors. Akron's helmets, likewise, have always been some shade of gold (sometimes mustard); an A was added to the side of the helmet in 1966 and still remains. In 2001, the school added a red stripe to the helmets in support of the Fire Truck Fund, an effort to raise money to purchase a new fire truck for the New York City Fire Department after 9/11. A year later, the school unveiled a new logo that maintained the A, and incorporated what the school described as "a sleek, determined kangaroo."

LORE After the 1892 season, Buchtel College students pleaded with the school's president, Reverend Orello Cone, to hire someone to coach the college's club teams. On Jan. 28, 1893, the school extended a one-year contract for a "gymnasium director" and "special teacher of gymnastics in baseball and football." The recipient of a lucrative $900 payment and a newly built baseball cage was John W. Heisman. After just one year, the faculty and board of trustees voted Heisman's job out of existence. Alas, the University of Akron hasn't come close to a Heisman since.

QUOTE "It probably put five to ten more years on my life. Akron's a tough job." —Gerry Faust, after his firing as Zips head coach after the 1994 season

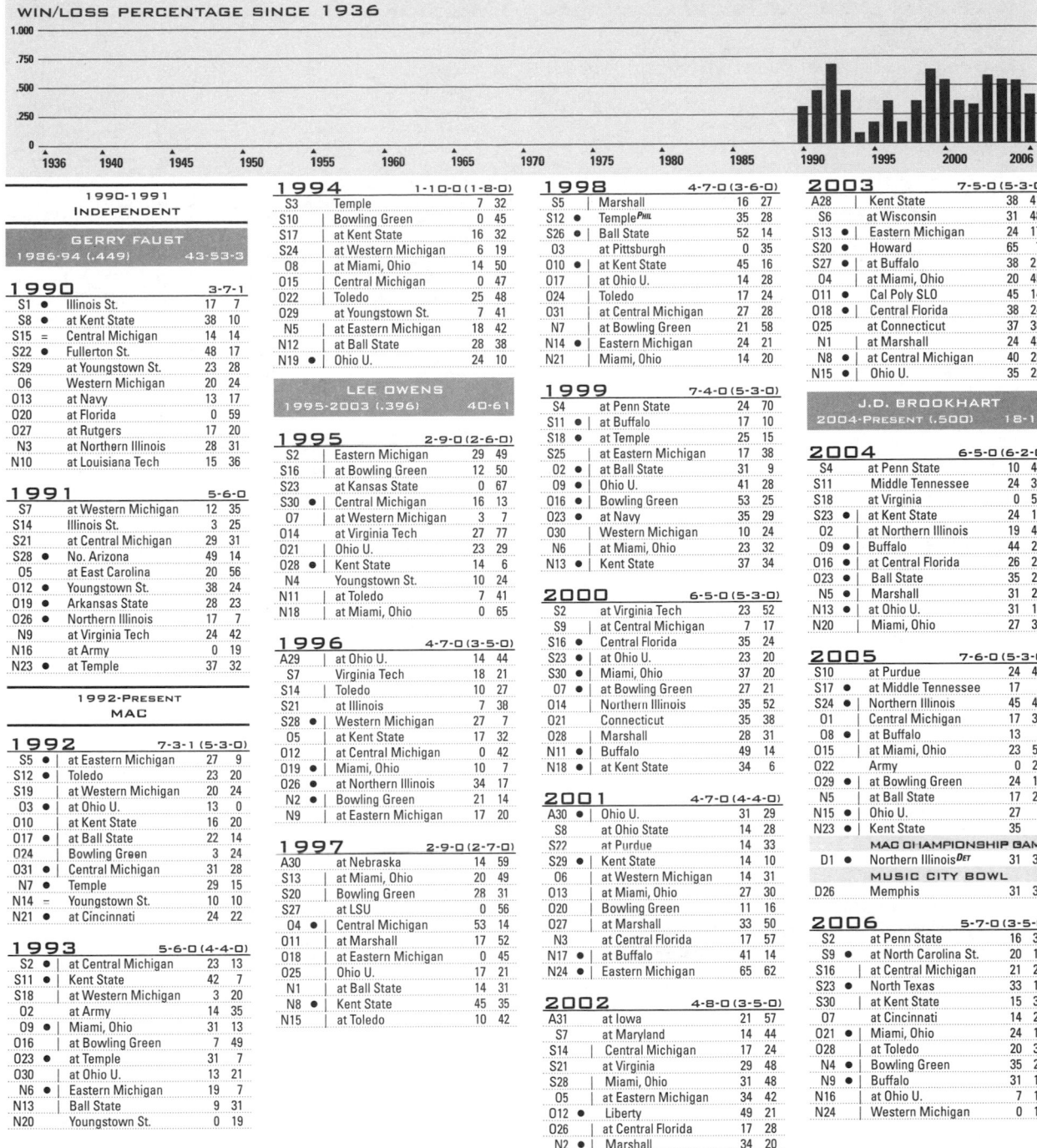

Akron All-Time Scores

Key: ƒ Forfeit † Game Later Forfieted # Disputed Victor * Disputed Score || Designated Conference Game 2 Counted Twice in Conference Standings

WIN/LOSS PERCENTAGE SINCE 1936

	1936	1940	1945	1950	1955	1960	1965	1970	1975	1980	1985	1990	1995	2000	2006

1990–1991 INDEPENDENT

GERRY FAUST
1986-94 (.449)   43-53-3

1990   3-7-1

S1	●	Illinois St.	17 7
S8	●	at Kent State	38 10
S15	=	Central Michigan	14 14
S22	●	Fullerton St.	48 17
S29		at Youngstown St.	23 28
O6		Western Michigan	20 24
O13		at Navy	13 17
O20		at Florida	0 59
O27		at Rutgers	17 20
N3		at Northern Illinois	28 31
N10		at Louisiana Tech	15 36

1991   5-6-0

S7		at Western Michigan	12 35
S14		Illinois St.	3 25
S21		at Central Michigan	29 31
S28	●	No. Arizona	49 14
O5		at East Carolina	20 56
O12	●	Youngstown St.	38 24
O19	●	Arkansas State	28 23
O26	●	Northern Illinois	17 7
N9		at Virginia Tech	24 42
N16		at Army	0 19
N23	●	at Temple	37 32

1992-PRESENT MAC

1992   7-3-1 (5-3-0)

S5	●	at Eastern Michigan	27 9
S12	●	Toledo	23 20
S19		at Western Michigan	20 24
O3	●	at Ohio U.	13 0
O10		at Kent State	16 20
O17	●	at Ball State	22 14
O24		Bowling Green	3 24
O31	●	Central Michigan	31 28
N7	●	Temple	29 15
N14	=	Youngstown St.	10 10
N21	●	at Cincinnati	24 22

1993   5-6-0 (4-4-0)

S2	●	at Central Michigan	23 13
S11	●	Kent State	42 7
S18		at Western Michigan	3 20
O2		at Army	14 35
O9	●	Miami, Ohio	31 13
O16		at Bowling Green	7 49
O23	●	at Temple	31 7
O30		at Ohio U.	13 21
N6	●	Eastern Michigan	19 7
N13		Ball State	9 31
N20		Youngstown St.	0 19

1994   1-10-0 (1-8-0)

S3		Temple	7 32
S10		Bowling Green	0 45
S17		at Kent State	16 32
S24		at Western Michigan	6 19
O8		at Miami, Ohio	14 50
O15		Central Michigan	0 47
O22		Toledo	25 48
O29		at Youngstown St.	7 41
N5		at Eastern Michigan	18 42
N12		at Ball State	28 38
N19	●	Ohio U.	24 10

LEE OWENS
1995-2003 (.396)   40-61

1995   2-9-0 (2-6-0)

S2		Eastern Michigan	29 49
S16		at Bowling Green	12 50
S23		at Kansas State	0 67
S30	●	Central Michigan	16 13
O7		at Western Michigan	3 7
O14		at Virginia Tech	27 77
O21		Ohio U.	23 29
O28	●	Kent State	14 6
N4		Youngstown St.	10 24
N11		at Toledo	7 41
N18		at Miami, Ohio	0 65

1996   4-7-0 (3-5-0)

A29		at Ohio U.	14 44
S7		Virginia Tech	18 21
S14		Toledo	10 27
S21		at Illinois	7 38
S28	●	Western Michigan	27 7
O5		at Kent State	17 32
O12		at Central Michigan	0 42
O19	●	Miami, Ohio	10 7
O26	●	at Northern Illinois	34 17
N2	●	Bowling Green	21 14
N9		at Eastern Michigan	17 20

1997   2-9-0 (2-7-0)

A30		at Nebraska	14 59
S13		at Miami, Ohio	20 49
S20		Bowling Green	28 31
S27		at LSU	0 56
O4	●	Central Michigan	53 14
O11		at Marshall	17 52
O18		at Eastern Michigan	0 45
O25		Ohio U.	17 21
N1		at Ball State	14 31
N8	●	Kent State	45 35
N15		at Toledo	10 42

1998   4-7-0 (3-6-0)

S5		Marshall	16 27
S12	●	Temple*PHIL*	35 28
S26	●	Ball State	52 14
O3		at Pittsburgh	0 35
O10	●	at Kent State	45 16
O17		at Ohio U.	14 28
O24		Toledo	17 24
O31		at Central Michigan	27 28
N7		at Bowling Green	21 58
N14	●	Eastern Michigan	24 21
N21	●	Miami, Ohio	14 20

1999   7-4-0 (5-3-0)

S4		at Penn State	24 70
S11	●	at Buffalo	17 10
S18	●	at Temple	25 15
S25		at Eastern Michigan	17 38
O2	●	at Ball State	31 9
O9	●	Ohio U.	41 28
O16	●	Bowling Green	53 25
O23	●	at Navy	35 29
O30		Western Michigan	10 24
N6		at Miami, Ohio	23 32
N13	●	Kent State	37 34

2000   6-5-0 (5-3-0)

S2		at Virginia Tech	23 52
S9		at Central Michigan	7 17
S16	●	Central Florida	35 24
S23	●	at Ohio U.	23 20
S30	●	Miami, Ohio	37 20
O7	●	at Bowling Green	27 21
O14	●	Northern Illinois	35 52
O21		Connecticut	35 38
O28		Marshall	28 31
N11	●	Buffalo	49 14
N18	●	at Kent State	34 6

2001   4-7-0 (4-4-0)

A30	●	Ohio U.	31 29
S8		at Ohio State	14 28
S22		at Purdue	14 33
S29	●	Kent State	14 10
O6		at Western Michigan	14 31
O13		at Miami, Ohio	27 30
O20		Bowling Green	11 16
O27		at Marshall	33 50
N3		at Central Florida	17 57
N17	●	at Buffalo	41 14
N24	●	Eastern Michigan	65 62

2002   4-8-0 (3-5-0)

A31		at Iowa	21 57
S7		at Maryland	14 44
S14		Central Michigan	17 24
S21		at Virginia	29 48
S28		Miami, Ohio	31 48
O5		at Eastern Michigan	34 42
O12	●	Liberty	49 21
O26		at Central Florida	17 28
N2	●	Marshall	34 20
N9		at Ohio U.	10 27
N16	●	Buffalo	21 10
N23	●	at Kent State	48 10

2003   7-5-0 (5-3-0)

A28		Kent State	38 41
S6		at Wisconsin	31 48
S13	●	Eastern Michigan	24 17
S20	●	Howard	65 7
S27	●	at Buffalo	38 21
O4		at Miami, Ohio	20 45
O11	●	Cal Poly SLO	45 14
O18	●	Central Florida	38 24
O25		at Connecticut	37 38
N1		at Marshall	24 42
N8	●	at Central Michigan	40 28
N15	●	Ohio U.	35 28

J.D. BROOKHART
2004-PRESENT (.500)   18-18

2004   6-5-0 (6-2-0)

S4		at Penn State	10 48
S11		Middle Tennessee	24 31
S18		at Virginia	0 51
S23	●	at Kent State	24 19
O2		at Northern Illinois	19 49
O9	●	Buffalo	44 21
O16	●	at Central Florida	26 21
O23	●	Ball State	35 23
N5	●	Marshall	31 28
N13	●	at Ohio U.	31 19
N20		Miami, Ohio	27 37

2005   7-6-0 (5-3-0)

S10		at Purdue	24 49
S17	●	at Middle Tennessee	17 7
S24	●	Northern Illinois	45 42
O1		Central Michigan	17 31
O8	●	at Buffalo	13 7
O15		at Miami, Ohio	23 51
O22		Army	0 20
O29	●	at Bowling Green	24 14
N5		at Ball State	17 23
N15	●	Ohio U.	27 3
N23	●	Kent State	35 8

MAC CHAMPIONSHIP GAME

D1	●	Northern Illinois*DET*	31 30

MUSIC CITY BOWL

D26		Memphis	31 38

2006   5-7-0 (3-5-0)

S2		at Penn State	16 34
S9	●	at North Carolina St.	20 17
S16	●	at Central Michigan	21 24
S23	●	North Texas	33 13
S30		at Kent State	15 37
O7		at Cincinnati	14 20
O21	●	Miami, Ohio	24 13
O28		at Toledo	20 35
N4	●	Bowling Green	35 28
N9	●	Buffalo	31 16
N16		at Ohio U.	7 17
N24		Western Michigan	0 17

MAC TEAMS

Neutral Site key: *DET* Detroit, MI / *PHIL* Philadelphia, PA

ƒ Forfeit † Game Later Forfieted # Disputed Victor * Disputed Score || Designated Conference Game 2 Counted Twice in Conference Standings

AKRON RECORD BOOK

SINGLE-GAME RECORDS

RUSHING YARDS

RANK	PLAYER	DATE	OPPONENT	ATT	AVG	YDS
1	James Black	Nov. 19, 1983	Austin Peay	52	5.7	295
2	Mike Clark	Sept. 27, 1986	UCF	31	8.2	255
3	James Black	Nov. 5, 1983	Youngstown State	40	6.2	246
4	Ron Tyson	Oct. 29, 1966	Northern Illinois	42	5.8	243
5	Bobby Hendry	Oct. 12, 2002	Liberty	26	9.2	240

PASSING YARDS

RANK	PLAYER	DATE	OPPONENT	ATT	COMP	YDS
1	Luke Getsy	Dec. 26, 2005	Memphis	59	34	455
2	Charlie Frye	Nov. 20, 2004	Miami	43	26	436
3	Charlie Frye	Nov. 8, 2003	Central Michigan	34	27	416
4	Luke Getsy	Dec. 1, 2005	Northern Illinois	50	30	413
5	Charlie Frye	Aug. 28, 2003	Kent State	46	36	407

RECEIVING YARDS

RANK	PLAYER	DATE	OPPONENT	REC	AVG	YDS
1	Willie Davis	Sept. 1, 1984	Kent State	9	22.3	201
2	Dan Ruff	Oct. 4, 1969	Ball State	10	19.5	195
3	Domenik Hixon	Nov. 5, 2004	Marshall	11	17.5	192
4	Matt Cherry	Oct. 13, 2001	Miami	10	18.9	189
5	Harold Robinson	Nov. 23, 1991	Temple	11	16.7	184

POINTS

RANK	PLAYER	DATE	OPPONENT	TOT
1	Bobby Hendry	Nov. 24, 2001	Eastern Michigan	30
	Terry Cameron	Nov. 18, 1978	Northern Iowa	30
	Art Bailey	Nov. 8, 1958	Denison	30

FIELD GOALS

RANK	PLAYER	DATE	OPPONENT	TOT
1	Daron Alcorn	Nov. 7, 1992	Temple	5
	Russ Klaus	Sept. 29, 1985	Bowling Green	5
	Andy Graham	Nov. 17, 1979	Eastern Illinois	5

TACKLES

RANK	PLAYER	DATE	OPPONENT	TOT
1	Brad Reese	Sept. 20, 1980	Western Kentucky	35

INTERCEPTIONS

RANK	PLAYER	DATE	OPPONENT	TOT
1	Dick Miller	Oct. 23, 1937	Baldwin-Wallace	6

RETIRED NUMBER

89 *Chris Angeloff*

SINGLE-SEASON RECORDS

RUSHING YARDS

RANK	PLAYER	SEASON	G	ATT	YDS
1	Mike Clark	1986	11	245	1,786
2	James Black	1983	11	351	1,568
3	Mike Clark	1985	11	301	1,299
4	Paul Winters	1979	11	318	1,298
5	Brett Biggs	2005	13	284	1,230

PASSING YARDS

RANK	PLAYER	SEASON	G	ATT	COMP	PCT	YDS
1	Charlie Frye	2003	12	421	273	64.8	3,549
2	Luke Getsy	2005	13	525	278	53.0	3,455
3	Charlie Frye	2002	12	380	250	65.8	2,824
4	Luke Getsy	2006	12	308	111	52.4	2,662
5	Charlie Frye	2004	11	346	220	63.6	2,623

RECEIVING YARDS

RANK	PLAYER	SEASON	G	REC	AVG	YDS
1	Domenik Hixon	2005	13	75	16.1	1,210
2	Dan Ruff	1968	10	52	20.0	1,041
3	Lavel Bailey	1999	11	42	22.4	941
4	David Harvey	2006	12	43	21.3	914
5	Matt Cherry	2003	12	66	13.4	904

SCORING

RANK	PLAYER	SEASON	TD	FG	PAT	P2	TOT
1	Jack Beidleman	1969	16	0	0	2	98
2	Brandon Payne	2000	16	0	0	0	96
3	Jason Swiger	2003	0	0	49	14	91
4	Bobby Hendry	2003	15	0	0	0	90
5	2 players tied at 86						

TOUCHDOWNS

RANK	PLAYER	SEASON	G	TOT
1	Jack Beidleman	1969	10	16
	Brandon Payne	2000	11	16
3	Bobby Hendry	2003	12	15
4	3 players tied at 14			

TACKLES

RANK	PLAYER	SEASON	TOT
1	Brad Reese	1980	221
2	Brad Reese	1979	214
3	Phil Dunn	1992	201
4	Steve Cockerham	1975	193
5	Steve Cockerham	1977	181

INTERCEPTIONS

RANK	PLAYER	SEASON	YDS	TOT
1	Dick Miller	1937	NA	13
2	Dwight Smith	2000	208	10
3	Curtis Howard	1977	91	8
4	4 players tied at 7			

PUNTING

RANK	PLAYER	SEASON	PUNTS	YDS	AVG
1	Ray Dodge	1948	42	1,886	44.9
2	Mike Hayes	1997	53	2,319	43.8

PUNT RETURNS

RANK	PLAYER	SEASON	RET	YDS	AVG
1	Domenik Hixon	2004	16	275	17.2
2	Matt Cherry	2001	10	163	16.3
	Jeff Sweitzer	1989	10	163	16.3

KICKOFF RETURNS

RANK	PLAYER	SEASON	RET	YDS	AVG
1	David Harvey	2006	17	510	30.0
2	Dan Ruff	1967	14	418	29.9

CAREER RECORDS

RUSHING YARDS

RANK	PLAYER	SEASONS	ATT	AVG	TD	YDS
1	Mike Clark	1984-86	804	5.3	25	4,257
2	James Black	1980-83	731	4.2	16	3,054
3	Jack Beidleman	1967-70	561	5.4	29	3,032
4	Brandon Payne	1999-2002	626	4.6	39	2,861
5	Bobby Hendry	2000-03	603	4.7	32	2,847
6	Billy Mills	1973-76	629	4.5	16	2,816
7	Paul Winters	1976-79	594	4.4	12	2,613
8	Dennis Brumfield	1979-81	625	3.7	18	2,314
9	Brett Biggs	2004-05	469	4.5	20	2,101
10	Torn Wilhelm	1972-75	436	4.6	13	2,003

PASSING YARDS

RANK	PLAYER	SEASONS	ATT	COMP	PCT	INT	TD	YDS
1	Charlie Frye	2001-04	1,436	913	63.6	32	64	11,049
2	Ja. Washington	1997-2000	931	471	50.6	33	38	6,699
3	Luke Getsy	2005-06	905	477	52.7	23	41	6,117
4	Mike Johnson	1988-89	598	281	47.0	26	20	3,989
5	Ve. Stewart	1983-86	596	263	44.1	44	20	3,945
6	Don Zwisler	1965-68	501	229	45.7	34	20	3,297
7	Mic Hutton	1969-71	439	185	42.1	28	25	3,142
8	Eric Schoch	1971-73	406	215	53.0	28	22	2,937
9	Jeff Sweitzer	1988-91	408	189	46.3	25	17	2,744
10	Marcel Weems	1991-93	387	184	47.5	20	8	2,736

RECEIVING YARDS

RANK	PLAYER	SEASONS	REC	AVG	TD	YDS
1	Lavel Bailey	1997-2000	138	18.7	21	2,577
2	Dan Ruff	1967-70	127	19.9	27	2,531
3	Domenik Hixon	2002-05	141	14.8	14	2,092
4	Matt Cherry	2000-03	149	13.4	10	1,997
5	Jake Schifino	1998-2001	131	15.2	10	1,986
6	Mac Thomas	1970-73	96	18.1	15	1,738
7	Willie Davis	1983-85	104	16.5	7	1,718
8	Ron Fuller	1974-77	87	17.6	6	1,531
9	Jabari Arthur	2004-06	98	15.1	7	1,482
10	Jack Beidleman	1967-70	86	16.4	7	1,414

SCORING

RANK	PLAYER	SEASONS	TD	FG	PAT	P2	TOT
1	Zac Derr	1998-2001	0	47	125	0	266
2	Brandon Payne	1999-02	43	0	0	2	260
3	Bob Dombroski	1986-89	0	51	253	0	253
4	Jason Swiger	2002-05	0	38	115	0	229
5	Jack Beidleman	1967-70	36	0	0	10	226

TOUCHDOWNS

RANK	PLAYER	SEASONS	TOT
1	Brandon Payne	1999-2002	43
2	Jack Beidleman	1967-70	36
3	Bobby Hendry	2000-03	33
4	Dan Ruff	1967-70	29
5	Art Bailey	1952, 1956-58	27

TACKLES

RANK	PLAYER	SEASONS	TOT
1	Steve Cockerham	1974-77	715
2	Brad Reese	1978-81	710

INTERCEPTIONS

RANK	PLAYER	SEASONS	YDS	TOT
1	Gary Tyler	1985-87	83	18
2	Dwight Smith	1997-2000	261	15
3	Shawn Vincent	1989-90	247	13
	Roosevelt Jewells	1979-81	109	13
	Dick Miller	1937	NA	13

PUNTING

RANK	PLAYER	SEASONS	PUNTS	YDS	AVG
1	Mike Hayes	1994-98	182	7,688	42.2
2	Andy Graham	1977-80	247	10,693	39.0

TEAM RECORDS

LONGEST WINNING STREAK
- 5, Oct. 9-Nov. 13, 2004

Streak broken vs. Miami (Ohio), 27-37, Nov. 20, 2004

LONGEST UNDEFEATED STREAK
- 6, Oct. 31, 1992-Sept. 11, 1993

Streak broken vs. Western Michigan, 3-20, Sept. 18, 1993

MOST CONSECUTIVE WINNING SEASONS
- 3, 2003-2005

MOST CONSECUTIVE BOWL APPEARANCES
- 1, 2005

MOST POINTS IN A GAME
- 65 (tie), vs. Eastern Michigan, Nov. 24, 2001; vs. Howard, Sept. 20, 2003

MOST POINTS ALLOWED IN A GAME
- 77, vs. Virginia Tech, Oct. 14, 1995

LARGEST MARGIN OF VICTORY
- 58 (65-7), vs. Howard, Sept. 20, 2003

LARGEST MARGIN OF DEFEAT
- 67 (0-67), vs. Kansas State, Sept. 23, 1995

LONGEST RUN FROM SCRIMMAGE
- 95 yards (tie), Jack Beidleman, vs. Eastern Kentucky, Oct. 18, 1969; Paul Winters, vs. Wayne State, Sept. 23, 1978

LONGEST PASS PLAY
- 92 yards, Tom Kot to Greg Thurman, vs. Indiana State, Nov. 2, 1974

LONGEST FIELD GOAL
- 56 yards, Daron Alcorn, vs. Toledo, Sept. 12, 1992

LONGEST PUNT
- 81, Jim Heyworth, vs. Northern Michigan, Oct. 12, 1974

LONGEST PUNT RETURN
- 85 yards, Domenik Hixon, vs. Ball State, Oct. 23, 2004

LONGEST INTERCEPTION RETURN
- 99 yards, Andre McCray, vs. Kent State, Oct. 10, 1998

PUNT RETURNS

RANK	PLAYER	SEASON	RET	YDS	AVG
1	Matt Cherry	2000-03	39	520	13.3

KICKOFF RETURNS

RANK	PLAYER	SEASON	RET	YDS	AVG
1	Jim Braccio	1964-66	21	548	26.2
2	Domenik Hixon	2002-05	48	1,154	24.0
3	Dan Ruff	1967-69	31	742	23.9

MAC TEAMS

AKRON ANNUAL STATISTICAL LEADERS

YR	RUSHING	YDS	ATT	AVG	PASSING	ATT	CMP	PCT	YDS	RECEIVING	REC	YDS	AVG
1990	Marcus Reliford	684	177	3.9	Jeff Sweitzer	186	87	.47	1,133	Bradford Jones	17	221	13.0
1991	Tyrone Nelson	769	142	5.4	Jeff Sweitzer	220	101	.46	1,599	Harold Robinson	37	779	21.1
1992	Marcel Weems	754	181	4.2	Marcel Weems	201	101	.50	1,383	Kenny Chapman	36	581	16.1
1993	Symeon Floyd	371	82	4.5	Marcel Weems	163	72	.44	1,157	Kenny Chapman	31	636	20.5
1994	DeShawn Brown	588	152	3.9	Brian Magrell	79	44	.56	548	DeShawn Brown	20	255	12.8
1995	Terrel Dixon	463	143	3.2	Mike Junko	148	78	.53	864	Eddie Alford	46	591	11.8
1996	Yasin Reeder	781	168	4.6	Mike Junko	125	60	.48	705	Devon Scott	30	399	13.3
1997	Greg Lomax	835	127	6.6	Greg Gromek	101	50	.50	715	Willie Spencer	43	521	12.1
1998	Greg Lomax	861	161	5.4	James Washington	300	148	.49	1,958	Lavel Bailey	41	558	13.6
1999	Brandon Payne	845	208	4.1	James Washington	240	131	.55	1,896	Lavel Bailey	42	941	22.4
2000	Brandon Payne	1,062	220	4.8	James Washington	283	143	.51	2,319	Lavel Bailey	44	876	19.9
2001	Bob Hendry	819	160	5.1	Charlie Frye	289	170	.59	2,053	Matt Cherry	48	630	13.1
2002	Bob Hendry	1,021	208	4.9	Charlie Frye	380	250	.66	2,824	Miquel Irvin	53	535	10.1
2003	Bob Hendry	981	231	4.2	Charlie Frye	421	273	.65	3,549	Matt Cherry	66	904	13.7
2004	Brett Biggs	871	185	4.7	Charlie Frye	346	220	.64	2,623	Domenik Hixon	66	882	13.4
2005	Brett Biggs	1,230	284	4.3	Luke Getsy	525	278	.53	3,455	Domenik Hixon	75	1,210	16.1
2006	Dennis Kennedy	914	226	4.0	Luke Getsy	380	199	.52	2,662	David Harvey	43	914	21.3

Receiving leaders by receptions
NCAA began including postseason stats in 2002

MAC TEAMS

BALL STATE

BY ED KRZEMIENSKI

IN 1918, FIVE BROTHERS, INDUSTRI-alists from Muncie, Ind., purchased the campus and buildings of the town's private normal school, renamed it after themselves and gave it to the state of Indiana. Whether George, Lucius, Frank, Edmund, and William paid much attention to athletics is difficult to say, but with a last name like Ball, it's nice to think that they did. But while Ball State has the most overtly athletic name in its state, football recruiting remains a challenge. The better players attend Indiana, Purdue, or Notre Dame; the best athletes play basketball. But in the Mid-American Conference, Ball State has more than held its own, winning the league title five times since joining, in 1975. Hoping to continue its winning ways, the school hired Brady Hoke as its new head coach before the start of the 2003 season. So far, though, it's been rough, and Hoke has yet to put together a winning season in Muncie. However, the 2006 team lifted spirits, winning three of its last four games, and challenged second-ranked Michigan in a 34–26 loss.

TRADITION Perhaps because the state is so generally enamored of basketball, Ball State's Cardinals have few football traditions. The team wears T-shirts and touches a sign, both sporting the motto "One at a Time," before games. But there are no trophy games nor even a heated rivalry. What the team does have, though, is a history of competitive play in the MAC and the distinction of sending many of its players to the NFL, including Tim Brown (1960-68), Shafer Suggs (1976-80), Bernie Parmalee (1991-2000), and Blaine Bishop (1993-2002).

BEST PLAYER From 1999 to 2002, Marcus Merriweather ran for more than 4,000 yards at Ball State. Entering his senior season, Merriweather needed 1,099 yards to become Ball State's career leading rusher. He eclipsed Parmalee's record with a 214-yard performance in the Cardinals' ninth game, against Western Michigan. Merriweather continued to add to his total, rushing for more than 1,600 yards in his record-setting season. All told, Merriweather holds the school rushing records for yards (career and single-season), attempts (career and

PROFILE

Ball State University
Muncie, Ind.
Founded: 1918
Enrollment: 17,728
Colors: Cardinal and White
Nickname: Cardinals
Stadium: Scheumann Stadium
     Opened in 1967
     FieldTurf; 22,500 capacity
First football game: 1924
All-time record: 381–345–32 (.524)
Bowl record: 0–3
Mid-American Conference championships:
5 (outright)
First-round draft choices: 0
Website: www.ballstatesports.com

THE BEST OF TIMES

From 1989 to 1996, the Cardinals had only one losing season with three MAC championships and three bowl appearances.

THE WORST OF TIMES

Two years after winning the 1996 MAC championship, the team began a 6–27 three-year slide, including a winless 1999 season and a streak of 21 consecutive losses.

CONFERENCE

Ball State became a member of the Mid-American Conference in 1973, began competition in 1975 and has remained in the MAC since. The Cardinals were previously affiliated with the Conference of Midwestern Universities (1968-72), the Indiana Collegiate Conference (1950-68) and the Indiana Intercollegiate Conference (1922-50).

DISTINGUISHED ALUMNI

David Letterman; Daniel Baldwin, actor; Jim Davis, creator of Garfield; John Schnatter, founder of Papa John's pizza; Bonzi Wells, NBA player

single-season), 100-yard games, and career touchdown runs.

BEST COACH John Magnabosco holds the Ball State coaching records for total games, victories, and tenure. From 1935 to 1952, with 1943 off for the war, Magnabosco led the Cardinals to nine winning seasons, 68 total victories, and a .586 winning percentage. In 1949, his squad went undefeated, a first in school history. In addition to his being a charter member of the Ball State Hall of Fame (begun in 1976), the football team's annual MVP award is also named for him.

BEST TEAM In 1978, Dwight Wallace took over as head coach of a Ball State team on a roll. In the previous three years, under coach Dave McClain, who left for a Big Ten job at Wisconsin, the Cardinals had put together an overall record of 26–7–0. The 1978 squad outdid them. The offense was led by quarterback Dave Wilson, who passed for more than 1,000 yards, and by running back Archie Currin, who tallied another 735 yards on

> *As might be expected, Ball State's original nickname, Hoosieroons, was not especially popular around campus.*

the ground. Finishing 10–1 (with a nonconference loss to Louisiana Tech), the Cardinals won the MAC and received some votes in the final AP poll, but no bowl invite. The MAC, however, named Wallace Coach of the Year.

BEST BACKFIELD Marcus Merriweather had his best season in 2002, but Ball State had its best backfield in 2001. That season, Merriweather had his typically great season, rushing for more than 1,200 yards and 12 touchdowns, and was joined by sophomore quarterback Tallmadge Hill. Hill threw for just under 2,000 yards and 13 touchdowns, including a MAC Player of the Week performance vs. Central Michigan (303 yards), as the Cardinals ended the conference season at 4–1 and tied for the lead in the West Division. Add to those two team leaders the brawny block of fullback Scott Volk and the triumvirate was complete.

BEST DEFENSE The 1978 Cardinals team was defined by its stifling defense. Spearheaded by MAC

FIGHT SONG

FIGHT, TEAM, FIGHT
Fight, team, fight for Ball State;
We must win this game.
Onward, now you Cardinals,
Bring glory to your name!
Rah! Rah! Rah!
Here's to both your colors—
Cardinal and white,
Praying for a victory—
So, FIGHT! FIGHT! FIGHT!

HIGHEST DRAFT CHOICE

| 1976 | Shafer Suggs, Jets (2nd/33) |

CONSENSUS ALL-AMERICANS

1967	Oscar Lubke, OT
1968	Amos Van Pelt, HB
1972	Douglas Bell, C
1973	Terry Schmidt, DB
1995-96	Brad Maynard, P

Defensive Player of the Year and future Kansas City Chief Ken Kremer, Ball State's defense dominated its opponents, shutting out four teams and never allowing more than 17 points in the 10-win season. Supporting Kremer on defense were five other All-MAC selections: Larry Williams, Al Rzepka, Bill Pindras, Bill Stahl, and the aptly named defensive tackle Rush Brown.

> *"Stand in front of a mirror and recite 'I am a fighting Cardinal, the fiercest robin-size bird in the world.'"*
> *—David Letterman*

BIGGEST GAME Bill Lynch's 1996 team started the season with two quick losses, to Kansas and Miami (Ohio), and the chances for turning things around looked pretty slim. Traveling to Minnesota to take on a Big Ten foe that one year earlier had routed the Cardinals 31-7 meant a likely 0–3 start. That much, in fact, was true. Minnesota defeated Ball State 26-23, but the Cardinals' performance that day did turn the season around. Ball State senior punter Brad Maynard kicked five times for a 52.6-yard average, an accomplishment that made him MAC Defensive Player of the Week and helped the Cardinals to a late lead, but with 15 seconds left, the Gophers won on an 18-yard touchdown pass. It may seem strange for a three-point loss to stand as the biggest game in school's history, but hanging with Minnesota launched Ball State into one of the greatest comeback seasons in MAC history. Beginning with Central Florida and ending with Toledo, Ball State ran off eight consecutive victories to capture its fifth league title before losing an 18-15 heartbreaker to Nevada in the Las Vegas Bowl. Never one to let the scoreboard stand in the way of recognizing a great team performance, Lynch said after the Minnesota game: "We did things to put ourselves in position to win. All we preach to them is to play hard with great effort; that's how you're supposed to play the game."

BIGGEST UPSET In 1997, the Cardinals looked dismal after seven games. Their only victory had been against Division I-AA James Madison, and the season seemed completely lost. Ball State stormed back, though, and won its final four games, including a 35-3 rout over No.18 Toledo in the season finale.

HEARTBREAKER For the next-to-last game of the 2001 season, Ball State traveled to Northern Illinois needing a victory to clinch the MAC West division and the right to play Marshall for the conference championship. The Cardinals held a 29-26 lead with three minutes left until Huskies quarterback Chris Finlen ran one in from 13 yards out, giving the game to Northern Illinois 33-29. Ball State, Northern Illinois, and Toledo ended in a first-place tie for the West. The tiebreaker sent Toledo, a team Ball State had earlier defeated, to the MAC championship game.

STADIUM In 1967, the Cardinals moved into Ball State Stadium (renamed in 2005 after former player John Scheumann), and they have played there ever since. After several upgrades in the 1990s and another in 2000, the stadium expanded to its current capacity of 22,500. In 1997, the school topped the 100,000 mark in total home attendance for the only time in its history. The school added permanent lights prior to the 2004 season opener. A student journalist recently suggested nicknaming the stadium The Nest.

RIVAL Ball State considers Miami (Ohio) its greatest rival, but Miami probably has more enmity toward Cincinnati. Ball State and Miami first met in 1931 but did not play each other consistently until Ball State joined the MAC in 1975. Ball State trails in the series 8–15–1. The Cardinals ended Miami's three-year, 16-game MAC winning streak when they beat the Redskins 23-6 on Sept. 18, 1976.

NICKNAME As might be expected, Ball State's original nickname, Hoosieroons, was not especially popular around campus. In 1927, the student newspaper *The Easterner* sponsored a contest to select a new name. On the line was $5 in gold and the school's reputation. Professor Paul Billy Williams, a loyal fan of the St. Louis Cardinals baseball team, expressed his admiration for the logo on Rogers Hornsby's sweatshirt and submitted the name. After a student vote on the issue, Ball State became the Cardinals, and Williams collected the prize. In 1989, another nationwide contest was held, this time to update the caricature of a running cardinal that served as the school logo. Inflation drove the prize to $2,000 but not in gold. Alumnus William Villarreal collected it for his drawing of a cardinal that displayed, in his words, "an attitude of strength, challenge, and intelligence."

MASCOT Charlie Cardinal has served as the official mascot for Ball State since 1969. Originally, students representing Charlie wore a papier-mâché, feathered, smiling head. Since then, Charlie's outfit has grown into a giant cardinal with a fiercer visage softened by an altogether fluffier composition.

UNIFORMS Perhaps not surprisingly, the school's colors are cardinal red and white. At home, the team

sports red jerseys with white numbers and red pants, both without stripes. On the road, the players don all-white outfits with red numbers. In 1971, having employed a red helmet design for much of the previous 25 years, Ball State switched to a white helmet with a red cardinal logo inspired by the St. Louis (now Arizona) Cardinals.

LORE It is doubtful that Ball State football will produce a player or event to match the national recognition of the Top Ten list or Garfield the cat, creations of Ball State alumni David Letterman and Jim Davis, respectively.

NUMBERS Maynard holds just about every punting record in Ball State history. For his career, he punted 242 times for 10,702 yards (including two 500-yard games) for a 44.2-yard average. As a professional, Maynard set a Super Bowl record with 11 punts for the New York Giants in 2001.

QUOTE "I want you to stand in front of a mirror and recite 'I am a fighting Cardinal, the fiercest robin-size bird in all the world.'" —David Letterman, referring to his alma mater on a 2000 episode of *The Late Show With David Letterman*

MAC TEAMS

BALL STATE ALL-TIME SCORES

WIN/LOSS PERCENTAGE SINCE 1936

PAUL (BILLY) WILLIAMS
1924-25, '29 (.188)   3-13

1924   1-3-0
O18		at Indiana State	0	47
O31		at Indianapolis	2	13
N7	●	Central Normal	9	6
N22		at Earlham	0	21

1925   2-5-0
O2		at Wabash	0	67
O16		at Central Normal	0	12
O20		Indianapolis	0	6
O30	●	at Manchester	13	7
N6		Indiana State	7	20
N13	●	Merom	32	0
N20		Earlham	6	20

NORMAN WANN
1926-27 (.733)   10-3-2

1926   5-1-1
O2		at Wabash	0	46
O15	●	Indianapolis	35	0
O20	●	Manchester	19	3
O29	=	Central Normal	0	0
N6	●	at Oakland City	54	7
N13	●	Hanover	13	0
N30	●	at Earlham	6	0

1927   5-2-1
S24		at Butler	12	46
O7	●	Franklin	13	0
O14		Central Normal	0	18
O22	=	at Indianapolis	12	12
O29	●	Oakland City	32	7
N5	●	Cedarville	43	0
N12	●	at Hanover	12	6
N19	●	Defiance	27	19

PAUL B. PARKER
1928 (.571)   3-2-2

1928   3-2-2
S29	●	Concordia	52	0
O6	=	at Franklin	6	6
O13	=	Indianapolis	6	6
O27	●	Central Normal	12	7
N3		at Butler	6	12
N10	●	Hanover	6	0
N17		at DePauw	0	19

PAUL (BILLY) WILLIAMS

1929   0-5-0
S28		Indianapolis	0	7
O5		at Western Kentucky	0	13
O12		Franklin	6	12
O18		at Central Normal	12	14
N16		at DePauw	6	46

LAWRENCE McPHEE
1930-34 (.397)   15-23-1

1930   6-1-0
S27	●	Valparaiso	14	0
O11	●	Oakland City	34	6
O17	●	at Central Normal	21	0
O24	●	at Wabash	14	12
N1		at Manchester	7	13
N8	●	at Franklin	20	0
N15	●	Indianapolis	20	7

1931   2-6-0
S25	●	Central Normal	12	0
O3		at Miami, Ohio	6	47	*
O9		at Butler	0	34
O17		at Wabash	0	21
O23		Manchester	6	14
O31	●	Earlham	22	6
N6		at Indiana State	7	13
N14		Franklin	12	26

1932   4-4-0
S23		at Butler	12	13
O1	●	at Earlham	26	12
O7	●	Central Normal	18	0
O14	●	Oakland City	34	12
O22		at Franklin	0	13
O29		at Manchester	0	20
N5		Valparaiso	0	20
N12	●	Indiana State	12	0

1933   1-6-1
S29		at Butler	2	19
O7		at DePauw	0	9
O13	●	Central Normal	6	0
O20		Valparaiso	0	20
O28		Manchester	0	7
N4		at Indiana State	6	9
N11	=	Franklin	6	6
N18		at Hanover	0	20

1934   2-6-0
S28		Butler	4	13
O5	●	at Central Normal	20	0
O13		DePauw	0	13
O18		at Franklin	0	6
O27		at Valparaiso	13	30
N3		at Manchester	0	13
N10	●	Indiana State	15	6
N17		Hanover	6	19

JOHN MAGNABOSCO
1935-52 (.586)   68-46-14

1935   3-4-1
S28	●	Franklin	7	0
O4	●	Central Normal	13	0
O12		Valparaiso	6	20
O19		at DePauw	7	14
O26	●	Oakland City	25	0
N2		at Indiana State	6	12
N9	=	Manchester	0	0
N16		at Hanover	13	20

1936   3-4-1
S26		at Eastern Michigan	0	6
O3		Central Normal	6	25
O10	●	at Franklin	12	0
O17		Indiana State	0	3
O24	●	Oakland City	40	0
O31		DePauw	0	0
N7		at Manchester	13	21
N14	●	Hanover	7	0

1937   5-2-1
S25		Eastern Michigan	6	13
O2	●	Oakland City	52	0
O9	●	Central Normal	26	0
O16		at DePauw	0	13
O23	●	at Hanover	12	0
O30	●	Manchester	26	6
N6	●	at Indiana State	7	0
N13	=	Franklin	6	6

1938   6-1-1
S24		at Butler	6	12
O1	●	at Central Normal	26	0
O8	●	Indiana State	13	9
O15	●	at Manchester	20	14
O22	=	St. Joseph's	13	13
O29	●	at Valparaiso	13	0
N5	●	Hanover	19	0
N12	●	Earlham	21	0

1939   6-2-0
S23	●	at Butler	0	16
S30	●	Grand Rapids	27	6
O7	●	St. Joseph's	6	0
O21	●	at Indiana State	29	6
O27		at Central Michigan	0	7
N4	●	at Earlham	14	13
N11	●	Valparaiso	16	7
N18	●	Manchester	20	14

1940   3-4-1
S21	=	at Miami, Ohio	0	0
S28	●	DeSales	12	0
O5		Central Michigan	0	7
O19		at Manchester	6	7
O26	●	at Valparaiso	26	0
N2	●	Central Normal	27	2
N9		at Butler	0	26
N16		Indiana State	7	27

1941   3-2-2
O4	=	at Northern Illinois	6	6
O10		at Butler	6	13
O18		Central Michigan	6	7
O25	●	at Valparaiso	40	0
N1	=	Manchester	0	0
N8	●	Central Normal	33	0
N15	●	at Indiana State	7	0

1942   6-2-0
S19	●	Franklin	38	0
S26	●	Central Normal	34	0
O10	●	Bowling Green	14	26
O17	●	at Northern Illinois	14	0
O24		at Central Michigan	13	19
O31	●	at Manchester	28	6
N7	●	Valparaiso	21	0
N14	●	Indiana State	16	7

1943
NO TEAM

1944   2-2-0
O14		Central Normal	6	13
O21	●	Franklin	19	6
N4		at Central Normal	6	25
N11	●	Earlham	27	7

1945   4-1-1
S29	●	Central Normal	28	6
O6	●	Franklin	29	6
O13	=	at Wabash	0	0
O20		Valparaiso	6	7
O27	●	at Earlham	40	6
N3	●	Butler	16	2

1946   3-4-1
S28	●	Central Normal	27	6
O5		at Bowling Green	0	13
O12		Wabash	0	6
O19	●	at Valparaiso	20	6
O26		at Butler	6	20
N2	●	Manchester	41	6
N9	=	Eastern Michigan	7	7
N16		at Indiana State	0	3

1947   5-1-2
S27	=	at Butler	6	6
O4	●	Eastern Illinois	21	13
O11	●	Valparaiso	18	14
O18	●	St. Joseph's	6	6
O23	●	at Anderson	9	0
N1	●	at Manchester	19	0
N6		at Eastern Michigan	7	14
N15	●	Indiana State	14	0

1948   6-2-0
S25		at St. Joseph's	0	33
O2		at Eastern Illinois	0	12
O9	●	Huntington	53	0
O16	●	Eastern Michigan	23	14
O23	●	Anderson	14	7
O30	●	at Valparaiso	20	0
N6	●	Manchester	35	0
N13	●	at Indiana State	10	7

1949   8-0-0
S24	●	St. Joseph's	28	14
O1	●	at DePauw	33	13
O8	●	Anderson	35	0
O15	●	at Eastern Michigan	33	2
O29	●	Valparaiso	16	6
N5	●	at Manchester	50	7
N12	●	Indiana State	34	6
N19	●	Eastern Illinois	47	13

1950   2-4-1
S23		at Eastern Illinois	6	35
O7	●	DePauw	27	13
O14		Butler	7	33
O21		Eastern Michigan	0	13
O28		at Valparaiso	7	21
N4	=	at St. Joseph's	7	7
N11	●	Indiana State	27	7

1951   0-6-1
S22		Evansville	21	35
S29		at Wabash	19	34
O6		at DePauw	7	14
O13		at Butler	14	20
O20	=	Indiana State	0	0
O26		Valparaiso	12	34
N3		St. Joseph's	21	39

1952   3-5-1
S20	=	at Hanover	7	7
S27		at Eastern Michigan	14	26
O4		DePauw	25	40
O11		Butler	6	28
O18	●	at Indiana State	33	0
O25		at Valparaiso	13	14
N1	●	at St. Joseph's	21	6
N8	●	Wabash	19	39
N15	●	at Evansville	26	7

GEORGE SERDULA
1953-55 (.604)   14-9-1

1953   5-2-1
S19	=	Hanover	13	13
S26	●	Millikin	19	13
O3	●	at DePauw	28	7
O10		at Butler	7	25
O17	●	Indiana State	33	6
* O22	●	Valparaiso *UNK*	7	27
O31	●	at St. Joseph's	14	6
N7	●	Evansville	42	28

1954   6-2-0
S18	●	at Hanover	40	6
S25	●	at Millikin	27	7
O2	●	DePauw	40	14
O9	●	Butler	26	13
O16		at Indiana State	13	14
O23	●	at Valparaiso	21	46
O30	●	St. Joseph's	26	6
N6	●	at Evansville	25	7

1955   3-5-0
S17	●	Hanover	39	0
S24	●	Indiana, (Pa.)	13	7
O1		at DePauw	6	19
O8		at Butler	13	20
O15	●	Indiana State	19	6
O22		Valparaiso	7	26
O29		at St. Joseph's	0	28
N5		Evansville	0	38

JIM FREEMAN — 1956-61 (.396) — 18-28-2

1956 4-4-0
S15	•	Hanover	12 7
S22	•	at Indiana, (Pa.)	26 0
O6	•	DePauw	19 6
O13		Butler	12 28
O20	•	at Indiana State	28 14
O27	•	at Valparaiso	12 49
N3		St. Joseph's	0 66
N10		at Evansville	7 33

1957 2-5-1
S14		at Hanover	6 34
S21		Illinois State	12 14
S28	=	Valparaiso	26 26
O12	•	at Evansville	27 13
O19		DePauw	14 40
O26		at Butler	7 27
N2		St. Joseph's	7 55
N9		at Indiana State	20 0

1958 6-2-0
S20	•	at Illinois State	31 14
S27		at Valparaiso	0 6
O4	•	Wooster	14 6
O11	•	Evansville	35 16
O18	•	at DePauw	20 6
O25	•	Butler	14 7
N1		at St. Joseph's	0 6
N8	•	Indiana State	26 8

1959 1-7-0
S19	•	Illinois State	6 22
S26	•	Valparaiso	6 24
O3		at Eastern Illinois	8 14
O10	•	at Evansville	0 10
O17	•	DePauw	30 24
O24	•	at Butler	0 27
O31	•	St. Joseph's	8 22
N7	•	at Indiana State	8 29

1960 3-5-0
S17	•	at Illinois State	3 7
S24	•	Valparaiso UNK	8 10
O1	•	Eastern Illinois	14 6
O8	•	Evansville	7 10
O15	•	at DePauw	24 20
O22	•	Butler	0 27
O29	•	at St. Joseph's	23 7
N5	•	Indiana State	23 26

1961 2-5-1
S23	=	Eastern Michigan	0 0
S30	•	at Butler	6 48
O7		DePauw	8 10
O14	•	at St. Joseph's	8 0
O21	•	Indiana State	0 41
O28	•	at Valparaiso	20 28
N4	•	Evansville	6 3
N11	•	at Ohio Northern	20 49

RAY LOUTHEN — 1962-67 (.726) — 37-13-3

1962 4-3-1
S21	•	at Eastern Michigan	14 0
S29	=	Butler	28 28
O6		at DePauw	6 7
O13	•	St. Joseph's	15 0
O20	•	at Indiana State	0 22
O27		Valparaiso	6 21
N3	•	at Evansville	27 7
N10	•	Bradley	42 22

1963 5-3-0
S21	•	Eastern Michigan	22 6
S28		at Butler	0 13
O5	•	DePauw	15 6
O12	•	at St. Joseph's	23 0
O19	•	Indiana State	15 7
O26	•	at Valparaiso	40 48
N2	•	Evansville	27 7
N9	•	at Bradley	14 28

1964 5-3-0
S19	•	Slippery Rock	26 7
S26	•	Butler	8 14
O3	•	at DePauw	23 20
O10	•	St. Joseph's	38 7
O17		at Indiana State	0 17
O24	•	Valparaiso	22 33
O31	•	at Evansville	23 16
N7		Akron	15 25

1965 9-0-1
S18	•	Indiana, (Pa.)	26 14
S25	•	at Valparaiso	14 6
O2	•	Evansville	42 13
O9	•	at Akron	16 14
O16	•	at DePauw	51 29
O23	•	Butler	22 7
O30	•	at Indiana State	52 15
N6	•	St. Joseph's	42 19
N13	•	Southern Illinois	30 19

GRANTLAND RICE BOWL
D11	=	Tennessee State UNK	14 14

1966 7-1-1
S17	•	at Indiana, (Pa.)	20 7
S24	•	Valparaiso	20 7
O1	=	at Evansville	21 21
O8	•	Northern Illinois	24 38
O15	•	DePauw	30 15
O22	•	at Butler	17 14
O29	•	Indiana State	31 20
N5	•	at St. Joseph's	29 16
N12	•	at Southern Illinois	15 14

1967 7-3-0
S16	•	Central Missouri	41 7
S23	•	at Valparaiso	39 7
S30	•	Evansville	31 10
O7		at Northern Illinois	14 28
O14	•	at DePauw	7 3
O21	•	Butler	65 7
O28	•	at Indiana State	26 24
N4		St. Joseph's	2 7
N11	•	Southern Illinois	24 6

GRANTLAND RICE BOWL
D9		Eastern Kentucky	13 27

WAVE MYERS — 1968-70 (.517) — 15-14

1968 5-4-0
S14		Northern Illinois	20 40
S21		at Bowling Green	8 62
S28	•	Valparaiso	26 11
O5	•	at Evansville	26 3
O12		Eastern Michigan	7 43
O19	•	DePauw	17 12
O26	•	at Butler	24 21
N2		Indiana State	14 20
N9	•	at St. Joseph's	47 6

1969 5-5-0
S13	•	Buffalo	10 7
S20		Eastern Kentucky	0 13
S27	•	Butler	36 7
O4		at Akron	9 49
O11		Indiana State	0 26
O18	•	at Evansville	38 0
O25		at Northern Illinois	13 17
N1	•	Middle Tennessee	14 12
N8	•	at Southern Illinois	27 48
N15	•	Eastern Michigan	31 22

1970 5-5-0
S12	•	at Buffalo	14 7
S19	•	Eastern Kentucky	12 13
S26	•	at Butler	26 13
O3		Akron	0 31
O10	•	at Indiana State	28 26
O17	•	Evansville	21 14
O24	•	Northern Illinois	14 31
O31	•	at Middle Tennessee	7 14
N7	•	Southern Illinois	24 17
N14	•	at Eastern Michigan	0 60

DAVE McCLAIN — 1971-77 (.642) — 46-25-3

1971 4-5-1
S11	•	Central Michigan	9 6
S18	•	Western Michigan	0 9
S25	•	Butler	27 0
O2		at Akron	7 10
O9	•	Indiana State	20 17
O16	•	at Southern Illinois	8 33
O23	=	at Northern Illinois	10 10
O30		at Middle Tennessee	7 28
N6	•	Wittenberg	28 21
N13	•	at Western Illinois	20 21

1972 5-4-1
S16	•	Central Michigan	30 12
S23	•	at Butler	50 41
S30	=	Akron	21 21
O7	•	at Indiana State	21 10
O14	•	Dayton	28 7
O21		at Southern Illinois	7 13
O28	=	Middle Tennessee	24 0
N4		Western Illinois	17 21
N11	•	at Western Michigan	14 31
N18	•	at Illinois State	23 24

1973 5-5-1
S8	•	at Eastern Michigan	14 17
S15	•	at Central Michigan	7 14
S22	•	Butler	52 14
S29	•	at Akron	16 14
O6	•	Indiana State	18 17
O13	•	at Dayton	12 13
O20	•	at Northern Illinois	17 45
O27	•	Middle Tennessee	34 3
N3	=	Southern Illinois	16 16
N10	•	at Western Michigan	13 30
N17	•	Illinois State	27 18

1974 6-4-0
S14		Central Michigan	17 24
S21	•	at Butler	45 0
S28	•	Akron	21 26
O5		at Indiana State	22 31
O12	•	Richmond	38 23
O19	•	Youngstown State	21 14
O26	•	at Eastern Michigan	9 17
N2	•	at Middle Tennessee	43 14
N9	•	Northern Illinois	31 21
N16	•	at Illinois State	18 7

1975-Present — MAC

1975 9-2-0 (4-2-0)
S6	•	Eastern Michigan	24 14
S13	•	Toledo	38 28
S20	•	at Ohio U.	0 10
S27	•	at Miami, Ohio	28 35
O4	•	Indiana State	20 16
O11	•	at Richmond	25 14
O18	•	Central Michigan	16 13
O25	•	at Northern Illinois	3 0
N1	•	at Bowling Green	27 20
N8	•	at Akron	17 14
N15	•	Illinois State	46 7

1976 8-3-0 (4-1-0)
S11	•	Louisiana Tech	41 28
S18	•	at Miami, Ohio	23 6
S25	•	at Toledo	27 14
O2	•	at Dayton	20 13
O9	•	at Illinois State	7 10
O16	•	Akron	0 3
O23	•	Appalachian State	20 7
O30	•	at Northern Illinois	33 7
N6	•	Indiana State	24 9
N13	•	Western Michigan	10 24
N20	•	at Eastern Michigan	52 3

1977 9-2-0 (5-1-0)
S10	•	at Toledo	43 3
S17	•	at Villanova	16 38
S24	•	at Kent State	12 13
O1	•	Central Michigan	28 12
O8	•	Illinois State	27 16
O15	•	Northern Illinois	31 6
O22	•	Cal Poly Pomona	66 10
O29	•	at Appalachian State	38 7
N5	•	at Indiana State	42 18
N12	•	at Western Michigan	29 25
N19	•	Eastern Michigan	45 21

DWIGHT WALLACE — 1978-84 (.519) — 40-37

1978 10-1-0 (8-0-0)
S9	•	Miami, Ohio	38 14
S16	•	Kent State	27 3
S23	•	Toledo	20 0
S30	•	at Central Michigan	27 0
O7	•	Indiana St.	7 0
O14	•	at Louisiana Tech	7 17
O21	•	at Illinois St.	14 7
O28	•	at Eastern Michigan	21 0
N4	•	at Bowling Green	39 14
N11	•	Western Michigan	20 14
N18	•	at Northern Illinois	31 13

1979 6-5-0 (4-4-0)
S8	•	at Miami, Ohio	3 27
S15	•	at Toledo	14 31
S22	•	at Kent State	35 10
S29	•	S.E. La.	17 7
O6	•	at Indiana St.	13 18
O13	•	Illinois St.	42 14
O20		Central Michigan	30 31
O27	•	Bowling Green	38 23
N3	•	Eastern Michigan	28 10
N10	•	at Western Michigan	10 20
N17	•	Northern Illinois	42 0

1980 6-5-0 (5-4-0)
S6	•	at Central Michigan	17 21
S13	•	at Northern Illinois	18 17
S20	•	Toledo	27 7
S27	•	Miami, Ohio	9 42
O4	•	at McNeese State	7 24
O18	•	Eastern Michigan	26 0
O25	•	Western Michigan	15 17
N1	•	at Bowling Green	21 24
N8	•	Kent State	34 7
N15	•	Ohio U.	37 18
N22	•	Indiana St.	28 21

1981 4-7-0 (2-6-0)
S12	•	McNeese State	24 21
S19	•	at Toledo	0 40
S26	•	at Ohio U.	27 30
O3	•	Northern Illinois	23 0
O10	•	at Indiana St.	7 31
O17	•	Kent State	7 17
O24	•	at Western Michigan	3 14
O31	•	Eastern Michigan	35 13
N7	•	Bowling Green	10 14
N14	•	Central Michigan	7 28
N21	•	at Illinois St.	14 10

1982 5-6-0 (4-4-0)
S11	•	Toledo	14 31
S18	•	at Wichita St.	20 33
S25	•	Indiana St.	0 17
O2	•	at Northern Illinois	14 7
O9	•	Ohio U.	7 34
O16	•	at Kent State	21 3
O23	•	Western Michigan	13 6
O30	•	at Eastern Michigan	16 7
N6	•	at Bowling Green	7 28
N13	•	at Central Michigan	13 24
N20	•	Illinois St.	52 17

1983 6-5-0 (4-4-0)
S3	•	Rhode Island	42 26
S10	•	Wichita St.	25 21
S17	•	at Ohio U.	31 14
S24	•	at Toledo	7 43
O1	•	Northern Illinois	14 27
O8	•	at Indiana St.	14 35
O15	•	at Kent State	17 13
O22	•	at Western Michigan	24 20
O29	•	Eastern Michigan	33 20
N5	•	at Bowling Green	30 45
N12	•	Central Michigan	10 38

1984 3-8-0 (3-5-0)
S1		at Massachusetts	10 26
S8		Toledo	2 20
S15	•	Ohio U.	17 31
S22		at Washington State	14 16
S29	•	at Northern Illinois	15 14
O6		Indiana St. IND	6 34
O13		Kent State	10 15
O20		Western Michigan	23 20
O27		at Eastern Michigan	17 10
N3		Bowling Green	13 38
N10		at Central Michigan	7 51

PAUL SCHUDEL — 1985-94 (.554) — 60-48-4

1985 4-7-0 (3-6-0)
S7		Bowling Green	6 31
S14		Miami, Ohio	13 17
S21		at Purdue	18 37
S28	•	at Toledo	23 19
O5		Northern Illinois	29 0
O12	•	at Ohio U.	36 23
O19		at Kent State	16 45
O26		at Western Michigan	0 34
N2		Eastern Michigan	24 27
N9		Indiana St. IND	29 27
N16		Central Michigan	9 23

1986 6-5-0 (4-4-0)
A30	•	at Northern Illinois	20 10
S6	•	at Miami, Ohio	7 45
S13	•	at Purdue	3 20
S27	•	Toledo	27 10
O4	•	Indiana St. IND	16 3
O11		Ohio U.	30 9
O18		Kent State	26 17
O25		Western Michigan	24 10
N1		at Eastern Michigan	7 14
N8		at Bowling Green	17 20
N15		at Central Michigan	22 43

1987   4-7-0 (3-5-0)

S12		at Toledo	17 21
S19		Bowling Green	0 24
S26		at Wisconsin	13 30
O3		at Miami, Ohio	20 30
O10	●	Kent State	24 23
O17		at Eastern Michigan	28 35
O24	●	Central Michigan	13 3
O31	●	Northern Illinois	42 17
N7	●	at Western Michigan	16 31
N14	●	Ohio U.	30 17
N21		Indiana St. *IND*	23 24

1988   8-3-0 (5-3-0)

S3		Toledo	13 3
S10	●	at Bowling Green	34 10
S17	●	Massachusetts	44 17
O1	●	Miami, Ohio	45 14
O8	●	at Kent State	31 20
O15		Eastern Michigan	12 16
O22	●	at Central Michigan	27 20
O29	●	at Northern Illinois	18 17
N5		Western Michigan	13 16
N12		at Ohio U.	25 27
N17	●	Indiana St. *IND*	24 10

1989   7-3-2 (6-1-1)

S2		at West Virginia	10 35
S9	=	at Rutgers	31 31
S16	●	at Bowling Green	28 3
S23		at Toledo	22 29
S30	●	Miami, Ohio	37 9
O7	●	at Kent State	23 21
O14	●	Western Michigan	14 13
O21	●	Indiana St. *IND*	34 27
O26	=	Central Michigan	13 13
N4	●	Eastern Michigan	23 17
N11	●	at Ohio U.	33 14

CALIFORNIA BOWL

D9		Fresno State *FRE*	6 27

1990   7-4-0 (5-3-0)

S8	●	at Illinois St.	13 3
S15		at Wisconsin	7 24
S22		Toledo	16 28
S29	●	Bowling Green	16 6
O6		at Miami, Ohio	10 24
O13	●	Kent State	31 0
O20		at Western Michigan	13 14
O27	●	Indiana St.	42 0
N3	●	at Central Michigan	13 3
N10	●	at Eastern Michigan	20 13
N17	●	Ohio U.	23 6

1991   6-5-0 (4-4-0)

A31		at Miami, Ohio	7 15
S7		at Navy	33 10
S14		at TCU	16 22
S21	●	Kent State	28 27
S28	●	at Indiana St.	14 10
O5		Western Michigan	16 25
O12	●	at Eastern Michigan	10 8
O26		at Central Michigan	3 10
N2	●	Ohio U.	10 6
N9	●	at Toledo	9 3
N16		Bowling Green	13 14

1992   5-6-0 (5-4-0)

S5		at Clemson	10 24
S12		at Kansas	10 62
S19	●	at Kent State	10 6
S26	●	Miami, Ohio	19 9
O3		at Western Michigan	14 21
O10	●	Eastern Michigan	31 7
O17		Akron	14 22
O24	●	Central Michigan	24 23
O31	●	at Ohio U.	24 21
N7		Toledo	9 10
N14		at Bowling Green	6 38

1993   8-3-1 (7-0-1)

S4		at Syracuse	12 35
S11	●	Illinois St.	45 30
S18	●	at Ohio U.	24 16
O2	●	at Central Michigan	20 17
O9	●	Toledo	31 30
O16		at Cincinnati	12 44
O23	=	Bowling Green	26 26
O30	●	at Eastern Michigan	18 13
N6	●	Miami, Ohio	21 0
N13	●	at Akron	31 9
N20	●	Kent State	28 3

LAS VEGAS BOWL

D17		Utah State *LV*	33 42

1994   5-5-1 (5-3-1)

S3		at West Virginia	14 16
S17		at Purdue	21 49
S24	●	Ohio U.	21 14
O1		Central Michigan	31 28
O8	=	at Toledo	24 24
O15		Western Michigan	16 13
O22		at Bowling Green	36 59
O29		Eastern Michigan	20 41
N5		at Miami, Ohio	21 24
N12		Akron	38 28
N19		at Kent State	34 0

BILL LYNCH
1995-2002 (.411)   37-53

1995   7-4-0 (6-2-0)

A31	●	at Miami, Ohio	17 15
S9	●	Western Illinois	20 7
S16		at Minnesota	7 31
S23		Western Michigan	10 0
S30		at Purdue	13 35
O7		at Toledo	14 17
O14	●	Bowling Green	30 10
O21		Eastern Michigan	35 40
O28	●	at Ohio U.	6 3
N4	●	at Kent State	28 13
N11	●	Central Michigan	24 16

1996   8-4 (7-1)

A29		at Kansas	10 35
S7		Miami, Ohio	6 16
S14		at Minnesota	23 26
S21	●	Central Florida	31 10
O5	●	at Western Michigan	28 5
O12	●	Ohio U.	30 27
O19	●	at Bowling Green	16 11
O26	●	at Central Michigan	24 17
N2	●	at Eastern Michigan	39 25
N9	●	Kent State	50 6
N16		Toledo	24 14

LAS VEGAS BOWL

D19		Nevada *LV*	15 18

1997   5-6 (4-4)

A30		at Miami, Ohio	10 27
S6	●	James Madison	24 6
S13		at Indiana	6 33
S20		at Purdue	14 28
S27		Marshall	16 42
O4		at Western Michigan	13 21
O11		at Eastern Michigan	32 38
O18	●	Central Michigan	37 34
O25	●	at Northern Illinois	21 14
N1	●	Akron	31 14
N8	●	Toledo	35 3

1998   1-10 (1-7)

S5		at South Carolina	20 38
S12		Eastern Michigan	7 13
S19		at Iowa State	0 38
S26		at Akron	14 52
O3	●	Northern Illinois	18 13
O10		at Toledo	6 27
O17		Miami, Ohio	17 28
O24		at Marshall	10 42
N7		Western Michigan	23 24
N14		at Central Florida	14 37
N21		at Central Michigan	21 31

1999   0-11 (0-8)

S4		at Indiana	9 21
S11		at Wisconsin	10 50
S18		Toledo	10 23
S25		at Army	21 41
O2		Akron	9 31
O9		at Northern Illinois	17 37
O23		at Western Michigan	0 28
O30		Ohio U.	25 37
N6		at Eastern Michigan	21 31
N13		at Bowling Green	14 35
N20		Central Michigan	21 27

2000   5-6 (4-3)

S2		at Florida	19 40
S9		Western Ill.	14 24
S16		at Kansas State	0 76
S30		Northern Illinois	14 43
O7	●	at Miami, Ohio	15 10
O14	●	Eastern Michigan	33 14
O21	●	at Buffalo	44 35
O28	●	at Central Michigan	38 34
N4		Western Michigan	3 42
N11	●	at Toledo	3 31
N18	●	Connecticut	29 0

2001   5-6 (4-3)

S1		at Auburn	0 30
S8		at Kentucky	20 28
S22		No. Iowa	39 42
S29		Miami, Ohio	20 28
O13	●	at Eastern Michigan	35 14
O20	●	Toledo	24 20
O27	●	at Connecticut	10 5
N3	●	Central Michigan	38 34
N10	●	Kent State	18 31
N17	●	at Northern Illinois	29 33
N24	●	at Western Michigan	35 31

2002   6-6 (4-4)

S7		at Missouri	6 41
S14	●	Indiana St.	23 21
S21		at Clemson	7 30
S28	●	at Connecticut	24 21
O5		Northern Illinois	29 41
O12		at Toledo	17 37
O19	●	Eastern Michigan	42 17
O26	●	at Bowling Green	20 38
N2	●	Western Michigan	17 7
N16	●	at Central Michigan	38 21
N23	●	Buffalo	41 21
N30	●	at Marshall	14 38

BRADY HOKE
2003-PRESENT (.341)   15-31

2003   4-8 (3-5)

A28	●	Indiana State	31 7
S6		Missouri	7 35
S13		at Pittsburgh	21 42
S20		Central Michigan	27 14
S27		at Boston College	29 53
O4	●	at Kent State	34 17
O18		Miami, Ohio	3 49
O25	●	Toledo	38 14
N1		at Northern Illinois	23 48
N8		at Western Michigan	20 28
N15		at Eastern Michigan	14 38
N22		Bowling Green	14 41

2004   2-9 (2-6)

S2		Boston College	11 19
S11		at Purdue	7 59
S18		at Missouri	0 48
S25	●	Western Michigan	41 14
O2		at Toledo	14 52
O9		Eastern Michigan	24 31
O16		at Bowling Green	13 51
O23		at Akron	23 35
O30		Northern Illinois	31 38
N13	●	Central Florida	21 17
N20		at Central Michigan	40 41

2005   4-7 (4-4)

S3		at Iowa	0 56
S10		Bowling Green	31 40
S17		at Auburn	3 63
O1		at Boston College	0 38
O8	●	at Western Michigan	60 57
O15		Toledo	14 34
O22		at Ohio U.	21 38
O29		at Northern Illinois	31 17
N5	●	Akron	23 17
N12	●	at Eastern Michigan	26 25
N19		Central Michigan	24 31

2006   5-7 (5-3)

A31	●	Eastern Michigan	38 20
S9		Indiana	23 24
S16		at Purdue	28 38
S23		N. Dakota St.	24 29
S30		Northern Illinois	28 40
O7	●	at Buffalo	55 25
O14		at Central Michigan	7 18
O21		Western Michigan	27 41
O28	●	at Miami, Ohio	20 17
N4	●	at Michigan	26 34
N14	●	at Toledo	20 17
N24	●	Kent State	30 6

BALL STATE RECORD BOOK

SINGLE-GAME RECORDS

RUSHING YARDS

RANK	PLAYER	DATE	OPPONENT	ATT	AVG	YDS
1	Earl Taylor	Nov. 20, 1976	Eastern Michigan	34	7.6	260
2	Marcus Merriweather	Oct. 28, 2000	Central Michigan	42	6.1	257
3	Corey Croom	Sept. 26, 1992	Miami Ohio	39	6.2	242
4	Amos Van Pelt	Nov. 5, 1966	St. Joseph's	24	9.5	228
5	Marcus Merriweather	Nov. 23, 2002	Buffalo	37	6.1	227

PASSING YARDS

RANK	PLAYER	DATE	OPPONENT	ATT	COMP	YDS
1	Mike Neu	Oct. 9, 1993	Toledo	40	28	469
2	Neil Britt	Nov. 5, 1983	Bowling Green	49	30	437
3	Joey Lynch	Nov. 20, 2004	Central Michigan	34	22	397
4	Robert Adams	Sept. 29, 1984	Northern Illinois	45	31	359
5	Phil Donahue	Nov. 11, 1972	Western Michigan	39	24	350

RECEIVING YARDS

RANK	PLAYER	DATE	OPPONENT	REC	AVG	YDS
1	Brian Oliver	Oct. 9, 1993	Toledo	12	24.8	297
2	Dave Naumcheff	Nov. 5, 1983	Bowling Green	12	19.8	237
3	Vic Comparetto	Oct. 9, 1971	Indiana State	6	36.5	219
4	Dante Ridgeway	Sept. 25, 2004	Western Michigan	9	24.1	217
5	Dante Ridgeway	Nov. 20, 2004	Central Michigan	10	21.5	215

POINTS

RANK	PLAYER	DATE	OPPONENT	TOT
1	Tim Brown	Sept. 20, 1958	Illinois State	25
2	Michael Blair	Nov. 12, 1994	Akron	24
	Bernie Parmalee	Nov. 14, 1987	Ohio	24
	Rick Morrison	Nov. 19, 1977	Eastern Michigan	24
	Larry Hamell	Oct. 26, 1963	Valparaiso	24

FIELD GOALS

RANK	PLAYER	DATE	OPPONENT	TOT
1	John Diettrich	Nov. 9, 1985	Indiana State	5
2	Several players tied with 4			

TACKLES

RANK	PLAYER	DATE	OPPONENT	TOT
1	Kevin Johnson	Oct. 29, 1994	Eastern Michigan	29
	Kevin Johnson	Sept. 18, 1993	Ohio U	29
	Kevin Johnson	Nov. 13, 1993	Akron	29
4	Kevin Johnson	Nov. 5, 1994	Miami (Ohio)	25
	Greg Garnica	Nov. 1, 1986	Eastern Michigan	25

INTERCEPTIONS

RANK	PLAYER	DATE	OPPONENT	TOT
1	Greg Garnica	Oct. 7, 1989	Miami (Ohio)	3
	Mike Lecklider	Oct. 11, 1975	Richmond	3
	Bob Burkhardt	Sept. 17, 1966	Indiana, Pa.	3
	Doc Heath	Sept. 24, 1966	Valparaiso	3

RETIRED NUMBERS

Ball State has no retired numbers

SINGLE-SEASON RECORDS

RUSHING YARDS

RANK	PLAYER	SEASON	ATT	YDS
1	Marcus Merriweather	2002	332	1,618
2	Marcus Merriweather	2001	268	1,244
3	Tony Nibbs	1994	221	1,210
4	Corey Croom	1992	301	1,157
5	Dave Blake	1974	263	1,125

PASSING YARDS

RANK	PLAYER	SEASON	ATT	COMP	PCT	YDS
1	Neil Britt	1983	348	206	59.2	2,377
2	Mike Neu	1993	283	186	65.7	2,148
3	Joey Lynch	2005	314	198	63.0	1,982
4	Nate Davis	2006	245	150	61.2	1,975
5	Talmadge Hill	2001	301	159	52.8	1,953

RECEIVING YARDS

RANK	PLAYER	SEASON	REC	AVG	YDS
1	Dante Ridgeway	2004	105	13.3	1,399
2	Dante Ridgeway	2003	89	12.1	1,075
3	Dave Naumcheff	1983	65	16.4	1,065
4	Brian Oliver	1993	62	16.3	1,010
5	Rick Morrison	1977	59	15.4	908

SCORING

RANK	PLAYER	SEASON	TD	FG	PAT	P2	TOT
1	Mark Bornholdt	1979	19	0	0	0	114
2	Bernie Parmalee	1987	15	0	0	0	90
3	Brian Jackson	2006	0	17	37	0	88
4	John Diettrich	1985	0	25	12	0	87
5	3 players tied with 84						

TOUCHDOWNS

RANK	PLAYER	SEASON	TOT
1	Mark Bornholdt	1979	19
2	Bernie Parmalee	1987	15
3	Fred Kehoe	1949	14
4	Marcus Merriweather	2001	13
	Michael Blair	1994	13

TACKLES

RANK	PLAYER	SEASON	TOT
1	Kevin Johnson	1993	204
2	Kevin Johnson	1993	196
3	Greg Garnica	1987	188
4	Greg Garnica	1986	185
5	Mark Parris	1992	178

INTERCEPTIONS

RANK	PLAYER	SEASON	YDS	TOT
1	Shafer Suggs	1974	60	8
	Nickey Baker	1965	142	8
3	5 players tied with 7			

PUNTING

RANK	PLAYER	SEASON	PUNTS	YDS	AVG
1	Brad Maynard	1995	66	3,071	46.5
2	Chris Miller	2006	48	2,637	46.3
3	Brad Maynard	1996	59	2,705	45.8
4	Brad Maynard	1994	59	2,684	45.5
5	Chris Miller	2005	68	2,917	43.8

PUNT RETURNS

RANK	PLAYER	SEASON	RET	YDS	AVG
1	Keyon Laws	1996	10	189	18.9
2	John Walker	1963	12	216	18.0

KICKOFF RETURNS

RANK	PLAYER	SEASON	RET	YDS	AVG
1	Jim Todd	1965	9	287	31.9

CAREER RECORDS

RUSHING YARDS

RANK	PLAYER	SEASONS	ATT	AVG	TD	YDS
1	Marcus Merriweather	1999-2002	851	4.7	34	4,002
2	Bernie Parmalee	1987-90	805	4.3	26	3,483
3	LeAndre Moore	1995-98	655	4.7	16	3,080
4	Michael Blair	1993-96	668	4.6	31	3,051
5	Corey Croom	1989-92	722	3.8	17	2,725
6	Amos Van Pelt	1966-68	442	5.0	23	2,209
7	Tony Nibbs	1992-94	427	4.9	8	2,098
8	Terry Lymon	1980-83	414	4.9	6	2,013
9	Tony Schmid	1971-73	NA	NA	NA	2,000

PASSING YARDS

RANK	PLAYER	SEASONS	ATT	COMP	PCT	INT	TD	YDS
1	Mike Neu	1990-93	970	580	59.8	40	43	6,271
2	Talmadge Hill	2000-03	901	524	58.2	42	44	5,884
3	David Riley	1986-89	670	398	59.4	26	25	4,730
4	Wade Kosakowski	1985-87	691	407	58.9	29	21	4,550
5	Joey Lynch	2003-06	613	391	63.8	12	37	4,292
6	Brent Baldwin	1993-96	597	392	65.7	20	35	4,256
7	Dave Wilson	1976-79	486	280	57.6	23	36	4,099
8	Willard Rice	1968-70	550	298	54.2	34	25	3,868
9	Neil Britt	1981-85	588	336	57.1	42	16	3,830

RECEIVING YARDS

RANK	PLAYER	SEASONS	REC	AVG	TD	YDS
1	Dante Ridgeway	2002-04	238	12.7	22	3,030
2	Deon Chester	1984-87	146	15.5	3	2,256
3	Brian Oliver	1991-94	138	15.3	24	2,111
4	Stevie Nelson	1979-82	120	15.6	9	1,874
5	Adrian Reese	1996-99	131	15.6	14	1,777
6	Rick Morrison	1976-78	NA	NA	12	1,736
7	Ricky George	1983-86	124	13.3	10	1,654
8	Mike LeSure	1989-92	108	13.3	6	1,439
9	Mike Andress	1974-77	NA	NA	15	1,436

SCORING

RANK	PLAYER	SEASONS	TD	FG	PAT	P2	TOT
1	Kenny Stucker	1988-91	0	62	93	0	279
2	Brian Jackson	2003-06	0	49	111	0	258
3	John Diettrich	1983-86	0	63	64	0	253
4	Michael Blair	1993-96	31	0	0	18	222
5	Brent Lockliear	1994-97	0	38	103	0	217

TOUCHDOWNS

RANK	PLAYER	SEASONS	TOT
1	Michael Blair	1993-96	37
2	Marcus Merriweather	1999-2001	35
3	Mark Bornholdt	1978-81	31
4	Bernie Parmalee	1987-90	29
5	Fred Kehoe	1946-49	26

TACKLES

RANK	PLAYER	SEASONS	TOT
1	Greg Garnica	1986-89	689

INTERCEPTIONS

RANK	PLAYER	SEASONS	YDS	TOT
1	Shafer Suggs	1972-75	NA	14
	Mike Lecklider	1974-76	148	14
3	Terry Schmidt	1971-73	150	13
4	Kevin Young	1983-85	131	12

PUNTING

RANK	PLAYER	SEASONS	PUNTS	YDS	AVG
1	Brad Maynard	1993-96	242	10,696	44.2
2	Jack Morse	1969-70	130	5,239	40.3
3	Reggie Hodges	2000-04	254	10,211	40.2

PUNT RETURNS

RANK	PLAYER	SEASON	RET	YDS	AVG
1	Juan Gorman	1992-94	26	395	15.2
2	Herb Jackson	1987-89	27	391	14.5

KICKOFF RETURNS

RANK	PLAYER	SEASON	RET	YDS	AVG
1	Stevie Nelson	1979-1982	58	1,440	24.8

TEAM RECORDS

LONGEST WINNING STREAK
• 14, Oct. 9, 1948-Nov. 19, 1949
Streak broken vs. Eastern Illinois, 6-35, Sept. 23, 1950

LONGEST UNDEFEATED STREAK
• 14, Oct. 9, 1948-Nov. 19, 1949
Streak broken vs. Eastern Illinois, 6-35, Sept. 23, 1950

MOST CONSECUTIVE WINNING SEASONS
• 7 (tie), 1962-68 and 1974-1980

MOST CONSECUTIVE BOWL APPEARANCES
• 1 (tie), 1965; 1967; 1989; 1993; 1996

MOST POINTS IN A GAME
• 66, vs. Cal Poly-Pomona, Oct. 22, 1977

MOST POINTS ALLOWED IN A GAME
• 76, vs. Kansas State, Sept. 16, 2000

LARGEST MARGIN OF VICTORY
• 58 (65-7), vs. Butler, Oct. 21, 1967

LARGEST MARGIN OF DEFEAT
• 76 (0-76), at Kansas State, Sept. 16, 2000

LONGEST RUN FROM SCRIMMAGE
• 85 yards, LeAndre Moore, vs. James Madison, Sept. 6, 1997

LONGEST PASS PLAY
• 98 yards, Mike Neu to Brian Oliver, vs. Toledo, Oct. 9, 1993

LONGEST FIELD GOAL
• 62 yards, John Diettrich, vs. Ohio, Oct. 11, 1986

LONGEST PUNT
• 78 yards (tie), Mark O'Connell, vs. Toledo, Sept. 20, 1980; Phillip Ems, vs. Kent, Oct. 4, 2003; Chris Miller, vs. North Dakota State, Sept. 23, 2006

LONGEST PUNT RETURN
• 95 yards, Bill Hajec, vs. Indiana State, Oct. 30, 1965

LONGEST INTERCEPTION RETURN
• 95 yards, Phil Faris, vs. Butler, Oct. 21, 1967

BALL STATE ANNUAL STATISTICAL LEADERS

YR	RUSHING	YDS	ATT	AVG	PASSING	ATT	CMP	PCT	YDS	RECEIVING	REC	YDS	AVG
1957	Tim Brown	419	42	10.0	Ed Corazzi	92	39	.42	884	Nat Pittman	10	255	25.5
1958	Tim Brown	551	112	4.9	Ed Corazzi	56	29	.52	557	Tim Brown	10	213	21.3
1959	Dave Hooten	285	76	3.8	Ed Corazzi	78	37	.47	527	Nat Pittman	13	247	19.0
1960	Joe Robinson	324	79	4.1	Phil Sullivan	90	35	.39	495	Roger Zabik	8	109	13.6
1961	Joe Burvan	278	54	5.1	Phil Sullivan	69	20	.29	269	Larry Hamell	9	145	16.1
1962	John Walker	631	110	5.7	Terry Bonta	27	13	.48	163	John Walker	6	90	15.0
1963	Merv Rettenmund	635	83	7.7	Marv Rettenmund	29	12	.41	190	Larry Hamell	9	146	16.2
1964	Jim Todd	672	98	6.9	Frank Houk	47	28	.60	283	Jim Todd	11	111	10.1
1965	Jim Todd	850	128	6.6	Frank Houk	62	30	.48	563	Steve Demuth	8	203	25.3
1966	Amos VanPelt	744	150	5.0	Frank Houk	138	74	.54	1,122	Tim Hostrawser	18	282	15.6
1967	Amos VanPelt	894	148	6.0	Doc Heath	74	31	.42	467	Tim Hostrawser	7	125	17.9
1968	Amos VanPelt	571	144	4.0	Willard Rice	209	124	.59	1,592	Ed Alley	38	528	13.9
1969	Dave Means	468	128	3.7	Willard Rice	223	117	.53	1,408	Phil Faris	27	431	16.0
1970	Dave Means	510	116	4.4	Phil Donahue	164	63	.38	868	Willie Lenzy	31	470	15.2
1971	Tony Schmid	666	129	5.2	Phil Donahue	97	39	.40	605	Vic Comparetto	20	381	19.1
1972	Tony Schmid	661	126	5.2	Phil Donahue	188	91	.48	1,481	Kevin Canfield	41	588	14.3
1973	Tony Schmid	673	152	4.4	Rick Scott	115	65	.57	858	Kevin Canfield	38	534	14.1
1974	Dave Blake	1,125	263	4.3	Rick Scott	88	45	.51	816	Rick Clark	33	643	19.5
1975	Earl Taylor	901	178	5.1	Art Yaroch	121	50	.41	720	Mike Andress	23	480	20.9
1976	Earl Taylor	1,017	203	5.0	Art Yaroch	157	78	.50	1,088	Rick Morrison	36	420	11.7
1977	George Jenkins	1,070	208	5.1	Dave Wilson	177	115	.65	1,589	Rick Morrison	59	908	15.4
1978	Archie Currin	735	161	4.6	Dave Wilson	143	75	.52	1,037	Tim Clary	26	362	13.9
1979	Mark Warlaumont	713	140	5.1	Dave Wilson	160	87	.54	1,452	Tim Clary	30	468	15.6
1980	Ken Currin	548	134	4.1	Mark O'Connell	295	175	.59	1,921	Stevie Nelson	38	487	12.8
1981	Terry Lymon	633	130	4.9	Doug Freed	256	137	.54	1,517	Stevie Nelson	37	635	17.2
1982	Terry Lymon	635	134	4.7	Doug Freed	182	85	.47	989	Stevie Nelson	25	265	10.6
1983	Terry Lymon	517	96	5.4	Neil Britt	348	206	.59	2,377	Mike Leuck	67	667	10.0
1984	Burt Austin	551	144	3.8	Neil Britt	189	107	.57	1,205	Mike Leuck	48	410	8.5
1985	Carlton Campbell	747	204	3.7	Wade Kosakowski	242	140	.58	1,614	Deon Chester	45	617	13.7
1986	Carlton Campbell	688	167	4.1	Wade Kosakowski	212	137	.65	1,459	Ricky George	55	569	10.3
1987	Bernie Parmalee	1,064	215	4.9	Wade Kosakowski	237	130	.55	1,477	Deon Chester	50	838	16.8
1988	Mark Stevens	774	185	4.2	David Riley	263	168	.64	1,886	Eugene Riley	41	457	11.1
1989	Bernie Parmalee	672	181	3.7	David Riley	256	149	.58	1,929	Sean Jones	30	518	17.3
1990	Bernie Parmalee	1,010	240	4.2	Mike Neu	180	91	.51	1,004	Bernie Parmalee	30	185	6.2
1991	Corey Croom	1,053	291	3.6	Mike Neu	225	141	.63	1,491	Mike LeSure	49	629	12.8
1992	Corey Croom	1,157	301	3.8	Mike Neu	282	162	.57	1,628	Brian Uliver	37	423	11.4
1993	Tony Nibbs	777	172	4.5	Mike Neu	283	186	.66	2,148	Brian Oliver	62	1,010	16.3
1994	Tony Nibbs	1,210	221	5.5	Brent Baldwin	188	100	.53	1,342	Juan Gorman	49	662	13.5
1995	Michael Blair	819	218	3.8	Brent Baldwin	202	119	.59	1,192	Ed Abernathy	31	288	9.3
1996	Michael Blair	680	147	4.6	Brent Baldwin	205	121	.59	1,703	Ed Abernathy	29	425	14.7
1997	LeAndre Moore	884	173	5.1	Jake Josetti	217	106	.49	1,569	Adrian Reese	30	526	17.5
1998	LeAndre Moore	909	217	4.2	Clay Walters	172	88	.51	969	Adrian Reese	27	341	12.6
1999	Nick Dunbar	590	163	3.6	Brian Conn	257	150	.58	1,525	Adrian Reese	58	664	11.4
2000	Marcus Merriweather	1,004	225	4.5	Talmadge Hill	212	130	.61	1,455	Sean Schembra	40	484	12.1
2001	Marcus Merriweather	1,244	268	4.6	Talmadge Hill	301	159	.53	1,953	Billy Lynch	40	419	10.5
2002	Marcus Merriweather	1,618	332	4.9	Andy Roesch	202	113	.56	1,341	Dante Ridgeway	44	556	12.6
2003	Scott Blair	640	137	4.4	Talmadge Hill	253	154	.61	1,691	Dante Ridgeway	89	1,075	12.1
2004	Adell Givens	963	202	4.8	Cole Stinson	179	91	.51	1,101	Dante Ridgeway	105	1,399	13.3
2005	Charles Wynn	533	127	4.2	Joey Lynch	314	198	.63	1,982	Terry Moss	36	420	11.7
2006	Larry Bostic	545	146	3.7	Nate Davis	245	150	.61	1,975	Dante Love	52	735	14.1

Receiving leaders by receptions
NCAA began including postseason stats in 2002

MAC TEAMS

BOWLING GREEN

BY ED KRZEMIENSKI

Bowling green, a name that evokes a proper English estate, competes only with Slippery Rock for the most picturesque moniker in college football. But don't be fooled: the Falcons are no strangers to winning. Coach Doyt Perry introduced the concept in the 1950s, Bob Gibson and Don Nehlen extended the winning ways through the mid-1970s, Denny Stolz reintroduced the art of the win in the first half of the 1980s, and Gary Blackney did the same at the beginning of the 1990s. Seventeen times since 1948 the Falcons have finished the season with no more than two losses. Such a strong gridiron history can be both scepter and burden. After six straight losing seasons, Bowling Green hired Urban Meyer as head coach in 2001. That seemed to do the trick, as the Falcons rebounded from a 2-9 season to go 8-3, Division I-A's top turnaround that year. Meyer left for Utah after the 2002 season, and won a national championship at Florida four years later. His successor, Gregg Brandon, kept the team "bowling" in each of his first two years, but hit harder times in the next two, including 2006's below-.500 performance, Bowling Green's first since 2000. If history is any indication, though, it should be a short stay below mediocrity. At Bowling Green, expectations are too high for that to persist.

TRADITION Bowling Green plays two award games. The Anniversary Award goes to the winner of the game between the Falcons and Kent State. Begun in 1985, the game commemorates the schools' shared founding date (1910). Nothing, though, compares to the Peace Pipe which goes to the winner of the Bowling Green-Toledo game. The game originated on the basketball court during the 1947-48 season and was later picked up on the football field in 1980. After the original Peace Pipe—a six-foot-long wooden pipe—disappeared, a new trophy was created with a smaller version of the pipe.

BEST PLAYER Brian McClure began his career as Bowling Green's quarterback in the third game of his freshman season, in 1982. Despite missing the last two regular-season games, McClure threw for more than 1,300 yards and was named MAC Freshman of the Year. But the best was still to come. In his sophomore season, McClure passed for 3,264 yards and was named MAC Offensive Player of the Year, the first of three consecutive years he

PROFILE

Bowling Green State University
Bowling Green, Ohio
Founded: 1910
Enrollment: 20,975
Colors: Orange and Brown
Nickname: Falcons
Stadium: Doyt L. Perry Stadium
   Opened in 1966
   FieldTurf; 28,599 capacity
First football game: 1919
All-time record: 469–311–52 (.595)
Bowl record: 4–3
Mid-American Conference championships:
10 (9 outright)
First-round draft choices: 1
Website: www.bgsufalcons.com

THE BEST OF TIMES

During the Doyt Perry era (1955-64), the Falcons had a 77–11–5 record, along with five MAC championships.

THE WORST OF TIMES

Moe Ankney inherited an 11–1 team in 1986. After five straight losing seasons, Ankney was replaced by Gary Blackney, whose first-year record in 1991 was ... 11–1.

CONFERENCE

Bowling Green joined the MAC in 1952 and has played there ever since. The Falcons also played in the Northwestern Ohio Intercollegiate Athletic Association from 1921 to 1931, in the Ohio Athletic Conference from 1933 to 1941, and as an independent from 1919 to 1920, in 1932, and from 1942 to 1951.

DISTINGUISHED ALUMNI

Tim Conway, comedian; Scott Hamilton, Olympic champion figure skater; Orel Hershiser, baseball player; Arnold Rampersad, author; Eva Marie Saint, Academy Award-winning actress; Nate Thurmond, Basketball Hall of Famer

Doyt Perry is not only the greatest football coach from Bowling Green, but also the most renowned person affiliated with the school's athletic program.

copped that award. McClure led the Falcons to an 11-0 regular season in his senior year before losing in the California Bowl. Overall, McClure led the Falcons to a 30-12 record, took them to two bowl games, and set virtually all the Bowling Green passing records and five NCAA marks. He threw for more than 300 yards in a game 12 times and, perhaps most impressive, became only the second collegiate quarterback, after Doug Flutie, to pass for more than 10,000 yards in his career, finishing with 10,280.

BEST COACH Perry stands as not only the greatest football coach from Bowling Green, but also as the most renowned person ever affiliated with the school's athletic program. Three decades after lettering nine times in three sports (1929 to 1931), Perry returned to Bowling Green to coach his alma mater. For the next 10 years, he led the football team to a 77-11-5 record that included two undefeated and five one-loss seasons, five MAC titles, and the 1959 College Division championship. Perry's .855

overall winning percentage ranks fifth on the all-time NCAA list. In 1964, Perry became Bowling Green's athletic director. In 1988, the National Football Foundation ushered Perry into the College Football Hall of Fame, making him, to date, the only full-time MAC representative as a coach to receive this honor.

BEST TEAM The 1959 Falcons went 9-0, outscored their opponents 274-83, and won the near-mythical College Division championship. Perry's team ended its perfect season with a 13-9 thriller at Ohio University. Besides the season-ending game, the 1959 Falcons won by an average score of 33-9. How they scored that many points is a mystery, considering that Bob Colburn led the team with 788 yards passing, Chuck Comer led with 361 yards rushing, and Bernie Casey paced Falcons receivers with 18 receptions. Colburn, Casey, end Ron Blackledge, and tackle Bob Zimpfer made the year's All-MAC team.

MAC TEAMS

FIGHT SONG

FORWARD FALCONS
(Played after a score)

Forward Falcons!
Forward Falcons!
Fight for victory,
Show our spirit,
Make them fear it,
Fight for ol' B-G.
Forward Falcons!
Forward Falcons!
Make the contest keen,
Hold up the fame
Of our mighty name
And win for Bowling Green!

AY ZIGGY ZOOMBA
(Played after a win)

Ay Ziggy Zoomba Zoomba Zoomba
Ay Ziggy Zoomba Zoomba Ze
Ay Ziggy Zoomba Zoomba Zoomba
Ay Ziggy Zoomba Zoomba Zi
Roll along, you B-G warriors
Roll along, and win for B-G-S-U.

FIRST-ROUND DRAFT CHOICE

1961	Bernie Casey, 49ers (9)	

CONSENSUS ALL-AMERICANS

1959	Bob Zimpfer, T	
1982	Andre Young, DL	

COLLEGE FOOTBALL HALL OF FAME INDUCTEES

NAME	YEARS	INDUCTED
Doyt Perry, COACH	1955-64	1988
Don Nehlen, COACH	1968-76	2005

BEST BACKFIELD In 2004, quarterback Omar Jacobs had a season for the ages, throwing for 4,002 yards, 41 touchdowns and only 7 interceptions. Jacobs' backfield mate was running back P.J. Pope, who ran for 1,098 yards and 15 touchdowns in the Falcons' 532-point offensive juggernaut. The two put an exclamation point on the end of the season at the GMAC Bowl. In a 52-35 win over Memphis, Pope ran for 151 yards and scored three touchdowns, while Jacobs threw for 365 yards and five touchdowns.

BEST DEFENSE The Falcons 1961 defense remains one of the best in MAC history. Ranked fourth in the nation during the regular season, Doyt Perry's defense gave up only 42 points, had three shutouts, and four six-point games, and gave up an average of 162.8 total yards per game. Ironically the season ended with a defensive collapse, when BG lost to Fresno State in the Mercy Bowl, 36-6.

BIGGEST GAME First-year head coach Blackney took his 10-1 Falcons to the 1991 California Bowl against Fresno State. In the same bowl game six years earlier, the Bulldogs had humiliated Bowling Green 51-7. Few gave the double-digit-underdog Falcons much of a chance. But the Falcons stunned Fresno State and won their first bowl game, 28-21, led by quarterback Erik White, who hooked up with receiver Mark Szlachcic a California Bowl-record 11 times. A year later, in the Las Vegas Bowl, Bowling Green repeated the feat when it upset Nevada. Ironically, the Falcons' only 1991 loss came in a 24-17 thriller against West Virginia, coached by former Falcons player and head coach Don Nehlen.

BIGGEST UPSET Most teams in the MAC would probably dread a trip to West Lafayette, Ind., to open Purdue's season. Bowling Green seems to relish it. In 1972, the Falcons upset Purdue 17-14. and in 2003 they beat the Boilermakers 27-26. On both occasions, Purdue was ranked in the Top 20.

HEARTBREAKER Powered by freshman phenom Brian McClure, Bowling Green played Fresno State in the 1982 California Bowl. With McClure passing for 246 yards and Chip Otten running for 136, the Falcons led the Bulldogs 28-7 at the beginning of the fourth quarter. But in the final quarter, Fresno State stormed back. With 11 seconds left, the Bulldogs scored their third touchdown of the period, added the extra point and snatched away a 29-28 victory.

STADIUM In 1966, Bowling Green replaced 43-year-old University Stadium with a new venue bearing a familiar name: Doyt L. Perry Stadium. The official capacity today is 28,599. Tell that to the more than 33,000 fans who packed the stadium for Bowling Green's game against Toledo in 1983.

RIVAL Bowling Green and Toledo first met in 1919 and haven't missed an annual game since 1948. On the line is the Peace Pipe Award, a counterpoint to the Nike-Ajax missile Toledo traditionally aims at the Bowling Green 50-yard line. Bowling Green leads the series 36-31-4 (through 2006). Seven of the top eight attendance records for Perry Stadium are for games against Toledo.

NICKNAME Until 1927, Bowling Green teams were called the Normals. After reading an article on falconry, alum Ivan "Doc" Lake suggested the team use Falcons as its nickname. Lake suggested the name because, as he reported in the *Bowling Green Sentinel-Tribune*, where he was a writer, falcons "often attacked birds two or three times their size." Also, the practical Lake noted, the name fit well into headlines.

MASCOT Frieda and Freddie Falcon, two giant, furry, earthbound falcons, serve as the official mascots of Bowling Green. Freddie was born in 1950 and finally got a date in 1966. Winners of the contest to embody the pair remain anonymous until the final home basketball and hockey game, when each is "beheaded" in front of the student body.

UNIFORMS The official colors at Bowling Green have been brown and burnt orange since 1914. In that year, Leon L. Winslow, a faculty member, got the idea for the combination from a woman's hat at a Toledo trolley station. Uniforms have tended toward the orange side of the combination, with brown highlights. Currently, jerseys are orange with white numbers; helmets are orange with the letters BG and a small falcon.

LORE Although Bowling Green will never be mistaken for a service academy, the school has an interesting relationship with the military on the football field. During World War II, the Falcons added several military-oriented schools to their schedule. In the three middle war years, the team played Miami Naval, Grosse Isle Navy, Patterson Field, and Bunker Hill Navy in addition to its regularly scheduled foes. Two decades later, during the Vietnam War, Bowling Green reprised its patriotism and played the Quantico Marines. The Falcons have a 4-2 record versus the military.

QUOTE "Ay Ziggy Zoomba Zoomba Zoomba!" —A loose translation of a Zulu war chant that Air Force bombardier Gilbert Fox brought back to Bowling Green after World War II; it serves as the school's unofficial fight song

BOWLING GREEN ALL-TIME SCORES

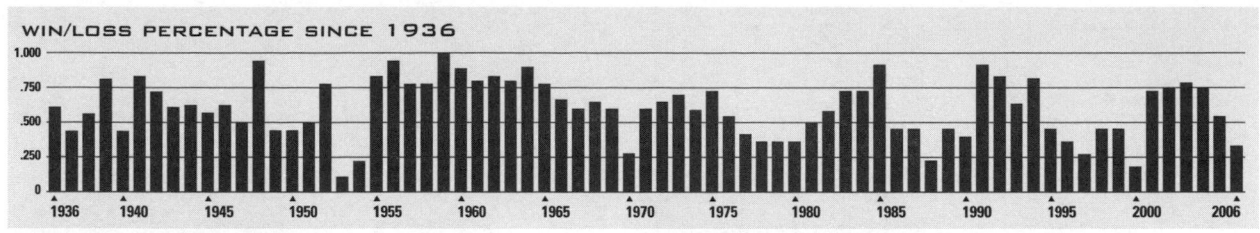

WIN/LOSS PERCENTAGE SINCE 1936

JOHN STITT
1919 (.000)   0-3

1919   0-3-0
O3		Toledo	0	6
O18		at Defiance	0	12
O23		Eastern Michigan	0	10

WALTER JEAN
1920 (.200)   1-4

1920   1-4-0
O5		at Findlay	6	10
O12		at Eastern Michigan	0	45 *
O16		Heidelberg	0	14
O23		Defiance	28	46
N6	●	at Kent State	7	0

EARL KRIEGER
1921 (.700)   3-1-1

1921   3-1-1
O1	=	Kent State	0	0
O7	●	at Defiance	7	0
O15	●	Findlay	151	0
O21		at Ashland	0	27
O29	●	at Toledo	20	7

ALLEN SNYDER
1922 (.643)   4-2-1

1922   4-2-1
S30		at Ohio Northern	0	27
O7		Adrian	0	7
O14	●	at Findlay	26	0
O19	●	Defiance	22	0
O28	●	at Huntington	38	6
N4	●	Toledo	6	6
N11	●	at Kent State	6	0

R.B. McCANDLESS
1923 (.375)   3-5

1923   3-5-0
S29		Ohio Northern	0	46
O6		at Heidelberg	12	3
O13	●	Bluffton	13	0
O19	●	Findlay	26	3
O27		at Toledo	0	27
N3		at Defiance	7	17
N10	●	Ashland	10	0
N24		at Baldwin-Wallace	0	25

WARREN STELLER
1924-34 (.619)   40-21-19

1924   3-4-0
O11		at Capital	0	19
O18	●	at Ashland	13	6
O25		at Toledo	7	12
O31		at Central Michigan	0	21
N8		Defiance	0	15
N15	●	at Bluffton	6	0
N24	●	Cedarville	34	0

1925   3-1-3
O3	=	at Otterbein	0	0
O10		Eastern Michigan	0	14
O16	=	Capital	0	0
O24	=	at Findlay	0	0
O31	●	at Defiance	2	0
N7	●	Bluffton	6	0
N20	●	Ashland	26	14

1926   4-3-1
S25	●	at Dayton	0	41
O2	●	at Bluffton	14	0
O9	●	Cedarville	25	0
O23		Findlay	6	7
O30	●	Central Michigan	13	0
N6	●	Defiance	30	7
N11		at Capital	0	15
N20	=	at Detroit CC	0	0

1927   5-1-1
S24	=	at Otterbein	0	0
O1	●	Ohio Northern	6	2
O15	●	at Kent State	13	0
O22	●	Detroit CC	6	0
O29	●	at Findlay	6	0
N11	●	at Defiance	15	0
N19		Bluffton	6	12

1928   5-0-2
S29	●	at Ohio Northern	7	0
O13	●	at Bluffton	6	0
O20	●	Toledo	14	0
N3	=	Defiance	12	12
N10	●	at Detroit CC	20	0
N19	●	Findlay	19	0
N26	=	Kent State	6	6

1929   4-2-1
S28		Baldwin-Wallace	0	18
O11		at Eastern Michigan	7	34
O18	●	Findlay	23	0
O26	=	at Toledo	0	0
N2	●	at Defiance	6	0
N9	●	Bluffton	15	0
N16	●	Detroit CC	25	2

1930   6-0-2
S27	●	Hope	19	0
O4	●	at Baldwin-Wallace	7	6
O11	●	at Bluffton	13	6
O18	●	Defiance	13	6
O25	=	at Findlay	6	6
N1	=	Toledo	0	0
N8	●	Albion	30	7
N15	●	at Detroit CC	19	7

1931   3-1-4
S26	=	at Baldwin-Wallace	0	0
O3	●	Mt. Union	6	0
O10	=	at Western Reserve	0	0
O17	●	Detroit CC	13	0
O24	=	Bluffton	0	0
O31		at Defiance	0	15
N7	=	Findlay	6	6
N14	●	Central Michigan	6	0

1932   3-3-1
S24		Baldwin-Wallace	0	24
O1	●	at Mt. Union	7	6
O14		at Bluffton	0	14
O22	●	Defiance	14	7
O29	=	at Hiram	0	0
N5	●	Toledo	12	6
N12		Ohio Northern	0	20

1933   2-3-2
S30		Mt. Union	6	7
O7	●	Bluffton	19	0
O14		at Baldwin-Wallace	6	58
O21	●	at Ohio Northern	6	0
O28		at Toledo	7	25
N4	=	Capital	0	0
N10	=	Hiram	0	0

1934   2-3-2
S29		at Mt. Union	0	12
O6	●	Otterbein	20	7
O13	=	Kent State	0	0
O20		at Hiram	3	13
O27	●	at Capital	13	0
N3		Toledo	0	22
N10	=	Ohio Northern	0	0

HARRY OCKERMAN
1935-40 (.510)   20-19-9

1935   1-6-0
O5		Capital	0	12
O12		Baldwin-Wallace	0	41
O19		at Ohio Northern	0	54
O26		at Kent State	0	45
N1		at Toledo	0	63
N9		Marietta	0	31
N16	●	Hiram	25	0

1936   4-2-3
S26		at Western Reserve	0	40
O3	=	at Capital	7	7
O10	●	Eastern Michigan	6	0
O17	●	at Wittenberg	13	0
O24		Kent State	0	6
O31	●	at Hiram	13	0
N7	●	at Ashland	20	0
N14	=	Ohio Northern	7	7
N20	=	Heidelberg	0	0

1937   3-4-1
S25	●	Hiram	12	0
O2		at Baldwin-Wallace	0	21
O9		at Eastern Michigan	0	25
O16	●	Capital	12	0
O23		Ohio Northern	7	9
O30	=	at Kent State	13	13
N6		Wittenberg	0	12
N11	●	at Heidelberg	12	0

1938   3-2-3
S24	=	at Capital	0	0
S30		at John Carroll	0	20
O8	●	Ashland	50	0
O15	●	Wittenberg	7	0
O22	=	at Ohio Northern	0	0
O29	=	Eastern Michigan	7	7
N5		Kent State	3	7
N12	●	at Hiram	28	7

1939   6-1-1
S30	●	Bluffton	35	0
O7	●	Wayne	9	0
O14		Capital	6	7
O21	●	Otterbein	26	6
O28	●	at Wittenberg	19	13
N4	●	at Kent State	34	0
N11	=	at Findlay	7	7
N18	●	at Eastern Michigan	23	13

1940   3-4-1
O5		Wittenberg	0	14
O11	●	at Findlay	14	7
O19	●	Eastern Michigan	15	0
O26	=	at Capital	7	7
N2		Kent State	0	13
N9	●	at Wooster	26	14
N16		at Eastern Kentucky	0	48
N21		at Wayne	0	19

ROBERT WHITTAKER
1941-54 (.565)   66-50-7

1941   7-1-1
S27	=	Wooster	14	14
O3		at Akron	0	8
O11	●	at Miami, Ohio	9	0
O18	●	at Eastern Michigan	20	6
O25	●	Heidelberg	39	6
N1	●	at Kent State	12	6
N8	●	at Wittenberg	13	0
N15	●	Findlay	47	0
N20	●	Wayne	19	0

1942   6-2-1
S26	●	Miami Naval	39	0
O3		at Ohio Wesleyan	14	15
O10		at Ball State	26	14
O17	●	at Wayne	20	6
O24	●	Miami, Ohio	7	6
O31		Kent State	0	7
N7	●	Wittenberg	10	0
N13	=	at Findlay	0	0
N21	●	Grosse Isle Navy	19	7

1943   5-3-1
S18	●	Ohio Wesleyan	18	7
S25	●	at Xavier	40	0
O2	●	Central Michigan	36	0
O9	●	Patterson Field	36	0
O16		Bunker Hill Navy	12	13
O23	=	at Baldwin-Wallace	7	7
O30	●	Alma	24	0
N6		at Miami, Ohio	6	45
N13		at Ohio Wesleyan	20	32

1944   5-3-0
S1	●	at Central Michigan	20	19
S9		Miami, Ohio	7	28
S16	●	at Ohio Wesleyan	13	6
S23		Baldwin-Wallace	6	13
S30	●	Alma	19	6
O7	●	Ohio Wesleyan	41	0
O14		at Case	20	18
O21		at Bunker Hill Navy	7	27

1945   4-3-0
A31	●	at Alma	15	0
S7	●	Central Michigan	19	6
S14	●	at Baldwin-Wallace	13	14
S22	●	at Miami, Ohio	0	26
S29	●	at Ohio U.	6	0
O6		at Oberlin	0	28
O13	●	Case	26	7

1946   5-3-0
S28		at Central Michigan	0	7
O5	●	Ball State	13	0 *
O12		Miami, Ohio	0	6
O19	●	at Kent State	13	0
O25	●	at Canisius	13	7
N2	●	Oberlin	14	0
N9		at St. Bonaventure	9	13
N16	●	Xavier	33	6

1947   5-5-0
S20		at Xavier	0	2
S27	●	Central Michigan	20	19
O4		at Dayton	13	20
O11		at Miami, Ohio	19	33
O18	●	Ohio U.	2	0
O25	●	Kent State	21	18
N1	●	Findlay	26	9
N8		at St. Bonaventure	14	21
N15	●	Northern Iowa	19	7
N22		at William & Mary	0	20

1948   8-0-1
S25	●	at Ohio U.	13	7
O2	●	at Central Michigan	13	12
O9	●	at Toledo	21	6
O16	●	Morris-Harvey	48	6
O23	●	Baldwin-Wallace	33	28
O30	●	at Findlay	28	7
N6	●	at Kent State	23	14
N13	●	Morningside	38	7
N20	=	John Carroll	13	13

1949   4-5-0
S24	●	Rider	47	14
O1	●	Central Michigan	20	0
O8		at Toledo	19	20
O15		at Morris-Harvey	0	21
O22		at Baldwin-Wallace	21	34
O28		at John Carroll	24	38
N5	●	Kent State	27	6
N12	●	at Mt. Union	35	7
N19		Eastern Kentucky	13	21

MAC TEAMS

1950 — 3-4-2

S23	=		at Rider	0	0
S30			Miami, Ohio	6	54
O7	•		Bradley	20	14
O14			at Central Michigan	0	12
O21	=		Baldwin-Wallace	34	34
O28	•		at Toledo	39	14
N4			at Kent State	6	19
N11	•		Youngstown	22	7
N18			at Eastern Kentucky	7	34

1951 — 4-4-1

S22	•		Ohio Wesleyan	23	13
S29			at Miami, Ohio	7	46
O6			Mt. Union	13	26
O13			at Ohio U.	7	28
O20	•		at Baldwin-Wallace	27	20
O27			Toledo	6	12
N3	=		Kent State	27	27
N10	•		at Youngstown	20	0
N17	•		at Bradley	20	6

1952-Present
MAC

1952 — 7-2-0 (2-2-0)

S20	•		Central Michigan	20	7
S27		|	Miami, Ohio	7	42
O4	•		at Ohio Wesleyan	45	0
O11	•		at Bradley	21	14
O18	•		Baldwin-Wallace	27	19
O25	•	|	at Toledo	29	19
N1	•	|	at Kent State	44	21
N8	•		Youngstown	50	0
N15		|	Ohio U.	14	33

1953 — 1-8-0 (0-4-0)

S18			at Youngstown	7	20
S26		|	at Miami, Ohio	0	47
O3			at Temple	0	27
O10	•		Bradley	39	13
O17			at Baldwin-Wallace	27	35
O24		|	Toledo	19	20
O31		|	Kent State	7	41
N7			Heidelberg	6	27
N14		|	at Ohio U.	14	22

1954 — 2-7-0 (0-6-0)

S18	•		at Dayton	18	0
S25		|	Miami, Ohio	7	46
O2			Waynesburg	7	12
O9		|	at Western Michigan	15	20
O16	•		Baldwin-Wallace	13	0
O23		|	at Toledo	7	38
O30		|	at Kent State	25	28
N6		|	Marshall	19	26
N13		|	Ohio U.	14	26

DOYT PERRY
1955-64 (.855) 77-11-5

1955 — 7-1-1 (4-1-1)

S17	•		Defiance	40	0
S23	=	|	at Kent State	6	6
O1	•	|	Western Michigan	35	0
O8	•		John Carroll	30	0
O15	•		at Baldwin-Wallace	34	14
O22	•	|	Toledo	39	0
O29	•	|	at Marshall	27	26
N5		|	at Miami, Ohio	0	7
N12	•	|	at Ohio U.	13	0

1956 — 8-0-1 (5-0-1)

S15	•		Defiance	73	0
S22	•	|	Kent State	17	0
S29	•	|	at Western Michigan	27	13
O6	•		at Drake	46	7
O13	•		at Baldwin-Wallace	32	21
O20	•	|	at Toledo	34	12
O27	•	|	Marshall	34	12
N3	=	|	Miami, Ohio	7	7
N10	•	|	Ohio U.	41	27

1957 — 6-1-2 (3-1-2)

S21	•		Baldwin-Wallace	60	7
S28	•		at Xavier	16	0
O5	•		at Delaware	7	0
O12	=	|	Western Michigan	14	14
O19	•	|	Toledo	29	0
O26	•	|	at Kent State	13	7
N2		|	Miami, Ohio	7	13
N9	=	|	at Ohio U.	7	7
N16	•	|	at Marshall	14	7

1958 — 7-2-0 (4-2-0)

S20	•		at Wichita State	20	14
S27	•		Lockbourne AFB	27	6
O4	•		at Dayton	25	0
O11	•	|	at Western Michigan	40	6
O18	•	|	at Toledo	31	16
O25		|	Kent State	7	8
N1		|	at Miami, Ohio	14	28
N8	•	|	Ohio U.	33	6
N15	•	|	Marshall	21	7

1959 — 9-0-0 (6-0-0)

S26	•	|	at Marshall	51	7
O3	•		Dayton	14	0
O10	•	|	Western Michigan	34	0
O17	•	|	Toledo	51	21
O24	•	|	at Kent State	25	8
O31	•	|	Miami, Ohio	33	16
N7	•		at Southern Illinois	23	14
N14	•		Delaware	30	8
N21	•	|	at Ohio U.	13	9

1960 — 8-1-0 (5-1-0)

S24	•	|	Marshall	14	7
O1	•	|	at Miami, Ohio	21	12
O8	•	|	at Western Michigan	14	13
O15	•	|	at Toledo	14	3
O22	•	|	Kent State	28	0
O29	•		Cal Poly SLO	50	6
N5	•		Southern Illinois	27	6
N12		|	Ohio U.	7	14
N19	•		at Texas-El Paso	21	0

1961 — 8-2-0 (5-1-0)

S23	•	|	at Marshall	40	0
S30	•		Dayton	28	11
O7	•	|	Western Michigan	21	0
O14	•	|	Toledo	17	6
O21	•	|	at Kent State	21	6
O28		|	Miami, Ohio	6	7
N4	•		West Texas State	28	6
N11	•	|	at Ohio U.	7	6
N18	•		at Southern Illinois	20	0
N23			Fresno State	6	36

1962 — 7-1-1 (5-0-1)

S22	•	|	Marshall	48	6
S29	•		at Dayton	14	7
O6	•	|	at Western Michigan	10	6
O13	•	|	at Toledo	28	13
O20	•	|	Kent State	45	6
O27	=	|	at Miami, Ohio	24	24
N3			at West Texas State	7	23
N10	•	|	Ohio U.	7	6
N17	•		Southern Illinois	21	0

1963 — 8-2-0 (4-2-0)

S21	•		Detroit	27	14
S28	•		at Southern Illinois	31	6
O5	•		Dayton	28	0
O12	•	|	Western Michigan	16	7
O19	•	|	Toledo	22	20
O26	•	|	at Kent State	18	3
N2		|	Miami, Ohio	12	21
N9	•	|	at Marshall	21	14
N16		|	at Ohio U.	0	16
N23	•		Xavier	26	15

1964 — 9-1-0 (5-1-0)

S19	•		Southern Illinois	35	12
S26	•		at North Texas	21	7
O3	•		Dayton	35	0
O10	•	|	at Western Michigan	28	8
O17	•	|	at Toledo	31	14
O24	•	|	Kent State	41	0
O31	•	|	at Miami, Ohio	21	18
N6	•	|	Marshall	28	0
N14		|	Ohio U.	0	21
N21	•		at Xavier	35	7

BOB GIBSON
1965-67 (.679) 19-9

1965 — 7-2-0 (5-1-0)

S18	•		Cal St. LA	21	0
S25			at West Texas State	0	34
O2	•		at Dayton	9	0
O9	•	|	Western Michigan	21	17
O16	•	|	Toledo	21	14
O23	•	|	at Kent State	7	6
O30		|	Miami, Ohio	7	23
N6	•	|	at Marshall	20	7
N13	•	|	at Ohio U.	17	7

1966 — 6-3-0 (4-2-0)

S17			at Tampa	13	20
S24	•		Dayton	13	0
O8		|	at Western Michigan	14	16
O15	•	|	at Toledo	14	13
O22		|	Kent State	12	35
O29	•	|	at Miami, Ohio	17	14
N5	•	|	Marshall	14	6
N12	•	|	Ohio U.	28	0
N19	•		at Temple	62	20

1967 — 6-4-0 (2-4-0)

S23	•		Quantico Marines	29	0
S30	•		at Dayton	7	0
O7		|	Western Michigan	6	10
O14		|	Toledo	0	33
O21	•	|	at Kent State	7	6
O28		|	Miami, Ohio	7	9
N4	•	|	at Marshall	9	7
N11		|	at Ohio U.	7	31
N18	•		Northern Illinois	17	7
N25	•		at Cal St. LA	42	27

DON NEHLEN
1968-76 (.598) 53-35-4

1968 — 6-3-1 (3-2-1)

S21	•		Ball State	62	8
S28	•		Dayton	20	14
O5	•	|	at Western Michigan	17	10
O12	=	|	at Toledo	0	0
O19	•	|	Kent State	30	7
O26		|	at Miami, Ohio	7	31
N2	•	|	Marshall	54	28
N9		|	Ohio U.	27	28
N16			at Northern Illinois	6	7
N23	•		at Xavier	44	14

1969 — 6-4-0 (4-1-0)

S20			Utah State	6	14
S27	•		at Dayton	27	7
O4	•	|	Western Michigan	21	10
O11		|	Toledo	26	27
O18	•	|	at Kent State	7	0
O25	•	|	Miami, Ohio	3	0
N1			at Marshall	16	21
N8	•	|	at Ohio U.	23	16
N15			at West Texas St.	12	28
N22	•		Northern Illinois	38	23

1970 — 2-6-1 (1-4-0)

S19			at Utah State	14	33
S26	=		Dayton	14	14
O3		|	at Western Michigan	3	23
O10		|	at Toledo	0	20
O17	•	|	Kent State	44	0
O24		|	at Miami, Ohio	3	7
O31	•		Marshall	26	24
N7		|	Ohio U.	7	34
N14			West Texas State	7	23

1971 — 6-4-0 (4-1-0)

S18	•	|	at Ohio U.	20	19
S25	•		East Carolina	47	21
O2	•	|	Western Michigan	23	6
O9		|	Toledo	7	24
O16	•	|	at Kent State	46	33
O23	•	|	Miami, Ohio	33	7
O30			at Marshall	10	12
N6	•		at Texas Arlington	34	17
N13			Xavier	27	42
N20			at Dayton	16	26

1972 — 6-3-1 (3-1-1)

S16	•		at Purdue	17	14
S23	•		at Miami, Ohio	16	7
S30	=	|	at Western Michigan	13	13
O7	•	|	at Toledo	19	8
O14		|	Kent State	10	14
O21			at San Diego State	19	35
O28	•		Marshall	46	7
N4	•	|	Ohio U.	17	0
N11	•		Dayton	17	0
N18			at Tampa	22	29

1973 — 7-3-0 (2-3-0)

S15	•		at Syracuse	41	14
S22	•		at Dayton	31	16
S29	•	|	Western Michigan	31	20
O6	•	|	Toledo	49	35
O13		|	at Kent State	7	21
O20		|	Miami, Ohio	8	31
O27	•		at Marshall	24	21
N3		|	at Ohio U.	23	24
N10	•		Eastern Michigan	31	7
N17	•		Northern Illinois	21	20

1974 — 6-4-1 (2-3-0)

S14			at East Carolina	6	24
S21	•		Dayton	41	21
S28	•	|	at Western Michigan	21	13
O5		|	at Toledo	19	24
O12	•	|	Kent State	26	10
O19		|	at Miami, Ohio	10	34
O26	•		Marshall	28	3
N2		|	Ohio U.	22	33
N9	•		Arkansas State	17	0
N16	•		Southern Miss[MBL]	38	20
N23	=		at San Diego State	21	21

1975 — 8-3-0 (4-2-0)

S13	•		at Brigham Young	23	21
S20	•		Southern Miss	16	14
S27	•		at Dayton	21	14
O4	•	|	Western Michigan	28	0
O11	•	|	Toledo	34	17
O18	•	|	Kent State[CLEV]	35	9
O25		|	Miami, Ohio	17	20
N1		|	Ball State	20	27
N8	•	|	at Ohio U.	19	17
N15	•		at Southern Illinois	48	6
N22			at Texas Arlington	17	21

1976 — 6-5-0 (4-3-0)

S11	•		at Syracuse	22	7
S18	•	|	Eastern Michigan	53	12
S25			San Diego State	15	27
O2	•	|	at Western Michigan	31	28
O9	•	|	at Toledo	29	28
O16	•	|	Kent State	17	13
O23		|	at Miami, Ohio	7	9
O30		|	Central Michigan	28	38
N6		|	Ohio U.	26	31
N13	•		Southern Illinois	35	7
N20			at U.T. Chattanooga	29	49

DENNY STOLZ
1977-85 (.554) 56-45-1

1977 — 5-7-0 (4-3-0)

S10	•		at Grand Valley St.	17	6
S17		|	at Eastern Michigan	6	16
S24			Iowa State	21	35
O1	•	|	Western Michigan	34	14
O8	•	|	Toledo	21	13
O15	•	|	at Kent State	14	10
O22		|	Miami, Ohio	13	33
O29		|	at Central Michigan	28	35
N5			U.T. Chattanooga	33	37
N12	•	|	at Ohio U.	39	27
N19			at Hawaii	21	41
N26			at Long Beach St.	28	29

1978 — 4-7-0 (3-5-0)

S9			at Villanova	28	35
S16	•	|	at Eastern Michigan	43	6
S23	•		Grand Valley St.	49	3
S30		|	at Western Michigan	20	24
O7	•	|	at Toledo	45	27
O14	•	|	Kent State	28	20
O21		|	at Miami, Ohio	7	18
O28		|	Central Michigan	7	38
N4		|	Ball State	14	39
N11			at Southern Miss	21	38
N18		|	Ohio U.	15	19

1979 — 4-7-0 (3-5-0)

S8	•	|	Eastern Michigan	32	6
S15			at Iowa State	10	38
S22		|	Central Michigan	0	24
S29	•	|	at Western Michigan	15	3
O6		|	Toledo	17	23
O13	•	|	at Kent State	28	17
O20		|	Miami, Ohio	3	21
O27		|	at Ball State	23	38
N3			at Kentucky	14	20
N10	•		Southern Miss	31	27
N17		|	at Ohio U.	21	48

1980 — 4-7-0 (4-4-0)

S6			at Richmond	17	20
S13		|	Eastern Michigan	16	18
S20			Long Beach St.	21	23
S27			at Kentucky	20	21
O4	•	|	at Western Michigan	17	14
O11	•	|	at Toledo	17	6
O18	•	|	Kent State	24	3
O25		|	at Miami, Ohio	3	7
N1	•	|	Ball State	24	21
N8		|	at Central Michigan	10	32
N22		|	Ohio U.	20	21

1981 — 5-5-1 (5-3-1)

S12		at Baylor	0	38
S19	|	at Ohio U.	21	23
S26		at Michigan State	7	10
O3	|	Western Michigan	7	21
O10	= |	Miami, Ohio	7	7
O17	● |	at Northern Illinois	17	10
O24	● |	Toledo	38	0
O31	● |	Kent State	13	7
N7	● |	at Ball State	14	10
N14	● |	at Eastern Michigan	28	0
N21	|	Central Michigan	3	6

1982 — 7-5-0 (7-2-0)

S4	● |	Ohio U.	40	0
S18	● |	at Central Michigan	34	30
O2	● |	Western Michigan	7	3
O9	|	at Miami, Ohio	12	17
O16	● |	Northern Illinois	20	18
O23	|	at Toledo	10	24
O30	● |	at Kent State	41	7
N6	● |	Ball State	28	7
N13	● |	Eastern Michigan	24	7
N20		at Long Beach St.	7	24
N25		at North Carolina	14	33
		CALIFORNIA BOWL		
D18		Fresno State	28	29

1983 — 8-3-0 (7-2-0)

S10	●	at Fresno State	35	27
S17		at Brigham Young	28	63
S24	● |	Miami, Ohio	17	14
O1	● |	at Eastern Michigan	26	21
O8	|	Toledo	3	6
O15	● |	at Western Michigan	23	20
O22	|	at Northern Illinois	23	24
O29	● |	Central Michigan	15	14
N5	● |	Ball State	45	30
N12	● |	at Ohio U.	24	20
N19	● |	Kent State	38	3

1984 — 8-3-0 (7-2-0)

S8	●	Richmond	55	28
S15		at Oklahoma State	14	31
S22	● |	at Miami, Ohio	41	10
S29	● |	Eastern Michigan	35	27
O6	|	at Toledo	6	17
O13	● |	Western Michigan	34	7
O20	● |	Northern Illinois	28	6
O27	|	at Central Michigan	21	42
N3	● |	at Ball State	38	13
N10	● |	Ohio U.	28	7
N17	● |	at Kent State	27	10

1985 — 11-1-0 (9-0-0)

S7	● |	at Ball State	31	6
S14	●	at Kentucky	30	26
S21	● |	Miami, Ohio	28	24
S28	●	Akron	27	22
O5	● |	at Western Michigan	48	7
O12	● |	at Eastern Michigan	42	24
O19	● |	Central Michigan	23	18
O26	● |	Kent State	26	14
N2	● |	at Northern Illinois	34	14
N16	● |	Toledo	21	0
N23	● |	at Ohio U.	38	17
		CALIFORNIA BOWL		
D14		Fresno State	7	51

MOE ANKNEY
1986-90 (.398) 20-31-3

1986 — 5-6-0 (5-3-0)

S6	● |	Ohio U.	21	16
S13		at Minnesota	7	31
S20	|	at Central Michigan	10	20
S27	|	at Miami, Ohio	7	24
O4	● |	Western Michigan	17	3
O11	● |	Eastern Michigan	24	10
O18		at Washington	0	48
O25	● |	at Kent State	31	15
N1		Northern Illinois	8	16
N8	● |	Ball State	20	17
N15	|	at Toledo	3	22

1987 — 5-6-0 (5-3-0)

S5		at Penn State	19	45
S12		Youngstown St.	17	20
S19	● |	at Ball State	24	0
S26	|	Western Michigan	27	34
O3		at Arizona	7	45
O10	● |	at Ohio U.	28	7
O17	● |	Toledo	20	6
O31	|	at Miami, Ohio	7	17
N7	● |	Kent State	30	20
N14	|	at Eastern Michigan	18	38
N21	● |	Central Michigan	18	17

1988 — 2-8-1 (1-6-1)

S3		at West Virginia	14	62
S10	|	Ball State	10	34
S17		at TCU	12	49
S24	|	at Toledo	5	34
O1	|	at Western Michigan	10	37
O8	● |	Ohio U.	42	0
O15	|	at Central Michigan	3	21
O22	●	Youngstown St.	20	16
O29	= |	Miami, Ohio	21	21
N5	|	at Kent State	19	31
N12	|	Eastern Michigan	3	28

1989 — 5-6-0 (5-3-0)

S9		at East Carolina	6	41
S16	|	Ball State	3	28
S23	● |	Central Michigan	24	20
S30		Akron	24	38
O7	● |	at Ohio U.	31	28
O14	● |	Toledo	27	23
O21	|	at Eastern Michigan	13	21
O28	|	at Miami, Ohio	13	17
N4	● |	Kent State	51	28
N11	● |	at Western MIchigan	31	30
N18		at Tulsa	10	45

1990 — 3-5-2 (2-4-2)

S2	●	at Cincinnati	34	20
S8		at Virginia Tech	7	21
S22	|	at Central Michigan	0	17
S29	|	at Ball State	6	16
O6	= |	Ohio U.	10	10
O13	|	at Toledo	13	19
O20	● |	Eastern Michigan	25	15
O27	= |	Miami, Ohio	10	10
N3	● |	at Kent State	20	16
N10	|	Western Michigan	13	19

GARY BLACKNEY
1991-2000 (.545) 60-50-2

1991 — 11-1-0 (8-0-0)

A31	● |	Eastern Michigan	17	6
S7		at West Virginia	17	24
S21	●	Cincinnati	20	16
S28	●	at Navy	22	19
O5	● |	Central Michigan	17	10
O12	● |	at Ohio U.	45	14
O19	● |	at Toledo	24	21
O26	● |	at Western Michigan	23	10
N2	● |	at Miami, Ohio	17	7
N9	● |	Kent State	35	7
N16	● |	at Ball State	14	13
		CALIFORNIA BOWL		
D14	●	Fresno State	28	21

1992 — 10-2-0 (8-0-0)

S3	● |	Western Michigan	29	19
S12		at Ohio State	6	17
S19		at Wisconsin	18	39
S26	●	East Carolina	44	34
O3	● |	at Central Michigan	17	14
O10	● |	Ohio U.	31	14
O17	● |	at Toledo	10	9
O24	● |	at Akron	24	3
O31	● |	Miami, Ohio	44	24
N7	● |	at Kent State	28	22
N14	● |	Ball State	38	6
		LAS VEGAS BOWL		
D18	●	Nevada	35	34

1993 — 6-3-2 (5-1-2)

S4		at Virginia Tech	16	33
S11	●	Cincinnati	21	7
S25		at Navy	20	27
O2	● |	Toledo	17	10
O9	● |	at Ohio U.	20	0
O16	● |	Akron	49	7
O23	= |	at Ball State	26	26
O30	● |	at Miami, Ohio	30	25
N6	● |	Kent State	40	7
N13	|	at Central Michigan	15	17
N20	= |	Western Michigan	14	14

1994 — 9-2-0 (7-1-0)

S1		at North Carolina St.	15	20
S10	● |	at Akron	45	0
S17	●	Navy	59	21
S24	● |	at Eastern Michigan	30	13
O1	●	at Cincinnati	38	0
O8	● |	Ohio U.	32	0
O15	● |	at Toledo	31	16
O22	● |	Ball State	59	36
O29	● |	Miami, Ohio	27	16
N5	● |	at Kent State	22	16
N12	|	Central Michigan	33	36

1995 — 5-6-0 (3-5-0)

A31		Louisiana Tech	21	28
S9	●	at Missouri	17	10
S16	● |	Akron	50	12
S23	|	at Central Michigan	16	22
S30	●	at Temple	37	31
O7	|	Miami, Ohio	0	21
O14	|	at Ball State	10	30
O21	|	Toledo	16	35
O28	|	at Western Michigan	0	17
N4	● |	Ohio U.	33	7
N11	● |	at Kent State	26	15

1996 — 4-7 (3-5)

A31		Alabama *BIRM*	7	21
S14	●	Temple	20	16
S21	● |	at Miami, Ohio	14	10
S28	● |	Central Michigan	31	27
O5	|	at Toledo	16	24
O12	● |	Kent State	31	24
O19	|	Ball State	11	16
O26	|	at Ohio U.	0	38
N2	|	at Akron	14	21
N9	|	Western Michigan	13	16
N16		at Central Florida	19	27

1997 — 3-8 (3-5)

A30		at Louisiana Tech	23	30
S6	● |	Miami, Ohio	28	21
S13		at Ohio State	13	44
S20	● |	at Akron	31	28
S27		at Kansas State	0	58
O4	● |	Northern Illinois	35	10
O11	|	Western Michigan	21	34
O18	|	at Ohio U.	0	24
O25	|	Toledo	20	35
N1	|	at Kent State	20	29
N8	|	at Marshall	0	28

1998 — 5-6 (5-3)

S5		at Missouri	0	37
S12		at Penn State	3	48
S26		Central Florida	31	38
O3	● |	Ohio U.	35	7
O10	|	at Miami, Ohio	12	24
O17	|	at Toledo	16	24
O24	● |	Kent State	42	21
O31	● |	Marshall	34	13
N7	● |	Akron	58	21
N14	|	at Western Michigan	27	56
N21	● |	at Northern Illinois	34	23

1999 — 5-6 (3-5)

S4		at Pittsburgh	10	30
S11	●	Tennessee Tech	40	15
S18	|	at Marshall	16	35
S25	|	at Kent State	27	41
O2	● |	Toledo	34	23
O9	|	Miami, Ohio	31	45
O16	|	at Akron	25	55
O23	|	at Ohio U.	14	17
O30	● |	Central Michigan	31	7
N13	● |	Ball State	35	14
N20	●	at Central Florida	33	30

2000 — 2-9 (2-6)

S2		at Michigan	7	42
S9		Pittsburgh	16	34
S16		at Temple	14	31
S23	|	at Buffalo	17	20
S30	● |	at Kent State	18	11
O7	|	Akron	21	27
O14	|	at Miami, Ohio	10	24
O21	● |	Eastern Michigan	20	6
N4	|	Marshall	13	20
N11	|	Ohio U.	21	23
N22	|	at Toledo	17	51

URBAN MEYER
2001-02 (.739) 17-6

2001 — 8-3 (5-3)

S1	●	at Missouri	20	13
S8	● |	Buffalo	35	0
S22	●	Temple	42	23
S29	|	at Marshall	31	37
O6	● |	Kent State	24	17
O13	|	at Western Michigan	28	37
O20	● |	at Akron	16	11
N3	|	Miami, Ohio	21	24
N10	● |	at Ohio U.	17	0
N17	●	at Northwestern	43	42
N23	● |	Toledo	56	21

2002 — 9-3 (6-2)

A29	●	Tennessee Tech	41	7
S14	●	Missouri	51	28
S21	●	at Kansas	39	16
O5	● |	Ohio U.	72	21
O12	● |	at Central Michigan	45	35
O19	● |	Western Michigan	48	45
O26	● |	Ball State	38	20
N2	● |	at Kent State	45	14
N9	|	at Northern Illinois	17	26
N16		at South Florida	7	29
N23	● |	Eastern Michigan	63	21
N30	|	at Toledo	24	42

GREGG BRANDON
2003-Present (.612) 30-19

2003 — 11-3 (7-1)

A28	●	Eastern Kentucky	63	13
S6	●	at Purdue	27	26
S13	●	Liberty	62	3
S20		at Ohio State	17	24
O4	● |	Central Michigan	23	3
O11	● |	at Western Michigan	32	21
O18	● |	at Eastern Michigan	33	20
O25	● |	Northern Illinois	34	18
N4	|	at Miami, Ohio	10	33
N15	● |	Kent State	42	33
N22	● |	at Ball State	41	14
N29	● |	Toledo	31	23
		MAC CHAMPIONSHIP GAME		
D4		Miami, Ohio	27	49
		MOTOR CITY BOWL		
D26	●	Northwestern	28	24

2004 — 9-3 (6-2)

S4		at Oklahoma	24	40
S11	●	S.E. Missouri St.	49	10
S24	|	at Northern Illinois	17	34
O2	●	at Temple	70	16
O9	● |	at Central Michigan	38	14
O16	● |	Ball State	51	13
O23	● |	at Ohio U.	41	16
O30	● |	Eastern Michigan	41	20
N6	● |	Western Michigan	52	0
N13	● |	Marshall	56	35
N23	|	at Toledo	41	49
		GMAC BOWL		
D22	●	Memphis	52	35

2005 — 6-5 (5-3)

S3		at Wisconsin	42	56
S10	● |	at Ball State	40	31
S21		at Boise State	20	48
O1	●	Temple	70	7
O8	● |	Ohio U.	38	14
O15	● |	at Buffalo	27	7
O22	|	Western Michigan	14	45
O29	|	Akron	14	24
N5	● |	at Kent State	24	14
N15	● |	at Miami, Ohio	42	14
N22	|	Toledo	41	44

2006 — 4-8 (3-5)

S2		Wisconsin *CLEV*	14	35
S9	● |	Buffalo	48	40
S16	●	at Florida Int.	33	28
S23	|	Kent State	3	38
S30	● |	at Ohio U.	21	9
O7		at Ohio State	7	35
O14	● |	Eastern Michigan	24	21
O19	|	at Central Michigan	14	31
O28		at Temple	14	28
N4	|	at Akron	28	35
N15	|	Miami, Ohio	7	9
N21	|	at Toledo	21	31

Neutral Site key: *BIRM* Birmingham, AL / *CLEV* Cleveland, OH / *MBL* Mobile, AL

ƒ **Forfeit** † **Game Later Forfieted** # **Disputed Victor** * **Disputed Score** || **Designated Conference Game** |2 **Counted Twice in Conference Standings**

BOWLING GREEN RECORD BOOK

SINGLE-GAME RECORDS

RUSHING YARDS

RANK	PLAYER	DATE	OPPONENT	ATT	AVG	YDS
1	Darryl Story	Nov. 5, 1983	Ball State	37	6.1	225
2	Steve Holmes	Oct. 24, 1998	Kent	NA	NA	220
3	Paul Miles	Oct. 28, 1972	Marshall	NA	NA	217
4	Bryant Jones	Oct. 30, 1981	Kent	46	4.6	212
5	Fred Durig	Nov. 17, 1951	Bradley	NA	NA	206

PASSING YARDS

RANK	PLAYER	DATE	OPPONENT	ATT	COMP	YDS
1	Brian McClure	Nov. 23, 1985	Ohio	NA	NA	479
2	Omar Jacobs	Sept. 3, 2005	Wisconsin	51	30	458
3	Josh Harris	Oct. 25, 2003	Northern Illinois	43	27	438
4	Brian McCLure	Oct. 1, 1983	Eastern Michigan	59	37	427
5	Omar Jacobs	Nov. 23, 2004	Toledo	60	36	415

RECEIVING YARDS

RANK	PLAYER	DATE	OPPONENT	REC	AVG	YDS
1	Robert Redd	Sept. 29, 2001	Marshall	9	23.9	215
2	Mark Szlachcic	Dec. 14, 1991	Fresno State	NA	NA	189
3	Jeff Groth	Oct. 14, 1978	Kent	NA	NA	188
4	Steve Sanders	Oct. 23, 2004	Ohio	9	20.6	185
	Charles Sharon	Oct. 8, 2005	Ohio	10	18.5	185

POINTS

RANK	PLAYER	DATE	OPPONENT	TOT
1	Dave Preston	Sept. 21, 1974	Dayton	30
2	7 players tied at 24			

FIELD GOALS

RANK	PLAYER	DATE	OPPONENT	TOT
1	Brian Leaver	Nov. 5, 1994	Kent State	5
2	Don Taylor	Oct. 5, 1974	Toledo	4

INTERCEPTIONS

RANK	PLAYER	DATE	OPPONENT	TOT
1	9 players tied at 3			

RETIRED NUMBERS

29 Paul Miles

SINGLE-SEASON RECORDS

RUSHING YARDS

RANK	PLAYER	SEASON	ATT	YDS
1	Fred Durig	1951	NA	1,444
2	Dave Preston	1974	324	1,414
3	Paul Miles	1971	274	1,185
4	Dan Saleet	1975	NA	1,114
5	P.J. Pope	2004	178	1,098

PASSING YARDS

RANK	PLAYER	SEASON	G	ATT	COMP	PCT	YDS
1	Omar Jacobs	2004	12	462	309	66.8	4,002
2	Josh Harris	2003	14	494	325	65.7	3,813
3	Brian McClure	1983	NA	466	298	63.9	3,264
4	Brian McClure	1984	NA	414	263	63.5	2,951
5	Rich Dackin	1989	NA	414	NA	NA	2,679

RECEIVING YARDS

RANK	PLAYER	SEASON	G	REC	AVG	YDS
1	Cole Magner	2003	14	99	11.5	1138
2	Stan Hunter	1983	NA	NA	NA	1107
3	Charles Sharon	2004	12	66	16.2	1070
4	Steve Sanders	2004	12	55	17.9	984
5	Robert Redd	2002	12	83	11.7	973

SCORING

RANK	PLAYER	SEASON	TD	FG	PAT	P2	TOT
1	Josh Harris	2002	22	0	0	1	134
2	P.J. Pope	2004	21	0	0	0	126
3	Bernard White	1985	19	0	0	0	114
	Dave Preston	1974	19	0	0	0	114
5	Shaun Suisham	2004	0	14	69	0	111

TOUCHDOWNS

RANK	PLAYER	SEASON	G	TOT
1	Josh Harris	2002	12	22
2	P.J. Pope	2004	12	21
3	Bernard White	1985	NA	19
	Dave Preston	1974	NA	19
5	2 players tied at 15			

TACKLES

RANK	PLAYER	SEASON	TOT
1	Richard Duetemeyer	1971	163
2	Mike Callesen	1977	160
	John Villapiano	1972	160
	John Villapiano	1971	160
5	Troy Dawson	1984	157

INTERCEPTIONS

RANK	PLAYER	SEASON	YDS	TOT
1	Max Minnich	1948	207	12

PUNTING

RANK	PLAYER	SEASON	AVG
1	Chris Shale	1990	46.8
2	Andy Pollock	1998	44.9
3	Bill Bradshaw	1953	44.0
4	Bill Bradshaw	1954	43.9
5	Norm Limpert	1964	42.1

PUNT RETURNS

RANK	PLAYER	SEASON	RET	YDS	AVG
1	Bob Zimpfer	1967	23	379	16.5
2	Bill Bradshaw	1954	NA	NA	14.4
3	Courtney Davis	1996	NA	NA	13.2
4	Allen Smith	1990	NA	NA	12.4
5	Robert Redd	2001	35	385	11.0

KICKOFF RETURNS

RANK	PLAYER	SEASON	RET	YDS	AVG
1	Joe Alls	2001	13	350	26.9
2	Zeb Jackson	1993	NA	NA	26.8
3	Kelly Lycan	1981	NA	NA	25.9
4	Steve Kuehl	1976	17	422	24.8
5	Joe Souliere	1966	NA	NA	24.5

CAREER RECORDS

RUSHING YARDS

RANK	PLAYER	SEASONS	ATT	AVG	TD	YDS
1	Dave Preston	1973-76	830	4.1	39	3,423
2	Paul Miles	1971-73	767	4.2	25	3,239
3	P.J. Pope	2002-05	595	5.2	33	3,116
4	Fred Durig	1950-52	NA	5.7	NA	2,564
5	Josh Harris	2000-03	596	4.1	43	2,473

PASSING YARDS

RANK	PLAYER	SEASONS	ATT	COMP	PCT	INT	TD	YDS
1	Brian McClure	1982-85	1,427	900	63.0	58	63	10,280
2	Josh Harris	2000-03	1,028	627	60.9	28	55	7,503
3	Omar Jacobs	2003-05	998	523	52.4	11	71	6,938
4	Rich Dackin	1986-89	1,073	591	55.0	44	NA	6,862
5	Erik White	1989-92	950	515	54.2	41	39	6,072

RECEIVING YARDS

RANK	PLAYER	SEASONS	REC	AVG	TD	YDS
1	Charles Sharon	2002-05	232	14.9	34	3,450
2	Robert Redd	1998-2002	211	12.9	26	2,726
3	Stan Hunter	1982-85	176	15.2	21	2,679
4	Mark Szlachcic	1989-93	182	13.8	18	2,507
5	Ronald Heard	1986-89	139	17.9	NA	2,491
6	Cole Magner	2001-04	215	11.1	18	2,385
7	Steve Sanders	2002-05	156	14.9	24	2,324
8	Jeff Groth	1975-78	NA	NA	NA	2,268
9	Reggie Thornton	1986-89	158	14.1	NA	2,231
10	Ronnie Redd	1991-94	NA	NA	27	2,196

SCORING

RANK	PLAYER	SEASONS	TD	FG	PAT	P2	TOT
1	Shaun Suisham	2001-04	0	45	226	0	361
2	Josh Harris	2000-03	47	0	0	1	284
3	Brian Leaver	1991-94	0	44	115	0	247
4	Dave Preston	1973-76	41	0	0	0	246
	P.J. Pope	2002-05	41	0	0	0	246

TOUCHDOWNS

RANK	PLAYER	SEASONS	TOT
1	Josh Harris	2000-03	47
2	Dave Preston	1973-76	41
	P.J. Pope	2002-05	41
4	Charles Sharon	2002-05	35
5	Bernard White	1984-85	34

TACKLES

RANK	PLAYER	SEASONS	TOT
1	Vince Palko	1991-94	478
2	Kevin O'Neill	1994-97	462
3	Troy Dawson	1982-85	455
4	John Villapiano	1971-73	439
5	Kyle Kramer	1985-88	399

INTERCEPTIONS

RANK	PLAYER	SEASONS	YDS	TOT
1	Martin Bayless	1980-83	NA	27
2	Janssen Patton	2000-03	229	18
3	Dave Bielinski	1989-92	NA	14
4	Jac Tomasello	1978-82	NA	13

PUNTING

RANK	PLAYER	SEASONS	PUNTS	YDS	AVG
1	Cris Shale	1988-1990	183	7,885	43.1
2	Andy Pollock	1996-98	191	8,066	42.3
3	Bill Bradshaw	1952-54	NA	NA	42.2
4	Greg A. Johnson	1984-86	189	7,731	40.9
	Jim Phelps	1981-83	219	8,955	40.9

TEAM RECORDS

LONGEST WINNING STREAK
• 18, Nov. 8, 1958-Nov. 5, 1960
Streak broken vs. Ohio, 7-14, Nov. 12, 1960

LONGEST UNDEFEATED STREAK
• 18 (tie), Oct. 18, 1929-Oct. 24, 1931
Streak broken vs. Defiance, 0-15, Oct. 31, 1931;
Nov. 8, 1958-Nov. 5, 1960
Streak broken vs. Ohio, 7-14, Nov. 12, 1960

MOST CONSECUTIVE WINNING SEASONS
• 15, 1955-1969

MOST CONSECUTIVE BOWL APPEARANCES
• 2 (tie), 1991-92; 2003-04

MOST POINTS IN A GAME
• 151, vs. Findlay, Oct. 15, 1921

MOST POINTS ALLOWED IN A GAME
• 63 (tie), vs. Toledo, Nov. 1, 1935; vs. Brigham Young,
Sept. 17, 1983

LARGEST MARGIN OF VICTORY
• 151 (151-0), vs. Findlay, Oct. 15, 1921

LARGEST MARGIN OF DEFEAT
• 63 (0-63), vs. Toledo, Nov. 1, 1935

LONGEST RUN FROM SCRIMMAGE
• 93 yards, Mike McGee, vs. Central Michigan, Sept. 26, 1987

LONGEST PASS PLAY
• 96 yards, Mark Minor to Dave Dudley, vs. San Diego State,
Sept. 25, 1976

LONGEST FIELD GOAL
• 60 yards, Derek Schorejs, vs. Toledo, Oct. 21, 1995

LONGEST PUNT
• 95 yards, Mars Lettman, vs. Bluffton, Oct. 13, 1928

LONGEST PUNT RETURN
• 100 yards, Courtney Davis, vs. Kent State, Oct. 12, 1996

LONGEST INTERCEPTION RETURN
• 90 yards, Rodney Cash, vs. Toledo, Oct. 9, 1948

PUNT RETURNS

RANK	PLAYER	SEASONS	RET	YDS	AVG
1	Bob Zimpfer	1967-69	72	958	13.3
2	Charles Sharon	2002-05	82	848	10.3
3	Robert Redd	1998-2002	105	823	7.8
4	Bill Pittman	1970-72	65	449	6.9

KICKOFF RETURNS

RANK	PLAYER	SEASONS	RET	YDS	AVG
1	Steve Kuehl	1973-76	49	1,078	22.0
2	Terry Nelson	1989-92	49	1,051	21.4
3	Darryl Story	1983-86	51	1,080	21.2
4	Joe Alls	1999-2000	55	1,147	20.9
5	Reggie Thornton	1988-89	65	1,222	18.8

BOWLING GREEN ANNUAL STATISTICAL LEADERS

YR	RUSHING	YDS	ATT	AVG	PASSING	ATT	CMP	PCT	YDS	RECEIVING	REC	YDS	AVG
1947	Jack Woodland	536	102	5.3	Ennis Walker	83	31	.37	476	Max Minnich	12	224	18.7
1948	Jack Woodland	522	108	4.8	Max Minnich	38	19	.50	405	Robert Schnelker	14	243	17.4
1949	Jack Woodland	694	133	5.2	Rod Lash	79	29	.37	599	Robert Schnelker	20	434	21.7
1950	Richard Pont	627	111	5.6	Rex Simonds	79	23	.29	319	Doug Mooney	8	36	4.5
1951	Fred Durig	1,444	214	6.7	Rex Simonds	95	36	.38	506	Jim Ladd	16	236	14.8
1952	Fred Durig	858	181	4.7	Bill Lyons	134	71	.53	915	Jim Ladd	43	632	14.7
1953	Bill Bradshaw	236	110	2.1	Bill Bradshaw	126	48	.38	865	Jim Ladd	31	473	15.3
1954	John Ladd	266	81	3.3	Bill Bradshaw	53	21	.40	414	Jack Hecker	12	274	22.8
1955	Carlos Jackson	505	86	5.9	Jim Bryan	64	45	.70	770	Jack Hecker	29	556	19.2
1956	Vic DeOrio	816	149	5.5	Don Nehlen	49	26	.53	362	Ray Reese	12	183	15.3
1957	Bob Ramlow	492	108	4.6	Don Nehlen	70	36	.51	499	Ray Reese	12	185	15.4
1958	Bob Ramlow	779	140	5.6	Bob Colburn	87	46	.53	685	Bernie Casey	16	310	19.4
1959	Chuck Comer	361	53	6.8	Bob Colburn	111	60	.54	788	Bernie Casey	18	264	14.7
1960	Don Lisbon	605	99	6.1	Jim Potts	71	44	.62	662	Clarence Mason	14	191	13.6
1961	Russ Hepner	637	137	4.6	Jim Potts	91	47	.52	712	Russ Hepner	14	187	13.4
1962	Don Lisbon	481	94	5.1	Tony Ruggiero	60	29	.48	393	Jay Cunningham	13	259	19.9
1963	Jay Cunningham	539	128	4.2	Jerry Ward	127	59	.47	858	Tom Sims	12	177	14.8
1964	Stew Williams	609	109	5.6	Jerry Ward	114	57	.50	726	Jay Cunningham	14	174	12.4
1965	Stew Williams	616	145	4.3	Dwight Wallace	66	34	.52	425	Dave Cranmer	16	180	11.3
1966	Dave Cranmer	374	81	4.6	P.J. Nyitray	79	38	.48	431	Eddie Jones	40	525	13.1
1967	Bob Zimpfer	538	128	4.2	P.J. Nyitray	164	73	.45	846	Eddie Jones	30	374	12.5
1968	Fred Mathews	733	207	3.6	P.J. Nyitray	144	78	.54	898	Eddie Jones	49	716	14.6
1969	Issac Wright	344	96	3.5	Vern Wireman	281	147	.52	1,666	Bob Zimpfer	48	785	16.3
1970	Julius Livas	279	109	2.6	Vern Wireman	174	60	.35	622	Bill Pittman	21	235	11.2
1971	Paul Miles	1,185	274	4.3	Reid Lamport	154	71	.46	1,006	Rick Newman	25	443	17.7
1972	Paul Miles	1,024	243	4.2	Reid Lamport	89	28	.32	430	Roger Wallace	16	242	15.1
1973	Paul Miles	1,030	250	4.1	Reid Lamport	161	70	.44	1,084	Roger Wallace	37	587	15.9
1974	Dave Preston	1,414	324	4.4	Mark Miller	134	67	.50	725	John Boles	25	291	11.6
1975	Dan Saleet	1,114	194	5.7	Mark Miller	187	98	.52	1,252	Dave Dudley	25	338	13.5
1976	Dave Preston	989	248	4.0	Mark Miller	245	126	.51	1,839	Jeff Groth	33	598	18.1
1977	Dan Saleet	572	137	4.2	Mark Miller	285	164	.58	2,103	Jeff Groth	39	693	17.8
1978	Dave Windatt	608	118	5.2	Mike Wright	259	134	.52	1,852	Jeff Groth	56	874	15.6
1979	Kevin Folkes	696	163	4.3	Mike Wright	210	104	.50	1,148	Dan Shetler	37	502	13.6
1980	Bryant Jones	806	174	4.6	Greg Taylor	77	43	.56	562	Dan Shetler	20	310	15.5
1981	Bryant Jones	1,051	253	4.2	Dayne Palsgrove	153	79	.52	732	Shawn Potts	31	391	12.6
1982	Chip Otten	673	157	4.3	Brian McClure	176	113	.64	1,391	Shawn Potts	50	841	16.8
1983	Darryl Story	724	166	4.4	Brian McClure	466	298	.64	3,264	Mark Dowdell	70	679	9.7
1984	Bernard White	1,036	247	4.2	Brian McClure	414	263	.64	2,951	Bernard White	56	400	7.1
1985	Bernard White	949	221	4.3	Brian McClure	371	226	.61	2,674	Stan Hunter	55	761	13.8
1986	Jeff Davis	825	180	4.3	Rich Dackin	194	114	.59	1,197	Gerald Bayless	34	300	8.8
1987	Shawn Daniels	423	121	3.5	Rich Dackin	330	189	.57	2,211	Reggie Thornton	47	698	14.9
1988	Mike McGee	538	146	3.5	Eric Smith	184	104	.57	1,306	Reggie Thornton	41	589	14.4
1989	LeRoy Smith	564	161	3.5	Rich Dackin	394	215	.55	2,679	Ronald Heard	51	916	18.0
1990	George Johnson	449	104	4.1	Erik White	262	127	.49	1,386	Mark Szlachcic	46	582	12.7
1991	LeRoy Smith	937	271	3.3	Erik White	323	185	.57	2,204	Mark Szlachcic	65	943	14.5
1992	Zeb Jackson	792	169	4.3	Erik White	344	195	.57	2,380	Mark Szlachcic	62	834	13.5
1993	Zeb Jackson	1,016	237	4.0	Ryan Henry	325	169	.49	2,242	Rameir Martin	56	876	15.6
1994	Keylan Cates	803	184	4.4	Ryan Henry	293	174	.59	2,368	Ronnie Redd	48	831	17.3
1995	Keylan Cates	910	220	3.9	Ryan Henry	177	90	.51	938	Eric Starks	32	433	13.5
1996	Courtney Davis	767	229	3.3	Bob Niemet	191	83	.44	1,129	Damron Hamilton	29	465	16.0
1997	Robbie Hollis	492	151	3.3	Bob Niemet	256	133	.52	1,723	Damron Hamilton	52	777	14.9
1998	Godfrey Lewis	753	163	4.6	Bob Niemet	144	68	.47	949	Kurt Gerling	34	656	19.3
1999	Joe Alls	592	117	5.1	Ricky Schneider	181	95	.53	1,121	Kurt Gerling	53	775	14.5
2000	John Gibson	514	155	3.3	Andy Sahm	244	123	.50	1,490	David Bautista	69	915	13.3
2001	Josh Harris	614	126	4.9	Andy Sahm	198	122	.62	1,326	Robert Redd	72	884	12.3
2002	Joe Alls	801	122	6.6	Josh Harris	353	198	.56	2,425	Robert Redd	83	973	11.7
2003	P.J. Pope	1,005	191	5.3	Josh Harris	494	325	.66	3,813	Cole Magner	99	1,138	11.5
2004	P.J. Pope	1,098	178	6.2	Omar Jacobs	462	309	.67	4,002	Cole Magner	77	746	9.7
2005	B.J. Lane	677	139	4.9	Omar Jacobs	321	195	.61	2590	Charles Sharon	74	1028	13.9
2006	Chris Bullock	769	160	4.8	Anthony Turner	252	144	.57	1596	Corey Partridge	55	658	12.0

Receiving leaders by receptions
All statistics include postseason

MAC TEAMS

BUFFALO

BY ED KRZEMIENSKI

THE STATE UNIVERSITY OF NEW York at Buffalo, now known as the University of Buffalo, dropped football as a varsity sport in January 1971 because of campus ambivalence and disputes over athletic expenses. The Bulls were not dead, though, only sleeping. In 1977, students and alumni persuaded the administration to resurrect the program. Shortly thereafter, the Bulls began what supporters termed the Run to Division I, a goal finally reached in 1999.

Getting there was the easy part. In its first five years in the MAC, Buffalo went 7–50 overall and 4–36 in the conference. With the rest of the MAC getting stronger by national standards and the conference's ongoing efforts to take on tougher opponents in out-of-conference games, the Bulls have a tough road ahead of them. But there are reasons for optimism. The school houses genuinely fine athletic facilities. It's located in a sports-crazy town that not only supports the NFL's Bills and NHL's Sabres but also sets attendance records for its minor league baseball team, the Bisons. Sure, it snows some in Buffalo. But the Bulls have a lot going for them.

In 2006, the school infused its team with some national pedigree when it hired former Nebraska standout quarterback Turner Gill as its new head coach. In his playing days, Gill never lost a conference game and was a finalist for the Heisman Trophy; as an assistant coach for his alma mater, Gill served on three national championship teams and coached a Heisman Trophy winner. At Buffalo, he quickly demonstrated a commanding presence, a gift for recruiting, and an unmistakable resolve to help mold the Bulls into a credible Division I team. Hopes—and expectations—have taken a huge jump for college football in Buffalo.

TRADITION Outside of Division I play, Buffalo has a long tradition. In 1894, 14 medical students practiced in a pasture heavily trodden by grazing horses before playing the school's first football game against Hobart College on a Buffalo baseball field. More than a century later on Sept. 23, 2000, Buffalo got its first Division I victory, beating Bowling Green 20-17. Traditions, then, are a work in progress. One of the recent additions—an a cappella rendition of the Bulls' fight song at halftime of home games—still has a ways to go before it becomes a permanent fixture.

BEST PLAYER Gerry Philbin played in the North-South All-Star Shrine Game after his senior season in 1963. The two-way tackle brutalized opponents for a Bulls team that went 5–3–1, and after graduation, Philbin went on to even bigger accomplishments when he joined the New York Jets of the AFL. There, utilized strictly as a defensive end, Philbin helped the Jets to their upset win in Super Bowl III; the following year he was inducted into the Bulls Athletic Hall of Fame. Philbin, who went on to the AFL, NFL, and World Football League for 11 seasons, was named to the All-Time AFL Team in 1969.

PROFILE

University of Buffalo
Buffalo, N.Y.
Founded: 1846
Enrollment: 27,220
Colors: Royal Blue and White
Nickname: Bulls
Stadium: UB Stadium
    Opened in 1993
    Artificial; 29,020 capacity
First football game: 1894
All-time record: 317–443–28 (.420)
First-round draft choices: 0
Website: www.buffalobulls.com

THE BEST OF TIMES

The Bulls put together five consecutive winning seasons from 1946 to 1950.

THE WORST OF TIMES

As expected, Buffalo faced a tough transition to Division I-A play in 1999 and 2000, going 2–20 in the MAC, including 14 consecutive losses out of the gate; in 1901, UB lost to Michigan 128–0.

CONFERENCE HISTORY

Buffalo joined the Mid-American Conference in 1999. From 1894 to 1998, the Bulls played as an independent.

DISTINGUISHED ALUMNI

Wolf Blitzer, CNN anchor; Brad Grey, TV producer, *The Sopranos*; Henry J. Nowak, Congressman; Ron Silver, actor

BEST COACH In 1955, Buffalo chancellor Clifford Furnas hired Dick Offenhamer to bring the Bulls back to respectability. Led by standout tackle Frank Woidzik, the Bulls posted a 4–4–1 record under the new head coach. Buffalo then reeled off four consecutive winning seasons, including back-to-back 8–1 seasons in 1958-59. In 11 seasons, Offenhamer's record was 58–37–5; his total victories rank second in school history, but his .605 winning percentage is the school's best for coaches with more than two seasons' service.

BEST TEAM The 1958 Bulls went 8–1, including a 6-3 win over powerful Harvard. Dick Offenhamer's team won the Lambert Cup for small eastern colleges and received a bid to the Tangerine Bowl. In a bold decision, the school declined the invitation to protest the bowl's discriminatory practices prohibiting black athletes from competing on its field. The team, however, received even greater publicity than the Tangerine Bowl could offer when, on Dec. 14, team captains Bottini and Lou Reale appeared on *The Ed Sullivan Show* to receive the Lambert Cup. In 1993, the school honored the 1958 team's accomplishments, both on and off the field, when it inducted the entire team into its athletic Hall of Fame.

BEST BACKFIELD In 1986, quarterback Ken Crosta and running back O.D. Underwood made up Buffalo's best backfield ever. Crosta threw for over 1,600 yards and 9 touchdowns for a 129.2 passer rating.

> *A band member recovered the original lyrics to the fight song, lost when football was eliminated in 1971.*

Underwood added 1,189 yards rushing, 15 touchdowns, five 100-yard games, and a monstrous 232-yard performance against Rochester. The team did well too, going 9–2.

BEST DEFENSE Except for a stellar two seasons in 1897 and 1899, two years when the team gave up a total of 12 points and lost no games, Buffalo's defensive strategy seems to that "the best defense is a good offense." Even in their best years, the Bulls have given up a lot of points. The 1959 defense stands out as an anomaly. Led by Nick Bottini and Gordon Bukaty (who intercepted six passes), the '59 Bulls defense held five opponents to under 10 points in their second consecutive 8–1 season.

BIGGEST GAME Riding a 14-game losing streak as a Division I school, Buffalo hosted Bowling Green for its fourth game of the 2000 season. With 1:27 remaining and the Bulls trailing by four points, Buffalo running back Marquis Dwarte managed to break off a 27-yard touchdown run, and the Bulls held on for a 20-17 win, their first Division I victory.

BIGGEST UPSET On Sept. 7, 2002, the Bulls traveled to Piscataway, N.J., to take on a Rutgers team that had beaten them by a combined score of 90-15 in their two most recent encounters. This particular evening, though, the Bulls dominated on both sides of the ball and scored a 34-11 victory.

MAC TEAMS

FIGHT SONG

BUFFALO VICTORY MARCH

Fight, fight for Buffalo, be proud
To fight for your dear Blue and White
So hit 'em high! Hit 'em low!
Throw 'em high! Throw 'em low!
Fight for your dear old Bulls!
Huh!
Cheer, cheer for Buffalo,
Our spirit will be with you 'til the end.
So play the game as best you can
For the glory of our dear Buffalo!

HIGHEST DRAFT CHOICE

1964	Gerry Philbin, Lions (3rd/30) and Jets (3rd/19)*

From 1960 to1966, the NFL and the AFL held separate, competing drafts.

CONSENSUS ALL-AMERICANS

1984	Gerry Quinlivan,	LB
1987	Steve Wojciechowski,	LB
1995	Pete Conley,	LB
1996	Michael Chichester,	DB

STADIUM In 1991, the New York State Dormitory Authority financed the construction of UB Stadium for $23 million. It quickly became a center for track and field, hosting the World University Games in 1993 and the NCAA Division I championships in 1998. Additional construction to the stadium brought it to its current capacity of 29,020.

MASCOT Big and blue, Victor E. Bull is one of the top mascots in the country. In 2002, Vic achieved what his favorite team could not when he was invited to a New Year's Day bowl. As one of the 12 All-America mascots chosen to compete for the inaugural national Mascot of the Year, Victor joined such heady company as Otto the Orange from Syracuse, Sebastian the Ibis from Miami, and the Penn State Nittany Lion.

UNIFORMS In Buffalo's first football game in 1894, Buffalo players wore blue jerseys, introducing one of the school's offical colors, which was paired with white. The uniforms have always used this color scheme, as have the helmets, with a bit of red thrown in at various times. The helmets have been white or blue, with numbers, the letters UB, or, more frequently, buffaloes in various poses: running, jumping, or snorting. In 2006, stylized horns were replaced on the Bulls' helmet by the interlocking block letters UB.

RIVAL At the Bowl Subdivision level, the Bulls still lack an intense rivalry. The most likely suspect is Rutgers. Close enough for unfriendly familiarity and on opposite sides of New York City condescension, the two schools have some necessary ingredients for a rivalry, and Rutgers' recent emergence as a Big East power has given the game an added appeal. The teams began playing regularly in 2000.

NICKNAME From 1915 to 1930, Buffalo was known as the Bisons. In 1931, though, the school changed its nickname to the Bulls in order to distinguish it from the city's professional teams.

LORE Buffalo owes some debt to *Sports Illustrated*. In the March 11, 1963, issue, a drawing of an enraged bull by artist Robert Riger appeared. The school requested, and received, permission to use the image of The Fighting Bull and unveiled it as its official logo one month later. More than three decades later, another issue of *Sports Illustrated* influenced the school. In his weekly column, Rick Reilly mentioned that "even Buffalo doesn't know the lyrics to Buffalo's" fight song. That spurred one of the members of the marching band to search for the original lyrics, lost when the school eliminated the football program in 1971 and the marching band in 1972. Tracking down the author, a retired professor of music, the student recovered a revised version of the song and renewed a tradition in Buffalo.

QUOTE "We finally did it."—Bulls senior linebacker Chris Gray, after the team won its first Division I-A game over Bowling Green in 2000.

BUFFALO ALL-TIME SCORES

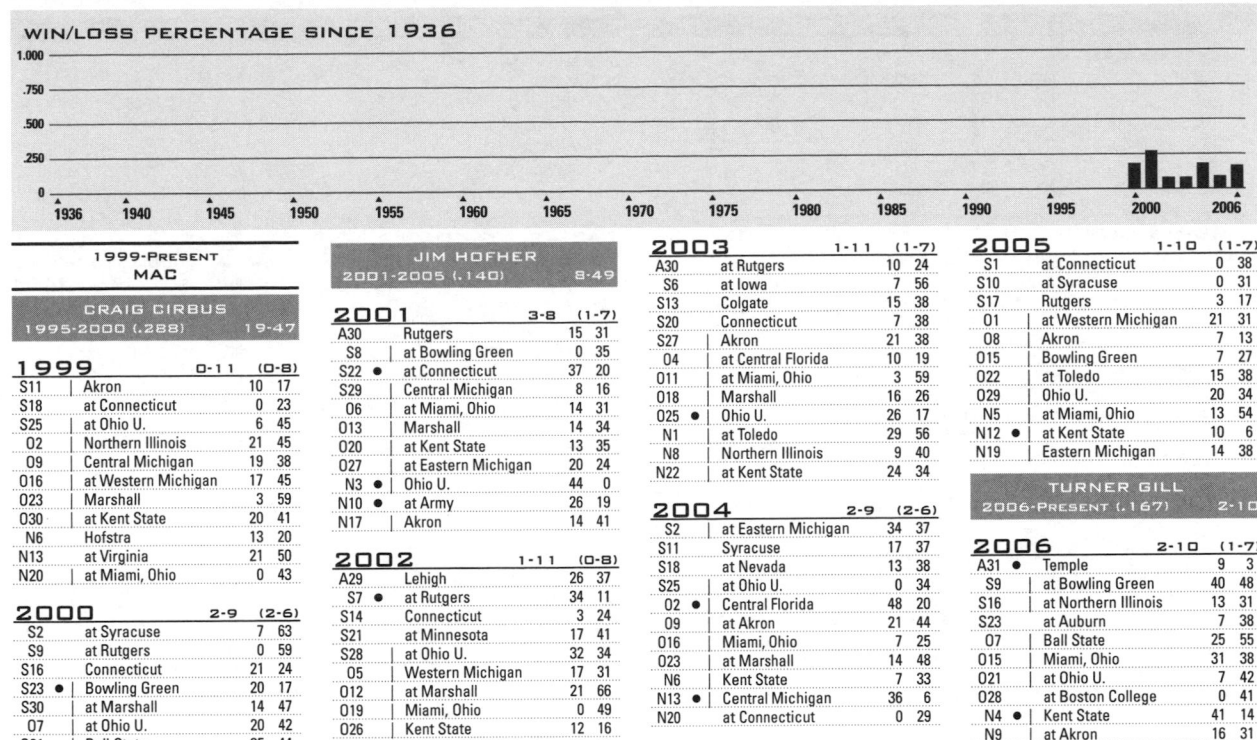

WIN/LOSS PERCENTAGE SINCE 1936

1999-PRESENT		
MAC		

CRAIG CIRBUS		
1995-2000 (.288)		19-47

1999   0-11   (0-8)

S11	Akron	10	17
S18	at Connecticut	0	23
S25	at Ohio U.	6	45
O2	Northern Illinois	21	45
O9	Central Michigan	19	38
O16	at Western Michigan	17	45
O23	Marshall	3	59
O30	at Kent State	20	41
N6	Hofstra	13	20
N13	at Virginia	21	50
N20	at Miami, Ohio	0	43

2000   2-9   (2-6)

S2	at Syracuse	7	63
S9	at Rutgers	0	59
S16	Connecticut	21	24
S23 ●	Bowling Green	20	17
S30	at Marshall	14	47
O7	at Ohio U.	20	42
O21	Ball State	35	44
O28	at Northern Illinois	10	73
N4 ●	Kent State	20	17
N11	at Akron	14	49
N18	Miami, Ohio	16	17

JIM HOFHER		
2001-2005 (.140)		8-49

2001   3-8   (1-7)

A30	Rutgers	15	31
S8	at Bowling Green	0	35
S22 ●	at Connecticut	37	20
S29	Central Michigan	8	16
O6	at Miami, Ohio	14	31
O13	Marshall	14	34
O20	at Kent State	13	35
O27	at Eastern Michigan	20	24
N3 ●	Ohio U.	44	0
N10 ●	at Army	26	19
N17	Akron	14	41

2002   1-11   (0-8)

A29	Lehigh	26	37
S7 ●	at Rutgers	34	11
S14	Connecticut	3	24
S21	at Minnesota	17	41
S28	at Ohio U.	32	34
O5	Western Michigan	17	31
O12	at Marshall	21	66
O19	Miami, Ohio	0	49
O26	Kent State	12	16
N9	Central Florida	21	45
N16	at Akron	10	21
N23	at Ball State	21	41

2003   1-11   (1-7)

A30	at Rutgers	10	24
S6	at Iowa	7	56
S13	Colgate	15	38
S20	Connecticut	7	38
S27	Akron	21	38
O4	at Central Florida	10	19
O11	at Miami, Ohio	3	59
O18	Marshall	16	26
O25 ●	Ohio U.	26	17
N1	at Toledo	29	56
N8	Northern Illinois	9	40
N22	at Kent State	24	34

2004   2-9   (2-6)

S2	at Eastern Michigan	34	37
S11	Syracuse	17	37
S18	at Nevada	13	38
S25	at Ohio U.	0	34
O2 ●	Central Florida	48	20
O9	at Akron	21	44
O16	Miami, Ohio	7	25
O23	at Marshall	14	48
N6	Kent State	7	33
N13 ●	Central Michigan	36	6
N20	at Connecticut	0	29

2005   1-10   (1-7)

S1	at Connecticut	0	38
S10	at Syracuse	0	31
S17	Rutgers	3	17
O1	at Western Michigan	21	31
O8	Akron	7	13
O15	Bowling Green	7	27
O22	at Toledo	15	38
O29	Ohio U.	20	34
N5	at Miami, Ohio	13	54
N12 ●	at Kent State	10	6
N19	Eastern Michigan	14	38

TURNER GILL		
2006-PRESENT (.167)		2-10

2006   2-10   (1-7)

A31 ●	Temple	9	3
S9	at Bowling Green	40	48
S16	at Northern Illinois	13	31
S23	at Auburn	7	38
O7	Ball State	25	55
O15	Miami, Ohio	31	38
O21	at Ohio U.	7	42
O28	at Boston College	0	41
N4 ●	Kent State	41	14
N9	at Akron	16	31
N18	at Wisconsin	3	35
N24	Central Michigan	28	55

BUFFALO RECORD BOOK

SINGLE-GAME RECORDS

RUSHING YARDS

RANK	PLAYER	DATE	OPPONENT	ATT	AVG	YDS
1	Alan Bell	Nov. 2, 1991	Duquesne	26	10.2	266
2	O.D. Underwood	Sept. 27, 1986	Rochester	36	6.4	232
3	Anthony Swan	Sept. 21, 1996	Lehigh	29	7.4	215
4	Anthony Swan	Sept. 2, 1995	Fordham	26	7.8	204
5	O.D. Underwood	Nov. 7, 1987	Albany State	30	6.7	201

PASSING YARDS

RANK	PLAYER	DATE	OPPONENT	ATT	COMP	YDS
1	Cliff Scott	Sept. 12, 1992	New Haven	51	29	490
2	Chad Salisbury	Oct. 18, 1997	Massachusetts	51	30	459
3	Chad Salisbury	Sept. 6, 1997	Illinois State	45	29	445
4	Chad Salisbury	Sept. 27, 1997	West Chester	46	29	418
5	Jim Rodriguez	Nov. 4, 1978	Coast Guard	41	30	417

RECEIVING YARDS

RANK	PLAYER	DATE	OPPONENT	REC	AVG	YDS
1	Joe D'Amico	Sept. 12, 1981	Cortland	5	43.6	218
2	Andre Forde	Sept. 28, 2002	Ohio	12	16.8	202
3	Gary Quatrani	Nov. 4, 1978	Coast Guard	10	19.6	196
4	Doc Smith	Sept. 12, 1992	New Haven	7	25.4	178
5	Chaz Ahmed	Oct. 27, 1990	Mercyhurst	13	13.5	175

POINTS

RANK	PLAYER	DATE	OPPONENT	TOT
1	Lou Corriere	Nov. 7, 1942	Hobart	36
2	Anthony Swan	Sept. 2, 1995	Fordham	30

FIELD GOALS

RANK	PLAYER	DATE	OPPONENT	TOT
1	Dallas Pelz	Nov. 1, 2003	Toledo	5
2	Dallas Pelz	Oct. 25, 2003	Ohio	4

TACKLES

RANK	PLAYER	DATE	OPPONENT	TOT
1	Craig Guest	Oct. 7, 1995	Maine	29
2	Lamar Wilcher	Aug. 30, 2003	Rutgers	16
3	Bryan Cummings	Nov. 20, 2004	Connecticut	15
	Mark Graham	Oct. 25, 2003	Ohio	15
	Craig Rohlfs	Oct. 21, 2000	Ball State	15

INTERCEPTIONS

RANK	PLAYER	DATE	OPPONENT	TOT
1	Pete Rao	Nov. 3, 1953	Cortland State	4

RETIRED NUMBERS

Buffalo has no retired numbers

SINGLE-SEASON RECORDS

RUSHING YARDS

RANK	PLAYER	SEASON	ATT	YDS
1	O.D. Underwood	1986	229	1,189
2	Anthony Swan	1996	244	1,117
3	Alan Bell	1991	225	1,017
4	Anthony Swan	1995	236	968
5	Aaron Leeper	2002	235	917

PASSING YARDS

RANK	PLAYER	SEASON	ATT	COMP	PCT	YDS
1	Chad Salisbury	1997	384	218	56.7	2,889
2	Marty Barrett	1983	366	207	56.5	2,504
3	Cliff Scott	1993	320	176	55.0	2,263
4	Marty Barrett	1981	267	131	49.0	2,155
5	Cliff Scott	1992	287	140	48.7	2,088

RECEIVING YARDS

RANK	PLAYER	SEASON	REC	AVG	YDS
1	Drew Haddad	1997	67	17.0	1,158
2	Drew Haddad	1999	85	12.0	1,058
3	Doc Smith	1992	47	21.0	996
4	Chris D'Amico	1983	56	17.0	929
5	Chaz Ahmed	1990	59	16.0	927

SCORING

RANK	PLAYER	SEASON	TD	FG	PAT	P2	TOT
1	Lee Jones	1966	16	0	0	0	96
2	Pat Whitehead	1982	15	0	0	2	94
3	O.D. Underwood	1986	15	0	0	0	90
4	Lee Jones	1967	12	0	0	0	72
5	Gerald Carlson	1995	0	17	0	17	68

TOUCHDOWNS

RANK	PLAYER	SEASON	TOT
1	Cliff Scott	1992	27
2	Marty Barrett	1983	18
3	4 players tied at 16		

TACKLES

RANK	PLAYER	SEASON	TOT
1	Craig Guest	1995	161
2	Pete Conley	1995	145
3	Steve Wojciechowski	1987	142
4	Craig Guest	1996	136
5	Mike Laipple	1985	127

INTERCEPTIONS

RANK	PLAYER	SEASON	YDS	TOT
1	Steve Nappo	1986	155	13
2	John Bernard	1983	143	12
3	Andy Hurley	1983	98	9
4	Jon Williams	1988	153	8
5	Andy Hurley	1984	110	7

PUNTING

RANK	PLAYER	SEASON	PUNTS	YDS	AVG
1	Mike Masucci	2000	38	1,575	41.4
2	Ben Woods	2004	72	2,964	41.2
3	Mike Masucci	1999	57	2,324	40.8
4	Scott McMahan	2002	81	3,258	40.2
5	Lawrence Hart	1969	51	2,035	40.0

PUNT RETURNS

RANK	PLAYER	SEASON	RET	YDS	AVG
1	Drew Haddad	1998	23	410	17.8
2	Naaman Roosevelt	2006	11	144	13.1
3	Drew Haddad	1999	21	254	12.1
4	Tom Hurd	1965	13	154	11.9
5	Andre Forde	2001	13	135	10.4

KICKOFF RETURNS

RANK	PLAYER	SEASON	RET	YDS	AVG
1	Naaman Roosevelt	2006	28	724	25.9
2	Rick Wells	1967	11	275	25.0
3	Gene Nance	1970	18	447	24.8
4	Alan Bell	1989	20	485	24.3
5	Keith Warren	1993	14	327	23.4

CAREER RECORDS

RUSHING YARDS

RANK	PLAYER	SEASONS	ATT	AVG	TD	YDS
1	Anthony Swan	1994-97	812	3.8	29	3,103
2	Alan Bell	1989-92	682	4.4	26	3,022
3	O.D. Underwood	1986-87	438	4.7	25	2,062
4	Lee Jones	1965-67	414	3.8	29	1,570
5	Willie Evans	1957-59	244	6.4	6	1,559
6	Derrick Gordon	1998-2001	347	4.4	9	1,528
7	Josh Roth	1996-99	330	4.5	14	1,488
8	Aaron Leeper	2002-04	357	4.0	12	1,439
9	Dave Dawson	2002-05	251	5.6	6	1,402
10	Pat Whitehead	1980-82	294	4.7	17	1,382

PASSING YARDS

RANK	PLAYER	SEASONS	ATT	COMP	PCT	INT	TD	YDS
1	Cliff Scott	1991-94	1,101	545	49.5	58	43	7,578
2	Marty Barrett	1980-83	956	513	53.7	53	44	6,945
3	Joe Freedy	1998-2001	1,008	522	51.8	45	32	5,912
4	Chad Salisbury	1997-98	671	372	55.4	30	31	4,947
5	Frank Reilly	1988-90	597	325	46.7	45	27	4,255
6	Ken Hyer	1981-84	529	275	51.6	26	22	3,420
7	Jim Rodriguez	1978-80	536	250	46.6	45	20	3,401
8	Randall Secky	2001-04	684	324	47.3	22	13	3,154
9	Mark Taylor	1993-96	544	248	45.6	30	14	3,143
10	Mick Murtha	1966-69	520	222	42.7	38	16	2,985

RECEIVING YARDS

RANK	PLAYER	SEASONS	REC	AVG	TD	YDS
1	Drew Haddad	1996-99	240	14.2	16	3,409
2	Chris D'Amico	1980-84	143	16.3	19	2,331
3	Kali Watkins	1995-98	145	15.6	15	2,260
4	Rusty Knapp	1990-93	129	16.3	5	2,105
5	Frank Price	1977-80	125	14.5	14	1,810
6	Andre Forde	1999-2002	125	14.2	15	1,775
7	Chaz Ahmed	1987-90	110	15.6	7	1,716
8	Jamie Gasparre	1996-97	102	15.5	19	1,581
9	Matt Knueven	2001-04	119	13.2	8	1,569
10	Gary Quatrani	1978-80	77	16.2	8	1,247

SCORING

RANK	PLAYER	SEASONS	TD	FG	PAT	P2	TOT
1	Alan Bell	1989-92	30	0	0	2	184
2	Anthony Swan	1994-97	30	0	0	0	180
3	Lee Jones	1965-67	29	0	0	0	174
4	O.D. Underwood	1986-87	25	0	0	1	152
5	Dallas Pelz	2000-03	0	35	42	0	147

TOUCHDOWNS

RANK	PLAYER	SEASONS	TOT
1	Cliff Scott	1991-94	63
2	Marty Barrett	1980-83	46
3	Gordon Bukaty	1958-60	37
4	Joe Freedy	1998-2001	34
5	3 players tied at 31		

TACKLES

RANK	PLAYER	SEASONS	TOT
1	Craig Guest	1993-96	455
2	Mike Laipple	1983-86	402
3	Pete Conley	1992-95	376
4	J.J. Gibson	2001-04	357
5	2 players tied at 300		

INTERCEPTIONS

RANK	PLAYER	SEASONS	YDS	TOT
1	Steve Nappo	1984-86	171	19
2	John Bernard	1980-83	221	18
3	Andy Hurley	1983-84	208	16
4	3 players tied at 12			

PUNTING

RANK	PLAYER	SEASONS	PUNTS	YDS	AVG
1	Scott McMahan	2001-02	149	5,900	39.6
2	Ben Woods	2004-	152	8,470	39.0
3	Mike Masucci	1997-2000	199	7,731	38.9
4	Dominic Milano	2003	78	2,977	37.7
5	Gerald Carlson	1993-96	260	9,732	37.4

PUNT RETURNS

RANK	PLAYER	SEASON	RET	YDS	AVG
1	Drew Haddad	1996-99	53	787	14.9
2	Naaman Roosevelt	2006-	11	144	13.1
3	Andre Forde	1999-2002	32	296	9.3
4	Dan Sella	1964-66	19	174	9.2
5	Craig Rohlfs	1998-2001	15	137	9.1

KICKOFF RETURNS

RANK	PLAYER	SEASON	RET	YDS	AVG
1	Naaman Roosevelt	2006-	28	724	25.9
2	Gene Nance	1970	18	447	24.8
3	Ruben Lindo	1991-92	17	417	24.5
4	Pat Patterson	1967-69	29	652	22.5
5	Bob Baker	1960-62	16	351	21.9

TEAM RECORDS

LONGEST WINNING STREAK
- 2, Nov. 3-10, 2001

Streak broken vs. Akron, 14-41, Nov. 17, 2001

LONGEST UNDEFEATED STREAK
- 2, Nov. 3-10, 2001

Streak broken vs. Akron, 14-41, Nov. 17, 2001

MOST CONSECUTIVE WINNING SEASONS
- None

MOST CONSECUTIVE BOWL APPEARANCES
- None

MOST POINTS IN A GAME
- 48, vs. Central Florida, Oct. 2, 2004

MOST POINTS ALLOWED IN A GAME
- 73, vs. Northern Illinois, Oct. 28, 2000

LARGEST MARGIN OF VICTORY
- 44 (44-0), vs. Ohio U., Nov. 3, 2001

LARGEST MARGIN OF DEFEAT
- 63 (10-73), vs. Northern Illinois, Oct. 28, 2000

LONGEST RUN FROM SCRIMMAGE
- 95 yards, Ed Malanowics, vs. Hobart, Nov. 16, 1929

LONGEST PASS PLAY
- 91 yards, Mark Taylor to Jamie Gasparre, vs. Hofstra, Nov. 2, 1996

LONGEST FIELD GOAL
- 54 yards, Gerald Carlson, vs. Edinboro, Sept. 28, 1996

LONGEST PUNT
- 86 yards (tie), Dana Loucks, vs. Frostburg State, Nov. 14, 1987; David Anastasi, vs. John Carroll, Sept. 2, 1989

LONGEST PUNT RETURN
- 94 yards, Drew Haddad, vs. Cornell, Oct. 3, 1998

LONGEST INTERCEPTION RETURN
- 90 yards, Gerry LaFountain, vs. Delaware, Nov. 6, 1965

MAC TEAMS

BUFFALO ANNUAL STATISTICAL LEADERS

YR	RUSHING	YDS	ATT	AVG	PASSING	ATT	CMP	PCT	YDS	RECEIVING	REC	YDS	AVG
1999	Josh Roth	519	124	4.2	Joe Freedy	299	151	.51	1,775	Drew Haddad	85	1,158	13.6
2000	Marquis Dwarte	611	129	4.7	Joe Freedy	338	184	.54	2,060	Andre Forde	36	590	16.4
2001	Marquis Dwarte	546	141	3.9	Joe Freedy	371	187	.51	2,077	Chad Bartoszek	42	441	10.5
2002	Aaron Leeper	917	235	3.9	Randall Secky	421	204	.48	2,015	Andre Forde	54	748	13.9
2003	Dave Dawson	678	128	5.3	P.J. Piskorik	162	85	.53	824	Matt Knueven	47	622	13.2
2004	Steven King	445	94	4.7	P.J. Piskorik	133	61	.46	616	Matt Knueven	29	415	14.3
2005	Steven King	532	136	3.9	Drew Willy	246	149	.61	1,481	Brett Hamlin	38	371	9.8
2006	James Starks	704	175	4.0	Drew Willy	231	138	.60	1,391	Terrance Breaux	32	444	13.9

Receiving leaders by receptions
NCAA began including postseason stats in 2002

CENTRAL MICHIGAN

BY ED KRZEMIENSKI

IT MIGHT NOT SURPRISE PEOPLE TO learn that through 2003, Texas A&M ranked 24th in all-time Division I-A winning percentage. It would probably surprise most, though, to find out that the team directly above the Aggies is Central Michigan. With an overall .609 mark, the Chippewas rank ahead of not just the Aggies but also Syracuse, Michigan State, and UCLA. From 1965 to 1991, Central Michigan ran off 27 consecutive nonlosing seasons, including an 8–2–1 mark in its first season in Division I-A. In recent years, the team rebuilt under Brian Kelly, who left nearby Division II powerhouse Grand Valley State University and brought quick success—a MAC championship and a bowl victory in 2006. Kelly left the Chippewas for the University of Cincinnati in 2007, when head coach Butch Jones took the reins.

TRADITION Each fall, the Central Michigan band teaches the school's fight song to newcomers on the football team, and the band accompanies the squad on the walk from a nearby motel to home games. The band also penned the school's most popular cheer: "CHIP-ooh-ah! FIGHT! FIGHT! FIGHT!"

BEST PLAYER Although QB Gary Hogeboom went on to the best pro career, running back Jim Podoley stands as the greatest Chippewa ever. From 1953 to 1956, Podoley ran for 2,775 yards and led the Chippewas to a combined record of 32–4–1. His 307 points, 51 touchdowns, and 29-yard punt-return average still stand as CMU career records. Perhaps most impressive, though, is Podoley's career average of 7.9 yards per carry. Despite playing in the NCAA College Division, Podoley was invited to the 1956 Senior Bowl and 1957 Blue-Gray Game. After college, Podoley played four seasons for the Washington Redskins and was inducted into the CMU Athletics Hall of Fame in 1984. He was the first and only Chippewa to have his number (62) retired.

BEST COACH Before retiring to become CMU's athletic director after the 1993 season, Herb Deromedi coached the Chippewas to a 110–55–10 record over 16 years. He owns the CMU record for wins and is tied with Bill Kelly for longest tenure. Under Deromedi, the Chippewas won or shared the MAC title three times and made their first Div. I postseason appearance in the 1990 California Raisin Bowl. Deromedi won MAC Coach of the Year twice and retired with a .657 winning percentage as the

PROFILE

Central Michigan University
Mount Pleasant, Mich.
Founded: 1892
Enrollment: 27,100
Colors: Maroon and Gold
Nickname: Chippewas
Stadium: Kelly/Shorts Stadium
   Opened in 1972
   FieldTurf; 30,255 capacity
First football game: 1896
All-time record: 542–342–36 (.609)
Bowl record: 1–2
Mid-American Conference championships:
5 (outright)
First-round draft choices: 1
Website: www.cmuchippewas.com

THE BEST OF TIMES

From 1979 to 1980, Central Michigan went 19–2–1 and won two MAC championships.

THE WORST OF TIMES

From 1995 to 2004, CMU had nine losing seasons in 10 years.

CONFERENCE

Central Michigan joined the MAC in 1975, when it moved up to Division I-A, and has been a member ever since.

DISTINGUISHED ALUMNI

Dick Enberg; Jeff Daniels, actor; John Grogan, author; Joseph Ralston, NATO Supreme Allied Commander General

FIGHT SONG

THE FIGHTING CHIPPEWA
(Chorus)
Come on and Fight! Central, down the field,
Fight for Victory,
Fight! Fellows never yield,
We're with you, oh Varsity,
Onward with banners bold,
To our colors we'll be true,
Fight for Maroon and Gold,
Down the field for CMU!
(Refrain)
Victory - Rah Rah!
Varsity - Rah Rah!
Chippewas we're proud of our nickname,
Hear our song - Rah Rah!
Loud and strong - Rah Rah!
Central is going to win this game!

The band penned the school's most popular cheer: "CHIP-ooh-ah! FIGHT! FIGHT! FIGHT!"

all-time MAC leader in victories. He was voted into the CMU Athletics Hall of Fame in 2000.

BEST TEAM In their final year in Division II, the 1974 Chippewas opened the season with a loss to Kent State—a future MAC rival— then won 12 straight. In the process, Roy Kramer's CMU team defeated Boise State, Louisiana Tech, and Delaware in the playoffs to win the D2 national championship. Seniors Mike Franckowiak and Matt Means led the team in passing and receiving, respectively, while junior running back Walt "Smoke" Hodges ran for 1,463 yards. Franckowiak and noseguard Rick Newsome were named Division II/Small College All-Americas. Franckowiak was also named a first-team Academic All-America.

BEST BACKFIELD The 1994 Chippewas relied on running back Brian Pruitt. Pruitt ran for a record 1,890 yards, which was more than 171 per game, including a 356-yard performance against Toledo. He averaged 12 points per game, which placed him second only to Colorado's Heisman Trophy winner Rashaan Salaam. Quarterbacking CMU was Eric Timpf. Timpf, understandably, did not need to throw the ball much that year. When he did, however, he did so accurately, completing over half of his passes for more than 1,300 yards. Together, Pruitt and Timpf led the Chippewas to the MAC crown and a berth in the Las Vegas Bowl against UNLV. Unfortunately, Pruitt suffered an injury and was unable to play, leaving CMU's offense empty-handed and with a 52-24 loss. Still, Pruitt was named first-team All-American and Timpf second-team all-MAC.

BEST DEFENSE In 1990, CMU's defense led the team to its first Division I bowl game, a California Bowl showdown against San Jose State. Led by J.J. Wierenga, Rich Curtiss, Ken Strong, and David Johnson—all first team all-MAC defenders—the Chippewas gave up an average of 8.9 points per game and pitched three shutouts. The D gave up only 2 first downs against Bowling Green and intercepted 6 passes against Miami. All told, six CMU defenders made either first or second team all-MAC.

BIGGEST GAME In 1974, the Chippewas went to the nationally televised Division II championship game, known then as the Camellia Bowl, as underdogs against powerhouse Delaware. The Blue Hens had won two of the last three College Division titles, and it looked as if the 1974

FIRST-ROUND DRAFT CHOICE

2007	Joe Staley, 49ers (28)

CONSENSUS ALL-AMERICANS

1942	Warren Schmakel, G
1959	Walter Beach, B
1962	Ralph Soffredine, G
1974	Rick Newsome, DL

COLLEGE FOOTBALL HALL OF FAME INDUCTEES

NAME	YEARS	INDUCTED
Herb Deromedi, COACH	1978-93	2007

game would be a runaway. It was, but not as expected: The Chippewas destroyed the Hens 54-14. CMU running backs Hodges and Dick Dunham each ran for over 100 yards and combined for six of the Chippewas' seven touchdowns. Neither, however, was named Offensive Player of the Game. That honor went to quarterback Mike Franckowiak, who not only completed 11 of 13 passes for 186 yards and a touchdown, but also accounted for 12 points with his foot, kicking two field goals and six extra points.

BIGGEST UPSET After tying Ohio and squeaking past Southwestern Louisiana (now Louisiana-Lafayette) to start the 1991 season, it looked as if Herb Deromedi's Chippewas might not make it back alive from East Lansing after their game with No. 18 Michigan State. But on this September day, it was the Spartans who needed help off the field. Controlling all facets of the game, CMU stunned MSU 20-3. Led by running back Billy Smith's 162 yards, the Chippewas outgained the Spartans 346-281 in a game dominated by the CMU defense. Setting the tone on the first series, CMU's defense stuffed a fourth-and-goal attempt at their own 1-yard line. Perhaps the game should not be regarded as much of an upset, though. One year later, the Chippewas, having lost their first game of the season to Kentucky, again traveled to East Lansing and again upset the Spartans, this time 24-20.

HEARTBREAKER In the 1994 Las Vegas Bowl, Central Michigan faced Nevada-Las Vegas in a rematch of the second game of the season, which CMU won 35-23 in Mount Pleasant. Prior to the game, however, Central's All-America tailback Brian Pruitt bruised his knee in practice and was unable to play. After one quarter of play, the score stood at 14-10 in favor of UNLV. By early in the fourth quarter, the Rebels were up 52-10. The final score, a discouraging cap on an otherwise stellar season, was 52-24.

STADIUM Kelly/Shorts Stadium opened in 1972 when Central Michigan defeated Illinois State in the first collegiate game ever played on Astroturf in Michigan. The arena was originally named Perry Shorts Stadium, after R. Perry Shorts, a 1900 graduate who became a banker and philanthropist. The school added "Kelly" in 1983 to honor former coach Bill Kelly. Several renovations brought the capacity to more than 30,000. Since its opening, Kelly/Shorts has been a sweet home indeed, as the Chippewas have won 72% of games played there.

> *At a home game, CMU freshman Jared Parko wore head feathers and a breastplate made of pasta.*

RIVAL Central Michigan is roughly equidistant—about 140 miles—from its MAC opponents, Western and Eastern Michigan. CMU's greater rival, though, is the Western Michigan Broncos. Six of the 10 biggest Kelly/Shorts Stadium crowds were at CMU-WMU games.

NICKNAME Originally known as the Normalites, CMU became the Dragons in 1925, then the Bearcats two years later. In 1942, the team became the Chippewas in consideration of a local Saginaw tribe. The school has kept that nickname despite the trend to avoid mascots derived from Native American tribes. The school states that it will "continue to use the Chippewa name with dignity and respect."

MASCOT So as not to dishonor the Saginaw Chippewa tribe, CMU has no mascot. That, however, has not kept students from breaking the rules. On Oct. 11, 2003, at a home game against Northern Illinois, Central Michigan freshman Jared Parko attended the game dressed in head feathers and a breastplate made of pasta, apparently of the penne rigate or mostaccioli variety. The following weekend, for a game against Toledo, school officials asked a similarly attired Parko to leave the stadium. Parko remarked that he meant no disrespect, and that "if we were the Bobcats, I would dress up as a Bobcat and try to get people going."

UNIFORMS From 1973 to 1988, CMU wore red helmets with a feathered spear on the side. At the end of the 1980s, though, the school edged away from Native American emblems and instituted blank red helmets. In the 1990s, the team went with red helmets adorned with the letters CMU, then in 1996 turned to the current design, featuring a gold C on the sides.

LORE Herb Deromedi beat most teams he faced as head coach of the Chippewas, but he really dominated his in-state rivals. Against Western Michigan, Deromedi posted a 13–2–1 career record and put up a 12–2–2 mark against Eastern Michigan. That kind of mastery will keep the alumni enthusiastic and future coaches looking pale.

NUMBERS In 1991, five years before the NCAA began its overtime system, Central Michigan ended the season with four ties. In fact, despite losing only one game all year, the team tied more MAC games than it won, finishing its conference schedule at 3–1–4.

QUOTE "I'm excited about the opportunity to wake up a sleeping giant." —Brian Kelly, on being hired head coach in 2004

MAC TEAMS

CENTRAL MICHIGAN ALL-TIME SCORES

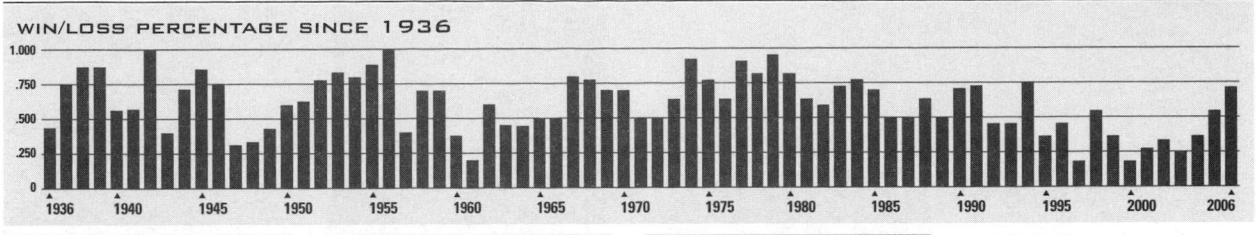

WIN/LOSS PERCENTAGE SINCE 1936

1936	1940	1945	1950	1955	1960	1965	1970	1975	1980	1985	1990	1995	2000	2006

PETE McCORMICK
1896 (.750)   3-1

1896   3-1-0
U		Alma HS^Unk	5 14
U	●	Bay City HS^Unk	14 4
U	●	Saginaw HS^Unk	35 0
U	●	Alma HS^Unk	8 4

CARL PRAY
1897-99 (.545)   6-5

1897   2-1-0
U		Alma^Unk	0 18
U	●	Bay City HS^Unk	10 0
U	●	Ithica HS^Unk	NA 10

1898   1-2-0
U		Alma^Unk	0 27
U	●	MP Indians^Unk	35 0
U		Mt. Pleasant HS^Unk	2 5

1899   3-2-0
U		Alma^Unk	0 12
U		Saginaw Stars^Unk	0 5
U	●	Cadillac HS^Unk	12 0
U	●	St. John's HS^Unk	27 5
U	●	Ferris State^Unk	6 0

NO HEAD COACH

1900   1-0-0
U	●	Cadillac HS^Unk	20 5

1901
NO TEAM

CHARLES TAMBLING
1902-05, '18 (.900)   18-2

1902   4-0-0
U	●	Marion HS^Unk	10 0
U	●	McBain HS^Unk	51 0
N1	●	Eastern Michigan^Unk	10 0
U	●	Ferris State^Unk	11 0

1903   6-0-0
U	●	Ferris State^Unk	12 0
U	●	Alma^Unk	23 5
U	●	Elsie Giants^Unk	15 0
U	●	Hillsdale^Unk	7 6
U	●	Clare HS	NA NA
U	●	Mount Pleasant HS	NA NA

1904   0-1-0
U		Ferris State^Unk	6 60

1905   7-1-0
U	●	Elsie Giants^Unk	5 0
U	●	Ferris State^Unk	35 2
U	●	Midland AC^Unk	51 0
U		Alma^Unk	6 12
N17	●	Eastern Michigan^Unk	13 0
U	●	Ferris State^Unk	10 0
U	●	W. Michigan JV^Unk	6 0
U	●	Kalamazoo	NA NA

1906
NO TEAM

RALPH THACKER
1907 (.333)   2-4

1907   2-4-0
U		Ferris State^Unk	0 45
U	●	Flint MSD^Unk	6 5
U	●	MP Indians^Unk	12 11
U		Western Michigan^Unk	0 27 *
N16		Eastern Michigan^Unk	0 39
U		Alma	NA NA

HUGH SUTHERLAND
1908 (.571)   4-3

1908   4-3-0
U		Alma^Unk	0 5
U	●	Alma^Unk	10 0
N7	●	Eastern Michigan^Unk	11 0
U	●	Western Michigan^Unk	5 11
U	●	Elsie Giants	NA NA
U		Hillsdale	NA NA
U	●	West Branch HS	NA NA

HARRY HELMER
1909-12 (.652)   14-7-2

1909   4-3-0
U	●	West Branch HS^Unk	23 0
U	●	Saginaw Arthur Hill HS^Unk	8 5
U	●	Alma^Unk	15 8
U		Michigan State JV^Unk	6 17
U	●	Ferris State^Unk	11 0
N5		at Eastern Michigan	0 17
U	●	Western Michigan^Unk	0 11

1910   6-1-1
U	●	MP Indians^Unk	18 0
U	●	West Branch HS^Unk	6 0
U	=	Michigan State JV^Unk	6 6
U	●	Flint MSD^Unk	40 0
U		Western Michigan^Unk	6 16
N12	●	Eastern Michigan^Unk	13 0
U	●	Ferris State^Unk	17 11
U	●	Elsie Giants	NA NA

1911   3-2-0
U	●	West Branch HS^Unk	17 6
U	●	Mount Pleasant HS	NA NA
U	●	Ithaca HS^Unk	3 0
U		Flint MSD	NA NA
U		Michigan State JV	NA NA

1912   1-1-1
U		Michigan State JV	NA NA
U	●	Flint MSD	NA NA
N8	=	Eastern Michigan^Unk	0 0

1913-15
NO TEAM

BLAKE MILLER
1916 (.167)   1-5

1916   1-5-0
U	●	West Branch HS^Unk	39 0
U		Bay City Western HS^Unk	0 12
U		Michigan State JV^Unk	0 14
U		Alma^Unk	0 39
U		Saginaw East^Unk	0 30
U		Alma^Unk	0 44

FRED JOHNSON
1917 (.333)   1-2

1917   1-2-0
U	●	Bay City Western HS^Unk	7 0
O20		at Eastern Michigan	0 63
U		Mount Pleasant HS^Unk	0 8

CHARLES TAMBLING
1918   1-0-0
U	●	Traverse City HS^Unk	41 6

GARLAND NEVITT
1919 (.500)   2-2-3

1919   2-2-3
U	●	Bay City Western HS^Unk	34 6
U	=	Saginaw East^Unk	13 13
U	●	Ferris State^Unk	7 0
U	=	Grand Rapids JC^Unk	7 7
N7	=	Eastern Michigan^Unk	7 7
U		Michigan State JV^Unk	0 13
U		Detroit JC^Unk	14 42

JOE SIMMONS
1920 (.563)   4-3-1

1920   4-3-1
U	●	Ferris State	80 0
O16		at Eastern Michigan	6 7
U	●	at Olivet	7 0
U	●	at Ferris State	34 0
U		Michigan State JV	6 14
U		at Hillsdale	10 14
U	●	at Hope	17 0
U	=	Detroit JC	6 6

WALLACE PARKER
1921-23, '26-28 (.729)   32-10-6

1921   5-1-1
U	●	at Ferris State	7 0
U	●	Olivet	35 0
O15		Eastern Michigan	6 7
U	●	Ferris State	60 0
U	●	at Alma	28 0
U	●	at Grand Rapids JC	7 0
U	=	at Detroit JC	0 0

1922   6-0-2
U	●	Ferris State	40 0
U	=	at St. Ignatius	6 6
U	●	Grand Rapids JC	39 0
N4	=	at Eastern Michigan	0 0
U	●	Northern Michigan	62 0
U	●	Michigan Mlty. Acad.	7 0
U	●	Alma	5 0
U	●	Detroit JC	20 7

1923   5-1-2
U	●	Bay City JC	37 0
U		at Albion	7 14
U	=	at Grand Rapids JC	0 0
O27	●	Eastern Michigan	27 3
U	●	at Northern Michigan	35 0
U	●	Olivet	40 0
U	=	at Alma	0 0
U	●	at Detroit City	21 7

LESTER BARNARD
1924-25 (.781)   11-2-3

1924   7-1-0
U	●	at Assumption	26 0
U		Albion	12 13
O25	●	at Eastern Michigan	13 0
O31	●	Bowling Green	21 0
U	●	Northern Michigan	22 0
U	●	at Valparaiso	13 0
U	●	Alma	13 0
U	●	Detroit City	38 6

1925   4-1-3
U	●	Carrollton AC	29 0
U		at Alma	0 14
U	●	at Northern Michigan	8 0
U	=	Detroit JV	0 0
U	=	at Western Michigan	0 0
U	●	Valparaiso	41 0
U	=	Albion	0 0
U	●	Detroit City	18 6

WALLACE PARKER

1926   3-4-1
O2		at Albion	14 20
O9		at Ferris State	6 7
O16	●	Northern Michigan	24 7
O23		at Eastern Michigan	0 41
O30		at Bowling Green	0 13
N13	●	Alma	13 2
N20	=	Battle Creek	0 0
U	●	Detroit City	9 0

1927   7-1-0
U	●	Adrian	26 0
U	●	Ferris State	20 0
O15	●	Olivet	7 0
O22	●	Western Michigan	18 12
O29		at Eastern Michigan	0 6
U	●	at Northern Michigan	6 0
N11	●	at Alma	14 13
U	●	at Detroit City	33 6

1928   6-3-0
S29	●	Detroit Tech	18 0
O6		at Adrian	0 9
O13	●	at Toledo	13 0
O20	●	Northern Michigan	26 0
O27		Eastern Michigan	0 36
N3	●	at Valparaiso	25 0
N10	●	at Ferris State	21 0
U		at Western Michigan	0 19
N29	●	Detroit City	23 0

A.J. NOWAK
1929-30 (.600)   8-5-2

1929   2-3-2
S28	●	Detroit Tech	28 7
O5	=	Michigan JV	0 0
O12	=	at Northern Michigan	6 6
O26		at Eastern Michigan	0 24
N9		Western Michigan	6 25
N16	●	Toledo	31 12
N28		at Detroit City	0 6

1930   6-2-0
U	●	Detroit Frosh	7 0
U	●	Michigan JV	13 7
U		at Western Michigan	0 54
U	●	at Ferris State	14 0
O25		Eastern Michigan	0 13
N8	●	at Alma	27 7
N15	●	Northern Michigan	34 0
N27	●	at Detroit City	13 0

GEORGE VAN BIBBER
1931-33 (.565)   12-9-2

1931   4-3-0
O3		at Michigan	0 27
O10	●	Ferris State	14 6
O24	●	at Eastern Michigan	20 12
O31	●	Detroit City	42 0
N7	●	Alma	13 0
N14		at Bowling Green	0 6
N21	●	Western Michigan	6 7

1932   3-4-1
O1	=	at Michigan JV	0 0
O8	●	Defiance	32 9
O15	●	Purdue JV	6 13
O22	●	Eastern Michigan	0 28
O29	●	at Detroit City	13 0
N5		at Western Michigan	0 7
N12	●	Michigan Coll. of Mines	46 0
N19		at Alma	0 9

1933   5-2-1
S30	●	Saint Mary's-Cal	52 0
O7		at Kalamazoo	18 13
O14	=	at Hillsdale	0 0
O21		at Eastern Michigan	7 13*
O28	●	Detroit City	26 13
N4		Western Michigan	0 13*
N11	●	at Ferris State	33 0
N18	●	Alma	27 0

MAC TEAMS

ALEX YUNEVICH
1934-36 (.438) 10-13-1

1934 — 5-3-0

S28		at Detroit	0	38
O6		Ferris State	2	6
O13	●	Hillsdale	15	6
O20	●	Eastern Michigan	13	12
O27	●	at Wayne State	13	7
N3		at Western Michigan	0	13
N10	●	Kalamazoo	12	0
N17	●	at Alma	26	0

1935 — 2-6-0

S27		at Detroit	0	43
O5		at Ferris State	7	12
O12		Wayne State	6	7
O19		at Eastern Michigan	0	7
O26	●	at Northern Michigan	7	0
N2	●	Assumption	19	0
N9		at Western Michigan	0	13
N16		Alma	0	13

1936 — 3-4-1

S26		at Baldwin-Wallace	2	65
O3	●	Ferris State	22	0
O10	=	at Wayne State	0	0
O17	●	at Northern State	7	6
O24		Eastern Michigan	7	13
O31	●	Saint Mary's-Cal	44	8
N7		at Western Michigan	0	33
N14		Detroit Tech	7	10

RON FINCH
1937-46 (.743) 53-18-1

1937 — 6-2-0

S25	●	Assumption	52	0
O2	●	at Ferris State	21	7
O9	●	Northern Michigan	32	0
O16		Wayne State	0	18
O23	●	at Eastern Michigan	27	10
O30	●	at Saint Mary's-Cal	38	0
N6		Western Michigan	0	7
N13	●	at Kalamazoo	30	0

1938 — 7-1-0

S23	●	at Lawrence Tech	44	0
O1	●	at Ferris State	68	0
O8	●	at Northern Michigan	47	0
O15	●	at Bluffton	45	0
O21	●	Eastern Michigan	7	6
O28	●	Saint Mary's-Cal	39	0
N5	●	at Wayne State	20	3
N12		at Western Michigan	0	35

1939 — 7-1-0

S22		at Detroit	7	20
S29	●	at Ferris State	20	0
S30	●	at Illinois State	14	0
O6	●	at Northern Michigan	6	0
O14	●	at Eastern Kentucky	18	14
O20	●	at Eastern Michigan	14	0
O27	●	Ball State	7	0
N11	●	at Wayne State	33	6

1940 — 4-3-1

S27	●	at Ferris State	37	0
O5	●	at Ball State	7	0
O12		at Northern Illinois	6	9
O19		at Bradley	0	19
O25	●	at Eastern Michigan	24	0
N2	=	at Wayne State	7	7
N9		Eastern Kentucky	0	25
N16	●	at DeSales	7	0

1941 — 4-3-0

O3	●	at Northern Michigan	7	6
O10		at Detroit	0	45
O18	●	at Ball State	7	6
O24	●	at Eastern Michigan	12	6
N1		at Wayne State	0	6
N8		at Grand Rapids U	6	7
N15	●	at DeSales	12	6

1942 — 6-0-0

O3	●	at Northern Michigan	21	0
O9	●	at Grand Rapids U	6	2
O15	●	at Eastern Michigan	14	0
O24	●	Ball State	19	13
O30	●	at Wayne State	13	0
N7	●	at Grand Rapids U	20	6

1943 — 2-3-0

O2		at Bowling Green	0	36
U		Western Michigan	0	19
U	●	at Alma	13	7
U		at Alma	0	8
U	●	at Alma	6	0

1944 — 5-2-0

U	●	at Alma	20	13
S1		Bowling Green	19	20
U	●	at Alma	33	13
U	●	at Michigan JV	25	12
O7		at Western Michigan	14	35
U	●	at Michigan JV	14	13
U	●	at Indiana State	25	0

1945 — 6-1-0

U	●	at Alma	13	0
S7		at Bowling Green	6	19
U	●	at Alma	26	0
S29	●	Western Michigan	6	0
O6	●	at Eastern Kentucky	14	7
U	●	at Wayne State	26	0
O20	●	at Albion	7	0

1946 — 6-2-0

S20		at Ohio Wesleyan	0	13
S28	●	at Bowling Green	7	0
O5	●	at Eastern Kentucky	20	7
O12	●	at Northern Michigan	60	0
O18	●	at Eastern Michigan	26	13
O25	●	Northern Illinois	58	7
N2		at Western Michigan	21	27
N9	●	at Great Lakes NAS	41	0

LYLE BENNETT
1947-49 (.354) 8-15-1

1947 — 2-5-1

S19		at Detroit	14	34
S27		at Bowling Green	19	20
O3	=	Northern Illinois	6	6
O11		Western Michigan	12	20
O17	●	at Northern Michigan	45	10
O24		at Youngstown	7	13
N1	●	Eastern Michigan	33	10 *
N15		at Milwaukee State	0	12

1948 — 3-6-0

S18	●	at Ferris State	27	6
O2		Bowling Green	12	13
O9		at Western Michigan	0	7
O14	●	at Northern Michigan	46	14
O16		Kent State	0	28
O23		at Youngstown	9	32
O30		Wayne State	12	27
N6		at Eastern Michigan	0	6
N13	●	at Milwaukee State	21	6

1949 — 3-4-0

S23	●	at Ferris State	33	7
O1		at Bowling Green	0	20
O8	●	at Michigan Mines	35	0
O14		at Kent State	12	26
O22		Western Michigan	8	35
O29		Hillsdale	0	8
N4	●	Eastern Michigan	18	7

WARREN SCHMAKEL
1950 (.600) 6-4

1950 — 6-4-0

S18	●	Alma	19	0
S23		at Western Illinois	7	28
S30		at Western Michigan	13	21
O7		Illinois State	13	14
O14	●	Bowling Green	12	0
O21	●	at DePauw	33	20
O28	●	at Eastern Michigan	26	7
N3	●	at Northern Illinois	27	14
N11	●	Ferris State	40	0
N18		at Hillsdale	20	21

BILL KELLY
1951-66 (.609) 91-58-2

1951 — 5-3-0

S22	●	at Southern Illinois	34	13
S28		Western Illinois	6	27
O13	●	Eastern Illinois	59	27
O20	●	at Eastern Michigan	19	13
O27	●	at Illinois State	26	0
N2		Northern Illinois	13	26
N9	●	at Ferris State	46	6
N17		at Western Michigan	25	46

1952 — 7-2-0

S13	●	at St. Ambrose	38	14
S20		at Bowling Green	7	20
S27	●	at Northern Illinois	56	7
O4		Western Michigan	0	18
O11	●	at Western Illinois	27	0
O18	●	Southern Illinois	55	7
O25	●	Eastern Michigan	26	7
N1	●	Illinois State	35	12
N8	●	at Eastern Illinois	41	0

1953 — 7-1-1

S19	●	Northern Iowa	34	20
S26	●	Western Michigan	21	0
O2	●	Eastern Illinois	33	6
O10		at Great Lakes NAS	16	39
O17	●	at Southern Illinois	19	6
O24	●	Western Illinois	13	6
O31	●	at Illinois State	29	19
N6	●	Northern Illinois	46	0
N14	=	at Eastern Michigan	33	33

1954 — 8-2-0

S11	●	at Milwaukee State	26	7
S18	●	Northern Iowa	42	21
S25	●	at Western Michigan	25	19
O2	●	at Eastern Illinois	60	0
O9		at Great Lakes NAS	28	32
O16	●	Southern Illinois	33	0
O23		at Western Illinois	7	14
O30	●	Illinois State	26	0
N6	●	at Northern Illinois	46	7
N13	●	Eastern Michigan	28	7

1955 — 8-1-0

S17	●	at Pittsburg State	33	0
S24	●	Western Michigan	27	12
O1		at Southern Illinois	13	14
O8	●	Northern Illinois	61	0
O15	●	Western Illinois	20	0
O22	●	at Illinois State	35	7
O29	●	at Milwaukee State	63	12
N5	●	at Eastern Michigan	27	20
N12	●	Eastern Illinois	48	14

1956 — 9-0-0

S15	●	at Bradley	38	33
S22	●	at Western Michigan	14	7
S29	●	Southern Illinois	32	13
O6	●	at Northern Illinois	41	0
O13	●	at Western Illinois	44	20
O20	●	Illinois State	20	0
O27	●	Milwaukee State	67	12
N3	●	Eastern Michigan	19	0
N10	●	at Eastern Illinois	38	7

1957 — 4-6-0

S14		at Bradley	7	14
S21		Western Michigan	0	33
S28		Hillsdale	14	35
O5		at Illinois State	20	24
O12		at Eastern Michigan	6	39
O19	●	Northern Illinois	52	12
O26		at Louisville	0	40
N2	●	Eastern Illinois	61	6
N9	●	at Southern Illinois	21	12
N16	●	Western Illinois	39	7

1958 — 7-3-0

S13	●	at Northern Michigan	27	14
S20	●	at Western Michigan	33	32
S27	●	at Hillsdale	19	13
O4	●	Illinois State	33	6
O11	●	Eastern Michigan	7	6
O18	●	at Northern Illinois	33	23
O25		Louisville	7	40
N1	●	at Eastern Illinois	27	8
N8		Southern Illinois	7	24
N15		at Western Illinois	23	38

1959 — 7-3-0

S12		at Bolling AFB	13	19
S19	●	Western Michigan	21	15
S25	●	at Drake	41	21
O3		Western Illinois	20	26
O10	●	at Illinois State	22	0
O17	●	at Eastern Michigan	21	8
O24	●	Northern Illinois	29	7
O31	●	Northern Michigan	20	8
N7	●	Eastern Illinois	26	0
N14		at Southern Illinois	20	51

1960 — 3-5-0

S17		at Western Michigan	0	31
S24		at Northern Michigan	3	20
O1		at Western Illinois	13	38
O8	●	Illinois State	50	0
O15	●	Eastern Michigan	28	0
O22		at Northern Illinois	15	36
N5	●	at Eastern Illinois	35	12
N12		Southern Illinois	17	28

1961 — 2-8-0

S9		at Northern Michigan	0	35
S16		Western Michigan	21	27
S21		at Youngstown	7	36
S30		at Southern Illinois	0	18
O7		Western Illinois	7	12
O14		at Illinois State	21	32
O21	●	at Eastern Michigan	13	11
O28		Northern Illinois	0	11
N4	●	Hillsdale	13	10
N11		Eastern Illinois	13	22

1962 — 6-4-0

S8		at Northern Michigan	12	20
S15		at Western Michigan	0	28
S22		Youngstown	7	14
S29		Southern Illinois	6	43
O6	●	at Western Illinois	17	8
O13	●	Illinois State	46	8
O20	●	Eastern Michigan	24	0
O27	●	at Northern Illinois	35	27
N3	●	at Hillsdale	9	0
N10	●	at Eastern Illinois	35	23

1963 — 4-5-1

S14		at Bradley	6	12
S21	=	at Youngstown	7	7
S28	●	Western Michigan	30	14
O5	●	Eastern Illinois	35	15
O12		at Northern Michigan	0	19
O19		at Western Illinois	7	28
O26	●	at Illinois State	24	22
N2	●	at Eastern Michigan	55	20
N9		Northern Illinois	22	27
N16		Hillsdale	23	31

1964 — 4-5-0

S12	●	at Whitewater State	13	7
S26	●	at Western Michigan	18	6
O3		at Eastern Illinois	14	17
O10		Northern Michigan	7	12
O17		Western Illinois	7	41
O24	●	Illinois State	12	0
O31	●	Youngstown	25	20
N7		at Northern Illinois	14	19
N14		at Hillsdale	7	26

1965 — 5-5-0

S11		at Whitewater State	13	35
S17		Youngstown	14	35
S25		Western Michigan	13	21
O2		Northern Illinois	14	19
O9	●	at Northern Michigan	13	0
O16		Hillsdale	0	13
O23	●	at Illinois State	32	8
O30	●	Western Illinois	9	6
N6	●	Eastern Illinois	48	6
N13	●	at Ferris State	37	0

1966 — 5-5-0

S10		Whitewater State	16	40
S17		Youngstown	6	7
S24		at Western Michigan	14	31
O1		at Northern Illinois	13	20
O8		Northern Michigan	14	35
O15	●	at Hillsdale	28	7
O22	●	Illinois State	20	6
O29	●	Western Illinois	28	3
N5	●	at Eastern Illinois	30	10
N19	●	Wayne State	44	0

ROY KRAMER
1967-77 (.718) 83-32-2

1967 — 8-2-0

S16	●	Bradley	23	21
S22	●	at Youngstown	24	20
S30		Northern Michigan	24	28
O7	●	Eastern Illinois	23	16
O14	●	Hillsdale	35	10
O21	●	at Central State	27	0
O28	●	at Illinois State	19	16
N4		at Western Illinois	28	30
N11	●	Morehead State	9	7
N18	●	at Wayne State	35	6

1968 7-2-0

S14	●	at Bradley	41	6
S21	●	Youngstown	24	20
S28		at Northern Michigan	24	28
O5	●	at Eastern Illinois	23	16
O12	●	at Hillsdale	35	10
O19	●	Central State	27	0
O26	●	at Illinois State	19	16
N2		Western Illinois	28	30
N16	●	Wayne State	35	6

1969 7-3-0

S13		at Western Michigan	0	24
S20	●	at Northern Iowa	28	10
S27	●	Wisconsin-Milwaukee	41	6
O4	●	at Illinois State	21	0
O11	●	Northern Michigan	40	37
O18		at Western Illinois	14	17
O25	●	Eastern Illinois	44	0
N1		Akron	6	9
N8	●	at Indiana State	25	24
N15	●	at Wayne State	35	20

1970 7-3-0

S12		Western Michigan	0	41
S19	●	Northern Iowa	27	9
S26	●	at Wisconsin-Milwaukee	27	0
O3	●	Illinois State	34	20
O10		at Northern Michigan	14	34
O17	●	Western Illinois	20	10
O24	●	at Eastern Illinois	58	34
O31		at Akron	19	35
N7	●	Indiana State	17	7
N14	●	at Hofstra	47	0

1971 5-5-0

S11		at Ball State	6	9
S18	●	Youngstown	47	19
S25		Northern Michigan	14	37
O2	●	at Indiana State	21	6
O9		at Western Illinois	0	28
O23	●	Eastern Illinois	47	14
O30	●	Akron	10	7
N6		at Illinois State	6	13
N13	●	Hofstra	24	13
N20		at Southern Illinois	8	35

1972 5-5-1

S9		at Ohio U.	21	26
S16		at Ball State	12	30
S23	●	at Northern Michigan	26	9
S30	●	Indiana State	34	0
O7		Western Illinois	19	20
O14	●	Eastern Kentucky	21	14
O21	●	at Eastern Illinois	63	0
O28		at Akron	10	14
N4	●	Illinois State	28	21
N11	=	at Youngstown	28	28
N18		Eastern Michigan	3	28

1973 7-4-0

S8		Western Michigan	13	18
S15	●	Ball State	14	7
S22		at Toledo	21	23
S29	●	at Dayton	15	6
O6	●	Illinois State	6	3
O13	●	at Indiana State	21	7
O20		at Western Illinois	18	24
N3	●	Eastern Michigan	31	21
N10	●	at Eastern Kentucky	21	7
N17	●	Northern Michigan	30	7
N24		at Kent State	7	28

1974 12-1-0

S7		Kent State	14	21
S14	●	at Ball State	24	17
S21	●	at Northern Michigan	21	7
S28	●	Dayton	42	8
O5	●	at Illinois State	21	14
O12	●	Indiana State	49	0
O19	●	Western Illinois	58	7
N2	●	at Eastern Michigan	28	13
N9	●	Western Michigan	42	6
N16	●	Southern Illinois	42	0
		DIVISION II PLAYOFFS		
N30	●	Boise State	20	6
D7	●	Louisiana Tech[WiFi]	35	14
D14	●	Delaware[SAC]	54	14

1975-Present MAC

1975 8-2-1 (4-1-1)

S6	● |	Western Michigan	34	0
S13	= |	Ohio U.	6	6
S20		Northern Michigan	16	17
S27	● |	at Toledo	34	27
O4	●	at Illinois State	42	7
O11	●	Eastern Michigan	20	7
O18	|	at Ball State	13	16
O25	● |	at Kent State	17	8
N1	●	Marshall	34	0
N8	●	at Western Illinois	24	7
N15	● |	Northern Illinois	69	7

1976 7-4-0 (4-3-0)

S11	|	Kent State	10	20
S18	● |	Toledo	9	7
S25	●	at Marshall	22	7
O2	●	Illinois State	26	7
O9	● |	Ohio U.	17	15
O16	●	Indiana State	16	13
O23		at Northern Michigan	13	41
O30	● |	at Bowling Green	38	28
N6	|	at Eastern Michigan	27	30
N13	● |	at Northern Illinois	31	9
N20	|	at Western Michigan	14	42

1977 10-1-0 (7-1-0)

S3	●	Alcorn State	37	7
S10	● |	Eastern Michigan	9	3
S17	●	at Illinois State	28	7
S24	● |	at Ohio U.	31	14
O1	|	at Ball State	12	28
O8	● |	at Northern Illinois	25	21
O15	●	Akron	17	14
O29	● |	Bowling Green	35	28
N5	● |	at Kent State	49	10
N12	● |	at Toledo	44	0
N19	● |	Western Michigan	28	23

HERB DEROMEDI
1978-93 (.657) 110-55-10

1978 9-2-0 (8-1-0)

S9	● |	Kent State	41	0
S16	● |	at Miami, Ohio	37	18
S23		at Alcorn St.	16	24
S30	|	Ball State	0	27
O7	● |	at Ohio U.	17	3
O14	●	Illinois St.	45	7
O21	● |	Northern Illinois	34	7
O28	● |	at Bowling Green	38	7
N4	● |	Toledo	27	3
N11	● |	at Eastern Michigan	41	9
N18	● |	at Western MIchigan	35	14

1979 10-0-1 (8-0-1)

S8	● |	Western Michigan	10	0
S22	● |	at Bowling Green	24	0
S29	● |	Miami, Ohio	19	18
O6	● |	Ohio U.	26	0
O13	● |	Northern Illinois	31	11
O20	● |	at Ball State	31	30
O27	● |	at Kent State	44	21
N3	= |	at Toledo	7	7
N10	● |	Eastern Michigan	37	14
N17	●	at Northwestern St.	28	0
N24	●	at San Jose State	34	32

1980 9-2-0 (7-2-0)

S6	● |	Ball State	21	17
S13	● |	at Miami, Ohio	15	14
S20	●	Illinois St.	16	0
S27	● |	Kent State	21	6
O4	● |	Toledo	14	10
O11	|	at Ohio U.	9	24
O18	|	at Northern Illinois	0	21
O25	●	Northwestern St.	17	0
N1	● |	at Eastern Michigan	51	15
N8	● |	Bowling Green	32	10
N15	● |	at Western Michigan	22	10

1981 7-4-0 (7-2-0)

S5		at Pacific	3	10
S19	● |	Northern Illinois	17	10
S26		Arkansas State	23	26
O3	● |	Eastern Michigan	63	14
O10	● |	at Western Michigan	15	13
O17	|	at Toledo	3	17
O24	● |	Kent State	24	3
O31	● |	at Ohio U.	38	21
N7	|	Miami, Ohio	3	7
N14	● |	at Ball State	28	7
N21	● |	at Bowling Green	6	3

1982 6-4-1 (5-3-1)

S4	●	Indiana St.	35	10
S18	|	Bowling Green	30	34
S25		at East Carolina	6	24
O2	● |	at Eastern Michigan	13	8
O9	= |	Western Michigan	18	18
O16	● |	Toledo	16	12
O23	● |	at Kent State	31	20
O30	● |	Ohio U.	42	18
N6	|	at Miami, Ohio	0	23
N13	● |	Ball State	24	13
N20	|	at Northern Illinois	13	19

1983 8-3-0 (7-2-0)

S3		at Kentucky	14	31
S10	●	No. Michigan	37	15
S24	● |	Western Michigan	32	14
O1	● |	Kent State	13	7
O8	● |	Eastern Michigan	24	3
O15	● |	at Ohio U.	14	9
O22	|	Miami, Ohio	7	12
O29	|	at Bowling Green	14	15
N5	● |	Northern Illinois	30	14
N12	● |	at Ball State	38	10
N19	● |	at Toledo	34	8

1984 8-2-1 (6-2-1)

S8	●	No. Michigan	45	22
S15	●	East Carolina	17	12
S22	● |	Western Michigan	38	19
S29	● |	at Kent State	14	10
O6	= |	at Eastern Michigan	16	16
O13	● |	Ohio U.	35	3
O20	● |	at Miami, Ohio	10	9
O27	● |	Bowling Green	42	21
N3	|	at Northern Illinois	7	8
N10	● |	Ball State	51	7
N17	|	Toledo	7	14

1985 7-3-0 (6-3-0)

S14	●	Pacific	27	10
S28	● |	at Ohio U.	13	7
O5	● |	Kent State	21	17
O12	● |	at Western Michigan	24	17
O19	|	at Bowling Green	18	23
O26	● |	Eastern Michigan	17	10
N2	|	Miami, Ohio	14	19
N9	|	at Toledo	7	10
N16	● |	at Ball State	23	9
N23	● |	Northern Illinois	30	21

1986 5-5-0 (4-4-0)

S13	●	Idaho	34	21
S20	● |	Bowling Green	20	10
S27	● |	Ohio U.	56	27
O4	|	at Kent State	30	33
O11	● |	at Western Michigan	18	10
O18		at Tulsa	6	42
O25	|	at Eastern Michigan	16	34
N1	|	at Miami, Ohio	21	59
N8	|	Toledo	14	26
N15	● |	Ball State	43	22

1987 5-5-1 (3-4-1)

S5	|	Miami, Ohio	6	15
S12	●	at Idaho	30	18
S26		at Minnesota	10	30
O3	|	at Kent State	21	24
O10	● |	Eastern MIchigan	16	6
O17	●	Tulsa	41	18
O24	|	at Ball State	3	13
O31	● |	Western Michigan	30	27
N7	● |	at Ohio U.	31	17
N14	= |	Toledo	17	17
N21	|	at Bowling Green	17	18

1988 7-4-0 (5-3-0)

S3		at Kentucky	7	18
S17	●	at Akron	27	16
S24	●	Montana St.	48	10
O1	● |	Kent State	31	7
O8	● |	at Eastern Michigan	20	6
O15	● |	Bowling Green	21	3
O22	|	Ball State	20	27
O29	|	at Western Michigan	24	42
N5	● |	Ohio U.	42	10
N12	|	at Toledo	13	20
N19	● |	at Miami, Ohio	34	17

1989 5-5-1 (5-2-1)

S9		at La. Lafayette	20	22
S16		Akron	26	27
S23	|	at Bowling Green	20	24
S30	● |	at Miami, Ohio	20	7
O7	● |	Kent State	38	0
O14	● |	at Western Michigan	34	6
O21		Youngstown St.	3	30
O26	● |	Eastern Michigan	24	9
N4	= |	at Ball State	13	13
N11	● |	Ohio U.	24	15
N18	|	at Toledo	6	29

1990 8-3-1 (7-1-0)

S1		at Kentucky	17	20
S8	●	Cincinnati	34	0
S15	=	at Akron	14	14
S22	● |	Bowling Green	17	0
S29	● |	Miami, Ohio	31	7
O6	● |	at Kent State	42	0
O13	● |	Western Michigan	20	13
O20	● |	Toledo	13	12
O27	● |	at Eastern Michigan	16	12
N3	|	Ball State	3	13
N10	● |	at Ohio U.	52	7
		CALIFORNIA BOWL		
D8		San Jose State	24	48

1991 6-1-4 (3-1-4)

A31	= |	at Ohio U.	17	17
S7	●	La. Lafayette	27	24
S14	●	at Michigan State	20	3
S21	●	Akron	31	29
S28	= |	at Toledo	16	16
O5	|	at Bowling Green	10	17
O12	= |	Miami, Ohio	10	10
O19	● |	at Kent State	23	7
O26	● |	Ball State	10	3
N2	= |	at Eastern Michigan	14	14
N16	● |	Western Michigan	27	17

1992 5-6-0 (4-5-0)

S5		at Kentucky	14	21
S12	●	at Michigan State	24	20
S19	● |	Ohio U.	24	0
S26	● |	Toledo	28	9
O3	|	Bowling Green	14	17
O10	|	at Miami, Ohio	13	16
O17	● |	Kent State	35	0
O24	|	at Ball State	23	24
O31	|	at Akron	28	31
N7	● |	Eastern Michigan	30	13
N14	|	at Western Michigan	14	19

1993 5-6-0 (5-4-0)

S2	|	Akron	13	23
S11	● |	Ohio U.	38	0
S18		at Nevada-Las Vegas	20	33
S25		at Michigan State	34	48
O2	|	Ball State	17	20
O9	● |	at Western Michigan	23	18
O16	|	Eastern Michigan	21	28
O23	● |	at Kent State	33	28
N6	● |	at Toledo	38	7
N13	● |	Bowling Green	17	15
N20	|	at Miami, Ohio	21	24

DICK FLYNN
1994-99 (.448) 30-37

1994 9-3-0 (8-1-0)

S3		at Iowa	21	52
S10	●	Nevada-Las Vegas	35	23
S17	● |	at Eastern Michigan	30	29
S24	● |	Kent State	45	0
O1	|	at Ball State	28	31
O8	● |	Western Michigan	35	28
O15	● |	at Akron	47	0
O22	● |	Miami, Ohio	32	30
O29	● |	at Ohio U.	22	10
N5	● |	Toledo	45	27
N12	● |	at Bowling Green	36	33
		LAS VEGAS BOWL		
D15		Nevada-Las Vegas	24	52

1995 4-7-0 (2-6-0)

S9	●	Weber St.	39	31
S16		at East Carolina	17	30
S23	● |	Bowling Green	22	16
S30	|	at Akron	13	16
O7	|	at Eastern Michigan	24	34
O14	●	at Yougstown St.	46	25
O21	● |	Kent State	27	16
O28	|	Miami, Ohio	13	17
N4	|	Toledo	7	19
N11	|	at Ball State	16	24
N18	|	at Western Michigan	31	48

1996   5-6   (4-4)

A31	●	at Boise State	42 21
S7		at Virginia	21 55
S14		Louisiana Tech	37 38
S21	●	Western Michigan	38 28
S28		at Bowling Green	27 31
O5		at Miami, Ohio	14 46
O12	●	Akron	42 0
O19	●	Eastern Michigan	41 36
O26		Ball State	17 24
N2	●	at Kent State	52 51
N9		at Toledo	20 23

1997   2-9   (1-7)

A28	●	Northern Illinois	44 10
S6		at Florida	6 82
S13	●	Boise State	44 26
S20		at Louisiana Tech	28 56
S27		Eastern Michigan	24 31
O4		at Akron	14 53
O11		Toledo	10 41
O18		at Ball State	34 37
O25		at Kent State	37 60
N1		Marshall	17 45
N8		at Western Michigan	24 38

1998   6-5   (5-3)

S5		at Iowa	0 38
S12	●	Western Illinois	35 14
S26	●	Kent State	46 7
O3		at Michigan State	7 38
O10	●	at Eastern Michigan	36 23
O17		at Northern Illinois	6 16
O24	●	Western Michigan	26 24
O31	●	Akron	28 27
N7		at Marshall	0 28
N14		at Toledo	14 17
N21	●	Ball State	31 21

1999   4-7   (3-5)

S2	●	Eastern Illinois	33 17
S11		at Syracuse	7 47
S18		at Purdue	16 58
S25		Miami, Ohio	16 24
O2		at Western Michigan	16 38
O9	●	at Buffalo	38 19
O16		Northern Illinois	27 31
O30		at Bowling Green	7 31
N6		Toledo	13 32
N13	●	Eastern Michigan	29 26
N20	●	at Ball State	27 21

MIKE DeBORD
2000-03 (.261)   12-34

2000   2-9   (2-6)

S2		at Purdue	0 48
S9	●	Akron	17 7
S16		at Wyoming	10 31
S23		Boise State	10 47
S30		at Toledo	0 41
O7		Kent State	21 24
O21		at Ohio U.	3 52
O28		Ball State	34 38
N4		at Eastern Michigan	15 31
N11	●	Western Michigan	21 17
N18		at Northern Illinois	6 40

2001   3-8   (2-6)

A30	●	Ea. Kentucky	42 28
S8		at Michigan State	21 35
S22		Toledo	28 52
S29	●	at Buffalo	16 8
O13		Ohio U.	3 34
O20		at Marshall	21 42
O27		Northern Illinois	24 33
N3		at Ball State	34 38
N10	●	Eastern Michigan	35 30
N17		at Western Michigan	17 20
N24		at Boise State	10 26

2002   4-8   (2-6)

A29	●	Sam Houston St.	34 10
S7	●	Wyoming	32 20
S14	●	at Akron	24 17
S21		at Indiana	29 39
S28		at Boston College	0 43
O12		Bowling Green	35 45
O19		at Northern Illinois	0 49
O26		Marshall	18 23
N2	●	at Eastern Michigan	47 21
N9		at Toledo	17 44
N16		Ball State	21 38
N23		Western Michigan	10 35

2003   3-9   (1-7)

A30		at Michigan	7 45
S6	●	New Hampshire	40 33
S13	●	Eastern Kentucky	42 41
S20		at Ball State	14 27
O4		at Bowling Green	3 23
O11		Northern Illinois	24 40
O18		Toledo	13 31
O25		at Central Florida	13 31
N1	●	Eastern Michigan	38 10
N8		Akron	28 40
N15		at Western Michigan	21 44
N22		at Navy	34 63

BRIAN KELLY
2004-06 (.543)   19-16

2004   4-7   (3-5)

S4		at Indiana	10 41
S11		at Michigan State	7 24
S18		S.E. Missouri St.	44 27
O2	●	Kent State	24 21
O9		Bowling Green	14 38
O16		at Northern Illinois	10 42
O23		at Toledo	22 27
O30	●	Western Michigan	24 21
N6		Eastern Michigan *DET*	58 61
N13		at Buffalo	6 36
N20	●	Ball State	41 40

2005   6-5   (5-3)

S2		Indiana	13 20
S10		at Miami, Ohio	38 37
S17		at Penn State	3 40
S24		Eastern Michigan	20 23
O1		at Akron	31 17
O8		at Army	14 10
O15	●	Ohio U.	37 10
O29	●	Toledo	21 17
N5		Northern Illinois	28 31
N12		at Western Michigan	24 31
N19	●	at Ball State	31 24

2006   10-4   (7-1)

A31		Boston College	24 31
S9		at Michigan	17 41
S16	●	Akron	24 21
S23	●	at Eastern Michigan	24 17
S30		at Kentucky	36 45
O7	●	at Toledo	42 20
O14	●	Ball State	18 7
O19	●	Bowling Green	31 14
N4		at Temple	42 26
N10	●	Western Michigan	31 7
N17		at Northern Illinois	10 31
N24	●	at Buffalo	55 28
		MAC CHAMPIONSHIP GAME	
N30	●	Ohio U. *DET*	31 10
		MOTOR CITY BOWL	
D26	●	Middle Tennessee	31 14

CENTRAL MICHIGAN RECORD BOOK

SINGLE-GAME RECORDS

RUSHING YARDS

RANK	PLAYER	DATE	OPPONENT	YDS
1	Robbie Mixon	Nov. 2, 2002	Eastern Michigan	377
2	Brian Pruitt	Nov. 5, 1994	Toledo	356
3	Jesse Lakes	Sept. 12, 1969	UW-Milwaukee	343
4	Silas Massey	Nov. 2, 1996	Kent State	292
5	Brian Pruitt	Sept. 10, 1994	UNLV	274

PASSING YARDS

RANK	PLAYER	DATE	OPPONENT	ATT	COMP	YDS
1	Kent Smith	Sept. 24, 2005	Western Michigan	70	46	460

RECEIVING YARDS

RANK	PLAYER	DATE	OPPONENT	REC	AVG	YDS
1	Norm Tellar	Nov. 16, 1929	Toledo	NA	NA	284

POINTS

RANK	PLAYER	DATE	OPPONENT	TOT
1	Rodney Stevenson	Nov. 15, 1986	Ball State	30
	Brian Pruit	Nov. 5, 1994	Toledo	30
	Chester Taylor	Sept. 22, 2001	Toledo	30

FIELD GOALS

RANK	PLAYER	DATE	OPPONENT	TOT
1	7 tied with 4			

TACKLES

RANK	PLAYER	DATE	OPPONENT	TOT
1	Brian Leigeb	Nov. 17, 2000	N. Illinois	26
2	3 tied with 23			

INTERCEPTIONS

RANK	PLAYER	DATE	OPPONENT	TOT
1	Steve Bograkos	Sept. 30, 1972	Indiana State	3

RETIRED NUMBERS

6 2 Jim Podoley

SINGLE-SEASON RECORDS

RUSHING YARDS

RANK	PLAYER	SEASON	ATT	YDS
1	Brian Pruitt	1994	292	1,890
2	Silas Massey	1996	312	1,544
3	Chuck Markey	1972	290	1,513
4	Walt Hodges	1974	NA	1,463
5	Billy Smith	1991	374	1,440

PASSING YARDS

RANK	PLAYER	SEASON	ATT	COMP	PCT	YDS
1	Dan LeFevour	2006	247	388	63.7	3,031
2	Chad Darnell	1996	348	189	54.3	2,921
3	Kent Smith	2005	420	255	60.7	2,799
4	Joe Youngblood	1993	287	167	55.1	2,466
5	Pete Shepherd	1999	320	171	53.4	2,295

RECEIVING YARDS

RANK	PLAYER	SEASON	YDS
1	Reggie Allen	1996	1,229
2	Jammarl O'Neal	1999	1,085
3	Ken Ealy	1990	916
4	Reggie Allen	1997	877
5	Bryan Schorman	1997	871

SCORING

RANK	PLAYER	SEASON	TD	FG	PAT	P2	TOT
1	Brian Pruitt	1994	22	0	0	0	132
2	Mike Franckowiak	1974	0	26	38	0	116
3	Jim Podoley	1954	18	0	1	0	109
4	Bernie Raterink	1955	18	0	0	0	108
5	Silas Massey	1996	18	0	0	0	98

TOUCHDOWNS

RANK	PLAYER	SEASON	TOT
1	Brian Pruitt	1994	22
2	Jim Podoley	1954	18
	Bernie Raterink	1955	18
4	3 players tied at 16		

TACKLES

RANK	PLAYER	SEASON	TOT
1	Ray Bentley	1982	173
2	Jim Schulte	1973	151
3	Mike Bevier	1984	148
4	Brian Leigeb	2000	147
5	Ray Bentley	1981	146

INTERCEPTIONS

RANK	PLAYER	SEASON	TOT
1	Jim Bowman	1983	8
2	5 players tied at 6		

PUNTING

RANK	PLAYER	SEASON	AVG
1	Art Texiera	1948	44.5
2	Brian Brandt	2003	43.1
3	Tony Mikulec	2006	42.0
4	Larry Moore	1963	41.0
5	Brian Brandt	2001	40.1

PUNT RETURNS

RANK	PLAYER	SEASON	AVG
1	Jim Podoley	1956	29.0
2	Damien Linson	2004	19.3
3	Bruce Wyman	1964	13.7
4	Ira Gooch	2000	13.2
5	Larry Adams	1968	13.1

KICKOFF RETURNS

RANK	PLAYER	SEASON	AVG
1	Bob Zilinski	1968	34.4
2	Chuck Markey	1972	30.0
	Mose Rison	1977	30.0
4	Asante White	2004	28.0
5	Silas Massey	1995	27.1

MAC TEAMS

CAREER RECORDS

RUSHING YARDS

RANK	PLAYER	SEASONS	ATT	AVG	TD	YDS
1	Curtis Adams	1981-84	761	5.5	44	4,162
2	Walt Hodges	1973-76	753	5.2	34	3,886
3	Jesse Lakes	1969-71	714	5.2	35	3,702
4	Brian Pruitt	1992-94	671	5.5	34	3,693
5	Eric Flowers	1996-99	737	4.2	35	3,122

PASSING YARDS

RANK	PLAYER	SEASONS	ATT	COMP	PCT	INT	TD	YDS
1	Jeff Bender	1988-91	960	502	.523	40	38	6,528
2	Pete Shepherd	1997-2000	879	455	.518	28	19	5,754
3	Derrick Vickers	2000-03	907	494	.545	23	34	5,358
4	Kent Smith	2002-05	785	453	.579	15	33	5,179
5	Joe Youngblood	1990-93	572	331	.529	38	35	4,718
6	Chad Darnell	1994-96	606	319	.526	23	33	4,705
7	Bob DeMarco	1981-84	496	264	.532	27	23	3,699
8	Pat Boyd	1962-65	528	259	.491	43	16	3,200
9	Andy MacDonald	1950-51	383	223	.582	NA	27	3,137
10	Gary Hogeboom	1976-79	355	208	NA	19	19	3,088

RECEIVING YARDS

RANK	PLAYER	SEASONS	REC	AVG	TD	YDS
1	Reggie Allen	1995-98	192	16.9	19	3,242
2	Bryan Schorman	1995-98	187	15.9	13	2,968
3	Damien Linson	2003-06	154	14.7	17	2,279
4	Ken Ealy	1988-1991	101	20.4	16	2,064
5	Matt Means	1972-74	130	15.4	12	2,004
6	John DeBoer	1982-85	93	21.2	19	1,975
7	Justin Harper	2002-05	167	10.4	11	1,744
8	Wally Hempton	1965-67	99	14.7	7	1,456
9	Terrance McMillan	1992-94	98	14.3	9	1,405
10	Rob Turner	1999-2002	112	12.2	5	1,363

SCORING

RANK	PLAYER	SEASONS	TD	FG	PAT	P2	TOT
1	Jim Podoley	1953-56	51	0	0	0	307
2	Rade Savich	1975-78	0	49	127	0	274
3	Kevin Nicholl	1986-89	0	56	105	0	273
4	Walt Beach	1956-59	NA	NA	NA	NA	268
5	Curtis Adams	1981-84	44	0	0	0	264

TOUCHDOWNS

RANK	PLAYER	SEASONS	TOT
1	Jim Podoley	1953-56	51
2	Curtis Adams	1981-84	44
3	Jesse Lakes	1969-71	35
	Willie Todd	1978-81	35
	Eric Flowers	1996-99	35

TACKLES

RANK	PLAYER	SEASONS	TOT
1	Brian Leigeb	1997-2000	486
2	Ray Bentley	1979-82	443
3	James King	2001-04	408
4	Rich Curtiss	1987-90	402
5	Bryan Gross	1976-78	396

INTERCEPTIONS

RANK	PLAYER	SEASONS	TOT
1	Jim Bowman	1981-84	16
2	Jamie Gent	1962-65	15
3	David Johnson	1987-90	14
	Steve Bograkos	1972-74	14
5	Joe Kellogg	1984-87	13

TEAM RECORDS

LONGEST WINNING STREAK
• 15, Oct. 8, 1955-Nov. 10, 1956
Streak broken vs. Bradley, 7-14, Sept. 14, 1957

LONGEST UNDEFEATED STREAK
• 23, Oct. 7, 1978-Oct. 4, 1980
Streak broken vs. Ohio, 9-24, Oct. 11, 1980

MOST CONSECUTIVE WINNING SEASONS
• 13, 1973-1985

MOST CONSECUTIVE BOWL APPEARANCES
• 1 (tie), 1990; 1994; 2006

MOST POINTS IN A GAME
• 80, vs. Ferris State, Oct. 9, 1920

MOST POINTS ALLOWED IN A GAME
• 82, vs. Florida, Sept. 6, 1997

LARGEST MARGIN OF VICTORY
• 80 (80-0), vs. Ferris State, Oct. 9, 1920

LARGEST MARGIN OF DEFEAT
• 76 (6-82), vs. Florida, Sept. 6, 1997

LONGEST RUN FROM SCRIMMAGE
• 98 yards, Eric Flowers, vs. Ball State, Nov. 21, 1998

LONGEST PASS PLAY
• 98 yards, Derrick Vickers to Rob Turner, vs. Ball State, Nov. 3, 2001

LONGEST FIELD GOAL
• 57 yards, Rade Savich, vs. Ball State, Oct. 18, 1975

LONGEST PUNT
• 85 yards, Wayne Schwalbach, vs. Ohio, Sept. 13, 1975

LONGEST PUNT RETURN
• 90 yards, Jim Podoley, vs. Northern Illinois, Nov. 6, 1953

LONGEST INTERCEPTION RETURN
• 100 yards (tie), Shawn Williams, vs. EMU, Oct. 10, 1998; Josh Gordy vs. Akron, Sept. 16, 2006

CENTRAL MICHIGAN ANNUAL STATISTICAL LEADERS

YR	RUSHING	YDS	ATT	AVG	PASSING	ATT	CMP	PCT	YDS	RECEIVING	REC	YDS	AVG
1951	Dave Clark	301	48	6.3	Andy MacDonald	183	114	.62	1,560	Porter Lewis	22	272	12.4
1952	Vern Hawes	540	69	7.8	Don Koleber	63	25	.40	417	Al Droth	16	302	18.9
1953	Chuck Miller	938	131	7.2	Lornie Kerr	70	27	.39	327	Jim Podoley	9	186	20.7
1954	Jim Podoley	1,079	110	9.8	Jim King	38	18	.47	399	Jerry Thomas	4	121	30.3
1955	Bernie Raterink	1,044	128	8.2	Mike Sweeney	31	15	.48	302	Ray Sine	6	140	23.3
1956	Jim Podoley	655	100	6.6	Herb Kipke	68	36	.53	490	Jim Podoley	12	211	17.6
1957	Walt Beach	1,084	140	7.7	Herb Kipke	75	34	.45	511	Walt Beach	27	313	11.6
1958	Walt Beach	929	129	7.2	Oarie Lemanski	73	33	.45	455	Walt Beach	16	264	16.5
1959	Jerry O'Neil	821	145	5.7	Oarie Lemanski	110	56	.51	962	Jerry O'Neil	12	296	24.7
1960	Bob Fisher	492	89	5.5	Wally Sadosty	112	51	.46	531	Len Jagello	10	150	15.0
1961	Chuck Koons	402	113	3.6	Gary Harrington	62	20	.32	239	Chuck Koons	21	130	6.2
1962	Bill Shuple	640	143	4.5	Dick Moffit	179	83	.46	1,109	Gary Finnin	31	361	11.6
1963	Bill Shuple	692	149	4.6	Pat Boyd	117	54	.46	817	Larry Moore	16	397	24.8
1964	Bruce Wyman	823	168	4.9	Pat Boyd	90	45	.50	607	Jamie Gent	19	422	22.2
1965	Jim Acitelli	445	99	4.5	Pat Boyd	283	146	.52	1,604	Wally Hempton	43	605	14.1
1966	Bob Rosso	662	168	3.9	Bob Miles	184	94	.51	1,368	Wally Hempton	34	574	16.9
1967	Craig Tefft	1,046	267	3.9	Gene Gilin	84	41	.49	611	Greg Hoefler	16	292	18.3
1968	Craig Tefft	1,126	239	4.7	Bob Miles	120	62	.52	918	Dave Lemere	15	325	21.7
1969	Jesse Lakes	1,263	253	5.0	Bob Miles	52	22	.42	305	Dave Lemere	18	239	13.3
1970	Jesse Lakes	1,296	250	5.2	Mick Brzezinski	123	50	.41	775	Rick Groth	31	451	14.5
1971	Jesse Lakes	1,143	211	5.4	Mick Brzezinski	162	69	.43	426	Ron Goodin	10	186	18.6
1972	Chuck Markey	1,513	290	5.2	Gary Bevington	162	69	.43	834	Matt Means	43	603	14.0
1973	Jim Sandy	1,168	209	5.6	Mike Franckowiak	88	41	.47	655	Matt Means	32	553	17.3
1974	Walt Hodges	1,463	251	5.8	Mike Franckowiak	122	63	.52	985	Matt Means	40	613	15.3
1975	Walt Hodges	1,025	186	5.5	Ron Rummel	98	37	.38	586	John Fossen	18	211	11.7
1976	Mike Gray	734	188	3.9	Ron Rummel	88	44	.50	761	Wayne Schwalbach	26	496	19.1
1977	Mose Rison	1,241	238	5.2	Ron Rummel	75	34	.45	638	Wayne Schwalbach	21	426	20.3
1978	Willie Todd	746	144	5.2	Gary Hogeboom	143	72	.50	1,095	Brian Blank	19	384	20.2
1979	Willie Todd	1,003	234	4.3	Gary Hogeboom	150	92	.61	1,404	Mike Ball	21	457	21.8
1980	Willie Todd	695	170	4.1	Kevin Northup	133	69	.52	1,011	Mike Hirn	22	388	17.6
1981	Reggie Mitchell	1,068	199	5.4	Bob DeMarco	162	85	.52	1,159	Mike Hirn	24	295	12.3
1982	Curtis Adams	1,090	204	5.3	Bob DeMarco	161	81	.50	1,113	Jaime Jackson	23	412	17.9
1983	Curtis Adams	1,431	267	5.4	Ron Fillmore	126	59	.47	915	John DeBoer	22	540	24.5
1984	Curtis Adams	1,204	222	5.4	Bob DeMarco	173	98	.57	1,427	John DeBoer	40	831	20.8
1985	Tony Brown	655	174	3.8	Ron Fillmore	185	94	.51	1,191	John DeBoer	26	494	19.0
1986	Rodney Stevenson	1,104	207	5.3	Marcelle Carruthers	138	64	.46	912	Melvin Houston	12	210	17.5
1987	John Hood	1,121	208	5.4	Marcelle Carruthers	191	108	.57	1,323	Eric Reed	43	652	15.2
1988	Donnie Riley	1,238	215	5.8	Jeff Bender	169	93	.55	1,309	Mark Hopkins	32	433	13.5
1989	Donnie Riley	1,187	269	4.4	Jeff Bender	232	108	.47	1,487	Ken Ealy	12	346	28.8
1990	Billy Smith	1,047	244	4.3	Jeff Bender	262	145	.55	1,978	Ken Ealy	44	916	20.8
1991	Billy Smith	1,440	374	3.9	Jeff Bender	297	156	.53	1,754	Ken Ealy	41	724	17.7
1992	Brian Pruitt	859	178	4.8	Joe Youngblood	278	161	.58	2,209	Terrance McMillan	43	649	15.1
1993	Brian Pruitt	944	201	4.7	Joe Youngblood	287	167	.58	2,466	D.J. Reid	47	693	14.7
1994	Brian Pruitt	1,890	292	6.5	Erik Timpf	174	90	.52	1,315	Terrance McMillan	28	398	14.2
1995	Silas Massey	1,089	225	4.8	Chad Darnell	258	130	.50	1,737	Bryan Schorman	38	604	15.9
1996	Silas Massey	1,544	312	4.9	Chad Darnell	348	189	.54	2,921	Reggie Allen	66	1,229	18.6
1997	Eric Flowers	909	216	4.2	Tim Crowley	321	148	.46	2,204	Reggie Allen	50	877	17.5
1998	Eric Flowers	1,302	292	4.5	Pete Shepherd	324	152	.47	2,005	Reggie Allen	61	832	13.6
1999	Eric Flowers	766	200	3.8	Pete Shepherd	320	171	.53	2,295	Jammarl O'Neal	59	1,085	18.4
2000	Vince Webber	458	130	3.5	Derrick Vickers	180	83	.46	1,059	David Hannah	34	411	12.1
2001	Terrence Jackson	1,194	252	4.7	Derrick Vickers	211	116	.55	1,156	Rob Turner	50	668	13.4
2002	Robbie Mixon	1,361	255	5.3	Derrick Vickers	320	175	.55	1,828	Rob Turner	43	506	11.8
2003	Jerry Seymour	1,117	205	5.4	Derrick Vickers	216	118	.55	1,345	Justin Harper	45	441	9.8
2004	Jerry Seymour	1,284	262	4.9	Kent Smith	333	188	.56	2,284	Jerry Seymour	47	413	8.8
2005	Ontario Sneed	1,065	220	4.8	Kent Smith	420	255	.61	2,799	Justin Harper	64	607	9.5
2006	Ontario Sneed	764	135	5.7	Dan LeFevour	388	247	.64	3,031	Bryan Anderson	73	867	11.9

Receiving leaders by receptions
All statistics include postseason

MAC TEAMS

EASTERN MICHIGAN

BY ED KRZEMIENSKI

It's not easy for a college football team to get a lot of attention when it plays just 11 miles from one of the greatest programs in the history of the sport. No one could blame Eastern Michigan if, every once in a while, it glances down the road from its home in Ypsilanti and ponders how sweet it would be to receive just half the attention that its neighbor in Ann Arbor gets. EMU, which in the early years of the 20th century scheduled opponents such as Ann Arbor High School, actually became something of a force in the 1920s and 1930s. But the team has struggled since its lone MAC championship in 1987. Since 1990, Eastern Michigan has had one nickname change (from Hurons to Eagles)—and the same number of winning seasons.

TRADITION It's indicative of the Eagles' slight success on the football field that their annual awards are named not for former players but former administrators. The James M. (Bingo) Brown Award for offensive MVP, the John Borowiec Award for the defensive MVP and the Harold Sponberg Award for Scholar-Lineman honor the former dean of men, an original member of the Bust Committee, and an ex-president of the school, respectively. Meanwhile, the stadium and an award for best scholar-athlete are named for former coach Elton J. Rynearson.

BEST PLAYER Gary Patton led the Hurons in rushing each of his four varsity seasons (1984-87). Running for 1,242 yards and 13 touchdowns his senior year, he led EMU to its only MAC championship and a victory in the California Bowl. By the end of his career, Patton held school records for rushing (3,497 yards) and touchdowns (31).

BEST COACH Elton J. Rynearson coached Eastern Michigan for a total of 26 seasons between 1917 and 1948. He led the school to an overall record of 114–58–15, for a .650 winning percentage. From 1925 to 1938, Rynearson compiled an amazing run during which his teams went 80–19–7, including a 6–1 mark in 1930, the only loss coming in a 7-0 thriller to powerhouse neighbor Michigan. During his 46 years of service to EMU, Rynie coached every varsity sport at one time or another.

BEST TEAM Led by Patton and 1,500-yard passer Ron Adams, Jim Harkema's 1987 team went 10–2 overall and 7–1 in the MAC. Four Hurons won all-conference honors: Patton, Adams, guard Brian Clouse, and defensive back Charles Gordon.

PROFILE

Eastern Michigan University
Ypsilanti, Mich.
Founded: 1849
Enrollment: 23,500
Colors: Dark green and white
Nickname: Eagles
Stadium: Rynearson Stadium
　　Opened in 1969
　　AstroTurf; 30,200 capacity
First football game: 1891
All-time record: 419–489–47 (.463)
Bowl record: 1–0
Mid-American Conference championships:
1 (outright)
First-round draft choices: 2
Website: www.emueagles.com

THE BEST OF TIMES

During the 1987 season, EMU posted a 10–2 record, taking the MAC championship and a victory in the California Bowl.

THE WORST OF TIMES

Eastern Michigan failed to achieve a single winning season from 1958 to 1963, going winless in 1960 and 1961.

CONFERENCE

EMU joined the Mid-American Conference in 1976 and has remained there since.

DISTINGUISHED ALUMNI

George "Iceman" Gervin, Basketball Hall of Famer; Shirley Spork, LPGA co-founder; Bob Welch, baseball player

FIGHT SONG

GO GREEN
Go Green, roll up the score
Go Green, let's get some more.
Raise a cheer for old Green and White
Let's show them we came here to fight.
Go Green, vict'ry we'll claim
Go Green, let's win this game.
We'll always fight for old EMU
Come on and let's go Green!

EAGLES FIGHT SONG
Eastern Eagles, hats off to you!
Fight, fight, fight for ole EMU.
Look to the sky, the Eagles will fly,
The bravest we'll defy!
Rah, rah, rah
Hold that line for ole Green and White,
Sons and daughters show your might,
So fight, fight for ole EMU and victory!

BEST BACKFIELD Eastern Michigan threw a party in the air in 1997 and everyone was invited. That season, Charlie Batch threw a school record 434 passes for 3,280 yards and 23 touchdowns. Joining him in the backfield were Savon Edwards and Mike Scott. Edwards led the team with a respectable 627 rushing yards and an excellent 4.9 yard-per-carry average. On the season, Edwards caught 47 passes and Scott another 39. No backfield in EMU history had more firepower.

BEST DEFENSE In 1970, junior defensive lineman Dave Pureifory and his teammates spent a lot of time on the other side of the line of scrimmage. That season, the Hurons tallied 88 tackles for loss, with Pureifory's 25 leading the bunch. With such pressure, it is not surprising that the defense also intercepted 19 passes. The defense gave up a total of just 1,832 yards, including an unbelievably stingy game against Ball State, which managed just 52 total yards in a 60-0 loss. Pete Kalogeras led the team with 120

In 1914, Olds had a special striped shirt made so that he would not be confused with the players. It caught on, and he is regarded as the originator of the officials' jersey.

tackles, but it was Pureifory who went on to the greatest glory as a College Division All-America and a sixth round draft pick of the Green Bay Packers.

BIGGEST GAME On Dec. 12, 1987, the 9–2 Hurons traveled to Fresno to take on the 10–1 San Jose State Spartans in the California Bowl. Playing as a 17-point underdog in front of a hostile crowd, Eastern Michigan came away with a 30-27 win in a seesaw offensive thriller that saw five lead changes. The Hurons went ahead for good on a 32-yard touchdown pass from Adams to Craig Ostrander with less than four minutes left in the game. The redoubtable Patton led the team with 130 yards rushing and was named Most Valuable Player.

BIGGEST UPSET Eastern Michigan's first season in the MAC was in 1976, and the Hurons got off to a horrid 1–7 start. A 30-27 home win over archrival Central Michigan, then 6–2, salvaged a modicum of pride. It was

FIRST-ROUND DRAFT CHOICES	
1978	Ron Johnson, Steelers (22)
1999	L.J. Shelton, Cardinals (21)

CONSENSUS ALL-AMERICANS	
1968	John Schmidt, C
1969	Robert Lints, MG
1970–71	Dave Pureifory, DT
1973	Jim Pietrzak, OT

PRO FOOTBALL HALL OF FAME INDUCTEES		
NAME	YEARS	INDUCTED
George Allen, COACH	1966-77	2002

EMU's only conference win of that first season, which saw the Hurons lose nine games by an average of more than 25 points.

STADIUM Eastern Michigan formally dedicated Rynearson Stadium on Oct. 25, 1969. Originally holding 15,500 spectators and a natural grass playing field, Rynearson now has a capacity of 30,200 (plus standing room in the south end zone) and AstroTurf.

RIVAL There's a huge three-way rivalry in Michigan not involving Wolverines and Spartans: Eastern, Central, and Western Michigan fight fiercely year-round for recruits and bragging rights. As former EMU head coach Rick Rasnick once noted, "The MAC is predominantly a regional conference, so wins against rivals can really help you when it comes to signing players." In this sense, Eastern considers Central its prime rival, and Central has clearly had the upper hand: Through 2004, Eastern trailed Central in their series 24–52–6.

NICKNAME EMU began its life on the football field known variously as the Normalites or Men from Ypsi. In 1929, the school held a contest for a new nickname. The winning entry of Hurons, a regional Native American tribe, came from two students, one of whom was additionally influenced by his place of employment, the Huron Hotel. EMU reconsidered its choice in 1988 when the Michigan Department of Civil Rights suggested schools drop the use of Native American names, logos, and mascots. Three years later, the school had another contest winner—the new and current nickname, Eagles.

UNIFORMS The school's official colors of dark green and white have remained consistent throughout the team's modern history, although the helmets have changed with the new nickname and mascot. Throughout its Huron history, the team periodically wore helmets with the profile of a Native American alongside "EMU." In 1991, as the school was trotting out its new name, helmets sported a "100" logo in honor of the team's 100th year of play. Currently, the team wears a large white E on both sides of a green helmet, with all white outfits on the road and all green at home.

MASCOT The school adopted an eagle named Swoop as its official mascot in 1994. A member of the EMU cheerleading squad, Swoop raised the fraternity of bird-oriented MAC mascots to five, not to mention his successor, the second Swoop.

LORE Dr. Lloyd W. Olds served as a football coach, professor, athletic director, and head of intramural sports, but his principal contribution to the world of sports spread well beyond Ypsilanti. You see, he invented the zebra. As a high school basketball referee in 1914, Olds had a special striped shirt made so that he would not be confused with the players. His striped shirt caught on in basketball. And in football, too.

QUOTE "Our economy is soaring higher than Swoop." —President Bill Clinton, in his keynote address at EMU's 2000 commencement ceremony

EASTERN MICHIGAN ALL-TIME SCORES

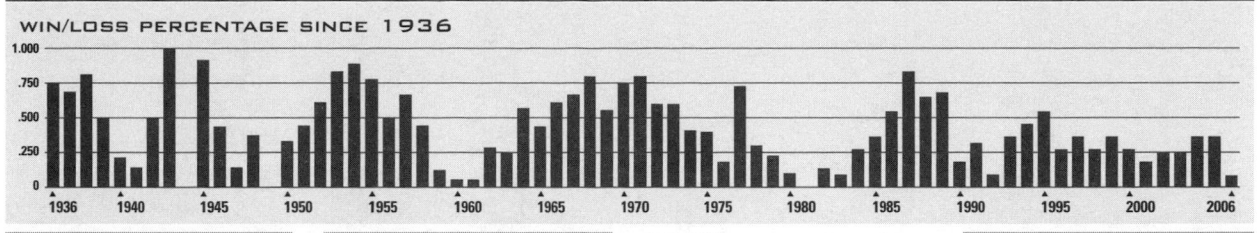

WIN/LOSS PERCENTAGE SINCE 1936

(Chart showing win/loss percentage with years marked: 1936, 1940, 1945, 1950, 1955, 1960, 1965, 1970, 1975, 1980, 1985, 1990, 1995, 2000, 2006; vertical axis: 0, .250, .500, .750, 1.000)

JAMES M. SWIFT
1891 (.000)   0-2

1891   0-2-0
O21		Ann Arbor HS	4 34
U		at Michigan Lit.	0 30

DEANE W. KELLEY
1892 (.667)   2-1

1892   2-1-0
O15		at Ann Arbor HS	0 16
O29		at Michigan Jr. Laws.	6 4
N2		Albion	30 10

ERNEST GOODRICH
1893 (.667)   4-2

1893   4-2-0
U	●	Lit. Students '96	16 8
U		at Hillsdale	0 28
U	●	at Detroit HS	14 10
U	●	at Ann Arbor HS	42 12
U		at Saint Mary's-Cal	22 30
U	●	at Fort Wayne	22 6

VERNE S. BENNETT
1894 (.714)   5-2

1894   5-2-0
S29	●	Ann Arbor HS	18 0
O6		at Olivet	0 48
O13	●	Michigan JV	18 4
O27	●	Ypsilanti HS	36 0
N3	●	Toledo AA	76 0
N17	●	at Detroit	18 6
N24	●	Ann Arbor HS	10 12

MARCUS CARTER
1895 (.500)   3-3

1895   3-3-0
O4	●	at Atlantis	9 8
O5	●	at Ann Arbor HS	32 0
O12	●	at Michigan JV	0 10
O26		at Saint Mary's-Cal	10 24
N2	●	Michigan Lits.	56 6
N16		at Detroit AC	12 16

FRED GREEN
1896 (.800)   4-1

1896   4-1-0
U	●	Hillsdale	18 0
O3		at Michigan	0 18
U	●	at Ann Arbor HS	30 0
U	●	at Albion	52 0
U	●	at Detroit AC	10 0

A. BIRD GLASPIE
1897 (.400)   2-3

1897   2-3-0
S25	●	Michigan Alumni	24 0
O2		at Michigan	0 24
O30		at Albion	0 18
N6	●	at Toledo YMCA	12 4
N30		Kalamazoo	0 16

ENOCH C. THORNE
1898 (.250)   1-5-2

1898   1-5-2
O1		at Michigan	0 21
O8		at Michigan State	6 11
U		at Toledo YMCA	0 16
U	=	Toledo YMCA	0 0
U	=	Alumni	0 0
U		at Hillsdale	0 24
N15	●	at Ypsilanti HS	7 0
N19		at Michigan State	6 24

DWIGHT WATSON
1899 (.500)   1-1-1

1899   1-1-1
O30	=	at Michigan JV	5 5
N11		at Michigan State	0 18
N18	●	Toledo YMCA	24 0

CLAYTON T. TEETZEL
1900-02 (.237)   4-14-1

1900   0-4-0
O20		Orchard Lake	0 17
O27		Michigan JV	0 41
N3		D.A.C. Reserves	0 11
N10		at Kalamazoo	0 12

1901   3-5-0
O5		at Michigan JV	20 28
O19	●	at Michigan Alkali Works	6 5
O26		Michigan JV	6 12
N2	●	at Michigan Alkali Works	12 10
N9		Kalamazoo	0 39
N16		Albion	0 29
N25		Albion	6 39
N30	●	Michigan School-Deaf	10 5

1902   1-5-1
O18		at Detroit Univ. School	0 18
O25	●	at Detroit Bus. Univ.	32 0
N1		at Central Michigan	0 10
N8	=	Detroit Cent. HS	6 6
N15		at Hillsdale	5 29
N22		Hillsdale	0 22
N29		at Michigan School-Deaf	0 40

* HUNTER FOREST
1903 (.500)   4-4

1903   4-4-0
O10		at Detroit	0 6
O17		Mt. Clemens	0 23
O24		Olivet	0 41
O31	●	Detroit Bus. Univ.	10 6
N7	●	at Adrian	16 0
N12	●	Detroit College	5 0
N14		at Hillsdale	11 12
N21	●	Adrian	36 0

DANIEL H. LAWRENCE
1904-05 (.625)   10-6

1904   6-2-0
O8		Detroit Bus. Univ.	24 5
O15		at Albion	0 68
O22	●	at Michigan School-Deaf	18 11
O29		at Michigan JV	0 43
N5	●	at Adrian	23 11
N12	●	Michigan School-Deaf	16 0
N19	●	Adrian	28 10
N24	●	Hillsdale	12 11

1905   4-4-0
S30		Michigan JV	0 20
O7	●	Detroit Bus. Univ.	30 0
O14		at Michigan Military Acad.	17 12
O21	●	Alumni Game	16 0
O28		at Olivet	0 69
N4	●	at Michigan School-Deaf	6 5
N17		at Central Michigan	0 13
N29		at Hillsdale	12 38

* HENRY F. SCHULTE
1906-08 (.594)   9-6-1

1906   5-0-1
O20	=	at Michigan School-Deaf	0 0
O25	●	Detroit	6 0
N3	●	at Adrian	6 0
N10	●	Flint	16 0
N17	●	at Western Michigan	14 5
N27	●	Hillsdale	10 6

1907   3-2-0
O12	●	Adrian	22 0
O26	●	Detroit	7 0
N9		at Western Michigan	0 6
N16	●	Central Michigan	39 0
N23		at Hillsdale	4 7

1908   1-4-0
O10	●	Michigan School-Deaf	5 0
O23		Alma	0 5
O31		at Adrian	0 4
N7		at Central Michigan	0 11
N21		Hillsdale	10 20

CLARE HUNTER
1909 (.333)   2-4

1909   2-4-0
O16		at Alma	0 5
O23		Cleary Business	0 19
O30		Adrian	2 6
N5	●	Central Michigan	17 0
N13		at Detroit	8 9
N20	●	at Hillsdale	17 6

CURRY HICKS
1910 (.083)   0-5-1

1910   0-5-1
O9	=	at Adrian	5 5
O22		Detroit Univ. School	0 6
O15		Alma	6 22
N5		at Detroit	0 16
N12		at Central Michigan	0 13
N19		Hillsdale	0 6

DWIGHT WILSON
1911 (.429)   3-4

1911   3-4-0
O14	●	at Detroit Univ. School	17 0
O21		Adrian	0 9
O28	●	Alumni	6 0
N4	●	Battle Creek Normal	17 0
N9		Detroit	0 16
U		at Culver Military Acad.	0 28
N25		at Hillsdale	6 28

LEROY BROWN
1912-13 (.538)   6-5-2

1912   4-2-1
O19	●	Michigan School-Deaf	20 7
O26	●	Alumni Game	9 0
O29	●	Cleary College	33 0
N2		at Assumption Coll.	0 12
N8	=	at Central Michigan	0 0
N15	●	Western Michigan	7 0
N23		Hillsdale	14 26

1913   2-3-1
O11		at Michigan JV	0 26
O18	●	Assumption Coll.	38 0
O25	=	Detroit	0 0
N1		at Western Michigan	6 12
N15		Alma	0 34
N22	●	at Hillsdale	6 0

DR. THOMAS RANSOM
1914 (.583)   3-2-1

1914   3-2-1
O10		at Michigan JV	0 7
O16	=	at Alma	0 0
O31	●	Assumption Coll.	32 10
N4	●	Saint Mary's-Cal	27 12
N14		Western Michigan	0 10
N21	●	Hillsdale	13 7

ELMER C. MITCHELL
1915-16 (.545)   5-4-2

1915   4-2-1
O9	●	at Assumption Coll.	33 0
O16	=	at Michigan JV	0 0
O23	●	Detroit	46 0
O30	●	Adrian	28 0
N6		at Western Michigan	0 19
N13	●	Battle Creek Tr.	47 0
N20		at Hillsdale	0 6

1916   1-2-1
O7		Alma	0 6
O14	=	at Michigan JV	0 0
O21		Kalamazoo	6 21
O28		at Detroit	12 6

ELTON J. RYNEARSON
1917, '19-20, '25-48 (.650) 114-58-15

1917   3-4-0
O13		at Michigan JV	0 18
O17	●	at Assumption Coll.	28 0
O20	●	Central Michigan	63 0
O27		Olivet	0 19
N3		at Alma	0 27
N10		Michigan State JV	7 13
N24	●	at Hillsdale	13 3

LYNN BELL
1918 (.333)   1-2

1918   1-2-0
O26		at Detroit JC	0 18
N2		at U-M Army Corps	6 7
N9	●	at Hillsdale	20 6

ELTON J. RYNEARSON

1919   4-2-1
O16	●	Assumption Coll.	12 0
O23		at Bowling Green	10 0
O25	●	Adrian	23 6
N1	●	Alma	14 0
N7		at Central Michigan	7 7
N15		Albion	7 30
N22		at Hillsdale	0 1

1920   6-2-0
O9	●	at Assumption Coll.	27 13
O12	●	Bowling Green	45 0
O16	●	Central Michigan	7 6
O23	●	at Alma	12 6
O30	●	Grand Rapids JC	20 0
N6	●	Detroit JC	21 7
N15		at Albion	0 28
* N29		Hillsdale	0 28

JOSEPH McCULLOCH
1921-22 (.538)   6-5-2

1921   3-3-0
O8	●	Assumption Coll.	48 0
O15	●	at Central Michigan	7 6
O22		Alma	0 7
N12	●	at Hillsdale	13 7
N18		Albion	14 27
N29		at Wayne State	0 3

1922   3-2-2
O7	●	at Assumption Coll.	13 0
O14	●	at Grand Rapids JC	12 0
O21		at Alma	0 14
O28	=	Wayne State	0 0
N4	=	Central Michigan	0 0
N11	●	Olivet	6 0
N18		Albion	0 14

JAMES BROWN
1923-24 (.313) 4-10-2

1923 2-5-1

S29	●	Adrian	13	0
O6		at Toledo	0	13
O13	=	Hillsdale	6	6
O20		Alma	0	19
O27		at Central Michigan	3	27
N3	●	at Kalamazoo	19	3
N17		Albion	7	21
N22		at Olivet	7	15

1924 2-5-1

S27	=	at Adrian	7	7
O4		Toledo	0	7
O11		at Hillsdale	13	14
O18		at Alma	0	9
O25		Central Michigan	0	13
N1	●	Kalamazoo	14	0
N15		at Albion	0	13
N22	●	Olivet	12	6

ELTON J. RYNEARSON

1925 8-0-0

O3	●	Detroit JV	8	0
O10	●	at Bowling Green	14	0
O17	●	Albion	6	0
O24	●	Hillsdale	20	0
O31	●	Ferris State	6	0
N8	●	at Olivet	20	0
N14	●	at Alma	25	0
N21	●	at Kalamazoo	7	6

1926 6-1-0

O2	●	Detroit JV	6	0
O9		at Alma	0	12
O16	●	at Detroit City College	6	0
O23	●	Central Michigan	41	0
O30	●	at Ferris State	21	0
N6	●	Olivet	20	0
N29	●	Kalamazoo	19	0

1927 8-0-0

O1	●	Olivet	20	0
O8	●	at Northern Illinois	25	6
O15	●	at Assumption Coll.	26	7
O22	●	Valparaiso	44	0
O29	●	Central Michigan	6	0
N5	●	at Adrian	20	0
N12	●	at Western Michigan	6	0
N19	●	Wayne State	39	0

1928 7-1-0

S29		at John Carroll	9	31
O6	●	Olivet	33	0
O13	●	Michigan JV	25	3
O19	●	Adrian	38	0
O27	●	at Central Michigan	36	0
N3	●	Northern Illinois	43	0
N10	●	Western Michigan	18	9
N17	●	at Wayne State	31	0

1929 5-1-2

O5	●	Bowling Green	34	7
O12	●	at DePaul	27	0
O19	●	Notre Dame JV	13	7
O26	●	Central Michigan	24	0
N2	=	at Western Michigan	7	7
N9		Michigan JV	14	18
N16	=	John Carroll	6	6
N23	●	at Detroit City Coll.	31	0

1930 6-1-0

S27		at Michigan	0	7
O11	●	Detroit City Coll.	33	7
O18	●	Western Michigan	19	0
O25	●	at Central Michigan	13	0
N1	●	Georgetown, Ky.	45	0
N8	●	Notre Dame JV	16	0
N15	●	at No. Iowa	19	0

1931 3-2-1

O3		at Michigan	0	34
O10	●	Ohio State JV	27	0
O17	=	at Notre Dame JV	0	0
O24		Central Michigan	12	20
N7	●	Ferris State	27	0
N14	●	No. Iowa	32	0

1932 5-2-0

S30		at Detroit	7	13
O7	●	at Northern Michigan	50	0
O15	●	Alma	27	0
O22	●	at Central Michigan	28	0
O29	●	Michigan JV	15	6
N5	●	South Dakota State	12	0
N13		No. Iowa	6	12

1933 6-2-0

S23	●	at Ferris State	20	0
S29		at Detroit	0	31
O7	●	at Northern Michigan	24	0
O13	●	St. Viator	13	8
O21	●	Central Michigan	13	*7
O28	●	Alma	19	6
N4		South Dakota State	7	13
N11	●	at No. Iowa	19	6

1934 5-2-0

O6	●	Northern Michigan	26	6
O13		at No. Iowa	0	33
O20		at Central Michigan	12	13
O27	●	Alma	15	6
N3	●	St. Viator	13	0
N10	●	Ferris State	9	7
N17	●	at Indiana State	34	14

1935 4-2-2

S28		at Northern Michigan	0	2
O5	●	at Wayne State	16	6
O12	●	No. Iowa	3	0
O19	●	Central Michigan	7	0
O26	=	at Illinois St.	0	0
N2		Valparaiso	0	19
N9	●	Indiana State	10	7
N16	=	at Hope	7	7

1936 6-2-0

S26	●	Ball State	6	0
O2	●	Northern Michigan	12	0
O10		at Bowling Green	0	6
O17		Wayne State	0	8
O24	●	at Central Michigan	13	7
O31	●	at Valparaiso	7	6
N7	●	Illinois St.	19	13
N14	●	at Indiana State	19	13

1937 5-2-1

S25	●	at Ball State	13	6
O2	●	at Northern Michigan	44	0
O9	●	Bowling Green	25	0
O15	=	at Alma	12	12
O23		Central Michigan	10	27
O30	●	at Hope	19	0
N6		at Wayne State	0	7
N13	●	Indiana State	33	7

1938 6-1-1

S24	●	at Indiana State	37	0
S30	●	at Alma	20	0
O7	●	at Illinois St.	12	6
O14	●	Wayne State	20	7
O21		at Central Michigan	6	7
O28	=	at Bowling Green	7	7
N4	●	Kalamazoo	39	7
N11	●	Northern Michigan	25	2

1939 3-3-1

O7	=	at Illinois St.	0	0
O13		Wayne State	7	9
O20		Central Michigan	0	14
O27	●	Kalamazoo	19	6
N4	●	at Wayne State	13	6
N10	●	Alma	16	6
N18		Bowling Green	13	23

1940 1-5-1

O4	=	Illinois St.	0	0
O11		at Detroit	0	47
O19		at Bowling Green	0	15
O25		at Central Michigan	0	24
N2	●	Alma	24	7
N9		Wayne State	7	19
N16		Kalamazoo	3	13

1941 0-5-2

S27	=	at Hope	0	0
O4	=	at Illinois St.	0	0
O11		at Kalamazoo	0	7
O18		Bowling Green	6	20
O24		Central Michigan	6	12
N1		Indiana State	0	14
N8		at Wayne State	0	12

1942 3-3-1

S25		at Alma	6	14
O1	●	Hope	13	9
O9	●	Illinois St.	14	7
O15		at Central Michigan	0	14
O23	=	Wayne State	12	12
O29	●	Hillsdale	19	13
N7		at Albion	0	12

1943 2-0-0

O18	●	at Wayne State	14	0
O28	●	Wayne State	14	0

1944

NO TEAM

1945 5-0-1

O6	●	Albion	6	0
O13	●	Hillsdale	13	0
O27	●	at Hillsdale	6	0
N3	●	at Albion	6	0
N9	●	at Wayne State	14	13
N16	=	Wayne State	0	0

1946 3-4-1

S28		at Illinois St.	0	10
O4		at Hope	0	13
O11	●	Alma	6	0
O18		Central Michigan	13	26
O26		at Hillsdale	7	18
N2	●	Albion	13	6
N9	=	at Ball State	7	7
N15	●	Great Lakes NAS	19	0

1947 1-6-0

S26		at Alma	0	12
O3		Illinois St.	0	6
O11		at Northern Illinois	6	21
O18		Hope	7	12
O24		Hillsdale	2	15
O31		at Central Michigan	10	33 *
N6	●	Ball State	14	7

1948 3-5-0

S24		at Hope	0	14
O2		at Illinois St.	7	40
O9	●	Northern Michigan	6	0
O16		at Ball State	14	23
O23		at Eastern Kentucky	0	20
O29		Northern Illinois	7	10
N6	●	Central Michigan	6	0
N12	●	Valparaiso	26	7

HARRY OCKERMAN
1949-51 (.269) 7-19

1949 0-8-0

S24		at Northern Michigan	0	6
O1		Akron	6	20
O8		at Northern Illinois	14	39
O15		Ball State	2	33
O21		Eastern Kentucky	6	27
O29		Hope	6	16
N4		at Central Michigan	7	18
N12		at Valparaiso	26	28

1950 3-6-0

S21	●	at Hope	19	6
S29		at Akron	7	40
O7		Northern Illinois	13	35
O14		Wayne State	6	26
O21	●	at Ball State	13	0
O28		Central Michigan	7	26
N4		at Illinois St.	0	14
N10		at Southern Illinois	13	44
N17	●	Northern Michigan	45	0

1951 4-5-0

S22	●	Hope	20	7
S29	●	Kalamazoo	20	6
O6		at Eastern Illinois	12	19
O13		at Northern Illinois	21	35
O20		Central Michigan	13	19
O27		at Western Illinois	28	63
N3	●	Illinois St.	12	0
N10	●	Southern Illinois	47	7
N17		at Wayne State	13	27

FRED TROSKO
1952-64 (.473) 50-56-4

1952 5-3-1

S19	●	at Hope	13	6
S27	●	Ball State	26	14
O4		Western Illinois	13	20
O11	●	Eastern Illinois	13	7
O18	●	Northern Illinois	19	7
O25		at Central Michigan	7	26
O31		at Wayne State	19	46
N7	=	at Illinois St.	14	14
N14	●	at Southern Illinois	30	6

1953 7-1-1

S19	●	Hope	20	7
S26	●	Hillsdale	28	13
O3	●	Wayne State	13	6
O10	●	at Eastern Illinois	34	6
O17	●	at Northern Illinois	20	14
O24	●	Southern Illinois	37	0
O31		at Western Illinois	0	20
N7	●	Illinois St.	27	6
N14	=	Central Michigan	33	33

1954 8-1-0

S17	●	at Hope	19	0
S25	●	Hillsdale	32	13
O1	●	Wayne State	7	0
O9	●	Eastern Illinois	33	0
O16	●	at Northern Illinois	34	0
O23	●	at Southern Illinois	20	0
O30	●	Western Illinois	33	19
N6	●	at Illinois St.	25	7
N13		at Central Michigan	7	28

1955 7-2-0

S17	●	Hope	27	0
S24		at Hillsdale	6	20
O1	●	at Baldwin-Wallace	20	0
O7	●	at Western Illinois	6	2
O15	●	Illinois St.	25	6
O22	●	Southern Illinois	7	2
O29	●	at Eastern Illinois	14	7
N5		Central Michigan	20	27
N12	●	at Northern Illinois	13	6

1956 4-4-0

S22		at Hillsdale	7	16
S29	●	Baldwin-Wallace	26	0
O6	●	Western Illinois	21	6
O13		at Illinois St.	7	22
O20		at Southern Illinois	7	14
O27	●	Eastern Illinois	65	0
N3		at Central Michigan	0	19
N10	●	at Northern Illinois	25	7

1957 6-3-0

S21		Hope	6	19
S28	●	at Illinois St.	33	14
O5		at Youngstown State	6	13
O12	●	Central Michigan	39	6
O19	●	at Eastern Illinois	39	0
O26	●	Southern Illinois	21	7
N2	●	at Northern Illinois	54	20
N9	●	Western Illinois	26	0
N16		at St. Joseph's	13	48

1958 4-5-0

S19		at Hope	7	19
S27	●	Illinois St.	13	0
O3	●	Youngstown State	21	12
O11		at Central Michigan	6	7
O18	●	Eastern Illinois	31	0
O25		at Southern Illinois	9	13
N1	●	at Northern Illinois	15	7
N8		Western Illinois	6	27
N15		St. Joseph's	0	3

1959 1-7-0

S30		Youngstown State	3	21
O7	●	Illinois St.	13	7
O14		at Northern Michigan	6	39
O17		Central Michigan	8	21
O24		at Eastern Illinois	6	32
O31		Southern Illinois	14	41
N7		at Northern Illinois	0	34
N14		at Western Illinois	0	22

1960 0-8-1

S17		Albion	7	21
S22		at Youngstown State	7	27
O1	=	at Illinois State	14	14
O7		Northern Michigan	0	21
O15		at Central Michigan	0	28
O22		Eastern Illinois	0	8
O29		at Southern Illinois	8	66
N5		Northern Illinois	0	19
N12		Western Illinois	2	26

1961 0-8-1

S16		at Albion	0	13
S23	=	at Ball State	0	0
S30		at Western Illinois	0	43
O6		at Illinois State	0	13
O13		Baldwin-Wallace	14	27
O21		Central Michigan	11	13
O28		at Eastern Illinois	0	7
N4		Southern Illinois	14	20
N11		at Northern Illinois	10	35

1962 2-5-0

S21		Ball State	0	14
S28		Kalamazoo	6	13
O6		at Illinois State	19	20
O13		at Baldwin-Wallace	15	27
O20		at Central Michigan	0	24
O27	●	Eastern Illinois	14	0
N10	●	Alma	30	6

1963 — 2-6-0

S21		at Ball State	6	22
S28	●	at Kalamazoo	13	12
O4		Ohio Northern	7	20
O11		Baldwin-Wallace	13	27
O19		at Findlay	18	48
O25	●	Adrian	13	0
N2		Central Michigan	20	55
N9		at Albion	6	17

1964 — 4-3-0

S26	●	Adrian	7	0
O10		at John Carroll	3	7
O17	●	Allegheny	28	7
O24		at Wayne State	0	13
O31	●	Western Reserve	17	7
N7	●	at Case Tech	48	26
N14		at Ashland	7	13

JERRY RAYMOND 1965-66 (.529) 8-7-2

1965 — 3-4-1

S25		Western Illinois	7	44
O1		Ohio Northern	0	7
O8		John Carroll	6	7
O16	●	at Allegheny	23	8
O23	●	Wayne State	20	0
O30	=	at Western Reserve	14	14
N6	●	Case Tech	41	20
N13		at Baldwin-Wallace	14	29

1966 — 5-3-1

S17		at Findlay	0	20
S24	=	Western Illinois	0	0
O1		Kentucky State	9	26
O8	●	at Western Reserve	16	3
O15	●	at John Carroll	12	2
O22	●	Ferris State	21	6
O29	●	Wayne State	16	0
N5		at Ohio Northern	9	17
N12	●	Eastern Illinois	17	13

DAN BOISTURE 1967-73 (.684) 45-20-3

1967 — 6-3-0

S16	●	Findlay	17	0
S23	●	Baldwin-Wallace	15	13
S30	●	at Eastern Illinois	28	12
O7	●	at Western Reserve	47	0
O14	●	John Carroll	34	0
O21	●	at Ferris State	13	6
O28		at Wayne State	3	20
N4		at La. Monroe	10	12
N11		at Northern Iowa	6	14

1968 — 8-2-0

S14	●	Morningside	46	16
S21	●	S. Connecticut	40	0
S28		at Arkansas State	7	26
O5	●	at Akron	16	7
O12	●	at Ball State	43	7
O19		at Tampa	0	21
O26	●	Kentucky State	7	0
N2	●	Northeastern	41	0
N9	●	Northern Iowa	34	7
N16	●	at Wittenberg	14	7

1969 — 5-4-0

S20		at Murray State	20	28
S27	●	Akron	10	3
O4		at Indiana State	13	14
O11	●	at Waynesburg	48	0
O18	●	Kentucky State	48	6
O25		Tampa	7	17
N1	●	at Northeastern	56	0
N8	●	Montana State	31	7
N15		at Ball State	22	31

1970 — 7-2-1

S12	=	at North Dakota State	14	14
S19	●	at Quantico Marines	23	0
S26	●	Waynesburg	30	0
O3	●	Indiana State	25	21
O10		at Western Kentucky	6	45
O17		at Eastern Kentucky	10	21
O24	●	Wisconsin-Milwaukee	35	0
O31	●	at Northern Michigan	14	8
N7	●	La. Monroe	20	0
N14	●	Ball State	60	0

1971 — 7-1-2

S11	●	Oshkosh State	50	0
S18	●	Quantico Marines	28	20
O2	●	at Idaho State	23	22
O9	●	Western Kentucky	17	14
O16	=	Eastern Kentucky	0	0
O23	●	at Wisconsin-Milwaukee	31	0
O30	●	Northern Michigan	31	3
N6	=	at La. Monroe	10	10
N13	●	South Dakota State	35	2
		PIONEER BOWL		
D11		Louisiana Tech	3	14

1972 — 6-4-0

S9	●	at Wisconsin-Oshkosh	26	14
S16		Toledo	0	16
S22		at Tampa	0	42
O7		Idaho State	14	21
O14	●	Quantico Marines	21	7
O21	●	at Northern Michigan	24	15
O28	●	New Mexico Highlands	30	6
N4	●	at St. Norbert	42	14
N11		at Louisiana Tech	17	24
N18	●	at Central Michigan	28	3

1973 — 6-4-0

S8	●	Ball State	17	14
S15	●	Louisiana Tech	21	19
S22	●	at Indiana State	25	14
S29	●	St. Norbert	47	14
O6		at Western Illinois	21	24
O20		at Kent State	20	34
O27	●	Youngstown State	42	2
N3		at Central Michigan	21	31
N10		at Bowling Green	7	31
N22	●	Weber State	44	7

GEORGE MANS 1974-75 (.405) 8-12-1

1974 — 4-6-1

S7		at Miami, Ohio	0	39
S14	●	Western Michigan	20	19
S21		La. Monroe	14	17
S28		Kent State	0	13
O5		at Arkansas State	7	14
O12	=	at McNeese State	6	6
O19	●	at Northern Michigan	24	0
O26	●	Ball State	17	9
N2		Central Michigan	13	28
N16		at Weber State	14	21
N23	●	at Toledo	28	12

1975 — 4-6-0

S6		at Ball State	14	24
S13	●	Indiana State	30	7
S20	●	at La. Monroe	27	24
S27	●	McNeese State	20	6
O11		at Central Michigan	7	20
O18		Northern Michigan	7	20
O25		Western Illinois	14	17
N1		at Youngstown State	14	15
N8	●	Illinois State	51	14
N15		at Western Michigan	14	24

1976-PRESENT MAC

ED CHLEBEK 1976-77 (.455) 10-12

1976 — 2-9-0 (1-5-0)

S4	|	Ohio U.	7	23
S11	|	at Western Michigan	13	31
S18	|	at Bowling Green	12	53
S26		at McNeese State	10	23
O2		Northern Michigan	6	28
O9	●	Arkansas State	32	30
O23		at Akron	0	36
O30	|	at Kent State	13	38
N6	● |	Central Michigan	30	27
N13		at Illinois State	6	14
N20	|	Ball State	3	52

1977 — 8-3-0 (4-3-0)

S3	● |	at Northern Illinois	25	2
S10		at Central Michigan	3	9
S17	● |	Bowling Green	16	6
S24	●	McNeese State	9	7
O1	● |	Toledo	17	7
O8	● |	Ohio U.	31	14
O22	|	Kent State	13	29
O29	●	at Akron	42	28
N5	●	at North Carolina A&T	21	20
N12	●	Illinois State	41	28
N19	|	at Ball State	21	45

MIKE STOCK 1978-82 (.144) 6-38-1

1978 — 3-7-0 (1-5-0)

S2		at No. Michigan	3	30
S9	|	at Ohio U.	22	23
S16	|	Bowling Green	6	43
S23	●	Indiana St.	27	8
S30	● |	at Toledo	17	12
O7	●	Akron	25	14
O21	|	at Western Michigan	0	32
O28	|	Ball State	0	21
N11	|	Central Michigan	9	41
N18		at Illinois St.	13	14

1979 — 2-8-1 (1-6-1)

S1	●	No. Michigan	21	7
S8	|	at Bowling Green	6	32
S15	|	at Ohio U.	7	20
S22		at Illinois St.	15	24
S29	|	Toledo	7	37
O6	= |	Northern Illinois	0	0
O13		Akron	12	24
O20	● |	Kent State	14	10
N3	|	at Ball State	10	28
N10	|	at Central Michigan	14	37
N17	|	Western Michigan	7	17

1980 — 1-9-0 (1-7-0)

S6	|	at Western Michigan	0	37
S13	● |	at Bowling Green	18	16
S20	|	at Ohio U.	6	34
S27	|	at Toledo	7	49
O11		at Akron	10	21
O18	|	Ball State	0	26
O25	|	at Kent State	12	35
N1	|	Central Michigan	15	51
N8		Illinois St.	7	15
N22	|	at Northern Illinois	6	38

1981 — 0-11-0 (0-9-0)

S12		Akron	7	14
S19		at Illinois St.	7	28
S26	|	Miami, Ohio	12	18
O3	|	at Central Michigan	14	63
O10	|	Toledo	7	42
O17	|	at Ohio U.	7	29
O24	|	Northern Illinois	7	30
O31	|	at Ball State	13	35
N7	|	at Kent State	7	13
N14	|	Bowling Green	0	28
N21	|	at Western Michigan	7	38

BOB LaPOINTE 1982 (.188) 1-6-1

1982 — 1-9-1 (1-7-1)

S11		at Akron	7	14
S18		at Louisiana Tech	12	49
S25	|	at Miami, Ohio	0	35
O2	|	Central Michigan	8	13
O9	|	at Toledo	19	20
O16	|	Ohio U.	13	14
O23	|	at Northern Illinois	0	10
O30	|	Ball State	7	16
N6	● |	Kent State	9	7
N13	|	at Bowling Green	7	24
N20	= |	Western Michigan	3	3

JIM HARKEMA 1983-92 (.422) 41-57-5

1983 — 1-10-0 (0-9-0)

S3	●	Marshall	7	3
S17		Akron	0	13
S24	|	at Ohio U.	14	31
O1	|	Bowling Green	21	26
O8	|	at Central Michigan	3	24
O15	|	Northern Illinois	15	34
O22	|	Toledo	9	37
O29	|	at Ball State	20	33
N5	|	at Kent State	13	37
N12	|	Miami, Ohio	12	24
N19	|	at Western Michigan	10	14

1984 — 2-7-2 (2-5-2)

S8		at Youngstown St.	7	31
S15		at Marshall	17	24
S22	|	Ohio U.	13	16
S29	|	at Bowling Green	27	35
O6	= |	Central Michigan	16	16
O13	= |	at Northern Illinois	10	10
O20	|	at Toledo	7	17
O27	|	Ball State	10	17
N3	● |	Kent State	20	18
N10	|	at Miami, Ohio	0	23
N17	● |	Western Michigan	24	14

1985 — 4-7-0 (3-6-0)

S7	●	Youngstown St.	27	22
S21		at Akron	12	16
S28	|	at Kent State	3	28
O5	● |	Toledo	21	10
O12	|	Bowling Green	24	42
O19	● |	at Ohio U.	27	21
O26	|	at Central Michigan	10	17
N2	● |	at Ball State	27	24
N9	|	Northern Illinois	0	3
N16	|	Miami, Ohio	16	31
N23	|	at Western Michigan	21	38

1986 — 6-5-0 (4-4-0)

S6	● |	Western Michigan	21	14
S13	●	at Youngstown St.	18	17
S20	●	Akron	24	21
S27	|	Kent State	16	20
O4	|	at Toledo	18	23
O11	|	at Bowling Green	10	24
O18	● |	Ohio U.	33	31
O25	● |	Central Michigan	34	16
N1	● |	Ball State	14	7
N8		at Northern Illinois	14	21
N15	|	at Miami, Ohio	20	34

1987 — 10-2-0 (7-1-0)

S5	●	Youngstown St.	35	20
S12	● |	at Miami, Ohio	33	17
S19		at Akron	16	17
S26	● |	at Kent State	23	21
O3	●	Northern Illinois	32	21
O10	|	at Central Michigan	6	16
O17	● |	Ball State	35	28
O24	● |	at Western Michigan	23	17
O31	● |	Ohio U.	34	16
N5	● |	at Toledo	38	9
N14	● |	Bowling Green	38	18
		CALIFORNIA BOWL		
D12	●	San Jose State	30	27

1988 — 6-3-1 (5-2-1)

S3	● |	Miami, Ohio	24	17
S10	●	at Youngstown St.	17	12
S17	● |	Kent State	21	14
S24		at Arizona	0	55
O8	|	Central Michigan	6	20
O15	● |	at Ball State	16	12
O22	|	Western Michigan	24	31
O29	= |	at Ohio U.	17	17
N5	● |	Toledo	20	19
N12	● |	at Bowling Green	28	3

1989 — 7-3-1 (6-2-0)

S2	● |	Kent State	30	7
S9	●	Youngstown St.	14	3
S16	● |	at Ohio U.	30	25
S23	=	at Colorado State	35	35
S30	● |	at Western Michigan	21	20
O7	● |	Toledo	31	14
O14		Liberty	24	25
O21	● |	Bowling Green	21	13
O28	|	at Central Michigan	9	24
N4	● |	Miami, Ohio	20	7
N11	|	at Ball State	17	23

1990 — 2-9-0 (2-6-0)

S1		at Fresno State	10	41
S8	● |	Western Michigan	27	24
S15	● |	Ohio U.	21	18
S22		at Youngstown St.	14	24
S29		at Indiana	6	37
O6	|	at Toledo	23	37
O20	|	at Bowling Green	15	25
O27	|	Central Michigan	12	16
N3	|	at Miami, Ohio	14	34
N10	|	Ball State	13	20
N17	|	at Kent State	24	25

1991 — 3-7-1 (3-4-1)

A31	|	at Bowling Green	6	17
S7		at Purdue	3	49
S14	|	at Miami, Ohio	3	29
S21		Louisiana Tech	14	17
S28		at Wisconsin	6	21
O5	● |	at Kent State	21	20
O12	|	Ball State	8	10
O19	● |	Western Michigan	42	24
N2	= |	Central Michigan	14	14
N9	● |	at Ohio U.	13	10
N16	|	Toledo	14	21

JAN QUARLESS
1992 (.143) 1-6

1992 1-10-0 (1-7-0)

S5		Akron	9 27
S12		at Louisiana Tech	17 31
S19		at Penn State	7 52
S26		Kent State	14 17
O3		Miami, Ohio	7 24
O10		at Ball State	7 31
O17		at Western Michigan	19 20
O24	●	Ohio U.	7 6
O31		at Army	17 57
N7		at Central Michigan	13 30
N14		at Toledo	0 41

RON COOPER
1993-94 (.409) 9-13

1993 4-7-0 (3-5-0)

S4		at West Virginia	6 48
S9		Temple	28 31
S18	●	Western Illinois	16 14
O2		at Miami, Ohio	15 7
O9	●	Kent State	20 15
O16	●	at Central Michigan	28 21
O23		Western Michigan	20 21
O30		Ball State	13 18
N6		at Akron	7 19
N13		Ohio U.	10 12
N19		at Toledo	0 14

1994 5-6-0 (5-4-0)

S3		at Nevada-Las Vegas	3 17
S10		at Wisconsin	0 56
S17		Central Michigan	29 30
S24		Bowling Green	13 30
O1		Miami, Ohio	17 21
O8	●	at Kent State	24 10
O22		at Western Michigan	14 33
O29	●	at Ball State	41 20
N5	●	Akron	42 18
N12	●	at Ohio U.	24 13
N19	●	Toledo	40 37

RICK RASNICK
1995-99 (.370) 20-34

1995 6-5-0 (5-3-0)

S2	●	at Akron	49 29
S9		at Pittsburgh	30 66
S16		Nevada-Las Vegas	51 6
S23	●	Ohio U.	31 20
O7	●	Central Michigan	34 24
O14		at Syracuse	24 52
O21	●	at Ball State	40 35
O28		at Toledo	28 34
N4		at Miami, Ohio	23 39
N11		Western Michigan	13 23
N18	●	at Kent State	40 7

1996 3-8 (3-5)

A31		Temple	24 28
S7		at Wisconsin	3 24
S14	●	at Western Michigan	19 12
S21		Toledo	7 24
S28		at Michigan State	0 47
O5		at Ohio U.	0 7
O12		Miami, Ohio	25 35
O19		at Central Michigan	36 41
O26	●	Kent State	51 10
N2		Ball State	25 39
N9	●	Akron	20 17

1997 4-7 (4-5)

S6		at Missouri	24 44
S13		at Toledo	35 38
S20		Kent State	38 41
S27	●	at Central Michigan	31 24
O4		Ohio U.	7 47
O11	●	Ball State	38 32
O18	●	Akron	45 0
O25		at Marshall	25 48
N1		Western Michigan	38 41
N8	●	at Northern Illinois	38 10
N15		at Central Florida	10 27

1998 3-8 (3-6)

S3		No. Iowa	10 13
S12	●	at Ball State	13 7
S19		at Michigan	20 59
S26		Marshall	23 26
O3	●	at Kent State	26 17
O10		Central Michigan	23 36
O17		at Western Michigan	35 45
O24		Northern Illinois	14 26
N7		at Ohio U.	21 49
N14		at Akron	21 24
N21	●	Toledo	10 7

TONY LOMBARDI
1999 (.000) 0-1

1999 4-7 (4-4)

S11		at Michigan State	7 51
S18		at Miami, Ohio	14 35
S25	●	Akron	38 17
O2		at Louisville	10 45
O9		Western Michigan	37 40
O16	●	Ohio U.	27 26
O23	●	at Toledo	20 13
O30		at Central Florida	6 31
N6	●	Ball State	31 21
N13		at Central Michigan	26 29
N20		at Northern Illinois	23 30

JEFF WOODRUFF
2000-03 (.209) 9-34

2000 3-8 (2-5)

S2	●	Connecticut	32 25
S9		Miami, Ohio	17 34
S16		at South Carolina	6 41
S23		at Temple	40 49
S30		Central Florida	10 31
O7		Toledo	14 42
O14		at Ball State	14 33
O21		at Bowling Green	6 20
N4	●	Central Michigan	31 15
N11	●	Northern Illinois	39 32
N18		at Western Michigan	0 28

2001 2-9 (1-6)

S1	●	S.E. Missouri St.	16 12
S8		at Maryland	3 50
S22		Indiana St.	14 21
S29		Western Michigan	10 31
O6		at Connecticut	0 19
O13		Ball State	14 35
O27	●	Buffalo	24 20
N3		at Northern Illinois	17 40
N10		at Central Michigan	30 35
N17		at Toledo	7 28
N24		at Akron	62 65

2002 3-9 (1-7)

A31		at Michigan State	7 56
S7		Toledo	13 65
S14	●	S.E. Missouri St.	35 32
S21		at Maryland	3 45
S28	●	So. Illinois	48 45
O5		Akron	42 34
O12		at Ohio U.	27 55
O19		at Ball State	17 42
N2		Central Michigan	21 47
N9		at Western Michigan	31 33
N16		Northern Illinois	21 49
N23		at Bowling Green	21 63

AL LAVAN
2003 (.667) 2-1

2003 3-9 (2-6)

A28	●	E. Tenn. St.	28 21
S4		Western Illinois	12 34
S13		at Akron	17 24
S20		at Navy	7 39
S27		Maryland	13 37
O4		Western Michigan	3 31
O11		at Toledo	14 49
O18		Bowling Green	20 33
N1		at Central Michigan	10 38
N8	●	Central Florida	19 13
N15	●	Ball State	38 14
N22	●	at Northern Illinois	24 38

JEFF GENYK
2004-Present (.265) 9-25

2004 4-7 (4-4)

S2	●	Buffalo	37 34
S11		at Florida	10 49
S18		Toledo	32 42
S25		Eastern Illinois	28 31
O2		Idaho	41 45
O9	●	at Ball State	31 24
O16	●	at Western Michigan	35 31
O30		at Bowling Green	20 41
N6	●	Central Michigan *Det*	61 58
N13		at Kent State	17 69
N20		Northern Illinois	16 34

2005 4-7 (3-5)

S1		at Cincinnati	26 28
S10	●	Louisiana-Lafayette	31 10
S17		at Michigan	0 55
S24	●	at Central Michigan	23 20
O1	●	Kent State	27 20
O8		at Toledo	3 30
O15		at Northern Illinois	8 24
O22		Miami, Ohio	23 24
N5		Western Michigan *Det*	36 44
N12		Ball State	25 26
N19		at Buffalo	38 14

2006 1-11 (1-7)

A31		at Ball State	20 38
S9		at Michigan State	20 52
S16		at Northwestern	6 14
S23		Central Michigan	17 24
S30		at Louisiana-Lafayette	14 33
O14		at Bowling Green	21 24
O21	●	Toledo	17 13
O28		at Western Michigan	15 18
N4		Ohio U.	10 16
N11		Navy	21 49
N17		at Kent State	6 14
N24		Northern Illinois	0 27

MAC TEAMS

Neutral Site key: *Det* Detroit, MI

f Forfeit   † Game Later Forfieted   # Disputed Victor   * Disputed Score   ‖ Designated Conference Game |2 Counted Twice in Conference Standings

EASTERN MICHIGAN RECORD BOOK

SINGLE-GAME RECORDS

RUSHING YARDS

RANK	PLAYER	DATE	OPPONENT	ATT	AVG	YDS
1	Larry Ratcliff	Oct. 16, 1971	Eastern Kentucky	40	7.3	291
	Larry Ratcliff	Oct. 2, 1971	Idaho State	34	7.4	251
	Ime Akpan	Sept. 28, 2002	Southern Illinois	37	6.8	251
4	Mike Scott	Oct. 12, 1996	Miami (Ohio)	27	9.2	248
5	Bobby Windom	Oct. 29, 1977	Akron	21	11.4	239

PASSING YARDS

RANK	PLAYER	DATE	OPPONENT	ATT	COMP	YDS
1	Walter Church	Oct. 19, 1996	Central Michigan	62	30	450
2	Charlie Batch	Oct. 18, 1997	Akron	23	20	439
	Walter Church	Oct. 17, 1998	Western Michigan	37	24	439
4	Charlie Batch	Nov. 1, 1997	Western Michigan	49	32	436
5	Charlie Batch	Oct. 28, 1995	Toledo	58	31	430

RECEIVING YARDS

RANK	PLAYER	DATE	OPPONENT	REC	AVG	YDS
1	Ontario Pryor	Oct. 19, 1996	Central Michigan	14	17.2	241
2	Kevin Walter	Oct. 5, 2002	Akron	9	25.0	225
3	Eric Deslauriers	Oct. 9, 2004	Ball State	10	20.9	209
4	Eric Deslauriers	Nov. 6, 2004	Central Michigan	14	14.8	207
5	Ontario Pryor	Aug. 31, 1996	Temple	7	28.9	202

POINTS

RANK	PLAYER	DATE	OPPONENT	TOT
1	Eric Deslauriers	Nov. 6, 2004	Central Michigan	26
2	11 players tied at 24			

FIELD GOALS

RANK	PLAYER	DATE	OPPONENT	TOT
1	7 players tied at 4			

RETIRED NUMBERS

Eastern Michigan has no retired numbers

SINGLE-SEASON RECORDS

RUSHING YARDS

RANK	PLAYER	SEASON	ATT	YDS
1	Anthony Sherrell	2003	338	1,531
2	Bobby Windom	1977	246	1,322
3	Gary Patton	1987	247	1,242
4	Stephen Whitfield	1994	284	1,232
5	Ime Akpan	2002	267	1,221

PASSING YARDS

RANK	PLAYER	SEASON	ATT	COMP	PCT	YDS
1	Charlie Batch	1997	434	247	56.9	3,280
2	Charlie Batch	1995	421	244	58.0	3,177
3	Matt Bohnet	2004	434	228	52.5	2,807
4	Troy Edwards	2002	410	237	55.9	2,762
5	Walter Church	1998	355	213	60.0	2,650

RECEIVING YARDS

RANK	PLAYER	SEASON	REC	AVG	YDS
1	Kevin Walter	2002	93	14.7	1,368
2	Eric Deslauriers	2004	84	15.0	1,257
3	Ontario Pryor	1996	62	16.6	1,031
4	Steve Clay	1995	63	15.9	999
5	Jermaine Sheffield	1998	62	15.4	953

SCORING

RANK	PLAYER	SEASON	TD	FG	PAT	P2	TOT
1	Andrew Wellock	2004	0	21	32	0	95
2	Kerry Keating	1957	15	0	0	0	90
	Ime Akpan	2002	15	0	0	0	90
4	Eric Deslauriers	2004	13	0	0	3	84
5	2 players tied at 78						

TOUCHDOWNS

RANK	PLAYER	SEASON	TOT
1	Kerry Keating	1957	15
	Ime Akpan	2002	15
3	Gary Patton	1987	13
	Anthony Sherrell	2003	13
	Eric Deslauriers	2004	13

TACKLES

RANK	PLAYER	SEASON	TOT
1	Alvin Sanders	1974	180
2	Joe Iliana	1982	160
3	Donald McCall	1999	156
4	Jim Durham	1984	155
	Brian Karol	1974	155

INTERCEPTIONS

RANK	PLAYER	SEASON	YDS	TOT
1	Bob Navarro	1989	73	12
2	Joe Clinton	1968	NA	10
3	Jeff Bixler	1973	85	7
	Richard Palmer	1991	219	7
5	3 players tied at 6			

PUNTING

RANK	PLAYER	SEASON	PUNTS	YDS	AVG
1	Rich Hanschu	1980	NA	2,487	43.6
2	Nick Avondet	1998	NA	2,695	42.8
3	Nick Avondet	2000	NA	2,954	41.6
	David Rysko	2002	NA	2,660	41.6
5	Bob Hirschmann	1985	NA	2,377	40.9

PUNT RETURNS

RANK	PLAYER	SEASON	RET	YDS	AVG
1	Craig Thmpson	1980	10	244	24.4
2	Chip Gooden	1969	16	367	22.9
3	Steve Clay	1995	8	166	20.8
4	Steve Clay	1994	14	278	19.9
5	Mike Strickland	1973	14	194	13.9

KICKOFF RETURNS

RANK	PLAYER	SEASON	RET	YDS	AVG
1	John White	1998	17	535	31.5
2	Steve Clay	1993	13	399	30.7
3	Clarence Chapman	1975	19	580	30.5
4	Clarence Chapman	1974	20	579	28.9
5	Steve Clay	1995	14	395	25.2

MAC TEAMS

CAREER RECORDS

RUSHING YARDS

RANK	PLAYER	SEASONS	ATT	AVG	YDS
1	Gary Patton	1984-87	702	5.0	3,497
2	Mike Strickland	1972-74	649	5.0	3,234
3	Anthony Sherrell	2002-05	635	4.5	2,888
4	Larry Ratcliff	1969-71	478	6.0	2,848
5	Ricky Calhoun	1980-83	629	4.2	2,665
6	Bobby Windom	1975-77	484	5.4	2,595
7	Stephen Whitfield	1991-94	502	4.3	2,167
8	Savon Edwards	1994-97	445	4.8	2,147
9	Doug Crisan	1976-79	481	3.9	1,886
10	Mike Scott	1993, 95-97	350	5.0	1,740

PASSING YARDS

RANK	PLAYER	SEASONS	ATT	COMP	PCT	INT	TD	YDS
1	Walter Church	1996-2000	1,441	807	56.0	49	43	9,142
2	Charlie Batch	1994-97	998	579	58.0	28	53	7,592
3	Matt Bohnet	2004-05	783	448	57.1	17	35	4,988
4	Ron Adams	1984-87	655	364	55.6	24	26	4,757
5	Tom Sullivan	1986-89	465	247	53.1	28	13	3,647
6	Troy Edwards	1999-2002	544	302	55.5	18	24	3,552
7	Scott Davis	1978-81	575	277	48.1	28	13	3,398
8	Steve Coulter	1981-83	556	257	46.2	27	10	3,242
9	Steve Raklovits	1973-77	508	238	46.9	34	18	3,103
10	Michael Armour	1993-95	415	233	56.1	19	18	2,983

RECEIVING YARDS

RANK	PLAYER	SEASONS	REC	AVG	TD	YDS
1	Eric Deslauriers	2003-06	322	10.1	32	3,250
2	Kevin Walter	1999-2002	211	13.5	20	2,838
3	Jermaine Sheffield	1997-99	126	16.2	14	2,043
4	Steve Clay	1992-95	133	13.9	14	1,846
5	Tom Parm	1976-79	101	16.9	NA	1,711
6	Brandon Campbell	1996-99	105	14.7	NA	1,548
7	Ontario Pryor	1993-96	93	15.6	NA	1,448
8	Chip Gooden	1968-70, 72	95	15.2	10	1,442
9	Derrin Powell	1983-84	NA	NA	NA	1,296
10	Savon Edwards	1994-97	135	9.5	NA	1,287

SCORING

RANK	PLAYER	SEASONS	TD	FG	PAT	P2	TOT
1	Andrew Wellock	2003-06	0	69	92	0	299
2	Justin Ventura	1995-98	0	42	113	0	239
3	Tim Henneghan	1986-89	0	38	92	0	206
4	Gary Patton	1984-87	31	0	0	0	186
5	3 players tied at 168						

TOUCHDOWNS

RANK	PLAYER	SEASONS	TOT
1	Gary Patton	1984-87	31
2	Anthony Sherrell	2002-05	28
3	Larry Ratcliff	1969-71	26
4	Kerry Keating	1954-57	25
	Anthony Sherrell	2002-	25

TACKLES

RANK	PLAYER	SEASONS	TOT
1	Reese McCaskill	1992-95	450
2	Scott Russell	1998-2001	423
3	Jeff Bixler	1972-75	375
4	David Marshall	1979-83	360
5	Kenny Philpot	1998-2001	357

INTERCEPTIONS

RANK	PLAYER	SEASONS	YDS	TOT
1	Joe Clinton	1966-69	NA	20
2	Jeff Bixler	1972-75	174	15
3	Darrell Mossburg	1970-72	187	14
4	Charles Gordon	1986-89	129	12
	Bob Navarro	1987-90	NA	12

PUNTING

RANK	PLAYER	SEASONS	PUNTS	YDS	AVG
1	Rich Hanschu	1979-80	63	2,738	43.4
2	Nick Avondet	1997-2000	262	10,618	40.5
3	David Rysko	2001-03	233	9,072	38.9
4	Wes Garner	1993	70	2,714	38.8
5	Bob Hirschmann	1982-85	259	10,025	38.7

TEAM RECORDS

LONGEST WINNING STREAK
• 13, Oct. 16, 1926-Nov. 19, 1927
Streak broken vs. John Carroll, 9-31, Sept. 29, 1928

LONGEST UNDEFEATED STREAK
• 13 (tie): Oct. 16, 1926-Nov. 19, 1927
Streak broken vs. John Carroll, 9-31, Sept. 29, 1928;
Oct. 24, 1970-Nov. 13, 1971
Streak broken vs. Louisiana Tech, 3-14, Dec. 11, 1971 (Pioneer Bowl)

MOST CONSECUTIVE WINNING SEASONS
• 14, 1925-38

MOST CONSECUTIVE BOWL APPEARANCES
• 1 (tie), 1971; 1987

MOST POINTS IN A GAME
• 76, vs. Toledo Athletic, Nov. 3, 1894

MOST POINTS ALLOWED IN A GAME
• 69 (tie), vs. Olivet, Oct. 28, 1905; vs. Kent State, Nov. 13, 2004

LARGEST MARGIN OF VICTORY
• 76 (76-0), vs. Toledo Athletic, Nov. 3, 1894

LARGEST MARGIN OF DEFEAT
• 69 (0-69) vs. Olivet, Oct. 28, 1905

LONGEST RUN FROM SCRIMMAGE
• 95 yards, Kerry Keating, vs. Illinois Normal, Sept. 28, 1957

LONGEST PASS PLAY
• 89 yards, Walter Church to Eric Powell, vs. Western Michigan, Oct. 17, 1998

LONGEST FIELD GOAL
• 52 yards (tie), Don Vesling, vs. Ohio, Oct. 19, 1985; Don Vesling, vs. Ball State, Nov. 2, 1985; Justin Ventura, vs. Marshall, Oct. 25, 1997; Andrew Wellock, vs. Idaho, Oct. 2, 2004; Andrew Wellock, vs. Buffalo, Nov. 19, 2005

LONGEST PUNT
• 90 yards (tie) , Charles Nemeth, vs. Alma, Nov. 4, 1940; Jack Baker, vs. Wayne State, Oct. 18, 1943

LONGEST PUNT RETURN
• 96 yards, Craig Thompson, vs. Western Michigan, Oct. 19, 1991

LONGEST INTERCEPTION RETURN
• 100 yards (tie), Jerry Warkentien, vs. Akron, Oct. 5, 1968; George Duranko, vs. Central Michigan, Nov. 18, 1972; Jim Johnston, vs. Northern Illinois, Oct. 13, 1951

EASTERN MICHIGAN ANNUAL STATISTICAL LEADERS

YR	RUSHING	YDS	ATT	AVG	PASSING	ATT	CMP	PCT	YDS	RECEIVING	REC	YDS	AVG
1952	Ed Skowneski	328	80	4.1		NA	NA	NA	NA		NA	NA	NA
1953	Tom Fagan	388	93	4.2		NA	NA	NA	NA		NA	NA	NA
1954	Virgil Windom	530	122	4.3		NA	NA	NA	NA		NA	NA	NA
1955	Tom McCormick	461	86	5.4		NA	NA	NA	NA		NA	NA	NA
1956	Kerry Keating	417	67	6.2	Herman Carroll	66	31	.47	413	Kerry Keating	8	126	15.8
1957	Kerry Keating	563	96	5.9	Bill Ameel	47	19	.40	328	Kerry Keating	5	153	30.6
1958	Al Day	296	80	3.7	John Kubiak	64	29	.45	452	Jerry Wedge	10	183	18.3
1959	Al Day	226	61	3.7	Dave Longridge	122	41	.34	513	Ron Gulyas	9	191	21.2
1960	Jim Dills	231	67	3.4	George Beaudette	60	25	.42	339	Bill Yanis	21	388	18.5
1961	Don Oboza	207	75	2.8	George Beaudette	155	50	.32	696	Pat Dignan	12	195	16.3
1962	Terry Hurley	261	84	3.1	Tom Prieur	148	61	.41	854	Terry Hurley	29	534	18.4
1963	Terry Hurley	366	101	3.6	Don Oboza	150	70	.47	885	Terry Hurley	31	345	11.1
1964	Pete DiMercurio	341	78	4.4	Bill MacGillivray	104	49	.47	760	Tom Grundner	21	333	15.9
1965	Bob Edelbrock	305	71	4.3	Ed Mass	120	58	.48	716	Tom Grundner	17	282	16.6
1966	Lonny Head	350	114	3.1	Rick Krumm	81	32	.40	351	Ted LeClaire	19	295	15.5
1967	John Vaccarelli	481	106	4.5	John Vaccarelli	78	22	.28	273	Gary Matsche	16	260	16.3
1968	Dennis Hewitt	607	157	3.9	Arnold Fontes	107	49	.46	725	Chip Gooden	23	463	20.1
1969	Larry Ratcliff	649	141	4.6	Donald Stewart	148	73	.49	1,042	Gary Matsche	34	513	15.1
1970	Larry Ratcliff	1,011	171	5.9	Donald Stewart	68	31	.46	499	Chip Gooden	26	430	16.5
1971	Larry Ratcliff	1,188	166	7.2	Bob Hill	53	20	.38	278	Tim Cogswell	10	209	20.9
1972	Mike Strickland	924	182	5.1	Houston Booth	62	29	.47	513	Chip Gooden	21	259	12.3
1973	Mike Strickland	1,105	185	6.0	Frank Kolch	124	71	.57	988	Reggie Garrett	43	693	16.1
1974	Mike Strickland	1,203	282	4.3	Jerry Mucha	56	27	.48	406	Clarence Chapman	17	296	17.4
1975	Clarence Chapman	643	119	5.4	Jerry Mucha	94	37	.39	526	Clarence Chapman	13	194	14.9
1976	Bobby Windom	824	147	5.6	Steve Raklovits	199	90	.45	954	Carlos Henderson	19	328	17.3
1977	Bobby Windom	1,322	246	5.4	Steve Raklovits	228	123	.54	1,784	James Hall	40	646	16.2
1978	Doug Crisan	485	103	4.7	Burt Beaney	133	62	.47	833	Tom Parm	21	363	17.3
1979	Doug Crisan	412	128	3.2	Scott Davis	254	131	.52	1,744	Tom Parm	41	701	17.1
1980	Albert Williams	456	121	3.8	Scott Davis	227	106	.47	1,143	Jeff Dackin	27	363	13.4
1981	Ricky Calhoun	971	235	4.1	J.F. Green	226	131	.58	1,391	Jeff Dackin	35	440	12.6
1982	Ricky Calhoun	656	139	4.7	Steve Coulter	258	117	.45	1,415	Ricky Simpson	32	385	12.0
1983	Ricky Calhoun	871	217	4.0	Steve Coulter	330	147	.45	1,827	Derrin Powell	34	582	17.1
1984	Gary Patton	566	103	5.5	Robert Gordon	189	89	.47	949	Derrin Powell	16	261	16.3
1985	Gary Patton	631	142	4.4	Ron Adams	167	91	.54	977	Don Vesling	19	354	18.6
1986	Gary Patton	1,058	210	5.0	Ron Adams	251	151	.60	1,995	Don Vesling	35	653	18.7
1987	Gary Patton	1,242	247	5.0	Ron Adams	202	107	.53	1,527	Mark Ziegler	26	486	18.7
1988	Bob Foster	762	169	4.5	Tom Sullivan	205	114	.56	1,664	Craig Ostrander	33	676	20.5
1989	Perry Foster	1,087	263	4.1	Tom Sullivan	253	129	.51	1,927	Todd Bell	20	515	25.8
1990	Ed Nwagbaraocha	402	110	3.7	Shane Jackson	245	113	.46	1,454	Patrick Walsh	29	385	13.3
1991	Cameron Moss	452	119	3.8	Kwame McKinnon	149	74	.50	849	Bryan Wauldron	14	213	15.2
1992	Stephen Whitfield	377	86	4.4	Kwesi Ramsey	129	43	.33	592	Craig Thompson	19	329	17.3
1993	Melvin Green	488	129	3.8	Michael Armour	165	93	.56	1,208	Anthony Cicchelli	31	616	19.9
1994	Stephen Whitfield	1,232	284	4.3	Michael Armour	230	135	.59	1,629	Steve Clay	46	589	12.8
1995	Savon Edwards	732	148	4.9	Charlie Batch	421	244	.58	3,177	Steve Clay	63	999	15.9
1996	Mike Scott	792	145	5.5	Walter Church	355	178	.50	2,151	Ontario Pryor	62	1,031	16.6
1997	Savon Edwards	627	128	4.9	Charlie Batch	434	247	.57	3,280	Ta-if Kumasi	39	710	18.2
1998	Eric Powell	473	152	3.1	Walter Church	355	213	.60	2,650	Jermaine Sheffield	62	953	15.4
1999	Eric Powell	583	151	3.9	Walter Church	332	178	.54	2,015	Brandon Campbell	53	764	14.4
2000	John White	561	155	3.6	Walter Church	399	238	.60	2,326	Kenny Christian	78	808	10.4
2001	Chris R. Roberson	755	167	4.5	Kainoa Akina	267	140	.52	1,504	Kevin Walter	62	748	12.1
2002	Ime Akpan	1,221	267	4.6	Troy Edwards	410	232	.57	2,762	Kevin Walter	93	1,368	14.7
2003	Anthony Sherrell	1,531	338	4.5	Chinedu Okoro	251	134	.53	1,360	Anthony Sherrell	44	304	6.9
2004	Anthony Sherrell	854	194	4.4	Matt Bohnet	434	228	.53	2,807	Eric Deslauriers	84	1,257	15.0
2005	Anthony Sherrell	442	89	5.0	Matt Bohnet	351	220	.63	2181	Eric Deslauriers	75	874	11.7
2006	Andy Schmitt	461	107	4.3	Andy Schmitt	213	131	.62	1182	Eric Deslauriers	74	898	12.1

Receiving leaders by receptions
All statistics include postseason

KENT STATE

BY ED KRZEMIENSKI

Kent state university sits in northeastern Ohio, one of the nation's premier regions for football recruiting. It maintains state-of-the-art athletic facilities and has a football-mad student body the size of most Big Ten schools—all of the ingredients necessary for a successful program.

Yet the Golden Flashes have been to just two bowl games, won just one conference title in 56 years, and own Division I-A football's lowest overall winning percentage. The latest coach to try to push Kent State to the top of the Mid-American Conference is Doug Martin, who was elevated from offensive coordinator to the head coaching job just before the 2004 season, inheriting a team that had won only 17 games over the previous six years. After winning just six games in his first two seasons, Martin's efforts began to pay off. In 2006, Kent State won its first four conference games en route to a 6–6 season, raising hopes for the future.

TRADITION Kent State plays two trophy games, one against Akron for the Wagon Wheel, and the other against Bowling Green for the Anniversary Award. Periodically, Kent and Youngstown State play in the Schwebel Challenge Series, named after the Schwebel Baking Company. The Flashes now play in front of a sea of gold, thanks in large part to a campaign to popularize the team's new logo, Flash the Golden Eagle. Since 2001, KSU has sold more than 30,000 gold T-shirts, worn by fans at KSU home games.

BEST PLAYER Recruited out of Crestwood (Ohio) High School as a quarterback, Jack Lambert played linebacker for the rest of his career. At Kent he led the Flashes in tackles in each of his three varsity years, from 1971 to 1973, was a unanimous All-MAC selection his last two years, and won the Vern Smith Award as MAC Player of the Year in 1972. Defensive coach Dennis Fitzgerald remarked that Lambert "had complete disdain for pain ... He played in one game with hip-pointers on both hips, a bruised chest and a swollen elbow." And head coach Don James summed up Lambert's intensity as well as anyone when he quipped, "Every time they gain an inch, he feels responsible."

BEST COACH Before heading west to become head coach at the University of Washington in 1975, Don James stopped off at Kent State to jump-start its floundering

PROFILE

Kent State University
Kent, Ohio
Founded: 1910
Enrollment: 22,317
Colors: Navy Blue and Gold
Nickname: Golden Flashes
Stadium: Dix Stadium
    Opened in 1969
    FieldTurf; 29,287 capacity
First football game: 1920
All-time record: 293–469–28 (.389)
Mid-American Conference championships:
1 (outright)
First-round draft choices: 0
Website: www.kentstatesports.com

THE BEST OF TIMES

From 1946 to 1956, the team had no losing and 10 winning seasons and an appearance in the 1954 Refrigerator Bowl (honest). In 1972, during the Jack Lambert and Larry Poole years, the school won its only MAC championship and a Tangerine Bowl berth.

THE WORST OF TIMES

Most others, but especially 1978-85, when the team went 20–68, and 1989-93, an even worse stretch with a cumulative record of 5–50. The former era ended tragically in 1986, when head coach Dick Scesniak died of a heart attack while running around the stadium.

CONFERENCE

KSU joined the Mid-American Conference in 1951, five years after the league's charter. Prior to joining the MAC, Kent State played independently from 1920 to 1930 as Kent State Normal College and in the Ohio Conference from 1931 to 1950 (as Kent State College until 1935 and as Kent State University afterward). The school is currently in the East Division of the MAC.

DISTINGUISHED ALUMNI

Lou Holtz; Drew Carey, comedian; Arsenio Hall, comedian; Chrissie Hynde, musician; Michael Keaton, actor; Joe Walsh, musician

football program. Inheriting a team that had gone 34–60–3 over the previous 10 years, James immediately led the Flashes to a 3–8 season in 1971. But he got better—in 1972, he coached the Flashes to a 6–5–1 season that included the school's first MAC championship, a Tangerine Bowl appearance, and MAC Coach of the Year honors for James. The next year the Flashes went 9–2; in 1974, they were 7–4. James left for Seattle with a 25–19–1 career record at Kent State—22 of those wins in his last three years. James was inducted into the College Football Hall of Fame in 1998.

BEST TEAM The 1972 Flashes won the MAC and appeared in the Tangerine Bowl, but the 1973 team was even better. Like the year before, Kent State went 4–1 in MAC play, but unlike the 1972 team, it had a winning record in out-of-conference games, including a 10-3 win over Louisville to begin the season. They finished with a 9–2 record, largely due to a combination of a dominant defense led by Lambert and a potent offense. Larry Poole

> *The 1954 team earned a trip to the Refrigerator Bowl—the players actually ran through a backless refrigerator placed on the field before the game.*

ran for over 1,000 yards and scored 18 touchdowns, and Greg Kokal threw for 1,776 yards. All told, the 1973 Flashes placed 18 players on the three All-MAC lists. KSU's only conference loss was 20-10 against undefeated Miami (Ohio), which finished 15th in the final AP poll. Had there been more bowl games in 1973, this Flashes team would have received a bid.

BEST BACKFIELD During its season-opening win over rival Akron in 1987, Kent State lost its starting quarterback. The remainder of Glen Mason's second season as head coach looked to be headed downhill. Eric Wilkerson had other ideas. The junior running back ran for 1,221 yards, had 10 touchdowns, led the NCAA in all-purpose yards, and was named MAC Offensive Player of the Year. Tim Phillips stepped in at quarterback admirably, completing 56 percent of his passes for over 1,600 yards, and Leroy Edmonds complemented Wilkerson, twice joining him with 100-yard games. With Mason's wide-open offensive system, the Flashes surprised everyone when they put together their

FIGHT SONG

KENT STATE FIGHT SONG
Fight on for KSU;
Fight for the Blue and Gold.
We're out to beat the foe;
Fight on brave and bold.
Fight on to victory;
Don't stop 'til we're through.
We're all together;
Let's go forward, KSU!

HIGHEST DRAFT CHOICES

1967	John Brooks, Eagles (2nd/44)
1970	Jim Corrigall, Cardinals (2nd/33)
1974	Gerald Tinker, Falcons (2nd/44)
1974	Jack Lambert, Steelers (2nd/46)
1998	Bob Hallen, Falcons (2nd/53)

CONSENSUS ALL-AMERICANS

1967	Oscar Lubke, OT
1968	Amos Van Pelt, HB
1972	Douglas Bell, C
1973	Terry Schmidt, DB
1995-96	Brad Maynard, P

COLLEGE FOOTBALL HALL OF FAME INDUCTEES

NAME	YEARS	INDUCTED
Don James, COACH	1971-74	1998

PRO FOOTBALL HALL OF FAME INDUCTEES

NAME	YEARS	INDUCTED
Jack Lambert, LB	1974-84	1990

first winning season in a decade. Other Kent State quarterbacks and running backs put up better numbers, but the school never had a better complete group.

BEST DEFENSE The 1973 Kent State defense was an immovable force. Lambert served as a senior captain, led the team in tackles with 205 (including 117 solos), and received unanimous first-team All-MAC honors. Joining him from a defense that gave up an average of 11.9 points per game on the first team All-MAC team defense were defensive linemen Walt Vrabel and Larry Faulk (the future Abdul Salaam of New York Jets Sack Exchange fame).

BIGGEST GAME The Flashes finished the 1972 season needing a victory over Toledo to claim the MAC championship. In front of a frenzied home crowd, Kent State held a 6-3 lead at the halftime break but blew the game open in the second half. Eddie Woodard started the half with a 95-yard kickoff return for a touchdown, Poole ran for a game-high 144 yards and two touchdowns, and Lambert had 15 tackles and 14 assists on defense. The final score was 27-9, and Kent State got its first and as yet only conference title.

BIGGEST UPSET In 1972, the Flashes traveled to Bowling Green with a 1–3–1 record and little hope of salvaging a successful season. Bowling Green, on the other hand, was 3–0–1, including an opening-game victory over Purdue. The Flashes won the game 14-10 and turned their season around, winning five of their last six games to claim the conference title.

HEARTBREAKER In 1972, following its MAC championship, Kent State traveled to Orlando to play the University of Tampa in the Tangerine Bowl—its first Division I postseason appearance. In what would have been a fitting conclusion to a great turnaround season (the Flashes went 0–5 in the MAC the previous year), Kent State fell short of victory by three points, losing 21-18.

STADIUM Kent State plays its games at Dix Stadium, a 29,287-capacity facility named for Robert C. Dix, a former member of the Kent State Board of Trustees. Although used the previous year, Dix Stadium was officially dedicated on Sept. 19, 1970, in a game against Ohio University. It had natural grass until 1997, when the school changed the surface to artificial turf.

> *What exactly is a Golden Flash and how does a team make a mascot from an intangible?*

RIVAL Located just 14 miles apart, the students of Kent State and the University of Akron share a lot of stomping grounds. Naturally, this interaction extends to the football field, where many players and fans rekindle rivalries at the collegiate level. Every year the teams play for the Wagon Wheel trophy, a game based on a legendary story in which the founder of the forerunner to the University of Akron lost a wheel in the mud at the present-day site of Kent State. Found in 1902, the wheel became the reward for the winner in 1946, when it was painted blue and gold. That neither team has played well in recent years makes the rivalry all the more significant. Akron leads the series 27–20–2 (through 2006).

NICKNAME Although it started out as Kent State Normal School, no one can accuse Kent State of normality when it comes to its nickname, the Golden Flashes. There is some debate as to who should be credited with its origin. Originally dubbed the Silver Foxes by university president John McGilvrey, when he was dismissed the school offered a $25 prize in a 1926 contest for a new name. Golden Flashes won and was first used by the basketball team in 1927. Another story reports that Oliver Wolcott, sports editor of the *Kent Courier Tribune*, thought the name Silver Foxes a bit delicate for the gridiron and began referring to the football team as the Golden Flashes beginning, conveniently for school historians, in 1927. Regardless of its true origin, 1927 saw the birth of one of collegiate football's most colorful and unique nicknames.

MASCOT Now the more important question: What exactly is a Golden Flash and how does a team create a mascot from such an intangible name? Moreover, how does one invest a Golden Flash with a sense of force? Whether prompted by a contest winner or a newspaper editor, the 1927 name change did not raise the bar much in terms of ferocity. Ultimately, though, the school came up with a choice both accurate and daunting. Flash the Golden Eagle is represented by a costumed student and was briefly symbolized by an actual eagle after 9/11.

UNIFORMS Thank God for hot water. In 1910, the school's official colors were, by state charter, purple and orange. When washing the basketball uniforms, though, a local laundry faded the obnoxious combination to a more palatable blue and gold. The athletes and student body found the harsh wash an undeniable improvement. With

the arrival of the moniker Golden Flashes 17 years later, the uniforms happily matched the team's nickname. As helmet technology improved, Kent State used, variously, Kent, KSU, and K on the side of the headgear. Most famously, Kent State used a golden lightning bolt that in various seasons mimicked precisely the helmet design of the NFL's San Diego Chargers. Currently, the team combines its three most prominent logos on a blue helmet: an uppercase K atop an image of Flash the Golden Eagle, who has a lightning bolt tail.

QUIRK After not fielding a team in the final two years of World War II, Kent State experienced a bit of a renaissance, racking up 13 winning seasons from 1946 to 1960. The 1954 team earned a trip to Evansville, Ind., to play the University of Delaware in the Refrigerator Bowl— before the game, the players actually ran through a backless refrigerator placed on the field. The Blue Hens defeated the Golden Flashes 19-7.

TRAGEDY It is impossible and improper to discuss any aspect of Kent State University without mentioning the events of May 4, 1970. That day, in the wake of a student protest over the American invasion of Cambodia, Ohio National Guardsmen shot into a crowd of students, killing four and wounding nine. Understandably, nothing will ever surpass this tragedy as the defining moment in Kent State's history. In 1986, the football team endured its own misfortune when head coach Dick Scesniak died of a heart attack while jogging around the stadium.

NUMBERS In 2001, Joshua Cribbs became the first freshman in Division I-A history to run and pass for 1,000 yards each in a single season. He repeated the feat in his sophomore season, and then attempted to become the first player to achieve a three-peat. Cribbs, however, fell short with 701 yards rushing in 2003.

QUOTE "You'd better hope he goes outside the Mid-American Conference, because someday he's gonna come back and beat you." —Gerry Myers, high school coach of Jack Lambert, to Miami (Ohio) head coach Bill Mallory, who rejected Lambert for being too slow; three years later, Lambert made four straight tackles inside the 2-yard line against the Redskins

KENT STATE ALL-TIME SCORES

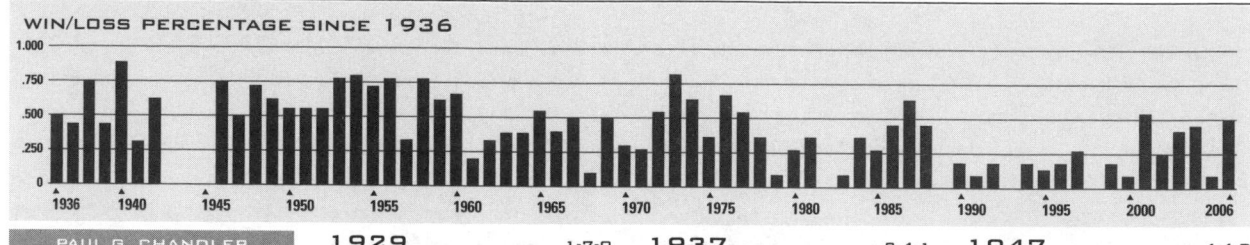

WIN/LOSS PERCENTAGE SINCE 1936

PAUL G. CHANDLER
1920-22 (.115)   1-11-1

1920   1-2-0
O30	at Ashland	0	6
N6	Bowling Green	0	7
U ●	St. Ignatius	1	0f

1921   0-2-1
O1 =	Bowling Green	0	0
U	John Carroll	0	13
U	Ashland	0	7

1922   0-7-0
U	at Hiram	0	14
U	at Mt. Union	0	32
U	St. Ignatius	0	34
U	Ashland	0	14
U	at Baldwin-Wallace	0	32
U	at California, Pa.	0	14
N11	Bowling Green	0	6

FRANK HARSH
1923-24 (.000)   0-9

1923   0-5-0
U	at Akron	0	32
U	at Baldwin-Wallace	0	118
U	West Liberty	6	7
U	Slippery Rock	0	82
U	Indiana STC	0	21

1924   0-4-0
U	Indiana STC	0	29
U	at Ashland	0	20
U	Hiram	0	14
U	at West Liberty	0	26

MERLE WAGONER
1925-32 (.342)   15-33-9

1925   1-1-1
U	Hiram	0	0
U =	at Edinboro	0	0
U =	at Indiana STC	6	6
N14 ●	West Liberty	7	6
U	Findlay	0	12

1926   2-6-0
S25	at Wittenberg	0	27
O9	West Liberty	2	25
O16	at Heidelberg	0	25
O23	at Ashland	0	55
O30 ●	Edinboro	12	0
N6	at Findlay	6	7
N13	Indiana STC	0	23
N20 ●	Wilmington	15	14

1927   1-5-1
S24 =	at Kenyon	6	6
O8	Slippery Rock	0	6
O15	Bowling Green	0	13
O22 ●	Cedarville	19	18
N5	Edinboro UNK	0	6
N12	at Indiana STC	0	7
N19	at Wilmington	0	24

1928   4-2-2
S29 ●	at Kenyon	25	6
O6	at John Carroll	0	12
O13 =	at Defiance	0	0
O20	at Akron	6	8
O27 ●	Cedarville	26	0
N3 ●	Rio Grande	13	0
N10 ●	Indiana STC	13	0
N26 =	at Bowling Green	6	6

1929   1-7-0
S28	at Oberlin	0	19
O5	at Akron	0	25
O12	at Heidelberg	2	25
O19	at Kenyon	15	21
O25	at John Carroll	0	32
N11 ●	Rio Grande	3	0
N16	Baldwin-Wallace	0	18
N23	at Indiana STC	0	21

1930   3-3-1
O3	at Mt. Union	6	18
O11	at Akron	6	12
O18	at Case Tech	0	6
O25 =	Ashland	0	0
N1 ●	Hiram	6	0
N8 ●	at Capital	33	0
N15 ●	Defiance	13	6

1931   3-4-0
O3	at Oberlin	6	12
O10	at Akron	6	12
O16	at Mt. Union	0	25
O31	at Baldwin-Wallace	0	31
N7 ●	Capital	33	0
N14 ●	Otterbein	6	0
N21 ●	Hiram	7	0

1932   0-5-2
S22	Hiram	0	6
O8	Otterbein	0	19
O15	Baldwin-Wallace	0	21
O22 =	at Akron	0	0
O29	at John Carroll	0	28
N5 =	at Capital	0	0
N12	Ashland	0	6

JOE BEGALA
1933-34 (.467)   4-5-6

1933   2-2-3
S29	at Muskingum	0	12
O7	Akron	6	19
O14 ●	Capital	13	0
O20 =	at Ashland	0	0
O28 =	at Hiram	0	0
N4 ●	Marietta	12	0
N18 =	Mt. Union	0	0

1934   2-3-3
S28 =	at Muskingum	6	6
O6	at Akron	0	26
O13 =	at Bowling Green	0	0
O20 ●	Otterbein	7	6
O27 =	Ashland	0	0
N3 ●	Hiram	26	6
N10	Baldwin-Wallace	0	39
N18	at Mt. Union	6	7

G. DONALD STARN
1935-42 (.546)   34-28-3

1935   3-5-0
S27	at Mt. Union	0	19
O5	Heidlberg	6	21
O11	at Akron	0	3
O19 ●	Otterbein	6	0
O26 ●	Bowling Green	45	0
N2 ●	at Hiram	45	6
N9	at Baldwin-Wallace	18	40
N16	at Ashland	7	19

1936   4-4-0
S25 ●	at John Carroll	34	7
O3	Heidelberg	0	19
O9	at Akron	0	6
O17	at Ohio U.	0	6
O24 ●	at Bowling Green	6	0
O30 ●	at Findlay	19	0
N7	Marrietta	12	14
N14 ●	Ashland	14	7

1937   3-4-1
S25	at Baldwin-Wallace	0	13
O2	Heidelberg	7	13
O9 ●	Otterbein	13	6
O16	at Wooster	6	15
O25	at Buffalo	0	13
O30 =	Bowling Green	13	13
N6 ●	Findlay	26	0
N11 ●	at Ashland	14	0

1938   6-2-0
S24 ●	Albion	17	0
O1 ●	at Heidelberg	22	6
O7 ●	at Findlay	13	7
O15 ●	Holbrook	49	0
O22 ●	Buffalo	54	0
O28	at John Carroll	6	27
N5 ●	at Bowling Green	7	3
N11	Baldwin-Wallace	6	26

1939   3-4-1
S30 ●	Lawrence Tech	20	6
O7 ●	Heidelberg	19	0
O14 =	at Mt. Union	6	6
O21	Findlay	7	10
O28 ●	at Hobart	8	6
N4	Bowling Green	0	34
N11	at Western Reserve	0	38
N18	at Baldwin-Wallace	6	40

1940   8-1-0
S21 ●	Bluffton	37	0
S28 ●	Assumption	26	0
O5 ●	Hiram	26	0
O12 ●	Mt. Union	26	0
O18 ●	at Findlay	13	0
O26 ●	at Wash & Jeff	31	0
N2 ●	at Bowling Green	13	0
N9	at Akron	7	23
N16 ●	at Baldwin-Wallace	14	7

1941   2-5-1
S27 ●	Bluffton	58	0
O3 ●	at Findlay	26	0
O10	at Case Tech	6	7
O17 ●	West Liberty	0	0
O24	at Western Reserve	0	28
N1 ●	Bowling Green	6	12
N8	John Carroll	0	12
N15	at Akron	13	41

1942   5-3-0
S26	at Toledo	14	26
O3 ●	Findlay	6	0
O10	at Miami, Ohio	7	53
O17 ●	Patterson Field	24	0
O24	Western Reserve	13	28
O31 ●	at Bowling Green	7	0
N7 ●	at Hiram	20	0
N14 ●	at Akron	23	6

1943-45
NO TEAM—WWII

TREVOR J. REES
1946-63 (.591)   92-63-5

1946   6-2-0
S28 ●	at Hiram	40	0
O5 ●	at John Carroll	20	7
O12 ●	Bluffton	39	0
O19	Bowling Green	0	13
O26	at Baldwin-Wallace	12	21
N2 ●	at Kalamazoo	12	0
N9 ●	at Ohio Wesleyan	7	0
N16 ●	at Akron	13	6

1947   4-4-0
S27 ●	at Mt. Union	13	6
O4	Miami, Ohio	7	35
O11	at Wooster	6	13
O18 ●	Kalamazoo	13	0
O25	at Bowling Green	18	21
N1 ●	John Carroll	26	7
N14 ●	Akron	6	0
N21	at Youngstown	0	13

1948   6-2-1
S24 ●	at Mt. Union	18	0
O2 ●	Wooster	39	0
O8 ●	Waynesburg	34	7
O16 ●	at Central Michigan	19	0
O23 =	at Western Reserve	14	14
O29 ●	Youngstown	7	19
N6	Bowling Green	14	23
N12 ●	at Akron	31	0
N20 ●	at Connecticut	42	26

1949   5-3-0
S23	Western Reserve	20	23
S30 ●	Mt. Union	13	11
O7	at Ohio U.	6	34
O14 ●	Central Michigan	26	12
O29 ●	Connecticut	27	0
N5	at Bowling Green	6	27
N12 ●	Akron	47	0
N18 ●	at Northern Illinois	21	19

1950   5-4-0
S22	at Morris-Harvey	0	7
S29 ●	at Mt. Union	14	19
O7	at John Carroll	7	48
O14 ●	Marietta	57	0
O21 ●	Ohio U.	35	13
O27 ●	Northern Illinois	56	7
N4 ●	Bowling Green	19	6
N11 ●	at Akron	19	7
N18	at New Hampshire	7	13

1951-PRESENT
MAC

1951   4-3-2 (2-1-0)
S22 ●	at Western Michigan	48	19
S28 ●	Mt. Union	28	27
O6 ●	at Western Reserve	42	20
O13	Bucknell	7	13
O20 =	Morris-Harvey	14	14
O27	at Ohio U.	27	28
N3 =	at Bowling Green	27	27
N10 ●	Akron	48	7
N17	New Hampshire	0	7

1952   5-4-0 (2-2-0)
S20 ●	Western Michigan	20	13
S26 ●	at Mt. Union	26	7
O3 ●	Western Reserve	25	19
O11	at Baldwin-Wallace	13	19
O18	Ohio U.	18	27
O25	at Marshall	26	14
N1	Bowling Green	21	44
N7 ●	at Akron	34	14
N15	at New Hampshire	21	23

1953   7-2-0 (3-1-0)
S19 ●	at Waynesburg	20	10
S25 ●	Fort Belvoir	6	7
O3 ●	at Western Reserve	27	0
O9 ●	Baldwin-Wallace	14	13
O17 ●	at Ohio U.	21	40
O24 ●	Marshall	27	7
O31 ●	at Bowling Green	41	7
N7 ●	Akron	54	19
N14 ●	at Western Michigan	40	7

1954 8-2-0 (4-1-0)

S18	●	Waynesburg	26	0
O1	● |	Western Reserve	65	0
O8	●	at Baldwin-Wallace	52	7
O16	|	Ohio U.	7	14
O23	● |	at Marshall	41	20
O30	● |	Bowling Green	28	25
N6	●	at Akron	58	18
N13	●	John Carroll	27	14
N20	● |	Western Michigan	20	13
		REFRIGERATOR BOWL		
D5		Delaware	7	19

1955 6-2-1 (4-1-1)

S23	= |	Bowling Green	6	6
O1		at Dayton	13	26
O7	●	Baldwin-Wallace	33	2
O15	● |	at Ohio U.	20	14
O22	● |	Marshall	39	6
O29	|	Miami, Ohio	7	19
N5	● |	at Toledo	27	0
N12	●	Waynesburg	14	0
N19	● |	at Western Michigan	25	14

1956 7-2-0 (4-2-0)

S22	|	at Bowling Green	0	17
S29	●	at Louisville	7	0
O6	●	Waynesburg	19	6
O13	● |	Ohio U.	32	13
O20	● |	at Marshall	25	7
O27	|	at Miami, Ohio	0	14
N3	● |	Toledo	52	6
N10	●	at Baldwin-Wallace	46	0
N17	● |	Western Michigan	27	13

1957 3-6-0 (1-5-0)

S21		at Xavier	7	13
S27	●	Baldwin-Wallace	26	13
O5	● |	at Ohio U.	14	9
O12	|	Miami, Ohio	14	27
O19	|	at Marshall	6	7
O26	|	Bowling Green	7	13
N2	|	at Toledo	7	21
N9	●	Louisville	13	7
N16	|	at Western Michigan	20	28

1958 7-2-0 (5-1-0)

S20	●	at Xavier	6	0
S27	●	at Baldwin-Wallace	21	14
O4	● |	Ohio U.	14	6
O11	|	at Miami, Ohio	0	35
O18	● |	Marshall	24	0
O25	● |	at Bowling Green	8	7
N1	● |	Toledo	32	6 *
N8		at Louisville	0	21
N15	● |	Western Michigan	32	6

1959 5-3-0 (3-3-0)

S25	●	Baldwin-Wallace	46	12
O3	|	at Ohio U.	0	46
O10	● |	Miami, Ohio	14	6
O17	● |	at Marshall	46	7
O24	|	Bowling Green	8	25
O31	● |	at Toledo	14	7
N7	|	at Western Michigan	0	7
N21	●	Louisville	16	14

1960 6-3-0 (4-2-0)

S24	●	at Baldwin-Wallace	16	6
O1	|	Ohio U.	8	25
O8	● |	at Miami, Ohio	22	19
O15	● |	Marshall	22	6
O22	|	at Bowling Green	0	28
O29	● |	Toledo	18	13
N5	● |	Western Michigan	10	3
N11		at Louisville	8	22
N19	●	at Dayton	14	7

1961 2-8-0 (1-5-0)

S16	●	Dayton	38	14
S23		at Xavier	8	16
S30	● |	at Ohio U.	23	17
O7	|	Miami, Ohio	0	21
O14	|	at Marshall	8	14
O21	|	Bowling Green	6	21
O28	|	at Toledo	22	31
N4	|	at Western Michigan	0	14
N11		Louisville	15	19
N18		Baldwin-Wallace	6	14

1962 3-6-0 (2-4-0)

S15	●	at Dayton	22	7
S22		Xavier	8	9
S29	|	Ohio U.	0	21
O6	|	at Miami, Ohio	14	23
O13	● |	Marshall	23	14
O20	|	at Bowling Green	6	45
O27	● |	Toledo	20	18
N3	|	Western Michigan	6	19
N10		at Louisville	8	29

1963 3-5-1 (1-5-0)

S28	=	at Xavier	7	7
O5	|	at Ohio U.	0	20
O12	|	Miami, Ohio	8	30
O19	|	at Western Michigan	12	26
O26	|	Bowling Green	3	18
N2	● |	at Toledo	20	0
N9	●	Louisville	26	7
N16	|	Marshall	8	14
N23	●	Dayton	23	0

LEO STRANG
1964-67 (.462) 17-20-2

1964 3-5-1 (1-4-1)

S26	●	Xavier	15	2
O3	= |	Ohio U.	3	3
O10	|	Miami, Ohio	14	17
O17	|	Western Michigan	9	12
O24	|	at Bowling Green	0	41
O31	● |	Toledo	14	11
N7	●	at Louisville	14	7
N14	|	at Marshall	7	12
N21		at Dayton	11	16

1965 5-4-1 (3-2-1)

S18		at Xavier	14	21
S25	●	Dayton	14	6
O2	● |	at Ohio U.	27	10
O9	● |	Miami, Ohio	24	13
O16	= |	at Western Michigan	10	10
O23	|	Bowling Green	6	7
O30	|	at Toledo	3	7
N6		at Penn State	6	21
N13	● |	Marshall	33	13
N20	●	Louisville	7	6

1966 4-6-0 (2-4-0)

S17		Buffalo	23	27
S25	●	at Northern Illinois	26	7
O1	|	Ohio U.	10	12
O8	|	at Miami, Ohio	0	7
O15	|	Western Michigan	20	23
O22	● |	at Bowling Green	35	12
O29	● |	Toledo	28	20
N5		at Louisville	20	23
N12	|	at Marshall	7	16
N19	●	Xavier	42	14

1967 5-5-0 (2-4-0)

S16		at Buffalo	6	30
S23	●	Northern Illinois	35	0
S30	● |	at Ohio U.	21	14 †
O7	|	Miami, Ohio	7	21
O14	|	at Western Michigan	7	16
O21	|	Bowling Green	6	7
O28	|	at Toledo	13	14
N4	●	Louisville	28	21
N11	● |	Marshall	41	2
N18	●	at Xavier	31	19

DAVE PUDDINGTON
1968-70 (.300) 9-21

1968 1-9-0 (1-5-0)

S14		at Dayton	10	24
S21		Buffalo	13	21
S28	|	Ohio U.	7	31
O5	|	at Miami, Ohio	0	24
O12	|	Western Michigan	0	14
O19	|	at Bowling Green	7	30
O26	|	Toledo	12	28
N2		at Louisville	9	23
N9	● |	at Marshall	36	12
N16		Xavier	7	23

1969 5-5-0 (1-4-0)

S13	●	Dayton	24	14
S20	|	at Ohio U.	0	35
S27	●	at Xavier	23	7
O4	●	at Buffalo	17	8
O11	|	at Western Michigan	13	33
O18	|	Bowling Green	0	7
O25	|	at Toledo	17	43
N1	●	Louisville	35	6
N8		Marshall	20	31
N15	● |	Miami, Ohio	17	14

1970 3-7-0 (1-4-0)

S19	|	Ohio U.	14	24
S26	●	Buffalo	27	21
O3		at Pittsburgh	6	27
O10	● |	Western Michigan	25	22
O17	|	at Bowling Green	0	44
O24	|	Toledo	17	34
O31		at Louisville	13	14
N7		at Marshall	17	20
N14	|	at Miami, Ohio	8	10
N21	●	Xavier	34	6

DON JAMES
1971-74 (.566) 25-19-1

1971 3-8-0 (0-5-0)

S11	●	at North Carolina St.	23	21
S18		at Cincinnati	20	42
S25	|	at Ohio U.	21	37
O2		Iowa State	14	17
O9	|	at Western Michigan	0	31
O16	|	Bowling Green	33	46
O23	●	at Xavier	24	13
O30		Northern Illinois	7	26
N6	●	Marshall	21	0
N13	|	Miami, Ohio	0	30
N20	|	at Toledo	6	41

1972 6-5-1 (4-1-0)

S9	=	at Akron	13	13
S16		at Louisville	0	34
S23	● |	Ohio U.	37	14
S30		San Diego State	0	14
O7	|	Western Michigan	12	13
O14	● |	at Bowling Green	14	10
O21	●	Xavier	26	16
O28		at Northern Illinois	7	28
N4	●	at Marshall	16	14
N11	● |	at Miami, Ohio	21	10
N18	● |	Toledo	27	9
		TANGERINE BOWL		
D29		Tampa	18	21

1973 9-2-0 (4-1-0)

S15	●	Louisville	10	3
S22	● |	at Ohio U.	35	7
S30		at San Diego State	9	17
O6	● |	at Western Michigan	39	15
O13	● |	Bowling Green	21	7
O20	●	Eastern Michigan	34	20
O27	●	at Utah State	27	16
N3	●	Marshall	35	3
N10	|	Miami, Ohio	10	20
N17	● |	at Toledo	52	16
N24	●	Central Michigan	28	7

1974 7-4-0 (2-3-0)

S7	●	at Central Michigan	21	14
S14	●	at Syracuse	20	14
S21	|	Ohio U.	0	20
S28	●	at Eastern Michigan	13	0
O5	● |	Western Michigan	28	6
O12	|	at Bowling Green	10	26
O19		Utah State	24	27
O26	●	Akron	51	14
N2	●	at Marshall	35	7
N9	|	at Miami, Ohio	17	19
N16	● |	Toledo	35	14

DENNIS FITZGERALD
1975-77 (.539) 18-16

1975 4-7-0 (1-6-0)

S13	●	at La. Monroe	31	29
S20	●	Virginia Tech	17	11
S27	|	at Ohio U.	21	23
O4	|	at Northern Illinois	15	38
O11	● |	at Western Michigan	22	17
O18	|	Bowling Green CLEV	9	35
O25	|	Central Michigan	8	17
N1		at West Virginia	13	38
N8	●	Marshall	30	21
N15	|	Miami, Ohio	8	27
N22	|	at Toledo	28	33

1976 8-4-0 (6-2-0)

S11	● |	at Central Michigan	20	10
S18	|	Ohio U.	12	14
S25		at Iowa State	7	47
O2	●	Air Force CLEV	24	19
O9	● |	Western Michigan	24	12
O16	|	at Bowling Green	13	17
O23		at Virginia Tech	14	42
O30	● |	Eastern Michigan	38	13
N6	●	at Hawaii	27	6
N13	● |	at Miami, Ohio	24	17
N20	● |	Toledo	35	9
N25	● |	Northern Illinois	42	0

1977 6-5-0 (5-4-0)

S12	●	Illinois St.	33	14
S17		at Colorado	0	42
S24	● |	Ball State	13	12
O1	● |	at Ohio U.	44	23
O8	● |	at Western Michigan	20	16
O15	|	Bowling Green	10	14
O22	● |	at Eastern Michigan	29	13
O29	|	Northern Illinois	18	21
N5	|	Central Michigan	10	49
N12	|	Miami, Ohio	0	25
N19	● |	at Toledo	23	12

RON BLACKLEDGE
1978-80 (.242) 8-25

1978 4-7-0 (2-6-0)

S9	|	at Central Michigan	0	41
S16	|	at Ball State	3	27
S23	●	Illinois St.	34	3
S30	● |	Ohio U.	20	14
O7	|	Western Michigan	0	14
O14	|	at Bowling Green	20	28
O21	●	Marshall	20	17
O28		at Air Force	10	26
N4	|	at Northern Illinois	21	27
N11	|	at Miami, Ohio	13	38
N18	● |	Toledo	17	13

1979 1-10-0 (1-7-0)

S8		Eastern Kentucky	14	17
S15		at Akron	13	15
S22		Ball State	10	35
S29	|	at Ohio U.	13	43
O6	● |	at Western Michigan	18	13
O13	|	Bowling Green	17	28
O20	|	at Eastern Michigan	10	14
O27	|	Central Michigan	21	44
N3	|	at Northern Illinois	0	25
N10	|	Miami, Ohio	8	35
N17	|	at Toledo	3	29

1980 3-8-0 (3-6-0)

S13		at Marshall	7	17
S20		at Navy	3	31
S27	|	at Central Michigan	6	21
O4	● |	Ohio U.	15	14
O11	|	Western Michigan	21	28
O18	|	at Bowling Green	3	24
O25	● |	Eastern Michigan	35	12
N1	|	Northern Illinois	14	35
N8	|	at Ball State	7	34
N15	|	at Miami, Ohio	14	49
N22	● |	Toledo	34	14

ED CHLEBEK
1981-82 (.182) 4-18

1981 4-7-0 (3-6-0)

S12	|	Western Michigan	17	20
S19	●	Akron	17	6
S26		at Iowa State	19	28
O3	|	at Miami, Ohio	13	20
O10	● |	Northern Illinois	31	10
O17	● |	at Ball State	17	7
O24	|	at Central Michigan	3	24
O31	|	at Bowling Green	7	13
N7	● |	Eastern Michigan	13	7
N14	|	at Toledo	0	17
N21	|	Ohio U.	7	20

1982 0-11-0 (0-9-0)

S4		at Marshall	21	30
S18	|	at Northern Illinois	15	23
S25	|	at Western Michigan	14	24
O2	|	Miami, Ohio	0	20
O9		at Iowa State	7	44
O16	|	Ball State	3	21
O23	|	Central Michigan	20	31
O30	|	Bowling Green	7	41
N6	|	at Eastern Michigan	7	9
N13	|	Toledo	0	3
N20	|	at Ohio U.	20	24

DICK SCESNIAK
1983-85 (.242) 8-25

1983 1-10-0 (1-8-0)

S3		at Akron	6	13
S10		at Syracuse	10	22
S24	|	Northern Illinois	7	38
O1	|	at Central Michigan	7	13
O8	|	at Miami, Ohio	7	27
O15	|	Ball State	13	17
O22	|	Ohio U.	20	21
O29	|	at Toledo	34	37
N5	● |	Eastern Michigan	37	13
N12	|	Western MIchigan	13	21
N19	|	at Bowling Green	3	38

1984 4-7-0 (3-6-0)

S1	●	Akron	24	17
S8		at Kentucky	0	42
S22	|	at Northern Illinois	10	24
S29	|	Central Michigan	10	14
O6	|	Miami, Ohio	3	19
O13	● |	at Ball State	15	10
O20	● |	at Ohio U.	19	7
O27	● |	Toledo	17	6
N3	|	at Eastern Michigan	18	20
N10	|	at Western Michigan	9	13
N17	|	Bowling Green	10	27

1985   3-8-0 (2-6-0)
S14	at Akron	0	24
S21	at Syracuse	0	34
S28 •	Eastern Michigan	28	3
O5	at Central Michigan	17	21
O12 •	Texas-El Paso	51	24
O19 •	Ball State	45	16
O26	at Bowling Green	14	26
N2	Ohio U.	23	33
N9	at Miami, Ohio	24	52
N16	Western Michigan	3	34
N23	at Toledo	7	10

GLEN MASON
1986-87 (.545)   12-10

1986   5-6-0 (5-3-0)
S6 •	Toledo	18	16
S13	Akron	7	17
S20	at Kentucky	12	37
S27 •	at Eastern Michigan	20	16
O4 •	Central Michigan	33	30
O11	at Florida	9	52
O18	at Ball State	17	26
O25	Bowling Green	15	31
N1 •	at Ohio U.	17	13
N8 •	Miami, Ohio	24	23
N15	at Western Michigan	7	27

1987   7-4-0 (5-3-0)
S12 •	at Akron	27	23
S19 •	at Kansas	31	17
S26	Eastern Michigan	21	23
O3 •	Central Michigan	24	21
O10	at Ball State	23	24
O17 •	Western Michigan	27	13
O24 •	at Ohio U.	24	10
O31	Toledo	17	13
N7	at Bowling Green	20	30
N14 •	Miami, Ohio	14	10
N21	at Pittsburgh	5	28

DICK CRUM
1988-90 (.212)   7-26

1988   5-6-0 (3-5-0)
S3 •	Youngstown St.	34	3
S10 •	Akron	32	12
S17	at Eastern Michigan	14	21
S24	at Kentucky	14	38
O1	at Central Michigan	7	31
O8	Ball State	20	31
O15 •	at Western Michigan	45	28
O22	Ohio U.	14	21
O29	at Toledo	28	35
N5	Bowling Green	31	19
N12 •	at Miami, Ohio	17	11

1989   0-11-0 (0-8-0)
S2	at Eastern Michigan	7	30
S9	at Akron	7	40
S16	at Kansas	21	28
S23	Western Michigan	4	26
S30	at North Carolina St.	22	42
O7	at Central Michigan	0	38
O14	Ball State	21	23
O21	at Ohio U.	14	37
O28	Toledo	42	47
N4	at Bowling Green	28	51
N11	Miami, Ohio	13	15

1990   2-9-0 (2-6-0)
S1	at West Virginia	24	35
S8	Akron	10	38
S22	at Western Michigan	10	37
S29	Cincinnati	24	27
O6	Central Michigan	0	42
O13	at Ball State	0	31
O20 •	Ohio U.	44	15
O27	at Toledo	14	28
N3	Bowling Green	16	20
N10	at Miami, Ohio	10	31
N17 •	Eastern Michigan	25	24

PETE CORDELLI
1991-93 (.091)   3-30

1991   1-10-0 (1-7-0)
A31	at Western Michigan	10	13
S14	at North Carolina St.	0	47
S21	at Ball State	27	28
S28	at Kentucky	6	24
O5	Eastern Michigan	20	21
O12	Cincinnati	19	38
O19	Central Michigan	7	23
O26	at Ohio U.	40	45
N2 •	Toledo	14	13
N9	at Bowling Green	7	35
N16	Miami, Ohio	9	20

1992   2-9-0 (2-7-0)
S5	at Pittsburgh	10	51
S12	Ohio U.	14	27
S19	Ball State	6	10
S26 •	at Eastern Michigan	17	14
O3	at Cincinnati	0	31
O10 •	Akron	20	16
O17	at Central Michigan	0	35
O24	Western Michigan	13	26
O31	at Toledo	17	32
N7	Bowling Green	22	28
N14	at Miami, Ohio	14	31

1993   0-11-0 (0-9-0)
S4	at Kentucky	0	35
S11	at Akron	7	42
S18	at Hawaii	17	49
O2	Western Michigan	21	27
O9	at Eastern Michigan	15	20
O16	at Ohio U.	10	15
O23	Central Michigan	28	33
O30	Toledo	27	45
N6	at Bowling Green	7	40
N13	Miami, Ohio	14	23
N20	at Ball State	3	28

JIM CORRIGALL
1994-97 (.193)   8-35-1

1994   2-9-0 (2-7-0)
S3	at Rutgers	6	28
S17 •	Akron	32	16
S24	at Central Michigan	0	45
O1	at Western Michigan	10	24
O8	Eastern Michigan	10	24
O15	at Youngstown St.	14	28
O22 •	Ohio U.	24	0
O29	at Toledo	14	48
N5	Bowling Green	16	22
N12	at Miami, Ohio	14	24
N19	Ball State	0	34

1995   1-9-1 (0-7-1)
S2 •	Youngstown St.	17	14
S9	Miami, Ohio	0	39
S16 =	at Ohio U.	28	28
S23	at West Virginia	6	45
S30	Western Michigan	6	52
O7	at South Carolina	14	77
O21	at Central Michigan	16	27
O28	at Akron	6	14
N4	Ball State	13	28
N11	Bowling Green	15	26
N18	Eastern Michigan	7	40

1996   2-9 (1-7)
A31	at Miami, Ohio	6	64
S7	at Pittsburgh	14	52
S14 •	Youngstown St.	28	12
S28	at Nevada	42	63
O5 •	Akron	32	17
O12	at Bowling Green	24	31
O19	Ohio U.	15	24
O26	at Eastern Michigan	10	51
N2	Central Michigan	51	52
N9	at Ball State	6	50
N16	at Western Michigan	27	76

1997   3-8 (3-5)
A28	at Ohio U.	7	31
S6	at Youngstown St.	23	44
S13	Marshall	17	42
S20 •	at Eastern Michigan	41	38
O4	Central Florida	43	59
O11	Miami, Ohio	26	62
O18	at Western Michigan	27	50
O25 •	Central Michigan	60	37
N1 •	Bowling Green	29	20
N8	at Akron	35	45
N22	at Navy	29	62

DEAN PEES
1998-2003 (.250)   17-51

1998   0-11 (0-8)
S5	at Georgia	3	56
S12	Youngstown St.	10	24
S19	at Navy	24	38
S26	at Central Michigan	7	46
O3	Eastern Michigan	17	26
O10	Akron	16	45
O17	at Marshall	7	42
O24	at Bowling Green	21	42
O31	Western Michigan	23	48
N14	at Miami, Ohio	0	56
N21	Ohio U.	21	31

1999   2-9 (2-6)
S4	at Cincinnati	3	41
S11	Navy	28	48
S18	at Pittsburgh	23	30
S25 •	Bowling Green	41	27
O2	at Ohio U.	3	31
O9	at Toledo	7	47
O16	Miami, Ohio	10	17
O23	at Northern Illinois	7	50
O30 •	Buffalo	41	20
N6	Marshall	16	28
N13	at Akron	34	37

2000   1-10 (1-7)
S2	at Pittsburgh	7	30
S9	at Purdue	10	45
S16	Youngstown St.	20	26
S23	at Miami, Ohio	14	45
S30	Bowling Green	11	18
O7 •	at Central Michigan	24	21
O14	Ohio U.	7	44
O21	at Marshall	12	34
O28	Western Michigan	0	42
N4	at Buffalo	17	20
N18	Akron	6	34

2001   6-5 (5-3)
S1	at Iowa	0	51
S8 •	Bucknell	38	17
S22	at West Virginia	14	34
S29	at Akron	10	14
O6	at Bowling Green	17	24
O13 •	Northern Illinois	44	34
O20 •	Buffalo	35	13
O27 •	at Ohio U.	24	14
N3	Marshall	21	42
N10 •	at Ball State	31	18
N24	Miami, Ohio	24	20

2002   3-9 (1-7)
A29 •	New Hampshire	34	7
S7	at Ohio State	17	51
S14 •	Cal Poly SLO	37	34
S21	at Miami, Ohio	20	27
S28	at Northern Illinois	6	13
O5	Marshall	21	42
O19	Ohio U.	0	50
O26 •	at Buffalo	16	12
N2	Bowling Green	14	45
N9	at Connecticut	21	63
N16	at Central Florida	6	32
N23	Akron	10	48

2003   5-7 (4-4)
A28 •	at Akron	41	38
S6	at Pittsburgh	3	43
S13 •	Youngstown St.	16	13
S20	at Penn State	10	32
S27 •	Central Florida	36	16
O4	Ball State	17	34
O11	at Marshall	33	49
O18	Connecticut	31	34
O25	Miami, Ohio	30	38
N8 •	at Ohio U.	37	33
N15	at Bowling Green	33	42
N22 •	Buffalo	34	24

DOUG MARTIN
2004-Present (.353)   12-22

2004   5-6 (4-4)
S4	at Iowa	7	39
S11 •	Liberty	38	10
S18	at Rutgers	21	29
S23	Akron	19	24
O2	at Central Michigan	21	24
O9	at Miami, Ohio	27	47
O16	Marshall	17	27
O30 •	Ohio U.	42	16
N6 •	at Buffalo	33	7
N13 •	Eastern Michigan	69	17
N23 •	at Central Florida	41	24

2005   1-10 (0-8)
S3	at Michigan State	14	49
S10 •	SE. Missouri St.	33	12
S17	Miami, Ohio	10	27
S24	at Ohio U.	32	35
O1	at Eastern Michigan	20	27
O15	at Navy	31	34
O22	Northern Illinois	3	34
O29	at Western Michigan	14	44
N5	Bowling Green	14	24
N12	Buffalo	6	10
N23	at Akron	3	35

2006   6-6 (5-3)
A31	Minnesota	0	44
S9	at Army	14	17
S16	at Miami, Ohio	16	14
S23	at Bowling Green	38	3
S30	Akron	37	15
O7	at Temple	28	17
O14 •	Toledo	40	14
O28	Ohio U.	7	17
N4	at Buffalo	14	41
N11	at Virginia Tech	0	23
N17 •	Eastern Michigan	14	6
N24	at Ball State	6	30

Neutral Site key: *Clev* Cleveland, OH / *Unk* Unknown
f Forfeit † Game Later Forfeited # Disputed Victor * Disputed Score || Designated Conference Game |2 Counted Twice in Conference Standings

MAC TEAMS

KENT STATE RECORD BOOK

SINGLE-GAME RECORDS

RUSHING YARDS

RANK	PLAYER	DATE	OPPONENT	ATT	AVG	YDS
1	Astron Whatley	Sept. 20, 1997	Eastern Michigan	42	8.9	373
2	Don Nottingham	Nov. 14, 1970	Dayton	43	6.4	275
3	Charles Chatman	Oct. 25, 1997	Central Michigan	32	8.0	257
4	Phil Witherspoon	Nov. 1, 1969	Louisville	29	8.3	242
5	Lou Mariano	Oct. 1, 1954	Western Reserve	10	22.6	226

PASSING YARDS

RANK	PLAYER	DATE	OPPONENT	ATT	COMP	YDS
1	Jose Davis	Oct. 4, 1997	UCF	51	32	551
2	Jose Davis	Nov. 8, 1997	Akron	59	34	419
	Stu Rayborn	Oct. 29, 1983	Toledo	40	23	419
4	Joshua Cribbs	Nov. 23, 2004	UCF	38	28	389
5	Kevin Shuman	Nov. 7, 1992	Bowling Green	53	28	371

RECEIVING YARDS

RANK	PLAYER	DATE	OPPONENT	REC	AVG	YDS
1	Eugene Baker	Nov. 16, 1996	Western Michigan	14	17.3	243
2	Darrell Dowery, Jr.	Nov. 23, 2004	UCF	13	18.5	240
3	Eugene Baker	Oct. 4, 1997	UCF	15	15.9	238
4	Eugene Baker	Nov. 8, 1997	Akron	15	15.7	236
5	Eugene Baker	Sept. 19, 1998	Navy	15	15.1	227

POINTS

RANK	PLAYER	DATE	OPPONENT	TOT
1	Jack Mancos	Sept. 22, 1951	Western Michigan	30
	Carmen Falcone	Oct. 22, 1938	Buffalo	30
3	David Alston	Nov. 6, 2004	Buffalo	26
4	5 players tied at 24			

FIELD GOALS

RANK	PLAYER	DATE	OPPONENT	TOT
1	Gordon Ober	Oct. 10, 1970	Western Michigan	4
2	11 players tied with 3			

TACKLES

RANK	PLAYER	DATE	OPPONENT	TOT
1	Jack Lambert	Nov. 18, 1972	Toledo	29
2	Bob Wallace	Oct. 28, 1978	Air Force	28
3	Jack Lazor	Nov. 12, 1977	Miami (Ohio)	27
4	Russ Hedderly	Oct. 3, 1981	Miami (Ohio)	25
5	3 players tied with 24			

INTERCEPTIONS

RANK	PLAYER	DATE	OPPONENT	TOT
1	Charles Kilbourne	Nov. 8, 1930	Capital	5
2	4 players tied with 3			

RETIRED NUMBERS

40	Eric Wilkerson
79	Jim Corrigall
99	Jack Lambert

SINGLE-SEASON RECORDS

RUSHING YARDS

RANK	PLAYER	SEASON	ATT	YDS
1	Eric Wilkerson	1988	247	1,325
2	Don Fitzgerald	1966	296	1,245
3	Eric Wilkerson	1987	244	1,221
4	Astron Whatley	1996	254	1,132
5	Larry Poole	1974	212	1,070

PASSING YARDS

RANK	PLAYER	SEASON	ATT	COMP	PCT	YDS
1	Jose Davis	1997	365	194	53.1	2,707
2	Joshua Cribbs	2003	364	178	48.9	2,424
3	Todd Goebbel	1996	354	188	53.1	2,419
4	Joshua Cribbs	2004	335	216	64.5	2,215
5	Michael Machen	2005	365	200	54.8	2,078

RECEIVING YARDS

RANK	PLAYER	SEASON	REC	AVG	YDS
1	Eugene Baker	1997	103	15.0	1,549
2	Eugene Baker	1996	69	17.6	1,215
3	Brian Dusho	1993	72	12.4	890
4	Najah Pruden	2006	39	20.7	808
5	James Kilbane	1985	53	15.2	806

SCORING

RANK	PLAYER	SEASON	TD	FG	PAT	P2	TOT
1	Eugene Baker	1997	18	0	0	1	110
2	Larry Poole	1973	18	0	0	0	108
3	Joshua Cribbs	2003	15	0	0	0	90
	Eric Wilkerson	1988	15	0	0	0	90
	Larry Poole	1974	15	0	0	0	90

TOUCHDOWNS

RANK	PLAYER	SEASON	TOT
1	Eugene Baker	1997	18
	Larry Poole	1973	18
3	Joshua Cribbs	2003	15
	Larry Poole	1974	15
5	2 players tied with 14		

TACKLES

RANK	PLAYER	SEASON	TOT
1	Jack Lambert	1972	233
2	Jack Lazor	1978	205
	Jack Lambert	1973	205
4	Jack Lazor	1977	197
5	Russell Hedderly	1981	191

INTERCEPTIONS

RANK	PLAYER	SEASON	YDS	TOT
1	Andrew Logan	1988	54	8
	Cedric Brown	1975	107	8
3	Lou Harris	1966	21	7
4	Charles Grandjean	1981	136	6
	Lou Harris	1967	49	6

PUNTING

RANK	PLAYER	SEASON	PUNTS	YDS	AVG
1	Joshua Brazen	2005	67	2,844	42.4
2	Tony DeLeone	1982	80	3,394	42.3
3	Matt Groff	1997	54	2.257	41.8
4	Jared Fritz	2002	59	2,409	40.8
5	Dan Brenning	1970	58	2,356	40.6

PUNT RETURNS

RANK	PLAYER	SEASON	RET	YDS	AVG
1	Fred Gissendaner	1965	10	175	17.5
2	Billy Blunt	1965	10	156	15.6
3	Jurron Kelly	1998	13	185	14.2

KICKOFF RETURNS

RANK	PLAYER	SEASON	RET	YDS	AVG
1	Eddie Woodard	1971	23	632	27.4
2	James Kovach	1968	12	323	26.9
3	Shawn Shoemaker	1999	14	374	26.7

CAREER RECORDS

RUSHING YARDS

RANK	PLAYER	SEASONS	ATT	AVG	TD	YDS
1	Astron Watley	1994-97	878	4.5	25	3,989
2	Eric Wilkerson	1985-88	739	5.2	36	3,830
3	Joshua Cribbs	2001-04	632	5.8	38	3,670
4	Larry Poole	1972-74	599	4.5	36	2,668
5	Don Nottingham	1968-70	602	4.2	19	2,515
6	Jack Mancos	1949-51	309	7.3	28	2,255
7	Don Fitzgerald	1965-67	557	4.0	NA	2,231
8	Jim Cullom	1951-53	420	5.1	18	2,146
9	Wilbur Little	1946-49	NA	NA	NA	2,109
10	Chante Murphy	1998-2000	457	4.4	NA	2,011

PASSING YARDS

RANK	PLAYER	SEASONS	ATT	COMP	PCT	INT	TD	YDS
1	Joshua Cribbs	2001-04	1,123	616	54.8	34	45	7,169
2	Jose Davis	1997-99	1,000	552	55.2	32	57	6,722
3	Greg Kokal	1972-75	786	405	51.5	49	30	5,587
4	Todd Goebbel	1995-97	605	304	50.2	25	25	3,747
5	Kevin Shuman	1991-93	611	295	48.3	30	16	3,483
6	Joe Dalpra	1988-91	500	239	47.8	26	21	2,991
7	Tim Phillips	1984-87	457	247	54.0	17	9	2,886
8	Stu Rayborn	1983-84	483	242	50.1	34	7	2,842
9	Michael Machen	2005-06	388	209	53.9	19	11	2,177
10	Ron Swartz	1965-67	349	161	46.1	26	16	2,122

RECEIVING YARDS

RANK	PLAYER	SEASONS	REC	AVG	TD	YDS
1	Eugene Baker	1995-98	229	15.3	35	3,513
2	Najah Pruden	2003-06	113	18.9	15	2,131
3	Darrell Dowery, Jr.	2001-04	152	12.7	8	1,931
4	Jurron Kelly	1998-2001	143	11.9	12	1,703
5	Todd Feldman	1981-84	86	19.3	8	1,663
6	Kim Featsent	1974-77	118	14.1	8	1,662
7	Shawn Barnes	1989-91	87	16.1	13	1,402
	Eric Dye	1984-87	92	15.2	5	1,402
9	Jason Gavadza	1996-99	86	15.3	13	1,312
10	Brian Dusho	1990-93	101	12.6	5	1,277

SCORING

RANK	PLAYER	SEASONS	TD	FG	PAT	P2	TOT
1	Joshua Cribbs	2001-04	41	0	0	0	246
2	Travis Mayle	2002-05	0	42	112	0	238
3	Eric Wilkerson	1985-88	38	0	0	0	228
	Larry Poole	1972-74	38	0	0	0	228
5	Eugene Baker	1995-98	35	0	0	0	210

TOUCHDOWNS

RANK	PLAYER	SEASONS	TOT
1	Joshua Cribbs	2001-04	41
2	Eric Wilkerson	1985-88	38
	Larry Poole	1972-74	38
4	Eugene Baker	1995-98	35
5	Michael Norcia	1952-55	29

TACKLES

RANK	PLAYER	SEASONS	TOT
1	Jack Lazor	1975-78	645
2	Jack Lambert	1971-73	593
3	Russ Hedderly	1980-83	548
4	Robert Wallace	1976-79	534
5	Mike Zele	1975-78	519

INTERCEPTIONS

RANK	PLAYER	SEASONS	YDS	TOT
1	Lou Harris	1965-67	106	19
2	Cedric Brown	1972-75	219	16
3	Tom McDonald	1969-71	198	13
	Pat Gucciardo	1963-65	162	13
5	Jamie Howell	1985-88	47	12

PUNTING

RANK	PLAYER	SEASONS	PUNTS	YDS	AVG
1	Matt Groff	1996-97	58	2,311	41.3
2	Joshua Brazen	2002-05	173	7,123	41.2
3	Dan Brenning	1969-70	96	3,874	40.4
4	Jared Fritz	1999-2002	191	7,583	39.7
5	Terry Schultz	1969-71	75	2,969	39.6

TEAM RECORDS

LONGEST WINNING STREAK
• 7 (tie), Nov. 6, 1937-Oct. 22, 1938

Streak broken vs. John Carroll, 6-27, Oct. 28, 1938;
Sept. 21-Nov. 2, 1940

Streak broken vs. Akron, 7-23, Nov. 9, 1940;
Oct. 24, 1953-Oct. 8, 1954

Streak broken vs. Ohio, 7-14, Oct. 16, 1954

LONGEST UNDEFEATED STREAK
• 8, Oct. 30, 1937-Oct. 22, 1938

Streak broken vs. John Carroll, 6-27, Oct. 28, 1938

MOST CONSECUTIVE WINNING SEASONS
• 9, 1948-1956

MOST CONSECUTIVE BOWL APPEARANCES
• 1, 1954

MOST POINTS IN A GAME
• 69, vs. Eastern Michigan, Nov. 13, 2004

MOST POINTS ALLOWED IN A GAME
• 118, vs. Baldwin-Wallace, Oct. 13, 1923

LARGEST MARGIN OF VICTORY
• 65 (65-0), vs. Western Reserve, Oct. 1, 1954

LARGEST MARGIN OF DEFEAT
• 118 (0-118), vs. Baldwin-Wallace, Oct. 13, 1923

LONGEST RUN FROM SCRIMMAGE
• 99 yards, Lou Mariano vs. Western Reserve, Oct. 1, 1954

LONGEST PASS PLAY
• 98 yards, Jose Davis to Eugene Baker, vs. UCF, Oct. 4, 1997

LONGEST FIELD GOAL
• 51 yards, Paul Marchese, vs. Bowling Green, Oct. 15, 1977

LONGEST PUNT
• 99 yards, Charles Kilbourne, vs. John Carroll, Oct. 25, 1929

LONGEST PUNT RETURN
• 87 yards, Gerald Tinker, vs. Toledo, Nov. 17, 1973

LONGEST INTERCEPTION RETURN
• 99 yards, Jack Williams, vs. Iowa, Sept. 4, 2004

PUNT RETURNS

RANK	PLAYER	SEASON	RET	YDS	AVG
1	Fred Gissendaner	1963-65	18	363	20.1
2	Gerald Tinker	1972-73	41	560	13.6

KICKOFF RETURNS

RANK	PLAYER	SEASON	RET	YDS	AVG
1	Norman Warren	1977-79	48	1,177	24.5
2	Orin Richburg	1968-69	13	313	24.1
3	Eddie Woodard	1971-73	63	1,509	24.0
4	Billy Blunt	1965-67	27	632	23.4
5	Derrick Nix	1983-86	63	1,365	21.7

KENT STATE ANNUAL STATISTICAL LEADERS

YR	RUSHING	YDS	ATT	AVG	PASSING	ATT	CMP	PCT	YDS	RECEIVING	REC	YDS	AVG
1946		NA	NA	NA	John Moore	74	45	.46	644		NA	NA	NA
1947	Wilbur Little	559	73	7.7	Neil Nelson	71	34	.48	360	Bob Evans	7	122	17.4
1948	Wilbur Little	758	108	7.0	Jerry Tuttle	91	40	.44	749		NA	NA	NA
1949	Jack Mancos	725	100	7.3		NA	NA	NA	NA	Jack Mancos	12	229	19.1
1950	Dick Pitts	757	128	5.9	Nick Dellerba	84	42	.50	574	Jim Betteker	17	227	13.4
1951	Jack Mancos	778	108	7.2		NA	NA	NA	NA	Bob Scott	10	154	15.4
1952	Jim Cullom	822	159	5.2		NA	NA	NA	NA	Jim Cullom	9	74	8.2
1953	Lou Mariano	816	98	8.3	Don Burke	78	26	.33	577	Gino Gioia	6	84	14.0
1954	Lou Mariano	1,037	95	10.9	Bob Stimac	36	17	.47	434	Bill Whitley	9	239	26.6
1955	Mike Norcia	600	82	7.3	Bob Stimac	66	26	.39	428	Ken Redin	6	102	17.0
1956	Ron Fowler	522	91	5.7	Ken Horton	61	35	.57	703	Dick Mihalus	9	238	26.4
1957	Ron Fowler	508	112	4.5	Ken Horton	71	23	.32	304	Dick Mihalus	7	100	14.3
1958	John Martin	386	85	4.5	Dick Mostardo	60	30	.50	542	Dick Mihalus	7	231	33.0
1959	John Martin	391	84	4.7	Dick Mostardo	43	12	.28	164	Lou Perry	5	141	28.2
1960	Marty Grosjean	482	90	5.4	Jim Flynn	79	38	.48	423	Bob Gusbar	25	301	12.0
1961	Cullen Bowen	275	80	3.4	George Jenkins	74	34	.46	387	Dick Wolf	18	288	16.0
1962	Dick Merschman	555	140	4.0	Jim Flynn	116	50	.43	605	Dick Wolf	12	119	9.9
1963	Bill Asbury	849	94	9.0	Ron Mollric	63	24	.38	293	Tom Zuppke	6	122	20.3
1964	Tom Clements	444	112	4.0	Ron Mollric	58	30	.52	384	Fred Gissendaner	17	258	15.2
1965	Bill Asbury	998	238	4.2	Ron Mollric	80	35	.44	407	Billy Blunt	30	337	11.2
1966	Don Fitzgerald	1,245	296	4.2	Ron Swartz	125	63	.50	879	Billy Blunt	26	287	11.0
1967	Don Fitzgerald	891	230	3.9	Ron Swartz	177	79	.45	1,029	Will Perry	45	601	13.4
1968	Don Nottingham	727	163	4.5	Steve Trustdorf	138	64	.46	773	Doug Smith	21	247	11.8
1969	Don Nottingham	990	231	4.3	Steve Trustdorf	81	35	.43	442	Doug Smith	15	166	11.1
1970	Don Nottingham	798	208	3.8	Steve Broderick	120	61	.51	757	Jeff Murrey	18	165	9.2
1971	Renard Harmon	566	115	4.9	Larry Hayes	155	67	.43	848	Jeff Murrey	23	259	11.3
1972	Larry Poole	588	126	4.7	Greg Kokal	107	54	.50	792	Gary Pinkel	34	477	14.0
1973	Larry Poole	1,010	261	3.9	Greg Kokal	234	133	.57	1,776	Gary Pinkel	36	409	11.4
1974	Larry Poole	1,070	212	5.0	Greg Kokal	169	85	.50	1,265	Ken Dooner	35	451	12.9
1975	Dan Watkins	916	189	4.8	Greg Kokal	276	133	.48	1,754	Kim Featsent	42	563	13.4
1976	Art Best	1,030	194	5.3	Mike Whalen	102	55	.54	822	Kim Featsent	26	415	16.0
1977	Tom Roper	630	122	5.2	Mike Whalen	91	46	.51	534	Kim Featsent	39	549	14.1
1978	Tom Delaney	440	144	3.1	Tom Delaney	79	25	.32	400	Mike Moore	13	250	19.2
1979	J.C. Stafford	497	130	3.8	Jeff Morrow	236	111	.47	1,284	Mike Moore	27	334	12.4
1980	Ron Pittman	485	115	4.2	Pat Gladfelter	162	72	.44	745	Darren Brown	27	419	15.5
1981	Ron Pittman	648	147	4.4	Bill Willows	146	65	.45	913	Darren Brown	19	333	17.5
1982	Dana Wright	363	123	3.0	Walter Kroan	259	113	.44	1,304	Todd Feldman	28	519	18.5
1983	O.D. Underwood	531	106	5.0	Stu Rayburn	217	117	.54	1,461	Joe Rucky	34	287	8.4
1984	Derrick Nix	720	212	3.4	Stu Rayburn	266	125	.47	1,381	Ken Hughes	40	621	15.5
1985	Eric Wilkerson	594	131	4.5	Steve Poth	184	98	.53	1,221	Jim Kilbane	53	806	15.2
1986	Patrick Young	779	190	4.1	Patrick Young	131	58	.44	756	Eric Dye	28	425	15.2
1987	Eric Wilkerson	1,221	244	5.0	Tim Phillips	248	141	.57	1,625	Eric Dye	40	606	15.2
1988	Eric Wilkerson	1,325	247	5.4	Patrick Young	103	41	.40	650	Fermin Olivera	10	180	18.0
1989	Terry Daniel	304	82	3.7	Joe Dalpra	191	86	.45	1,089	Andre Palmer	26	417	16.0
1990	Marcus Haywood	672	178	3.8	Joe Dalpra	252	125	.50	1,533	Tony Gucciardo	29	339	11.7
1991	Brad Smith	645	142	4.5	Kevin Shuman	164	82	.50	943	Shawn Barnes	33	558	16.9
1992	Troy Robinson	422	107	3.9	Kevin Shuman	281	124	.44	1,518	Jimmie Woody	54	714	13.2
1993	Raeshaun Jernigan	856	169	5.1	Kevin Shuman	166	89	.54	1,022	Brian Dusho	72	890	12.4
1994	Astron Whatley	1,003	241	4.2	Mike Challenger	162	81	.50	842	Chris Amill	9	247	27.4
1995	Astron Whatley	978	231	4.2	Todd Goebbel	164	75	.46	792	Kantroy Walker	28	328	11.7
1996	Astron Whatley	1,132	254	4.5	Todd Goebbel	354	188	.53	2,419	Eugene Baker	69	1,215	17.6
1997	Astron Whatley	876	152	5.8	Jose Davis	365	194	.53	2,707	Eugene Baker	103	1,549	15.0
1998	DeMarlo Rozier	621	185	3.4	Jose Davis	320	178	.56	2,046	Eugene Baker	49	685	14.0
1999	Chante Murphy	676	162	4.2	Jose Davis	315	180	.57	1,969	Jason Gavadza	47	654	13.9
2000	Chante Murphy	800	199	4.0	Zach Williams	213	114	.54	1,120	Jurron Kelly	37	393	10.6
2001	Joshua Cribbs	1,019	164	6.2	Joshua Cribbs	238	131	.55	1,516	Jurron Kelly	37	479	12.9
2002	Joshua Cribbs	1,057	137	7.7	Joshua Cribbs	186	91	.49	1,014	Darrell Dowery	34	348	10.2
2003	Joshua Cribbs	701	161	4.4	Joshua Cribbs	364	178	.49	2,424	Darrell Dowery	41	783	19.1
2004	Joshua Cribbs	893	170	5.3	Joshua Cribbs	335	216	.64	2,215	Darrell Dowery	68	712	10.5
2005	Jerry Flowers	304	96	3.2	Michael Machen	365	200	.55	2,078	Derrick Bush	39	388	9.9
2006	Eugene Jarvis	798	185	4.3	Julian Edelman	242	134	.55	1,859	Najah Pruden	39	808	20.7

Receiving leaders by receptions
The NCAA began including postseason stats in 2002

MAC TEAMS

MIAMI (OHIO)

BY ED KRZEMIENSKI

WHEN ROBERT FROST REFERS TO a school as "the most beautiful college there is," it must have something going for it. Along with Frost's praise, Miami University in Oxford, Ohio, consistently receives accolades as one of the nation's "public Ivies" for its strong academics. But where Miami sheds any resemblance to the Ivy League is on the football field, where the RedHawks stand tall in the Football Bowl subdivision. In total, Miami (Ohio) has more victories and the same winning percentage as its more celebrated namesake to the south, the University of Miami. The school also has perhaps the greatest coaching bloodlines in the sport. Often called the Cradle of Coaches, Miami played a part in the development of more than two dozen successful head coaches, including such legends as Paul Brown, Sid Gillman, Weeb Ewbank, Bo Schembechler, Ara Parseghian, Woody Hayes and the group's most recent national champion, Jim Tressel. In 2003, Miami head coach Terry Hoeppner became the latest to make his mark. In his fifth year at the helm, Hoeppner led the RedHawks to a No. 10 national ranking, the Mid-American Conference championship, a GMAC Bowl win and the nation's longest winning streak—13 straight victories. He left for Indiana following the 2004 season (and died of a brain tumor in the summer of 2007). Offensive coordinator Shane Montgomery took over as head coach.

TRADITION Miami and Cincinnati play each year for the Victory Bell, a traveling trophy that originally hung in Miami's Harrison Hall (Old Main). The two teams met for the first time in 1888 and began the Victory Bell tradition sometime in the 1890s when some Cincinnati fans "borrowed" the bell from the Miami campus. The game is one of the most-played rivalries and is the oldest rivalry west of the Allegheny Mountains.

BEST PLAYER In three magical seasons from 2001 to 2003, quarterback Ben Roethlisberger rewrote all of Miami's passing records. After one season at the helm, Roethlisberger passed his way into sixth place on the school's career list with 3,105 yards. Following his 3,238-yard sophomore season, Roethlisberger was less than

PROFILE

Miami University
Oxford, Ohio
Founded: 1809
Enrollment: 16,300
Colors: Red and White
Nickname: RedHawks
Stadium: Yager Stadium
  Opened in 1983
  FieldTurf; 24,286 capacity
First football game: 1888
All-time record: 641–362–44 (.633)
Bowl record: 6–3
Mid-American Athletic Conference championships: 14 (12 outright)
First-round draft choices: 2
Website: www.muredhawks.com

THE BEST OF TIMES

From 1973 to 1975, the then-Redskins had a great run: a 32–1–1 record, three consecutive MAC championships, three consecutive Tangerine Bowl victories, and final AP rankings of 15, 10, and 12. The only loss was a 14-13 heartbreaker to Michigan State.

THE WORST OF TIMES

Sandwiched between two one-loss MAC championship seasons, in 1976 the Redskins went 3–8, marking the school's first losing season in 34 years.

CONFERENCE

Miami was a charter member of the Mid-American Conference in 1946 (the conference began play in 1947) but did not compete in football until 1948.

DISTINGUISHED ALUMNI

R. Michael DeWine, U.S. senator; Rita Dove, U.S. poet laureate; Benjamin Harrison, U.S. president; P.J. O'Rourke, political satirist; Paul Smucker, jelly company founder

> *There is no Miami, Ohio. The school is in Oxford, Ohio.*

200 yards behind Mike Bath's career lead. As a junior, the 6'5" QB shattered the school record, passing for 4,486 yards with a 165.8 passer rating. (His junior season's total alone would have placed him third on the all-time list.) MAC opponents let out a collective sigh of relief when Roethlisberger announced his plan to forego his senior season and enter the NFL draft in 2004. Bowling Green coach Gregg Brandon articulated the feeling after Roethlisberger threw for 440 yards against his Falcons, saying, "I can't wait to play them when he's gone." Roethlisberger passed for 10,829 yards and 84 touchdowns in his career, led Miami to a 27–11 overall record and took the RedHawks to their first bowl game in 17 years—the 2003 GMAC Bowl, in which Miami beat Louisville 49-28.

BEST COACH Although he was not in Oxford as long as many of his celebrated brethren, Dick Crum did as much at Miami as any head coach. From 1974 to 1977, Crum won 34 games and built a .767 winning percentage. Neither of those marks constitutes a record for the school, but sometimes wins need to be weighed as well as counted. In his three winning seasons at Miami, Crum led the then-Redskins to three MAC titles, two Tangerine Bowl victories, two appearances in the final national rankings (No. 10 in 1974 and No. 12 in 1975) and compiled a gaudy 31–2–1 record. Crum ended his Miami career with a 34–10–1 record before leaving in 1978 to become the head coach at North Carolina.

BEST TEAM Bill Mallory's last season in Oxford was the school's best—not only did the team go undefeated in 1973, but they did so against some serious competition. Out of conference, Miami won at Purdue, at South Carolina, and at Florida in the Tangerine Bowl. Senior Bob Hitchens led in rushing with 591 yards, but the strength of this team was its defense. Miami was No. 15 in the final AP poll, but arguably deserved a higher place. Mallory left after the season to take over Colorado's program.

BEST BACKFIELD Ben Roethlisberger's monstrous 37-touchdown 2003 season was just the spearhead of a complete offensive juggernaut. Despite the second-game season-ending injury of his leading rusher, Nate Clemens, Roethlisberger had a lot of support from his backfield mates. Cal Murray stepped in and ran for 1,030 yards, including six 100-yard games, and Mike Smith

FIGHT SONG

MIAMI FIGHT SONG
Love and honor to Miami,
Our college old and grand.
Proudly we shall ever hail thee,
Over all the land.
Alma mater now we praise thee,
Sing joyfully this lay.
Love and honor to Miami,
Forever and a day.

FIRST-ROUND DRAFT CHOICES

1969	Bob Babich, Chargers (18)
2004	Ben Roethlisberger, Steelers (11)

CONSENSUS ALL-AMERICANS

1982	Brian Pillman, MG

COLLEGE FOOTBALL HALL OF FAME INDUCTEES

NAME	YEARS	INDUCTED
George Little, COACH	1916, 1919-21	1955
Ara Parseghian, COACH	1951-55	1980
Woody Hayes, COACH	1949-50	1983
Sid Gillman, COACH	1944-47	1989
Bo Schembechler, COACH	1963-68	1993
Bob Babich, LB	1966-68	1994

PRO FOOTBALL HALL OF FAME INDUCTEES

NAME	YEARS	INDUCTED
Paul Brown, COACH	1946-62	1967
Weeb Ewbank, COACH	1954-73	1978

added another pair of 100-yard efforts. All told, the running game averaged 160 yards per game and scored 36 touchdowns. That running attack plus Miami's seemingly-unstoppable quarterback equals a 2003 backfield that is the best in school history, and perhaps the best in MAC history.

BEST DEFENSE
In 1973, Miami gave up an average of 161.3 yards per game and a total of just 76 points in 11 games. Most impressively, the defense gave up an average of only 1.8 yards per carry while forcing 35 turnovers. The defensive standout was middle guard Brad Cousino, who had 195 tackles, including a team-leading 32 for loss. For his efforts, Cousino was named the MAC Player of the Year. The defense culminated its undefeated season by holding Florida to 90 rushing yards in a 16-7 Tangerine Bowl victory.

BIGGEST GAME
On Nov. 10, 1973, Miami traveled to Kent State to play the Golden Flashes in a game that would determine the MAC championship. Both teams were undefeated in league play, and for the first time in the history of the MAC, two of its members were meeting as nationally ranked teams. At 7–1, defending conference champion Kent State was ranked No. 19 while the undefeated Redskins were No. 17. Miami got all of the scoring it needed from fullback Chuck Varner, who scored on a two-yard run and a nine-yard pass. Leading 17-10 after three quarters, Miami finished off the Flashes when sophomore David Draudt kicked a school-record 52-yard field goal in the final quarter. It took 30 years for two MAC opponents to be simultaneously ranked again.

BIGGEST UPSET
Defeating Northwestern is usually not something even a MAC team regards as an upset. But in 1995, Northwestern had beaten Notre Dame in its opening game and was ranked No. 25 in the nation, so 1–1 Miami entered as an underdog. Randy Walker's Redskins won a close one, 30-28, but the enormity of the upset became clear only after Northwestern completed the rest of its regular season without a loss. Commenting on his team's improbable run, Northwestern head coach Gary Barnett said that the only game he felt for certain

the Wildcats would win going into the regular season was the one against Miami. After losing in the Rose Bowl, Northwestern ended the season 10–2 and ranked No. 8. Miami ended its year 8–2–1 and unranked.

ALL-CENTURY TEAM	
The greatest RedHawks as chosen by The Cincinnati Enquirer in 1999.	
1951-55	Ara Parseghian, coach
OFFENSE	
1946-47	Paul Dietzel, OL
1952-54	Tom Jones, OL
1972-74	Mike Biehle, OL
1995-97	Mike Bird, G
1983-86	Dan Dalrymple, T
1947-50	Doc Urich, TE
1967-69	Gary Arthur, TE
1995-98	Jay Hall, WR
1949-51	John Pont, RB
1996-99	Travis Prentice, TB
1972-75	Sherman Smith, QB
1984-87	Gary Gussman, K
DEFENSE	
1974-77	Jack Glowik, DL
1988-91	Jon Wauford, DE
1966-68	Bob Babich, LB
1972-74	Brad Cousino, LB
1980-83	Brian Pillman, LB
1989-92	Curt McMillan, LB
1993-96	Dee Osborne, LB
1968-70	Dick Adams, DB
1977-79	Kirk Springs, S
1984-87	Sheldon White, CB
1990-92	Ron Carpenter, S
1991-94	Gary Layton, P

HEARTBREAKER
On Sept. 20, 1975, Miami traveled to East Lansing to play Michigan State riding not only a three-game undefeated streak against Big Ten opponents, but also a 24-game unbeaten streak. Leading 13-7 with 1:08 left in the game, it looked as if the Redskins would continue their roll. But Michigan State ended that dream with a late rally capped by a 56-yard touchdown pass for a 14-13 win. Miami won the rest of its games, though, and ended up No. 12 in the final AP poll.

STADIUM
Fred C. Yager Stadium came into being in 1983. Named in honor of a 1914 graduate who supported the stadium project, it holds 24,286 people. The facilities include a Cradle of Coaches room on the second level honoring all coaches once affiliated with Miami, including more than 40 from football programs around the nation.

RIVAL
Miami's first game was against Cincinnati in 1888, a 0-0 tie that constituted Miami's entire season. Since then, the teams have met 108 times. Perhaps most memorable was the 1973 meeting in Oxford. After Miami's Larry Harper returned the opening kickoff 95 yards for a touchdown, the offense took the day off. Fortunately, Miami's top-ranked defense shut down the Bearcats and the Redskins won 6-0, preserving their undefeated season. Through the 2004 season, Miami leads the series with a record of 58–44–7.

DISPUTE
Following a last-second loss to Marshall in 2002, Miami defensive coordinator Jon Wauford was arrested by West Virginia state troopers for shoving a fan who had rushed the field. Wauford wasn't the only out-of-control Miami coach that night. In the box, Miami's linebackers coach, Taver Johnson, destroyed a desk and sent several chairs through the walls after the game. Making matters significantly worse—it was the RedHawks' first game on national television.

NICKNAME At the urging of the Oklahoma-based Miami Tribe, for whom the school is named, Miami abandoned its traditional nickname of Redskins and became the RedHawks in 1997. Official use of the name Redskins began in the 1930-31 school year, because Big Red, a common appellation for Miami, caused some confusion with Denison University. Previously, the team was also known as the Miami Boys, the Big Reds, the Reds and Whites, and the Big Red-Skinned Warriors.

MASCOT When Miami switched its nickname to RedHawks, it needed a new mascot as well. Enter a giant red bird named Swoop that, according to school lore, was born in the spring of 1972 and watched the games from afar (actually from above) until the fortuitous 1997 nickname shift when Swoop was officially adopted as the mascot. The costumed-student Swoop brought the total number of bird-oriented MAC mascots to five and, defying all probability, the number of MAC mascots named Swoop to two.

UNIFORMS As Redskins and RedHawks, Miami has always maintained its red-and-white color scheme. Just about as consistent have been the team's helmets; since 1960, the helmets have been white with a red insignia. Except for a brief period in the latter half of the 1960s, when each player had his number on the side of his helmet, Miami helmets sported a red uppercase M of varying thickness on both. From 1966 to 1971 and then again in the early 1980s, a silhouette of an Indian appeared near the front of the headgear.

QUIRK The school is very particular as to how others refer to it. When referring to Miami, the school advises, one is to use Miami University, Miami University (Ohio) or Miami (Ohio). (How to speak parenthetically, the school doesn't say.) More specifically, Miami of Ohio is not proper. Also, there is no Miami, Ohio; the school is in Oxford, Ohio. Sportscasters will likely take heed of these distinctions when America goes metric. Incidentally, Miami (Ohio) has played Miami (Fla.) on three occasions: Miami leads the series 3–0 … the Florida one, that is.

NUMBERS Miami represents one of two mid-major programs (the other is Army) in the top 25 for all-time NCAA Division I-A victories. Most successful was the school's three-year run from 1973 to 1975, which ended with a 32–1–1 record, a mark surpassed only by Oklahoma during that span.

QUOTE "People keep calling us the giant killers. But today we proved we're the giants." —Kicker John Scott in 1998, after unranked Miami beat No. 12 North Carolina 13-10 on a 37-yard Scott field goal with one second left to play

MAC TEAMS

MIAMI (OHIO) ALL-TIME SCORES

WIN/LOSS PERCENTAGE SINCE 1936

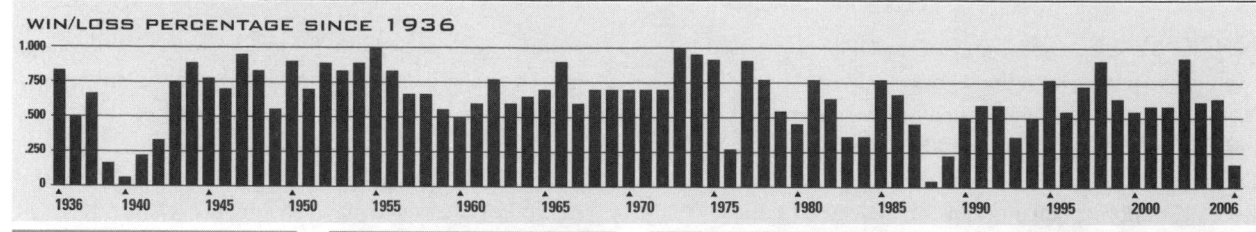

NO HEAD COACH

1888 — 0-0-1
D8	=	Cincinnati	0	0

1889 — 4-0-0
U	•	at Cincinnati	34	0
U	•	at Dayton HS	44	0
U	•	at Earlham	8	0
U	•	Dayton AC	14	4

1890
NO TEAM

1891 — 1-1-0
U		at Ohio Wesleyan	0	104
U	•	Hamilton AC	38	0

1892 — 2-2-0
U		at Earlham	0	12
U		at Centre	6	12
U	•	Cincinnati YMCA *Unk*	8	0
U	•	Hamilton AC	28	0

1893 — 3-0-0
U	•	Cincinnati	24	6
U	•	Earlham	28	6
U	•	at Cincinnati	6	0

1894 — 1-2-0
U	•	at Hamilton AC	18	0
U		at Cincinnati	0	6
O13		at Kentucky	6	28

C.K. FAUVER
1895 (1.000) — 3-0

1895 — 3-0-0
N16	•	at Cincinnati	12	0
U	•	at Wittenberg	12	4
U	•	Butler	6	0

ERNEST MERRILL
1896 (.750) — 3-1

1896 — 3-1-0
U	•	at Cincinnati	6	4
U	•	at Dayton	10	0
U	•	Earlham	26	0
U		Butler	4	16

HERBERT McINTYRE
1897 (.357) — 2-4-1

1897 — 2-4-1
U		Cincinnati	0	6
U		Cincinnati *Unk*	6	10
U	=	Dayton AC *Unk*	0	0
U	•	at Earlham	10	0
U	•	Nashville Guards	10	0
U		at Indiana	6	22
U		at Centre	0	18

NO HEAD COACH

1898 — 0-2-0
U		Cincinnati	0	22
U		Dayton HS	6	11

1899 — 1-5-0
U		Cincinnati *Unk*	0	22
U		at Centre	12	15
U	•	Wittenberg	6	0
U		Earlham	0	6
O13		at Vanderbilt	0	12
O18		at Kentucky	5	18

ALONZO BRANCH
1900 (.000) — 0-2

1900 — 0-2-0
U		at Wittenberg	0	33
U		at Cincinnati	12	16

THOMAS HAZZARD
1901 (.300) — 1-3-1

1901 — 1-3-1
U		Denison *Unk*	0	6
U		Wittenberg	0	12
U	=	at Earlham	0	0
U		Dayton AC *Unk*	0	5
U	•	Antioch	23	6

PETER McPHERSON
1902-03 (.500) — 6-6-1

1902 — 5-2-1
U	•	Denison *Unk*	24	5
O4		at Kentucky	5	11
U	•	Earlham	12	0
U	=	at Xavier	0	0
U		at Centre	6	12
U	•	at Wittenberg	11	0
U	•	Otterbein *Unk*	6	5
U	•	at Earlham	22	0

1903 — 1-4-0
U		at Ohio Wesleyan	6	19
U		at DePauw	6	11
U	•	at Cincinnati	15	0
O24		at Kentucky	0	47
U		at Xavier	0	33

ARTHUR SMITH
1904 (.167) — 1-5

1904 — 1-5-0
O1		at Ohio State	0	80
U	•	Hamilton AC	12	6
U		at Cincinnati	0	46
U		Butler	0	32
U		at Indiana Medics	0	51
U		at Wittenberg	0	68

NO HEAD COACH

1905 — 4-3-0
U	•	Hamilton AC	52	0
U	•	Georgetown, Ky.	42	0
U		at Butler	0	17
U		at Wittenberg	0	35
U		at Centre	0	24
U	•	Antioch	9	0
N30		at Marshall	35	5	*

ARTHUR PARMALEE
1906 (.214) — 1-5-1

1906 — 1-5-1
U	•	Georgetown, Ky.	16	0
U	=	at Cincinnati	0	0
U		Wittenberg	0	11
U		at Centre	0	8
U		Marietta	0	6
U		at Earlham	0	11
U		at DePauw	0	19

AMOS FOSTER
1907-08 (.929) — 13-1

1907 — 6-1-0
U	•	Antioch	38	0
U	•	at Earlham	11	10
U	•	at DePauw	6	17
U	•	Centre *Unk*	10	0
U	•	Otterbein	32	0
U	•	at Marietta	12	10
U	•	at Cincinnati Gym	6	0

1908 — 7-0-0
O3	•	Wilmington	34	0
O10	•	at Centre	6	0
O17	•	at Ohio U.	5	0
O31	•	at Oberlin	11	10
N7	•	Wabash	6	0
N21	•	Ohio Wesleyan	24	0
N26	•	at Transylvania	27	0

HAROLD IDDINGS
1909-10 (.393) — 5-8-1

1909 — 3-4-0
O2	•	Wilmington	35	2
O9		at Western Reserve	0	3
O16	•	Ohio U.	45	0
O23	•	Marietta	10	0
N6		at St. Louis	0	22
N16		at Notre Dame	0	46
N25		at Cincinnati	6	10

1910 — 2-4-1
U	•	Wilmington	5	0
U		at Centre	2	12
U		DePauw	0	10
U		at Cincinnati	0	3
U		at Marietta	0	17
U	=	at Butler	0	0
U	•	Wittenberg	19	0

EDWIN SWEETLAND
1911 (.375) — 2-4-2

1911 — 2-4-2
S30	•	Wilmington	46	0
O7		at Ohio State	0	3
O14		Kentucky	0	12
O21	•	at Wittenberg	6	3
N4		at Ohio Wesleyan	0	11
N11	=	at DePauw	0	0
N18		at Cincinnati	0	11
N25	=	Western Reserve	5	5

JAMES DONNELLY
1912-14 (.625) — 14-8-2

1912 — 3-3-2
S28	•	Wilmington	30	0
O5	=	at Wittenberg	0	0
O12		at Kentucky	13	8
O26		at St. Louis	0	35
N2		at DePauw	7	23
N9	•	Ohio U.	18	6
N16		Denison	0	13
N28	=	at Cincinnati	21	21

1913 — 6-2-0
S27	•	Wilmington	33	0
O4	•	Georgetown, Ky.	26	0
O11		at Oberlin	7	48
O25	•	at Denison	19	0
N1	•	Ohio Wesleyan	12	0
N8	•	Ohio U.	44	6
N15		at Western Reserve	0	7
N27	•	at Cincinnati	13	7

1914 — 5-3-0
S26	•	Otterbein	40	0
O3	•	at Oberlin	9	0
O10	•	at Ohio U.	0	6
O24	•	at Mount Union	16	14
O31	•	at Indiana	3	48
N7	•	at Ohio Wesleyan	10	3
N14	•	Denison	33	40
N27	•	at Cincinnati	20	13

C.J. ROBERTS
1915 (.750) — 6-2

1915 — 6-2-0
S25	•	Ohio Northern	41	0
O2	•	at Akron	23	6
O9	•	at Indiana	0	41
O23	•	at Mount Union	17	0
O30	•	Ohio Wesleyan	19	7
N6		Denison *Unk*	0	14
N13	•	Ohio U.	13	7	*
N25	•	at Cincinnati	24	12

GEORGE LITTLE
1916, '19-21 (.875) — 27-3-2

1916 — 7-0-1
S30	•	Ohio Northern	27	0
O7	•	Earlham	58	0
O14	•	at Wooster	10	6
O21	•	Kenyon	66	0
N4	=	Denison *Unk*	0	0
N11	•	at Ohio Wesleyan	9	0
N18	•	Western Reserve	35	6
N30	=	at Cincinnati	33	0	*

GEORGE RIDER
1917-18 (.893) — 11-0-3

1917 — 6-0-2
O6	•	Ohio Northern	32	0
O13	•	at Kentucky	0	0
O20	•	Earlham	91	0
O27	•	Ohio Wesleyan	20	0
N3	•	Denison *Unk*	13	0
N10	•	at Mount Union	6	0
N17	•	Wooster	0	0
N29	•	at Cincinnati	40	0

1918 — 5-0-1
S28	•	Ohio Northern	47	0
N2	•	Kenyon	62	0
N9	•	at Ohio Wesleyan	14	7
N16	•	Denison	20	6
N23	•	Butler	52	0
N28	=	at Cincinnati	0	0

GEORGE LITTLE

1919 — 7-1-0
O4	•	Kenyon	26	0
O11	•	at Case	7	2
O18	•	Ohio Wesleyan	13	7
O25	•	Oberlin	0	13
N1	•	Denison *Unk*	14	0
N8	•	Ohio Northern	60	0
N15	•	at Mount Union	13	10
N28	•	at Cincinnati	14	0

1920 — 5-2-1
O2	•	Xavier	31	0
O9	•	Kenyon	41	7
O16	•	Kentucky	14	0
O23	•	at Wittenberg	0	17
O30	=	Denison *Unk*	7	7
N6	•	at Ohio Wesleyan	7	0
N17	•	Mount Union	14	0
N25	•	at Cincinnati	0	7

1921 — 8-0-0
O1	•	Dayton	55	0
O8	•	Wittenberg	14	0
O15	•	at Ohio Northern	27	0
O22	•	Ohio Wesleyan	56	0
O29	•	Denison *Unk*	21	6
N5	•	Otterbein	21	0
N12	•	at Mount Union	29	0
N24	•	Cincinnati	15	7

HARRY EWING
1922-23 (.500) — 7-7-2

1922 — 4-3-1
U	=	Alumni	0	0
U	•	Akron	20	12
U	•	Ohio Northern	6	0
U		Denison *Unk*	6	12
U		at Ohio Wesleyan	0	6
U	•	Mount Union	20	6
U		at Oberlin	0	3
N30	•	Cincinnati *Unk*	9	6

1923 3-4-1

S29	●	Georgetown, Ky.	22	0
O6	●	Alumni & JV	25	6
O13		at Wooster	0	13
O20		Oberlin	7	13
O27	●	Denison UNK	9	6
N10		at Mount Union	6	7
N17	=	Akron	13	13
N23		at Cincinnati	0	23

CHESTER PITTSER
1924-31 (.618) 41-25-2

1924 2-6-0

S27	●	Georgetown, Ky.	7	0
O4		at Michigan	0	55
O11		Mount Union	6	15
O18		Wooster	6	20
N1	●	Denison UNK	13	12
N8		Western Reserve	21	24
N15		at Oberlin	2	13
N27		at Cincinnati	7	8

1925 5-3-0

O3	●	Georgetown, Ky.	19	0
O10	●	Wittenberg	30	0
O17	●	Transylvania	19	0
O24		at Indiana	7	25
O31		Denison UNK	0	6
N7	●	at Mount Union	8	6
N14		Oberlin	7	18
N26	●	at Cincinnati	33	0

1926 5-2-1

S25	●	Wilmington	9	0
O2		Ohio Wesleyan	7	14
O9	●	Ohio Northern	34	12
O16		at Wittenberg	0	7
O30	●	Denison UNK	16	0
N6	●	Mount Union	27	19
N13	●	at Oberlin	13	0
N25	=	at Cincinnati	6	6

1927 8-1-0

S24	●	Hanover	80	0
O1	●	Otterbein	33	0
O8	●	at Ohio Wesleyan	35	7
O15	●	Denison	26	0
O22	●	Oberlin	23	0
O29		Wittenberg	0	23
N5	●	at Ohio Northern	34	6
N12	●	at Dayton	7	6
N24	●	at Cincinnati	17	14

1928 6-2-0

S29	●	Defiance	42	0
O6	●	Transylvania	8	0
O13		at Denison	0	21
O20		Ohio Wesleyan	0	12
N3	●	Ohio U.	20	13
N10	●	at Oberlin	18	0
N17	●	at Wittenberg	18	0
N29	●	at Cincinnati	34	0

1929 7-2-0

S28	●	Earlham	57	0
O5	●	at Western Reserve	18	0
O12	●	Kentucky Wesleyan	24	0
O19		at Ohio Wesleyan	12	20
O26	●	Wittenberg	3	0
N2		at Ohio U.	0	14
N9	●	Oberlin	20	0
N16	●	Denison	31	0
N28	●	at Cincinnati	14	6

1930 4-4-1

S27		at Indiana	0	14
O4	=	Illinois JV	6	6
O11	●	Kentucky Wesleyan	20	0
O18	●	at Denison	19	6
O25		Ohio U.	6	27
N1	●	Ashland	48	0
N8		Ohio Wesleyan	20	23
N15	●	at Oberlin	12	0
N27		at Cincinnati	0	6

1931 4-5-0

S26		at Pittsburgh	0	61
O3	●	Ball State	47	6 *
O10	●	Wabash	37	0
O17	●	Georgetown, Ky.	45	0
O24		at Ohio Wesleyan	7	12
O31	●	Denison	19	0
N7		Wittenberg	6	10
N14		at Ohio U.	0	13
N26		at Cincinnati	0	20

FRANK WILTON
1932-41 (.528) 44-39-5

1932 7-1-0

O1		at Illinois	7	20
O8	●	DePauw	33	13
O15	●	at Denison	27	7
O22	●	Ohio U.	16	0
O29	●	at Wabash	33	0
N5	●	Ohio Wesleyan	26	3
N12	●	at Wittenberg	19	0
N24	●	at Cincinnati	21	13

1933 7-2-0

S30		at Indiana	0	7
O7	●	Hanover	14	0
O14	●	Marshall	42	14
O21		at Ohio U.	0	6
O28	●	Wittenberg	44	7
N4	●	Georgetown, Ky.	51	0
N11	●	at Ohio Wesleyan	24	0
N18	●	Heidelberg	42	0
N30	●	at Cincinnati	6	2

1934 5-4-0

S29	●	Eastern Kentucky	19	0
O6		at Carnegie Tech	7	13
O13	●	Hanover	39	6
O20	●	Ohio U.	7	0
O26		at John Carroll	0	20
N3		Ohio Wesleyan	6	10
N10	●	at Wittenberg	33	0
N17	●	at Marshall	7	0
N29		at Cincinnati	0	21

1935 5-3-1

S28	●	Eastern Kentucky	33	7
O5	●	at Case	21	6
O12		Ohio Wesleyan	0	8
O19	●	John Carroll	28	12
O26	●	Marshall	20	13
N2		at Ohio U.	0	20
N9	●	Adrian	59	0
N16	=	at Dayton	6	6
N28		at Cincinnati	7	8

1936 7-1-1

S26	●	DePauw	14	6
O3	●	at Case	20	7
O10	●	Western Michigan	6	0
O17	●	Dayton	14	7 *
O24	●	Ohio U.	3	0
O31		at Ohio Wesleyan	0	13
N7	●	Toledo	13	0
N14	●	at Marshall	14	7
N26	=	at Cincinnati	0	0

1937 4-4-1

S25	●	Alma	27	0
O2	●	Marietta	75	6
O9		Marshall	0	7
O16		at Ohio U.	0	19
O23		at Toledo	7	13
O30	=	Case	13	13
N6	●	Ohio Wesleyan	32	0
N13		at Dayton	7	21
N25	●	at Cincinnati	14	6

1938 6-3-0

S24	●	Alma	51	0
O1	●	at Mount Union	40	0
O8		at Marshall	0	41
O15	●	Findlay	53	0
O22	●	Dayton	14	0
O29		at Ohio Wesleyan	16	20
N5		Ohio U.	12	20
N12	●	at Case	27	12
N24	●	at Cincinnati	16	7

1939 1-7-1

S30	●	Mount Union	7	0
O7		at Western Michigan	0	6
O14		Marshall	0	21
O21		Akron	0	14
O28	=	Ohio Wesleyan	0	0
N4		Detroit Tech	7	19
N11		at Ohio U.	7	20
N18		at Dayton	0	20
N23		at Cincinnati	0	13

1940 0-7-1

S21	=	Ball State	0	0
S28		Case	0	10
O5		at Ohio Wesleyan	7	24
O19		Dayton	6	28
O26		at Western Reserve	6	47
N2		Ohio U.	0	27
N9		Western Michigan	13	20
N21		at Cincinnati	0	44

1941 2-7-0

S20	●	Hanover	53	0
S27	●	Wabash	26	0
O4		at Illinois	0	45
O11		Bowling Green	0	9
O18		at Dayton	0	16
O25		Ohio Wesleyan	6	26
N1		at Ohio U.	0	26
N8		Western Reserve	13	28
N20		at Cincinnati	0	26

STU HOLCOMB
1942-43 (.553) 10-8-1

1942 3-6-0

S26	●	Centre	28	6
O3		at Dartmouth	7	58
O10	●	Kent State	53	7
O17		Dayton	0	20
O24		at Bowling Green	6	7
O31		Ohio U.	13	39
N7	●	at Ohio Wesleyan	28	25
N14		at Western Reserve	7	12
N26		at Cincinnati	12	21

1943 7-2-1

S18	=	at Indiana	7	7
S25	●	Bethany	34	12
O2	●	at Xavier	60	6
O9	●	Wooster UNK	20	6
O16		at Western Michigan	0	6
O23	●	Ohio Wesleyan	35	0
O30		Arkansas Monticello UNK	0	35
N6	●	Bowling Green	45	6
N13	●	at Baldwin Wallace	40	6
N20	●	Xavier UNK	52	7

SID GILLMAN
1944-47 (.829) 31-6-1

1944 8-1-0

S9	●	at Bowling Green	28	7
S23	●	Oberlin	13	7
S30	●	Western Michigan	32	6
O7	●	at Rochester	19	7
O14	●	DePauw	12	0
O21	●	at Murray St.	26	14
N4	●	Denison UNK	16	0
N11	●	at Ohio Wesleyan	32	20
N18		at DePauw	7	13

1945 7-2-0

S22	●	Bowling Green	26	0
S29	●	Notre Dame JV	13	0
O6	●	Wright Field UNK	14	0
O13	●	at Western Michigan	21	13
O20	●	Ohio U.	34	0
O26		at Miami, Fla.	13	27
N3	●	Indiana Normal	51	0
N10		at Purdue	7	21
N22	●	at Cincinnati	28	14

1946 7-3-0

S21		at Purdue	7	13
S28	●	Memphis NATC	42	0
O5	●	at Dayton	35	0
O12	●	at Bowling Green	6	0
O19	●	Xavier	28	6
O26	●	at Ohio U.	23	14
N2	●	Bradley	35	6
N8		at Miami, Fla.	17	20
N16	●	Western Michigan	20	0
N28		at Cincinnati	7	13

1947 9-0-1

S27	●	Murray St.	28	12
O4	●	at Kent State	35	7
O11	●	Bowling Green	33	19
O18	=	at Xavier	6	6
O25	●	Ohio U.	21	0
N1	●	at Bradley	32	27
N8	●	Dayton	12	0
N15	●	at Wichita	22	7
N27	●	at Cincinnati	38	7
		SUN BOWL		
J1	●	Texas Tech	13	12

1948-PRESENT
MAC

GEORGE BLACKBURN
1948 (.833) 7-1-1

1948 7-1-1 (4-0-0)

S18	●	Marshall	38	6
S25	=	at Virginia	14	14
O2	● |	at Western Reserve	49	0
O16	●	Xavier	9	0
O23	● |	at Ohio U.	21	0
O30	● |	Western Michigan	34	28
N6		at Dayton	0	7
N13	●	Wichita	41	16
N25	● |	at Cincinnati	43	19

WOODY HAYES
1949-50 (.737) 14-5

1949 5-4-0 (3-1-0)

S24	●	at Wichita	23	6
O1		at Virginia	18	21
O8		Xavier	19	27
O15		at Pittsburgh	26	35
O22	● |	Ohio U.	26	0
O29	● |	at Western Michigan	34	20
N5	● |	Western Reserve	46	7
N12	●	Dayton	52	20
N24	|	at Cincinnati	6	27

1950 9-1-0 (4-0-0)

S30	●	at Bowling Green	54	6
O7		Xavier	0	7
O14	● |	Western Michigan	35	0
O21	●	at Butler	42	7
O28	● |	at Ohio U.	28	20
N4	●	Wichita	39	13
N11	●	Dayton	27	12
N18	● |	at Western Reserve	69	14
N25	● |	at Cincinnati	28	0
		SALAD BOWL		
J1	●	Arizona State	34	21

ARA PARSEGHIAN
1951-55 (.859) 39-6-1

1951 7-3-0 (3-1-0)

S22	●	at Wichita	21	13
S29	●	Bowling Green	46	7
O6		Xavier	14	32
O13	● |	at Western Michigan	34	27
O20	● |	Ohio U.	7	0
O27		at Marquette	7	27
N3	●	Buffalo	27	7
N10	●	at Dayton	21	20
N17	● |	Western Reserve	34	7
N24	|	at Cincinnati	14	19

1952 8-1-0 (4-1-0)

S27	● |	at Bowling Green	42	7
O4	●	Xavier	26	7
O11	● |	Western Michigan	55	6
O18	●	at Wichita	56	7
O25	● |	at Ohio U.	20	0
N1	● |	Toledo	27	13
N7	●	at Marquette	22	21
N15	●	Dayton	27	13
N27	|	at Cincinnati	9	34

1953 7-1-1 (3-0-1)

S26	● |	Bowling Green	47	0
O3	●	Xavier	28	6
O10	● |	at Western Michigan	52	6
O17	●	at Marshall	48	6
O24	= |	Ohio U.	7	7
O31	● |	at Toledo	81	0
N7	●	Tennessee Tech	44	6
N14	●	at Dayton	20	7
N26		at Cincinnati	0	14

1954 8-1-0 (4-0-0)

S25	● |	at Bowling Green	46	7
O2	●	at Marquette	27	26
O9	●	Xavier	42	7
O16	● |	Marshall	46	0
O23	● |	at Ohio U.	46	13
O31	● |	Western Michigan	48	0
N6	●	at Indiana	6	0
N13		Dayton	12	20
N25	●	at Cincinnati	21	9

1955 9-0-0 (5-0-0)

S24	●	at Northwestern	25	14
O1	●	Xavier	13	12
O8	● |	Toledo	47	0
O15	● |	at Marshall	46	7
O22	● |	Ohio U.	34	7
O29	● |	at Kent State	19	7
N5	● |	Bowling Green	7	0
N12	●	at Dayton	21	0
N24	●	at Cincinnati	14	0

JOHN PONT
1956-62 (.657) 43-22-2

1956 7-1-1 (4-0-1)

S22		George Washington	6	7
S29	●	Xavier	14	7
O6	● |	Toledo	33	14
O13	● |	Marshall	21	14
O20	● |	at Ohio U.	16	7
O27	● |	Kent State	14	0
N3	= |	at Bowling Green	7	7
N10	●	Dayton	21	14
N22	●	at Cincinnati	27	13

1957 6-3-0 (5-0-0)

S28	● |	at Western Michigan	20	0
O5		Xavier	19	39
O12	● |	at Kent State	27	14
O19	● |	Ohio U.	26	0
O26		at Purdue	6	37
N2	● |	at Bowling Green	13	7
N9	● |	Marshall	25	13
N16		at Dayton	7	13
N28	●	at Cincinnati	20	14

1958 6-3-0 (5-0-0)

S27	● |	Western Michigan	34	20
O4		Xavier	8	22
O11	● |	Kent State	35	0
O18	● |	at Ohio U.	14	10
O25		at Indiana	7	12
N1	● |	Bowling Green	28	14
N8	● |	at Marshall	26	0
N15	●	Dayton	34	0
N27		at Cincinnati	7	18

1959 5-4-0 (3-2-0)

S26	● |	at Western Michigan	21	0
O3	●	Xavier	33	7
O10	|	at Kent State	6	14
O17	●	Villanova	26	6
O24	● |	Ohio U.	24	0
O31	|	at Bowling Green	16	33
N7	● |	Toledo	25	7
N14		at Dayton	0	13
N26		at Cincinnati	7	14

1960 5-5-0 (2-3-0)

S17		at Xavier	6	17
S24	● |	Western Michigan	15	14
O1	|	Bowling Green	12	21
O8	|	Kent State	19	22
O15	●	at Villanova	17	7
O22	|	at Ohio U.	0	21
O29		at Army	7	30
N5	● |	at Toledo	30	13
N12	●	Dayton	23	8
N19	●	at Cincinnati	10	6

1961 6-4-0 (3-2-0)

S16		Villanova	0	33
S23	●	Xavier	3	0
S30	|	at Western Michigan	3	6
O7	● |	at Kent State	21	0
O14		at Purdue	6	19
O21	|	Ohio U.	18	28
O28	● |	at Bowling Green	7	6
N4	● |	Toledo	40	14
N11	●	at Dayton	48	6
N18	●	at Cincinnati	7	3

1962 8-2-1 (3-1-1)

S15	●	at Xavier	23	14
S22	●	Quantico Marines	16	0
S29	● |	Western Michigan	17	7
O6	● |	Kent State	23	14
O13	●	at Purdue	10	7
O20	|	at Ohio U.	6	12
O27	= |	Bowling Green	24	24
N3	● |	at Toledo	21	12
N10	●	Dayton	42	10
N17	●	at Cincinnati	38	16
TANGERINE BOWL				
D22		Houston	21	49

BO SCHEMBECHLER
1963-68 (.692) 40-17-3

1963 5-3-2 (4-1-1)

S21		Xavier	12	21
S28	= |	Marshall	14	14
O5	● |	at Western Michigan	27	19
O12	● |	at Kent State	30	8
O19		at Northwestern	6	37
O26	|	Ohio U.	10	13
N2	● |	at Bowling Green	21	12
N9	● |	Toledo	40	8
N16	=	at Dayton	27	27
N28	●	at Cincinnati	21	19

1964 6-3-1 (4-2-0)

S19	=	at Xavier	7	7
S26	● |	at Marshall	21	0
O3	● |	Western Michigan	35	0
O10	● |	Kent State	17	14
O17	●	at Northwestern	28	27
O24	|	at Ohio U.	7	10
O31	|	Bowling Green	18	21
N7	● |	at Toledo	35	14
N14	●	Dayton	27	21
N21		at Cincinnati	14	28

1965 7-3-0 (5-1-0)

S18		at Purdue	0	38
S25		Xavier	28	29
O2	● |	at Western Michigan	36	9
O9	|	at Kent State	13	24
O16	● |	Marshall	28	7
O23	● |	Ohio U.	34	0
O30	● |	at Bowling Green	23	7
N6	● |	Toledo	20	16
N13	●	at Dayton	28	0
N20	●	at Cincinnati	37	7

1966 9-1-0 (5-1-0)

S17	●	at Indiana	20	10
S24	●	at Xavier	27	3
O1	● |	Western Michigan	26	7
O8	● |	Kent State	7	0
O15	● |	at Marshall	12	0
O22	● |	at Ohio U.	33	13
O29	|	Bowling Green	14	17
N5	● |	at Toledo	24	12
N12	●	Dayton	38	6
N26	●	at Cincinnati	28	8

1967 6-4-0 (4-2-0)

S16	|	at Western Michigan	14	24
S23	●	at Tulane	14	3
S30		Xavier	6	7
O7	● |	at Kent State	21	7
O14	● |	Marshall	48	6
O21	● |	Ohio U.	22	15
O28	● |	at Bowling Green	9	7
N4	|	Toledo	14	24
N11		at Dayton	6	7
N18	●	at Cincinnati	27	14

1968 7-3-0 (5-1-0)

S14	●	at Xavier	28	7
S21		at Pacific	20	21
S28	● |	Western Michigan	28	0
O5	● |	Kent State	24	0
O12	● |	at Marshall	46	0
O19	|	at Ohio U.	7	24
O26	● |	Bowling Green	31	7
N2	● |	at Toledo	21	17
N9	●	Dayton	14	0
N23		at Cincinnati	21	23

BILL MALLORY
1969-73 (.765) 39-12

1969 7-3-0 (2-3-0)

S13	●	Xavier	35	7
S20	●	at Dayton	19	9
S27	● |	at Western Michigan	24	20
O11	●	Marshall	35	7
O18	● |	Ohio U.	24	21
O25	|	at Bowling Green	0	3
N1	|	Toledo	10	14
N8	●	at Maryland	34	21
N15	|	at Kent State	14	17
N22	●	at Cincinnati	36	20

1970 7-3-0 (3-2-0)

S19	●	at Xavier	28	7
S26	● |	Western Michigan	23	12
O3	●	Northern Illinois	48	0
O10	●	at Marshall	19	12
O17	|	at Ohio U.	22	23
O24	● |	Bowling Green	7	3
O31	|	at Toledo	13	14
N7	●	Dayton	17	0
N14	● |	Kent State	10	8
N21		at Cincinnati	0	33

1971 7-3-0 (2-3-0)

S11	●	at Pacific	17	10
S18	●	at Xavier	17	7
S25	●	at Dayton	14	0
O2	●	Marshall	66	6
O16	|	Ohio U.	0	3
O23	|	at Bowling Green	7	33
O30	|	Toledo	6	45
N6	● |	at Western Michigan	7	6
N13	● |	at Kent State	30	0
N20	●	Cincinnati	43	7

1972 7-3-0 (2-3-0)

S16	●	Dayton	34	7
S23	|	Bowling Green	7	16
S30	●	Xavier	25	7
O7	●	at Marshall	22	7
O14	● |	at Ohio U.	31	7
O21	●	at South Carolina	21	8
O28	|	at Toledo	21	35
N4	● |	Western Michigan	38	8
N11	|	Kent State	10	21
N18	●	at Cincinnati	23	0

1973 11-0-0 (5-0-0)

S15	●	Dayton	32	0
S22	●	at Purdue	24	19
S29	●	at South Carolina	13	11
O6	●	Marshall	31	6
O13	● |	Ohio U.	10	6
O20	● |	at Bowling Green	31	8
O27	● |	Toledo	16	0
N3	● |	at Western Michigan	24	9
N10	● |	at Kent State	20	10
N17	●	Cincinnati	6	0
TANGERINE BOWL				
D22	●	Florida	16	7

DICK CRUM
1974-77 (.767) 34-10-1

1974 10-0-1 (5-0-0)

S7	●	Eastern Michigan	39	0
S21	=	at Purdue	7	7
S28	●	at Marshall	42	0
O5	●	at Kentucky	14	10
O12	● |	at Ohio U.	31	3
O19	● |	Bowling Green	34	10
O26	● |	at Toledo	38	22
N2	● |	Western Michigan	31	0
N9	● |	Kent State	19	17
N16	●	at Cincinnati	27	7
TANGERINE BOWL				
D21	●	Georgia	21	10

1975 11-1-0 (6-0-0)

S13	●	Marshall	50	0
S20		at Michigan State	13	14
S27	● |	Ball State	35	28
O4	●	at Purdue	14	3
O11	●	at Dayton	10	0
O18	● |	Ohio U.	17	9
O25	● |	at Bowling Green	20	17
N1	● |	Toledo	35	21
N8	● |	at Western Michigan	44	21
N15	● |	at Kent State	27	8
N22	●	Cincinnati	21	13
TANGERINE BOWL				
D20	●	South Carolina	20	7

1976 3-8-0 (2-4-0)

S4		at North Carolina	10	14
S11		at Marshall	16	21
S18	|	Ball State	6	23
S25		at Cincinnati	0	17
O2		at Purdue	20	42
O16	|	at Ohio U.	14	28
O23	● |	Bowling Green	9	7
O30	|	at Toledo	9	24
N6	● |	Western Michigan	31	0
N13	|	Kent State	17	24
N20	●	Dayton	28	8

1977 10-1-0 (5-0-0)

S3	●	Dayton	26	23
S17		at South Carolina	19	42
S24	●	at Indiana	21	20
O1	●	at Yale	28	14
O8	●	Marshall	29	19
O15	● |	Ohio U.	28	24
O22	● |	at Bowling Green	33	13
O29	● |	Toledo	27	3
N5	● |	at Western Michigan	14	8
N12	● |	at Kent State	25	0
N24	●	at Cincinnati	12	7

TOM REED
1978-82 (.636) 34-19-2

1978 8-2-1 (5-2-0)

S9	|	at Ball State	14	38
S16	|	Central Michigan	18	37
S23	● |	Western Michigan	7	3
S30	=	Dayton	10	10
O7	●	at North Carolina	7	3
O14	●	at Marshall	29	3
O21	● |	Bowling Green	18	7
O28	● |	at Toledo	28	7
N4	● |	at Ohio U.	31	16
N11	● |	Kent State	38	13
N18	●	Cincinnati	28	24

1979 6-5-0 (3-4-0)

S8	● |	Ball State	27	3
S15	●	at Kentucky	15	14
S22		at Michigan State	21	24
S29	|	at Central Michigan	18	19
O6	●	at Marshall	28	0
O13	|	Ohio U.	7	9
O20	● |	at Bowling Green	21	3
O27	|	Toledo	21	24
N3	|	at Western Michigan	3	24
N10	● |	at Kent State	35	8
N17	●	Cincinnati	27	14

1980 5-6-0 (4-3-0)

S13	|	Central Michigan	14	15
S20		at Syracuse	24	36
S27	● |	at Ball State	42	9
O4		at Purdue	3	28
O11	●	Marshall	34	6
O18	|	at Ohio U.	7	17
O25	● |	Bowling Green	7	3
N1	|	at Toledo	14	17
N8	● |	Western Michigan	34	24
N15	● |	Kent State	49	14
N22		at Cincinnati	13	23

1981 8-2-1 (6-1-1)

S12	●	at William & Mary	33	14
S19		at North Carolina	7	49
S26	● |	at Eastern Michigan	18	12
O3	● |	Kent State	20	13
O10	= |	at Bowling Green	7	7
O17	● |	Western Michigan	20	19
O24	● |	Ohio U.	40	14
O31	|	at Toledo	10	17
N7	● |	at Central Michigan	7	3
N14	● |	Northern Illinois	30	3
N21	●	Cincinnati	7	3

1982 7-4-0 (5-3-0)

S11	●	William & Mary	35	17
S18	●	at Northwestern	27	13
S25	● |	Eastern Michigan	35	0
O2	● |	at Kent State	20	0
O9	● |	Bowling Green	17	12
O16	|	at Western Michigan	0	10
O23	|	at Ohio U.	0	20
O30	● |	Toledo	21	17
N6	● |	Central Michigan	23	0
N13	|	at Northern Illinois	7	12
N18		at Cincinnati	10	20

TIM ROSE
1983-89 (.417) 31-44-3

1983 4-7-0 (3-5-0)

S10		at South Carolina	3	24
S17		at North Carolina	17	48
S24	|	at Bowling Green	14	17
O1	|	Western Michigan	18	20
O8	● |	Kent State	27	7
O15	|	at Toledo	9	10
O22	● |	at Central Michigan	12	7
O29	|	Northern Illinois	0	17
N5	|	Ohio U.	14	17
N12	● |	at Eastern Michigan	24	12
N19	●	Cincinnati	14	10

1984 4-7-0 (3-5-0)

S8	|	at Western Michigan	13	17
S15		at Houston	17	30
S22	|	Bowling Green	10	41
S29		at Washington	7	53
O6	● |	at Kent State	19	3
O13	|	Toledo	7	10
O20	|	Central Michigan	9	10
O27	● |	at Northern Illinois	20	7
N3	|	at Ohio U.	19	24
N10	● |	Eastern Michigan	23	0
N22	●	at Cincinnati	31	26

1985 8-2-1 (7-1-1)

S14	● |	at Ball State	17	13
S21	|	at Bowling Green	24	28
S28		at Oklahoma State	10	45
O5	● |	Ohio U.	29	22
O12	● |	at Toledo	26	14
O19	= |	Western Michigan	10	10
O26	● |	Northern Illinois	32	15
N2	● |	at Central Michigan	19	14
N9	● |	Kent State	52	24
N16	● |	at Eastern Michigan	31	16
N23	●	Cincinnati	16	10

1986 8-4-0 (6-2-0)

Date		Opponent		
S6	●	Ball State	45	7
S13		at Cincinnati	38	45
S20		at LSU	21	12
S27	●	Bowling Green	24	7
O4		at Ohio U.	34	14
O11	●	Toledo	24	8
O18	●	at Western Michigan	17	27
O25	●	at Northern Illinois	20	6
N1	●	Central Michigan	59	21
N8	●	at Kent State	23	24
N15	●	Eastern Michigan	34	20
		CALIFORNIA BOWL		
D13		San Jose State	7	37

1987 5-6-0 (5-3-0)

Date		Opponent		
S5	●	at Central Michigan	15	6
S12	●	Eastern Michigan	17	33
S19		at Syracuse	10	24
S26		at Cincinnati	26	31
O3	●	Ball State	30	20
O10	●	at Western Michigan	17	0
O17	●	Ohio U.	10	9
O24	●	at Toledo	25	37
O31	●	Bowling Green	17	7
N7		at Miami, Fla.	3	54
N14	●	at Kent State	10	14

1988 0-10-1 (0-7-1(

Date		Opponent		
S3		at Eastern Michigan	17	24
S10		at Oklahoma State	20	52
S17		at Minnesota	3	35
S24		Cincinnati	18	34
O1		at Ball State	14	45
O8		Western Michigan	18	41
O15		at Ohio U.	21	38
O22		Toledo	7	20
O29	=	at Bowling Green	21	21
N12		Kent State	11	17
N19		Central Michigan	17	34

1989 2-8-1 (2-5-1)

Date		Opponent		
S9		at Purdue	10	27
S16		at Michigan State	0	49
S23		Cincinnati	14	30
S30		Central Michigan	7	20
O7		at Ball State	9	37
O14	=	Ohio U.	22	22
O21		at Toledo	14	17
O28	●	Bowling Green	17	13
N4		at Eastern Michigan	7	20
N11		at Kent State	15	13
N18		Western Michigan	7	14

RANDY WALKER
1990-98 (.611)   58-36-5

1990 5-5-1 (4-3-1)

Date		Opponent		
S1		at North Carolina	0	34
S8		Toledo	14	20
S15		at LSU	7	35
S22	●	at Cincinnati	16	12
S29	●	at Central Michigan	7	31
O6	●	Ball State	24	10
O13	●	at Ohio U.	40	18
O27	=	at Bowling Green	10	10
N3	●	Eastern Michigan	34	14
N10	●	Kent State	31	10
N17	●	at Western Michigan	17	31

1991 6-4-1 (4-3-1)

Date		Opponent		
A31	●	Ball State	15	7
S7		at Kentucky	20	23
S14	●	Eastern Michigan	29	3
S28	●	at Cincinnati	22	9
O5	●	at La. Lafayette	27	14
O12	=	at Central Michigan	10	10
O19	●	Ohio U.	34	0
O26	●	at Toledo	7	24
N2	●	Bowling Green	7	17
N9	●	at Western Michigan	23	24
N16	●	at Kent State	20	9

1992 6-4-1 (5-3-0)

Date		Opponent		
S5	=	at West Virginia	29	29
S12		at Indiana	0	16
S19	●	Cincinnati	17	14
S26	●	at Ball State	9	19
O3	●	at Eastern Michigan	24	7
O10	●	Central Michigan	16	13
O17	●	at Ohio U.	23	21
O24	●	Toledo	17	20
O31	●	at Bowling Green	24	44
N7	●	Western Michigan	20	7
N14	●	Kent State	31	14

1993 4-7-0 (3-6-0)

Date		Opponent		
S11	●	La. Lafayette	29	28
S18	●	at Cincinnati	23	30
S25	●	at Western Michigan	0	17
O2	●	Eastern Michigan	7	15
O9	●	at Akron	13	31
O16	●	at Toledo	22	19
O23	●	Ohio U.	20	22
O30	●	Bowling Green	25	30
N6	●	at Ball State	0	21
N13	●	at Kent State	23	14
N20	●	Central Michigan	24	21

1994 5-5-1 (5-3-0)

Date		Opponent		
S3	●	Western Michigan	25	28
S10	●	at Indiana	14	35
S17	=	Cincinnati	17	17
S24	●	at Michigan State	10	45 †
O1	●	at Eastern Michigan	21	17
O8	●	Akron	50	14
O15	●	at Ohio U.	31	10
O22	●	at Central Michigan	30	32
O29	●	at Bowling Green	16	27
N5	●	Ball State	24	21
N12	●	Kent State	24	14

1995 8-2-1 (6-1-1)

Date		Opponent		
A31		Ball State	15	17
S9	●	at Kent State	39	0
S16	●	at Northwestern	30	28
S23	●	Cincinnati	23	16
S30	●	at Michigan	19	38
O7	●	at Bowling Green	21	0
O14	=	Toledo	28	28
O28	●	at Central Michigan	17	13
N4	●	Eastern Michigan	39	23
N11	●	at Ohio U.	30	2
N18	●	Akron	65	0

1996 6-5 (6-2)

Date		Opponent		
A31	●	Kent State	64	6
S7	●	at Ball State	16	6
S14	●	at Indiana	14	21
S21	●	Bowling Green	10	14
S28	●	at Cincinnati	23	30
O5	●	Central Michigan	46	14
O12	●	at Eastern Michigan	35	25
O19	●	at Akron	7	10
O26	●	Army	7	27
N2	●	at Toledo	27	7
N9	●	Ohio U.	24	8

1997 8-3 (6-2)

Date		Opponent		
A30	●	Ball State	27	10
S6		at Bowling Green	21	28
S13	●	Akron	49	20
S27	●	at Army	38	14
O4	●	at Virginia Tech	24	17
O11	●	at Kent State	62	26
O18	●	Marshall	45	21
O25	●	Cincinnati	31	34
N1	●	at Toledo	28	35
N8	●	at Ohio U.	45	21
N15	●	Northern Illinois	42	0

1998 10-1 (7-1)

Date		Opponent		
S5	●	at North Carolina	13	10
S12	●	at Army	14	13
S26	●	Toledo	28	14
O3		at Marshall	17	31
O10	●	Bowling Green	24	12
O17	●	at Ball State	28	17
O24	●	at Cincinnati	41	0
O31	●	Ohio U.	35	21
N7	●	at Northern Illinois	41	10
N14	●	Kent State	56	0
N21	●	at Akron	20	14

TERRY HOEPPNER
1999-2004 (.658)   48-25

1999 7-4 (6-2)

Date		Opponent		
S4	●	at Northwestern	28	3
S11	●	at West Virginia	27	43
S18	●	Eastern Michigan	35	14
S25	●	at Central Michigan	24	16
O2	●	Marshall	14	32
O9	●	at Bowling Green	45	31
O16	●	at Kent State	17	10
O30	●	Cincinnati	42	52
N6	●	Akron	32	23
N13	●	at Ohio U.	28	40
N20	●	Buffalo	43	0

2000 6-5 (5-3)

Date		Opponent		
S2	●	at Vanderbilt	33	30
S9	●	at Eastern Michigan	34	17
S16		at Ohio State	16	27
S23	●	Kent State	45	14
S30	●	at Akron	20	37
O7		Ball State	10	15
O14	●	Bowling Green	24	10
O28	●	at Cincinnati	15	45
N4	●	Ohio U.	27	24
N11	●	at Marshall	31	51
N18	●	at Buffalo	17	16

2001 7-5 (6-2)

Date		Opponent		
S1		at Michigan	13	31
S8		at Iowa	19	44
S22	●	Cincinnati	21	14
S29	●	at Ball State	28	20
O6	●	Buffalo	31	14
O13	●	Akron	30	27
O20	●	at Ohio U.	36	14
O27	●	Western Michigan	25	11
N3	●	at Bowling Green	24	21
N10	●	Marshall	21	27
N17	●	at Hawaii	51	52
N24	●	at Kent State	20	24

2002 7-5 (5-3)

Date		Opponent		
A31	●	at North Carolina	27	21
S7		Iowa	24	29
S14	●	at LSU	7	33
S21	●	Kent State	27	20
S28	●	at Akron	48	31
O5	●	at Cincinnati	31	26
O12		Northern Illinois	41	48
O19	●	at Buffalo	49	0
O26	●	at Toledo	27	13
N2	●	Ohio U.	38	20
N12	●	at Marshall	34	36
N23	●	Central Florida	31	48

2003 13-1 (8-0)

Date		Opponent		
A30		at Iowa	3	21
S13	●	at Northwestern	44	14
S20	●	at Colorado State	41	21
S27	●	Cincinnati	42	37
O4	●	Akron	45	20
O11	●	Buffalo	59	3
O18	●	at Ball State	49	3
O25	●	at Kent State	38	30
N4	●	Bowling Green	33	10
N12	●	Marshall	45	6
N22	●	at Ohio U.	49	31
N28	●	at Central Florida	56	21
		MAC CHAMPIONSHIP GAME		
D4	●	at Bowling Green	49	27
		GMAC BOWL		
D18	●	Louisville	49	28

2004 8-5 (7-1)

Date		Opponent		
A28	●	Indiana St.	49	0
S4	●	at Michigan	10	43
S11	●	at Cincinnati	26	45
S18	●	Ohio U.	40	20
S29	●	at Marshall	25	33
O9	●	Kent State	47	24
O16	●	at Buffalo	25	7
O23	●	Central Florida	43	7
N3	●	Toledo	23	16
N13	●	at Western Michigan	42	21
N20	●	at Akron	37	27
		MAC CHAMPIONSHIP GAME		
D2		Toledo _Det_	27	35
		INDEPENDENCE BOWL		
D28		Iowa State	13	17

SHANE MONTGOMERY
2005-PRESENT (.391)   9-14

2005 7-4 (5-3)

Date		Opponent		
S3		at Ohio State	14	34
S10		Central Michigan	37	38
S17	●	at Kent State	27	10
S28	●	Cincinnati	44	16
O5		at Northern Illinois	27	38
O15	●	Akron	51	23
O22	●	at Eastern Michigan	24	23
O29	●	at Temple	41	14
N5	●	Buffalo	54	13
N15	●	Bowling Green	14	42
N21	●	at Ohio U.	38	7

2006 2-10 (2-6)

Date		Opponent		
A31		Northwestern	3	21
S9		at Purdue	31	38
S16		Kent State	14	16
S23		at Syracuse	14	34
S30		at Cincinnati	10	24
O8		Northern Illinois	25	28
O15	●	at Buffalo	38	31
O21	●	at Akron	13	24
O28	●	Ball State	17	20
N4	●	at Western Michigan	24	27
N15	●	at Bowling Green	9	7
N24		Ohio U.	24	34

MAC TEAMS

Neutral Site key: _Det_ Detroit, MI / _Unk_ Unknown
ƒ **Forfeit** † **Game Later Forfieted** # **Disputed Victor** * **Disputed Score** || **Designated Conference Game** |2 **Counted Twice in Conference Standings**

MIAMI (OHIO) RECORD BOOK

SINGLE-GAME RECORDS

RUSHING YARDS

RANK	PLAYER	DATE	OPPONENT	ATT	AVG	YDS
1	Travis Prentice	Nov. 6, 1999	Akron	41	9.2	376
2	George Swarn	Nov. 16, 1985	Eastern Michigan	41	8.0	326
3	Terry Carter	Oct. 13, 1990	Ohio	26	9.6	250
4	Travis Prentice	Nov. 15, 1997	Northern Illinois	22	10.9	239
	George Swarn	Sept. 8, 1984	Western Michigan	29	8.2	239

PASSING YARDS

RANK	PLAYER	DATE	OPPONENT	ATT	COMP	YDS
1	Ben Roethlisberger	Oct. 12, 2002	Northern Illinois	61	41	525
2	Ben Roethlisberger	Nov. 17, 2001	Hawaii	53	40	452
3	Ben Roethlisberger	Dec. 4, 2003	Bowling Green	35	26	440
4	Josh Betts	Sept. 11, 2004	Cincinatti	43	26	416
5	Ben Roethlisberger	Oct. 25, 2003	Kent State	44	28	409

RECEIVING YARDS

RANK	PLAYER	DATE	OPPONENT	REC	AVG	YDS
1	Jeremy Patterson	Sept. 11, 1993	SW Louisiana	10	19.8	198
2	Sly Johnson	Sept. 18, 2001	Eastern Michigan	6	30.7	184
3	Martin Nance	Oct. 25, 2003	Kent State	10	18.1	181
	Tom Murphy	Sept. 24, 1983	Bowling Green	9	20.1	181
5	Ryne Robinson	Nov. 11, 2006	Western Michigan	10	18.0	180

POINTS

RANK	PLAYER	DATE	OPPONENT	TOT
1	Wilbur Cartwright	Nov. 1, 1930	Ashland	31
2	Travis Prentice	Nov. 14, 1998	Kent State	30

FIELD GOALS

RANK	PLAYER	DATE	OPPONENT	TOT
1	Gary Gussman	Sept. 5, 1987	Central Michigan	5

TACKLES

RANK	PLAYER	DATE	OPPONENT	TOT
1	Craig Guest	Oct. 7, 1995	Maine	29

INTERCEPTIONS

RANK	PLAYER	DATE	OPPONENT	TOT
1	Dan Rebsch	Nov. 4, 1972	Western Michigan	5

RETIRED NUMBERS

40 Bob Hitchens

42 John Pont

SINGLE-SEASON RECORDS

RUSHING YARDS

RANK	PLAYER	SEASON	G	ATT	YDS
1	Travis Prentice	1998	11	365	1,787
2	Travis Prentice	1999	11	354	1,659
3	Deland McCullough	1995	NA	321	1,627
4	Travis Prentice	1997	11	296	1,549
5	George Swarn	1985	NA	309	1,511

PASSING YARDS

RANK	PLAYER	SEASON	ATT	COMP	PCT	YDS
1	Ben Roethlisberger	2003	495	342	68.1	4,486
2	Josh Betts	2004	442	267	60.4	3,495
3	Ben Roethlisberger	2002	428	271	63.3	3,238
4	Josh Betts	2005	434	248	57.1	3,178
5	Ben Roethlisberger	2001	381	241	63.3	3,105

RECEIVING YARDS

RANK	PLAYER	SEASON	REC	AVG	YDS
1	Martin Nance	2003	90	16.6	1,498
2	Ryne Robinson	2005	75	14.9	1,119
3	Martin Nance	2005	81	13.7	1,107
4	Trevor Gaylor	1999	53	19.4	1,028
5	Andy Schillinger	1986	50	19.1	955

SCORING

RANK	PLAYER	SEASON	TD	FG	PAT	P2	TOT
1	Travis Prentice	1997	25	0	0	0	150
2	Travis Prentice	1999	17	0	0	12	126
3	Travis Prentice	1998	19	0	0	3	120
4	Mike Smith	2003	28	0	0	0	108
5	Luke Clemens	2002	16	0	0	3	102

TOUCHDOWNS

RANK	PLAYER	SEASON	G	TOT
1	Travis Prentice	1997	11	25
2	Travis Prentice	1999	11	21
3	Travis Prentice	1998	11	20
4	Mike Smith	2003	NA	18
5	Luke Clemens	2002	NA	17

TACKLES

RANK	PLAYER	SEASON	TOT
1	Marc Smith	1970	223
2	Mike Monos	1973	210
3	Curt McMillan	1991	204
4	Brad Cousino	1974	195
5	Joe Farais	1978	189

INTERCEPTIONS

RANK	PLAYER	SEASON	G	YDS	TOT
1	6 players tied at 7				

PUNTING

RANK	PLAYER	SEASON	PUNTS	YDS	AVG
1	Gary Layton	1994	NA	NA	45.0

PUNT RETURNS

RANK	PLAYER	SEASON	RET	YDS	AVG
1	Ryne Robinson	2003	38	654	17.2

KICKOFF RETURNS

RANK	PLAYER	SEASON	RET	YDS	AVG
1	Milt Bowen	2000	32	706	22.1

CAREER RECORDS

RUSHING YARDS

RANK	PLAYER	SEASONS	ATT	AVG	TD	YDS
1	Travis Prentice	1996-99	1,138	4.9	73	5,596
2	Deland McCullough	1992-95	949	4.6	36	4,368
3	George Swarn	1983-86	881	4.7	22	4,172
4	Bob Hitchens	1971-73	773	4.0	34	3,118
5	Jay Peterson	1980-83	702	4.1	21	2,874
6	Greg Jones	1978-81	597	4.8	20	2,839
7	Rob Carpenter	1973-76	623	4.5	26	2,789
8	John Pont	1949-51	355	6.9	25	2,457
9	Terry Carter	1990-04	571	4.2	9	2,400
10	Mark Hunter	1976-79	526	4.6	24	2,396

PASSING YARDS

RANK	PLAYER	SEASONS	ATT	COMP	PCT	INT	TD	YDS
1	Ben Roethlisberger	2001-03	1,304	854	63.3	34	84	10,829
2	Josh Betts	2002-05	929	541	58.2	30	54	7,029
3	Mike Bath	1997-2000	903	444	49.2	NA	49	6,524
4	Sam Ricketts	1994-97	885	484	54.7	NA	44	5,870
5	Neil Dougherty	1991-95	678	365	53.8	NA	27	4,074
6	Terry Morris	1985-86	510	314	61.6	NA	25	3,836
7	Larry Fortner	1975-78	564	277	50.0	NA	27	3,667
8	Mel Olix	1946-49	409	197	48.2	NA	28	3,035
9	Ernie Kellermann	1962-64	416	217	52.2	NA	23	3,011
10	Jim Bengala	1968-70	446	218	48.9	NA	NA	2,649

RECEIVING YARDS

RANK	PLAYER	SEASONS	REC	AVG	TD	YDS
1	Ryne Robinson	2003-06	258	14.3	22	3,697
2	Martin Nance	2002-05	208	15.1	26	3,131
3	Michael Larkin	2001-04	200	13.9	32	2,772
4	Trevor Gaylor	1996-99	128	16.6	20	2,131
5	Jay Hall	1995-98	121	14.7	17	1,787
6	Tremayne Banks	1994-96	118	13.7	10	1,622
7	Jason Branch	1999-2002	121	13.3	18	1,611
8	Andy Schillinger	1984-87	96	16.8	15	1,609
9	Milt Stegall	1988-91	106	14.9	8	1,581
10	Sly Johnson	1997-2000	84	18.8	12	1,576

SCORING

RANK	PLAYER	SEASONS	TD	FG	PAT	P2	TOT
1	Travis Prentice	1996-99	73	0	0	15	468
2	Gary Gussman	1984-87	0	68	102	0	306
3	Jared Parseghian	2001-04	0	36	154	0	262
4	Chad Seitz	1992-95	0	47	97	0	238
5	Deland McCullough	1992-95	36	0	0	5	226

TOUCHDOWNS

RANK	PLAYER	SEASONS	TOT
1	Travis Prentice	1996-99	78
2	Deland McCullough	1992-95	37
3	Bob Hitchens	1971-73	34
4	Luke Clemens	2001-04	33
5	Michael Larkin	2001-04	32

TACKLES

RANK	PLAYER	SEASONS	TOT
1	Curt McMillan	1989-92	575
2	Mark Hatgas	1975-78	526
3	Johnnie Williams	1992-95	524
4	Brad Cousino	1972-74	515
5	Kent McCormick	1977-80	488

INTERCEPTIONS

RANK	PLAYER	SEASONS	YDS	TOT
1	Ron Carpenter	1990-92	361	16
2	David Thomas	1991-94	232	15
3	Dave Williams	1980-82	260	14
	Dick Adams	1969-70	154	14
	Dick Boron	1966-68	237	14

PUNTING

RANK	PLAYER	SEASONS	PUNTS	YDS	AVG
1	Gary Layton	1991-94	240	9,998	41.7
2	Jason Cheney	1995-96	119	4,938	41.5
3	Mike Wafzig	2001-04	185	7,548	40.8
4	Kent McCullough	1997-2000	232	9,419	40.6
5	Jake Richardson	2005-	104	4,149	39.9

TEAM RECORDS

LONGEST WINNING STREAK
• 14, Sept. 13, 2003-Aug. 28, 2004
Streak broken vs. Michigan, 10-42, Sept. 4, 2004

LONGEST UNDEFEATED STREAK
• 27: Nov. 13, 1915-Oct. 18, 1919
Streak broken vs. Oberlin, 0-13, Oct. 25, 1919

MOST CONSECUTIVE WINNING SEASONS
• 17, 1943-1959

MOST CONSECUTIVE BOWL APPEARANCES
• 3, 1973-1975

MOST POINTS IN A GAME
• 91, vs. Earlham, Oct. 20, 1917

MOST POINTS ALLOWED IN A GAME
• 104, vs. Ohio Wesleyan, Date Unknown, 1891

LARGEST MARGIN OF VICTORY
• 91 (91-0), vs. Earlham, Oct. 20, 1917

LARGEST MARGIN OF DEFEAT
• 104 (0-104), vs. Ohio Wesleyan, date unknown, 1891

LONGEST RUN FROM SCRIMMAGE
• 98 yards, George Swarn, vs. Western Michigan, Sept. 8, 1984

LONGEST PASS PLAY
• 94 yards, Mike Bath to Sly Johnson, vs. Eastern Michigan, Sept. 18, 1999

LONGEST FIELD GOAL
• 54 yards, Chad Seitz, vs. Michigan, Sept. 30, 1995

LONGEST PUNT
• 78 yards, Gary Layton, vs. Bowling Green, Oct. 29, 1994

LONGEST PUNT RETURN
• 96 yards, Bill Neumeier, vs. Bowling Green, Oct. 27, 1962

LONGEST INTERCEPTION RETURN
• 97 yards, Ernie Bremer, vs. Dayton, Nov. 16, 1963

PUNT RETURNS

RANK	PLAYER	SEASON	RET	YDS	AVG
1	Ryne Robinson	2003-06	121	1,677	13.9

KICKOFF RETURNS

RANK	PLAYER	SEASON	RET	YDS	AVG
1	Milt Bowen	1999-2002	81	1,826	22.5

MIAMI (OHIO) ANNUAL STATISTICAL LEADERS

YR	RUSHING	YDS	ATT	AVG	PASSING	ATT	CMP	PCT	YDS	RECEIVING	REC	YDS	AVG
1957	Dave Thelen	755	115	6.6	Ernie Jarvis	35	13	.37	197	Harold Williams	9	118	13.1
1958	Harold Williams	566	87	6.5	Nick Mourouzis	32	14	.44	191	David Girbert	6	65	10.8
1959	David Girbert	332	55	6.0	Thomas Kilmurray	79	42	.53	454	Howie Millisor	11	132	12.0
1960	John Moore	616	94	6.5	Jack Gayheart	87	34	.39	441	Howie Millisor	17	261	15.4
1961	Bill Triplett	648	145	4.5	Jack Gayheart	77	34	.44	551	Robert Jencks	20	359	18.0
1962	Scott Tyler	538	77	7.0	Ernie Kellerman	133	61	.46	856	Robert Jencks	26	426	16.4
1963	Tom Longsworth	642	173	3.7	Ernie Kellerman	134	68	.51	895	Jack Himebauch	15	226	15.1
1964	Don Peddie	691	162	4.3	Ernie Kellerman	149	88	.59	1,260	Jack Himebauch	27	379	14.0
1965	Al Moore	677	155	4.4	Bruce Matte	146	70	.48	1,016	John Erisman	32	433	13.5
1966	Joe Kozar	633	178	3.6	Bruce Matte	111	60	.54	845	John Erisman	41	600	14.6
1967	Al Moore	717	135	5.3	Kent Thompson	106	38	.36	460	Gary Arthur	14	145	10.4
1968	Cleve Dickerson	736	161	4.6	Kent Thompson	159	76	.48	970	Mike Palija	22	334	15.2
1969	Cleve Dickerson	622	169	3.7	Jim Bengala	187	101	.54	1,276	Mike Palija	43	567	13.2
1970	Tim Fortney	1,063	265	4.0	Jim Bengala	236	107	.45	1,265	Mike Palija	41	639	15.6
1971	Bob Hitchens	1,192	271	4.4	Stu Showalter	109	43	.39	464	John Viher	24	251	10.5
1972	Bob Hitchens	1,370	326	4.3	Steve Williams	93	49	.53	676	John Viher	29	414	14.3
1973	Bob Hitchens	591	176	3.4	Steve Sanna	149	76	.51	927	John Wiggins	27	414	15.3
1974	Randy Walker	873	214	4.1	Steve Sanna	106	60	.57	724	Larry Harper	25	352	14.1
1975	Rob Carpenter	1,082	235	4.3	Sherman Smith	123	54	.44	592	Steve Joecken	17	225	13.2
1976	Rob Carpenter	1,064	240	4.4	Larry Fortner	202	88	.44	1,219	Steve Joecken	23	404	17.6
1977	Mark Hunter	809	170	4.8	Larry Fortner	186	109	.59	1,473	Paul Warth	26	450	17.3
1978	Mark Hunter	1,046	210	5.0	Larry Fortner	166	80	.48	975	Mark Angelo	21	299	14.2
1979	Paul Drennan	503	128	3.9	Chuck Hauck	207	97	.47	1,258	Keith Dummitt	17	395	23.2
1980	Greg Jones	952	201	4.7	Mark Kelly	86	41	.48	517	Don Treadwell	30	661	22.0
1981	Greg Jones	1,134	253	4.5	John Appold	171	80	.47	929	Don Treadwell	21	391	18.6
1982	Jay Peterson	1,250	271	4.3	John Appold	191	104	.54	1,051	Keith Dummitt	25	333	13.3
1983	Jay Peterson	842	224	3.8	Todd Rollins	212	110	.52	1,262	Tom Murphy	39	610	15.6
1984	George Swarn	1,281	269	4.8	Todd Rollins	140	77	.55	951	Tom Murphy	32	492	15.4
1985	George Swarn	1,511	309	4.9	Terry Morris	202	121	.60	1,471	George Swarn	29	430	14.8
1986	George Swarn	1,112	251	4.4	Terry Morris	308	193	.63	2,365	George Swarn	46	955	20.8
1987	Jon Gist	429	117	3.7	Mike Bates	359	218	.61	2,218	Chris Thomas	39	574	14.7
1988	Chris Alexander	816	164	5.0	Chris Ondrula	219	128	.58	1,304	John Stofa	32	450	14.1
1989	Chris Alexander	551	126	4.4	Joe Napoli	342	191	.56	1,988	Steve Fumi	25	426	17.0
1990	Terry Carter	858	197	4.4	Jim Clement	196	84	.43	1,184	Milt Stegall	32	590	18.4
1991	Kevin Ellerbe	708	184	3.8	Jim Clement	178	81	.46	938	Milt Stegall	45	489	10.9
1992	Deland McCullough	1,026	227	4.5	Neil Dougherty	291	148	.51	1,486	Jeremy Patterson	31	370	11.9
1993	Deland McCullough	612	174	3.5	Danny Smith	195	92	.47	982	Jim Clement	42	426	10.1
1994	Deland McCullough	1,103	227	4.9	Neil Dougherty	201	120	.60	1,431	Eric Henderson	43	560	13.0
1995	Deland McCullough	1,627	321	5.1	Sam Ricketts	211	108	.51	1,337	Tremayne Banks	44	733	16.7
1996	Ty King	1,065	247	4.3	Sam Ricketts	234	125	.53	1,333	Tremayne Banks	52	617	11.9
1997	Travis Prentice	1,549	296	5.2	Sam Ricketts	324	188	.58	2,466	Jay Hall	54	861	15.9
1998	Travis Prentice	1,787	365	4.9	Mike Bath	209	108	.52	1,500	Trevor Gaylor	38	653	17.2
1999	Travis Prentice	1,659	354	4.7	Mike Bath	295	138	.47	2,525	Trevor Gaylor	53	1,028	19.4
2000	Steve Little	986	189	5.2	Mike Bath	384	189	.49	2,415	Sly Johnson	37	620	16.8
2001	Steve Little	587	135	4.3	Ben Roethlisberger	381	241	.63	3,105	Mike Larkin	37	672	18.2
2002	Luke Clemens	1,009	223	4.5	Ben Roethlisberger	428	271	.63	3,238	Jason Branch	40	505	12.6
2003	Cal Murray	1,056	186	5.5	Ben Roethlisberger	495	342	.69	4,486	Martin Nance	90	1,498	16.6
2004	Luke Clemens	899	213	4.2	Josh Betts	444	268	.60	3,518	Ryne Robinson	64	932	14.6
2005	Brandon Murphy	1,070	226	4.7	Josh Betts	434	248	.57	3178	Martin Nance	81	1,107	13.7
2006	Andre Bratton	63	285	4.5	Mike Kokal	355	208	.59	2419	Ryne Robinson	91	1,178	12.9

Receiving leaders by receptions
NCAA began including postseason stats in 2002

NORTHERN ILLINOIS

BY ED KRZEMIENSKI

NORTHERN ILLINOIS KNOWS THE perils of being a successful conference-affiliated mid-major. In 2003, after upsetting two perennial powerhouses, the Huskies found themselves in the middle of the annual Bowl Championship Series controversy. They made a push for consideration in a major bowl but losses to MAC opponents left 10–2 NIU out of the Motor City Bowl. However, under head coach Joe Novak NIU has become one of the top teams in a now-powerful conference.

TRADITION In addition to the team's gridiron success, the Huskies faithful have had much to celebrate. NIU's cheerleading squad is often among the top contenders in the national championships. Band Day brings 20 or so groups to DeKalb, where they play a high-decibel version of the "Huskie Fight Song." Longtime Huskies fans shake their car keys during kickoff, perhaps letting their "dogs" know it's time to go for a ride.

BEST PLAYER In 2006, Garrett Wolfe just missed breaking Leshon Johnson's single-season rushing mark for NIU, but his 1,928 yards, 148 yards per game, and 6.2 per carry were still enough to lead the nation. Wolfe, 5'7" and known as Little Big Man, scored 18 TDs during his senior year and ran wild over Ball State, gaining 353 yards. No one-hit wonder, Williams ran for 1,656 yards as a sophomore, and as a junior finished second in the nation in rushing with 1,580 yards, despite missing three games with a knee injury. As coach Joe Novak said, "What I am sure of is that I'm a better coach with Garrett running the football."

BEST COACH Howard Fletcher coached NIU for 13 years from 1956 to 1968 and won 74 games. More significant than his seven winning seasons, though, was the excitement Fletcher brought to the DeKalb campus. Three of his squads played in the Mineral Water Bowl for the NCAA College Division Championship, and in 1963, Fletcher's Huskies won that title. Innovative in his approach to the game, Fletch taught his '63 squad the blitz-T formation, which resulted in their leading the nation in passing. Fletcher corresponded regularly on the intricacies of this shotgun-style offense with a coaching friend of his named Tom Landry.

PROFILE

Northern Illinois University
DeKalb, Ill.
Founded: 1895
Enrollment: 25,208
Colors: Cardinal and black
Nickname: Huskies
Stadium: Brigham Field at Huskie Stadium
    Opened in 1965
    FieldTurf; 24,000 capacity
First football game: 1899
All-time record: 486–434–51 (.527)
Bowl record: 2–1
Mid-American Conference championships:
    1 (outright)
First-round draft choices: 0
Website: www.niu.edu/athletics

THE BEST OF TIMES

The threes have it: In 1963, undefeated NIU won the college division national title; in 1973, Mark Kellar led the nation in rushing; in 1983, NIU won a MAC title and the California Bowl; in 1993, LeShon Johnson led the nation in rushing; in 2003, the Huskies dropped Maryland, Alabama, and Iowa State in a 10–2 campaign.

THE WORST OF TIMES

1996 to 1998: The team went 3–30, bookending a 23-game losing streak.

CONFERENCE HISTORY

Northern Illinois entered the MAC in 1975 but left after a decade. The Huskies returned in 1997 to stay. NIU played as an independent (1899-21, 1926-27, 1966-74, 1986-92 and 1996); in the Little 19 Conference (1922-25, 1928-46); the Illinois Intercollegiate Athletic Conference (1947-49); the Interstate Intercollegiate Athletic Conference (1950-65); and the Big West (1993-95).

> *Huskies fans shake car keys during kickoff, letting their "dogs" know it's time for a ride.*

BEST TEAM The 1963 Huskies went undefeated and won the NCAA College Division Championship by defeating Southwest Missouri State 21-14 in the Mineral Water Bowl at Excelsior Springs, Mo. In an era of the rushing play, the 1963 Huskies became synonymous with the forward pass. George Bork led the offense and was the first collegiate passer to reach 3,000 yards in a single season. The Huskies put up some amazing numbers: final scores of 55-7 and 61-0, a 445-yard passing game, a seven-touchdown passing game and a 17-reception game for Gary Stearns. Fletcher summed up his philosophy succinctly: "We believe in putting the ball in the air and spreading out our opponents." In 1986, the school inducted the entire 1963 squad into its Huskies Hall of Fame.

BEST BACKFIELD Garrett Wolfe generated most of the headlines in 2005, averaging 175 yards per game and scoring 16 touchdowns. But quarterback Phil Horvath, a junior from Naperville, Ill., put up some gaudy numbers of his own. Horvath threw for 2,001 yards, 18 touchdowns, and, most impressively, completed over 70% of his passes (first in the NCAA). Against Akron, he completed 39 of 52 passes for 486 yards and six touchdowns in rallying the Huskies from a 21-point deficit to send the game into overtime. Unfortunately, Horvath broke his non-throwing arm in the ninth game of the season. With Horvath out for the MAC championship game, a rematch with Akron, Wolfe shouldered the load, running for 270 yards and two touchdowns in a thrilling, but ultimately disappointing 31-30 loss.

BEST DEFENSE The 1983 MAC champions naturally included NIU's best defense. The team lost early to Wisconsin, but under the leadership of defensive coordinator and future head coach Joe Novak, NIU began to dominate opponents with its powerful front line led by Gary Schlinger and Scott Kellar. The defense shut out Miami (Ohio) in late October, for NIU's sixth straight win, then bounced back from a loss to Central Michigan to wrap up the MAC with easy wins over Toledo and Ohio U.

BIGGEST GAME Bill Mallory's 1983 Huskies brought NIU its only MAC championship and

---

DISTINGUISHED ALUMNI

Joan Allen, actress; Dan Castellaneta, actor and voice of Homer Simpson; J. Dennis Hastert, politician; Paul Sereno, paleontologist

FIGHT SONG

HUSKIE FIGHT SONG
Huskies, come on you Huskies
And make a score or two
Huskies, you're Northern Huskies
The team to pull us through
Forward, together forward
There's victory in view
Come on you Huskies, Fight on you
Huskies and win for NIU.

HIGHEST DRAFT CHOICES

1969	John Spilis, Packers (3rd/64)
1994	LeShon Johnson, Packers (3rd/84)
2007	Garrett Wolfe, Bears (3rd/93)

CONSENSUS ALL-AMERICANS

1962-63	George Bork, QB
1993	LeShon Johnson, TB

COLLEGE FOOTBALL HALL OF FAME INDUCTEES

NAME	YEARS	INDUCTED
George Bork, QB	1960-63	1999

California Bowl bid when they were pitted against Cal State-Fullerton on Dec. 17. The Huskies won a thriller 20-13. Lou Wicks, the NIU fullback who gained a career-best 119 yards on 14 carries and won the game's MVP, led the Huskies to victory. The NIU defense stopped CSF on a fourth-and-one with 35 seconds left in the game and ended the season at 10–2 and just outside the Top 20. Moreover, the California Bowl team sent 19 players to several professional leagues and was inducted en masse into the Huskie Hall of Fame in 1995.

BIGGEST UPSET

On Aug. 28, 2003, the Huskies hosted No. 15 Maryland. Falling behind twice, NIU battled back to tie the game with an 18-play, 84-yard drive late in the fourth quarter. In overtime, NIU prevailed, 20-13, when Randee Drew intercepted a pass that ricocheted off a Maryland receiver's foot. The upset set the tone for the season. NIU won at Alabama, started the year with a 7–0 run, and advanced to 12 in the AP poll, before winding up with a 10–2 record.

HEARTBREAKER

In 1992, Northern Illinois led Wisconsin 17-3 in the fourth quarter and looked to be on its way to a second straight win over the Badgers. But Wisconsin cut the lead to 17-16, and then, in the final seconds of the game, attempted a two-point conversion for the win. Badgers quarterback Darrell Bevell sneaked into the end zone to give Wisconsin an 18-17 win.

STADIUM

In 1965, Huskie Stadium, a.k.a. The Doghouse, a.k.a. The House That George Bork Built (the last in honor of the school's former little All-America quarterback), replaced cozy but outdated Glidden Field as the home for NIU football. Originally seating 20,257, the structure curiously remained half built. Beginning with head coach Howard Fletcher in the mid-1960s and continuing with his seven immediate successors, the notion of a completed stadium served as a recruiting promise. "Son," the mantra went, "by the time you graduate, we will have built the other side of the stadium." That dream became reality in 1995, when the

east grandstand extended the existing superstructure and raised the capacity; it's currently 24,000. In 2003, the name was changed to Brigham Field at Huskie Stadium, to honor onetime player, coach, and athletic director Bob Brigham.

RIVAL

Because it reentered competition in the MAC in 1997 and remains the only conference school from Illinois, NIU has yet to establish much in the way of an in-conference rivalry. It's traditional in-state rivals, moreover, fell off the schedule as NIU rose to Division I-A play. Historically, Illinois State has served as the Huskies' greatest foe. The schools began meeting in 1906 and have played 55 times since. Maintaining the rivalry has been difficult, as NIU plays in the Bowl Subdivision and Illinois State in the Championship Subdivision, and the teams have not met since 2000. NIU holds a 25–22–9 advantage in the series. Perhaps an annual game with the University of Illinois could create a new tradition. Certainly, the Huskies have no reason to fear being outclassed by the Illini on the gridiron.

DISPUTE

At the end of the 2003 season, Northern Illinois was overlooked for a bowl game. Miami and Bowling Green represented the MAC in postseason play, but the 10–2 Huskies stayed home. Joe Novak was hot: "I don't think a .500 team should get in over a team that won 10 games. Are you telling me they had a better season than us? Baloney." The .500 team was a reference to a 6–6 Northwestern team that received a bid to the Motor City Bowl.

DUBIOUS DISTINCTION

In 1982, Northern Illinois lost to Northwestern 31-6, allowing the Wildcats to end their 34-game losing streak.

NICKNAME

Northern Illinois ran through a series of nicknames before finally solidifying its moniker. Early on, the teachers college teams became known as The Profs. Later the school was the Cardinals, Evansmen (for head coach Chick Evans), Northerners and Teachers, before a committee was appointed to find "a term with a trifle

ALL-CENTURY TEAM	
The team was selected in 1999 by an NIU committee chaired by sports information director Michael Korcek.	
OFFENSE	
1977-79	Randy Clark, OL
1983-86	Todd Peat, OG
1984-87	Ted Karamanos, OG
1980-83	Scott Bolzan, OT
1988-90	Eric Wenckowski, C
1977-80	Jim Hannula, TE
1960-63	Hugh Rohrschneider, WR
1966-68	John Spilis, WR
1960-63	George Bork, QB
1992-93	LeShon Johnson, TB
1985-88	Rodney Taylor, HB
1971-73	Mark Kellar, FB
1980-83	Vince Scott, PK
1948-51	Fran Cahill, KR
DEFENSE	
1945-47	Larry Brink, DL
1982-85	Scott Kellar, DT
1983-86	Doug Bartlett, DT
1993-95	Hollis Thomas, NG
1970-72	Larry Clark, LB
1973-75	Bob Gregolunas, LB
1976-79	Frank Lewandoski, ILB
1959-61	Tom Beck, HB
1971-73	Rich Marks, SS
1977-80	Dave Petway, FS
1985, 87-89	Brett Tucker, CB
1969-71	Tom Wittum, P

more dash" in 1940. The winning entry was a pretty and powerful dog, and the nickname Huskies, regarded as apt for the school's varsity teams. A notable stipulation is that the team should be known, in its singular form, as Husk*ie* instead of the traditional Husk-Y form.

MASCOT NIU's mascot is Victor E. Huskie, a student-in-costume chosen as part of the cheerleading squad. Laura Schlembach, 2002's Victor E. Huskie, noted that the job was not all Milk Bones and fire hydrants, though, especially in the dog days of summer. Commenting on the first day she was issued the outfit, Schlembach remarked, "They just handed me this large bag ... and it was the worst smell ever. The next game I came prepared. I brought Febreze. I brought dryer sheets. I made that thing smell so nice." In previous years, the school kept a series of real dogs for mascots.

UNIFORMS The Huskies wear a mix of red (cardinal), white, and black. Throughout most of its history, "NIU" has been emblazoned its helmets with a block "N" overlaid with an "I." Currently, the team wears black helmets with a cardinal NIU and a white mascot profile on the side. The team jerseys are cardinal at home and white on the road; pants are solid black both at home and on the road.

TRAGEDY On the second day of conditioning drills in February 2002, Jawan Jackson collapsed and died. The 19-year-old freshman was attempting to make the Huskies squad as a walk-on.

LORE In 1983, the city of Chicago experienced its own Heidi Bowl. With temperatures below zero, the local television station carrying the California Bowl game between NIU and Cal State-Fullerton lost its signal when the transmitter on top of the John Hancock Center froze in the third quarter. A station spokesman said they received thousands of complaints.

NUMBERS From 1911-13, Beloit defeated Northern Illinois on opening day by scores of 42-0, 65-0, and 115-0. In 1914, with Beloit removed from the schedule, the team gave up a total of 13 points in a 6–0–1 season. The next year, St. Viator's roughed up NI-not-yet-U, 96-0. In 1916, the school returned to its better ways and gave up just 19 points in a 6–1–1 season.

QUOTE "I thought I was in Norman, Oklahoma." — Fresno State coach Jim Sweeney in 1990, after NIU's wishbone offense shredded his team by a score of 73-18

MAC TEAMS

NORTHERN ILLINOIS ALL-TIME SCORES

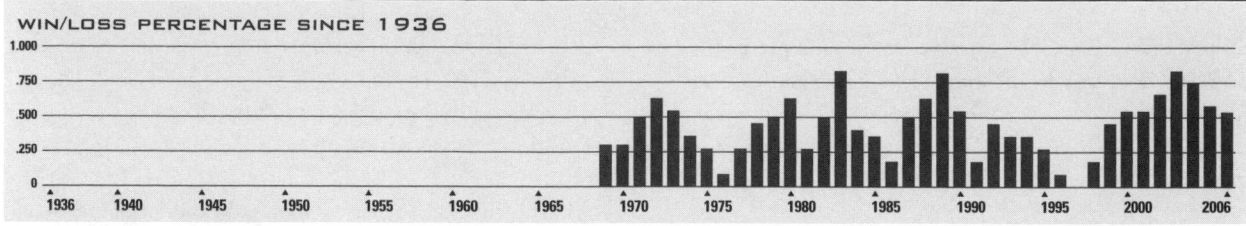

WIN/LOSS PERCENTAGE SINCE 1936

RICHARD URICH
1969-70 (.300)   6-14

1969   3-7-0
S13		at N. Dakota St.	0 28
S20	●	Idaho	47 30
S27		at West Texas St.	7 22
O4		at Marshall	18 17
O11		Western Kentucky	12 14
O18		at Dayton	24 56
O25		Ball State	17 13
N8		Toledo	21 35
N15		Western Michigan	22 31
N22		at Bowling Green	23 38

1970   3-7-0
S12		San Diego State	3 35
S19		Montana	6 30
S26	●	at Xavier	18 0
O3		Miami, Ohio	0 48
O10		West Texas St.	22 24
O24	●	at Ball State	31 14
O31		Dayton	20 21
N7		at Toledo	7 45
N14		at Western Michigan	18 38
N21	●	Buffalo	43 26

JERRY IPPOLITI
1971-75 (.464)   25-29-1

1971   5-5-1
S11		at Wisconsin	0 31
S18	●	Long Beach St.	48 38
S25		at Western Michigan	17 27
O2		at San Diego State	10 30
O9	●	Marshall	33 18 *
O16		at West Texas St.	22 19
O23	=	Ball State	10 10
O30	●	at Kent State	26 7
N6		Toledo	8 23
N13		at Boston College	10 20
N20	●	Xavier	14 9

1972   7-4-0
S9	●	Illinois St.	21 7
S16		at Wisconsin	7 31
S23		Western Michigan	10 14
S30	●	at Marshall	24 7
O7	●	Xavier	20 7
O14		at Idaho	13 31
O21	●	West Texas State	17 8
O28	●	Kent State	28 7
N4	●	at Toledo	30 7
N11	●	Fresno State	6 9
N17	●	at Long Beach St.	22 13

1973   6-5-0
S8	●	Indiana St.	42 24
S15	●	So. Illinois	34 28
S22		at Western Michigan	14 28
S29	●	at West Texas St.	21 14
O6	●	at Fresno State	24 15
O13		Marshall	36 39
O20	●	Ball State	45 17
O27	●	at Illinois St.	28 14
N3		Western Illinois	27 30
N10	●	at Xavier	36 40
N17		at Bowling Green	20 21

1974   4-7-0
S7		at McNeese State	16 19
S14	●	Long Beach St.	16 14
S21		Western Michigan	13 30
S28		Indiana St.	14 23
O5		at Ohio U.	14 31
O12	●	at Marshall	20 17
O19	●	at So. Illinois	17 7
O26		Illinois St.	14 24
N2		at Toledo	14 44
N9	●	at Ball State	21 31
N16	●	Idaho	27 21

1975-1985 MAC

1975   3-8-0 (2-3-0)
S13		Long Beach St.	7 24
S20		at Northwestern	3 10
S27	●	at Western Michigan	20 0
O4		Kent State	38 15
O11		at Indiana St.	10 21
O18		So. Illinois	52 12
O25		Ball State	0 3
N1		at Illinois St.	10 27
N8		Toledo	22 24
N15		at Central Michigan	7 69
N22		at Idaho	24 25

PAT CULPEPPER
1976-79 (.330)   14-29-1

1976   1-10-0 (0-6-0)
S11		at Wichita St.	0 21
S18		Western Michigan	6 37
S25		at Long Beach St.	0 37
O9		at Indiana St.	10 28
O16		Illinois St.	7 3
O23		at So. Illinois	0 54
O30		Ball State	7 33
N6		at Toledo	2 17
N13		Central Michigan	9 31
N20		at Ohio U.	15 63
N25		at Kent State	0 42

1977   3-8-0 (2-5-0)
S3		Eastern Michigan	2 25
S10		at Louisville	0 38
S17		at Wisconsin	3 14
S24		at Western Michigan	21 49
O1		at Illinois St.	7 16
O8		Central Michigan	21 25
O15		at Ball State	6 31
O22	●	So. Illinois	28 0
O29	●	at Kent State	21 18
N5		Toledo	9 27
N19	●	Ohio U.	20 6

1978   5-6-0 (2-4-0)
S16		Western Michigan	30 44
S23		at La. Monroe	10 27
S30	●	Illinois St.	49 21
O7		at Long Beach St.	19 24
O14	●	Western Illinois	24 20
O21		at Central Michigan	7 34
O28	●	at So. Illinois	14 13
N4	●	Kent State	27 21
N11		at Toledo	16 35
N18		Ball State	13 31
N25	●	at Ohio U.	23 14

1979   5-5-1 (3-3-1)
S15	●	E. Tennessee St.	21 14
S22		at Western Michigan	17 45
S29		Long Beach St.	3 9
O6	=	at Eastern Michigan	0 0
O13		at Central Michigan	11 31
O20	●	at Illinois St.	33 7
O27		So. Illinois	11 21
N3	●	Kent State	25 0
N10	●	Toledo	28 10
N17		at Ball State	0 42
N24	●	Ohio U.	28 27

BILL MALLORY
1980-83 (.568)   25-19

1980   7-4-0 (4-3-0)
S5	●	at Long Beach St.	16 9
S13		Ball State	17 18
S20		Western Michigan	6 35
S27	●	at Ohio U.	22 21
O4	●	at So. Illinois	20 17
O11		Illinois St.	18 28
O18	●	Central Michigan	21 0
O25	●	at Wichita St.	17 14
N1	●	at Kent State	35 14
N8	●	at Toledo	6 13
N22	●	Eastern Michigan	38 6

1981   3-8-0 (2-7-0)
S12		Long Beach St.	7 17
S19		at Central Michigan	10 17
S26	●	Illinois St.	40 7
O3		at Ball State	0 23
O10		at Kent State	10 31
O17		Bowling Green	10 17
O24	●	at Eastern Michigan	30 7
O31		Western Michigan	12 23
N7	●	Ohio U.	38 14
N14		at Miami, Ohio	3 30
N21		Toledo	0 31

1982   5-5-0 (5-4-0)
S4		at Toledo	3 9
S18	●	Kent State	23 15
S25	●	at Northwestern	6 31
O2	●	Ball State	7 14
O16		at Bowling Green	18 20
O23	●	Eastern Michigan	10 0
O30		at Western Michigan	3 27
N6	●	at Ohio U.	36 0
N13	●	Miami, Ohio	12 7
N20	●	Central Michigan	19 13

1983   10-2-0 (8-1-0)
S3	●	at Kansas	37 34
S10		at Wisconsin	9 37
S24	●	at Kent State	38 7
O1	●	at Ball State	27 14
O8	●	Western Michigan	27 3
O15	●	at Eastern Michigan	34 15
O22	●	Bowling Green	24 23
O29	●	at Miami, Ohio	17 0
N5		at Central Michigan	14 30
N12	●	Toledo	26 10
N19		Ohio U.	41 17

CALIFORNIA BOWL
D17		Fullerton St.	20 13

LEE CORSO
1984 (.409)   4-6-1

1984   4-6-1 (3-5-1)
S1	●	West Texas St.	40 33
S8		at Wisconsin	14 27
S22	●	Kent State	24 10
S29		Ball State	14 15
O6		at Western Michigan	20 15
O13	=	Eastern Michigan	10 10
O20		at Bowling Green	6 28
O27		Miami, Ohio	7 20
N3	●	Central Michigan	8 7
N10		at Toledo	7 13
N17		at Ohio U.	3 10

JERRY PETTIBONE
1985-90 (.508)   33-32-1

1985   4-7-0 (4-4-0)
S7	●	Western Michigan	17 0
S14		at Wisconsin	17 38
S21		at Iowa	20 48
S28		at Northwestern	16 38
O5		at Ball State	0 29
O19	●	Toledo	16 3
O26		at Miami, Ohio	15 32
N2		Bowling Green	14 34
N9	●	at Eastern Michigan	3 0
N16	●	Ohio U.	35 7
N23		at Central Michigan	21 30

1986-1992 INDEPENDENT

1986   2-9-0
A30		Ball State	10 20
S6		at West Virginia	14 47
S13		at Wisconsin	20 35
S20		at Iowa	3 57
S27		Western Illinois	0 10
O4		at Miami, Fla.	0 34
O18		at Toledo	28 29
O25		at Miami, Ohio	6 20
N1	●	at Bowling Green	16 8
N8	●	Eastern Michigan	21 14
N15		at Ohio U.	26 34

1987   5-5-1
S12		Lamar	35 39
S19		at Western Michigan	34 14
S26	=	at Northwestern	16 16
O3		at Eastern Michigan	31 32
O10	●	Toledo	41 5
O17	●	S.W. Missouri St.	27 21
O24	●	Fullerton St.	20 21
O31		at Ball State	17 42
N7	●	Western Illinois	29 14
N14		Akron	21 27
N28		at Nevada-Las Vegas	34 31

1988   7-4-0
S3		Akron	7 6
S10		Middle Tennessee	14 10
S17	●	at Wisconsin	19 17
S24		at Minnesota	20 31
O1	●	S.W. Missouri St.	17 3
O8		at Toledo	20 33
O15		at La. Lafayette	0 45
O22	●	at So. Illinois	10 9
O29		Ball State	17 18
N5	●	Western Illinois	16 6
N12	●	Western Michigan	15 7

1989   9-2-0
S2	●	Fullerton St.	26 17
S9		at Nebraska	17 48
S23	●	at Kansas State	37 20
S30	●	Western Illinois	34 27
O7	●	So. Illinois	29 24
O14		at Louisiana Tech	21 42
O21	●	Nevada-Las Vegas	42 24
O28	●	at Temple	20 17
N4	●	La. Lafayette	23 20
N11	●	Toledo	39 27
N18	●	at Cincinnati	56 3

1990   6-5-0
S1	●	Ea. Illinois	28 17
S8		at Nebraska	14 60
S15		at Toledo	14 23
S22	●	Kansas State	42 35
S29		at Northwestern	7 24
O6	●	Fresno State	73 18
O13	●	Arkansas State	35 0
O20	●	Murray St.	49 7
N3	●	at Akron	31 28
N10		at East Carolina	20 24
N17		at La. Lafayette	20 24

CHARLIE SADLER
1991-95 (.327)   18-37

1991   2-9-0
S7		at Fresno State	7 55
S14	●	Arkansas State	22 21
S21		at Kansas State	17 34
S28		at Iowa	7 58
O5		Louisiana Tech	3 37
O12		Western Michigan	10 22
O19		at Florida	10 41
O26		at Akron	7 17
N2		La. Lafayette	12 13
N16	●	Illinois St.	27 24
N23		at Toledo	21 42

1992   5-6-0

S5		at Illinois	14 30
S12	●	Illinois St.	26 19
S19	●	at Arkansas State	31 0
S26		at Wisconsin	17 18
O3		Middle Tennessee	13 21
O10	●	Southern Miss	23 10
O24	●	Liberty	27 21
O31		at Western Michigan	7 13
N7	●	at La. Lafayette	23 15
N14		at Army	14 21
N21		Toledo	8 25

1993-1995
BIG WEST

1993   4-7-0 (3-3-0)

S2		at Iowa State	10 54
S11		at Indiana	10 28
S18	● |	Arkansas State	23 7
S25	● |	at Nevada	46 42
O2	● |	So. Illinois	45 15
O9		at New Mexico State	17 24
O16	● |	Pacific	21 16
O23	|	La. Lafayette	19 33
O30	|	at Louisiana Tech	16 17
N6		at Iowa	20 54
N13		at Mississippi	0 44

1994   4-7-0 (3-3-0)

S1		Oklahoma State	14 31
S10		at La. Lafayette	9 29
S17		at Illinois	10 34
S24	●	Ea. Illinois	49 17
O1	|	Nevada	31 35
O8	● |	New Mexico State	48 27
O15	|	at Pacific	32 41
O22	● |	Louisiana Tech	27 17
O29	|	at Vanderbilt	16 17
N5	● |	at Arkansas State	38 16
N12	|	at Arkansas	27 30

1995   3-8-0 (3-3-0)

A31		at Southern Miss	13 45
S9		Louisville	21 34
S16	● |	at San Jose State	18 17
S23	● |	La. Lafayette	25 24
S30		at Kansas State	0 44
O7	● |	Nevada-Las Vegas	62 14
O14	|	at Utah State	7 42
O28		Cincinnati	19 55
N4		at Florida	20 58
N11	|	Arkansas State	21 28
N18	|	at Louisiana Tech	14 59

1996
INDEPENDENT

JOE NOVAK
1996-PRESENT (.480)   61-66

1996   1-10

A31		at Maryland	6 30
S7		Western Ill.	0 17
S14		at Penn State	0 49
S21	●	at Arkansas State	31 30
S28		Texas-El Paso	6 37
O5		North Texas	21 24
O19		at Louisville	3 27
O26		Akron	17 34
N2		Louisiana Tech	14 40
N9		at La. Lafayette	31 45
N16		at Oregon State	28 67

1997-PRESENT
MAC

1997   0-11 (0-8)

A28	|	at Central Michigan	10 44
S6		Kansas State	7 47
S13	|	Western Michigan	13 21
S20		at North Carolina St.	14 41
O4	|	at Bowling Green	10 35
O11		Vanderbilt	7 17
O18	|	at Toledo	14 41
O25	|	Ball State	14 21
N1	|	Ohio U.	30 35
N8	|	Eastern Michigan	10 38
N15	|	at Miami, Ohio	0 42

1998   2-9 (2-6)

S3		at Western Michigan	23 37
S12		at Kansas State	7 73
S19		Eastern Illinois	10 24
O3	|	at Ball State	13 18
O10		at Central Florida	17 38
O17	● |	Central Michigan	16 6
O24	● |	at Eastern Michigan	26 14
O31	|	Toledo	3 16
N7	|	Miami, Ohio	10 41
N14	|	at Ohio U.	12 28
N21	|	Bowling Green	23 34

1999   5-6 (5-3)

S2		Western Illinois	21 27
S11		at Vanderbilt	31 34
S18		at Iowa	0 24
S25		Western Michigan	21 24
O2	● |	at Buffalo	45 21
O9	|	Ball State	37 17
O16	|	at Central Michigan	31 27
O23	|	Kent State	50 7
O30	|	at Marshall	9 41
N13	|	at Toledo	14 44
N20	● |	Eastern Michigan	30 23

2000   6-5 (4-3)

A31		at Northwestern	17 35
S9		Illinois St.	52 0
S23		at Auburn	14 31
S30	|	at Ball State	43 14
O7	|	Central Florida	40 20
O14	|	at Akron	52 35
O21	|	at Western Michigan	22 52
O28	● |	Buffalo	73 10
N4	|	Toledo	24 38
N11	|	at Eastern Michigan	32 39
N18	● |	Central Michigan	40 6

2001   6-5 (4-3)

A30	●	South Florida	20 17
S8		at Illinois	12 17
S22		Sam Houston St.	41 16
S29	|	at Toledo	20 41
O6	|	Marshall	15 37
O13	|	at Kent State	34 44
O20	|	Western Michigan	20 12
O27	|	at Central Michigan	33 24
N3	|	Eastern Michigan	40 17
N17	● |	Ball State	33 29
N24	|	at Wake Forest	35 38

2002   8-4 (7-1)

A29	●	Wake Forest	42 41
S7		at South Florida	6 37
S14		at Wisconsin	21 24
S21		Western Illinois	26 29
S28	● |	Kent State	13 6
O5	● |	at Ball State	41 29
O12	● |	at Miami, Ohio	48 41
O19	|	Central Michigan	49 0
O26	● |	at Western Michigan	24 20
N9	● |	Bowling Green	26 17
N16	● |	at Eastern Michigan	49 21
N23	|	Toledo	30 33

2003   10-2 (6-2)

A28	●	Maryland	20 13
S6	●	Tenn. Tech	42 17
S20	●	at Alabama	19 16
S27	●	Iowa State	24 16
O4	● |	Ohio U.	30 23
O11	● |	at Central Michigan	40 24
O18	● |	Western Michigan	37 10
O25	|	at Bowling Green	18 34
N1	● |	Ball State	48 23
N8	● |	at Buffalo	40 9
N15	|	at Toledo	30 49
N22	● |	Eastern Michigan	38 24

2004   9-3 (7-1)

S4		at Maryland	20 23
S11	●	So. Illinois	23 22
S18		at Iowa State	41 48
S24	● |	Bowling Green	34 17
O2	● |	Akron	49 19
O9	● |	at Central Florida	30 28
O16	● |	Central Michigan	42 10
O23	● |	at Western Michigan	59 38
O30	|	at Ball State	38 31
N10	|	Toledo	17 31
N20	● |	at Eastern Michigan	34 16
		SILICON VALLEY BOWL	
D30	●	Troy State	34 21

2005   7-5 (6-2)

S3		at Michigan	17 33
S10		at Northwestern	37 38
S17	●	Tenn. Tech	42 3
S24		at Akron	42 48
O5	●	Miami, Ohio	38 27
O15	● |	Eastern Michigan	24 8
O22	● |	at Kent State	34 3
O29	|	Ball State	17 31
N5	● |	at Central Michigan	31 28
N16	● |	at Toledo	35 17
N22	● |	Western Michigan	42 7
		MAC CHAMPIONSHIP GAME	
D1		Akron*DET*	30 31

2006   7-6 (5-3)

S2		at Ohio State	12 35
S9		Ohio U.	23 35
S16	● |	Buffalo	31 13
S23	● |	Indiana St.	48 14
S30	|	at Ball State	40 28
O8	● |	at Miami, Ohio	28 25
O14	|	at Western Michigan	14 16
O21	● |	Temple	43 21
O28	|	at Iowa	14 24
N7	|	Toledo	13 17
N17	● |	Central Michigan	31 10
N24	● |	at Eastern Michigan	27 0
		POINSETTIA BOWL	
D19		TCU	7 37

NORTHERN ILLINOIS RECORD BOOK

SINGLE-GAME RECORDS

RUSHING YARDS

RANK	PLAYER	DATE	OPPONENT	ATT	AVG	YDS
1	Garrett Wolfe	Sept. 30, 2006	Ball State	31	11.4	353
2	Garrett Wolfe	Nov. 20, 2004	Eastern Michigan	43	7.6	325
3	LeShon Johnson	Oct. 2, 1993	Southern Illinois	20	16.1	322
4	Stacey Robinson	Oct. 6, 1990	Fresno State	22	14.0	308
5	LeShon Johnson	Nov. 6, 1993	Iowa	32	9.6	306

PASSING YARDS

RANK	PLAYER	DATE	OPPONENT	ATT	COMP	YDS
1	Phil Horvath	Sept. 24, 2005	Akron	52	39	486
2	George Bork	Oct. 19, 1963	Illinois State	NA	NA	445
3	George Bork	Nov. 3, 1962	Illinois State	NA	NA	435

RECEIVING YARDS

RANK	PLAYER	DATE	OPPONENT	REC	AVG	YDS
1	Sam Hurd	Nov. 5, 2005	Central Michigan	12	21.8	266
2	P.J. Fleck	Oct. 4, 2003	Ohio	14	16.7	234
3	Sam Hurd	Oct. 5, 2005	Miami (Ohio)	7	31.9	223
4	Hugh Rohrschneider	Nov. 3, 1962	Illinois State	NA	NA	221

POINTS

RANK	PLAYER	DATE	OPPONENT	TOT
1	Bill Anderson	Oct. 19, 1912	Wheaton	42
2	Reino Nori	Nov. 23, 1935	Eastern Illinois	35
3	8 players tied at 30			

FIELD GOALS

RANK	PLAYER	DATE	OPPONENT	TOT
1	Vince Scott	Nov. 6, 1982	Ohio	5
2	10 players tied at 4			

TACKLES

RANK	PLAYER	DATE	OPPONENT	TOT
1	Frank Lewandoski	Sept. 16, 1978	Western Michigan	33
2	Derril Corbett	Oct. 25, 1958	Illinois State	30
3	Larry Clark	Nov. 11, 1972	Fresno State	29

INTERCEPTIONS

RANK	PLAYER	DATE	OPPONENT	TOT
1	Dan Mojica	Oct. 20, 1951	Illinois State	4
	Dan Meyer	Oct. 22, 1966	Hillsdale	4

RETIRED NUMBERS

6	Dave Petzke
11	George Bork
12	Bob Heimerdinger
31	Mark Kellar

SINGLE-SEASON RECORDS

RUSHING YARDS

RANK	PLAYER	SEASON	G	ATT	YDS
1	LeShon Johnson	1993	11	327	1,976
2	Garrett Wolfe	2006	13	309	1,928
3	Michael Turner	2002	12	338	1,915
4	Mark Kellar	1973	11	291	1,719
5	Garrett Wolfe	2004	11	256	1,656

PASSING YARDS

RANK	PLAYER	SEASON	G	ATT	COMP	PCT	YDS
1	George Bork	1963	NA	374	244	65.2	3,077
2	Josh Haldi	2003	12	336	199	59.2	2,544
3	George Bork	1962	NA	356	232	65.2	2,506
4	Ron Christian	1965	NA	323	173	53.6	2,101
5	Chris Finlen	2001	11	331	166	50.2	2,036

RECEIVING YARDS

RANK	PLAYER	SEASON	REC	AVG	YDS
1	Dave Petzke	1978	91	13.4	1,215
2	Justin McCareins	2000	66	17.7	1,168
3	Sam Hurd	2005	65	16.5	1,074
4	Hugh Rohrschneider	1963	75	13.8	1,036
5	PJ Fleck	2003	77	13.4	1,028

SCORING

RANK	PLAYER	SEASON	TD	PAT	P2	FG	TOT
1	Garrett Wolfe	2004	21	0	0	0	126
2	Stacey Robinson	1990	13	0	3	0	120
	Michael Turner	2002	20	0	0	0	120
4	Garrett Wolfe	2006	19	2	0	0	116
5	Stacey Robinson	1989	19	0	0	0	114

TOUCHDOWNS

RANK	PLAYER	SEASON	G	TOT
1	Garrett Wolfe	2004	11	21
2	Michael Turner	2002	12	20
3	Stacey Robinson	1989	11	19
	Stacey Robinson	1990	NA	19
	Garrett Wolfe	2006	13	19

TACKLES

RANK	PLAYER	SEASON	TOT
1	Steve Henriksen	1991	191
2	Larry Clark	1972	189
3	Frank Lewandoski	1977	179
4	Frank Lewandoski	1979	173
5	Ron Delisi	1988	171

INTERCEPTIONS

RANK	PLAYER	SEASON	YDS	TOT
1	Al Jones	1951	92	10
2	Dan Meyer	1965	149	8
3	Al Eck	1960	108	7
	Randee Drew	2002	103	7
5	11 players tied with 6			

PUNTING

RANK	PLAYER	SEASON	PUNTS	YDS	AVG
1	Jimmy Erwin	2001	60	2,507	41.8
2	Todd Van Keppel	1984	67	2,798	41.8
3	Mike Kent	1985	52	2,170	41.7
4	Todd VanKeppel	1982	58	2,397	41.3
5	Tom Wittum	1970	76	3,104	40.8

PUNT RETURNS

RANK	PLAYER	SEASON	RET	YDS	AVG
1	Dan Sheldon	2002	21	477	22.7
2	Justin McCareins	2000	19	362	19.1
3	Dan Sheldon	2004	24	394	16.4
4	Jack Dean	1962	12	164	13.7
5	Jack Dean	1963	14	183	13.1

KICKOFF RETURNS

RANK	PLAYER	SEASON	RET	YDS	AVG
1	John Spills	1968	24	690	28.8
2	A.J. Harris	2005	15	480	27.2
3	Byron Florence	1972	16	422	26.4
4	Randee Drew	2002	15	392	26.1
5	Raymond Patterson	1989	15	390	26.0

CAREER RECORDS

RUSHING YARDS

RANK	PLAYER	SEASONS	ATT	AVG	TD	YDS
1	Garrett Wolfe	2004-06	807	6.4	52	5,164
2	Michael Turner	2000-03	940	5.3	43	4,941
3	Mark Kellar	1971-73	744	5.0	32	3,745
4	Allen Ross	1977-80	867	4.0	30	3,500
5	Adam Dach	1987-91	665	5.2	19	3,438
6	LeShon Johnson	1992-93	592	5.6	18	3,314
7	Charles Talley	1993-96	661	4.8	27	3,155
8	Stacey Robinson	1988-90	428	6.4	38	2,727
9	Thomas Hammock	1999-2002	544	4.5	25	2,432
10	John Lalonde	1968-70	509	4.4	14	2,227

PASSING YARDS

RANK	PLAYER	SEASONS	ATT	COMP	PCT	TD	YDS
1	George Bork	1960-63	902	577	63.4	60	6,782
2	Chris Finlen	1997, 99-2001	910	502	55.2	42	6,551
3	Josh Haldi	2001-04	776	427	55.0	55	6,015
4	Phil Horvath	2004-06	630	397	62.5	35	4,887
5	Marshall Taylor	1985-88	582	300	51.5	NA	4,167
6	Bob Heimerdinger	1948-51	552	251	45.5	38	4,076
7	Pete Kraker	1976-81	618	284	46.0	18	3,290
8	Lew Flinn	1957-59	414	197	47.6	35	3,233
9	Ron Christian	1963-65	470	239	50.9	36	2,933
10	Mike Griesman	1965-67	443	218	49.2	26	2,811

RECEIVING YARDS

RANK	PLAYER	SEASONS	REC	AVG	TD	YDS
1	Justin McCareins	1997-2000	204	14.7	29	2,991
2	Sam Hurd	2002-05	143	16.2	21	2,322
3	Hugh Rohrschneider	1960-63	183	12.2	19	2,224
4	P.J. Fleck	1999-2003	179	12.1	11	2,162
5	Dan Sheldon	2001-04	94	21.1	18	1,986
6	Gary Stearns	1960-63	142	13.8	17	1,958
7	Dave Petzke	1977-78	148	13.2	16	1,958
8	Deon Mitchell	1995-98	143	13.6	6	1,951
9	John Spills	1966-68	138	13.2	22	1,815
10	Al Eck	1958-60	111	16.3	19	1,812

SCORING

RANK	PLAYER	SEASONS	TD	FG	PAT	P2	TOT
1	Steve Azar	2000-03	0	73	151	0	370
2	Garrett Wolfe	2004-06	57	0	2	0	344
3	Michael Turner	2000-03	48	0	0	0	288
4	Chris Nedick	2004-	0	45	136	0	271
5	John Ivanic	1987-90	0	43	115	0	244

TOUCHDOWNS

RANK	PLAYER	SEASONS	TOT
1	Michael Turner	2000-03	48
2	Stacey Robinson	1988-90	38
	Garrett Wolfe	2004-05	38
4	Mark Kellar	1971-73	33
5	Reino Nori	1932-35	31

TACKLES

RANK	PLAYER	SEASONS	TOT
1	Frank Lewandoski	1976-79	616
2	Tim Griffin	1982-85	471
3	Larry Clark	1970-72	446
4	Ron Delisi	1986-89	437
5	Larry Williams	1999-2002	434

INTERCEPTIONS

RANK	PLAYER	SEASONS	YDS	TOT
1	Dan Meyer	1964-66	178	16
2	Al Eck	1958-60	221	15
	Vince Thompson	1999-2002	109	15
4	Chris Blake	1971-73	208	14
	Randee Drew	2000-03	184	14

PUNTING

RANK	PLAYER	SEASONS	PUNTS	YDS	AVG
1	Mike Kent	1985-86	112	4,544	40.6
2	Todd Van Keppel	1981-84	225	10,312	40.4
3	Tom Wittum	1969-71	228	9,210	40.4
4	Jimmy Irwin	2000-02	167	6,594	39.5
5	Jim Hannula	1977-80	229	8,796	38.4

PUNT RETURNS

RANK	PLAYER	SEASON	RET	YDS	AVG
1	Dan Sheldon	2001-04	57	1,021	17.9
2	Justin McCareins	1997-2000	49	609	12.4
3	Jack Dean	1962-64	31	376	12.1
4	Jeff Sanders	1982-83	39	382	9.8
5	Leon Moody	1995-96	30	260	8.7

KICKOFF RETURNS

RANK	PLAYER	SEASON	RET	YDS	AVG
1	Darrell Hill	1998-2001	28	695	24.8
2	Byron Florence	1971-73	45	1,103	24.5
3	Deon Mitchell	1995-98	100	2,349	23.5
4	Mike Pickney	1979-80	35	807	23.1
5	Bob Florence	1974-75	29	665	22.9

TEAM RECORDS

LONGEST WINNING STREAK
• 7 (tie), Sept. 28-Nov. 16, 2002
Streak broken vs. Toledo, 30-33, Nov. 23, 2002,
Aug. 28-Oct. 18, 2003
Streak broken vs Bowling Green, 18-34, Oct. 25, 2003

LONGEST UNDEFEATED STREAK
• 7 (twice): Sept. 28-Nov. 16, 2002
Streak broken vs. Toledo, 30-33, Nov. 23, 2002,
Aug. 28-Oct. 18, 2003
Streak broken vs Bowling Green, 18-34, Oct. 25, 2003

MOST CONSECUTIVE WINNING SEASONS
• 7, 2000-present

MOST CONSECUTIVE BOWL APPEARANCES
• 1 (tie), 1983, 2004, 2006

MOST POINTS IN A GAME
• 73 (tie), vs. Fresno State, Oct. 6, 1990 vs.
Buffalo, Oct. 28, 2000

MOST POINTS ALLOWED IN A GAME
• 73, vs. Kansas State, Sept. 12, 1998

LARGEST MARGIN OF VICTORY
• 63 (73-10), vs. Buffalo, Oct. 28, 2000

LARGEST MARGIN OF DEFEAT
• 66 (7-73), vs. Kansas State, Sept. 12, 1998

LONGEST RUN FROM SCRIMMAGE
• 99 yards, Reino Nori, vs. UW-Whitewater, Nov. 17, 1934

LONGEST PASS PLAY
• 99 yards, Dan Urban to Justin McCareins, vs. Ball State, Sept. 30, 2000

LONGEST FIELD GOAL
• 52 yards (tie), Steve Azar, vs. Maryland, Aug. 28, 2003; Chris Nendick, vs. Akron, Dec. 1, 2005

LONGEST PUNT
• 98 yards, Toimi Jarvi, vs. Illinois State, Oct. 11, 1941

LONGEST PUNT RETURN
• 90 yards, Dan Sheldon, vs. Kent State, Sept. 28, 2002

LONGEST INTERCEPTION RETURN
• 100 yards, Dave Petway, vs. Southern Illinois, Oct. 22, 1977

MAC TEAMS

NORTHERN ILLINOIS ANNUAL STATISTICAL LEADERS

YR	RUSHING	YDS	ATT	AVG	PASSING	ATT	CMP	PCT	YDS	RECEIVING	REC	YDS	AVG
1948	Bob Brigham	786	138	5.7	Don Fortunato	164	66	.40	1,214	Floyd Hunsberger	22	401	18.2
1949	Ernie Wickstrom	452	63	7.2	Bob Heimerdinger	115	45	.54	779	Bill Russell	19	334	17.6
1950	Hugh Helms	506	94	5.4	Bob Heimerdinger	210	102	.49	1,597	Ernie Wickstrom	29	504	17.4
1951	Bill Graham	395	64	6.2	Bob Heimerdinger	225	103	.46	1,710	Fran Cahill	40	876	21.9
1952	Jack Pheanis	339	69	4.9	Jim Harmes	106	46	.43	694	Jim McKinzie	44	703	16.0
1953	Wes Luedeking	330	97	3.4	Paul Smith	62	23	.37	275	Wes Luedeking	24	247	10.3
1954	Bill Graham	236	91	2.6	Ron Hicks	108	45	.42	617	Tom Skubich	14	147	10.5
1955	Bob Snider	242	66	3.7	Don Coulom	90	37	.41	402	Bob Snider	16	202	12.6
1956	Tom Skubich	404	89	4.5	Joe Plaskas	44	12	.27	154	Bob Soltis	6	117	19.5
1957	Ron Hansen	211	41	5.1	Lew Flinn	103	40	.39	897	Jim Caldwell	16	497	31.1
1958	Joe Plaskas	511	136	3.8	Lew Flinn	137	64	.47	916	Al Eck	32	486	15.2
1959	Joe Plaskas	698	140	5.0	Lew Flinn	174	93	.53	1,420	Al Eck	34	586	17.2
1960	Bob Soltis	559	77	7.3	Tom Beck	156	77	.49	1,176	Al Eck	45	740	16.4
1961	Mickey Stevens	225	50	4.5	George Bork	121	72	.60	841	Rich Bader	33	430	13.0
1962	Jack Dean	504	100	5.0	George Bork	356	232	.65	2,506	Hugh Rohrschneider	76	795	10.5
1963	Jack Dean	516	78	6.6	George Bork	374	244	.65	3,077	Hugh Rohrschneider	75	1,036	13.8
1964	Jack Dean	733	160	4.6	Jack Dean	110	59	.54	716	Bill Pelkey	26	436	16.8
1965	Leigh Gilbert	473	97	4.9	Ron Christian	323	173	.54	2,101	Bob Stark	58	525	9.1
1966	Jim Wendler	358	78	4.6	Mike Griesman	283	141	.50	1,899	Jack Frost	48	796	16.6
1967	Bruce Bray	344	76	4.5	Bob Carpenter	203	88	.43	1,169	John Spilis	46	620	13.5
1968	John Lalonde	866	177	4.9	Bob Carpenter	259	128	.49	1,421	John Spilis	46	629	13.7
1969	John Lalonde	813	187	4.3	Steve Parker	181	85	.47	827	Tom Bastable	26	357	13.7
1970	John Lalonde	548	145	3.8	Terry Drugan	117	58	.50	561	Willie Hatter	35	418	11.9
1971	Mark Kellar	710	168	4.2	Terry Drugan	174	77	.44	957	Willie Hatter	50	615	12.3
1972	Mark Kellar	1,316	285	4.6	Terry Drugan	77	34	.44	390	Willie Hatter	17	268	15.8
1973	Mark Kellar	1,719	291	5.9	Bob Gregolunas	58	27	.47	362	Dan Gentile	15	319	21.3
1974	Vince Smith	720	131	5.5	Jerry Golsteyn	138	62	.45	712	Gary Hosier	27	375	13.9
1975	Ed Johnson	814	179	4.5	Jerry Golsteyn	221	117	.53	1,539	Ken Moore	30	425	14.2
1976	Vince Smith	448	105	4.3	Pete Kraker	152	47	.31	525	Scott Paplham	15	208	13.9
1977	Allen Ross	1,043	273	3.8	Pete Kraker	183	103	.56	1,034	Dave Petzke	57	743	13.0
1978	Allen Ross	1,033	259	4.0	Pete Kraker	283	134	.47	1,731	Dave Petzke	91	1,215	13.4
1979	Allen Ross	751	194	3.9	John Gibbons	124	44	.35	747	Mike Pinckney	34	601	17.7
1980	Allen Ross	673	141	4.8	John Gibbons	179	102	.57	1,119	Jim Latanski	30	421	14.0
1981	Joe Law	596	143	4.2	Rick Bridges	104	49	.47	636	Joe Law	20	156	7.8
1982	Pete Roth	1,008	220	4.6	Tim Tyrrell	93	38	.41	458	Greg Spicher	14	208	14.9
1983	Darryl Richardson	1,204	235	5.1	Tim Tyrrell	189	91	.48	1,260	Reggie Sims	27	279	10.3
1984	Pete Roth	557	137	4.1	Darryl Taylor	132	62	.47	938	Reggie Sims	39	475	12.2
1985	Darryl Richardson	585	121	4.8	Marshall Taylor	186	94	.51	1,162	Curt Pardridge	26	409	15.7
1986	Antonio Davis	648	141	4.6	Marshall Taylor	130	67	.52	993	Virgil Gerin	18	210	11.7
1987	Marshall Taylor	826	157	5.3	Marshall Taylor	139	76	.55	1,039	Virgil Gerin	28	366	13.1
1988	Adam Dach	906	192	4.7	Marshall Taylor	127	63	.50	973	Mark Clancy	13	315	24.2
1989	Stacey Robinson	1,443	223	6.5	Stacey Robinson	128	65	.51	863	Kurt Cassidy	12	137	11.4
1990	Stacey Robinson	1,238	193	6.4	Stacey Robinson	118	58	.49	861	Kurt Cassidy	13	198	15.2
1991	Adam Dach	847	165	5.1	Rob Rugai	86	47	.55	624	Larry Wynn	21	415	19.8
1992	LeShon Johnson	1,338	265	5.0	Rob Rugai	132	76	.58	987	Larry Wynn	37	538	14.5
1993	LeShon Johnson	1,976	327	6.0	Scott Crabtree	141	80	.57	1,163	Raymond Roberts	31	401	12.9
1994	Brian Grimes	876	169	5.2	Aaron Gilbert	185	93	.50	1,437	Vaurice Patterson	34	578	17.0
1995	Charles Talley	1,540	285	5.4	Aaron Gilbert	184	79	.43	1,057	Ralph Strickland	38	664	17.5
1996	Charles Talley	1,008	241	4.2	Brandon Barker	203	105	.52	1,223	Deon Mitchell	36	524	14.6
1997	Ivory Bryant	828	224	3.7	Chris Finlen	149	87	.58	1,107	Deon Mitchell	45	588	13.1
1998	Ivory Bryant	655	187	3.5	Craig Harmon	172	81	.47	795	Justin McCareins	54	486	9.0
1999	William Andrews	1,127	240	4.7	Chris Finlen	199	118	.59	1,551	Justin McCareins	57	906	15.9
2000	Thomas Hammock	1,083	215	5.0	Chris Finlen	231	131	.57	1,857	Justin McCareins	66	1,168	17.7
2001	Thomas Hammock	1,096	268	4.1	Chris Finlen	331	166	.50	2,036	P.J. Fleck	59	732	12.4
2002	Michael Turner	1,915	338	5.7	Josh Haldi	254	130	.51	2,027	Dan Sheldon	40	783	19.6
2003	Michael Turner	1,648	310	5.3	Josh Haldi	336	199	.59	2,544	P.J. Fleck	77	1,028	13.4
2004	Garrett Wolfe	1,656	256	6.5	Josh Haldi	179	94	.53	1,384	Dan Sheldon	40	936	23.4
2005	Garrett Wolfe	1,580	242	6.5	Phil Horvath	238	168	.71	2001	Sam Hurd	65	1074	16.5
2006	Garrett Wolfe	1,928	309	6.2	Phil Horvath	269	257	.58	1932	Britt Davis	57	731	12.8

Receiving leaders by receptions
NCAA began including postseason stats in 2002

MAC TEAMS

MAC TEAMS

OHIO

BY ED KRZEMIENSKI

LIKE EVERY COLLEGE IN THE STATE, Ohio University looks with a degree of envy at the football monster in Columbus. For Ohio U., though, there is a bit of spite added to the envy, since the Ohio State University not only drains the state of recruits but also hijacked the name Ohio itself— both for its stadium and as its band's halftime signature. While Athens may not be the seat of Western civilization or hold the best football team in the state, the university there still has a fairly rich football tradition. From the late 1920s through World War II, the Bobcats dominated the Buckeye conference, going undefeated three times. In the 1960s, Ohio frequently stood atop the MAC, winning or sharing the conference title four times in that decade. After four consecutive losing seasons, the school hired former Nebraska coach Frank Solich after the 2004 season. In just his second year, Solich guided the team to a MAC East title, a seven-game win streak, and the team's first bowl appearance in 38 seasons.

TRADITION The team had until 2005 played Marshall University annually in the Battle for the Bell. The teams first faced off in 1905 when they competed for a mounted bell from an Ohio River steamboat. The game has been played off and on until Marshall left the MAC before the 2005 season.

BEST PLAYER Vince Costello certainly became the greatest Ohio football alum, playing 12 years as a linebacker in the NFL, but his collegiate accolades include only a second-team All-MAC selection at center in his 1952 senior season. But for accomplishments as a Bobcat, no one surpasses Todd Snyder, who set school records for receptions and yards in each of his varsity seasons, 1967 to 1969: 33 catches for 629 yards, 46 for 777 and 62 for 835, respectively. He also led the team in scoring his senior season and remains at or near the top of every school receiving record.

BEST COACH No one comes close to Don Peden, after whom Ohio's football stadium is now named. An Ohio alum (class of 1914), Peden compiled a 121–46–11 record from 1924 to 1946, with the 1943 and 1944 seasons canceled. That is a .711 winning percentage (Bear Bryant's, in comparison, is .780). His teams went undefeated three times, and his only losing season was in 1945.

BEST TEAM The competition was of a lesser caliber, the players were smaller, the ball was rounder, and the stock market crashed midseason. Still, it's difficult to overlook the accomplishment of Ohio's 1929 squad. That season, Don Peden's team won the Buckeye A.A. championship with a 9–0 record, including a victory over the Big Ten's Indiana.

Most amazingly, though, the team gave up only seven points all season. Only Ohio Wesleyan scored on the Bobcats, who finished the season with a 305-7 scoring margin. From 1929 to 1931, Ohio went 24–1–1, outscoring its opponents 704 to 53. In the modern era, the 1968 squad stands out. That team won the MAC with an undefeated regular season before losing to Richmond by seven points in the Tangerine Bowl. While defense set the 1929 team apart, offense made the 1968 Bobcats go. Dave LeVeck ran for 850 yards, Cleve Bryant passed for 1,524, Todd Snyder caught 46 passes for 777 yards, and Bob Houmard scored 19 touchdowns, each school records at the time. Houmard's mark of 114 points still stands.

Although Marshall and Ohio have long played in the Battle for the Bell, Ohio vs. Miami (Ohio) has a more consistent history.

when he ran for 282 yards and 4 touchdowns against Bowling Green. He also threw for 567 yards. Hookfin averaged 5.8 yards per carry in his 1,125-yard season. The two ended their careers as Ohio's top two career rushers.

BEST DEFENSE In 1962, Ohio did not win the MAC but still went to a bowl game, mostly because of its outstanding defense. The 1962 Bobcats shut out three opponents and held another four to single digits. In its first bowl game ever, Ohio faced West Texas State in the Sun Bowl. In a 15-14 loss, the Bobcats defense kept the game close when All-MAC lineman Skip Hoovler returned an interception 91 yards for a touchdown.

BEST BACKFIELD In 1968, Ohio's backfield of Cleve Bryant, Dave LeVeck, and Bob Houmard each made first team All-MAC. But even that great backfield did not accomplish what Kareem Wilson and Steveland Hookfin did in 1996. That season, quarterback Wilson and running back Hookfin each ran for more than 1,000 yards. Wilson set an NCAA record for a quarterback with 275 rushing attempts

BIGGEST GAME On Nov. 12, 1960, the Bobcats traveled to Bowling Green for a MAC clash of titans. Both teams were undefeated for the year, and the Falcons were riding an 18-game winning streak that included an undefeated 1959 season. In a thriller, Ohio won the game 14-7 and dethroned Bowling Green as MAC and National College Division champions.

MAC TEAMS

FIGHT SONG

STAND UP AND CHEER
Stand up and cheer,
Cheer loud and long for old Ohio,
For today we raise the Green and White above the rest.
Our team is fighting
And we are bound to win the fray.
We've got the team,
We've got the steam,
For this is old Ohio's day!
Rah! Rah! Rah!

FIRST-ROUND DRAFT CHOICE

1936	Art Lewis, Giants (9)

CONSENSUS ALL-AMERICANS

1935	Art Lewis, T
1960	Dick Grecni, C

BIGGEST UPSET The cover of the September 9, 2005, program for the Ohio-Pitt game in Athens read, A NEW ERA BEGINS. It was the first home game under coach Frank Solich, but having lost 38-14 a week before to Northwestern made it seem as if it were business as usual for the Bobcats. Playing in front of 24,545 fans and in their first national television audience in nearly 40 years, the Bobcats looked outclassed by the defending Big East champions when Pitt's LaRod Stephens returned the opening kickoff for a TD. But Ohio bounced back, when Dion Byrum returned an interception 38 yards for a touchdown. With seven seconds left in the game, Ohio's Josh Cummings kicked a 27-yard field goal to tie the game at 10. In the first overtime, Byrum again played the hero, intercepting another pass, and returning it 85 yards for the game-winning touchdown. A new era had begun.

HEARTBREAKER After riding the most powerful offense in school history to an undefeated regular season and Top 20 rankings in the AP and UPI polls, the 1968 Bobcats faced the Richmond Spiders in the Tangerine Bowl, a game that promised to be a shootout. And it was. Cleve Bryant threw four touchdown passes, including three to Todd Snyder, who caught 11 passes for 214 yards. In the end, the Bobcats put up 42 points on the scoreboard. But Richmond scored 49 to end Ohio's undefeated season.

WILDEST FINISH In 1968, Ohio defeated Cincinnati 60-48. Combined, the teams produced 1,175 total yards and 67 first downs. They accomplished these feats in 59 minutes, 46 seconds of game time. With 14 seconds left, a massive fight between the Bobcats and Bearcats (one might say a cat fight) broke out and officials stopped the game.

BEST COMEBACK With the clock winding down, Ohio trailed Bowling Green 27-14; it looked as if Ohio's 1968 unbeaten season would end. Ohio, however, scored two touchdowns in the game's final 4:20, winning 28-27.

STADIUM In its 74th season of hosting the Bobcats, Peden Stadium stands as one of college football's bucolic jewels. The 24,000 capacity makes Ohio's home field cozy, but recent renovations added state-of-the-art practice and training facilities to the old house. The stadium was originally known as Ohio University's Athletic Plant but was renamed in 1946 for longtime head coach Don Peden.

RIVAL Although Marshall and Ohio have long played in the Battle for the Bell, Ohio vs. Miami (Ohio) has a more consistent history. The Bobcats and RedHawks first played in 1908 and began a series of uninterrupted annual meetings beginning in 1928 (with a break for two years during World War II). Ohio trails the series against Miami by a 29–50–2 margin.

NICKNAME In 1925, Hal Rowland won $10 for proposing Bobcats as the new Ohio nickname. The animal was chosen due to its reputation as sly, wily, and scrappy. Any animal would have been an improvement: Prior to that year, the team was known as the Green and White.

MASCOT In addition to the costumed Bobcat, a live bobcat, Sir Winsalot, was introduced in 1983. Owned by an Ohio alum and kept at his house, Sir Winsalot was joined by Paws and both were moved to the Columbus Zoo in 1986. Sir Winsalot died in 1999 and Paws in 2002. There have been no official replacements, athough a plaque commemorating the cats still stands at the zoo.

UNIFORMS Hunter-green home jerseys with white numbers and the player's name on the back over white pants with a double-green stripe up the side mark the Bobcats on their home field. On the road, the colors are flipped: white jerseys and green or white pants. The team wears white helmets with an arched Ohio across the side. In years past, the helmets sported a paw print and an outline of the state of Ohio.

QUIRK Which side are you on? Two of the greatest players in Ohio Bobcats history—Vince Costello and Dick Grecni—played both ways in college, and each made All-MAC squads at center. Both spent their entire professional careers as linebackers—Costello with the Cleveland Browns and New York Giants, and Grecni with the Minnesota Vikings.

LORE The man given credit for introducing football—not just the game, but the first football—to the Ohio campus is John Brough, who, in 1826, was fond of kicking the ball over the Center Building, now Cutler Hall. Kicking a ball over a building is impressive, but more impressively, Brough was inaugurated as governor of Ohio on Jan. 11, 1864.

QUOTE "That will be enough of that s—! We're going after their asses!" —Coach Bill Hess, shouting at staff members in 1959 after 15 winless years against Miami. It worked. Ohio won in 1960, kick-starting a five-year winning streak versus its rival

OHIO ALL-TIME SCORES

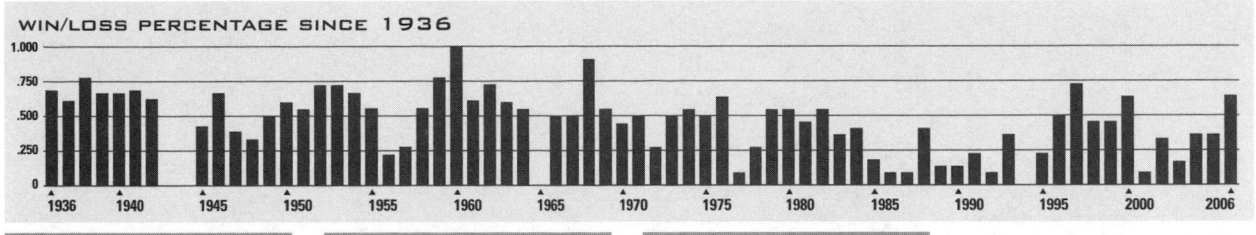

WIN/LOSS PERCENTAGE SINCE 1936

| 1936 | 1940 | 1945 | 1950 | 1955 | 1960 | 1965 | 1970 | 1975 | 1980 | 1985 | 1990 | 1995 | 2000 | 2006 |

NO HEAD COACH

1894   0-1-0
| U | Marietta *Unk* | 0 | 8 |

HARVEY DEME
1895 (.400)   2-3

1895   2-3-0
U •	Parker HS *Unk*	18	0
U	Ohio Wesleyan *Unk*	0	38
U	Marietta *Unk*	0	24
U	Marietta *Unk*	0	66
U •	Lancaster *Unk*	60	0

FRANK REMSBURG
1896 (.643)   4-2-1

1896   4-2-1
U	Marietta *Unk*	10	22
U •	Chillicothe *Unk*	12	6
U	Cincinnati *Unk*	0	52
U =	Parker HS *Unk*	0	0
U •	Portsmouth *Unk*	18	0
U •	Denison *Unk*	18	12
U •	Chillicothe YMCA *Unk*	22	8

WARWICK FORD
1897 (.778)   7-2

1897   7-2-0
S25	Cincinnati *Unk*	0	12
U	Marietta *Unk*	0	4
U •	Muskingum *Unk*	32	0
U •	Denison *Unk*	28	0
O30 •	Ohio Medical *Unk*	12	0
U •	Otterbein *Unk*	24	0
U •	Marietta *Unk*	6	4
N5 •	West Virginia *Unk*	12	0
U •	D&D Institute *Unk*	36	6

PETER McLAREN
1898 (.375)   1-2-1

1898   1-2-1
O1 =	Cincinnati *Unk*	12	12
U •	Dayton YMCA *Unk*	11	5
N12	Ohio Medical *Unk*	0	12
N15	West Virginia *Unk*	0	16

FRED SULLIVAN
1899, 1903 (.400)   4-6

1899   2-2-0
U •	Muskingum *Unk*	33	0
U	Ohio Medical *Unk*	0	36
O21	Ohio State *Unk*	0	41
U •	Nelsonville *Unk*	45	0

KARL CORE
1900 (.438)   3-4-1

1900   3-4-1
U •	Nelsonville *Unk*	45	0
U	Parkersburg AC *Unk*	0	5
O6	at Ohio State	0	20
U •	Otterbein *Unk*	12	0
U •	Ohio Wesleyan *Unk*	17	0
U	Wash. & Jeff. *Unk*	0	49
U =	Wittenberg *Unk*	5	5
U	Ohio Wesleyan *Unk*	5	6

ART JONES
1901 (.778)   6-1-2

1901   6-1-2
U •	Ohio Wesleyan *Unk*	6	5
U •	Parkersburg HS *Unk*	35	0
O12	at Ohio State	0	17
U •	Denison *Unk*	12	0
U •	Marietta *Unk*	11	5
U •	Cincinnati *Unk*	16	0
U =	Otterbein *Unk*	0	0
U •	Muskingum *Unk*	17	5
U =	Marietta *Unk*	11	11

HAROLD MONOSMITH
1902 (.083)   0-5-1

1902   0-5-1
U =	at Pittsburgh	0	0
O4	at Ohio State	0	17
U	Parkersburg AC *Unk*	0	31
U	W. Pennsylvania *Unk*	0	34
U	Bethany *Unk*	0	11
U	Marietta *Unk*	0	50

FRED SULLIVAN

1903   2-4-0
U •	Gallipolis *Unk*	28	0
U •	Mercer Bus. Coll. *Unk*	5	0
U	Marietta *Unk*	5	28
U	Wittenberg *Unk*	0	40
U	Otterbein *Unk*	0	22
U	Marietta *Unk*	0	54

HENRY HART
1904 (.357)   2-4-1

1904   2-4-1
U •	Mercer Bus. Coll. *Unk*	34	0
U	Marietta *Unk*	0	31
U	Wittenberg *Unk*	5	10
U	Otterbein *Unk*	0	18
U	Buckhannon *Unk*	0	18
U •	Athens HS *Unk*	12	0
U =	Bethany *Unk*	6	6

JOSEPH RAILSBACK
1905 (.333)   2-5-2

1905   2-5-2
U =	Marietta *Unk*	0	0
O7	at Wash. & Jeff.	0	57
O14	West Virginia *Unk*	0	28
U	Otterbein *Unk*	5	6
U	Ohio Northern *Unk*	0	44
U =	Muskingum *Unk*	0	0
N11	at Marshall	5	6
U •	Marietta *Unk*	6	0
U •	Muskingum *Unk*	32	0

ARTHUR McFARLAND
1906-08 (.563)   13-10-1

1906   7-1-0
U •	Columbus East HS *Unk*	20	0
S29 •	at West Virginia	9	6
U •	Otterbein *Unk*	10	0
U •	Buckhannon *Unk*	65	0
U •	Muskingum *Unk*	16	5
U •	Cincinnati *Unk*	16	5
U •	Denison *Unk*	20	0
U	Marietta *Unk*	2	12

1907   3-4-1
U =	Parkersburg YMCA *Unk*	6	6
S28	at West Virginia	5	35
U •	D&D Inst. *Unk*	47	0
U	Ohio Wesleyan *Unk*	0	6
U •	Parkersburg YMCA *Unk*	10	0
U	Mount Union *Unk*	0	30
U •	Ohio Northern *Unk*	8	0
U	Marietta *Unk*	0	60

1908   3-5-0
O3 •	Marshall	59	0
U	Ohio Northern *Unk*	0	10
O17	Miami, Ohio	0	5
U	Denison *Unk*	0	12
U •	Mount Union *Unk*	14	11
U •	Wittenberg *Unk*	25	5
U •	Otterbein *Unk*	5	6
U	Parkersburg HS *Unk*	0	15

ROBERT WOODS
1909-10 (.233)   2-10-3

1909   2-4-2
U	W.V. Wesleyan *Unk*	0	11
U	Otterbein *Unk*	3	18
O16	at Miami, Ohio	0	45
U =	Ohio Northern *Unk*	0	0
U •	Willmington *Unk*	17	3
U •	Muskingum *Unk*	6	0
U	Ohio Northern *Unk*	0	29
U =	Heidelberg *Unk*	0	0

1910   0-6-1
S24	at Kentucky	0	10
U	Denison *Unk*	0	12
U	Marietta *Unk*	0	12
U	Wilmington *Unk*	0	6
O29	Pittsburgh *Unk*	0	71
U =	Muskingum *Unk*	0	0
U	Otterbein *Unk*	0	12

ARTHUR HINAMAN
1911-12 (.324)   4-10-3

1911   3-3-2
O7	at Ohio Wesleyan	0	10
O14	at West Virginia	0	3
O21 =	Marshall	5	5
O28 =	at Otterbein	11	11
U •	Kenyon *Unk*	16	0
U •	Muskingum *Unk*	50	0
U	Wittenberg *Unk*	0	10
N30 •	at Marietta	6	5

1912   1-7-1
U =	Kenyon *Unk*	7	7
U	Ohio Wesleyan *Unk*	6	8
U	Wittenberg *Unk*	12	27
O26	at West Virginia	0	6
U	Buchtel *Unk*	0	27
N9	Miami, Ohio *Unk*	6	18
U •	Otterbein *Unk*	10	7
U	West Reston *Unk*	7	41
U	Marietta *Unk*	0	27

MARK BANKS
1913-17 (.561)   22-17-2

1913   2-5-1
U •	Wilmington *Unk*	30	0
U	Cincinnati *Unk*	2	20
U =	Muskingum *Unk*	3	3
U	Otterbein *Unk*	0	21
U	Denison *Unk*	0	52
N8	at Miami, Ohio	6	44
U •	Wooster *Unk*	7	6
U	Marietta *Unk*	7	13

1914   4-4-0
U •	Otterbein *Unk*	36	0
O10 •	Miami, Ohio	6	0
U	Denison *Unk*	0	20
U •	Ohio Wesleyan *Unk*	16	7
U •	Marietta *Unk*	19	23
U •	Wooster *Unk*	36	6
U	Mount Union *Unk*	6	28
U	Cincinnati *Unk*	0	15

1915   8-1-0
U •	Transylvania *Unk*	5	0
O2 •	Ohio Northern	16	0
O9 •	at Cincinnati	15	0
U •	Muskingum *Unk*	36	0
U •	Otterbein *Unk*	48	7
U •	Marietta *Unk*	16	6
U •	Wittenberg *Unk*	12	0
N13	Miami, Ohio *Unk*	7	13 *
N20 •	Marshall	18	7

1916   5-2-1
U =	Ohio Wesleyan *Unk*	0	0
O7	at Syracuse	0	73
U •	Otterbein *Unk*	13	7
U •	Kenyon *Unk*	6	0
U •	Wittenberg *Unk*	89	3
U •	Cincinnati *Unk*	33	10
U	Wooster *Unk*	0	9
U •	Oberlin *Unk*	13	7

1917   3-5-0
U	Wooster *Unk*	0	20
U	Ohio Wesleyan *Unk*	0	14
U	Carnegie Tech *Unk*	0	21
U •	Cincinnati *Unk*	22	0
U •	Baldwin Wallace *Unk*	43	0
U •	Kenyon *Unk*	20	0
U	Oberlin *Unk*	0	46
U	Marietta *Unk*	0	6

FRANK GULLUM
1918-19 (.577)   7-5-1

1918   4-0-1
U •	Ohio State JV *Unk*	13	6
N9 =	Cincinnati	6	6
U •	Denison *Unk*	7	0
U •	Camp Sherman *Unk*	62	0
U •	Marietta *Unk*	52	7

1919   3-5-0
U •	Muskingum *Unk*	13	6
U	Akron *Unk*	6	10
U	Heidelberg *Unk*	6	7
U •	Kenyon *Unk*	19	7
U	Ohio Wesleyan *Unk*	0	6
U •	Baldwin Wallace *Unk*	80	0
U	Wittenberg *Unk*	7	33
U	Denison *Unk*	16	32

RUSS FINSTERWALD
1920-22 (.563)   13-10-1

1920   4-3-0
U •	Bethany *Unk*	7	0
O9	at Cincinnati	0	6
O16 •	at Marshall	55	0
U •	Otterbein *Unk*	54	14
U	Denison *Unk*	0	17
U	Heidelberg *Unk*	0	7
U •	Akron *Unk*	39	0

1921   4-4-1
S24	Morris-Harvey	40	0
O1	at Syracuse	0	38
O8	Bethany	0	13
O15	at West Virginia	0	7
O22	at Denison	7	14
O29 •	Baldwin Wallace	35	0
N5	Cincinnati	7	6
N12	at Columbia	23	21
N19 =	Marietta	0	0

1922   5-3-0
U •	Baldwin Wallace *Unk*	28	0
U •	Marietta *Unk*	3	0
N25	at West Virginia	0	28
U	Bethany *Unk*	0	7
U	Xavier *Unk*	7	13
U •	Western Reserve *Unk*	35	0
U •	Denison *Unk*	7	0
U •	Otterbein *Unk*	20	0

---

440 OHIO

F.B. HELDT
1923 (.389) 3-5-1

1923 3-5-1

S29	●	Rio Grande	20	0
O6		at Oberlin	0	6
O13		at Xavier	7	15
O20		Cincinnati	6	13
O26	●	Western Reserve	7	0
N3	●	Kenyon	14	0
N10		at Ohio Wesleyan	0	40
N17	=	at Denison	7	7
N29		Marietta	3	7

DON PEDEN
1924-46 (.711) 121-46-11

1924 4-4-0

S27	●	Rio Grande	10	0
O4		at Wittenberg	0	3
O11		Oberlin	7	13
O24	●	Kenyon	6	0
U		Ohio Northern UNK	7	12
N8	●	at Marietta	21	17
N15		Denison	7	14
N22	●	at Ohio Wesleyan	6	0

1925 6-2-0

O3	●	Rio Grande	19	6
O10	●	at Denison	26	0
O17	●	at Toledo	7	0
O24		Ohio Wesleyan	0	26
O31		at Ohio Northern	0	6
N7	●	Marietta	10	0
N14	●	at Cincinnati	13	2
U	●	Wittenberg UNK	20	0

1926 5-2-1

O2	●	Rio Grande	40	0
O9		Akron	0	3
O16	●	at Denison	6	0
O23	●	Cincinnati	38	7
O30	=	at Ohio Wesleyan	0	0
N6	●	Ohio Northern	9	0
N12	●	at Marietta	12	0
N20		at Wittenberg	6	7

1927 4-2-2

S24	●	Rio Grande	21	0
O1		at Michigan State	0	27
O8	●	Ohio Northern	25	0
O15	●	Marietta	20	0
O22		Wittenberg	0	28
N5	●	at Denison	12	7
N12	=	at Cincinnati	7	7
N18	=	Ohio Wesleyan	0	0

1928 6-3-0

S29	●	Rio Grande	45	7
U	●	West Liberty	14	6
O13		at Wittenberg	12	13 *
O20	●	Cincinnati	65	0
O27	●	at Ohio Northern	39	0
N3		at Miami, Ohio	13	20
N10	●	Marietta	40	0
N17		at Ohio Wesleyan	0	7
N24	●	Denison	27	13

1929 9-0-0

S28	●	at Indiana	18	0
O5	●	West Liberty	26	0
O12	●	Ohio Wesleyan	21	7
O19	●	at Muskingum	59	0
O26	●	at Cincinnati	35	0
N2	●	Miami, Ohio	14	0
N9	●	at Denison	54	0
N16	●	at Marietta	45	0
N22	●	Wittenberg	33	0

1930 8-0-1

S27	●	Wilmington	27	0
O3	●	at Butler	12	7
O11	=	West Liberty	13	13
O18	●	at Western Reserve	47	0
O25	●	at Miami, Ohio	27	6
N1	●	at Cincinnati	48	0
N8	●	Denison	36	0
N15	●	Dayton	10	6
N22	●	at Ohio Wesleyan	7	0

1931 7-1-0

S26		at Indiana	6	7
O3	●	Butler	40	0
O10	●	at Denison	33	0
O17	●	Simpson	22	0
O24	●	at Cincinnati	13	7
O31	●	Ohio Wesleyan	18	0
N7	●	at DePauw	27	0
N14	●	Miami, Ohio	13	0

1932 7-2-0

S24	●	Rio Grande	19	0
O1		at Indiana	6	7
O8	●	Franklin	39	0
O15	●	at Navy	14	0
O22		at Miami, Ohio	0	16
O28	●	Georgetown	27	0
N5	●	Wittenberg	19	6
N12	●	Cincinnati	23	0
N19	●	at Ohio Wesleyan	25	0

1933 6-2-1

S30	●	Morris-Harvey	61	0
O7		at Purdue	6	13
O14	●	Franklin	78	0
O21	●	Miami, Ohio	6	0
O28	●	Transylvania	68	0
N4	●	at Wittenberg	39	0
N11	=	at Marshall	0	0
N18		at Cincinnati	0	2
N25	●	Ohio Wesleyan	19	13

1934 4-4-1

S22	●	Rio Grande	53	0
S29		at Indiana	0	27
O13	●	Georgetown	36	6
O20		at Miami, Ohio	0	7
O27	●	Marshall	8	0
N3		at West Virginia	2	7
N10	=	Cincinnati	0	0
N17	●	at Dayton	17	0
N24		at Ohio Wesleyan	0	20

1935 8-0-0

S28	●	at Illinois	6	0
O11	●	at John Carroll	49	0
O19	●	Marshall	20	13
O26	●	Dayton	26	0
N2	●	Miami, Ohio	20	0
N9	●	Muskingum	20	17
N16	●	Cincinnati	16	6
N23	●	Ohio Wesleyan	13	0

1936 5-2-1

S26		at Purdue	0	47
O10	=	Marshall	13	13
O17	●	Kent State	6	0
O24		at Miami, Ohio	0	3
O31	●	Cincinnati	10	7
U	●	Muskingum	32	0
N14	●	Ohio Wesleyan	20	0
N21	●	John Carroll	21	0

1937 5-3-1

S18	●	Rio Grande	80	0
S25		at Illinois	6	20
O9		at Western Reserve	0	7
O16	●	Miami, Ohio	19	0
O23		Dayton	0	6
O30	=	at Marshall	13	13
N6	●	at Cincinnati	17	0
N13	●	at Rutgers	13	0
N20	●	Ohio Wesleyan	20	6

1938 7-2-0

S24	●	at Illinois	6	0
O1	●	at Xavier	14	12
O8		at Western Reserve	14	26
O15	●	at Ohio Wesleyan	28	0
O22	●	Wayne St.	52	7
O29	●	Cincinnati	13	12
N5	●	Miami, Ohio	20	12
N12		at Dayton	0	13
N19	●	Marshall	14	7

1939 6-3-0

S23		Western Kentucky	7	14
S30		at Butler	7	12
O7	●	Western Reserve	14	12
O14		Ohio Wesleyan	7	12
O21	●	at Xavier	20	6
O28	●	Dayton	14	0
N4	●	at Morris-Harvey	14	13
N11	●	Miami, Ohio	20	7
N18	●	at Western Michigan	13	6

1940 5-2-2

S28	●	Youngstown St.	13	0
O5	=	Butler	7	7
O12	●	Western Michigan	20	7
O19	●	Furman	15	6
O26	=	at Ohio Wesleyan	0	0
N2	●	at Miami, Ohio	27	0
N9		at Western Reserve	0	6
N16	●	at Dayton	7	0
N21		at Xavier	0	6

1941 5-2-1

S26		at Youngstown St.	0	14
O4		Western Reserve	0	7
O11	●	Western Kentucky	20	7
O18	=	at Akron	0	0
O25	●	at Butler	20	7
N1	●	Miami, Ohio	26	0
N8	●	Ohio Wesleyan	21	0
N20	●	at Dayton	21	7

1942 5-3-0

O3	●	Akron	39	0
O10	●	Butler	6	0
O17		at Cincinnati	7	26
O24	●	Ohio Wesleyan	26	14
O31	●	at Miami, Ohio	39	13
N7		at Western Reserve	7	20
N14	●	Xavier	20	14
N26		at Dayton	0	20

1943-44

NO TEAM

1945 3-4-0

S29		Bowling Green	0	6
O6		Western Michigan	20	21
O13	●	Cincinnati	20	19
N20		at Miami, Ohio	0	34
U		Murray St.	13	19
U	●	Baldwin Wallace	33	7
N17	●	at West Virginia	14	0

1946 6-3-0

S28	●	Murray St.	27	7
O5	●	at Western Michigan	25	7
O12	●	Muskingum	38	0
O19		at Cincinnati	0	19
O26		Miami, Ohio	14	23
N2	●	at Ohio Wesleyan	49	7
N9	●	Baldwin Wallace	21	14
N16		Dayton	7	14
N23	●	at Xavier	25	6

1947-PRESENT
MAC

HAROLD WISE
1947-48 (.361) 6-11-1

1947 3-5-1 (1-3-0)

S27	●	Ohio Northern	34	0
O4	● |	Butler	14	7
O11	|	at Western Reserve	7	20
O18		at Bowling Green	0	2
O25	|	at Miami, Ohio	0	21
N1	|	Cincinnati	0	34
N8	=	Ohio Wesleyan	7	7
N15		at Dayton	6	18
N22	●	Xavier	12	7

1948 3-6-0 (2-3-0)

S25		Bowling Green	7	13
O2		at Wash. & Lee	0	13
O9	|	at Cincinnati	13	18
O16	● |	at Western Reserve	37	7
O23	|	Miami, Ohio	0	21
O30	|	Duquesne	14	13
N6		at West Virginia	6	48
N13	● |	at Butler	14	6
N20	|	Western Michigan	7	40

CARROLL WIDDOES
1949-57 (.536) 42-36-5

1949 4-4-1 (2-2-1)

S24	●	West Virginia	17	7
O1	● |	at Western Michigan	16	6
O7	●	at Kent State	34	6
O15	= |	at Western Reserve	7	7
O22	|	at Miami, Ohio	0	26
O29		at Marshall	6	14
N5	|	Cincinnati	13	34
N12	● |	Butler	14	0
N19		Buffalo	7	20

1950 6-4-0 (2-2-0)

S23	●	at Akron	28	6
S30		at Illinois	2	28
O7	●	at Butler	21	14
O14	● |	Western Reserve	35	0
O21		at Kent State	13	35
O28	|	at Miami, Ohio	20	28
N4	|	at Cincinnati	0	23
N11	●	at Buffalo	22	14
N18	● |	Western Michigan	10	7
N23	●	Marshall	14	6

1951 5-4-1 (2-2-0)

S22	●	at Morris-Harvey	26	0
S29	●	Akron	40	7
O6	● |	at Western Michigan	13	0
O13	●	Bowling Green	28	7
O20	|	at Miami, Ohio	0	7
O27	● |	Kent State	28	27
N3		at Toledo	6	13
N10	|	Cincinnati	0	40
N17		Eastern Kentucky	13	27
N22	=	at Marshall	13	13

1952 6-2-1 (5-2-0)

S25	●	at Morris-Harvey	20	6
O4	● |	Toledo	22	20
O11	● |	at Western Reserve	22	7
O18	● |	at Kent State	27	18
O25	|	Miami, Ohio	0	20
N1	● |	Western Michigan	28	13
N8	|	at Cincinnati	7	41
N15	● |	at Bowling Green	33	14
N22	=	Marshall	21	21

1953 6-2-1 (5-0-1)

S19	● |	at Toledo	26	0
O3		at Harvard	0	16
O10	● |	Western Reserve	39	0
O17	● |	Kent State	40	21
O24	= |	at Miami, Ohio	7	7
O31	● |	at Western Michigan	67	12
N7	●	Morris-Harvey	38	7
N14	● |	Bowling Green	22	14
N21		at Marshall	6	9

1954 6-3-0 (5-2-0)

S25	●	Xavier	12	0
O2	● |	Toledo	28	20
O9	● |	at Western Reserve	37	0
O16	● |	at Kent State	14	7
O23	|	Miami, Ohio	13	46
O30		at Harvard	13	27
N6	|	at Western Michigan	6	19
N13	● |	at Bowling Green	26	14
N20	● |	Marshall	26	25

1955 5-4-0 (3-3-0)

S15	●	at Youngstown St.	6	0
S24	● |	Marshall	13	6
O1	● |	at Toledo	34	13 *
O15	|	Kent State	14	20
O22	|	at Miami, Ohio	7	34
O29		at Indiana	14	21
N5	● |	Western Michigan	40	14
N12	|	Bowling Green	0	13
N19	●	Morris-Harvey	32	13

1956 2-7-0 (2-4-0)

S22		at Florida State	7	47
S29	|	Toledo	13	19
O6		at Xavier	7	31
O13	|	at Kent State	13	32
O20	|	Miami, Ohio	7	16
O27		Louisville	19	25
N3	● |	at Western Michigan	27	0
N10	|	at Bowling Green	27	41
N17	● |	Marshall	16	0

1957 2-6-1 (1-4-1)

S21	●	at Indiana, Pa.	50	0
S28	|	at Toledo	6	14
O5	|	Kent State	9	14
O12		at Harvard	7	14
O19	|	at Miami, Ohio	0	26
O26	|	at Marshall	28	34
N2	● |	Western Michigan	20	7
N9	= |	Bowling Green	7	7
N16		at Louisville	7	40

BILL HESS
1958-77 (.537) 107-92-4

1958 5-4-0 (2-4-0)

S20	●	Youngstown St.	38	0
S27	● |	Toledo	13	6
O4	|	at Kent State	6	14
O11	●	at Dayton	27	8
O18	|	Miami, Ohio	10	14
O25	● |	Marshall	22	0
N1	|	at Western Michigan	14	21
N8	|	at Bowling Green	6	33
N15	●	Louisville	23	6

1959 7-2-0 (4-2-0)

S26	● |	at Toledo	36	7
O3	● |	Kent State	46	0
O10	●	Xavier	25	7
O17	●	at Youngstown St.	44	12
O24	|	Miami, Ohio	0	24
O31	● |	Western Michigan	12	9
N7	● |	Marshall	21	14
N14	●	at Louisville	22	15
N21	|	Bowling Green	9	13

MAC TEAMS

OHIO 441

1960 10-0-0 (6-0-0)

S17	●		at Dayton	28	0
S24	●	|	Toledo	48	7
O1	●	|	at Kent State	25	8
O8	●		at Boston U.	36	6
O15	●		at Xavier	6	0
O22	●	|	Miami, Ohio	21	0
O29	●	|	at Western Michigan	24	0
N5	●	|	Marshall	19	0
N12	●	|	at Bowling Green	14	7
N19	●		So. Illinois	48	6

1961 5-3-1 (3-2-1)

S23	●	|	at Toledo	10	6
S30		|	Kent State	17	23
O7	●		at Dayton	14	13
O14			Xavier	3	6
O21	●	|	at Miami, Ohio	28	18
O28	●		at Delaware	17	16
N4	●	|	at Marshall	14	7
N11		|	Bowling Green	6	7
N18	=	|	Western Michigan	20	20

1962 8-3-0 (5-1-0)

S22	●	|	Toledo	31	0
S29	●	|	at Kent State	21	0
O6	●		Dayton	27	25
O13	●		Xavier	20	6
O20	●	|	Miami, Ohio	12	6
O27	●		at Buffalo	41	6
N3	●	|	Marshall	35	0
N10		|	at Bowling Green	6	7
N17	●	|	at Western Michigan	32	16
N24			at Iowa State	22	31
			SUN BOWL		
D31			West Texas St.	14	15

1963 6-4-0 (5-1-0)

S21			Buffalo	0	7
S28	●		at Dayton	13	6
O5	●	|	Kent State	20	0
O12		|	at Toledo	17	18
O19			Delaware	12	29
O26	●	|	at Miami, Ohio	13	10
N2			at Xavier	0	20
N9	●	|	Western Michigan	27	13
N16	●	|	Bowling Green	16	0
N23	●	|	at Marshall	17	0

1964 5-4-1 (3-2-1)

S19	●		at West Texas St.	16	14
S26			at Purdue	0	17
O3	=	|	at Kent State	3	3
O10	●	|	Toledo	21	12
O17			Xavier	19	23
O24	●	|	Miami, Ohio	10	7
O31	●		Dayton	24	0
N7		|	at Western Michigan	8	13
N14	●	|	at Bowling Green	21	0
N21		|	Marshall	0	10

1965 0-10-0 (0-6-0)

S18			at West Texas St.	0	7
S25			at Maryland	7	24
O2		|	Kent State	10	27
O9		|	at Toledo	7	21
O16			Xavier	19	21
O23		|	at Miami, Ohio	0	34
O30			at Dayton	7	13
N6		|	Western Michigan	6	17
N13		|	at Bowling Green	7	17
N20		|	at Marshall	14	29

1966 5-5-0 (3-3-0)

S17			at Purdue	3	42
S24	●		at Boston College	23	14
O1	●	|	at Kent State	12	10
O8	●	|	Toledo	21	6
O15	●		Xavier	24	10
O22		|	Miami, Ohio	13	33
O29			Dayton	12	20
N5		|	at Western Michigan	13	20
N12		|	at Bowling Green	0	28
N19	●	|	Marshall	28	6

1967 5-5-0 (4-2-0)

S16	●	|	at Toledo	20	14
S23	●	|	at Marshall	48	14
S30		|	at Kent State	14	21 †
O7	●		at Kansas	30	15
O14			William & Mary	22	25
O21		|	at Miami, Ohio	15	22
O28			at Dayton	9	10
N4	●	|	Western Michigan	20	10
N11	●	|	Bowling Green	31	7
N18			at Penn State	14	35

1968 10-1-0 (6-0-0)

S21	●	|	at Marshall	48	8
S28	●	|	at Kent State	31	7
O5	●	|	Toledo	40	31
O12	●		at William & Mary	41	0
O19	●	|	Miami, Ohio	24	7
O26	●		Dayton	42	12
N2	●	|	at Western Michigan	34	27
N9	●	|	at Bowling Green	28	27
N16	●		at Cincinnati	60	48
N23	●		Northern Illinois	28	12
			TANGERINE BOWL		
D27			Richmond	42	49

1969 5-4-1 (2-3-0)

S20	●	|	Kent State	35	0
S27	=		at Minnesota	35	35
O4		|	at Toledo	9	34
O11	●		Xavier	31	6
O18		|	Miami, Ohio	21	24
O25			at Penn State	3	42
N1	●	|	Western Michigan	22	17
N8		|	Bowling Green	16	23
N15	●		Cincinnati	46	6
N22	●		at Marshall	38	35

1970 4-5-0 (3-2-0)

S19	●	|	at Kent State	24	14
S26			at Minnesota	7	49
O3		|	Toledo	7	42
O10	●		Dayton	17	14
O17	●	|	Miami, Ohio	23	22
O24			at Cincinnati	21	29
O31		|	at Western Michigan-	23	52
N7	●	|	at Bowling Green	34	7
N14			at Penn State	22	32

1971 5-5-0 (2-3-0)

S18		|	Bowling Green	19	20
S25	●	|	Kent State	37	21
O2		|	at Toledo	28	31
O9	●		at Kentucky	35	6
O16	●	|	at Miami, Ohio	3	0
O23			at Virginia Tech	29	37
O30		|	Western Michigan	14	28
N6	●		at Tulane	30	7
N13			Cincinnati	15	23
N20	●		at Marshall	30	0

1972 3-8-0 (1-4-0)

S9	●		Central Michigan	26	21
S16			at Idaho	14	17
S23		|	at Kent State	14	37
S30	●	|	Toledo	38	22
O7	●		at Cincinnati	28	14
O14		|	at Miami, Ohio	7	31
O21			Virginia Tech	21	53
O28		|	at Western Michigan	17	34
N4		|	at Bowling Green	0	17
N11			at Tulane	6	44
N18			Marshall	14	31

1973 5-5-0 (2-3-0)

S22		|	Kent State	7	35
S29		|	at Toledo	8	35
O6	●		at Northwestern	14	12
O13		|	at Miami, Ohio	6	10
O20			at South Carolina	22	38
O27	●	|	Western Michigan	16	0
N3	●	|	Bowling Green	24	23
N10	●		Cincinnati	14	8
N17			at Penn State	10	49
N22	●		at Marshall	35	21

1974 6-5-0 (3-2-0)

S14			at North Carolina	7	42
S21	●	|	at Kent State	20	0
S28		|	Toledo	16	19
O5	●		Northern Illinois	31	14
O12		|	Miami, Ohio	3	31
O19	●		Morehead St.	49	10
O26	●	|	at Western Michigan	26	3
N2	●	|	at Bowling Green	33	22
N9			at Cincinnati	13	35
N16			at Penn State	16	35
N23	●		Marshall	35	0

1975 5-5-1 (3-3-1)

S13	=	|	at Central Michigan	6	6
S20	●	|	Ball State	10	0
S27	●	|	Kent State	23	21
O4			at Minnesota	0	21
O11	●		at William & Mary	22	8
O18		|	at Miami, Ohio	9	17
O25		|	at Toledo	10	14
N1	●	|	Western Michigan	24	10
N8		|	Bowling Green	17	19
N15			Cincinnati	5	6
N22	●		at Marshall	38	21

1976 7-4-0 (6-2-0)

S4	●	|	at Eastern Michigan	23	7
S18	●	|	at Kent State	14	12
S25	●		Idaho	35	0
O2	●	|	Toledo	34	8
O9		|	at Central Michigan	15	17
O16	●	|	Miami, Ohio	28	14
O23			William & Mary	0	20
O30		|	at Western Michigan	10	21
N6	●	|	at Bowling Green	31	26
N13			at Cincinnati	0	35
N20	●	|	Northern Illinois	63	15

1977 1-10-0 (0-8-0)

S10	●		at Marshall	49	27
S17			at Purdue	7	44
S24		|	Central Michigan	14	31
O1		|	Kent State	23	44
O8		|	at Eastern Michigan	14	31
O15		|	at Miami, Ohio	24	28
O22		|	at Toledo	29	31
O29		|	Western Michigan	22	28
N5			Cincinnati	26	38
N12		|	Bowling Green	27	39
N19		|	at Northern Illinois	6	20

BOB KAPPES
1978 (.273) 3-8

1978 3-8-0 (3-5-0)

S9	●	|	Eastern Michigan	23	22
S23			at Purdue	0	24
S30		|	at Kent State	14	20
O7		|	Central Michigan	3	17
O14			at South Carolina	7	24
O21		|	Toledo	14	28
O28	●	|	at Western Michigan	10	7
N4		|	Miami, Ohio	16	31
N11			at Cincinnati	0	35
N18	●	|	at Bowling Green	19	15
N25		|	Northern Illinois	14	23

BRIAN BURKE
1979-84 (.477) 31-34-1

1979 6-5-0 (4-4-0)

S8			at Minnesota	10	24
S15	●	|	Eastern Michigan	20	7
S22	●		Marshall	35	0
S29	●	|	Kent State	43	13
O6		|	at Central Michigan	0	26
O13	●	|	at Miami, Ohio	9	7
O20		|	at Toledo	13	21
O27		|	Western MIchigan	6	20
N10	●		at Cincinnati	27	7
N17	●	|	Bowling Green	48	21
N24		|	at Northern Illinois	27	28

1980 6-5-0 (5-4-0)

S13			at Minnesota	14	38
S20	●	|	Eastern Michigan	34	6
S27		|	Northern Illinois	21	22
O4		|	at Kent State	14	15
O11	●	|	Central Michigan	24	9
O18	●	|	Miami, Ohio	17	7
O25	●	|	Toledo	24	9
N1		|	at Western Michigan	7	13
N8	●		Marshall	28	20
N15		|	at Ball State	18	37
N22	●	|	at Bowling Green	21	20

1981 5-6-0 (5-4-0)

S12			at Minnesota	17	19
S19	●	|	Bowling Green	23	21
S26	●	|	Ball State	30	27
O3		|	at Toledo	14	21
O10			Cincinnati	9	19
O17	●	|	Eastern Michigan	29	7
O24		|	at Miami, Ohio	14	40
O31		|	Central Michigan	21	38
N7		|	at Northern Illinois	14	38
N14	●	|	Western Michigan	37	20
N21	●	|	at Kent State	20	7

1982 6-5-0 (5-4-0)

S4		|	at Bowling Green	0	40
S11			at Minnesota	3	57
S18	●		Richmond *CoLO*	23	14
O2	●	|	Toledo	17	14
O9	●	|	at Ball State	34	7
O16	●	|	at Eastern Michigan	14	13
O23	●	|	Miami, Ohio	20	0
O30		|	at Central Michigan	18	42
N6		|	Northern Illinois	0	36
N13		|	at Western Michigan	7	16
N20	●	|	Kent State	24	20

1983 4-7-0 (3-6-0)

S3			at West Virginia	3	55
S10	●		at Richmond	17	10
S17		|	Ball State	14	31
S24	●	|	Eastern Michigan	31	14
O1		|	at Toledo	0	31
O15		|	Central Michigan	9	14
O22	●	|	at Kent State	21	20
O29		|	Western Michigan	14	16
N5	●	|	at Miami, Ohio	17	14
N12		|	Bowling Green	20	24
N19		|	at Northern Illinois	17	41

1984 4-6-1 (4-4-1)

S1			at West Virginia	0	38
S8			at North Carolina St.	6	43
S15	●	|	at Ball State	31	17
S22	●	|	at Eastern Michigan	16	13
S29	=	|	Toledo	16	16
O13		|	at Central Michigan	3	35
O20		|	Kent State	7	19
O27		|	at Western Michigan	14	33
N3	●	|	Miami, Ohio	24	19
N10		|	at Bowling Green	7	28
N17	●	|	Northern Illinois	10	3

CLEVE BRYANT
1985-89 (.182) 9-44-2

1985 2-9-0 (2-7-0)

S14			at Marshall	7	31
S21			at Duke	13	34
S28		|	Central Michigan	7	13
O5		|	at Miami, Ohio	22	29
O12		|	Ball State	23	36
O19		|	Eastern Michigan	21	27
O26		|	at Toledo	10	24
N2	●	|	at Kent State	33	23
N9	●	|	Western Michigan	21	15
N16		|	at Northern Illinois	7	35
N23		|	Bowling Green	17	38

1986 1-10-0 (0-8-0)

S6		|	at Bowling Green	16	21
S13			Marshall	7	21
S20			at Duke	7	22
S27		|	at Central Michigan	27	56
O4		|	Miami, Ohio	14	34
O11		|	at Ball State	9	30
O18		|	at Eastern Michigan	31	33
O25		|	Toledo	21	24
N1		|	Kent State	13	17
N8		|	at Western Michigan	17	45
N15	●		Northern Illinois	34	26

1987 1-10-0 (0-8-0)

S5			at West Virginia	3	23
S12	●		Marshall	23	15
S19		|	at Toledo	12	17
O3			at Kentucky	0	28
O10		|	Bowling Green	7	28
O17		|	at Miami, Ohio	9	10
O24		|	Kent State	10	24
O31		|	at Eastern Michigan	16	34
N7		|	Central Michigan	17	31
N14		|	at Ball State	17	30
N21		|	Western Michigan	13	31

1988 4-6-1 (4-3-1)

S10			at Marshall	14	31
S17			at Purdue	10	33
S24			at Nevada-Las Vegas	18	26
O1	●	|	Toledo	24	14
O8		|	at Bowling Green	0	42
O15	●	|	Miami, Ohio	38	21
O22	●	|	at Kent State	21	14
O29	=	|	Eastern Michigan	17	17
N5		|	at Central Michigan	10	42
N12	●	|	Ball State	27	25
N19		|	at Western Michigan	16	23

1989 1-9-1 (1-6-1)

S2		|	at Toledo	18	27
S9			at Iowa State	3	28
S16		|	Eastern Michigan	25	30
S23			at Vanderbilt	10	54
S30			at LSU	6	57
O7		|	Bowling Green	28	31
O14	=	|	at Miami, Ohio	22	22
O21	●	|	Kent State	37	14
O28		|	at Western Michigan	13	28
N11		|	at Central Michigan	15	24
N18		|	Ball State	14	33

MAC TEAMS

TOM LICHTENBERG
1990-94 (.164)   8-45-2

1990   1-9-1 (0-7-1)
S1	at Pittsburgh	3	35
S15	at Eastern Michigan	18	21
S22 ●	Tennessee Tech	42	32
S29	Toledo	20	27
O6 =	at Bowling Green	10	10
O13	Miami, Ohio	18	40
O20	at Kent State	15	44
O27	Western Michigan	23	31
N3	at Youngstown St.	0	27
N10	Central Michigan	7	52
N17	at Ball State	6	23

1991   2-8-1 (1-6-1)
A31 =	Central Michigan	17	17
S14 ●	Tenn. Tech	35	14
S21	at Mississippi	14	38
S28	at Western Michigan	9	35
O5	at Toledo	13	17
O12	Bowling Green	14	45
O19	at Miami, Ohio	0	34
O26 ●	Kent State	45	40
N2	at Ball State	6	10
N9	Eastern Michigan	10	13
N23	at Tulsa	13	45

1992   1-10-0 (1-7-0)
S5	at Iowa State	9	35
S12 ●	at Kent State	27	14
S19	at Central Michigan	0	24
S26	Western Michigan	3	19
O3	Akron	0	13
O10	at Bowling Green	14	31
O17	Miami, Ohio	21	23
O24	at Eastern Michigan	6	7
O31	Ball State	21	24
N7	Youngstown St.	20	28
N14	at Colorado State	24	35

1993   4-7-0 (4-5-0)
S4	at North Carolina	3	44
S11	at Central Michigan	0	38
S18	Ball State	16	24
S25	at Toledo	10	28
O2	at Virginia	7	41
O9	Bowling Green	0	20
O16 ●	Kent State	15	10
O23 ●	at Miami, Ohio	22	20
O30 ●	Akron	21	13
N6	Western Michigan	28	34
N13 ●	at Eastern Michigan	12	10

1994   0-11-0 (0-9-0)
S10	at Pittsburgh	16	30
S17	Utah State	0	5
S24	at Ball State	14	21
O1	Toledo	6	31
O8	at Bowling Green	0	32
O15	Miami, Ohio	10	31
O22	at Kent State	0	24
O29	Central Michigan	10	22
N5	at Western Michigan	3	15
N12	Eastern Michigan	13	24
N19	at Akron	10	24

JIM GROBE
1995-2000 (.500)   33-33-1

1995   2-8-1 (1-6-1)
A31	at Iowa State	21	36
S9 ●	Illinois St.	14	6
S16 =	Kent State	28	28
S23	at Eastern Michigan	20	31
S30	at North Carolina	0	62
O14	Western Michigan	17	34
O21 ●	at Akron	29	23
O28	Ball State	3	6
N4	at Bowling Green	7	33
N11	Miami, Ohio	2	30
N18	at Toledo	20	31

1996   6-6 (5-3)
A29 ●	Akron	44	14
S7 ●	at Hawaii	21	10
S14	at Army	20	37
S21	at Northwestern	7	28
O5 ●	Eastern Michigan	7	0
O12	at Ball State	27	30
O19 ●	at Kent State	24	15
O26 ●	Bowling Green	38	0
N2 ●	at Western Michigan	38	0
N9	at Miami, Ohio	8	24
N16	at East Carolina	45	55
N23	Toledo	23	24

1997   8-3 (6-2)
A28 ●	Kent State	31	7
S6 ●	at Maryland	21	14
S13	at Kansas State	20	23
S20 ●	Buffalo	50	0
S27 ●	Western Michigan	31	7
O4 ●	at Eastern Michigan	47	7
O18 ●	Bowling Green	24	0
O25	at Akron	21	17
N1 ●	at Northern Illinois	35	30
N8 ●	Miami, Ohio	21	45
N15	at Marshall	0	27

1998   5-6 (5-3)
S3	at North Carolina St.	31	34
S12	at Wisconsin	0	45
S19	East Carolina	14	21
S26 ●	at Western Michigan	37	35
O3	at Bowling Green	7	35
O10	Marshall	23	30
O17 ●	Akron	28	14
O31	at Miami, Ohio	21	35
N7 ●	Eastern Michigan	49	21
N14 ●	Northern Illinois	28	12
N21 ●	at Kent State	31	21

1999   5-6 (5-3)
S4	at Minnesota	7	33
S11	No. Iowa	21	36
S18	at Ohio State	16	40
S25	Buffalo	45	6
O2 ●	Kent State	31	3
O9	at Akron	28	41
O16	at Eastern Michigan	26	27
O23 ●	Bowling Green	17	14
O30 ●	at Ball State	37	25
N13 ●	Miami, Ohio	40	28
N26	at Marshall	3	34

2000   7-4 (5-3)
S2	at Iowa State	15	25
S9 ●	at Minnesota	23	17
S16	Tenn. Tech	52	14
S23	Akron	20	23
S30	at Western Michigan	10	23
O7 ●	Buffalo	42	20
O14 ●	at Kent State	44	7
O21 ●	Central Michigan	52	3
N4	at Miami, Ohio	24	27
N11 ●	at Bowling Green	23	21
N18 ●	Marshall	38	28

BRIAN KNORR
2001-04 (.239)   11-35

2001   1-10 (1-7)
A30	at Akron	29	31
S8	at West Virginia	3	20
S22	Iowa State	28	31
O6	Toledo	41	48
O13 ●	at Central Michigan	34	3
O20	Miami, Ohio	24	36
O27	Kent State	14	24
N3	at Buffalo	0	44
N10	Bowling Green	0	17
N17	at Marshall	18	42
N24	at North Carolina St.	20	27

2002   4-8 (4-4)
A31	at Pittsburgh	14	27
S7	Northeastern	0	31
S14	at Florida	6	34
S21	at Connecticut	19	37
S28 ●	Buffalo	34	32
O5	at Bowling Green	21	72
O12 ●	Eastern Michigan	55	27
O19 ●	at Kent State	50	0
N2	at Miami, Ohio	20	38
N9 ●	Akron	27	10
N23	Marshall	21	24
N30	at Central Florida	32	42

2003   2-10 (1-7)
A28	S.E. Missouri St.	17	3
S6	at Iowa State	20	48
S13	Minnesota	20	42
S27	Western Michigan	32	39
O4	at Northern Illinois	23	30
O11 ●	Central Florida	28	0
O18	at Kentucky	14	35
O25	at Buffalo	17	26
N8	Kent State	33	37
N15	at Akron	28	35
N22	Miami, Ohio	31	49
N28	at Marshall	0	28

2004   4-7 (2-6)
S4 ●	VMI	42	14
S11	at Pittsburgh	3	24
S18	at Miami, Ohio	20	40
S25 ●	Buffalo	34	0
O2 ●	at Kentucky	28	16
O9	Marshall	13	16
O16	at Toledo	13	31
O23	Bowling Green	16	41
O30	at Kent State	16	42
N6 ●	at Central Florida	17	16
N13	Akron	19	31

FRANK SOLICH
2005-Present (.520)   13-12

2005   4-7 (3-5)
S3	at Northwestern	14	38
S9 ●	Pittsburgh	16	10
S17	at Virginia Tech	0	45
S24 ●	Kent State	35	32
O8	at Bowling Green	14	38
O15	at Central Michigan	10	37
O22 ●	Ball State	38	21
O29 ●	at Buffalo	34	20
N4	Toledo	21	30
N15	at Akron	3	27
N21	Miami, Ohio	7	38

2006   9-5 (7-1)
S2 ●	Tenn-Martin	29	3
S9 ●	at Northern Illinois	35	23
S16	at Rutgers	7	24
S23	at Missouri	6	31
S30	Bowling Green	9	21
O7 ●	Western Michigan	27	20
O14	at Illinois	20	17
O21 ●	Buffalo	42	7
O28 ●	at Kent State	17	7
N4 ●	at Eastern Michigan	16	10
N16 ●	Akron	17	7
N24 ●	at Miami, Ohio	34	24

MAC CHAMPIONSHIP GAME
N30	Central Michigan_Det_	10	31

GMAC BOWL
J7	Southern Miss	7	28

Neutral Site key: _CoLO_ Columbus, OH / _Det_ Detroit, MI / _Unk_ Unknown
_f_ Forfeit † Game Later Forfieted # Disputed Victor * Disputed Score || Designated Conference Game |2 Counted Twice in Conference Standings

OHIO RECORD BOOK

SINGLE-GAME RECORDS

RUSHING YARDS

RANK	PLAYER	DATE	OPPONENT	ATT	AVG	YDS
1	Kareem Wilson	Oct. 26, 1996	Bowling Green	NA	NA	282
2	Dick Conley	Nov. 19, 1966	Marshall	36	7.6	275
3	Kalvin McRae	Oct. 22, 2005	Ball State	NA	NA	264
4	Arnold Welcher	Nov. 22, 1975	Marshall	NA	NA	257
5	Tim Worner	Sept. 30, 1972	Toledo	38	6.6	252

PASSING YARDS

RANK	PLAYER	DATE	OPPONENT	ATT	COMP	YDS
1	Donny Harrison	Oct. 15, 1983	Kent State	45	20	409
2	Andy Vetter	Oct. 1, 1977	Kent State	43	28	394
3	Donny Harrison	Nov. 5, 1983	Bowling Green	64	32	380
4	Dennis Swearingen	Oct. 12, 1985	Ball State	58	31	355

RECEIVING YARDS

RANK	PLAYER	DATE	OPPONENT	REC	AVG	YDS
1	Todd Snyder	Dec. 28, 1968	Richmond	11	19.5	214
2	Todd Snyder	Oct. 26, 1968	Dayton	11	18.5	203
3	Tom Compernolle	Nov. 15, 1986	Northern Illinois	11	16.0	176

POINTS

RANK	PLAYER	DATE	OPPONENT	TOT
1	Eller Armbrust	Sept. 18, 1937	Rio Grande	33
2	6 players tied at 24			

FIELD GOALS

RANK	PLAYER	DATE	OPPONENT	TOT
1	16 players tied at 3			

TACKLES

RANK	PLAYER	DATE	OPPONENT	TOT
1	Benny King	Sept. 18, 1993	Ball State	23
2	Benny King	Oct. 30, 1993	Akron	22
3	Jabaar Thompson	Sept. 17, 1994	Utah State	21
4	Jabaar Thompson	Oct. 30, 1993	Akron	20
5	2 players tied at 19			

INTERCEPTIONS

RANK	PLAYER	DATE	OPPONENT	TOT
1	9 players tied at 3			

RETIRED NUMBERS

Ohio has no retired numbers

SINGLE-SEASON RECORDS

RUSHING YARDS

RANK	PLAYER	SEASON	ATT	YDS
1	Steveland Hookfin	1998	273	1,315
2	Kalvim McRae	2006	258	1,252
3	Arnold Welcher	1975	236	1,175
4	Kalvin McRae	2005	209	1,153
5	Steveland Hookfin	1996	192	1,125

PASSING YARDS

RANK	PLAYER	SEASON	ATT	COMP	PCT	YDS
1	Sammy Shon	1981	320	175	54.7	2,366
2	Donny Harrison	1983	357	203	56.9	2,309
3	Bruce Porter	1986	383	216	56.4	2,281
4	Dennis Swearingen	1985	383	195	50.9	2,056
5	Tom Dubs	1991	264	144	54.5	1,855

RECEIVING YARDS

RANK	PLAYER	SEASON	REC	AVG	YDS
1	Eddie Washington	1983	68	12.7	866
2	Richard Hill	1991	49	17.6	863
3	Todd Snyder	1969	62	13.5	835
4	Todd Snyder	1968	46	16.9	777
5	Bob Allen	1970	48	14.6	699

SCORING

RANK	PLAYER	SEASON	TD	FG	PAT	P2	TOT
1	Bob Houmard	1968	19	0	0	0	114
2	Kalvin McRae	2006	16	0	0	1	98
3	Kareem Wilson	1996	14	0	0	2	88
4	Kareem Wilson	1998	13	0	0	0	78
	Andy Vetter	1976	13	0	0	0	78

TOUCHDOWNS

RANK	PLAYER	SEASON	TOT
1	Bob Houmard	1968	19
2	Kareem Wilson	1996	14
3	Kareem Wilson	1998	13
	Andy Vetter	1976	13
5	3 players tied at 12		

TACKLES

RANK	PLAYER	SEASON	TOT
1	David Terry	1988	177
2	Mike Mangen	1983	171
3	Jack LeVeck	1971	169
4	3 players tied at 159		

INTERCEPTIONS

RANK	PLAYER	SEASON	YDS	TOT
1	Joe Callan	1979	110	9
2	Tevell Jones	1997	NA	7
	John Dickason	1960	173	7
	Jim McKenna	1949	NA	7
5	3 players tied at 6			

PUNTING

RANK	PLAYER	SEASON	PUNTS	YDS	AVG
1	Dave Zastudil	2001	50	2,280	45.6
2	Dave Zastudil	1998	NA	NA	45.3
3	Dave Zastudil	2000	47	2,084	44.3
4	Dave Zastudil	1999	60	2,595	43.3
5	Dave Green	1971	NA	NA	43.0

PUNT RETURNS

RANK	PLAYER	SEASON	RET	YDS	AVG
1	Dick Phillips	1950	NA	NA	20.7
2	Larry Hargrove	1989	NA	NA	18.4
3	Chris Garrett	2006	NA	378	14.5
4	Bob Anderson	1964	NA	NA	13.6
5	Courtney Burton	1992	NA	NA	12.3

KICKOFF RETURNS

RANK	PLAYER	SEASON	RET	YDS	AVG
1	Bob Allen	1971	NA	NA	30.1
2	Scott Mayle	2005	21	572	27.2
3	Dave LeVeck	1968	NA	NA	27.1
4	Courtney Burton	1992	NA	NA	26.4
	Sean Williams	1997	NA	NA	26.4

MAC TEAMS

CAREER RECORDS

RUSHING YARDS

RANK	PLAYER	SEASONS	ATT	AVG	TD	YDS
1	Steveland Hookfin	1995-98	767	5.2	29	3,972
2	Kareem Wilson	1995-98	885	4.1	49	3,597
3	Tim Curtis	1990-93	750	4.0	19	2,995
4	Kalvin McRae	2004-	609	4.9	26	2,964
5	Chad Brinker	1999-2002	549	5.1	27	2,826
6	Kevin Babcock	1976-79	675	3.9	NA	2,614
7	Arnold Welcher	1974-77	544	4.6	NA	2,525
8	Bob Brooks	1958-60	498	4.7	21	2,364
9	Dontrell Jackson	1999-2002	540	4.1	13	2,201
10	Jamel Patterson	1999-2001	321	6.4	19	2,056

PASSING YARDS

RANK	PLAYER	SEASONS	ATT	COMP	PCT	INT	TD	YDS
1	Sammy Shon	1978-81	805	452	56.1	46	24	5,412
2	Anthony Thornton	1987-90	889	408	45.9	40	17	5,199
3	Donny Harrison	1979-83	591	334	56.5	26	18	3,856
4	Austen Everson	2003-06	608	305	50.2	25	18	3,586
5	Dennis Swearingen	1982-85	603	330	54.7	38	NA	3,475
6	Cleve Bryant	1967-69	507	226	44.6	27	29	3,414
7	Rich Bevly	1972-74	452	189	41.8	23	20	2,873
8	Tom Dubs	1990-93	428	214	50.0	NA	NA	2,666
9	Andy Vetter	1974-77	NA	195	NA	23	19	2,529
10	Dontrell Jackson	1999-2002	370	176	47.5	21	16	2,452

RECEIVING YARDS

RANK	PLAYER	SEASONS	REC	AVG	TD	YDS
1	Todd Snyder	1967-69	140	16.0	15	2,241
2	Scott Mayle	2002-06	107	17.3	11	1,847
3	Eddie Washington	1980-83	127	13.9	8	1,761
4	Tom Compernolle	1983-86	144	11.3	12	1,620
5	Bob Allen	1969-71	103	14.2	9	1,459
6	Scott Mayle	2002-06	107	13.4	11	1,436
7	Courtney Burton	1990-93	102	13.5	10	1,374
8	Mike Green	1972-75	88	14.6	8	1,288
9	Mark Geisler	1976-79	105	11.3	NA	1,188
10	Lance Pickens	1980-83	NA	NA	NA	1,145

SCORING

RANK	PLAYER	SEASONS	TD	FG	PAT	P2	TOT
1	Kareem Wilson	1995-98	49	0	0	4	302
2	Kevin Kerr	1999-2002	0	38	115	0	229
3	Chad Brinker	1999-2002	30	0	0	2	184
4	3 tied at 176.						

TOUCHDOWNS

RANK	PLAYER	SEASONS	TOT
1	Kareem Wilson	1995-98	49
2	Chad Brinker	1999-2002	30
3	Steveland Hookfin	1995-98	29
	Kalvin McRae	2004-	29
4	Bob Houmard	1966-68	27

TACKLES

RANK	PLAYER	SEASONS	TOT
1	Mike Mangen	1981-84	513
2	Benny King	1992-95	462
3	Brian Mays	1982-85	458
4	Bill Garrett	1986-89	450
5	Jabaar Thompson	1992-95	447

INTERCEPTIONS

RANK	PLAYER	SEASONS	YDS	TOT
1	Joe Callan	1975-79	179	18
2	Bop White	1999-2002	114	17
3	Bert Dampier	1970-72	247	13
4	Mike Schott	1967-69	140	12
5	4 players tied at 11			

PUNTING

RANK	PLAYER	SEASONS	PUNTS	YDS	AVG
1	Dave Zastudil	1998-2001	207	9,225	44.6
2	Matthew Miller	2002-05	203	8,155	40.2
3	Mike Green	1973-75	176	7,026	40.0
4	Steve Green	1976-79	183	7,069	38.6
5	Paul Hamilton	1994-95	127	4,862	38.3

TEAM RECORDS

LONGEST WINNING STREAK
• 12, Nov. 24, 1928-Oct. 3, 1930
Streak broken vs. West Liberty State, 13-13, Oct. 11, 1930

LONGEST UNDEFEATED STREAK
• 19, Nov. 24, 1928-Nov. 22, 1930
Streak broken vs. Indiana, 6-7, Sept. 26, 1931

MOST CONSECUTIVE WINNING SEASONS
• 19, 1924-42

MOST CONSECUTIVE BOWL APPEARANCES
• 1 (tie), 1962; 1968; 2006

MOST POINTS IN A GAME
• 89, vs. Wittenburg, 1916

MOST POINTS ALLOWED IN A GAME
• 73, vs. Syracuse, Oct. 7, 1916

LARGEST MARGIN OF VICTORY
• 86 (89-3), vs. Wittenberg, 1916

LARGEST MARGIN OF DEFEAT
• 73 (0-73), vs. Syracuse, Oct. 7, 1916

LONGEST RUN FROM SCRIMMAGE
• 93 yards, Glenn Hunter, vs. Eastern Michigan, Sept. 24, 1983

LONGEST PASS PLAY
• 98 yards, Tom Dubs to Richard Hill, vs. Kent State, Oct. 26, 1991

LONGEST FIELD GOAL
• 57 yards, Gary Homer, vs. Penn State, Nov. 17, 1973

LONGEST PUNT
• 75 yards (tie), Dave Zastudil, vs. Akron, Oct. 17, 1998; Mike Green, vs. Bowling Green, Nov. 8, 1975

LONGEST PUNT RETURN
• 87 yards, Larry Grimes, vs. Marshall, Sept. 13, 1986

LONGEST INTERCEPTION RETURN
• 95 yards, Jim Albert, vs. Western Michigan, Nov. 9, 1963

PUNT RETURNS

RANK	PLAYER	SEASON	RET	YDS	AVG
1	Chris Garrett	2006-	NA	378	14.5
2	Dick Phillips	1950-52	47	646	13.7
3	Larry Hargrove	1987-89	54	629	11.7
4	Stafford Owens	2001-04	64	713	11.1
5	Raynald Ray	1997-00	64	699	10.9

KICKOFF RETURNS

RANK	PLAYER	SEASON	RET	YDS	AVG
1	Bob Allen	1969-71	NA	NA	25.1
2	Sean Williams	1995-97	NA	NA	24.4
3	Andrew Greer	1988-89	62	1,448	23.4
4	Courtney Burton	1990-93	47	1,084	23.1
5	Scott Mayle	2003-06	50	1,375	22.7

OHIO ANNUAL STATISTICAL LEADERS

YR	RUSHING	YDS	ATT	AVG	PASSING	ATT	CMP	PCT	YDS	RECEIVING	REC	YDS	AVG
1962	Jim Albert	397	88	4.5	Bob Babbitt	113	57	.50	1,010	Jim Albert	14	304	21.7
1963	Jim Albert	707	122	5.8	Wes Dayno	108	42	.39	635	Jim Albert	13	186	14.3
1964	Wash Lyons	835	192	4.3	Larry Bainter	79	30	.38	443	Jim Dorna	15	162	10.8
1965	Sam Bogan	308	75	4.1	Sam Fornsaglio	51	26	.51	305	Dick Conley	15	305	20.3
1966	Bob Houmard	641	189	3.4	Ron DeLucca	111	44	.40	655	Jay Maupin	26	447	17.2
1967	Dick Conley	841	226	3.7	Cleve Bryant	180	68	.38	1,157	Todd Snyder	33	629	19.1
1968	Dave LeVeck	850	175	4.9	Cleve Bryant	200	98	.49	1,524	Todd Snyder	46	777	16.9
1969	Dave LeVeck	464	106	4.4	Steve Skiver	109	47	.43	749	Todd Snyder	62	835	13.5
1970	Bill Gary	1,064	265	4.0	Steve Skiver	229	107	.47	1,417	Bob Allen	48	699	14.6
1971	Dave Juenger	646	211	3.1	Dave Juenger	163	80	.49	922	Bob Allen	37	485	13.1
1972	L.C. Lyons	554	161	3.4	Rich Bevly	132	56	.42	865	Dave Juenger	32	508	15.9
1973	Dave Houseton	731	209	3.5	Rich Bevly	147	62	.42	1,007	Mike Green	22	425	19.3
1974	L.C. Lyons	928	231	4.0	Rich Bevly	173	71	.41	1,001	Rick Lilienthal	22	315	14.3
1975	Arnold Welcher	1,175	236	5.0	Rick Lilienthal	215	84	.39	982	Mike Green	50	642	12.8
1976	Arnold Welcher	1,034	213	4.9	Andy Vetter	135	71	.53	877	Phil Buckner	12	226	18.8
1977	Kevin Babcock	585	147	4.0	Andy Vetter	202	116	.57	1,548	Nigel Turpin	46	624	13.6
1978	Kevin Babcock	866	232	3.7	Mike Scimeca	93	40	.43	483	Mark Geisler	25	244	9.8
1979	Tony Carifa	727	156	4.7	Sammy Shon	220	133	.60	1,336	Tony Carifa	45	380	8.4
1980	Tony Carifa	853	198	4.3	Sammy Shon	235	131	.56	1,527	Mark Green	30	489	16.3
1981	Todd Yoho	500	113	4.4	Sammy Shon	320	175	.55	2,366	Shawn Silcott	39	573	14.7
1982	Orvell Johns	451	130	3.5	Donny Harrison	198	114	.58	1,308	Eddie Washington	37	524	14.2
1983	Glenn Hunter	338	92	3.7	Donny Harrison	357	203	.57	2,309	Eddie Washington	68	866	12.7
1984	Glenn Hunter	800	228	3.5	Dennis Swearingen	185	117	.63	1,211	Tom Compernolle	36	459	12.8
1985	Jesse Owens	709	209	3.4	Dennis Swearingen	383	195	.51	2,056	Tom Compernolle	46	524	11.4
1986	Jesse Owens	557	161	3.5	Bruce Porter	383	216	.56	2,281	Tom Compernolle	61	626	10.3
1987	John Caldwell	950	238	4.0	Anthony Thornton	180	75	.42	949	Cyle Feldman	21	302	14.4
1988	Andrew Greer	863	193	4.5	Anthony Thornton	187	78	.42	1,162	Byron Cross	20	342	17.1
1989	Andrew Greer	905	192	4.7	Anthony Thornton	234	120	.51	1,502	Jim Swanson	37	503	13.6
1990	Rickey Howell	832	192	4.3	Anthony Thornton	228	125	.55	1,586	Gerald Harris	33	497	15.1
1991	Tim Curtis	1,085	271	4.0	Tom Dubs	264	144	.55	1,835	Richard Hill	49	863	17.6
1992	Tim Curtis	825	213	3.9	Tom Dubs	139	57	.41	712	Chris Jenkins	38	550	14.5
1993	Tim Curtis	829	217	3.9	D.R. Robinson	148	81	.55	844	Courtney Burton	31	366	11.8
1994	Lakarlos Townsend	676	199	3.4	Sam Vink	195	90	.46	944	Jason Goss	23	357	15.5
1995	Kareem Wilson	893	244	3.7	Kareem Wilson	130	48	.37	657	Shawn Smith	8	192	24.0
1996	Steveland Hookfin	1,125	195	5.8	Kareem Wilson	90	38	.42	567	Damion Maxwell	17	184	10.8
1997	Steveland Hookfin	864	159	5.4	Kareem Wilson	54	14	.26	369	Damion Maxwell	7	180	18.0
1998	Steveland Hookfin	1,315	273	4.8	Kareem Wilson	71	26	.37	512	Damion Maxwell	14	194	13.9
1999	Chad Brinker	600	121	5.0	Dontrell Jackson	113	52	.46	745	Raynald Ray	22	466	21.2
2000	Dontrell Jackson	864	155	5.6	Dontrell Jackson	119	54	.45	881	Raynald Ray	15	308	20.5
2001	Jamel Patterson	638	117	5.5	Dontrell Jackson	83	44	.53	559	Joe Mohler	21	269	12.8
2002	Chad Brinker	1,099	228	4.8	Fred Ray	100	56	.56	712	Stafford Owens	17	259	15.2
2003	Fred Ray	382	77	5.0	Ryan Hawk	100	49	.49	765	Anthony Hackett	26	452	17.4
2004	Kalvin McRae	559	142	3.9	Ryan Hawk	262	137	.52	1,585	Chris Jackson	39	390	10.0
2005	Kalvin McRae	1,153	209	5.5	Austen Everson	220	105	.48	1,151	Scott Mayle	21	338	16.1
2006	Kalvin McRae	1,252	258	4.9	Austen Everson	253	137	.54	1,356	Kalvin McRae	29	280	9.7

Receiving leaders by receptions
The NCAA began including postseason stats in 2002

TEMPLE

BY MIKE VACCARO

PHILADELPHIA IS A FOOTBALL town. Ask the thousands of rabid Eagles fans who fill Lincoln Financial Field on fall Sundays. Ask the thousands more on the waiting list for seats. When the Phillies are playing well, fans ask each other about the Eagles between innings. When the Sixers or the Flyers win, again fans are really thinking about the Eagles. Temple, the only Bowl Subdivision program in this football-mad city, has yet to seize its place in the football grid. But Al Golden, named coach in 2006, believes now is the time. "Sometimes you get to inherit traditions and sometimes you get to build your own," he says. "Both are equally exciting. I want the young men playing for me now to be able to look back in 20 years and say, 'We were a part of starting something outstanding.'"

TRADITION Temple believes walk-ons should be an integral part of the football program, and the results have been fruitful. Russell Newman walked onto the program in 1998, was an all-conference defensive tackle two years later and made the Denver Broncos' roster as a rookie. Sean Dillard walked on to the team in 1999; by 2001, he was an All-Big East wide receiver who would go on to play for the Washington Redskins. "Recruiting will never be an exact science," former Temple coach Bobby Wallace said. "We figure we owe it to certain kids who may be overlooked in the recruiting process to give them a look. More often than you might imagine, it works out wonderfully for everyone."

BEST PLAYER Bill Cosby is the most famous running back ever to wear the cherry and white, but Paul Palmer rules the Owls' record book. Even though Palmer was considered too small and too slight coming out of high school in 1983, coach Bruce Arians figured he was "a guy who could carry the ball eight, 10 times a game, a solid guy who could be a contributor." In the fourth game of his freshman year, the kid got his shot against Boston College, carrying 11 times for 98 yards. In 1986, Palmer rushed for a team-record 349 yards against East Carolina. Over his career, he gained 4,895 yards—1,500 more than any other Owl. "I never imagined this," Palmer said after his senior year, in which he finished second to Vinny Testaverde for the Heisman Trophy. "I wanted to leave a mark. But I never dreamed it would be this kind of impression."

PROFILE

Temple University
Philadelphia, Pa.
Founded: 1884
Enrollment: 34,000
Colors: Cherry and White
Nickname: Owls
Stadium: Lincoln Financial Field
    Opened in 2003
    Grass; 68,532 capacity
First football game: 1894
All-time record: 389–515–52 (.434)
Bowl record: 1–1
First-round draft choices: 2
Website: www.owlsports.com

THE BEST OF TIMES

Temple's positive football history can be summed up in two names: Glenn "Pop" Warner and Wayne Hardin. Warner finished his legendary career at Temple, going 31–18–9 from 1933 to 1938, guiding the Owls to their first-ever bowl appearance, a 20-14 loss to Tulane in the inaugural Sugar Bowl, in 1935. Hardin, 80–52–3 from 1970 to 1982, led the Owls to their only 10-win season and their only bowl victory (28-17 over Cal in the Garden State Bowl) in 1979.

THE WORST OF TIMES

From 1989 to 1999, covering the coaching tenures of Jerry Berndt and Ron Dickerson and the first two years of Bobby Wallace, the Owls went 23–98—including 8–58 from 1991 to 1996—losing 27 straight Big East games at one point.

CONFERENCE

From the program's inception in 1894 through 1957, Temple played as an independent. From 1957 through 1970, while playing in the NCAA's small-college division, the Owls were a member of the Middle Atlantic States Collegiate Athletic Conference. After moving up to Division I in 1970, the Owls again played as an independent for 20 years. In 1991 they joined the Big East, which expelled them after the 2004 season. Temple played as an independent from 2005 to 2006 before joining the MAC in 2007.

> *Bill Cosby is the most famous running back ever to wear the cherry and white, but Paul Palmer rules the Owls' record book.*

BEST COACH Glenn "Pop" Warner had already built powerhouses at Pittsburgh and Stanford, when Temple lured the Old Fox to Philadelphia to breathe life into the Owls program. Warner did, leading Temple to a 31–18–9 record from 1933 to 1938. In 1934, a 7–1–2 record earned the Owls an invite to the first Sugar Bowl, where Temple battled Tulane. The game was tied for three quarters until a late TD gave Tulane a 20-14 win. Warner's tenure ended on Dec. 3, 1938, when the Owls upset Florida 20-12 in the heat and humidity of Gainesville. It was the last of Pop's 319 career coaching victories.

BEST TEAM Temple hadn't received a bowl bid in more than 40 years when Wayne Hardin's team bolted out of the gate 8–1 in 1979. Penn State put a dent into those dreams, beating Temple 22-7. But the Owls bounced back with a 42-10 rout of Villanova in the season finale, earning a spot in the Garden State Bowl on Dec. 15, 1979, against California. Temple jumped out to a 21-0 lead in the first quarter, but the Golden Bears came roaring back to score 17 unanswered points. Then, in a fitting conclusion to the best season in Owls history, quarterback Brian Broomell engineered a 14-play, 78-yard scoring drive late in the game, cementing a 10–2 season and No. 17 final ranking in both polls, the high-water mark in school history on both counts.

BEST BACKFIELD In the mid-1980s, Paul Palmer set record upon record as Temple's best running back. Palmer broke onto the national scene when he ran for 206 yards against Penn State in his junior year. When he ran for a school record 1,866 yards during his senior campaign, he did so behind the powerful blocks of fullback Shelly Poole, who received honorable mention as all-East by the Associated Press. Perhaps more surprising, though, is that this was not just a "ground chuck" offense. QB Lee Saltz, another all-East honorable mention, threw for a respectable 1,729 yards and 12 TDs to go along with Palmer's 15 scores. Whatever head coach Bruce Arians learned in guiding this potent backfield must have

---

DISTINGUISHED ALUMNI

Bill Cosby; Norman Braman, owner, Philadelphia Eagles; David Brenner, comedian; Robert Merton, sociologist; Bob Saget, actor; Patricia Wettig, actress

FIGHT SONG

T FOR TEMPLE U
U-ni-versity!
Fight, fight fight!
For the Cherry and the White,
For the Cherry and the White,
We'll fight, fight, fight!

FIRST-ROUND DRAFT CHOICES

| 1986 | John Rienstra, Steelers (9) |
| 1987 | Paul Palmer, Chiefs (19) |

CONSENSUS ALL-AMERICANS

| 1985 | John Rienstra, OL |
| 1986 | Paul Palmer, RB |

COLLEGE FOOTBALL HALL OF FAME INDUCTEES

NAME		YEARS	INDUCTED
Pop Warner, COACH		1933-38	1951
Ray Morrison, COACH		1940-48	1954

worked—he is now the offensive coordinator for the Pittsburgh Steelers.

BEST DEFENSE The 1979 Owls who went 10–2 and qualified for their second (and most recent) bowl bid were built around a hard-hitting defense anchored by all-time tackles leader Steve Conjar, pass-rush specialist Guy Peters, and future Eagle, Giant, and Packer LB Mike Curcio. All three played important roles in the Owls' 28-17 win in the Garden State Bowl. After jumping out to a 21-0 lead, Temple relied on its defense to keep the pressure on Cal. They did, allowing only 23 total rushing yards. The game remains the only postseason victory in Temple football history. Possibly more impressive than the bowl victory, though, was an early-season loss to Pitt. Led by Dan Marino, Pitt went 11–1 in 1979, but managed to score only 10 points against Temple's ferocious defense.

BIGGEST GAME The Mid-Winter Sports Association of New Orleans was created in 1934 to establish an annual New Year's Day football game. On Dec. 2 of that year, the association selected Tulane, 9–1, and Temple, 7–0–2 under Warner, to compete in the first Sugar Bowl. Some 28,000 people saw Temple's Danny Testa score the first touchdown in Sugar Bowl history off a Glenn Frey pass. The Owls' Dave Smukler (who played all 60 minutes) later added a 25-yard touchdown run to give the Owls a 14-0 lead. Tulane battled back to a 20-14 victory, but Temple earned the lasting admiration of its legendary coach: "This is a game that people will remember for many, many years, and this is a team that Temple University will be proud of forever."

BIGGEST UPSET Bobby Wallace had lost his first six games as Temple coach to start the 1998 season, and Temple had lost every one of the 25 conference road games it had played since joining the Big East in 1991. Before a homecoming crowd, Virginia Tech, ranked No. 14, seized a 17-7 halftime lead. But Temple refused to go away. Midway through the fourth, Carlos Johnson hauled in an 80-yard pass from Devin Scott to give the Owls a 21-17 lead. Later, a one-yard plunge by Scott made the score 28-24. But the Hokies drove to the Temple 3, where they had second and two with less than a minute to play. Temple's defense stiffened and Tech turned the ball over on downs.

HEARTBREAKER Temple was in the midst of another long, awful season (1–8, 0–4 in Big East play) when 12th-ranked Virginia Tech came to Lincoln Financial Field on Nov. 15, 2003. The Hokies looked rusty, but led 17-0 with 14:23 to go. Then Temple quarterback Walter Washington led the Owls on drives of 82 and 80 yards, narrowing the gap to 17-14. A revitalized Owl defense was stopping Tech, and a 37-yard field goal by Temple kicker Jared Davis tied the game with 40

seconds left. After an interception, Davis had a chance to win it, but he missed a 50-yard attempt. In OT, Tech jumped to a 24-17 lead, but Temple answered with a 22-yard hookup from Washington to Zamir Cobb that should have sent the game into double overtime, except Davis missed the extra point. Game over: Virginia Tech 24, Temple 23. "They didn't play like a team that's won just one ball game," Hokies coach Frank Beamer said. "I've never felt so bad about winning a game in my life."

STADIUM In 2003, Temple started playing its games at Lincoln Financial Field—the 68,532-seat, natural-grass, state-of-the-art home of the Philadelphia Eagles—a giant step in the right direction for the program. Before that, Temple had been a co-tenant at Veterans Stadium since 1975. The Owls had an on-campus stadium, Temple Stadium, which they called home from 1928 to 1975.

RIVAL Temple used to battle Bucknell every year for the Old Shoe, but that game was discontinued in 1971 after Temple jumped to Division I-A status. Temple and Villanova also used to play an annual game for intracity bragging rights, but after Villanova dropped to I-AA in 1980, that also dissolved. In the Big East, Temple's natural rival was Rutgers, which for many years shared the bottom of the league with the Owls. With the move to the MAC in 2007, there are no natural geographic rivals, but of their new foes the Owls have played Akron the most, boasting a 9–7 all-time mark against the Zips heading into 2007.

NICKNAME Temple was the first school to adopt an owl as its official mascot in 1884. Legend has it that the owl, a nocturnal hunter, was originally proposed as the school mascot because Temple began as a night school, and its founder, Russell Conwell, urged his students on with the remark, "The owl of the night makes the eagle of the day."

UNIFORMS Temple was also the first school in the nation to officially adopt cherry as its primary color. The combination of red and white for football uniforms is quite common, but only one other school (Rensselaer Polytechnic Institute) uses cherry and white. The helmet has undergone many changes through the years.

QUOTE "Football at Temple—Division I-A football—is as important in maintaining a national institution as things like our health system, as our Research I status … It gives you identity. In the 1920s, there were the same issues at Temple. They brought in Pop Warner as the coach. The academics here said, 'You're killing Temple. You're making it a sports factory.' Well, we went to the first Sugar Bowl. Anybody who lived in that period said it was the greatest period that Temple ever had." —Temple president Peter Liacouras, 2000

TEMPLE ALL-TIME SCORES

WIN/LOSS PERCENTAGE SINCE 1936

| | 1936 | 1940 | 1945 | 1950 | 1955 | 1960 | 1965 | 1970 | 1975 | 1980 | 1985 | 1990 | 1995 | 2000 | 2006 |

CHARLES M. WILLIAMS
1894-98 (.466)   13-15-1

1894   4-1-0
U	●	Phil. Dental Coll. Unk	14	6
U	●	First Regiment Unk	26	0
U	●	Ursinus Unk	0	16
U	●	Crescent AC Unk	12	10
U	●	Central Pa. Coll. Unk	18	0

1895   1-4-1
U	=	Schuylkill Navy Unk	0	0
U		Trenton Unk	0	8
U	●	Central Pa. Coll. Unk	30	0
U		Stevens Unk	0	10
U		Pratt Inst. Unk	0	15
U		Ursinus Unk	0	56

1896   3-2-0
U		Brooklyn Poly Unk	8	16
U		Loyola-Baltimore Unk	6	14
U		Trenton Unk	4	2
U	●	Phil. Dental Coll. Unk	6	0
U	●	Central Pa. Coll. Unk	26	0

1897   3-3-0
U		Eastburn Acad. Unk	18	3
U		Phil. Dental Canisius Unk	22	0
U		Loyola-Baltimore Unk	6	22
U		Central Pa. Coll. Unk	54	10
U		St. Francis Unk	0	30
U		Phil. Pharmacy Unk	0	20

1898   2-5-0
U		Oak Lane AC Unk	0	12
U		West Chester Unk	6	20
U	●	U. of Phil. Unk	3	0
U	●	Schuylkill Navy Unk	12	8
U		Widener Unk	8	15
U		Trenton Unk	3	40
U		Beverly AC Unk	0	38

JOHN T. ROGERS
1899-1900 (.357)   4-8-2

1899   1-4-1
U		St. Joseph's Unk	0	10
U		Phil. Pharmacy Unk	0	15
U		Ursinus Unk	0	1 f
U	●	Eastburn Acad. Unk	22	0
U	=	U. of Phil. Unk	5	5
U		Franklin & Marshall Unk	0	96

1900   3-4-1
U	=	St. Joseph's Unk	0	0
U		W. Chester Teachers Unk	0	5
U	●	U. of Phil. Unk	40	3
U	●	La Salle Unk	12	3
U	●	Eastburn Acad. Unk	25	6
U		Medico Unk	0	5
U		Jefferson Unk	6	11
U		Widener Unk	12	36

H. SHINDLE WINGERT
1901-05 (.583)   13-9-2

1901   3-2-0
U		Trenton Unk	0	15
U	●	La Salle Unk	6	5
U		St. Joseph's Unk	0	32
U	●	Phil. Dental Coll. Unk	10	0
U	●	Central Pa. Coll. Unk	21	13

1902   1-4-1
U		Phil. Pharmacy Unk	6	11
U		Trenton Unk	0	12
U	=	St. Joseph's Unk	0	0
U	●	Phil. Dental Coll. Unk	18	12
U		Pratt Inst. Unk	0	21
U		Medico Unk	5	6

1903   4-1-0
U	●	Tioga AC Unk	13	6
U	●	Medico Unk	13	6
U	●	Trenton Unk	0	6
U	●	St. Joseph's Unk	12	0
U	●	La Salle Unk	18	6

1904   3-2-0
U	●	Phil. Dental Coll. Unk	21	0
U	●	Medico Unk	30	6
O22	●	La Salle Unk	14	0
U		Widener Unk	0	3
U		Pratt Inst. Unk	0	14

1905   2-0-1
U	=	La Salle Unk	12	12
U	●	Phil. Dental Coll. Unk	30	0
U	●	Medico Unk	6	0

1906
NO TEAM

HORACE BUTTERWORTH
1907 (.833)   4-0-2

1907   4-0-2
U	●	Schuylkill Navy Unk	21	5
U	●	Widener Unk	17	6
U	●	Girard Coll. Unk	14	0
U	=	St. Joseph's Unk	5	5
U	●	Loyola-Baltimore Unk	13	12
U	=	Phil. Pharmacy Unk	12	12

DR. FRANK W. WHITE
1908 (.583)   3-2-1

1908   3-2-1
U		Widener Unk	0	22
U	=	La Salle Unk	12	12
U	●	Phil. Pharmacy Unk	6	5
U	●	Girard Coll. Unk	25	12
U	●	Loyola-Baltimore Unk	12	10
U		Villanova Unk	0	5

WILLIAM J. SCHATZ
1909-13 (.500)   13-13-3

1909   0-4-1
U		Lebanon Unk	0	45
U		Widener Unk	0	12
U		Muhlenberg Unk	0	24
U		Phil. Pharmacy Unk	0	18
U	=	Schuylkill Navy Unk	0	0

1910   3-3-0
U		Ursinus Unk	0	53
U		Widener Unk	6	18
U	●	St. Joseph's Unk	9	6
U	●	Girard Coll. Unk	21	13
U	●	Phil. Osteopathy Unk	22	6
U		Wenonah Military Unk	6	27

1911   6-1-0
U	●	Phil. Osteopathy Unk	21	6
U	●	La Salle Unk	25	0
U		Widener Unk	0	30
U	●	New York Aggies Unk	18	12
U	●	Pratt Inst. Unk	6	0
U	●	Phil. Navy Unk	13	6
U	●	West Chester Unk	7	0

1912   3-2-0
U		Widener Unk	0	28
U	●	New York Aggies Unk	7	6
U	●	Phil. Normal Unk	18	0
U		Pratt Inst. Unk	7	13
U	●	La Salle Unk	6	0

1913   1-3-2
U	●	Widener Unk	0	18
O18		at Delaware	0	28
U	=	Albright Unk	0	0
U	●	Camden BC Unk	12	0
U	=	St. Joseph's Unk	13	13
U		La Salle Unk	6	22

WILLIAM NICHOLAI
1914-16 (.618)   9-5-3

1914   3-3-0
U	●	Phil. Normal Unk	24	12
U	●	La Salle Unk	6	0
U	●	Bloomsburg Unk	13	6
O17		Delaware	7	20
U		St. Joseph's Unk	7	14
U		Albright Unk	12	28

1915   3-1-1
U		Schuylkill Navy Unk	0	21
U	●	Phil. Navy Unk	6	0
U	●	La Salle Unk	13	12
U	=	Phil. Normal Unk	0	0
U	●	St. Joseph's Unk	13	7

1916   3-1-2
U	=	La Salle Unk	0	0
U	=	Millersville Unk	0	0
U	●	Bryn Athyn Unk	0	7
U	●	Coatesville Unk	20	7
U	●	Phil. Normal Unk	35	0
U	●	Phil. Navy Unk	6	0

ELWOOD GEIGES
1917 (.071)   0-6-1

1917   0-6-1
U		Widener Unk	0	1 f
U		Franklin & Marshall Unk	0	1 f
U		Albright Unk	0	1 f
U		Moravian Unk	0	1 f
U		Susquehanna Unk	0	1 f
U		Lebanon Valley Unk	0	1 f
U	=	Temple Prep Unk	6	6

1918-1919
NO TEAM WWI

1920-1921
NO TEAM

FRANCOIS M. D'ELISCU
1922-23 (.136)   1-9-1

1922   1-4-1
U	●	East Stroudsburg Unk	14	0
U	=	Trenton Unk	0	0
U		New York Aggies Unk	0	40
U		Millersville Unk	0	31
U		Gallaudet Unk	6	31
U		St. Joseph's Unk	6	20

1923   0-5-0
O6		at Haverford	0	3
O20		at Juniata	6	14
O27		at Ursinus	0	52
N10		at Susquehanna	7	25
N17		Drexel	0	7

ALBERT BARRON
1924 (.200)   1-4

1924   1-4-0
O4		at East Stroudsburg	6	40
O18		at St. Thomas	0	19
N1		at Wyoming Seminary	0	34
N8		at West Chester	3	13
N22	●	Drexel	6	0

HENRY J. MILLER
1925-32 (.740)   50-15-8

1925   5-2-2
O2	●	Upsala	19	0
O10	●	at Schuylkill	3	0
O17	●	at St. John's	18	0
O24	●	at Widener	0	13
O31	=	Lebanon Valley	0	0
N7	●	at George Washington	0	0
N14	●	St. Joseph's	32	0
N21	●	at Susquehanna	26	10
N25	●	at Schuylkill Navy	6	16

1926   5-3-0
S25	●	at Ursinus	12	0
O9	●	Lebanon Valley	13	3
O16	●	Susquehanna	14	0
O23	●	Schuylkill Navy	12	0
O30		Albright	0	19
N6		at Muhlenberg	12	29
N11		Quantico Marines	12	42
N20	●	Washington Coll.	13	0

1927   7-1-0
O1	●	Blue Ridge	110	0
O8	●	Juniata	58	0
O15		at Dartmouth	7	47
O22	●	Gallaudet	62	0
O29	●	at Brown	7	0
N5	●	Albright	13	0
N12	●	Washington Coll.	75	0
N19	●	Bucknell	19	13

1928   7-1-2
S29	●	St. Thomas	12	0
O6	●	Gallaudet	39	0
O13	●	W. Maryland	7	0
O20	●	Albright	32	0
O27	●	Providence	41	0
N3		at Schuylkill Navy	7	10
N10	=	Villanova	0	0
N17	●	Geneva	6	0
N24	●	Washington Coll.	73	6
N29	=	Bucknell	7	7

1929   6-3-1
S28	●	Thiel	25	0
O5	●	St. Thomas	20	0
O12	●	St. Bonaventure	28	0
O19		W. Maryland	0	23
O26	=	Wash. & Jeff.	0	0
N2		Bucknell	0	13
N9	●	Gallaudet	31	0
N16	●	Lafayette	13	0
N23	●	Drake	16	14
N30		Villanova	0	15

1930   7-3-0
S26	●	Thiel	13	6
O3	●	St. Thomas	28	2
O10	●	Bucknell	7	6
O18	●	Wash. & Jeff.	20	7
O25		Villanova Phil	7	8
N1	●	Wake Forest	36	0
N8	●	Miami, Fla.	34	0
N15	●	Lafayette	46	0
N22		Carnegie Tech	13	32
N29	●	Drake	20	49

1931   8-1-1
S25	●	Mt. St. Mary's	33	0
O2	●	Albright	19	7
O10	●	Penn State	12	0
O16	=	Bucknell	0	0
O23	●	Haskell	6	0
O30	●	Wash. & Jeff.	6	3
N7	●	Villanova	13	7
N14		Carnegie Tech	13	19
N21	●	at Denver	18	0
N28	●	Missouri KC	38	6

1932 — 5-1-2

S30	●	Thiel	31	0
O7	●	West Virginia	14	13
O14	●	Bucknell	12	0
O21	●	Denver	14	0
O28	=	Carnegie Tech	7	7
N4	=	Haskell	14	14
N12	●	Penn State	13	12
N19		Villanova	0	7

GLENN "POP" WARNER 1933-38 (.612) 31-18-9

1933 — 5-3-0

S29	●	South Carolina	26	6
O7		at Carnegie Tech	0	25
O13	●	Haskell	31	0
O20	●	West Virginia	13	7
O28		at Bucknell	7	20
N4	●	Drake	20	14
N18	●	Wash. & Jeff.	13	0
N25		Villanova	0	24

1934 — 7-1-2

S29	●	Virginia Tech	34	0
O6	●	Texas A&M	40	6
O13	=	Indiana	6	6
O19	●	West Virginia	28	13
O27	●	at Marquette	28	6
N3	●	Holy Cross	14	0
N10	●	at Carnegie Tech	34	6
N24	●	Villanova	22	0
D1	=	Bucknell	0	0
		SUGAR BOWL		
J1		Tulane	14	20

1935 — 7-3-0

S20	●	St. Joseph's	51	0
S27	●	Centre	25	13
O5	●	at Texas A&M	14	0
O12	●	Vanderbilt	6	3
O19	●	at Carnegie Tech	13	0
O26	●	at West Virginia	19	6
N2		Michigan State	7	12
N16	●	Marquette	26	6
N23		Villanova	14	21
N30		Bucknell	6	7

1936 — 6-3-2

S19	●	at St. Joseph's	18	0
S26	●	Centre	50	7
O2	●	Mississippi	12	7
O12	●	at Boston Collge	14	0
O17		at Carnegie Tech	0	7
O31	●	Holy Cross	3	0
N7	=	Michigan State	7	7
N14	●	Villanova	6	0
N21		Iowa	0	25
N28	=	Bucknell	0	0
D5		at Saint Mary's-Cal	7	13

1937 — 3-2-4

S25	●	VMI	18	7
O1	=	Mississippi	0	0
O8	●	Florida	7	6
O12	=	at Boston College	0	0
O23	●	Carnegie Tech	7	0
O30	=	at Holy Cross	0	0
N6		Michigan State	6	13
N13	=	at Bucknell	0	0
N20		Villanova	0	33

1938 — 3-6-1

S24	●	Albright	6	0
O1		Pittsburgh	6	28
O8		TCU	6	28
O15	●	Bucknell	26	0
O21	=	Boston College	26	26
O29		Georgetown	0	13
N5		at Holy Cross	0	33
N12		Villanova	7	20
N19		at Michigan State	0	10
D3	●	at Florida	20	12

FRED H. SWAN 1939 (.222) 2-7

1939 — 2-7-0

S29		Georgetown	2	3
O7		Carnegie Tech	0	6
O14	●	TCU	13	11
O21		at Boston College	0	19
O27	●	Bucknell	16	0
N4		Pittsburgh	7	13
N11		at Holy Cross	0	14
N18		Villanova	6	12
N25		at Michigan State	7	18

RAY MORRISON 1940-48 (.455) 31-38-9

1940 — 4-4-1

S27	●	Muhlenberg	64	7
O4		Georgetown	0	14
O12		at Boston College	20	33
O18	●	Michigan State	21	19
O26		Penn State	0	18
N2	●	at Bucknell	10	7
N9	●	Villanova	28	0
N16	=	at Holy Cross	6	6
N23		at Oklahoma	6	9

1941 — 7-2-0

S26	●	Kansas	31	9
O4	●	VMI	28	13
O10	●	Georgetown	17	7
O18	●	Penn State	14	0
O25	●	Bucknell	41	14
N1		at Boston College	0	31
N8	●	Villanova	14	13
N15		at Michigan State	0	46
N22	●	at Holy Cross	31	13

1942 — 2-5-3

S25		Georgetown	0	7
O2	●	VMI	7	6
O9	=	Bucknell	7	7
O16	=	at SMU	6	6
O23		N.C. Pre-Flight	0	34
O31	=	Michigan State	7	7
N7		at Boston College	0	28
N14		Holy Cross	0	13
N21	●	Oklahoma	14	7
N28		Villanova	7	20

1943 — 2-6-0

S24	●	VMI	27	0
O1	●	Swarthmore	13	6
O9		at Army	0	51
O15		Ursinus	6	10
O22		Bucknell	6	7
N6		at Holy Cross	6	42
N13		at Penn State	0	13
N20		Villanova	7	34

1944 — 2-4-2

S29	●	Swarthmore	34	12
O6		Holy Cross	0	30
O14	●	at NYU	25	0
O20	=	Syracuse	7	7
O27	=	Bucknell	7	7
N4		at West Virginia	0	6
N11		Penn State	6	7
N18		at Tennessee	14	27

1945 — 7-1-0

S28	●	Syracuse	7	6
O5	●	NYU	59	0
O12	●	Bucknell	64	0
O19	●	West Virginia	28	12
O27	●	at Pittsburgh	6	0
N3	●	Lafayette	20	0
N10		at Penn State	0	27
N17	●	at Holy Cross	14	6

1946 — 2-4-2

S27	=	SMU	7	7
O4		Georgia	7	35
O12	=	at Pittsburgh	0	0
O18	●	West Virginia	6	0
N2		at Syracuse	7	28
N9		at Penn State	0	26
N16	●	Bucknell	27	6
N23		Holy Cross	7	12

1947 — 3-6-0

S26	●	NYU	32	7
O4		at Holy Cross	13	19
O11		at Syracuse	12	28
O17	●	Muhlenberg	7	6
O25	●	at Bucknell	21	0
N1		Oklahoma State	0	26
N8		Penn State	0	7
N15		at Michigan State	6	14
N22		at West Virginia	0	21

1948 — 2-6-1

S24	=	Lebanon Valley	7	7
O2		West Virginia *HER*	7	27
O9		at Rutgers	20	34
O15		Boston U.	7	13
O23		at Oklahoma State	7	41
O29	●	Bucknell	20	0
N6	●	Syracuse	20	0
N13		at Penn State	0	47
N20		Holy Cross	7	13

ALBERT P. KAWAL 1949-54 (.464) 24-28-3

1949 — 5-4-0

S24		Texas	0	54
O1	●	Rutgers	14	7
O7	●	at Syracuse	27	14
O14	●	Bucknell	20	19
O21	●	Rhode Island	47	6
O29		at Michigan State	14	62
N5		at Boston U.	7	28
N19	●	at Holy Cross	20	7
N28		Penn State	7	28

1950 — 4-4-1

S22	●	Albright	32	6
S29	●	Syracuse	7	6
O14		at Rutgers	20	26
O21	●	Wayne St.	26	0
O28	=	at Penn State	7	7
N4	●	Delaware	39	0
N11		Bucknell	0	35
N18		Fordham	21	26
N25		at Holy Cross	21	26

1951 — 6-4-0

S21		at Syracuse	0	19
S29	●	at Brown	20	4
O6	●	Rutgers	14	7
O12	●	Albright	47	6
O20	●	at Delaware	13	7
O26	●	Boston U.	20	13
N3		at Bucknell	7	28
N10	●	NYU	34	6
N17		Fordham	6	35
N24		at Holy Cross	7	41

1952 — 2-7-1

S20		at Penn State	13	20
S26	●	Albright	21	0
O3		Syracuse	0	27
O10		Bucknell	12	19
O18		at Indiana	0	33
O25	●	NYU	34	7
N1		at Rutgers	28	40
N6	=	at Boston U.	14	14
N15		Fordham	6	33
N22		Holy Cross	0	28

1953 — 4-4-1

S18	●	Albright	34	0
S26		at Syracuse	0	42
O3	●	Bowling Green	27	0
O17	●	at Bucknell	27	21
O24	●	Scranton	33	7
O31	=	Bainbridge	7	7
N7		at Yale	6	32
N14		at Fordham	0	28
N21		Boston U.	0	20

1954 — 3-5-0

O2		Boston College	9	21
O9		at Delaware	13	51
O16		Bucknell	0	27
O23	●	at Brown	19	14
O30		at Rutgers	0	25
N6	●	Brandeis	27	0
N13	●	at Scranton	20	0
N20		Boston U.	7	19

JOSH CODY 1955 (.000) 0-8

1955 — 0-8-0

S24		at Holy Cross	7	42
O1		Scranton	6	20
O15		at Bucknell	0	38
O22		at Carnegie Tech	16	18
O29		at Lehigh	14	27
N5		Muhlenberg	6	7
N12		Delaware	0	46
N19		at Boston U.	0	25

PETER P. STEVENS 1956-59 (.125) 4-28

1956 — 3-5-0

S29		at Lafayette	0	20
O6	●	at Muhlenberg	19	14
O13	●	Scranton	28	20
O20	●	Carnegie Tech	27	12
O27		Bucknell	6	12
N3		Lehigh	0	21
N10		Gettysburg	7	13
N17		at Delaware	7	14

1957 — 1-6-0

O5		at Bucknell	6	19
O12		at Hofstra	7	13
O19	●	Lafayette	13	12
N2		Muhlenberg	16	40
N9		at Delaware	7	71
N16		at Gettysburg	7	42
N23		Buffalo	6	13

1958 — 0-8-0

O4		Delaware	14	35
O11		at Muhlenberg	18	21
O18		at Lafayette	0	35
O25		at Scranton	0	6
N1		at Buffalo	6	54
N8		Bucknell	6	44
N15		Gettysburg	6	22
N22		Hofstra	6	34

1959 — 0-9-0

S26		Buffalo	14	28
O3		Scranton	12	26
O10		Muhlenberg	13	14
O17		Lafayette	20	52
O24		Hofstra	0	15
O31		at Drexel	8	12
N7		at Delaware	0	62
N14		at Bucknell	6	26
N21		at Gettysburg	0	35

GEORGE MAKRIS 1960-69 (.505) 45-44-4

1960 — 2-7-0

S24	●	Kings Point	26	13
O1		Buffalo	12	21
O8		at Muhlenberg	14	17
O15		at Lafayette	7	9
O22		at Hofstra	4	6
O29	●	Drexel	30	8
N5		Delaware	12	26
N12		at Bucknell	0	23
N19		Gettysburg	8	14

1961 — 2-5-2

S23		at Kings Point	0	12
S30		Bucknell	7	8
O7	●	Muhlenberg	36	12
O14	=	Lafayette	12	12
O21		at Buffalo	3	30
O28	●	Hofstra	14	12
N4		at Delaware	0	28
N11	=	at Gettysburg	0	0
N18		Toledo	14	15

1962 — 3-6-0

S22	●	Kings Point	14	3
S29		Bucknell	14	15
O6	●	at Muhlenberg	38	7
O13	●	at Lafayette	21	0
O20		Buffalo	13	16
O27		at Hofstra	10	19
N3		Delaware	8	20
N10		at Toledo	0	13
N17		Gettysburg	15	22

1963 — 5-3-1

S21	●	Ithaca	30	21
S28	=	at Kings Point	20	20
O5	●	Connecticut	9	7
O12	●	Muhlenberg	29	0
O19	●	Lafayette	31	0
O26	●	Hofstra	46	14
N2		at Bucknell	3	14
N9		at Delaware	23	32
N16		at Susquehanna	18	22

1964 — 7-2-0

S26	●	Kings Point	34	9
O3	●	So. Connecticut	22	6
O10	●	at Boston U.	44	13
O17	●	at Lafayette	38	18
O24		at Connecticut	7	25
O31		Bucknell	28	31
N7	●	at Delaware	21	0
N14	●	Gettysburg	32	20
N21	●	Hofstra	21	6

1965 — 5-5-0

S18		George Washington	13	21
S25		at Kings Point	21	27
O2		Boston U.	7	14
O9		at Bucknell	14	40
O16	●	Lafayette	27	12
O23	●	at Connecticut	12	11
O30	●	Delaware	31	22
N6	●	Rhode Island	28	0
N13	●	Gettysburg	22	21
N20		Hofstra	28	42

MAC TEAMS

1966 — 6-3-0
S24	•	at Kings Point	48 8
O1	•	Boston U.	9 6
O8	•	Bucknell	82 28
O15	•	at Hofstra	18 7
O22	•	Connecticut	35 25
O29	•	Delaware	14 20
N5	•	at Rhode Island	21 19
N12	•	at Gettysburg	19 21
N19	•	Bowling Green	20 62

1967 — 7-2-0
S23	•	at Kings Point	18 12
S30	•	Boston U.	22 16
O7	•	at Buffalo	14 44
O14	•	Hofstra	35 23
O21	•	at Dayton	6 56
O28	•	at Delaware	26 17
N4	•	at Bucknell	13 8
N11	•	Gettysburg	45 27
N18	•	Akron	22 21

1968 — 4-6-0
S21	•	Rhode Island	28 0
S28	•	at Wayne St.	26 6
O5	•	at Boston U.	0 7
O12	•	Bucknell	26 29
O19	•	at Hofstra	20 12
O26	•	Delaware	27 50
N2	•	Buffalo	40 50
N9	•	at Gettysburg	30 11
N16	•	Northeastern	26 41
N23	•	Dayton	17 35

1969 — 4-5-1
S20	•	at Rhode Island	47 3
S27		William & Mary	6 7
O4	•	Wayne St.	34 0
O11	=	at Bucknell	7 7
O18	•	Hofstra	34 7
O25	•	at Delaware	0 33
N1	•	at Buffalo	0 33
N8		Gettsburg	14 16
N15	•	at Northeastern	35 17
N22	•	Boston U.	3 21

WAYNE HARDIN
1970-82 (.604) 80-52-3

1970 — 7-3-0
S12	•	Akron	0 21
S19	•	at Bucknell	10 3
S26	•	at Holy Cross	23 13
O3	•	at Boston U.	10 7
O10	•	Connecticut	41 23
O17	•	at Xavier	28 15
O31	•	Delaware	13 15
N7	•	Rhode Island	18 15
N14	•	Buffalo	21 8
N26	•	Villanova	26 31

1971 — 6-2-1
S18	•	Boston College	3 17
O2	•	Boston U.	34 10
O9	•	at Connecticut	38 0
O16	•	Xavier	38 0
O23	•	at West Virginia	33 43
O30	•	at Delaware	32 27
N6	•	Rhode Island	40 13
N13	•	William & Mary	17 13
N20	=	Villanova	13 13

1972 — 5-4-0
S9	•	at Syracuse	10 17
S16	•	at Xavier	16 12
S23	•	at Boston College	27 49
S30	•	Holy Cross	15 7
O14	•	West Virginia	39 36
O20	•	at Boston U.	14 17
O28	•	Delaware	9 28
N11	•	Rhode Island	22 0
N18	•	at Villanova	12 10

1973 — 9-1-0
S8	•	Xavier	49 7
S15	•	at Boston College	0 45
S22	•	Akron	47 33
S29	•	at Holy Cross	63 34
O6	•	Cincinnati	16 15
O13	•	Boston U.	35 15
O27	•	at Delaware	31 8
N3	•	Rhode Island	43 0
N17	•	at Drake	35 10
N24	•	at Villanova	34 0

1974 — 8-2-0
S14	•	Rhode Island	38 7
S28	•	Boston College	34 7
O5	•	Marshall	31 10
O12	•	So. Illinois	59 16
O19	•	Holy Cross	56 0
O26	•	Delaware	21 17
N2	•	at Cincinnati	20 22
N9	•	at Pittsburgh	24 35
N16	•	at West Virginia	35 21
N23	•	Villanova PHIL	17 7

1975 — 6-5-0
S6		Penn State PHIL	25 26
S13	•	at West Virginia	7 50
S20	•	Boston College	9 27
O4	•	Cincinnati	21 17
O11	•	Pittsburgh	6 55
O18	•	Akron	23 24
O25	•	at Delaware	45 0
N1	•	Dayton	23 10
N8	•	Rhode Island	45 6
N22	•	Drake	44 7
N29	•	Villanova PHIL	41 3

1976 — 4-6-0
S11	•	at Akron	23 13
S18	•	Grambling	31 30
S25	•	at Pittsburgh	7 21
O2	•	Delaware	16 18
O9	•	West Virginia	0 42
O23	•	at Syracuse	16 24
O30	•	Penn State	30 31
N6	•	at Drake	31 7
N13	•	at Dayton	35 6
N20	•	Villanova PHIL	7 24

1977 — 5-5-1
S10	•	So. Illinois	20 24
S17	•	Drake	42 0
S24	•	Pittsburgh	0 76
O1	•	at Delaware	6 3
O8	•	at West Virginia	16 38
O22	•	La. Lafayette	27 20
O29	=	at Cincinnati	17 17
N5	•	Rutgers	24 14
N12	•	at Penn State	7 44
N19	•	at Villanova	38 15
D11	•	Grambling TOK	32 35

1978 — 7-3-1
S1	•	Penn State	7 10
S16	•	at Drake	36 29
S23	•	at Pittsburgh	12 20
S30	•	Delaware	38 7
O7	=	at William & Mary	22 22
O14	•	Cincinnati	16 13
O21	•	West Virginia	28 27
O28	•	at Akron	56 21
N11	•	at Rutgers	10 13
N18	•	Villanova PHIL	27 17
D9	•	Boston College TOK	28 24

1979 — 10-2-0
S8	•	at West Virginia	38 16
S15	•	Drake	43 21
S22	•	at Delaware	31 14
S29	•	Pittsburgh	9 10
O6	•	at Rutgers	41 20
O13	•	Syracuse PHIL	49 17
O20	•	Cincinnati	35 14
N3	•	at Hawaii	34 31
N10	•	Akron	42 6
N17	•	at Penn State	7 22
N24	•	at Villanova	42 10

GARDEN STATE BOWL
D15	•	California	28 17

1980 — 4-7-0
S13	•	Rutgers	3 21
S20	•	Delaware	7 28
S27	•	at Pittsburgh	2 36
O4	•	Boston U.	53 6
O11	•	at Syracuse	7 31
O18	•	Akron	16 7
O25	•	Cincinnati	23 7
N1	•	at Louisville	17 12
N8	•	West Virginia	28 41
N15	•	Penn State	7 50
N22	•	at Villanova	7 23

1981 — 5-5-0
S5	•	William & Mary	42 0
S12	•	Syracuse PHIL	31 19
S19	•	at Delaware	7 13
O3	•	at Penn State	0 30
O10	•	Colgate	31 0
O17	•	at Rutgers	24 12
O24	•	at Cincinnati	24 13
O31	•	at Georgia	3 49
N7	•	at West Virginia	19 24
N21	•	Pittsburgh	0 35

1982 — 4-7-0
S4	•	at Penn State	14 31
S11	•	at Syracuse	23 18
S18	•	Delaware	22 0
S25	•	Rutgers	7 10
O2	•	at Boston College	7 17
O9	•	at Louisville	55 14
O16	•	at Pittsburgh	7 38
O30	•	Cincinnati	41 7
N6	•	West Virginia	17 20
N13	•	at Colgate	17 24
N20	•	East Carolina	10 23

BRUCE ARIANS
1983-88 (.409) 27-39

1983 — 4-7-0
S2	•	Syracuse PHIL	17 6
S10	•	at Pittsburgh	0 35
S24	•	Penn State PHIL	18 23
O1	•	Boston College	15 18
O8	•	at Cincinnati	16 31
O15	•	East Carolina	11 24
O22	•	at Delaware	23 16
O29	•	at Georgia	14 31
N5	•	at West Virginia	9 27
N12	•	Louisville	24 7
N19	•	at Rutgers	24 23

1984 — 6-5-0
S8	•	East Carolina	17 0
S15	•	at Rutgers	9 10
S22	•	Pittsburgh	13 12
S29	•	at Florida State	27 44
O6	•	at William & Mary	28 14
O13	•	at Boston College	10 24
O20	•	Delaware	19 34
O27	•	Virginia Tech	7 9
N3	•	Cincinnati	42 10
N17	•	West Virginia	19 17
N30	•	Toledo	35 6

1985 — 4-7-0
S7	•	at Boston College	25 28
S14	•	at Penn State	25 27
S21	•	Brigham Young	24 26
S28	•	at East Carolina	21 7
O5	•	at Cincinnati	28 16
O12	•	Rutgers	14 13
O19	•	William & Mary	45 16
O26	•	at Syracuse	14 29
N2	•	at Delaware	10 17
N9	•	Pittsburgh	17 21
N16	•	at West Virginia	10 23

1986 — 6-5-0
S6	•	at Penn State	15 45
S13	•	at Western Michigan	49 17
S20	•	Florida A&M	38 17
S27	•	at Brigham Young	17 27
O4	•	at Pittsburgh	19 13
O11	•	East Carolina	45 28
O18	•	Virginia Tech NOR	29 13
O25	•	Syracuse PHIL	18 28
N8	•	Boston College	29 38
N15	•	at Alabama	14 24
N22	•	at Rutgers	29 22

1987 — 3-8-0
S5	•	at Toledo	13 12
S12	•	at Boston College	7 28
S19	•	at Pittsburgh	24 21
S26	•	Akron	23 3
O3	•	at Penn State	13 27
O10	•	Tulsa	17 24
O17	•	at Florida	3 34
O31	•	at Army	7 17
N7	•	at East Carolina	26 31
N14	•	Houston	7 37
N21	•	Rutgers	14 17

1988 — 4-7-0
S3	•	at Syracuse	21 31
S10	•	Alabama	0 37
S17	•	at Navy	12 7
O1	•	Penn State PHIL	9 45
O15	•	at Pittsburgh	7 42
O22	•	at California	14 31
O29	•	at Rutgers	35 30
N5	•	East Carolina	17 34
N12	•	at Akron	37 17
N19	•	at Tulsa	10 15
N26	•	Boston College	45 28

JERRY BERNDT
1989-92 (.250) 11-33

1989 — 1-10-0
S2	•	at Western Michigan	24 31
S9	•	Syracuse PHIL	3 43
S16	•	at Penn State	3 42
S23	•	at Virginia Tech	0 23
S30	•	at Houston	7 65
O7	•	Pittsburgh	3 27
O14	•	at Boston College	14 35
O28	•	Northern Illinois	17 20
N4	•	at Georgia	10 37
N11	•	at East Carolina	24 31
N18	•	Rutgers	36 33

1990 — 7-4-0
S1	•	at Wyoming	23 38
S8	•	at Syracuse	9 19
S15	•	Austin Peay	28 0
S22	•	at Wisconsin	24 18
O6	•	at Penn State	10 48
O20	•	Virginia Tech	31 28
O27	•	East Carolina	30 27
N3	•	at Tennessee	20 41
N10	•	at Pittsburgh	28 18
N17	•	Rutgers	29 22
N24	•	at Boston College	29 10

1991-2004 BIG EAST

1991 — 2-9-0 (0-5-0)
S7	•	Alabama BIRM	3 41
S14		at Pittsburgh	7 26
S21		at Clemson	7 37
S28	•	Samford	40 0
O5		Penn State PHIL	7 24
O12		at West Virginia	9 10
O19	•	Navy	21 14
N2		at Syracuse	6 27
N9		Boston College	13 33
N16		at Rutgers	0 41
N23		Akron	32 37

1992 — 1-10-0 (0-6-0)
S5	•	Boston U.	35 0
S12		at Penn State	8 49
S19		Virginia Tech	7 26
S26		at Kansas State	14 35
O3		at Washington State	10 51
O17		Pittsburgh	20 27
O24		Syracuse PHIL	7 38
O31		at Boston College	6 45
N7		at Akron	15 29
N14		at Miami, Fla.	0 48
N21		Rutgers	10 35

RON DICKERSON
1993-97 (.145) 8-47

1993 — 1-10-0 (0-7-0)
S9	•	at Eastern Michigan	31 28
S18		California	0 58
S25		at Boston College	14 66
O2		Rutgers ERUT	0 62
O9		Army	21 56
O16		at Virginia Tech	7 55
O23		Akron	7 31
O30		at Miami, Fla.	7 42
N6		at Syracuse	3 52
N13		West Virginia	7 49
N20		Pittsburgh	18 28

1994 — 2-9-0 (0-7-0)
S3	•	at Akron	32 7
S17	•	East Carolina	14 31
S24	•	at Army	23 20
O1		Penn State	21 48
O8		at Virginia Tech	13 41
O15		at Boston College	28 45
O22		Syracuse PHIL	42 49
O29		at Pittsburgh	19 45
N5		at Rutgers	21 38
N12		West Virginia	17 55
N19		Miami, Fla.	14 38

MAC TEAMS

1995 — 1-10-0 (1-6-0)

S2		at Kansas State	7	34
S9		at West Virginia	13	24
S16		at Penn State	14	66
S30		Bowling Green	31	37
O7		at Syracuse	14	31
O14	●	Pittsburgh	29	27
O21		at East Carolina	22	32
O28		at Miami, Fla.	12	36
N4		Boston College	9	10
N11		Virginia Tech DC	16	38
N18		Rutgers	20	23

1996 — 1-10-0 (0-7-0)

A31	●	at Eastern Michigan	28	24
S7		Washington State	34	38
S14		at Bowling Green	16	20
S21		Penn State ERut	0	41
O5		at Pittsburgh	52	53
O12		at Virginia Tech	0	38
O19		West Virginia	10	30
O26		at Rutgers	17	28
N2		Miami, Fla.	26	57
N16		at Boston College	20	21
N23		Syracuse Phil	15	36

1997 — 3-8-0 (3-4-0)

A28		at Western Michigan	14	34
S6	●	Boston College	28	21
S13		at Penn State	10	52
S20		Virginia Tech	13	23
S27		Maryland Phil	21	24
O4	●	Pittsburgh	17	13
O18		at Syracuse	7	60
O25		at Miami, Fla.	15	47
N1	●	Rutgers	49	7
N8		at Navy	17	49
N15		at West Virginia	21	41

BOBBY WALLACE
1998-2005 (.211) — 19-71

1998 — 2-9-0 (2-5-0)

S5		at Toledo	12	24
S12		Akron Phil	28	35
S19		at Boston College	7	31
S26		at Maryland	20	30
O3		William & Mary	38	45
O10		West Virginia	7	37
O17	●	at Virginia Tech	28	24
O31		at Rutgers	10	21
N7	●	at Pittsburgh	34	33
N14		Miami, Fla.	7	42
N21		Syracuse Phil	7	38

1999 — 2-9-0 (2-5-0)

S2		Maryland	0	6
S11		at Kansas State	0	40
S18		at Akron	15	25
S25		at Marshall	0	34
O2		at Pittsburgh	24	55
O9	●	Boston College	24	14
O23		at West Virginia	17	20
O30	●	Rutgers	56	28
N6		at Syracuse	10	27
N20		Virginia Tech	7	62
D4		at Miami, Fla.	0	55

2000 — 4-7-0 (1-6-0)

S2	●	at Navy	17	6
S9		at Maryland	10	17
S16	●	Bowling Green	31	14
S23	●	Eastern Michigan	49	40
S28		West Virginia	24	29
O7		at Virginia Tech	13	35
O14	●	at Rutgers	48	14
O21		Miami, Fla.	17	45
N4		at Boston College	3	31
N11		Syracuse	12	31
N18		Pittsburgh	0	7

2001 — 4-7-0 (2-5-0)

A30	●	Navy	45	26
S8		Toledo	7	33
S22		at Bowling Green	23	42
O6		at Boston College	10	23
O13	●	Rutgers	30	5
O20		at Syracuse	3	45
O27		Pittsburgh	7	33
N3		at Miami, Fla.	0	38
N10		Virginia Tech	0	35
N17	●	at West Virginia	17	14
N24	●	Connecticut	56	7

2002 — 4-8-0 (2-5-0)

A29	●	Richmond	34	7
S7		Oregon State	3	35
S14		Miami, Fla.	21	44
S21		at South Carolina	21	42
S28		Cincinnati	22	35
O12	●	Syracuse	17	16
O19		at Connecticut	38	24
O26		at Virginia Tech	10	20
N2		West Virginia	20	46
N9		at Pittsburgh	22	29
N16	●	at Rutgers	20	17
N23		Boston College	14	36

2003 — 1-11-0 (0-7-0)

A30		at Penn State	10	23
S6		Villanova	20	23
S20		at Cincinnati	24	30
S27		at Louisville	12	21
O4	●	at Middle Tennessee	44	36
O11		Boston College	13	38
O18		at Miami, Fla.	14	52
O25		Rutgers	14	30
N8		at Syracuse	17	41
N15		Virginia Tech	23	24
N22		Pittsburgh	16	30
N29		at West Virginia	28	45

2004 — 2-9-0 (1-5-0)

S4		Virginia	14	44
S11		at Maryland	22	45
S18	●	Florida A&M	38	7
S25		at Toledo	17	45
O2		Bowling Green	16	70
O9		Pittsburgh	22	27
O16		at Rutgers	6	16
O23		at Connecticut	31	45
N6		at West Virginia	21	42
N13	●	Syracuse	34	24
N20		Boston College	17	34

2005-2006
INDEPENDENT

2005 — 0-11-0

S1		at Arizona State	16	63
S10		at Wisconsin	0	65
S17		Toledo	17	42
S24		Western Michigan	16	19
O1		at Bowling Green	7	70
O8		Maryland	7	38
O15		Miami, Fla.	3	34
O22		at Clemson	7	37
O29		Miami, Ohio	14	41
N5		at Virginia	3	51
N19		at Navy	17	38

AL GOLDEN
2006-Present (.083) — 1-11

2006 — 1-11-0

A31		at Buffalo	3	9
S9		Louisville	0	62
S16		at Minnesota	0	62
S23		at Western Michigan	7	41
S30		at Vanderbilt	14	43
O7		Kent State	17	28
O12		Clemson	9	63
O21		at Northern Illinois	21	43
O28	●	Bowling Green	28	14
N4		Central Michigan	26	42
N11		at Penn State	0	47
N18		at Navy	6	42

Neutral Site key: Birm Birmingham, AL / ERut East Rutherford, NJ / Her Hershey, PA / KC Kansas City, MO / Nor Norfolk, VA / Phil Philadelphia, PA / Tok Tokyo, Japan / Unk Unknown Unknown / DC Washington, DC
ƒ Forfeit † Game Later Forfieted # Disputed Victor * Disputed Score ‖ Designated Conference Game |2 Counted Twice in Conference Standings

TEMPLE RECORD BOOK

SINGLE-GAME RECORDS

RUSHING YARDS

RANK	PLAYER	DATE	OPPONENT	ATT	AVG	YDS
1	Paul Palmer	Oct. 11, 1986	East Carolina	43	8.1	349
2	Paul Palmer	Oct. 19, 1985	William & Mary	28	10	281
3	Zachary Dixon	Oct. 14, 1978	Cincinnati	33	7.3	241
4	Paul Palmer	Oct. 18, 1986	Virginia Tech	44	5.4	239
5	Tanardo Sharps	Oct. 19, 2002	Connecticut	35	6.4	223

PASSING YARDS

RANK	PLAYER	DATE	OPPONENT	ATT	COMP	YDS
1	Henry Burris	Oct. 5, 1996	Pittsburgh	41	25	445
2	Henry Burris	Oct. 22, 1994	Syracuse	53	32	392
3	Mike McGann	Oct. 12, 2002	Syracuse	38	20	340
4	Mike McGann	Sept. 20, 2003	Cincinnati	46	26	338
5	Devin Scott	Sept. 9, 2000	Maryland	34	24	336

RECEIVING YARDS

RANK	PLAYER	DATE	OPPONENT	REC	AVG	YDS
1	Van Johnson	Oct. 5, 1996	Pittsburgh	7	30.6	214
2	Travis Shelton	Oct. 21, 2006	Northern Illinios	7	29.1	204
3	Rich Drayton	Oct. 29, 1988	Rutgers	6	30.7	184
4	Willie Marshall	Sept. 22, 1985	Pittsburgh	7	26.1	183
5	Troy Kersey	Aug. 31, 1996	E. Michigan	7	25.4	178

POINTS

RANK	PLAYER	DATE	OPPONENT	TOT
1	Jim Callahan	Oct. 8, 1966	Bucknell	30
	Sherman Myers	Oct. 13, 1979	Syracuse	30

FIELD GOALS

RANK	PLAYER	DATE	OPPONENT	TOT
1	Cap Poklemba	Nov. 9, 2002	Pittsburgh	5
	Bob Wright	Nov. 24, 1990	Boston College	5
	Bob Clauser	Sept. 18, 1982	Delaware	5
4	17 players tied with 3			

TACKLES

RANK	PLAYER	DATE	OPPONENT	TOT
1	Lorenzo Square	Nov. 5, 1988	East Carolina	23
	Taylor Suman	Nov. 6, 1999	Syracuse	23

INTERCEPTIONS

RANK	PLAYER	DATE	OPPONENT	TOT
1	Mark McCants	Oct. 18, 1980	Akron	3

RETIRED NUMBERS

64 Bill Singletary

SINGLE-SEASON RECORDS

RUSHING YARDS

RANK	PLAYER	SEASON	ATT	YDS
1	Paul Palmer	1986	346	1,866
2	Paul Palmer	1985	275	1,516
3	Tanardo Sharps	2002	311	1,267
4	Zachary Dixon	1978	223	1,153
5	Todd McNair	1987	249	1,058

PASSING YARDS

RANK	PLAYER	SEASON	ATT	COMP	PCT	YDS
1	Henry Burris	1994	409	215	52.6	2,716
2	Walter Washington	2004	332	187	56.3	2,207
3	Brian Broomell	1979	214	120	56.1	2,103
4	Henry Burris	1996	280	142	51.0	2,084
5	Henry Burris	1995	300	139	46.3	2,004

RECEIVING YARDS

RANK	PLAYER	SEASON	REC	AVG	YDS
1	Gerald Lucear	1979	45	21.4	964
2	Van Johnson	1996	50	18.0	902
3	Willie Marshall	1985	40	22.3	893
4	Zamir Cobb	2003	74	11.7	866
5	Sean Dillard	2001	51	14.6	747

SCORING

RANK	PLAYER	SEASON	TD	FG	PAT	P2	TOT
1	Don Bitterlich	1975	0	21	32	0	95
2	Walter Washington	2004	15	0	0	1	92
3	Paul Palmer	1986	15	0	0	0	90
4	Bob Wright	1990	0	19	28	0	85
5	Gerald Lucear	1978	13	0	0	0	78

TOUCHDOWNS

RANK	PLAYER	SEASON	TOT
1	Brian Broomell	1979	26
2	Walter Washington	2004	25
3	Henry Burris	1994	24
4	Steve Joachim	1974	20
5	3 players tied with 15		

TACKLES

RANK	PLAYER	SEASON	TOT
1	Steve Conjar	1980	174
2	Steve Conjar	1979	163
3	Mike Curcio	1979	154
4	Lance Johnstone	1995	153
5	Al Singleton	1995	151

INTERCEPTIONS

RANK	PLAYER	SEASON	YDS	TOT
1	Sam Shaffer	1981	76	9
2	Kevin Harvey	1999	55	6
	Anthony Young	1982	111	6
	Mark McCants	1980	151	6
	Bob Mizia	1974	37	6

PUNTING

RANK	PLAYER	SEASON	PUNTS	YDS	AVG
1	Kip Shenefelt	1983	65	2,859	44.0
2	Casey Murphy	1979	40	1,718	43.0
3	Casey Murphy	1978	52	2,227	42.8
4	Trent Thompson	1990	42	1,795	42.7
5	Kip Shenefelt	1985	51	2,149	42.1

PUNT RETURNS

RANK	PLAYER	SEASON	RET	YDS	AVG
1	Marc Baxter	1992	12	167	13.9
2	Rich Drayton	1990	15	196	13.1

KICKOFF RETURNS

RANK	PLAYER	SEASON	RET	YDS	AVG
1	Paul Loughran	1971	15	502	33.5
2	Lew Lawhorn	1992	30	600	30.0
3	Travis Shelton	2006	27	778	28.8
4	Makonnen Fenton	2002	14	380	27.1
5	Makonnen Fenton	2001	20	522	26.1

CAREER RECORDS

RUSHING YARDS

RANK	PLAYER	SEASONS	ATT	AVG	TD	YDS
1	Paul Palmer	1983-86	935	5.2	39	4,895
2	Tanardo Sharps	1999-2002	687	4.7	20	3,260
3	Anthony Anderson	1975-78	583	4.5	22	2,610
4	Todd McNair	1985-88	576	4.1	16	2,383
5	Henry Hynoski	1972-74	439	5.1	16	2,218
6	Mark Bright	1976-79	351	5.5	17	1,943
7	Harold Harmon	1980-83	371	4.7	6	1,730
8	Stacey Mack	1997-98	298	5.3	14	1,591
9	Zachary Dixon	1977-78	312	4.9	12	1,522
10	Umar Ferguson	2003-05	364	4.2	11	1,513

PASSING YARDS

RANK	PLAYER	SEASONS	ATT	COMP	PCT	INT	TD	YDS
1	Henry Burris	1993-96	1,136	558	.491	45	49	7,495
2	Mike McGann	2001-05	1,050	511	.487	50	25	5,967
3	Lee Saltz	1983-86	655	339	.518	33	29	5,371
4	Devin Scott	1998-2001	681	401	.589	22	23	3,947
5	Doug Shobert	1970-72	598	341	.570	43	26	3,913
6	Brian Broomell	1976-79	500	263	.526	31	35	3,902
7	Tim Riordan	1981-83	403	313	.777	22	20	3,679
8	Matt Baker	1987-90	511	285	.558	23	24	3,651
9	Walter Washington	2003-04	539	297	.551	12	18	3,262
10	Steve Joachim	1973-74	380	208	.547	23	31	3,262

RECEIVING YARDS

RANK	PLAYER	SEASONS	REC	AVG	TD	YDS
1	Willie Marshall	1983-86	111	20.5	16	2,272
2	Gerald Lucear	1978-81	126	14.9	18	1,882
3	Van Johnson	1992-96	106	17.6	15	1,869
4	Zamir Cobb	2000-03	165	11.2	14	1,856
5	Troy Kersey	1994-97	89	20.0	10	1,780
6	Rich Drayton	1987-90	122	13.9	5	1,693
7	Sean Dillard	1999-2002	130	12.6	7	1,632
8	Steve Watson	1975-78	98	16.6	7	1,629
9	Randy Grossman	1971-1973	79	19.0	10	1,505
10	Keith Gloster	1984-87	57	26.0	11	1,483

SCORING

RANK	PLAYER	SEASONS	TD	FG	PAT	P2	TOT
1	Paul Palmer	1983-86	43	0	0	3	264
2	Bill Wright	1985-88	0	46	90	0	228
3	Don Bitterlich	1973-75	0	35	115	0	220
4	Cap Poklemba	1999-2002	0	36	82	0	190
5	Nick Mike-Mayer	1970-72	0	33	57	0	156

TOUCHDOWNS

RANK	PLAYER	SEASONS	TOT
1	Henry Burris	1993-96	49
2	Paul Palmer	1983-86	43
3	Brian Broomell	1976-79	35
4	Steve Joachim	1973-74	31
5	Lee Saltz	1983-86	29

TACKLES

RANK	PLAYER	SEASONS	TOT
1	Steve Conjar	1978-81	492
2	Lance Johnstone	1992-95	429
3	Al Singleton	1993-96	390
4	Taylor Suman	1998-2001	389
5	Joe Klecko	1973-76	373

INTERCEPTIONS

RANK	PLAYER	SEASONS	YDS	TOT
1	Anthony Young	1981-84	232	20
2	Mark McCants	1977-80	297	15
3	Kevin Ross	1980-83	107	13
	Bob Salla	1975-77	149	13
5	2 players tied at 11			

PUNTING

RANK	PLAYER	SEASONS	PUNTS	YDS	AVG
1	Trent Thompson	1990-91	96	4,028	42.0
2	Casey Murphy	1976-79	197	8,194	41.5
3	Kip Shenefelt	1982-85	194	8,017	41.3
4	Josh Boies	1996-97	86	3,442	40.0
5	Ed Liberati	1986-89	245	9,731	39.7

TEAM RECORDS

LONGEST WINNING STREAK
- 14, Sept. 22, 1973-Oct. 26, 1974
Streak broken vs. Cincinnati, 20-22, Nov. 2, 1974

LONGEST UNDEFEATED STREAK
- 14, Sept. 22, 1973-Oct. 26, 1974
Streak broken vs. Cincinnati, 20-22, Nov. 2, 1974

MOST CONSECUTIVE WINNING SEASONS
- 13, 1925-37

MOST CONSECUTIVE BOWL APPEARANCES
- 1 (tie), 1934; 1979

MOST POINTS IN A GAME
- 110, vs. Blue Ridge, Oct. 1, 1927

MOST POINTS ALLOWED IN A GAME
- 96, vs. Franklin & Marshall, Date Unknown, 1899

LARGEST MARGIN OF VICTORY
- 110 (110-0), vs. Blue Ridge, Oct. 1, 1927

LARGEST MARGIN OF DEFEAT
- 96 (0-96), vs. Franklin & Marshall, Date Unknown, 1899

LONGEST RUN FROM SCRIMMAGE
- 84 yards, Kevin Grady, vs. Akron, Oct. 18, 1975

LONGEST PASS PLAY
- 96 yards, Lee Saltz to Keith Gloster, vs. Cincinnati, Oct. 5, 1985

LONGEST FIELD GOAL
- 56 yards, Don Bitterlich, vs. Akron, Oct. 18, 1975

LONGEST PUNT
- 76 yards, Kip Shenefelt, vs. Louisville, Nov. 12, 1983

LONGEST PUNT RETURN
- 95 yards, Rich Drayton, vs. Austin Peay, Sept. 15, 1990

LONGEST INTERCEPTION RETURN
- 92 yards, Rich Lee, vs. Delaware, Oct. 30, 1971

PUNT RETURNS

RANK	PLAYER	SEASON	RET	YDS	AVG
1	Zamir Cobb	2000-03	NA	NA	10.4

KICKOFF RETURNS

RANK	PLAYER	SEASON	RET	YDS	AVG
1	Paul Loughran	1970-72	NA	NA	29.0

TEMPLE ANNUAL STATISTICAL LEADERS

YR	RUSHING	YDS	ATT	AVG	PASSING	ATT	CMP	PCT	YDS	RECEIVING	REC	YDS	AVG
1971	Paul Loughran	468	108	4.3	Doug Shobert	191	120	.63	1,513	Randy Grossman	27	473	17.5
1972	Paul Loughran	593	125	4.7	Doug Shobert	238	130	.55	1,416	Clint Graves	63	707	11.2
1973	Tom Sloan	1,036	173	6.0	Steve Joachim	159	80	.50	1,312	Randy Grossman	39	683	17.5
1974	Henry Hynoski	1,006	206	4.9	Steve Joachim	221	128	.58	1,950	Pete Righi	35	608	17.4
1975	Tom Duff	752	146	5.2	Pat Carey	198	103	.52	1,304	Jeff Stempel	30	510	17.0
1976	Anthony Anderson	803	176	4.6	Pat Carey	126	62	.49	839	Ken Williams	35	580	16.6
1977	Anthony Anderson	756	195	3.9	Pat Carey	163	77	.47	1,074	Steve Watson	31	573	18.5
1978	Zachary Dixon	1,153	223	5.2	Brian Broomell	209	112	.54	1,362	Steve Watson	41	637	15.5
1979	Mark Bright	1,036	193	5.4	Brian Broomell	214	120	.56	2,103	Gerald Lucear	45	964	21.4
1980	Kevin Duckett	651	129	5.0	Tink Murphy	191	90	.47	1,097	Gerald Lucear	29	387	13.3
1981	Jim Brown	883	163	5.4	Tink Murphy	245	128	.52	1,589	Gerald Lucear	47	493	10.5
1982	Harold Harmon	883	165	5.4	Tim Riordan	247	157	.64	1,840	Reggie Brown	43	591	13.7
1983	Paul Palmer	628	141	4.5	Tim Riordan	277	143	.52	1,732	Russell Carter	31	482	15.5
1984	Paul Palmer	885	182	4.9	Lee Saltz	184	97	.53	1,337	Willie Marshall	22	503	22.9
1985	Paul Palmer	1,516	275	5.5	Lee Saltz	229	107	.47	1,875	Willie Marshall	40	893	22.3
1986	Paul Palmer	1,866	346	5.4	Lee Saltz	203	117	.58	1,729	Willie Marshall	30	514	17.1
1987	Todd McNair	1,058	249	4.2	James Thompson	153	66	.43	985	Rich Drayton	18	286	15.9
1988	Todd McNair	761	197	3.9	Matt Baker	193	101	.52	1,539	Rich Drayton	26	460	17.7
1989	Ventres Stevenson	841	173	4.9	Anthony Richardson	126	68	.54	812	Maurice Johnson	31	290	9.4
1990	Scott McNair	623	116	5.4	Matt Baker	222	134	.60	1,462	Rich Drayton	48	564	11.8
1991	Scott McNair	605	152	4.0	Trent Thompson	172	79	.46	927	Leslie Shepherd	26	436	16.8
1992	Sam Jenkins	524	146	3.6	Chris Paliscak	137	65	.47	691	Wilbur Washington	22	285	13.0
1993	Ralphiel Mack	570	107	5.3	Henry Burris	149	62	.42	691	Ramondo Davidson	25	266	10.6
1994	Juan Gaddy	285	103	2.8	Henry Burris	409	215	.53	2,716	Sidney Morse	39	261	6.7
1995	Eugene Culbreath	451	103	4.4	Henry Burris	300	139	.46	2,004	Troy Kersey	20	469	23.5
1996	Ramod Lee	526	130	4.0	Henry Burris	280	142	.51	2,084	Van Johnson	50	902	18.0
1997	Stacey Mack	842	173	4.9	Pat Bonner	202	107	.53	1,561	Kevin Walker	34	688	20.2
1998	Stacey Mack	749	125	6.0	Devin Scott	69	25	.36	459	Carlos Johnson	18	378	21.0
1999	Marcus Godfrey	332	84	4.0	Devin Scott	369	222	.60	1,815	Carlos Johnson	51	520	10.2
2000	Tanardo Sharps	1,038	201	5.2	Devin Scott	216	136	.63	1,456	Greg Muckerson	41	487	11.9
2001	Tanardo Sharps	771	150	5.1	Mike McGann	190	87	.46	934	Sean Dillard	51	747	14.6
2002	Tanardo Sharps	1,267	311	4.1	Mike McGann	353	173	.49	1,994	Zamir Cobb	45	483	10.7
2003	Walter Washington	579	156	3.7	Mike McGann	234	123	.52	1,405	Zamir Cobb	74	866	11.7
2004	Walter Washington	889	222	4.0	Walter Washington	332	187	.56	2,207	Phil Goodman	47	677	14.4
2005	Umar Ferguson	710	191	3.7	Mike McGann	250	122	.49	1,469	Bruce Gordon	42	601	14.3
2006	Tim Brown	731	182	4.0	Adam Dimichele	220	135	.61	1,518	Tim Brown	33	218	6.6

Receiving leaders by receptions
The NCAA began including postseason stats in 2002

MAC TEAMS

TOLEDO

BY ED KRZEMIENSKI

ALTHOUGH BEST KNOWN FOR ITS minor league baseball team, the Mud Hens, and its fictional son, M*A*S*H's Max Klinger, the city of Toledo also boasts an excellent football team. Along with fellow Mid-American Conference members Miami of Ohio and Marshall, the University of Toledo stands as one of the giants of the MAC—nationally ranked eight times in the polls and the owner of the second-longest winning streak in Division I-A history, a 35-game run that encompassed three entire seasons from 1969 through 1971. Thirty years later, Toledo hired alum and hometown boy Tom Amstutz as head coach and, in six years, "Toledo Tom" led the Rockets to a 50–25 overall record, two MAC championships, four bowl berths, and four wins over Top 25 teams.

TRADITION Every time the Rockets score, the Phi Kappa Phi fraternity fires a cannon. It was fired off the northeast stone tower in the Glass Bowl until 1989, when it was moved to the field. Not to be outdone by a cannon, Toledo players bang their helmets on the doorway when entering or leaving any locker room. No word as to whether the players have to be wearing their helmets when adhering to this tradition. Students, meanwhile, gather around the Spirit Rock for pep rallies. Since 1968, the rock has been burned, painted, and tarred and feathered hundreds of times. Traditionally, the Spirit Rock only gets painted during twilight hours.

BEST PLAYER In 1968, Toledo recruited a quarterback named Chuck Ealey from Portsmouth, Ohio, a small town on the Kentucky border. Ealey had an impressive résumé, to say the least, having gone 30–0 in his prep career. In college, Ealey just got better. Continuing his unbeaten streak in the first game of his sophomore season at Toledo, Ealey led the Rockets to victory in all 35 of his college games from 1969 to 1971. Dubbed the Wizard of Oohs and Ahs, Ealey led the Rockets to a 35-game winning streak, bested only by Oklahoma's 47-game streak from 1953 to 1957. Ealey won MAC Back of the Year in each of his three varsity seasons and was the first MAC player to place in the top 10 in Heisman Trophy voting, when he finished eighth in 1971.

PROFILE

University of Toledo
Toledo, Ohio
Founded: 1872
Enrollment: 19,374
Colors: Midnight Blue and Gold
Nickname: Rockets
Stadium: Glass Bowl
    Opened in 1937
    NeXturf; 26,248 capacity
First football game: 1917
All-time record: 452–369–24 (.549)
Bowl record: 7–3
Mid-American Conference championships:
10 (8 outright)
First-round draft choices: 1
Website: www.utrockets.com

THE BEST OF TIMES

From 1969 to 1971, the Rockets went 35–0, winning three consecutive MAC championships and Tangerine Bowls.

THE WORST OF TIMES

From 1956 to 1964, UT won only 24 games while losing 57 and tying two. UT also had one of the worst beginnings in the history of the game, losing the first three of its inaugural season's games by a combined 262-0.

CONFERENCE

Toledo joined the Mid-American Conference in 1952, and has remained there since. Previously, UT played as an independent from 1917 to 1920, 1936 to 1937, and 1948 to 1951; in the Northwestern Ohio Intercollegiate Athletic Association from 1921 to 1930; and in the Ohio Athletic Conference from 1932 to 1935 and 1938 to 1947.

DISTINGUISHED ALUMNI

Seth Abraham, president, Madison Square Garden/Radio City Entertainment; Jon Hendricks, jazz singer; John Neff, investment legend; Karl Ronn, inventor of the Swiffer; Mildred Taylor, children's author

> ## Toledo and Bowling Green play for the Peace Pipe, but they rarely choose to smoke it.

One of Ealey's performances against Western Michigan was so amazing that WMU's coach Bill Doolittle remarked, "I think God was throwing some of those passes. I know he [Ealey] had to have some help." Part of a generation of gifted black quarterbacks ignored by the NFL, Ealey went on to a seven-year career in the Canadian Football League, where he led the Hamilton Tiger-Cats to the Grey Cup championship in his rookie season.

BEST COACH Gary Pinkel holds Toledo records for victories (73) and years served (10). Before taking over at Missouri in 2001, Pinkel coached the Rockets to eight winning seasons in ten years, including an 11–0–1 mark in 1995 and a 10–1 record in 2000. In the 1995 season, Toledo won the MAC, defeated Nevada in the Las Vegas Bowl and ended up ranked No. 24 in the nation. Pinkel's Rockets finished the 2000 season ranked No. 25.

BEST TEAM An argument could be made for any of the three consecutive undefeated teams from 1969 to 1971, but the 1970 squad deserves the nod. Led by junior quarterback Ealey, who threw for 1,898 yards and 16 touchdowns, the 1970 Rockets outscored their opponents 344-76 in their 12–0 season. Most impressive was the fact that except for a 14-13 thriller against a strong Miami of Ohio team, no one even challenged this Toledo squad. Colorado State put up the next-best effort and they lost by 10 points. The Rockets' average margin of victory was more than 24 points per game, including a 40-12 rout of William & Mary in the Tangerine Bowl. Four players from this team ended up in the NFL, and one of those, defensive tackle Mel Long, was a consensus All-American. Toledo was No. 12 in the final AP poll.

BEST BACKFIELD As the quarterback who led Toledo to 35 consecutive victories, it would seem like Chuck Ealey and two tackling dummies could have served as the Rockets' best ever backfield. That, of course, is not how it works—Ealey could not have led Toledo to its unprecedented success alone. In 1971, Ealey put together a typically superb season, throwing for 1,821 yards and 15 touchdowns. That year, Joe Schwartz became Toledo's first 1,000-yard running back when he rushed for 1,130 yards in the Rockets' third consecutive undefeated season.

FIGHT SONG

U OF TOLEDO
U of Toledo, we'll fight for you
(Fight! Fight! Fight!)
U of Toledo, we love the gold and blue
(Let's go blue!)
Men of the varsity, the enemy must yield,
We'll fight just like our ancestors
And march right down the field!
T-O-L-E-D-O, Toledo!

FIRST-ROUND DRAFT CHOICE

1993	Dan Williams, Broncos (11)	

CONSENSUS ALL-AMERICANS

1938	Dan Buckwick, G	
1971	Mel Long, DT	

COLLEGE FOOTBALL HALL OF FAME INDUCTEES

NAME	YEARS	INDUCTED
Merle Gulick, QB	1924-25	1965
Mel Long, DT	1969-71	1998

The junior Schwartz certainly made his presence felt in the season opener, running for 206 yards—including an 82-yard jaunt—against East Carolina. The fun had just begun.

BEST DEFENSE The 1971 Rockets' defense ranked No. 1 in the nation, but the previous year's squad was actually a bit better. Led by defensive tackle Mel Long, who a year later became the MAC's first consensus All-America, Toledo allowed an average of 185 yards per game in 1970. The real strength of the 1970 defense, though, was its ball-hawking nature. The team averaged almost 4 turnovers a game, 26 interceptions, including 7 by Gary Hinkson alone—versus a single touchdown pass allowed. The result was some very long afternoons for Toledo opponents, who managed only 88 points in 12 games. Toledo placed four more defenders (including Long and Hinkson) on the all-MAC first team defense.

BIGGEST GAME On Dec. 14, 1995, in the Las Vegas Bowl, Toledo and Nevada played the first overtime game in Division I history. It looked dark for the Rockets late in the game when Nevada recovered a fumble at the Toledo 4-yard line. Leading 34-31, the Toledo defense held the Wolf Pack to a field goal, and did the same in overtime, as Nevada took its first—very fragile—lead of the game. Running back Wasean Tait proved to be the Toledo hero when he scored on his third consecutive carry of the overtime to give the Rockets a 40-37 victory. It was a fitting end. Tait ran for 185 yards and four touchdowns, and accounted for 238 all-purpose yards, all Las Vegas Bowl records at the time. (In a rare regular-season meeting earlier in the year, Tait ran for 176 yards against the Wolf Pack on his way to a season total of 1,905 yards.)

BIGGEST UPSET In its fourth game of the 2003 season, Toledo faced a home game against Pitt—a rare visit to the MAC from a major power, and by a team that had spanked the Rockets 37-19 the previous season. Toledo entered the late-September game with little hope, and the chances of an upset seemed even more remote by the fourth quarter, with Pitt leading 31-21 and the Rockets on their own 2-yard line. Toledo quarterback Bruce Gradkowski, however, led the team on a 98-yard touchdown drive that cut the lead to 31-28 with 6:45 left. With 43 seconds to go, Gradkowski finished the comeback with a nine-yard touchdown pass to Lance Moore.

BIGGEST COMEBACK In the 2001 MAC championship, it looked like Toledo would waste its

> *Astronaut John Glenn gave the school an authentic space suit, helmet and boots in 1977.*

opportunity to impress a national television audience. Midway through the second quarter, the Rockets trailed the Byron Leftwich-led Marshall Thundering Herd 23-0 in front of a discouraged home crowd. But Toledo scored 10 quick points before the half and another 25 in the third, and led Marshall 35-29 at the start of the final quarter. Marshall took back the lead by a point when Leftwich threw an 18-yard touchdown pass to Denero Marriott early in the fourth quarter. But Toledo running back Chester Taylor, who ran for 152 of his 188 yards in the second half, answered back, scoring the game's final touchdown to give the Rockets a 41-36 victory and end Marshall's four-year run of MAC championships.

STADIUM Toledo's Glass Bowl is widely regarded as the best football stadium in the MAC. It was constructed almost entirely with federal funds made available by FDR's Works Progress Administration, and completed in 1937. In honor of the local companies that donated glass for the stadium's towers and press box, the school officially named it the Glass Bowl. Unfortunately, Toledo attempted to christen the Glass Bowl during a heavy rainstorm. With no grass yet planted around the stadium, the deluge flooded the area and mud blocked the gates. The school was forced to postpone its opening game until the following Monday, Sept. 27, 1937. Despite the fact that the listed capacity for the Glass Bowl is 26,248, a crowd of 36,852 jammed in to watch the Rockets host Navy in 2001.

RIVAL Without question, Toledo's greatest rival is Bowling Green. The teams play annually for the Peace Pipe, but they rarely choose to smoke it. The week of the game is known as BG Week in Toledo, since it is considered in bad taste to utter the words Bowling Green. Diehard Rocket fans refrain from uttering so much as their rival's initials, preferring "that school down the road." Making matters even more intense is the Nike-Ajax missile that the school received from the U.S. Army in 1961. Known simply as The Rocket, the missile resides on the northeast corner of the Glass Bowl. It is pointed on a trajectory 25 miles to the south of Toledo. Were it to be fired, The Rocket would land directly on the 50-yard line of Bowling Green's Doyt L. Perry Stadium. Despite the continuing possibility of a preemptive missile attack, Toledo trails in the series, 29–36–4.

NICKNAME In 1923, Carnegie Tech played against a Toledo team without a nickname. Pressed by Pittsburgh sportswriters to come up with one, James Neal, a UT

student working in the press box, labeled the team Skyrockets in honor of their high-flying performance against the stronger Techsters. The sportswriters shortened the name to Rockets, which has been used ever since. Prior to 1923, writers referred to the team variously as the Blue and Gold, Munies (for municipal university), and Dwyer's boys (for coach Joseph Dwyer).

MASCOT Rocky the Rocket's career began in 1966 when the student government's spirit and traditions committee began selecting students to periodically dress up as the mascot. In 1968, the "uniform" consisted of a wastepaper basket with a pointed top. In 1977, U.S. senator and former astronaut John Glenn helped the school upgrade to an authentic space suit, helmet, and boots from the NASA Space Center in Houston. Beginning in 1998, Rocky the Rocket appeared in a blue-and-gold rocket-man costume with a jet pack and helmet.

UNIFORMS At an organizational meeting of the Varsity T booster club on Dec. 1, 1919, 10 of Toledo's varsity football lettermen chose midnight blue and gold as the school's official colors. Ever since, the Rockets have appeared in a combination of these two colors, as well as white. Currently, the team wears midnight blue jerseys with matching pants at home and white jerseys on the road. Except for a period in the mid-1960s, when the helmets were white with a rocket on the side, Toledo's headgear has been blue with gold or white lettering—spelling either UT or the word Toledo. Since 1997, the helmets have been blue, with Toledo written across the side in white, and a gold rocket in flight overhead.

NUMBERS Two years after Ealey ended his career at Toledo, the Rockets put another sensation behind center. Although Gene Swick never matched Ealey's winning ways, he put up some gaudy numbers when it came to throwing the ball. In his final game at Toledo, against Kent State in 1975, Swick passed for 283 yards to send his career mark for total offense to 8,074, surpassing the NCAA Division I-A record held previously by Stanford's Jim Plunkett. Swick was the first to break the 8,000-yard mark.

QUOTE "Nobody else wanted the job." —Team member Charles Morgan, on how John Brandeberry became Toledo's first head coach. The Rockets failed to score in their 1917 debut season, losing their first game to Detroit 145-0.

TOLEDO ALL-TIME SCORES

WIN/LOSS PERCENTAGE SINCE 1936

1936	1940		1945		1950		1955		1960		1965		1970		1975	
1980		1985		1990		1995		2000		2006						

JOHN BRANDEBERRY
1917 (.000)   0-3-0

1917   0-3-0
O10	at Detroit	0	145
O20	at Ohio Northern	0	90
U	at Findlay	0	27

JAMES BAXTER
1918 (.500)   1-1

1918   1-1-0
U ●	Defiance *Unk*	19	12
U	Hillsdale *Unk*	18	31

WALT HOBT
1919-20 (.222)   2-7

1919   2-4-0
S27	Ohio Northern *Unk*	0	13
O3 ●	at Bowling Green	6	0
U	Western Reserve *Unk*	0	19
O19	Adrian *Unk*	6	27
U ●	Defiance *Unk*	12	6
U	Wayne St.	7	8

1920   0-3-0
S25	at Western Reserve	7	17
O1	Wooster	0	36
O7	at Wayne St.	0	14

JOSEPH DWYER
1921-22 (.433)   5-7-3

1921   3-5-0
S24	at Cincinnati	0	20
O8 ●	at Findlay	46	0
O15 ●	Defiance	40	0
O22	at Adrian	0	1 *f*
O29	Bowling Green	7	20
N5 ●	Baldwin-Wallace	1	0 *f*
N11	at Bluffton	0	14
N19	Wayne St.	0	13

1922   2-2-3
O7	at Defiance	0	7
O14 =	Alma	0	0
O20 ●	Hillsdale	6	0
N4 =	at Bowling Green	6	6
N11 ●	Muskingum	3	0
N18 ●	at Wayne St.	2	6
N24 =	Baldwin-Wallace	0	0

JAMES DWYER
1923-25 (.444)   12-15

1923   6-4-0
S29	at Carnegie Tech	12	32
O6 ●	Eastern Michigan	13	0
O13	at Akron	3	10
O19 ●	Defiance	26	0
O27 ●	Bowling Green	27	0
N3 ●	Findlay	87	0
N10 ●	Grand Rapids	32	0
N17 ●	Wayne St.	38	0
N24	at Hillsdale	19	32
D1	Notre Dame JV	0	31

1924   5-3-0
O4 ●	at Eastern Michigan	7	0
O11	at Carnegie Tech	0	54
O25 ●	at Bowling Green	12	7
U ●	Hillsdale	19	0
N1 ●	Assumption	6	0
N8	at Dayton	6	52
N15 ●	at Wayne St.	27	0
N22	at Akron	7	14

1925   1-8-0
S6	Western Reserve	0	14
O3	at Buffalo	0	2
O10	Dayton	6	29
O17	Ohio U.	0	7
O31	at Assumption	2	6
N7	at Michigan State	0	58
N11 ●	at Findlay	20	0
N14	Wayne St.	0	23
N21	at Louisville	0	33 *

BONI PETCOFF
1926-29 (.466)   13-15-1

1926   3-5-0
O2	at Alma	0	19
O9	Hillsdale	14	26
O16	at Defiance	0	12
O23	Bluffton	7	13
O30 ●	Findlay	7	0
N6	at Xavier	6	69
N13 ●	at Wayne St.	14	7
N20 ●	Bufflao	33	7

1927   5-2-0
O1	Alma	0	30
O8 ●	Hillsdale	19	0
O15 ●	Wayne St.	13	0
O22 ●	at Bluffton	6	0
N4 ●	Defiance	16	7
N11 ●	at Findlay	34	0
N18	at Wittenberg	0	25

1928   1-6-0
O5 ●	Findlay	31	9
O13	at Central Michigan	0	13
O20	at Bowling Green	0	14
O27	at Defiance	0	15
N3	at Wayne St.	6	13
N9	Bluffton	9	33
N17	Michigan JV	0	33

1929   4-2-1
S28	Akron	0	26
O12 ●	at Findlay	7	0
O26 =	Bowling Green	0	0
N2 ●	at Bluffton	7	0
N9 ●	Wayne St.	17	0
N16	at Central Michigan	12	31
N23 ●	Defiance	25	13

JIM NICHOLSON
1930-35 (.550)   20-16-4

1930   2-5-1
S27	at Akron	0	41
O4	at Ohio Northern	0	6
O11 ●	Defiance	12	13
O17	at Findlay	6	20
O24	Heidelberg	0	58
N1 =	at Bowling Green	0	0
N8 ●	Bluffton	14	0
N22 ●	at Wayne St.	18	0

1931

NO TEAM

1932   3-4-0
O1 ●	Capital	18	0
O8 ●	Wayne St.	0	3
O15 ●	at Heidelberg	0	12
O22 ●	Marietta	6	0
O28 ●	Ohio State JV	0	6
N5 ●	at Bowling Green	6	12
N12 ●	Otterbein	12	7

1933   4-2-2
S30	at Capital	2	27
O7 =	at Wayne St.	0	0
O14 ●	Defiance	29	6
O21 ●	at Kenyon	12	0
O28 ●	Bowling Green	25	7
N4 =	Heidelberg	6	6
N11 ●	John Carroll	13	33
N18 ●	Otterbein	12	7

1934   5-3-0
S29 ●	Capital	20	0
O6 ●	Western Reserve	0	7
O13 ●	Louisville	19	7
O20 ●	Kenyon	40	0
O27 ●	at Buffalo	0	8
N3 ●	at Bowling Green	22	0
N10 ●	at Muskingum	9	0
N23 ●	Case	13	33

1935   6-2-1
S28 ●	Capital	0	6
O5 ●	at Boston U.	0	6
O12 =	Haskell	0	0
O19 ●	at Case	18	7
O26 ●	Denison	13	0
N1 ●	Bowling Green	63	0
N9 ●	at Louisville	41	7
N16 ●	Buffalo	19	6
N23 ●	Heidelberg	31	0

DOC SPEARS
1936-42 (.591)   38-26-2

1936   2-6-0
O3 ●	Findlay	32	0
O10	Boston U.	0	6
O17 ●	at Denison	6	9
O24 ●	Western Reserve	0	14
O31 ●	Wayne St.	6	9
N7	at Miami, Ohio	0	13
N14 ●	at Heidelberg	0	7
N21 ●	Otterbein	50	0

1937   6-3-0
S27 ●	Bluffton	26	0
O2 ●	Georgetown, Ky.	19	0
O9 ●	at Ohio Wesleyan	6	0
O16 ●	Akron	7	21
O23 ●	Miami, Ohio	13	7
O30 ●	at Wayne St.	39	19
N6 ●	Dayton	12	7
N13 ●	at West Virginia	0	34
N20 ●	at Xavier	6	8

1938   6-3-1
S24 ●	West Liberty	13	0
O1 ●	St. Joseph	26	0
O8 ●	Ohio Wesleyan	26	0
O15 ●	at Dayton	13	17
O22 ●	Marshall	13	7
O29 ●	at Wayne St.	39	20
N5 =	John Carroll	6	6
N12 ●	at Akron	7	13
N24 ●	at Xavier	0	13
D2 ●	at St. Mary's, Texas	13	7

1939   7-3-0
S23 ●	Valparaiso	39	0
S30 ●	Detroit Tech	19	6
O7 ●	St. Mary's, Texas	20	12
O14 ●	North Dakota	26	7
O20 ●	at Scranton	6	7
O28 ●	Western Michigan	6	0
N4 ●	at John Carroll	20	0
N11 ●	at Marshall	12	14
N18 ●	Long Island	12	13
N23 ●	at Xavier	20	0

1940   6-3-0
S28 ●	Detroit Tech	21	3
O5 ●	Davis & Elkins	34	12
O12 ●	Marshall	7	6
O19 ●	Scranton	0	6
O26 ●	at Western Michigan	12	0
N2 ●	John Carroll	33	12
N8 ●	at Baldwin-Wallace	12	14
N16 ●	at Butler	20	6
N23 ●	at Long Island	7	19

1941   7-4-0
S27	St. Joseph	0	3
O4 ●	Detroit Tech	55	0
O11 ●	at Marshall	7	33
O18 ●	at John Carroll	20	0
O25 ●	at Western Michigan	0	34
N2 ●	at Illinois Wesleyan	9	0
U ●	Camp Shelby	39	0
N8 ●	Butler	2	18
N15 ●	Baldwin-Wallace	27	7
N22 ●	at Bradley	14	6
N27 ●	at Jefferson Barracks	22	21

1942   4-4-1
S26 ●	Kent State	26	14
O3 ●	Illinois Wesleyan	26	0
O10 ●	Western Michigan	0	13
O16 =	at John Carroll	6	6
O24 ●	Marshall	7	0
O31 ●	US Coast Guard	0	26
N7 ●	at Butler	0	12
N14 ●	at Youngstown St.	12	30
N21 ●	Bradley	14	13

1943-45

NO TEAM – WWII

BILL ORWIG
1946-47 (.762)   15-4-2

1946   6-2-2
S28 =	Western Reserve	14	14
O5 ●	Case	42	14
O12 =	at Marshall	14	14
O19 ●	Dayton	13	20
O26 ●	at Akron	33	19
N2 ●	John Carroll	28	19
N11 ●	Wayne St.	14	6
N16 ●	at Baldwin-Wallace	14	7
N23 ●	at Wichita St.	7	13
	GLASS BOWL		
D7 ●	Bates	21	12

1947   9-2-0
S20 ●	Great Lakes NAS	40	0
S27 ●	Case	41	0
O4 ●	John Carroll	14	35
O11 ●	Youngtown St.	21	7
O18 ●	at Dayton	14	13
O25 ●	Akron	38	7
N1 ●	Baldwin-Wallace	14	6
N8 ●	at Wayne St.	7	0
N15 ●	South Dakota St.	33	12
N22 ●	at Canisius	13	21
	GLASS BOWL		
D6 ●	Hampshire	20	14

J.N. STAHLEY
1948-49 (.524)   11-10

1948   5-6-0
S18 ●	Bates	42	0
S24 ●	at Detroit	0	36
O2 ●	John Carroll	20	46
O9 ●	Bowling Green	6	21
O16 ●	Dayton	0	20
O23 ●	at Springfield	21	14
O30 ●	Baldwin-Wallace	14	20
N6 ●	Wayne St.	27	14
N13 ●	Canisius	21	26
N20 ●	at New Hampshire	28	14
	GLASS BOWL		
D4 ●	Oklahoma City	27	14

TOLEDO 461

1949 6-4-0

S25		Loras	26	35
O1		JohnCarroll	14	28
O8	●	Bowling Green	20	19
O15		at Dayton	14	47
O22	●	Springfield	42	14
O29	●	Oklahoma City	48	7
N5	●	at Wayne St.	37	7
N12	●	North Dakota	56	6
N19	●	at New Hampshire	48	14
		GLASS BOWL		
D3		Cincinnati	13	33

ROBERT SNYDER
1950 (.444) 4-5

1950 4-5-0

S24	●	Pittsburgh, Kansas	32	14
S30		John Carroll	0	41
O7		at Western Michigan	19	54
O14		Dayton	13	14
O21	●	at Bradley	32	20
O28		Bowling Green	14	39
N4	●	Western Reserve	27	7
N10		at St. Bonaventure	7	38
N17	●	Wayne St.	56	7

DON GREENWOOD
1951 (.571) 4-3

CLAIR DUNN
1951-53 (.429) 9-12

1951 6-4-0

S15	●	Davis & Elkins	88	0
S22		at Detroit	32	34
S29		Western Michigan	6	14
O6	●	John Carroll	26	12
O13		at Dayton	7	47
O20	●	Marshall	32	14
O27	●	at Bowling Green	12	6
N3	●	Ohio U.	13	6
N10	●	Bradley	38	13
N22		at Xavier	6	32

1952-PRESENT
MAC

1952 4-5-0 (1-4-0)

S20		Eastern Kentucky	6	7
S27	● |	Western Reserve	10	9
O4	|	at Ohio U.	20	22
O11	●	John Carroll	6	3
O18	|	at Western Michigan	14	19
O25	|	Bowling Green	19	29
N1	|	at Miami, Ohio	13	27
N8	●	Bradley	20	14
N15	●	at Youngstown St.	24	21

1953 3-6-0 (2-3-0)

S19	|	Ohio U.	0	26
S26	|	at Western Reserve	20	21
O3		Fort Belvoir	13	62
O10		at Cincinnati	7	41
O17	● |	Western Michigan	19	7
O24	● |	at Bowling Green	20	19
O31	|	Miami, Ohio	0	81
N7	●	at Bradley	27	12
N14		John Carroll	7	36

FORREST ENGLAND
1954-55 (.556) 9-7-2

1954 6-2-1 (3-2-0)

S18	●	Muskingum	27	6
S25	|	Western Reserve	7	12
O2	|	at Ohio U.	20	28
O9	●	John Carroll	7	6
O16	● |	at Western Michigan	19	7
O23	● |	Bowling Green	38	7
O30	=	at Eastern Kentucky	13	13
N6	●	Baldwin-Wallace	47	13
N12	● |	at Marshall	27	21

1955 3-5-1 (2-4-0)

S17	=	Eastern Kentucky	6	6
S23	●	at Detroit	12	7
O1	|	Ohio U.	13	34 *
O8	|	at Miami, Ohio	0	47
O15	● |	Western Michigan	6	0
O22	|	at Bowling Green	0	39
N5	|	Kent State	0	27
N12	● |	Marshall	27	13
N19		at Louisville	13	33

JACK MORTON
1956 (.167) 1-7-1

1956 1-7-1 (1-5-0)

S15		Eastern Kentucky	6	12
S22		Louisville	12	27
S29	● |	at Ohio U.	19	13
O6	|	Miami, Ohio	14	33
O13	|	at Western Michigan	15	26
O20	|	Bowling Green	12	34
N3	|	at Kent State	6	52
N9	|	at Marshall	13	32
N17	=	Brandeis	21	21

HARRY LARCHE
1957-59 (.426) 11-15-1

1957 5-4-0 (3-2-0)

S21	●	at Eastern Kentucky	7	0
S28	● |	Ohio U.	14	6
O5		at Louisville	20	48
O12	|	Marshall	7	14
O19	|	at Bowling Green	0	29
O26	● |	Western Michigan	27	16 *
N2	● |	Kent State	21	7
N9		at Xavier	7	20
N16	●	Muskingum	33	7

1958 4-5-0 (1-4-0)

S20	●	Eastern Kentucky	19	2
S27	|	at Ohio U.	6	13
O4	●	Louisville	13	7
O11	|	at Marshall	12	35
O18	|	Bowling Green	16	31
O25	● |	at Western Michigan	21	6
N1	|	at Kent State	6	32 *
N8		Xavier	8	34
N15	●	Youngtown St.	21	8

1959 2-6-1 (0-6-0)

S19	●	Eastern Kentucky	20	2
S26	|	Ohio U.	7	36
O3	●	Baldwin-Wallace	26	20
O10	|	Marshall	13	20
O17	|	at Bowling Green	21	51
O24	|	Western Michigan	14	24
O31	|	Kent State	7	14
N7	|	at Miami, Ohio	7	25
N12	=	at Youngstown St.	8	8

CLIVE RUSH
1960-62 (.286) 8-20

1960 2-7-0 (0-6-0)

S17	●	Youngstown St.	34	30
S24	|	at Ohio U.	7	48
O1	|	at Marshall	0	14
O8		Hillsdale	25	31
O15	|	Bowling Green	3	14
O22	|	at Western Michigan	3	7
O29	|	at Kent State	13	18
N5	|	Miami, Ohio	13	30
N12	●	Bradley	28	0

1961 3-7-0 (2-4-0)

S16		Wichita St.	7	12
S23	|	Ohio U.	6	10
S30		at Youngstown St.	12	14
O7	● |	Marshall	33	6
O14	|	at Bowling Green	6	17
O21	|	Western Michigan	0	7
O28	● |	Kent State	31	22
N4	|	at Miami, Ohio	14	40
N11		at Bradley	22	28
N18	●	at Temple	15	14

1962 3-6-0 (1-5-0)

S15		South Dakota St.	14	25
S22	|	at Ohio U.	0	31
O6	● |	at Marshall	42	12
O13	|	Bowling Green	13	28
O20	|	at Western Michigan	0	21
O27	|	at Kent State	18	20
N3	|	Miami, Ohio	12	21
N10	●	Temple	13	0
N17	●	at Tulsa	21	18

FRANK LAUTERBUR
1963-70 (.598) 48-32-2

1963 2-7-0 (1-5-0)

S21		at Dayton	19	22
S28		Villanova	14	18
O5	|	at Marshall	18	19
O12	● |	Ohio U.	18	17
O19	|	at Bowling Green	20	22
O26	|	Western Michigan	7	18
N2	|	Kent State	0	20
N9	|	at Miami, Ohio	8	40
N16	●	So. Illinois	14	0

1964 2-8-0 (1-5-0)

S19		Villanova	6	22
S25		at Detroit	6	22
O3	|	Marshall	0	13
O10	|	at Ohio U.	12	21
O17	|	Bowling Green	14	31
O24	● |	at Western Michigan	21	13
O31	|	at Kent State	11	14
N7	|	Miami, Ohio	14	35
N14	●	at So. Illinois	27	8
N21		Tulsa	16	39

1965 5-5-0 (2-4-0)

S18	●	at Villanova	9	7
S25	●	Quantico Marines	9	0
O2	|	at Marshall	0	14
O9	● |	Ohio U.	21	7
O16	|	at Bowling Green	14	21
O23	|	Western Michigan	0	3
O30	● |	Kent State	7	3
N6	|	at Miami, Ohio	16	20
N13		at Xavier	7	14
N20	●	Dayton	21	7

1966 2-7-1 (1-5-0)

S17	●	Xavier	9	0
S24		at Villanova	11	20
O1	● |	Marshall	23	7
O8	|	at Ohio U.	6	21
O15	|	Bowling Green	13	14
O22	|	at Western Michigan	13	14
O29	|	at Kent State	20	28
N5	|	Miami, Ohio	12	24
N12	=	Quantico Marines	14	14
N19		at Dayton	16	20

1967 9-1-0 (5-1-0)

S16	|	Ohio U.	14	20
S23	●	at Xavier	24	7
S30	● |	at Marshall	14	7
O14	● |	at Bowling Green	33	0
O21	● |	Western Michigan	35	9
O28	● |	Kent State	14	13
N4	● |	at Miami, Ohio	24	14
N11	●	Northern Illinois	35	0
N18	●	Dayton	21	7
N23	●	Villanova	52	6

1968 5-4-1 (3-2-1)

S14	●	Richmond	31	14
S21	●	at Villanova	45	21
S28	● |	Marshall	35	12
O5	|	at Ohio U.	31	40
O12	= |	Bowling Green	0	0
O19	● |	at Western Michigan	30	6
O26	● |	at Kent State	28	12
N2	|	Miami, Ohio	17	21
N9		Xavier	10	20
N16		at Dayton	3	10

1969 11-0-0 (5-0-0)

S20	●	Villanova	45	18
S27	●	at Marshall	38	13
O4	● |	Ohio U.	34	9
O11	● |	at Bowling Green	27	26
O18	● |	Western Michigan	38	13
O25	● |	Kent State	43	17
N1	● |	at Miami, Ohio	14	10
N8	●	at Northern Illinois	35	21
N15	●	Dayton	20	0
N22	●	at Xavier	35	0
		TANGERINE BOWL		
D26	●	Davidson	56	33

1970 12-0-0 (5-0-0)

S12	●	East Carolina	35	2
S19	●	at Buffalo	27	6
S26	●	Marshall	52	3
O3	● |	at Ohio U.	42	7
O10	● |	Bowling Green	20	0
O17	● |	at Western Michigan	20	0
O24	● |	at Kent State	34	17
O31	● |	Miami, Ohio	14	13
N7	●	Northern Illinois	45	7
N14	●	at Dayton	31	7
N21	●	Colorado State	24	14
		TANGERINE BOWL		
D28	●	William & Mary	40	12

JOHN MURPHY
1971-76 (.522) 35-32

1971 12-0-0 (5-0-0)

S11	●	at East Carolina	45	0
S18	●	Villanova	10	7
S25	●	at Texas- Arlington	23	0
O2	● |	Ohio U.	31	28
O9	● |	at Bowling Green	24	7
O16	● |	Western Michigan	35	24
O23	●	Dayton	35	7
O30	● |	at Miami, Ohio	45	6
N6	●	at Northern Illinois	23	8
N13	●	at Marshall	43	0
N20	● |	Kent State	41	6
		TANGERINE BOWL		
D28	●	Richmond	28	3

1972 6-5-0 (2-3-0)

S9		at Tampa	0	21
S16	●	at Eastern Michigan	16	0
S23	●	Texas- Arlington	38	24
S30	|	at Ohio U.	22	38
O7	|	Bowling Green	8	19
O14	● |	at Western Michigan	20	13
O21	●	at Dayton	20	17
O28	● |	Miami, Ohio	35	21
N4		Northern Illinois	7	30
N11	●	Marshall	21	0
N18	|	at Kent State	9	27

1973 3-8-0 (1-4-0)

S15		at Tampa	25	35
S22	●	Central Michigan	23	21
S29	● |	Ohio U.	35	8
O6	|	at Bowling Green	35	49
O13	|	Western Michigan	22	24
O20	●	Dayton	14	10
O27	|	at Miami, Ohio	0	16
N3		at Colorado State	14	21
N10		at Marshall	14	17
N17	|	Kent State	16	52
N24		at Xavier	31	35

1974 6-5-0 (3-2-0)

S14		at Tampa	13	47
S21		Villanova	0	7
S28	● |	at Ohio U.	19	16
O5	● |	Bowling Green	24	19
O12	● |	at Western Michigan	31	24
O19	●	at Dayton	38	27
O26	|	Miami, Ohio	22	38
N2	●	Northern Illinois	44	14
N9	●	Marshall	45	14
N16	|	at Kent State	14	35
N23		Eastern Michigan	12	28

1975 5-6-0 (4-4-0)

S6	●	Western Carolina	32	31
S13	|	at Ball State	28	38
S20		at Villanova	10	14
S27	|	Central Michigan	27	34
O4		Dayton	13	24
O11	|	at Bowling Green	17	34
O18	● |	Western Michigan CLEV	25	7
O25	● |	Ohio U.	14	10
N1	|	at Miami, Ohio	21	35
N8	● |	at Northern Illinois	24	22
N22	● |	Kent State	33	28

1976 3-8-0 (2-6-0)

S11		at Massachusetts	14	28
S18	|	at Central Michigan	7	9
S25	|	Ball State	14	27
O2	|	at Ohio U.	8	34
O9	|	Bowling Green	28	29
O16	|	at Western Michigan	21	34
O23		at Dayton	14	17
O30	● |	Miami, Ohio	24	9
N6	● |	Northern Illinois	17	2
N13	●	Marshall	39	8
N20	|	at Kent State	9	35

CHUCK STOBART
1977-81 (.438) 24-31-1

1977 2-9-0 (2-7-0)

S10	|	Ball State	3	43
S17		East Carolina	9	22
S24		at Marshall	0	24
O1	|	at Eastern Michigan	7	17
O8	|	at Bowling Green	13	21
O15	|	Western Michigan	7	28
O22	● |	Ohio U.	31	29
O29	|	at Miami, Ohio	3	27
N5	● |	at Northern Illinois	27	9
N12	|	Central Michigan	0	44
N19	|	Kent State	12	23

MAC TEAMS

1978 — 2-9-0 (2-7-0)

S9		Marshall	0	17
S16		at Minnesota	12	38
S23	|	at Ball State	0	20
S30	|	Eastern Michigan	12	17
O7	|	Bowling Green	27	45
O14	|	at Western Michigan	7	17
O21	● |	at Ohio U.	28	14
O28	|	Miami, Ohio	7	28
N4	|	at Central Michigan	3	27
N11	● |	Northern Illinois	35	16
N18	|	at Kent State	13	17

1979 — 7-3-1 (7-1-1)

S8		at Marshall	14	31
S15	● |	Ball State	31	14
S22		at Arizona State	0	49
S29	● |	at Eastern Michigan	37	7
O6	● |	at Bowling Green	23	17
O13	● |	Western Michigan	17	0
O20	● |	Ohio U.	21	13
O27	● |	at Miami, Ohio	24	21
N3	= |	Central Michigan	7	7
N10	|	at Northern Illinois	10	28
N17	● |	Kent State	29	3

1980 — 4-7-0 (3-6-0)

S13		McNeese St.	17	20
S20	|	at Ball State	7	27
S27	● |	Eastern Michigan	49	7
O4	|	at Central Michigan	10	14
O11	|	Bowling Green	6	17
O18	|	at Western Michigan	7	17
O25	|	at Ohio U.	9	24
N1	● |	Miami, Ohio	17	14
N8	● |	Northern Illinois	13	6
N15	●	at Marshall	38	10
N22	|	at Kent State	14	34

1981 — 9-3-0 (8-1-0)

S12		at Louisville	6	31
S19	● |	Ball State	40	0
S26		at East Carolina	24	28
O3	● |	Ohio U.	21	14
O10	● |	at Eastern Michigan	42	7
O17	● |	Central Michigan	17	3
O24	|	at Bowling Green	0	38
O31	● |	Miami, Ohio	17	10
N7	● |	at Western Michigan	28	14
N14	● |	Kent State	17	0
N21	● |	at Northern Illinois	31	0
		CALIFORNIA BOWL		
D19	●	San Jose State	27	25

DAN SIMRELL
1982-89 (.562) 49-38-2

1982 — 6-5-0 (5-4-0)

S4	● |	Northern Illinois	9	3
S11	● |	at Ball State	31	14
S18	●	Marshall	17	9
S25		at Wisconsin	27	36
O2	|	at Ohio U.	14	17
O9	● |	Eastern Michigan	20	19
O16	|	at Central Michigan	12	16
O23	● |	Bowling Green	24	10
O30	|	at Miami, Ohio	17	21
N6	|	Western Michigan	10	17
N13	● |	at Kent State	3	0

1983 — 9-2-0 (7-2-0)

S10	●	Massachusetts	45	13
S17	●	at Richmond	31	6
S24	● |	Ball State	43	7
O1	● |	Ohio U.	31	0
O8	● |	at Bowling Green	6	3
O15	● |	Miami, Ohio	10	9
O22	● |	at Eastern Michigan	37	9
O29	● |	Kent State	37	34
N5	● |	at Western MIchigan	20	16
N12	|	at Northern Illinois	10	26
N19	|	Central Michigan	8	34

1984 — 8-3-1 (7-1-1)

S8	● |	at Ball State	20	2
S22	●	Ea. Illinois	38	17
S29	= |	at Ohio U.	16	16
O6	● |	Bowling Green	17	6
O13	● |	at Miami, Ohio	10	7
O20	● |	Eastern Michigan	17	7
O27	|	at Kent State	6	17
N3	● |	Western Michigan	17	13
N10	● |	Northern Illinois	13	7
N17	● |	at Central Michigan	14	7
N30		at Temple	6	35
		CALIFORNIA BOWL		
D15		Nevada-Las Vegas	13	30 †

1985 — 4-7-0 (3-6-0)

S7		at Arizona	10	23
S21	●	at Wichita St.	22	15
S28	|	Ball State	19	23
O5	|	at Eastern Michigan	10	21
O12	|	Miami, Ohio	14	26
O19	|	at Northern Illinois	3	16
O26	● |	Ohio U.	24	10
N2	|	at Western Michigan	13	18
N9	● |	Central Michigan	10	7
N16	|	at Bowling Green	0	21
N23	● |	Kent State	10	7

1986 — 7-4-0 (5-3-0)

A30		at Florida State	0	24
S6	|	at Kent State	16	18
S13	●	Wichita St.	30	13
S27	|	at Ball State	10	27
O4	● |	Eastern Michigan	23	18
O11	|	at Miami, Ohio	8	24
O18	●	Northern Illinois	29	28
O25	● |	at Ohio U.	24	21
N1	● |	Western Michigan	28	7
N8	● |	at Central Michigan	26	14
N15	● |	Bowling Green	22	3

1987 — 3-7-1 (3-4-1)

S5		Temple	12	13
S12	● |	Ball State	21	17
S19	● |	Ohio U.	17	12
O3	|	at Western Michigan	14	21
O10	|	at Northern Illinois	5	41
O17	|	at Bowling Green	6	20
O24	● |	Miami, Ohio	37	25
O31	|	at Kent State	13	17
N5	|	Eastern Michigan	9	38
N14	= |	at Central Michigan	17	17
N21		at Miami, Fla.	14	24

1988 — 6-5-0 (4-4-0)

S3	|	at Ball State	3	13
S10	|	Western Michigan	9	31
S17		at McNeese St.	19	46
S24	● |	Bowling Green	34	5
O1	|	at Ohio U.	14	24
O8	●	Northern Illinois	33	20
O15	●	Austin Peay	38	14
O22	● |	at Miami, Ohio	20	7
O29	● |	Kent State	35	28
N5	|	at Eastern Michigan	19	20
N12	● |	Central Michigan	20	13

1989 — 6-5-0 (6-2-0)

S2	● |	Ohio U.	27	18
S16		at Wisconsin	10	23
S23	● |	Ball State	29	22
S30		at Indiana	12	32
O7	|	at Eastern Michigan	14	31
O14	|	at Bowling Green	23	27
O21	● |	Miami, Ohio	17	14
O28	● |	at Kent State	47	42
N4	● |	Western Michigan	19	18
N11		at Northern Illinois	27	39
N18	● |	Central Michigan	29	6

NICK SABAN
1990 (.818) 9-2

1990 — 9-2-0 (7-1-0)

S8	● |	at Miami, Ohio	20	14
S15	●	Northern Illinois	23	14
S22	● |	at Ball State	28	16
S29	● |	at Ohio U.	27	20
O6	● |	Eastern Michigan	37	23
O13	● |	Bowling Green	19	13
O20	|	at Central Michigan	12	13
O27	● |	Kent State	28	14
N3	● |	at Western Michigan	37	9
N10		Navy	10	14
N17	●	Arkansas State	43	28

GARY PINKEL
1991-2000 (.659) 73-37-3

1991 — 5-5-1 (4-3-1)

S7		Kansas	7	30
S21	● |	at Western Michigan	23	13
S28	= |	Central Michigan	16	16
O5	● |	Ohio U.	17	13
O12		at Washington	0	48
O19	|	at Bowling Green	21	24
O26	● |	Miami, Ohio	24	7
N2	|	at Kent State	13	14
N9	|	Ball State	3	9
N16	● |	at Eastern Michigan	21	14
N23	●	Northern Illinois	42	21

1992 — 8-3-0 (5-3-0)

S5	●	Arkansas State	49	0
S12	|	at Akron	20	23
S19	●	at Purdue	33	29
S26	|	at Central Michigan	9	28
O10	● |	Western Michigan	21	12
O17	|	Bowling Green	9	10
O24	● |	at Miami, Ohio	20	17
O31	● |	Kent State	32	17
N7	● |	at Ball State	10	9
N14	● |	Eastern Michigan	41	0
N21	●	at Northern Illinois	25	8

1993 — 4-7-0 (3-5-0)

S4		at Indiana	0	27
S18	●	So. Illinois	49	28
S25	● |	Ohio U.	28	10
O2	|	at Bowling Green	10	17
O9	|	at Ball State	30	31
O16	|	Miami, Ohio	19	22
O23		Cincinnati	24	31
O30	● |	at Kent State	45	27
N6	|	Central Michigan	7	38
N13	|	at Western Michigan	26	39
N19	● |	Eastern Michigan	14	0

1994 — 6-4-1 (4-3-1)

S3	●	Indiana St.	20	17
S10		at Purdue	17	51
S17	●	Liberty	47	37
O1	● |	at Ohio U.	31	6
O8	= |	Ball State	24	24
O15	|	Bowling Green	16	31
O22	● |	at Akron	48	25
O29	● |	Kent State	48	14
N5	|	at Central Michigan	27	45
N12	● |	Western Michigan	37	34
N19	|	at Eastern Michigan	37	40

1995 — 11-0-1 (7-0-1)

S9	●	East Tenn. St.	41	20
S14	● |	at Western Michigan	31	21
S23	●	at Nevada	49	35
S30	●	at Cincinnati	45	31
O7	● |	Ball State	17	14
O14	= |	at Miami, Ohio	28	28
O21	● |	at Bowling Green	35	16
O28	● |	Eastern Michigan	34	28
N4	● |	at Central Michigan	19	7
N11	● |	Akron	41	7
N18	● |	Ohio U.	31	20
		LAS VEGAS BOWL		
D14	●	Nevada	40	37

1996 — 7-4 (6-2)

S7		Indiana	6	40
S14	● |	at Akron	27	10
S21	● |	at Eastern Michigan	24	7
S28	●	Weber St.	31	24
O5	● |	Bowling Green	24	16
O19		at Louisiana Tech	20	61
O26	● |	Western Michigan	10	7
N2	|	Miami, Ohio	7	27
N9	● |	Central Michigan	23	20
N16	|	at Ball State	14	24
N23	● |	at Ohio U.	24	23

1997 — 9-3 (7-1)

S6	●	Purdue	36	22
S13	● |	Eastern Michigan	38	35
S20	● |	at Western Michigan	23	13
S27	●	Nevada	31	13
O11	● |	at Central Michigan	41	10
O18	● |	Northern Illinois	41	14
O25	● |	at Bowling Green	35	20
N1	● |	Miami, Ohio	35	28
N8	|	at Ball State	3	35
N15	● |	Akron	42	10
N22		at Central Florida	17	34
		MAC CHAMPIONSHIP GAME		
D5		at Marshall	14	34

1998 — 7-5 (6-2)

S5	●	Temple	24	12
S12		at Ohio State	0	49
S19	● |	Western Michigan	35	7
S26	|	at Miami, Ohio	14	28
O3		Central Florida	24	31
O10	● |	Ball State	27	6
O17	● |	Bowling Green	24	16
O24	● |	at Akron	24	17
O31	● |	at Northern Illinois	16	3
N14	● |	Central Michigan	17	14
N21	|	at Eastern Michigan	7	10
		MAC CHAMPIONSHIP GAME		
D4		at Marshall	17	23

1999 — 6-5 (5-3)

S2		Syracuse	12	35
S18	● |	at Ball State	23	10
S25	●	Massachusetts	24	3
O2	|	at Bowling Green	23	34
O9	● |	Kent State	47	7
O14	|	at Marshall	13	38
O23	|	Eastern Michigan	13	20
O30		Louisiana Tech	17	34
N6	● |	at Central Michigan	32	13
N13	● |	Northern Illinois	44	14
N20	● |	Western Michigan	45	21

2000 — 10-1 (6-1)

S2	●	at Penn State	24	6
S9	●	Weber St.	51	0
S16	●	Eastern Ill.	31	26
S23	|	at Western Michigan	14	21
S30	● |	Central Michigan	41	0
O7	● |	at Eastern Michigan	42	14
O14	● |	Marshall	42	0
O28	●	at Navy	35	14
N4	● |	at Northern Illinois	38	24
N11	● |	Ball State	31	3
N22	● |	Bowling Green	51	17

TOM AMSTUTZ
2001-PRESENT (.667) 50-25

2001 — 10-2 (5-2)

A30	●	Minnesota	38	7
S8	●	at Temple	33	7
S22	● |	at Central Michigan	52	28
S29	● |	Northern Illinois	41	20
O6	● |	at Ohio U.	48	41
O20	|	at Ball State	20	24
O27	●	Navy	21	20
N6	● |	Western Michigan	41	35
N17	● |	Eastern Michigan	28	7
N23	|	at Bowling Green	21	56
		MAC CHAMPIONSHIP GAME		
N30	●	Marshall	41	36
		MOTOR CITY BOWL		
D29	●	Cincinnati	23	16

2002 — 9-5 (7-1)

A29	●	Cal Poly SLO	44	16
S7	● |	at Eastern Michigan	65	13
S14		at Minnesota	21	31
S21	●	Nevada-Las Vegas	38	21
S28		at Pittsburgh	19	37
O12	● |	Ball State	37	17
O19	● |	at Central Florida	27	24
O26	|	Miami, Ohio	13	27
N9	● |	Central Michigan	44	17
N16	● |	at Western Michigan	42	21
N23	● |	at Northern Illinois	33	30
N30	● |	Bowling Green	42	24
		MAC CHAMPIONSHIP GAME		
D7		at Marshall	45	49
		MOTOR CITY BOWL		
D26		Boston College	25	51

2003 — 8-4 (6-2)

A29		at Nevada-Las Vegas	18	28
S6	●	Liberty	49	3
S12	● |	at Marshall	24	17
S20	●	Pittsburgh	35	31
S27		at Syracuse	7	34
O11	● |	Eastern Michigan	49	14
O18	● |	at Central Michigan	31	13
O25	|	at Ball State	13	38
N1	● |	Buffalo	56	29
N15	● |	Northern Illinois	49	30
N22	● |	Western Michigan	34	17
N29	|	at Bowling Green	23	31

2004 — 9-4 (7-1)

S4		at Minnesota	21	63
S11		at Kansas	14	63
S18	● |	at Eastern Michigan	42	32
S25	●	Temple	45	17
O2	● |	Ball State	52	14
O9	● |	at Western Michigan	59	33
O16	● |	Ohio U.	31	13
O23	● |	Central Michigan	27	22
N3	|	at Miami, Ohio	16	23
N10	● |	at Northern Illinois	31	17
N23	● |	Bowling Green	49	41
		MAC CHAMPIONSHIP GAME		
D2	●	Miami, Ohio DET	35	27
		MOTOR CITY BOWL		
D27		Connecticut	10	39

2005   9-3   (6-2)

S1	●	Western Illinois	62	14
S10	● |	Western Michigan	56	23
S17	● |	at Temple	42	17
S27		at Fresno State	14	44
O8	● |	Eastern Michigan	30	3
O15	● |	at Ball State	34	14
O22	● |	Buffalo	38	15
O29	|	at Central Michigan	17	21
N4	● |	at Ohio U.	30	21
N16	|	Northern Illinois	17	35
N22	● |	at Bowling Green	44	41
		GMAC BOWL		
D21	●	Texas-El Paso	45	13

2006   5-7   (3-5)

A31		at Iowa State	43	45
S9	|	at Western Michigan	10	31
S15	●	Kansas	37	31
S23	●	McNeese St.	41	7
S30		at Pittsburgh	3	45
O7	|	Central Michigan	20	42
O14	|	at Kent State	14	40
O21	|	at Eastern Michigan	13	17
O28	● |	Akron	35	20
N7	● |	at Northern Illinois	17	13
N14	|	Ball State	17	20
N21	● |	Bowling Green	31	21

MAC TEAMS

TOLEDO RECORD BOOK

SINGLE-GAME RECORDS

RUSHING YARDS

RANK	PLAYER	DATE	OPPONENT	ATT	AVG	YDS
1	Casey McBeth	Oct. 22, 1994	Akron	36	8.4	304
2	Asa Jenkins	Sept. 15, 1951	Davis & Elkins	14	20.6	289
3	Emerson Cole	Nov. 12, 1949	North Dakota	15	15.3	230
4	Chester Taylor	Nov. 4, 2000	Northern Illinois	30	7.7	230
5	Wasean Tait	Oct. 21, 1995	Bowling Green	41	5.5	224

PASSING YARDS

RANK	PLAYER	DATE	OPPONENT	YDS
1	Bruce Gradkowski	Sept. 20, 2003	Pitt	461
2	Bruce Gradkowski	Oct. 2, 2004	Ball State	455
3	Bruce Gradkowski	Nov. 1, 2003	Buffalo	435
4	Jim Kelso	Sept. 25, 1982	Wisconsin	382
5	Chuck Ealey	Oct. 16, 1971	Western Michigan	381

RECEIVING YARDS

RANK	PLAYER	DATE	OPPONENT	YDS
1	Kenny Higgins	Nov. 23, 2004	Bowling Green	233
2	Jeff Calabrese	Oct. 28, 1972	Miami (Ohio)	203
3	Lance Moore	Nov. 1, 2003	Buffalo	195
4	Jeff Hepinstall	Sept. 6, 1975	Western Carolina	181
	Capus Robinson	Oct. 29, 1983	Kent State	181

POINTS

RANK	PLAYER	DATE	OPPONENT	TOT
1	Casey McBeth	Oct. 22, 1994	Akron	32
2	Gib Stick	Nov. 3, 1923	Findlay	30
	Joe Schwartz	Nov. 20, 1971	Kent State	30
	Chester Taylor	Sept. 22, 2001	CMU	30

FIELD GOALS

RANK	PLAYER	DATE	OPPONENT	TOT
1	Rusty Hanna	Nov. 21, 1992	N. Illinois	6
2	Rusty Hanna	Sept. 23, 1989	Ball State	5
	Todd France	Sept. 16, 2000	E. Illinois	5
4	4 players tied at 4			

TACKLES

RANK	PLAYER	DATE	OPPONENT	TOT
1	Jim Walser	Nov. 13, 1976	Marshall	29
2	Larry Macek	Nov. 8, 1975	N. Illinois	28
3	Ed Scott	Oct. 5, 1973	Bowling Green	26
	Aaron Bivens	Sept. 10, 1977	Ball State	26
	Darrell Mossburg	Sept. 26, 1992	CMU	26

INTERCEPTIONS

RANK	PLAYER	DATE	OPPONENT	TOT
1	Jerry Palmer	Nov. 4, 1950	Western Reserve	4
2	5 players tied at 3			

RETIRED NUMBERS

16	Chuck Ealey
18	Gene Swick
66	Mel Triplett
77	Mel Long

SINGLE-SEASON RECORDS

RUSHING YARDS

RANK	PLAYER	SEASON	ATT	YDS
1	Wasean Tait	1995	370	2,090
2	Chester Taylor	2001	299	1,620
3	Kelvin Farmer	1986	299	1,532
4	Chester Taylor	2000	250	1,470
5	Trinity Dawson	2005	232	1,294

PASSING YARDS

RANK	PLAYER	SEASON	ATT	COMP	PCT	YDS
1	Bruce Gradkowski	2004	399	280	70.2	3,518
2	Brian Jones	2002	423	297	70.2	3,446
3	Bruce Gradkowski	2003	389	277	71.2	3,210
4	Chris Wallace	1997	433	232	53.6	2,955
5	Gene Swick	1975	308	190	61.7	2,487

RECEIVING YARDS

RANK	PLAYER	SEASON	REC	AVG	YDS
1	Lance Moore	2003	103	11.6	1,194
2	Lance Moore	2004	90	13.2	1,189
3	Carl Ford	2002	79	13.4	1,062
4	Don Fair	1970	81	11.7	949
5	2 players tied at 886				

SCORING

RANK	PLAYER	SEASON	TD	FG	PAT	P2	TOT
1	Chester Taylor	2001	24	0	0	0	144
	Wasean Tait	1995	24	0	0	0	144
3	Joe Schwartz	1971	20	0	0	0	120
4	Chester Taylor	2000	19	0	0	0	114
5	3 players tied at 96						

TOUCHDOWNS

RANK	PLAYER	SEASON	TOT
1	Chester Taylor	1995	24
	Wasean Tait	2001	24
3	Joe Schwartz	2000	20
4	Chester Taylor	1971	19
5	2 players tied at 16		

TACKLES

RANK	PLAYER	SEASON	TOT
1	Barry Sneed	1964	240
2	Lee Emery	1964	207
3	Ed Scott	1973	204
4	John Niezgoda	1969	201
5	Larry Macek	1975	200

INTERCEPTIONS

RANK	PLAYER	SEASON	TOT
1	Mark Brandon	1983	9
2	Scott Resseguie	1974	7
	Curtis Johnson	1969	7
	Gary Hinkson	1970	7
	Mark Brandon	1984	7

PUNTING

RANK	PLAYER	SEASON	PUNTS	YDS	AVG
1	Brandon Hannum	2003	NA	NA	43.5
2	Ty Grude	1996	63	2,701	42.9
3	Ty Grude	1995	NA	NA	42.5
4	Brett Kern	2006	NA	NA	41.7
5	Gabe Lindstrom	1998	78	3,195	41.0

PUNT RETURNS

RANK	PLAYER	SEASON	RET	YDS	AVG
1	Donta Greene	2002	30	444	14.8
2	Steve Banks	1971	37	155	14.2
3	Mike Slater	1976	31	93	13.0
4	Jameel Turner	1997	31	322	10.4
5	Dan Crockett	1969	30	267	8.9

KICKOFF RETURNS

RANK	PLAYER	SEASON	RET	YDS	AVG
1	Ainsworth Morgan	1993	29	713	24.6
2	Dontà Greene	2002	36	809	22.5
3	Renza Hughley	1986	28	622	22.2
4	Richard Davis	2006	32	701	21.9
5	Eddie Harris	1984	28	554	19.8

CAREER RECORDS

RUSHING YARDS

RANK	PLAYER	SEASONS	ATT	AVG	TD	YDS
1	Chester Taylor	1998-2001	834	5.8	56	4,849
2	Wasean Tait	1993-98	837	5.2	38	4,338
3	Trinity Dawson	2002-05	674	5.2	NA	3,474
4	Casey McBeth	1991-94	540	5.0	NA	2,719
5	Steve Morgan	1981-84	638	4.0	NA	2,540
6	Kelvin Farmer	1983-86	574	4.3	NA	2,483
7	Roland Moss	1966-68	655	3.7	32	2,421
8	Joe Schwartz	1970-72	554	4.2	35	2,337
9	Mike Alston	1976-79	457	4.8	NA	2,180
10	Neil Trotter	1987-90	NA	NA	NA	2,168

PASSING YARDS

RANK	PLAYER	SEASONS	ATT	COMP	PCT	INT	TD	YDS
1	Bruce Gradkowski	2002-05	1,123	766	68.2	27	85	9,225
2	Gene Swick	1993-96	938	556	59.3	44	43	7,266
3	Ryan Huzjak	1972-75	1,067	600	56.2	31	52	6,926
4	Kevin Meger	1999-2001	892	465	52.1	34	23	6,023
5	Chris Wallace	1989-92	848	454	53.5	NA	44	5,454
6	Tavares Bolden	1995-98	831	498	59.9	NA	34	5,417
7	Chuck Ealey	1983-86	697	385	55.2	29	45	5,275
8	Jim Kelso	1969-71	681	354	52.0	36	24	4,773
9	A.J. Sager	1980-83	753	391	51.9	39	NA	4,165
10	John Schneider	2001-02	626	NA	NA	30	20	3,785

RECEIVING YARDS

RANK	PLAYER	SEASONS	REC	AVG	TD	YDS
1	Lance Moore	2001-04	222	12.5	25	2,776
2	Steve Odom	2003-06	216	12.2	19	2,631
3	Don Fair	1969-71	171	12.8	13	2,191
4	Mel Long	1997-2000	175	12.5	21	2,188
5	Dontà Greene	1999-2002	188	10.5	NA	1,979
6	Carl Ford	1999-2002	149	13.2	17	1,966
7	Rick Isaiah	1987-90	126	15.4	NA	1,939
8	Don Seymour	1972-74	NA	NA	17	1,758
9	Brock Kreitzburg	1995-98	134	12.5	NA	1,676
10	Eric Hutchinson	1984-87	NA	NA	NA	1,567

SCORING

RANK	PLAYER	SEASONS	TD	FG	PAT	P2	TOT
1	Chester Taylor	1998-2001	61	0	0	0	366
2	Todd France	1998-2001	0	59	154	0	337
3	Jason Robbins	2002-05	0	38	211	0	325
4	Rusty Hanna	1989-92	0	68	94	0	298
5	Joe Schwartz	1970-72	42	0	0	0	252

TOUCHDOWNS

RANK	PLAYER	SEASONS	TOT
1	Chester Taylor	1998-2001	61
2	Joe Schwartz	1970-72	42
3	Wasean Tait	1993-98	40
4	Roland Moss	1966-68	36
	Trinity Dawson	2002-05	36

TACKLES

RANK	PLAYER	SEASONS	TOT
1	Aaron Bivins	1975-77	508
2	Joe Conroy	1974, 76-78	490
3	Jack Laraway	1978-81	459
	Tim Inglis	1983-86	459
5	Doug Williams	1977-79	427

INTERCEPTIONS

RANK	PLAYER	SEASONS	YDS	TOT
1	Gary Hinkson	1969-71	NA	18
2	Mark Brandon	1981-84	178	17
3	Brandon Hefflin	2000-03	NA	16
4	Curtis Johnson	1967-69	173	14
5	2 players tied at 12			

PUNTING

RANK	PLAYER	SEASONS	PUNTS	YDS	AVG
1	Brett Kern	2004-	NA	NA	40.8
2	Gabe Lindstrom	1997-98	NA	NA	40.8
3	Ty Grude	1993-96	215	8,449	39.3
4	Roland Moss	1966-68	NA	NA	39.3
5	Brandon Hannum	2000-03	164	6,632	39.2

TEAM RECORDS

LONGEST WINNING STREAK
- 35, Sept. 20, 1969-Dec. 28, 1971
Streak broken vs. Tampa, 0-21, Sept. 9, 1972

LONGEST UNDEFEATED STREAK
- 35, Sept. 20, 1969-Dec. 28, 1971
Streak broken vs. Tampa, 0-21, Sept. 9, 1972

MOST CONSECUTIVE WINNING SEASONS
- 11, 1995-2005

MOST CONSECUTIVE BOWL APPEARANCES
- 3, 1969-1971

MOST POINTS IN A GAME
- 88, vs. Davis & Elkins, Sept. 15, 1951

MOST POINTS ALLOWED IN A GAME
- 145, vs. Detroit, Oct. 10, 1917

LARGEST MARGIN OF VICTORY
- 88 (88-0), vs. Davis & Elkins, Sept. 15, 1951

LARGEST MARGIN OF DEFEAT
- 145 (0-145), vs. Detroit, Oct. 10, 1917

LONGEST RUN FROM SCRIMMAGE
- 95 yards, Ben Tombaugh, vs. Austin Peay, Oct. 15, 1988

LONGEST PASS PLAY
- 96 yards, Bruce Gradkowski to Kenny Higgins, vs. Ball State, Oct. 2, 2004

LONGEST FIELD GOAL
- 55 yards, Todd France, vs. Western Michigan, Nov. 6, 2001

LONGEST PUNT
- 92 yards, Brandon Hannum, vs. Bowling Green, Nov. 23, 2001

LONGEST PUNT RETURN
- 98 yards, Jim Gray, vs. Dayton, Sept. 21, 1963

LONGEST INTERCEPTION RETURN
- 93 yards, Tom Duncan, vs. Marshall, Sept. 28, 1968

PUNT RETURNS

RANK	PLAYER	SEASON	RET	YDS	AVG
1	James Turner	1996-99	83	657	7.9
2	Eddie Harris	1982-85	88	625	7.1

KICKOFF RETURNS

RANK	PLAYER	SEASON	RET	YDS	AVG
1	Ainsworth Morgan	1990-93	45	1,041	23.1
2	Richard Davis	2005-06	49	1,088	22.2
3	Renza Hughly	1986-87	54	1,134	21.0
4	Eddie Harris	1982-85	80	1,662	20.8
5	Donta Greene	1999-2002	60	914	15.2

MAC TEAMS

TOLEDO ANNUAL STATISTICAL LEADERS

YR	RUSHING	YDS	ATT	AVG	PASSING	ATT	CMP	PCT	YDS	RECEIVING	REC	YDS	AVG
1951	A.C. Jenkins	899	116	7.8	Steve Piskach	86	27	.31	493		NA	NA	NA
1952	Bob Carson	322	110	2.9	Dave Andrzejewski	106	41	.39	582	Bob Carson	18	428	23.8
1953	Mel Triplett	479	81	5.9	Dave Andrzejewski	84	28	.33	403	Rick Kaser	11	189	17.2
1954	Mel Triplett	803	149	5.4	Jerry Nowak	53	25	.47	393	Dick Basich	14	255	18.2
1955	Julius Taormina	449	83	5.4	Sam Tisci	58	22	.38	404	Gene Cook	10	230	23.0
1956	Don Wright	498	112	4.4	Sam Tisci	64	22	.34	354	Dan Howell	13	218	16.8
1957	Norm Billingslea	565	104	5.4	Sam Tisci	131	56	.43	760	Gene Cook	30	495	16.5
1958	Occie Burt	618	124	5.0	Jerry Stoltz	75	29	.39	403	Jack Campbell	16	214	13.4
1959	Occie Burt	437	91	4.8	Dennis Wilkie	122	47	.39	723	Bob Smith	18	455	25.3
1960	John Murray	608	142	4.3	Jerry Stoltz	50	16	.32	277	Bob Smith	14	268	19.1
1961	Frank Baker	739	169	4.4	Phil Yenrick	95	37	.39	563	Pete Jolliff	18	330	18.3
1962	Frank Baker	613	147	4.2	Phil Yenrick	97	37	.38	552	Jim Thibert	11	198	18.0
1963	Jim Gray	645	114	5.7	Dan Simrell	118	48	.41	608	Jim Gray	15	168	11.2
1964	Jim Berkey	408	103	4.0	Dan Simrell	215	115	.53	1,239	Henry Burch	47	412	8.8
1965	Jim Berkey	440	142	3.1	John Schneider	108	54	.50	598	Henry Burch	36	325	9.0
1966	Roland Moss	443	175	2.5	John Schneider	273	130	.48	1,537	Henry Burch	38	480	12.6
1967	Roland Moss	833	213	3.9	John Schneider	245	127	.52	1,650	Pete Kramer	34	556	16.4
1968	Roland Moss	1,145	267	4.3	Steve Jones	243	98	.40	1,197	Dennis Tobias	27	294	10.9
1969	Tony Harris	889	153	5.8	Chuck Ealey	175	98	.56	1,428	Don Fair	33	469	14.2
1970	Charles Cole	774	196	3.9	Chuck Ealey	285	161	.56	2,026	Don Fair	81	949	11.7
1971	Joe Schwartz	1,130	226	5.0	Chuck Ealey	237	126	.53	1,821	Don Fair	57	773	13.6
1972	Joe Schwartz	776	223	3.5	Bruce Arthur	171	83	.49	1,168	Jeff Calabrese	62	886	14.3
1973	Herman Price	595	168	3.5	Gene Swick	301	165	.55	2,234	Don Seymour	44	773	17.6
1974	Mike Taormina	609	161	3.8	Gene Swick	287	178	.62	2,234	John Ross	77	866	11.2
1975	Tim Zimmerman	496	126	3.9	Gene Swick	308	190	.62	2,487	Scott Resseguie	39	683	17.5
1976	Skip McCulley	578	102	5.7	Jeff Hepinstall	198	89	.45	1,299	Scott Resseguie	32	530	16.6
1977	Mike Alston	772	154	5.0	Jeff Hepinstall	72	26	.36	359	Frank Jarm	12	204	17.0
1978	Mike Alston	460	101	4.6	Maurice Hall	110	39	.35	610	Butch Hunyadi	19	494	26.0
1979	Mike Alston	806	166	4.9	Maurice Hall	122	53	.43	648	Butch Hunyadi	29	500	17.2
1980	Melvin Tucker	563	120	4.7	Jim Kelso	82	41	.50	589	Rod Achter	10	269	26.9
1981	Arnold Smiley	1,013	197	5.1	Jim Kelso	121	58	.48	875	Rod Achter	14	361	25.8
1982	Steve Morgan	598	143	4.2	Jim Kelso	281	149	.53	1,963	Capus Robinson	43	709	16.5
1983	Steve Morgan	630	145	4.3	Jim Kelso	197	106	.54	1,346	Capus Robinson	31	499	16.1
1984	Steve Morgan	1,271	336	3.8	A.J. Sager	290	156	.54	1,647	Eric Hutchinson	26	451	17.3
1985	Kelvin Farmer	748	229	3.3	A.J. Sager	253	130	.51	1,335	Jay Walsh	27	284	10.5
1986	Kelvin Farmer	1,532	299	5.1	A.J. Sager	189	96	.51	1,107	Eric Hutchinson	33	504	15.3
1987	David Rohrs	681	178	3.8	Bill Bergan	130	72	.55	908	Eric Hutchinson	29	431	14.9
1988	Neil Trotter	783	163	4.8	Steve Keene	128	66	.52	793	Rick Isaiah	25	389	15.6
1989	Wayne Goodwin	859	196	4.4	Mark Melfi	237	131	.55	1,632	Rick Isaiah	46	743	16.2
1990	Troy Parker	879	233	3.8	Kevin Meger	257	139	.54	1,861	Rick Isaiah	49	717	14.6
1991	Steve Cowan	748	162	4.6	Kevin Meger	276	147	.53	1,787	Marcus Goodwin	42	600	14.3
1992	Casey McBeth	1,037	223	4.7	Kevin Meger	285	139	.49	1,727	Marcus Goodwin	58	738	12.7
1993	Wasean Tait	680	139	4.9	Tim Kubiak	146	70	.48	970	Scott Brunswick	41	571	13.9
1994	Casey McBeth	1,053	180	5.9	Ryan Huzjak	289	170	.59	1,928	Scott Brunswick	44	572	13.0
1995	Wasean Tait	2,090	370	5.6	Ryan Huzjak	314	179	.57	2,134	Steve Rosi	44	546	12.4
1996	Kevin Kidd	453	127	3.6	Ryan Huzjak	332	183	.55	2,058	James Spriggs	53	754	14.2
1997	Dwayne Harris	1,278	254	5.0	Chris Wallace	433	232	.54	2,955	Mel Long	47	556	11.8
1998	Wasean Tait	625	151	4.1	Chris Wallace	400	219	.55	2,476	Ray Curry	45	513	11.4
1999	Chester Taylor	1,176	182	6.5	Tavares Bolden	229	123	.54	1,354	Mel Long	47	599	12.7
2000	Chester Taylor	1,470	250	5.9	Tavares Bolden	283	161	.57	1,597	Mel Long	50	587	11.7
2001	Chester Taylor	1,620	299	5.4	Tavares Bolden	319	214	.67	2,466	Donta Greene	64	643	10.0
2002	Astin Martin	785	135	5.8	Brian Jones	423	297	.70	3,446	Carl Ford	79	1,062	13.4
2003	Trinity Dawson	999	199	5.0	Bruce Gradkowski	389	277	.71	3,210	Lance Moore	103	1,194	11.6
2004	Scooter McDougle	620	146	4.2	Bruce Gradkowski	399	280	.70	3,518	Lance Moore	90	1,189	13.2
2005	Trinity Dawson	1,294	232	5.6	Bruce Gradkowski	332	207	.62	2469	Steve Odom	55	690	12.5
2006	Jalen Parmele	1,131	207	5.5	Clint Cochran	169	96	.57	960	Chris Hopkins	54	565	10.5

Receiving leaders by receptions
The NCAA began including postseason stats in 2002

WESTERN MICHIGAN

BY ED KRZEMIENSKI

WHEN MICHIGAN DECIDED IN 1903 that it needed a third school for training teachers, it chose Kalamazoo and named the school Western State Normal College. Thus, Western Michigan University was born. In recent years, WMU has spread its recruiting net beyond the Midwest. Though still dependent on the talent pools of Michigan and Illinois, Western Michigan has brought in players from Florida, California, and even Hawaii and American Samoa. It paid off initially, as WMU won or shared the MAC West title in two of coach Gary Darnell's first four years. What goes up must come down, though, and in 2004, Darnell's squad lost 10 straight to end the season 1–10. The school named Darnell's former offensive coordinator Bill Cubit as its new coach following that season.

TRADITION Before home games, the team touches a sign above the exit door to the field that reads "Our House." During home games, the PA announcer at Waldo Stadium announces, "Here comes Amtrak!" when a train passes by.

BEST PLAYER At the end of his career as a Bronco running back in 1978, Jerome Persell held the gold, silver, and bronze medals of seasonal rushing records at Western. Although those records and his career mark of 4,190 yards have been surpassed, Persell still ranks as the greatest Bronco of all time. In 1976, he placed second nationally with an average of 150.5 yards rushing per game; the following year he ranked fourth in the nation in rushing and ninth in scoring. For his efforts, Persell was first-team All-MAC and was named the MAC Offensive Player of the Year and team MVP in each of his three varsity seasons. Persell never played professionally.

BEST COACH Al Molde didn't take long to turn around the struggling Western Michigan football program. In 1987, his first season, Molde won five games with a team that had won only three the year before. One year later WMU won the MAC outright. That year, Molde took the Broncos to the California Bowl (only the second postseason appearance Western Michigan made after the 1961 Aviation Bowl), and won MAC Coach of the Year

PROFILE

Western Michigan University
Kalamazoo, Mich.
Founded: 1903
Enrollment: 24,481
Colors: Brown and Gold
Nickname: Broncos
Stadium: Waldo Stadium
    Opened in 1939
    FieldTurf; 30,200 capacity
First football game: 1906
All-time record: 490–381–24 (.561)
Bowl record: 0–3
Mid-American Conference championships: 2 (1 outright)
First-round draft choices: 1
Website: www.wmubroncos.com

THE BEST OF TIMES

From 1988 to 1995, Western Michigan had seven winning seasons, including a MAC championship in 1988.

THE WORST OF TIMES

From 1951 to 1960, Western Michigan did not experience a single winning season.

CONFERENCE

Except for a brief stint in the Michigan Collegiate Conference (from 1927 to 1930), Western Michigan was an independent through the early decades of its program. The Broncos joined the Mid-American Conference in 1948, and have remained there since.

DISTINGUISHED ALUMNI

Tim Allen, comedian; Dennis Archer, Detroit mayor; Jim Bouton, baseball pitcher and best-selling author; Neil Smith, New York Rangers general manager; Luther Vandross, singer

MAC TEAMS

Buster Bronco belongs to the goofy phylum of the college mascot kingdom.

honors. From 1987 to 1996, Molde went 62–47–2, tying him with William Spaulding for the most victories in school history.

BEST TEAM The 1988 Broncos began their season with five straight wins, including a season-opening upset of Wisconsin. Led by six first-team All-MAC players, including MAC offensive Player of the Year QB Tony Kimbrough, Western ended its regular season at 9–2 overall and 7–1 in the MAC. With its first and only outright conference championship (Western shared a title with Miami in 1966), the Broncos traveled to Fresno for the California Bowl. Before a hostile crowd of 31,272, they rolled up 503 total yards, including 366 in the air by Kimbrough, and 30 points but fell to Fresno State 35–30. Five players from that team went pro, including Kimbrough, who played in the Canadian Football League, and defensive end Joel Smeenge, who went on to a successful career with the NFL's New Orleans Saints and Jacksonville Jaguars.

BEST BACKFIELD The 1999 Broncos broke 41 school records and clinched the division title by October. Quarterback Tim Lester led the stampede, setting records for pass attempts, completions, and yards and touchdowns. His backfield mate, running back Robert Sanford, ran for 1,092 yards to provide a dose of balance to the offense, which averaged 31 points a game. Lester and Sanford led WMU to the MAC championship game, where WMU lost to heavily favored Marshall.

BEST DEFENSE In 1982, Western Michigan offered its last scholarship—a partial one—to a 185-pound linebacker named John Offerdahl. Offerdahl was so impressive during camp that his scholarship became full and he became a starter. It turns out the scholarship was worth it: the Broncos led the nation in scoring defense, giving up only 7.1 points per game, and ranked ninth overall. Seven opponents were held to single digits, and only one team scored more than 14 points: Central Michigan who scored 18 points. It was Jack Harbaugh's first year as coach and, thanks to the defense, his best.

BIGGEST GAME Needing a victory to secure a MAC title in 1988, the Broncos traveled to Muncie, Ind.,

FIGHT SONG
WMU FIGHT
Fight on, fight on for Western,
Take the ball, make a score, win the game,
Onward for the brown and gold,
Push 'em back, push 'em back,
Bring us fame!
Fight on, fight on for Western,
Over one, over all we will reign,
Fight, Broncos, fight,
Fight with all your might,
Western win this game!
B-R-O-N-C-O, B-R-O-N-C-O, GOOO
BRONCOS! W-M-U!

FIRST-ROUND DRAFT CHOICE	
2004	Jason Babin, Texans (27)

CONSENSUS ALL-AMERICANS	
1982	Matt Meares, OL

to take on the Cardinals of Ball State. Cold, wet, and windy, the day saw the Cardinals take an early lead before WMU quarterback Tony Kimbrough tied the score on a pass to Bruce Boyko. Kicker John Creek emerged as the Broncos' hero, though, as he connected on three short field goals to give Western a 16-7 lead. Ball State added a late touchdown to shave the gap to 16-13, but it wasn't enough. The game and the conference title went to the Broncos.

A batch of brown-eyed Susans served as WMU's inspiration for their color scheme.

BIGGEST UPSET In 1988, Western set the tone for two teams when it defeated Wisconsin 24-14 to open the season. For the Broncos, it marked the school's first victory over a Big Ten team in the modern era. For the Badgers, it began a three-year nightmare that resulted in just four wins.

HEARTBREAKER Losing to rival Central Michigan is never easy, but doing so after entering the game as a 20-point favorite is even more painful. That's exactly what happened when Western Michigan traveled to Mount Pleasant to face the woeful Chippewas in 2000. The Broncos entered the game with an 8–1 record, while the Chippewas, at 1–8, were in the midst of a mirror-image season. Nevertheless, behind a stifling defense, the Chippewas upset the Broncos 21–17. And sadly, it seems to be a tradition, with Western Michigan 1–12–1 at Mount Pleasant since 1977.

STADIUM Built for an original outlay of $250,000 in 1939, Waldo Stadium was constructed as part of an athletic complex and named for the school's first president, Dwight B. Waldo. From 1973 to 1991, the stadium had artificial turf, then Prescription Athletic Turf, before returning to the fake stuff (NeXturf) in 2001. Although Waldo Stadium seats a maximum of 30,200 fans, the school set the MAC home-attendance mark in 2000 with 36,361. In fact, Western Michigan has broken the MAC single-game home attendance record four times and has exploited that support, going 21–4 at home from 1997 to 2001.

RIVAL Western Michigan considers Central Michigan its prime rival, and the feeling is mutual. The teams first met in 1907 but did not play each other consistently or even annually until 1943. Then Central joined Western in the MAC in 1975, and their meetings and rivalry were guaranteed. Despite being only a short bus ride away, the trip to Mount Pleasant has been a painfully long journey for the Broncos. Since the teams began to play in the MAC together, the Broncos have had just one win at Central Michigan's Kelly/Shorts Stadium.

NICKNAME Located on Prospect Hill, later known as Normal Hill, Western Michigan first used Hilltoppers as its nickname. In an effort to distinguish itself from Western Kentucky, which also used the moniker, the school held a contest in 1939 to come up with a new name. Assistant coach John Gill suggested Broncos, and the W club's semiannual publication *The Hilltopper* was renamed *The Bronco*.

MASCOT Buster Bronco, a cheerleader in horse's clothing, debuted in 1988 and has appeared at all Western Michigan games ever since. Buster is a darkbrown horse clad in basketball high-tops and a WMU shirt. With bipedal ability and a Bullwinkle-esque face, Buster belongs to the lovable and goofy phylum of the college mascot kingdom.

UNIFORMS Legend has it that Waldo chose the school's colors in 1906 at the behest of his only assistant, Josephine Wing. Pointing to a batch of brown-eyed Susans outside the window, Wing suggested their gold-and-brown scheme for the school. That much has remained unchanged. The helmets, on the other hand, have undergone several incarnations. For awhile, a brown bucking bronco appeared on a white shell; at other times, helmets have been plain white or yellow. Currently, the helmets are gold with the profile of a bronco on the side. The team wears brown home and white away jerseys, both with gold numbers and gold pants. In 1998, black was added as an accent color.

QUIRK From the don't-try-this-at-home file comes Jason Babin, a Western Michigan defensive end with a strange pregame ritual. On Friday nights before games, Babin ate an entire bucket of fried chicken—bones and all—to psych himself up. It worked: Babin won MAC defensive Player of the Year honors following his junior and senior seasons in 2002 and 2003, respectively.

LORE In 1916, Western Michigan lost to Notre Dame's JV 10–6. During the game George Gipp drop-kicked a record-breaking 62-yard field goal. Contrary to legend, it wasn't a spontaneous decision by Gipp; he had announced his intent to kick in advance. Maybe he'd felt the wind pick up.

NUMBERS Western Michigan opened its 1916 season with a 93-0 win over the Grand Rapids Veterinary school. Too bad the team was not yet known as the Broncos.

QUOTE "It was time for us to win one of those games or quit opening our mouths." —Gary Darnell, after WMU upset Iowa in the second game of 2000. He had earlier said that it was his intention to compete with Big Ten teams.

WESTERN MICHIGAN ALL-TIME SCORES

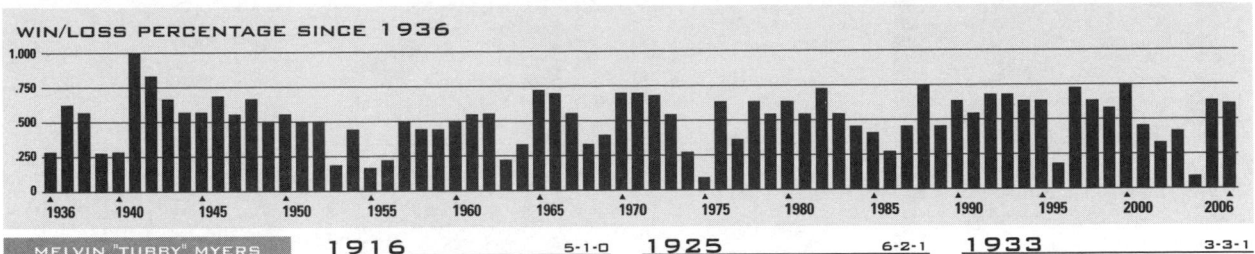

WIN/LOSS PERCENTAGE SINCE 1936

MELVIN "TUBBY" MYERS
1906 (.333)   1-2

1906   1-2-0
N17		Eastern Michigan	5 14
U		Kalamazoo Unk	0 14
U	●	Wayland HS Unk	21 0

WILLIAM SPAULDING
1907-21 (.706)   62-25-3

1907   3-2-1
U	●	Grand Rapids HS Unk	9 0
U		Albion Unk	0 5
U		Olivet Unk	0 3
U	●	Central Michigan Unk	27 0*
N9		Eastern Michigan	6 0
U	=	Ferris St. Unk	0 0

1908   3-3-0
U	●	Mc Fadden's PC Unk	20 0
O10		Michigan State	0 35
U		Olivet Unk	0 34
U		Albion Unk	0 24
U	●	Central Michigan Unk	11 5
U	●	Kalamazoo Unk	2 0

1909   7-0-0
U	●	Otsego Indy's Unk	61 0
U	●	Albion Unk	6 0
U	●	Battle Creek HS Unk	15 0
U	●	Dowagiac HS Unk	47 0
U	●	Benton Harbor Coll. Unk	28 3
U	●	Kalamazoo Unk	26 5
U	●	Central Michigan Unk	11 0

1910   4-1-1
U	=	Hillsdale Unk	3 3
U		Albion Unk	0 6
U	●	Culver Military Acad. Unk	22 5
U	●	Central Michigan Unk	16 6
U	●	Hope Unk	6 0
U	●	Kalamazoo Unk	28 0

1911   2-3-0
U		Hillsdale Unk	6 14
U		Albion Unk	5 12
U	●	Culver Military Acad. Unk	3 27
U	●	Battle Creek TS	62 6
U	●	Hope Unk	34 0

1912   3-2-1
U	●	Culver Military Acad. Unk	19 13
U	●	Albion Unk	6 3
U		Michigan State JV Unk	0 20
U	●	Hope Unk	54 0
U	=	Hillsdale Unk	7 7
N15		at Eastern Michigan	0 7*

1913   4-0-0
U	●	Albion Unk	20 3
U	●	Culver Military Acad. Unk	13 6
U	●	Hope Unk	14 0
N1		Eastern Michigan	12 6

1914   6-0-0
U	●	Battle Creek TS Unk	28 0
U	●	Olivet Unk	3 0
U	●	Albion Unk	43 0
U	●	Ferris St. Unk	68 0
U	●	Hillsdale Unk	28 7
N14		at Eastern Michigan	10 0

1915   5-1-0
U		Hillsdale Unk	16 20
U	●	Albion Unk	54 7
U	●	Alma Unk	79 0
U	●	Olivet Unk	40 0
N6		Eastern Michigan	19 0
U	●	Culver Military Acad. Unk	83 16

1916   5-1-0
U	●	Grand Rapids Veterinary Unk	93 0
U	●	Albion Unk	37 0
U	●	Indiana, Pa. Unk	94 6
U	●	Michigan State JV Unk	77 3
U	●	Notre Dame JV Unk	6 10
U	●	Ohio Northern Unk	82 19

1917   4-3-0
U	●	Albion Unk	26 6
O10		Michigan	13 17
U	●	Notre Dame JV Unk	83 0
N3	●	Michigan State	14 0
U	●	Camp Custer Unk	61 7
U		Detroit Unk	6 35
U		Indiana, Pa. Unk	0 40

1918   3-2-0
U		Albion Unk	12 14
N2		Michigan State	7 16
U	●	Hillsdale Unk	103 0
U	●	Hop Unk	62 0
U	●	Notre Dame JV Unk	39 0

1919   4-1-0
U	●	Wayne St. Unk	88 0
O11		Michigan State	21 18
U	●	Wabash Unk	27 13
O25		Notre Dame Unk	0 53
U	●	Albion Unk	20 7

1920   3-4-0
U	●	Olivet Unk	47 7
O9		at Notre Dame	0 42*
U		Chicago YMCA Unk	6 10
U	●	Marquette Unk	7 46
U	●	Jope Unk	46 0
U	●	Earlham Unk	6 0
U		Wabash Unk	7 27

1921   6-2-0
U	●	Ferris St.	49 0
U	●	at Albion	20 9
U	●	Notre Dame JV	7 0
U		Chicago YMCA	3 7
O22		at Michigan State	14 17
U	●	Earlham	42 7
U	●	Hope	65 0
U	●	Milwaukee Engineers	62 0

MILTON OLANDER
1922-23 (.893)   12-1-1

1922   6-0-0
U	●	Defiance	19 0
U	●	at Valparaiso	7 0
U	●	Albion	10 0
U	●	Chicago YMCA	13 0
U	●	Notre Dame JV	44 0
U	●	at Earlham	67 0

1923   6-1-1
S29		Notre Dame JV	15 0
O6	●	Valparaiso	7 0
O13	●	Alma	21 7
O20	=	at St. Viator	7 7
O29	●	Western Kentucky	26 0
N10	●	Earlham	46 0
N17	●	Chicago YMCA	32 0
N29		at Albion	6 7

EARL MARTINEAU
1924-28 (.711)   26-10-2

1924   5-1-0
U	●	Alma	7 0
O4		Notre Dame JV	7 15
O11	●	St. Viator	6 0
O25		at Western Kentucky	14 0
N1	●	Wisconsin-Oshkosh	23 7
U	=	Chicago YMCA	18 18
N27	●	Albion	26 6

1925   6-2-1
S26	●	Western Kentucky Unk	20 0
O3		Bradley Unk	2 6
O10		St. Thomas Unk	13 27
O17	●	Valparaiso Unk	45 0
U	●	Notre Dame JV Unk	21 0
U	●	Wisconsin-Oshkosh Unk	7 6
U	=	Central Michigan	0 0
U	●	Chicago YMCA Unk	14 6
N26	●	Albion Unk	3 2

1926   7-1-0
S25	●	Olivet	25 0
O2		Bradley	0 12
O9	●	Albion	28 0
O16		at Western Kentucky	3 2
O23		Chicago YMCA	7 0
O30	●	Valparaiso	37 0
N13	●	Notre Dame JV	12 6
N20	●	Wisconsin-Oshkosh	20 0

1927   3-4-0
O8		at Lombard	6 18
O15		Notre Dame JV	0 18
O22		at Central Michigan	12 18
O29	●	Wayne St.	44 0
N5	●	at Wisconsin-Oshkosh	19 6
N12		Eastern Michigan	0 6
N26	●	Albion	19 6

1928   5-2-0
U	●	Chicago YMCA Unk	26 0
O6	●	Ferris St. Unk	14 0
O13		Lombard Unk	0 14
O27	●	Wayne St. Unk	45 0
U	●	Michigan JV Unk	6 0
N10		at Eastern Michigan	9 18
U	●	Central Michigan	19 0

MITCHELL "MIKE" GARY
1929-41 (.628)   59-34-5

1929   5-2-1
U	●	Ferris St. Unk	41 0
U	●	Illinois JV Unk	20 0
U		Notre Dame JV Unk	7 13
U	●	Lombard Unk	14 6
O26	●	Wayne St. Unk	40 0
N2		Eastern Michigan	7 7
N9	●	at Central Michigan	25 6
U		Michigan JV Unk	7 12

1930   5-1-1
U	●	Ferris St.	46 0
U	●	Central Michigan	54 0
O18		at Eastern Michigan	0 19
U	●	at Wayne St.	52 0
U	●	Michigan JV	14 6
N8	●	at No. Iowa	26 0
N27	=	Western Kentucky	0 0

1931   5-2-0
S26	●	Ferris St.	25 0
O2		at Detroit	0 20
U		at Michigan JV	0 19
U	●	Notre Dame JV	27 6
N7	●	at No. Iowa	14 0
N14	●	Western Kentucky	13 0
N21	●	at Central Michigan	7 6

1932   6-0-1
S24	●	Hope	31 6
O1	●	at North Central	27 0
O8	=	DePaul	0 0
O15	●	at St. Viator	7 0
O29	●	No. Iowa	26 0
N5	●	Central Michigan	7 0
N12	●	Adrian	76 0

1933   3-3-1
S30		North Central	0 7
O6		at Detroit	0 26
O14		at No. Iowa	8 6
O21	=	Carroll	0 0
O28		DePaul	6 25
N4	●	at Central Michigan	13 0*
N11		St. Viator	33 0

1934   7-1-0
O5		at Detroit	7 25
O13	●	at Carroll	25 7
O20		No. Iowa	7 0
O27	●	DePaul	13 0
N3	●	Central Michigan	13 0
N9	●	at St. Viator	19 7
N24		West Chester St.	13 7
N29		at Western Kentucky	7 6

1935   5-3-0
S28	●	Illinois Coll. Unk	13 0
O5	●	Western Kentucky Unk	6 0
O12	●	Chicago Unk	6 31
O19	●	No. Iowa	14 21
O26	●	DePaul Unk	0 26
N9	●	Central Michigan	13 0
N16	●	Butler Unk	19 7
N23	●	West Chester St. Unk	7 6

1936   2-5-0
S25		at Detroit	0 40
O10	●	Miami, Ohio	0 6*
O17	●	Valparaiso	7 0
O24	●	No. Iowa	6 12
O31	●	at DePaul	7 19
N7	●	Central Michigan	33 0
N14	●	at Butler	7 13

1937   5-3-0
O1		at Detroit	7 20
O9	●	Illinois Coll.	37 0
O16	●	at No. Iowa	7 0
O23		St. Viator	7 13
O30	●	Western Kentucky	13 7
N6	●	at Central Michigan	7 0
N13	●	at Butler	14 13
N20		DePaul	0 12

1938   4-3-0
S24	●	Illinois Coll.	28 0
S30		at Detroit	0 7
O8	●	No. Iowa	20 0
O15		at Akron	0 6
O29	●	Western Kentucky	6 13
N5	●	at Butler	13 0
N12	●	Central Michigan	35 0

1939   2-6-1
S29		at Detroit	0 14
O7	●	Miami, Ohio	6 0
O14		Akron	6 0
O21	=	at No. Iowa	13 13
O28		at Toledo	0 6
N4		Western Kentucky	14 20
N11		Butler	0 12
N18		Ohio U.	6 13
U		at Wayne St.	6 7

1940   2-5-0
O5		Wayne St.	6 13
O12		at Ohio U.	7 20
O19		No. Iowa	19 20
O26		Toledo	0 12
N2		at Western Kentucky	6 25
N9	●	at Miami, Ohio	20 13
N16	●	Manchester	19 14

MAC TEAMS

1941 · 8-0-0
S27	•	at Western Reserve	7	0
O3	•	Butler	14	6
O18	•	at No. Iowa	28	7
O25	•	Toledo	34	0
N1	•	Western Kentucky	21	7
N8	•	Manchester	12	0
N15	•	at Wayne St.	34	0
N20	•	Ripon	35	7

JOHN GILL
1942-52 (.594)   50-34-1

1942 · 5-1-0
S26		at Dayton	0	21
O10	•	Toledo	13	0
O17	•	No. Iowa	14	7
O24	•	Butler	13	7
U	•	Grosse Isle Navy	13	2
N14	•	Wayne St.	13	0

1943 · 4-2-0
U	•	at Central Michigan	19	0
S25		at Michigan	6	57
U	•	Alma	54	0
U	•	Xavier	60	0
O16	•	Miami, Ohio	6	0
N6		Great Lakes NAS	6	32

1944 · 4-3-0
U	•	Fort Sheridan	67	0
U	•	Wabash	20	0
U		Bunker Hill Navy	7	33
S30	•	at Miami, Ohio	6	32
O7	•	Central Michigan	35	14
O14		at Great Lakes NAS	0	38
U	•	at Wooster	27	0

1945 · 4-3-0
S22	•	Alma	21	13
S29		at Central Michigan	0	6
O6	•	at Ohio U.	21	20
O13	•	Miami, Ohio	13	21
O27		Great Lakes NAS	0	39
N3	•	at Valparaiso	26	6
N10	•	Wooster	66	0

1946 · 5-2-1
S28	•	Ripon	47	0
O5		Ohio U.	7	25
O12	•	Butler	19	0
O19	=	at No. Iowa	0	0
O26	•	at Western Kentucky	32	21
N2	•	Central Michigan	27	21
N9	•	Valparaiso	26	13
N16		at Miami, Ohio	0	20

1947 · 5-4-0
S26	•	at Xavier	0	19
O4	•	Washington, Mo.	14	0
O11	•	at Central Michigan	20	12
O18	•	No. Iowa	14	0
O25	•	at Butler	20	21
N1	•	Western Kentucky	38	0
N8	•	at Illinois	14	60
N27	•	at Oklahoma City	7	35
U	•	Beloit	12	0

1948-PRESENT
MAC

1948 · 6-3-0 (3-1-0)
S25	•		Western Reserve	26	0
O2	•		at Beloit	33	0
O9	•		Central Michigan	7	0
O16	•		at No. Iowa	6	13
O23	•		Xavier	20	39
O30	•		at Miami, Ohio	28	34
N6	•		Butler	20	7
N13	•		at Washington, Mo.	19	6
N20	•		at Ohio U.	40	7

1949 · 4-4-0 (2-3-0)
S24	•		No. Iowa	20	6
O1			Ohio U.	6	16
O8	•		at Cincinnati	6	27
O15	•		Washington, Mo.	0	12
O22	•		at Central Michigan	35	8
O29			Miami, Ohio	20	34
N5	•		at Butler	40	6
N12	•		at Western Reserve	21	14

1950 · 5-4-0 (1-3-0)
S23	•		Northern Illinois	40	13
S30	•		Central Michigan	21	13
O7	•		Toledo	54	19
O14			at Miami, Ohio	0	35
O21	•		at Washington, Mo.	26	7
O28			Cincinnati	6	27
N4	•		Butler	34	13
N11			Western Reserve	0	26
N18			at Ohio U.	7	10

1951 · 4-4-0 (0-4-0)
S22			Kent State	19	48
S29	•		at Toledo	14	6
O6			Ohio U.	0	13
O13			Miami, Ohio	27	34
O20	•		Washington, Mo.	12	7
N3	•		at Butler	20	0
N10			at Western Reserve	26	27
N17	•		Central Michigan	46	25

1952 · 4-4-0 (1-4-0)
S20			at Kent State	13	20
S27	•		Illinois Wesleyan	44	6
O4	•		at Central Michigan	18	0
O11			at Miami, Ohio	6	55
O18	•		Toledo	19	14
O25	•		at Washington, Mo.	28	20
N1			Ohio U.	13	28
N8			Western Reserve	13	16

JACK PETOSKEY
1953-56 (.257)   8-25-2

1953 · 1-6-1 (0-4-1)
S26			at Central Michigan	0	21
O3	•		at Illinois Wesleyan	20	7
O10			Miami, Ohio	6	52
O17			at Toledo	7	19
O24			Washington, Mo.	7	18
O31			Ohio U.	12	67
N7	=		at Western Reserve	14	14
N14			Kent State	0	40

1954 · 4-5-0 (3-4-0)
S25			Central Michigan	19	25
O2			at Marshall	13	47
O9	•		Bowling Green	20	15
O16			Toledo	7	19
O23	•		at Washington, Mo.	7	6
O31			at Miami, Ohio	0	48
N6	•		Ohio U.	19	6
N13	•		Western Reserve	38	0
N20			at Kent State	13	20

1955 · 1-7-1 (0-5-0)
S17	=		Great Lakes NAS	13	13
S24			at Central Michigan	12	27
O1			Bowling Green	0	35
O8			Marshall	0	28
O15			at Toledo	0	6
O22			Washington, Mo.	14	26
N5			at Ohio U.	14	40
N12	•		Western Reserve	13	0
N19			Kent State	14	25

1956 · 2-7-0 (1-4-0)
S22			Central Michigan	7	14
S29			Bowling Green	13	27
O6			at Marshall	0	13
O13	•		Toledo	26	15
O20			at Washington, Mo.	7	13
O27			at Great Lakes NAS	6	13
N3			Ohio U.	0	27
N10	•		at Western Reserve	42	19
N17			Kent State	13	27

MERLE SCHLOSSER
1957-63 (.461)   28-33-3

1957 · 4-4-1 (1-4-1)
S21	•		at Central Michigan	33	0
S28			Miami, Ohio	0	20
O5			Marshall	7	12
O12	=		at Bowling Green	14	14
O19	•		Youngstown St.	25	14
O26			at Toledo	16	27
N2			at Ohio U.	7	20
N9	•		Western Reserve	20	0
N16	•		Kent State	28	20

1958 · 4-5-0 (2-4-0)
S20			Central Michigan	32	33
S27			at Miami, Ohio	20	34
O4	•		at Marshall	30	24
O11			Bowling Green	6	40
O18	•		at Washington, Mo.	34	2
O25			Toledo	6	21
N1	•		Ohio U.	21	14
N8	•		Western Reserve	33	0
N15			at Kent State	6	32

1959 · 4-5-0 (3-3-0)
S19			at Central Michigan	15	21
S26	•		Miami, Ohio	0	21
O3	•		Marshall	51	0
O10			at Bowling Green	0	34
O17	•		Washington, Mo.	78	0
O24	•		at Toledo	24	14
O31			at Ohio U.	9	12
N7	•		Kent State	7	0
N14			Detroit	0	14

1960 · 4-4-1 (2-4-0)
S17	•		Central Michigan	31	0
S24	•		at Miami, Ohio	14	15
O1	=		Baldwin-Wallace	28	28
O8			Bowling Green	13	14
O15	•		at Washington, Mo.	43	0
O22	•		Toledo	7	3
O29	•		Ohio U.	0	24
N5			at Kent State	3	10
N12	•		Marshall	34	12

1961 · 5-4-1 (4-1-1)
S16	•		at Central Michigan	27	21
S23	•		at Detroit	14	21
S30	•		Miami, Ohio	6	3
O7			at Bowling Green	0	21
O21	•		at Toledo	7	0
O28	•		Marshall	20	0
N4	•		Kent State	14	0
N11			Utah State	22	65
N18	=		at Ohio U.	20	20

AVIATION BOWL
| D9 | | | New Mexico | 12 | 28 |

1962 · 5-4-0 (3-3-0)
S15	•		Central Michigan	28	0
S22			at Louisville	21	27
S29	•		at Miami, Ohio	7	17
O6			Bowling Green	6	10
O20	•		Toledo	21	0
O27	•		at Marshall	12	0
N3	•		at Kent State	19	6
N10	•		Brigham Young	28	20
N17			Ohio U.	16	32

1963 · 2-7-0 (2-4-0)
S21	•		at Wisconsin	0	41
S28	•		at Central Michigan	14	30
O5			Miami, Ohio	19	27
O12	•		at Bowling Green	7	16
O19	•		Kent State	26	12
O26	•		at Toledo	18	7
N2			Marshall	7	20
N9			at Ohio U.	13	27
N16			Louisville	7	21

BILL DOOLITTLE
1964-74 (.541)   58-49-2

1964 · 3-6-0 (2-4-0)
S19	•		at Louisville	10	7
S26			Central Michigan	6	18
O3			at Miami, Ohio	0	35
O10			Bowling Green	8	28
O17	•		at Kent State	12	9
O24			Toledo	13	21
O31			at Marshall	7	16
N7			Ohio U.	13	8
N14			at Brigham Young	8	43

1965 · 6-2-1 (3-2-1)
S18	•		Louisville	17	13
S25	•		at Central Michigan	21	13
O2			Miami, Ohio	9	36
O9	•		at Bowling Green	17	21
O16	=		Kent State	10	10
O23	•		at Toledo	3	0
O30	•		Marshall	17	14
N6	•		at Ohio U.	17	6
N13	•		Montana	17	14

1966 · 7-3-0 (5-1-0)
S17	•		Lamar Tech	16	14
S24	•		Central Michigan	31	14
O1			at Miami, Ohio	9	26
O8	•		Bowling Green	16	14
O15	•		at Kent State	23	20
O22	•		Toledo	14	13
O29	•		at Marshall	35	29
N5	•		Ohio U.	20	13
N12	•		at Xavier	6	21
N19	•		at West Texas St.	7	30

1967 · 5-4-0 (4-2-0)
S16	•		Miami, Ohio	24	14
S23	•		Arkansas State	8	21
S29	•		at Brigham Young	19	44
O7	•		at Bowling Green	10	6
O14	•		Kent State	16	7
O21	•		at Toledo	9	35
O28	•		Marshall	42	10
N4	•		at Ohio U.	10	20
N11	•		Xavier	18	7

1968 · 3-6-0 (2-4-0)
S14	•		Arkansas State	20	0
S21	•		Brigham Young	7	17
S28	•		at Miami, Ohio	0	28
O5	•		Bowling Green	10	17
O12	•		at Kent State	14	0
O19	•		Toledo	6	30
O26	•		at Marshall	40	12
N2	•		Ohio U.	27	34
N9			at West Texas St.	36	53

1969 · 4-6-0 (1-4-0)
S13	•		Central Michigan	24	0
S20	•		at Pacific	0	21
S27	•		Miami, Ohio	20	24
O4	•		at Bowling Green	10	21
O11	•		Kent State	33	13
O18	•		at Toledo	13	38
O25	•		Marshall	48	14
N1			at Ohio U.	17	22
N8			West Texas St.	20	28
N15	•		at Northern Illinois	31	22

1970 · 7-3-0 (2-3-0)
S12	•		at Central Michigan	41	0
S19	•		Brigham Young	35	17
S26	•		at Miami, Ohio	12	23
O3	•		Bowling Green	23	3
O10	•		at Kent State	22	25
O17	•		Toledo	0	20
O24	•		at Marshall	34	3
O31	•		Ohio U.	52	23
N7	•		at West Texas St.	20	0
N14			Northern Illinois	38	18

1971 · 7-3-0 (2-3-0)
S11	•		Illinois St.	35	7
S18	•		at Ball State	9	0
S25	•		Northern Illinois	27	17
O2	•		at Bowling Green	6	23
O9	•		Kent State	31	0
O16	•		at Toledo	24	35
O23	•		Marshall	37	0
O30	•		at Ohio U.	28	14
N6	•		Miami, Ohio	6	7
N13	•		Pacific	25	21

1972 · 7-3-1 (2-2-1)
S9	•		Long Beach St.	28	20
S16	•		at Fresno State	14	41
S23	•		at Northern Illinois	14	10
S30	=		Bowling Green	13	13
O7	•		at Kent State	13	12
O14	•		Toledo	13	20
O21	•		at Marshall	34	0
O28	•		Ohio U.	34	17
N4	•		at Miami, Ohio	8	38
N11	•		Ball State	31	14
N18	•		Idaho	27	16

1973 · 6-5-0 (1-4-0)
S8	•		at Central Michigan	18	13
S15	•		Long Beach St.	13	8
S22	•		Northern Illinois	28	14
S29			at Bowling Green	20	31
O6			Kent State	15	39
O13	•		at Toledo	24	22
O20	•		Marshall	21	7
O27			at Ohio U.	0	16
N3	•		Miami, Ohio	9	24
N10	•		Ball State	30	13
N17			at Texas-Arlington	12	31

1974 — 3-8-0 (0-5-0)

S7	●	Texas-Arlington	33	6
S14		at Eastern Michigan	19	20
S21	●	at Northern Illinois	30	13
S28	|	Bowling Green	13	21
O5	|	at Kent State	6	28
O12	|	Toledo	24	31
O19	●	at Marshall	20	17
O26	|	Ohio U.	3	26
N2	|	at Miami, Ohio	0	31
N9		Central Michigan	6	42
N16		at Long Beach St.	33	34

ELLIOT UZELAC
1975-81 (.494) 38-39

1975 — 1-10-0 (0-7-0)

S6	|	at Central Michigan	0	34
S13		Akron	21	27
S20		at Minnesota	0	38
S27	|	Northern Illinois	0	20
O4	|	at Bowling Green	0	28
O11	|	Kent State	17	22
O18	|	Toledo Clev	7	25
O25		at Marshall	19	21
N1	|	at Ohio U.	10	24
N8	|	Miami, Ohio	21	44
N15	●	Eastern Michigan	24	14

1976 — 7-4-0 (6-3-0)

S11	● |	Eastern Michigan	31	13
S18	● |	at Northern Illinois	37	6
S25		at Minnesota	10	21
O2	|	Bowling Green	28	31
O9	|	at Kent State	12	24
O16	● |	Toledo	34	21
O23	●	Marshall	31	21
O30	● |	Ohio U.	21	10
N6	|	at Miami, Ohio	0	31
N13	● |	at Ball State	24	10
N20	● |	Central Michigan	42	14

1977 — 4-7-0 (3-5-0)

S10		at Minnesota	7	10
S17		Texas-Arlington	10	17
S24	● |	Northern Illinois	49	21
O1	|	at Bowling Green	14	34
O8	|	Kent State	16	20
O15	● |	at Toledo	28	7
O22	●	Marshall	53	29
O29	● |	at Ohio U.	28	22
N5	|	Miami, Ohio	8	14
N12	|	Ball State	25	29
N19	|	at Central Michigan	23	28

1978 — 7-4-0 (5-4-0)

S9	●	Illinois St.	27	17
S16	● |	at Northern Illinois	44	30
S23	|	at Miami, Ohio	3	7
S30	● |	Bowling Green	24	20
O7	● |	at Kent State	14	0
O14	● |	Toledo	17	7
O21	● |	Eastern Michigan	32	0
O28	|	Ohio U.	7	10
N4	●	at Marshall	24	6
N11	|	at Ball State	14	20
N18	|	Central Michigan	14	35

1979 — 6-5-0 (5-4-0)

S8	|	at Central Michigan	0	10
S15		at South Carolina	7	24
S22	● |	Northern Illinois	45	17
S29	|	Bowling Green	3	15
O6	|	Kent State	13	18
O13	|	at Toledo	0	17
O20	●	Grand Valley St.	37	0
O27	● |	at Ohio U.	20	6
N3	● |	Miami, Ohio	24	3
N10	● |	Ball State	20	10
N17	● |	at Eastern Michigan	17	7

1980 — 7-4-0 (6-3-0)

S6	● |	Eastern Michigan	37	0
S13	●	at Illinois St.	31	17
S20	● |	at Northern Illinois	35	6
S27		at Michigan State	7	33
O4	|	Bowling Green	14	17
O11	● |	at Kent State	28	21
O18	● |	Toledo	17	7
O25	● |	at Ball State	17	15
N1	● |	Ohio U.	13	7
N8	|	at Miami, Ohio	24	34
N15	|	Central Michigan	10	22

1981 — 6-5-0 (5-4-0)

S12	● |	at Kent State	20	17
S19	●	Marshall	14	3
S26		at Wisconsin	10	21
O3	● |	at Bowling Green	21	7
O10	|	Central Michigan	13	15
O17	|	at Miami, Ohio	19	20
O24	● |	Ball State	14	3
O31	● |	at Northern Illinois	23	12
N7	|	Toledo	14	28
N14	|	at Ohio U.	20	37
N21	● |	Eastern Michigan	38	7

JACK HARBAUGH
1982-86 (.482) 25-27-3

1982 — 7-2-2 (5-2-2)

S4	●	Grand Valley St.	28	3
S11	●	at Marshall	34	0
S25	● |	Kent State	24	14
O2	|	at Bowling Green	3	7
O9	= |	at Central Michigan	18	18
O16	● |	Miami, Ohio	10	0
O23	|	at Ball State	6	13
O30	● |	Northern Illinois	27	3
N6	● |	at Toledo	17	10
N13	● |	Ohio U.	16	7
N20	= |	at Eastern Michigan	3	3

1983 — 6-5-0 (4-5-0)

S10	●	at Texas-Arlington	21	14
S17	●	at Illinois St.	14	13
S24	|	Central Michigan	14	32
O1	● |	at Miami, Ohio	20	18
O8	|	at Northern Illinois	3	27
O15	|	Bowling Green	20	23
O22	|	Ball State	20	24
O29	● |	at Ohio U.	16	14
N5	|	Toledo	16	20
N12	● |	at Kent State	21	13
N19	● |	Eastern Michigan	14	10

1984 — 5-6-0 (3-6-0)

S8	● |	Miami, Ohio	17	13
S15	●	Illinois St.	41	14
S22	|	at Central Michigan	19	38
S29	●	Marshall	42	7
O6	|	Northern Illinois	15	20
O13	|	at Bowling Green	7	34
O20	|	at Ball State	20	23
O27	● |	Ohio U.	33	14
N3	|	at Toledo	13	17
N10	● |	Kent State	13	9
N17	|	at Eastern Michigan	14	24

1985 — 4-6-1 (4-4-1)

S7	|	at Northern Illinois	0	17
S14		at Army	6	48
S28		at Michigan State	3	7
O5	|	Bowling Green	7	48
O12	|	Central Michigan	17	24
O19	= |	at Miami, Ohio	10	10
O26	● |	Ball State	34	0
N2	● |	Toledo	18	13
N9	|	at Ohio U.	15	21
N16	● |	at Kent State	34	3
N23	● |	Eastern Michigan	38	21

1986 — 3-8-0 (3-5-0)

S6	|	at Eastern Michigan	14	21
S13		Temple	17	49
S20		Long Beach St.	13	14
S27		at Michigan State	10	45
O4	|	at Bowling Green	3	17
O11	|	Central Michigan	10	18
O18	● |	Miami, Ohio	27	17
O25	|	at Ball State	10	24
N1	|	at Toledo	7	28
N8	● |	Ohio U.	45	17
N15	● |	Kent State	27	7

AL MOLDE
1987-96 (.568) 62-47-2

1987 — 5-6-0 (4-4-0)

S5	●	Akron	24	19
S12		at Illinois St.	6	20
S19		Northern Illinois	14	34
S26	● |	at Bowling Green	34	27
O3	● |	Toledo	21	14
O10	|	Miami, Ohio	0	17
O17	|	at Kent State	13	27
O24	|	Eastern Michigan	17	23
O31	|	at Central Michigan	27	30
N7	● |	Ball State	31	16
N21	● |	at Ohio U.	31	13

1988 — 9-3-0 (7-1-0)

S3	●	at Wisconsin	24	14
S10	● |	at Toledo	31	9
S17	●	Illinois St.	44	14
O1	● |	Bowling Green	37	10
O8	● |	at Miami, Ohio	41	18
O15	|	Kent State	28	45
O22	● |	at Eastern Michigan	31	24
O29	● |	Central Michigan	42	24
N5	● |	at Ball State	16	13
N12	|	at Northern Illinois	7	15
N19	● |	Ohio U.	23	16
CALIFORNIA BOWL				
D10		Fresno State	30	35

1989 — 5-6-0 (3-5-0)

S2	●	Temple	31	24
S9	●	Louisiana Tech	24	20
S16		at Maryland	0	23
S23	● |	at Kent State	26	4
S30	|	Eastern Michigan	20	21
O14	|	Central Michigan	6	34
O21	|	at Ball State	13	14
O28	● |	Ohio U.	28	13
N4	|	at Toledo	18	19
N11	|	Bowling Green	30	31
N18	● |	at Miami, Ohio	14	7

1990 — 7-4-0 (5-3-0)

S8	|	at Eastern Michigan	24	27
S15	●	Louisiana Tech	27	21
S22	● |	Kent State	37	10
S29		at Iowa State	20	34
O6	●	at Akron	24	20
O13	|	at Central Michigan	13	20
O20	● |	Ball State	14	13
O27	● |	at Ohio U.	31	23
N3	|	Toledo	9	37
N10	● |	at Bowling Green	19	13
N17	● |	Miami, Ohio	31	17

1991 — 6-5-0 (4-4-0)

A31	● |	Kent State	13	10
S7	●	Akron	35	12
S14		at Florida State	0	58
S21	|	Toledo	13	23
S28	● |	Ohio U.	35	9
O5	● |	at Ball State	25	16
O12	●	at Northern Illinois	22	10
O19	|	at Eastern Michigan	24	42
O26	|	Bowling Green	10	23
N9	● |	Miami, Ohio	24	23
N16	|	at Central Michigan	17	27

1992 — 7-3-1 (6-3-0)

S3	|	at Bowling Green	19	29
S12	=	at TCU	17	17
S19	● |	Akron	24	20
S26	● |	at Ohio U.	19	3
O3	● |	Ball State	21	14
O10	|	at Toledo	12	21
O17	● |	Eastern Michigan	20	19
O24	● |	at Kent State	26	13
O31	● |	Northern Illinois	13	7
N7	|	at Miami, Ohio	7	20
N14	● |	Central Michigan	19	14

1993 — 7-3-1 (6-1-1)

S2		Youngstown St.	13	17
S11		at Purdue	13	28
† S18	● |	Akron	20	3
S25	● |	Miami, Ohio	17	0
O2	● |	at Kent State	27	21
O9	|	Central Michigan	18	23
O23	● |	at Eastern Michigan	21	20
O30	●	at Army	20	7
N6	● |	at Ohio U.	34	28
N13	● |	Toledo	39	26
N20	= |	at Bowling Green	14	14

1994 — 7-4-0 (5-3-0)

S3	● |	at Miami, Ohio	28	25
S8	●	Western Illinois	43	7
S17	●	at Iowa State	23	19
S24	● |	Akron	19	6
O1	● |	Kent State	24	10
O8	|	at Central Michigan	28	35
O15	|	at Ball State	13	16
O22	● |	Eastern Michigan	33	14
N5	● |	Ohio U.	15	3
N12	|	at Toledo	34	37
N19		at La. Lafayette	14	17

1995 — 7-4-0 (6-2-0)

A31	●	Weber St.	28	21
S9		at Indiana	10	24
S14	|	Toledo	21	31
S23	|	at Ball State	0	10
S30	● |	at Kent State	52	6
O7	● |	Akron	7	3
O14	● |	at Ohio U.	34	17
O21		at Auburn	13	34
O28	● |	Bowling Green	17	0
N11	● |	at Eastern Michigan	23	13
N18	● |	Central Michigan	48	31

1996 — 2-9 (2-6)

A29		Eastern Illinois	20	28
S7		at West Virginia	9	34
S14	|	Eastern Michigan	12	19
S21	|	at Central Michigan	28	38
S28	|	at Akron	7	27
O5	|	Ball State	5	28
O12		at Wyoming	28	42
O26	|	at Toledo	7	10
N2	|	Ohio U.	0	38
N9	● |	at Bowling Green	16	13
N16	● |	Kent State	76	27

GARY DARNELL
1997-2004 (.500) 46-46

1997 — 8-3 (6-2)

A28	●	Temple	34	14
S6		at Michigan State	10	42
S13	● |	at Northern Illinois	21	13
S20	|	Toledo	13	23
S27	|	at Ohio U.	7	31
O4	● |	Ball State	21	13
O11	● |	at Bowling Green	34	21
O18	● |	Kent State	50	27
N1	● |	at Eastern Michigan	41	38
N8	● |	Central Michigan	38	24
N15	●	at La. Monroe	32	19

1998 — 7-4 (5-3)

S3	● |	Northern Illinois	37	23
S12		at Indiana	30	45
S19	|	at Toledo	7	35
S26	|	Ohio U.	35	37
O3	●	La. Monroe	27	14
O10	●	at Vanderbilt	27	24
O17	● |	Eastern Michigan	45	35
O24	|	at Central Michigan	24	26
O31	● |	at Kent State	48	23
N7	● |	at Ball State	24	23
N14	● |	Bowling Green	56	27

1999 — 7-5 (6-2)

S4		at Florida	26	55
S11	●	Youngstown St.	46	28
S18		at Missouri	34	48
S25	● |	at Northern Illinois	24	21
O2	● |	Central Michigan	38	16
O9	● |	at Eastern Michigan	40	37
O16	● |	Buffalo	45	17
O23	● |	Ball State	28	0
O30	● |	at Akron	24	10
N13	|	Marshall	17	31
N20	|	at Toledo	21	45
MAC CHAMPIONSHIP GAME				
D3		Marshall HUN	30	34

2000 — 9-3 (7-1)

A31		at Wisconsin	7	19
S9	●	at Iowa	27	21
S16	●	Indiana St.	56	0
S23	● |	Toledo	21	14
S30	● |	Ohio U.	23	10
O5	● |	at Marshall	30	10
O21	● |	Northern Illinois	52	22
O28	● |	at Kent State	42	0
N4	● |	at Ball State	42	3
N11	|	at Central Michigan	17	21
N18	● |	Eastern Michigan	28	0
MAC CHAMPIONSHIP GAME				
D2		Marshall HUN	14	19

2001 — 5-6 (4-4)

A30	●	Illinois St.	48	7
S8		at Virginia Tech	0	31
S22		at Michigan	21	38
S29	● |	at Eastern Michigan	31	10
O6	● |	Akron	31	14
O13	● |	Bowling Green	37	28
O20	|	at Northern Illinois	12	20
O27	|	at Miami, Ohio	11	25
N6	|	at Toledo	35	41
N17	● |	Central Michigan	20	17
N24	|	Ball State	31	35

2002　4-8 (3-5)

A29	●	Indiana St.	48	17
S7		at Michigan	12	35
S14		at Purdue	24	28
S28		Virginia Tech	0	30
O5	● |	at Buffalo	31	17
O12	|	Central Florida	27	31
O19	|	at Bowling Green	45	48
O26	|	Northern Illinois	20	24
N2	|	at Ball State	7	17
N9	● |	Eastern Michigan	33	31
N16	|	Toledo	21	42
N23	|	at Central Michigan	35	10

2003　5-7 (4-4)

A30		at Michigan State	21	26
S6	●	William & Mary	56	24
S13		Virginia	16	59
S27	● |	at Ohio U.	39	32
O4	● |	at Eastern Michigan	31	3
O11	|	Bowling Green	21	32
O18	|	at Northern Illinois	10	37
O25	|	Marshall	21	41
N1		at Connecticut	27	41
N8	● |	Ball State	28	20
N15	● |	Central Michigan	44	21
N22	|	at Toledo	17	34

2004　1-10 (0-8)

S2	●	Tenn-Martin	42	0
S11		at Virginia Tech	0	63
S18		at Illinois	27	30
S25	|	at Ball State	14	41
O9	|	Toledo	33	59
O16	|	Eastern Michigan	31	35
O23	|	Northern Illinois	38	59
O30	|	at Central Michigan	21	24
N6	|	at Bowling Green	0	52
N13	|	Miami, Ohio	21	42
N20	|	at Marshall	21	31

BILL CUBIT
2005-PRESENT (.625)　15-9

2005　7-4 (5-3)

S3		at Virginia	19	31
S10	|	at Toledo	23	56
S17	●	So. Illinois	34	28
S24	●	at Temple	19	16
O1	● |	Buffalo	31	21
O8	|	Ball State	57	60
O22	● |	at Bowling Green	45	14
O29	● |	Kent State	44	14
N5	● |	Eastern Michigan*DET*	44	36
N12	● |	Central Michigan	31	24
N22	|	at Northern Illinois	7	42

2006　8-5 (6-2)

S2		at Indiana	20	39
S9	● |	Toledo	31	10
S16	●	at Virginia	17	10
S23	●	Temple	41	7
O7	|	at Ohio U.	20	27
O14	● |	Northern Illinois	16	14
O21	● |	at Ball State	41	27
O28	● |	Eastern Michigan	18	15
N4	● |	Miami, Ohio	27	24
N10	|	at Central Michigan	7	31
N18		at Florida State	20	28
N24	● |	at Akron	17	0
		INTERNATIONAL BOWL		
J6		Cincinnati	24	27

Neutral site key: *Clev* Cleveland, OH / *Det* Detroit, MI / *Hun* Huntington, WV / *Unk* Unkown
ƒ Forfeit　† Game Later Forfieted　# Disputed Victor　* Disputed Score　‖ Designated Conference Game　|2 Counted Twice in Conference Standings

WESTERN MICHIGAN RECORD BOOK

SINGLE-GAME RECORDS

RUSHING YARDS

RANK	PLAYER	DATE	OPPONENT	YDS
1	Lovell Coleman	Sept. 20, 1958	Central Michigan	279
2	Sam Dunlap	Date unknown, 1916	Ohio Northern	247
3	Jerome Persell	Sept. 11, 1976	Eastern Michigan	241

PASSING YARDS

RANK	PLAYER	DATE	OPPONENT	YDS
1	Chad Munson	Sept. 6, 2003	William & Mary	450
2	Tim Lester	Nov. 14, 1998	Bowling Green	435
3	Tim Lester	Oct. 17, 1998	Eastern Michigan	432
4	Tim Lester	Oct. 10, 1999	Buffalo	407
5	Tim Lester	Sept. 4, 1999	Florida	405

RECEIVING YARDS

RANK	PLAYER	DATE	OPPONENT	REC	AVG	YDS
1	Corey Alston	Nov. 1, 1997	Eastern Michigan	9	29.2	263
2	Greg Jennings	Oct. 8, 2005	Ball State	11	22.2	244
3	Bob Phillips	Nov. 14, 1981	Ohio	NA	NA	203
4	Kelly Spielmaker	Nov. 15, 1983	Toledo	NA	NA	186
5	Steve Neal	Oct. 17, 1998	Eastern Michigan	9	20.4	184

POINTS

RANK	PLAYER	DATE	OPPONENT	TOT
1	Walt Olsen	1916	Grand Rapids Veterinary	52
2	Sam Dunlap	1916	Ohio Northern	42
3	Walt Olsen	1916	Michigan State Frosh	31

FIELD GOALS

RANK	PLAYER	DATE	OPPONENT	TOT
1	Mike Prindle	Sept. 29, 1984	Marshall	7
2	Nate Meyer	Sept. 3, 2005	Virginia	4
	Mike Prindle	Oct. 27, 1984	Ohio	4
	Jay Barresi	Nov. 4, 1989	Toledo	4
	Brad Selent	Nov. 7, 1998	Ball State	4

TACKLES

RANK	PLAYER	DATE	OPPONENT	TOT
1	Willie Berrios	Oct. 31, 1987	Central Michigan	27
2	Greg Igaz	Sept. 19, 1970	Brigham Young	25
3	Van Dickerson	Nov. 19, 1977	Central Michigan	24
	John Offerdahl	Oct. 20, 1984	Ball State	24

INTERCEPTIONS

RANK	PLAYER	DATE	OPPONENT	TOT
1	Bill Yambrick	Nov. 14, 1942	Wayne State	4
	Sam Antonazzo	Oct. 26, 1968	Marshall	4
3	Tony Carr	Sept. 9, 2002	Eastern Michigan	3
	George Ihler	Oct. 27, 1962	Marshall	3
	Dick Trudeau	Nov. 19, 1966	West Texas State	3

SINGLE-SEASON RECORDS

RUSHING YARDS

RANK	PLAYER	SEASON	ATT	YDS
1	Shawn Faulkner	1983	394	1,668
2	Robert Sanford	2000	293	1,571

PASSING YARDS

RANK	PLAYER	SEASON	ATT	COMP	PCT	YDS
1	Tim Lester	1999	470	282	60.0	3,639

RECEIVING YARDS

RANK	PLAYER	SEASON	REC	AVG	YDS
1	Greg Jennings	2005	98	12.8	1,259

SCORING

RANK	PLAYER	SEASON	TD	FG	PAT	P2	TOT
1	Walt Olsen	1916	17	0	36	0	138

TOUCHDOWNS

RANK	PLAYER	SEASON	TOT
1	Sam Dunlap	1916	19
	Jerome Persell	1976	19
3	Robert Sanford	2000	18
4	Walt Olsen	1916	17

TACKLES

RANK	PLAYER	SEASON	TOT
1	John Offerdahl	1983	192
2	Eric Manns	1978	186
3	John Offerdahl	1984	182

INTERCEPTIONS

RANK	PLAYER	SEASON	YDS	TOT
1	Brad Tayles	1989	370	25

PUNTING

RANK	PLAYER	SEASON	PUNTS	YDS	AVG
1	Adam Anderson	2003	72	3,162	43.9
2	Dale Livingston	1967	49	2,123	43.3
3	Todd Rawsthorne	1990	35	1,502	42.9
4	Jim Klapthor	1985	77	3,161	41.1

PUNT RETURNS

RANK	PLAYER	SEASON	RET	YDS	AVG
1	Josh Bush	2000	35	526	15.0

KICKOFF RETURNS

RANK	PLAYER	SEASON	RET	YDS	AVG
1	Rashad McDade	1999	37	898	24.3

MAC TEAMS

RETIRED NUMBERS

44 Jerome Persell

49 John Offerdahl

74 Bob Rowe

CAREER RECORDS

RUSHING YARDS

RANK	PLAYER	SEASONS	ATT	AVG	TD	YDS
1	Robert Stanford	1997-2000	838	5.0	43	4,219
2	Jerome Persell	1976-78	842	5.0	39	4,190
3	Shawn Faulkner	1980-83	761	4.4	NA	3,341
4	Jim Vackaro	1992-95	625	4.9	NA	3,045

PASSING YARDS

RANK	PLAYER	SEASONS	ATT	COMP	PCT	INT	TD	YDS
1	Tim Lester	1996-99	1,507	875	58.0	NA	87	11,299
2	Brad Tayles	1989-92	1,370	663	48.4	67	49	8,717
3	Jay McDonagh	1993-95	892	529	59.3	NA	45	6,148
4	Jeff Welsh	1997-2001	NA	382	59.0	NA	34	4,849

RECEIVING YARDS

RANK	PLAYER	SEASONS	REC	AVG	TD	YDS
1	Steve Neal	1997-2000	235	15.3	27	3,599
2	Greg Jennings	2002-05	238	14.9	39	3,539
3	Corey Alston	1997-2000	NA	NA	25	2,456
4	Kendrick Mosley	1999-2003	163	12.5	NA	2,042
5	Allan Boyko	1987-90	NA	NA	19	1,957
6	Josh Bush	1998-2001	150	12.6	NA	1,889
7	Bob Phillips	1979-82	NA	NA	16	1,802

SCORING

RANK	PLAYER	SEASONS	TD	FG	PAT	P2	TOT
1	Brad Selent	1997-2000	0	50	157	0	307
2	Robert Sanford	1997-2000	43	0	0	0	258
3	Walt Olsen	1916-17, 19	32	NA	NA	NA	253
4	Jerome Persell	1976-78	39	0	0	3	240
5	Mike Prindle	1981-84	0	54	77	0	239

TOUCHDOWNS

RANK	PLAYER	SEASONS	TOT
1	Robert Sanford	1997-2000	43
2	Jerome Persell	1976-78	39
3	Walt Olsen	1916-17, 19	32
4	Lovell Coleman	1957-59	30

TACKLES

RANK	PLAYER	SEASONS	TOT
1	John Offerdahl	1982-85	694
2	Sean Mulhearn	1987-90	435
3	Eric Hoffman	1985-88	406
4	Peter Tuffo	1990-94	382
5	Greg Igaz	1969-71	346

INTERCEPTIONS

RANK	PLAYER	SEASONS	YDS	TOT
1	Dave Krebs	1937-39	NA	24
2	Floyd Stolsteimer	1951-53	223	15
	Ron Karles	1970-72	313	15
4	Ronald Rogers	1997-2001	NA	14

PUNTING

RANK	PLAYER	SEASONS	PUNTS	YDS	AVG
1	Todd Rawsthorne	1990-91	NA	NA	40.8
	Adam Anderson	2001-03	NA	NA	40.8
3	Dale Livingston	1965-66	NA	NA	39.9
4	Nate Meyer	2005-06	NA	NA	39.5
5	Lesli Gratton	1948-50	NA	NA	39.4

TEAM RECORDS

LONGEST WINNING STREAK
- 12, 1921 (date unknown)-Oct. 13, 1923
Streak broken vs. St. Viator, 7-7, Oct. 20, 1923

LONGEST UNDEFEATED STREAK
- 16, 1921(date not available)-Nov. 17, 1923
Streak broken vs. Albion, 6-7, Nov. 29, 1923

MOST CONSECUTIVE WINNING SEASONS
- 8 (twice), 1912-19 and 1941-48

MOST CONSECUTIVE BOWL APPEARANCES
- 1 (tie), 1961, 1988, 2006

MOST POINTS IN A GAME
- 103, vs. Hillsdale, November, 1918

MOST POINTS ALLOWED IN A GAME
- 67, vs. Ohio, Oct. 31, 1953

LARGEST MARGIN OF VICTORY
- 103 (103-0), vs. Hillsdale, November, 1918

LARGEST MARGIN OF DEFEAT
- 63 (0-63), vs. Virginia Tech, Sept. 11, 2004

LONGEST RUN FROM SCRIMMAGE
- 95 yards, Clarence Frendt, vs. Detroit City, 1930

LONGEST PASS PLAY
- 94 yards, Jon Drach to Greg Jennings, vs. Central Michigan, Nov. 15, 2003

LONGEST FIELD GOAL
- 56 yards (tie), Mike Prindle, vs. Marshall, Sept. 29, 1984; Brad Selent, vs. Central Michigan, Oct. 24, 1998

LONGEST PUNT
- 86 yards (tie), Dale Morris, vs. Butler, Nov. 5, 1938; Dale Livingston, vs. Kent State, Oct. 15, 1966

LONGEST PUNT RETURN
- 95 yards, Paul Agema, vs. Akron, Oct. 6, 1990

LONGEST INTERCEPTION RETURN
- 100 yards, Vern Brown, vs. BYU, Sept. 19, 1970

PUNT RETURNS

RANK	PLAYER	SEASON	RET	YDS	AVG
1	Kendrick Mosley	1999-2003	NA	869	NA

KICKOFF RETURNS

RANK	PLAYER	SEASON	RET	YDS	AVG
1	Lovell Coleman	1957-59	NA	NA	27.8

WESTERN MICHIGAN ANNUAL STATISTICAL LEADERS

YR	RUSHING	YDS	ATT	AVG	PASSING	ATT	CMP	PCT	YDS	RECEIVING	REC	YDS	AVG
1947	Arthur Gillespie	436	129	3.4	Nick Milosevich	105	49	.47	580	Carl Schiller	47	327	7.0
1948	Harry Hildreth	396	77	5.1	Hilton Foster	58	28	.48	436	George Mesko	15	305	20.3
1949	Arnold Thompson	243	56	4.3	Robert White	146	54	.37	870	Pat Clysdale	19	291	15.3
1950	Bob Morse	369	60	6.2	Norm Harris	135	40	.30	684	Chas Atkcounis	7	201	28.7
1951	Earl Montross	556	105	5.3	Owen Bennett	102	38	.37	661	Len Johnston	21	405	19.3
1952	Bill Brown	364	85	4.3	Charles Higgins	142	57	.40	868	John Smith	17	336	19.8
1953	John Kelder	220	66	3.3	Louis Fierens	31	9	.29	116	Bernard Porter	9	190	21.1
1954	Charles Nidiffer	271	85	3.2	Jerry Ganzel	115	41	.36	624	John Berryman	11	208	18.9
1955	Charles Nidiffer	478	107	4.5	Robert Mason	74	23	.31	254	John Berryman	13	185	14.2
1956	Buryl Breed	493	119	4.1	Robert Mason	74	28	.38	427	Joe Grigg	7	153	21.9
1957	Lovell Coleman	384	80	4.8	Jim Kolk	45	25	.56	473	Jesse Madden	7	228	32.6
1958	Lovell Coleman	1,068	174	6.1	Jim Kolk	28	12	.43	158	Jesse Madden	7	101	14.4
1959	Lovell Coleman	466	126	3.7	Ed Chlebek	67	32	.48	555	Jesse Madden	12	297	24.8
1960	Lloyd Swelnis	479	79	6.1	Ed Chlebek	72	51	.71	626	Dennis Holland	10	149	14.9
1961	Bob White	278	70	4.0	Ed Chlebek	79	45	.57	577	Dennis Holland	10	96	9.6
1962	Bill Schlee	599	120	5.0	Roger Theder	124	58	.47	824	Jim Bedner	12	255	21.3
1963	George Archer	397	90	4.4	Ken Barnhill	93	36	.39	668	Tom Patterson	15	269	17.9
1964	Troy Allen	195	67	2.9	Bob Radlinski	93	38	.41	469	Stan Williams	7	77	11.0
1965	Steve Terlep	361	105	3.4	Ron Seifert	116	55	.47	660	Dave Mollard	25	269	10.8
1966	Tim Majerle	731	204	3.6	Jim Boreland	118	47	.40	756	Dave Mollard	27	361	13.4
1967	Jack Foster	377	90	4.2	Jim Boreland	90	42	.47	620	Marty Barski	28	392	14.0
1968	Kenneth Woodside	474	134	3.5	Mark Bordeax	171	83	.49	1,143	Alan Bellile	30	394	13.1
1969	Paul Schneider	554	112	4.9	Ted Grignon	109	47	.43	549	Greg Flaska	37	433	11.7
1970	Roger Lawson	1,205	168	7.2	Ted Grignon	123	62	.50	1,001	Greg Flaska	17	372	21.9
1971	Larry Cates	819	162	5.1	Ted Grignon	129	68	.53	912	Dave Hallabrin	22	294	13.4
1972	Larry Cates	660	122	5.4	Steve Doolittle	101	40	.40	518	Bob Gavinski	17	290	17.1
1973	Paul Jorgensen	482	111	4.3	Paul Jorgensen	106	41	.39	664	Frank Mumford	13	225	17.3
1974	Dan Matthews	769	142	5.4	Paul Jorgensen	119	53	.45	701	Greg Cowser	32	403	12.6
1975	Dan Matthews	873	181	4.8	Sollie Boone	77	23	.30	318	Ted Forrest	21	286	13.6
1976	Jerome Persell	1,505	269	5.6	Pepper Powers	103	46	.45	571	Tom Henry	17	225	13.2
1977	Jerome Persell	1,339	264	5.1	Albert Little	121	50	.41	802	Tim Clysdale	19	228	12.0
1978	Jerome Persell	1,346	309	4.4	Albert Little	138	61	.44	828	Tim Clysdale	18	213	11.8
1979	Larry Caper	844	168	5.0	Albert Little	67	32	.48	342	Tim Clysdale	16	207	12.9
1980	Craig Morrow	778	150	5.2	Tom George	124	59	.48	644	Reggie Hinton	29	429	14.8
1981	Shawn Faulkner	701	155	4.5	Tom George	207	104	.50	1,419	Bob Phillips	53	809	15.3
1982	Shawn Faulkner	910	206	4.4	Chris Conklin	137	76	.55	853	Bob Phillips	39	577	14.8
1983	Shawn Faulkner	1,668	394	4.2	Steve Hoffman	213	125	.59	1,407	Kelly Spielmaker	48	653	13.6
1984	Otis Cheathem	778	190	4.1	Steve Hoffman	265	151	.57	1,732	Cliff Read	47	591	12.6
1985	Lewis Howard	819	177	4.6	Chris Conklin	244	133	.55	1,574	Paul Sorce	47	567	12.1
1986	Joe Glenn	602	152	4.0	Chris Conklin	261	127	.49	1,668	Kelly Spielmaker	43	575	13.4
1987	Robert Davis	477	115	4.1	Dave Kruse	278	125	.45	1,592	Jamie Hence	50	858	17.2
1988	Robert Davis	1,054	226	4.7	Tony Kimbrough	324	186	.57	2,465	Bruce Boyko	44	583	13.3
1989	Dan Boggan	744	208	3.6	Brad Tayles	321	147	.46	1,909	Ulric King	32	435	13.6
1990	Corey Sylve	840	147	5.7	Brad Tayles	345	171	.50	2,397	Paul Agema	57	785	13.8
1991	Corey Sylve	711	176	4.0	Brad Tayles	328	162	.49	1,949	John Morton	39	588	15.1
1992	Jim Vackaro	893	183	4.9	Brad Tayles	376	183	.49	2,462	Ulric King	48	732	15.3
1993	Dave Madsen	571	140	4.1	Jay McDonagh	283	174	.61	1,974	Andre Wallace	55	599	10.9
1994	Jim Vackaro	910	187	4.9	Jay McDonagh	293	172	.59	2,136	Andre Wallace	68	758	11.1
1995	Jim Vackaro	702	128	5.5	Jay McDonagh	316	183	.58	2,038	Tony Knox	43	430	10.0
1996	Bruno Heppell	700	160	4.4	Tim Lester	363	203	.56	2,189	Tony Knox	71	754	10.6
1997	Robert Sanford	1,033	216	4.8	Tim Lester	268	154	.57	2,160	Jake Moreland	36	406	11.3
1998	Darnell Fields	1,016	189	5.4	Tim Lester	406	236	.58	3,311	Steve Neal	63	1,121	17.8
1999	Robert Sanford	1,092	221	4.9	Tim Lester	470	282	.60	3,639	Steve Neal	74	1,113	15.0
2000	Robert Sanford	1,571	293	5.4	Jeff Welsh	354	207	.58	2,537	Steve Neal	67	848	12.7
2001	Philip Reed	539	122	4.4	Jeff Welsh	213	134	.63	1,702	Josh Bush	48	617	12.9
2002	Philip Reed	1,053	221	4.8	Chad Munson	309	162	.52	2,160	Antonio Thomas	45	439	9.8
2003	Philip Reed	744	189	3.9	Chad Munson	266	150	.56	2,123	Kendrick Mosley	77	1,019	13.2
2004	Trovon Riley	691	172	4.0	Ryan Cubit	290	170	.59	1,887	Greg Jennings	74	1,092	14.8
2005	Trovon Riley	1,004	220	4.6	Tim Hiller	150	98	.65	1334	Greg Jennings	98	1259	12.8
2006	Mark Bonds	1,082	252	4.3	Ryan Cubit	365	224	.61	2138	Jamarko Simmons	61	668	11.0

Receiving leaders by receptions
All statistics include postseason

MAC TEAMS

MAC ANNUAL REVIEW

What follows is a year-by-year rundown of 60 seasons of Mid-American conference football, incorporating final poll rankings when a MAC team appears on it, MAC players on All-American teams, bowl game results, all-conference teams, Heisman Trophy balloting, other award winners, and instances in which MAC teams and players ranked among NCAA team and individual statistical leaders.

Final Polls. Each season's review begins with the final writers' and, eventually, coaches poll of the season when a MAC team appears on it, with the MAC teams highlighted in bold.

Consensus All-Americans and All-Conference Teams. Beginning with the 1947 all-MAC team which featured Miami of Ohio's halfback Ara Parseghian, we've collected each season's all-conference team as well as an annual listing of MAC players who placed among the consensus All-Americans, along with the names of all other conference players who received first-team All-America mention from selectors recognized by the NCAA.

Conference Standings. Beginning with 1934, when original MAC member Cincinnati went 3–1 to unofficially capture the first conference title, we run an annual review of MAC standings through the years, assembled through NCAA records and Richard Billingsley's all-time scores database.

NCAA Statistical Leaders. Reliable statistics to determine top 10 category leaders in college football's first 60 seasons simply don't exist. It wasn't until Homer Cooke, founder of what would become the NCAA Statistics Service, began contacting every school in the country in 1937 that the NCAA began to tabulate national statistical rankings. Even in Cooke's early years, leaders were often determined with one or more games for a team being unreported. Those discrepancies as well as missing data for part of the '50s, makes the first few decades of the NCAA's recordkeeping a somewhat rough guide to the era. Progress began in earnest in 1970, when the NCAA began determining most categorical champions on a per-game basis rather than by accumulated totals. At any rate, we've isolated MAC performers who landed on the NCAA lists throughout.

The MAC has had a fairly fluid roster of member teams, with some like Marshall and Northern Illinois dropping out, rejoining, and even re-dropping out. On these pages we've included players and results from the teams from that year, and also from future conference members like Temple (which joined for 2007), though when they are featured prior to their inclusion, the references carry an asterisk (*) to note that the team was not yet a member of the MAC.

KEY TO ALL-AMERICA TEAMS

AA – All-America Board
AP – Associated Press
CF – Walter Camp Foundation
CM – *Collier's* magazine (selections by Grantland Rice, 1925 to '47; published American Football Coaches Association teams, 1948 to '56, listed under FC)
CN – CNN, SI.com
CP – Central Press
CW – Caspar Whitney (published in *The Week's Sport* in association with Walter Camp, 1889 to '90; published in *Harper's Weekly*, 1891 to '96, and in *Outing* magazine, which he owned, 1898 to 1908; Walter Camp substituted for Whitney, who was on a world sports tour, and selected *Harper's Weekly's* team for 1897)

FC – American Football Coaches Association (published in *The Saturday Evening Post*, 1945 to '47; in *Collier's* magazine, 1948 to '56; sponsored by General Mills from 1957 to '59 and by Eastman Kodak from 1960 to '93)
FM – *Football World* magazine
FN – *Football News*
FW – Football Writers Association of America (published in *Look* magazine, 1946 to '70)
IN – International News Service (merged with United Press in 1958 to form UPI)
LK – *Look* magazine (published Football Writers Association of America teams, 1946 to '70, listed under FW)
LM – *Liberty* magazine
MS – Frank Menke Syndicate

NA – North American Newspaper Alliance
NE – Newspaper Enterprise Association
NW – *Newsweek*
PI – United Press International
SN – *The Sporting News*
UP – United Press (merged with International News Service in 1958 to form UPI)
WC – Walter Camp (published in *Harper's Weekly*, 1897; in *Collier's* magazine, 1898 to 1924)

1947

CONFERENCE STANDINGS

	CONFERENCE			OVERALL		
	W	L	T	W	L	T
Cincinnati	3	1	0	7	3	0
Case Western Reserve	2	1	0	4	5	0
Butler	1	3	0	5	3	1
Ohio U	1	3	0	3	5	1
Miami (Ohio)*				9	0	1
Toledo*				9	2	0
Ball State*				5	1	2
Western Michigan*				5	4	0
Bowling Green*				5	5	0
Kent State*				4	4	0
Temple*				3	6	0
Central Michigan*				2	5	1
Eastern Michigan*				1	6	0

BOWL GAMES

DATE	GAME	SCORE
J1	Sun	Miami (Ohio)* 13, Texas Tech 12

ALL-CONFERENCE TEAM

POS	Name	School
QB	Mel Olix	Miami (Ohio)#
HB	Ara Parseghian	Miami (Ohio)#
HB	Warren Lahr	Case Western Reserve
C	Paul Dietzel	Miami (Ohio)#
G	Ed Zednik	Ohio U
G	John Vilkowski	Cincinnati
T	John Weaver	Miami (Ohio)#
T	Dick Langenbeck	Cincinnati
E	Bill Hoover	Miami (Ohio)#
E	Cass Sisler	Case Western Reserve

1948

CONFERENCE STANDINGS

	CONFERENCE			OVERALL		
	W	L	T	W	L	T
Miami (Ohio)	4	0	0	7	1	1
Western Michigan	3	1	0	6	3	0
Cincinnati	3	1	0	3	6	1
Ohio U	2	3	0	3	6	0
Case Western Reserve	1	4	0	1	8	1
Butler	0	4	0	3	5	0
Bowling Green*				8	0	1
Ball State*				6	2	0
Kent State*				6	2	1
Toledo*				5	6	0
Eastern Michigan*				3	5	0
Central Michigan*				3	6	0
Temple*				2	6	1

ALL-CONFERENCE TEAM

POS	Name	School
QB	Mel Olix	Miami (Ohio)
HB	Paul Shoults	Miami (Ohio)
HB	Francis Moriarty	Butler
FB	Jim Dougherty	Cincinnati
C	Chuck Schoolmaster	Western Michigan
G	John Vilkowski	Cincinnati
G	Ed Lewis	Case Western Reserve
T	Jack Murphy	Butler
T	Jim Weaver	Miami (Ohio)
E	Doc Urich	Miami (Ohio)
E	John Marco	Ohio U

NCAA STATISTICAL LEADERS

INDIVIDUAL

KICKOFF RETURNS	KR	YDS	AVG
9 Leonard Corbin, Case Western Reserve	15	378	25.2

TEAM

TOTAL OFFENSE	G	P	YDS	AVG	YPG
8 Miami (Ohio)	9	546	3412	6.2	379.1

#Miami (Ohio), a founding member of the MAC, didn't play in the conference until 1948 but its players were named to the all-conference team
*Independent or other conference affiliation

1949

CONFERENCE STANDINGS

	CONFERENCE			OVERALL		
	W	L	T	W	L	T
Cincinnati	4	0	0	7	4	0
Miami (Ohio)	3	1	0	5	4	0
Ohio U	2	2	1	4	4	1
Western Michigan	2	3	0	4	4	0
Case Western Reserve	1	3	1	4	5	1
Butler	0	3	0	2	6	0
Ball State*				8	0	0
Toledo*				6	4	0
Kent State*				5	3	0
Temple*				5	4	0
Bowling Green*				4	5	0
Central Michigan*				3	4	0
Eastern Michigan*				0	8	0

ALL-CONFERENCE TEAM

POS	Name	School
QB	Tom O'Malley	Cincinnati
HB	John Pont	Miami (Ohio)
HB	Jack Bickel	Miami (Ohio)
C	Chuck Schoolmaster	Western Michigan
G	Milt Taylor	Ohio U
G	Lee Hasinger	Cincinnati
T	Ernie Plank	Miami (Ohio)
T	Al Schneider	Ohio U
E	Doc Urich	Miami (Ohio)
E	Pat Clysdale	Western Michigan
E	Jim Kelly	Cincinnati

NCAA STATISTICAL LEADERS

INDIVIDUAL

PASSING	G	ATT	COM	PCT	INT	I%	YDS	YPA	TD	TD%	COM.PG
2 Tom O'Malley, Cincinnati	10	225	108	48.0	15	6.7	1617	7.2	16	7.1	10.8

RUSHING/YARDS PER GAME			G	ATT	YDS	AVG	YPG
4 John Pont, Miami (Ohio)			9	128	977	7.6	108.6

RUSHING/YARDS PER CARRY			G	ATT	YDS	YPC
1 John Pont, Miami (Ohio)			9	128	977	7.8

RECEIVING	G	REC	YDS	TD	YPR	RPG	YPG
6 Jim Kelly, Cincinnati	10	42	478	2	11.4	4.2	47.8

PUNT RETURNS		PR	YDS	AVG
2 Gene Gibson, Cincinnati		21	438	20.9

KICKOFF RETURNS		KR	YDS	AVG
7 John Pont, Miami (Ohio)		13	385	29.6

TEAM

PASSING OFFENSE	G	ATT	COM	INT	PCT	YDS	YPA	TD	YPG	I%	YPC
6 Cincinnati	10	234	111	18	47.4	1664	7.1	16	166.4	7.7	15.0

TOTAL OFFENSE			G	P	YDS	AVG	YPG
10 Miami (Ohio)			9	592	3421	5.8	380.1

PASSING DEFENSE	G	ATT	COM	PCT	YPC	INT	I%	YDS	YPA	TD	YPG
2 Miami (Ohio)	9	127	39	30.7	12.7	20	15.8	495	3.9	5	55.0

1950

CONFERENCE STANDINGS

	CONFERENCE			OVERALL		
	W	L	T	W	L	T
Miami (Ohio)	4	0	0	9	1	0
Cincinnati	3	1	0	8	4	0
Ohio U	2	2	0	6	4	0
Western Michigan	1	3	0	5	4	0
Case Western Reserve	1	3	0	2	8	0
Central Michigan*				6	4	0
Kent State*				5	4	0
Temple*				4	4	1
Toledo*				4	5	0
Bowling Green*				3	4	2
Eastern Michigan*				3	6	0
Ball State*				2	4	1

BOWL GAMES

DATE	GAME	SCORE
J1	Salad	Miami (Ohio) 34, Arizona State 21
J1	Sun	West Texas State 14, Cincinnati 13

ALL-CONFERENCE TEAM

POS	Offense	School
QB	Gene Rossi	Cincinnati
HB	John Pont	Miami (Ohio)
C	Frank Middendorf	Cincinnati
G	Bill Shalosky	Cincinnati
G	Dale Doland	Miami (Ohio)
T	Don Green	Miami (Ohio)
T	Al Schneider	Ohio U
E	Jim Bailey	Miami (Ohio)
E	Don Urich	Miami (Ohio)
E	Jim Kelly	Cincinnati

POS	Defense	School
DB	Bob Stratton	Cincinnati

NCAA STATISTICAL LEADERS

INDIVIDUAL

PUNT RETURNS		PR	YDS	AVG
7 Gene Gibson, Cincinnati		16	322	20.1

1951

CONFERENCE STANDINGS

	CONFERENCE			OVERALL		
	W	L	T	W	L	T
Cincinnati	3	0	0	10	1	0
Miami (Ohio)	3	1	0	7	3	0
Kent State	2	1	0	4	3	2
Ohio U	2	2	0	5	4	1
Case Western Reserve	1	3	0	2	6	1
Western Michigan	0	4	0	4	4	0
Temple*				6	4	0
Toledo*				6	4	0
Central Michigan*				5	3	0
Bowling Green*				4	4	1
Eastern Michigan*				4	5	0
Ball State*				0	6	1

ALL-CONFERENCE TEAM

POS	Offense	School
QB	Gene Rossi	Cincinnati
HB	John Pont	Miami (Ohio)
HB	Ed Roberts	Ohio U
FB	Jim Daugherty	Cincinnati
C	Frank Middendorf	Cincinnati
G	Jay Fry	Miami (Ohio)
T	Al Schneider	Ohio U
T	Andy Matto	Cincinnati
T	Don Green	Miami (Ohio)
E	Dick Jarvis	Cincinnati
E	Clive Rush	Miami (Ohio)
E	Jim Baily	Miami (Ohio)

POS	Defense	School
DE	Al Feeney	Case Western Reserve
DB	Floyd Stollsteimer	Western Michigan
DB	Tom Morris	Western Michigan
DB	Glenn Sample	Cincinnati
DB	Bob Stratton	Cincinnati

NCAA STATISTICAL LEADERS

TEAM

TOTAL OFFENSE		G	P	YDS	AVG	YPG
5	Cincinnati	11	796	4491	5.6	408.3

1952

CONFERENCE STANDINGS

	CONFERENCE			OVERALL		
	W	L	T	W	L	T
Cincinnati	3	0	0	8	1	0
Miami (Ohio)	4	1	0	8	1	0
Ohio U	5	2	0	6	2	1
Bowling Green	2	2	0	7	2	0
Kent State	2	2	0	5	4	0
Case Western Reserve	1	4	0	5	4	0
Western Michigan	1	4	0	4	4	0
Toledo	1	4	0	4	5	0
Central Michigan*				7	2	0
Eastern Michigan*				5	3	1
Ball State*				3	5	1
Temple*				2	7	1

ALL-CONFERENCE TEAM

POS	Offense	School
QB	Gene Rossi	Cincinnati
HB	Tom Pagna	Miami (Ohio)
HB	Rick Kaser	Toledo
HB	Dom DelBene	Cincinnati
C	John Mcvay	Miami (Ohio)
G	Al Sanders	Miami (Ohio)
G	Lloyd Williams	Miami (Ohio)
G	Bill Shalosky	Cincinnati
T	Don Grammer	Cincinnati
T	Dick Gordon	Toledo
T	Tom Jones	Miami (Ohio)
T	Al Kilgore	Kent State
E	Jim Ladd	Bowling Green
E	Dick Delaney	Case Western Reserve

POS	Defense	School
LB	Vince Costello	Ohio U
LB	John Turk	Ohio U
DE	Don Fritz	Cincinnati
DE	Al Feeney	Western Reserve
DB	Tom Asani	Ohio U
DB	Floyd Stollsteimer	Western Michigan
DB	Dick Goist	Cincinnati
DB	Glen Sample	Cincinnati
DB	Harold Carroll	Case Western Reserve
DB	Len Corbin	Case Western Reserve
DG	Terry Boyle	Cincinnati

NCAA STATISTICAL LEADERS

TEAM LEADERS

PASSING OFF./YPG		G	ATT	COM	INT	PCT	YDS	YPA	TDYPG	I%	YPC
5	Cincinnati	10	194	116	9	59.8	1864	9.6	15 186.4	4.6	16.1

TOTAL OFFENSE		G	P	YDS	AVG	YPG
7	Cincinnati	10	658	3882	5.9	388.2

1953

CONFERENCE STANDINGS

	CONFERENCE			OVERALL		
	W	L	T	W	L	T
Ohio U	5	0	1	6	2	1
Miami (Ohio)	3	0	1	7	1	1
Kent State	3	1	0	7	2	0
Toledo	2	3	0	3	6	0
Case Western Reserve	1	2	1	5	3	1
Western Michigan	0	4	1	1	6	1
Bowling Green	0	4	0	1	8	0
Central Michigan*				7	1	1
Eastern Michigan*				7	1	1
Ball State*				5	2	1
Temple*				4	4	1

ALL-CONFERENCE TEAM

POS	Player	School
QB	Bill Rederick	Ohio U
HB	Tom Pagna	Miami (Ohio)
FB	Jim Cullom	Kent State
C	Lowell Andemon	Ohio U
G	Ralph Zurbrugg	Miami (Ohio)
G	Bob Penrod	Ohio U
T	Al Kilgore	Kent State
T	Tom Jones	Miami (Ohio)
E	Jim Ladd	Bowling Green
E	Lou Sawchik	Ohio U

*Independent or other conference affiliation

1954

CONFERENCE STANDINGS

	CONFERENCE			OVERALL		
	W	L	T	W	L	T
Miami (Ohio)	4	0	0	8	1	0
Kent State	4	1	0	8	2	0
Ohio U	5	2	0	6	3	0
Toledo	3	2	0	6	2	1
Western Michigan	3	4	0	4	5	0
Case Western Reserve	2	3	0	3	4	1
Marshall	2	5	0	4	5	0
Bowling Green	0	6	0	2	7	0
Eastern Michigan*				8	1	0
Central Michigan*				8	2	0
Ball State*				6	2	0
Temple*				3	5	0

ALL-CONFERENCE TEAM

POS	Offense	School
QB	Dick Hunter	Miami (Ohio)
HB	Bob Wallace	Miami (Ohio)
HB	Erland Ahlberg	Ohio U
FB	Mel Triplett	Toledo
C	George Machoukas	Toledo
G	Albie Maier	Marshall
G	Stan Jones	Miami (Ohio)
T	Joe Barbee	Kent State
T	Tom Jones	Miami (Ohio)
E	Mel Baker	Miami (Ohio)
E	Jack Hecker	Bowling Green

1955

FINAL POLL

UP	AP	TEAM	RECORD
1	1	Oklahoma	11-0-0
2	2	Michigan State	9-1-0
3	3	Maryland	10-1-0
4	4	UCLA	9-2-0
6	5	Ohio State	7-2-0
5	6	TCU	9-2-0
7	7	Georgia Tech	9-1-1
10	8	Auburn	8-2-1
8	9	Notre Dame	8-2-0
9	10	Mississippi	10-1-0
11	11	Pittsburgh	7-4-0
13	12	Michigan	7-2-0
12	13	USC	6-4-0
18	14	Miami, Fla.	6-3-0
20	15	Miami (Ohio)	9-0-0
20	16	Stanford	6-3-1
14	17	Texas A&M	7-2-1
20	18	Navy	6-2-1
17	19	West Virginia	8-2-0
15	20	Army	6-3-0
15		Duke	7-2-1
19		Iowa	3-5-1

CONFERENCE STANDINGS

	CONFERENCE			OVERALL		
	W	L	T	W	L	T
Miami (Ohio)	5	0	0	9	0	0
Bowling Green	4	1	1	7	1	1
Kent State	4	1	1	6	2	1
Ohio U	3	3	0	5	4	0
Toledo	2	4	0	3	5	1
Marshall	1	5	0	3	6	0
Western Michigan	0	5	0	1	7	1
Central Michigan*				8	1	0
Eastern Michigan*				7	2	0
Ball State*				3	5	0
Temple*				0	8	0

ALL-CONFERENCE TEAM

POS	Offense	School
QB	Tom Dimitroff	Miami (Ohio)
HB	Tirrel Burton	Miami (Ohio)
HB	Len Hellyer	Marshall
RB	Mike Norcia	Kent State
C	Dick Mattern	Miami (Ohio)
G	Russ Giganti	Miami (Ohio)
G	Bob McCollins	Marshall
T	Kenneth Russell	Bowling Green
T	Fred Koch	Bowling Green
T	Roger Siesel	Miami (Ohio)
E	Jack Hecker	Bowling Green
E	Pres Bliss	Miami (Ohio)

1956

CONFERENCE STANDINGS

	CONFERENCE			OVERALL		
	W	L	T	W	L	T
Bowling Green	5	0	1	8	0	1
Miami (Ohio)	4	0	1	7	1	1
Kent State	4	2	0	7	2	0
Marshall	2	4	0	3	6	0
Ohio U	2	4	0	2	7	0
Western Michigan	1	4	0	2	7	0
Toledo	1	5	0	1	7	1
Central Michigan*				9	0	0
Ball State*				4	4	0
Eastern Michigan*				4	4	0
Temple*				3	5	0

ALL-CONFERENCE TEAM

POS	Player	School
QB	Tom Dimitroff	Miami (Ohio)
HB	Vic DeOrio	Bowling Green
FB	Dean Porter	Miami (Ohio)
FB	Jack Giroux	Bowling Green
FB	Dave Thelen	Miami (Ohio)
C	Harold Peek	Bowling Green
G	Clayton Umbles	Toledo
G	Tim Murnen	Bowling Green
T	Kenneth Russell	Bowling Green
T	Luke Owens	Kent State
E	Gino Gioia	Kent State
E	Bill Mallory	Miami (Ohio)

1957

CONFERENCE STANDINGS

	CONFERENCE			OVERALL		
	W	L	T	W	L	T
Miami (Ohio)	5	0	0	6	3	0
Marshall	4	2	0	6	3	0
Bowling Green	3	1	2	6	1	2
Toledo	3	2	0	5	4	0
Western Michigan	1	4	1	4	4	1
Ohio U	1	4	1	2	6	1
Kent State	1	5	0	3	6	0
Eastern Michigan*				6	3	0
Central Michigan*				4	6	0
Ball State*				2	5	1
Temple*				1	6	0

ALL-CONFERENCE TEAM

POS	Player	School
QB	Bob Wagner	Marshall
T	Ron Fenik	Ohio U
HB	Cagle Curtis	Marshall
FB	Dave Thelen	Miami (Ohio)
C	Jim Wahlke	Miami (Ohio)
G	Ray Reese	Bowling Green
G	Tim Murnen	Bowling Green
G	Pat Orloff	Miami (Ohio)
T	Larry Baker	Bowling Green
E	Mack Yoho	Miami (Ohio)
E	Gene Cook	Toledo
E	Roy Hodge	Toledo

1958

CONFERENCE STANDINGS

	CONFERENCE			OVERALL		
	W	L	T	W	L	T
Miami (Ohio)	5	0	0	6	3	0
Kent State	5	1	0	7	2	0
Bowling Green	4	2	0	7	2	0
Ohio U	2	4	0	5	4	0
Western Michigan	2	4	0	4	5	0
Toledo	1	4	0	4	5	0
Marshall	1	5	0	3	6	0
Central Michigan*				7	3	0
Ball State*				6	2	0
Eastern Michigan*				4	5	0
Temple*				0	8	0

ALL-CONFERENCE TEAM

POS	Player	School
QB	Dick Mostardo	Kent State
T	Ron Kackc	Miami (Ohio)
HB	Harold Williams	Miami (Ohio)
HB	Occie Burt	Toledo
HB	Lovell Coleman	Western Michigan
G	Ed Hill	Miami (Ohio)
G	Ray Reese	Bowling Green
G	Gary Cobb	Miami (Ohio)
T	Bob Zimpfer	Bowling Green
E	Tom Colaner	Bowling Green
E	Jerry Nowell	Miami (Ohio)
E	Frank Haladik	Toledo

1959

CONFERENCE STANDINGS

	CONFERENCE			OVERALL		
	W	L	T	W	L	T
Bowling Green	6	0	0	9	0	0
Ohio U	4	2	0	7	2	0
Miami (Ohio)	3	2	0	5	4	0
Kent State	3	3	0	5	3	0
Western Michigan	3	3	0	4	5	0
Marshall	1	4	0	1	8	0
Toledo	0	6	0	2	6	1
Central Michigan*				7	3	0
Ball State*				1	7	0
Eastern Michigan*				1	7	0
Temple*				0	9	0

ALL-CONFERENCE TEAM

POS	Player	School
QB	Bob Colburn	Bowling Green
T	Bob Zimpfer	Bowling Green
HB	Bernie Casey	Bowling Green
G	Gary Cobb	Miami (Ohio)
E	Jim Massarelli	Ohio U
E	Ron Blackledge	Bowling Green

1960

CONFERENCE STANDINGS

	CONFERENCE			OVERALL		
	W	L	T	W	L	T
Ohio U	6	0	0	10	0	0
Bowling Green	5	1	0	8	1	0
Kent State	4	2	0	6	3	0
Miami (Ohio)	2	3	0	5	5	0
Western Michigan	2	4	0	4	4	1
Marshall	1	4	0	2	7	1
Toledo	0	6	0	2	7	0
Ball State*				3	5	0
Central Michigan*				3	5	0
Temple*				2	7	0
Eastern Michigan*				0	8	1

ALL-CONFERENCE TEAM

POS	Player	School
QB	Dave Wagner	Ohio U
T	Jerry Croft	Bowling Green
HB	John Moore	Miami (Ohio)
HB	Bob Harrison	Ohio U
FB	Bob Brooks	Ohio U
C	Dick Grecni	Ohio U
G	Jerry Colaner	Bowling Green
G	Joe Dean	Ohio U
T	John Lomokowski	Western Michigan
E	Bob Gusbar	Kent State

1961

CONFERENCE STANDINGS

	CONFERENCE			OVERALL		
	W	L	T	W	L	T
Bowling Green	5	1	0	8	2	0
Western Michigan	4	1	1	5	4	1
Miami (Ohio)	3	2	0	6	4	0
Ohio U	3	2	1	5	3	1
Toledo	2	4	0	3	7	0
Marshall	1	4	0	2	7	1
Kent State	1	5	0	2	8	0
Ball State*				2	5	1
Temple*				2	5	2
Central Michigan*				2	8	0
Eastern Michigan*				0	8	1

BOWL GAMES

DATE	GAME	SCORE
N23	**Mercy**	Fresno State 36, Bowling Green 6
D9	**Aviation**	New Mexico 28, Western Michigan 12

ALL-CONFERENCE TEAM

POS	Player	School
QB	Ed Chlebek	Western Michigan
T	Jerry Croft	Bowling Green
T	Tom Nomina	Miami (Ohio)
RB	Millard Fleming	Marshall
RB	Frank Baker	Toledo
FB	Bill Triplett	Miami
C	Rucker Wickline	Marshall
E	Dennis Holland	Western Michigan
E	Dick Newsome	Bowling Green
G	Gary Sherman	Bowling Green

*Independent or other conference affiliation

NCAA Statistical Leaders

Team Leaders

RUSHING OFFENSE

		G	ATT	YDS	AVG	YPG
8	Bowling Green	9	519	2132	4.1	236.9

RUSHING DEFENSE

		G	ATT	YDS	AVG	YPG
7	Bowling Green	9	317	780	2.5	86.7

TOTAL DEFENSE

		G	P	YDS	AVG	YPG
4	Bowling Green	9	460	1456	3.2	161.8

SCORING DEFENSE

			G	PTS	AVG
3	Bowling Green		9	42	4.7

1962

Conference Standings

	Conference			Overall		
	W	L	T	W	L	T
Bowling Green	5	0	1	7	1	1
Ohio U	5	1	0	8	3	0
Miami (Ohio)	3	1	1	8	2	1
Western Michigan	3	3	0	5	4	0
Kent State	2	4	0	3	6	0
Toledo	1	5	0	3	6	0
Marshall	0	5	0	4	6	0
Central Michigan*				6	4	0
Ball State*				4	3	1
Temple*				3	6	0
Eastern Michigan*				2	5	0

Bowl Games

DATE	GAME	SCORE
D22	**Tangerine**	Houston 49, Miami (Ohio) 21
D31	**Sun**	West Texas State 15, Ohio U 14

All-Conference Team

POS	**Player**	**School**
FB	Bob Babbitt	Ohio U
FB	Dick Merschman	Kent State
HB	Scott Tyler	Miami (Ohio)
HB	Don Libson	Bowling Green
T	Tom Nomina	Miami (Ohio)
T	Bob Reynolds	Bowling Green
T	Dick Schultz	Ohio U
C	Ed Bettridge	Bowling Green
G	Gary Sherman	Bowling Green
E	Bob Jencks	Miami (Ohio)
E	Jim Cure	Marshall
K	Asa Elsea	Bowling Green
LB	Skip Hoovler	Ohio U

NCAA Statistical Leaders

Individual Leaders

RECEIVING/RECEPTIONS

		G	REC	YDS	TD	YPR	YPG	RPG
5	Jim Cure, Marshall	10	46	667	3	14.5	66.7	4.6

KICKOFF RETURNS/YARDS

					KR	YDS	AVG
8	Larry Coyer, Marshall				13	393	30.2

SCORING

					TDS	XPT	FG	PTS
7	Bob Jencks, Miami (Ohio)				6	24	8	84

KICK SCORING

					XPA	XP	FG	PTS
1	Bob Jencks, Miami (Ohio)				26	24	8	48
8	Jim McKee, Ohio U				31	25	4	37

Team Leaders

RUSHING DEFENSE

		G	ATT	YDS	AVG	YPG
6	Bowling Green	9	316	788	2.5	87.6

TOTAL DEFENSE

		G	P	YDS	AVG	YPG
6	Bowling Green	9	467	1664	3.6	184.9

1963

Conference Standings

	Conference			Overall		
	W	L	T	W	L	T
Ohio U	5	1	0	6	4	0
Miami (Ohio)	4	1	1	5	3	2
Bowling Green	4	2	0	8	2	0
Marshall	3	2	1	5	4	1
Western Michigan	2	4	0	2	7	0
Kent State	1	5	0	3	5	1
Toledo	1	5	0	2	7	0
Ball State*				5	3	0
Eastern Michigan*				2	6	0
Central Michigan*				4	5	1
Temple*				5	3	1

All-Conference Team

POS	**Player**	**School**
QB	Ernie Kellerman	Miami (Ohio)
FB	Tom Longsworth	Miami (Ohio)
HB	Jay Cunnigham	Bowling Green
HB	Tom Reicosky	Bowling Green
HB	Jim Albert	Ohio U
T	Wynn Lembright	Toledo
T	Mike Hicks	Marshall
G	Dave Mallory	Miami (Ohio)
G	Chuck Liedtke	Western Michigan
E	Ron Fowlkes	Ohio U
LB	Skip Hoovler	Ohio U

NCAA Statistical Leaders

Individual Leaders

RUSHING/YARDS

		G	ATT	YDS	AVG	YPG
4	Jack Mahone, Marshall	10	163	884	5.4	88.4

RECEIVING/RECEPTIONS

		G	REC	YDS	TD	YPR	YPG	RPG
8	Jim Cure, Marshall	10	40	534	2	13.4	53.4	4.0

PUNTING

					PUNT	YDS	AVG
6	Norm Limpert, Bowling Green				42	1735	41.3

PUNT RETURNS/YARDS

					PR	YDS	AVG
8	Jim Gray, Toledo				13	212	16.3

Team Leaders

PASSING DEFENSE

		G	ATT	COM	PCT	YPC	INT	I%	YDS	YPA	TD	YPG
4	Ohio U	10	125	49	39.2	12.7	6	4.8	621	5.0	5	62.1
5	Toledo	9	101	38	37.6	15.0	6	5.9	569	5.6	5	63.2

1964

CONFERENCE STANDINGS

	CONFERENCE			OVERALL		
	W	L	T	W	L	T
Bowling Green	5	1	0	9	1	0
Marshall	4	2	0	7	3	0
Miami (Ohio)	4	2	0	6	3	1
Ohio U	3	2	1	5	4	1
Western Michigan	2	4	0	3	6	0
Kent State	1	4	1	3	5	1
Toledo	1	5	0	2	8	0
Ball State*				5	3	0
Eastern Michigan*				4	3	0
Central Michigan*				4	5	0
Temple*				7	2	0

ALL-CONFERENCE TEAM

POS	Offense	School
QB	Ernie Kellerman	Miami (Ohio)
FB	Stew Williams	Bowling Green
FB	Jim Wisser	Bowling Green
HB	Tom Reicosky	Bowling Green
HB	Jay Cunningham	Bowling Green
RB	Jack Mahone	Marshall
T	Jerry Jones	Bowling Green
T	John Frick	Ohio U
T	Ron Stepsis	Ohio U
G	Booker Collins	Kent State
G	Lance Tigyer	Ohio U
C	Heath Wingate	Bowling Green
E	Jamie Rivers	Bowling Green
E	Ron Fowlkes	Ohio U
E	Chuck Turner	Ohio U
E	Jim Cure	Marshall

POS	Defense	School
LB	Skip Hoovler	Ohio U
LB	Tom Good	Marshall
LB	Bill Winter	Marshall
DB	Pat Gucciardo	Kent State
DB	Jim Gray	Toledo
DB	Larry Coyer	Marshall
DE	Ken Moon	Western Michigan

NCAA STATISTICAL LEADERS

INDIVIDUAL LEADERS

PASSING/COMP.	G	ATT	COM	PCT	INT	I%	YDS	YPA	TD	TD%	COM.PG
10 Dan Simrell, Toledo	10	215	115	53.5	13	6.1	1239	5.8	4	1.9	11.5

RUSHING/YARDS			G	ATT	YDS	AVG	YPG
10 Jack Mahone, Marshall			10	190	878	4.6	87.8

RUSHING/YARDS PER CARRY			G	ATT	YDS	YPC
2 Stew Williams, Bowling Green			10	109	609	5.6
Based on top 42 rushers						

RECEIVING/RECEPTIONS	G	REC	YDS	TD	YPR	YPG	RPG
8 Henry Burch, Toledo	9	47	420	1	8.9	46.7	5.2

PUNTING			PUNT	YDS	AVG
7 Norm Limpert, Bowling Green			31	1305	42.1

KICKOFF RETURNS/YARDS			KR	YDS	AVG
9 Willie Loper, Toledo			16	399	24.9

TEAM LEADERS

RUSHING OFFENSE	G	ATT	YDS	AVG	YPG
2 Bowling Green	10	491	2393	4.9	239.3

TOTAL OFFENSE	G	P	YDS	AVG	YPG
10 Bowling Green	10	637	3343	5.2	334.3

PASSING DEFENSE	G	ATT	COM	PCT	YPC	INT	I%	YDS	YPA	TD	YPG
1 Kent State	9	118	41	34.7	11.8	7	5.9	482	4.1	4	53.6
8 Ohio U	10	155	64	41.3	12.3	7	4.5	789	5.1	4	78.9

TOTAL DEFENSE	G	P	YDS	AVG	YPG
7 Bowling Green	10	527	1883	3.6	188.3

SCORING OFFENSE			G	PTS	AVG
4 Bowling Green			10	275	27.5

1965

CONFERENCE STANDINGS

	CONFERENCE			OVERALL		
	W	L	T	W	L	T
Bowling Green	5	1	0	7	2	0
Miami (Ohio)	5	1	0	7	3	0
Western Michigan	3	2	1	6	2	1
Kent State	3	2	1	5	4	1
Marshall	2	4	0	5	5	0
Toledo	2	4	0	5	5	0
Ohio U	0	6	0	0	10	0
Ball State*				9	0	1
Eastern Michigan*				3	4	1
Central Michigan*				5	5	0
Temple*				5	5	0

ALL-CONFERENCE TEAM

POS	Offense	School
QB	Bruce Matte	Miami (Ohio)
T	Tony Fire	Bowling Green
T	Ed Philpott	Miami (Ohio)
HB	Al Moore	Miami (Ohio)
HB	Joe Souliere	Bowling Green
FB	Stew Williams	Bowling Green
FB	Bill Asbury	Kent State
C	Heath Wingate	Bowling Green
C	Tom Stillwagon	Miami (Ohio)
G	Jon Brooks	Kent State
G	Ed Musbach	Kent State
G	Steve Erickson	Toledo
E	Jamie Rivers	Bowling Green
E	Gary Durchik	Miami
E	John Erisman	Miami

POS	Defense	School
LB	Tom Good	Marshall
LB	Tom Beutler	Toledo
DB	Mike Weger	Bowling Green
DB	Pat Gucciardo	Kent State
DB	Marty Barski	Western Michigan
DE	Fred Zimmeran	Toledo
LB	Jim Bright	Miami (Ohio)

NCAA STATISTICAL LEADERS

INDIVIDUAL LEADERS

RUSHING/YARDS	G	ATT	YDS	AVG	YPG
8 Bill Asbury, Kent State	10	238	998	4.2	99.8

PUNT RETURNS/YARDS			PR	YDS	AVG
9 Joe Souliere, Bowling Green			18	372	20.7

SCORING			TDS	XPT	FG	PTS
4 Mickey Jackson, Marshall			16	0	0	96

TEAM LEADERS

RUSHING DEFENSE	G	ATT	YDS	AVG	YPG
2 Buffalo*	10	421	737	1.8	73.7
10 Miami (Ohio)	10	373	898	2.4	89.8

PASSING DEFENSE	G	ATT	COM	PCT	YPC	INT	I%	YDS	YPA	TD	YPG
1 Toledo	10	146	57	39.0	12.2	13	8.9	698	4.8	2	69.8
4 Bowling Green	9	144	65	45.1	11.2	8	5.6	730	5.1	4	81.1

TOTAL DEFENSE	G	P	YDS	AVG	YPG
3 Toledo	10	593	1820	3.1	182.0
4 Buffalo*	10	621	1831	2.9	183.1
5 Bowling Green	9	499	1680	3.4	186.7
9 Miami (Ohio)	10	544	2088	3.8	208.8

SCORING DEFENSE			G	PTS	AVG
4 Buffalo*			10	78	7.8

*Independent or other conference affiliation

1966

CONFERENCE STANDINGS

	Conference			Overall		
	W	L	T	W	L	T
Miami (Ohio)	5	1	0	9	1	0
Western Michigan	5	1	0	7	3	0
Bowling Green	4	2	0	6	3	0
Ohio U	3	3	0	5	5	0
Kent State	2	4	0	4	6	0
Toledo	1	5	0	2	7	1
Marshall	1	5	0	2	8	0
Ball State*				7	1	1
Eastern Michigan*				5	3	1
Central Michigan*				5	5	0
Temple*				6	3	0

ALL-CONFERENCE TEAM

POS	Offense	School
QB	Bruce Matte	Miami (Ohio)
T	John Shafer	Miami (Ohio)
T	Ken Carmon	Ohio U
RB	Andy Socha	Marshall
FB	Don Fitzgerald	Kent State
FB	Joe Kozar	Miami (Ohio)
C	Heath Wingate	Bowling Green
G	Dave Tsaloff	Miami (Ohio)
G	Jon Brooks	Kent State
E	Jamie Rivers	Bowling Green
E	John Erisman	Miami (Ohio)
K	Bob Brown	Ohio U
K	Dale Livingston	Western Michigan

POS	Defense	School
DT	Bob Rowe	Western Michigan
LB	Barry Sneed	Toledo
LB	Tom Beutler	Toledo
DB	Dick Wagoner	Bowling Green
DB	Mike Weger	Bowling Green
DB	Bob Smith	Miami (Ohio)

NCAA STATISTICAL LEADERS

INDIVIDUAL LEADERS

RUSHING/YARDS	G	ATT	YDS	TD	AVG	YPG
2 Don Fitzgerald, Kent State	10	296	1245	12	4.2	124.5

SCORING			TDS	XPT	FG	PTS
3 Lealand Jones, Buffalo*			16	0	0	96

TEAM LEADERS

PASSING DEFENSE	G	ATT	COM	PCT	YPC	INT	I%	YDS	YPA	TD	YPG
1 Toledo	10	142	56	39.4	12.6	9	6.3	704	5.0	8	70.4

TOTAL DEFENSE				G		P	YDS	AVG	TD	YPG
9 Toledo				10		607	2097	3.5	21	209.7

SCORING DEFENSE							G	PTS	AVG
8 Miami (Ohio)							10	76	7.6

1967

CONFERENCE STANDINGS

	Conference			Overall		
	W	L	T	W	L	T
Toledo	5	1	0	9	1	0
Miami (Ohio)	4	2	0	6	4	0
Western Michigan	4	2	0	5	4	0
Ohio U	4	2	0	5	5	0
Bowling Green	2	4	0	6	4	0
Kent State	2	4	0	5	5	0
Marshall	0	6	0	0	10	0
Ball State*				7	3	0
Eastern Michigan*				6	3	0
Central Michigan*				8	2	0
Temple*				2	7	0

CONSENSUS ALL-AMERICANS

POS	Defense	HT	WT	School	AP	CP	FC	FW	NE	PI
None										

OTHERS RECEIVING FIRST-TEAM HONORS		
LB	Tom Beutler	Toledo •

ALL-CONFERENCE TEAM

POS	Offense	School
QB	John Schneider	Toledo
T	Don Wyper	Toledo
T	Ken Carmon	Ohio U
HB	Dick Conley	Ohio U
HB	Al Moore	Miami (Ohio)
HB	Roland Moss	Toledo
FB	Don Fitzgerald	Kent State
C	Gene Hamlin	Western Michigan
C	Paul Krasula	Miami (Ohio)
G	John Brown	Toledo
G	Dave Tsaloff	Miami (Ohio)
SE	Eddie Jones	Bowling Green
E	Pete Kramer	Toledo
E	Gary Arthur	Miami (Ohio)
K	Dale Livingston	Western Michigan

POS	Defense	School
DE	Mel Tucker	Toledo
DE	Jerry Collins	Western Michigan
DT	Jim Corrigall	Kent State
DT	Ray Hayes	Toledo
LB	Paul Elzey	Toledo
LB	Charles Burley	Bowling Green
LB	Bob Babich	Miami (Ohio)
LB	Tom Beutler	Toledo
DB	John Flynn	Toledo
DB	Lou Harris	Kent State
DB	Bob Smith	Miami (Ohio)
DB	Dave Hudson	Western Michigan

NCAA STATISTICAL LEADERS

INDIVIDUAL LEADERS

PASSING/COMP	G	ATT	COM	PCT	INT	I%	YDS	YPA	TD	TD%	COM.PG
8 John Schneider, Toledo	10	245	127	51.8	11	4.5	1650	6.7	10	4.1	12.7

RUSHING/YARDS PER CARRY							G	ATT	YDS	YPC
9 Al Moore, Miami (Ohio)							10	135	717	5.3
Based on top 34 rushers										

PUNTING								PUNT	YDS	AVG
4 Dale Livingston, Western Michigan								49	2122	43.3

SCORING								TDS	XPT	FG	PTS
2 Roland Moss, Toledo								16	0	0	96

TEAM LEADERS

PASSING DEFENSE	G	ATT	COM	PCT	YPC	INT	I%	YDS	YPA	TD	YPG
6 Kent State	10	229	92	40.2	10.7	15	6.6	986	4.3	5	98.6
10 Toledo	10	206	84	40.8	12.1	16	7.8	1014	4.9	4	101.4

TOTAL DEFENSE				G		P	YDS	AVG	TD	YPG
5 Toledo				10		618	1984	3.2	9	198.4

SCORING DEFENSE							G	PTS	AVG
3 Toledo							10	83	8.3

1968

FINAL POLL

AP	FINAL POLL	RECORD
1	Ohio State	10-0-0
2	Penn State	11-0-0
3	Texas	9-1-1
4	USC	9-1-1
5	Notre Dame	7-2-1
6	Arkansas	10-1-0
7	Kansas	9-2-0
8	Georgia	8-1-2
9	Missouri	8-3-0
10	Purdue	8-2-0
11	Oklahoma	7-4-0
12	Michigan	8-2-0
13	Tennessee	8-2-1
14	SMU	8-3-0
15	Oregon State	7-3-0
16	Auburn	7-4-0
17	Alabama	8-3-0
18	Houston	6-2-2
19	LSU	8-3-0
20	**Ohio U**	10-1-0

CONFERENCE STANDINGS

	CONFERENCE			OVERALL		
	W	L	T	W	L	T
Ohio U	6	0	0	10	1	0
Miami (Ohio)	5	1	0	7	3	0
Bowling Green	3	2	1	6	3	1
Toledo	3	2	1	5	4	1
Western Michigan	2	4	0	3	6	0
Kent State	1	5	0	1	9	0
Marshall	0	6	0	0	9	1
Ball State*				5	4	0
Eastern Michigan*				8	2	0
Central Michigan*				7	2	0
Temple*				4	6	0

BOWL GAMES

DATE	GAME	SCORE
D27	**Tangerine**	Richmond 49, Ohio U 42

CONSENSUS ALL-AMERICANS

POS	Defense	HT	WT	School	AP	CP	FC	FW	NE	PI
None										

OTHERS RECEIVING FIRST-TEAM HONORS

LB	Bob Babich	Miami (Ohio)	•

ALL-CONFERENCE TEAM

POS	Offense	School
QB	Cleve Bryant	Ohio U
T	Ken Carmon	Ohio U
HB	Dave LeVeck	Ohio U
HB	Roland Moss	Toledo
FB	Bob Houmard	Ohio U
C	Jeff Robinson	Ohio U
G	Mel Miller	Toledo
G	Larry Thompson	Miami (Ohio)
s	Todd Snyder	Ohio U
e	Gary Arthur	Miami (Ohio)
K	Ken Crots	Toledo

POS	Defense	School
DE	Mel Tucker	Toledo
DE	Jerry Collins	Western Michigan
DT	Merv Nugent	Miami (Ohio)
DT	Errol Kahoun	Miami (Ohio)
DT	Dave Hutchins	Miami (Ohio)
DT	Jim Corrigall	Kent State
LB	Bob Babich	Miami (Ohio)
LB	Bob Reiber	Miami (Ohio)
LB	Steve Robinson	Ohio U
LB	Joe Green	Bowling Green
DB	Dave Hudson	Western Michigan
DB	Curtis Johnson	Toledo
DB	Dick Boron	Miami (Ohio)
SE	Eddie Jones	Bowling Green

NCAA STATISTICAL LEADERS

INDIVIDUAL LEADERS

PUNT RETURNS/YARDS		PR	YDS	TD	AVG
9	Bob Zimpfer, Bowling Green	24	332	1	13.8

SCORING		TDS	XPT	FG	PTS
5	Bob Houmard, Ohio U	19	0	0	114

KICK SCORING		XPA	XP	FGA	FG	PTS
10	Kenneth Crots, Toledo	29	29	17	9	56

TEAM LEADERS

RUSHING DEFENSE			G	ATT	YDS	AVG	TD	YPG
2	Miami (Ohio)		10	359	775	2.2	5	77.5

PASSING DEFENSE	G	ATT	COM	PCT	YPC	INT	I%	YDS	YPA	TD	YPG
1 Kent State	10	183	75	41.0	14.3	10	5.5	1076	5.9	9	107.6
2 Toledo	10	249	106	42.6	10.8	17	6.8	1141	4.6	8	114.1
3 Western Michigan	9	200	80	40.0	12.9	20	10.0	1034	5.2	3	114.9
9 Bowling Green	10	239	110	46.0	11.4	20	8.4	1250	5.2	7	125.0

TOTAL DEFENSE		G	P	YDS	AVG	TD	YPG
2	Miami (Ohio)	10	632	2324	3.7	13	232.4
9	Bowling Green	10	675	2452	3.6	19	245.2

SCORING OFFENSE		G	PTS	AVG
4	Ohio U	10	376	37.6

SCORING DEFENSE		G	PTS	AVG
2	Miami (Ohio)	10	99	9.9

1969

CONFERENCE STANDINGS

	CONFERENCE			OVERALL		
	W	L	T	W	L	T
Toledo	5	0	0	11	0	0
Bowling Green	4	1	0	6	4	0
Miami (Ohio)	2	3	0	7	3	0
Ohio U	2	3	0	5	4	1
Kent State	1	4	0	5	5	0
Western Michigan	1	4	0	4	6	0
Ball State*				5	5	0
Eastern Michigan*				5	4	0
Central Michigan*				7	3	0
Temple*				4	5	1
Northern Illinois*				3	7	0

BOWL GAMES

DATE	GAME	SCORE
D26	**Tangerine**	Toledo 56, Davidson 33

CONSENSUS ALL-AMERICANS

POS	Defense	HT	WT	School	AP	CP	FC	FW	NE	PI
None										

OTHERS RECEIVING FIRST-TEAM HONORS

LB	Jim Corrigall	Kent State	•
DB	Curtis Johnson	Toledo	•

*Independent or other conference affiliation

ALL-CONFERENCE TEAM

POS	Offense	School
QB	Chuck Ealey	Toledo
HB	Tony Harris	Toledo
HB	Don Nottingham	Kent State
T	Jim Rance	Toledo
T	Dave Hutchins	Miami (Ohio)
E	Todd Snyder	Ohio U
C	Fred Blosser	Kent State
E	Gary Arthur	Miami (Ohio)
FL	Bob Zimpfer	Bowling Green
G	Larry Thompson	Miami (Ohio)
G	Keith Volk	Western Michigan

POS	Defense	School
LB	Steve Robinson	Ohio U
LB	John Niezgoda	Toledo
LB	Joe Green	Bowling Green
DT	Mike Siwek	Western Michigan
DT	Mel Long	Toledo
DT	Jim Corrigall	Kent State
DB	Dick Adams	Miami (Ohio)
DB	Honester Davidson	Bowling Green
DB	Curtis Johnson	Toledo
DE	Jim Tyler	Toledo
DE	Phil Villapiano	Bowling Green
K	Ken Crots	Toledo

NCAA STATISTICAL LEADERS

INDIVIDUAL LEADERS

RUSHING/YARDS PER CARRY		G	ATT	YDS	YPC
5	Tony Harris, Toledo	10	146	849	5.8

*-Based on top 32 rushers

RECEIVING/RECEPTIONS		G	REC	YDS	TD	YPR	YPG	RPG
8	Todd Snyder, Ohio U	10	62	835	8	13.5	83.5	6.2
10	Fred Mathews, Bowling Green	10	57	528	6	9.3	52.8	5.7

TEAM LEADERS

RUSHING DEFENSE		G	ATT	YDS	AVG	TD	YPG
5	Toledo	10	453	838	1.8	7	83.8
7	Miami (Ohio)	10	410	858	2.1	11	85.8

PASSING DEFENSE	G	ATT	COM	PCT	YPC	INT	I%	YDS	YPA	TD	YPG
6 Buffalo*	9	157	71	45.2	12.8	6	3.8	911	5.8	4	101.2

TOTAL DEFENSE		G	P	YDS	AVG	TD	YPG
1	Toledo	10	703	2,091	3.0	18	209.1
8	Buffalo*	9	565	2,065	3.7	11	229.4

SCORING DEFENSE		G	PTS	AVG
4	Buffalo*	9	89	9.9

1970

FINAL POLL

AP	FINAL POLL	RECORD
1	Nebraska	11-0-1
2	Notre Dame	10-1-0
3	Texas	10-1-0
4	Tennessee	11-1-0
5	Ohio State	9-1-0
6	Arizona State	11-0-0
7	LSU	9-3-0
8	Stanford	9-3-0
9	Michigan	9-1-0
10	Auburn	9-2-0
11	Arkansas	9-2-0
12	Toledo	12-0-0
13	Georgia Tech	9-3-0
14	Dartmouth	9-0-0
15	USC	6-4-1
16	Air Force	9-3-0
17	Tulane	8-4-0
18	Penn State	7-3-0
19	Houston	8-3-0
20	Mississippi	7-4-0
20	Oklahoma	7-4-1

CONFERENCE STANDINGS

	CONFERENCE			OVERALL		
	W	L	T	W	L	T
Toledo	5	0	0	12	0	0
Miami (Ohio)	3	2	0	7	3	0
Ohio U	3	2	0	4	5	0
Western Michigan	2	3	0	7	3	0
Kent State	1	4	0	3	7	0
Bowling Green	1	4	0	2	6	1
Ball State*				5	5	0
Eastern Michigan*				7	2	1
Central Michigan*				7	3	0
Temple*				7	3	0
Northern Illinois*				3	7	0

BOWL GAMES

DATE	GAME	SCORE
D28	Tangerine	Toledo 40, William & Mary 12

CONSENSUS ALL-AMERICANS

POS	Defense	HT	WT	School	AP	CP	FC	FW	NE	PI
None										

OTHERS RECEIVING FIRST-TEAM HONORS
T	Mel Long	Toledo	•

ALL-CONFERENCE TEAM

POS	Offense	School
QB	Chuck Ealey	Toledo
FB	Roger Lawson	Western Michigan
FB	Charlie Cole	Toledo
TB	Tim Founty	Miami (Ohio)
WR	Don Fair	Toledo
E	Al Benton	Ohio U
E	Greg Flaska	Western Michigan
E	Bob Allen	Ohio U
C	Fred Blosser	Kent State
E	Mike Palija	Miami (Ohio)
T	Ken Wilson	Toledo
G	Bob Caverly	Toledo
G	Dave Finley	Bowling Green

POS	Defense	School
LB	Tom Elias	Western Michigan
LB	John Niezgoda	Toledo
DT	Mel Long	Toledo
DT	Dick Dougherty	Miami (Ohio)
MG	Steve Schnitkey	Toledo
DB	Vern Davis	Western Michigan
DB	Dick Adams	Miami (Ohio)
DB	Gary Hinkson	Toledo
DB	Tom Duncan	Toledo
DE	Phil Villapiano	Bowling Green
DE	Bob Rose	Toledo

NCAA STATISTICAL LEADERS

INDIVIDUAL LEADERS

RUSHING/YARDS PER GAME		G	ATT	YDS	TD	AVG	YPG
7	Roger Lawson, Western Michigan	10	168	1205	13	7.2	120.5
8	Bill Gary, Ohio U	9	265	1064	11	4.0	118.2

RUSHING/YARDS PER CARRY		G	ATT	YDS	YPC
1	Roger Lawson, Western Michigan	10	168	1205	7.2

Based on top 24 rushers

RECEIVING		G	REC	YDS	TD	YPR	YPG	RPG
3	Don Fair, Toledo	11	76	893	4	11.8	81.2	6.9

KICK SCORING		XPA	XP	FGA	FG	PTS	PTPG
5	Tom Duncan, Toledo	44	36	21	12	72	6.5

TEAM LEADERS

RUSHING OFFENSE

		G	ATT	YDS	AVG	TD	YPG
10	Western Michigan	10	558	2631	4.7	22	263.1

RUSHING DEFENSE

		G	ATT	YDS	AVG	TD	YPG
7	Miami (Ohio)	10	504	1050	2.1	8	105.0

PASSING DEFENSE

		G	ATT	COM	PCT	YPC	INT	I%	YDS	YPA	TD	YPG
1	Toledo	11	251	88	35.1	9.7	24	9.6	856	3.4	1	77.8
3	Miami (Ohio)	10	191	84	44.0	10.5	14	7.3	881	4.6	6	88.1
7	Bowling Green	9	164	77	47.0	12.1	12	7.3	935	5.7	5	103.9

TOTAL DEFENSE

		G	P	YDS	AVG	TD	YPG
1	Toledo	11	727	2044	2.8	8	185.8
3	Miami (Ohio)	10	695	1931	2.8	14	193.1

SCORING DEFENSE

		G	PTS	AVG
2	Toledo	11	76	6.9

1971

FINAL POLL

AP	FINAL POLL	RECORD
1	Nebraska	13-0-0
2	Oklahoma	11-1-0
3	Colorado	10-2-0
4	Alabama	11-1-0
5	Penn State	11-1-0
6	Michigan	11-1-0
7	Georgia	11-1-0
8	Arizona State	11-1-0
9	Tennessee	10-2-0
10	Stanford	9-3-0
11	LSU	9-3-0
12	Auburn	9-2-0
13	Notre Dame	8-2-0
14	Toledo	12-0-0
15	Mississippi	10-2-0
16	Arkansas	8-3-1
17	Houston	9-3-0
18	Texas	8-3-0
19	Washington	8-3-0
20	USC	6-4-1

CONFERENCE STANDINGS

	Conference			Overall		
	W	L	T	W	L	T
Toledo	5	0	0	12	0	0
Bowling Green	4	1	0	6	4	0
Western Michigan	2	3	0	7	3	0
Miami (Ohio)	2	3	0	7	3	0
Ohio U	2	3	0	5	5	0
Kent State	0	5	0	3	8	0
Ball State*				4	5	1
Eastern Michigan*				7	1	2
Central Michigan*				5	5	0
Temple*				6	2	1
Northern Illinois*				5	5	1

BOWL GAMES

DATE	GAME	SCORE
D28	Tangerine	Toledo 28, Richmond 3

CONSENSUS ALL-AMERICANS

POS	Defense	HT	WT	School	AP	FC	FW	NE	PI
T	Mel Long	6-1	230	Toledo	•		•	•	•

ALL-CONFERENCE TEAM

POS	Offense	School
QB	Chuck Ealey	Toledo
RB	Paul Miles	Bowling Green
RB	Bob Hitchens	Miami (Ohio)
RB	Joe Schwartz	Toledo
HB	Larry Cates	Western Michigan
WR	Don Fair	Toledo
E	Al Baker	Toledo
E	Bob Allen	Ohio U
C	Dennis Maupin	Bowling Green
E	Al Benton	Ohio U
T	John Czerwinski	Bowling Green
T	Don Caldwell	Ohio U
G	Larry Ulmer	Western Michigan

POS	Defense	School
LB	Tom Elias	Western Michigan
LB	Marc Smith	Miami (Ohio)
LB	Jack LeVeck	Ohio U
LB	John Niezgoda	Toledo
DT	Mel Long	Toledo
DT	Bernard Thomas	Western Michigan
MG	Doug Krause	Miami (Ohio)
DB	Tim Raybuck	Miami (Ohio)
DB	Gary Hinkson	Toledo
DB	John Saunders	Toledo
DE	Bill Slater	Western Michigan
DE	Bob Rose	Toledo

HEISMAN TROPHY VOTING

	PLAYER	POS	SCHOOL	TOTAL
8	Chuck Ealey	QB	Toledo	137

NCAA STATISTICAL LEADERS

INDIVIDUAL LEADERS

ALL-PURPOSE

		GRUSH	REC	PR	KR	YDS	YPG
9	Paul Loughran, Temple*	468	198	291	502	1459	162.1

RUSHING/YARDS PER GAME

		G	ATT	YDS	TD	AVG	YPG
10	Paul Miles, Bowling Green	10	274	1185	7	4.3	118.5

RECEIVING

		G	REC	YDS	TD	YPR	YPG	RPG
8	Willie Hatter, Northern Illinois*	10	50	615	1	12.3	61.5	5.0

PUNTING

		PUNT	YDS	AVG
4	Dave Green, Ohio U	33	1416	42.9

KICKOFF RETURNS

		KR	YDS	TD	AVG
1	Paul Loughran, Temple*	15	502	1	33.5
2	Bob Allen, Ohio U	14	421	0	30.1
9	Eddie Woodard, Kent State	23	632	1	27.5

SCORING

		TDS	XPT	FG	PTS	PTPG
5	Joe Schwartz, Toledo	18	0	0	108	9.8

KICK SCORING

		XPA	XP	FGA	FG	PTS	PTPG
2	Nick Mike-Mayer, Temple*	28	26	17	12	62	6.9

TEAM LEADERS

RUSHING DEFENSE

		G	ATT	YDS	AVG	TD	YPG
4	Western Michigan	10	407	932	2.3	7	93.2
5	Miami (Ohio)	10	408	953	2.3	4	95.3
7	Toledo	11	539	1199	2.2	11	109.0

PASSING DEFENSE

		G	ATT	COM	PCT	YPC	INT	I%	YDS	YPA	TD	YPG
3	Toledo	11	195	68	34.9	11.4	18	9.2	776	4.0	2	70.5
6	Miami (Ohio)	10	211	92	43.6	10.2	14	6.6	940	4.5	4	94.0
8	Kent State	11	177	82	46.3	12.9	11	6.2	1054	6.0	5	95.8

TOTAL DEFENSE

		G	P	YDS	AVG	TD	YPG
1	Toledo	11	734	1975	2.7	13	179.5
3	Miami (Ohio)	10	619	1893	3.1	8	189.3

SCORING OFFENSE

		G	PTS	AVG
9	Toledo	11	355	32.3

SCORING DEFENSE

		G	PTS	AVG
4	Toledo	11	91	8.3

*Independent or other conference affiliation

1972

CONFERENCE STANDINGS

	CONFERENCE			OVERALL		
	W	L	T	W	L	T
Kent State	4	1	0	6	5	1
Bowling Green	3	1	1	6	3	1
Western Michigan	2	2	1	7	3	1
Miami (Ohio)	2	3	0	7	3	0
Toledo	2	3	0	6	5	0
Ohio U	1	4	0	3	8	0
Ball State*				5	4	1
Eastern Michigan*				6	4	0
Central Michigan*				5	5	1
Temple*				5	4	0
Northern Illinois*				7	4	0

BOWL GAMES

DATE	GAME	SCORE
D29	**Tangerine**	Tampa 21, Kent State 18

CONSENSUS ALL-AMERICANS

POS	Offense	HT	WT	School	AP	CF	FC	FW	NE	PI
None										

	OTHERS RECEIVING FIRST-TEAM HONORS		
G	Bill Singletary	Temple*	•

ALL-CONFERENCE TEAM

POS	Offense	School
QB	Bruce Arthur	Toledo
RB	Paul Miles	Bowling Green
RB	Bob Hitchens	Miami (Ohio)
RB	Joe Schwartz	Toledo
HB	Larry Cates	Western Michigan
WR	Jeff Calabrese	Toledo
C	Fred Hicks	Western Michigan
T	Don Caldwell	Ohio U
T	John Czerwinski	Bowling Green
G	Fred Sturt	Bowling Green
G	Larry Ulmer	Western Michigan

POS	Defense	School
LB	Jack Lambert	Kent State
DI	Bernard Thomas	Western Michigan
DT	Willie Duke	Toledo
DT	Steve Kovacs	Miami (Ohio)
DT	Tom Hall	Bowling Green
DB	Dan Rebsch	Miami (Ohio)
DB	Bert Dampier	Ohio U
DB	Pete Alsup	Toledo
DB	Ron Karlis	Western Michigan
DE	Dan Arbour	Western Michigan

INDIVIDUAL LEADERS

ALL-PURPOSE		G	RUSH	REC	PR	KR	YDS	YPG
9	Paul Loughran, Temple*	9	593	196	146	438	1373	152.6

RUSHING/YARDS PER GAME		G	ATT	YDS	TD	AVG	YPG
2	Bob Hitchens, Miami (Ohio)	10	326	1370	15	4.2	137.0

RECEIVING		G	REC	YDS	TD	YPR	YPG	RPG
2	Clinton Graves, Temple*	9	63	707	3	11.2	78.6	7.0
5	Jeff Calabrese, Toledo	11	62	886	2	14.3	80.5	5.6

PUNT RETURNS		PR	YDS	TD	AVG
5	Gerald Tinker, Kent State	19	268	1	14.1

KICKOFF RETURNS		KR	YDS	TD	AVG
2	Byron Florence, Northern Illinois*	16	456	1	28.5
8	Eddie Woodard, Kent State	21	516	1	24.6

SCORING		TDS	XPT	FG	PTS	PTPG
9	Bob Hitchens, Miami (Ohio)	15	0	0	90	9.0

INTERCEPTIONS		INT	YDS	TD	INT/GM
5	Denny Costello, Miami (Ohio)	7	52	0	0.78
7	Ron Karlis, Western Michigan	8	247	2	0.73

TEAM LEADERS

RUSHING OFFENSE		G	ATT	YDS	AVG	TD	YPG
8	Miami (Ohio)	10	683	2806	4.1	25	280.6

RUSHING DEFENSE		G	ATT	YDS	AVG	TD	YPG
2	Western Michigan	11	454	980	2.2	14	89.1
4	Miami (Ohio)	10	365	961	2.6	8	96.1
9	Bowling Green	10	458	1134	2.5	8	113.4

PASSING DEFENSE		G	ATT	COM	PCT	YPC	INT	I%	YDS	YPA	TD	YPG
5	Toledo	11	177	70	39.5	13.5	13	7.3	947	5.4	8	86.1

TOTAL DEFENSE		G	P	YDS	AVG	TD	YPG
6	Miami (Ohio)	10	596	2276	3.8	15	227.6
10	Bowling Green	10	661	2437	3.7	17	243.7

SCORING DEFENSE		G	PTS	AVG
10	Miami (Ohio)	10	116	11.6

1973

FINAL POLL

UP	AP	TEAM	RECORD
1	1	Notre Dame	11-0-0
5	2	Ohio State	10-0-1
2	3	Oklahoma	10-0-1
4	4	Alabama	11-1-0
3	5	Penn State	12-0-0
6	6	Michigan	10-0-1
9	7	Nebraska	9-2-1
7	8	USC	9-2-1
12	9	Arizona State	11-1-0
10	9	Houston	11-1-0
11	11	Texas Tech	11-1-0
13	12	UCLA	9-2-0
8	13	LSU	9-3-0
17	14	Texas	8-3-0
NR	15	Miami (Ohio)	11-0-0
18	16	North Carolina St.	9-3-0
16	17	Missouri	8-4-0
19	18	Kansas	7-4-1
14	19	Tennessee	8-4-0
23	20	Maryland	8-4-0
21	20	Tulane	9-3-0

CONFERENCE STANDINGS

	CONFERENCE			OVERALL		
	W	L	T	W	L	T
Miami (Ohio)	5	0	0	11	0	0
Kent State	4	1	0	9	2	0
Bowling Green	2	3	0	7	3	0
Ohio U	2	3	0	5	5	0
Western Michigan	1	4	0	6	5	0
Toledo	1	4	0	3	8	0
Temple*				9	1	0
Central Michigan*				7	4	0
Northern Illinois*				6	5	0
Eastern Michigan*				6	4	0
Ball State*				5	5	1

BOWL GAMES

DATE	GAME	SCORE
D22	**Tangerine**	Miami (Ohio) 16, Florida 7

ALL-CONFERENCE TEAM

POS	Offense	School
QB	Gene Swick	Toledo
QB	Greg Kokal	Kent State
RB	Paul Miles	Bowling Green
FB	Phil Polak	Bowling Green
WR	Randy Whatley	Toledo
T	Jeff Beams	Ohio U
C	Dan Cunningham	Miami
G	Keith Young	Toledo
TE	Garry Pinkel	Kent State
SE	Gerald Tinker	Kent State

POS	Defense	School
DB	Mike Carter	Western Michigan
DB	Dan Rebsch	Miami (Ohio)
DB	Bernard Harmon	Kent State
LB	Dom Riggio	Western Michigan
LB	Mike Monos	Miami (Ohio)
LB	Jack Lambert	Kent State
DT	Walt Vrabel	Kent State
DT	Larry Faulk	Kent State
DE	Herman Jackson	Miami (Ohio)
DE	Bill Blind	Miami (Ohio)

NCAA STATISTICAL LEADERS

INDIVIDUAL

PASSING		G	ATT	COM	PCT	INT	I%	YDS	YPA	TD	TD%	COM.PG
6	Gene Swick, Toledo	11	301	165	54.8	17	5.7	2234	7.4	15	5.0	15.0

ALL-PURPOSE		G	RUSH	REC	PR	KR	YDS	YPG
9	Mark Kellar, Northern Illinois*	11	1719	17	0	0	1736	157.8

RUSHING/YARDS PER GAME		G	ATT	YDS	TD	AVG	YPG
1	Mark Kellar, Northern Illinois*	11	291	1719	16	5.9	156.3

RUSHING/YARDS PER CARRY		G	ATT	YDS	YPC
8	Tom Sloan, Temple*	10	173	1036	6.0
10	Mark Kellar, Northern Illinois*	11	291	1719	5.9
	Based on top 25 rushers				

SCORING		TD	XPT	FG	PTS	PTPG
2	Larry Poole, Kent State	18	0	0	108	9.8
8	Mark Kellar, Northern Illinois*	16	2	0	98	8.9

KICK SCORING		XPA	XPT	FGA	FG	PTS	PTPG
9	Dave Draudt, Miami (Ohio)	21	20	27	14	62	6.2

INTERCEPTIONS		INT	YDS	TD	INT/GM
7	Joe Spicer, Miami (Ohio)	7	64	0	0.70

TEAM

RUSHING OFFENSE		G	ATT	YDS	AVG	TD	YPG
8	Northern Illinois*	11	664	3465	5.2	39	315.0

PASSING OFFENSE		G	ATT	COM	INT	PCT	YDS	YPA	TD	I%	YPC	YPG
6	Toledo	11	303	163	17	53.8	2234	7.4	15	5.6	13.7	203.1

TOTAL OFFENSE		G	P	YDS	AVG	TD	YPG
6	Temple*	10	786	4555	5.8	46	455.5

RUSHING DEFENSE		G	ATT	YDS	AVG	TD	YPG
1	Miami (Ohio)	10	424	770	1.8	2	77.0

TOTAL DEFENSE		G	P	YDS	AVG	TD	YPG
1	Miami (Ohio)	10	645	1774	2.8	6	177.4

SCORING OFFENSE		G	PTS	AVG
9	Temple*	10	353	35.3

SCORING DEFENSE		G	PTS	AVG
4	Miami (Ohio)	10	69	6.9

*Independent or other conference affiliation

1974

FINAL POLL

UP	AP	TEAM	RECORD
PB	1	Oklahoma	11-0-0
1	2	USC	10-1-1
5	3	Michigan	10-1-0
3	4	Ohio State	10-2-0
2	5	Alabama	11-1-0
4	6	Notre Dame	10-2-0
7	7	Penn State	10-2-0
6	8	Auburn	10-2-0
8	9	Nebraska	9-3-0
10	10	Miami (Ohio)	10-0-1
9	11	North Carolina St.	9-2-1
18	12	Michigan State	7-3-1
13	13	Maryland	8-4-0
14	14	Baylor	8-4-0
12	15	Florida	8-4-0
15	16	Texas A&M	8-3-0
17	17	Mississippi State	9-3-0
	17	Texas	8-4-0
11	19	Houston	8-3-1
15	20	Tennessee	7-3-2

CONFERENCE STANDINGS

	CONFERENCE			OVERALL		
	W	L	T	W	L	T
Miami (Ohio)	5	0	0	10	0	1
Kent State	4	1	0	9	2	0
Bowling Green	2	3	0	7	3	0
Ohio U	2	3	0	5	5	0
Western Michigan	1	4	0	6	5	0
Toledo	1	4	0	3	8	0
Central Michigan*				12	1	0
Temple*				8	2	0
Ball State*				6	4	0
Eastern Michigan*				4	6	1
Northern Illinois*				4	7	0

BOWL GAMES

DATE	GAME	SCORE
D21	Tangerine	Miami (Ohio) 21, Georgia 10

CONSENSUS ALL-AMERICANS

POS	Offense	HT	WT	School		AP	CF	FC	FW	PI
None										

OTHERS RECEIVING FIRST-TEAM HONORS

QB	Steve Joachim*			Temple	•					

POS	Defense	HT	WT	School		AP	CF	FC	FW	PI
None										

OTHERS RECEIVING FIRST-TEAM HONORS

LB	Brad Cousino			Miami (Ohio)			•			

AWARD WINNERS

PLAYER	POS	SCHOOL	AWARD NAME
Steve Joachim	QB	Temple*	Maxwell

ALL-CONFERENCE TEAM

POS	Offense	School
QB	Gene Swick	Toledo
RB	Dave Preston	Bowling Green
RB	Larry Poole	Kent State
RB	L.C. Lyons	Ohio U
G	Larry Wiggins	Kent State
G	Pat Kief	Miami (Ohio)
T	Mike Biehle	Miami (Ohio)
T	Ed Madison	Ohio U
TE	Don Seymour	Toledo
TE	Ken Dooner	Kent State
SE	John Ross	Toledo
PK	Dave Druadt	Miami (Ohio)

POS	Defense	School
LB	Ed Scott	Toledo
LB	Brad Cousino	Miami (Ohio)
LB	Chuck Varner	Miami (Ohio)
T	Larry Faulk	Kent State
T	Gary Dourm	Ohio U
DE	Marvin Elliot	Kent State
DB	Mike Nugent	Ohio U
DB	Cedric Brown	Kent State
DB	John Mcvay	Miami (Ohio)
DB	Joe Spicer	Miami (Ohio)
DE	Jay Fry	Miami (Ohio)
P	Jeff Rowlands	Miami (Ohio)

NCAA STATISTICAL LEADERS

INDIVIDUAL

PASSING

		G	ATT	COM	PCT	INT	I%	YDS	YPA	TD	TD%	COM.PG
3	Gene Swick, Toledo	11	287	178	62.0	14	4.9	2235	7.8	13	4.5	16.2
10	Steve Joachim, Temple*	10	221	128	57.9	13	5.9	1950	8.8	20	9.0	12.8

RUSHING/YARDS PER GAME

		G	ATT	YDS	TD	AVG	YPG
5	Dave Preston, Bowling Green	11	324	1414	19	4.4	128.5

RECEIVING

		G	REC	YDS	TD	YPR	YPG	RPG
2	John Ross, Toledo	11	77	866	2	11.2	78.7	7.0

SCORING

		TD	XPT	FG	PTS	PTPG
5	Dave Preston, Bowling Green	19	0	0	114	10.4
10	Larry Poole, Kent State	15	0	0	90	8.2

KICK SCORING

		XPA	XPT	FGA	FG	PTS	PTPG
2	Don Bitterlich, Temple*	44	44	15	9	71	7.1

TEAM

PASSING OFFENSE

		G	ATT	COM	INT	PCT	YDS	YPA	TD	I%	YPC	YPG
6	Toledo	11	309	187	14	60.5	2335	7.6	13	4.5	12.5	212.3
8	Temple*	10	233	134	16	57.5	2027	8.7	20	6.9	15.1	202.7

TOTAL OFFENSE

		G	P	YDS	AVG	TD	YPG
3	Temple*	10	738	4473	6.1	44	447.3

RUSHING DEFENSE

		G	ATT	YDS	AVG	TD	YPG
5	Miami (Ohio)	10	454	1153	2.5	6	115.3

TOTAL DEFENSE

		G	P	YDS	AVG	TD	YPG
4	Miami (Ohio)	10	640	2190	3.4	9	219.0

SCORING OFFENSE

		G	PTS	AVG
4	Temple*	10	335	33.5

SCORING DEFENSE

		G	PTS	AVG
4	Miami (Ohio)	10	76	7.6

MAC ANNUAL REVIEW & BOWLS

1975

FINAL POLL

UP	AP	TEAM	RECORD
1	1	Oklahoma	11-1-0
2	2	Arizona State	12-0-0
3	3	Alabama	11-1-0
4	4	Ohio State	11-1-0
5	5	UCLA	9-2-1
7	6	Texas	10-2-0
6	7	Arkansas	10-2-0
8	8	Michigan	8-2-2
9	9	Nebraska	10-2-0
10	10	Penn State	9-3-0
12	11	Texas A&M	10-2-0
16	12	Miami (Ohio)	11-1-0
11	13	Maryland	9-2-1
15	14	California	8-3-0
13	15	Pittsburgh	8-4-0
	16	Colorado	9-3-0
19	17	USC	8-4-0
13	18	Arizona	9-2-0
19	19	Georgia	9-3-0
17	20	West Virginia	9-3-0

CONFERENCE STANDINGS

	CONFERENCE			OVERALL		
	W	L	T	W	L	T
Miami (Ohio)	6	0	0	11	1	0
Central Michigan	4	1	1	8	2	1
Ball State	4	2	0	9	2	0
Bowling Green	4	2	0	8	3	0
Toledo	4	4	0	5	6	0
Ohio U	3	3	1	5	5	1
Northern Illinois	2	3	0	3	8	0
Kent State	1	6	0	4	7	0
Western Michigan	0	7	0	4	6	0
Temple*				6	5	0
Eastern Michigan*				4	6	0

BOWL GAMES

DATE	GAME	SCORE
D20	**Tangerine**	Miami (Ohio) 20, South Carolina 7

CONSENSUS ALL-AMERICANS

POS	Offense	HT	WT	School	AP	FC	FW	PI
None								

OTHERS RECEIVING FIRST-TEAM HONORS

| QB | Gene Swick | | | Toledo | | | • | |

HEISMAN TROPHY VOTING

	Player	POS	School	1ST	2ND	3RD	TOTAL
10	Gene Swick	QB	Toledo	5	19	20	73

ALL-CONFERENCE TEAM

POS	Offense	School
QB	Gene Swick	Toledo
RB	Walt Hodges	Central Michigan
RB	Rob Carpenter	Miami (Ohio)
RB	Sherman Smith	Miami (Ohio)
WR	Mike Green	Northern Illinois
G	Mitch Hoban	Ball State
C	Steve Studer	Bowling Green
T	Ed Madison	Ohio U
T	Mike Szymarek	Central Michigan
T	Chuck Benjamin	Miami (Ohio)
TE	Ricky Taylor	Miami (Ohio)
PK	Jim Neddeff	Ball State

POS	Defense	School
LB	Bill Schmidt	Central Michigan
LB	Bob Gregolunas	Northern Illinois
DE	Mel Edwards	Miami (Ohio)
DE	Art Stringer	Ball State
MG	Rod Day	Ohio U
DB	Ron Zook	Miami (Ohio)
DB	Shafer Suggs	Ball State
DB	Jimmy Jones	Central Michigan
DB	Cedric Brown	Kent State
T	Jim Feucht	Miami (Ohio)

NCAA STATISTICAL LEADERS

INDIVIDUAL

PASSING	G	ATT	COM	PCT	INT	I%	YDS	YPA	TD	TD%	COM.PG
2 Gene Swick, Toledo	11	308	190	61.7	12	3.9	2487	8.1	15	4.9	17.3

ALL-PURPOSE			GRUSH	REC	PR	KR	YDS	YPG
6 Dan Watkins, Kent State			10	916	59	47	508	1530	153.0

RUSHING/YARDS PER CARRY				G	ATT	YDS	YPC
7 Dan Saleet, Bowling Green				10	194	1114	5.7
Based on top 27 rushers							

SCORING			TD	XPT	FG	PTS	PTPG
2 Dave Preston, Bowling Green			14	0	0	84	9.3
5 Don Bitterlich, Temple*			0	32	21	95	8.6
8 Walt Hodges, Central Michigan			12	0	0	72	8.0

FIELD GOALS				FGA	FGM	PCT	FGG
1 Don Bitterlich, Temple*				31	21	0.68	1.91

INTERCEPTIONS					INT	YDS	TD	INT/GM
2 Cedric Brown, Kent State					8	107	1	0.89
5 Mike Lecklider, Ball State					7	61	0	0.64

TEAM

RUSHING OFFENSE				G	ATT	YDS	AVG	TD	YPG
5 Central Michigan				11	740	3613	4.9	32	328.5

PASSING OFFENSE	G	ATT	COM	INT	PCT	YDS	YPA	TD	I%	YPC	YPG
4 Toledo	11	312	190	12	60.9	2487	8.0	15	3.8	13.1	226.1

RUSHING DEFENSE				G	ATT	YDS	AVG	TD	YPG
2 Miami (Ohio)				11	462	947	2.0	8	86.1
3 Central Michigan				11	435	993	2.3	4	90.3

PASSING DEFENSE	G	ATT	COM	PCT	YPC	INT	I%	YDS	YPA	TD	YPG
8 Bowling Green	11	196	78	39.8	11.7	17	8.7	914	4.7	5	83.1

TOTAL DEFENSE				G	P	YDS	AVG	TD	YPG
5 Central Michigan				11	625	2268	3.6	12	206.2
6 Miami (Ohio)				11	679	2353	3.5	18	213.9

SCORING DEFENSE				G	PTS	AVG
6 Central Michigan				11	102	9.3

*Independent or other conference affiliation

1976

CONFERENCE STANDINGS

	Conference			Overall		
	W	L	T	W	L	T
Ball State	4	1	0	8	3	0
Kent State	6	2	0	8	4	0
Ohio U	6	2	0	7	4	0
Western Michigan	6	3	0	7	4	0
Central Michigan	4	3	0	7	4	0
Bowling Green	4	3	0	6	5	0
Miami (Ohio)	2	4	0	3	8	0
Toledo	2	6	0	3	8	0
Eastern Michigan	1	5	0	2	9	0
Northern Illinois	0	6	0	1	10	0
Temple*				4	6	0

ALL-CONFERENCE TEAM

POS	Offense	School
QB	Art Yaroch	Ball State
RB	Ron Carpenter	Miami (Ohio)
RB	Arnold Welcher	Ohio U
RB	Jerome Persell	Western Michigan
WR	Rick Morrison	Ball State
WR	Kim Featsent	Kent State
G	Bob Weidaw	Ohio U
G	Mitch Hoban	Ball State
T	John Obrock	Bowling Green
T	Rocco Moore	Western Michigan
C	Mike Sitko	Western Michigan
K	Paul Marchese	Kent State

POS	Defense	School
T	John Wunderlich	Central Michigan
T	John Neuman	Central Michigan
T	Glenn Deadmon	Kent State
LB	Greg Locket	Ohio U
LB	Jack Lazor	Kent State
LB	Jack Glowik	Miami (Ohio)
DB	Maurice Harvey	Ball State
DB	Ed Rykulski	Central Michigan
DB	Ron Johnson	Eastern Michigan
DB	Dave Gapinski	Western Michigan

NCAA STATISTICAL LEADERS

INDIVIDUAL

ALL-PURPOSE

		GRUSH	REC	PR	KR	YDS	YPG
3	Jerome Persell, Western Michigan	10	1505	38	0	18	1561	156.1
10	Anthony Anderson, Temple*	10	803	174	0	367	1344	134.4

RUSHING/YARDS PER GAME

		G	ATT	YDS	TD	AVG	YPG
2	Jerome Persell, Western Michigan	10	269	1505	19	5.6	150.5

RUSHING/YARDS PER CARRY

		G	ATT	YDS	YPC
9	Jerome Persell, Western Michigan	10	269	1505	5.6
	Based on top 38 rushers				

PUNT RETURNS

		PR	YDS	TD	AVG
8	Rick Morrison, Ball State	19	234	0	12.3

KICKOFF RETURNS

		KR	YDS	TD	AVG
6	Steve Kuehl, Bowling Green	14	359	0	25.6

SCORING

		TD	XPT	FG	PTS	PTPG
2	Jerome Persell, Western Michigan	19	4	0	118	11.8

FIELD GOALS

		FGA	FGM	PCT	FGG
7	Paul Marchese, Kent State	25	16	0.64	1.33
8	Rade Savich, Central Michigan	24	14	0.58	1.27

TEAM

RUSHING OFFENSE

		G	ATT	YDS	AVG	TD	YPG
9	Western Michigan	11	677	3,136	4.6	32	285.1

TOTAL OFFENSE

		G	P	YDS	AVG	TD	YPG
10	Bowling Green	11	890	4425	5.0	38	402.3

PASSING DEFENSE

		G	ATT	COM	PCT	YPC	INT	I%	YDS	YPA	TD	YPG
1	Western Michigan	11	175	74	42.3	11.7	10	5.7	863	4.9	6	78.5
5	Ohio U	11	196	70	35.7	13.2	15	7.7	921	4.7	9	83.7

SCORING DEFENSE

		G	PTS	AVG
8	Ball State	11	124	11.3

1977

CONFERENCE STANDINGS

	Conference W	L	T	Overall W	L	T
Miami (Ohio)	5	0	0	10	1	0
Central Michigan	7	1	0	10	1	0
Ball State	5	1	0	9	2	0
Eastern Michigan	4	3	0	8	3	0
Bowling Green	4	3	0	5	7	0
Kent State	5	4	0	6	5	0
Western Michigan	3	5	0	4	7	0
Northern Illinois	2	5	0	3	8	0
Toledo	2	7	0	2	9	0
Ohio U	0	8	0	1	10	0
Temple*				5	5	1

ALL-CONFERENCE TEAM

POS	Offense	School
QB	Mark O'Connell	Ball State
QB	Andy Vetter	Northern Illinois
WR	Kim Featsent	Kent State
WR	Rick Morrison	Ball State
G	Tim Sopha	Central Michigan
G	Rollie Hanson	Eastern Michigan
T	Tom Jesko	Kent State
T	Jack Streicher	Miami (Ohio)
TE	Wayne Schwalbach	Central Michigan
TB	Bobbie Windom	Eastern Michigan
TB	Jerome Persell	Western Michigan
PK	Paul Marchese	Kent State

POS	Defense	School
T	Ken Kremer	Ball State
T	Mike Zele	Kent State
MG	Jack Glowik	Miami (Ohio)
LB	Jack Lazor	Kent State
LB	Mose Rison	Central Michigan
DB	Maurice Harvey	Ball State
DB	Vondell Robertson	Central Michigan
DB	Ron Johnson	Eastern Michigan
DB	Kirk Springs	Miami (Ohio)
DB	Dave Hausfeld	Toledo
DE	Tom Williams	Eastern Michigan
DE	Greg Sullivan	Miami (Ohio)

NCAA STATISTICAL LEADERS

INDIVIDUAL

ALL-PURPOSE	G	RUSH	REC	PR	KR	YDS	YPG
4 Mose Rison, Central Michigan	10	1241	59	0	330	1630	163.0

RUSHING/ YARDS PER GAME	G	ATT	YDS	TD	AVG	YPG
4 Jerome Persell, Western Michigan	10	264	1339	14	5.1	133.9
7 Mose Rison, Central Michigan	10	238	1241	11	5.2	124.1
9 Bobby Windom, Eastern Michigan	11	246	1322	9	5.4	120.2

RECEIVING	G	REC	YDS	TD	YPR	YPG	RPG
5 Rick Morrison, Ball State	11	59	908	8	15.4	82.5	5.4
7 Dave Petzke, Northern Illinois	11	57	746	5	13.1	67.8	5.2

PUNT RETURNS	PR	YDS	TD	AVG
7 Vondell Robertson, Central Michigan	22	269	0	12.2

KICKOFF RETURNS	KR	YDS	TD	AVG
9 Norman Warren, Kent State	22	569	1	25.9

SCORING	TD	XPT	FG	PTS	PTPG
9 Jerome Persell, Western Michigan	14	0	0	84	8.4

FIELD GOALS	FGA	FGM	PCT	FGg
1 Paul Marchese, Kent State	27	18	0.67	1.80

TEAM

RUSHING OFFENSE	G	ATT	YDs	AVG	TD	YPG
10 Central Michigan	11	741	3213	4.3	31	292.1

RUSHING DEFENSE	G	ATT	YDS	AVG	TD	YPG
7 Central Michigan	11	475	1209	2.5	13	109.9

PASSING DEFENSE	G	ATT	COM	PCT	YPC	INT	I%	YDS	YPA	TD	YPG
3 Northern Illinois	11	165	74	44.8	13.2	9	5.5	974	5.9	8	88.5

TOTAL DEFENSE	G	P	YDS	AVG	TD	YPG
4 Central Michigan	11	671	2422	3.6	19	220.2

SCORING OFFENSE	G	PTS	AVG
8 Ball State	11	377	34.3

*Independent or other conference affiliation

1978

CONFERENCE STANDINGS

	CONFERENCE			OVERALL		
	W	L	T	W	L	T
Ball State	8	0	0	10	1	0
Central Michigan	8	1	0	9	2	0
Miami (Ohio)	5	2	0	8	2	1
Western Michigan	5	4	0	7	4	0
Bowling Green	3	5	0	4	7	0
Ohio U	3	5	0	3	8	0
Northern Illinois	2	4	0	5	6	0
Kent State	2	6	0	4	7	0
Toledo	2	7	0	2	9	0
Eastern Michigan	1	5	0	3	7	0
Temple*				7	3	1

ALL-CONFERENCE TEAM

POS	Offense	School
QB	Mike Wright	Bowling Green
RB	Mark hunter	Miami (Ohio)
RB	Kevin Babcock	Ohio U
WR	Jeff Groth	Bowling Green
G	Dave Bordine	Western Michigan
G	Tim Sopha	Central Michigan
T	Steve Milano	Ohio U
T	Jack Streicher	Miami (Ohio)
TE	Ray Hinton	Ball State
TB	Jerome Persell	Western Michigan
PK	Rade Savich	Central Michigan

POS	Defense	School
T	Mike Zele	Kent State
T	Rush Brown	Ball State
LB	Jack Lazor	Kent State
LB	Eric Manns	Western Michigan
DB	Pat Hume	Western Michigan
DB	Kirk Springs	Miami (Ohio)
DB	Bill Stahl	Ball State
DB	Robert Jackson	Central Michigan
DE	Mike McKibben	Kent State
DE	Greg Sullivan	Miami (Ohio)
DE	Stewe Groves	Ohio U
DE	Jim Conroy	Toledo

NCAA STATISTICAL LEADERS

INDIVIDUAL

RUSHING/YARDS PER GAME

		G	ATT	YDS	TD	AVG	YPG
10	Jerome Persell, Western Michigan	11	309	1346	6	4.4	122.4

RECEIVING

		G	REC	YDS	TD	YPR	YPG	RPG
1	Dave Petzke, Northern Illinois	11	91	1217	11	13.4	110.6	8.3
9	Jeff Groth, Bowling Green	11	56	874	8	15.6	79.5	5.1

PUNT RETURNS

		PR	YDS	TD	AVG
9	James Johnson, Eastern Michigan	24	287	2	12.0

SCORING

		TD	XPT	FG	PTS	PTPG
8	Willie Todd, Central Michigan	13	2	0	80	8.0

FIELD GOALS

		FGA	FGM	PCT	FGG
10	Rade Savich, Central Michigan	24	15	0.63	1.40

TEAM

RUSHING DEFENSE

		G	ATT	YDS	AVG	TD	YPG
5	Ball State	11	472	1124	2.4	4	102.2

PASSING DEFENSE

		G	ATT	COM	PCT	YPC	INT	I%	YDS	YPA	TD	YPG
3	Miami (Ohio)	11	213	85	39.9	12.2	15	7.0	1039	4.9	5	94.5
7	Northern Illinois	11	175	80	45.7	13.8	16	9.1	1100	6.3	2	100.0
9	Central Michigan	11	215	81	37.7	13.7	22	10.2	1111	5.2	6	101.0

TOTAL DEFENSE

		G	P	YDS	AVG	TD	YPG
3	Ball State	11	719	2333	3.2	7	212.1
7	Central Michigan	11	738	2645	3.6	15	240.5

SCORING OFFENSE

		G	PTS	AVG
8	Central Michigan	11	331	30.1

SCORING DEFENSE

		G	PTS	AVG
1	Ball State	11	82	7.5
6	Central Michigan	11	119	10.8

1979

FINAL POLL

UP	AP	TEAM	RECORD
1	1	Alabama	12-0-0
2	2	USC	11-0-1
3	3	Oklahoma	11-1-0
4	4	Ohio State	11-1-0
5	5	Houston	11-1-0
8	6	Florida State	11-1-0
6	7	Pittsburgh	11-1-0
9	8	Arkansas	10-2-0
7	9	Nebraska	10-2-0
10	10	Purdue	10-2-0
11	11	Washington	9-3-0
13	12	Texas	9-3-0
12	13	Brigham Young	11-1-0
15	14	Baylor	8-4-0
14	15	North Carolina	8-3-1
PB	16	Auburn	8-3-0
17	17	Temple*	10-2-0
19	18	Michigan	8-4-0
16	19	Indiana	8-4-0
18	20	Penn State	8-4-0

CONFERENCE STANDINGS

	CONFERENCE			OVERALL		
	W	L	T	W	L	T
Central Michigan	8	0	1	10	0	1
Toledo	7	1	1	7	3	1
Western Michigan	5	4	0	6	5	0
Ball State	4	4	0	6	5	0
Ohio U	4	4	0	6	5	0
Northern Illinois	3	3	1	5	5	1
Miami (Ohio)	3	4	0	6	5	0
Bowling Green	3	5	0	4	7	0
Eastern Michigan	1	6	1	2	8	1
Kent State	1	7	0	1	10	0
Temple*				10	2	0

BOWL GAMES

DATE	GAME	SCORE
D15	**Garden State**	Temple* 28, California 17

ALL-CONFERENCE TEAM

POS	**Offense**	
QB	Gary Hogeboom	Central Michigan
RB	Kevin Babcock	Ohio U
RB	Willie Todd	Central Michigan
WR	Mike Ball	Central Michigan
WR	Tom Parm	Eastern Michigan
C	Doug Lantz	Miami (Ohio)
C	Randy Clark	Northern Illinois
G	Mark Lootens	Western Michigan
G	Dave Crowder	Miami (Ohio)
T	Marty Smallbone	Central Michigan
TE	Mark Geisler	Ohio U
PK	John Spengler	Bowling Green
PK	Steve Green	Ohio U
P	Jeff Morrow	Kent State

POS	**Defense**	**School**
OLB	Matt Murphy	Western Michigan
T	Rush Brown	Ball State
LB	Frank Lewandoski	Northern Illinois
LB	Eric Manns	Western Michigan
LB	Bill White	Central Michigan
LB	Tim Hollandsworth	Central Michigan
DB	Robert Jackson	Central Michigan
DB	Joe Catlan	Ohio U
DE	Stewe Groves	Ohio U
DE	Steve Claussen	Northern Illinois

NCAA STATISTICAL LEADERS

INDIVIDUAL

PASSING	G	ATT	COM	PCT	INT	I%	YDS	YPA	TD	TD%	RATING
2 Brian Broomell, Temple*	11	214	120	56.1	11	5.1	2103	9.8	22	10.3	162.3

PUNTING								PUNT	YDS	AVG
7 Casey Murphy, Temple*								40	1718	42.9

KICKOFF RETURNS								KR	YDS	TD	AVG
1 Stevie Nelson, Ball State								18	565	1	31.4

SCORING							TD	XPT	FG	PTS	PTPG
2 Mark Bornholdt, Ball State							19	0	0	114	11.4

INTERCEPTIONS								INT	YDS	TD	INT/GM
1 Joe Callan, Ohio U								9	110	0	1.00

TEAM

RUSHING OFFENSE				G	ATT	YDS	AVG	TD	YPG
8 Central Michigan				11	741	3183	4.3	29	289.4

TOTAL OFFENSE				G	P	YDS	AVG	TD	YPG
6 Temple*				11	770	4815	6.3	49	437.7

RUSHING DEFENSE				G	ATT	YDS	AVG	TD	YPG
3 Western Michigan				11	435	1091	2.5	7	99.2
9 Central Michigan				11	446	1224	2.7	11	111.3

PASSING DEFENSE	G	ATT	COM	PCT	YPC	INT	I%	YDS	YPA	TD	YPG
8 Ohio U	11	185	76	41.1	13.9	17	9.2	1055	5.7	10	95.9

TOTAL DEFENSE				G	P	YDS	AVG	TD	YPG
6 Western Michigan				11	651	2398	3.7	12	218.0
9 Central Michigan				11	689	2646	3.8	17	240.5

SCORING OFFENSE								G	PTS	AVG
6 Temple*								11	371	33.7

TURNOVER MARGIN				G	FR	INT	TOT	FL	INTL	TOT	MAR
1 Toledo				11	28	18	46	14	6	20	2.4

MAC ANNUAL REVIEW & BOWLS

1980

CONFERENCE STANDINGS

	CONFERENCE			OVERALL		
	W	L	T	W	L	T
Central Michigan	7	2	0	9	2	0
Western Michigan	6	3	0	7	4	0
Northern Illinois	4	3	0	7	4	0
Miami (Ohio)	4	3	0	5	6	0
Ohio U	5	4	0	6	5	0
Ball State	5	4	0	6	5	0
Bowling Green	4	4	0	4	7	0
Toledo	3	6	0	4	7	0
Kent State	3	6	0	3	8	0
Eastern Michigan	1	7	0	1	9	0
Temple*				4	7	0

ALL-CONFERENCE TEAM

POS	Offense	School
QB	Mark O'Connell	Ball State
RB	Bobby Howard	Western Michigan
RB	Tony Carifa	Ohio U
RB	Greg Jones	Miami (Ohio)
WR	Don Treadwell	Miami (Ohio)
WR	Stevie Nelson	Ball State
C	Don Puthoff	Ohio U
G	Don Petrosius	Ball State
G	Joe Maiorana	Central Michigan
T	Bud Sitko	Western Mchigan
T	Marty Smallbone	Central Michigan
TE	Ray Hinton	Ball State
PK	John Spengler	Bowling Green

POS	Defense	School
L	Chuck Stiver	Central Michigan
LB	Kent McCormick	Miami (Ohio)
LB	Mike Terna	Northern Illinois
LB	Allen Hughes	Western Michigan
DT	Todd Gates	Bowling Green
DB	George Bullock	Western Michigan
DB	Robert Jackson	Central Michigan
DB	Charlie Grandjean	Central Michigan
DB	Dave Petway	Northern Illinois
DB	Mike Kennedy	Toledo
DE	Kurt Dobronski	Central Michigan
DE	Jim Hinkle	Western Michigan
P	Alton Laupp	Western Michigan

NCAA STATISTICAL LEADERS

INDIVIDUAL

	PUNTING	CL	PUNT	YDS	AVG
8	Rick Hanschu, Eastern Michigan	SO	57	2487	43.6

TEAM

	RUSHING DEFENSE			G	ATT	YDS	AVG	TD	YPG
9	Ohio U			11	481	1269	2.6	11	115.4

	PASSING DEFENSE	G	ATT	COM	PCT	YPC	INT	I%	YDS	YPA	TD	YPG
4	Western Michigan	11	219	92	42.0	11.6	13	5.9	1063	4.9	5	96.6
9	Toledo	11	211	96	45.5	12.4	17	8.1	1189	5.6	5	108.1
9	Northern Illinois	11	199	106	53.3	11.2	13	6.5	1189	6.0	4	108.1

	SCORING DEFENSE				G	PTS	AVG
10	Central Michigan				11	127	11.5

1981

CONFERENCE STANDINGS

	CONFERENCE			OVERALL		
	W	L	T	W	L	T
Toledo	8	1	0	9	3	0
Miami (Ohio)	6	1	1	8	2	1
Central Michigan	7	2	0	7	4	0
Bowling Green	5	3	1	5	5	1
Western Michigan	5	4	0	6	5	0
Ohio U	5	4	0	5	6	0
Kent State	3	6	0	4	7	0
Ball State	2	6	0	4	7	0
Northern Illinois	2	7	0	3	8	0
Eastern Michigan	0	9	0	0	11	0
Temple*				5	5	0

BOWL GAMES

DATE	GAME	SCORE
D19	California	Toledo 27, San Jose State 25

ALL-CONFERENCE TEAM

POS	Offense	School
QB	Sam Shone	Ohio U
E	John Lyons	Miami (Ohio)
RB	Jay Peterson	Miami (Ohio)
RB	Reggie Mitchell	Central Michigan
RB	Bryant Jones	Bowling Green
RB	Greg Jones	Miami (Ohio)
WR	Stevie Nelson	Ball State
WR	Bob Phillips	Western Michigan
OT	Dave Pyles	Miami (Ohio)
DT	John Zupancic	Miami (Ohio)
C	Matt Meares	Western Michigan
G	Mike Chelovich	Northern Illinois
G	Kavid Menefee	Toledo
T	Tony Vitale	Central Michigan
TE	Mike Hirn	Central Michigan
K	Ron Harter	Ohio U

POS	Defense	School
LB	Allan Hughes	Western Michigan
LB	Craig Newburg	Ball State
LB	Ray Bentley	Central Michigan
LB	Russ Hedderly	Kent State
DB	Bruce Brownie	Central Michigan
DB	Charlie Grandjean	Kent State
DB	Mike Kennedy	Toledo
DE	Kurt Dobronski	Central Michigan
P	Jim Phelps	Bowling Green

NCAA STATISTICAL LEADERS

INDIVIDUAL

INTERCEPTIONS	CL	INT	YDS	TD	INT/GM
1 Sam Shaffer, Temple*	SR	9	76	0	0.90
4 Martin Bayless, Bowling Green	SO	7	55	1	0.64

TEAM

PASSING DEFENSE	G	ATT	COM	PCT	YPC	INT	I%	YDS	YPS	TD	YPG
2 Northern Illinois	11	195	91	46.7	12.4	14	7.2	1125	5.8	10	102.3
5 Kent State	11	213	104	48.8	11.5	16	7.5	1195	5.6	4	108.6
9 Central Michigan	11	232	121	52.2	10.6	11	4.7	1281	5.5	6	116.5

TOTAL DEFENSE	G	P	YDS	AVG	TD	YPG
4 Central Michigan	11	704	2621	3.7	14	238.3

SCORING DEFENSE	G	PTS	AVG
9 Central Michigan	11	131	11.9
10 Bowling Green	11	132	12.0

TURNOVER MARGIN	G	FR	INT	TOT	FL	INTL	TOT	MAR
2 Bowling Green	11	19	19	38	4	12	16	2.0

1982

CONFERENCE STANDINGS

	CONFERENCE			OVERALL		
	W	L	T	W	L	T
Bowling Green	7	2	0	7	5	0
Western Michigan	5	2	2	7	2	2
Miami (Ohio)	5	3	0	7	4	0
Central Michigan	5	3	1	6	4	1
Toledo	5	4	0	6	5	0
Ohio U	5	4	0	6	5	0
Northern Illinois	5	4	0	5	5	0
Ball State	4	4	0	5	6	0
Eastern Michigan	1	7	1	1	9	1
Kent State	0	9	0	0	11	0
Temple*				4	7	0

BOWL GAMES

DATE	GAME	SCORE
D18	California	Fresno State 29, Bowling Green 28

ALL-CONFERENCE TEAM

POS	Offense	School
QB	Brian McClure	Bowling Green
RB	Curtis Adams	Central Michigan
RB	Pete Roth	Northern Illinois
WR	Shawn Potts	Bowling Green
WR	Bob Phillips	Western Michigan
C	Matt Meares	Western Michigan
G	Chris McKay	Central Michigan
G	Rich Barrent	Northern Illinois
T	Chuck Towland	Toledo
T	Duanne Wilson	Western Michigan
TE	Brian Glasgow	Northern Illinois
PK	Tony Lee	Toledo

POS	Defense	School
DT	Max Gill	Northern Illinois
MG	Brian Pillman	Miami (Ohio)
LB	Mark Emans	Bowling Green
LB	Ray Bentley	Central Michigan
DB	Mark Kujacznski	Western Michigan
DB	Dave Williams	Miami (Ohio)
DB	Andre Young	Bowling Green
DB	Martin Bayless	Bowling Green
DB	Sel Drain	Ball State
DE	Kelly George	Ball State
DE	Darryl Meadows	Toledo
P	Jim Phelps	Bowling Green

NCAA STATISTICAL LEADERS

INDIVIDUAL

PASSING	CL	G	ATT	COM	PCT	INT	I%	YDS	YPA	TD	TD%	RATING
7 Tim Riordan, Temple*	JR	11	247	157	63.6	7	2.8	1840	7.5	13	5.3	137.8

TEAM

TOTAL DEFENSE	G	P	YDS	AVG	TD	YPG
5 Central Michigan	11	731	2731	3.7	18	248.3

*Independent or other conference affiliation

1983

NCAA Statistical Leaders

Conference Standings

	Conference			Overall		
	W	L	T	W	L	T
Northern Illinois	8	1	0	10	2	0
Toledo	7	2	0	9	2	0
Central Michigan	7	2	0	8	3	0
Bowling Green	7	2	0	8	3	0
Ball State	4	4	0	6	5	0
Western Michigan	4	5	0	6	5	0
Miami (Ohio)	3	5	0	4	7	0
Ohio U	3	6	0	4	7	0
Kent State	1	8	0	1	10	0
Eastern Michigan	0	9	0	1	10	0
Temple*				4	7	0

Bowl Games

DATE	GAME	SCORE
D17	California	No. Illinois 20, Cal St.-Fullerton 13

All-Conference Team

POS	Offense	School
QB	Brian McClure	Bowling Green
RB	Curtis Adams	Central Michigan
RB	Darryl Richardson	Northern Illinois
RB	Shawn Faulkner	Western Michigan
WR	Ed Washington	Ohio U
WR	Dave Naumcheff	Ball State
C	Rick Chitwood	Ball State
G	Chris McKay	Central Michigan
G	John Berlan	Toledo
T	Scott Bolzan	Northern Illinois
T	Brian Vehar	Toledo
TE	Mark Dowdell	Bowling Green
PK	Vince Scott	Northern Illinois

POS	Defense	School
L	Pat Brackett	Central Michigan
LB	Jeff Offerdahl	Western Michigan
LB	Brian Pillman	Miami (Ohio)
LB	Mark Emans	Bowling Green
LB	Kevin Egnatuk	Central Michigan
DE	Mike Russell	Toledo
DT	Mike Mills	Central Michigan
DB	Mark Brandon	Toledo
DB	Martin Bayless	Bowling Green
DB	Jim Bowman	Central Michigan
DB	Jeff Sanders	Northern Illinois
P	Jim Phelps	Bowling Green

Individual

ALL-PURPOSE

		CL	G	RUSH	REC	PR	KR	YDS	YPG
3	Shawn Faulkner, Western Michigan	SR	11	1,668	221	0	0	1,889	171.7
4	Curtis Adams, Central Michigan	JR	11	1,431	86	0	234	1,751	159.2

RUSHING/YARDS PER GAME

		CL	G	ATT	YDS	TD	AVG	YPG
2	Shawn Faulkner, Western Michigan	SR	11	394	1668	7	4.2	151.6
4	Curtis Adams, Central Michigan	JR	11	267	1431	15	5.4	130.1

RECEIVING

		CL	G	REC	YDS	TD	YPR	YPG	RPG
4	Mark Dowdell, Bowling Green	JR	11	70	679	5	9.7	61.7	6.4
6	Ed Washington, Ohio U	SR	11	68	866	5	12.7	78.8	6.2
7	Mike Leuck, Ball State	JR	11	67	667	4	10.0	60.6	6.1
10	Dave Naumcheff, Ball State	SR	11	65	1065	6	16.4	96.8	5.9

PUNTING

		CL	PUNT	YDS	AVG
4	Kip Shenefelt, Temple*	SO	65	2860	44.0

KICKOFF RETURNS

		CL	KR	YDS	TD	AVG
7	Eddie Harris, Toledo	SO	11	290	0	26.4
10	Terrell Smith, Ball State	JR	22	519	0	23.6

SCORING

		CL	TD	XPT	FG	PTS	PTPG
7	Curtis Adams, Central Michigan	JR	16	0	0	96	8.7

INTERCEPTIONS

		CL	INT	YDS	TD	INT/GM
1	Martin Bayless, Bowling Green	SR	10	64	0	0.91
2	Mark Brandon, Toledo	JR	9	66	1	0.82
3	Jim Bowman, Central Michigan	JR	8	87	1	0.73
7	Kevin Young, Ball State	JR	7	72	0	0.64

Team

RUSHING OFFENSE

		G	ATT	YDS	AVG	TD	YPG
6	Central Michigan	11	591	3048	5.2	24	277.1

PASSING OFFENSE

		G	ATT	COM	INT	PCT	YDS	YPA	TD	I%	YPC	YPG
2	Bowling Green	11	480	305	17	63.5	3320	6.9	16	3.5	10.9	301.8

RUSHING DEFENSE

		G	ATT	YDS	AVG	TD	YPG
10	Toledo	11	437	1142	2.6	10	103.8

PASSING DEFENSE

		G	ATT	COM	PCT	YPC	INT	I%	YDS	YPA	TD	YPG
1	Ohio U	11	221	112	50.7	11.3	7	3.2	1268	5.7	5	115.3
9	Eastern Michigan	11	238	138	58.0	11.6	9	3.8	1603	6.7	10	145.7

SCORING DEFENSE

		G	PTS	AVG
6	Central Michigan	11	136	12.4

1984

Conference Standings

	Conference			Overall		
	W	L	T	W	L	T
Toledo	7	1	1	8	3	1
Bowling Green	7	2	0	8	3	0
Central Michigan	6	2	1	8	2	1
Ohio U	4	4	1	4	6	1
Northern Illinois	3	5	1	4	6	1
Miami (Ohio)	3	5	0	4	7	0
Ball State	3	5	0	3	8	0
Western Michigan	3	6	0	5	6	0
Kent State	3	6	0	4	7	0
Eastern Michigan	2	5	2	2	7	2
Temple*				6	5	0

Bowl Games

DATE	GAME	SCORE
D15	**California**	Nevada-Las Vegas 30, Toledo 13

All-Conference Team

POS	**Offense**	**School**
QB	Brian McClure	Bowling Green
RB	Bernard White	Bowling Green
RB	Curtis Adams	Central Michigan
RB	Steve Morgan	Toledo
WR	Stan Hunter	Bowling Green
WR	John DeBoer	Central Michigan
C	Brian Johnson	Bowling Green
G	Todd Peat	Northern Illinois
G	John Berlan	Toledo
T	Brian Vehar	Toledo
T	Tom Toth	Western Michigan
TE	Mark Dowdell	Bowling Green
PK	Mike Prindle	Western Michigan

POS	**Defense**	**School**
DT	Pat Brackett	Central Michigan
DT	Scott Kellar	Northern Illinois
LB	John Offerdahl	Western Michigan
LB	Mike Bevier	Central Michigan
DB	Melvin Marshall	Bowling Green
DB	Jim Bowman	Central Michigan
DB	Derrick Samuels	Kent State
DB	Mark Brandon	Toledo
DE	Steve Hoyt	Toledo
DE	Steve Sklenar	Central Michigan
P	Todd Van Keppel	Northern Illinois

NCAA Statistical Leaders

Individual Leaders

PASSING		CL	G	ATT	COM	PCT	INT	I%	YDS	YPA	TD	TD%	RAT
9	Bob DeMarco, CMU	SR	11	173	98	56.7	4	2.3	1427	8.3	12	6.9	144.2

ALL-PURPOSE		CL	G	RUSH	REC	PR	KR	YDS	YPG
6	George Swarn, Miami (Ohio)	SO	11	1,282	187	0	147	1,616	146.9
9	Curtis Adams, Central Michigan	SR	10	1,204	55	0	168	1,427	142.7

RUSHING/YARDS PER GAME		CL	G	ATT	YDS	TD	AVG	YPG
4	Curtis Adams, Central Michigan	SR	10	222	1204	13	5.4	120.4
6	George Swarn, Miami (Ohio)	SO	11	269	1282	5	4.8	116.5

RUSHING/YARDS PER CARRY		CL	G	ATT	YDS	YPC
7	Curtis Adams, Central Michigan	SR	10	222	1204	5.4
	Based on top 23 rushers					

RECEIVING		CL	G	REC	YDS	TD	YPR	YPG	RPG
10	Bernard White, Bowling Green	JR	11	56	400	0	7.1	36.4	5.1

FIELD GOALS		CL	FGA	FGM	PCT	FG/GM
2	Mike Prindle, Western Michigan	SR	30	24	0.80	2.18

Team

PASSING OFFENSE		G	ATT	COM	INT	PCT	YDS	YPA	TD	I%	YPC	YPG
8	Bowling Green	11	416	265	13	63.7	2960	7.1	21	3.1	11.2	269.1

RUSHING DEFENSE		G	ATT	YDS	AVG	TD	YPG
7	Central Michigan	11	424	1102	2.6	5	100.2
9	Toledo	11	411	1181	2.9	6	107.4

TOTAL DEFENSE		G	P	YDS	AVG	TD	YPG
4	Central Michigan	11	746	2899	3.9	14	263.5
5	Toledo	11	745	2908	3.9	12	264.4

SCORING DEFENSE		G	PTS	AVG
4	Toledo	11	134	12.2
8	Central Michigan	11	141	12.8

*Independent or other conference affiliation

1985

CONFERENCE STANDINGS

	Conference			Overall		
	W	L	T	W	L	T
Bowling Green	9	0	0	11	1	0
Miami (Ohio)	7	1	1	8	2	1
Central Michigan	6	3	0	7	3	0
Western Michigan	4	4	1	4	6	1
Northern Illinois	4	4	0	4	7	0
Toledo	3	6	0	4	7	0
Eastern Michigan	3	6	0	4	7	0
Ball State	3	6	0	4	7	0
Kent State	2	6	0	3	8	0
Ohio U	2	7	0	2	9	0
Temple*				4	7	0

BOWL GAMES

DATE	GAME	SCORE
D14	**California**	Fresno State 51, Bowling Green 7

CONSENSUS ALL-AMERICANS

POS	Offense	HT	WT	School	AP	CF	FC	FW	PI
L	John Rienstra	6-4	280	Temple*	•			•	

HEISMAN TROPHY VOTING

	Player	POS	School	1ST	2ND	3RD	TOTAL
10	Brian McClure	QB	Bowling Green	7	10	13	54

ALL-CONFERENCE TEAM

POS	Offense	School
QB	Brian McClure	Bowling Green
RB	Bernard White	Bowling Green
RB	George Swarn	Miami (Ohio)
RB	Jesse Owens	Ohio U
WR	Jim Kilbane	Kent State
WR	Stan Hunter	Bowling Green
G	Rick Poljan	Central Michigan
G	Mike Estep	Bowling Green
G	Todd Peat	Northern Illinois
C	Craig Kantner	Ball State
T	Dal Dalrymple	Miami (Ohio)
TE	Glen Hirschfeld	Miami (Ohio)
PK	John Diettrich	Ball State

POS	Defense	School
LB	Tim Inglis	Toledo
LB	John Offerdahl	Western Michigan
DE	Steve Sklenar	Central Michigan
DT	Doug Bartlett	Northern Illinois
DT	Lee Bullington	Kent State
DT	Brent Williams	Toledo
DT	Mark Garalczyk	Western Michigan
DB	Melvin Marshall	Bowling Green
DB	Carl Kloosterman	Central Michigan
DB	Harold McGuire	Toledo
DB	Ken Luckett	Western Michigan
DE	Bob Beemer	Toledo
P	Greg A. Johnson	Bowling Green

INDIVIDUAL

	ALL-PURPOSE	CL	G	RUSH	REC	PR	KR	YDS	YPG
2	Paul Palmer, Temple*	JR	9	1,516	131	0	96	1,743	193.7
3	George Swarn, Miami (Ohio)	JR	11	1,511	424	0	17	1,952	177.5

	RUSHING/YARDS PER GAME	CL	G	ATT	YDS	TD	AVG	YPG
2	Paul Palmer, Temple*	JR	9	279	1516	9	5.4	168.4

	RUSHING/YARDS PER CARRY	CL	G	ATT	YDS	YPC
8	Paul Palmer, Temple*	JR	9	279	1516	5.4
	Based on top 23 rushers					

	SCORING	CL	TD	XPT	FG	PTS	PTPG
1	Bernard White, Bowling Green	SR	19	0	0	114	10.4
9	George Swarn, Miami (Ohio)	JR	16	0	0	96	8.7

	FIELD GOALS	CL	FGA	FGM	PCT	FGG
1	John Diettrich, Ball State	SR	29	25	0.86	2.27
9	Gary Gussman, Miami (Ohio)	SO	26	18	0.69	1.64

TEAM

	PASSING DEFENSE	G	ATT	COM	PCT	YPC	INT	I%	YDS	YPA	TD	YPG
7	Central Michigan	10	233	128	54.9	10.8	14	6.0	1,377	5.9	2	137.7
8	Western Michigan	11	263	141	53.6	10.8	15	5.7	1,520	5.8	7	138.2
9	Toledo	11	301	144	47.8	10.6	17	5.6	1,523	5.1	6	138.5

	TOTAL DEFENSE		G	P	YDS	AVG	TD	YPG
3	Toledo		11	763	2,880	3.8	17	261.8
4	Central Michigan		10	672	2,658	4.0	16	265.8

	SCORING OFFENSE		G	PTS	AVG
10	Bowling Green		11	348	31.6

1986

CONFERENCE STANDINGS

	Conference			Overall		
	W	L	T	W	L	T
Miami (Ohio)	6	2	0	8	4	0
Toledo	5	3	0	7	4	0
Kent State	5	3	0	5	6	0
Bowling Green	5	3	0	5	6	0
Eastern Michigan	4	4	0	6	5	0
Ball State	4	4	0	6	5	0
Central Michigan	4	4	0	5	5	0
Western Michigan	3	5	0	3	8	0
Ohio U	0	8	0	1	10	0
Temple*				6	5	0
Northern Illinois*				2	9	0

BOWL GAMES

DATE	GAME	SCORE
D13	California	San Jose State 37, Miami (Ohio) 7

CONSENSUS ALL-AMERICANS

POS	Offense	HT	WT	School	AP	CF	FC	FW	PI
RB	Paul Palmer*	5-10	180	Temple	•	•	•	•	•

ALL-CONFERENCE TEAM

POS	Offense	School
QB	Terry Morris	Miami (Ohio)
TB	Kelvin Farmer	Toledo
TB	Gary Patton	Eastern Michigan
TB	Rodney Stevenson	Central Michigan
WR	Ricky George	Ball State
WR	Andy Schillinger	Miami (Ohio)
C	Brett Petersmark	Eastern Michigan
G	Mike Estep	Bowling Green
G	Rick Poljan	Central Michigan
T	Brian Williams	Central Michigan
T	Dan Dalrymple	Miami (Ohio)
TE	Ron Duncan	Ball State
PK	John Diettrich	Ball State

POS	Defense	School
LB	Steve Huffman	Toledo
LB	Tim Walton	Ball State
LB	Paul Schweitzer	Bowling Green
OLB	John Hunter	Bowling Green
OLB	Dave Brown	Miami (Ohio)
DT	Andy Marlatt	Miami (Ohio)
DT	Greg Johnson	Bowling Green
DT	Troy Schultz	Ball State
DT	Mark Garalczyk	Western Michigan
DB	Harold McGuire	Toledo
DB	Sheldon White	Miami (Ohio)
DB	Stuart Sims	Kent State
DB	Mike Skiver	Eastern Michigan
P	Greg A. Johnson	Bowling Green

HEISMAN TROPHY VOTING

PLAYER	POS	SCHOOL	1ST	2ND	3RD	TOTAL
2 Paul Palmer*	TB	Temple	28	207	174	672

NCAA STATISTICAL LEADERS

INDIVIDUAL

PASSING	CL	G	ATT	COM	PCT	INT	I%	YDS	YPA	TD	TD%	RAT
8 Lee Saltz, Temple*	SR	11	203	117	57.6	7	3.5	1,727	8.5	12	5.9	141.7

ALL-PURPOSE	CL	G	RUSH	REC	PR	KR	YDS	YPG
1 Paul Palmer, Temple*	SR	11	1,866	110	0	657	2,633	239.4
5 Gary Patton, Eastern Michigan	JR	11	1,058	371	0	384	1,813	164.8
8 Kelvin Farmer, Toledo	SR	11	1,532	203	0	0	1,735	157.7

RUSHING/YARDS PER GAME	CL	G	ATT	YDS	TD	AVG	YPG
1 Paul Palmer, Temple*	SR	11	346	1,866	15	5.4	169.6
2 Kelvin Farmer, Toledo	SR	11	299	1,532	16	5.1	139.3
6 Rodney Stevenson, Central Michigan	SO	9	208	1,104	14	5.3	122.7

RUSHING/YARDS PER CARRY	CL	G	ATT	YDS	YPC
10 Paul Palmer, Temple*	SR	11	346	1,866	5.4

KICKOFF RETURNS	CL	KR	YDS	TD	AVG
7 Chris Thomas, Miami (Ohio)	JR	17	441	1	25.9

SCORING	CL	TDS	XP	FG	PTS	PTPG
2 Rodney Stevenson, Central Michigan	SO	14	0	0	84	9.3
6 Kelvin Farmer, Toledo	SR	16	0	0	96	8.7

FIELD GOALS	CL	FGA	FGM	PCT	FGG
8 John Diettrich, Ball State	SR	23	17	0.74	1.55

INTERCEPTIONS	CL	INT	YDS	TD	INT/GM
6 Chris Wagner, Western Michigan	FR	7	17	0	0.64

TEAM

RUSHING OFFENSE	G	ATT	YDS	AVG	TD	YPG
4 Central Michigan	10	591	2,798	4.7	26	279.8

PASSING DEFENSE	G	ATT	COM	PCT	YPC	INT	I%	YDS	YPA	TD	YPG
3 Bowling Green	11	221	109	49.3	11.5	20	9.0	1,257	5.7	4	114.3
7 Toledo	11	263	146	55.5	10.0	16	6.1	1,464	5.6	8	133.1

1987

CONFERENCE STANDINGS

	Conference			Overall		
	W	L	T	W	L	T
Eastern Michigan	7	1	0	10	2	0
Kent State	5	3	0	7	4	0
Miami (Ohio)	5	3	0	5	6	0
Bowling Green	5	3	0	5	6	0
Western Michigan	4	4	0	5	6	0
Central Michigan	3	4	1	5	5	1
Toledo	3	4	1	3	7	1
Ball State	3	5	0	4	7	0
Ohio U	0	8	0	1	10	0
Northern Illinois*				5	5	1
Temple*				3	8	0

BOWL GAMES

DATE	GAME	SCORE
D12	California	Eastern Michigan 30, San Jose State 27

*Independent or other conference affiliation

1988

ALL-CONFERENCE TEAM

POS	Offense	School
QB	Ron Adams	Eastern Michigan
TB	John Hood	Central Michigan
TB	Eric Wilkerson	Kent State
WR	Eric Dye	Kent State
WR	Jamie Hence	Western Michigan
TB	Gary Patton	Eastern Michigan
C	Craig Kantner	Ball State
C	Chip Curtis	Kent State
G	Brian Clouse	Eastern Michigan
T	Joe Churches	Central Michigan
T	Ken Moyer	Toledo
TE	Ron Duncan	Ball State
PK	Gary Gussman	Miami (Ohio)

POS	Defense	School
T	Andy Marlatt	Miami (Ohio)
T	Paul Sandor	Toledo
LB	Chris Wise	Central Michigan
LB	Pete Mather	Miami (Ohio)
OLB	John Hunter	Bowling Green
OLB	Phil Zielinski	Central Michigan
DE	Joel Smeenge	Western Michigan
DE	Joe Foley	Bowling Green
DB	Kyle Kramer	Bowling Green
DB	Howard Young	Central Michigan
DB	Charles Gordon	Eastern ichigan
DB	Sheldon White	Miami (Ohio)

NCAA STATISTICAL LEADERS

INDIVIDUAL

ALL-PURPOSE

	CL	G	RUSH	REC	PR	KR	YDS	YPG
1 Eric Wilkerson, Kent State	JR	11	1221	269	0	584	2,074	188.6

PUNT RETURNS

	CL	PR	YDS	TD	AVG
10 Rodney Taylor, Northern Illinois*	JR	23	282	1	12.3

KICKOFF RETURNS

	CL	KR	YDS	TD	AVG
8 John Hood, Central Michigan	SO	19	489	1	25.7

SCORING

	CL	TDS	XP	FG	PTS	PTPG
8 Bernie Parmalee, Ball State	FR	15	0	0	90	9.0

FIELD GOALS

	CL	FGA	FGM	PCT	FGG
3 Gary Gussman, Miami (Ohio)	SR	25	20	.80	1.82
8 John Ivanic, Northern Illinois*	FR	24	18	.75	1.64

TEAM

RUSHING OFFENSE

	G	ATT	YDS	AVG	TD	YPG
6 Northern Illinois*	11	701	3,246	4.6	31	295.1

CONFERENCE STANDINGS

	CONFERENCE			OVERALL		
	W	L	T	W	L	T
Western Michigan	7	1	0	9	3	0
Eastern Michigan	5	2	1	6	3	1
Ball State	5	3	0	8	3	0
Central Michigan	5	3	0	7	4	0
Ohio U	4	3	1	4	6	1
Toledo	4	4	0	6	5	0
Kent State	3	5	0	5	6	0
Bowling Green	1	6	1	2	8	1
Miami (Ohio)	0	7	1	0	10	1
Northern Illinois*				7	4	0
Temple*				4	7	0

BOWL GAMES

DATE	GAME	SCORE
D10	California	Fresno State 35, Western Michigan 30

ALL-CONFERENCE TEAM

POS	Offense	School
QB	Tony Kimbrough	Western Michigan
RB	Bernie Parmalee	Ball State
RB	Don Riley	Central Michigan
TB	Eric Wilkerson	Kent State
WR	Reggie Thornton	Bowling Green
WR	Robert Oliver	Western Michigan
C	Chip Curtis	Kent State
G	Chuck Pellegrini	Central Michigan
G	George Linberger	Toledo
G	Todd Olson	Toledo
T	Ken Moyer	Toledo
T	Kevin Haverdink	Western Michigan
TE	Eugen Riley	Ball State
PK	Bruce Nichols	Toledo

POS	Defense	School
NG	Mose Carter	Ball State
L	Scott Alferink	Central Michigan
L	Bert Weidner	Kent State
DE	Joel Smeenge	Western Michigan
LB	Eric Hoffman	Western Michigan
OLB	Mike McCreary	Toledo
OLB	Mark Dennis	Central Michigan
DB	Willie Berrios	Western Michigan
DB	Jamie Howell	Kent State
DB	Tom Menard	Eastern Michigan
DB	Kyle Kramer	Bowling Green
P	Chuck Konrad	Miami (Ohio)

NCAA Statistical Leaders

1989

Individual

ALL-PURPOSE

		CL	G	RUSH	REC	PR	KR	YDS	YPG
3	Eric Wilkerson, Kent State	SR	11	1,325	73	0	502	1,900	172.7
7	Andrew Greer, Ohio U	JR	11	863	114	0	810	1,787	162.5

RUSHING/YARDS PER GAME

		CL	G	ATT	YDS	TD	AVG	YPG
8	Eric Wilkerson, Kent State	SR	11	247	1,325	14	5.4	120.5
10	Don Riley, Central Michigan	JR	11	215	1,238	7	5.8	112.6

RUSHING/YARDS PER CARRY

		CL	G	ATT	YDS	YPC
7	Don Riley, Central Michigan	JR	11	215	1,238	5.8
	Based on top 23 rushers					

PUNTING

		CL	PUNT	YDS	AVG
6	Bill Rudison, Akron*	JR	58	2,511	43.3

PUNT RETURNS

		CL	PR	YDS	TD	AVG
9	Larry Hargrove, Ohio U	JR	21	253	1	12.1

FIELD GOALS

		CL	FGA	FGM	PCT	FGG
9	Kenny Stucker, Ball State	FR	23	18	.78	1.64

INTERCEPTIONS

		CL	INT	YDS	TD	INT/GM
1	Andy Logan, Kent State	SR	8	54	0	0.73
4	Tony McCorvey, Bowling Green	SR	7	33	0	0.64
8	David Johnson, Central Michigan+	SO	6	56	0	0.55

+Nine tied with 0.55

Team

RUSHING OFFENSE

		G	ATT	YDS	AVG	TD	YPG
8	Kent State	11	624	3,073	4.9	28	279.4

PASSING OFFENSE

		G	ATT	COM	INT	PCT	YDS	YPA	TD	I%	YPC	YPG
10	Western Michigan	11	397	221	18	55.7	2,863	7.2	22	4.5	13.0	260.3

RUSHING DEFENSE

		G	ATT	YDS	AVG	TD	YPG
7	Central Michigan	11	441	1,165	2.6	10	105.9

PASSING DEFENSE

		G	ATT	COM	PCT	YPC	INT	I%	YDS	YPA	TD	YPG
9	Eastern Michigan	10	212	124	58.5	11.3	11	5.2	1,395	6.6	7	139.5

TOTAL DEFENSE

		G	P	YDS	AVG	TD	YPG
6	Ball State	11	664	2,887	4.3	18	262.5

Conference Standings

	Conference			Overall		
	W	L	T	W	L	T
Ball State	6	1	1	7	3	2
Eastern Michigan	6	2	0	7	3	1
Toledo	6	2	0	6	5	0
Central Michigan	5	2	1	5	5	1
Bowling Green	5	3	0	5	6	0
Western Michigan	3	5	0	5	6	0
Miami (Ohio)	2	5	1	2	8	1
Ohio U.	1	6	1	1	9	1
Kent State	0	8	0	0	11	0
Northern Illinois*				9	2	0
Temple*				1	10	0

Bowl Games

DATE	GAME	SCORE
D9	California	Fresno State 27, Ball State 6

All-Conference Team

POS	Offense	School
QB	David Riley	Ball State
RB	Perry Foster	Eastern Michigan
RB	Donnie Riley	Central Michigan
RB	Andrew Greer	Ohio U
WR	Rick Isaiah	Toledo
WR	Ron Heard	Bowling Green
C	Ralph Newland	Central Michigan
G	Todd Wright	Ball State
T	Steve Brockelbank	Eastern Michigan
T	Craig Kuligowski	Toledo
TE	Eugene Riley	Ball State
PK	Kevin Nicholl	Central Michigan

POS	Defense	School
L	Ralph Wize	Ball State
L	J.J. Wierenga	Central Michigan
L	Doug Spidel	Toledo
DE	Joel Smeenge	Western Michigan
LB	Greg Garnica	Ball State
LB	Bill Garrett	Ohio U
OLB	Mark Dennis	Central Michigan
OLB	Ronald Tatum	Toledo
DB	David Haugh	Ball State
DB	David Johnson	Central Michigan
DB	Bob Navarro	Eastern Michigan
DB	Larry Hargrove	Ohio U
P	Cris Shale	Bowling Green

*Independent or other conference affiliation

NCAA Statistical Leaders

1990

Individual

ALL-PURPOSE

	CL	G	RUSH	REC	PR	KR	YDS	YPG
8 Andrew Greer, Ohio U	SR	11	903	227	0	598	1,728	157.1

RUSHING/Yards Per Game

	CL	G	ATT	YDS	TD	AVG	YPG
6 Stacey Robinson, Northern Illinois*	JR	11	223	1,443	19	6.5	131.2

RUSHING/Yards Per Carry

	CL	G	ATT	YDS	YPC
3 Stacey Robinson, Northern Illinois*	JR	11	223	1,443	6.5
Based on top 23 rushers					

PUNT RETURNS

	CL	PR	YDS	TD	AVG
1 Larry Hargrove, Ohio U	SR	17	309	2	18.2
2 Herb Jackson, Ball State	JR	16	262	0	16.4

KICKOFF RETURNS

	CL	KR	YDS	TD	AVG
8 Raymond Patterson, Northern Illinois*	FR	15	390	0	26.0

SCORING

	CL	TDS	XP	FG	PTS	PTPG
9 Stacey Robinson, Northern Illinois*	JR	19	0	0	114	10.4

FIELD GOALS

	CL	FGA	FGM	PCT	FGG
6 Kevin Nicholl, Central Michigan	SR	24	20	.83	1.82

INTERCEPTIONS

	CL	INT	YDS	TD	INT/GM
1 Bob Navarro, Eastern Michigan	JR	12	73	0	1.09

Team

RUSHING OFFENSE

	G	ATT	YDS	AVG	TD	YPG
6 Northern Illinois*	11	680	3,638	5.3	40	330.7

TOTAL DEFENSE

	G	P	YDS	AVG	TD	YPG
7 Eastern Michigan	11	740	3,014	4.1	20	274.0

Conference Standings

	CONFERENCE			OVERALL		
	W	L	T	W	L	T
Toledo	7	1	0	9	2	0
Central Michigan	7	1	0	8	3	1
Western Michigan	5	3	0	7	4	0
Ball State	5	3	0	7	4	0
Miami (Ohio)	4	3	1	5	5	1
Bowling Green	2	4	2	3	5	2
Kent State	2	6	0	2	9	0
Eastern Michigan	2	6	0	2	9	0
Ohio U	0	7	1	1	9	1
Temple*				7	4	0
Northern Illinois*				6	5	0
Akron*				3	7	1

Bowl Games

DATE	GAME	SCORE
D8	California	San Jose State 48, Central Michigan 24

Consensus All-Americans

POS	Defense	HT	WT	School	AP	CF	FC	FW	PI
None									

OTHERS RECEIVING FIRST-TEAM HONORS
P	Cris Shale	Bowling Green	•

All-Conference Team

POS	Offense	School
QB	Jeff Bender	Central Michigan
RB	Corey Sylve	Western Michigan
RB	Bernie Parmalee	Ball State
WR	Ken Ealy	Central Michigan
C	Andy Billman	Miami (Ohio)
G	Paul Jacobson	Central Michigan
G	Todd Wright	Ball State
T	Craig Kuligowski	Toledo
T	Scott Thomas	Western Michigan
TE	Jerry Evans	Toledo
PK	Kenny Stucker	Ball State

POS	Defense	School
L	Mark Ross	Bowling Green
L	J.J. Wierenga	Central Michigan
L	Andy Harmon	Kent State
L	Jon Wauford	Miami (Ohio)
LB	Toby Beegle	Ball State
LB	Rich Curtiss	Central Michigan
LB	Sean Mulhearn	Western Michigan
OLB	Matt Eberflus	Toledo
DB	Terry Wilson	Bowling Green
DB	Ken Strong	Central Michigan
DB	David Johnson	Central Michigan
DB	Ron Carpenter	Miami (Ohio)
P	Cris Shale	Bowling Green

NCAA STATISTICAL LEADERS

1991

INDIVIDUAL

RUSHING/YARDS PER GAME

		CL	G	ATT	YDS	TD	AVG	YPG
10	Stacey Robinson, Northern Illinois*	SR	11	193	1,238	19	6.4	112.6

RUSHING/YARDS PER CARRY

		CL	G	ATT	YDS	YPC
3	Stacey Robinson, Northern Illinois*	SR	11	193	1,238	6.4
	Based on top 22 rushers					

PUNTING

		CL	PUNT	YDS	AVG
1	Cris Shale, Bowling Green	SR	66	3,087	46.8
9	Todd Rawsthorne, Western Michigan	JR	35	1,502	42.9
10	Trent Thompson, Temple*	JR	42	1,795	42.7

KICKOFF RETURNS

		CL	KR	YDS	TD	AVG
7	Milt Stegall, Miami (Ohio)	JR	18	497	1	27.6

SCORING

		CL	TDS	XP	FG	PTS	PTPG
1	Stacey Robinson, Northern Illinois*	SR	19	6	0	120	10.9

FIELD GOALS

		CL	FGA	FGM	PCT	FGG
4	Bob Wright, Temple*	SR	25	19	.76	1.73
9	Rusty Hanna, Toledo	SO	29	18	.62	1.64

INTERCEPTIONS

		CL	INT	YDS	TD	INT/GM
3	Shawn Vincent, Akron*	SR	7	191	0	0.64
3	Ron Carpenter, Miami (Ohio)	JR	7	164	1	0.64
3	Ozzie Jackson, Akron*	SR	7	50	0	0.64
9	Dave Bielinski, Bowling Green	SO	6	63	0	0.60

TEAM

RUSHING OFFENSE

		G	ATT	YDS	AVG	TD	YPG
1	Northern Illinois*	11	619	3,791	6.1	36	344.6

RUSHING DEFENSE

		G	ATT	YDS	AVG	TD	YPG
9	Central Michigan	11	392	1,097	2.8	2	99.7
10	Ball State	11	461	1,120	2.4	8	101.8

PASSING DEFENSE

		G	ATT	COM	PCT	INT	I%	YDS	YPA	TD	TD%	RAT
2	Central Michigan	11	289	129	44.6	15	5.2	1,462	5.1	6	2.1	83.6
3	Ball State	11	247	116	47.0	17	6.9	1,329	5.4	4	1.6	83.7
4	Miami (Ohio)	11	244	106	43.4	15	6.2	1,327	5.4	8	3.3	87.7

TOTAL DEFENSE

		G	P	YDS	AVG	TD	YPG
2	Ball State	11	708	2,449	3.5	12	222.6
4	Central Michigan	11	681	2,559	3.8	8	232.6
9	Miami (Ohio)	11	765	3,036	4.0	26	276.0

SCORING DEFENSE

		G	PTS	AVG
1	Central Michigan	11	98	8.9
3	Ball State	11	121	11.0

CONFERENCE STANDINGS

	CONFERENCE			OVERALL		
	W	L	T	W	L	T
Bowling Green	8	0	0	11	1	0
Central Michigan	3	1	4	6	1	4
Miami (Ohio)	4	3	1	6	4	1
Toledo	4	3	1	5	5	1
Ball State	4	4	0	6	5	0
Western Michigan	4	4	0	6	5	0
Eastern Michigan	3	4	1	3	7	1
Ohio U	1	6	1	2	8	1
Kent State	1	7	0	1	10	0
Akron*				5	6	0
Temple*				2	9	0
Northern Illinois*				2	9	0

BOWL GAMES

DATE	GAME	SCORE
D14	California	Bowling Green 28, Fresno State 21

ALL-CONFERENCE TEAM

POS	Offense	School
QB	Erik White	Bowling Green
RB	Billy Smith	Central Michigan
RB	Tim Curtis	Ohio U
WR	Marcus Goodwin	Toledo
C	Albert Thigpen	Toledo
G	Bobby Pandelidis	Eastern Michigan
G	Andy McCollum	Toledo
T	Paul Hutchins	Western Michigan
T	James Wyatt	Central Michigan
PK	Kenny Stucker	Ball State

POS	Defense	School
L	Mike Nettie	Central Michigan
L	Jon Wauford	Miami (Ohio)
L	Dan Williams	Toledo
L	Henry Hall	Ball State
LB	Mark Parris	Ball State
LB	Curt McMillan	Miami (Ohio)
OLB	Matt Eberflus	Toledo
DB	Richard Palmer	Eastern Michigan
DB	Ron Carpenter	Miami (Ohio)
DB	Darren Anderson	Toledo
P	Damon Keller	Ball State

NCAA STATISTICAL LEADERS

INDIVIDUAL

RUSHING/YARDS PER GAME

		CL	G	ATT	YDS	TD	AVG	YPG
8	Billy Smith, Central Michigan	SR	11	374	1,440	6	3.9	130.9

KICKOFF RETURNS

		CL	KR	YDS	TD	AVG
2	Ronald Rice, Eastern Michigan	FR	11	319	0	29.0

INTERCEPTIONS

		CL	INT	YDS	TD	INT/GM
6	Richard Palmer, Eastern Michigan	SO	7	219	1	0.64
6	Ron Carpenter, Miami (Ohio)	JR	7	197	1	0.64

TEAM

TOTAL DEFENSE

		G	P	YDS	AVG	TD	YPG
5	Miami (Ohio)	11	747	2,980	4.0	15	270.9
7	Central Michigan	11	741	3,001	4.0	16	272.8

SCORING DEFENSE

		G	PTS	AVG
5	Miami (Ohio)	11	140	12.7
9	Bowling Green	11	147	13.4

*Independent or other conference affiliation

1992

CONFERENCE STANDINGS

	CONFERENCE			OVERALL		
	W	L	T	W	L	T
Bowling Green	8	0	0	10	2	0
Western Michigan	6	3	0	7	3	1
Toledo	5	3	0	8	3	0
Akron	5	3	0	7	3	1
Miami (Ohio)	5	3	0	6	4	1
Ball State	5	4	0	5	6	0
Central Michigan	4	5	0	5	6	0
Kent State	2	7	0	2	9	0
Ohio U	1	7	0	1	10	0
Eastern Michigan	1	7	0	1	10	0
Northern Illinois*				5	6	0
Temple*				1	10	0

BOWL GAMES

DATE	GAME	SCORE
D18	Las Vegas	Bowling Green 35, Nevada 34

ALL-CONFERENCE TEAM

POS	Offense	School
QB	Erik White	Bowling Green
RB	Corey Croom	Ball State
RB	Tim Curtis	Ohio U
RB	Casey McBeth	Toledo
RB	Henry Hall	Ball State
WR	Mark Szlachcic	Bowling Green
WR	Marcus Goodwin	Toledo
C	Art Droski	Central Michigan
G	Marty Malcolm	Central Michigan
G	Andy McCollum	Toledo
T	Joe Wyse	Bowling Green
T	Paul Hutchins	Western Michigan
TE	James Patton	Miami (Ohio)

POS	Defense	School
L	Mike Nettie	Central Michigan
L	Jason Carthen	Ohio U
L	Maurice Bulls	Toledo
L	Dan Williams	Toledo
LB	Kevin O'Brein	Bowling Green
LB	Artie Mangham	Bowling Green
LB	Curt McMillan	Miami (Ohio)
DB	Joe Bair	Bowling Green
DB	Richard Palmer	Eastern Michigan
DB	Ron Carpenter	Miami (Ohio)
DB	Mark Ricks	Western Michigan
DB	Vic Green	Akron
P	Daron Alcorn	Akron

INDIVIDUAL

PASSING

		CL	G	ATT	COM	PCT	INT	I%	YDS	YPA	TD	TD%	RAT
9	Joe Youngblood, CMU	JR	11	278	161	57.9	13	4.7	2,209	8.0	18	6.5	136.7

RUSHING/YARDS PER GAME

		CL	G	ATT	YDS	TD	AVG	YPG
8	LeShon Johnson, Northern Illinois*	JR	11	265	1,338	6	5.0	121.6
10	Deland McCullough, Miami (Ohio)	FR	9	227	1,026	6	4.5	114.0

PUNT RETURNS

		CL	PR	YDS	TD	AVG
8	Marc Baxter, Temple*	FR	12	167	0	13.9

KICKOFF RETURNS

		CL	KR	YDS	TD	AVG
3	Lew Lawhorn, Temple*	SO	20	600	2	30.0
6	Craig Thompson, Eastern Michigan	JR	18	490	1	27.2
9	Courtney Burton, Ohio U	JR	21	545	1	26.0

SCORING

		CL	TDS	XP	FG	PTS	PTPG
10	Rusty Hanna, Toledo	SR	0	26	21	89	8.1

FIELD GOALS

		CL	FGA	FGM	PCT	FGG
5	Rusty Hanna, Toledo	SR	29	21	.72	1.90
9	Daron Alcorn, Akron*	SR	26	18	.69	1.60

INTERCEPTIONS

		CL	INT	YDS	TD	INT/GM
2	Joe Bair, Bowling Green	JR	7	51	0	0.64
2	Chris Owens, Akron*	SR	7	49	0	0.64

TEAM

RUSHING DEFENSE

		G	ATT	YDS	AVG	TD	YPG
10	Toledo	11	466	1,248	2.7	8	113.5

PASSING DEFENSE

		G	ATT	COM	PCT	INT	I%	YDS	YPA	TD	TD%	RAT
1	Western Michigan	11	283	121	42.8	15	5.3	1,522	5.4	5	1.8	83.2
9	Toledo	11	325	148	45.5	13	4.0	1,880	5.8	7	2.2	93.2

SCORING DEFENSE

		G	PTS	AVG
8	Toledo	11	153	13.9

TURNOVER MARGIN

		G	FR	INT	TOT	FL	INTL	TOT	MAR
2	Akron*	11	10	24	34	7	11	18	1.5

1993

CONFERENCE STANDINGS

	Conference			Overall		
	W	L	T	W	L	T
Ball State	7	0	1	8	3	1
Western Michigan	6	1	1	7	3	1
Bowling Green	5	1	2	6	3	2
Central Michigan	5	4	0	5	6	0
Akron	4	4	0	5	6	0
Ohio U	4	5	0	4	7	0
Eastern Michigan	3	5	0	4	7	0
Toledo	3	5	0	4	7	0
Miami (Ohio)	3	6	0	4	7	0
Kent State	0	9	0	0	11	0
Northern Illinois*				4	7	0
Temple*				1	10	0

BOWL GAMES

DATE	GAME	SCORE
D17	**Las Vegas**	Utah State 42, Ball State 33

CONSENSUS ALL-AMERICANS

POS	Offense	HT	WT	School	AP	CF	FC	FN	FW	PI	SN
RB	**LeShon Johnson***	6-0	201	Northern Illinois	•	•	•	•	•	•	•

ALL-CONFERENCE TEAM

POS	Offense	School
QB	Mike Neu	Ball State
RB	Tim Curtis	Ohio U
RB	Zeb Jackson	Bowling Green
WR	Brian Oliver	Ball State
WR	Rameer Martin	Bowling Green
C	Matt Foley	Bowling Green
OL	Jose Munoz	Ball State
TB	Mike Blair	Ball State
OL	Darrell McCaul	Central Michigan
T	Joe Wyse	Bowling Green
TE	Ted Freeman	Ball State
K	Chuck Selinger	Central Michigan

POS	Defense	School
L	Walter Campbell	Eastern Michigan
L	Clint Frazier	Bowling Green
L	Bob Dudley	Bowling Green
LB	Vince Palko	Bowling Green
OLB	Rich Yurkiewicz	Kent State
LB	Mike Kyler	Central Michigan
DB	Richard Palmer	Eastern Michigan
DB	David Thomas	Miami (Ohio)
DB	Pierre Hixon	Western Michigan
P	Gary Layton	Miami (Ohio)

HEISMAN TROPHY VOTING

	PLAYER	POS	SCHOOL	1ST	2ND	3RD	TOTAL
6	LeShon Johnson*	RB	Northern Illinois	5	51	59	176

NCAA STATISTICAL LEADERS

INDIVIDUAL

ALL-PURPOSE		CL	G	RUSH	REC	PR	KR	YDS	YPG
1	LeShon Johnson, Northern Illinois*	SR	11	1,976	106	0	0	2,082	189.3

RUSHING/YARDS PER GAME		CL	G	ATT	YDS	TD	AVG	YPG
1	LeShon Johnson, Northern Illinois*	SR	11	327	1,976	12	6.0	179.6

RUSHING/YARDS PER CARRY		CL	G	ATT	YDS	YPC
7	LeShon Johnson, Northern Illinois*	SR	11	327	1,976	6.0
	Based on top 21 rushers					

RECEIVING		CL	G	REC	YDS	TD	RPG	YPR	YPG
10	Brian Oliver, Ball State	JR	11	62	1,010	10	5.6	16.3	91.8

INTERCEPTIONS		CL	INT	YDS	TD	INT/GM
7	David Thomas, Miami (Ohio)	JR	6	63	0	0.55

TEAM

PASSING DEFENSE	G	ATT	COM	PCT	INT	I%	YDS	YPA	TD	TD%	RAT
7 Central Michigan	11	302	151	.500	13	4.3	1,730	5.7	6	2.0	96.1

TOTAL DEFENSE	G	P	YDS	AVG	TD	YPG
7 Bowling Green	11	715	3,285	4.6	22	298.6

Independent or other conference affiliation

1994

CONFERENCE STANDINGS

	CONFERENCE			OVERALL		
	W	L	T	W	L	T
Central Michigan	8	1	0	9	3	0
Bowling Green	7	1	0	9	2	0
Western Michigan	5	3	0	7	4	0
Miami (Ohio)	5	3	0	5	5	1
Ball State	5	3	1	5	5	1
Toledo	4	3	1	5	5	1
Eastern Michigan	5	4	0	5	6	0
Kent State	2	7	0	2	9	0
Akron	1	8	0	1	10	0
Ohio U	0	9	0	0	11	0
Northern Illinois*				4	7	0
Temple*				2	9	0

BOWL GAMES

DATE	GAME	SCORE
D15	**Las Vegas**	Nevada-Las Vegas 52, Central Michigan 24

ALL-CONFERENCE TEAM

POS	**Offense**	**School**
QB	Ryan Henry	Bowling Green
RB	Tony Nibbs	Ball State
RB	Brian Pruitt	Central Michigan
RB	Casey McBeth	Toledo
WR	Andre Walllace	Western Michigan
WR	Ronnie Redd	Bowling Green
C	Jeff Chabot	Miami (Ohio)
L	Tom Nutten	Western Michigan
T	Chris O'Brien	Central Michigan
L	Chad Bukey	Bowling Green
G	Matt Nastally	Central Michigan
TE	Jerremy Dunlap	Central Michigan
PK	Brian Leaver	Bowling Green

POS	**Defense**	**School**
L	Greg Cepek	Bowling Green
L	Bill Atha	Miami (Ohio)
L	Jason Phillips	Miami (Ohio)
L	Dion Powell	Western Michigan
LB	Vince Palko	Bowling Green
LB	Peter Tuffo	Western Michigan
OLB	Yusef Dibbles	Eastern Michigan
DB	George Johnson	Bowling Green
DB	Quincy Writh	Central Michigan
DB	Ron Rice	Eastern Michigan
DB	David Thomas	Miami (Ohio)
P	Gary Layton	Miami (Ohio)

INDIVIDUAL

PASSING	CL	G	ATT	COM	PCT	INT	I%	YDS	YPA	TD	TD%	RAT
10 Ryan Henry, Bowling Green	SO	11	293	174	59.4	11	3.8	2,368	8.1	25	8.5	147.9

ALL-PURPOSE	CL	G	RUSH	REC	PR	KR	YDS	YPG
2 Brian Pruitt, Central Michigan	SR	11	1,890	69	0	330	2,289	208.1

RUSHING/YARDS PER GAME	CL	G	ATT	YDS	TD	AVG	YPG
2 Brian Pruitt, Central Michigan	SR	11	292	1,890	20	6.5	171.8

RUSHING/YARDS PER CARRY	CL	G	ATT	YDS	YPC
3 Brian Pruitt, Central Michigan	SR	11	292	1,890	6.5
Based on top 30 rushers					

PUNTING	CL	PUNT	YDS	AVG
3 Brad Maynard, Ball State	JR	59	2,684	45.5
5 Gary Layton, Miami (Ohio)	SR	55	2,477	45.0

PUNT RETURNS	CL	PR	YDS	TD	AVG
1 Steve Clay, Eastern Michigan	JR	14	278	1	19.9

SCORING	CL	TDS	XP	FG	PTS	PTPG
3 Brian Pruitt, Central Michigan	SR	22	0	0	132	12.0
4 Brian Leaver, Bowling Green	SR	0	42	21	105	9.6

FIELD GOALS	CL	FGA	FGM	PCT	FGG
3 Brian Leaver, Bowling Green	SR	24	21	.88	1.91

TEAM

RUSHING OFFENSE	G	ATT	YDS	AVG	TD	YPG
4 **Central Michigan**	11	571	3,132	5.5	37	284.7
9 **Toledo**	11	509	2,667	5.2	28	242.5

TOTAL DEFENSE	G	P	YDS	AVG	TD	YPG
8 **Western Michigan**	11	726	3,047	4.2	23	277.0

SCORING OFFENSE	G	PTS	AVG
8 **Bowling Green**	11	391	35.5
10 **Central Michigan**	11	376	34.2

TURNOVER MARGIN	G	FR	INT	TOT	FL	INTL	TOT	MAR
8 **Northern Illinois***	11	16	15	31	13	7	20	1.0

1995

FINAL POLLS

CNN	AP	TEAM	RECORD
1	1	Nebraska	12-0-0
3	2	Florida	12-1-0
2	3	Tennessee	11-1-0
5	4	Florida State	10-2-0
4	5	Colorado	10-2-0
8	6	Ohio State	11-2-0
6	7	Kansas State	10-2-0
7	8	Northwestern	10-2-0
10	9	Kansas	10-2-0
9	10	Virginia Tech	10-2-0
13	11	Notre Dame	9-3-0
11	12	USC	9-2-1
12	13	Penn State	9-3-0
14	14	Texas	10-2-1
15	15	Texas A&M	9-3-0
17	16	Virginia	9-4-0
19	17	Michigan	9-4-0
18	18	Oregon	9-3-0
16	19	Syracuse	9-3-0
PB	20	Miami, Fla.	8-3-0
PB	21	Alabama	8-3-0
21	22	Auburn	8-4-0
20	23	Texas Tech	9-3-0
24	24	**Toledo**	11-0-1
22	25	Iowa	8-4-0
23		East Carolina	9-3-0
25		LSU	7-4-1

CONFERENCE STANDINGS

	CONFERENCE			OVERALL		
	W	L	T	W	L	T
Toledo	7	0	1	11	0	1
Miami (Ohio)	6	1	1	8	2	1
Ball State	6	2	0	7	4	0
Western Michigan	6	2	0	7	4	0
Eastern Michigan	5	3	0	6	5	0
Bowling Green	3	5	0	5	6	0
Central Michigan	2	6	0	4	7	0
Akron	2	6	0	2	9	0
Ohio U	1	6	1	2	8	1
Kent State	0	7	1	1	9	1

Northern Illinois*				3	8	0
Temple*				1	10	0

BOWL GAMES

DATE	GAME	SCORE
D14	**Las Vegas**	Toledo 40, Nevada 37 OT

CONSENSUS ALL-AMERICANS

POS	Defense	HT	WT	School	AP	CF	FC	FN	FW	PI	SN
P	Brad Maynard	6-1	175	Ball State	•	•					

ALL-CONFERENCE TEAM

POS	Offense	School
QB	Charlie Batch	Eastern Michigan
WR	Steve Clay	Eastern Michigan
RB	Deland McCullough	Miami (Ohio)
RB	Wasean Tait	Toledo
L	Chad Bukey	Bowling Green
L	Barry Stokes	Eastern Michigan
C	Brock Gutierrez	Central Michigan
TE	Steve Rosi	Toledo
K	Derek Schorejs	Bowling Green

POS	Defense	School
L	Dion Powell	Western Michigan
L	Keith McKenzie	Ball State
L	Greg Cepek	Bowling Green
L	Steve Haynes	Toledo
LB	Dee Osborne	Miami (Ohio)
LB	Andre Vaughn	Western Michigan
LB	Kenyon Harper	Miami (Ohio)
LB	Jason Woullard	Bowling Green
DB	Quincy Writh	Central Michigan
DB	Johnnie Williams	Miami (Ohio)
DB	Tristan Moss	Western Michigan

NCAA STATISTICAL LEADERS

INDIVIDUAL

ALL-PURPOSE		CL	G	RUSH	REC	PR	KR	YDS	YPG
3	Wasean Tait, Toledo	JR	11	1,905	183	0	0	2,088	189.8

RUSHING/YARDS PER GAME		CL	G	ATT	YDS	TD	AVG	YPG
2	Wasean Tait, Toledo	JR	11	357	1,905	20	5.3	173.2
6	Deland McCullough, Miami (Ohio)	SR	11	321	1,627	14	5.1	147.9
10	Charles Talley, Northern Illinois*	JR	11	285	1,540	7	5.4	140.0

PUNTING		CL	PUNT	YDS	AVG
1	Brad Maynard, Ball State	JR	66	3,071	46.5

KICKOFF RETURNS		CL	KR	YDS	TD	AVG
4	Steve Clay, Eastern Michigan	SR	14	395	1	28.2
7	Silas Massey, Central Michigan	FR	16	434	0	27.1

SCORING		CL	TDS	XP	FG	PTS	PTPG
3	Wasean Tait, Toledo	JR	20	0	0	120	10.9

TEAM

RUSHING OFFENSE		G	ATT	YDS	AVG	TD	YPG
5	Toledo	11	564	2,690	4.8	32	244.5
10	Northern Illinois*	11	546	2,497	4.6	18	227.0

PASSING OFFENSE		G	ATT	COM	INT	PCT	YDS	YPA	TD	I%	YPC	YPG
7	Eastern Michigan	11	441	254	19	.576	3,323	7.5	23	4.3	13.1	302.1

PASSING DEFENSE		G	ATT	COM	PCT	INT	I%	YDS	YPA	TD	TD%	RAT
1	Miami (Ohio)	11	303	137	45.2	22	7.3	1,544	5.1	11	3.6	85.5
4	Ball State	11	303	128	42.2	10	3.3	1,469	4.9	14	4.6	91.6

TOTAL DEFENSE		G	P	YDS	AVG	TD	YPG
2	Miami (Ohio)	11	738	2,764	3.7	15	251.3
4	Ball State	11	712	2,850	4.0	22	259.1
8	Western Michigan	11	686	3,092	4.5	23	281.1

SCORING DEFENSE		G	PTS	AVG
7	Miami (Ohio)	11	165	15.0

TURNOVER MARGIN		G	FR	INT	TOT	FL	INTL	TOT	MAR
1	Toledo	11	16	18	34	6	6	12	2.0
7	Miami (Ohio)	11	9	22	31	8	11	19	1.1

*Independent or other conference affiliation

1996

CONFERENCE STANDINGS

	CONFERENCE			OVERALL		
	W	L	T	W	L	T
Ball State	7	1	0	8	4	0
Toledo	6	2	0	7	4	0
Miami (Ohio)	6	2	0	6	5	0
Ohio U	5	3	0	6	6	0
Central Michigan	4	4	0	5	6	0
Akron	3	5	0	4	7	0
Bowling Green	3	5	0	4	7	0
Eastern Michigan	3	5	0	3	8	0
Western Michigan	2	6	0	2	9	0
Kent State	1	7	0	2	9	0
Northern Illinois*				1	10	0
Temple*				1	10	0

BOWL GAMES

DATE	GAME	SCORE
D19	**Las Vegas**	Nevada 18, Ball State 15

CONSENSUS ALL-AMERICANS

POS	Defense	HT	WT	School	CL	AP	CF	FC	FN	FW	SN
P	Brad Maynard	6-1	176	Ball State	SR	•	•				

ALL-CONFERENCE TEAM

POS	Offense	School
QB	Chad Darnell	Central Michgan
TB	Ty King	Miami (Ohio)
TB	Astron Whatley	Eastern Michigan
TB	Silas Massey	Central Michigan
WR	Tony Knox	Western Michigan
C	Matt Cravens	Miami (Ohio)
L	Jason Caudill	Ohio U
L	Mike Bird	Miami (Ohio)
L	Tony Roush	Ball State
L	Scott Rehberg	Central Michigan
TE	Adam Simonson	Central Michigan

POS	Defense	School
L	Mario Daniel	Ohio U
L	Damon Hummel	Ball State
L	Lional Dalton	Eastern Michigan
LB	Dee Osborne	Miami (Ohio)
LB	Jason Taylor	Akron
LB	Aaron Gralak	Ball State
DB	Raphael Ball	Ball State
DB	Cory Gilliard	Ball State
DB	Jamie Tayler	Miami (Ohio)
DB	Mark Heron	Toledo
PK	Brent Locklear	Ball State
P	Brad Maynard	Ball State

INDIVIDUAL

PASSING
		CL	G	ATT	COM	PCT	INT	I%	YDS	YPA	TD	TD%	RAT
10	Brent Baldwin, Ball State	SR	11	205	121	59.0	5	2.4	1,703	8.3	14	6.8	146.5

ALL-PURPOSE
		CL	G	RUSH	REC	PR	KR	YDS	YPG
5	Silas Massey, Central Michigan	SO	10	1,544	103	0	159	1,806	180.6

RUSHING/YARDS PER GAME
		CL	G	ATT	YDS	TD	AVG	YPG
5	Silas Massey, Central Michigan	SO	10	312	1,544	16	4.9	154.4

RECEIVING
		CL	G	REC	YDS	TD	RPG	YPR	YPG
5	Reggie Allen, Central Michigan	SO	10	66	1,229	9	6.6	18.6	122.9
8	Eugene Baker, Kent State	SO	11	69	1,215	13	6.3	17.6	110.5

PUNTING
		CL	PUNT	YDS	AVG
6	Brad Maynard, Ball State	SR	59	2,705	45.9

PUNT RETURNS
		CL	PR	YDS	TD	AVG
5	Keijuan Douglas, Eastern Michigan	FR	12	183	1	15.3
10	Tremayne Banks, Miami (Ohio)	SR	29	395	0	13.6

KICKOFF RETURNS
		CL	KR	YDS	TD	AVG
8	Tony Knox, Western Michigan	SR	25	690	1	27.6
10	Tremayne Banks, Miami (Ohio)	SR	19	518	1	27.3

SCORING
		CL	TDS	XP	FG	PTS	PTPG
10	Silas Massey, Central Michigan	SO	16	2	0	98	9.8

TEAM

RUSHING OFFENSE
		G	ATT	YDS	AVG	TD	YPG
6	Ohio U	12	685	3,286	4.8	29	273.8

TOTAL OFFENSE
		G	P	YDS	AVG	TD	YPG
7	Central Michigan	11	871	5,252	6.0	45	477.5

PASSING DEFENSE
		G	ATT	COM	PCT	INT	I%	YDS	YPA	TD	TD%	RAT
2	Miami (Ohio)	11	260	104	40.0	11	4.2	1,323	5.1	6	2.3	81.9

SCORING DEFENSE
		G	PTS	AVG
9	Miami (Ohio)	11	168	15.3

TURNOVER MARGIN
		G	FR	INT	TOT	FL	INTL	TOT	MAR
9	Bowling Green	11	13	13	26	1	14	15	1.0

1997

CONFERENCE STANDINGS

	CONFERENCE			OVERALL		
	W	L	T	W	L	T
EAST						
Marshall	7	1	0	10	3	0
Miami (Ohio)	6	2	0	8	3	0
Ohio U	6	2	0	8	3	0
Kent State	3	5	0	3	8	0
Bowling Green	3	5	0	3	8	0
Akron	2	7	0	2	9	0
WEST						
Toledo	7	1	0	9	3	0
Western Michigan	6	2	0	8	3	0
Ball State	4	4	0	5	6	0
Eastern Michigan	4	5	0	4	7	0
Central Michigan	1	7	0	2	9	0
Northern Illinois	0	8	0	0	11	0

Championship **Marshall 34 Toledo 14**

Temple*				3	8	0

BOWL GAMES

DATE	GAME	SCORE
D26	**Motor City**	Mississippi 34, Marshall 31

CONSENSUS ALL-AMERICANS

POS	Offense	HT	WT	School	CL	AP	CF	FC	FN	FW	SN
WR	**Randy Moss**	6-5	210	Marshall	So.	•	•	•	•	•	•

ALL-CONFERENCE TEAM

POS	Offense	School
QB	Chad Pennington	Marshall
TB	Astron Whatley	Kent State
RB	Travis Prentice	Miami (ohio)
RB	Dwayne Harris	Toledo
WR	Eugene Baker	Kent State
WR	Lavorn Colclough	Marshall
WR	Randy Moss	Marshall
L	Mike Bird	Miami (ohio)
C	John Wade	Marshall
G	Bob Hallen	Kent State
T	Steve Zahursky	Kent State
TE	Damian Vaughn	Miami (Ohio)
K	John Scott	Miami (Ohio)

POS	Defense	School
DL	B.J. Cohen	Marshall
L	Lional Dalton	Eastern Michigan
L	Chad Brightman	Miami (Ohio)
L	Jason Richards	Toledo
LB	Larry McCloud	Marshall
LB	Kevin O'Neill	Bowling Green
LB	JoJuan Armour	Miami (Ohio)
LB	Marcus Matthews	Toledo
DB	Paris Johnson	Miami (Ohio)
DB	Jamie Taylor	Miami (Ohio)
DB	Tevell Jones	Ohio U
DB	Clarence Love	Toledo
P	Kent McCullough	Miami (Ohio)

HEISMAN TROPHY VOTING

	PLAYER	POS	SCHOOL	1ST	2ND	3RD	TOTAL
4	Randy Moss	WR	Marshall	17	56	90	253

AWARD WINNERS

PLAYER	POS	SCHOOL	AWARD
Randy Moss	WR	Marshall	Biletnikoff

NCAA STATISTICAL LEADERS

INDIVIDUAL

PASSING		CL	G	ATT	COM	PCT	INT	I%	YDS	YPA	TD	TD%	RAT
10	Chad Pennington, Marshall	SO	12	428	253	59.1	12	2.8	3480	8.1	39	9.1	151.9

ALL-PURPOSE		CL	G	RUSH	REC	PR	KR	YDS	YPG
4	Randy Moss, Marshall	SO	12	2	1647	266	263	2178	181.5

RUSHING/YARDS PER GAME		CL	G	ATT	YDS	TD	AVG	YPG
6	Travis Prentice, Miami (Ohio)	SO	11	296	1549	25	5.2	140.8
7	Dwayne Harris, Toledo	JR	10	254	1278	10	5.0	127.8

RECEIVING		CL	G	REC	YDS	TD	RPG	YPR	YPG
2	Eugene Baker, Kent	JR	11	103	1549	18	9.4	15.0	140.8
3	Randy Moss, Marshall	SO	12	90	1647	25	7.5	18.3	137.3

PUNT RETURNS		CL	PR	YDS	TD	AVG
4	Nod Washington, Miami (Ohio)	JR	12	185	0	15.4
9	Steve Neal, Western Michigan	SO	14	204	1	14.6

SCORING		CL	TDS	XP	FG	PTS	PTPG
2	Travis Prentice, Miami (Ohio)	SO	25	0	0	150	13.6
4	Randy Moss, Marshall	SO	25	2	0	152	12.7
10	Eugene Baker, Kent	JR	18	2	0	110	10.0

INTERCEPTIONS		CL	INT	YDS	TD	INT/GM
2	Tevell Jones, Ohio U	SR	7	36	0	0.64

TEAM

RUSHING OFFENSE		G	ATT	YDS	AVG	TD	YPG
4	Ohio U	11	649	3321	5.1	32	301.9

PASSING OFFENSE		G	ATT	COM	INT	PCT	YDS	YPA	TD	I%	YPC	YPG
7	Marshall	12	450	264	13	58.7	3688	8.2	41	2.9	14.0	307.3
8	Eastern Michigan	11	438	250	11	57.1	3314	7.6	23	2.5	13.3	301.3
10	Kent	11	451	235	16	52.1	3243	7.2	35	3.6	13.8	294.8

TOTAL OFFENSE		G	P	YDS	AVG	TD	YPG
10	Marshall	12	832	5339	6.4	58	444.9

PASSING DEFENSE		G	ATT	COM	PCT	INT	I%	YDS	YPA	TD	TD%	RAT
7	Marshall	12	322	146	45.3	15	4.7	1948	6.1	8	2.5	95.0

SCORING OFFENSE		G	PTS	AVG
5	Marshall	12	453	37.8
6	Miami (Ohio)	11	412	37.5

SCORING DEFENSE		G	PTS	AVG
10	Ohio U	11	177	16.1

*Independent or other conference affiliation

1998

NCAA Statistical Leaders

Conference Standings

	CONFERENCE			OVERALL		
	W	L	T	W	L	T
EAST						
Marshall	7	1	0	12	1	0
Miami (Ohio)	7	1	0	10	1	0
Ohio U	5	3	0	5	6	0
Bowling Green	5	3	0	5	6	0
Akron	3	6	0	4	7	0
Kent State	0	8	0	0	11	0
WEST						
Toledo	6	2	0	7	5	0
Western Michigan	5	3	0	7	4	0
Central Michigan	5	3	0	6	5	0
Eastern Michigan	3	6	0	3	8	0
Northern Illinois	2	6	0	2	9	0
Ball State	1	7	0	1	10	0

Championship **Marshall 23 Toledo 1**

Temple*				2	9	0

Bowl Games

DATE	GAME	SCORE
D23	**Motor City**	Marshall 48, Louisville 29

All-Conference Team

POS	**Offense**	**School**
QB	Chad Pennington	Marshall
RB	Doug Chapman	Marshall
RB	Travis Prentice	Miami (Ohio)
RB	Steveland Hookfin	Ohio U
WR	Reggie Allen	Central Michigan
WR	Steve Neal	Western Michigan
WR	LaVorn Colclough	Marshall
OL	L.J. Shelton	Eastern Michigan
OL	Dustin Cohen	Miami (Ohio)
OL	Colin Westrich	Toledo
OL	Mike Guilliams	Marshall
OL	Kevin Kuntz	Akron
C	Mike Varone	Ohio U
TE	Jake Moreland	Western Michigan
PK	Brad Selent	Western Michigan

POS	**Defense**	**School**
L	Dan Falcon	Western Michigan
L	Jon McCall	Central Michigan
L	Lincoln Dupree	Eastern Michigan
L	Girardie Mercer	Marshall
L	Ricky Hall	Marshall
ILB	Tom Carder	Ohio U
LB	JoJuan Armour	Miami (Ohio)
ILB	Jason Lamar	Toledo
DB	Jay Baker	Miami (Ohio)
DB	Rogers Beckett	Marshall
DB	Daninelle Derricott	Marshall
P	Dave Zastudil	Ohio U

INDIVIDUAL

ALL-PURPOSE		CL	GRUSH	REC	PR	KR	YDS	YPG
8	Travis Prentice, Miami (Ohio)	JR	11	1787	107	0	0	1894	172.2

RUSHING/YARDS PER GAME		CL	G	ATT	YDS	TD	AVG	YPG
2	Travis Prentice, Miami (Ohio)	JR	11	365	1787	19	4.9	162.5
10	Steve Hookfin, Ohio U	SR	11	273	1315	11	4.8	119.6

PUNTING		CL	PUNT	YDS	AVG
4	Dave Zastudil, Ohio U	FR	50	2266	45.3
6	Andy Pollock, Bowling Green	SR	50	2243	44.9

SCORING		CL	TDS	XP	FG	PTS	PTPG
4	Travis Prentice, Miami (Ohio)	JR	20	0	0	120	10.9

FIELD GOALS		CL	FGA	FGM	PCT	FGG
10	Brad Selent, Western Michigan	SO	26	18	0.69	1.64

INTERCEPTIONS		CL	INT	YDS	TD	INT/GM
8	Daninelle Derricott, Marshall	JR	6	118	0	0.50

TEAM

RUSHING OFFENSE		G	ATT	YDS	AVG	TD	YPG
2	Ohio U	11	680	3044	4.5	27	276.7

PASSING OFFENSE	G	ATT	COM	INT	PCT	YDS	YPA	TD	I%	YPC	YPG
9 Western Michigan	11	409	238	16	58.2	3414	8.3	24	3.9	14.3	310.4

PASSING DEFENSE	G	ATT	COM	PCT	INT	I%	YDS	YPA	TD	TD%	RAT
5 Miami (Ohio)	11	298	142	47.7	13	4.4	1659	5.6	6	2.0	92.3

SCORING DEFENSE		G	PTS	AVG
4	Miami (Ohio)	11	142	12.9

1999

FINAL POLLS

ESPN	AP	TEAM	RECORD
1	1	Florida State	12-0
3	2	Virginia Tech	11-1
2	3	Nebraska	12-1
4	4	Wisconsin	10-2
5	5	Michigan	10-2
6	6	Kansas State	11-1
7	7	Michigan State	10-2
8	8	Alabama	10-3
9	9	Tennessee	9-3
10	10	**Marshall**	13-0
11	11	Penn State	10-3
14	12	Florida	9-4
12	13	Mississippi State	10-2
13	14	Southern Miss	9-3
15	15	Miami, Fla.	9-4
16	16	Georgia	8-4
19	17	Arkansas	8-4
17	18	Minnesota	8-4
18	19	Oregon	9-3
21	20	Georgia Tech	8-4
23	21	Texas	9-5
22	22	Mississippi	8-4
20	23	Texas A&M	8-4
25	24	Illinois	8-4
	25	Purdue	7-5
24		Stanford	8-4

CONFERENCE STANDINGS

	CONFERENCE			OVERALL		
	W	L	T	W	L	T
EAST						
Marshall	8	0	0	13	0	0
Miami (Ohio)	6	2	0	7	4	0
Akron	5	3	0	7	4	0
Ohio U	5	3	0	5	6	0
Bowling Green	3	5	0	5	6	0
Kent State	2	6	0	2	9	0
Buffalo	0	8	0	0	11	0
WEST						
Western Michigan	6	2	0	7	5	0
Toledo	5	3	0	6	5	0
Northern Illinois	5	3	0	5	6	0
Eastern Michigan	4	4	0	4	7	0
Central Michigan	3	5	0	4	7	0
Ball State	0	8	0	0	11	0

Championship **Marshall 34 Western Michigan 30**

Temple*		2	9	0

BOWL GAMES

DATE	GAME	SCORE
D27	**Motor City**	Marshall 21, Brigham Young 3

ALL-CONFERENCE TEAM

POS	Offense	School
QB	Chad Pennington	Marshall
RB	Travis Prentice	Miami (Ohio)
RB	Chester Taylor	Toledo
RB	Doug Chapman	Marshall
WR	Steve Neal	Western Michigan
WR	Nate Poole	Marshall
WR	James Williams	Marshall
OL	Ryan Diem	Northern Illinois
OL	Colin Westrich	Toledo
OL	Jimmy Cabellos	Marshall
OL	Mike Guilliams	Marshall
C	Jason Starkey	Marshall
TE	Jason Gavadza	Kent State

POS	Defense	School
L	Andy Aracri	Miami (Ohio)
L	DeJuan Goulde	Toledo
L	Girardie Mercer	Marshall
OLB	Dustin Cohen	Miami (Ohio)
ILB	Jason Lamar	Toledo
LB	Scott Niles	Western Michigan
LB	Paul Toviessi	Marshall
LB	John Grace	Marshall
DB	Donald McCall	Eastern Michigan
DB	Maurice Hines	Marshall
DB	Rogers Beckett	Marshall
PK	Kent Baker	Northern Illinois
P	Dave Zastudil	Ohio U

HEISMAN TROPHY VOTING

PLAYER	POS	SCHOOL	1ST	2ND	3RD	TOTAL
5 Chad Pennington	QB	Marshall	21	45	94	247

NCAA STATISTICAL LEADERS

INDIVIDUAL

PASSING

	CL	G	ATT	COM	PCT	INT	I%	YDS	YPA	TD	TD%	RAT
3 Chad Pennington, Marshall	SR	12	405	275	67.9	11	2.7	3799	9.4	37	9.1	171.4
10 Tim Lester, Western Michigan	SR	12	470	282	60.0	13	2.8	3639	7.7	34	7.2	143.4

ALL-PURPOSE

	CL	G	RUSH	REC	PR	KR	YDS	YPG
5 Travis Prentice, Miami (Ohio)	SR	11	1659	270	0	0	1929	175.4

RUSHING/YARDS PER GAME

	CL	G	ATT	YDS	TD	AVG	YPG
4 Travis Prentice, Miami (Ohio)	SR	11	354	1659	17	4.7	150.8

RUSHING/YARDS PER CARRY

	CL	G	ATT	YDS	YPC
2 Chester Taylor, Toledo	JR	11	182	1176	6.5

*-Based on top 50 rushers

RECEIVING

	CL	G	REC	YDS	TD	RPG	YPR	YPG
5 Drew Haddad, Buffalo	SR	11	85	1158	6	7.7	13.6	105.3

KICKOFF RETURNS

	CL	KR	YDS	TD	AVG
1 James Williams, Marshall	SR	15	493	1	32.9

SCORING

	CL	TDS	XP	FG	PTS	PTPG
2 Travis Prentice, Miami (Ohio)	SR	21	0	0	126	11.5

FIELD GOALS

	CL	FGA	FGM	PCT	FGG
6 Todd France, Toledo	SO	26	18	0.69	1.64

INTERCEPTIONS

	CL	INT	YDS	TD	INT/GM
7 Kevin Harvey, Temple	SR	6	55	1	0.60

TEAM

RUSHING OFFENSE

	G	ATT	YDS	AVG	TD	YPG
6 Ohio U	11	624	2883	4.6	26	262.1
10 Toledo	11	492	2631	5.3	21	239.2

PASSING OFFENSE

	G	ATT	COM	INT	PCT	YDS	YPA	TD	I%	YPC	YPG
7 Marshall	12	427	286	11	67.0	3901	9.1	37	2.6	13.6	325.1

TOTAL OFFENSE

	G	P	YDS	AVG	TD	YPG
7 Marshall	12	841	5584	6.6	57	465.3

PASSING DEFENSE

	G	ATT	COM	PCT	INT	I%	YDS	YPA	TD	TD%	RAT
3 Marshall	12	432	226	52.3	24	5.6	2308	5.3	8	1.9	92.2

TOTAL DEFENSE

	G	P	YDS	AVG	TD	YPG
7 Marshall	12	882	3516	4.0	11	293.0

SCORING OFFENSE

	G	PTS	AVG
7 Marshall	12	442	36.8

SCORING DEFENSE

	G	PTS	AVG
2 Marshall	12	134	11.2

TURNOVER MARGIN

	G	FR	INT	TOT	FL	INTL	TOT	MAR
4 Marshall	12	6	24	30	6	11	17	1.1

*Independent or other conference affiliation

2000

NCAA Statistical Leaders

Individual

Conference Standings

	Conference			Overall		
	W	L	T	W	L	T
MAC EAST						
Marshall	5	3	0	8	5	0
Ohio U	5	3	0	7	4	0
Miami (Ohio)	5	3	0	6	5	0
Akron	5	3	0	6	5	0
Buffalo	2	6	0	2	9	0
Bowling Green	2	6	0	2	9	0
Kent State	1	7	0	1	10	0
WEST						
Western Michigan	7	1	0	9	3	0
Toledo	6	1	0	10	1	0
Northern Illinois	4	3	0	6	5	0
Ball State	4	3	0	5	6	0
Eastern Michigan	2	5	0	3	8	0
Central Michigan	2	6	0	2	9	0

Championship **Marshall 19 Western Michigan 14**

Temple*				4	7	0

Bowl Games

DATE	GAME	SCORE
D27	**Motor City**	Marshall 25, Cincinnati 14

Consensus All-Americans

POS	DEFENSE	HT	WT	SCHOOL	CL	AP	CF	FC	FN	FW	SN
DB	**Dwight Smith**	5-11	205	Akron	Sr.	•	•	•		•	•

All-Conference Team

POS	**Offense**	**School**
QB	Traueres Bolden	Toledo
RB	Thomas Hammock	Northern Illinois
RB	Chester Taylor	Toledo
RB	Robert Sanford	Western Michigan
WR	Steve Neal	Western Michigan
WR	Justin McCareins	Northern Illinois
WR	Nate Poole	Marshall
C	McCallister Collins	Northern Illinois
OL	Ryan Diem	Northern Illinois
OL	Jim Harding	Toledo
OL	Paul Lambert	Western Michigan
OL	Jimmy Cabellos	Marshall
TE	Mobolaji Afariogun	Western Michigan
P/K	Todd France	Toledo

POS	**Defense**	**School**
L	DeJuan Gold	Toledo
L	Anthony Allsbury	Western Michigan
L	Jimmy Parker	Marshall
L	Paul Toviessi	Marshall
ILB	Garrett Soldano	Western Michigan
ILB	Max Yates	Marshall
OLB	Larry Williams	Northern Illinois
OLB	Ira Singleton	Toledo
DB	Dwight Smith	Akron
DB	Jermaine Hampton	Northern Illinois
DB	Maurice Hines	Marshall
DB	Daninelle Derricott	Marshall
P	Dave Zastudil	Ohio U

Individual

ALL-PURPOSE		POS	CL	G	RUSH	REC	PR	KR	YDS	YPG
5	Justin McCareins, Northern Illinois	FL	SR	11	73	1168	362	411	2014	183.1

RUSHING/YARDS PER GAME		POS	CL	G	ATT	YDS	TD	AVG	YPG
7	Chester Taylor, Toledo	TB	SR	11	250	1470	18	5.9	133.6
8	Robert Sanford, Western Michigan	TB	SR	12	293	1571	18	5.4	130.9

RECEIVING		POS	CL	G	REC	YDS	TD	RPG	YPR	YPG
4	Justin McCareins, Northern Illinois	FL	SR	11	66	1168	10	6.0	17.7	106.2

PUNTING		POS	CL	PUNT	YDS	AVG
5	Dave Zastudil, Ohio U	P	JR	47	2084	44.3

PUNT RETURNS		POS	CL	PR	YDS	TD	AVG
3	Justin McCareins, Northern Illinois	FL	SR	19	362	1	19.1

SCORING		POS	CL	TDS	XP	FG	PTS	PTPG
6	Thomas Hammock, Northern Illinois	TB	SO	16	0	0	96	10.7
7	Chester Taylor, Toledo	TB	SR	19	0	0	114	10.4

FIELD GOALS		POS	CL	FGA	FGM	PCT	FGG
9	Steve Azar, Northern Illinois	K	FR	15	14	0.93	1.56

INTERCEPTIONS		POS	CL	INT	YDS	TD	INT/GM
1	Dwight Smith, Akron	DB	SR	10	208	2	0.91

Team

RUSHING OFFENSE		G	ATT	YDS	AVG	TD	YPG
2	Ohio U	11	646	3553	5.5	32	323.0
9	Toledo	11	514	2792	5.4	29	253.8

PASSING OFFENSE		G	ATT	COM	INT	PCT	YDS	YPA	TD	I%	YPC	YPG
10	Marshall	12	483	293	10	60.7	3584	7.4	24	2.1	12.2	298.7

RUSHING DEFENSE		G	ATT	YDS	AVG	TD	YPG
5	Toledo	11	365	897	2.5	10	81.5

TOTAL DEFENSE		G	P	YDS	AVG	TD	YPG
3	Toledo	11	703	2959	4.2	16	269.0
9	Western Michigan	12	803	3399	4.2	16	283.3

SCORING DEFENSE		G	PTS	AVG
3	Toledo	11	125	11.4
4	Western Michigan	12	139	11.6

TURNOVER MARGIN		G	FR	INT	TOT	FL	INTL	TOT	MAR
1	Toledo	11	16	15	31	5	4	9	2.00

2001

FINAL POLLS

ESPN	AP	TEAM	RECORD
1	1	Miami, Fla.	12-0
2	2	Oregon	11-1
3	3	Florida	10-2
4	4	Tennessee	11-2
5	5	Texas	11-2
6	6	Oklahoma	11-2
8	7	LSU	10-3
7	8	Nebraska	11-2
9	9	Colorado	10-3
11	10	Washington State	10-2
10	11	Maryland	10-2
12	12	Illinois	10-2
13	13	South Carolina	9-3
14	14	Syracuse	10-3
15	15	Florida State	8-4
17	16	Stanford	9-3
16	17	Louisville	11-2
18	18	Virginia Tech	8-4
19	19	Washington	8-4
20	20	Michigan	8-4
23	21	Boston College	8-4
25	22	Georgia	8-4
22	23	Toledo	10-2
	24	Georgia Tech	8-5
24	25	Brigham Young	12-2
21		**Marshall**	11-2

CONFERENCE STANDINGS

	CONFERENCE			OVERALL		
	W	L	T	W	L	T
EAST						
Marshall	8	0	0	11	2	0
Miami (Ohio)	6	2	0	7	5	0
Bowling Green	5	3	0	8	3	0
Kent State	5	3	0	6	5	0
Akron	4	4	0	4	7	0
Buffalo	1	7	0	3	8	0
Ohio U	1	7	0	1	10	0
WEST						
Toledo	5	2	0	10	2	0
Northern Illinois	4	3	0	6	5	0
Ball State	4	3	0	5	6	0
Western Michigan	4	4	0	5	6	0
Central Michigan	2	6	0	3	8	0
Eastern Michigan	1	6	0	2	9	0

Championship **Toledo 41 Marshall 36**

Temple*				4	7	0

BOWL GAMES

DATE	GAME	SCORE
D19	**GMAC**	Marshall 64, East Carolina 61, 2 OT
D29	**Motor City**	Toledo 23, Cincinnati 16

CONSENSUS ALL-AMERICANS

POS	**Offense**	HT	WT	**School**	CL	AP	CF	FC	FN	FW	SN
None											

OTHERS RECEIVING FIRST-TEAM HONORS
P	**Dave Zastudil**	Ohio U	•

ALL-CONFERENCE TEAM

POS	**Offense**	**School**
QB	Bryon Leftwich	Marshall
RB	Chester Taylor	Toledo
RB	Thomas Hammock	Northern Illinois
RB	Marcus Merriweather	Ball State
WR	Robert Redd	Bowling Green
WR	Josh Davis	Marshall
WR	Darius Watts	Marshall
C	Paul Thaler	Miami (Ohio)
OL	Konrad Dean	Akron
OL	Brian Hallett	Kent State
OL	Nathan McPeek	Marshall
OL	Steve Sciuilo	Marshall
TE	Greg Kellett	Marshall
K	Steve Azar	Northern Illinois

POS	**Defense**	**School**
L	Brandon Hicks	Bowling Green
L	David Bockmore	Toledo
L	Anthony Allsbury	Western Michigan
L	Ralph Street	Marshall
ILB	Terrell Jones	Miami
ILB	Ralph Street	Marshall
ILB	Max Yates	Marshall
OLB	James Harrison	Kent State
OLB	Matt Robillard	Miami
OLB	Larry Williams	Northern Illinois
DB	Tedaro France	Central Michigan
DB	Vince Thompson	Northern Illinois
DB	Ronald Rogers	Western Michigan
DB	Chris Crocker	Marshall
K	Steve Azar	Northern Illinois
P	Dave Zastudil	Ohio U

NCAA STATISTICAL LEADERS

INDIVIDUAL

	PASSING	POS	CL	G	ATT	COM	PCT	INT	I%	YDS	YPA	TD	TD%	RAT
5	Byron Leftwich, Marshall	QB	JR	12	470	315	67.0	7	1.5	4132	8.79	38	8.1	164.6

	RUSHING/YARDS PER GAME	POS	CL	G	ATT	YDS	TD	AVG	YPG
7	Chester Taylor, Toledo	TB	JR	11	268	1430	20	5.3	130.0
10	Marcus Merriweather, Ball State	TB	SR	10	268	1244	12	4.6	124.4

	RUSHING/YARDS PER CARRY	POS	CL	G	ATT	YDS	YPC
9	Joshua Cribbs, Kent State	QB	FR	11	164	1019	6.2

	RECEIVING	POS	CL	G	REC	YDS	TD	RPG	YPR	YPG
6	Darius Watts, Marshall	WR	SO	12	91	1417	18	7.6	15.6	118.1

	PUNTING	POS	CL	PUNT	YDS	AVG
2	Dave Zastudil, Ohio U	P	SR	50	2280	45.6
9	Curtis Head, Marshall	P	JR	45	1996	44.4

	KICKOFF RETURNS	POS	CL	KR	YDS	TD	AVG
5	Corey Parchman, Ball State	WR	SR	15	465	2	31.0

	SCORING	POS	CL	TDS	XP	FG	PTS	PTPG
3	Chester Taylor, Toledo	TB	JR	23	0	0	138	12.6

	FIELD GOALS	POS	CL	FGA	FGM	PCT	FGG
3	Steve Azar, Northern Illinois	K	SO	26	20	0.77	1.82

TEAM

	RUSHING OFFENSE	G	ATT	YDS	AVG	TD	YPG
6	Ohio U	11	567	2641	4.7	20	240.1

	PASSING OFFENSE	G	ATT	COM	INT	PCT	YDS	YPA	TD	I%	YPC	YPG
3	Marshall	12	477	319	7	66.9	4201	8.8	40	3.2	13.2	350.1

	TOTAL OFFENSE	G	P	YDS	AVG	TD	YPG
3	Marshall	12	880	6060	6.9	61	505.0

	RUSHING DEFENSE	G	ATT	YDS	AVG	TD	YPG
4	Bowling Green	11	372	949	2.6	5	86.3

	SCORING OFFENSE	G	PTS	AVG
8	Marshall	12	448	37.3

	TURNOVER MARGIN	G	FR	INT	TOT	FL	INTL	TOT	MAR
3	Bowling Green	11	17	18	35	5	13	18	1.6

*Independent or other conference affiliation

2002

FINAL POLLS

ESPN	AP	TEAM	RECORD
1	1	Ohio State	14-0
2	2	Miami, Fla.	12-1
3	3	Georgia	13-1
4	4	USC	11-2
5	5	Oklahoma	12-2
7	6	Texas	11-2
6	7	Kansas State	11-2
8	8	Iowa	11-2
9	9	Michigan	10-3
10	10	Washington State	10-3
PB	11	Alabama	10-3
11	12	North Carolina St.	11-3
13	13	Maryland	11-3
16	14	Auburn	9-4
12	15	Boise State	12-1
15	16	Penn State	9-4
17	17	Notre Dame	10-3
14	18	Virginia Tech	10-4
18	19	Pittsburgh	9-4
21	20	Colorado	9-5
23	21	Florida State	9-5
25	22	Virginia	9-5
22	23	TCU	10-2
19	24	**Marshall**	11-2
20	25	West Virginia	9-4
24		Florida	8-4

CONFERENCE STANDINGS

	CONFERENCE			OVERALL		
	W	L	T	W	L	T
EAST						
Marshall	7	1	0	11	2	0
Central Florida	6	2	0	7	5	0
Miami (Ohio)	5	3	0	7	5	0
Ohio U	4	4	0	4	8	0
Akron	3	5	0	4	8	0
Kent State	1	7	0	3	9	0
Buffalo	0	8	0	1	11	0
WEST						
Northern Illinois	7	1	0	8	4	0
Toledo	7	1	0	9	5	0
Bowling Green	6	2	0	9	3	0
Ball State	4	4	0	6	6	0
Western Michigan	3	5	0	4	8	0
Central Michigan	2	6	0	4	8	0
Eastern Michigan	1	7	0	3	9	0
Championship **Marshall 49 Toledo 45**						
Temple*				4	8	0

BOWL GAMES

DATE	GAME	SCORE
D18	**GMAC**	Marshall 38, Louisville 15
D26	**Motor City**	Boston College 51, Toledo 25

ALL-CONFERENCE TEAM

POS	Offense	School
QB	Byron Leftwich	Marshall
RB	Marcus Merriweather	Ball State
WR	Robert Redd	Bowling Green
WR	Kevin Walter	Eastern Michigan
WR	Darius Watts	Marshall
OL	Steve Sciuilo	Marshall
OL	Nick Kaczur	Toledo
OL	Kyle Croskey	Central Michigan
OL	Chris Tuminello	Toledo
TE	Mobolaji Afariogun	Western Michigan

POS	Defense	School
L	Jason Babin	Western Michigan
L	Chris Browning	Western Michigan
L	Elton Patterson	Central Florida
LB	Tom Ward	Toledo
LB	David Gardner	Toledo
OLB	Matt Robillard	Miami (Ohio)
OLB	Larry Williams	Northern Illinois
DB	Vince Thompson	Northern Illinois
DB	Asante Samuel	Central Florida
DB	Atari Bigby	Central Florida
P	Curtis Head	Marshall
P/K	Jared Parseghian	Miami (Ohio)

HEISMAN TROPHY VOTING

	PLAYER	POS	SCHOOL	1ST	2ND	3RD	TOTAL
6	**Byron Leftwich**	QB	Marshall	22	26	34	152

NCAA STATISTICAL LEADERS

INDIVIDUAL

PASSING		CL	G	ATT	COM	PCT	INT	I%	YDS	YPA	TD	TD%	RAT
2	Byron Leftwich, Marshall	SR	12	491	331	67.4	10	2.0	4268	8.7	30	6.1	156.5
3	Brian Jones, Toledo	SR	14	423	297	70.2	9	2.1	3446	8.2	23	5.4	152.3
4	Ryan Schneider, Central Florida	JR	12	430	265	61.6	16	3.7	3770	8.8	31	7.2	151.6

ALL-PURPOSE		POS	CL	G	RUSH	REC	PR	KR	YDS	YPG
2	Michael Turner, No. Illinois	RB	JR	12	1915	100	0	269	2284	190.3
3	Robbie Mixon, Central Michigan	RB	SR	12	1361	253	0	524	2138	178.2

RUSHING/YARDS PER GAME		POS	CL	G	ATT	YDS	TD	AVG	YPG
2	Michael Turner, No. Illinois	RB	JR	12	338	1915	19	5.7	159.6
5	Marcus Merriweather, Ball State	RB	SR	12	332	1618	12	4.9	134.8

RUSHING/YARDS PER CARRY		POS	CL	G	ATT	YDS	YPC
1	Joshua Cribbs, Kent State	QB	SO	10	137	1057	7.7
6	Joe Alls, Bowling Green	RB	SR	10	122	801	6.6

RECEIVING		POS	CL	G	REC	YDS	TD	RPG	YPR	YPG
7	Kevin Walter, Eastern Michigan	WR	SR	12	93	1368	9	7.8	14.7	114.0

PUNT RETURNS		POS	CL	PR	YDS	TD	AVG
1	Dan Sheldon, Northern Illinois	WR	SO	21	477	3	22.7
10	Kendrick Mosley, Western Michigan	WR	SR	29	440	2	15.2

KICKOFF RETURNS		POS	CL	KR	YDS	TD	AVG
9	Makonnen Fenton, Temple*	RB	JR	14	380	1	27.1

SCORING		POS	CL	TDS	XP	FG	PTS	PTPG
3	Josh Harris, Bowling Green	QB	JR	22	0	0	134	11.2
8	Michael Turner, Northern Illinois	RB	JR	20	0	0	120	10.0

INTERCEPTIONS		POS	CL	INT	YDS	TD	INT/GM
8	Randee Drew, Northern Illinois	DB	JR	7	103	0	0.58
9	Vince Thompson, Northern Illinois	DB	SR	5	4	0	0.56
10	Bop White, Ohio U	DB	SR	6	52	0	0.55

TEAM

RUSHING OFFENSE		G	ATT	YDS	AVG	TD	YPG
8	Ohio U	12	649	2878	4.4	30	239.8

PASSING OFFENSE		G	ATT	COM	INT	PCT	YDS	YPA	TD	I%	YPC	YPG
3	Marshall	13	575	383	15	66.6	4804	8.4	35	2.6	12.5	369.5
6	Central Florida	12	442	270	17	61.1	3837	8.7	31	3.9	14.2	319.8

TOTAL OFFENSE		G	P	YDS	AVG	TD	YPG
3	Marshall	13	991	6439	6.5	59	495.3
5	Toledo	14	1033	6611	6.4	66	472.2
9	Bowling Green	12	898	5387	6.0	65	448.9

PASSING DEFENSE		G	ATT	COM	PCT	INT	I%	YDS	YPA	TD	TD%	RAT
8	Marshall	13	366	175	47.8	15	4.1	2099	5.7	10	2.7	96.8

SCORING OFFENSE		G	PTS	AVG
3	Bowling Green	12	490	40.8

2003

FINAL POLLS

ESPN	AP	TEAM	RECORD
2	1	USC	12-1
1	2	LSU	13-1
3	3	Oklahoma	12-2
4	4	Ohio State	11-2
5	5	Miami, Fla.	11-2
7	6	Michigan	10-3
6	7	Georgia	11-3
8	8	Iowa	10-3
9	9	Washington State	10-3
12	10	Miami (Ohio)	13-1
10	11	Florida State	10-3
11	12	Texas	10-3
14	13	Mississippi	10-3
13	14	Kansas State	11-4
16	15	Tennessee	10-3
15	16	Boise State	13-1
20	17	Maryland	10-3
19	18	Purdue	9-4
18	19	Nebraska	10-3
17	20	Minnesota	10-3
21	21	Utah	10-2
22	22	Clemson	9-4
23	23	Bowling Green	11-3
25	24	Florida	8-5
24	25	TCU	11-2

CONFERENCE STANDINGS

	CONFERENCE			OVERALL		
	W	L	T	W	L	T
EAST						
Miami (Ohio)	8	0	0	13	1	0
Marshall	6	2	0	8	4	0
Akron	5	3	0	7	5	0
Kent State	4	4	0	5	7	0
Central Florida	2	6	0	3	9	0
Ohio U	1	7	0	2	10	0
Buffalo	1	7	0	1	11	0
WEST						
Bowling Green	7	1	0	11	3	0
Northern Illinois	6	2	0	10	2	0
Toledo	6	2	0	8	4	0
Western Michigan	4	4	0	5	7	0
Ball State	3	5	0	4	8	0
Eastern Michigan	2	6	0	3	9	0
Central Michigan	1	7	0	3	9	0

Championship **Miami (Ohio) 49 Bowling Green 27**

Temple*				1	11	0

BOWL GAMES

DATE	GAME	SCORE
D18	**GMAC**	Miami (Ohio) 49, Louisville 28
D26	**Motor City**	Bowling Green 28, Northwestern 24

ALL-CONFERENCE TEAM

POS	**Offense**	**School**
QB	Ben Roethlisberger	Miami (Ohio)
RB	Anthony Sherrell	Eastern Michigan
RB	P.J. Pope	Bowling Green
RB	Michael Turner	Northern Illinois
WR	P.J. Fleck	Northern Illinois
WR	Lance Moore	Toledo
WR	Darius Watts	Marshall
C	Scott Mruczkowski	Bowling Green
OL	Jacob Bell	Miami (Ohio)
OL	Jake VerStraete	Northern Illinois
OL	Nick Kaczur	Toledo
OL	Nathan McPeek	Marshall
TE	Andrew Clarke	Toledo
P/K	Steve Azar	Northern Illinois

POS	**Defense**	**School**
L	Phil Smith	Miami (Ohio)
L	Vinson Reynolds	Northern Illinois
L	Jason Babin	Western Michigan
L	Jamus Martin	Marshall
ILB	David Lusky	Eastern Michigan
ILB	Terrell Jones	Miami (Ohio)
OLB	Brian Atkinson	Northern Illinois
OLB	Lorenzo Scott	Ball State
DB	Justin Beriault	Ball State
DB	Janssen Patton	Bowling Green
DB	Randee Drew	Northern Illinois
DB	Atari Bigby	University of Central Florida
P	Adam Anderson	Western Michigan

HEISMAN TROPHY VOTING

PLAYER	POS	SCHOOL	1ST	2ND	3RD	TOTAL
9 **Ben Roethlisberger**	QB	Miami (Ohio)	5	9	14	47

NCAA STATISTICAL LEADERS

INDIVIDUAL

PASSING	CL	G	ATT	COM	PCT	INT	I%	YDS	YPA	TD	TD%	RAT
2 Ben Roethlisberger, Miami (Ohio)	JR	14	495	342	69.1	10	2.0	4486	9.1	37	7.5	165.8
6 Bruce Gradkowski, Toledo	SO	12	389	277	71.2	7	1.8	3210	8.3	29	7.5	161.5

ALL-PURPOSE	POS	CL	G	RUSH	REC	PR	KR	YDS	YPG
3 Jerry Seymour, Central Michigan	RB	FR	9	1117	103	0	330	1550	172.2
5 Michael Turner, Northern Illinois	RB	SR	12	1648	230	0	58	1936	161.3
7 Lance Moore, Toledo	WR	JR	12	26	1194	219	456	1895	157.9
10 Anthony Sherrell, Eastern Michigan	RB	JR	12	1531	304	0	0	1835	152.9

RUSHING/YARDS PER GAME	POS	CL	G	ATT	YDS	TD	AVG	YPG
2 Michael Turner, Northern Illinois	RB	SR	12	310	1648	14	5.3	137.3
7 Anthony Sherrell, Eastern Michigan	RB	JR	12	338	1531	12	4.5	127.6
9 Jerry Seymour, Central Michigan	RB	FR	9	205	1117	8	5.5	124.1

RECEIVING	POS	CL	G	REC	YDS	TD	RPG	YPR	YPG
4 Martin Nance, Miami (Ohio)	WR	JR	14	90	1498	11	6.4	16.6	107.0

PUNTING	POS	CL	PUNT	YDS	AVG
1 Matt Prater, Central Florida	P	SO	58	2781	48.0

PUNT RETURNS	POS	CL	PR	YDS	TD	AVG
2 Ryne Robinson, Miami (Ohio)	WR	FR	38	654	3	17.2

FIELD GOALS	POS	CL	FGA	FGM	PCT	FGG
8 Steve Azar, Northern Illinois	K	SR	26	21	0.81	1.75

TEAM

PASSING OFFENSE	G	ATT	COM	INT	PCT	YDS	YPA	TD	I%	YPC	YPG
4 Miami (Ohio)	14	535	363	11	67.9	4772	8.9	38	2.1	13.2	340.9
7 Akron	12	449	287	10	63.9	3736	8.3	22	2.2	13.0	311.3
8 Western Michigan	12	450	272	20	60.4	3701	8.2	31	4.4	13.6	308.4
9 Bowling Green	14	528	345	13	65.3	4206	8.0	32	2.5	12.2	300.4

TOTAL OFFENSE	G	P	YDS	AVG	TD	YPG
2 Miami (Ohio)	14	1053	7016	6.7	82	501.1
3 Bowling Green	14	1111	6954	6.3	61	496.7
9 Akron	12	923	5643	6.1	55	470.3

SCORING OFFENSE	G	PTS	AVG
1 Miami (Ohio)	14	602	43.0
10 Akron	12	435	36.3

TURNOVER MARGIN	G	FR	INT	TOT	FL	INTL	TOT	MAR
3 Miami (Ohio)	14	18	21	39	8	11	19	1.4
6 Northern Illinois	12	8	23	31	7	10	17	1.2
9 Toledo	12	10	15	25	6	8	14	0.9

*Independent or other conference affiliation

2004

NCAA Statistical Leaders

Conference Standings

EAST	Conference		Overall	
	W	L	W	L
Miami (Ohio)	7	1	8	5
Akron	6	2	6	5
Marshall	6	2	6	6
Kent State	4	4	5	6
Ohio U	2	6	4	7
Buffalo	2	6	2	8
Central Florida	0	8	0	11
WEST				
Toledo	7	1	9	4
Northern Illinois	7	1	9	3
Bowling Green	6	2	9	3
Eastern Michigan	4	4	4	7
Central Michigan	3	5	4	7
Ball State	2	6	2	9
Western Michigan	0	8	1	10

Championship **Toledo 35 Miami (Ohio) 27**

Temple*			2	9

Bowl Games

DATE	GAME	SCORE
D22	**GMAC**	Bowling Green 52, Memphis 35
D23	**Fort Worth**	Cinncinnati 32, Marshall 14
D27	**Motor City**	Connecticut 39, Toledo 10
D28	**Independence**	Iowa State 17, Miami (Ohio) 13
D30	**Silicon Valley Classic**	Northern Illinois 34, Troy 21

Consensus All-Americans

POS	Defense	HT	WT	CL	School	AP	CF	FC	FN	FW
None										

OTHERS RECEIVING FIRST-TEAM HONORS
DL	Jonathan Goddard		Marshall	•

All-Conference Team

POS	**Offense**	School
QB	Omar Jacobs	Bowling Green
RB	Adell Givens	Ball State
RB	Garrett Wolfe	Northern Illinois
WR	Dante Ridgeway	Ball State
WR	Lance Moore	Toledo
WR	Greg Jennings	Western Michigan
OL	Rob Warren	Bowling Green
OL	Jake VerStraete	Northern Illinois
OL	Nick Kaczur	Toledo
OL	Adam Kieft	Central Michigan
C	Brian VanAcker	Northern Illinois
TE	Tony Scheffler	Western Michigan
TE	Brad Cieslak	Northern Illinois
K	Andrew Wellock	Eastern Michigan

POS	**Defense**	School
L	Marcus Johnson	Miami (Ohio)
L	Travis Moore	Northern Illinois
ILB	Jovan Burkes	Bowling Green
LB	Javan Lee	Northern Illinois
OLB	Lorenzo Scott	Ball State
OLB	Brian Atkinson	Northern Illinois
OLB	Terna Nande	Miami (Ohio)
DB	Justin Beriault	Ball State
DB	Keon Newson	Bowling Green
DB	Lionel Hickenbottom	Northern Illinois
DB	Patrick Body	Toledo
P	Reggie Hodges	Ball State

Individual

PASSING		CL	G	ATT	COM	PCT	INT	I%	YDS	YPA	TD	TD%	RAT
4	Omar Jacobs, Bowling Green	SO	12	462	309	66.9	4	0.9	4002	8.7	41	8.9	167.2
5	Bruce Gradkowski, Toledo	JR	13	399	280	70.2	8	2.0	3518	8.8	27	6.8	162.6

ALL-PURPOSE		POS	CL		GRU	SREC	PR	KR		YDS		YPG
3	Garrett Wolfe, Northern Illinois	RB	SO	11	1656	117	0	231		2004		182.2
9	Jerry Seymour, Central Michigan	RB	SO	11	1284	413	0	105		1802		163.8

RUSHING/YARDS PER GAME		POS	CL	G	ATT	YDS		TD	AVG		YPG
5	Garrett Wolfe, Northern Illinois	RB	SO	11	256	1656		18	6.5		150.6

RUSHING/YARDS PER CARRY		POS	CL	G	ATT	YDS					YPC
5	Garrett Wolfe, Northern Illinois	RB	SO	11	256	1656					6.5

RECEIVING		POS	CL	G	REC	YDS	TD	RPG	YPG		YPG
1	Dante Ridgway, Ball State	WR	JR	11	105	1399	8	9.6	13.3		127.2
4	Eric Deslauriers, Eastern Michigan	WR	JR	11	84	1257	13	7.6	15.0		114.3
8	Greg Jennings, Western Michigan	WR	SR	11	74	1092	11	6.7	14.8		99.3

PUNT RETURNS		POS	CL	PR	YDS	TD	AVG
5	Domenik Hixon, Akron	WR	JR	16	275	1	17.2
7	Dan Sheldon, Northern Illinois	WR	SR	24	394	1	16.4

KICKOFF RETURNS		POS	CL	KR	YDS	TD	AVG
7	Asante White, Central Michigan	WR	FR	12	336	0	28.0

SCORING		POS	CL	TDS	XP	FG	PTS	PTPG
3	Garrett Wolfe, Northern Illinois	RB	SO	21	0	0	126	11.5
4	P.J. Pope, Bowling Green	RB	JR	21	0	0	126	10.5

FIELD GOALS		POS	CL	FGA	FGM	PCT	FGG
3	Andrew Wellock, Eastern Michigan	K	SO	23	21	0.91	1.91

INTERCEPTIONS		POS	CL	INT	YDS	TD	INT/GM
4	Keon Newson, Bowling Green	DB	SR	6	107	2	0.50
4	Chris Royal, Marshall	DB	JR	6	103	1	0.50

Team

PASSING OFFENSE		G	ATT	COM	INT	PCT	YDS	YPA	TD	I%	YPC	YPG
3	Bowling Green	12	472	313	4	66.3	4057	8.6	41	0.9	13.0	338.1
8	Toledo	13	449	308	10	68.6	3879	8.6	28	2.2	12.6	298.4

TOTAL OFFENSE		G	P	YDS	AVG	TD	YPG
2	Bowling Green	12	904	6076	6.7	69	506.3

SCORING OFFENSE		G	PTS	AVG
4	Bowling Green	12	532	44.3

TURNOVER MARGIN		G	FR	INT	TOT	FL	INTL	TOT	MAR
3	Bowling Green	12	11	14	25	6	4	10	1.3

2005

CONFERENCE STANDINGS

	CONFERENCE		OVERALL	
MAC EAST	W	L	W	L
Akron	5	3	7	6
Miami (Ohio)	5	3	7	4
Bowling Green	5	3	6	5
Ohio U	3	5	4	7
Buffalo	1	7	1	10
Kent State	0	8	1	10
WEST				
Northern Illinois	6	2	7	5
Toledo	6	2	9	3
Western Michigan	5	3	7	4
Central Michigan	5	3	6	5
Ball State	4	4	4	7
Eastern Michigan	3	5	4	7

Championship **Akron 31 Northern Illinois 30**

Temple*			0	11

BOWL GAMES

DATE	GAME	SCORE
D21	**GMAC**	Toledo 45, UTEP 13
D26	**Motor City**	Memphis 38, Akron 31

CONSENSUS ALL-AMERICANS

POS	DEFENSE	HT	WT	CL	SCHOOL	AP	CF	FC	SN	FW
None										

OTHERS RECEIVING FIRST-TEAM HONORS
DB	**Dion Bynum**	Ohio	•

ALL-CONFERENCE TEAM

POS	**Offense**	**School**
QB	Bruce Gradkowski	Toledo
RB	Trinity Dawson	Toledo
RB	Kalvin McRae	Ohio
RB	Garrett Wolfe	Northern Illinois
WR	Sam Hurd	Northern Illinois
WR	Martin Nance	Miami (Ohio)
WR	Greg Jennings	Western Michigan
C	Brian VanAcker	Northern Illinois
OL	Nate Bunce	Miami (Ohio)
OL	Doug Free	Northern Illinois
OL	Ben Leuck	Northern Illinois
OL	John Greco	Toledo
TE	Tony Scheffler	Western Michigan
K	Andrew Wellock.	Eastern Michigan

POS	**Defense**	**School**
L	Dan Bazuin	Central Michigan
L	Justin Parrish	Kent State
L	Marcus Johnson	Miami (Ohio)
ILB	Matt Muncy	Ohio U.
ILB	Ameer Ismail	Western Michigan
OLB	Terna Nande	Miami (Ohio)
OLB	John Busing	Miami (Ohio)
OLB	Mike Alston	Toledo
DB	Ray Smith	Northern Illinois
DB	Darrell Hunter	Miami (Ohio)
DB	Dion Byrum	Ohio
DB	Keon Jackson	Toledo
NIU	Quince Holman	Northern Illinois
P	Chris Miller	Ball State

NCAA STATISTICAL LEADERS

INDIVIDUAL

PASSING		CL	G	ATT	COM	PCT	INT	I%	YDS	YPA	TD	TD%	RTG
6	Phil Horvath, Northern Illinois	Jr.	9	238	168	70.6	8	3.4	2001	8.4	18	7.6	159.2

ALL-PURPOSE		POS	CL	G	RUSH	REC	PR	KR	YDS	YPG
2	Garrett Wolfe, Northern Illinois	RB	Jr.	9	1580	222	0	0	1802	200.2
7	Domenik Hixon, Akron	WR	Sr.	13	24	1210	200	705	2139	164.5

RUSHING/YARDS PER GAME		POS	CL	G	ATT	YDS	TD	AVG	YPG
2	Garrett Wolfe, Northern Illinois	RB	Jr.	9	242	1580	16	6.5	175.6

RECEIVING		POS	CL	G	REC	YDS	TD	RPG	YPG
2	Greg Jennings, Western Mich.	WR	Sr.	11	98	1259	14	8.9	114.5
8	Ryan Robinson, Miami (Ohio)	WR	Jr.	11	75	1119	8	6.8	101.7

FIELD GOALS		POS	CL	FGA	FGM	PCT	FGG
9	Todd Soderquist, Miami (Ohio)	K	Sr.	27	19	0.70	1.73

INTERCEPTIONS		POS	CL	INT	YDS	TD	INT/GM
2	Dion Bynum, Ohio U	DB	Sr.	6	153	2	.55
2	Jelani Jordan, Bowling Green	DB	Sr.	6	66	0	.55

TEAM

TURNOVER MARGIN		G	FR	INT	TOT	FL	INTL	TOT	MAR
5	Miami (Ohio)	11	15	20	35	8	14	22	1.2

Independent or other conference affiliation

2006

CONFERENCE STANDINGS

	CONFERENCE		OVERALL	
	W	L	W	L
EAST				
Ohio U	7	1	9	5
Kent State	5	3	6	6
Akron	3	5	5	7
Bowling Green	3	5	4	8
Miami (Ohio)	2	6	2	10
Buffalo	1	7	2	10
WEST				
Central Michigan	7	1	10	4
Western Michigan	6	2	8	5
Northern Illinois	5	3	7	6
Ball State	5	3	5	7
Toledo	3	5	5	7
Eastern Michigan	1	7	1	11

Championship **Central Michigan 31 Ohio 10**

Temple*			1	11

BOWL GAMES

DATE	GAME	SCORE
D19	**Poinsettia**	TCU 37, No. Illinois 7
J6	**International**	Cincinnati 27, Western Michigan 24
J7	**GMAC**	Southern Miss 28, Ohio 7

ALL-CONFERENCE TEAM

POS	Offense	School
QB	Dan LeFevour	Central Michigan
RB	Garrett Wolfe	Northern Illinois
RB	Kalvin McRae	Ohio U.
RB	Jalen Parmele	Toledo
WR	Bryan Anderson	Central Michigan
WR	Eric Deslauriers	Eastern Michigan
WR	Ryne Robinson	Miami (Ohio)
WR	Chris Hopkins	Toledo
C	Kory Lichtensteiger	Bowling Green
OL	Matt Coppage	Ohio U.
OL	John Greco	Toledo
OL	Doug Free	Northern Illinois
K	Andrew Wellock	Eastern Michigan

POS	Defense	School
L	Dan Muir	Kent State
L	Larry English	Northern Illinois
LB	Red Keith	Central Michigan
LB	Matt Muncy	Ohio U.
LB	Ameer Ismail	Western Michigan
OLB	Mike Alston	Toledo
DB	Joey Card	Miami (Ohio)
DB	T.J. Wright	Ohio U.
DB	Barry Church	Toledo
DB	Londen Fryar	Western Michigan
P	Chris Miller	Ball State

NCAA STATISTICAL LEADERS

INDIVIDUAL

ALL-PURPOSE		POS	CL	GRUSH	REC	PR	KR	YDS	YPG
1	Garrett Wolfe, Northern Illinois	RB	Sr.	13 1928	249	0	0	2177	167.5

RUSHING/YARDS PER GAME		POS	CL	G	ATT	YDS	TD	AVG	YPG
1	Garrett Wolfe, Northern Illinois	RB	Sr.	13	309	1928	18	6.2	148.3

RUSHING/YARDS PER CARRY		POS	CL	G	ATT	YDS	YPC
10	Garrett Wolfe, Northern Illinois	RB	Sr.	13	309	1928	6.2

RECEIVING		POS	CL	G	REC	YDS	TD	RPG	YPG
5	Ryne Robinson, Miami (Ohio)	WR	Sr.	12	91	1178	8	7.6	98.2

PUNTING		POS	CL	PUNT	YDS	AVG
2	Chris Miller, Ball State	P	Jr.	57	2637	46.3

PUNT RETURNS		POS	CL	PR	YDS	TD	AVG
7	Chris Garrett, Ohio	WR	Fr.	26	378	1	14.5
8	Joe Chapple, Western Michigan	WR	Sr.	16	230	0	14.4

KICKOFF RETURNS		POS	CL	KR	YDS	TD	AVG
2	David Harvey, Akron	WR	Fr.	17	510	0	30.0
8	Brandon West, Western Michigan	RB	Fr.	22	615	1	28.0

SCORING		POS	CL	TDS	XP	FG	PTS	PTPG
7	Garrett Wolfe, Northern Illinois	RB	Sr.	19	0	0	116	8.9

FIELD GOALS		POS	CL	FGA	FGM	PCT	FGG
9	Chris Nendick, Northern Illinois	K	Jr.	27	20	0.74	1.54

TEAM

RUSHING DEFENSE		G	ATT	YDS	AVG	TD	YPG
6	Western Michigan	13	380	989	2.6	11	76.1

PASSING DEFENSE		G	ATT	COM	PCT	INT	I%	YDS	YPA	TD	TD%	RAT
5	Kent State	12	326	171	52.5	16	4.9	1907	5.9	8	2.5	99.9

TURNOVER MARGIN		G	FR	INT	TOT	FL	INTL	TOT	MAR
7	Western Michigan	13	10	24	34	9	13	22	0.92

MAC BOWLS

What follows is a compendium of every bowl game in which a Mid-American Conference team ever played, along with a record of the pre- and (when recorded) postgame national rankings for each team. When possible, we have also included the MVPs cited in media guides, on the bowls' websites, or in reported accounts of the game.

Those looking for the former Tangerine Bowl—which featured MAC champions in the late 1960s and early '70s—can find it under the Capital One Bowl, the game's new corporate name.

These summaries were assembled from a variety of sources, including bowl records, local libraries, newspapers, media guides, books, and the Pro Football Hall of Fame (for the College All-Star Game). If a scoring summary does not appear, we were unable to piece one together from published accounts of the game.

The first section is comprised of bowl games currently certified by the NCAA in which MAC teams have played. Defunct bowls—excluding unsanctioned games involving lesser quality opponents or squads of servicemen—appear following that. In both sections, bowls appear in alphabetical order.

ARMED FORCES BOWL

PROFILE

Site: Fort Worth, Texas
Stadium: Amon G. Carter
Capacity: 44,008
Surface: Grass

PLAYING SITES

Amon G. Carter Stadium, since 2003

NAME CHANGES

PlainsCapital Fort Worth Bowl, 2003-2004
Fort Worth Bowl, 2005
Bell Helicopter Armed Forces Bowl, since 2006

SEASON	DATE	PRE-GAME RANK	TEAMS	SCORE	FINAL RANK	MOST VALUABLE PLAYERS	ATT.
2004	Dec. 23, 2004		**Cincinnati**	32		Gino Guidugli, Cincinnati, QB	27,902
			Marshall	14		Josh Davis, Marshall, WR	

DECEMBER 23, 2004
CINCINNATI 32, MARSHALL 14

	1ST	2ND	3RD	4TH	FINAL
CIN	10	14	0	8	32
MAR	14	0	0	0	14

SCORING SUMMARY
CIN Giddens 9 blocked punt return (Lovell kick)
CIN FG Lovell 23
MAR Davis 14 pass from Hill (O'Connor kick)
MAR Smith 32 interception return (O'Connor kick)
CIN Celek 15 pass from Guidugli (Lovell kick)
CIN Jackson 8 pass from Guidugli (Lovell kick)
CIN FG Lovell 19
CIN FG Lovell 35

CIN	TEAM STATISTICS	MAR
24	First Downs	11
168	Rushing Yards	(-3)
24-39-2	Passing	14-32-1
231	Passing Yards	137
399	Total Yards	134
3-53	Punt Returns - Yards	1-8
2-41	Kickoff Returns - Yards	7-133
2-40.0	Punts - Average	5-25.6
1-0	Fumbles - Lost	2-1
6-60	Penalties - Yards	1-5
38:27	Possession Time	21:33

INDIVIDUAL LEADERS
RUSHING
CIN: Hall 23-62; Glatthaar 10-48.
MAR: Charles 7-9; Hill 5-4.
PASSING
CIN: Guidugli 24-36-1, 231 yards, 2 TD.
MAR: Hill 14-30-1, 137 yards, 1 TD.
RECEIVING
CIN: Thomas 9-102; Hall 5-38.
MAR: Davis 5-67, 1 TD; Deifel 1-30.

CAPITAL ONE BOWL

PROFILE

Site: Orlando, Fla.
Stadium: Florida Citrus Bowl
Capacity: 70,000
Surface: Grass

PLAYING SITES

Tangerine Bowl, 1947-72
Florida Field, 1973
Tangerine Bowl, now Florida Citrus Bowl, 1974-82
Orlando Stadium, now Florida Citrus Bowl, 1983-85
Florida Citrus Bowl, since 1986

NAME CHANGES

Tangerine Bowl, 1947-82
Florida Citrus Bowl, 1983-93
CompUSA Florida Citrus Bowl, 1994-99
OurHouse.com Florida Citrus Bowl, 2000
Capital One/Florida Citrus Bowl, 2001-02
Capital One Bowl, since 2003

SEASON	DATE	PRE-GAME RANK	TEAMS	SCORE	FINAL RANK	MOST VALUABLE PLAYERS	ATT.
1962	Dec. 22, 1962		**Houston**	49		Joe Lopasky, Houston	7,500
			Miami (Ohio)	21		Billy Roland, Houston	
1968	Dec. 27, 1968		**Richmond**	49		Buster O'Brien, Richmond, B	16,114
		15	**Ohio U.**	42	20	Walker Gillette, Richmond, L	
1969	Dec. 26, 1969	20	**Toledo**	56		Chuck Ealey, Toledo, QB	16,311
			Davidson	33		Dan Crockett, Toledo, L	
1970	Dec. 28, 1970	15	**Toledo**	40	12	Chuck Ealey, Toledo, QB	15,164
			William & Mary	12		Vince Hublen, William & Mary, L	
1971	Dec. 28, 1971	14	**Toledo**	28	14	Chuck Ealey, Toledo, QB	16,750
			Richmond	3		Mel Long, Toledo, L	
1972	Dec. 29, 1972		**Tampa**	21		Freddie Solomon, Tampa, B	20,062
			Kent State	18		Jack Lambert, Kent State, L	
1973	Dec. 22, 1973	15	**Miami (Ohio)**	16	15	Chuck Varner, Miami, B	37,234
			Florida	7		Brad Cousino, Miami, L	
1974	Dec. 21, 1974	15	**Miami (Ohio)**	21	10	Sherman Smith, Miami, B	15,897
			Georgia	10		Brad Cousino and John Roudebush, Miami, L	
1975	Dec. 20, 1975	16	**Miami (Ohio)**	20	12	Rob Carpenter, Miami, B	20,247
			South Carolina	7		Jeff Kelly, Miami, L	

DECEMBER 22, 1962
HOUSTON 49, MIAMI (OHIO) 21

	1ST	2ND	3RD	4TH	FINAL
HOU	7	28	7	7	49
MIA	7	0	7	7	21

SCORING SUMMARY
MIA Myers 9 pass from Kellerman (Jencks kick)
HOU Lopasky 3 run (McMillan kick)
HOU Brezena 1 run (McMillan kick)
HOU Brezena 44 pass from Roland (McMillan kick)
HOU Lopasky 70 punt return (McMillan kick)
HOU McMillan 5 pass from Roland (McMillan kick)
MIA Kellerman 1 run (Jencks kick)
HOU Lopasky 4 run (McMillan kick)
MIA Neumeier 10 run (Jencks kick)
HOU Lopasky 13 pass from Roland (McMillan kick)

HOU	TEAM STATISTICS	MIA
17	First Downs	18
207	Rushing Yards	54
13-19-1	Passing	17-40-2
206	Passing Yards	265
413	Total Yards	319
3-41.3	Punts - Average	5-38.8
7-83	Penalties - Yards	7-65

INDIVIDUAL LEADERS
RUSHING
HOU: Brezena 11-55, 1 TD; Roland 7-48.
MIA: Longsworth 6-27; Neumeier 3-14, 1 TD.
PASSING
HOU: Roland 11-17-1, 199 yards, 3 TD.
MIA: Kellermann 17-40-2, 265 yards, 1 TD.
RECEIVING
HOU: Lopasky 3-81, 1 TD; Brewer 2-58.
MIA: Jencks 5-75; Myers 5-75.

DECEMBER 27, 1968
RICHMOND 49, OHIO 42

	1ST	2ND	3RD	4TH	FINAL
UR	7	21	14	7	49
OU	7	14	13	8	42

SCORING SUMMARY
OU Snyder 40 pass from Bryant (Pataki kick)
UR Livesay 24 pass from O'Brien (Dussault kick)
UR O'Brien 31 run (Dussault kick)
OU Bryant 7 run (Pataki kick)
UR Kellum 1 run (Dussault kick)
UR Gillette 5 pass from O'Brien (Dussault kick)
OU Snyder 2 pass from Bryant (Pataki kick)
UR Kellum 9 run (Dussault kick)
UR Crenshaw 12 pass from O'Brien (Dussault kick)
OU LeVeck 1 run (run failed)
OU Snyder 4 pass from Bryant (Pataki kick)
UR Livesay 15 pass from O'Brien (Dussault kick)
OU Houmard 3 pass from Bryant (LeVeck run)

INDIVIDUAL LEADERS
RUSHING
UR: O'Brien 7-39, 1 TD; Kellum 15-36, 2 TD.
OU: LeVeck 20-85, 1 TD; Bryant 17-74, 1 TD.
PASSING
UR: O'Brien 39-58-1, 447 yards, 4 TD.
OU: Bryant 17-33-2, 233 yards, 4 TD.
RECEIVING
UR: Gillette 20-242, 1 TD; Livesay 10-127, 2 TD.
OU: Snyder 11-214, 3 TD; Swindell 3-28.

DECEMBER 26, 1969
TOLEDO 56, DAVIDSON 33

	1ST	2ND	3RD	4TH	FINAL
TOL	14	28	0	14	56
DAV	7	0	14	12	33

SCORING SUMMARY
TOL	Ealey 52 run (Crots kick)
DAV	Zaharov 1 run (Terry kick)
TOL	Cole 1 run (Crots kick)
TOL	Seymour 10 pass from Ealey (Crots kick)
TOL	Crockett 34 pass from Ealey (Crots kick)
TOL	Seymour 5 pass from Ealey (Crots kick)
TOL	Cole 11 run (Crots kick)
DAV	Hannen 12 pass from Slade (kick failed)
DAV	Hannen 16 pass from Slade (Mikolayunas pass from Slade)
DAV	Hannen 8 pass from Slade (pass failed)
TOL	Cole 16 run (Crots kick)
DAV	Lyon 29 pass from Slade (pass failed)
TOL	Aschliman recovered fumble in end zone (Crots kick)

TOL	TEAM STATISTICS	DAV
22	First Downs	24
334	Rushing Yards	101
11-14-0	Passing	22-38-0
147	Passing Yards	305
481	Total Yards	406
4-28.0	Punts - Average	5-36.0
6-65	Penalties - Yards	2-17

DECEMBER 28, 1970
TOLEDO 40, WILLIAM & MARY 12

	1ST	2ND	3RD	4TH	FINAL
TOL	0	7	13	20	40
W&M	6	0	0	6	12

SCORING SUMMARY
W&M	Bushnell 10 run (kick failed)
TOL	Cole 1 run (Duncan kick)
TOL	Harris 15 run (Duncan kick)
TOL	Schwartz 9 run (kick failed)
TOL	Fair 4 pass from Ealey (Duncan kick)
TOL	Ealey 3 run (Duncan kick)
TOL	Niezgoda 52 interception return (kick failed)
W&M	Regan 2 run (pass failed)

TOL	TEAM STATISTICS	W&M
26	First Downs	15
326	Rushing Yards	139
12-22-0	Passing	13-22-2
128	Passing Yards	127
454	Total Yards	266
2-38.5	Punts - Average	7-38.4
9-100	Penalties - Yards	7-66

DECEMBER 28, 1971
TOLEDO 28, RICHMOND 3

	1ST	2ND	3RD	4TH	FINAL
TOL	0	14	0	14	28
UR	3	0	0	0	3

SCORING SUMMARY
UR	FG Clark 27
TOL	Long recovered fumble in end zone (Keim kick)
TOL	Schwartz 1 run (Keim kick)
TOL	Ealey 1 run (Keim kick)
TOL	Schwartz 3 run (Keim kick)

TOL	TEAM STATISTICS	UR
25	First Downs	7
206	Rushing Yards	114
15-24-0	Passing	2-11-2
189	Passing Yards	24
395	Total Yards	138
4-34.7	Punts - Average	7-46.4
1-1	Fumbles - Lost	1-1
5-51	Penalties - Yards	10-70

INDIVIDUAL LEADERS
RUSHING
TOL: Schwartz 20-51, 2 TD; Ealey 12-38, 1 TD.
UR: Meyers 13-32; Smith 10-51.
PASSING
TOL: Ealey 14-23-0, 176 yards.
UR: Nichols 2-11-2, 24 yards.
RECEIVING
TOL: Fair 8-100; Baker 2-37.
UR: Popovich 1-12; Smith 1-12.

DECEMBER 29, 1972
TAMPA 21, KENT STATE 18

	1ST	2ND	3RD	4TH	FINAL
TAM	14	7	0	0	21
KENT	0	0	6	12	18

SCORING SUMMARY
TAM	Orndorff 15 pass from Carter (Cooper kick)
TAM	Orndorff 35 pass from Carter (Cooper kick)
TAM	Solomon 2 run (Cooper kick)
KENT	Tinker 76 pass from Kokal (kick failed)
KENT	Dooner 10 pass from Kokal (run failed)
KENT	Harmon 78 punt return (kick failed)

DECEMBER 22, 1973
MIAMI (OHIO) 16, FLORIDA 7

	1ST	2ND	3RD	4TH	FINAL
MIA	3	0	10	3	16
UF	0	0	0	7	7

SCORING SUMMARY
MIA	FG Draudt 26
MIA	FG Draudt 45
MIA	Varner 3 run (Draudt kick)
UF	Moore 1 run (Williams kick)
MIA	FG Draudt 27

MIA	TEAM STATISTICS	UF
14	First Downs	12
239	Rushing Yards	90
1-8-0	Passing	9-21-4
6	Passing Yards	99
245	Total Yards	189
10-33.3	Punts - Average	6-34.3
2-1	Fumbles - Lost	4-3
3-39	Penalties - Yards	3-27

INDIVIDUAL LEADERS
RUSHING
MIA: Varner 28-157, 1 TD; Hitchens 20-62.
UF: Moore 16-101, 1 TD; Richards 7-49.
PASSING
MIA: Sanna 1-8-0, 6 yards.
UF: Bowden 5-9-1, 66 yards.
RECEIVING
MIA: Williams 1-6.
UF: Moore 3-30; Foldberg 2-25.

DECEMBER 21, 1974
MIAMI (OHIO) 21, GEORGIA 10

	1ST	2ND	3RD	4TH	FINAL
MIA	14	7	0	0	21
UGA	3	0	7	0	10

SCORING SUMMARY
MIA	Carpenter 1 run (Draudt kick)
UGA	FG Leavitt 20
MIA	Taylor 7 pass from Smith (Draudt kick)
MIA	Smith 8 run (Draudt kick)
UGA	Goff 1 run (Leavitt kick)

MIA	TEAM STATISTICS	UGA
18	First Downs	17
228	Rushing Yards	74
3-8-0	Passing	11-24-0
39	Passing Yards	200
267	Total Yards	274
5-36.0	Punts - Average	4-30.0
3-3	Fumbles - Lost	5-2
3-25	Penalties - Yards	20-24

INDIVIDUAL LEADERS
RUSHING
MIA: Carpenter 30-114, 1 TD; Smith 22-90, 1 TD.
UGA: Harrison 17-69.
PASSING
MIA: Smith 1-2-0, 7 yards; Sanna 2-24-0, 22 yards.
UGA: Robinson 11-24-0, 190 yards.
RECEIVING
MIA: Schulte 1-15; Taylor 1-7, 1 TD.
UGA: Appleby 6-102; Wilson 3-45.

DECEMBER 20, 1975
MIAMI (OHIO) 20, SOUTH CAROLINA 7

	1ST	2ND	3RD	4TH	FINAL
MIA	7	7	3	3	20
USC	0	0	7	0	7

SCORING SUMMARY
MIA	Carpenter 5 run (Johnson kick)
MIA	Carpenter 1 run (Johnson kick)
MIA	FG Johnson 47
USC	Amrein 3 run (Marino kick)
MIA	FG Johnson 33

MIA	TEAM STATISTICS	USC
19	First Downs	17
238	Rushing Yards	56
10-13-1	Passing	18-29-1
137	Passing Yards	228
375	Total Yards	284
4-35.8	Punts - Average	6-44.8
0-0	Fumbles - Lost	1-0
5-35	Penalties - Yards	3-24

INDIVIDUAL LEADERS
RUSHING
MIA: Carpenter 29-120, 2 TD; Smith 17-64.
USC: Williams 9-57; Long 11-19.
PASSING
MIA: Smith 10-13-1, 137 yards.
USC: Grantz 18-29-1, 228 yards.
RECEIVING
MIA: Joecken 3-68; Walker 4-44.
USC: Logan 9-109; Stephens 4-51.

GMAC BOWL

PROFILE

Site: Mobile, Ala.
Stadium: Ladd-Peebles Stadium
Capacity: 40,686
Surface: FieldTurf

PLAYING SITES

Ladd-Peebles Stadium, since 1999

NAME CHANGES

Mobile Alabama Bowl, 1999
GMAC Mobile Alabama Bowl,
  2000
GMAC Bowl, since 2001

SEASON	DATE	PRE-GAME RANK	TEAMS	SCORE	FINAL RANK	MOST VALUABLE PLAYERS	ATT.
2001	Dec. 19, 2001		**Marshall**	64 2 OT		Byron Leftwich, Marshall, QB	40,139
			East Carolina	61			
2002	Dec. 18, 2002		**Marshall**	38	24	Byron Leftwich, Marshall, QB	40,646
			Louisville	15			
2003	Dec. 18, 2003	14	Miami (Ohio)	49	10	Ben Roethlisberger, Miami (Ohio), QB	40,620
			Louisville	28			
2004	Dec. 22, 2004		**Bowling Green**	52		Omar Jacobs, Bowling Green, QB	40,160
			Memphis	35			
2005	Dec. 21, 2005		**Toledo**	45		Bruce Gradkowski, Toledo, QB	35,422
			UTEP	13			
2006	Jan. 7, 2007		**Southern Mississippi**	28		Damion Fletcher, Southern Mississippi, RB	38,751
			Ohio	7			

DECEMBER 19, 2001
MARSHALL 64, EAST CAROLINA 61

	1ST	2ND	3RD	4TH	OT	OT	FINAL
MAR	0	8	28	15	7	6	64
ECU	21	17	3	10	7	3	61

SCORING SUMMARY

ECU	Hunt 12 interception return (Miller kick)
ECU	Steward 43 fumble return (Miller kick)
ECU	Garrard 9 run (Miller kick)
ECU	FG Miller 25
MAR	Watts 35 pass from Leftwich (Buggs run)
ECU	Henry 7 run (Miller kick)
ECU	Garrard 6 run (Miller kick)
MAR	Street 25 interception return (Head kick)
MAR	Leftwich 9 run (Head kick)
ECU	FG Miller 22
MAR	Tarpley 25 interception return (Head kick)
MAR	Wallace 15 run (Head kick)
ECU	FG Miller 32
MAR	Marriott 30 pass from Leftwich (pass failed)
ECU	Henry 55 run (Miller kick)
MAR	FG Head 27
MAR	Watts 11 pass from Leftwich (kick failed)
MAR	Wallace 2 run (Head kick)
ECU	Leonard 25 run (Miller kick)
ECU	FG Miller 37
MAR	Davis 8 pass from Leftwich

MAR	TEAM STATISTICS	ECU
36	First Downs	23
73	Rushing Yards	331
41-70-2	Passing	11-23-2
576	Passing Yards	161
649	Total Yards	492
1-5	Punt Returns - Yards	2-12
6-88	Kickoff Returns - Yards	2-(-3)
4-35.5	Punts - Average	4-38.3
3-2	Fumbles - Lost	1-1
7-59	Penalties - Yards	5-32
46:49	Possession Time	28:11

INDIVIDUAL LEADERS

RUSHING
MAR: Wallace 17-86, 2 TD.
ECU: Henry 29-195, 2 TD; Alston 6-91; Garrard 14-40, 2 TD.

PASSING
MAR: Leftwich 41-70-2, 576 yards, 4 TD.
ECU: Garrard 11-23-2, 161 yards.

RECEIVING
MAR: Marriott 15-234, 1 TD; Watts 7-133, 2 TD; Davis 8-87, 1 TD.
ECU: Collier 4-75; Alston 2-44.

DECEMBER 18, 2002
MARSHALL 38, LOUISVILLE 15

	1ST	2ND	3RD	4TH	FINAL
LOU	0	7	0	8	15
MAR	7	10	7	14	38

SCORING SUMMARY

MAR	Marriott 9 pass from Leftwich (Head kick)
MAR	FG Head 23
MAR	Doss 8 pass from Leftwich (Head kick)
LOU	Patterson 2 run (Smith kick)
MAR	Doss 12 pass from Leftwich (Head kick)
MAR	Marriott 26 pass from Leftwich (Head kick)
MAR	Wallace 15 run (Head kick)
LOU	Jones 11 pass from Ragone (Jones pass from Ragone)

LOU	TEAM STATISTICS	MAR
20	First Downs	23
56	Rushing Yards	99
21-48-1	Passing	22-44-1
205	Passing Yards	249
261	Total Yards	348
2-15	Punt Returns - Yards	3-5
6-76	Kickoff Returns - Yards	2-24
7-43.7	Punts - Average	6-50.2
4-2	Fumbles - Lost	0-0
10-88	Penalties - Yards	17-147
26:59	Possession Time	33:01

INDIVIDUAL LEADERS

RUSHING
LOU: Ragone 9-31; Patterson 6-19, 1 TD.
MAR: Wallace 14-75, 1 TD; Carey 9-15.

PASSING
LOU: Ragone 20-45-1, 193 yards, 1 TD.
MAR: Leftwich 22-44-1, 249 yards, 4 TD.

RECEIVING
LOU: Owens 5-39; Glenn 2-26; Jones 2-25, 1 TD.
MAR: Marriott 10-137, 2 TD; Watts 3-32; Doss 3-26, 2 TD.

DECEMBER 18, 2003
MIAMI (OHIO) 49, LOUISVILLE 28

	1ST	2ND	3RD	4TH	FINAL
MIA	21	14	0	14	49
LOU	0	21	7	0	28

SCORING SUMMARY

MIA	Larkin 28 pass from Roethlisberger (Parseghian kick)
MIA	Murray 2 run (Parseghian kick)
MIA	Nance 12 pass from Roethlisberger (Parseghian kick)
LOU	Gates 1 run (Smith kick)
MIA	Brandt 16 pass from Roethlisberger (Parseghian kick)
MIA	Larkin 26 pass from Roethlisberger (Parseghian kick)
LOU	Russell 31 pass from Bush (Smith kick)
LOU	Russell 2 pass from LeFors (Smith kick)
LOU	Russell 24 pass from LeFors (Smith kick)
MIA	Smith 3 run (Parseghian kick)
MIA	Pusateri 35 interception return (Parseghian kick)

MIA	TEAM STATISTICS	LOU
28	First Downs	22
221	Rushing Yards	237
21-33-0	Passing	18-27-3
376	Passing Yards	255
597	Total Yards	492
4-17	Punt Returns - Yards	2-18
4-36	Kickoff Returns - Yards	7-92
4-30.0	Punts - Average	4-42.3
2-0	Fumbles - Lost	1-0
8-73	Penalties - Yards	5-58
30:52	Possession Time	29:08

INDIVIDUAL LEADERS

RUSHING
MIA: Murray 15-142, 1 TD; Smith 12-82, 1 TD.
LOU: Gates 12-128, 1 TD; LeFors 8-49.

PASSING
MIA: Roethlisberger 21-33-0, 376 yards, 4 TD.
LOU: LeFors 17-26-3, 224 yards, 2 TD.

RECEIVING
MIA: Nance 9-169 ,1 TD; Larkin 5-88, 2 TD.
LOU: Russell 7-144, 3 TD; Ghent 2-45.

DECEMBER 22, 2004
BOWLING GREEN 52, MEMPHIS 35

	1ST	2ND	3RD	4TH	FINAL
BG	21	14	7	10	52
MEM	7	21	0	7	35

SCORING SUMMARY

BG	Pope 1 run (Suisham kick)
BG	Sharon 18 pass from Jacobs (Gostkowski kick)
MEM	Doucette 42 pass from Wimprine (Gostkowski kick)
BG	Sharon 36 pass from Jacobs (Suisham kick)
MEM	Kelley 60 pass from Wimprine (Gostkowski kick)
BG	Sanders 31 pass from Jacobs (Suisham kick)
MEM	Avery 38 pass from Wimprine (Gostkowski kick)
MEM	Williams 31 run (Gostkowski kick)
BG	Sanders 17 pass from Jacobs (Suisham kick)
BG	Pope 13 pass from Jacobs (Suisham kick)
BG	FG Suisham 37
BG	Pope 1 run (Suisham kick)
MEM	Doucette 14 pass from Wimprine (Gostkowski kick)

BG	TEAM STATISTICS	MEM
29	First Downs	21
193	Rushing Yards	90
26-44-1	Passing	26-39-1
365	Passing Yards	324
558	Total Yards	414
2-0	Punt Returns - Yards	2-11
1-26	Kickoff Returns - Yards	3-57
4-31.8	Punts - Average	6-32.8
1-1	Fumbles - Lost	2-1
2-14	Penalties - Yards	4-28
33:23	Possession Time	26:37

INDIVIDUAL LEADERS

RUSHING
BG: Pope 28-151, 2 TD; Lane 5-36.
MEM: Williams 18-120, 1 TD.

PASSING
BG: Jacobs 26-44-1, 365 yards, 5 TD.
MEM: Wimprine 26-39-1, 324 yards, 4 TD.

RECEIVING
BG: Sanders 7-123, 2 TD; Sharon 5-117, 2 TD.
MEM: Kelley 4-108, 1 TD; Doucette 2-56, 2 TD.

DECEMBER 21, 2005
TOLEDO 45, UTEP 13

	1ST	2ND	3RD	4TH	FINAL
TOL	7	21	3	14	45
UTEP	3	10	0	0	13

SCORING SUMMARY

TOL	Allen 10 pass from Gradkowski (Robbins kick)
UTEP	FG Schneider 34
TOL	Washington 33 pass from Gradkowski (Robbins kick)
TOL	Thomas 37 interception return (Robbins kick)
UTEP	Higgins Jr. 18 pass from Palmer (Schneider kick)
UTEP	FG Schneider 23
TOL	Odom 31 pass from Gradkowski (Robbins kick)
TOL	FG Robbins 29
TOL	Powell 22 pass from Gradkowski (Robbins kick)
TOL	Hopkins 13 pass from Gradkowski (Robbins kick)

TOL	TEAM STATISTICS	UTEP
25	First Downs	16
164	Rushing Yards	63
19-32-2	Passing	17-41-2
304	Passing Yards	192
468	Total Yards	255
1-4	Punt Returns - Yards	1-1
3-112	Kickoff Returns - Yards	6-80
1-35.0	Punts - Average	5-35.4
1-1	Fumbles - Lost	1-0
9-80	Penalties - Yards	4-45
32:05	Possession Time	27:55

INDIVIDUAL LEADERS

RUSHING
TOL: Dawson 24-124; Parmele 5-19.
UTEP: Thomas 18-71; Higgins Jr. 1-15.

PASSING
TOL: Gradkowski 18-30-2, 298 yards, 5 TD.
UTEP: Palmer 14-33-1, 163 yards, 1 TD.

RECEIVING
TOL: Odom 5-97, 1 TD; Moore 4-84.
UTEP: West 6-88; Higgins Jr. 2-30, 1 TD.

JANUARY 7, 2007
SOUTHERN MISS 28, OHIO 7

	1ST	2ND	3RD	4TH	FINAL
OHIO	0	0	0	7	7
USM	0	21	7	0	28

SCORING SUMMARY

USM	Harrison 43 run (McCaleb kick)
USM	Fletcher 2 run (McCaleb kick)
USM	Denley 18 interception return (McCaleb kick)
USM	Fletcher 9 run (McCaleb kick)
OHIO	Christy 13 pass from Everson (Lasher kick)

OHIO	TEAM STATISTICS	USM
12	First Downs	17
47	Rushing Yards	124
15-37-2	Passing	14-22-1
177	Passing Yards	160
224	Total Yards	284
3-27	Punt Returns - Yards	0-0
3-32	Kickoff Returns - Yards	0-0
5-37.0	Punts - Average	4-41.8
0-0	Fumbles - Lost	1-0
6-39	Penalties - Yards	6-50
24:55	Possession Time	35:05

INDIVIDUAL LEADERS

RUSHING
OHIO: McRae 10-37; Bower 3-9.
USM: Harrison 9-68, 1 TD; Fletcher 20-58, 2 TD.

PASSING
OHIO: Everson 14-34-1, 175 yards, 1 TD; Bower 1-3-1, 2 yards.
USM: Young 14-22-1, 160 yards.

RECEIVING
OHIO: Mayle 4-56; Norwood 3-36.
USM: Barnes 4-59; Perine 3-37.

INDEPENDENCE BOWL

PROFILE

Site: Shreveport, La.
Stadium: Independence Stadium
Capacity: 50,459
Surface: Grass

PLAYING SITES

Independence Stadium, since 1976

NAME CHANGES

Independence Bowl, 1976-90
Poulan/Weed Eater Independence Bowl, 1991-97
Sanford Independence Bowl, 1998-2000
MainStay Independence Bowl, 2001-03
Independence Bowl, 2004-05
PetroSun Independence Bowl, since 2006

SEASON	DATE	PRE-GAME RANK	TEAMS	SCORE	FINAL RANK	MOST VALUABLE PLAYERS	ATT.
2004	Dec. 28, 2004		Iowa State	17		Bret Meyer, Iowa State, QB	43,000
			Miami (Ohio)	13		Nick Moser, Iowa State, DB	

DECEMBER 28, 2004
IOWA STATE 17, MIAMI (OHIO) 13

	1ST	2ND	3RD	4TH	FINAL
ISU	7	3	0	7	17
MIA	0	7	6	0	13

SCORING SUMMARY

ISU	Hicks 4 run (Culbertson kick)
ISU	FG Culbertson 23
MIA	Clemens 28 pass from Betts (Parseghian kick)
MIA	Smith 2 run (kick failed)
ISU	Kock 1 run (Culbertson kick)

ISU	TEAM STATISTICS	MIA
22	First Downs	18
295	Rushing Yards	60
10-28-0	Passing	20-44-1
114	Passing Yards	240
409	Total Yards	300
3-34	Punt Returns - Yards	3-72
1-21	Kickoff Returns - Yards	3-22
7-37.9	Punts - Average	8-45.4
0-0	Fumbles - Lost	1-0
7-71	Penalties - Yards	7-48
30:33	Possession Time	29:27

INDIVIDUAL LEADERS

RUSHING
ISU: Hicks 27-159, 1 TD; Meyer 23-122.
MIA: Smith 9-46, 1 TD.

PASSING
ISU: Meyer 10-28-0, 114 yards.
MIA: Betts 20-44-1, 240 yards, 1 TD.

RECEIVING
ISU: Blythe 3-42; Davis 3-30.
MIA: Robinson 7-101.

INTERNATIONAL BOWL

PROFILE

Site: Toronto, Ontario
Stadium: Rogers Centre
Capacity: 53,506
Surface: FieldTurf

PLAYING SITES

Rogers Centre, since 2006

NAME CHANGES

International Bowl, since 2006

SEASON	DATE	PRE-GAME RANK	TEAMS	SCORE	FINAL RANK	MOST VALUABLE PLAYERS	ATT.
2006	Jan. 6, 2007		Cincinnati	27		Dominick Goodman, Cincinnati, WR	26,717
			Western Michigan	24			

JANUARY 6, 2007
CINCINNATI 27, WESTERN MICHIGAN 24

	1ST	2ND	3RD	4TH	FINAL
WMU	0	17	0	7	24
CIN	14	10	0	3	27

SCORING SUMMARY

CIN	Bowie 25 interception return (Lovell kick)
CIN	Goodman 21 pass from Davila (Lovell kick)
CIN	Goodman 21 pass from Davila (Lovell kick)
CIN	FG Lovell 37
WMU	Simmons 76 pass from Biggers (Meyer kick)
WMU	Martin 30 pass from Cubit (Meyer kick)
WMU	FG Meyer 29
WMU	West 7 run (Meyer kick)
CIN	FG Lovell 33

WMU	TEAM STATISTICS	CIN
19	First Downs	21
108	Rushing Yards	126
24-45-2	Passing	20-37-2
260	Passing Yards	221
368	Total Yards	347
0-0	Punt Returns - Yards	1-13
2-33	Kickoff Returns - Yards	4-57
7-41.6	Punts - Average	5-43.6
0-0	Fumbles - Lost	2-1
3-19	Penalties - Yards	2-20
29:45	Possession Time	30:15

INDIVIDUAL LEADERS

RUSHING
WMU: West 21-109, 1 TD; Thompson 6-9.
CIN: Benton 10-62; Moore 10-57.

PASSING
WMU: Cubit 23-42-2, 184 yards, 1 TD; Biggers 1-1-0, 76 yards, 1 TD.
CIN: Davila 19-35-2, 214 yards, 2 TD.

RECEIVING
WMU: Simmons 13-172, 1 TD; Ledbetter 5-38.
CIN: Goodman 7-109, 2 TD; Celek 4-21.

LAS VEGAS BOWL

MAC ANNUAL REVIEW & BOWLS

PROFILE

Site: Las Vegas, Nev.
Stadium: Sam Boyd Stadium
Capacity: 36,800
Surface: TurfTech

PLAYING SITES

Sam Boyd Stadium, since 1992

NAME CHANGES

Las Vegas Bowl, 1992-98
EA Sports Las Vegas Bowl, 1999
Las Vegas Bowl, 2000
Sega Sports Las Vegas Bowl,
   2001-2002
Las Vegas Bowl, 2003
Pioneer PureVision Las Vegas
   Bowl, since 2004

SEASON	DATE	PRE-GAME RANK	TEAMS	SCORE	FINAL RANK	MOST VALUABLE PLAYERS	ATT.
1992	Dec. 18, 1992		**Bowling Green**	35		Erik White, Bowling Green, QB	15,476
			Nevada	34			
1993	Dec. 17, 1993		**Utah State**	42		Anthony Calvillo, Utah State, QB	15,508
			Ball State	33			
1994	Dec. 15, 1994		**UNLV**	52		Henry Bailey, UNLV, WR	17,562
			Central Michigan	24			
1995	Dec. 14, 1995	25	**Toledo**	40	OT 24	Wasean Tait, Toledo, RB	11,127
			Nevada	37			
1996	Dec. 18, 1996		**Nevada**	18		Mike Crawford, Nevada, LB	10,118
			Ball State	15			

DECEMBER 18, 1992
BOWLING GREEN 35, NEVADA 34

	1ST	2ND	3RD	4TH	FINAL
BG	14	14	0	7	35
NEV	3	0	21	10	34

SCORING SUMMARY
BG Smith 10 pass from White (Leaver kick)
NEV FG Terelak 30
BG Jackson 4 run (Leaver kick)
BG White 8 pass from Smith (Leaver kick)
BG Jackson 17 run (Leaver kick)
NEV Senior 5 pass from Vargas (Terelak kick)
NEV Holmes 5 run (Terelak kick)
NEV Matter 3 pass from Vargas (Terelak kick)
NEV Reeves 3 run (Terelak kick)
NEV FG Terelak 19
BG Hankins 3 pass from White (Leaver kick)

BG	TEAM STATISTICS	NEV
21	First Downs	25
157	Rushing Yards	94
25-41-0	Passing	29-49-0
253	Passing Yards	344
410	Total Yards	438
5-43.2	Punts - Average	4-36.7
0-0	Fumbles - Lost	3-2
5-56	Penalties - Yards	3-10
33:35	Possession Time	26:25

INDIVIDUAL LEADERS
RUSHING
BG: Jackson 22-113, 2 TD; Smith 12-27.
NEV: Holmes 18-62, 1 TD; Vargas 4-22.
PASSING
BG: White 24-40-0, 245 yards, 2 TD; Smith 1-1-0, 8 yards, 1 TD.
NEV: Vargas 24-40-0, 283 yards, 2 TD.
RECEIVING
BG: Smith 7-68, 1 TD; Szlachcic 5-51.
NEV: Reeves 8-92; King 5-88.

DECEMBER 17, 1993
UTAH STATE 42, BALL STATE 33

	1ST	2ND	3RD	4TH	FINAL
USU	14	7	14	7	42
BSU	0	0	17	16	33

SCORING SUMMARY
USU McMahon 22 pass from Calvillo (Morrealle kick)
USU Grier 3 run (Morrealle kick)
USU Thompson 3 pass from Calvillo (Morrealle kick)
BSU McCray 7 pass from Neu (Swart kick)
BSU FG Swart 31
USU Grier 15 run (Morrealle kick)
USU Lee 16 pass from Calvillo (Morrealle kick)
BSU Blair 2 pass from Neu (Swart kick)
BSU Safety (Calvillo forced out of end zone)
USU Toomer 32 interception return (Morrealle kick)
BSU Nibbs 2 run (Oliver pass from Neu)
BSU Oliver 2 pass from Neu (pass failed)

USU	TEAM STATISTICS	BSU
25	First Downs	14
205	Rushing Yards	73
25-39-2	Passing	21-38-2
286	Passing Yards	241
491	Total Yards	314
3-39.3	Punts - Average	5-41.0
2-1	Fumbles - Lost	1-1
15-150	Penalties - Yards	5-30
35:11	Possession Time	24:49

INDIVIDUAL LEADERS
RUSHING
USU: Grier 33-142, 2 TD; Calvillo 8-50.
BSU: Kent 1-27; Nibbs 6-18, 1 TD.
PASSING
USU: Calvillo 25-29-2, 286 yards, 3 TD.
BSU: Neu 20-37-2, 239 yards, 3 TD.
RECEIVING
USU: Jenkins 5-94; McMahon 4-54, 1 TD.
BSU: Oliver 5-114, 1 TD; Blair 10-66, 1 TD.

DECEMBER 15, 1994
UNLV 52, CENTRAL MICHIGAN 24

	1ST	2ND	3RD	4TH	FINAL
UNLV	14	17	14	7	52
CMU	10	0	0	14	24

SCORING SUMMARY
UNLV Bailey 46 pass from Brown (Garritano kick)
UNLV Bailey 1 run (Garritano kick)
CMU FG Blasy 20
CMU McMillan 53 pass from Timpf (Blasy kick)
UNLV Bailey 49 run (Garritano kick)
UNLV Washington 15 fumble return (Garritano kick)
UNLV FG Garritano 38
UNLV Bailey 1 run (Garritano kick)
UNLV Keener 33 pass from Brown (Garritano kick)
UNLV Gatewood 45 pass from Davis (Garritano kick)
CMU McMillan 24 pass from Darnell (Blasy kick)
CMU Tolbert 4 run (Blasy kick)

UNLV	TEAM STATISTICS	CMU
26	First Downs	22
301	Rushing Yards	152
15-27-0	Passing	13-25-2
288	Passing Yards	224
589	Total Yards	376
2-45.0	Punts - Average	5-41.2
3-1	Fumbles - Lost	5-2
8-89	Penalties - Yards	6-50
23:29	Possession Time	36:34

INDIVIDUAL LEADERS
RUSHING
UNLV: Branch 13-125; Bailey 7-79, 3 TD.
CMU: Tolbert 11-79, 1 TD; King 6-51.
PASSING
UNLV: Brown 11-21-0, 195 yards, 2 TD.
CMU: Timpf 7-12-1, 122 yards, 1 TD.
RECEIVING
UNLV: Gatewood 6-104, 1 TD; Bailey 5-101, 1 TD.
CMU: McMillan 4-100, 2 TD; Korytkowski 3-44.

DECEMBER 14, 1995
TOLEDO 40, NEVADA 37

	1ST	2ND	3RD	4TH	OT	FINAL
TOL	7	14	6	7	6	40
NEV	7	7	10	10	3	37

SCORING SUMMARY
TOL Huzjak 31 run (Spring kick)
NEV Minor 2 run (Shea kick)
TOL Tait 18 run (Spring kick)
TOL Tait 31 run (Spring kick)
NEV Minor 1 run (Shea kick)
NEV FG Shea 34
TOL Harris 16 run (kick failed)
NEV Bennett 4 run (Shea kick)
TOL Tait 26 run (Spring kick)
NEV Minor 1 run (Shea kick)
NEV FG Shea 26
NEV FG Shea 22
TOL Tait 2 run

TOL	TEAM STATISTICS	NEV
33	First Downs	23
307	Rushing Yards	83
23-41-1	Passing	27-51-0
254	Passing Yards	330
561	Total Yards	413
3-37.3	Punts - Average	5-49.8
4-3	Fumbles - Lost	2-0
9-84	Penalties - Yards	3-15
34:29	Possession Time	25:31

INDIVIDUAL LEADERS
RUSHING
TOL: Tait 31-185, 4 TD; Huzjak 13-59, 1 TD.
NEV: Minor 16-38, 3 TD; Wilson 10-34.
PASSING
TOL: Huzjak 23-41-1, 254 yards.
NEV: Maxwell 27-49-0, 330 yards.
RECEIVING
TOL: Tait 6-53; Kreitzburg 4-49.
NEV: Van Dyke 14-176; West 4-46.

DECEMBER 18, 1996
NEVADA 18, BALL STATE 15

	1ST	2ND	3RD	4TH	FINAL
NEV	9	3	0	6	18
BSU	0	7	0	8	15

SCORING SUMMARY
NEV Wilkins 16 pass from Dutton (kick blocked)
NEV FG Shea 26
BSU Moore 62 run (Locklear kick)
NEV FG Shea 33
NEV Wilkins 11 pass from Bennett (pass failed)
BSU Reese 27 pass from Baldwin (Abernathy pass from Baldwin)

NEV	TEAM STATISTICS	BSU
24	First Downs	12
84	Rushing Yards	112
26-48-2	Passing	11-31-1
376	Passing Yards	106
460	Total Yards	218
6-39.0	Punts - Average	12-41.1
1-0	Fumbles - Lost	1-0
6-51	Penalties - Yards	7-49

INDIVIDUAL LEADERS
RUSHING
NEV: Lemon 24-96.
BSU: Moore 8-74, 1 TD; Blair 14-44.
PASSING
NEV: Dutton 18-33-2, 224, 1 TD; Bennett 8-15-0, 152, 1 TD.
BSU: Baldwin 11-31-1, 106 yards, 1 TD.

MOTOR CITY BOWL

PROFILE

Site: Detroit, Mich.
Stadium: Ford Field
Capacity: 65,000
Surface: FieldTurf

PLAYING SITES

Pontiac Silverdome, 1997-2001
Ford Field, since 2002

NAME CHANGES

Motor City Bowl, since 1997

SEASON	DATE	PRE-GAME RANK	TEAMS	SCORE	FINAL RANK	MOST VALUABLE PLAYERS	ATT.
1997	Dec. 26, 1997		**Mississippi**	34	22	Stewart Patridge, Mississippi, QB	43,340
			Marshall	31			
1998	Dec. 23, 1998		**Marshall**	48		Chad Pennington, Marshall, QB	32,206
			Louisville	29			
1999	Dec. 27, 1999	11	**Marshall**	21	10	Doug Chapman, Marshall, RB	44,449
			BYU	3			
2000	Dec. 27, 2000		**Marshall**	25		Byron Leftwich, Marshall, QB	44,911
			Cincinnati	14			
2001	Dec. 29, 2001	25	**Toledo**	23	23	Chester Taylor, Toledo, RB	44,164
			Cincinnati	16			
2002	Dec. 26, 2002		**Boston College**	51		Brian St. Pierre, Boston College, QB	45,761
			Toledo	25			
2003	Dec. 26, 2003		**Bowling Green**	28	23	Josh Harris, Bowling Green, QB	51,286
			Northwestern	24		Jason Wright, Northwestern, RB	
2004	Dec. 27, 2004		**Connecticut**	39		Dan Orlovsky, Connecticut, QB	52,552
			Toledo	10			
2005	Dec. 26, 2005		**Memphis**	38		DeAngelo Williams, Memphis, RB	50,616
			Akron	31			
2006	Dec. 26, 2006		**Central Michigan**	31		Dan LeFevour, Central Michigan, QB	54,113
			Middle Tennessee	14			

DECEMBER 26, 1997
MISSISSIPPI 34, MARSHALL 31

	1ST	2ND	3RD	4TH	FINAL
MISS	7	0	14	13	34
MAR	10	7	0	14	31

SCORING SUMMARY
MISS Avery 1 run (Lindsey kick)
MAR Moss 80 pass from Pennington (Malashevich kick)
MAR FG Malashevich 36
MAR Colclough 19 pass from Pennington (Malashevich kick)
MISS Rone 13 pass from Patridge (Lindsey kick)
MISS McAllister 20 pass from Patridge (Lindsey kick)
MAR Chapman 6 pass from Pennington (Malashevich kick)
MISS Heard 19 pass from Patridge (kick failed)
MAR Chapman 9 run (Malashevich kick)
MISS McAllister 1 run (Lindsey kick)

MISS	TEAM STATISTICS	MAR
29	First Downs	23
179	Rushing Yards	170
29-48-1	Passing	23-45-0
332	Passing Yards	337
511	Total Yards	507
4-41.8	Punts - Average	7-39.7
0-0	Fumbles - Lost	3-2
7-71	Penalties - Yards	10-93
34:21	Possession Time	25:39

INDIVIDUAL LEADERS
RUSHING
MISS: Avery 27-110, 1 TD; McAllister 8-71, 1 TD.
MAR: Chapman 19-152, 1 TD.

PASSING
MISS: Patridge 29-47-1, 332 yards, 3 TD.
MAR: Pennington 23-45-0, 337 yards, 3 TD.

RECEIVING
MISS: Heard 3-81, 1 TD; Peterson 7-66.
MAR: Moss 6-173, 1 TD; Colclough 8-84, 1 TD.

DECEMBER 23, 1998
MARSHALL 48, LOUISVILLE 29

	1ST	2ND	3RD	4TH	FINAL
LOU	0	21	0	8	29
MAR	7	14	17	10	48

SCORING SUMMARY
MAR Williams 29 pass from Pennington (Malashevich kick)
LOU Collins 2 run (Hilbert kick)
MAR Washington 14 pass from Pennington (Malashevich kick)
LOU Sheffield 21 pass from Redman (Hilbert kick)
MAR Williams 26 pass from Pennington (Malashevich kick)
LOU Collins 13 run (Hilbert kick)
MAR Long 50 pass from Pennington (Malashevich kick)
MAR Chapman 1 run (Malashevich kick)
MAR FG Malashevich 22
MAR Chapman 1 run (Malashevich kick)
LOU Collins 1 run (Hilbert kick)
MAR FG Malashevich 32

LOU	TEAM STATISTICS	MAR
26	First Downs	27
66	Rushing Yards	202
35-54-1	Passing	18-24-0
336	Passing Yards	411
402	Total Yards	613
0-0	Punt Returns - Yards	4-62
4-78	Kickoff Returns - Yards	2-38
4-49.3	Punts - Average	1-58.0
3-0	Fumbles - Lost	2-0
13-109	Penalties - Yards	14-123
28:49	Possession Time	31:11

INDIVIDUAL LEADERS
RUSHING
LOU: Collins 14-94, 3 TD.
MAR: Turner 13-94; Chapman 26-76, 2 TD.

PASSING
LOU: Redman 35-54-1, 336 yards, 1 TD.
MAR: Pennington 18-24-0, 411 yards, 4 TD.

RECEIVING
LOU: Jackson 8-96; Boyd 8-84; Sheffield 8-75, 1 TD.
MAR: Chapman 2-69; Williams 3-68, 2 TD; Cooper 5-67.

DECEMBER 27, 1999
MARSHALL 21, BYU 3

	1ST	2ND	3RD	4TH	FINAL
BYU	3	0	0	0	3
MAR	0	7	7	7	21

SCORING SUMMARY
BYU FG Pochman 28
MAR Chapman 30 pass from Pennington (Malashevich kick)
MAR Chapman 87 run (Malashevich kick)
MAR Chapman 1 run (Malashevich kick)

BYU	TEAM STATISTICS	MAR
12	First Downs	14
-16	Rushing Yards	147
16-29-2	Passing	17-28-1
220	Passing Yards	207
204	Total Yards	354
7-48.3	Punts - Average	5-42.8
2-2	Fumbles - Lost	0-0
8-81	Penalties - Yards	11-84
30:31	Possession Time	29:29

INDIVIDUAL LEADERS
RUSHING
BYU: Atuaia 4-35.
MAR: Chapman 14-133, 2 TD; Turner 7-15.

PASSING
BYU: Feterik 6-11-0, 125 yards; Peterson 4-7-1, 50 yards.
MAR: Pennington 17-28-1, 207 yards, 1 TD.

RECEIVING
BYU: Hooks 4-108; Atuaia 4-25.
MAR: Williams 5-95; Chapman 4-40, 1 TD.

DECEMBER 27, 2000
MARSHALL 25, CINCINNATI 14

	1ST	2ND	3RD	4TH	FINAL
CIN	7	7	0	0	14
MAR	9	0	13	3	25

SCORING SUMMARY
MAR Watts 77 pass from Leftwich (Jenkins kick)
CIN McCleskey 2 run (Ruffin kick)
MAR Safety (Jackson tackled by Owens in end zone)
CIN McCleskey 2 run (Ruffin kick)
MAR Leftwich 1 run (pass failed)
MAR Wallace 4 run (Jenkins kick)
MAR FG Jenkins 25

CIN	TEAM STATISTICS	MAR
24	First Downs	13
96	Rushing Yards	101
19-39-2	Passing	17-30-1
189	Passing Yards	221
285	Total Yards	322
5-29.8	Punts - Average	6-37.5
1-0	Fumbles - Lost	1-1
11-80	Penalties - Yards	14-110
35:59	Possession Time	24:01

INDIVIDUAL LEADERS
RUSHING
CIN: McCleskey 20-72, 2 TD; Jackson 14-61.
MAR: Wallace 20-78, 1 TD; Leftwich 9-21, 1 TD.

PASSING
CIN: Kenner 19-39-2, 189 yards.
MAR: Leftwich 17-30-1, 221 yards, 1 TD.

RECEIVING
CIN: Collins-Baker 4-55; Chatman 3-42; Vann 3-42.
MAR: Watts 3-90, 1 TD; Poole 3-65.

DECEMBER 29, 2001
TOLDEO 23, CINCINNATI 16

	1ST	2ND	3RD	4TH	FINAL
CIN	0	13	0	3	16
TOL	3	0	10	10	23

SCORING SUMMARY
TOL	FG France 28
CIN	FG Ruffin 29
CIN	Walker 28 pass from Guidugli (Ruffin kick)
CIN	FG Ruffin 46
TOL	FG France 42
TOL	Bolden 28 run (France kick)
TOL	FG France 30
CIN	FG Ruffin 25
TOL	Taylor 24 run (France kick)

CIN	TEAM STATISTICS	TOL
19	First Downs	24
13	Rushing Yards	322
29-47-0	Passing	14-28-1
283	Passing Yards	135
296	Total Yards	457
7-49.1	Punts - Average	4-39.3
1-0	Fumbles - Lost	0-0
6-48	Penalties - Yards	8-75
25:44	Possession Time	34:16

INDIVIDUAL LEADERS
RUSHING
CIN: McClesky 11-18.
TOL: Taylor 31-190, 1 TD; Bolden 7-99, 1 TD.

PASSING
CIN: Guidugli 29-46-0, 283 yards, 1 TD.
TOL: Bolden 14-28-1, 135 yards.

RECEIVING
CIN: Vann 8-78; Keith 9-63.
TOL: Ford 5-73.

DECEMBER 26, 2002
BOSTON COLLEGE 51, TOLEDO 25

	1ST	2ND	3RD	4TH	FINAL
BC	14	28	6	3	51
TOL	3	15	7	0	25

SCORING SUMMARY
BC	Knight 2 run (Sciortino kick)
BC	Adams 17 pass from St. Pierre (Sciortino kick)
TOL	FG Robbins 35
BC	Hazard 40 pass from St. Pierre (Sciortino kick)
TOL	Dawson 2 run (Robbins kick)
BC	Dodd 5 run (Sciortino kick)
BC	Adams 40 pass from St. Pierre (Sciortino kick)
BC	Brokaw 1 run (Sciortino kick)
TOL	Ford 9 pass from Jones (Dawson run)
BC	FG Sciortino 23
BC	FG Sciortino 35
TOL	Johnson 30 pass from Jones (Robbins kick)
BC	FG Sciortino 45

BC	TEAM STATISTICS	TOL
30	First Downs	21
149	Rushing Yards	102
25-35-0	Passing	27-41-2
342	Passing Yards	331
491	Total Yards	433
1-3	Punt Returns - Yards	1-2
5-112	Kickoff Returns - Yards	8-173
1-39.0	Punts - Average	3-23.3
0-0	Fumbles - Lost	3-0
4-26	Penalties - Yards	11-96
29:59	Possession Time	30:01

INDIVIDUAL LEADERS
RUSHING
BC: Knight 19-65, 1 TD; Dodd 7-33, 1 TD; Brokaw 7-20, 1 TD.
TOL: Jones 9-32; Martin 6-31; Dawson 10-28, 1 TD.

PASSING
BC: St. Pierre 25-35-0, 342 yards, 3 TD.
TOL: Jones 27-41-2, 331 yards, 2 TD.

RECEIVING
BC: Adams 5-92, 2 TD; Hemmings 4-71; Hazard 5-66, 1 TD.
TOL: Ford 10-112, 1 TD; Greene 4-63; Johnson 3-49, 1 TD.

DECEMBER 26, 2003
BOWLING GREEN 28, NORTHWESTERN 24

	1ST	2ND	3RD	4TH	FINAL
BG	0	7	7	14	28
NU	7	3	7	7	24

SCORING SUMMARY
NU	Herron 40 run (Huffman kick)
NU	FG Huffman 31
BG	Harris 4 run (Suisham kick)
NU	Wright 77 run (Huffman kick)
BG	Magner 7 pass from Harris (Suisham kick)
BG	Sanders 11 pass from Harris (Suisham kick)
NU	Herron 2 run (Huffman kick)
BG	Magner 3 pass from Harris (Suisham kick)

BG	TEAM STATISTICS	NU
30	First Downs	16
88	Rushing Yards	357
38-51-3	Passing	7-15-0
386	Passing Yards	58
474	Total Yards	415
2-21	Punt Returns - Yards	2-3
3-46.0	Punts - Average	5-34.4
0-0	Fumbles - Lost	2-2
1-15	Penalties - Yards	3-40
34:08	Possession Time	25:52

INDIVIDUAL LEADERS
RUSHING
BG: Harris 21-68, 1 TD; Pope 11-23.
NU: Wright 21-237, 1 TD; Herron 12-80, 2 TD.

PASSING
BG: Harris 38-50-2, 386 yards, 3 TD.
NU: Basanez 7-15-0, 58 yards.

RECEIVING
BG: Magner 12-97, 2 TD; Sharon 7-93; Sanders 5-74, 1 TD.
NU: Philmore 3-43; Wright 2-11.

DECEMBER 27, 2004
CONNECTICUT 39, TOLEDO 10

	1ST	2ND	3RD	4TH	FINAL
UCONN	17	13	3	6	39
TOL	0	7	3	0	10

SCORING SUMMARY
UCONN	FG Nuzie 35
UCONN	Williams 32 pass from Orlovsky (Nuzie kick)
UCONN	Taylor 68 punt return (Nuzie kick)
TOL	Gradkowski 1 run (Robbins kick)
UCONN	Sparks 7 pass from Orlovsky (Nuzie kick)
UCONN	FG Nuzie 37
UCONN	FG Nuzie 25
TOL	FG Robbins 27
UCONN	FG Nuzie 36
UCONN	Lawrence 11 run (kick failed)

UCONN	TEAM STATISTICS	TOL
20	First Downs	20
159	Rushing Yards	78
20-41-1	Passing	22-40-2
239	Passing Yards	203
398	Total Yards	281
2-69	Punt Returns - Yards	1-7
3-101	Kickoff Returns - Yards	5-83
3-30.3	Punts - Average	6-32.3
0-0	Fumbles - Lost	2-1
5-44	Penalties - Yards	4-35
28:18	Possession Time	31:42

INDIVIDUAL LEADERS
RUSHING
UCONN: Brockington 15-72; Bellamy 9-55.
TOL: Dawson 19-78.

PASSING
UCONN: Orlovsky 20-41-1, 239 yards, 2 TD.
TOL: Council 16-28-2, 160 yards.

RECEIVING
UCONN: Henry 9-109; Cutaia 2-47.
TOL: Moore 5-48; Holmes 4-47.

DECEMBER 26, 2005
MEMPHIS 38, AKRON 31

	1ST	2ND	3RD	4TH	FINAL
MEM	0	13	7	18	38
AKR	3	0	7	21	31

SCORING SUMMARY
AKR	FG Swiger 43
MEM	FG Gostkowski 32
MEM	D. Williams 1 run (Gostkowski kick)
MEM	FG Gostkowski 25
MEM	D. Williams 2 run (Gostkowski kick)
AKR	Arthur 46 pass from Getsy (Swiger kick)
MEM	FG Gostkowski 50
AKR	Biggs 72 pass from Getsy (Swiger kick)
MEM	D. Williams 2 run (Avery run)
MEM	E. Williams 5 run (Gostkowski kick)
AKR	Hixon 14 pass from Getsy (Swiger kick)
AKR	Arthur 18 pass from Getsy (Swiger kick)

MEM	TEAM STATISTICS	AKR
39	First Downs	45
346	Rushing Yards	47
7-14-0	Passing	34-59-0
170	Passing Yards	455
516	Total Yards	502
5-39	Punt Returns - Yards	0-0
3-97	Kickoff Returns - Yards	2-39
5-45.6	Punts - Average	8-40.5
1-1	Fumbles - Lost	0-0
7-62	Penalties - Yards	10-61
29:48	Possession Time	30:12

INDIVIDUAL LEADERS
RUSHING
MEM: D. Williams 30-233, 3 TD; Doss 9-56.
AKR: Biggs 14-46; Kennedy 3-13.

PASSING
MEM: Avery 7-13-0, 170 yards.
AKR: Getsy 34-59-0, 455 yards, 4 TD.

RECEIVING
MEM: Scott 3-103; E. Williams 1-42.
AKR: Arthur 8-180, 2 TD; Biggs 4-79, 1 TD.

DECEMBER 26, 2006
CMU 31, MIDDLE TENNESSEE 14

	1ST	2ND	3RD	4TH	FINAL
MT	0	7	0	7	14
CMU	14	7	7	3	31

SCORING SUMMARY
CMU	Sneed 1 run (Albreski kick)
CMU	Sneed 29 pass from LeFevour (Albreski kick)
MT	Gross 3 run (Smith kick)
CMU	LeFevour 9 run (Albreski kick)
CMU	Kress 56 interception return (Albreski kick)
MT	McNair 6 run (Smith kick)
CMU	FG Albreski 43

MT	TEAM STATISTICS	CMU
19	First Downs	22
61	Rushing Yards	149
27-41-2	Passing	16-26-0
259	Passing Yards	162
320	Total Yards	311
1-39	Punt Returns - Yards	1-3
4-61	Kickoff Returns - Yards	3-46
5-40.0	Punts - Average	4-47.0
0-0	Fumbles - Lost	0-0
10-103	Penalties - Yards	4-55
36:41	Possession Time	23:19

INDIVIDUAL LEADERS
RUSHING
MT: Gross 12-37, 1 TD; McNair 11-23, 1 TD.
CMU: LeFevour 15-69, 1 TD; Sneed 11-48, 1 TD.

PASSING
MT: Marks 25-37-2, 251 yards; Craddock 2-4-0, 8 yards.
CMU: LeFevour 16-26-0, 162 yards, 1 TD.

RECEIVING
MT: Gee 9-63; Grigsby 5-86.
CMU: Anderson 6-51; Sneed 6-48, 1 TD.

POINSETTIA BOWL

Site: San Diego, Calif.
Stadium: Qualcomm Stadium
Capacity: 71,400
Surface: Grass

Qualcomm Stadium, since 2005

San Diego County Credit Union Poinsettia Bowl, since 2005

SEASON	DATE	PRE-GAME RANK	TEAMS	SCORE	FINAL RANK	MOST VALUABLE PLAYERS	ATT.
2006	Dec. 19, 2006	25	**Texas Christian Univ.**	37	22	Jeff Ballard, TCU, QB	29,709
			Northern Illinois	7		Tommy Blake, TCU, DE	

DECEMBER 19, 2006
TCU 37, NORTHERN ILLINOIS 7

	1ST	2ND	3RD	4TH	FINAL
NIU	0	0	0	7	7
TCU	6	10	14	7	37

SCORING SUMMARY

TCU	Hobbs 4 run (kick blocked)
TCU	Ballard 10 run (Manfredini kick)
TCU	FG Manfredini 25
TCU	Ballard 1 run (Manfredini kick)
TCU	Ballard 6 run (LoCoco kick)
NIU	Tranchitella 32 blocked punt return (Nendick kick)
TCU	Hecht 6 pass from Ballard (LoCoco kick)

NIU	TEAM STATISTICS	TCU
5	First Downs	23
-20	Rushing Yards	198
6-19-1	Passing	19-29-0
80	Passing Yards	258
60	Total Yards	456
1-42	Punt Returns - Yards	6-89
6-80	Kickoff Returns - Yards	1-38
9-40.6	Punts - Average	6-27.3
1-0	Fumbles - Lost	2-0
0-0	Penalties - Yards	7-80
27:36	Possession Time	32:24

INDIVIDUAL LEADERS

RUSHING
NIU: Wolfe 20-28; Anderson 3-4.
TCU: Hobbs 18-109, 1 TD; Brown 14-52.

PASSING
NIU: Nicholson 6-18-1, 80 yards; Morris 0-1-0, 0 yards.
TCU: Ballard 19-29-0, 258 yards, 1 TD.

RECEIVING
NIU: Carter 2-14; Wolfe 2-2; Simon 1-62.
TCU: Hobbs 3-61; Harmon 6-94.

SUGAR BOWL

Site: New Orleans, La.
Stadium: Louisiana Superdome
Capacity: 72,003
Surface: Momentum Turf

Tulane Stadium, 1935-74
Louisiana Superdome, 1975-2005
Georgia Dome, 2006

Sugar Bowl Football Classic, 1935-87
USF&G Sugar Bowl, 1988-95
Nokia Sugar Bowl, since 1996

SEASON	DATE	PRE-GAME RANK	TEAMS	SCORE	FINAL RANK	MOST VALUABLE PLAYERS	ATT.
1934	Jan. 1, 1935		**Tulane**	20			22,026
			Temple*	14			

JANUARY 1, 1935
TULANE 20, TEMPLE* 14

	1ST	2ND	3RD	4TH	FINAL
TUL	0	7	7	6	20
TEM	7	7	0	0	14

SCORING SUMMARY

TEM	Tester 7 pass from Smukler (Smukler kick)
TEM	Smukler 3 run (Smukler kick)
TUL	Simons 85 kickoff return (Mintz kick)
TUL	Hardy 11 pass from Bryan (Mintz kick)
TUL	Hardy 25 pass from Mintz (kick failed)

TUL	TEAM STATISTICS	TEM
10	First Downs	13
140	Rushing Yards	182
8-16-1	Passing	3-13-1
88	Passing Yards	19
228	Total Yards	201
3-2	Fumbles - Lost	2-1
2-20	Penalties - Yards	2-7

*Played as an independent or with other conference affiliation

SUN BOWL

PROFILE

Site: El Paso, Texas
Stadium: Sun Bowl Stadium
Capacity: 50,426
Surface: AstroPlay

PLAYING SITES

El Paso High School Stadium, 1935-37
Kidd Field, 1938-62
Sun Bowl Stadium, since 1963

NAME CHANGES

Sun Bowl, 1935-85
John Hancock Sun Bowl, 1986-89
John Hancock Bowl, 1990-93
Sun Bowl, 1994-95
Norwest Sun Bowl, 1996-98
Wells Fargo Sun Bowl, 1999-2003
Vitalis Sun Bowl, 2004-05
Brut Sun Bowl, since 2006

SEASON	DATE	PRE-GAME RANK	TEAMS	SCORE	FINAL RANK	MOST VALUABLE PLAYERS	ATT.
1947	Jan. 1, 1948		Miami (Ohio)*	13			18,000
			Texas Tech	12			
1950	Jan. 1, 1951		West Texas A&M	14		Bill Cross, West Texas A&M, E	16,000
			Cincinnati	13			
1962	Dec. 31, 1962		West Texas A&M	15		Jerry Logan, West Texas A&M, HB	16,000
			Ohio	14		Don Hoovler, Ohio U., G	

JANUARY 1, 1948
MIAMI (OHIO)* 13, TEXAS TECH 12

	1ST	2ND	3RD	4TH	FINAL
MIA	6	0	0	7	13
TT	0	6	0	6	12

SCORING SUMMARY
MIA Parseghian 1 run (kick failed)
TT Conley 3 run (kick failed)
MIA Shoults 1 run (Speelman kick)
TT Winkler 30 interception return (kick blocked)

MIA	TEAM STATISTICS	TT
21	First Downs	5
294	Rushing Yards	194
11-22-2	Passing	5-14-2
120	Passing Yards	83
414	Total Yards	277
6-11	Punt Returns - Yards	1-33
3-11	Kickoff Returns - Yards	2-35
7-35.0	Punts - Average	7-25.0
1-1	Fumbles - Lost	1-0
9-65	Penalties - Yards	6-50

JANUARY 1, 1951
WEST TEXAS A&M 14, CINCINNATI 13

	1ST	2ND	3RD	4TH	FINAL
WT A&M	0	7	7	0	14
CIN	0	6	7	0	13

SCORING SUMMARY
WT A&M Cross 4 run (Dunn kick)
CIN McKeever 3 run (kick failed)
CIN Stratton 17 pass from Rossi (Shalonsky kick)
WT A&M Cross 62 pass from Mayfield (Dunn kick)

WT A&M	TEAM STATISTICS	CIN
19	First Downs	12
238	Rushing Yards	106
6-15-3	Passing	14-30-3
123	Passing Yards	170
361	Total Yards	276
4-44.0	Punts - Average	5-30.0
3-0	Fumbles - Lost	3-0
8-80	Penalties - Yards	8-70

INDIVIDUAL LEADERS
RUSHING
WT A&M: Wright 23-135; Cross 15-53.
CIN: Stratton 8-59; McKeever 9-40, 1 TD.
PASSING
WT A&M: Mayfield 5-14-3, 103 yards, 1 TD.
CIN: Rossi 14-29-3, 170 yards, 1 TD.

DECEMBER 31, 1962
WEST TEXAS A&M 15, OHIO 14

	1ST	2ND	3RD	4TH	FINAL
WT A&M	0	7	0	8	15
OHIO	0	3	8	3	14

SCORING SUMMARY
OHIO FG McGee 52
WT A&M Logan 13 pass from Dawson (Gibson kick)
OHIO Hoovler 91 interception return (Smith pass from Babbitt)
OHIO FG McGee 24
WT A&M Richardson 32 pass from Dawson (Ostander pass from Dawson)

WT A&M	TEAM STATISTICS	OHIO
18	First Downs	14
343	Rushing Yards	167
7-10-0	Passing	12-29-0
105	Passing Yards	157
448	Total Yards	324
5-41.0	Punts - Average	4-41.0
6-4	Fumbles - Lost	1-0
97	Penalty Yards	40

*Played as an independent or with other conference affiliation

DEFUNCT BOWLS
AVIATION BOWL

PROFILE

Site: Dayton, Ohio
Stadium: Welcome Stadium
Capacity: 10,000
Surface: Grass

SEASON	DATE	PRE-GAME RANK	TEAMS	SCORE	FINAL RANK	MOST VALUABLE PLAYERS	ATT.
1961	Dec. 9, 1961		**New Mexico**	28		Bobby Santiago, New Mexico, RB	3,694
			Western Michigan	12		Chuck Cummings, New Mexico, G	

DECEMBER 9, 1961
NEW MEXICO 28, WESTERN MICHIGAN 12

	1ST	2ND	3RD	4TH	FINAL
UNM	14	0	14	0	28
WMU	6	0	0	6	12

SCORING SUMMARY
UNM   Cromartie 2 run (kick failed)
UNM   Santiago 10 run (Morgan run)
WMU   White 4 run (run failed)
UNM   Morgan 10 run (run failed)
UNM   Cummings 43 interception return (Bradford run)
WMU   Cooke 5 pass from Chlebeck (pass failed)

UNM	TEAM STATISTICS	WMU
20	First Downs	18
339	Rushing Yards	96
0-4-0	Passing	18-33-2
0	Passing Yards	207
339	Total Yards	303
7-33.0	Punts - Average	4-36.0

INDIVIDUAL LEADERS
RUSHING
UNM: Santiago 10-83, 1 TD.
WMU: White 10-43, 1 TD.

CALIFORNIA BOWL

PROFILE

Site: Fresno, Calif.
Stadium: Bulldog Stadium
Capacity: 30,000
Surface: Grass

SEASON	DATE	PRE-GAME RANK	TEAMS	SCORE	FINAL RANK	MOST VALUABLE PLAYERS	ATT.
1981	Dec. 19, 1981		**Toledo**	27		Arnold Smiley, Toledo, RB	15,565
			San Jose State	25		Marlin Russell, Toledo, LB	
1982	Dec. 18, 1982		**Fresno State**	29		Chip Otten, Bowling Green, TB	30,000
			Bowling Green	28		Jac Tomasello, Bowling Green, DB	
1983	Dec. 17, 1983		**No. Illinois**	20		Lou Wicks, No. Illinois, FB	20,464
			Cal. St. Fullerton	13		James Pruitt, Cal. St. Fullerton, WR	
1984	Dec. 15, 1984		**Nevada-Las Vegas+**	30		Randall Cunningham, Nevada-Las Vegas, QB	21,741
			Toledo	13		Steve Morgan, Toledo, TB	
1985	Dec. 14, 1985		**Fresno State**	51		Mike Mancini, Fresno State, P	32,554
		20	**Bowling Green**	7		Greg Meehan, Bowling Green, FL	
1986	Dec. 13, 1986		**San Jose State**	37		Mike Perez, San Jose State, QB	10,743
			Miami (Ohio)	7		Andrew Marlatt, Miami (Ohio), DT	
1987	Dec. 12, 1987		**Eastern Michigan**	30		Gary Patton, Eastern Michigan, TB	24,000
			San Jose State	27		Mike Perez, San Jose State, QB	
1988	Dec. 10, 1988		**Fresno State**	35		Darrell Rosette, Fresno State, RB	31,272
			Western Michigan	30		Tony Kimbrough, Western Michigan, QB	
1989	Dec. 9, 1989		**Fresno State**	27		Ron Cox, Fresno State, LB	31,610
			Ball State	6		Sean Jones, Ball State, WR	
1990	Dec. 8, 1990		**San Jose State**	48		Sheldon Canley, San Jose State, TB	25,431
			Central Michigan	24		Ken Ealy, Central Michigan, WR	
1991	Dec. 14, 1991		**Bowling Green**	28		Mark Szlachcic, Bowling Green, WR	34,825
			Fresno State	21		Mark Barsotti, Fresno State, QB	

+ Game later forfeited to Toledo because of the use of ineligible players by UNLV

DECEMBER 19, 1981
TOLEDO 27, SAN JOSE STATE 25

	1ST	2ND	3RD	4TH	FINAL
TOL	7	7	7	6	27
SJSU	0	3	8	14	25

SCORING SUMMARY
TOL   Achter 45 run (Lee kick)
SJSU FG Berg 24
TOL   Smiley 7 run (Lee kick)
TOL   Schafer 12 pass from Hall (Lee kick)
SJSU Fernandez 12 pass from Clarkson (Fernandez pass from Clarkson)
TOL   FG Lee 27
SJSU Fernandez 22 pass from Clarkson (kick blocked)
SJSU Fernandez 35 pass from Clarkson (Taylor pass from Willhite)
TOL   FG Lee 41

TOL	TEAM STATISTICS	SJSU
21	First Downs	29
221	Rushing Yards	54
11-22-1	Passing	43-63-5
265	Passing Yards	467
486	Total Yards	521
3-39.3	Punts - Average	2-47.0
7-2	Fumbles - Lost	4-1
3-25	Penalties - Yards	10-85

DECEMBER 18, 1982
FRESNO STATE 29, BOWLING GREEN 28

	1ST	2ND	3RD	4TH	FINAL
FRES	0	0	7	22	29
BG	0	14	14	0	28

SCORING SUMMARY
BG   Otten 4 run (Youssef kick)
BG   Meek 1 pass from McClure (Youssef kick)
BG   Potts 5 pass from McClure (Youssef kick)
FRES Paige 11 pass from Tedford (Darrow kick)
BG   Potts 6 fumble recovery (Youssef kick)
FRES Paige 4 run (Darrow kick)
FRES Paige 27 pass from Tedford (Carter pass from Tedford)
FRES Wesson 2 pass from Tedford (Darrow kick)

FRES	TEAM STATISTICS	BG
27	First Downs	17
80	Rushing Yards	126
31-50-4	Passing	22-32-1
373	Passing Yards	246
453	Total Yards	372
2-39.5	Punts - Average	7-39.9
4-3	Fumbles - Lost	2-0
24:20	Possession Time	35:40

INDIVIDUAL LEADERS
RUSHING
FRES: Thomas 5-48; Carter 6-41.
BG: Otten 31-136, 1 TD; Wagner 5-18.
PASSING
FRES: Tedford 31-50-4, 373 yards, 3 TD.
BG: McClure 22-32-1, 246 yards, 2 TD.
RECEIVING
FRES: Paige 15-246, 2 TD; Griever 4-43.
BG: Otten 11-76; Taylor 3-74.

DECEMBER 17, 1983
NO. ILLINOIS 20, CAL ST. FULLERTON 13

	1ST	2ND	3RD	4TH	FINAL
NIU	3	7	7	3	20
CSF	3	7	0	3	13

SCORING SUMMARY
NIU   FG Scott 23
CSF   FG Steinke 26
NIU   Richardson 3 run (Scott kick)
CSF   Redick 25 pass from Allen (Steinke kick)
NIU   Richardson 4 run (Scott kick)
NIU   FG Scott 42
CSF   FG Steinke 40

NIU	TEAM STATISTICS	CSF
15	First Downs	15
253	Rushing Yards	146
10-18-0	Passing	18-32-0
119	Passing Yards	233
372	Total Yards	379
3-42.0	Punts - Average	3-36.3
1-0	Fumbles - Lost	2-0
9-75	Penalties - Yards	9-85
33:33	Possession Time	26:27

INDIVIDUAL LEADERS
RUSHING
NIU: Wicks 14-117, Richardson 21-67, 2TD.
CSF: Calhoun 5-55.
PASSING
NIU: Tyrell 10-18-0, 119 yards.
CSF: Allen 18-32-0, 323 yards, 1 TD.
RECEIVING
SJSU: Sims 4-42
CSF: Pruitt 6-133, Pitts 6-60.

December 15, 1984
UNLV[+] 30, Toledo 13

	1ST	2ND	3RD	4TH	FINAL
UNLV	7	6	17	0	30
TOL	3	3	7	0	13

[+] Game later forfeited to Toledo because of the use of ineligible players by UNLV

SCORING SUMMARY

UNLV	Gladney 19 pass from Cunningham (DiGiovanna kick)
TOL	FG Walker 22
UNLV	Jones 7 pass from Cunningham (kick failed)
TOL	FG Walker 36
UNLV	FG DiGiovanna 44
TOL	Poure 38 pass from Sager (Walker kick)
UNLV	Woods 16 run (DiGiovanna kick)
UNLV	Cunningham 10 run (DiGiovanna kick)

UNLV	TEAM STATISTICS	TOL
18	First Downs	20
127	Rushing Yards	203
18-28-1	Passing	12-31-0
270	Passing Yards	137
397	Total Yards	340
3-27.7	Punts - Average	5-34.6
2-2	Fumbles - Lost	3-1
8-77	Penalties - Yards	6-40

December 14, 1985
Fresno State 51, Bowling Green 7

	1ST	2ND	3RD	4TH	FINAL
FRES	7	16	14	14	51
BG	0	0	0	7	7

SCORING SUMMARY

FRES	Williams 10 run (Belli kick)
FRES	Mosley 1 run (Belli kick)
FRES	Taylor 33 pass from Sweeney (Belli kick)
FRES	Safety (McClure tackled in end zone)
FRES	Taylor 53 pass from Sweeney (Belli kick)
FRES	Skipper 29 run (Belli kick)
BG	Davis 18 run (Silvi kick)
FRES	Baker 40 pass from Sweeney (Belli kick)
FRES	Skipper 13 run (Belli kick)

FRES	TEAM STATISTICS	BG
15	First Downs	21
225	Rushing Yards	89
10-20-1	Passing	23-48-3
194	Passing Yards	259
419	Total Yards	348
7-47.4	Punts - Average	6-35.3
2-1	Fumbles - Lost	6-5
27:51	Possession Time	32:09

INDIVIDUAL LEADERS

RUSHING
FRES: Williams 18-94, 1 TD; Skipper 5-77, 2 TD.
BG: Davis 7-78, 1 TD; Story 9-41.

PASSING
FRES: Sweeney 9-19-1, 185 yards, 3 TD.
BG: McClure 22-42-3, 254 yards.

RECEIVING
FRES: Taylor 2-86, 2 TD; Baker 2-49, 1 TD.
BG: Schmelzle 7-84; Meehan 7-65.

December 13, 1986
San Jose State 37, Miami (Ohio) 7

	1ST	2ND	3RD	4TH	FINAL
SJSU	3	14	7	13	37
MIA	7	0	0	0	7

SCORING SUMMARY

SJSU	FG Olivarez 45
MIA	Stofa 20 pass from Morris (Gussman kick)
SJSU	Saxon 1 run (Olivarez kick)
SJSU	Liggins 36 pass from Perez (Olivarez kick)
SJSU	Malaulu 4 pass from Perez (Olivarez kick)
SJSU	Liggins 31 pass from Perez (Olivarez kick)
SJSU	Alexander 39 interception return (kick failed)

SJSU	TEAM STATISTICS	MIA
23	First Downs	22
113	Rushing Yards	24
22-40-0	Passing	18-41-5
313	Passing Yards	208
426	Total Yards	232
4-29.3	Punts - Average	5-34.4
6-1	Fumbles - Lost	1-1
14-163	Penalties - Yards	10-101

INDIVIDUAL LEADERS

RUSHING
SJSU: Saxon 25-92, 1 TD; Jackson 6-18.
MIA: Swarn 12-46; Morris 6-12.

PASSING
SJSU: Perez 21-37-0, 291 yards, 3 TD.
MIA: Morris 15-33-4, 166 yards, 1 TD.

RECEIVING
SJSU: Liggins 8-133, 2 TD; McCloud 2-41.
MIA: Stofa 5-71, 1 TD; Marhofer 5-69.

December 12, 1987
Eastern Michigan 30, San Jose St 27

	1ST	2ND	3RD	4TH	FINAL
EMU	10	7	0	13	30
SJSU	7	7	7	6	27

SCORING SUMMARY

EMU	Foster 1 run (Henneghan kick)
SJSU	Jackson 6 run (Olivarez kick)
EMU	FG Henneghan 42
EMU	Foster 1 run (Henneghan kick)
SJSU	Klump 1 pass from Saxon (Olivarez kick)
SJSU	Johnson 12 pass from Perez (Olivarez kick)
EMU	Patton 15 run (kick failed)
SJSU	Saxon 16 run (pass failed)
EMU	Ostrander 32 pass from Adams (Henneghan kick)

December 10, 1988
Fresno St 35, Western Michigan 30

	1ST	2ND	3RD	4TH	FINAL
FRES	7	7	21	0	35
WMU	0	17	7	6	30

SCORING SUMMARY

FRES	Alexander 55 pass from Barsotti (Loop kick)
FRES	Alexander 38 pass from Barsotti (Loop kick)
WMU	Oliver 31 pass from Kimbrough (Creek kick)
WMU	Davis 51 run (Creek kick)
WMU	FG Creek 29
FRES	Rosette 65 run (Loop kick)
WMU	Davis 15 pass from Kimbrough (Creek kick)
FRES	Rosette 4 run (Loop kick)
FRES	Jones 26 run (Loop kick)
WMU	Kimbrough 6 run (pass failed)

FRES	TEAM STATISTICS	WMU
17	First Downs	24
200	Rushing Yards	137
15-29-3	Passing	24-57-0
240	Passing Yards	366
440	Total Yards	503
9-36.0	Punts - Average	10-37.0
1-1	Fumbles - Lost	3-2
20-166	Penalties - Yards	8-65
32:34	Possession Time	27:26

INDIVIDUAL LEADERS

RUSHING
FRES: Rosette 23-149, 2 TD; Jones 6-69, 1 TD.
WMU: Davis 15-71, 1 TD; Kimbrough 17-65, 1 TD.

PASSING
FRES: Barsotti 15-29-3, 240 yards, 2 TD.
WMU: Kimbrough 24-57-0, 366 yards, 2 TD.

RECEIVING
FRES: Alexander 3-103, 2 TD; Jones 5-76.
WMU: Boyko 5-120; Oliver 7-119, 1 TD.

December 9, 1989
Fresno State 27, Ball State 6

	1ST	2ND	3RD	4TH	FINAL
FRES	0	10	3	14	27
BSU	0	6	0	0	6

SCORING SUMMARY

FRES	FG Loop 34
BSU	Barbee 1 run (kick failed)
FRES	Shelley 91 pass from Barsotti (Loop kick)
FRES	FG Loop 27
FRES	Cox 58 interception return (Loop kick)
FRES	Thornton 5 pass from Buechele (Loop kick)

FRES	TEAM STATISTICS	BSU
18	First Downs	16
116	Rushing Yards	61
17-28-0	Passing	15-32-4
309	Passing Yards	160
425	Total Yards	221
2-2	Punt Returns - Yards	3-10
2-19	Kickoff Returns - Yards	6-149
6-31.7	Punts - Average	7-34.0
0-0	Fumbles - Lost	0-0
9-57	Penalties - Yards	4-30
31:41	Possession Time	29:18

INDIVIDUAL LEADERS

RUSHING
FRES: Craver 22-65; Cooks 8-31.
BSU: Parmalee 21-77; Hammersley 1-3.

PASSING
FRES: Barsotti 14-23-0, 246 yards, 1 TD.
BSU: Riley 13-29-3, 138 yards.

RECEIVING
FRES: Jones 7-70; Pickens 2-66.
BSU: Wilson 5-46; Parmalee 4-18.

December 8, 1990
San Jose St 48, Central Michigan 24

	1ST	2ND	3RD	4TH	FINAL
SJSU	7	19	15	7	48
CMU	0	7	3	14	24

SCORING SUMMARY

SJSU	Canley 5 run (Bowen kick)
SJSU	FG Bowen 37
CMU	Ealy 55 pass from Bender (Nicholl kick)
SJSU	Canley 22 run (kick failed)
SJSU	Blackmon 25 pass from Marrini (run failed)
SJSU	FG Bowen 25
CMU	FG Nicholl 27
SJSU	Canley 59 run (Blackmon pass from Marrini)
SJSU	Canley 5 run (Bowen kick)
SJSU	Canley 5 pass from Marrini (Bowen kick)
CMU	Ealy 48 pass from Bender (Nicholl kick)
CMU	Ealy 17 pass from Bender (Nicholl kick)

SJSU	TEAM STATISTICS	CMU
28	First Downs	13
200	Rushing Yards	63
32-43-1	Passing	14-25-1
442	Passing Yards	220
642	Total Yards	283
2-1	Fumbles - Lost	1-1
12-118	Penalties - Yards	4-30
37:11	Possession Time	22:49

INDIVIDUAL LEADERS

RUSHING
SJSU: Canley 23-164, 4 TD; Barbosa 8-16.
CMU: Smith 20-37; Rush 3-10.

PASSING
SJSU: Marrini 27-36-1, 404 yards, 2 TD.
CMU: Bender 14-25-1, 220 yards, 3 TD.

RECEIVING
SJSU: Blakes 4-95; Jackson 4-69.
CMU: Ealy 7-161, 3 TD; Kench 4-36.

December 14, 1991
Bowling Green 28, Fresno State 21

	1ST	2ND	3RD	4TH	FINAL
BG	14	7	0	7	28
FRES	7	7	0	7	21

SCORING SUMMARY

BG	Landman 5 pass from Smith (Leaver kick)
BG	Szlachcic 29 pass from White (Leaver kick)
FRES	Barsotti 3 run (Mahoney kick)
BG	Szlachcic 9 pass from White (Leaver kick)
FRES	Daigle 57 run (Mahoney kick)
BG	Smith 1 run (Leaver kick)
FRES	Thompson 5 pass from Barsotti (Mahoney kick)

BG	TEAM STATISTICS	FRES
22	First Downs	24
115	Rushing Yards	198
19-31-1	Passing	25-36-1
268	Passing Yards	286
383	Total Yards	484
4-31.6	Punts - Average	3-32.0
2-1	Fumbles - Lost	2-2
3-36	Penalties - Yards	11-86
30:46	Possession Time	29:14

INDIVIDUAL LEADERS

RUSHING
BG: Jackson 16-59; Smith 13-46, 1 TD.
FRES: Neal 14-78; Daigle 8-77, 1 TD.

PASSING
BG: White 18-30-1, 263 yards, 2 TD.
FRES: Barsotti 25-36-1, 286 yards, 1 TD.

receiving
BG: Szlachcic 11-189, 2 TD; Redd 2-47.
FRES: Rivers 6-84; Winans 3-66.

GARDEN STATE BOWL

Site: East Rutherford, N.J.
Stadium: Giants Stadium
Capacity: 77,716
Surface: AstroTurf

SEASON	DATE	PRE-GAME RANK	TEAMS	SCORE	FINAL RANK	MOST VALUABLE PLAYERS	ATT.
1979	Dec. 15, 1979	20	Temple*	28	17	Mark Bright, Temple, RB	55,493
			California	17			

DECEMBER 15, 1979
TEMPLE* 28, CALIFORNIA 17

	1ST	2ND	3RD	4TH	FINAL
TU	21	0	0	7	28
CAL	0	14	0	3	17

SCORING SUMMARY
TU	Duckett 8 run (Fioravanti kick)
TU	Duckett 4 run (Fioravanti kick)
TU	Pitts 7 pass from Broomell (Fioravanti kick)
CAL	Bouza 12 pass from Campbell (Luckhurst kick)
CAL	Rose 14 pass from Campbell (Luckhurst kick)
CAL	FG Luckhurst 34
TU	Lucear 5 pass from Broomell (Fioravanti kick)

TU	TEAM STATISTICS	CAL
21	First Downs	15
300	Rushing Yards	23
9-20-0	Passing	25-39-1
81	Passing Yards	241
381	Total Yards	264
6-34.2	Punts - Average	6-37.0
1-1	Fumbles - Lost	3-1

INDIVIDUAL LEADERS
RUSHING
TU: Bright 19-112; Duckett 22-92, 2 TD.
CAL: Jones 14-49; Campbell 6-29.
PASSING
TU: Broomell 9-20-0, 81 yards, 2 TD.
CAL: Campbell 25-38-1, 241 yards, 2 TD.
RECEIVING
TU: Lucear 3-41, 1 TD; Wesnak 1-20.
CAL: Bouza 7-114, 1 TD; Rose 8-62, 1 TD.

MERCY BOWL

Site: Los Angeles, Calif.
Stadium: Memorial Coliseum
Capacity: 94,000
Surface: Grass

SEASON	DATE	PRE-GAME RANK	TEAMS	SCORE	FINAL RANK	MOST VALUABLE PLAYERS	ATT.
1961	Nov. 23, 1961		Fresno State	36		Beau Carter, Fresno State, QB	33,145
			Bowling Green	6			

NOVEMBER 23, 1961
FRESNO STATE 36, BOWLING GREEN 6

	1ST	2ND	3RD	4TH	FINAL
FRES	3	7	20	6	36
BG	0	6	0	0	6

SCORING SUMMARY
FRES	FG Masich 29
BG	Bell 2 run (kick failed)
FRES	Barrett 45 pass from Carter (Masich kick)
FRES	Seifert 1 run (Masich kick)
FRES	Barrett 23 pass from Carter (Masich kick)
FRES	Carter 4 run (Masich kick)
FRES	Carter 8 run (Masich kick)

FRES	TEAM STATISTICS	BG
23	First Downs	17
100	Rushing Yards	111
22-43-1	Passing	11-22-3
368	Passing Yards	208
468	Total Yards	319
4-32.0	Punts - Average	4-34.0
1-0	Fumbles - Lost	5-3
7-75	Penalties - Yards	4-20

*Played as an independent or with other conference affiliation

SALAD BOWL

Site: Phoenix
Stadium: Montgomery Stadium
Surface: Grass

SEASON	DATE	PRE-GAME RANK	TEAMS	SCORE	FINAL RANK	MOST VALUABLE PLAYERS	ATT.
1950	Jan. 1, 1951		**Miami (Ohio)**	34		Jim Bailey, Miami (Ohio), RB	23,000
			Arizona State	21			

JANUARY 1, 1951
MIAMI (OHIO) 34, ARIZONA STATE 21

	1ST	2ND	3RD	4TH	FINAL
MIA	7	14	6	7	34
ASU	0	7	7	7	21

SCORING SUMMARY
MIA — Pont 1 run (Sautter kick)
MIA — Beckrest 8 pass from Wirkowski (Sautter kick)
MIA — Bailey 2 run (Sautter kick)
ASU — White 29 pass from Aja (Fuller kick)
MIA — Maccioli 7 pass from Wirkowski (kick failed)
ASU — Wahlin 4 run (Fuller kick)
MIA — Bailey 50 run (Sautter kick)
ASU — White 16 run (Fuller kick)

MIA	TEAM STATISTICS	ASU
22	First Downs	21
225	Rushing Yards	240
16-24-2	Passing	10-22-2
231	Passing Yards	171
456	Total Yards	411
5-28.5	Punts - Average	5-33.2
4-20	Penalties - Yards	6-32

INDIVIDUAL LEADERS
RUSHING
MIA: Bailey 21-108, 2 TD; Pont 15-67, 1 TD.
ASU: White 17-106, 1 TD; Wahlin 14-76, 1 TD.
PASSING
MIA: Wirkowski 16-24-2, 231 yards, 2 TD.
ASU: Aja 8-18-2, 139 yards, 1 TD.
RECEIVING
MIA: Maccioli 4-73, 1 TD; Urich 3-48.
ASU: White 4-87, 1 TD; Rippel 3-52.

SILICON VALLEY CLASSIC

Site: San Jose, Calif.
Stadium: Spartan Stadium
Capacity: 31,500
Surface: Grass

Spartan Stadium, since 2000

Silicon Valley Football Classic,
2000-2004

SEASON	DATE	PRE-GAME RANK	TEAMS	SCORE	FINAL RANK	MOST VALUABLE PLAYERS	ATT.
2004	Dec. 30, 2004		**Northern Illinois**	34		DeWitt Betterson, No. Illinois, RB	21,456
			Troy State	21			

DECEMBER 30, 2004
NORTHERN ILLINOIS 34, TROY STATE 21

	1ST	2ND	3RD	4TH	FINAL
NI	14	10	3	7	34
TS	14	0	0	7	21

SCORING SUMMARY
TS — McDowell 1 run (Whibbs kick)
TS — Richardson 23 pass from McDowell (Whibbs kick)
NI — Wolfe 50 run (Nendick kick)
NI — Haldi 1 run (Nendick kick)
NI — FG Nendick 30
NI — Haldi 1 run (Nendick kick)
NI — FG Nendick 39
NI — Harris 3 run (Nendick kick)
TS — McDowell 4 run (whibbs kick)

NI	TEAM STATISTICS	TS
17	First Downs	13
213	Rushing Yards	170
8-24-0	Passing	6-22-1
146	Passing Yards	122
359	Total Yards	292
0	Fumbles Lost	0
4-40	Penalties - Yards	4-29
32:8	Possession Time	27:52

INDIVIDUAL LEADERS
RUSHING
NI: Harris 23-120, 1 TD; Wolfe 15-84, 1 TD.
TS: Betterson 25-150; McDowell 13-18, 2 TD.
PASSING
NI: Haldi 8-24-0, 146 yards.
TS: McDowell 6-20-1, 122 yards, 1 TD.
RECEIVING
NI: Powers 1-47; Cieslak 2-35.
TS: Samples 3-87; Richardson 1-23, 1 TD.

POSTGAME WRAP-UP

ACKNOWLEDGMENTS

Talking about football games, Woody Hayes once said, "You win with people."

The same goes with book publishing, and the *ESPN Big Ten Football Encyclopedia* couldn't have been accomplished without the contributions of dozens of skilled writers, editors, designers, proofreaders, and fact-checkers.

That we finished in time is a tribute to the expert organizational and editing skills of project coordinator Bill Vourvoulias, who directed the book's editorial production flow in New York City. Jaime Lowe joined us during the final month and helped in numerous editorial aspects as well.

Laura Smyth of Smythtype oversaw the design, remaining true to the clean, crisp look of the *ESPN College Football Encyclopedia*, while improving on specific elements of the book's appearance at several turns, especially with our new Annual Statistical Leaders charts. Once again, Eric Baker was responsible for the sharp, readable cover design. Gabriel Ruegg helped us in the later stages with his mastery of all things Quark-related.

Chris Raymond of ESPN Books wanted this book to happen, and not just so he could have further documentation of Penn State, his alma mater, and its glory years. Chris is one of the most talented people in the book business, and his belief in the Encyclopedia series has been our greatest asset over the years.

Todd Jones and Ed Krzemienski ably updated their histories of the teams of the Big Ten and MAC, respectively (with Mike Vaccaro revisiting his entry for the newest MAC member, Temple), and Chuck Culpepper and Mark Wangrin contributed a pair of lucid new essays on the Big Ten's rich history.

Richard Billingsley once again provided his all-time scores database—newly updated—and Pat Porter returned as well, helping us update the winning percentage charts that accompany each team's all-time scores.

Copyediting work was handled by Beth Adelman, Steve Horne, Dave Sutter, Ethan Lipton, Roseann Marulli, and Margaret McNicol Robbins. Overseeing the production and operation headaches of getting a 500-page book to press on time was John W. Glenn, who gave us the answers we needed, even when we weren't giving him the answers he wanted.

Checking and coordinating this latest torrent of information were Craig Winston, chief of research for *ESPN The Magazine*; the redoubtable Roger Jackson, who oversaw the data on first-round draft choices, and Gueorgui Milkov, who supervised the dizzying amount of fresh copy that came through in the final week. We also received invaluable checking help from Doug Mittler, Amanda Angel, Max Klinger, Jim Weber, Anthony Tao, Dale Brauner, and Anna K. Clemmons. Michael Steiner provided an able assist as well.

We're indebted to Lou Monaco, Andrew Webb, Michael Morrison, and Gerry Brown, who compiled much of the new information on school records, all-conference teams, first-round draft choices, and Hall of Fame inductees. And we certainly want to thank the sports-information staffs at the Big Ten Conference, the Mid-American Conference, and each of their member schools for their assistance in the earliest stages of this project.

Each of the books in the *ESPN College Football Encyclopedia* series owe a lasting debt of gratitude to patron saints John Skipper and John Walsh.

Finally, I would be remiss if I didn't give personal thanks for support, guidance, and sustenance along the way to: Sloan Harris; Rick Pappas; Joe Posnanski; Gerald Early; Robert Minter; Robert Draper; Ernie Accorsi; Joel Bussert; David Zivan; Vahe Gregorian; Larry Kindbom; David Hale; Denise Lieberman; my mother, Lois MacCambridge; my children, Miles and Ella MacCambridge; and my girlfriend, Ivy Tominack.

MJM
St. Louis, September 2007

CONTRIBUTORS

Historian, freelance writer, and Bowl Championship Series pollster, **Richard Billingsley** has been ranking college football teams for more than 35 years. Since being selected by the BCS in 1999, Billingsley has been instrumental in shaping the formula used to determine the national championship game. He currently serves as the designated representative of the computer group to the BCS.

Chuck Culpepper grew up following college football in Virginia in the 1970s, when Virginia went 32–77–1 and Virginia Tech went 47–61–2, yet he somehow came to adore the sport. A graduate of the University of Virginia, he worked as a football-minded sports columnist at the *Lexington* (Ky.) *Herald-Leader* in the 1990s and the *Oregonian* in Portland in the early 2000s, before becoming in October 2002 the college football writer at *Newsday* in New York. There, he would revel in walking out into Times Square at 5 a.m. on a Saturday, catching a taxi to an airport, and winding up in some glorious den of din like Auburn. He has covered seven Rose Bowls and 27 bowl games overall and is believed to be one of the few humans in history to have witnessed both a Music City Bowl and a Motor City Bowl. Since 2006, he has lived in London, working on a book, checking college football scores in the wee hours of Sunday morning, and writing for the *Los Angeles Times*.

Todd Jones is a narrative-projects reporter and sports blogger for *The Columbus Dispatch*, which nominated him for the 2006 Pulitzer Prize in feature writing. The Associated Press of Ohio named him best sportswriter in Ohio in 2003, and awarded him second place for sports column writing in 2004 and 2006. The Press Club of Cleveland awarded him first place for feature writing in 2006 and first place for sports columnist in 2004. The University of Kentucky graduate has also worked for the *Cincinnati Post* and *Los Angeles Times*, and has been a freelance contributor for *The New York Times*. He lives in Columbus with his wife, Deborah Bertsch, a college English instructor, and their two daughters, Anna and Kate.

Ed Krzemienski is a professor of history. He has taught at Purdue, The Citadel, and Indiana University-Purdue University Indianapolis. He is currently working on a book about college football in the south during the 1960s. He lives with his wife, Beth, and his son, Edward Joseph, in Lafayette, Ind.

Mike Vaccaro is the lead sports columnist for the *New York Post* and has been a newspaper columnist for close to 20 years. A St. Bonaventure University graduate, he is the author of two books: *Emperors & Idiots*, a history of the Yankees-Red Sox rivalry, and *1941: The Greatest Year in Sports*, which was released in June 2007. He lives in Hillsdale, N.J.

Mark Wangrin is an Austin, Texas-based freelance writer who's written two books, including a history of University of Texas football, and contributed to numerous ESPN book projects, including *ESPN SportsCentury* and the *ESPN College Football Encyclopedia*. He is a frequent contributor to ESPN.com. A Chicago native, he attended Northwestern during the Purple's dark ages—1978-81—when the Wildcats won only one of 44 games. Wangrin lives with his wife Barbara, daughter Makala, son Ben, dog Elvis, and the haunting memory of how that roughing-the-kicker call almost cost those '79 Wildcats their win over Wyoming.